Machine-Learning-Based Hyperspectral Image Processing

IEEE Press
445 Hoes Lane
Piscataway, NJ 08854

Machine-Learning-Based Hyperspectral Image Processing

Edited by

Bing Zhang
Aerospace Information Research Institute
Chinese Academy of Sciences
Beijing, China

College of Resources and Environment
University of Chinese Academy of Sciences
Beijing, China

IEEE Press

WILEY

Published by John Wiley & Sons, Inc., Hoboken, New Jersey.

Library of Congress Cataloging-in-Publication Data

Names: Zhang, Bing, 1969–
Title: Machine-learning-based hyperspectral image processing / Bing Zhang.
Description: Hoboken, New Jersey : Wiley, [2026] | Includes index.
Identifiers: LCCN 2025023045 (print) | LCCN 2025023046 (ebook) | ISBN 9781394267859 hardback | ISBN 9781394267873 adobe pdf | ISBN 9781394267866 epub
Subjects: LCSH: Hyperspectral imaging | Machine learning
Classification: LCC TR267.73 .Z43 2025 (print) | LCC TR267.73 (ebook) | DDC 006.4/2–dc23/eng/20250730
LC record available at https://lccn.loc.gov/2025023045
LC ebook record available at https://lccn.loc.gov/2025023046

Cover Design: Wiley
Cover Image: © SEAN GLADWELL/Getty Images

Set in 9.5/12.5pt STIXTwoText by Straive, Pondicherry, India

Contents

About the Editor

Professor Bing Zhang is the Deputy Director of the Aerospace Information Research Institute, the Chinese Academy of Sciences. He is a member of the Chinese Academy of Sciences, an IEEE Fellow, and a fellow of the Geographical Society of China. He has long been engaged in research on the hyperspectral remote sensing technology and its applications. He has published more than 400 journal papers. His creative achievements were rewarded more than 10 important prizes from the international institutions and Chinese government, including the IEEE Geoscience and Remote Sensing Society (GRSS) Regional Leader Award, the National Science and Technology Advance Award of China, the Outstanding Scientific Achievement Award of the Chinese Academy of Sciences, and the Qian Xuesen Outstanding Contribution Award of China Space Foundation. Prof. Zhang has provided a long-term service to the international remote sensing community, the Student Paper Competition Committee Member in the IEEE Geoscience and Remote Sensing Society from 2015 to 2019, the Best Paper Competition Committee Member in IEEE Geoscience and Remote Sensing Society, and Associate Editor for *IEEE Journal of Selected Topics in Applied Earth Observations and Remote Sensing* from 2012 to 2022. Currently, he serves as an Associate Editor for *IEEE Transactions on Geoscience and Remote Sensing*, the Editor-in-Chief of the *National Remote Sensing Bulletin*, which is the top Chinese journal in the remote sensing field, and a Technical Committee Member of *IEEE Workshop on Hyperspectral Image and Signal Processing* (WHISPERS).

List of Contributors

Jon Atli Benediktsson
Faculty of Electrical and Computer Engineering, University of Iceland, Reykjavik Iceland

Chein-I Chang
Center of Hyperspectral Imaging in Remote Sensing, Information Science and Technology College, Dalian Maritime University Dalian, China

Department of Computer Science and Electrical Engineering, University of Maryland Baltimore, MD, USA

Jocelyn Chanussot
GIPSA-Laboratory, University Grenoble Alpes, Grenoble, France

Bowen Chen
Image Processing Centre, School of Astronautics, Beihang University, Beijing, China

Hongyu Chen
School of Computer Science, China University of Geosciences, Wuhan, China

Kaiyuan Chen
The Institute of Optics and Electronics, the State Key Laboratory Cultivation Base of Atmospheric Optoelectronic Detection and Information Fusion, Jiangsu International Joint Laboratory on Meteorological Photonics and Optoelectronic Detection, and Jiangsu Engineering Research Center for Intelligent Optoelectronic Sensing Technology of Atmosphere, Nanjing University of Information Science and Technology Nanjing, China

Yong Chen
School of Artificial Intelligence, Jiangxi Normal University Nanchang, China

Zhonghao Chen
School of Computer and Information Hohai University, Nanjing, China

Kecheng Du
College of Surveying and Geo-Informatics Tongji University, Shanghai, China

Peijun Du
School of Geography and Ocean Science Nanjing University, Nanjing, China

Qian Du
Department of Electrical and Computer Engineering, Mississippi State University Mississippi State, MS, USA

Ruitong Du
Aerospace Information Research Institute, Chinese Academy of Sciences, Beijing, China

Leyuan Fang
College of Electrical and Information Engineering, Hunan University Changsha, China

Wei Feng
Department of Remote Sensing Science and Technology, School of Electronic Engineering, Xi'an, Shaanxi, China

Paolo Gamba
Laboratory of Telecommunications and Remote Sensing, Department of Electrical Computer and Biomedical Engineering
University of Pavia, Pavia, Italy

Hongmin Gao
School of Computer Application Technology
Hohai University, Nanjing, China

Kun Gao
School of Optics and Photonics, Beijing Institute of Technology, Beijing, China

Lianru Gao
Aerospace Information Research Institute, Chinese Academy of Sciences, Beijing, China

Center of Hyperspectral Imaging in Remote Sensing, Information Science and Technology College, Dalian Maritime University
Dalian, China

Yanfeng Gu
School of Electronics and Information Engineering, Harbin Institute of Technology
Harbin, China

Wangquan He
College of Computer Science and Software Engineering, Shenzhen University
Shenzhen, China

Wei He
State Key Laboratory of Information Engineering in Surveying, Mapping and Remote Sensing, Wuhan University
Wuhan, China

Jiaochan Hu
Center of Hyperspectral Imaging in Remote Sensing, Information Science and Technology College, Dalian Maritime University
Dalian, China

Jia Jia
Center of Hyperspectral Imaging in Remote Sensing, Information Science and Technology College, Dalian Maritime University
Dalian, China

Sen Jia
College of Computer Science and Software Engineering, Shenzhen University
Shenzhen, China

Licheng Jiao
School of Artificial Intelligence, Xidian University, Xi'an, China

Chiman Kwan
Applied Research LLC, Rockville, MD, Rockville, USA

Chong Li
Faculty of Mathematics and Statistics
Ningbo University, Ningbo, China

Jiaxin Li
Aerospace Information Research Institute
Chinese Academy of Sciences, Beijing, China

College of Resources and Environment
University of Chinese Academy of Sciences
Beijing, China

Jun Li
School of Computer Science and Hubei Key Laboratory of Intelligent Geo-Information Processing, University of Geosciences
Wuhan, China

Wei Li
School of Information and Electronics, Beijing Institute of Technology, Beijing
China

Yunsong Li
State Key Laboratory of Integrated Services Networks, Xidian University, Xi'an, China

Liqin Liu
Image Processing Centre, School of Astronautics, Beihang University, Beijing, China

Sicong Liu
College of Surveying and Geo-Informatics
Tongji University, Shanghai, China

Wenfei Luo
School of Geographical Science
South China Normal University
Guangzhou, China

Li Ma
School of Mechanical Engineering and Electronic Information, China University of Geosciences, Wuhan, China

Jiangtao Peng
Faculty of Mathematics and Statistics
Hubei University, Wuhan, China

Antonio Plaza
Hyperspectral Computing Laboratory
Department of Technology of Computers and Communications, Escuela Politécnica, University of Extremadura Cáceres, Spain

Hairong Qi
Department of Electrical Engineering and Computer Science, Advanced Imaging and Collaborative Information Processing Group
The University of Tennessee, Knoxville
TN, USA

Ying Qu
State Key Laboratory of Remote Sensing and Digital Earth, Faculty of Geographical Science, Beijing Normal University, Beijing, China

Kai Ren
Faculty of Electrical Engineering and Computer Science, Ningbo University
Ningbo, China

Qi Ren
College of Computer Science and Software Engineering, Shenzhen University
Shenzhen, China

Chuhan Shen
Center of Hyperspectral Imaging in Remote Sensing, Information Science and Technology College, Dalian Maritime University
Dalian, China

Zhenwei Shi
Image Processing Centre, School of Astronautics, Beihang University
Beijing, China

Jakob Sigurdsson
Faculty of Electrical and Computer Engineering, University of Iceland, Reykjavik
Iceland

Yuanchao Su
College of Geomatics, Xi'an University of Science and Technology, Xi'an, China

He Sun
Aerospace Information Research Institute
Chinese Academy of Sciences, Beijing, China

Weiwei Sun
Department of Geography and Spatial Information Techniques, Ningbo University
Ningbo, China

Xiaohua Tong
College of Surveying and Geo-Informatics
Tongji University, Shanghai, China

Bing Tu
The Institute of Optics and Electronics, the State Key Laboratory Cultivation Base of Atmospheric Optoelectronic Detection and Information Fusion, Jiangsu International Joint Laboratory on Meteorological Photonics and Optoelectronic Detection, and Jiangsu Engineering Research Center for Intelligent Optoelectronic Sensing Technology of Atmosphere, Nanjing University of Information Science and Technology
Nanjing, China

Magnus O. Ulfarsson
Faculty of Electrical and Computer Engineering, University of Iceland, Reykjavik
Iceland

Bin Wang
Key Laboratory for Information
Science of Electromagnetic Waves (MoE)
Fudan University, Shanghai, China

Image and Intelligence Laboratory
School of Information Science and Technology
Fudan University, Shanghai, China

Guanchun Wang
School of Artificial Intelligence, Xidian
University, Xi'an, China

Jian-Li Wang
School of Computing and Artificial
Intelligence, Southwest Jiaotong University
Chengdu, China

Yuebin Wang
School of Land Science and Technology
China University of Geosciences
Beijing, China

Zhicheng Wang
Department of Earth Sciences and the
Laboratory for Space Research
The University of Hong Kong
Hong Kong, China

Jie Wu
College of Electrical and Information
Engineering, Hunan University
Changsha, China

Rui Wu
School of Geographical Science,
South China Normal University
Guangzhou, China

Jie Xie
School of Rail Transportation, Soochow
University, Suzhou, China

Weiying Xie
State Key Laboratory of Integrated Services
Networks, Xidian University, Xi'an
China

Mengdao Xing
Academy of Advanced Interdisciplinary
Research, Xidian University, Xi'an
Shaanxi, China

Meng Xu
College of Computer Science and Software
Engineering, Shenzhen University
Shenzhen, China

Ruoqing Xu
College of Geomatics, Xi'an University of
Science and Technology, Xi'an, China

Shufang Xu
School of Applied Electronic Technology
Anhui Normal University, Wuhu, China

Bin Yang
School of Computer Science and Technology
Donghua University, Shanghai, China

Xianchang Yang
School of Information Science and
Engineering, Hunan Institute of Science and
Technology, Yueyang, China

Haoyang Yu
Center of Hyperspectral Imaging in Remote
Sensing, Information Science and Technology
College, Dalian Maritime University
Dalian, China

Bing Zhang
Aerospace Information Research Institute,
Chinese Academy of Sciences, Beijing, China

College of Resources and Environment,
University of Chinese Academy of Sciences
Beijing, China

Jingyan Zhang
School of Artificial Intelligence, Xidian
University, Xi'an, China

Liqiang Zhang
State Key Laboratory of Remote Sensing and Digital Earth, Faculty of Geographical Science, Beijing Normal University, Beijing, China

Shaoquan Zhang
Jiangxi Province Key Laboratory of Water Information Cooperative Sensing and Intelligent Processing, School of Information Engineering, Nanchang Institute of Technology, Nanchang, China

Shuyu Zhang
College of Computer Science and Software Engineering, Shenzhen University
Shenzhen, China

Xiangrong Zhang
School of Artificial Intelligence, Xidian University, Xi'an, China

Xin Zhang
State Key Laboratory of Integrated Services Networks, Xidian University, Xi'an, China

Yiyan Zhang
School of Computer and Information
Hohai University, Nanjing, China

Bin Zhao
School of Information Science and Engineering, Shandong Agricultural University, Taian, China

Jiangsan Zhao
Department of Agricultural Technology
Norwegian Institute of Bioeconomy Research (NIBIO), Ås, Norway

Xi-Le Zhao
School of Mathematical Sciences, University of Electronic Science and Technology of China, Chengdu, China

Ke Zheng
College of Geography and Environment
Liaocheng University, Liaocheng, China

Yu-Bang Zheng
School of Information Science and Technology, Southwest Jiaotong University, Chengdu, China

Jiasong Zhu
College of Computer Science and Software Engineering, Shenzhen University
Shenzhen, China

Xiao Xiang Zhu
Chair of Data Science in Earth Observation
Technical University of Munich, Munich
Germany

Zhiqing Zhu
Department of Remote Sensing, The College of Geomatics, and The College of Geology and Environment, Xi'an University of Science and Technology, Xi'an, China

Lina Zhuang
Aerospace Information Research Institute
Chinese Academy of Sciences, Beijing, China

Zhengxia Zou
Department of Guidance, Navigation and Control, School of Astronautics
Beihang University, Beijing, China

1

Review for Machine-Learning-Based Hyperspectral Image Analysis

He Sun and Ruitong Du

Aerospace Information Research Institute, Chinese Academy of Sciences, Beijing, China

1.1 Overview

Hyperspectral imaging is a powerful remote-sensing technique that captures and analyzes the reflectance or radiance of a scene across a large number of continuous spectral bands, ranging from the visible to the near-infrared regions of the electromagnetic spectrum. Compared to other remote-sensing imaging modalities (such as multispectral or panchromatic imaging), hyperspectral imaging provides more detailed and accurate information about the spectral response of materials and objects in a scene, enabling precise identification and differentiation of different materials or objects, even those that may appear similar to the naked eye or in other imaging modalities. Hyperspectral imaging finds wide applications in fields such as agriculture, environmental monitoring, geology, oceanography, and military surveillance. For example, in agriculture, hyperspectral imaging can be used for crop monitoring, disease detection, and yield estimation. In environmental monitoring, it can be used for water quality assessment, land-cover mapping, and pollution detection. In geology and mineral exploration, it can be used for mineral identification and mapping. In military surveillance, it can be used for target detection and tracking. However, hyperspectral imaging is challenged by high data volume, complex noise, low spatial resolution, atmospheric interference, high acquisition cost, as well as the need for accurate calibration and validation.

To address these challenges, machine learning techniques have been widely employed. Machine learning techniques can be divided into two categories: traditional machine learning and deep learning. Traditional machine learning is a statistical learning method based on statistical learning theory. Algorithms such as support vector machines (SVMs), random forests, decision trees, and naive Bayes are used to establish a prediction model based on the relationship between the features and labels of the sample data. In hyperspectral imaging, traditional machine learning techniques are commonly used for classification and regression tasks. For example, SVMs and random forests can be used for object classification and spectral curve analysis. Deep learning is a machine learning method based on artificial neural networks. Deep learning models usually consist of multiple layers of neurons, which can establish a prediction model by learning the relationship between the features and labels of the input data. In hyperspectral imaging, deep learning techniques are commonly used for feature extraction and image processing. For example, convolutional neural networks (CNNs) can be used for image denoising and feature extraction, autoencoders (AEs) can be used for data compression and dimensionality reduction, and generative adversarial networks (GANs) can be used for image super-resolution processing.

Machine-Learning-Based Hyperspectral Image Processing, First Edition. Edited by Bing Zhang.

1.2 Denoising

Hyperspectral images (HSIs), acquired by hyperspectral imaging sensors, contain hundreds of spectral bands. The spectral information an HSI provides makes it possible to discriminate different materials in a scene. Therefore, HSIs have been used in applications such as agricultural production, mineral exploration, and environmental protection [1–4]. However, due to photon effects, atmospheric absorption, and sensor disturbance, HSIs are corrupted by different kinds of noise, such as quantization noise, thermal noise, and shot noise. Therefore, denoising is an essential preprocessing step for HSI analysis and applications.

HSI denoising has evolved considerably in recent years [5–12]. Grayscale image 2-D denoising methods can be extended to HSI denoising by treating each spectral band separately. Examples are the non-local means (NLMs) filter [13], the 2-D wavelet denoising [14], the block-matching and 3-D filter (BM3D) [15], and the weighted nuclear norm minimization (WNNM) [16]. Single-band methods utilize only spatial information leading to spectral distortion.

HSIs are spectrally correlated. Therefore, denoising methods should jointly exploit spatial and spectral information [17]. Several spectral–spatial denoising methods have been proposed [18]. Yuan et al. [19] suggested a spectral–spatial adaptive total variation denoising method for removing Gaussian noise. Chen et al. [20] proposed a denoising method based on spectral–spatial domain mixing prior. Huang et al. [21] used a spatial–spectral weighted nuclear minimization denoising method for removing mixed types of noise in HSI. Besides all these methods, there are other methods based on transforming HSI to the wavelet domain and utilizing wavelet-based spatial and spectral information to remove the noise [22]. Chen and Qian [23] used principal component analysis (PCA) of the HSI and then transformed the low-energy PCA output channels to the wavelet domain to remove the noise using 2-D spatial and 1-D spectral wavelet shrinkage denoising. Othman and Qian [24] suggested a hybrid of spatial and spectral wavelet shrinkage by using a spectral derivative to elevate noise and then utilize wavelet-based spatial and spectral denoising. Rasti et al. [25] presented a wavelet-domain-based spectral–spatial penalty method for HSI denoising. These wavelet-based spectral–spatial methods use spatial and spectral information of HSI to remove noise and utilize wavelet transform to provide a sparse representation (SR) for clean HSI to further remove noise in the wavelet domain.

Recently, many low-rank model-based methods have been proposed for HSI denoising [26–32]. Zhang et al. [33] presented a low-rank matrix recovery (LRMR) method for removing mixed types of noise in HSI. An extension of the LRMR method [34] was proposed using an adaptive iteration regularization framework for HSI denoising. Chen et al. [35] presented a nonconvex low-rank matrix approximation method using a nonconvex regularizer. These low-rank model-based methods exploit the low-dimensional structures in the HSIs. HSIs are usually self-similar and have sparse characteristics in the spatial domain and hence can be denoised using SR. Lu et al. [36] and Li et al. [37] suggested an HSI denoising method based on SR using the high similar spatial information of HSI. More recently, several denoising methods based on a combination of low-rank and SR have been presented. Liu et al. [38] used group sparse and nuclear norm low-rank penalties for removing stripe noise. Zhuang and Bioucas-Dias [39] utilized similar patches in the low-dimensional subspace to exploit the sparse and low-rank characteristics of HSI. Rasti et al. [40] used a sparse low-rank model, which utilizes sparse penalized least squares for estimating the unknown signal for denoising.

While HSIs are high dimensional, they can usually be represented using a few elements from a basis or dictionary [41]. A sparse image model often exploits this important characteristic. Noise-free HSIs can thus be represented by a sparse linear combination of the basis features [42, 43].

Therefore, SR is often used in model-based HSI denoising. An SR, based on sparse coding [44], is used in [36, 37, 45] to denoise HSIs. However, the noise in HSIs can usually not be sufficiently removed by denoising methods that rely either on the low rank or the sparse characteristics of HSIs [46].

Denoising performance can be improved by considering both the low rank and the sparsity of HSIs [47]. In [39], a fast hyperspectral denoising method (FastHyDe) was proposed. FastHyDe used singular value decomposition (SVD) to obtain the low-rank eigenimages and then used patch-based block-matching and 3-D filter (BM3D) [15] based on the SR for the eigenimages to remove noise. In [30], the Non-local meets Global (NGmeet) denoising method was proposed. NGmeet split the spectral bands of the HSI into groups and used the NLM on these groups to extract eigenimages that are used as an SR of HSI to remove Gaussian noise. In [47], a spectral–spatial transform-based sparse and low-rank representations (SSSLRR) method was proposed. SSSLRR utilized the sparse and low-rank model in the transform domain to remove the Gaussian noise, salt and pepper noise, and stripes. FastHyDe, NGmeet, and SSSLRR use the sparse and low-rank characteristics of HSIs to construct a denoising model to obtain good denoising results.

In addition, to exploit the low rank and sparsity of HSIs, many researchers extend the HSI model by including regularizers. These regularizers can use the characteristics of HSIs. The total variation (TV) regularizer [48, 49] is commonly used to promote piecewise smoothness. Many HSI denoising methods have been proposed that use TV or variants of TV [19, 50–54]. Aggarwal and Majumdar [50] utilized the spatio-spectral total variation to explore the 2-D total variation along the spatial dimension and the 1-D total variation along the spectral dimension to inherit the structure of HSI and used the split-Bregman approach to obtain the optimal solution. He et al. [51] proposed the spatial–spectral total variation regularized local low-rank matrix recovery (LLRSSTV) method to remove mixed noise. LLRSSTV divided the original HSI into local overlapping patches and separated the low-rank clean HSI patches from the sparse noise by using the rank-constrained low-rank matrix recovery, and then a global spatial–spectral total variation regularized image reconstruction strategy is utilized to ensure the global spatial–spectral smoothness of the reconstructed image from the low-rank patches. Fan et al. [52] utilized the spatial–spectral TV regularized low-rank tensor factorization (SSTV-LRTF) method to remove mixed noise in HSIs. SSTV-LRTF used the SSTV regularization to simultaneously consider the local spatial structure and spectral correlation of neighboring bands for removing Gaussian noise and used the LRTF to separate the LR low-rank clean image from sparse noise.

Another way to exploit the spectral–spatial correlation in HSIs is by using tensors [55–58]. Model-based methods based on tensor are much easier and more efficient than model-based methods based on matrix to exploit the spectral–spatial information of HSIs for HSI denoising. Tensor-based dictionary learning [59] and tensor-based subspace representation [60] yield better denoising performance than the matrix-based dictionary learning and matrix-based subspace representation, respectively. Zhang et al. [55] used the double low-rank (DLR) matrix decomposition method for HSI denoising. DLR simultaneously explored the low-rank characteristic of the lexicographically ordered noise-free HSI and the low-rank structure of the stripe noise on each band of the HSI to achieve separation of the noise-free HSI, stripe noise, and other mixed noise. He et al. [56] utilized the tensor subspace low-rank learning with non-local prior (TSLRLN) method to exploit the low rankness of both spatial and spectral modes of an HSI tensor to realize complete tensor operations for subspace low-rank learning and to avoid the correlation loss brought about by tensor flattening. Chen et al. [57] used the factor group sparsity-regularized nonconvex low-rank approximation (FGSLR) method to capture the spectral correlation via low-rank factorization and utilized the factor group sparsity regularization to further enhance the low-rank property. Lin et al.

[58] utilized the non-convex low-rank tensor approximation (NonLRTA) model for mixed noise removal. NonLRTA estimated the intrinsic structure of the underlying HSI from its noisy observation and used the augmented Lagrange multiplier (ALM) algorithm to solve the proposed model.

Instead of using subjective physical assumptions of HSIs for model-based HSI denoising, deep-learning-based methods have emerged that use data-driven features learned from noisy and noise-free HSI pairs. In [61], a dual-attention denoising network was proposed combining spatial and spectral attention modules. A deep spatial–spectral global reasoning network considering both the local and global information for removing noise was proposed in [62]. A deep neural denoising network is used in [63] to remove mixed noise and generate high-quality denoised HSIs. In [64], a low-rank spatial–spectral denoising network was proposed. The network concatenates spatial–spectral atrous and multiatrous blocks into a plug-and-play low-rank module for HSI denoising. In [65], a spectral–spatial cross-attention network combines group convolutions and attention modules for HSI denoising. These deep-learning-based methods can give competitive results using a large number of noisy-clean (noisy and noiseless) HSI pairs for training.

1.3 Super-resolution

Hyperspectral image super-resolution (HSI-SR) aims to merge high spatial resolution panchromatic/multispectral images (PAN/MSI) with low-resolution hyperspectral images (LR-HSI) of the same area. This compensates for the limitations of their respective spectral and spatial resolutions, resulting in a high-resolution hyperspectral image (HR-HSI). There are several methods available, including pansharpening, Bayesian analysis, matrix/tensor decomposition, and deep learning methods.

1.3.1 Pansharpening-based Methods

One example of HSI-SR is pansharpening, which transforms an LR-HSI to HR-HSI by fusing it with a PAN. There are four main categories of pansharpening methods: component substitution (CS), multiresolution analysis (MRA), variational methods, and hybrid approaches. Among them, the fusion methods based on CS and MRA have been developed earlier. Various methods have been introduced into professional remote-sensing software such as ENVI and ERDAS IMAGING. One of the most widely used methods for pansharpening is Brovey transform [66] which utilizes spectral modeling to enhance the visual contrast of data's histogram in areas with high and low ends, such as shadows, water bodies, and highly reflective regions. The Gram–Schmidt method [67] is another commonly used technique for pansharpening. This method involves subtracting the synthetic PAN image from the original image to obtain spatial details, which are then injected into upsampled HS bands to create pansharpened images. The intensity hue saturation [68] method is a commonly used CS technique. It was developed with the assumption that hue and saturation components contain most of the spectral information, while the intensity component retains spatial information.

The method based on pansharpening extension is developed from the PAN and HSI fusion method, which uses pansharpening approach to fuse MSI and HSI [69]. When it comes to pansharpening extension methods, one approach is to divide the HSI into discrete bands and then group and merge them using a pansharpening technique. However, this method does not fully take into account the inherent characteristics of HSI. As a result, achieving highly precise reconstruction results can be challenging. Based on this issue regarding MSI–HSI imaging fusions wavelet-transform-based method [70], component replacement-based method [71], multiresolution analysis-based method [72], etc. have been proposed since pansharpening-extension-based methods lack degradation model establishment and optimization, making it difficult to balance between space details and spectral fidelity during reconstruction.

1.3.2 Bayesian-based Methods

Based on Bayesian methods, appropriate prior information is first applied to regularize the inverse problem to be solved in the target scene. The target parameters are then solved by maximizing the posterior probability or minimizing the negative logarithm of the posterior probability. Such methods often solve problems within subspaces. MAP–SMM method [73] is proposed using a random mixture model to solve unknown parameters, which has been successfully used to solve high/panchromatic and high/multispectral image super-resolution fusion problems. Hardie et al. [74] established an objective function by maximizing the posterior probability while satisfying degradation model constraints, effectively mining potential relationships between panchromatic images and target images. Subsequently, Zhang et al. [75] applied this idea in wavelet domains and impose Gaussian mixture scale priors to enhance model robustness against noise. Although these methods have achieved ideal results in image restoration, they are computationally inefficient. Therefore, Wei et al. [76, 77] transformed maximum likelihood probability problems into closed-form solutions for solving Sylvester equations to effectively reduce computational pressure on models and proposed a more robust R-FUSE method. In addition, these authors subsequently introduced strategies for introducing sparse Gaussian priors into subspace expression coefficients and used them for complete dictionary SR [78].

1.3.3 Matrix/Tensor-decomposition-based Methods

Matrix-decomposition-based methods decompose HSI and solve target image-based matrices and coefficient matrices through inter-image correlation properties before fusing them into target images. Matrix decomposition is where three-dimensional cubes are stretched into two-dimensional matrices, assuming that the target image can be decomposed into the product of two matrices; this process usually uses linear spectral unmixing or SR modeling. Coupled Nonnegative Matrix Factorization (CNMF) [79] obtained high-resolution abundance and endmember spectra by alternately using non-negative matrix factorization for input images in order to fuse them as target images; building upon this idea, Dong et al. [80] proposed non-negative dictionary learning strategies which jointly solved dictionaries containing spectral information with sparse coefficients to obtain target images.

The method, based on tensor representation, regards the original data as a third-order tensor, retaining the original data arrangement of the cube. Therefore, it has received widespread attention in the field of image fusion in recent years. The Tucker decomposition assumes that the target HSI can be decomposed into a core tensor and three matrices. Li et al. assumed that the target HSI can be sparsely represented under three tensor dictionaries and used an alternating optimization strategy to solve four parameters [81]. Based on this, multiple methods have been improved upon it. For example, Wan et al. considered non-local spatial self-similarity and dictionary non-negativity constraints [82], Xu et al. [83] recovered the spatial and spectral smoothness of images by introducing total variation regularization term and Laplacian regularization term, respectively, while Wang et al. also took into account characteristics such as low-rank spectra and non-local self-similarity [84].

Although tensor-decomposition-based fusion methods can mine spatial–spectral low-rank characteristics of hyperspectral imaging effectively, their time complexity is typically high; furthermore, as more prior regularization terms are included in models, there may be significant impacts on other data's generalizability.

1.3.4 Deep-learning-based Methods

Deep-learning-based approaches have been widely applied in remote-sensing fields due to their powerful feature extraction and characterization capabilities. High-spatial-resolution HSI spatial–spectral fusion methods mainly include supervised learning- and unsupervised learning-based approaches.

Supervised learning methods are divided into two stages: training and testing. In the training stage, a large number of low spatial resolution high spectral datasets and high spatial resolution multispectral datasets are generated by using spatial and spectral downsampling on the reference HSI. The generated data is used as network input to construct the mapping relationship to the reference image. In the testing stage, the mapping relationship is applied to test data to achieve super-resolution fusion of new data. CNNs have been widely used in high/multispectral image super-resolution fusion due to their excellent feature extraction capabilities.

We can divide supervised methods into three types: single-stream networks, multistream networks, and hybrid networks. Single-stream methods often concatenate upsampled hyperspectral data with multispectral data into a new three-dimensional cube for learning in the network. Palsson et al. [85] used 3D convolutional networks and residual networks to learn mapping functions; Han et al. [86] used skip connections for deep mining of multispectral spatial information. However, single-stream methods ignore differences between two types of data which makes it difficult to effectively extract features from different modalities of data, while multistream methods use different sub-networks to extract information from both types of data separately before fusing them together at later stages. Xu et al. [87] first learnt features at different scales for multispectral images before fusing them with corresponding scale HSIs; Yang et al. used two sub-networks that extract features on spatial and spectral dimensions before reconstructing target images pixel by pixel [88]. Spatial and spectral attention mechanisms have also been introduced into high/multispectral image super-resolution fusion field for better feature correction [89]. Additionally, in recent years there have been papers proposing combining traditional methods with deep models in order to solve problems related to poor interpretability of deep learning methods. For example, Sun et al. combined deep models with detail injection models to achieve spatial resolution enhancement by separately learning missing detail components and high-resolution intensity components [90].

Compared with supervised learning methods, unsupervised learning methods do not require the construction of a large training set to learn the mapping relationship between input images and reference images. Only one pair of LR-HSI and HR-MSI can be used to reconstruct the target HR-HSI. The reference image in the figure refers to the already-available high/multispectral image pairs. We divide this type of method into two categories: encoding–decoding method and generation–constraint method.

The encoding–decoding method introduces linear spectral unmixing ideas into deep learning, using AEs to learn abundance and endmembers for reconstructing target images. Qu et al. [91] assumed that the abundance of input images follows a Dirichlet distribution so that it satisfies a constraint where all abundances sum up to one, but this method assumes prior knowledge about spectral response functions. Based on this assumption, HyCoNet [92] achieved adaptive learning for degradation models without relying on prior knowledge about degradation functions. Furthermore, Yao et al. [93] introduced cross-modal attention mechanisms to efficiently utilize information between multispectral and hyperspectral data. Wang et al. [94] proposed a variational probabilistic AE framework composed of CNNs with three sub-networks that can be jointly trained for reconstructing spatial information. Subsequently, Qu et al. and Zheng et al. [95, 96] proposed a unified framework for image registration and fusion which achieves high-quality reconstruction for unregistered input images.

The generation–constraint approach utilizes a powerful generative network with strong feature extraction capabilities to reconstruct the input image into the target image under the constraints of external information and degraded models. The input image can be an existing multispectral or random noise image or even a preprocessed initial image. For example, Fu et al. [97] used a specially designed network structure to selectively or learn spectral responses to assist in generating target images from multispectral inputs. Li et al. [98] introduced a three-stage training strategy to achieve adaptive learning of degenerate functions.

In recent years, significant progress has been made in the field of hyperspectral remote-sensing image super-resolution due to the continuous development of related theories. This has resulted in a substantial improvement in reconstruction quality both spatially and spectrally. With the impetus of artificial intelligence technology, earth observation platforms, and related application demands, it is expected that this field will continue to flourish in the future.

1.4 Unmixing

1.4.1 Linear Unmixing

Spectral unmixing is a useful technique of hyperspectral imagery exploration, which explores precise information extraction from the subpixel perspective. To deal with mixed pixels, many algorithms have been proposed for spectral unmixing by separating the pixel spectra into a collection of endmember spectra, and a set of abundance fractions. As the general and prevalent unmixing benchmark, the linear spectral mixing model (LSMM) assumes the existence of pure pixels in the hyperspectral scene where physical interactions between the light scattered by different materials are directly received by the sensor. However, LSMM usually relies on the specific distribution of simplex architecture to guarantee sufficiently scattered characteristics, which may not be satisfied in reality due to the effect of endmember variability and nonlinear interactions. Based on the existing research work, this project presents a novel geometric unmixing model, namely the affine simplicial cone (ASC) model, to fully capture the local geometric features of hyperspectral imagery and alleviate the error propagation between turbulent endmembers from a geometric view. In addition, with great advances in computer technology, neural networks have become popular and emerging tools for spectral unmixing, which provides an intelligent and automatic way for the joint extraction of endmembers and corresponding abundances. This project develops a robust deep autoencoder network (DAEN) for spectral unmixing, including stacked autoencoder (SAE) for initialization and a variational autoencoder (VAE) for non-negative matrix factorization, which effectively addresses the presence of outliers in hyperspectral data and enhances unmixing accuracy compared with state-of-the-art approaches. The peculiarity of the proposed ASC and DAEN will be investigated and substantiated via experiments with both simulated and real hyperspectral datasets in the following sections.

1.4.2 Nonlinear Unmixing

The linear spectral mixture model assumes that the endmember signatures interact linearly with the incident radiation at a subpixel level. Nevertheless, the linear model is a rough assumption that may not hold in practice [99]. Conversely, nonlinear mixture models consider and characterize the interactions between the sunlight scattered by multiple materials, being at an intimate or multilayered levels [100].

For the intimate level, the interactions consist of photons emitted from molecules of one material absorbed by molecules of another material, in turn emitting more photons. Generally, the models that assume intimate mixtures are more faithful to the imaging mechanism of the instrument. However, these models are strongly sensitive to some inherent parameters, which are often determined by the knowledge of the geometric positioning of the sensor [101]. The dependence upon external parameters brings great difficulties when implementing the inversion. For multilayered level, the corresponding models hold that multiple interactions among the scatterers are at different layers, leading to an infinite sequence of powers of products of reflectance. In form, the multilayered level model can be regarded as a combination of the LMM and additional high-order terms, where high-order scattering is negligibly weak [101].

Unfortunately, most nonlinear mixture models are too complex and difficult to exploit in real scenarios because they require detailed knowledge about the physical interactions between the sunlight scattered by multiple materials [102]. To facilitate the application, bilinear mixture models have been proposed and used more commonly in practice. These bilinear mixture models consider the second-order scattering of photons between two materials. Although high-order scattering is neglected, bilinear mixture models can provide very good approximations of the sunlight scattering mechanism in real scenarios [99]. Bilinear mixture models can formulize as a combination of linear and bilinear terms, where the linear components explain endmembers and abundances, and bilinear components (or nonlinear components) reflect the second-order scattering interactions [101]. Besides obtaining endmembers and abundances, nonlinear-mixture-based unmixing approaches generally estimate the impact of the scattering interactions. The related traditional approaches include the generalized bilinear model (GBM) unmixing [103], semi-non-negative matrix factorization (semi-NMF) [104], or robust NMF (rNMF) [105].

Recently, the development of deep learning has facilitated advances in nonlinear unmixing, which brings many new nonlinear unmixing methods, such as nonlinear unmixing via DAENs [106], plug-and-play prior [107], deep AEs with multitask learning for bilinear unmixing [108], LSTM-DNN-based AE network [109], additive 3-D-CNN AE network [110], unsupervised nonlinear AEs [111], endmember-guided unmixing network (EGU-Net) [112], intimate mixtures using Hapke model, and CNN [113], and graph regularized multilinear mixing model [114]. Deep-learning-based nonlinear unmixing methods have significantly improved the accuracy and performance of unmixing, indicating that deep learning will continue to play an essential role in subpixel interpretation.

1.5 Classification

1.5.1 Classical Machine Learning

The syncretic form of image and spectrum brings HSI more details of terrestrial objects and benefits the precision land-use and land-cover mapping [99, 115]. HSI classification (HSIC) uses a classifier to determine the class of each pixel based on its spectral and spatial features. Like remote-sensing image classification, HSIC can be divided into supervised and unsupervised models [116, 117]. Compared to unsupervised classification, supervised models have been widely studied and applied due to their advantages in accuracy and stability [118, 119]. Under the supervision mode, a series of classic classification methods have emerged in the field.

The early classic classification approach is based on the spectral curves of ground objects for recognition. These methods mainly utilize spectrum in the spectral library and use matching algorithms to identify the type of ground coverage. Classic models include matching algorithms based on the minimum distance between spectrum, spectral waveform matching, spectral encoding matching, envelope analysis, and spectral angle mapping (SAM) [120–122]. Some of these methods are sensitive to noise, while others have high requirements for spectral calibration and reflectance conversion. Some methods may even lose spectral information, so most are only suitable for rough and fast classification.

In subsequent research, another classic classification approach was gradually developed, which is based on the feature space [123]. It mainly utilizes the statistical characteristics of data to establish models. One of the classic methods is the maximum likelihood classification (MLC), which is a Bayesian statistical model estimated based on the probability distribution of samples [124]. Another classic method is the random forest classification, which is a machine learning model with tree structure developed from the decision tree algorithm [125, 126]. In addition, the SVM is also a classic model. Its main principle is to find the optimal hyperplane that can maximize the margin between boundary samples [127]. And it is suitable for classifying high-dimensional limited samples like HSI [18, 128]. With the deepening of research, based on the classic models that mainly deal with spectral features mentioned above, the spatial features and their combination have gradually become the key to improving classification. The representative one is the Markov random field (MRF) framework, which combines spectral and spatial features through the form of probability transformation to effectively improve the misclassification caused by complex spectral character [129]. However, due to the relatively independent processing of spatial and spectral features, there is still an imbalance in feature utilization in this post-processing framework.

For the purpose of classification, hyperspectral data actually contains high correlation between adjacent bands, and redundancy in both the spectral and spatial domains. Therefore, it has been demonstrated that HSI is essentially low rank and can be represented sparsely [39, 130]. In this context, the SR-based models have been introduced and rapidly promoted [131–133]. The main principle is that the sample to be classified should be determined as a class with less error when using linear representation of training samples [134, 135]. Under the constraints of different weight coefficients, classical models for processing spectral features can be divided into SR-based classification (SRC) and collaborative representation-based classification (CRC) [136, 137]. And in terms of combining and processing spatial and spectral features, such frameworks also have good scalability. Second generations of SRC have appeared in the literature [138–140]. These models are basically under a common sparsity shared framework, with spatial consistency in consideration [141, 142]. Based on the inherent group-structured property, Group Sparse Representation Classifier (GSRC) is designed to reconstruct the dictionary composed of several class-dependent sub-dictionaries such that a testing sample is represented by group atoms rather than individual ones [143, 144]. In addition to the expansion of sparsity constraints, the representation model framework is constantly evolving around three main aspects. Firstly, at the level of spectral features, a series of research work focusing on feature and sample transformation has been carried out [145, 146]. Secondly, at the level of spatial features, research work is oriented toward expanding by combining different levels of spatial information, such as nonlocal spatial similarity [147, 148]. Thirdly, at the mining level of the model mechanism, a more simplified judgment mechanism and a multilevel feature integration framework have emerged [149, 150].

1.5.2 Deep Learning

HSI classification refers to the process of classifying and identifying surface objects using hyperspectral remote-sensing image data. HSIs consist of several consecutive spectral bands, each corresponding to a narrowband frequency band, which can provide more detailed and richer spectral information than the common RGB images. These rich features, like fingerprint information of imaged objects, can realize accurate detection (pixel level) of objects. Therefore, HSI has been widely used in many fields and has achieved promising results, such as agricultural application, water quality monitoring, mineral distribution and composition analysis, natural disaster prediction, and military field. Among them, HSIC is an extremely important research direction in HSI analysis. The goal of HSIC is to classify the pixel in the image into different categories, such as water bodies, vegetation, buildings, and roads, in order to obtain a comprehensive understanding of surface features. However, the nature of high dimension of HSI and limited labeled samples bring great challenges to HSIC.

In the past decade, due to the outstanding abstract features, extraction ability of convolution neural network (CNN) has been widely studied for HSIC and has achieved promising performances. Generally, depending on the type of features utilized for classification, CNN-based classification methods are mainly grouped into three categories: (i) spectral-feature-based (pixel-wise) models [151], (ii) spatial-feature-based (patch-wise) models [152], (iii) models based on spectral–spatial feature-based (cube-wise) models [153]. Among them, the limited labeled samples make it difficult for CNN to give full play to the performance when only spectral features are utilized [154]. Furthermore, the intraclass variability of spectral features will lead to a large amount of salt and pepper noise in the classification results [155]. For methods employing spatial features, the spatial neighborhood information of the pixels to be classified is used as the input of the model [156]. Due to the introduction of neighborhood information, CNN-based models can obtain more training data to a certain extent to improve classification performance. Furthermore, the assumption of consistent neighborhood pixel categories makes the model more robust in the classification process and alleviates the noise problem in the spectral-feature-based models. Accordingly, to obtain more realistic classification results, the comprehensive exploitation of spectral and spatial features for HSIC has been widely studied in recent years [157].

There are three main ideas of spectral–spatial feature extraction based on CNN. The first category methods employ 3D convolution kernels directly to extract spectral–spatial features simultaneously. For instance, Chen et al. constructed the model of spectral–spatial joint extraction by 3D convolutional filters [158]. However, the joint spectral–spatial feature extraction using 3D convolution kernels brings more training parameters.

Accordingly, the second kind of feature extraction methods by extracting spectral and spatial features hierarchically is introduced. For example, using the structural flexibility of the 3D convolutional kernel, a spectral–spatial residual network (SSRN) was designed to extract spectral features first and then spatial features subsequently [159]. Meanwhile, HybridSN was constructed to mine spectral and spatial features hierarchically in a lighter way by mixing 3D and 2D convolution operations [160]. Although the above- mentioned sequential feature extraction idea reduces the model parameters while ensuring the classification effect, these methods will destroy the original characteristic of the later extracted information (spatial or spectral).

Recently, methods of extracting spectral and spatial features separately and then fusing them for classification have been widely studied. For instance, the classification performance in the case of limited training samples is improved by constructing a two-branch deep CNN for spectral and spatial feature extraction [161]. Subsequently, the dual-channel spectral–spatial fusion capsule generative adversarial network (DcCapsGAN) was proposed to improve classification performance by generating pseudo-samples while extracting features in parallel [162]. In terms of the practical performance of the methods described above, parallel extraction of spectral features and spatial features can obtain promising classification performance.

1.6 Target Detection

1.6.1 Anomaly Detection

In contrast to the hyperspectral target detection task, hyperspectral anomaly detection can identify anomalous objects deviating from the background distribution in the scene without using any prior information. This technology has high application value and has been extensively applied to various civil and military fields. There is no clear definition of anomalous targets, and, in general, anomalies are considered to have the following characteristics: (i) anomalous targets are significantly different from the surrounding background objects at both spatial and spectral levels; (ii) the proportion of anomalous pixels in the whole image is relatively small; and (iii) the occurrence probability of anomalous targets is also low. It has been a key challenge for researchers in this field to separate anomalies from the background using only the intrinsic information of HSIs. Meanwhile, a plethora of anomaly detection algorithms equipped with diverse design ideas have been proposed. The existing methods are mainly divided into two categories: traditional machine-learning-based and deep-learning-based methods.

Among all the traditional methods, the core idea of the statistical-model-based approaches is to construct the background model using the global or local information of the image, and those pixels that are far from the background distribution are deemed as anomalous targets. As a benchmark method for hyperspectral anomaly detection, the Reed-Xiaoli (RX) detector takes the background modeling as a multivariate Gaussian distribution [163]. It utilizes the Mahalanobis distance between the testing pixel and the estimated background to detect potential anomalies. The global-RX version and the local-RX version are derived by estimating the background from the whole information of the image or the neighborhood information of the pixel to be measured [164]. To improve the separability of the background and anomalies in HSIs, various techniques have been introduced, such as density peak clustering [165, 166], spectral–spatial graph theory [167], quaternion frequency domain [168], and quantum domain [169] analysis. These methods enhance the capability of models to recognize anomalies from different viewpoints. Subsequently, compressed sensing theory has also attracted considerable attention. The representation-based methods mainly reconstruct each pixel using a constructed dictionary and apply the reconstruction residual to indicate the anomaly degree of each pixel. Such methods are mainly subdivided into SR, collaborative representation, and low-rank representation. In particular, the methods based on SR assume that background samples can be linearly represented by a small number of atoms from an overcomplete background dictionary, while anomalous samples cannot [170]. The collaborative representation, in contrast, emphasizes the collaboration among dictionary atoms. Therefore, this approach holds that normal background pixels can be linearly represented by all atoms from the background dictionary, but anomalous pixels cannot [135, 171, 172]. The reconstruction residuals also serve as the anomalous values of the testing pixels. The low-rank representation describes the global structure of the data, and the HSIs can be decomposed into low-rank background components and sparse anomaly components. Hence, many matrix decomposition and tensor decomposition methods are presented to identify anomalies in images [173].

Deep learning has been extensively employed in the hyperspectral anomaly detection field due to its powerful feature mining and nonlinear fitting capability. Deep-learning-based approaches typically use AEs or GANs to learn deep background characteristics in HSIs, so that a favorable background reconstruction model can be built [174]. The models imposing various constraints enable learning the background distribution in the image, enhancing the representation of the background features. Moreover, the ability of networks to fit anomalies is relatively weak owing to the low percentage of anomalous pixels in the HSI, which causes the reconstruction error of anomalous targets to be higher than that of the background. Eventually, the reconstruction error is taken for measuring the anomaly level of each pixel. Recently, weakly supervised learning technology has been introduced into this field, and such methods require a prior screening of coarse background samples from the HSI and treating them as training samples for the network, aiming to strengthen the background learning ability of the model [175, 176]. Very recently, the self-supervised learning-based blind-spot reconstruction network enables the model to reconstruct each pixel using only its neighbors by designing blind spots in the center of the receptive field (the network is unable to see the information of the central pixel) [177]. Since anomalous pixels are significantly different from the surrounding background, they have larger reconstruction errors, which contribute to detecting potential anomalies from HSIs.

1.6.2 Spectral Match

With the availability of the prior information of target, target detection aims to locate objects of interest within a specific scene [178, 179]. As one of the most active topics in hyperspectral remote-sensing, target detection has been widely used and has exerted its unique advantages in a variety of military and civilian fields, such as exposing camouflage, identifying small targets, and determining the category of land cover [180]. For practical considerations, it is necessary to develop target detection methods suitable for HSIs to meet the performance requirements of low false-alarm rate, high detection rate, and robustness [181, 182].

Since the 1990s, scholars have applied signal processing theories to HSI processing and established a basic design framework for target detection in HSIs. The general processing flow of such traditional methods is to derive a decision function through specific model assumptions and decision criteria, and then to substitute testing pixels into the function to obtain the detection output for determining the existence of the target [183]. The effectiveness of the detectors designed according to this flow as well as its variations has been proven. The probability statistics (white-space) model and the subspace projection model are the most classic and important model assumptions in the field of signal processing [184, 185]. Algorithms developed based on such models have shown stable detection effects in many cases. Constrained energy minimization (CEM) is one of the most widely used detectors derived from a linearly constrained minimum-variance beamformer in digital signal processing [186]. It extracts target signals in a specific direction by suppressing background signals in other directions using the Fisher linear discriminant criterion [187, 188]. It is worth noting that a series of derivative versions developed based on CEM, such as sparse CEM (SparseCEM) [189], hierarchical CEM (hCEM) [190], ensemble-based CEM (E-CEM) [191], transform domain adaptive CEM (FACEM) [192], have been widely used and manifested stable performance. The generalized likelihood ratio test (GLRT) depends on the assumptions of the conditional probability distribution for the target and the background. Its detection performance has the properties of high signal-to-noise ratio (SNR) and constant false-alarm rate (CFAR), which makes the algorithm more robust in the use of HSIs in various real scenes. There are two adaptive versions of GLRT, the adaptive coherence/cosine estimator (ACE) and the adaptive matched filter (AMF). Their decision functions are derived using the correlation or covariance matrix of the given HSI [193]. The orthogonal subspace projection (OSP) and its derivative algorithms use mathematical projection operators to project the testing pixels into the orthogonal subspace of the background to highlight the target and eliminate interference [194]. In general, traditional signal-processing-based target detection has established a mature theoretical system and various algorithms.

Over the last few decades, the rapid development of machine learning has inspired a new surge of activities in hyperspectral target detection. Although it is quite challenging to learn from and apply machine learning on the basis of existing theoretical systems to adapt to target detection for HSIs in various scenes with complexity, machine-learning-based methods stand out for their ability to tap into the wealth of detailed information contained in HSI data. Several machine-learning-based techniques have gained significant attention, including SR, kernel methods, discriminative subspace analysis, self-learning of spectral data, manifold learning, tensor decomposition, and deep learning. Recently, a great number of machine-learning-based methods have emerged in the field of hyperspectral target detection and achieved impressive performance. For example, representation-based methods, such as sparse representation-based detector (SRD) [195], combined sparse and collaborative representation-based detector (CSCR) [196], sparse and low-rank matrix decomposition (SLRMD) [197], adaptive iterated shrinkage thresholding method (AISTM) [198], and weighted Cauchy distance graph and local adaptive collaborative representation-based detector (CGCRD) [199], achieve a more accurate separation by constructing various forms of target or background dictionaries to represent testing pixels.

In addition, deep learning has grown significantly as an important branch of machine learning. The massive amount of algorithms derived from CNN [200], AE [201], deep belief network (DBN) [202], and GAN [176] continue to drive the development of high-precision detection. So far, the tremendous amount of research on data-driven training networks have gradually revealed the great potential of deep learning in the field of hyperspectral target detection. Particularly, there are a series of methods based on background learning models to overcome the insufficiency of target samples and accurately estimate the background distribution, achieving higher detection accuracy [203]. The migration of machine learning theories in hyperspectral target detection has yielded various representative algorithms with excellent performance, exhibiting strong parsing ability for real data with complexity.

In summary, the research on target detection for HSIs tackles core technical difficulties, trying to find a simple, straightforward, and effective way to measure the spectral differences between different classes of land cover to solve the problem of highlighting the target and suppressing the background. Such issues provide a wide space for the migration of methods from various fields. Besides, all the existing methods focus on different application problems and satisfy different usage requirements, which also helps to inspire more thinking modes and problem-solving viewpoints.

1.7 Change Detection

Change detection (CD) in remote sensing denotes the large-scale land surface change information by analyzing two or more images taken at different times, and is a powerful means in remote sensing to reveal ecological and human activities on the land surface. With the growing amount of available remote-sensing data and the development of remote-sensing sensors, CD has attracted growing research, and is becoming more important for a great number of fields and applications, such as land-use and land-cover monitoring, disaster prevention and post-damage analysis, ecological monitoring, precision agriculture, and ice-melt assessment. The spectral information of HSIs can fully reflect the differences in physical structure and chemical composition within the sample. Hyperspectral image change detection (HSI-CD) can uniquely separate more subtle and varied changes. Thus, CD in hyperspectral remote-sensing images is a rapidly evolving area of interest. However, HSI also brings with it the disadvantage of high data dimension, redundant information, and accurate data preprocessing, which makes change analysis more complex and challenging.

In recent years, a multitude of methodologies have been developed in HSI-CD. In terms of algorithm development, HSI-CD can be divided into algebraic operation based, transformation based, classification comparison based, and deep learning based. Algebraic operation methods are used to extract change information by algebraically calculating the changes of spectral features in the corresponding wavebands of multitemporal images. The main methods include image difference, image ratio, image log ratio, absolute average difference (AAD), Euclidean distance (ED), vector angle (VA), and change vector analysis (CVA) [204]. Despite being a classic and easy to use, a major problem with the performance of algebraic operation methods is the dependence on threshold settings. The image transformation methods explore more representative feature information by re-selecting and combining bands or projection transformations of images, which improve the accuracy and efficiency of CD. The main methods include multivariate alteration detection (MAD), iteratively reweighted MAD (IR-MAD), differential principal component analysis (DPCA), and iterative slow feature analysis (ISFA) [205]. Classification comparison methods, such as post classification comparison (PCC) and compound classification, usually consist of two steps. The first step is to select samples and classify features of multitemporal images separately. The second step is to get detailed information on changes in features by comparing classification maps. Although PCC methods enrich the "from–to" land-cover change information, these methods have the effect of error accumulation and often ignore the correlation between bitemporal HSIs, resulting in unsatisfactory results. While the compound classification methods improve the correlation of bitemporal images, they are highly demanding on the training samples. Deep learning is a stronger feature extraction algorithm than traditional machine learning in most vision tasks. There have been many well-recognized works on deep-learning-based HSI-CD, such as CNNs, 3-D CNNs, AEs, recurrent neural networks (RNNs), graph convolutional networks (GCNs), GANs, and transformers, and they have achieved good performance [206].

For different CD application purposes, HSI-CD methods can be divided into three categories: binary, multiclass, and time-series CD [207]. Binary CD only divides images into changed class and unchanged class, and does not pay attention to what changes. It is the most typical and popular method in HSI-CD. Due to the spectral properties of HSIs, many methods of comparing spectral information have been proposed, such as CVA and spectral information divergence. For the high dimensionality and redundancy of HSIs, a number of transform-based methods have also been devised for the compression and highlighting of HSI changes. Many extensions and iterations of MAD have been proposed and applied in practice.

Multiclass CD focuses on the type of change, such as a house flattening and a flat house being different classes. Bovolo proposed the compressed change vector analysis (C2VA), which is an improved model of CVA [208]. This method provides a two-dimensional change representation to solve the problem of multiple CD. Compared with binary CD, multiclass CD methods are more challenging and lack comprehensive multitemporal ground reference data. Therefore, to adapt to multiclass CD task, many unsupervised and semi-supervised methods based on C2VA are proposed to solve the problem of complex structure of HSIs and lack of training samples [3]. The idea of unmixing has also been introduced to CD, taking into account the characteristics of mixed pixels in HSIs. Analyzing the changes of endmembers and abundances, sparse unmixing methods demonstrate advantages in HSI-CD [209].

Time series CD is to discover the change law of objects through remote-sensing images of the same area at multiple times, and realize the rapid positioning of changing areas in large-scale time series images. The construction of long time series for change analysis is important for the observation of subtle changes in the land surface. There are some time series CD algorithms, such as 3-D spectral modeling and multilinear algebra. The methods of modeling temporal changes of features are well suited to modeling surface changes associated with seasonal variations. More methods combining hyperspectral spectral features in abundance have also been proposed, effectively addressing the complexity of multiple time tasks.

In conclusion, HSI-CD is widely used and is becoming increasingly important in remote-sensing applications. There are different HSI-CD methods for different tasks. This book will introduce the classic HSI-CD algorithm in detail.

1.8 Experimental Datasets

1.8.1 Chikusei Data, Houston Data, and GF-YR Data

The Chikusei data contains HSIs of Chikusei, Ibaraki, Japan, acquired by the Hyperspec-VNIR-CIRIS spectrometer. With a ground sampling distance (GSD) of 2.5 m, the image size is 2517 × 2335 pixels. Chikusei contains a total of 512 bands, and there are 128 bands in the spectral range from 363 to 1018 nm. The dataset collected ground truth for 19 categories. In the experiment, we cropped the Chikusei HS image to a size of 1290 × 1508, and 16 categories are contained in the cropped image. The original HSI is displayed as bands 64, 42, and 23 for channels R, G, and B, respectively.

The Houston 2013 data were released by the IEEE GRSS Data Fusion Contest (DFC) in 2013, which was acquired by the ITRES CASI-1500 sensor at the Houston University campus and nearby area. The LR-HSI and the HR-MSI were obtained from spatial and spectral down-sampling of the raw Houston data, respectively. The raw image data size is 349 × 1905 with a total of 144 bands, covering the spectral range of 364–1046 nm.

The HS and MS data of GF-YR were acquired by GF-5 and GF-1 satellites, respectively. We obtained the GF-5 hyperspectral and labeling data from the First Marine Institute, Department of Natural Resources, which was acquired over the Yellow River Delta National Nature Reserve in China. A 16-m multispectral camera carried by GF-1 can provide MS data with four bands at the ranges of 450–520, 520–590, 630–690, and 770–890 nm. The full-band spectral imager on GF-5 produces imaging data with a spatial resolution of 30 m. And imaging spectrum spans a range of 400–2500 nm, encompassing a total of 330 bands. Notably, the spectral resolution of the visible band can achieve 5 nm. After preprocessing the data to eliminate defective bands, the image retains 295 bands for analysis.

1.8.2 Washington DC Mall, the University of Houston Data, Indian Pines, and Pavia Data

The first simulated dataset (i.e., Washington DC Mall) was widely used in HSI analysis. It was acquired by the HYDICE sensor in 1995 in Washington DC, United States. This full Washington DC Mall image has a region of 1280 × 307 pixels, and the spatial resolution is 3 m. The image consists of 210 bands, and spectral wavelength is ranging from 0.4 to 2.5 μm. After removing the low SNRs and atmospheric absorption bands, 191 bands were kept. The subregion consisting of 304 × 304 × 191 pixels was clipped from the full dataset as a reference HR-HSI.

The second dataset (i.e., Indian Pines) was acquired by the airborne visible/infrared imaging spectrometer (AVIRIS) sensor over the Indian Pines test site in Northwestern Indiana. The image has 224 spectral bands with the size of 145 × 145 pixels, and the spectral wavelength range is from 0.4 to 2.5 μm. After removing bands caused by water vapor absorption and low SNRs, the subregion consisting of 144 × 144 × 191 pixels was chosen from the full dataset as a reference HR-HSI.

The third dataset is University of Houston data, which was used in the 2018 IEEE Geoscience and Remote Sensing Society (GRSS) Data Fusion Contest. The image contains 601 × 2384 pixels and 48 bands ranging from 0.38 to 1.05 μm. The subimage consisting of 320 × 320 × 46 pixels was chosen from the whole dataset as a reference HR-HSI for our experiments.

The fourth Pavia University data was collected by the reflective optics system imaging spectrometer (ROSIS-3) optical airborne sensor. This image contains 115 bands and with the size of 610 × 340 × 115. After removing bands caused by water vapor absorption and low SNRs, the subregion consisting of 304 × 304 × 191 pixels was clipped from the full dataset as a reference HR-HSI in this study.

1.8.3 ARAH HS Dataset and Houston University Dataset

The ARAH HS dataset consists of 480 pairs of HSIs and MSIs (i.e., RGB images), which were distributed in the NTIRE 2020 Spectral Recovery Challenge. All images have the same spatial size of 512 × 482 and their spectral coverage ranges from 400 to 700 nm, where all HSIs contain 31 spectral bands. In the challenge, 480 pairs of images are selected for training, and the rest are used for validation. Next, the red and blue bands of all MSI are interchanged in the RARAH data to construct the VARAH dataset.

The Houston University dataset was distributed in the 2018 IEEE GRSS Data Fusion Contest consisting of an HSI and an MSI (i.e., RGB image). The HSI and the MSI are aligned, covering Houston University campus and its neighborhood. The HSI with a GSD of 1 m has a spatial size of 1202 × 4172 and contains 50 spectral bands ranging from 380 to 1050 nm. The original MSI with a GSD of 0.05 m has a spatial size of 24,040 × 83,440 and is downsampled to a spatial size of 1202 × 4172 for matching the HSI.

1.8.4 Indian Pines Dataset

Indian Pines dataset was acquired by the AVIRIS instrument over the agricultural area of Northwestern Indiana in 1992, which has a spatial dimension of 145 × 145 and 224 spectral bands. The spatial resolution of the data is 20 m per pixel. Due to atmospheric absorption, 4 zero bands and 35 lower SNR bands are discarded, and 185 channels are preserved. The ground truth contains 10,366 labeled pixels and 16 ground-truth classes.

1.8.5 Botswana Dataset

Hyperspectral dataset Botswana was acquired by the NASA EO-1 satellite over the Okavango Delta, Botswana, in 2001–2004. The spatial resolution of data is 30 m per pixel. The spatial and spectral dimensions are 1476 × 256 and 242. After removing the uncalibrated and noisy bands associated with water absorption features, the remaining 145 bands are reserved for analysis. The dataset contains 14 ground-truth classes and 3248 labeled samples.

1.8.6 University of Pavia Dataset

The PU image was acquired by ROSIS sensor over the University of Pavia in northwestern Italy. It has 610 × 340 pixels with spatial resolution of 1.3 m and 115 bands covering the spectral wavelength range from 0.43 to 0.86. After removing the 12 noisy bands, the other 103 high SNR bands were retained for experiments. Furthermore, it contains 42,776 labeled pixels and can be divided into nine ground-truth classes.

1.8.7 Center of Pavia Dataset

The PC image was captured by the ROSIS sensor over Pavia City in northern Italy. It has 1096 × 1096 pixels with a spatial resolution of 1.3 m and 115 spectral bands covering from 400 to 1000 nm. After removing a black region of 1096 × 381 pixels and 13 noise-affected bands, the remaining region becomes a two-part image with 102 spectral bands, and the right part of 1096 × 492 pixels is used for our experiments. There are nine land-cover classes and 103,539 labeled pixels within this image.

1.8.8 Salinas Dataset

The third dataset is SA, which was captured by the AVIRIS spectral sensor at SA Valley in California. It contains 224 bands and 512 × 217 pixels with spatial resolution of 3.7 m. Similar to the IP dataset, 20 water absorption attenuation bands were removed, and the remaining 204 spectral bands with wavelength coverage range from 0.36 to 2.5 μm. In addition, 16 land-cover types with 54,129 annotated pixels are available in the SA dataset.

1.8.9 Houston Dataset

The Houston dataset consists of Houston 2013 (called SD) and Houston 2018 (called TD). The former includes 349 × 1905 pixels and 144 spectral bands. The latter includes 209 × 955 pixels and 48 spectral bands. These datasets were captured using different sensors and at different acquisition times in Houston, TX, United States. To align with the Houston 2018 dataset, we selected an overlapping region of 209 × 955 pixels from the Houston 2013 dataset and extracted 48 spectral bands from it.

1.8.10 Washington DC Mall Dataset

The image totally consists of 280 × 307 pixels, with a spatial resolution of 3 m per pixel. The original image contains 210 spectral bands, with the spectral coverage ranging from 0.4 to 2.5 μm. In practice, 191 bands are preserved, while the spectral bands ranging from 0.9 to 1.4 μm are removed due to the atmospheric absorption. The reference of this image includes six classes of interests, with a total of 10,190 labeled samples.

1.8.11 Hyperspectral Mapper (HyMap)

The data is acquired from the Rochester Institute of Technology Hyperspectral Target Detection Blind Test website. The HyMap data has 126 bands covering the wavelength range of 0.45–2.5 μm, with a spatial size of 280 × 800. The scene is Cooke City, Montana, United States, with three car pixels as target, which cannot be distinguished in the image with the naked eye.

1.8.12 San Diego

This dataset was acquired by the AVIRIS covering the area of San Diego in the spectral range of 370~2510 nm with a spatial resolution of 3.5 m. The water absorption and low SNR bands are removed from the original 224 spectral channels, and 189 bands are reserved for experiments. The full image contains 400 × 400 pixels. The AVIRIS-1 is a cropped sub-image containing 100 × 100 pixels. Three planes occupying 20, 22, and 22 pixels are regarded as anomalies. The AVIRIS-2 dataset is also cropped from the above-mentioned full AVIRIS image. Its spatial size is 128 × 128 and contains 189 bands. In this sub-image, three planes occupying 34, 42, and 44 pixels are regarded as anomalies.

1.8.13 BIT-HSI-I

The prior target spectrum is obtained from the close-range camouflage car spectrum of the corresponding scene collected in advance. Here, a center pixel spectrum is chosen as the prior. The dataset was acquired using the Dualix spectral imager GaiaSkymini2 on the campus of the Beijing Institute of Technology (BIT). The spectral range is 400–1000 nm, and the spectral resolution is 3.5 nm. The spatial resolution at a distance of 500 m is 0.14 m. The collected target is a camouflage vehicle model. The backgrounds are wet grassland, dry grassland, shaded grassland, and leaf ground.

1.8.14 Airport-Beach-Urban (ABU)

This dataset includes airport, beach, and urban scenes. Each image is a 100 × 100 pixel section from larger images on the AVIRIS website. Anomalies are manually labeled using Environment for Visualizing Images (ENVI) software. Airport images were taken in Los Angeles and Gulfport, with resolutions of 7.1 and 3.4 m per pixel, respectively. Beach images were captured in various locations, with resolutions ranging from 1.3 to 17.2 m per pixel. Urban images, from Texas Coast, Gainesville, and Los Angeles, have resolutions between 3.5 and 17.2 m per pixel. All images were captured by AVIRIS, except Beach (4) by the ROSIS-03 sensor.

1.8.15 Viareggio

This dataset was collected during the "Viareggio 2013 trial" hyperspectral data collection campaign, in Viareggio, Italy. It has a size of 375 × 450 pixels with a 0.6-m spatial resolution and contains 511 spectral bands with a 2.3-nm spectral resolution. In the scene, three vehicles, four panels, and two reference calibration tarps with 135 anomalous pixels are labeled anomalies.

1.8.16 Umatilla

This dataset consisted of a pair of real bitemporal hyperspectral remote-sensing images acquired by the Hyperion sensor mounted on the EO-1 satellite on 1 May, 2004 ($\mathbf{X}_1$) and 8 May, 2007 ($\mathbf{X}_2$). The study area is an agricultural land of Hermiston city in Umatilla County, Oregon, United States. The selected area, which has a size of 180 × 225 pixels, is a subset of the original whole image. The original images contain 242 spectral channels, whose wavelength range is from 350 to 2580 nm. The images are characterized by a spectral resolution of 10 nm and a spatial resolution of 30 m. After the pre-processing phase (e.g., uncalibrated and noisiest bands removal, bad stripes repairing, atmospheric corrections, and co-registration), 159 pre-processed bands (i.e., bands 8–57, 82–119, 131–164, 182–184, 187–220) were used for testing the proposed CD approach.

The dataset is available for download from the following website: https://github.com/SicongLiuRS/Hyperspectral-Change-Detection-dataset-Irrigated-Agricultural-Area.

1.8.17 Yancheng

This dataset is made up of a pair of real bitemporal hyperspectral EO-1 Hyperion remote-sensing images acquired over a wetland agricultural land in Yancheng, Jiangsu Province, China. Images were acquired on 3 May, 2006 ($\mathbf{X}_1$) and 23 April, 2007 ($\mathbf{X}_2$), respectively. A subset of the original images is selected with a size of 430×220 pixels. The original Hyperion images contain 242 bands ranging from 350 to 2580 nm, characterized by a spectral resolution of 10 nm and a spatial resolution of 30 m. Pre-processing was applied on the original images including uncalibrated and noisiest bands removal, bad stripes repairing, atmospheric correction, and image co-registration, with a residual error of 0.5 pixel. After removing the low SNR bands, 128 pre-processed bands (i.e., 13–53, 85–96, 103–118, 135–164, 188–199, and 202–218) were used in the experiments. The dataset is available for download from the following website: https://github.com/SicongLiuRS/Hyperspectral-Change-Detection-dataset-Wetland-Area.

1.9 Chapter Arrangement and Writing Purpose

Since the 1980s, HSI has become an emerging technique in various tasks due to its strong ability to identify different materials in the spectral domain. The success of HSI analysis largely depends on the rapid development of machine learning methodologies, which has provided an effective tool for analyzing the 3D spatial–spectral data cube. For future work in the HSI analysis community, it is believed that the machine-learning-based approaches will play a more significant role with their enormous potential for many aspects of HSI applications. During the last several years, the publications in the HSI area have covered the rapid advances of machine-learning-based HSI analysis. Apart from those journal and conference publications, textbooks still play an important role in reviewing the recent advances and pointing out the future direction of HSI analysis. The detailed chapter arrangement will be given as follows.

Part I of this book focuses more on the denoising and super-resolution work in the HSI area, which includes Chapters 2 to 8. In these chapters, the state-of-the-art hyperspectral denoising and super-resolution methods have been carefully reviewed and summarized. For the hyperspectral denoising methods, low-rank-based methods have been given to fully investigate the data property of HSI. As for the hyperspectral super-resolution methods, both supervised and unsupervised methods have been given to improve the spatial and spectral characteristics of HSI. With the development of deep learning technique, the deep feature extraction methods have been utilized to improve the performance of hyperspectral denoising and super-resolution methods.

Part II of this book presents the hyperspectral unmixing methods in the last several years. In these chapters, the novel unmixing methods have been given in detail. In Chapter 9, non-negative matrix factorization has been utilized in unsupervised hyperspectral unmixing due to its strong ability of blind signal separation. Chapter 10 presents a hyperspectral unmixing method based on the low-rank property. Chapter 11 selects the best endmember to improve the unmixing performance. In Chapters 12 and 13, a deep-learning-based and a model-based unmixing method have been proposed, respectively.

In the third part of this book, different classification methods have been proposed for the HSI. Due to the strong ability of deep learning technique and SR, most methods have been designed based on these two machine learning strategies, which includes Chapters 14 to 20. To solve the problem of domain shift in the classification task, Chapters 15 and 16 have proposed two different domain adaption methods for hyperspectral classification task. Another trend of current classification methods is to train a model without too much samples; Chapter 20 has designed a classification method with limited samples.

The last part of this book is about the hyperspectral target and CD methods. In this part, both spectral matching and anomaly detection methods have been given for the target detection task. Chapters 21 and 22 summarize the commonly used CEM method and collaborative representation method for the spectral matching. Chapters 23 and 24 have proposed two novel deep learning methods for the anomaly detection task. In the last chapter of this part and this book, a spectral change analysis method has been presented for hyperspectral CD task.

References

1 Zhang, H., Liu, L., He, W., and Zhang, L. (2019). Hyperspectral image denoising with total variation regularization and nonlocal low-rank tensor decomposition. *IEEE Trans. Geosci. Remote Sens.* 58 (5): 3071–3084.

2 Bioucas-Dias, J.M., Plaza, A., Camps-Valls, G. et al. (2013). Hyperspectral remote sensing data analysis and future challenges. *IEEE Geosci. Remote Sens. Mag.* 1 (2): 6–36.

3 Chang, Y., Yan, L., Fang, H. et al. (2018). HSI-DeNet: hyperspectral image restoration via convolutional neural network. *IEEE Trans. Geosci. Remote Sens.* 57 (2): 667–682.

4 Rasti, B., Scheunders, P., Ghamisi, P. et al. (2018). Noise reduction in hyperspectral imagery: overview and application. *Remote Sens.* 10 (3): 482.

5 Yuan, Q., Zhang, Q., Li, J. et al. (2018). Hyperspectral image denoising employing a spatial–spectral deep residual convolutional neural network. *IEEE Trans. Geosci. Remote Sens.* 57 (2): 1205–1218.

6 Zhao, X.L., Xu, W.H., Jiang, T.X. et al. (2020). Deep plug-and-play prior for low-rank tensor completion. *Neurocomputing* 400: 137–149.

7 He, W., Yokoya, N., Yuan, L., and Zhao, Q. (2019). Remote sensing image reconstruction using tensor ring completion and total variation. *IEEE Trans. Geosci. Remote Sens.* 57 (11): 8998–9009.

8 Zhao, B., Sveinsson, J.R., Ulfarsson, M.O. et al. (2020). Hyperspectral images denoising based on mixtures of factor analyzers. *IGARSS 2020 – 2020 IEEE International Geoscience and Remote Sensing Symposium*, 1516–1519, Waikoloa, HI, USA (26 September 2020). IEEE.

9 Zhuang, L. and Ng, M.K. (2020). Hyperspectral mixed noise removal by l1-norm-based subspace representation. *IEEE J. Sel. Top. Appl. Earth Obs. Remote Sens.* 13: 1143–1157.

10 Zhao, B., Sveinsson, J.R., Ulfarsson, M.O. et al. (2020). Local spatial-spectral correlation based mixtures of factor analyzers for hyperspectral denoising. *IGARSS 2020 – 2020 IEEE International Geoscience and Remote Sensing Symposium*, 1488–1491, Waikoloa, HI, USA (26 September 2020). IEEE.

11 Wang, M., Wang, Q., Chanussot, J., and Hong, D. (2021). l_0-l_1 hybrid total variation regularization and its applications on hyperspectral image mixed noise removal and compressed sensing. *IEEE Trans. Geosci. Remote Sens.* 59: 7695–7710.

12 Maffei, A., Haut, J.M., Paoletti, M.E. et al. (2020). A single model CNN for hyperspectral image denoising. *IEEE Trans. Geosci. Remote Sens.* 58 (4): 2516–2529.

13 Buades, A., Coll, B., and Morel, J.M. (2005). A non-local algorithm for image denoising. *2005 IEEE Computer Society Conference on Computer Vision and Pattern Recognition (CVPR'05)*, 60–65, San Diego, CA, USA (20–25 June 2005). IEEE.

14 Donoho, D.L. and Johnstone, I.M. (1995). Adapting to unknown smoothness via wavelet shrinkage. *J. Am. Stat. Assoc.* 90 (432): 1200–1224.

15 Dabov, K., Foi, A., Katkovnik, V., and Egiazarian, K. (2007). Image denoising by sparse 3-D transform-domain collaborative filtering. *IEEE Trans. Image Process.* 16 (8): 2080–2095.

16 Gu, S., Zhang, L., Zuo, W. et al. (2014). Weighted nuclear norm minimization with application to image denoising. *2014 IEEE Conference on Computer Vision and Pattern Recognition*, 2862–2869, Columbus, OH, USA (23–28 June 2014). IEEE.

17 Qian, Y. and Ye, M. (2013). Hyperspectral imagery restoration using nonlocal spectral-spatial structured sparse representation with noise estimation. *IEEE J. Sel. Top. Appl. Earth Obs. Remote Sens.* 6 (2): 499–515.

18 Gao, L., Zhao, B., Jia, X. et al. (2017). Optimized kernel minimum noise fraction transformation for hyperspectral image classification. *Remote Sens.* 9 (6): 548.

19 Yuan, Q., Zhang, L., and Shen, H. (2012). Hyperspectral image denoising employing a spectral–spatial adaptive total variation model. *IEEE Trans. Geosci. Remote Sens.* 50 (10): 3660–3677.

20 Chen, S., Hu, X., and Peng, S. (2012). Hyperspectral imagery denoising using a spatial-spectral domain mixing prior. *J. Comput. Sci. Technol.* 27 (4): 851–861.

21 Huang, X., Du, B., Tao, D., and Zhang, L. (2020). Spatial-spectral weighted nuclear norm minimization for hyperspectral image denoising. *Neurocomputing* 399: 271–284.

22 Chang, S.G., Bin, Y., and Vetterli, M. (2000). Spatially adaptive wavelet thresholding with context modeling for image denoising. *IEEE Trans. Image Process.* 9 (9): 1522–1531.

23 Chen, G. and Qian, S. (2010). Denoising of hyperspectral imagery using principal component analysis and wavelet shrinkage. *IEEE Trans. Geosci. Remote Sens.* 49 (3): 973–980.

24 Othman, H. and Qian, S. (2006). Noise reduction of hyperspectral imagery using hybrid spatial-spectral derivative-domain wavelet shrinkage. *IEEE Trans. Geosci. Remote Sens.* 44 (2): 397–408.

25 Rasti, B., Sveinsson, J.R., Ulfarsson, M.O., and Benediktsson, J.A. (2013). Wavelet based hyperspectral image restoration using spatial and spectral penalties. *SPIE* 8892: 135–142.

26 Du, B., Huang, Z., Wang, N. et al. (2018). Joint weighted nuclear norm and total variation regularization for hyperspectral image denoising. *Int. J. Remote Sens.* 39 (2): 334–355.

27 Huang, Z., Li, S., Fang, L. et al. (2018). Hyperspectral image denoising with group sparse and low-rank tensor decomposition. *IEEE Access* 6: 1380–1390.

28 Xie, T., Li, S., and Sun, B. (2020). Hyperspectral images denoising via nonconvex regularized low-rank and sparse matrix decomposition. *IEEE Trans. Image Process.* 29: 44–56.

29 Chang, Y., Yan, L., Fang, H., and Liu, H. (2014). Simultaneous destriping and denoising for remote sensing images with unidirectional total variation and sparse representation. *IEEE Geosci. Remote Sens. Lett.* 11 (6): 1051–1055.

30 He, W., Yao, Q., Li, C. et al. (2020). Non-local meets global: an integrated paradigm for hyperspectral image restoration. *IEEE Trans. Pattern Anal. Mach. Intell.* 44 (4): 2089–2107.

31 Zhang, Q., Yuan, Q., Li, J. et al. (2019). Hybrid noise removal in hyperspectral imagery with a spatial–spectral gradient network. *IEEE Trans. Geosci. Remote Sens.* 57 (10): 7317–7329.

32 Wang, M., Yu, J., Xue, J., and Sun, W. (2016). Denoising of hyperspectral images using group low-rank representation. *IEEE J. Sel. Top. Appl. Earth Obs. Remote Sens.* 9 (9): 4420–4427.

33 Zhang, H., He, W., Zhang, L. et al. (2013). Hyperspectral image restoration using low-rank matrix recovery. *IEEE Trans. Geosci. Remote Sens.* 52 (8): 4729–4743.

34 He, W., Zhang, H., Zhang, L., and Shen, H. (2015). Hyperspectral image denoising via noise-adjusted iterative low-rank matrix approximation. *IEEE J. Sel. Top. Appl. Earth Obs. Remote Sens.* 8 (6): 3050–3061.

35 Chen, Y., Guo, Y., Wang, Y. et al. (2017). Denoising of hyperspectral images using nonconvex low rank matrix approximation. *IEEE Trans. Geosci. Remote Sens.* 55 (9): 5366–5380.

36 Lu, T., Li, S., Fang, L. et al. (2015). Spectral–spatial adaptive sparse representation for hyperspectral image denoising. *IEEE Trans. Geosci. Remote Sens.* 54 (1): 373–385.

37 Li, J., Yuan, Q., Shen, H., and Zhang, L. (2016). Noise removal from hyperspectral image with joint spectral–spatial distributed sparse representation. *IEEE Trans. Geosci. Remote Sens.* 54 (9): 5425–5439.

38 Liu, N., Li, W., Tao, R., and Fowler, J.E. (2019). Wavelet-domain low-rank/group-sparse destriping for hyperspectral imagery. *IEEE Trans. Geosci. Remote Sens.* 57 (12): 10310–10321.

39 Zhuang, L. and Bioucas-Dias, J.M. (2018). Fast hyperspectral image denoising and inpainting based on low-rank and sparse representations. *IEEE J. Sel. Top. Appl. Earth Obs. Remote Sens.* 11 (3): 730–742.

40 Rasti, B., Ulfarsson, M.O., and Ghamisi, P. (2017). Automatic hyperspectral image restoration using sparse and low-rank modeling. *IEEE Geosci. Remote Sens. Lett.* 14 (12): 2335–2339.

41 Willett, R.M., Duarte, M.F., Davenport, M.A., and Baraniuk, R.G. (2014). Sparsity and structure in hyperspectral imaging: sensing, reconstruction, and target detection. *IEEE Signal Process. Mag.* 31 (1): 116–126.

42 Yang, J., Wright, J., Huang, T.S., and Ma, Y. (2010). Image super-resolution via sparse representation. *IEEE Trans. Image Process.* 19 (11): 2861–2873.

43 Ma, G., Huang, T.Z., Huang, J., and Zheng, C.C. (2019). Local low-rank and sparse representation for hyperspectral image denoising. *IEEE Access* 7: 79850–79865.

44 Hoyer, P.O. (2002). Non-negative sparse coding. *Proceedings of the 12th IEEE Workshop on Neural Networks for Signal Processing*, 557–565, Martigny, Switzerland (6 September 2002). IEEE.

45 Wei, W., Zhang, L., Tian, C. et al. (2017). Structured sparse coding-based hyperspectral imagery denoising with intracluster filtering. *IEEE Trans. Geosci. Remote Sens.* 55 (12): 6860–6876.

46 Cai, J., He, W., and Zhang, H. (2022). Anisotropic spatial–spectral total variation regularized double low-rank approximation for HSI denoising and destriping. *IEEE Trans. Geosci. Remote Sens.* 60: 5536619.

47 Zhao, B., Ulfarsson, M.O., Sveinsson, J.R., and Chanussot, J. (2022). Hyperspectral image denoising using spectral-spatial transform-based sparse and low-rank representations. *IEEE Trans. Geosci. Remote Sens.* 60: 1–25.

48 Rudin, L.I., Osher, S., and Fatemi, E. (1992). Nonlinear total variation based noise removal algorithms. *Phys. D: Nonlinear Phenom.* 60 (1–4): 259–268.

49 Chambolle, A. (2004). An algorithm for total variation minimization and applications. *J. Math. Imaging Vis.* 20: 89–97.

50 Aggarwal, H.K. and Majumdar, A. (2016). Hyperspectral image denoising using spatio-spectral total variation. *IEEE Geosci. Remote Sens. Lett.* 13 (3): 442–446.

51 He, W., Zhang, H., Shen, H., and Zhang, L. (2018). Hyperspectral image denoising using local low-rank matrix recovery and global spatial–spectral total variation. *IEEE J. Sel. Top. Appl. Earth Obs. Remote Sens.* 11 (3): 713–729.

52 Fan, H., Li, C., Guo, Y. et al. (2018). Spatial–spectral total variation regularized low-rank tensor decomposition for hyperspectral image denoising. *IEEE Trans. Geosci. Remote Sens.* 56 (10): 6196–6213.

53 Wang, M., Wang, Q., and Chanussot, J. (2021). Tensor low-rank constraint and l0 total variation for hyperspectral image mixed noise removal. *IEEE J. Sel. Top. Signal Process.* 15 (3): 718–733.

54 Peng, C., Liu, Y., Kang, K. et al. (2022). Hyperspectral image denoising using non-convex local low-rank and sparse separation with spatial-spectral total variation regularization. *IEEE Trans. Geosci. Remote Sens.* 60: 5538617.

55 Zhang, H., Cai, J., He, W. et al. (2021). Double low-rank matrix decomposition for hyperspectral image denoising and destriping. *IEEE Trans. Geosci. Remote Sens.* 60: 1–19.

56 He, C., Sun, L., Huang, W. et al. (2021). TSLRLN: tensor subspace low-rank learning with non-local prior for hyperspectral image mixed denoising. *Signal Process.* 184: 108060.

57 Chen, Y., Huang, T.Z., He, W. et al. (2021). Hyperspectral image denoising using factor group sparsity-regularized nonconvex low-rank approximation. *IEEE Trans. Geosci. Remote Sens.* 60: 1–16.

58 Lin, J., Huang, T.Z., Zhao, X.L. et al. (2021). A novel non-convex low-rank tensor approximation model for hyperspectral image restoration. *Appl. Math. Comput.* 408: 126342.

59 Gong, X., Chen, W., and Chen, J. (2020). A low-rank tensor dictionary learning method for hyperspectral image denoising. *IEEE Trans. Geosci. Remote Sens.* 68: 1168–1180.

60 Lin, J., Huang, T., Zhao, X. et al. (2020). A tensor subspace representation-based method for hyperspectral image denoising. *IEEE Trans. Geosci. Remote Sens.* 59: 7739–7757.

61 Shi, Q., Tang, X., Yang, T. et al. (2021). Hyperspectral image denoising using a 3-d attention denoising network. *IEEE Trans. Geosci. Remote Sens.* 59 (12): 10348–10363.

62 Cao, X., Fu, X., Xu, C., and Meng, D. (2021). Deep spatial-spectral global reasoning network for hyperspectral image denoising. *IEEE Trans. Geosci. Remote Sens.* 60: 1–14.

63 Zhuang, L. and Ng, M.K. (2021). FastHyMix: fast and parameter-free hyperspectral image mixed noise removal. *IEEE Trans. Neural Netw. Learn. Syst.* 34: 4702–4716.

64 Zhang, H., Chen, H., Yang, G., and Zhang, L. (2021). LR-Net: low-rank spatial-spectral network for hyperspectral image denoising. *IEEE Trans. Image Process.* 30: 8743–8758.

65 Wang, Z., Shao, Z., Huang, X. et al. (2021). SSCAN: a spatial–spectral cross attention network for hyperspectral image denoising. *IEEE Geosci. Remote Sensi. Lett.* 19: 1–5.

66 Gillespie, A.R., Kahle, A.B., and Walker, R.E. (1987). Color enhancement of highly correlated images. II. Channel ratio and "chromaticity" transformation techniques. *Remote Sens. Environ.* 22 (3): 343–365.

67 Laben, C.A. and Brower, B.V. (2000). Process for enhancing the spatial resolution of multispectral imagery using pan-sharpening. United States patent US 6,011,875.

68 Tu, T.-M., Su, S.-C., Shyu, H.-C., and Huang, P.S. (2001). A new look at IHS-like image fusion methods. *Inf. Fusion* 2 (3): 177–186.

69 Sara, D., Mandava, A.K., Kumar, A. et al. (2021). Hyperspectral and multispectral image fusion techniques for high resolution applications: a review. *Earth Sci. Inf.* 14 (4): 1685–1705.

70 Gomez, R.B., Jazaeri, A., and Kafatos, M. (2001). Wavelet-based hyperspectral and multispectral image fusion. In: *Geo-Spatial Image and Data Exploitation II*, vol. 4383, 36–42. SPIE.

71 Aiazzi, B., Baronti, S., and Selva, M. (2007). Improving component substitution pansharpening through multivariate regression of MS + Pan data. *IEEE Trans. Geosci. Remote Sens.* 45 (10): 3230–3239.

72 Selva, M., Aiazzi, B., Butera, F. et al. (2015). Hyper-sharpening: a first approach on SIM-GA data. *IEEE J. Sel. Top. Appl. Earth Obs. Remote Sens.* 8 (6): 3008–3024.

73 Eismann, M.T. and Hardie, R.C. (2005). Hyperspectral resolution enhancement using high-resolution multispectral imagery with arbitrary response functions. *IEEE Trans. Geosci. Remote Sens.* 43 (3): 455–465.

74 Hardie, R.C., Eismann, M.T., and Wilson, G.L. (2004). MAP estimation for hyperspectral image resolution enhancement using an auxiliary sensor. *IEEE Trans. Image Process.* 13 (9): 1174–1184.

75 Zhang, Y., Mei, S., and He, M. (2011). Bayesian fusion of hyperspectral and multispectral images using Gaussian scale mixture prior, *2011 IEEE International Geoscience and Remote Sensing Symposium*, 2531–2534, Vancouver, BC, Canada (24–29 July 2011). IEEE.

76 Wei, Q., Dobigeon, N., and Tourneret, J.-Y. (2015). Fast fusion of multi-band images based on solving a Sylvester equation. *IEEE Trans. Image Process.* 24 (11): 4109–4121.

77 Wei, Q., Dobigeon, N., Tourneret, J.-Y. et al. (2016). R-FUSE: robust fast fusion of multiband images based on solving a Sylvester equation. *IEEE Signal Process. Lett.* 23 (11): 1632–1636.

78 Wei, Q., Bioucas-Dias, J., Dobigeon, N., and Tourneret, J.-Y. (2015). Hyperspectral and multispectral image fusion based on a sparse representation. *IEEE Trans. Geosci. Remote Sens.* 53 (7): 3658–3668.

79 Yokoya, N., Yairi, T., and Iwasaki, A. (2011). Coupled nonnegative matrix factorization unmixing for hyperspectral and multispectral data fusion. *IEEE Trans. Geosci. Remote Sens.* 50 (2): 528–537.

80 Dong, W., Fu, F., Shi, G. et al. (2016). Hyperspectral image super-resolution via non-negative structured sparse representation. *IEEE Trans. Image Process.* 25 (5): 2337–2352.

81 Li, S., Dian, R., Fang, L., and Bioucas-Dias, J.M. (2018). Fusing hyperspectral and multispectral images via coupled sparse tensor factorization. *IEEE Trans. Image Process.* 27 (8): 4118–4130.

82 Wan, W., Guo, W., Huang, H., and Liu, J. (2020). Nonnegative and nonlocal sparse tensor factorization-based hyperspectral image super-resolution. *IEEE Trans. Geosci. Remote Sens.* 58 (12): 8384–8394.

83 Xu, T., Huang, T.-Z., Deng, L.-J. et al. (2020). Hyperspectral image superresolution using unidirectional total variation with tucker decomposition. *IEEE J. Sel. Top. Appl. Earth Obs. Remote Sens.* 13: 4381–4398.

84 Wang, K., Wang, Y., Zhao, X.-L. et al. (2020). Hyperspectral and multispectral image fusion via nonlocal low-rank tensor decomposition and spectral unmixing. *IEEE Trans. Geosci. Remote Sens.* 58 (11): 7654–7671.

85 Palsson, F., Sveinsson, J.R., and Ulfarsson, M.O. (2017). Multispectral and hyperspectral image fusion using a 3-D-convolutional neural network. *IEEE Geosci. Remote Sens. Lett.* 14 (5): 639–643.

86 Han, X.-H., Shi, B., and Zheng, Y. (2018). SSF-CNN: spatial and spectral fusion with CNN for hyperspectral image super-resolution, *2018 25th IEEE International Conference on Image Processing (ICIP)*, 2506–2510, Athens, Greece (7–10 October 2018). IEEE.

87 Xu, S., Amira, O., Liu, J. et al. (2020). HAM-MFN: hyperspectral and multispectral image multiscale fusion network with RAP loss. *IEEE Trans. Geosci. Remote Sens.* 58 (7): 4618–4628.

88 Yang, J., Zhao, Y.-Q., and Chan, J.C.-W. (2018). Hyperspectral and multispectral image fusion via deep two-branches convolutional neural network. *Remote Sens.* 10 (5): 800.

89 Hu, J.-F., Huang, T.-Z., Deng, L.-J. et al. (2021). Hyperspectral image super-resolution via deep spatiospectral attention convolutional neural networks. *IEEE Trans. Neural Netw. Learn. Syst.* 33 (12): 7251–7265.

90 Sun, W., Ren, K., Meng, X. et al. (2021). A band divide-and-conquer multispectral and hyperspectral image fusion method. *IEEE Trans. Geosci. Remote Sens.* 60: 1–13.

91 Qu, Y., Qi, H., and Kwan, C. (2018). Unsupervised sparse dirichlet-net for hyperspectral image super-resolution, *IEEE/CVF Conference on Computer Vision and Pattern Recognition*, 2511–2520, Salt Lake City, UT, USA (18–23 June 2018). IEEE.

92 Zheng, K., Gao, L., Liao, W. et al. (2020). Coupled convolutional neural network with adaptive response function learning for unsupervised hyperspectral super resolution. *IEEE Trans. Geosci. Remote Sens.* 59 (3): 2487–2502.

93 Yao, J., Hong, D., Chanussot, J. et al. (2000). Cross-attention in coupled unmixing nets for unsupervised hyperspectral super-resolution, *ECCV 2020: 16th European Conference*, 208–224, Glasgow, UK (23–28 August 2020).

94 Wang, Z., Chen, B., Lu, R. et al. (2020). FusionNet: an unsupervised convolutional variational network for hyperspectral and multispectral image fusion. *IEEE Trans. Image Process.* 29: 7565–7577.

95 Qu, Y., Qi, H., Kwan, C. et al. (2021). Unsupervised and unregistered hyperspectral image super-resolution with mutual Dirichlet-Net. *IEEE Trans. Geosci. Remote Sens.* 60: 1–18.

96 Zheng, K., Gao, L., Hong, D. et al. (2021). NonRegSRNet: a nonrigid registration hyperspectral super-resolution network. *IEEE Trans. Geosci. Remote Sens.* 60: 1–16.

97 Fu, Y., Zhang, T., Zheng, Y. et al. (2019). Hyperspectral image super-resolution with optimized RGB guidance, *Proceedings of the IEEE/CVF Conference on Computer Vision and Pattern Recognition*, 11661–11670, Long Beach, CA, USA (15–20 June 2019), IEEE.

98 Li, J., Zheng, K., Yao, J. et al. (2022). Deep unsupervised blind hyperspectral and multispectral data fusion. *IEEE Geosci. Remote Sens. Lett.* 19: 1–5.

99 Bioucas-Dias, J.M., Plaza, A., Dobigeon, N. et al. (2012). Hyperspectral unmixing overview: geometrical, statistical, and sparse regression-based approaches. *IEEE J. Sel. Top. Appl. Earth Obs. Remote Sens.* 5 (2): 354–379.

100 Dobigeon, N., Tourneret, J.Y., Richard, C. et al. (2014). Nonlinear unmixing of hyperspectral images: models and algorithms. *IEEE Signal Process. Mag.* 31 (1): 82–94.

101 Heylen, R., Parente, M., and Gader, P. (2014). A review of nonlinear hyperspectral unmixing methods. *IEEE J. Sel. Top. Appl. Earth Obs. Remote Sens.* 7 (6): 1844–1868.

102 Chen, J., Zhao, M., Wang, X. et al. (2023). Integration of physics-based and data-driven models for hyperspectral image unmixing: a summary of current methods. *IEEE Signal Process. Mag.* 40 (2): 61–74.

103 Halimi, A., Altmann, Y., Dobigeon, N., and Tourneret, J.-Y. (2011). Nonlinear unmixing of hyperspectral images using a generalized bilinear model. *IEEE Trans. Geosci. Remote Sens.* 49 (11): 4153–4162.

104 Yokoya, N., Chanussot, J., and Iwasaki, A. (2014). Nonlinear unmixing of hyperspectral data using semi-nonnegative matrix factorization. *IEEE Trans. Geosci. Remote Sens.* 52 (2): 1430–1437.

105 Fevotte, C. and Dobigeon, N. (2015). Nonlinear hyperspectral unmixing with robust nonnegative matrix factorization. *IEEE Trans. Image Process.* 24 (12): 4810–4819.

106 Wang, M., Zhao, M., Chen, J., and Rahardja, S. (2019). Nonlinear unmixing of hyperspectral data via deep autoencoder networks. *IEEE Geosci. Remote Sens. Lett.* 16 (9): 1467–1471.

107 Wang, Z., Zhuang, L., Gao, L. et al. (2020). Hyperspectral nonlinear unmixing by using plug-and-play prior for abundance maps. *Remote Sens.* 12 (24): 4117.

108 Su, Y., Xu, X., Li, J. et al. (2020). Deep autoencoders with multitask learning for bilinear hyperspectral unmixing. *IEEE Trans. Geosci. Remote Sens.* 59 (10): 8615–8629.

109 Zhao, M., Yan, L., and Chen, J. (2021). LSTM-DNN based autoencoder network for nonlinear hyperspectral image unmixing. *IEEE J. Sel. Top. Signal Process.* 15 (2): 295–309.

110 Zhao, M., Wang, M., Chen, J., and Rahardja, S. (2021). Hyperspectral unmixing for additive nonlinear models with a 3-D-CNN autoencoder network. *IEEE Trans. Geosci. Remote Sens.* 60: 1–15.

111 Shahid, K.T. and Schizas, I.D. (2021). Unsupervised hyperspectral unmixing via nonlinear autoencoders. *IEEE Trans. Geosci. Remote Sens.* 60: 1–13.

112 Hong, D., Gao, L., Yao, J. et al. (2021). Endmember-guided unmixing network (EGU-Net): a general deep learning framework for self-supervised hyperspectral unmixing. *IEEE Trans. Neural Netw. Learn. Syst.* 33 (11): 6518–6531.

113 Rasti, B., Koirala, B., and Scheunders, P. (2022). HapkeCNN: blind nonlinear unmixing for intimate mixtures using Hapke model and convolutional neural network. *IEEE Trans. Geosci. Remote Sens.* 60: 1–15.

114 Li, M., Zhu, F., Guo, A.J.X., and Chen, J. (2019). A graph regularized multilinear mixing model for nonlinear hyperspectral unmixing. *Remote Sens.* 11 (19): 2188.

115 Plaza, A., Benediktsson, J.A., Boardman, J.W. et al. (2009). Recent advances in techniques for hyperspectral image processing. *Remote Sens. Environ.* 113: S110–S122.

116 Hong, D., Yokoya, N., Xia, G.-S. et al. (2020). X-ModalNet: a semi-supervised deep cross-modal network for classification of remote sensing data. *ISPRS J. Photogramm. Remote Sens.* 167: 12–23.

117 Yu, C., Liu, C., Song, M. et al. (2022). Unsupervised domain adaptation with content-wise alignment for hyperspectral imagery classification. *IEEE Geosci. Remote Sens. Lett.* 19: 1–5.

118 Li, J., Bioucas-Dias, J.M., and Plaza, A. (2013). Semisupervised hyperspectral image classification using soft sparse multinomial logistic regression. *IEEE Geosci. Remote Sens. Lett.* 10 (2): 318–322.

119 Ghamisi, P., Plaza, J., Chen, Y. et al. (2017). Advanced spectral classifiers for hyperspectral images: a review. *IEEE Geosci. Remote Sens. Mag.* 5 (1): 8–32.

120 Goetz, A. (1990). Hyperspectral imaging: advances in a spectrum of applications. *Proceedings of the 5th Australasian Remote Sensing Conference* (pp. 49–53). Perth, Australia, October 8–12, 1990.

121 Clark, C. and Clark, A. (1998). Spectral identification by singular value decomposition. *Int. J. Remote Sens.* 19 (12): 2317–2329.

122 Liu, Y., Lu, S., Lu, X. et al. (2019). Classification of urban hyperspectral remote sensing imagery based on optimized spectral angle mapping. *J. Indian Soc. Remote Sens.* 47: 289–294.

123 Fauvel, M., Tarabalka, Y., Benediktsson, J.A. et al. (2013). Advances in spectral-spatial classification of hyperspectral images. *Proc. IEEE* 101 (3): 652–675.

124 McIver, D. and Friedl, M. (2002). Using prior probabilities in decision-tree classification of remotely sensed data. *Remote Sens. Environ.* 81 (2–3): 253–261.

125 Tong, F. and Zhang, Y. (2022). Spectral–spatial and cascaded multilayer random forests for tree species classification in airborne hyperspectral images. *IEEE Trans. Geosci. Remote Sens.* 60: 1–11.

126 Belgiu, M. and Drăguţ, L. (2016). Random forest in remote sensing: a review of applications and future directions. *ISPRS J. Photogramm. Remote Sens.* 114: 24–31.

127 Melgani, F. and Bruzzone, L. (2004). Classification of hyperspectral remote sensing images with support vector machines. *IEEE Trans. Geosci. Remote Sens.* 42 (8): 1778–1790.

128 Yu, H., Gao, L., Liao, W. et al. (2017). Multiscale superpixel-level subspace-based support vector machines for hyperspectral image classification. *IEEE Geosci. Remote Sens. Lett.* 14 (11): 2142–2146.

129 Yu, H., Gao, L., Li, J. et al. (2016). Spectral-spatial hyperspectral image classification using subspace-based support vector machines and adaptive Markov random fields. *Remote Sens.* 8 (4): 355.

130 Gao, L., Yao, D., Li, Q. et al. (2017). A new low-rank representation based hyperspectral image denoising method for mineral mapping. *Remote Sens.* 9 (11): 1145.

131 Chen, Y., Nasrabadi, N.M., and Tran, T.D. (2013). Hyperspectral image classification via kernel sparse representation. *IEEE Trans. Geosci. Remote Sens.* 51 (1): 217–231.

132 Fang, L., Li, S., Kang, X. et al. (2014). Spectral–spatial hyperspectral image classification via multiscale adaptive sparse representation. *IEEE Trans. Geosci. Remote Sens.* 52 (12): 7738–7749.

133 Li, W., Liu, J., and Du, Q. (2016). Sparse and low rank graph-based discriminant analysis for hyperspectral image classification. *IEEE Trans. Geosci. Remote Sens.* 54 (7): 4094–4105.

134 Li, W., Du, Q., Zhang, F. et al. (2016). Hyperspectral image classification by fusing collaborative and sparse representations. *IEEE J. Sel. Top. Appl. Earth Obs. Remote Sens.* 9 (9): 4178–4187.

135 Li, W. and Du, Q. (2015). Collaborative representation for hyperspectral anomaly detection. *IEEE Trans. Geosci. Remote Sens.* 53 (3): 1463–1474.

136 Dundar, T. and Ince, T. (2019). Sparse representation-based hyperspectral image classification using multiscale superpixels and guided filter. *IEEE Geosci. Remote Sens. Lett.* 16 (2): 246–250.

137 Su, H., Yu, Y., Du, Q. et al. (2020). Ensemble learning for hyperspectral image classification using tangent collaborative representation. *IEEE Trans. Geosci. Remote Sens.* 58 (6): 3778–3790.

138 Jia, S., Xie, Y., Tang, G. et al. (2016). Spatial-spectral-combined sparse representation-based classification for hyperspectral imagery. *Soft. Comput.* 20 (12): 4659–4668.

139 Zou, J., Li, W., Chen, C. et al. (2016). Scene classification using local and global features with collaborative representation fusion. *Inf. Sci.* 348: 209–226.

140 Yu, H., Gao, L., Liao, W. et al. (2018). Group sparse representation based on nonlocal spatial and local spectral similarity for hyperspectral imagery classification. *Sensors* 18 (6): 1695.

141 Chen, Y., Nasrabadi, N.M., and Tran, T.D. (2011). Hyperspectral image classification using dictionary-based sparse representation. *IEEE Trans. Geosci. Remote Sens.* 49 (10): 3973–3985.

142 Zhang, H., Zhang, Y., Nasrabadi, N.M. et al. (2012). Joint-structured-sparsity-based classification for multiple-measurement transient acoustic signals. *IEEE Trans. Syst. Man. Cybern. B* 42 (6): 1586–1598.

143 Sun, X., Qu, Q., Nasrabadi, N.M. et al. (2014). Structured priors for sparse-representation-based hyperspectral image classification. *IEEE Geosci. Remote Sens. Lett.* 11 (7): 1235–1239.

144 Li, W. and Du, Q. (2015). A survey on representation-based classification and detection in hyperspectral remote sensing imagery. *Pattern Recogn. Lett.* 83 (2): 115–123.

145 Gao, L., Yu, H., Zhang, B. et al. (2016). Locality-preserving sparse representation-based classification in hyperspectral imagery. *J. Appl. Remote. Sens.* 10 (4): 042004.

146 Yu, H., Gao, L., Li, W. et al. (2017). Locality sensitive discriminant analysis for group sparse representation-based hyperspectral imagery classification. *IEEE Geosci. Remote Sens. Lett.* 14 (8): 1358–1362.

147 Yu, H., Gao, L., Liao, W. et al. (2020). Global spatial and local spectral similarity-based manifold learning group sparse representation for hyperspectral imagery classification. *IEEE Trans. Geosci. Remote Sens.* 58 (5): 3043–3056.

148 Li, J., Zhang, H., and Zhang, L. (2014). Column-generation kernel nonlocal joint collaborative representation for hyperspectral image classification. *ISPRS J. Photogramm. Remote Sens.* 94: 25–36.

149 Yu, H., Shang, X., Zhang, X. et al. (2021). Hyperspectral image classification based on adjacent constraint representation. *IEEE Geosci. Remote Sens. Lett.* 18 (4): 707–711.

150 Yu, H., Shang, X., Song, M. et al. (2021). Union of class-dependent collaborative representation based on maximum margin projection for hyperspectral imagery classification. *IEEE J. Sel. Top. Appl. Earth Obs. Remote Sens.* 14: 553–566.

151 Chen, Y., Lin, Z., Zhao, X. et al. (2014). Deep learning-based classification of hyperspectral data. *IEEE J. Sel. Top. Appl. Earth Obs. Remote Sens.* 7 (6): 2094–2107. https://doi.org/10.1109/JSTARS.2014.2329330.

152 Paoletti, M.E., Haut, J.M., Fernandez-Beltran, R. et al. (2019). Deep pyramidal residual networks for spectral-spatial hyperspectral image classification. *IEEE Trans. Geosci. Remote Sens.* 57 (2): 740–754. https://doi.org/10.1109/TGRS.2018.2860125.

153 Ben Hamida, A., Benoit, A., Lambert, P., and Ben Amar, C. (2018). 3-D deep learning approach for remote sensing image classification. *IEEE Trans. Geosci. Remote Sens.* 56 (8): 4420–4434. https://doi.org/10.1109/TGRS.2018.2818945.

154 Gao, L., Gu, D., Zhuang, L. et al. (2020). Combining t-distributed stochastic neighbor embedding with convolutional neural networks for hyperspectral image classification. *IEEE Geosci. Remote Sens. Lett.* 17 (8): 1368–1372. https://doi.org/10.1109/LGRS.2019.2945122.

155 Hong, D., Gao, L., Hang, R. et al. (2020). Deep encoder-decoder networks for classification of hyperspectral and LiDAR data. *IEEE Geosci. Remote Sens. Lett.* 19: 1–5. https://doi.org/10.1109/LGRS.2020.3017414.

156 Zhang, B., Sun, X., Gao, L., and Yang, L. (2011). Endmember extraction of hyperspectral remote sensing images based on the ant colony optimization (ACO) algorithm. *IEEE Trans. Geosci. Remote Sens.* 49 (7): 2635–2646. https://doi.org/10.1109/TGRS.2011.2108305.

157 Xue, Z., Yu, X., Liu, B. et al. (2021). HResNetAM: hierarchical residual network with attention mechanism for hyperspectral image classification. *IEEE J. Sel. Top. Appl. Earth Obs. Remote Sens.* 14: 3566–3580. https://doi.org/10.1109/JSTARS.2021.3065987.

158 Chen, Y., Jiang, H., Li, C. et al. (2016). Deep feature extraction and classification of hyperspectral images based on convolutional neural networks. *IEEE Trans. Geosci. Remote Sens.* 54 (10): 6232–6251. https://doi.org/10.1109/TGRS.2016.2584107.

159 Zhong, Z., Li, J., Luo, Z., and Chapman, M. (2018). Spectral-spatial residual network for hyperspectral image classification: a 3-D deep learning framework. *IEEE Trans. Geosci. Remote Sens.* 56 (2): 847–858. https://doi.org/10.1109/TGRS.2017.2755542.

160 Roy, S.K., Krishna, G., Dubey, S.R., and Chaudhuri, B.B. (2020). HybridSN: exploring 3-D–2-D CNN feature hierarchy for hyperspectral image classification. *IEEE Geosci. Remote Sens. Lett.* 17 (2): 277–281. https://doi.org/10.1109/LGRS.2019.2918719.

161 Li, X., Ding, M., and Pizurica, A. (2020). Deep feature fusion via two-stream convolutional neural network for hyperspectral image classification. *IEEE Trans. Geosci. Remote Sens.* 58 (4): 2615–2629. https://doi.org/10.1109/TGRS.2019.2952758.

162 Wang, J., Guo, S., Huang, R. et al. (2022). Dual-channel capsule generation adversarial network for hyperspectral image classification. *IEEE Trans. Geosci. Remote Sens.* 60: 1–16. https://doi.org/10.1109/TGRS.2020.3044312.

163 Reed, I.S. and Yu, X. (1990). Adaptive multiple-band CFAR detection of an optical pattern with unknown spectral distribution. *IEEE Trans. Acoust. Speech Signal Process.* 38 (10): 1760–1770.

164 Molero, J.M., Garzon, E.M., Garcia, I., and Plaza, A. (2013). Analysis and optimizations of global and local versions of the RX algorithm for anomaly detection in hyperspectral data. *IEEE J. Sel. Top. Appl. Earth Obs. Remote Sens.* 6 (2): 801–814.

165 Tu, B., Yang, X., Li, N. et al. (2020). Hyperspectral anomaly detection via density peak clustering. *Pattern Recogn. Lett.* 129: 144–149.

166 Tu, B., Yang, X., Zhou, C. et al. (2020). Hyperspectral anomaly detection using dual window density. *IEEE Trans. Geosci. Remote Sens.* 58 (12): 8503–8517.

167 Tu, B., Wang, Z., Ouyang, H. et al. (2022). Hyperspectral anomaly detection using the spectral-spatial graph. *IEEE Trans. Geosci. Remote Sens.* 60: 5542814.

168 Tu, B., Yang, X., He, W. et al. (2023). Hyperspectral anomaly detection using reconstruction fusion of quaternion frequency domain analysis. *IEEE Trans. Neural Netw. Learn. Syst.* 35: 8358–8372. https://doi.org/10.1109/TNNLS.2022.3227167.

169 Tu, B., Wang, Z., Yang, X. et al. (2022). Hyperspectral anomaly detection using quantum potential clustering. *IEEE Trans. Instrum. Meas.* 71: 5025913.

170 Huyan, N., Zhang, X., Zhou, H., and Jiao, L. (2019). Hyperspectral anomaly detection via background and potential anomaly dictionaries construction. *IEEE Trans. Geosci. Remote Sens.* 57 (4): 2263–2276.

171 Zhang, G., Li, N., Tu, B. et al. (2020). Hyperspectral anomaly detection via dual collaborative representation. *IEEE J. Sel. Top. Appl. Earth Obs. Remote Sens.* 13: 4881–4894.

172 Tu, B., Li, N., Liao, Z. et al. (2019). Hyperspectral anomaly detection via spatial density background purification. *Remote Sens.* 11 (22): 2618.

173 Li, L., Li, W., Du, Q., and Tao, R. (2021). Low-rank and sparse decomposition with mixture of Gaussian for hyperspectral anomaly detection. *IEEE Trans. Cybern.* 51 (9): 4363–4372.

174 Wang, D., Gao, L., Qu, Y. et al. (2023). Frequency-to-spectrum mapping GAN for semisupervised hyperspectral anomaly detection. *CAAI Trans. Intell. Technol.* 8: 1258–1273. https://doi.org/10.1049/cit2.12154.

175 Xie, W., Zhang, X., Li, Y. et al. (2021). Weakly supervised low-rank representation for hyperspectral anomaly detection. *IEEE Trans. Cybern.* 51 (8): 3889–3900.

176 Jiang, T., Xie, W., Li, Y. et al. (2022). Weakly supervised discriminative learning with spectral constrained generative adversarial network for hyperspectral anomaly detection. *IEEE Trans. Neural Netw. Learn. Syst.* 33 (11): 6504–6517.

177 Gao, L., Wang, D., Zhuang, L. et al. (2023). BS3LNet: a new blind-spot self-supervised learning network for hyperspectral anomaly detection. *IEEE Trans. Geosci. Remote Sens.* 61: 5504218.

178 Manolakis, D. and Shaw, G. (2002). Detection algorithms for hyperspectral imaging applications. *IEEE Signal Process. Mag.* 19 (1): 29–43.

179 Nasrabadi, N.M. (2014). Hyperspectral target detection: an overview of current and future challenges. *IEEE Signal Process. Mag.* 31 (1): 34–44.

180 Du, B. and Zhang, L. (2014). Target detection based on a dynamic subspace. *Pattern Recogn.* 47 (1): 344–358.

181 Du, Q. and Chang, C. (2004). A signal-decomposed and interference-annihilated approach to hyperspectral target detection. *IEEE Trans. Geosci. Remote Sens.* 42 (4): 892–906.

182 Yang, S. and Shi, Z. (2016). Hyperspectral image target detection improvement based on total variation. *IEEE Trans. Image Process.* 25 (5): 2249–2258.

183 Brumbley, C.M. and Chang, C. (1999). An unsupervised vector quantization-based target subspace projection approach to mixed pixel detection and classification in unknown background for remotely sensed imagery. *Pattern Recogn.* 32 (7): 1161–1174.

184 Scharf, L.L. and Friedlander, B. (1994). Matched subspace detectors. *IEEE Trans. Signal Process.* 42 (8): 2146–2157.

185 Kraut, S. and Scharf, L.L. (1999). The CFAR adaptive subspace detector is a scale-invariant GLRT. *IEEE Trans. Signal Process.* 47 (9): 2538–2541.

186 Harsany, J.C. (1993). Detection and classification of subpixel spectral signatures in hyperspectral image sequences. Ph.D. thesis. University of Maryland, Baltimore County, 116 pp.

187 Farrand, W.H. and Harsanyi, J.C. (1997). Mapping the distribution of mine tailings in the Coeur d'Alene River Valley, Idaho, through the use of a constrained energy minimization technique. *Remote Sens. Environ.* 59 (1): 64–76.

188 Du, Q., Ren, H., and Chang, C.-I. (2003). A comparative study for orthogonal subspace projection and constrained energy minimization. *IEEE Trans. Geosci. Remote Sens.* 41 (6): 1525–1529.

189 Yang, S. and Shi, Z. (2014). SparseCEM and SparseACE for hyperspectral image target detection. *IEEE Geosci. Remote Sens. Lett.* 11 (12): 2135–2139.

190 Zou, Z. and Shi, Z. (2016). Hierarchical suppression method for hyperspectral target detection. *IEEE Trans. Geosci. Remote Sens.* 54 (1): 330–342.

191 Zhao, R., Shi, Z., Zou, Z. et al. (2019). Ensemble based cascaded constrained energy minimization for hyperspectral target detection. *Remote Sens.* 11 (11): 1310.

192 Zhao, X., Hou, Z., Wu, X. et al. (2021). Hyperspectral target detection based on transform domain adaptive constrained energy minimization. *Int. J. Appl. Earth Obs. Geoinf.* 103: 102461.

193 Bakhshi, G., Shahtalebi, K., and Momeni, M. (2019). A new adaptive algorithm for target detection in hyperspectral images. *Infrared Phys. Technol.* 99: 222–230.

194 Chang, C. (2005). Orthogonal subspace projection (OSP) revisited: a comprehensive study and analysis. *IEEE Trans. Geosci. Remote Sens.* 43 (3): 502–518.

195 Chen, Y., Nasrabadi, N.M., and Tran, T.D. (2011). Sparse representation for target detection in hyperspectral imagery. *IEEE J. Sel. Top. Signal Process.* 5 (3): 629–640.

196 Li, W., Du, Q., and Zhang, B. (2015). Combined sparse and collaborative representation for hyperspectral target detection. *Pattern Recogn.* 48 (12): 3904–3916.

197 Bitar, A.W., Cheong, L., and Ovarlez, J. (2019). Sparse and low-rank matrix decomposition for automatic target detection in hyperspectral imagery. *IEEE Trans. Geosci. Remote Sens.* 57 (8): 5239–5251.

198 Zhao, X., Li, W., Zhang, M. et al. (2020). Adaptive iterated shrinkage thresholding-based Lp-norm sparse representation for hyperspectral imagery target detection. *Remote Sens.* 12: 3991.

199 Zhao, X., Li, W., Zhao, C. et al. (2022). Hyperspectral target detection based on weighted Cauchy distance graph and local adaptive collaborative representation. *IEEE Trans. Geosci. Remote Sens.* 60: 1–13.

200 Li, W., Wu, G., and Du, Q. (2017). Transferred deep learning for anomaly detection in hyperspectral imagery. *IEEE Geosci. Remote Sens. Lett.* 14 (5): 597–601.

201 Shi, Y., Li, J., Yin, Y. et al. (2019). Hyperspectral target detection with macro-micro feature extracted by 3-D residual autoencoder. *IEEE J. Sel. Top. Appl. Earth Obs. Remote Sens.* 12 (12): 4907–4919.

202 Chen, Y., Zhao, X., and Jia, X. (2015). Spectral–spatial classification of hyperspectral data based on deep belief network. *IEEE J. Sel. Top. Appl. Earth Obs. Remote Sens.* 8 (6): 2381–2392.

203 Xie, W., Zhang, X., Li, Y. et al. (2020). Background learning based on target suppression constraint for hyperspectral target detection. *IEEE J. Sel. Top. Appl. Earth Obs. Remote Sens.* 13: 5887–5897.

204 Bovolo, F., Marchesi, S., and Bruzzone, L. (2012). A framework for automatic and unsupervised detection of multiple changes in multitemporal images. *IEEE Trans. Geosci. Remote Sens.* 50 (6): 2196–2212. https://doi.org/10.1109/TGRS.2011.2171493.

205 Kwan, C. (2019). Methods and challenges using multispectral and hyperspectral images for practical change detection applications. *Inf.* 10 (11): 353. https://doi.org/10.3390/info10110353.

206 Wang, Y., Hong, D., Sha, J. et al. (2022). Spectral–spatial–temporal transformers for hyperspectral image change detection. *IEEE Trans. Geosci. Remote Sens.* 60: 1–14. https://doi.org/10.1109/TGRS.2022.3203075.

207 Liu, S., Marinelli, D., Bruzzone, L., and Bovolo, F. (2019). A review of change detection in multitemporal hyperspectral images: current techniques, applications, and challenges. *IEEE Geosci. Remote Sens. Mag.* 7 (2): 140–158. https://doi.org/10.1109/MGRS.2019.2898520.

208 Liu, S., Bruzzone, L., Bovolo, F. et al. (2015). Sequential spectral change vector analysis for iteratively discovering and detecting multiple changes in hyperspectral images. *IEEE Trans. Geosci. Remote Sens.* 53 (8): 4363–4378. https://doi.org/10.1109/TGRS.2015.2396686.

209 Liu, S., Bruzzone, L., Bovolo, F., and Du, P. (2016). Unsupervised multitemporal spectral unmixing for detecting multiple changes in hyperspectral images. *IEEE Trans. Geosci. Remote Sens.* 54 (5): 2733–2748. https://doi.org/10.1109/TGRS.2015.2505183.

2

Hyperspectral Image Denoising Based on Low-rank Regularization

Yong Chen[1], *Hongyu Chen*[2], *and Wei He*[3]

[1] *School of Artificial Intelligence, Jiangxi Normal University, Nanchang, China*
[2] *School of Computer Science, China University of Geosciences, Wuhan, China*
[3] *State Key Laboratory of Information Engineering in Surveying, Mapping and Remote Sensing, Wuhan University, Wuhan, China*

Mathematical Symbols Used in This Chapter

$\mathcal{X} \in \mathbb{R}^{M \times N \times B}$	Clean $M \times N$ HSI with B spectral bands.
$\mathcal{Y} \in \mathbb{R}^{M \times N \times B}$	HSI degraded by various mixed noises.
$\mathcal{S}$	Sparse noise.
$\mathcal{N}$	Gaussian noise.
$\mathcal{R}(\mathcal{X})$ and $\mathcal{R}(\mathcal{S})$	Regularization terms.
λ_1 and λ_2	Regularization parameters.
$\mathbf{U} \in \mathbb{R}^{M \times r}$	Spatial coefficient matrix.
$\mathbf{V} \in \mathbb{R}^{N \times r}$	Spectral basis matrix.

2.1 Introduction

Hyperspectral image (HSI) has been extensively employed in practical applications due to the abundant spectral information, such as unmixing [1, 2], recognition [3], and classification [4]. Although HSI techniques have excelled in capturing imagery of large areas with high spectral resolution, they fall short of satisfying practical demands for high-quality HSI with the desired signal-to-noise ratios (SNRs) [5]. Influenced by weather conditions, sensor instability, calibration error, and physical mechanisms, the collected HSI is inevitably polluted by various noises during the imaging process, which destroys the image vision and constrains the advanced application tasks [6]. Therefore, HSI restoration is regarded as a meaningful preprocessing step in remote-sensing image processing, which refers to the process of restoring a high-quality HSI to obtain detailed and accurate information about the surface.

For HSI restoration, the global spectral correlation is the most important property. The global spectral correlation is derived from the fact that each spectral signature can be approximately represented by a linear combination of a small number of pure spectral endmembers, and the

Machine-Learning-Based Hyperspectral Image Processing, First Edition. Edited by Bing Zhang.

number of endmembers is much less than the spectral band [7]. Up to now, numerous methods have been dedicated to designing low-rank characterization to explore the spectral correlation of HSI, which can be roughly divided into two categories: model-driven approaches and data-driven approaches. Model-driven approaches regard the restoration from noisy HSI as an ill-posed inverse problem and design corresponding spectral low-rank regularization for HSI restoration, such as low-rank matrix approximation, low-rank tensor approximation (LRTA), and nonlocal modeling. Despite the generally good interpretability and satisfactory performance of these spectral low-rank regularizations, the significant computational cost they entail remains a major obstacle when applied to generate higher-level products from operational satellites collecting large-scale data.

Recently, data-driven approaches have been proven to be a powerful tool in various image-processing tasks. Different from model-driven approaches designing the spectral low-rank prior manually, data-driven approaches adaptively learn the spectral low-rank prior from external training datasets via a deep neural network, which can achieve state-of-the-art restoration results and are highly computationally efficient. However, their generalization ability is relatively limited. When the noise distribution of the test data is not present in the training dataset, their performance may decrease. This chapter provides an overview of state-of-the-art model-driven and data-driven approaches for HSI restoration based on spectral low-rank regularization, as well as comparative experiments to show their advantages and characteristics. This is followed by a discussion of the future challenges and research directions.

2.2 Model-driven Approaches

Let $\mathcal{X} \in \mathbb{R}^{M \times N \times B}$ be a clean $M \times N$ HSI with B spectral bands, and $\mathcal{Y} \in \mathbb{R}^{M \times N \times B}$ be the observed HSI degraded by various mixed noises, including Gaussian noise, impulse noise, stripes, and deadlines; then the degradation model between these two HSIs can be formulated as:

$$\mathcal{Y} = \mathcal{X} + \mathcal{S} + \mathcal{N} \tag{2.1}$$

where $\mathcal{S}$ and $\mathcal{N}$ are with the same size as $\mathcal{X}$ and denote sparse noise (mixture of impulse noise, stripes, and deadlines) and Gaussian noise, respectively.

Model-driven approaches regard the restoration of clean HSI $\mathcal{X}$ from noisy HSI $\mathcal{Y}$ is an ill-posed inverse problem and explore the intrinsic characteristics of $\mathcal{X}$. The general HSI restoration framework of model-driven approaches can be formulated as:

$$\min_{\mathcal{X},\mathcal{S}} \frac{1}{2} \|\mathcal{Y} - \mathcal{X} - \mathcal{S}\|_F^2 + \lambda_1 \mathcal{R}(\mathcal{X}) + \lambda_2 \mathcal{R}(\mathcal{S}), \tag{2.2}$$

where $\mathcal{R}(\mathcal{X})$ and $\mathcal{R}(\mathcal{S})$ represent two regularization terms, characterizing the internal priors of clean HSI $\mathcal{X}$ and sparse noise $\mathcal{S}$. λ_1 and λ_2 are two regularization parameters employed to balance the data-fidelity term and regularization terms. As the mixture of impulse noise, stripes, and deadlines only corrupts a few parts or bands in HSI, they are regarded as sparse noise [8]. That is to say, the regularization term $\mathcal{R}(\mathcal{S})$ of sparse noise can be consistently designed as $\|\mathcal{S}\|_1$, which is employed to isolate the sparse noise from the clean image. How to exploit prior knowledge of HSI and design corresponding regularization terms is crucial. For HSI restoration, the global spectral correlation is the most important prior. In the following sections, we first provide an overview of the most recent model-driven approaches based on spectral low-rank regularization for HSI restoration and subsequently present and discuss some related experimental results.

2.2.1 Survey of Model-driven HSI Restoration Approaches Employing Spectral Low-rank Regularization

HSI has a high correlation in the spectral dimension, and spectral low-rank regularization is an effective tool to describe it. In recent years, there have been many spectral low-rank regularization terms available for HSI restoration, and the mainstream spectral low-rank regularization terms include low-rank matrix approximation, LRTA, and nonlocal low-rank matrix/tensor approximation.

2.2.1.1 Low-rank Matrix Approximation

By unfolding the HSI along the spectral dimension into a two-dimensional matrix, the matrix exhibits a low-rank property. Therefore, low-rank matrix approximation can be employed to design the spectral low-rank regularization. To the best of our knowledge, the first spectral low-rank regularization method based on low-rank matrix approximation was proposed in [8], and it was named as LRMR. Later, the noise-adjusted iterative low-rank matrix approximation (NAILRMA) model is proposed in [9]. Since low-rank matrix approximation based on nuclear norm minimization is that all the singular values are simultaneously minimized, it is not a very tight low-rank approximation way. To improve the performance of LRMR, many nonconvex low-rank matrix approximation functions, such as weighted Schatten p-norm [10, 11], γ-norm [12], and smooth rank approximation [13], have been proposed to formulate the low-rank matrix approximation instead of the original nuclear norm minimization. Both matrix nuclear norm and nonconvex low-rank matrix approximation functions need to perform singular value decomposition (SVD) in each iteration, which results in plenty of computation cost. To apply the SVD-free rank surrogate, a low-rank factorization strategy can be used to describe the low-rank matrix minimization, because any low-rank matrix can be factorized into the product of two low-dimension matrices. References [14–23] proposed to use a low-rank factorization on the clean HSI, which decomposes the clean HSI as the spectral basis matrix and spatial representation coefficient (reduced image).

Because of the lack of spatial regularization, spectral low-rank regularization alone cannot restore the HSI efficiently. Therefore, spatial-based regularizations are embedded into the spectral low-rank regularization to simultaneously restore the HSI. In the framework of low-rank matrix approximation, common spatial regularization includes total variation (TV) regularization. Reference [24] incorporated the band-by-band TV regularization into a low-rank matrix approximation framework to boost the restoration result. Reference [25] further integrated spatial–spectral TV regularization to improve the performance of local low-rank matrix approximation. Reference [22] proposed a representative coefficient TV to simultaneously characterize the low-rank and local smooth properties of HSI. Reference [19] employed double-factor TV-regularized low-rank matrix factorization for HSI restoration.

In summary, low-rank matrix approximation-based approaches can capture the global spectral correlation, and additional spatial regularization can boost the restoration result. However, these methods need to reshape the original 3-D HSI into a 2-D matrix and destroy the original 3-D structure. To preserve the 3-D cube structure of HSI, the LRTA framework has been widely developed in these years.

2.2.1.2 Low-rank Tensor Approximation

HSI could be naturally treated as 3-D tensor data, and tensor modeling methods can effectively preserve its structure. Research has shown that HSI exhibits a strong correlation not only in the spectral dimension but also in the spatial dimension. Therefore, an LRTA-based strategy can be employed for HSI restoration. Common low-rank approximation methods include canonical polyadic (CP) decomposition, Tucker decomposition, block term decomposition (BTD), tensor singular value decomposition (*t*-SVD), and tensor ring (TR) decomposition. CP decomposition employs a summation format with several rank-1 tensors to approximate the original tensor. Reference [26] presented the rank-1 tensor decomposition for HSI restoration. Tucker decomposition approximates a tensor into a core tensor multiplied (or transformed) by a matrix along each mode. Reference [27, 28] developed the LRTA method for HSI restoration, which explores the spatial–spectral correlation via Tucker decomposition. BTD approximates a tensor by several component tensors, with each one represented by Tucker decomposition. T-SVD approximates a 3-D tensor as three components through tensor SVD, which is generalized from matrix-based SVD. References [29, 30] formulated the LRTA method for HSI restoration based on t-SVD and three-directional *t*-SVD. TR decomposition approximates a high-dimensional tensor by circular multilinear products on a series of third-order factor tensors. Reference [31] developed the TR decomposition to approximate the HSI more accurately.

Similar to low-rank matrix approximation, LRTA only characterizes the intrinsic spatial–spectral correlation of HSI, while neglecting the spatial local smoothness prior. Therefore, TV and enhanced TV priors have also been widely incorporated into an LRTA framework. Reference [32] introduced spatial–spectral TV regularization to the low-rank Tucker decomposition framework for HSI restoration. Reference [33] designed the group sparsity-based TV regularization and embedded it into the low-rank Tucker decomposition framework. Reference [34] combined the spatial–spectral TV regularization with BTD for HSI restoration. Reference [35] introduced the spatial–spectral TV regularization within the t-SVD framework to enhance the local spatial smoothness of the restoration results. Reference [36] introduced a factor TV regularization for TR decomposition to capture the spatial–spectral continuity of HSI.

Compared with low-rank matrix approximation methods, LRTA methods can effectively preserve the original tensor structure and exploit the global spatial–spectral correlation of HSI. However, directly approximating the original HSI with LRTA ignores the nonlocal self-similarity prior of HSI, which is a better prior for characterizing the spectral low-rank property of HSI.

2.2.1.3 Nonlocal Low-rank Matrix/Tensor Approximation

Nonlocal self-similarity illustrates that there are many repeated local patches in HSI. Nonlocal-based methods are focused on the correlation representation of the grouped tensor, namely local spatial, global spectral, and nonlocal self-similarity correlations. Since low-rank matrix/tensor approximation is an effective strategy to capture the data correlation, nonlocal low-rank matrix/tensor approximation-based approaches are widely used for HSI restoration. Reference [37] firstly proposed a tensor dictionary learning (TDL), which is based on low-rank Tucker decomposition, to jointly model the spatial–spectral correlation and nonlocal self-similarity of HSI. Based on the TDL architecture, many state-of-the-art nonlocal low-rank matrix/tensor approaches were proposed for HSI restoration, including the Kronecker-basis-representation-based tensor sparsity measure (KBR) method [38], hyper-Laplacian regularized unidirectional low-rank tensor recovery (LLRT) method [39], weighted low-rank tensor recovery (WLRTR) method [40], and nonlocal tensor ring decomposition (NLTR) method [41]. Although these methods achieve satisfactory restoration results, the computational burden is heavy as the number of spectral bands increases. To alleviate this problem, the subspace representation is first employed to project the HSI into a low-dimensional subspace, and then the reduced HSI is restored by a nonlocal low-rank matrix/tensor approximation strategy. Reference [17] adopted the nonlocal weighted low-rank matrix approximation to restore the reduced HSI. Reference [42] employed the nonlocal LRTA for the reduced HSI. Reference [21] proposed a nonlocal group sparsifying transform learning for reduced HSI restoration.

Nonlocal low-rank matrix/tensor approximation can achieve state-of-the-art restoration results since they simultaneously depict the correlation between the spatial, spectral, and nonlocal dimensions of HSI. Nevertheless, these methods are relatively time consuming and sensitive to sparse noise.

2.2.2 Experimental Results

In this section, the simulated and real HSI restoration experiments are carried out to illustrate the performance of representative model-driven methods. Additionally, experiments for Gaussian noise and mixed noise are considered separately.

2.2.2.1 Gaussian Noise Degradation Experiments

Simulated Gaussian Noise Experimental Design

We choose one noise-free HSI dataset Washington DC (WDC) Mall data set as simulated data, whose size is $256 \times 256 \times 191$, with complex texture and boundary information. The noise settings are additive Gaussian noise $N(0,\sigma^2\mathbf{I})$ with $\sigma = 10, 30, 80, 100$, and Gaussian noise $N(0,\Sigma^2)$, where Σ is a diagonal matrix with diagonal elements sampled from a Uniform distribution U[10,100]. Three quantitative indices, including peak signal-to-noise ratio (PSNR), structure similarity (SSIM), and spectral angle mapper (SAM), are employed to evaluate the restoration performance of different methods. The PSNR and SSIM are mainly employed to measure spatial information, while SAM measures the ability of spectral information preservation. The better restoration results are reflected by the larger PSNR and SSIM, and the smaller SAM values.

Moreover, 10 representative state-of-the-art HSI restoration methods have also been conducted for comparison, including the LRTA method [27], TDL [37], low-rank tensor approximation with TV regularization (LRTDTV) method [32], fast HSI restoration (FastHyDe) method [14], global local factorization (GLF) method [42], KBR [38], LLRT [39], WLRTR [40], nonlocal meets global (NGmeet) method [17], and nonlocal group sparsifying transform learning (TLNLGS) method [21]. Note that these methods involve low-rank matrix approximation methods, LRTA methods, and nonlocal low-rank approximation methods for a comprehensive comparison.

Quantitative and Visual Comparison in Simulated Gaussian Noise Experiments

The quantitative results of different methods on WDC datasets under different Gaussian noise cases are listed in Table 2.1. We highlight the top two methods in bold and underline. From the results, we can observe that nonlocal low rank approximation methods generally outperform low-rank matrix/tensor approximation methods. In particular, the combination of low-rank matrix decomposition with nonlocal low-rank approximation outperforms directly using nonlocal low-rank approximation on the original HSI. These methods first learn a global spectral low-rank orthogonal basis and subsequently exploit the spatial nonlocal similarity of reduced HSI on this basis, which can enhance the global spectral low-rank property. TLNLGS considerably outperforms other methods in most indices and noise cases since the group sparsifying transform can simultaneously capture the nonlocal self- similarity and local smooth structure of the reduced image.

Figure 2.1 presents the restoration results of Gaussian noise with $\sigma = 100$. Since LRTA and LRTDTV directly employ the LRTA for the original HSI, the performance is limited. Although the noise removal effects by nonlocal low-rank approximation methods TDL, KBR, LLRT, and WLRTR are improved, the restored spectral signatures are distorted. Subspace representation with

Table 2.1 Quantitative results of comparison methods on the WDC dataset under different Gaussian noise cases.

σ	Index	Noisy	LRTA	TDL	LRTDTV	FastHyDe	GLF	KBR	LLRT	WLRTR	NGmeet	TLNLGS
10	PSNR	28.13	38.61	41.90	38.40	41.40	41.61	40.60	41.99	<u>42.61</u>	42.44	**42.90**
	SSIM	0.781	0.973	0.989	0.977	0.989	0.990	0.986	<u>0.991</u>	0.990	<u>0.991</u>	**0.992**
	SAM	16.40	5.55	3.39	4.48	3.87	3.80	2.94	3.43	<u>2.91</u>	3.20	**2.70**
30	PSNR	18.59	32.75	35.07	34.44	37.19	37.47	34.83	36.33	36.99	<u>37.76</u>	**37.84**
	SSIM	0.368	0.916	0.954	0.943	0.971	0.973	0.953	0.967	0.970	<u>0.974</u>	**0.975**
	SAM	36.44	8.09	6.11	6.14	5.22	4.99	4.96	5.16	4.71	<u>4.40</u>	**4.29**
80	PSNR	10.07	27.81	29.38	29.94	32.29	<u>32.52</u>	29.43	31.04	31.30	32.32	**32.71**
	SSIM	0.093	0.782	0.850	0.861	0.920	<u>0.923</u>	0.845	0.894	0.899	0.918	**0.926**
	SAM	59.51	10.59	8.84	8.69	7.41	7.10	7.96	7.10	7.89	<u>6.73</u>	**6.57**
100	PSNR	8.13	26.71	27.73	28.86	31.25	<u>31.32</u>	28.45	29.94	29.77	31.16	**31.56**
	SSIM	0.062	0.733	0.799	0.828	<u>0.901</u>	<u>0.901</u>	0.810	0.864	0.860	0.895	**0.905**
	SAM	64.28	11.24	9.85	9.31	8.055	7.75	8.69	7.63	9.05	<u>7.27</u>	**7.08**
[10,100]	PSNR	14.06	21.91	22.14	30.57	**37.17**	<u>36.82</u>	30.77	29.37	29.96	30.57	36.62
	SSIM	0.229	0.492	0.511	0.866	**0.972**	<u>0.970</u>	0.884	0.820	0.835	0.883	**0.972**
	SAM	54.37	29.75	31.57	7.10	<u>5.253</u>	5.29	7.98	12.44	15.94	13.40	**5.00**

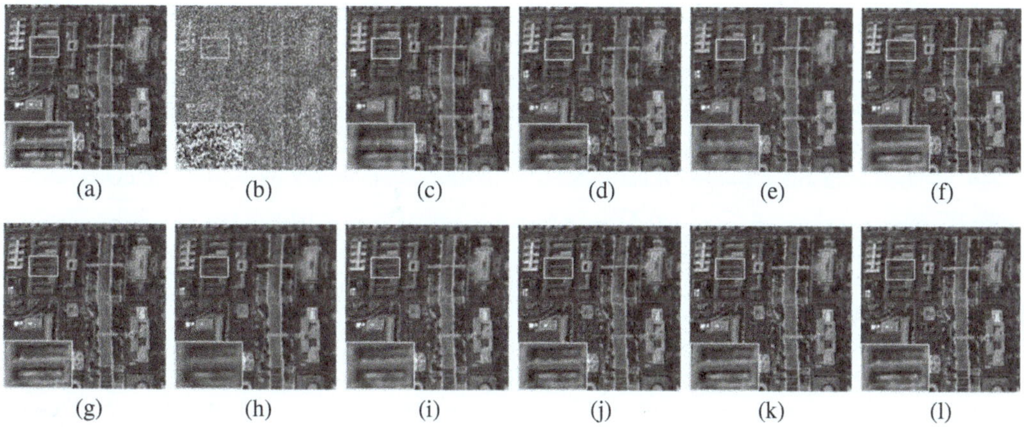

Figure 2.1 Restoration results of band 108 from the WDC dataset at $\sigma = 100$. (a) Original, (b) noisy, (c) LRTA, (d) TDL, (e) LRTDTV, (f) FastHyDe, (g) GLF, (h) KBR, (i) LLRT, (j) WLRTR, (k) NGmeet, and (l) TLNLGS.

nonlocal low-rank approximation methods FastHyDe, GLF, and NGmeet obtain satisfactory results compared with other methods, but the restoration results are slightly smoothed. On the contrary, by exploring the group sparsity on the nonlocal image, TLNLGS removes heavy Gaussian noises while preserving the image details.

Real Experiment

One representative real-world data is selected for the real noisy HSI dataset, i.e., the airborne visible/infrared imaging spectrometer (AVIRIS) Indian Pines dataset. The spatial size of the Indian Pines dataset is 145×145, and the spectral dimension is 220. Due to the influence of the atmosphere (water absorption), the Indian Pines dataset is seriously degraded by noise.

Figure 2.2 shows the restoration results of the real Indian Pines dataset. As shown in Figure 2.2a, the noise seriously influences the image quality. LRTA, TDL, and LLRT can obtain satisfactory

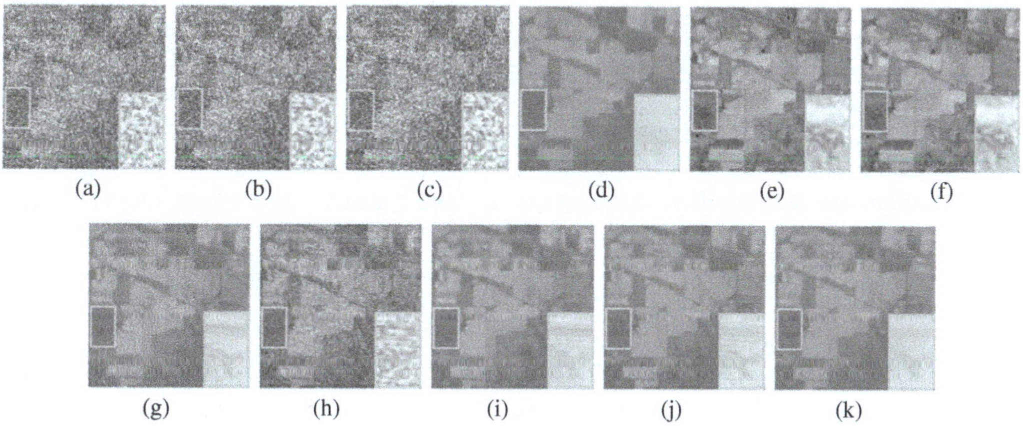

Figure 2.2 Restoration results of band 220 from the real Indian Pines dataset. (a) Noisy, (b) LRTA, (c) TDL, (d) LRTDTV, (e) FAstHyDe, (f) GLF, (g) KBR, (h) LLRT, (i) WLRTR, (j) NGmeet, and (k) TLNLGS.

denoising results in simulated noise, but they fail to remove the high-intensity noise in real data. Although LRTDTV removes the noise by the combination of TV regularization and LRTA, the restored result is over-smoothed. FastHyDe and GLF can remove the obvious noise. KBR, WLRTR, and NGmeet effectively remove the noise and preserve most of the image detail. However, since they ignore the sparse prior of the nonlocal image, some stripe artifacts remain in the denoised results as shown in the enlarged box. TLNLGS eliminates all noises as well as achieves better visual quality.

2.2.2.2 Mixed Noise Degradation Experiments

Simulated Mixed Noise Experimental Design

To evaluate the mixed noise removal effect of different methods, we also select the WDC as the simulated dataset. Seven representative methods are considered for quantitative and visual comparison, i.e., low-rank matrix approximation with TV regularization (LRTV) method [24], weighted low-rank matrix approximation with spatial–spectral TV regularization (LSSTV) method [10], Schatten p-norm-based low-rank matrix approximation (WSNM) method [11], low-rank matrix factorization approximation (NMoG) method [23], low-rank tensor approximation with spatial–spectral TV regularization (LRTDTV) method [32], low-rank tensor approximation with group sparse regularization (LRTDGS) method [33], and factor group sparsity-regularized nonconvex low-rank matrix approximation (FGSLR) method [20]. The PSNR, SSIM, and SAM are employed as quantitative evaluation indices. Moreover, five different mixed noise cases are simulated, i.e.,

Case 1. (Gaussian noise): Zero-mean Gaussian noise with noise variance 0.15 is added to all bands.

Case 2. (Gaussian noise + impulse noise): Mixtures of zero-mean Gaussian noise and impulse noise are added to all bands. The variances of Gaussian noise and percentages of impulse noise are randomly sampled within the range of [0.05,0.2] and [0,0.2], respectively.

Case 3. (Gaussian noise + impulse noise + deadlines): Mixtures of zero-mean Gaussian noise, impulse noise, and deadlines are added to HSI. The variances of Gaussian noise are randomly sampled within the range of [0.05,0.2], and the percentages of impulse noise are set as 0.05 for all bands. Moreover, 40% of bands are added deadlines whose numbers are from 5 to 12.

Case 4. (Gaussian noise + impulse noise + stripes): Mixtures of zero-mean Gaussian noise, impulse noise, and stripes are added to HSI. The distributions of Gaussian and impulse noises are the same as in Case 3. Moreover, 40% of bands are added stripes whose number is from 5 to 12.

Case 5. (Gaussian noise + impulse noise + deadlines + stripes): Mixtures of zero-mean Gaussian noise, impulse noise, deadlines, and stripes are added to HSI. The distributions of Gaussian and impulse noises are the same as in Case 2. Moreover, we select 20% of bands in which to add deadlines and stripes whose numbers are all from 5 to 12. Furthermore, the number of overlapped bands of deadlines and stripes is set as 5% of bands.

Quantitative and Visual Comparison in Simulated Mixed Noise Experiments

Table 2.2 lists the three quantitative indices comparison of different HSI restoration methods on the simulated WDC dataset. The best results among all methods are highlighted in bold. From the table, we can see that LRTA methods outperform low-rank matrix approximation methods. Although LRTDTV and LRTDGS employ the LRTA to capture the high spatial–spectral correlation of HSI, they cannot dynamically adjust the rank with the iteration increase, and the results are

Table 2.2 Quantitative results of comparison methods on the WDC dataset under different mixed noise cases.

Cases	Index	Noisy	LRTV	SSTV	WSNM	NMoG	LRTDTV	LRTDGS	FGSLR
Case 1	PSNR	16.48	31.55	32.67	33.21	33.35	33.47	34.03	**34.38**
	SSIM	0.273	0.883	0.912	0.921	0.926	0.926	0.935	**0.942**
	SAM	0.626	0.121	0.101	0.091	0.093	0.080	0.081	**0.076**
Case 2	PSNR	13.84	32.36	33.88	33.37	30.45	34.08	34.73	**35.64**
	SSIM	0.205	0.907	0.932	0.935	0.882	0.937	0.945	**0.955**
	SAM	0.719	0.112	0.090	0.152	0.148	0.075	0.076	**0.068**
Case 3	PSNR	15.19	32.43	33.67	34.06	30.03	34.06	34.37	**35.54**
	SSIM	0.254	0.911	0.937	0.943	0.878	0.939	0.946	**0.959**
	SAM	0.654	0.113	0.091	0.102	0.157	0.073	0.085	**0.067**
Case 4	PSNR	14.97	32.24	33.55	34.03	32.03	34.03	34.75	**35.43**
	SSIM	0.244	0.907	0.930	0.937	0.921	0.937	0.947	**0.955**
	SAM	0.659	0.113	0.093	0.106	0.147	0.075	0.074	**0.068**
Case 5	PSNR	13.75	32.05	33.52	33.07	30.21	33.90	34.12	**35.03**
	SSIM	0.204	0.902	0.931	0.933	0.876	0.936	0.941	**0.954**
	SAM	0.728	0.117	0.094	0.152	0.150	0.075	0.095	**0.071**

largely determined by the rank selection. FGSLR can significantly outperform other methods with respect to the three evaluation indices since it is a tighter rank approximation than the matrix nuclear norm and can dynamically adjust the rank.

Figure 2.3 presents the restoration results of the simulated WDC dataset under mixed noise Case 5. As shown in Figure 2.3b, the image is seriously contaminated by a mixture of Gaussian,

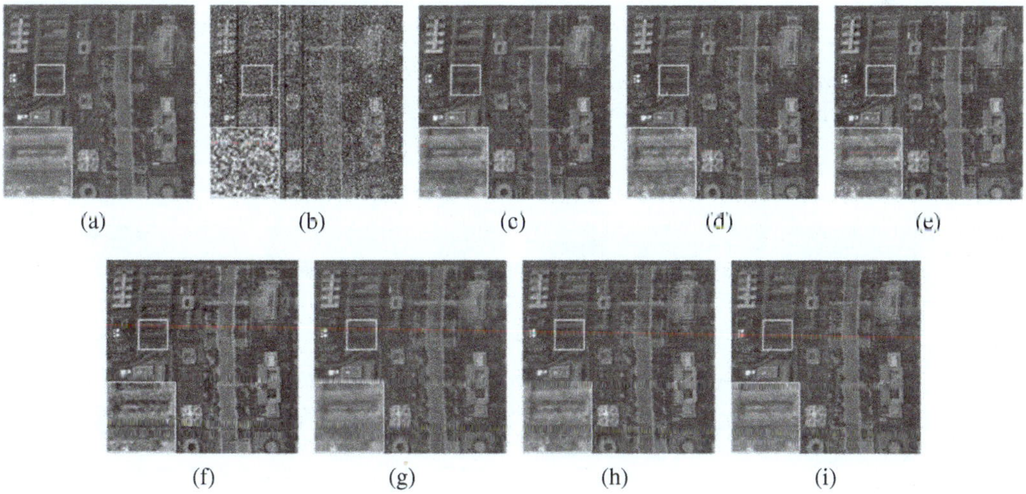

Figure 2.3 Restoration results of band 100 from the WDC dataset at case 5. (a) Original, (b) noisy, (c) LRTV, (d) LSSTV, (e) WSNM, (f) NMoG, (g) LRTDTV, (h) LRTDGS, and (i) FGSLR.

impulse, deadlines, and stripes noises. After being restored by all methods, the mixed noises are largely damped. However, LRTV, LSSTV, WSNM, and NMoG cannot thoroughly remove the noises, and some Gaussian noises are left in the results as shown in the enlarged box. Although LRTDTV successfully removes the mixture noise, it obtains the over-smoothed restoration results. LRTDGS performs satisfactory results, but image details are slightly destroyed shown in the enlarged box. In contrast, we can observe that FGSLR effectively removes the mixture noise as well as restores the image details and structures.

Real Experiment

The GF-5 dataset is selected as a real noisy HSI dataset. The GF-5 dataset was acquired by the GF-5 satellite, which was developed by the Chinese Aerospace Science and Technology Corporation and launched in 2018. The original size of the GF-5 dataset is $2100 \times 2048 \times 180$, and 25 bands are missing information. After removing the missing bands and extracting a small region, a sub-HSI with the size of $256 \times 256 \times 155$ is chosen for experiments. This dataset is seriously degraded by the mixture of Gaussian, stripes, and deadlines noises as shown in Figure 2.4a.

Figure 2.4 shows the restoration results of different methods on band 154. From the results of the enlarged box, we can easily observe that most methods can remove the Gaussian noise but fail to remove the stripes and deadlines. As displayed in Figure 2.4h, the FGSLR method successfully eliminates the mixture noise as well as restores the underlying image structures.

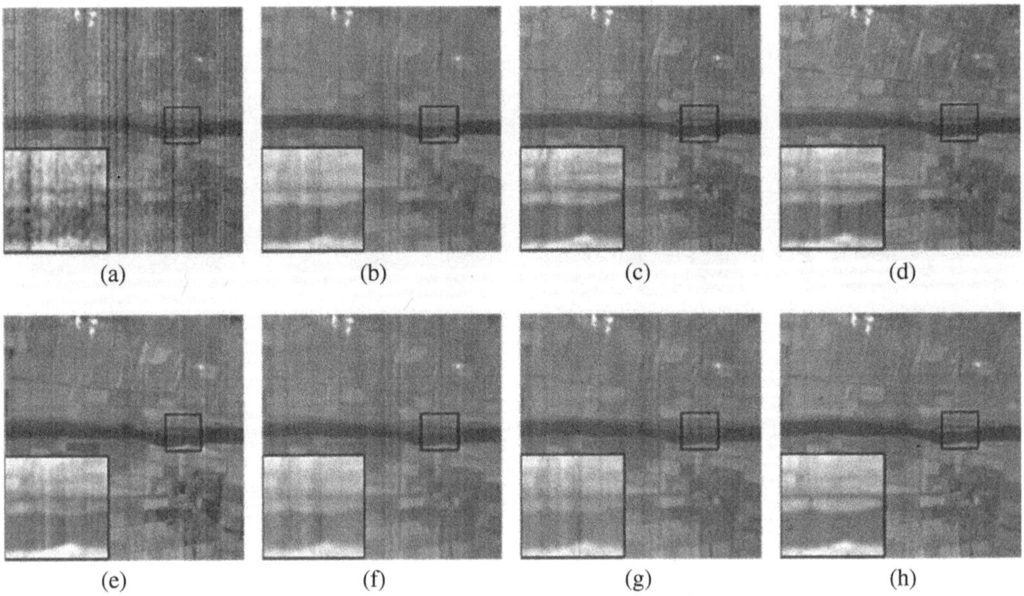

Figure 2.4 Restoration results of band 154 from the real GF-5 dataset. (a) Noisy, (b) LRTV, (c) LSSTV, (d) WSNM, (e) NMoG, (f) LRTDTV, (g) LRTDGS, and (h) FGSLR.

2.3 Data-driven Approaches

Model-driven methods formulate the HSI restoration problem as an optimization task by applying hand-crafted priors, where one of the commonly used regularizations is the spectral low-rank prior. However, the restoration performance of these model-driven methods is overly dependent on the hand-crafted priors [38, 43]. Therefore, in recent years, data-driven deep learning hyperspectral restoration networks have been proposed successively, which utilize the powerful feature representation capabilities of deep convolutional neural networks [44–46]. Although these data-driven deep learning methods achieve competitive restoration performance, poor interpretability and generalization of these networks lead to unstable restoration results in large-scale real scenarios, due to the neglect of the prior properties of HSIs. To address these issues, some model–data-driven methods combine the spectral low-rank property of the HSIs with deep learning networks to improve the interpretability and generalization capability [47, 48]. LR-Net [49] designed and embedded a Low-Rank Module into an end-to-end convolutional restoration network to integrate the spectral low-rank property into the data-driven model. To train these networks, simulated images with different intensities and types of noise need to be generated for supervision. The supervised learning model-data-driven methods achieve degradation removal of HSIs by learning the latent prior properties of simulated noisy data. Due to the distribution difference between simulated mixed noise and real mixed complex noise, have a restoration performance drop, when applying to the real noisy HSIs. In terms of this, some unsupervised deep spectral low-rank decomposition networks have been developed. In the following sections, we first provide an overview of the most recent unsupervised deep spectral low-rank decomposition approaches for HSI noise removal and subsequently present and discuss a few related experimental results.

2.3.1 Survey of Unsupervised Deep Spectral Low-rank Regularization

To achieve unsupervised image restoration, the deep image prior method [50] was proposed to reconstruct the desired images in a self-supervised learning manner. DIP model uses the deep learning networks as a data-driven regularization, called the untrained neural network prior (UNNP), for image restoration [51, 52]. The neural network tends to fit the image data first and then the degradations, when feeding a random vector into the network and using a single degraded image for supervision. Therefore, self-supervised image restoration can be achieved by performing an early stopping strategy in the training phase. To our best knowledge, the Deep Hyperspectral Prior model [53] is the first unsupervised network to adopt the UNNP to address HSI restoration tasks. The restoration processing is presented as shown in Figure 2.5.

Following that, some other DIP-based unsupervised methods have been proposed for HSI restoration [54–56]. The 2-D U-Net and 3-D U-Net were often applied as the DIP network for hyperspectral restoration. Besides the improvement of the architecture of DIP networks, combining unsupervised neural networks with spectral low-rank prior knowledge is an important research topic.

To utilize the spectral low-rank regularization, low-rank approximation-based methods aim to find two matrices, spatial coefficient $\mathbf{U} \in \mathbb{R}^{M\times r}$ and spectral basis $\in \mathbb{R}^{N\times r}$, where $r = \min(M, N)$, to represent the hyperspectral spatial–spectral matrix $\mathbf{X} \in \mathbb{R}^{M\times N}$ (M and N denote the number of spatial pixels and spectral bands) by their product:

$$\min_{\mathbf{U},\mathbf{V}} \|\mathbf{X} - \mathbf{U}\mathbf{V}^T\|_F + R(\mathbf{U}, \mathbf{V}), \tag{2.3}$$

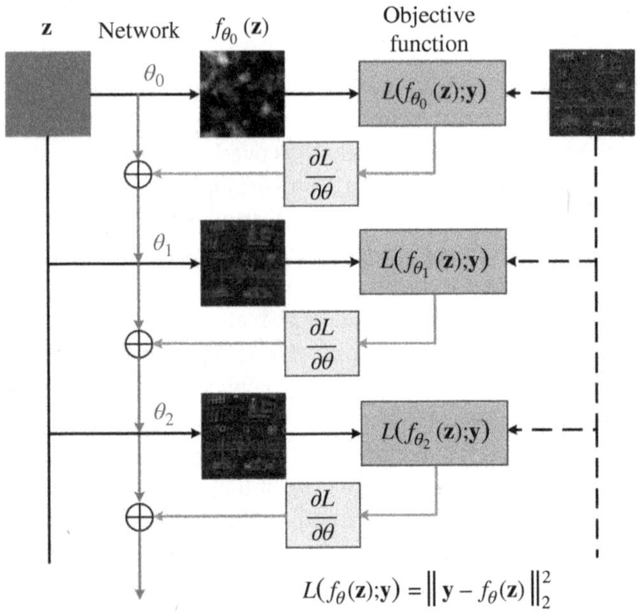

Figure 2.5 Untrained neural network priors. The unsupervised training process of the deep image prior.

where the function $R(\mathbf{U}, \mathbf{V})$ is a regularizer for $\mathbf{U}$ and $\mathbf{V}$. This low-rank approximation is frequently used in the recovery of HSIs by principal component analysis (PCA) [57], nonnegative matrix factorization (NMF) [58], and k-means [59]. However, these low-rank approximations are not usually robust enough to learn low-rank matrices with outliers for the non-Gaussian signal. To address the limitation, on the one hand, some improved low-rank decomposition methods ameliorate this shortcoming [60, 61]. On the other hand, related work applying deep networks for matrix factorization in a self-supervised manner has also emerged as an important way to integrate spectral low-rank prior with data-driven deep learning [62].

Therefore, the deep networks can be adopted as implicit regularizers for $\mathbf{U}$ and $\mathbf{V}$. Two generative networks $f_\mathbf{U}$ and $f_\mathbf{V}$ in DeepTensor [63] are utilized to model spatial coefficient $\mathbf{U}$ and spectral basis $\mathbf{V}$ for imposing data-driven regularization:

$$\min_{\mathbf{U},\mathbf{V}} \|\mathbf{X} - f_\mathbf{U}(\mathbf{z}_\mathbf{U}) f_\mathbf{V}(\mathbf{z}_\mathbf{V})^T\|_F \tag{2.4}$$

where $\mathbf{z}_\mathbf{U}$ and $\mathbf{z}_\mathbf{V}$ are random vectors as inputs of the 2-D spatial network $f_\mathbf{U}$ and the 1-D spectral network $f_\mathbf{V}$. Based on the linear mixture model for HSIs, several 2-D U-Net models were designed to generate abundance maps, and several 1-D fully connected networks were used to model endmembers in DS2DP [64] for HSI restoration. Taking the above optimization problem as the loss function, DIP-based deep low-rank decomposition networks use the noisy HSI $\mathbf{X}$ as the supervision and generate the latent spatial coefficient and spectral basis to obtain the restoration result by early stopping in an unsupervised manner.

The data structure of degraded HSIs is complex and the mixed noise distribution is diverse. It is challenging to directly learn DIP networks from raw noisy observation data to restore fine HSIs. To mitigate the self-supervised training challenge, integrating the DIP networks with the iterative optimization framework is an effective strategy to benefit from the interpretable model-driven methods and efficient data-driven networks. To further enhance the unsupervised training stability, some traditional handcrafted prior regularization can be imposed into the iterative optimization framework as well, such as TV regularization, and non-local prior. The alternating direction method of multipliers (ADMM) or half-quadratic splitting (HQS) optimization algorithm can be leveraged to solve the HSI restoration problem with deep spectral low-rank regularization.

By lexicographically ordering the HSI tensors, the degradation observe model can be formulated as:

$$\mathbf{Y} = \mathbf{X} + \mathbf{S} + \mathbf{N}, \tag{2.5}$$

where $\mathbf{Y}, \mathbf{X}, \mathbf{S}, \mathbf{N} \in R^{W \times B}$ denote the vectorized form of $\mathcal{Y}, \mathcal{X}, \mathcal{S}, \mathcal{N}$, and $W = M \times N$. Based on the maximum-a-posteriori (MAP) estimation, the HSI mixed noise removal problem can be formulated to solve the optimization problem:

$$\hat{\mathbf{X}} = \arg\min_{\mathbf{X}} \|\mathbf{Y} - \mathbf{X} - \mathbf{S}\|_F^2 + \lambda_1 R_1(\mathbf{X}) + \lambda_2 R_2(\mathbf{S}), \tag{2.6}$$

where λ_1 and λ_2 indicates the regularization weight, and $R_1(\mathbf{X})$ is the deep spectral low-rank regularizer of clean HSIs. $R_2(\mathbf{S})$ is the sparse regularization term. To impose deep spectral low-rank regularization, Flex-DLD [65] developed an ADMM-based iterative optimization framework and built two generative neural networks to introduce spectral low-rank prior. The loss function is formulated as:

$$\mathcal{L} = \left\|\mathbf{Y} - f_{\mathbf{U}}(Z_{\mathbf{U}}) f_{\mathbf{V}}(\mathbf{z}_{\mathbf{V}})^T\right\|_F^2 + \lambda \left\|f_{\mathbf{U}}(\mathbf{z}_{\mathbf{U}})^T f_{\mathbf{U}}(\mathbf{z}_{\mathbf{U}}) - \mathbf{I}\right\|_F^2, \tag{2.7}$$

where $\mathbf{I}$ denotes the identity matrix. Adam optimizer is leveraged to optimize parameters of the deep low-rank networks $f_{\mathrm{U}}(\cdot)$ and $f_{\mathrm{V}}(\cdot)$. To further introduce spatial regularization, the spatial–spectral TV regularization can also added into the loss function to improve the restoration performance of deep spectral low-rank decomposition-based approaches.

2.3.2 Experimental Results

2.3.2.1 Comparison Methods and Evaluation Measures

We select the following four unsupervised deep spectral low-rank regularization methods: disentangled spatiospectral deep priors (DS2DP) [64], deep sparse and low-rank model (DIP-SLR) [62], DeepTensor [63], deep low-rank decomposition model With flexible priors (Flex-DLD) [65]. We use the PSNR, SAM, and SSIM as evaluation criteria for the HSI restoration results of different methods.

2.3.2.2 Gaussian Noise Degradation Experiments

Experimental Settings

The CAVE dataset with 32 images of size $512 \times 512 \times 31$ is selected as the testing dataset, divided into five sections, which consist of different scenes and objects. Each band of the images is normalized into [0,1] for processing and evaluation. For the Gaussian noise case, the noise settings are additive Gaussian noise $N(0,\sigma^2\mathbf{I})$ with σ = 10, 30, 50, 100 to fully validate different deep spectral low-rank methods.

Quantitative and Visual Comparison in Gaussian Noise Experiments

The quantitative results of different methods on the CAVE datasets under different Gaussian noise cases are listed in Table 2.3. The evaluation indices of the best methods are highlighted by using

Table 2.3 Quantitative results of comparison methods on the CAVE dataset under different Gaussian noise cases.

Intensity	Index	Noisy	DIP-SLR	DS2DP	DeepTensor	Flex_DLD
10	PSNR	28.131	40.408	38.789	40.743	**42.795**
	SSIM	0.784	0.985	0.960	0.985	**0.990**
	SAM	31.512	4.963	9.367	5.164	**4.284**
30	PSNR	18.588	37.112	34.977	36.063	**39.279**
	SSIM	0.358	0.968	0.912	0.943	**0.976**
	SAM	52.131	6.255	11.227	11.254	**5.501**
50	PSNR	14.152	34.965	33.185	34.469	**37.335**
	SSIM	0.208	0.949	0.886	0.929	**0.963**
	SAM	61.132	7.366	12.050	10.211	**6.296**
100	PSNR	8.130	32.348	30.765	31.083	**34.086**
	SSIM	0.087	0.903	0.781	0.847	**0.933**
	SAM	71.732	10.063	16.571	15.260	**8.050**

bold. As shown in Table 2.3, combining the self-supervised DIP model with the spectral low-rank prior knowledge, these unsupervised hyperspectral denoising methods can handle the Gaussian noise with different intensities well. Figure 2.6 shows the restoration results of different unsupervised deep denoising methods with the Gaussian noise variance 50. DIP-SLR removed the heavy Gaussian noise but left some chessboard artifacts. DS2DP and DeepTensor achieved better restoration results. However, the detailed local area has some noise. Flex-DLD obtain satisfactory denoising results compared with other methods, but the restoration results are slightly smoothed.

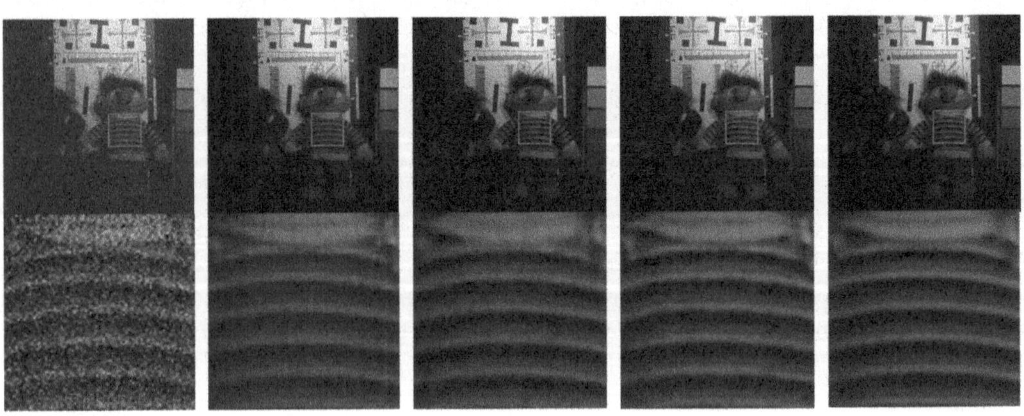

Noisy (14.149)	DIP-SLR (32.835)	DS2DP (31.082)	DeepTensor (32.723)	Flex-DLD (35.218)

Figure 2.6 Restoration results of band 28 from the CAVE-toy image with the noise variance 50.

2.3.2.3 Mixed Noise Degradation Experiments

Experimental Settings

To evaluate the mixed noise removal effect of these deep low-rank unsupervised methods, the CAVE dataset was also chosen as the simulated dataset. Moreover, four different mixed noise cases with Gaussian noise, impulse noise, stripes and deadlines are simulated, i.e.,

Case 1. (Gaussian noise + impulse noise): Different intensities of zero-mean Gaussian noise and impulse noise are simulated to all bands. The variances of Gaussian noise and percentages of impulse noise are randomly sampled within the range of [0,0.2].

Case 2. (Gaussian noise + impulse noise + stripes): Mixtures of zero-mean Gaussian noise, impulse noise, and stripes are added to the CAVE images. The variances of Gaussian noise and percentages of impulse noise are also randomly sampled within the range of [0,0.2] same as Case1. In addition, 11 bands are added stripes whose numbers are from 20 to 40.

Case 3. (Gaussian noise + impulse noise + deadlines): Each band is simulated by the Gaussian and impulse noise as in Case 1. 11 bands are added deadlines whose numbers are from 3 to 10.

Case 4. (Gaussian noise + impulse noise + stripes + deadlines): Mixtures of zero-mean Gaussian noise, impulse noise, deadlines, and stripes are added to HSI. The distributions of Gaussian and impulse noises are the same as in Case 1. Stripes and deadlines are added as Cases 2 and 3, respectively.

Quantitative and Visual Comparison in Mixed Noise Experiments

Table 2.4 lists four mixed noisy comparisons of different HSI restoration methods on the CAVE datasets. The best results among all methods are highlighted in bold. Due to the good generalizability of the DIP-based model for different degradations, these unsupervised methods can eliminate the complex mixed noise, benefiting from the utilization of spectral low-rank property of clean HSIs. However, the denoising performance of the DIP-SLR method in mixed noisy cases is not as well as its performance in the Gaussian noise. DIP-SLR directly adopts SVD to obtain the eigenimages of noisy HSIs for self-supervision of a 2-D DIP network, ignoring the noise in spectral basis.

Table 2.4 Quantitative results of comparison methods on the CAVE dataset under different mixed noise cases.

Cases	Index	Noisy	DIP-SLR	DS2DP	DeepTensor	Flex_DLD
Case 1	PSNR	12.974	21.711	35.873	37.513	**39.718**
	SSIM	0.181	0.552	0.918	0.967	**0.980**
	SAM	54.749	31.504	9.785	6.978	**5.218**
Case 2	PSNR	12.938	21.705	35.774	37.235	**39.465**
	SSIM	0.179	0.552	0.916	0.962	**0.976**
	SAM	54.921	31.505	10.002	7.651	**5.831**
Case 3	PSNR	12.972	21.725	35.959	37.467	**39.467**
	SSIM	0.180	0.552	0.926	0.966	**0.978**
	SAM	54.788	31.457	9.497	6.846	**5.351**
Case 4	PSNR	12.935	21.734	35.669	37.189	**39.250**
	SSIM	0.178	0.552	0.918	0.961	**0.975**
	SAM	54.958	31.460	10.003	7.500	**6.008**

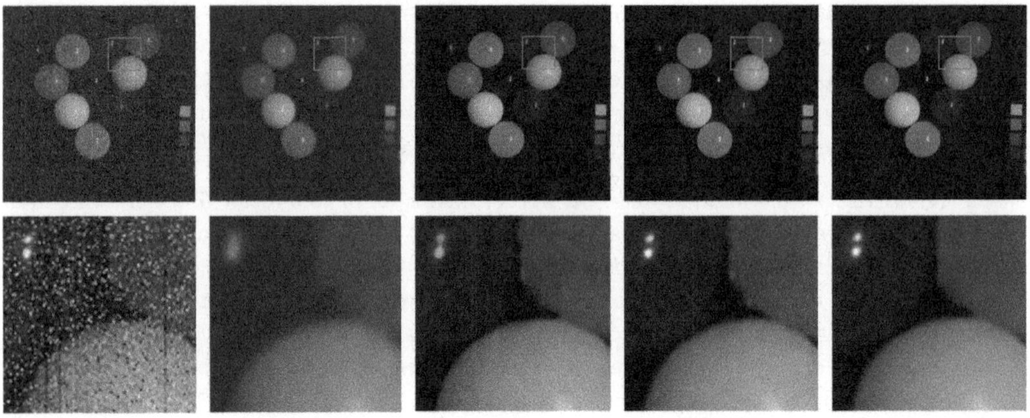

Figure 2.7 Restoration results of band 28 from the CAVE-superballs image with the mixed noisy Case 6.

By simultaneously generating the spectral basis and spatial coefficient by DIP networks, DS2DP and DeepTensor can obtain better denoising performance. Flex_DLD utilizes the ADMM-based plug-and-play framework and introduces spatial–spectral TV loss to achieve competitive denoising results.

The mixed noise removal results in Case 6 are presented in Figure 2.7. DIP-SLR removed the Gaussian noise, impulse noise, stripes, and deadlines, but spectral distortion occurs in the denoising result. DS2DP and DeepTensor maintained the original spectral information. Compared with DS2DP and DeepTensor, Flex-DLD obtained better mixed-noise restoration results, but some spatial details were lost.

2.4 Conclusion and Outlook

This chapter presents a review of state-of-the-art model-driven and data-driven spectral low-rank regularization methods for HSI restoration. Model-driven spectral low-rank optimization methods fully utilize the physical degradation process of hyperspectral imaging and hand-crafted expert prior knowledge of HSIs to achieve the high generalization restoration in complex scenarios. Deep learning techniques have demonstrated its efficient performance on various hyperspectral restoration tasks, by automatically learning implicit prior properties using data-driven strategies. However, data-driven approaches often overly rely on training simulated HSIs, leading to its lack of interpretability and generalization capabilities. Therefore, some deep low-rank decomposition-based networks have been applied for the HSI mixed noise removal and have achieved competitive performance. Hence, spectral low-rank regularization is suitable for HSI restoration.

A limitation of spectral low-rank regularization is that the iterative optimization framework has many hyper-parameters that need to select and high time consumptions. Moreover, the training process and restoration performance of unsupervised deep low-rank decomposition based on DIP models are usually not stable enough in complex noisy scenarios, which remains a key challenge from a practical point of view. Therefore, a self-supervised strategy with Large Language Model or Large Vision Model can be a direction for future research.

References

1 Green, R.O., Eastwood, M.L., Sarture, C.M. et al. (1998). Imaging spectroscopy and the airborne visible/infrared imaging spectrometer (AVIRIS). *Remote Sens. Environ.* 65 (3): 227–248.

2 Hong, D., Yokoya, N., Chanussot, J., and Zhu, X.X. (2018). An augmented linear mixing model to address spectral variability for hyperspectral unmixing. *IEEE Trans. Image Process.* 28 (4): 1923–1938.

3 Uzair, M., Mahmood, A., and Mian, A. (2015). Hyperspectral face recognition with spatiospectral information fusion and PLS regression. *IEEE Trans. Image Process.* 24 (3): 1127–1137.

4 Hong, D., Wu, X., Ghamisi, P. et al. (2020). Invariant attribute profiles: a spatial-frequency joint feature extractor for hyperspectral image classification. *IEEE Trans. Geosci. Remote Sens.* 58 (6): 3791–3808.

5 Ghamisi, P., Yokoya, N., Li, J. et al. (2017). Advances in hyperspectral image and signal processing: a comprehensive overview of the state of the art. *IEEE Geosci. Remote Sens. Mag.* 5 (4): 37–78.

6 Rasti, B., Chang, Y., Dalsasso, E. et al. (2021). Image restoration for remote sensing: overview and toolbox. *IEEE Geosci. Remote Sens. Mag.* 10 (2): 201–230.

7 Bioucas-Dias, J.M., Plaza, A., Dobigeon, N. et al. (2012). Hyperspectral unmixing overview: geometrical, statistical, and sparse regression-based approaches. *IEEE J. Sel. Top. Appl. Earth Obs. Remote Sens.* 5 (2): 354–379.

8 Zhang, H., He, W., Zhang, L. et al. (2013). Hyperspectral image restoration using low-rank matrix recovery. *IEEE Trans. Geosci. Remote Sens.* 52 (8): 4729–4743.

9 He, W., Zhang, H., Zhang, L., and Shen, H. (2015). Hyperspectral image denoising via noise-adjusted iterative low-rank matrix approximation. *IEEE J. Sel. Top. Appl. Earth Obs. Remote Sens.* 8 (6): 3050–3061.

10 Wang, Q., Wu, Z., Jin, J. et al. (2018). Low rank constraint and spatial spectral total variation for hyperspectral image mixed denoising. *Signal Process.* 142: 11–26.

11 Xie, Y., Qu, Y., Tao, D. et al. (2016). Hyperspectral image restoration via iteratively regularized weighted schatten p-norm minimization. *IEEE Trans. Geosci. Remote Sens.* 54 (8): 4642–4659.

12 Chen, Y., Guo, Y., Wang, Y. et al. (2017). Denoising of hyperspectral images using nonconvex low rank matrix approximation. *IEEE Trans. Geosci. Remote Sens.* 55 (9): 5366–5380.

13 Ye, H., Li, H., Yang, B. et al. (2019). A novel rank approximation method for mixture noise removal of hyperspectral images. *IEEE Trans. Geosci. Remote Sens.* 57 (7): 4457–4469.

14 Zhuang, L. and Bioucas-Dias, J.M. (2018). Fast hyperspectral image denoising and inpainting based on low-rank and sparse representations. *IEEE J. Sel. Top. Appl. Earth Obs. Remote Sens.* 11 (3): 730–742.

15 Chen, Y., Huang, T.Z., Zhao, X.L., and Deng, L.J. (2018). Hyperspectral image restoration using framelet-regularized low-rank nonnegative matrix factorization. *Appl. Math. Model.* 63: 128–147.

16 Cao, C., Yu, J., Zhou, C. et al. (2019). Hyperspectral image denoising via subspace-based nonlocal low-rank and sparse factorization. *IEEE J. Sel. Top. Appl. Earth Obs. Remote Sens.* 12 (3): 973–988.

17 He, W., Yao, Q., Li, C. et al. (2019). Non-local meets global: an integrated paradigm for hyperspectral denoising. *IEEE/CVF Conference on Computer Vision and Pattern Recognition (CVPR)*, 6868–6877, Long Beach, CA, USA (15–20 June 2019), IEEE.

18 Jiang, T.X., Zhuang, L., Huang, T.Z. et al. (2021). Adaptive hyperspectral mixed noise removal. *IEEE Trans. Geosci. Remote Sens.* 60: 1–13.

19 Zheng, Y.B., Huang, T.Z., Zhao, X.L. et al. (2020). Double-factor-regularized low-rank tensor factorization for mixed noise removal in hyperspectral image. *IEEE Trans. Geosci. Remote Sens.* 58 (12): 8450–8464.

20 Chen, Y., Huang, T.Z., He, W. et al. (2021). Hyperspectral image denoising using factor group sparsity-regularized nonconvex low-rank approximation. *IEEE Trans. Geosci. Remote Sens.* 60: 1–16.

21 Chen, Y., He, W., Zhao, X.L. et al. (2022). Exploring nonlocal group sparsity under transform learning for hyperspectral image denoising. *IEEE Trans. Geosci. Remote Sens.* 60: 1–18.

22 Peng, J., Wang, H., Cao, X. et al. (2022). Fast noise removal in hyperspectral images via representative coefficient total variation. *IEEE Trans. Geosci. Remote Sens.* 60: 1–17.

23 Chen, Y., Cao, X., Zhao, Q. et al. (2017). Denoising hyperspectral image with non-iid noise structure. *IEEE Trans. Cybern.* 48 (3): 1054–1066.

24 He, W., Zhang, H., Zhang, L., and Shen, H. (2015). Total-variation-regularized low-rank matrix factorization for hyperspectral image restoration. *IEEE Trans. Geosci. Remote Sens.* 54 (1): 178–188.

25 He, W., Zhang, H., Shen, H., and Zhang, L. (2018). Hyperspectral image denoising using local low-rank matrix recovery and global spatial–spectral total variation. *IEEE J. Sel. Top. Appl. Earth Obs. Remote Sens.* 11 (3): 713–729.

26 Guo, X., Huang, X., Zhang, L., and Zhang, L. (2013). Hyperspectral image noise reduction based on rank-1 tensor decomposition. *ISPRS J. Photogramm. Remote Sens.* 83: 50–63.

27 Renard, N., Bourennane, S., and Blanc-Talon, J. (2008). Denoising and dimensionality reduction using multilinear tools for hyperspectral images. *IEEE Geosci. Remote Sens. Lett.* 5 (2): 138–142.

28 Karami, A., Yazdi, M., and Asli, A.Z. (2011). Noise reduction of hyperspectral images using kernel non-negative tucker decomposition. *IEEE J. Sel. Top. Signal Process.* 5 (3): 487–493.

29 Fan, H., Chen, Y., Guo, Y. et al. (2017). Hyperspectral image restoration using low-rank tensor recovery. *IEEE J. Sel. Top. Appl. Earth Obs. Remote Sens.* 10 (10): 4589–4604.

30 Zheng, Y.B., Huang, T.Z., Zhao, X.L. et al. (2019). Mixed noise removal in hyperspectral image via low-fibered-rank regularization. *IEEE Trans. Geosci. Remote Sens.* 58 (1): 734–749.

31 He, W., Chen, Y., Yokoya, N. et al. (2022). Hyperspectral super-resolution via coupled tensor ring factorization. *Pattern Recogn.* 122: 108280.

32 Wang, Y., Peng, J., Zhao, Q. et al. (2017). Hyperspectral image restoration via total variation regularized low-rank tensor decomposition. *IEEE J. Sel. Top. Appl. Earth Obs. Remote Sens.* 11 (4): 1227–1243.

33 Chen, Y., He, W., Yokoya, N., and Huang, T. (2020). Hyperspectral image restoration using weighted group sparsity-regularized low-rank tensor decomposition. *IEEE Trans. Cybern.* 50 (8): 3556–3570.

34 Xiong, F., Zhou, J., and Qian, Y. (2019). Hyperspectral restoration via l_0 gradient regularized low-rank tensor factorization. *IEEE Trans. Geosci. Remote Sens.* 57 (12): 10410–10425.

35 Fan, H., Li, C., Guo, Y. et al. (2018). Spatial–spectral total variation regularized low-rank tensor decomposition for hyperspectral image denoising. *IEEE Trans. Geosci. Remote Sens.* 56 (10): 6196–6213.

36 Chen, Y., Zeng, J., He, W. et al. (2022). Hyperspectral and multispectral image fusion using factor smoothed tensor ring decomposition. *IEEE Trans. Geosci. Remote Sens.* 60: 1–17.

37 Peng, Y., Meng, D., Xu, Z. et al. (2014). Decomposable nonlocal tensor dictionary learning for multispectral image denoising. *2014 IEEE Conference on Computer Vision and Pattern Recognition*, 2949–2956, Columbus, OH, USA (23–28 June 2014). IEEE.

38 Xie, Q., Zhao, Q., Meng, D., and Xu, Z. (2017). Kronecker-basis-representation based tensor sparsity and its applications to tensor recovery. *IEEE Trans. Pattern Anal. Mach. Intell.* 40 (8): 1888–1902.

39 Chang, Y., Yan, L., and Zhong, S. (2017). Hyper-laplacian regularized unidirectional low-rank tensor recovery for multispectral image denoising. *IEEE Conference on Computer Vision and Pattern Recognition (CVPR)*, 4260–4268, Honolulu, HI, USA (21–26 July 2017). IEEE.

40 Chang, Y., Yan, L., Zhao, X.L. et al. (2020). Weighted low-rank tensor recovery for hyperspectral image restoration. *IEEE Trans. Cybern.* 50 (11): 4558–4572.

41 Chen, Y., He, W., Yokoya, N. et al. (2019). Nonlocal tensor-ring decomposition for hyperspectral image denoising. *IEEE Trans. Geosci. Remote Sens.* 58 (2): 1348–1362.

42 Zhuang, L., Fu, X., Ng, M.K., and Bioucas-Dias, J.M. (2021). Hyperspectral image denoising based on global and nonlocal low-rank factorizations. *IEEE Trans. Geosci. Remote Sens.* 59 (12): 10438–10454.

43 Lu, T., Li, S.T., Fang, L.Y. et al. (2016). Spectral-spatial adaptive sparse representation for hyperspectral image denoising. *IEEE Trans. Geosci. Remote Sens.* 54 (1): 373–385.

44 Dong, W.S., Wang, H., Wu, F.F. et al. (2019). Deep spatial-spectral representation learning for hyperspectral image denoising. *IEEE Trans. Comput. Imaging* 5 (4): 635–648.

45 Wei, K.X., Fu, Y., and Huang, H. (2021). 3-D quasi-recurrent neural network for hyperspectral image denoising. *IEEE Trans. Neural Netw. Learn. Syst.* 32 (1): 363–375.

46 Yuan, Q.Q., Zhang, Q., Li, J. et al. (2019). Hyperspectral image denoising employing a spatial-spectral deep residual convolutional neural network. *IEEE Trans. Geosci. Remote Sens.* 57 (2): 1205–1218.

47 Xiong, F.C., Zhou, J., Tao, S.Y. et al. (2022). SMDS-Net: model guided spectral-spatial network for hyperspectral image denoising. *IEEE Trans. Image Process.* 31: 5469–5483.

48 Bodrito, T., Zouaoui, A., Chanussot, J., and Mairal, J. (2021). A trainable spectral-spatial sparse coding model for hyperspectral image restoration. *Adv. Neural Inf. Proces. Syst.* 34: 5430–5442.

49 Zhang, H.Y., Chen, H.Y., Yang, G.Y., and Zhang, L.P. (2021). LR-Net: low-rank spatial-spectral network for hyperspectral image denoising. *IEEE Trans. Image Process.* 30: 8743–8758.

50 Ulyanov, D., Vedaldi, A., and Lempitsky, V. (2018). Deep image prior. *2018 IEEE/CVF Conference on Computer Vision and Pattern Recognition*, 9446–9454, Salt Lake City, UT, USA (18–23 June 2018). IEEE.

51 Qayyum, A., Ilahi, I., Shamshad, F. et al. (2023). Untrained neural network priors for inverse imaging problems: a survey. *IEEE Trans. Pattern Anal.* 45 (5): 6511–6536.

52 Shi, Z.L., Mettes, P., Maji, S., and Snoek, C.G.M. (2022). On measuring and controlling the spectral bias of the deep image prior. *Int. J. Comput. Vis.* 130 (4): 885–908.

53 Sidorov, O. and Hardeberg, J. (2019). Deep hyperspectral prior: single-image denoising, inpainting, super-resolution. *2019 IEEE/CVF International Conference on Computer Vision Workshop (ICCVW)*, 3844–3851, Seoul, Korea (South) (27–28 October 2019). IEEE.

54 Lin, B.H., Tao, X.M., and Lu, J.H. (2020). Hyperspectral image denoising via matrix factorization and deep prior regularization. *IEEE Trans. Image Process.* 29: 565–578.

55 Shen, W.L., Liu, J.M., Li, J.H., and Tian, C. (2023). Deep tensor attention prior network for hyperspectral image denoising. *IEEE J. Sel. Top. Appl. Earth Obs. Remote Sens.* 16: 6448–6462.

56 Wu, W.H., Huang, T.Z., Zhao, X.L. et al. (2022). Hyperspectral image denoising via tensor low-rank prior and unsupervised deep spatial-spectral prior. *IEEE Trans. Geosci. Remote Sens.* 60: https://doi.org/10.1109/TGRS.2022.3228927.

57 Chen, G.Y. and Qian, S.E. (2011). Denoising of hyperspectral imagery using principal component analysis and wavelet shrinkage. *IEEE Trans. Geosci. Remote Sens.* 49 (3): 973–980.

58 Xu, Y.Y. and Qian, Y.T. (2016). Group sparse nonnegative matrix factorization for hyperspectral image denoising. *2016 IEEE International Geoscience and Remote Sensing Symposium (IGARSS)*, 6958–6961, Beijing, China (10–15 July 2016). IEEE.

59 Cohen, M.B., Elder, S., Musco, C. et al. Dimensionality reduction for k-means clustering and low rank approximation. *Proceedings of the Forty-seventh Annual ACM Symposium on Theory of Computing*, Portland, OR, USA, June 14–17, 2015, pp. 163–172.

60 Bahri, M., Panagakis, Y., and Zafeiriou, S. (2019). Robust Kronecker component analysis. *IEEE Trans. Pattern Anal.* 41 (10): 2365–2379.

61 Chen, X., Han, Z., Wang, Y. et al. (2018). A generalized model for robust tensor factorization with noise modeling by mixture of Gaussians. *IEEE Trans. Neural Netw. Learn Syst.* 29 (11): 5380–5393.

62 Nguyen, H.V., Ulfarsson, M.O., Sigurdsson, J. et al. (2022). Deep sparse and low-rank prior for hyperspectral image denoising. *2022 IEEE International Geoscience and Remote Sensing Symposium*, 1217–1220, Kuala Lumpur, Malaysia (17–22 July 2022). IEEE.

63 Saragadam, V., Balestriero, R., Veeraraghavan, A., and Baraniuk, R.G. (2024). Deeptensor: low-rank tensor decomposition with deep network priors. *IEEE Trans. Pattern Anal. Mach. Intell.* 46: 10337–10348.

64 Miao, Y.C., Zhao, X.L., Fu, X. et al. (2021). Hyperspectral denoising using unsupervised disentangled spatiospectral deep priors. *IEEE Trans. Geosci. Remote Sens.* 60: 5513916.

65 Chen, Y., Zhang, H., Wang, Y. et al. (2024). Flex-DLD: deep low-rank decomposition model with flexible priors for hyperspectral image denoising and restoration. *IEEE Trans. Image Process.* 33: 1211–1226.

3

Hyperspectral Image Denoising Based on Tensor Models

Yu-Bang Zheng[1], *Jian-Li Wang*[2], *and Xi-Le Zhao*[3,*]

[1] *School of Information Science and Technology, Southwest Jiaotong University, Chengdu, China*
[2] *School of Computing and Artificial Intelligence, Southwest Jiaotong University, Chengdu, China*
[3] *School of Mathematical Sciences, University of Electronic Science and Technology of China, Chengdu, China*

Mathematical Symbols Used in This Chapter

$\mathcal{Y}$	Degraded HSI.
$\mathcal{X}$	High-quality HSI.
A	Degradation operator.
$\mathcal{E}$	Noise.
Ω	Index set for the known elements.
λ	Regularization parameter.
$\mathcal{N}$	Gaussian noise.
$\mathcal{S}$	Sparse noise.
$\mathbf{g}_r^{(k)} \in \mathbb{R}^{I_k}$ for $k = 1, 2, \ldots, N$	CP factors.
$\mathcal{G} \in \mathbb{R}^{r_1 \times r_2 \times \ldots \times r_N}$	Core tensor.
$\mathbf{U}_k \in \mathbb{R}^{I_k \times r_k}$ for $k = 1, 2, \ldots, N$	Matrices.
τ	Regularization parameters.
$\mathbf{D}_k$	Difference matrix.

3.1 Introduction

Hyperspectral images (HSIs) present intricate, multi-dimensional representations capturing a wide spectrum of spectral data for each pixel within a scene [1, 2], making HSIs invaluable for various applications, including natural disaster monitoring, terrain detection, and land use analysis [3–6]. However, real-world HSIs commonly encounter issues such as noise contamination (e.g., Gaussian noise, salt and pepper noise, deadlines, and stripes) and information loss (e.g., due to cloud cover, as depicted in Figure 3.1), stemming from limitations in imaging mechanisms and conditions. These factors significantly degrade the quality of HSIs, impacting the accuracy and reliability of subsequent analysis tasks such as classification, target recognition, and change detection. HSI reconstruction aims to restore a complete and high-quality HSI from a degraded version. In recent

*Corresponding author for this chapter.

Machine-Learning-Based Hyperspectral Image Processing, First Edition. Edited by Bing Zhang.

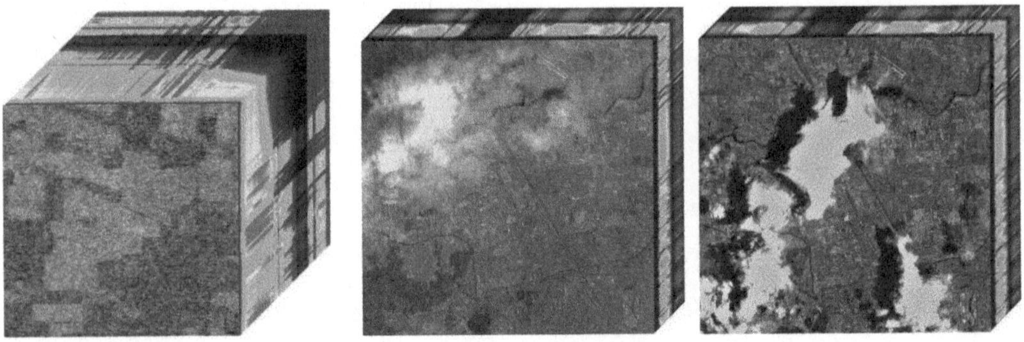

Figure 3.1 An example of noisy image and cloud-contaminated image.

years, tensor modeling methods have emerged as potent tools for HSI reconstruction, achieving notable success in improving image quality and facilitating more accurate analysis.

This chapter will first introduce the fundamental framework for HSI reconstruction. Subsequently, it will delve into the application of tensor modeling-based methods for addressing HSI reconstruction challenges, providing a comprehensive understanding of underlying concepts, models, and algorithms. Finally, experiments on representative datasets will be conducted to evaluate and compare the performance of various HSI reconstruction methods.

3.2 HSI Reconstruction

As a natural extension of vectors and matrices, tensors can effectively represent HSIs. For instance, an HSI can be depicted as a third-order tensor $\mathcal{X} \in \mathbb{R}^{I_1 \times I_2 \times I_3}$ (I_1: spatial height, I_2: spatial width, I_3: spectral band). Therefore, the problem of HSI reconstruction can be mathematically modeled as a tensor optimization problem. HSI reconstruction involves the inversion of the data degradation process, making the assumptions of the degradation model crucial for research in this problem. Under the assumption of additive noise, the degradation model of HSIs can be uniformly represented as follows:

$$\mathcal{Y} = A(\mathcal{X}) + \mathcal{E}, \tag{3.1}$$

where $\mathcal{Y}$ represents the degraded HSI, $\mathcal{X}$ denotes the high-quality HSI, A stands for the degradation operator, and $\mathcal{E}$ is the noise. This chapter primarily focuses on two common types of HSI reconstruction problems: mixed noise removal and completion.

HSI mixed noise removal aims to recover the clean HSI from a noise-contaminated HSI, where the noise positions are unknown. Assuming that the observed HSI $\mathcal{Y} \in \mathbb{R}^{I_1 \times I_2 \times I_3}$ is corrupted by additive Gaussian noise $\mathcal{N}$ and additive sparse noise $\mathcal{S}$ (such as salt and pepper noise, deadlines, and stripes), the degradation of the HSI can be expressed as follows:

$$\mathcal{Y} = \mathcal{X} + \mathcal{N} + \mathcal{S}. \tag{3.2}$$

For this problem, the degradation operator A in Eq. (3.1) is an identity operator, and the noise term $\mathcal{E}$ is decomposed into two parts: Gaussian noise $\mathcal{N}$ and sparse noise $\mathcal{S}$.

HSI completion aims to estimate the missing elements from an incomplete HSI, where the positions of missing elements are known. Assuming that $\mathcal{Y} \in \mathbb{R}^{I_1 \times I_2 \times I_3}$ is a partial observation of the target HSI $\mathcal{X}$, the degradation operator A in Eq. (3.1) can be specifically represented as the following projection operator:

$$A(\mathcal{X}) = \mathcal{P}_{\Omega}(\mathcal{X}) = \begin{cases} \mathcal{X}(i_1, i_2, i_3), & \text{if } (i_1, i_2, i_3) \in \Omega, \\ 0, & \text{otherwise} \end{cases} \tag{3.3}$$

where Ω is the index set for the known elements. Therefore, under the assumption of no noise, the degradation model of HSI completion can be explicitly expressed as follows:

$$\mathcal{Y} = \mathcal{P}_{\Omega}(\mathcal{X}), \tag{3.4}$$

where we assume that the missing elements in the observed HSI are all zeros.

As HSI reconstruction involves the inversion of the data degradation process, the corresponding tensor optimization problem is a typical ill-posed inverse problem. Inverse problems exhibit ill-posedness in their solution, mainly manifested in non-uniqueness and instability of the solution. Regularization methods are the primary tools for addressing ill-posed problems, aiming to effectively narrow down the feasible solution space or enhance the stability of the solution by introducing prior knowledge of the true HSI and noise term. Based on regularization methods, the HSI reconstruction problem corresponding to the degradation model Eq. (3.1) can be uniformly modeled as the following tensor optimization problem:

$$\min_{\mathcal{X},\mathcal{E}} L_1(\mathcal{X}) + \lambda L_2(\mathcal{E}), \quad \mathcal{Y} = A(\mathcal{X}) + \mathcal{E}, \tag{3.5}$$

where λ is the regularization parameter; $L_1(\mathcal{X})$ and $L_2(\mathcal{E})$ are regularization terms, used to reflect the prior knowledge of the high-quality HSI and the noise term, respectively, i.e., the inherent characteristics of the true HSI and the noise term. This chapter mainly considers common additive mixture of Gaussian and sparse noises. We employ the Frobenius norm-based regularization term and the ℓ_1 norm-based regularization to characterize the Gaussian and the sparse components, respectively, since they follow Gaussian and Laplace distributions, respectively. Therefore, exploring the prior knowledge of HSI and designing effective regularization terms to characterize this prior knowledge are crucial for solving HSI reconstruction problems.

Among existing HSI reconstruction methods, global correlation, local continuity, nonlocal self-similarity, and deep prior are commonly used priors. As mentioned earlier, tensors serve as the mathematical representation tool for HSIs. Therefore, in the following sections, we will focus on tensor modeling-based HSI reconstruction methods and explain how to capture the aforementioned prior information of HSIs within the framework of tensor modeling.

3.3 Tensor Modeling-based HSI Reconstruction Methods

We summarize notations used in this chapter in Table 3.1 [7]. A *tensor* is a multi-dimensional array, where the count of dimensions (referred to as *modes*) is termed the *tensor order*. Given a third-order tensor $\mathcal{X} \in \mathbb{R}^{I_1 \times I_2 \times I_3}$, its *fibers* are defined as a vector obtained by fixing indexes in two modes and its *slices* are defined as a matrix obtained by fixing indexes in one mode. Figure 3.2 presents a visualization display of the fibers and slices of a third-order tensor $\mathcal{X} \in \mathbb{R}^{8 \times 9 \times 6}$. Next, we review the definitions of several important tensor operations. i.e., mode-k unfolding, mode-k tensor–matrix product, and t-product.

Table 3.1 Notation declarations.

Notations	Interpretations
$x, \mathbf{x}, \mathbf{X}, \mathcal{X}$	Scalar, vector, matrix, tensor
x_{i_1,i_2,i_3} or $\mathcal{X}(i_1, i_2, i_3)$	The (i_1, i_2, i_3)th element of a third-order tensor $\mathcal{X}$
$\mathbf{x}_{:,i_2,i_3}$ or $\mathcal{X}(:, i_2, i_3)$	The (i_2, i_3)th column of a third-order tensor $\mathcal{X}$
$\mathbf{x}_{\mathbf{i_1},:,\mathbf{i_3}}$ or $\mathcal{X}(\mathbf{i_1}, :, \mathbf{i_3})$	The (i_1, i_3)th row of a third-order tensor $\mathcal{X}$
$\mathbf{x}_{\mathbf{i_1},\mathbf{i_2},:}$ or $\mathcal{X}(\mathbf{i_1}, \mathbf{i_2}, :)$	The (i_1, i_2)th tube of a third-order tensor $\mathcal{X}$
$\|\mathcal{X}\|_F$	Frobenius norm $\|\mathcal{X}\|_F = \sqrt{\sum_{i_1,i_2,\ldots,i_N} \|x_{i_1,i_2,\ldots,i_N}\|^2}$
$\|\mathcal{X}\|_1$	ℓ_1 norm $\|\mathcal{X}\|_1 = \sum_{i_1,i_2,\ldots,i_N} \| x_{i_1,i_2,\ldots,i_N} \|$
$\mathbf{X}_{(\mathbf{k})}$	The mode-k unfolding of $\mathcal{X}$
$\langle \cdot, \cdot \rangle$	Inner product
$\otimes$	Kronecker product
$\odot$	Component-wise multiplication
$\oslash$	Component-wise division
$*$	t-product
$\circ$	Vector outer product
$\star$	Circular convolution

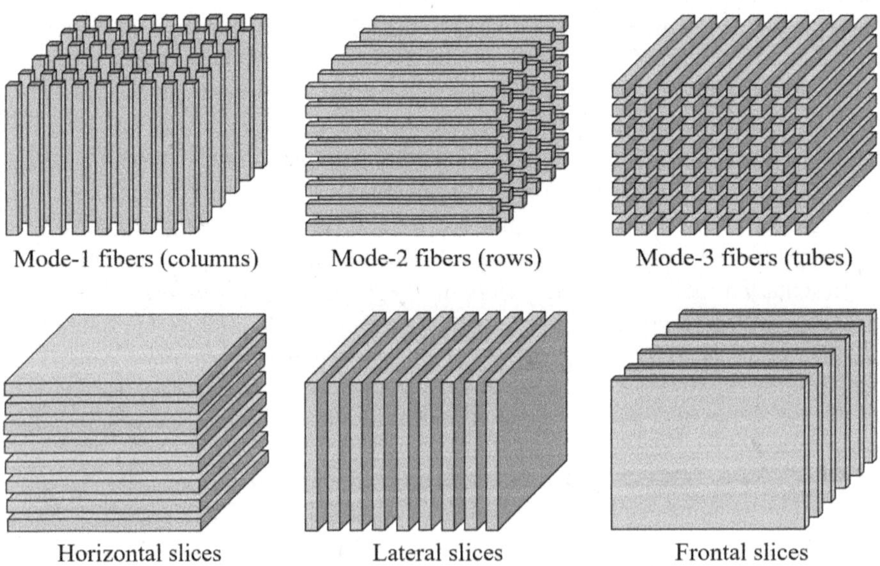

Figure 3.2 An illustration of the fibers and slices of a third-order tensor.

Definition 3.1 (Mode-k unfolding [7]).
Let $\mathcal{X} \in \mathbb{R}^{I_1 \times I_2 \times \dots \times I_N}$ be an Nth-order tensor, then its mode-k unfolding, denoted by $\mathbf{X}_{(k)}$, is defined as an $I_k \times \prod_{i \neq k} I_i$ matrix, the (i_k, j)th element of which maps to the $(i_1, i_2, \dots, i_N)$th element of $\mathcal{X}$, where

$$j = 1 + \sum_{s=1, s \neq k}^{N} (i_s - 1) J_s \text{ with } J_s = \sum_{m=1, m \neq k}^{s-1} I_m. \tag{3.6}$$

The corresponding operator and inverse operator are denoted as $\mathbf{X}_{(k)} = \text{Unfold}_k(\mathcal{X})$ and $\mathcal{X} = Fold_k(\mathbf{X}_{(k)})$, respectively.

Definition 3.2 (Mode-k tensor–matrix product [7]).
Let $\mathcal{X} \in \mathbb{R}^{I_1 \times I_2 \times \dots \times I_N}$ be an Nth-order tensor and $\mathbf{A} \in \mathbb{R}^{J \times I_k}$ be a matrix, then the mode-k tensor–matrix product between $\mathcal{X}$ and $\mathbf{A}$, denoted by $\mathcal{X} \times_k \mathbf{A}$, yields an $I_1 \times \dots \times I_{k-1} \times J \times I_{k+1} \times \dots \times I_N$ tensor $\mathcal{Y}$, whose elements are formulated as

$$\mathcal{Y}_{i_1,\dots,i_{k-1},j,i_{k+1},\dots,i_N} = \sum_{i_k=1}^{I_k} x_{i_1,i_2,\dots,i_N} a_{j,i_k}. \tag{3.7}$$

Remark 3.1 According to above two definitions, we have $\mathcal{Y} = \mathcal{X} \times_k \mathbf{A} \Leftrightarrow \mathbf{Y}_{(k)} = \mathbf{A}\mathbf{X}_{(k)}$.

Definition 3.3 (t-product [8]).
Let $\mathcal{X} \in \mathbb{R}^{I_1 \times I_2 \times I_3}$ and $\mathcal{Y} \in \mathbb{R}^{I_2 \times I_4 \times I_3}$ be third-order tensors, then the t-product between $\mathcal{X}$ and $\mathcal{Y}$, denoted by $\mathcal{X} * \mathcal{Y}$, yields an $I_1 \times I_4 \times I_3$ tensor $\mathcal{Z}$, whose tubes are formulated as

$$\mathcal{Z}(i,j,:) = \sum_{t=1}^{I_2} \mathcal{X}(i,t,:) \star \mathcal{Y}(t,j,:). \tag{3.8}$$

where $\star$ denotes the circular convolution between two tubes.

Remark 3.2 The t-product can be seen as an extension of matrix–matrix multiplication, with the key distinction being that scalar multiplication is replaced by circular convolution between tensor tubes. The circular convolution of two tubes in the spatial domain is equivalent to the point-wise multiplication of their Fourier transforms, and thus $\mathcal{Z} = \mathcal{X} * \mathcal{Y}$ is equivalent to $\bar{\mathbf{Z}}^{(i)} = \bar{\mathbf{X}}^{(i)}\bar{\mathbf{Y}}^{(i)}$ for $i = 1, 2, \dots, I_3$, where $\bar{\mathcal{Z}} = \mathcal{Z} \times_3 \mathbf{F}$ and $\mathbf{F}$ is a one-dimensional discrete Fourier transform (DFT) matrix.

3.3.1 Tensor Decomposition

Tensor decomposition represents target HSIs as a collection of smaller-scale factor matrices or tensors and establishes interaction operations among these factors. Over the past decade, tensor decomposition has exhibited remarkable capability in capturing the global correlations within HSIs and has proven to be an invaluable mathematical tool for tackling the challenging HSI reconstruction problem. Unlike matrices, tensor decomposition comes in various forms, each corresponding to a different tensor rank. Popular tensor decompositions and ranks include the CANDECOMP/PARAFAC (CP) decomposition and CP rank, the Tucker decomposition and Tucker rank, the block-term decomposition (BTD) with rank-(L,L,1) (also known as LL1 decomposition), the tensor singular value decomposition (SVD) and tubal rank, the tensor train (TT) decomposition and TT rank, the tensor ring (TR) decomposition and TR rank, and the fully connected tensor network (FCTN) decomposition and FCTN rank. Below, we offer definitions of the aforementioned tensor decompositions along with a discussion of their respective strengths and weaknesses.

Definition 3.4 (CP decomposition [7]).
Let $\mathcal{X} \in \mathbb{R}^{I_1 \times I_2 \times \dots \times I_N}$ be an Nth-order tensor and can be decomposed into

$$\mathcal{X} := \sum_{r=1}^{R} \lambda_r \mathbf{g}_r^{(1)} \circ \mathbf{g}_r^{(2)} \circ \dots \circ \mathbf{g}_r^{(N)}, \tag{3.9}$$

where λ_r for $r = 1, 2, \dots, R$ are the weights of the rth rank-1 tensors, $\mathbf{g}_r^{(k)} \in \mathbb{R}^{I_k}$ for $k = 1, 2, \dots, N$ are CP factors, and $\circ$is the vector outer product. Then we call Eq. (3.6) a CP decomposition of $\mathcal{X}$, denoted by $\mathcal{X} = CP\left(\{\lambda_r\}_{r=1:R}, \left\{\mathbf{g}_r^{(k)}\right\}_{r=1:R}^{k=1:N}\right)$. The minimum number of rank-1 tensors required to express the tensor $\mathcal{X}$ is called the CP rank, i.e.,

$$rank_{CP}(\mathcal{X}) := \min\left\{R \mid \mathcal{X} = \sum_{r=1}^{R} \lambda_r \mathbf{g}_r^{(1)} \circ \mathbf{g}_r^{(2)} \circ \dots \circ \mathbf{g}_r^{(N)}, \mathbf{g}_r^{(k)} \in \mathbb{R}^{I_k}\right\}. \tag{3.10}$$

The CP decomposition (Figure 3.3) has desirable mathematical properties like matrices. However, minimizing the CP rank is an NP-hard problem, and establishing a solvable relaxed form for CP rank is challenging. Therefore, in practical applications, researchers often employ low-rank CP decomposition to describe the low-rank structure of HSIs. Moreover, since the CP rank is a scalar, the CP decomposition cannot capture the different correlations between different dimensions of HSIs.

Definition 3.5 (Tucker decomposition [7]).
Let $\mathcal{X} \in \mathbb{R}^{I_1 \times I_2 \times \dots \times I_N}$ be an Nth-order tensor and can be decomposed into

$$\mathcal{X} := \mathcal{G} \times_1 \mathbf{U}_1 \times_2 \mathbf{U}_2 \times_3 \dots \times_N \mathbf{U}_N, \tag{3.11}$$

where $\mathcal{G} \in \mathbb{R}^{r_1 \times r_2 \times \dots \times r_N}$ is the core tensor, $\mathbf{U}_k \in \mathbb{R}^{I_k \times r_k}$ for $k = 1, 2, \dots, N$ are matrices, and $\times_k$ is the mode-k tensor–matrix product. Then we call Eq. (3.8) a Tucker decomposition of $\mathcal{X}$, denoted by $\mathcal{X} = \text{Tucker}(\mathcal{G}, \{\mathbf{U}_k\}_{k=1}^{N})$. The vector $(rank(\mathbf{X}_{(1)}), rank(\mathbf{X}_{(2)}), \dots, rank(\mathbf{X}_{(N)})) = (r_1, r_2, \dots, r_N)$ is called the Tucker rank, where $\mathbf{X}_{(k)}$ for $k = 1, 2, \dots, N$ are the mode-k unfolding of $\mathcal{X}$.

The Tucker decomposition (Figure 3.3), renowned for its flexibility in capturing diverse correlations across dimensions, finds extensive applications in HSI mixed noise removal. However, with the increasing dimensionality of the tensor, the computational complexity of the Tucker decomposition grows exponentially. Consequently, when handling high-order tensors, it may encounter substantial computational burdens.

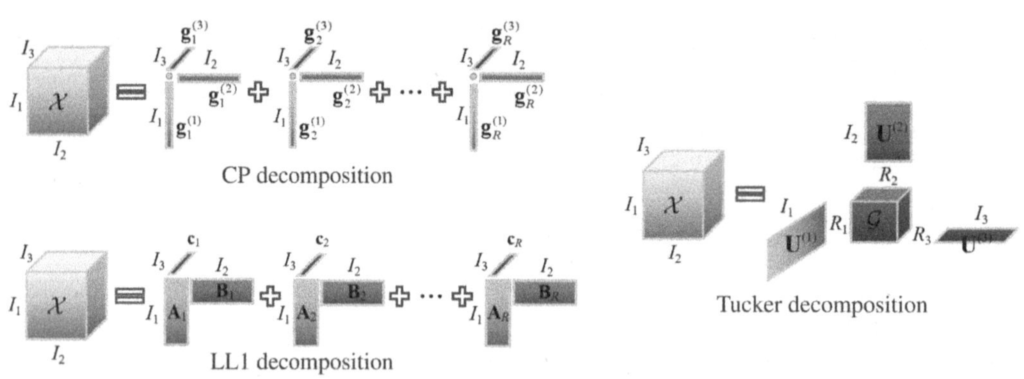

Figure 3.3 An illustration of CP, Tucker, and LL1 decompositions on a third-order tensor.

Definition 3.6 (BTD with rank-(L, L, 1) [7]).

Let $\mathcal{X} \in \mathbb{R}^{I_1 \times I_2 \times I_3}$ be a third-order tensor and can be decomposed into

$$\mathcal{X} := \sum_{r=1}^{R} \mathbf{A}_r \mathbf{B}_r \circ \mathbf{c}_r, \tag{3.12}$$

where $\mathbf{A}_r \in \mathbb{R}^{I_1 \times L}, \mathbf{B} \in \mathbb{R}^{L \times I_2}$, and $\mathbf{c}_r \in \mathbb{R}^{I_3}$ for $r = 1, 2, ..., R$ are BTD factors. Then we call Eq. (3.9) a BTD with rank-(L, L, 1) (also called LL1 decomposition) of $\mathcal{X}$, denoted by $\mathcal{X} = BTD(\{\mathbf{A}_r\}_{r=1}^{R}, \{\mathbf{B}_r\}_{r=1}^{R}, \{\mathbf{c}_r\}_{r=1}^{R})$.

The LL1 decomposition (Figure 3.3) can capture both spectral and spatial correlations in HSIs simultaneously. In particular, the LL1 decomposition has a clear physical interpretation, where $\mathbf{c}_r$ for $r = 1, 2, ..., R$ represents spectral signatures and $\mathbf{A}_r\mathbf{B}_r$ for $r = 1, 2, ..., R$ represents the abundance matrix. This allows LL1 decomposition to effectively extract spectral features and capture spatial information.

Definition 3.7 (Tensor SVD [8, 9]).

Let $\mathcal{X} \in \mathbb{R}^{I_1 \times I_2 \times I_3}$ be a third-order tensor and can be decomposed into

$$\mathcal{X} := \mathcal{U} * \mathcal{S} * \mathcal{V}^T, \tag{3.13}$$

where $\mathcal{S} \in \mathbb{R}^{I_1 \times I_2 \times I_3}$ is an f-diagonal tensor whose frontal slices are diagonal matrices, $\mathcal{U} \in \mathbb{R}^{I_1 \times I_1 \times I_3}$ and $\mathcal{V} \in \mathbb{R}^{I_2 \times I_2 \times I_3}$ are orthogonal tensors, $*$ is the t-product, and $\mathcal{V}^T$ is the transposition of tensor $\mathcal{V}$. Then we call Eq. (3.10) a tensor SVD of $\mathcal{X}$, denoted by $\mathcal{X} = tSVD(\mathcal{U}, \mathcal{S}, \mathcal{V})$. The number of non-zero tubes of $\mathcal{S}$ is called the tubal rank of $\mathcal{X}$, i.e., $rank_{tubal}(\mathcal{X}) := \#\{i : \mathcal{S}(i, i, :) \neq 0\}$.

Based on Remark 3.2, we can easily obtain that tensor SVD is equivalent to a series of matrix. SVDs in the Fourier domain mathematically, i.e.,

$$\bar{\mathcal{X}} = \mathcal{X} \times_3 \mathbf{F} \text{ and } \bar{\mathbf{X}}^{(i)} = \bar{\mathbf{U}}^{(i)} \bar{\mathbf{S}}^{(i)} \left(\bar{\mathbf{V}}^{(i)}\right)^T \text{ for } i = 1, 2, ..., I_3, \tag{3.14}$$

where $\bar{\mathbf{X}}^{(i)}$ denotes the ith frontal slice of $\bar{\mathcal{X}}$. Therefore, many researchers explored various transforms to replace the Fourier transform and proposed a series of variants of tensor SVD (Figure 3.4). The evolution of transforms can be summarized as a progression from unitary [10] to invertible [11], then from invertible to semi-invertible [12], and finally from linear to nonlinear transforms

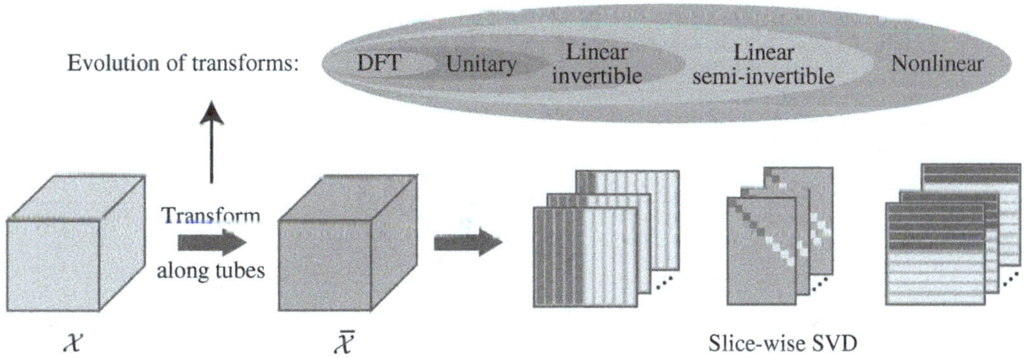

Figure 3.4 An illustration and evolution of transform-based tensor SVD.

[13, 14]. The progressive evolution of transforms has bolstered the representation capability of tensor SVD, yielding increasingly effective performance of the corresponding HSI processing methods. However, the above tensor SVD and its variants lack the flexibility necessary to address different correlations along different modes of HSIs. For example, when setting the band of an HSI to be the frontal slice of a third-order tensor, the tensor SVD characterizes its spatial correlations via SVDs, while describes its spectral correlation by the embedded transforms. However, the correlation of an HSI along its spectral mode should be much stronger than those along its spatial modes. Thus, treating each mode flexibly similar to the Tucker decomposition is expected to compensate for this defect. To solve this issue, Zheng et al. [15, 16] extend the tensor SVD in multiple modes and proposed the tensor fibered rank. Compared to the tubal rank, the fibered rank can more flexibly characterize the correlation of different dimensions in HSIs, thereby enabling the corresponding methods to achieve better performance.

Definition 3.8 (TT decomposition [17]).
Let $\mathcal{X} \in \mathbb{R}^{I_1 \times I_2 \times \ldots \times I_N}$ be an Nth-order tensor and can be decomposed into

$$\mathcal{X}(i_1, i_2, \ldots, i_N) = \sum_{r_1=1}^{R_1} \sum_{r_2=1}^{R_2} \ldots \sum_{r_{N-1}=1}^{R_{N-1}} \mathbf{G}_1(i_1, r_1)\mathcal{G}_2(r_1, i_2, r_2)\ldots\mathbf{G}_N(r_{N-1}, i_N), \tag{3.15}$$

where $\mathbf{G}_1 \in \mathbb{R}^{I_1 \times R_1}$, $\mathbf{G}_N \in \mathbb{R}^{R_{N-1} \times I_N}$, and $\mathcal{G}_k \in \mathbb{R}^{R_{k-1} I_k \times R_k}$ for $k = 2, 3, \ldots, N-1$ are TT cores. Then we call Eq. (3.12) a TT decomposition of $\mathcal{X}$, denoted by $\mathcal{X} = TT(\{\mathcal{G}_k\}_{k=1}^{N})$. The vector $(R_1, R_2, \ldots, R_{N-1}) \in \mathbb{R}^{N-1}$ is called the TT rank.

Based on the TT decomposition, the TR decomposition replaces the first and last TT cores ($\boldsymbol{G}_1$ and $\boldsymbol{G}_N$) with two third-order tensors and conducts an additional operation between them. Mathematically, the definition of the TR decomposition is as follows.

Definition 3.9 (TR decomposition [18]).
Let $\mathcal{X} \in \mathbb{R}^{I_1 \times I_2 \times \ldots \times I_N}$ be an Nth-order tensor and can be decomposed into

$$X = \sum_{r_1=1}^{R_1} \sum_{r_2=1}^{R_2} \cdots \sum_{r_N=1}^{R_N} G_1(r_N, i_1, r_1)G_2(r_1, i_2, r_2)\cdots G_N(r_{N-1}, i_N, r_N) \tag{3.16}$$

where $\mathcal{G}_1 \in \mathbb{R}^{R_N \times I_N \times R_1}$ and $\mathcal{G}_k \in \mathbb{R}^{R_{k-1} \times I_k \times R_k}$ for $k = 2, 3, \ldots, N$ are TR cores. Then we call Eq. (3.13) a TR decomposition of $\mathcal{X}$, denoted by $\mathcal{X} = TR(\{\mathcal{G}_k\}_{k=1}^{N})$. The vector $(R_1, R_2, \ldots, R_N) \in \mathbb{R}^N$ is called the TR rank.

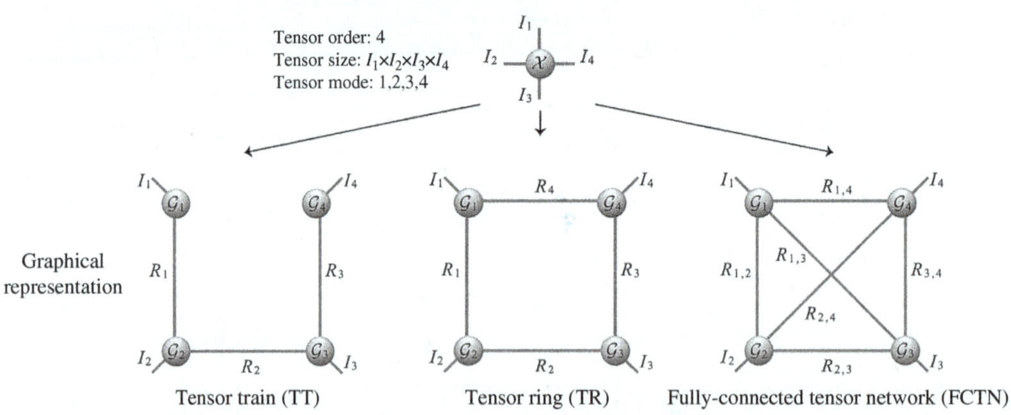

Figure 3.5 A graphical representation of TT, TR, and FCTN decompositions on a fourth-order tensor.

TT and TR decompositions (Figure 3.5) offer efficient storage and computational capabilities for high-order tensors by confining the TT and TR cores to second- and third-order tensors, respectively. However, TT and TR decompositions exclusively involve tensor operations between adjacent two cores, thus directly capturing only the correlation between adjacent modes of a tensor. Consequently, their capacity to capture the global correlation of higher-order tensors is limited. Additionally, the TT decomposition maintains invariance only under a converse transposition of a tensor, while the TR decomposition retains invariance under a converse transposition or a circular transposition. For other generalized transpositions, such as when an $I_1 \times I_2 \times I_3 \times I_4$ tensor is transposed to an $I_2 \times I_1 \times I_3 \times I_4$ tensor, the corresponding TT and TR decompositions vary accordingly. In summary, TT and TR decompositions offer advantages in storage and computational efficiency, but struggle with limitations in correlation characterization and transpositional invariance.

To break through the limitations of TT and TR decompositions, Zheng et al. [19] proposed an FCTN decomposition, whose mathematical definition is as follows.

Definition 3.10 (FCTN Decomposition [19]).
Let $\mathcal{X} \in \mathbb{R}^{I_1 \times I_2 \times \ldots \times I_N}$ be an Nth-order tensor and can be decomposed into

$$\begin{aligned}\mathcal{X}(i_1, i_2, \ldots, i_N) = &\sum_{r_{1,2}=1}^{R_{1,2}} \sum_{r_{1,3}=1}^{R_{1,3}} \cdots \sum_{r_{1,N}=1}^{R_{1,N}} \sum_{r_{2,3}=1}^{R_{2,3}} \cdots \sum_{r_{2,N}=1}^{R_{2,N}} \cdots \sum_{r_{N-1,N}=1}^{R_{N-1,N}} \\ &\mathcal{G}_1(i_1, r_{1,2}, r_{1,3}, \ldots, r_{1,N}) \\ &\mathcal{G}_2(r_{1,2}, i_2, r_{2,3}, \ldots, r_{2,N}) \ldots \\ &\mathcal{G}_k(r_{1,k}, r_{2,k}, \ldots, r_{k-1,k}, i_k, r_{k,k+1}, \ldots, r_{k,N}) \ldots \\ &\mathcal{G}_N(r_{1,N}, r_{2,N}, \ldots, r_{N-1,N}, i_N),\end{aligned} \tag{3.17}$$

where $\mathcal{G}_k \in \mathbb{R}^{R_{1,k} \times R_{2,k} \times \ldots \times R_{k-1,k} \times I_k \times R_{k,k+1} \times \ldots \times R_{k,N}}$ for $k = 1, 2, \ldots, N$ are Nth-order tensors and called FCTN cores. Then we call Eq. (3.14) an FCTN decomposition of $\mathcal{X}$, denoted by $\mathcal{X} = FCTN(\{\mathcal{G}_k\}_{k=1}^N)$. The vector $(R_{1,2}, R_{1,3}, \ldots, R_{1,N}, R_{2,3}, R_{2,4}, \ldots, R_{2,N}, \ldots, R_{N-1,N}) \in \mathbb{R}^{\frac{N(N-1)}{2}}$ is called the FCTN rank.

Compared to the TT and TR decompositions, the FCTN decomposition considers operations between any pairs of FCTN cores (Figure 3.5), enabling it to adequately capture global tensor correlations and maintain invariance under arbitrary tensor transpositions. However, one limitation of FCTN decomposition is that it requires the FCTN cores to be designed as Nth-order tensors. This may lead to increased computational complexity and memory requirements compared to the TT and TR decompositions.

3.3.2 Tensor Decomposition for HSI Reconstruction

As delineated in Section 3.2, prevalent prior knowledge in HSIs encompasses global correlation, local continuity, non-local self-similarity, and deep prior. Of these, global correlation stands out as a pivotal prior knowledge due to its integral role in reconstructing the fundamental global structural information of HSIs.

Tensor Decomposition for Global Correlation: Global correlation implies that HSIs contain a significant amount of redundant and correlated information, facilitating the approximation of the overall data structure through a low-rank tensor. Mathematically, enforcing the global correlation of HSIs can be effectively achieved through low-rank tensor decomposition or tensor rank minimization. Consequently, we present frameworks for HSI reconstruction based on tensor decomposition and tensor rank minimization, respectively.

Tensor decomposition represents an HSI through a collection of small-sized factor matrices/tensors, particularly adept at capturing global correlation [20–25]. Considering an observed HSI $\mathcal{Y} \in \mathbb{R}^{I_1 \times I_2 \times I_3}$, the tensor decomposition-based HSI reconstruction model can be formulated as

$$\begin{aligned} \min_{\mathcal{X},\mathcal{E}} \ & \left\| \mathcal{X} - TD\left(\{\mathcal{G}_k\}_{k=1}^{d}\right) \right\|_F^2 + \lambda L(\mathcal{E}) \\ \text{s.t.} \ & \mathcal{Y} = A(\mathcal{X}) + \mathcal{E}, \end{aligned} \tag{3.18}$$

where $TD\left(\{\mathcal{G}\}_{k=1}^{d}\right)$ is the tensor decomposition defined in Section 3.1. Specifically, for the HSI mixed noise removal problem, the tensor decomposition-based model can be formulated as

$$\begin{aligned} \min_{\mathcal{X},\mathcal{N},\mathcal{S}} \ & \left\| \mathcal{X} - TD\left(\{\mathcal{G}_k\}_{k=1}^{d}\right) \right\|_F^2 + \|\mathcal{N}\|_F^2 + \mu\|\mathcal{S}\|_1 \\ \text{s.t.} \ & \mathcal{Y} = \mathcal{X} + \mathcal{N} + \mathcal{S}. \end{aligned} \tag{3.19}$$

For example, within the framework Eq. (3.16), Guo et al. [24] proposed a CP decomposition-based model, Karami et al. [23] suggested a Tucker decomposition-based model, and Xiong et al. [25] introduced an LL1 decomposition-based model.

For the HSI completion problem, the tensor decomposition-based model can be formulated as

$$\begin{aligned} \min_{\mathcal{X}} \ & \left\| \mathcal{X} - TD\left(\{\mathcal{G}_k\}_{k=1}^{d}\right) \right\|_F^2 \\ \text{s.t.} \ & \mathcal{P}_\Omega(\mathcal{Y}) = \mathcal{P}_\Omega(\mathcal{X}). \end{aligned} \tag{3.20}$$

For example, within the framework Eq. (3.17), Zhao et al. [26] proposed a CP decomposition-based model, Lin et al. [27] introduced a Tucker decomposition-based model for thick cloud removal, Rontogiannis et al. [28] suggested an LL1 decomposition-based model, Zhou et al. [29] developed a tensor SVD-based model, Li et al. [30] presented a TR decomposition-based model for thick cloud removal, and Zheng et al. [19] constructed an FCTN decomposition-based model. All of the aforementioned tensor decomposition-based models can be effectively solved using alternating least squares (ALS), alternating gradient descent (AGD), or proximal alternating minimization (PAM) algorithms.

Another approach to capture the global correlation of HSIs involves minimizing the tensor rank. Considering an observed HSI $\mathcal{Y} \in \mathbb{R}^{I_1 \times I_2 \times I_3}$, the tensor rank minimization-based HSI reconstruction model can be formulated as

$$\begin{aligned} \min_{\mathcal{X},\mathcal{E}} \ & R(\mathcal{X}) + \lambda L(\mathcal{E}) \\ \text{s.t.} \ & \mathcal{Y} = A(\mathcal{X}) + \mathcal{E}, \end{aligned} \tag{3.21}$$

where $R(\mathcal{X})$ is the tensor rank defined in Section 3.1. It should be pointed out that if the tensor rank is a vector, then $R(\mathcal{X})$ is the sum or product of its elements. The optimization problem associated with directly minimizing the rank function is NP-hard, and thus researchers designed many convex and non-convex relaxations for various tensor rank. For example, for the tubal rank defined in Definition 3.7, Semerci et al. [31] proposed a tensor nuclear norm (TNN) as its convex relaxation and then Fan et al. [32] applied TNN for HSI mixed noise removal. Besides, many non-convex relaxations, such as the logarithmic-based TNN [15] and the Laplace-based TNN [33], were introduced to better approximate the tubal rank and achieved competitive results in HSI reconstruction. For the Tucker rank defined in Definition 3.5, researchers usually select the sum or product of elements of the Tucker rank as the objective function because their relaxation forms are easy to formulate. Examples of such convex or non-convex relaxations include the sum of the nuclear norm (SNN)

[34, 35], the logarithmic-based nuclear norm [36], and the ϵ-based nuclear norm [37]. All of these relaxations have been successfully applied to HSI reconstruction problems and obtained competitive results [15, 32, 37–42]. All of the above tenor rank minimization-based models can be well solved by augmented Lagrange multiplier (ALM) or alternating direction method of multipliers (ADMM)-based algorithms.

Tensor decomposition with local continuity. Local continuity indicates that neighboring points in HSIs are likely to share similar values, characteristics, or properties [43–55]. In other words, local continuity corresponds to a low variation or sparsity in the gradient values within local regions. Therefore, local continuity can be seen as a form of sparsity in the gradient domain. 3D total variation (3DTV) regularization is a powerful tool to promote smooth variations within the data while penalizing abrupt changes in HSIs. Its mathematical formulation can be written as

$$3DTV(\mathcal{X}) = \sum_{k=1}^{3} \alpha_k \left\| \mathbf{D}_k \mathbf{X}_{(k)} \right\|_1, \tag{3.22}$$

where $\alpha_k \geq 0$ satisfying $\sum_{k=1}^{3} \alpha_k = 1$ and $\mathbf{D}_k$ for $k = 1, 2, 3$ are first-order difference matrices, i.e.,

$$\mathbf{D}_k = \begin{pmatrix} -1 & 1 & \dots & 0 & 0 \\ 0 & -1 & \dots & 0 & 0 \\ \vdots & \vdots & \ddots & \vdots & \vdots \\ 0 & 0 & \dots & -1 & 1 \\ 1 & 0 & \dots & 0 & -1 \end{pmatrix} \in \mathbb{R}^{I_k \times I_k}. \tag{3.23}$$

Not limited to 3DTV, several other forms of TV-based regularization terms have also been applied to capture the local continuity of HSIs. Examples include spatiospectral adaptive hyperspectral TV [56], spectral adaptive multidimensional nonlocal TV [57], spatiospectral TV [58], isotropic spectral–spatial TV [59], hybrid spatiospectral TV [60], weighted group TV [54], weighted cross 3DTV [61], and enhanced 3DTV [62]. For uniformity, we will denote the above TV-based regularization terms collectively by $TV(\mathcal{X})$.

With the definition of TV-based regularization terms, the tensor decomposition- and tensor rank minimization-based HSI reconstruction models can be formulated as

$$\begin{aligned} \min_{\mathcal{X},\mathcal{E}} \; & \left\| \mathcal{X} - TD\left(\{\mathcal{G}_k\}_{k=1}^{d}\right) \right\|_F^2 + \lambda L(\mathcal{E}) + \tau TV(\mathcal{X}) \\ \text{s.t.} \; & \mathcal{Y} = A(\mathcal{X}) + \mathcal{E}, \end{aligned} \tag{3.24}$$

and

$$\begin{aligned} \min_{\mathcal{X},\mathcal{E}} \; & R(\mathcal{X}) + \lambda L(\mathcal{E}) + \tau TV(\mathcal{X}) \\ \text{s.t.} \; & \mathcal{Y} = A(\mathcal{X}) + \mathcal{E}, \end{aligned} \tag{3.25}$$

respectively, where λ and τ are regularization parameters. For example, within the framework of Eq. (3.21), Wang et al. [53] proposed a Tucker decomposition and 3DTV-based HSI mixed noise removal model, Xiong et al. [63] introduced an LL1 decomposition and 3DTV-based HSI mixed noise removal model, and He et al. [64] suggested a TR decomposition and 3DTV-based HSI completion model. Within the framework of Eq. (3.22), Fan et al. [49] proposed a tensor tubal rank and 3DTV-based HSI mixed noise removal model, and Wang et al. [51] introduced a tensor fibered rank and 3DTV-based HSI mixed noise removal model.

Considering the high computational complexity of directly applying regularization on large-sized HSIs, several researchers instead introduced regularization on small-sized factors obtained by tensor decomposition to encourage a smoother representation of HSIs [65, 66]. Mathematically, the factor regularization-based HSI reconstruction model can be formulated as

Minimize $\|\mathbf{D}_k\mathbf{U}_k\|_1$

$\Downarrow$ $\mathbf{D}_k$ is the difference matrix

Enhance the local continuity within each column of $\mathbf{U}_k$

$\Downarrow$ Each column of $\mathbf{X}_{(k)}$ is a linear combination of columns of $\mathbf{U}_k$

Figure 3.6 An illustration of why regularization achieves local continuity in the target tensor $\mathcal{X}$.

$$\min_{\mathcal{X},\mathcal{E}} \left\|\mathcal{X} - TD\left(\{\mathcal{G}_k\}_{k=1}^{d}\right)\right\|_F^2 + \lambda L(\mathcal{E}) + \tau \sum_{k=1}^{d} \alpha_k \phi(\mathcal{G}_k) \quad \text{s.t. } \mathcal{Y} = A(\mathcal{X}) + \mathcal{E}, \tag{3.26}$$

where $\alpha_k \geq 0$ satisfying $\sum_{k=1}^{d} \alpha_k = 1$; λ and τ are regularization parameters. For example, within Tucker decomposition, the factor regularization-based HSI reconstruction model can be formulated as

$$\min_{\mathcal{X},\mathcal{E}} \|\mathcal{X} - \mathcal{G} \times_1 \mathbf{U}_1 \times_2 \mathbf{U}_2 \times_3 \mathbf{U}_3\|_F^2 + \lambda L(\mathcal{E}) + \tau \sum_{k=1}^{3} \alpha_k \|\mathbf{D}_k\mathbf{U}_k\|_1 \quad \text{s.t. } \mathcal{Y} = A(\mathcal{X}) + \mathcal{E}. \tag{3.27}$$

Below, we explain the working mechanism behind the factor regularization in problem Eq. (3.24). Firstly, given that $\mathbf{D}_k$ represents a difference matrix, the minimization of $\|\mathbf{D}_k\mathbf{U}_k\|_1$ serves to enhance local continuity within each column of $\mathbf{U}_k$. Secondly, building upon the relationship $\mathbf{X}_{(k)} = \mathbf{U}_k\mathbf{M}_{k(k)}$, where $\mathcal{M}_k = \mathcal{G}\prod_{i=1, i\neq k}^{3} \times_i \mathbf{U}_i$, we can deduce that each column of $\mathbf{X}_{(k)}$ can be interpreted as a linear combination of columns from $\mathbf{U}_k$. Consequently, reinforcing local continuity within each column of $\mathbf{U}_k$ propagates an analogous enhancement in local continuity within each column of $\mathbf{X}_{(k)}$; other forms of factor regularization have also been proposed and applied to promote the local continuity, such as $\sum_{k=1}^{3} \alpha_k \|\mathbf{D}_k\mathbf{U}_k\|_F^2$ and $\sum_{k=1}^{3} \alpha_k \|\mathbf{Q}_k\|_1$ with $\mathbf{D}_k\mathbf{U}_k = \mathbf{Q}_k\mathbf{V}_k$ and $\mathbf{V}_k\mathbf{V}_k^T = \mathbf{I}_k$ (Figure 3.6).

Tensor decomposition with non-local self-similarity. Non-local self-similarity indicates that patterns or structures within HSIs exhibit similarity not only within a local neighborhood but also across different regions [55, 67–77]. The methodological framework for exploiting non-local self-similarity typically entails the segmentation of data into multiple small patches, the recovery of the tensor composed of similar patches, and the aggregation of the recovered patches back into the data. In particular, all the mentioned tensor modeling-based methods above can be used for the recovery of the tensor composed of similar patches. Below, we take an HSI $\mathcal{Y} \in \mathbb{R}^{I_1 \times I_2 \times I_3}$ as an example to introduce the detailed process of the non-local self-similarity-based method.

1) **Segmentation:** Partition the observed HSI $\mathcal{Y}$ into a set of overlapped full-band patches denoted as $\{\mathcal{Y}_t \in \mathbb{R}^{p \times p \times I_3}\}_{t=1}^{T}$ where the patches are extracted with a row and column stride of 1, $p \ll \min\{I_1, I_2\}$, and $T = (I_1 - p + 1) \times (I_2 - p + 1)$ is the number of total patches. Similarly, derive key patches by adjusting the row and column stride to $p - 1$. Therefore, the number of key patches is $L = ((I_1 - p)/(p - 1) + 1) \times ((I_2 - p)/(p - 1) + 1)$ and the set of all key patches is a subset of $\{\mathcal{Y}_t \in \mathbb{R}^{p \times p \times I_3}\}_{t=1}^{T}$.
2) **Similar patch matching:** Evaluate the similarity between each key patch and every patch in the set $\{\hat{\mathcal{Y}}_t \in \mathbb{R}^{p \times p \times I_3}\}_{t=1}^{T}$, choose the top s similar patches for each key patch to form a new

fourth-order tensor with size of $p \times p \times I_3 \times s$, and reshape the fourth-order tensor into a third-order tensor with size of $p^2 \times I_3 \times s$.

3) **Matched patch recovering:** Utilize tensor modeling-based methods, such as Eqs. (3.15) and (3.17), to reconstruct each newly formed third-order tensor.
4) **Aggregation:** Reshape all recovered third-order tensors into fourth-order tensors and aggregate them back into the HSI.

Figure 3.7 presents a flowchart of the tensor modeling-based method for non-local self-similarity. Within this framework, Zhang et al. [55] proposed a nonlocal Tucker decomposition-based HSI mixed noise removal model and Zheng et al. [78] introduced a nonlocal FCTN decomposition-based HSI completion model, where the unfolding and folding operations in Figure 3.7 are removed to cleverly leverage the remarkable ability of FCTN decomposition for dealing with higher-order tensors.

3.3.3 Tensor Modeling Meets Deep Learning

Despite the significant success achieved by the tensor modeling-based methods for HSI reconstruction, they usually rely on hand crafted priors, which cannot fully capture the details and textures in HSIs, leaving room for improvement in their performance. As an emerging paradigm, deep learning (DL)-based methods directly learn an end-to-end mapping between the degraded and clean HSI from a large number of paired data for HSI reconstruction, rather than making subjective physical assumptions (e.g., tensor low-rankness) on the underlying HSIs. Attributing to the powerful representation ability of neural networks, DL-based methods provide competitive performance in addressing HSI reconstruction problem.

Over the past decade, a large number of DL-based methods have been developed specifically for HSI reconstruction. For instance, Yuan et al. [79] proposed a spatial–spectral deep convolutional neural network (HSID-CNN) model for HSI denoising, where the high correlation of the current band and its neighboring bands is fully exploited. Zhang et al. [80] developed a spatial–spectral gradient network (SSGN) for HSI mixed noise removal, which can simultaneously deal with the different types of noise. Guan et al. [81] developed an innovative deep recurrent convolutional neural network (DnRCNN) model for HSI destriping, which studies destriping from the perspective of inner band and interband correlation explorations with the recurrent convolutional neural network (CNN). Dong et al. [82] proposed a 3-D HSI denoising CNN (3D-DCNN), which decomposes the 3-D filters as 2-D spatial filters and 1-D spectral filters to effectively reduce the computing complexity. Cao et al. [83] proposed a deep spatial–spectral global reasoning network to consider both the local and global information for HSI noise removal. Liu and Lee [84] put forward the 3-D atrous

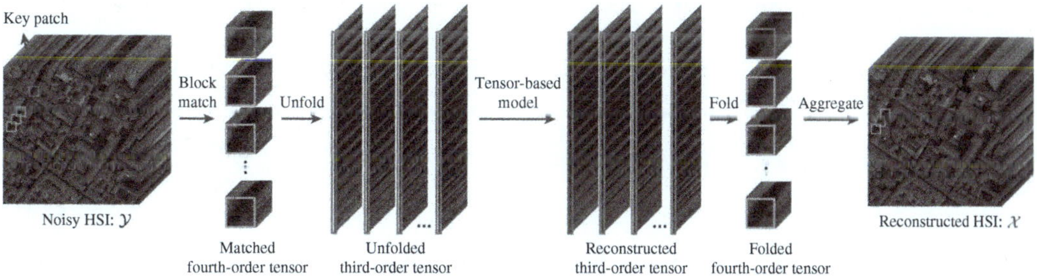

Figure 3.7 A flowchart of the tensor modeling-based HSI reconstruction model with non-local self-similarity.

denoising CNN (3DADCNN) for HSI denoising. Chen et al. [85] proposed an efficient end-to-end transformer, named HSI denoising transformer (Hider), for mixed HSI noise removal. However, these methods often ignore the intrinsic prior structure of HSI (e.g., tensor low-rankness), hindering potential performance enhancements. To overcome this problem, some methods have also been proposed for HSI reconstruction through integrating tensor model and DL.

3.3.3.1 Tensor Modeling Meets Supervised Learning

There has been a significant surge in research on the integration of tensor modeling with DL to boost HSI reconstruction performance in recent years. A popular approach among these is the integration of tensor modeling with supervised learning through a so-called plug-and-play (PnP) framework. Below we describe PnP in detail.

Plug-and-play framework. PnP is a highly flexible framework [86, 87] that leverages the power of off-the-shelf denoisers in half-quadratic splitting (HQS) or other proximal algorithms. After variable splitting technique, the optimization problem is decoupled into easier subproblems, one of which is the proximal operator of regularization. The proximal operator of regularization $Prof_{\Phi} : \mathbb{R}^n \rightarrow \mathbb{R}^n$ is defined as

$$prox_{\Phi}(\mathbf{y}) = \underset{x}{\text{argmin}}\ \Phi(\mathbf{x}) + \frac{1}{2\sigma^2} \| \mathbf{x} - \mathbf{y} \|^2, \tag{3.28}$$

which maps the input $\mathbf{y}$ to the minimizer of Eq. (3.25). Under the PnP framework, the proximal operator of regularization is replaced by the denoising algorithm (termed as denoiser), which maps the noisy image to the clean image. Here, the denoiser serves as an implicit regularizer to express image priors.

Combining an implicit regularization term, the HSI reconstruction problem can be uniformly modeled as the following optimization problem:

$$\begin{aligned} \min_{\mathcal{X},\mathcal{E}}\ & L_1(\mathcal{X}) + \lambda L_2(\mathcal{E}) + \tau\Phi(\mathcal{X}) \\ \text{s.t.}\ & \mathcal{Y} = A(\mathcal{X}) + \mathcal{E}, \end{aligned} \tag{3.29}$$

where λ and τ are regularization parameters; $\Phi(\mathcal{X})$ is an implicit regularizer, used to reflect the prior knowledge of the high-quality HSI. The minimization problem Eq. (3.26) can be solved by the HQS or other proximal algorithms under the PnP framework. Next, we develop the HQS algorithm to solve it as an example.

By introducing an auxiliary variable $\mathcal{Z}$, Eq. (3.26) can be reformulated as the following optimization problem, i.e.,

$$\begin{aligned} \min_{\mathcal{X},\mathcal{E},\mathcal{Z}}\ & L_1(\mathcal{X}) + \lambda L_2(\mathcal{E}) + \tau\Phi(\mathcal{Z}) \\ \text{s.t.}\ & \mathcal{Y} = A(\mathcal{X}) + \mathcal{E}, \mathcal{X} = \mathcal{Z}. \end{aligned} \tag{3.30}$$

Under the HQS algorithm framework, Eq. (3.27) can be transformed as the following unconstrained problem:

$$\mathcal{L}_{\beta,\mu}(\mathcal{X},\mathcal{E},\mathcal{Z}) = L_1(\mathcal{X}) + \lambda L_2(\mathcal{E}) + \tau\Phi(\mathcal{Z}) + \frac{\beta}{2} \| \mathcal{Y} - A(\mathcal{X}) - \mathcal{E} \|_F^2 + \frac{\mu}{2} \| \mathcal{X} - \mathcal{Z} \|_F^2, \tag{3.31}$$

where β and μ are penalty parameters. Such problem can be addressed by iteratively solving a sequence of subproblems, one of which is the proximal operator of regularization. To be specific, the $\mathcal{Z}$-subproblem is

$$\min_{\mathcal{Z}} \tau\Phi(\mathcal{Z}) + \frac{\mu}{2}\|\mathcal{X}_k - \mathcal{Z}\|_F^2. \tag{3.32}$$

Let $\sigma = \sqrt{\tau/\mu}$, Eq. (3.28) can be rewritten as

$$prox_{\Phi}(\mathcal{Z}) = \underset{\mathcal{Z}}{\operatorname{argmin}}\, \Phi(\mathcal{Z}) + \frac{1}{2\left(\sqrt{\tau/\mu}\right)^2}\|\mathcal{X}_k - \mathcal{Z}\|_F^2. \tag{3.33}$$

Under the PnP framework, the proximal operator of regularization Eq. (3.29) can be replaced by the off-the-shelf denoisers (e.g., deep denoisers [87, 88]), which corresponds to Gaussian denoising on $\mathcal{X}$ with noise level $\sqrt{\tau/\mu}$.

Based on PnP framework, researchers proposed a number of models that combine tensor modeling with supervised learning, which simultaneously benefit from the HSI's domain knowledge and the powerful representation capability of neural networks. For example, under the framework Eq. (3.26), Zeng et al. [89] proposed a CNN denoiser prior regularized HSI mixed noise removal model by combining tensor Tucker decomposition and an implicit regularizer expressed by FFDNet [88]. Li et al. [90] proposed a PnP robust low-rank tensor completion model with the deep prior denoiser for HSI completion, which combines the transformed TNN and deep prior to explore the global low rankness and local details of the underlying HSI simultaneously.

3.3.3.2 Tensor Modeling Meets Unsupervised Learning

Although PnP technique can effectively integrate tensor modeling and supervised learning, PnP-based methods often require a pre-trained deep Gaussian denoiser. This reliance on pretraining may result in insufficient generalization capability across diverse datasets. To address this issue, some methods that combine tensor modeling with unsupervised learning have also been proposed. For example, Wu et al. [91] proposed a novel model for HSI mixed noise removal by organically combining TR decomposition and the deep spatial–spectral prior. Mathematically, the proposed model can be formulated as

$$\begin{aligned} &\min_{\mathcal{X},\mathcal{S},\{\mathcal{G}_k\}_{k=1}^d,\{\theta_k,\xi_k\}_{k=1}^m} \left\|\mathcal{X} - TD\left(\{\mathcal{G}_k\}_{k=1}^d\right)\right\|_F^2 + \lambda \,\|\,\mathcal{N}\|_F^2 + \mu \,\|\,\mathcal{S}\|_1 \\ &\text{s.t. } \mathcal{Y} = \mathcal{X} + \mathcal{N} + \mathcal{S}, \mathcal{X} = \sum_{m=1}^{M} \mathbf{A}_{\theta_m}(\mathbf{z}_m) \circ \mathbf{c}_{\xi_m}(\mathbf{w}_m), \end{aligned} \tag{3.34}$$

where λ and μ are regularizer parameters, and $\mathbf{A}_{\theta_m}(\mathbf{z}_m) \in \mathbb{R}^{I_1 \times I_2}$ and $\mathbf{c}_{\xi_m}(\mathbf{w}_m) \in \mathbb{R}^{I_3}$ are mth abundance map and corresponding signature of endmember, which are generated by the U-Net network and fully connected networks (FCN), respectively. $\mathbf{z}_m$ and $\mathbf{w}_m$ represent random input of the U-Net network and FCN, respectively.

Luo et al. [92] introduced a hierarchical low-rank tensor factorization (HLRTF) to capture the underlying low-rank structure of HSI with compact representation ability. They achieved this by embedding a deep neural network as a nonlinear transform into the t-SVD framework. Mathematically, the optimization model of the proposed HLRTF for HSI reconstruction can be formulated as

$$\min_{\hat{\mathcal{A}},\hat{\mathcal{B}},\{\mathbf{H}_k\}_{k=1}^l} L\left(g\left(\hat{\mathcal{A}}\Delta\hat{\mathcal{B}}\right),\mathcal{Y}\right), \tag{3.35}$$

where $\hat{\mathcal{A}} \in \mathbb{R}^{I_1 \times r \times I_3}$ and $\hat{\mathcal{B}} \in \mathbb{R}^{r \times I_2 \times I_3}$ are tensor factors and g(·)is a deep neural network with parameters $\{\mathbf{H}_k\}_{k=1}^l$. L is the fidelity loss between the recovered result and the degraded HSI.

3.4 Numerical Experiments

In this section, we compare the performance of various methods by taking the HSI mixed noise removal task as an example. We employ one public HSI as the test data, which is the Washington DC Mall dataset (http://lesun.weebly.com/hyperspectral-data-set.html) with the size of $256 \times 256 \times 191$. We select LRMR [38], LRTR [32], LRTDTV [53], 3DLogTNN [15],

HLRTF [92], and LRTF-DFR [65] as the compared methods. We employ three quantitative evaluation indexes, including the mean of peak signal-to-noise rate (MPSNR) over all bands, the mean of structural similarity (MSSIM) over all bands, and the mean of spectral angle mapping (MSAM) over all spectral vectors, to evaluate the overall quality of the restored results quantitatively.

Since the noise in HSIs usually manifests as a mixture of several kinds of noise in real noise scenarios, we consider the following three cases:

Case 1. *Gaussian Noise:* Gaussian noise with zero mean is added to all bands, and the noise standard deviation in each band is randomly sampled from the interval [0.1,0.2].

Case 2. *Gaussian Noise + Salt and Pepper Noise:* Gaussian noise is added in the same way as Case 1. Furthermore, salt and pepper noise is added to all bands, and the noise proportion in each band is randomly sampled from the interval [0.1,0.2].

Case 3. *Gaussian Noise + Salt and Pepper Noise + Stripe:* Gaussian noise and salt and pepper noise are added in the same way as Case 2. Furthermore, 20% of all bands are randomly selected to add stripes, and the number of stripes in each selected band is randomly sampled from the set {6, 7,..., 15}. In particular, if a column is selected to add the stripe, all elements of that column will become a certain value randomly sampled from the interval [0.6,0.8]. In Table 3.2, we present the MPSNR, MSSIM, MSAM, and the running time values obtained by all compared methods on the HSI Washington DC Mall. It can be seen that LRTF-DFR achieves the best PSNR, SSIM, and SAM values, primarily because this method more comprehensively explores the prior information of HSIs. HLRTF achieves the second-best results for different noise cases, this is because

Table 3.2 The quantitative comparison of all compared methods for cases.

Cases	Indexes	Noise	LRMR	LRTR	LRTDTV	3DLogTNN	HLRTF	LRTF-DFR
Case 1	MPSNR	16.658	31.786	30.136	31.762	34.053	34.565	35.727
	MSSIM	0.2916	0.9059	0.8824	0.8956	0.9480	0.9475	0.9588
	MSAM	42.476	10.310	10.226	6.7906	6.1617	5.5929	5.1281
	Time (s)	—	21.236	29.111	62.916	226.74	12.804	35.122
Case 2	MPSNR	11.055	30.128	27.722	29.684	32.542	33.231	34.651
	MSSIM	0.1258	0.8761	0.8097	0.8521	0.9296	0.9316	0.9498
	MSAM	51.271	10.483	11.785	8.0123	6.6611	6.3432	5.4430
	Time (s)	—	21.428	30.095	62.294	230.11	12.855	35.132
Case 3	MPSNR	10.964	29.716	26.121	29.194	29.682	32.860	34.562
	MSSIM	0.1234	0.8706	0.7634	0.8408	0.8796	0.9283	0.9487
	MSAM	51.110	10.718	16.334	9.1195	16.756	6.6642	5.6147
	Time (s)	—	21.210	31.470	62.660	230.86	12.871	35.094

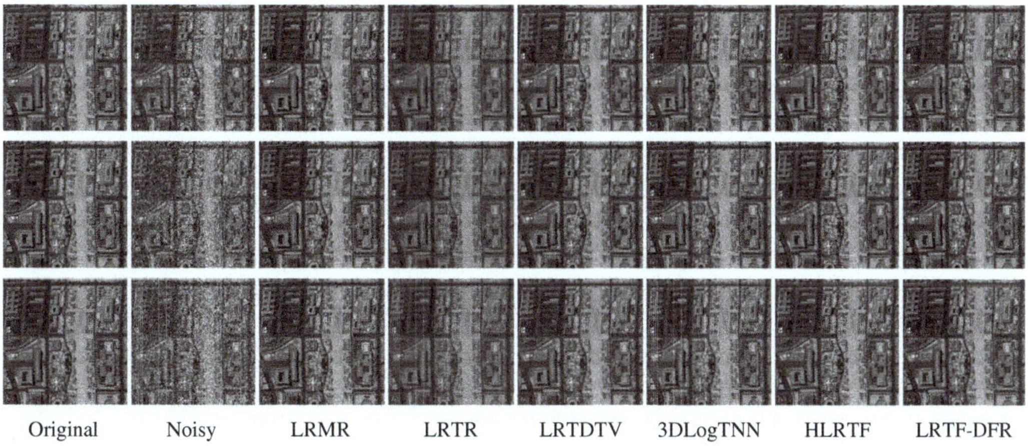

Figure 3.8 Restoration results at band 83 of the Washington DC Mall. From top to bottom: the results under Cases 1, 2, and 3, respectively. From left to right: the original image, the noisy image, the results of LRMR, LRTR, LRTDTV, 3DLogTNN, HLRTF, and LRTF-DFR, respectively.

it simultaneously utilizes the HSI's domain knowledge (e.g., the global low-rankness) and the powerful representation capability of unsupervised neural network, which can perform well on different data. On the other hand, LRTR obtains poorer results, primarily because this method only directly utilizes the spatial correlation of HSIs, and this spatial correlation is not very significant as compared to the spectral correlation. Although 3DLogTNN achieves better results in Cases 1 and 2, this method is relatively time consuming. This is because 3DLogTNN considers tensor SVD in multiple dimensions, which requires more computational time.

To visually compare the restoration results, Figure 3.8 shows band 83 of the HSI Washington DC Mall obtained by different compared methods in all cases. As observed, the visual results achieved by LRTF-DFR surpass those of all the other methods in terms of noise removal as well as the restoration of global structure and local details. HLRTF can simultaneously remove the random noise without obvious residual noise. Comparatively, the results obtained by LRMR still present some residual noise, the results of LRTR and 3DLogTNN contain larger amounts of stripes in Case 3, and the results obtained by LRTDTV exhibit an issue of oversmoothing compared to the original image.

3.5 Conclusion

In this chapter, we introduced tensor modeling-based methods for HSI reconstruction. Specifically, the chapter begins by introducing the degradation model for HSI reconstruction. Then, we offer definitions of the various tensor decompositions along with a discussion of their respective strengths and weaknesses. Based on tensor decompositions, we introduced the application of tensor modeling-based methods for addressing HSI reconstruction problems, providing a comprehensive understanding of underlying concepts, models, and algorithms. Moreover, we compared the performance of various methods by taking the HSI mixed noise removal task as an example.

References

1 Bioucas-Dias, J.M., Plaza, A., Camps-Valls, G. et al. (2013). Hyperspectral remote sensing data analysis and future challenges. *IEEE Geosci. Remote Sens. Mag.* 1 (2): 6–36.

2 Bioucas-Dias, J.M., Plaza, A., Dobigeon, N. et al. (2012). Hyperspectral unmixing overview: geometrical, statistical, and sparse regression-based approaches. *IEEE J. Sel. Top. Appl. Earth Obs. Remote Sens.* 5 (2): 354–379.

3 Su, H., Wu, Z., Zhang, H., and Du, Q. (2022). Hyperspectral anomaly detection: a survey. *IEEE Geosci. Remote Sens. Mag.* 10 (1): 64–90.

4 Patro, R.N., Subudhi, S., Biswal, P.K., and Dell'acqua, F. (2021). A review of unsupervised band selection techniques: land cover classification for hyperspectral earth observation data. *IEEE Geosci. Remote Sens. Mag.* 9 (3): 72–111.

5 Hong, D., He, W., Yokoya, N. et al. (2021). Interpretable hyperspectral artificial intelligence: when nonconvex modeling meets hyperspectral remote sensing. *IEEE Geosci. Remote Sens. Mag.* 9 (2): 52–87.

6 Rasti, B., Chang, Y., Dalsasso, E. et al. (2022). Image restoration for remote sensing: overview and toolbox. *IEEE Geosci. Remote Sens. Mag.* 10 (2): 201–230.

7 Kolda, T.G. and Bader, B.W. (2009). Tensor decompositions and applications. *SIAM Rev.* 51 (3): 455–500.

8 Kilmer, M.E. and Martin, C.D. (2011). Factorization strategies for third-order tensors. *Linear Algebra Appl.* 435 (3): 641–658.

9 Kilmer, M.E., Braman, K., Hao, N., and Hoover, R.C. (2013). Third-order tensors as operators on matrices: a theoretical and computational framework with applications in imaging. *SIAM J. Matrix Anal. Appl.* 34 (1): 148–172.

10 Song, G., Ng, M.K., and Zhang, X. (2020). Robust tensor completion using transformed tensor singular value decomposition. *Numer. Linear Algebra Appl.* 27 (3): e2299.

11 Lu, C., Peng, X., and Wei, Y. (2019). Low-rank tensor completion with a new tensor nuclear norm induced by invertible linear transforms. *2019 IEEE/CVF Conference on Computer Vision and Pattern Recognition (CVPR)*, 5989–5997, Long Beach, CA, USA (15–20 June 2019). IEEE.

12 Jiang, T.-X., Ng, M.K., Zhao, X.-L., and Huang, T.-Z. (2020). Framelet representation of tensor nuclear norm for third-order tensor completion. *IEEE Trans. Image Process.* 29: 7233–7244.

13 Li, B.-Z., Zhao, X.-L., Ji, T.-Y. et al. (2022). Nonlinear transform induced tensor nuclear norm for tensor completion. *J. Sci. Comput.* 92: 83.

14 Luo, Y.-S., Zhao, X.-L., Jiang, T.-X. et al. (2022). Self-supervised nonlinear transform-based tensor nuclear norm for multi-dimensional image recovery. *IEEE Trans. Image Process.* 31: 3793–3808.

15 Zheng, Y.-B., Huang, T.-Z., Zhao, X.-L. et al. (2020). Mixed noise removal in hyperspectral image via low-fibered-rank regularization. *IEEE Trans. Geosci. Remote Sens.* 58 (1): 734–749.

16 Zheng, Y.-B., Huang, T.-Z., Zhao, X.-L. et al. (2020). Tensor N-tubal rank and its convex relaxation for low-rank tensor recovery. *Inf. Sci.* 532: 170–189.

17 Oseledets, I.V. (2011). Tensor-train decomposition. *SIAM J. Sci. Comput.* 33 (5): 2295–2317.

18 Zhao, Q., Zhou, G., Xie, S. et al. (2016). Tensor ring decomposition. *arXiv preprint* 1606.05535.

19 Zheng, Y.-B., Huang, T.-Z., Zhao, X.-L. et al. (2021). Fully-connected tensor network decomposition and its application to higher-order tensor completion. *AAAI Conf. Artif. Intell.* 35: 11071–11078.

20 Ye, M., Qian, Y., and Zhou, J. (2015). Multitask sparse nonnegative matrix factorization for joint spectral–spatial hyperspectral imagery denoising. *IEEE Trans. Geosci. Remote Sens.* 53 (5): 2621–2639.

21 Xu, F., Chen, Y., Peng, C. et al. (2017). Denoising of hyperspectral image using low-rank matrix factorization. *IEEE Geosci. Remote Sens. Lett.* 14 (7): 1141–1145.

22 Du, B., Huang, Z., and Wang, N. (2018). A bandwise noise model combined with low-rank matrix factorization for hyperspectral image denoising. *IEEE J. Sel. Top. Appl. Earth Obs. Remote Sens.* 11 (4): 1070–1081.

23 Karami, A., Yazdi, M., and Zolghadre Asli, A. (2011). Noise reduction of hyperspectral images using kernel non-negative tucker decomposition. *IEEE J. Sel. Top. Signal Process.* 5 (3): 487–493.

24 Guo, X., Huang, X., Zhang, L., and Zhang, L. (2013). Hyperspectral image noise reduction based on rank-1 tensor decomposition. *ISPRS J. Photogramm. Remote Sens.* 83: 50–63.

25 Xiong, F., Zhou, J., and Qian, Y. (2018). Hyperspectral imagery denoising via reweighed sparse low-rank nonnegative tensor factorization. *2018 25th IEEE International Conference on Image Processing (ICIP)*, 3219–3223, Athens, Greece (7–10 October 2018). IEEE.

26 Zhao, Q., Zhang, L., and Cichocki, A. (2015). Bayesian CP factorization of incomplete tensors with automatic rank determination. *IEEE Trans. Pattern Anal. Mach. Intell.* 37 (9): 1751–1763.

27 Lin, J., Huang, T.-Z., Zhao, X.-L. et al. (2022). Robust thick cloud removal for multitemporal remote sensing images using coupled tensor factorization. *IEEE Trans. Geosci. Remote Sens.* 60: 1–16.

28 Rontogiannis, A.A., Giampouras, P.V., and Kofidis, E. (2021). Rank-revealing block-term decomposition for tensor completion. *2021 IEEE International Conference on Acoustics, Speech and Signal Processing (ICASSP)*, 2915–2919, Toronto, ON, Canada (6–11 June 2021). IEEE.

29 Zhou, P., Lu, C., Lin, Z., and Zhang, C. (2018). Tensor factorization for low-rank tensor completion. *IEEE Trans. Image Process.* 27 (3): 1152–1163.

30 Li, L.-Y., Huang, T.-Z., Zheng, Y.-B. et al. (2023). Thick cloud removal for multitemporal remote sensing images: when tensor ring decomposition meets gradient domain fidelity. *IEEE Trans. Geosci. Remote Sens.* 61: 1–14.

31 Semerci, O., Hao, N., Kilmer, M.E., and Miller, E.L. (2014). Tensor-based formulation and nuclear norm regularization for multienergy computed tomography. *IEEE Trans. Image Process.* 23 (4): 1678–1693.

32 Fan, H., Chen, Y., Guo, Y. et al. (2017). Hyperspectral image restoration using low-rank tensor recovery. *IEEE J. Sel. Top. Appl. Earth Obs. Remote Sens.* 10 (10): 4589–4604.

33 Xu, W.-H., Zhao, X.-L., Ji, T.-Y. et al. (2019). Laplace function based non-convex surrogate for low-rank tensor completion. *Signal Process. Image Commun.* 73: 62–69.

34 Liu, J., Musialski, P., Wonka, P., and Ye, J. (2013). Tensor completion for estimating missing values in visual data. *IEEE Trans. Pattern Anal. Mach. Intell.* 35 (1): 208–220.

35 Ng, M.K., Yuan, Q., Yan, L., and Sun, J. (2017). An adaptive weighted tensor completion method for the recovery of remote sensing images with missing data. *IEEE Trans. Geosci. Remote Sens.* 55 (6): 3367–3381.

36 Ji, T.-Y., Huang, T.-Z., Zhao, X.-L. et al. (2017). A non-convex tensor rank approximation for tensor completion. *Appl. Math. Model.* 48: 410–422.

37 Lin, J., Huang, T.-Z., Zhao, X.-L. et al. (2021). A novel non-convex low-rank tensor approximation model for hyperspectral image restoration. *Appl. Math. Comput.* 408: 126342.

38 Zhang, H., He, W., Zhang, L. et al. (2014). Hyperspectral image restoration using low-rank matrix recovery. *IEEE Trans. Geosci. Remote Sens.* 52 (8): 4729–4743.

39 Zhang, H., Cai, J., He, W. et al. (2022). Double low-rank matrix decomposition for hyperspectral image denoising and destriping. *IEEE Trans. Geosci. Remote Sens.* 60: 1–19.

40 Fan, F., Ma, Y., Li, C. et al. (2017). Hyperspectral image denoising with superpixel segmentation and low-rank representation. *Inf. Sci.* 397–398: 48–68.

41 Wei, W., Zhang, L., Jiao, Y. et al. (2019). Intracluster structured low-rank matrix analysis method for hyperspectral denoising. *IEEE Trans. Geosci. Remote Sens.* 57 (2): 866–880.

42 Xie, T., Li, S., and Sun, B. (2020). Hyperspectral images denoising via nonconvex regularized low-rank and sparse matrix decomposition. *IEEE Trans. Image Process.* 29: 44–56.

43 He, W., Zhang, H., Zhang, L., and Shen, H. (2016). Total-variation-regularized low-rank matrix factorization for hyperspectral image restoration. *IEEE Trans. Geosci. Remote Sens.* 54 (1): 178–188.

44 Sun, L., Jeon, B., Zheng, Y., and Wu, Z. (2017). Hyperspectral image restoration using low-rank representation on spectral difference image. *IEEE Geosci. Remote Sens. Lett.* 14 (7): 1151–1155.

45 He, W., Zhang, H., Shen, H., and Zhang, L. (2018). Hyperspectral image denoising using local low-rank matrix recovery and global spatial–spectral total variation. *IEEE J. Sel. Top. Appl. Earth Obs. Remote Sens.* 11 (3): 713–729.

46 Wang, Q., Wu, Z., Jin, J. et al. (2018). Low rank constraint and spatial spectral total variation for hyperspectral image mixed denoising. *Signal Process.* 142: 11–26.

47 Liu, H., Sun, P., Du, Q. et al. (2019). Hyperspectral image restoration based on low-rank recovery with a local neighborhood weighted spectral–spatial total variation model. *IEEE Trans. Geosci. Remote Sens.* 57 (3): 1409–1422.

48 Yang, Y., Zheng, J., Chen, S., and Zhang, M. (2020). Hyperspectral image restoration via local low-rank matrix recovery and moreau-enhanced total variation. *IEEE Geosci. Remote Sens. Lett.* 17 (6): 1037–1041.

49 Fan, H., Li, C., Guo, Y. et al. (2018). Spatial–spectral total variation regularized low-rank tensor decomposition for hyperspectral image denoising. *IEEE Trans. Geosci. Remote Sens.* 56 (10): 6196–6213.

50 Zeng, H., Xie, X., Cui, H. et al. (2021). Hyperspectral image restoration via global l1-2 spatial–spectral total variation regularized local low-rank tensor recovery. *IEEE Trans. Geosci. Remote Sens.* 59 (4): 3309–3325.

51 Wang, M., Wang, Q., Chanussot, J., and Li, D. (2021). Hyperspectral image mixed noise removal based on multidirectional low-rank modeling and spatial–spectral total variation. *IEEE Trans. Geosci. Remote Sens.* 59 (1): 488–507.

52 Wang, M., Wang, Q., and Chanussot, J. (2021). Tensor low-rank constraint and l_0 total variation for hyperspectral image mixed noise removal. *IEEE J. Sel. Top. Signal Process.* 15 (3): 718–733.

53 Wang, Y., Peng, J., Zhao, Q. et al. (2018). Hyperspectral image restoration via total variation regularized low-rank tensor decomposition. *IEEE J. Sel. Top. Appl. Earth Obs. Remote Sens.* 11 (4): 1227–1243.

54 Chen, Y., He, W., Yokoya, N., and Huang, T.-Z. (2020). Hyperspectral image restoration using weighted group sparsity-regularized low-rank tensor decomposition. *IEEE Trans. Cybern.* 50 (8): 3556–3570.

55 Zhang, H., Liu, L., He, W., and Zhang, L. (2020). Hyperspectral image denoising with total variation regularization and nonlocal low-rank tensor decomposition. *IEEE Trans. Geosci. Remote Sens.* 58 (5): 3071–3084.

56 Yuan, Q., Zhang, L., and Shen, H. (2012). Hyperspectral image denoising employing a spectral–spatial adaptive total variation model. *IEEE Trans. Geosci. Remote Sens.* 50 (10): 3660–3677.

57 Li, J., Yuan, Q., Shen, H., and Zhang, L. (2015). Hyperspectral image recovery employing a multidimensional nonlocal total variation model. *Signal Process.* 111: 230–248.

58 Aggarwal, H.K. and Majumdar, A. (2016). Hyperspectral image denoising using spatio-spectral total variation. *IEEE Geosci. Remote Sens. Lett.* 13 (3): 442–446.

59 Chang, Y., Yan, L., Fang, H., and Luo, C. (2015). Anisotropic spectral-spatial total variation model for multispectral remote sensing image destriping. *IEEE Trans. Image Process.* 24 (6): 1852–1866.

60 Takeyama, S., Ono, S., and Kumazawa, I. (2017). Hyperspectral image restoration by hybrid spatio-spectral total variation. *2017 IEEE International Conference on Acoustics, Speech and Signal Processing (ICASSP)*, 4586–4590, New Orleans, LA, USA (5–9 March 2017). IEEE.

61 Sun, L., Jeon, B., Zheng, Y., and Wu, Z. (2017). A novel weighted cross total variation method for hyperspectral image mixed denoising. *IEEE Access* 5: 27172–27188.

62 Peng, J., Xie, Q., Zhao, Q. et al. (2020). Enhanced 3DTV regularization and its applications on HSI denoising and compressed sensing. *IEEE Trans. Image Process.* 29: 7889–7903.

63 Xiong, F., Zhou, J., and Qian, Y. (2019). Hyperspectral restoration via l_0 gradient regularized low-rank tensor factorization. *IEEE Trans. Geosci. Remote Sens.* 57 (12): 10410–10425.

64 He, W., Yokoya, N., Yuan, L., and Zhao, Q. (2019). Remote sensing image reconstruction using tensor ring completion and total variation. *IEEE Trans. Geosci. Remote Sens.* 57 (11): 8998–9009.

65 Zheng, Y.-B., Huang, T.-Z., Zhao, X.-L. et al. (2020). Double-factor-regularized low-rank tensor factorization for mixed noise removal in hyperspectral image. *IEEE Trans. Geosci. Remote Sens.* 58 (12): 8450–8464.

66 Zheng, Y.-B., Huang, T.-Z., Zhao, X.-L., and Zhao, Q. (2022). Tensor completion via fully-connected tensor network decomposition with regularized factors. *J. Sci. Comput.* 92: 1–35.

67 Chang, Y., Yan, L., and Zhong, S. (2017). Hyper-Laplacian regularized unidirectional low-rank tensor recovery for multispectral image denoising. *2017 IEEE Conference on Computer Vision and Pattern Recognition (CVPR)*, 5901–5909, Honolulu, HI, USA (21–26 July 2017). IEEE.

68 Zhuang, L. and Bioucas-Dias, J.M. (2018). Fast hyperspectral image denoising and inpainting based on low-rank and sparse representations. *IEEE J. Sel. Top. Appl. Earth Obs. Remote Sens.* 11 (3): 730–742.

69 Zhuang, L., Fu, X., Ng, M.K., and Bioucas-Dias, J.M. (2021). Hyperspectral image denoising based on global and nonlocal low-rank factorizations. *IEEE Trans. Geosci. Remote Sens.* 59 (12): 10438–10454.

70 Cao, C., Yu, J., Zhou, C. et al. (2019). Hyperspectral image denoising via subspace-based nonlocal low-rank and sparse factorization. *IEEE J. Sel. Top. Appl. Earth Obs. Remote Sens.* 12 (3): 973–988.

71 Zhuang, L. and Ng, M.K. (2020). Hyperspectral mixed noise removal by l_1-norm-based subspace representation. *IEEE J. Sel. Top. Appl. Earth Obs. Remote Sens.* 13: 1143–1157.

72 He, W., Yao, Q., Li, C. et al. (2022). Non-local meets global: an iterative paradigm for hyperspectral image restoration. *IEEE Trans. Pattern Anal. Mach. Intell.* 44 (4): 2089–2107.

73 Xue, J., Zhao, Y., Liao, W., and Chan, J.C.-W. (2019). Nonlocal low-rank regularized tensor decomposition for hyperspectral image denoising. *IEEE Trans. Geosci. Remote Sens.* 57 (7): 5174–5189.

74 Bai, X., Xu, F., Zhou, L. et al. (2018). Nonlocal similarity based nonnegative tucker decomposition for hyperspectral image denoising. *IEEE J. Sel. Top. Appl. Earth Obs. Remote Sens.* 11 (3): 701–712.

75 Chang, Y., Yan, L., Zhao, X.-L. et al. (2020). Weighted low-rank tensor recovery for hyperspectral image restoration. *IEEE Trans. Cybern.* 50 (11): 4558–4572.

76 Gong, X., Chen, W., and Chen, J. (2020). A low-rank tensor dictionary learning method for hyperspectral image denoising. *IEEE Trans. Signal Process.* 68: 1168–1180.

77 Chen, Y., He, W., Yokoya, N. et al. (2020). Nonlocal tensor-ring decomposition for hyperspectral image denoising. *IEEE Trans. Geosci. Remote Sens.* 58 (2): 1348–1362.

78 Zheng, W.-J., Zhao, X.-L., Zheng, Y.-B., and Pang, Z.-F. (2022). Nonlocal patch-based fully connected tensor network decomposition for multispectral image inpainting. *IEEE Geosci. Remote Sens. Lett.* 19: 1–5.

79 Yuan, Q., Zhang, Q., Li, J. et al. (2019). Hyperspectral image denoising employing a spatial-spectral deep residual convolutional neural network. *IEEE Trans. Geosci. Remote Sens.* 57 (2): 1205–1218.

80 Zhang, Q., Yuan, Q., Li, J. et al. (2019). Hybrid noise removal in hyperspectral imagery with a spatial-spectral gradient network. *IEEE Trans. Geosci. Remote Sens.* 57 (10): 7317–7329.

81 Guan, J., Lai, R., Li, H. et al. (2023). DnRCNN: deep recurrent convolutional neural network for HSI destriping. *IEEE Trans. Neural Netw. Learn. Syst.* 34 (7): 3255–3268.

82 Dong, W., Wang, H., Wu, F. et al. (2019). Deep spatial-spectral representation learning for hyperspectral image denoising. *IEEE Trans. Comput. Imaging* 5 (4): 635–648.

83 Cao, X., Fu, X., Xu, C., and Meng, D. (2022). Deep spatial-spectral global reasoning network for hyperspectral image denoising. *IEEE Trans. Geosci. Remote Sens.* 60: 1, 5504714–14.

84 Liu, W. and Lee, J. (2019). A 3-D atrous convolution neural network for hyperspectral image denoising. *IEEE Trans. Geosci. Remote Sens.* 57 (8): 5701–5715.

85 Chen, H., Yang, G., and Zhang, H. (2022). Hider: a hyperspectral image denoising transformer with spatial–spectral constraints for hybrid noise removal. *IEEE Trans. Neural Netw. Learn. Syst.*, https://doi.org/10.1109/TNNLS.2022.3215751.

86 Venkatakrishnan, S.V., Bouman, C.A., and Wohlberg, B. (2013). Plug-and-play priors for model based reconstruction. *2013 IEEE Global Conference on Signal and Information Processing*, 945–948, Austin, TX, USA (3–5 December 2013). IEEE.

87 Zhang, K., Li, Y., Zuo, W. et al. (2022). Plug-and-play image restoration with deep denoiser prior. *IEEE Trans. Pattern Anal. Mach. Intell.* 44 (10): 6360–6376.

88 Zhang, K., Zuo, W., and Zhang, L. (2018). FFDNet: toward a fast and flexible solution for CNN-based image denoising. *IEEE Trans. Image Process.* 27 (9): 4608–4622.

89 Zeng, H., Xie, X., Cui, H. et al. (2020). Hyperspectral image restoration via CNN denoiser prior regularized low-rank tensor recovery. *Comput. Vis. Image Underst.* 197–198: 103004.

90 Li, Y., Qiu, D., and Zhang, X. (2023). Robust low transformed multi-rank tensor completion with deep prior regularization for multi-dimensional image recovery. *IEEE Trans. Big Data.* 9 (5): 1288–1301.

91 Wu, W.-H., Huang, T.-Z., Zhao, X.-L. et al. (2022). Hyperspectral image denoising via tensor low-rank prior and unsupervised deep spatial–spectral prior. *IEEE Trans. Geosci. Remote Sens.* 60: 5545514.

92 Luo, Y., Zhao, X., Meng, D. et al. (2022). HLRTF: hierarchical low-rank tensor factorization for inverse problems in multi-dimensional imaging. *2022 IEEE/CVF Conference on Computer Vision and Pattern Recognition (CVPR)*, 19281–19290, New Orleans, LA, USA (18–24 June 2022). IEEE.

4

Hyperspectral Image Denoising Based on Spatial–Spectral Joint Constraints

Bin Zhao[1], *Magnus O. Ulfarsson*[2], *Jakob Sigurdsson*[2], *Jon Atli Benediktsson*[2], *and Jocelyn Chanussot*[3]

[1] *School of Information Science and Engineering, Shandong Agricultural University, Taian, China*
[2] *Faculty of Electrical and Computer Engineering, University of Iceland, Reykjavik, Iceland*
[3] *GIPSA-Laboratory, University Grenoble Alpes, Grenoble, France*

Mathematical Symbols Used in This Chapter

$\mathbf{X} = [\mathbf{x}_1, \mathbf{x}_2, ..., \mathbf{x}_n]^T \in \mathbb{R}^{n \times B}$	Clean HSI with n pixels and B spectral bands.
$\mathbf{Y}, \mathbf{N} \in \mathbb{R}^{n \times B}$	Observed noisy HSI and noise.
m	The number of similar patches.
$w_{i,j}$	Patch-based weighting function.
$\mathbf{I}_n$	$n \times n$ identity matrix.
$\mathbf{D} \in \mathbb{R}^{n \times n}$	3-D orthogonal wavelet basis.
$\mathbf{W} \in \mathbb{R}^{n \times B}$	Wavelet coefficients matrix.

4.1 Non-local Means Low-rank Approximation

4.1.1 Introduction

Non-local means (NLM) is a single-band image denoising method, which uses the spatial self-similarity of image to denoise. NLM utilizes the patch-based weighted function to get the denoised results. The denoising operator of NLM is constructed from patches of the corrupted noisy image. Thus, the denoising operator is affected by noise. Non-local means low-rank approximation (NLMLRA) [1] is an extension of the idea of [2], which focuses on grayscale images. The distinction of our proposed method is that we use full band pixel-based patches to calculate the weighting function to take full advantage of the high spatial and spectral correlation and constructs a low-rank approximation (LRA) function for denoising operator to improve the NLM denoised performance rather than only using spatial information alone as in [1–10]. To improve the practicability and reduce computational cost, Chebyshev polynomials are used in the NLMLRA.

Machine-Learning-Based Hyperspectral Image Processing, First Edition. Edited by Bing Zhang.

4.1.2 Problem Formulation

Let $\mathbf{X} = [\mathbf{x}_1, \mathbf{x}_2, \ldots, \mathbf{x}_n]^T \in \mathbb{R}^{n \times B}$ denote a clean HSI with n pixels and B spectral bands. Here, $\mathbf{x}_i \in \mathbb{R}^B$ is the ith pixel. The additive noise is assumed in hyperspectral denoising problem, the observational model can be described as

$$\mathbf{Y} = \mathbf{X} + \mathbf{N}, \tag{4.1}$$

where $\mathbf{Y}$, $\mathbf{N} \in \mathbb{R}^{n \times B}$ represent the observed noisy HSI and noise, respectively. Therefore, HSI denoising problem is to find an estimate $\hat{\mathbf{X}} \in \mathbb{R}^{n \times B}$ of $\mathbf{X}$ from $\mathbf{Y}$.

NLM is a classical image denoising method and can be expressed as

$$\hat{\mathbf{x}}_i = \frac{\sum_{j=1}^{m} w_{i,j}\mathbf{y}_j}{\sum_{j=1}^{m} w_{i,j}}, \tag{4.2}$$

where m is the number of similar patches, $w_{i,j}$ is a patch-based weighting function, i.e.,

$$w_{i,j} = \exp\left(-\frac{\|\mathcal{Y}_j - \mathcal{Y}_i\|_2^2}{2h^2}\right), \tag{4.3}$$

where $\mathcal{Y}_i \in \mathbb{R}^{p \times B}$ is a patch and is centered around $\mathbf{y}_i$, p is the size of the patch, and $h > 0$ is filtering parameter. In matrix notation NLM is

$$\hat{\mathbf{X}} = \mathbf{A}\mathbf{Y}, \tag{4.4}$$

where $\mathbf{A} = \mathbf{D}^{-1}\mathbf{W}$ is an NLM operator of $\mathbf{Y}$, $\mathbf{D} \in \mathbb{R}^{n \times n}$ is a diagonal matrix given by $\mathbf{D}_{ii} = \sum_{j=1}^{m} w_{i,j}$, and $w_{i,j}$ are the elements of $\mathbf{W}$.

Image $\mathbf{Y}$ is noisy, $\mathbf{A}$ is constructed from noisy data, and is thus noisy as well [11]. We would like to replace $\mathbf{A}$ with an operator which is less noisy. In particular, we look for replacing $\mathbf{A}$ with its LRA. A simple way to construct the LRA is to use truncated singular-value decomposition (SVD). However, directly calculating the SVD of $\mathbf{A}$ is computationally expensive and often impractical. The slanted Butterworth (SB) function [2] is a filter function that can suppress eigenvalues with small magnitude when applied to a matrix and accurately approximate the remaining low-rank operator, while preserving the fundamental properties of the original operator. Therefore, we use SB function to construct an LRA for NLM operator.

4.1.2.1 Constructing LRA for the NLM Operator Based on Chebyshev Polynomials

The SB function can be expressed as

$$f_{\omega,d}^{sb}(x) = x\left(1 + \left(\frac{1-x}{1-\omega}\right)^{2d}\right)^{-(1/2)}, \quad x \in [0,1] \tag{4.5}$$

where $0 \leq \omega \leq 1$ is filter cutoff and $d \in \mathbb{N}$ is the order of the filter.

The SB function based on NLM operator $\mathbf{A}$ becomes

$$f_{\omega,d}^{sb}(\mathbf{A}) = \mathbf{A}\left(\mathbf{I}_n + \left(\frac{\mathbf{I}_n - \mathbf{A}}{1-\omega}\right)^{2d}\right)^{-(1/2)}, \tag{4.6}$$

where $\mathbf{I}_n$ is the $n \times n$ identity matrix. The direct evaluation of the matrix function $f^{sb}_{\omega,d}(\mathbf{A})$ for a large matrix $\mathbf{A}$ is infeasible. Here, we use Chebyshev polynomials to evaluate the $f^{sb}_{\omega,d}(\mathbf{A})$ function.

The Chebyshev polynomials of the first kind of degree k are given by

$$T_k(x) = \cos(k\arccos(x)), \quad x \in [-1,1], \quad k = 0,1,2,.... \tag{4.7}$$

The Chebyshev expansion is

$$f(x) = \sum_{j=0}^{\infty} \alpha_j T_j(x) \tag{4.8}$$

$$\alpha_0 = \frac{1}{2}\langle f, T_0\rangle_T, \quad \alpha_n = \langle f, T_n\rangle_T, \qquad n \in \mathbb{N}, \tag{4.9}$$

where α_i is Chebyshev coefficient for $f(x), \langle f, T_j\rangle_T = \frac{1}{N+1}\sum_{k=1}^{N+1} f(x_k)T_j(x_k),\ j = 0, ..., N,$ and $x_k = \cos\left(\pi\left(k - \frac{1}{2}\right)/N\right)$.

We evaluate $f^{sb}_{\omega,d}$: [0,1] $\rightarrow \mathbb{R}$ by truncating Eq. (4.8), i.e.,

$$f^{sb}_{\omega,d}(z) \approx \sum_{j=0}^{N} \alpha_j T_j(y), \tag{4.10}$$

where N is the length of the truncation and is set to 50 as a default value, and $y = 2z - 1$ maps $f^{sb}_{\omega,d}$ from [0,1] to [−1,1]. Thus $f^{sb}_{\omega,d}(\mathbf{A})$ is approximated by

$$f^{sb}_{\omega,d}(\mathbf{A}) \approx S_N\left(f^{sb}_{\omega,d}, \mathbf{A}\right) = \sum_{j=0}^{N} \alpha_j T_j(2\mathbf{A} - \mathbf{I}_n). \tag{4.11}$$

Finally, the clean image of $\bf Y$ is estimated as

$$\hat{\mathbf{X}} = S_N\left(f^{sb}_{\omega,d}, \mathbf{A}\right)\mathbf{Y}. \tag{4.12}$$

4.1.3 Experiments and Results

In the following experiments, we use two simulated and one real noisy HSI datasets. The simulated datasets are Washington DC Mall (WDCM) dataset and University of Pavia (UP) dataset. In the experiments, two small parts of the WDCM and UP datasets are used. Their sizes are 200 × 200 × 191 for the WDCM dataset and 200 × 200 × 103 for the UP dataset. Both datasets are assumed to be noise-free HSIs. The datasets are normalized band by band between [0,1] before adding noise. The Gaussian noise with zero-mean and standard deviation σ was added to the clean WDCM and UP datasets. In the experiments, we set σ to two different values 0.05 and 0.1.

To evaluate the denoised results of the simulated datasets, the quantitative metrics are peak signal-to-noise ratio (PSNR) and mean structural similarity (MSSIM) are used.

Here, we evaluate the performance of NLMLRA and NLM for both quantitative metrics and visualization of the denoised WDCM and UP HSIs. The PSNR and SSIM of each band are calculated and depicted in Figure 4.1 for quantitative assessment. Table 4.1 gives the denoising results in terms

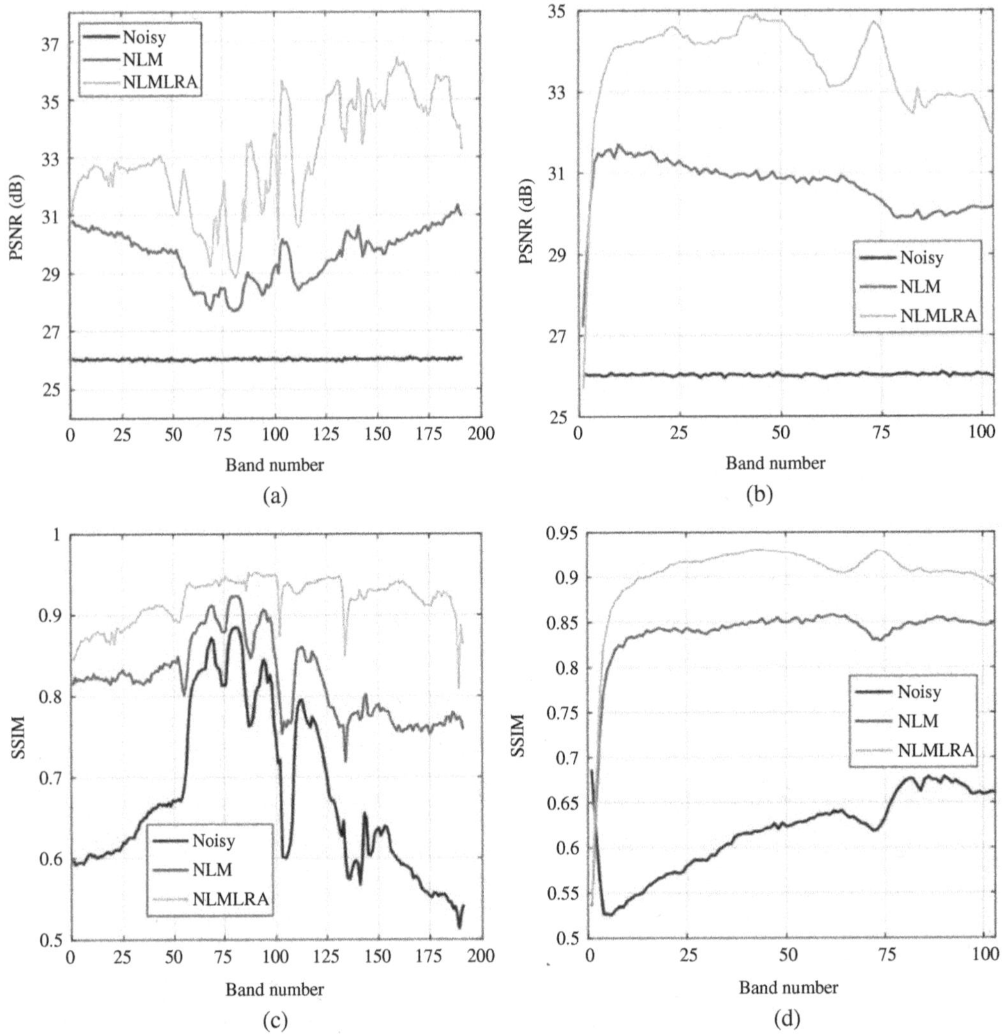

Figure 4.1 PSNR (a–b), and SSIM (c–d) values of each band of denoised WDCM and UP datasets (σ = 0.05).

of PSNR, MSSIM, and Time for both the WDCM and UP datasets. From the figure and table, it can be seen that the obtained PSNR, SSIM, and MSSIM of NLMLRA are higher than for NLM method. The denoising methods are implemented using MATLAB R2019a on a computer having Intel Core i7-67000 processor (3.40 GHz), 8.00 GB of memory, and 64-bit Windows 10 Operating System. The running times for NLMLRA are faster than NLM.

We choose σ = 0.05for both the WDCM and UP datasets to demonstrate visual quality. Figures 4.2 and 4.3 show the denoised results for band 1 of the WDCM dataset and band 32 of the UP dataset, respectively. NLM cannot completely remove the noise as there is still noise in the denoised images. NLMLRA works well in filtering out the noise and provides cleaner denoised images.

For the experiments based on the real dataset, the Indian Pines dataset is used. Figure 4.4 presents the denoised results for bands 2 and 105. It can be clearly observed that NLM gives oversmooth denoised images. The proposed NLMLRA method gives better denoised images.

Table 4.1 The quantitative evaluation results (PSNR (dB), MSSIM, and Time (second)) for the different denoising methods for the Washington DC Mall (WDCM) and the University of Pavia (UP) datasets. The best results are in bold typeface.

Dataset	Noisy level	Metric	Noisy	NLM	NLMLRA
WDCM	$\sigma = 0.05$	PSNR	26.02	29.52	32.83
		MSSIM	0.6750	0.8198	0.9069
		Time	—	11.24	9.07
	$\sigma = 0.1$	PSNR	20.01	25.79	28.56
		MSSIM	0.4081	0.6549	0.7793
		Time	—	11.96	9.16
UP	$\sigma = 0.05$	PSNR	26.03	30.65	33.69
		MSSIM	0.6184	0.8381	0.9060
		Time	—	5.59	4.60
	$\sigma = 0.1$	PSNR	20.01	26.69	29.56
		MSSIM	0.3427	0.6828	0.8036
		Time	—	5.61	4.61

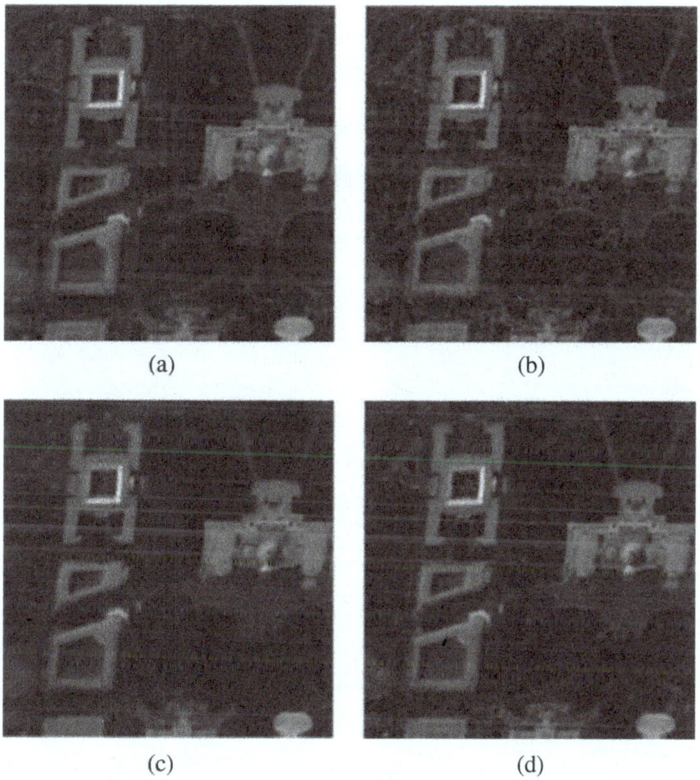

Figure 4.2 The results for the different denoising methods for the WDCM dataset. (a) Original band 1, (b) noisy band 1, (c) NLM, and (d) NLMLRA.

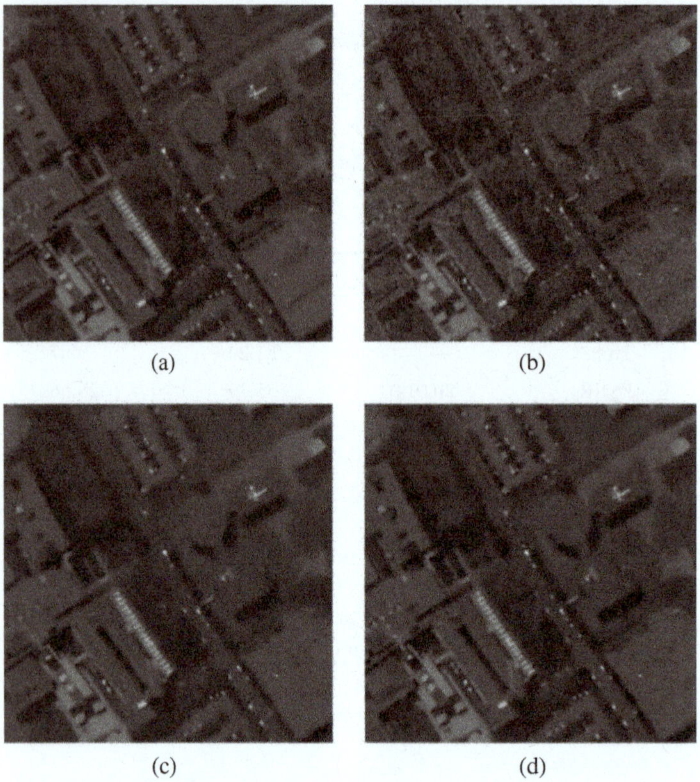

Figure 4.3 The results for the different denoising methods for the UP dataset. (a) Original band 32, (b) noisy band 32, (c) NLM, and (d) NLMLRA.

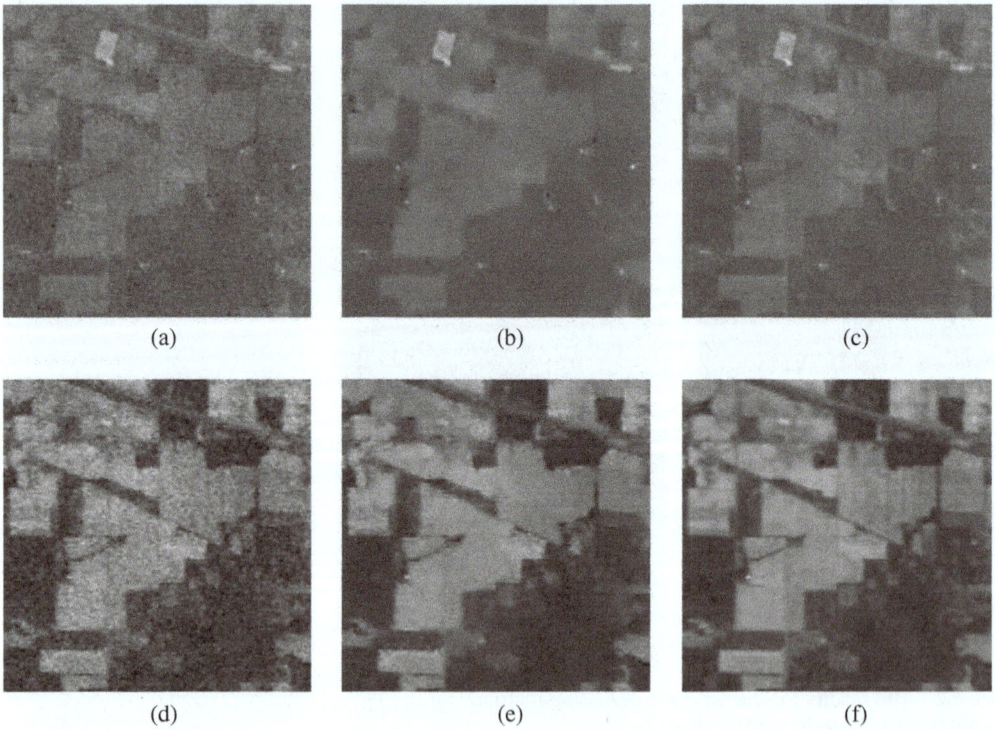

Figure 4.4 The results for the different denoising methods for the Indian Pines dataset. (a) Original band 2, (b) NLM, (c) NLMLRA, (d) original band 105, (e) NLM, and (f) NLMLRA.

4.2 Wavelet-based Block Low-rank Representations

4.2.1 Introduction

HSI can be represented by LRA owing to the high correlation in the spectral–spatial domain [12–19]. Using this characteristic, singular value thresholding (SVT) and block SVT (BSVT) denoising methods were proposed in [20]. SVT uses SVD for noisy HSI and then utilizes soft thresholding for singular value and finally uses inverse SVD for a low-rank matrix to obtain the denoised HSI. BSVT is an extended denoising method of SVT that segments HSI to different blocks and then uses SVT for each block. In this chapter, we propose the wavelet-based block low-rank representation (WBBLRR) denoising method [21] for HSIs. WBBLRR mainly includes three steps for HSI denoising. First, the noisy HSI is decomposed to different sub-images blocks in wavelet domain using 3-D wavelet decomposition. Second, each block uses low-rank representations model to obtain the denoised block. Third, the denoising HSI is obtained using inverse 3-D wavelet transformation for all the denoised blocks.

4.2.2 Problem Formulation

Let $\mathbf{X} \in \mathbb{R}^{n \times B}$ denote a clean HSI with n pixels and B spectral bands. The additive noise is assumed in hyperspectral denoising problem; the observational model can be described as

$$\mathbf{Y} = \mathbf{X} + \mathbf{N}, \tag{4.13}$$

where $\mathbf{Y}, \mathbf{N} \in \mathbb{R}^{n \times B}$represents the observed noisy HSI and noise, respectively. The HSI denoising problem is to find an estimate $\hat{\mathbf{X}} \in \mathbb{R}^{n \times B}$ of $\mathbf{X}$ from $\mathbf{Y}$. Using 3-D discrete wavelet transform (3-D DWT) decomposition, the model can be expressed as

$$\mathbf{Y} = \mathbf{D}\mathbf{W} + \mathbf{N}, \tag{4.14}$$

where $\mathbf{D} \in \mathbb{R}^{n \times n}$ is the 3-D orthogonal wavelet basis and $\mathbf{W} \in \mathbb{R}^{n \times B}$ is a wavelet coefficients matrix.

To enforce the low rank, nuclear norm penalty is used on the wavelet coefficients $\mathbf{W}$. Here, the wavelet-based low-rank denoising problem can be expressed as

$$\hat{\mathbf{W}} = \arg\min_{\mathbf{W}} \quad \|\mathbf{H} - \mathbf{W}\|_F^2 + \lambda\|\mathbf{W}\|_*, \tag{4.15}$$

where $\mathbf{H} = \mathbf{D}^T\mathbf{Y}$, $\|\cdot\|_F^2$ is the Frobenius norm, and $\|\mathbf{W}\|_*$is the nuclear norm of $\mathbf{W}$. The solution of the abovementioned optimization Eq. (4.15) is

$$\hat{\mathbf{W}} - \mathbf{U}\mathbf{S}_{\mathrm{w}}(\boldsymbol{\Sigma})\mathbf{V}^T \tag{4.16}$$

where $\mathbf{W} = \mathbf{U}(\boldsymbol{\Sigma})\mathbf{V}^T$ is the SVD of $\mathbf{W}$, and for each diagonal element $\boldsymbol{\Sigma}_{ii}$ of $\boldsymbol{\Sigma}$, $\mathbf{S}_{\mathbf{w}}(\boldsymbol{\Sigma})$ is the generalized soft-thresholding operator with $\boldsymbol{\lambda}$.

$$\mathbf{S}_{\mathbf{W}}(\boldsymbol{\Sigma})_{ii} = \max\left((\boldsymbol{\Sigma})_{ii} - \lambda, 0\right). \tag{4.17}$$

HSI can be decomposed into different sub-images (approximation coefficients sub-image and detail coefficients sub-images) using 3-D DWT decomposition. Each sub-image can be considered as a block. Here, the main idea of WBBLRR is to apply different regularization parameters for different blocks. Therefore, the WBBLRR problem can be expressed as

$$\hat{\mathbf{W}} = \arg\min_{\mathbf{W}} \sum_{k=1}^{7L+1} \|\mathbf{H}_k - \mathbf{W}_k\|_F^2 + \lambda_k\|\mathbf{W}_k\|_*, \tag{4.18}$$

where $\mathbf{H} = [\mathbf{H}_1; \mathbf{H}_2; \ldots; \mathbf{H}_{7L+1}]$ (the notation ";" shows vertical concatenation) and L is the level of the 3-D DWT decomposition, and $\mathbf{W} = [\mathbf{W}_1; \mathbf{W}_2; \ldots; \mathbf{W}_{7L+1}]$. Therefore, the solution to each block optimization problem is given by

$$\hat{\mathbf{W}}_k = \mathbf{U}_k \mathbf{S}_{\mathbf{w}}(\mathbf{\Sigma}_k)\mathbf{V}_k^T, \tag{4.19}$$

where $\mathbf{W}_k = \mathbf{U}_k(\mathbf{\Sigma}_k)\mathbf{V}_k{}^T$ is the SVD of $\mathbf{W}_k$\$, \$$k = 1, 2, \ldots, 7L + 1$, and $\mathbf{S}_{\mathbf{w}}(\mathbf{\Sigma}_k) = \max((\mathbf{\Sigma}_k)_{ii} - \lambda_k, 0)$.

Finally, the clean image of $\mathbf{Y}$ is estimated as

$$\hat{\mathbf{X}} = \mathbf{D}\hat{\mathbf{W}}. \tag{4.20}$$

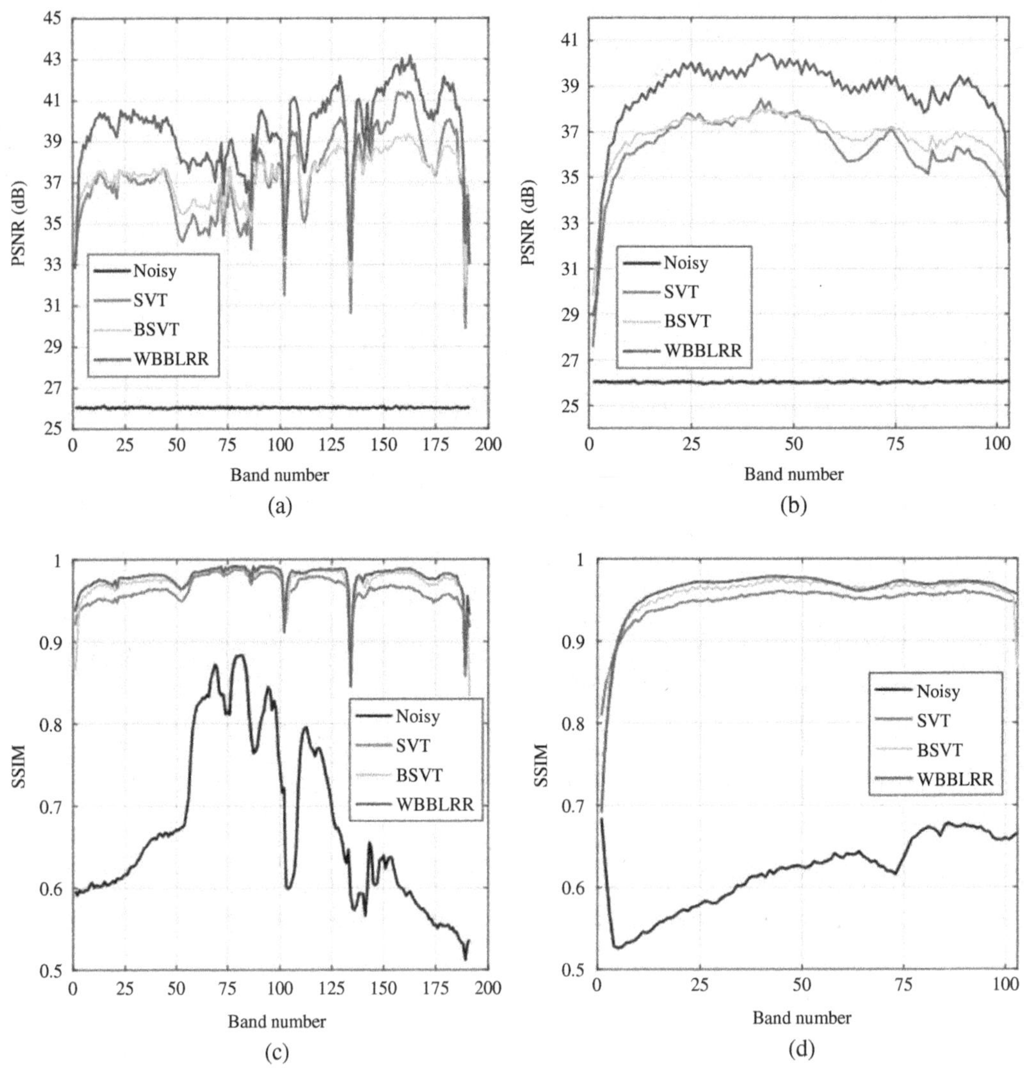

Figure 4.5 PSNR (a–b), and SSIM (c–d) values of each band of denoised WDCM and UP datasets (σ = 0.05).

4.2.3 Experiments and Results

In the following experiments, SVT, BSVT, and WBBLRR denoising methods are compared on two simulated and one real noisy HSI datasets. The simulated datasets are WDCM dataset and UP dataset. In the experiments, two small parts of the WDCM and UP datasets are used. Their sizes are $200 \times 200 \times 191$ for the WDCM dataset and $200 \times 200 \times 103$ for the UP dataset. Both datasets are assumed to be noise-free HSIs. The datasets are normalized band by band between [0,1] before adding noise. The Gaussian noise with zero-mean and standard deviation σ was added to the clean WDCM and UP datasets. In the experiments, we set σ to two different values 0.05, and 0.1.

To evaluate the denoised results of the simulated datasets, the quantitative metrics are PSNR and MSSIM are used.

Here, we evaluate the performance of SVT, BSVT, and WBBLRR for both quantitative metrics and visualization of the denoised WDCM and UP HSIs. The PSNR and SSIM of each band are calculated and depicted in Figure 4.5 for quantitative assessment. Table 4.2 gives the denoising results in terms of PSNR, MSSIM, and Time for both the WDCM and UP datasets. From the figure and table, it can be seen that the obtained PSNR, SSIM, and MSSIM of WBBLRR are higher than for BSVT and SVT methods. The denoising methods are implemented using MATLAB R2019a on a computer having Intel Core i7-67000 processor (3.40 GHz), 8.00 GB of memory, and 64-bit Windows 10 Operating System. The running times for WBBLRR are faster than BSVT and SVT.

We choose $\sigma = 0.05$ for both the WDCM and UP datasets to demonstrate visual quality. Figures 4.6 and 4.7 show the denoised results for band 5 of the WDCM dataset and the UP dataset, respectively. WBBLRR works well in filtering out the noise and provides cleaner denoised images.

For the experiments based on the real dataset, the Indian Pines dataset is used. Figure 4.8 presents the denoised results for bands 4, 5, and 200, respectively. It can be clearly observed that the noise is suppressed by all the denoising methods and the proposed WBBLRR method gives good denoised images.

Table 4.2 The quantitative evaluation results (PSNR (dB), MSSIM, and Time (second)) for the different denoising methods for the Washington DC Mall (WDCM) and the University of Pavia (UP) datasets. The best results are in bold typeface.

Dataset	Noisy level	Metric	Noisy	SVT	BSVT	WBBLRR
WDCM	$\sigma = 0.05$	PSNR	26.02	36.84	37.14	39.11
		MSSIM	0.6750	0.9688	0.9705	0.9731
		Time	—	25.19	71.24	16.13
	$\sigma = 0.1$	PSNR	20.01	28.94	31.34	35.33
		MSSIM	0.4081	0.9293	0.9388	0.9425
		Time	—	24.74	71.36	16.13
UP	$\sigma = 0.05$	PSNR	26.03	35.94	36.62	38.07
		MSSIM	0.6184	0.9406	0.9469	0.9562
		Time	—	11.86	34.28	8.84
	$\sigma = 0.1$	PSNR	20.01	27.74	30.30	34.30
		MSSIM	0.3427	0.8744	0.8859	0.9070
		Time	—	11.68	34.21	9.19

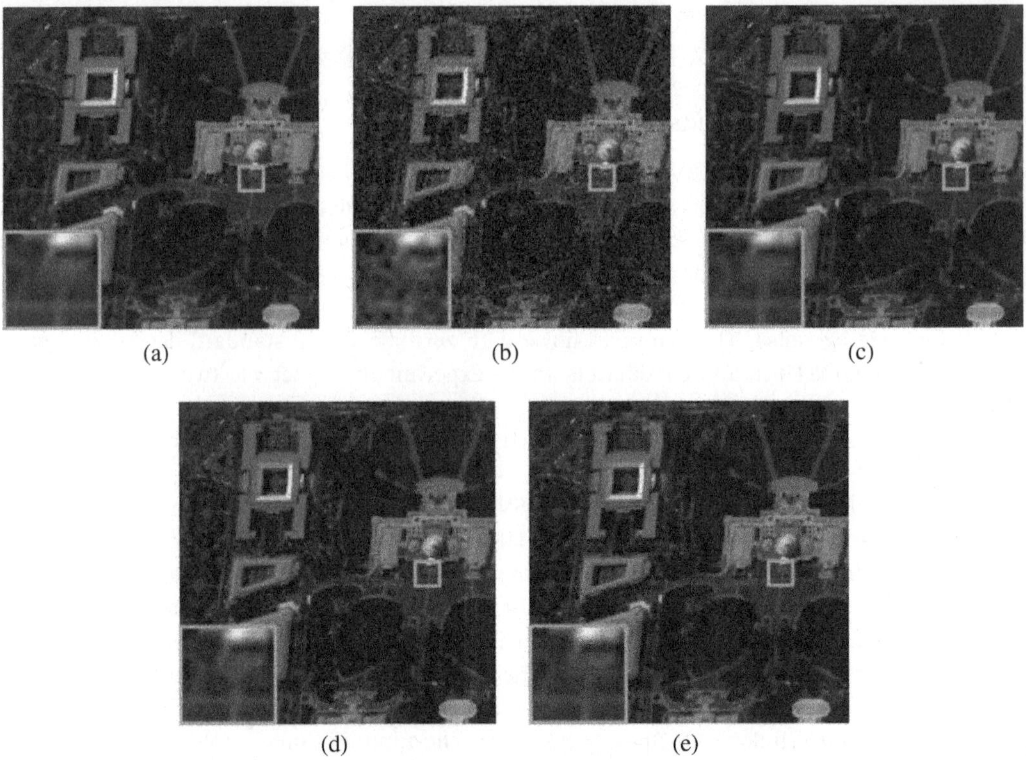

Figure 4.6 The results for the different denoising methods for the WDCM dataset. (a) Original band 5, (b) noisy band 5, (c) SVT, (d) BSVT, and (e) WBBLRR.

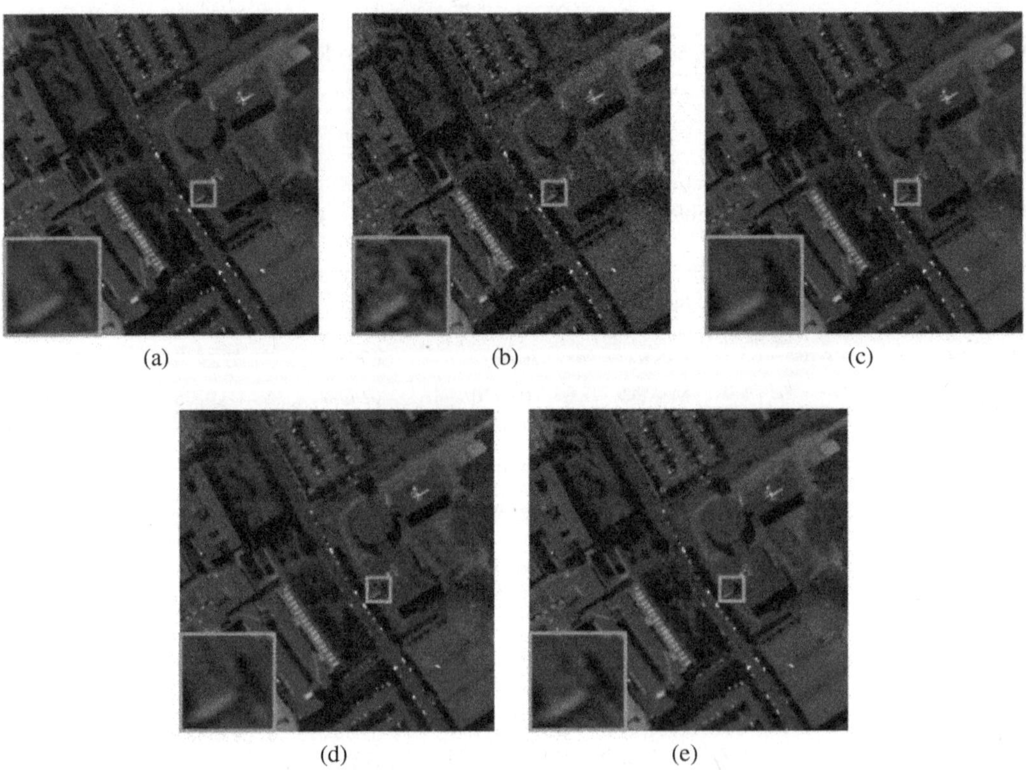

Figure 4.7 The results for the different denoising methods for the UP dataset. (a) Original band 5, (b) noisy band 5, (c) SVT, (d) BSVT, and (e) WBBLRR.

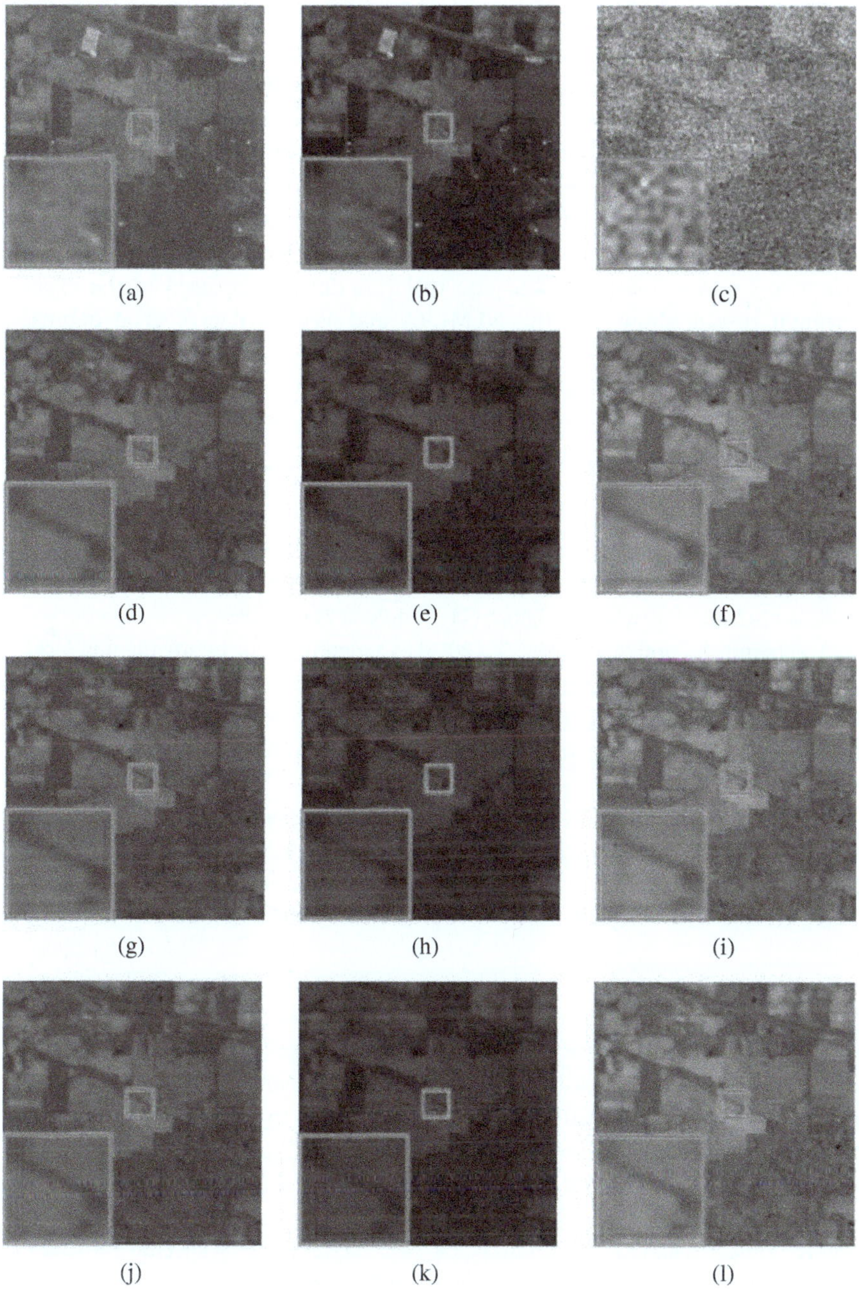

Figure 4.8 The results for the different denoising methods for the Indian Pines dataset, (a) Original band 4, (b) Original band 5, (c) Original band 200, (d) SVT based on band 4, (e) SVT based on band 5, (f) SVT based on band 200, (g) BSVT based on band 4, (h) BSVT based on band 5, (i) BSVT based on band 200, (j) WBBLRR based on band 4, (k) WBBLRR based on band 5, and (l) WBBLRR based on band 200.

4.3 Conclusions

In this chapter, we propose two new low-rank based denoising methods for HSI. These are NLMLRA and WBBLRR denoising method. NLMLRA uses the patch-based similarity weighting function to construct the NLM denoising operator. To improve the practicability and reduce computational cost, Chebyshev polynomials are used in the NLMLRA. WBBLRR is a block low-rank representations method that uses 3-D wavelet transformation to segment HSI to different blocks and utilizes low-rank representations to obtain denoised blocks. To validate the performance of denoising methods, two simulated datasets and one real HSI dataset are used in the experiments. The experiment results show that the NLMLRA and WBBLRR give good denoised results.

References

1 Zhao, B., Sveinsson, J.R., Ulfarsson, M.O., and Chanussot, J. 2021. Non-local means low-rank approximation for hyperspectral denoising. *2021 IEEE International Geoscience and Remote Sensing Symposium IGARSS*, 4147–4150, Brussels, Belgium (11–16 July 2021). IEEE.

2 May, V., Keller, Y., Sharon, N., and Shkolnisky, Y. (2016). An algorithm for improving non-local means operators via low-rank approximation. *IEEE Trans. Image Process.* 25 (3): 1340–1353.

3 Zhao, B., Ulfarsson, M.O., Sveinsson, J.R., and Chanussot, J. (2022). Hyperspectral image denoising using spectral-spatial transform-based sparse and low-rank representations. *IEEE Trans. Geosci. Remote Sens.* 60: 1–25.

4 Bioucas-Dias, J.M., Plaza, A., Camps-Valls, G. et al. (2013). Hyperspectral remote sensing data analysis and future challenges. *IEEE Geosci. Remote Sens. Mag.* 1 (2): 6–36.

5 Yuan, Q., Zhang, Q., Li, J. et al. (February 2019). Hyperspectral image denoising employing a spatial-pectral deep residual convolutional neural network. *IEEE Trans. Geosci. Remote Sens.* 57 (2): 1205–1218.

6 Dabov, K., Foi, A., Katkovnik, V., and Egiazarian, K. (August 2007). Image denoising by sparse 3-D transform-domain collaborative filtering. *IEEE Trans. Image Process.* 16 (8): 2080–2095.

7 Yuan, Q., Zhang, L., and Shen, H. (October 2012). Hyperspectral image denoising employing a spectral–spatial adaptive total variation model. *IEEE Trans. Geosci. Remote Sens.* 50 (10): 3660–3677.

8 Zhang, Q., Yuan, Q., Li, J. et al. (October 2019). Hybrid noise removal in hyperspectral imagery with a spatial–spectral gradient network. *IEEE Trans. Geosci. Remote Sens.* 57 (10): 7317–7329.

9 Zhuang, L. and Ng, M.K. (2021). FastHyMix: fast and parameter-free hyperspectral image mixed noise removal. *IEEE Trans. Neural Netw. Learn. Syst.* 34: 4702–4716.

10 Zhang, H., Chen, H., Yang, G., and Zhang, L. (2021). LR-Net: low-rank spatial-spectral network for hyperspectral image denoising. *IEEE Trans. Image rocess.* 30: 8743–8758.

11 Meyer, F.G. and Shen, X. (2014). Perturbation of the eigenvectors of the graph Laplacian: application to image denoising. *Appl. Comput. Harmon. Anal.* 36 (2): 326–334.

12 Wang, Z., Shao, Z., Huang, X. et al. (2021). SSCAN: a spatial-spectral cross attention network for hyperspectral image denoising. *IEEE Geosci. Remote Sensi. Lett.* 19: 1–5.

13 Monga, V., Li, Y., and Eldar, Y.C. (2021). Algorithm unrolling: Interpretable, Efficient deep learning for signal and image processing. *IEEE Signal rocess. Mag.* 38 (2): 18–44.

14 He, W., Zhang, H., Zhang, L., and Shen, H. (June 2015). Hyperspectral image denoising via noise-adjusted iterative low-rank matrix approximation. *IEEE J. Sel. Topics Appl. Earth Observ. Remote Sens.* 8 (6): 3050–3061.

15 Wang, J.-L., Huang, T.-Z., Zhao, X.-L. et al. (2021). Multi-dimensional visual data completion via low-rank tensor representation under coupled transform. *IEEE Trans. Image Process.* 30: 3581–3596.

16 Xiong, F., Zhou, J., Tao, S. et al. (2022). SMDS-Net: model guided spectral-spatial network for hyperspectral image denoising. *IEEE Trans. Image Process.* 31: 5469–5483.

17 Gkillas, A., Ampeliotis, D., and Berberidis, K. (2023). Connections between deep equilibrium and sparse representation models with application to hyperspectral image denoising. *IEEE Trans. Image Process.* 32: 1513–1528.

18 Fu, G., Xiong, F., Lu, J. et al. (2024). Hyperspectral image denoising via spatial-spectral recurrent transformer. *IEEE Trans. Geosci. Remote Sens.* 62: 5511214.

19 Dong, Y., Gao, D., Li, Y. et al. (2024). Degradation estimation recurrent neural network with local and non-local priors for compressive spectral imaging. *IEEE Trans. Geosci. Remote Sens.* 62: 5520115.

20 Candes, E.J., Sing-Long, C.A., and Trzasko, J.D. (2013). Unbiased risk estimates for singular value thresholding and spectral estimators. *IEEE Trans. Signal Process.* 61 (19): 4643–4657.

21 Zhao, B., Sveinsson, J.R., Ulfarsson, M.O., and Chanussot, J. 2021. Wavelet-based block low-rank representations for hyperspectral denoising. *2021 IEEE International Geoscience and Remote Sensing Symposium IGARSS*, 2484–2487, Brussels, Belgium (11–16 July 2021). IEEE.

5

Hyperspectral Image Reconstruction Based on Spectral Super-resolution

Prof. Yanfeng Gu

School of Electronics and Information Engineering, Harbin Institute of Technology, Harbin, China

Mathematical Symbols Used in This Chapter

u Original HSI.
$\hat{u}$ Reconstructed HSI.
H LR-HSI.
M HR-MSI.
$\mathbf{B} \in \mathbb{R}^{v \times v}$ Blurring matrix on a spatial dimension.
$\mathbf{P} = [p_1, \ldots, p_v] \in \mathbb{R}^{p \times v}$ Sparse coefficient for sub-pixels.
$\mathbf{N}_1$ Additive noise.
$\mathbf{D} = [d_1, \ldots, d_n] \in \mathbb{R}^{v \times n}$ Spatial down-sampling matrix.
$\mathbf{M}'$ Multispectral dictionary.
$\mathbf{R} \in \mathbb{R}^{b_m \times b_h}$ Spectral down-sampling matrix.
$\mathbf{Y}_{in}$ Large-scene MSI.
$\mathbf{X}$ Sparse representation coefficients encoded on MSI.
$\boldsymbol{\Delta}$ Lagrange multiplier.
ρ Lagrangian penalty parameters.

5.1 Introduction

5.1.1 Background

At present, HSIs are increasingly being utilized in various fields, including feature class identification [1], resource investigation [2], environmental monitoring [3–6], meteorology [7–10], agriculture [11–15], geology [16], military [17–20], and numerous other domains with a wide range of promising application prospects. However, due to the constraints of the sensor's imaging ability and the law of energy conservation, satellite HSIs generally have low spatial resolution (LR) and narrow imaging swaths. In contrast, satellite MSIs usually contain a few to dozens of bands, and they have higher spatial resolution compared with HSIs, but lower spectral resolution, resulting in limited ability to identify land covers. The limited spatial resolution of HSIs often leads to mixed pixels, which hinders precise data classification and accurate object recognition. Moreover, the narrow imaging width results in the limited image coverage of HSI, and large-scene HSI can only be acquired by stitching, which requires complicated pre-processing to minimize stitching

Machine-Learning-Based Hyperspectral Image Processing, First Edition. Edited by Bing Zhang.

errors and thus complicates data acquisition for large scenes. Consequently, to overcome the limitations of HSIs and MSIs, and capture spectral information from low-spatial-resolution HSIs (LR-HSIs) and spatial information from high-spatial-resolution MSIs (HR-MSIs), two combined utilization methods of HSI and MSI are explored in the chapter to generate high-spatial-resolution HSIs (HR-HSIs) for large scenes.

At this stage, image fusion and image super-resolution are the two main implementation methods in the study of MS-HS co-utilization. The former generates fused HR-HSI with the same scene as the input LR-HSI [21]; however, the latter is not limited by the input imaging width and can obtain large-scene HR-HSIs that are consistent with the scene of input HR-MSIs. Image super-resolution methods are categorized into hyperspectral spatial super-resolution and multispectral spectral super-resolution, where spatial super-resolution aims at introducing spatial information to LR-HSIs and then obtain HR-HSIs, while spectral super-resolution aims to introduce spectral information to low-spectral-resolution MSIs to generate corresponding HSIs.

Dictionary learning and deep learning are the primary super-resolution techniques. Dictionary learning extracts a spectral dictionary from LR-HSI, representing the reflectance. The dictionary comprises spectral vectors, which capture the properties of a specific object. By combining spectral dictionary with sparse representation coefficients from LR-HSI and HR-MSI, HR-HSI can be reconstructed in the wavelengths of visible and near-infrared [22]. Dictionary learning often sets priors manually to standardize reconstruction, and thus the quality of the reconstructed images is often limited by prior knowledge and computational resources. Furthermore, it is mainly based on a linear model, and its representation ability and the generalization ability of the model are relatively limited. Deep learning learns the nonlinear mapping between MSIs and HSIs through a data-driven strategy [23–26]. The mapping relationship is represented by the parameters of the neural network, which are optimized by backpropagation algorithms during training to minimize the difference between the predicted HSI and the real HSI. However, most studies focus on the limited range of 400–1000 nm, in the visible and near-infrared bands, which is the same spectral range as the input MSI and is limited by the input image. More significantly, both deep-learning and dictionary-learning methods overlook spatial resolution disparities between MSI and HSI, leading to information loss during preprocessing and compromising reconstruction quality.

In this topic, we innovatively propose two image super-resolution methods for acquiring HSIs with high spatial resolution in large scenes, given dictionary learning and deep learning, respectively.

For the first approach, we innovatively combine sub-pixel representation with the construction of coupled dictionaries and propose a novel large-scale and high-spatial-resolution satellite hyperspectral image reconstruction based on MSI–HSI collaborative representation. By considering spectral resolution disparities between HSI and MSI, we utilize a sub-pixel dictionary that combines HSI and MSI characteristics for learning, and the accuracy of the spatial reconstruction is enhanced by incorporating additional spatial information from overlapping MSI. Furthermore, since the narrower coverage of HSI compared to MSI, we design a sub-pixel coupled dictionary to effectively capture the coherence information between MS–HS images, and finally a large-scale HR-HSI is reconstructed. Specifically, sub-pixel dictionary, spatial down-sampling matrix, and spatial blur matrix are used to overcome the spatial-resolution differences between HSIs and MSIs and ensure the accuracy of spatial reconstruction, and the spectral-resolution differences are resolved by using spectral response function (SRF).

For the second approach, to avoid the manual setting of a priori information and the complex parameter selection in multispectral–hyperspectral image collaborative mapping based on dictionary learning, and to adjust the network parameters automatically, distinguished from traditional convolutional neural networks, a collaborative mapping model based on adaptive learning is proposed, including an image fusion module, spectral super-resolution network, and adaptive learning network. Spectral super-resolution networks learn the mapping between multispectral and hyperspectral images based on the attention mechanism. The image fusion module leverages spatial and spectral consistency in training data, providing pseudo labels for spectral super-resolution training. The adaptive learning network incorporates spectral response priors via unsupervised learning, adjusting the output of the super-resolution network to preserve spectral information in reconstructed data. Through the experiment, the model eliminates the need for the manual setting of image prior information and complex parameter selection, and can adjust the network structure and parameters dynamically, eventually enhancing the reconstructed image quality, and enabling the fine classification of large-scale scenes with high spatial resolution.

5.1.2 Related Works

5.1.2.1 Dictionary Learning in Image Super-resolution

Dictionary learning methods mainly rely on manually setting priors to standardize reconstruction, which depicts the structure of hyperspectral images. Initially, Arad and Ben-Shahar [27] proposed a spectral super-resolution model based on sparse representation, using RGB and hyperspectral training data to estimate sparse coefficients and obtain high-resolution hyperspectral images. Aeschbacher et al. [28] improved this method with a new shallow learning approach. Reference [29] used sparse representation to recover large-scale hyperspectral images from partially overlapping hyperspectral and multispectral data. Fotiadou et al. [30] proposed a coupled dictionary learning model that jointly learns low- and high-spectral-resolution features to enhance spectral super-resolution. Gao et al. [31] adopted a joint sparse low-rank learning approach for more accurate reconstruction. Han et al. [32] introduced a spectral library to improve spectral super-resolution quality through joint utilization of multi-hyperspectral images via dictionary learning.

Liu et al. [33] proposed a class-guided coupled dictionary-learning method that incorporates training sample labels to create discriminative regularization terms for HSI reconstruction. In Reference [34], Liu et al. introduced a method that constructs class-specific and mutually coupled dictionaries using sample labels, emphasizing class-specificity for improved classification. To capitalize on HSI's inherent features such as spectral correlation, local sparsity, nonlocal self-similarity, and spatial piecewise smoothness, Rostami and Beheshti Shirazi [35] decomposed the HSI-SR problem into multiple identical SC–SR tasks. To archive spectral-SR, Yan et al. [36] created a spectral library and fused MSI spatial information with its hyperspectral data to get a latent HSI. By learning a low-rank HSI dictionary, get an adaptive sparse MSI coefficients. Nie et al. [37] archived fine classification by maintaining data structures with low-rank and sparsity constraints introducing a discriminative incremental dictionary method to improve dictionary representation.

In conclusion, dictionary-learning-based methods canonically reconstruct the data by introducing an inherent image prior, whereas it is necessary to set the relevant parameters manually in dictionary learning, and the changes of parameters often have a significant impact on the experimental results. Due to its complex iterative approach, dictionary learning often requires a long time.

5.1.2.2 Deep Learning in Image Super-resolution

The image super-resolution methods based on deep learning rely on the mapping relationship between LR-HSIs and HR-MSIs by constructing a suitable deep network. In these methods, three-dimensional multispectral data are often used as input, and the network reconstructs hyperspectral images by extracting spatial and spectral features from the data. Yan et al. [38] proposed a multi-scale deep convolutional neural network that symmetrically down-samples and up-samples intermediate feature maps through a cascaded paradigm, enabling joint encoding of local and non-local image information for spectral reconstruction. Han et al. [39] proposed a cluster-based multi-branch neural network for end-to-end learning. In addition to spectral similarity, an improved super-pixel segmentation is also introduced to jointly consider spatial contextual information. Hu et al. [40] proposed a high-resolution learning network for hyperspectral data reconstruction, which utilizes a spatial–spectral attention module in high-resolution space to extract pixel-level features and introduces frequency domain learning to reduce frequency domain differences.

Similarly, Li et al. [41] also considered feature extraction of channels or frequency bands and proposed a hybrid attention network with structural information consistency, combining spectral gradient constraint loss with mean absolute error as a new loss function. Zamir et al. [42] designed a multi-stage architecture and achieved information exchange between different stages through horizontal and vertical connections.

Moreover, DRCRNet [43] is used to remove the contamination of images by noise, shadows, and other factors. And a dual-channel recalibration module is embedded to adaptively recalibrate channel feature responses, thereby achieving high-fidelity spectrum restoration. The DsTer network [44] combines Transformer and ResNet networks, considering the learning of remote interaction information in images, and finally achieves spectral super-resolution of multispectral remote sensing images. Li et al. [22] proposed a multi-sensor SR framework (MSSRF) based on a two-step approach in which the problems of amplitude inconsistency and band information extraction are solved using an ideal projection network and an ideal multi-sensor SR network, respectively. And Li and Gu introduced a progressive spatial–spectral joint network (PSJN) composed of a 2-D spatial feature extraction module, a 3-D progressive spatial–spectral feature construction module, and a spectral postprocessing module [24].

In addition, a multitemporal spectral reconstruction network (MTSRN) [25] is proposed to reconstruct HS images from multitemporal MS images, which contains a reconstruction network and a temporal features extraction, and a multitemporal fusion network that can independently reconstruct the MS data of a single phase into HS data and can improve the reconstruction effect by combining neighboring phase information, respectively. Du et al. [25] proposed a novel convolution and transformer joint network (CTJN) including cascaded shallow-feature extraction modules (SFEMs) and deep-feature extraction modules (DFEMs), which can explore local spatial features and global spectral features.

In conclusion, since the wavelength of multispectral sensors is roughly 400–1000 nm, while it is 400–2500 nm in hyperspectral sensors, the deep learning method cannot accurately reconstruct large-scene HR-HSI in the range of 1000–2500 nm, leading to an inaccurate mapping relationship, which may compromise the reconstruction quality.

5.2 Experimental Datasets and Evaluation Indicators

5.2.1 Experimental Datasets

We use Chikusei data, Houston data, and GF-YR data in the experiment.

The Chikusei data contains hyperspectral images of Chikusei, Ibaraki, Japan, acquired by the Hyperspec-VNIR-CIRIS spectrometer. With a ground sampling distance of 2.5 m, the image size is 2517×2335 pixels. Chikusei contains a total of 512 bands, and there are 128 bands in the spectral range from 363 to 1018 nm. The dataset collected ground truth for 19 categories. In the experiment,

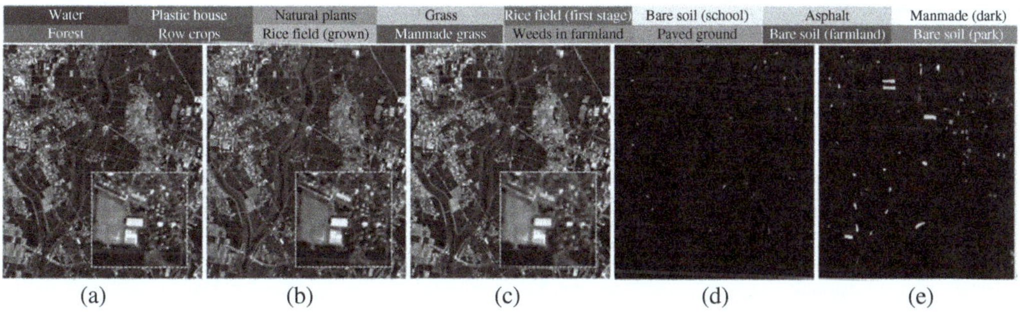

Figure 5.1 The Chikusei data. (a) Original HSI, (b) Chikusei HR-MSI data, (c) Chikusei LR-HSI data, (d) labels of training set, and (e) Labels of test set.

we cropped the Chikusei HS image to a size of 1290 × 1508, and 16 categories are contained in the cropped image. The original HSI is displayed as shown in Figure 5.1a. And we got the HR-MSI and LR-HSI by spectrally and spatially down-sampling the original HSI. Assuming that the full width at half maximum (FWHM) is 6, the SRF is simulated by the Gaussian function centered on wavelength. Subsequently, the indicators of MS and HS Chikusei data, such as bands, source, and image size, are listed in Table 5.1. Moreover, Figure 5.1d and e shows the training set and test set labels. The number of labels for training sets and test sets during the classification of Chikusei data is listed in Table 5.2.

The Houston data were released by the IEEE GRSS Data Fusion Contest (DFC) in 2013, which was acquired by the ITRES CASI-1500 sensor at the Houston University campus and nearby area. The LR-HSI and the HR-MSI were obtained from spatial and spectral down-sampling of the raw Houston data, respectively. Table 5.1 lists the image size, source, spatial resolution, band number, and other indicators of the experimental data. The raw image data size is 349 × 1905 with a total of 144 bands, covering the spectral range of 364–1046 nm. The original HSI is displayed as shown in Figure 5.2a. Moreover, Figure 5.2b and c shows the training set and test set labels. The number of labels for class training sets and test sets during the classification of Houston data is listed in Table 5.3.

Table 5.1 Experimental datasets.

Dataset		Source	Image size	Number of bands	Spatial resolution (m)
Houston	Original HR-HSI	CASI	342 × 1902	144	2.5
	HR-MSI	Simulate	342 × 1902	4	2.5
	LR-HSI	Simulate	171 × 951	144	5
Chikusei	Original HR-HSI	Hyperspec-VNIR-CIRIS	1290 × 1508	128	2.5
	HR-MSI	Simulate	1290 × 1508	10	2.5
	LR-HSI	Simulate	645 × 754	128	5
GF-YR	LR-HSI	GF5	734 × 763	295	30
	HR-MSI	GF1	1468 × 1526	4	15

Table 5.2 The number of labels for training and test sets in Chikusei data.

Labels	Categories	Number of training labels	Number of testing labels
1	Rice field (first stage)	87	862
2	Rice field (grown)	56	503
3	Natural plant	767	2158
4	Row crops	237	1011
5	Asphalt	52	218
6	Forest	245	2142
7	Water	410	2360
8	Plastic house	86	576
9	Bare soil (school)	258	455
10	Bare soil (farmland)	518	3405
11	Manmade grass	67	251
12	Paved ground	104	377
13	Manmade (dark)	116	985
14	Weeds in farm	136	1530
15	Bare soil (park)	108	1156
16	Grass	102	306

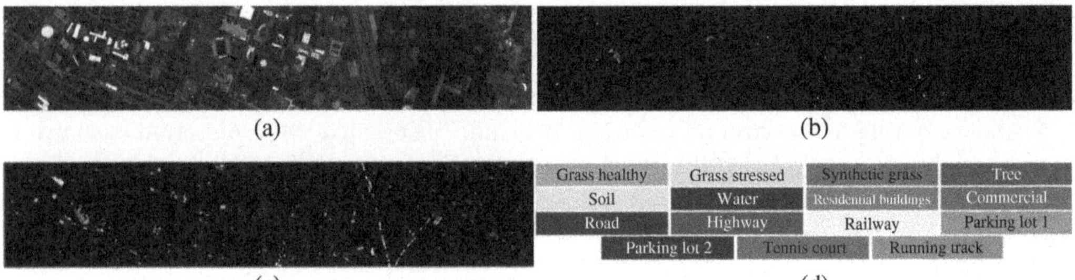

Figure 5.2 The Houston data. (a) The original HSI (selecting 71, 39, and 16 bands), (b) labels of the training set, (c) labels of the test set, and (d) all feature categories.

The HS and MS data of GF-YR were acquired by GF-5 and GF-1 satellites, respectively. We obtained the GF-5 hyperspectral and labeling data from the First Marine Institute, Department of Natural Resources, which was acquired over the Yellow River Delta National Nature Reserve in China. As shown in Table 5.1, a 16-m multispectral camera carried by GF-1 can provide MS data with four bands at the ranges of 450–520, 520–590, 630–690, and 770–890 nm. The full-band spectral imager on GF-5 produces imaging data with a spatial resolution of 30 m. And imaging spectrum spans a range of 400–2500 nm, encompassing a total of 330 bands. Notably, the spectral resolution of the visible band can achieve 5 nm. After preprocessing the data to eliminate defective bands, the image retains 295 bands for analysis. Figure 5.3 shows the GF-5 LR-HSI and GF-1 HR-MSI, respectively. The number of labels for each category in GF-YR is represented in Table 5.4.

Table 5.3 The number of labels for training and test sets in Houston data.

Labels	Categories	Number of training labels	Number of testing labels
1	Grass healthy	537	699
2	Grass stressed	61	1154
3	Synthetic grass	340	357
4	Tree	209	1035
5	Soil	74	1168
6	Water	22	303
7	Residential buildings	52	1203
8	Commercial	320	924
9	Road	76	1149
10	Highway	279	948
11	Railway	33	1185
12	Parking lot 1	329	904
13	Parking lot 2	20	449
14	Tennis court	665	162
15	Running track	279	381

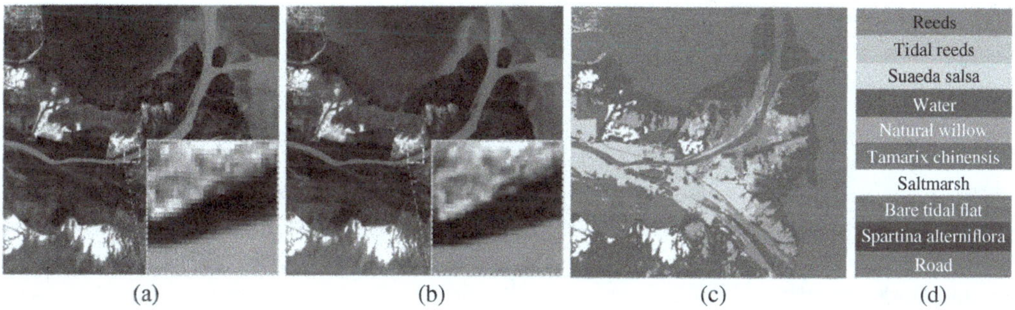

Figure 5.3 The GF-YR data. (a) LR-HSI acquired by GF-5 (displayed in 56, 39, 25 bands), (b) HR-MSI acquired by GF-1(displayed in 3, 2, 1 bands), (c) classification results for labeling data, and (d) all feature categories.

Table 5.4 GF-YR labeling data.

Labels	Categories	Number of global labels
1	Reeds	171,779
2	Tamarix chinensis	104,809
3	Tidal reeds	83,161
4	Saltmarsh	76,206
5	Suaeda salsa	102,579
6	Naked tidal flat	436,015
7	Water	1,066,570
8	Spartina alterniflora	180,186
9	Nature willow	13,492
10	Road	5371

5.2.2 Evaluation Indicators

We gauge the resemblance and the classification precision between the reconstructed HR-HSI and the original HSI in the experiment.

Firstly, a range of metrics are used to undergo a thorough evaluation of reconstruction similarity. We use peak signal-to-noise ratio (PSNR) to measure the distortion after reconstruction, spectral angle index (SAM) and structural similarity (SSIM) are applied to measure spectral similarity and structural similarity, respectively. Moreover, spectral distortion index (D_λ), spatial distortion index (D_s), and global image quality (QNR) are introduced to evaluate the quality of reconstructed HSI in these aspects.

Secondly, we adopt overall accuracy (OA) and Kappa coefficient to assess the accuracy in classifying different features or classes.

The calculation formulas are as follows:

$$RMSE = \sqrt{\frac{1}{HWN}\sum_{l=1}^{N}\sum_{i=1}^{H}\sum_{j=1}^{W}(u_l(i,j) - \hat{u}_l(i,j))^2}$$
$$PSNR = 20\lg\frac{1}{RMSE} \tag{5.1}$$

$$SAM = \frac{1}{HW}\sum_{i=1}^{H}\sum_{j=1}^{W}\arccos\left(\frac{\langle u(i,j), \hat{u}(i,j)\rangle}{|u(i,j)||\hat{u}(i,j)|}\right) \tag{5.2}$$

$$SSIM = \frac{(2\mu_u\mu_{\hat{u}} + c_1)(2\sigma_u\sigma_{\hat{u}} + c_2)}{\left(\mu_u^2 + \mu_{\hat{u}}^2 + c_1\right)\left(\sigma_u^2 + \sigma_{\hat{u}}^2 + c_2\right)}$$
$$c_1 = (k_1L)^2, \quad c_2 = (k_2L)^2, \quad c_3 = c_2/2 \tag{5.3}$$

where u represents the original HSI, $\hat{u}$ represents the reconstructed HSI. N, H, and W represent the number of bands, height, and width of HSI, respectively. c_1, c_2, and $c_3$are constants to avoid the denominator tending to a zero. Default $k_1 = 0.01, \quad k_2 = 0.03$, L is the range of pixel values in the image.

$$Q(\hat{u}_i, \hat{u}_j) = \frac{4\sigma_{\hat{u}_i\hat{u}_j}\bar{\hat{u}}_i\bar{\hat{u}}_j}{\left(\sigma_{\hat{u}_i}^2 + \sigma_{\hat{u}_j}^2\right)\left(\bar{\hat{u}}_i^2 + \bar{\hat{u}}_j^2\right)} \tag{5.4}$$

$$D_\lambda = \sqrt[q]{\frac{1}{N(N-1)}\sum_{i=1}^{N}\sum_{j=1, j\neq i}^{N}|Q(\hat{u}_i, \hat{u}_j) - Q(H_i, H_j)|^q} \tag{5.5}$$

$$D_s = \sqrt[q]{\frac{1}{N}\sum_{i=1}^{N}|Q(\hat{u}_i, M) - Q(H_i, \tilde{M})|^q} \tag{5.6}$$

$$QNR = (1 - D_\lambda)^\mu(1 - D_s)^\rho \tag{5.7}$$

where H and M represent LR-HSI and HR-MSI, respectively. $\tilde{M}$ is an MSI after the down-sampling of M, which has the same spatial resolution as H.

5.3 A Learning Subpixel Super-resolution Model Based on Coupled Dictionary

5.3.1 Proposed Method

In this section, we constructed a multi-hyperspectral collaborative sub-pixel representation model called Sub-CDL based on coupled dictionary learning. The consistency information between MS and HS images is fully learned by designing coupled dictionaries to complete a high-resolution hyperspectral sub-pixel image (HR-HSI) in large scenes covered by MSI, where spatial-resolution disparities between HSI and MSI are addressed by using the sub-pixel dictionary, spatial down-sampling matrix, and spatial blur matrix. Additionally, spectral-resolution differences are resolved by SRF. More specifically, the method utilizes spatial regularization constraint and sub-pixel coupled dictionary low-rank constraint as restrictive conditions, and the alternating direction method of multipliers (ADMM) is used to optimize the model. Ultimately, high-resolution reconstruction of HSIs with large scenes is enabled.

5.3.1.1 The Overall Structure of Sub-CDL

In Sub-CDL, to address the differences in spatial resolution and spectral resolution between LR-HSI and HR-MSI, we integrate spatial down-sampling and spatial blurred matrices to solve spatial resolution disparities in MS-HS data. We employ SRF to reconcile spectral resolution differences.

Spatial regularization constraint and sub-pixel coupled dictionary low-rank constraint are utilized to facilitate the learning and optimization of multi-hyperspectral coupled dictionaries. As shown in Figure 5.4, the proposed methodology proceeds as follows:

Initially, overlapping MSI and HSI are leveraged to establish a coupled sub-pixel dictionary learning model, to fully utilize the spectral and spatial information in LR-HSI and HR-MSI and learn a sub-pixel HS dictionary. The sub-pixel HS dictionary is firstly initialized, and spatial down-sampling matrix and spatial blur matrix are used to connect the information in LR-HSI with the sub-pixel HS dictionary, SRF is used to connect the sub-pixel HS dictionary with the information

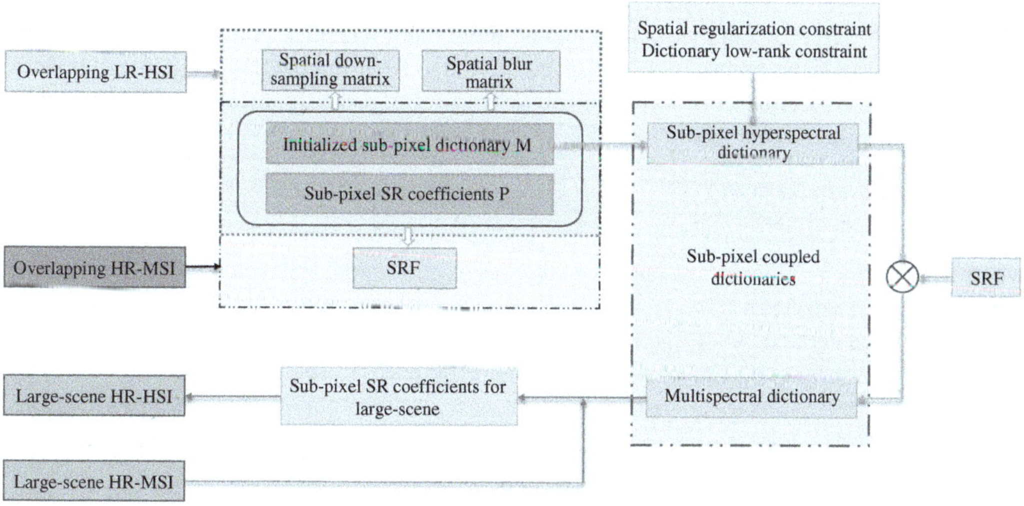

Figure 5.4 The overall structure of Sub-CDL.

in HR-MSI. With spatial regularization constraint and sub-pixel dictionary low-rank constraint, the model is subsequently optimized through the ADMM. The approach enables the comprehensive learning of the coupled sub-pixel dictionary and the extraction of collaborative features from MS-HS data.

Subsequently, SRF is employed to craft a multispectral dictionary. The sub-pixel representation coefficient within extensive scenes is learned by integrating large-scene MSI. The process enables high-resolution reconstruction of HSI within large scenes, thus refining and enhancing the quality of HSIs.

5.3.1.2 Coupled Subpixel Dictionary Learning Model

Firstly, reorganize LR-HSI in overlapping regions into a two-dimensional matrix consisting of single-pixel vectors $\mathbf{Y}_h = [y_{h1}, \ldots, y_{hn}] \in \mathbb{R}^{b_h \times n}$, where b_h represents the number of bands of LR-HSI and n represents the number of pixels in LR-HSI. We defined $\mathbf{M} = [m_1, \ldots, m_p] \in \mathbb{R}^{b_h \times p}$ as an initialized sub-pixel hyperspectral dictionary to be learned and updated which has p dictionary atoms and b_h spectral channels.

Furthermore, $\mathbf{S} = [s_1, \ldots, s_n] \in \mathbb{R}^{p \times n}$ is defined to represent the sparse representation coefficient for HS data $\mathbf{Y}_h$ with n pixels, and $\mathbf{S}$ needs to satisfy the constraints: $\mathbf{S} \geq 0$ and $\mathbf{1}_p^T\mathbf{S} = \mathbf{1}_n^T$, $\mathbf{1}_p^T = [1, 1, \ldots, 1]^T$, which keeps the sparse representation coefficient matrix non-negative and ensures the sum of all coefficients is 1, respectively. Adding spatial resolution differences between HS and MS into consideration, $\mathbf{P} = [p_1, \ldots, p_v] \in \mathbb{R}^{p \times v}$can be introduced as the sub-pixel sparse representation coefficient matrix for HS data, where the number of sub-pixels in $\mathbf{P}$ is $v = n \times s^2$, and s is a scaling factor. Assuming $\mathbf{D} = [d_1, \ldots, d_n] \in \mathbb{R}^{v \times n}$ as a spatial down-sampling matrix, we can establish a precise sub-pixel representation relationship $\mathbf{S} = \mathbf{PD}$ between the sparse and the sub-pixel sparse representation coefficient.

Subsequently, by incorporating the sub-pixel representation relationship along with the spatial blur matrix and the spatial down-sampling matrix, and taking the fidelity term of HS data into account, we can derive the following sub-pixel representation model in overlapping LR-HSI:

$$\mathbf{Y}_h = \mathbf{MPBD} + \mathbf{N}_1 \tag{5.8}$$

where $\mathbf{B} \in \mathbb{R}^{v \times v}$ is a blurring matrix on a spatial dimension, namely a point expansion function during the real imaging process, which can be estimated from the overlapping HS–MS images; $\mathbf{P} = [p_1, \ldots, p_v] \in \mathbb{R}^{p \times v}$represents the sparse coefficient for sub-pixels. $\mathbf{N}_1$ means the additive noise.

If the average filtering method is adopted, then $\mathbf{D}$ can be defined as:

$$\mathbf{D} = \frac{(\mathbf{I}_l \otimes \mathbf{1}_s^T)^T \otimes (\mathbf{I}_r \otimes \mathbf{1}_s^T)^T}{s^2} \tag{5.9}$$

where l and r represent the sizes of rows and columns in the original HSI, respectively. The number of pixels n in HSI satisfies $n = l \times r$, $\otimes$ represents the Cronecker product, and $\mathbf{I}$ represents the identity matrix of the corresponding size.

The overlapping MSI and HSI have simultaneous differences in spatial and spectral resolution. For HR-MSI of the overlapping areas, $\mathbf{Y}_m = [y_{m1}, \ldots, y_{mn}] \in \mathbb{R}^{b_m \times v}$ represents an image with b_m bands and v pixels, where $b_m < b_h$, $v = n \times s^2$. s is a scaling factor. $\mathbf{M}'$ represents a multispectral dictionary. The overlapping MSI can also be represented as:

$$\mathbf{Y}_m = \mathbf{M}'\mathbf{P} + \mathbf{N}_2 \tag{5.10}$$

where $\mathbf{M}' = \mathbf{RM}$ represents the relationship between the HS and MS dictionary. $\mathbf{R} \in \mathbb{R}^{b_m \times b_h}$ is a spectral down-sampling matrix, which can be calculated from the SRF of the HS sensor. Similarly, $\mathbf{N}_2$represents the additive noise in the process.

Due to the ill-posedness of the problem, spatial prior information is introduced to regularize the model in the task of image reconstruction:

$$\varphi(\nabla_x\mathbf{P}, \nabla_y\mathbf{P})^{def} = \sum_{j=1}^{v}\sqrt{\sum_{i=1}^{p}\left\{\left[(\nabla_x\mathbf{P})_{ij}\right]^2 + \left[(\nabla_y\mathbf{P})_{ij}\right]^2\right\}} \tag{5.11}$$

where $(\nabla_x\mathbf{P})_{ij}$ represents the elements in the row i and column j of the matrix, $\nabla_x\mathbf{P}$ and $\nabla_y\mathbf{P}$ represent the image horizontal and vertical discretization difference calculated by using the periodic boundary conditions, respectively. The spatial prior information retains the edges and the detailed spatial information in the image, aiming at imposing sparsity in the distribution of the absolute gradient of the image, which means that the transition between the pixels of the image should be smooth in the spatial dimension, except for a few pixels consistent with the edges.

Based on the considerations mentioned above, the proposed method of coupled sub-pixel dictionary learning can be represented by the following optimization problems:

$$\min_{\mathbf{Z,M}}\left\{\begin{array}{l}\frac{1}{2}\|\mathbf{Y}_h - \mathbf{MPBD}\|_F^2 + \frac{\lambda}{2}\|\mathbf{Y}_m - \mathbf{RMP}\|_F^2 \\ + \mu\varphi(\nabla_x\mathbf{P}, \nabla_y\mathbf{P}) + \gamma\|\mathbf{M}\|_*\end{array}\right\} \tag{5.12}$$

where the first two terms are data fidelity, the latter two are the spatial regularization constraint on representation coefficient and the low rank constraint on coupled subpixel dictionary, respectively; $\|\|_F^2$ and $\|\|_*$ represent the calculation of the F norm and kernel norm of the matrix, respectively.

5.3.1.3 Model Optimization Based on ADMM

In the proposed method, we optimize the problem through variable separation by using ADMM. Firstly, introduce auxiliary variables to divide the original optimization variable $\mathbf{P}$ into a total of six variables. One is still called $\mathbf{P}$, five auxiliary variables $\mathbf{U}_1$, $\mathbf{U}_2$, $\mathbf{U}_3$, $\mathbf{U}_4$, $\mathbf{J}$, respectively. The optimization problem is as follows:

$$\underset{\mathbf{P,M,U_1,U_2,U_3,U_4,J}}{\text{minimize}}\left\{\begin{array}{l}\frac{1}{2}\|\mathbf{Y}_h - \mathbf{MU}_1\mathbf{D}\|_F^2 + \frac{\lambda}{2}\|\mathbf{Y}_m - \mathbf{RMU}_2\|_F^2 \\ + \mu\varphi(\mathbf{U}_3, \mathbf{U}_4) + \gamma\|\mathbf{J}\|_*\end{array}\right\} \tag{5.13}$$

$$s.t.\ \ \mathbf{U}_1 = \mathbf{PB},\quad \mathbf{U}_2 = \mathbf{P},\quad \mathbf{U}_3 = \nabla_x\mathbf{P},\quad \mathbf{U}_4 = \nabla_y\mathbf{P},\quad \mathbf{J} = \mathbf{M}$$

The augmented Lagrangian function of the optimization model is:

$$\begin{aligned}&\mathcal{L}(\mathbf{P}, \mathbf{M}, \mathbf{U}_1, \mathbf{U}_2, \mathbf{U}_3, \mathbf{U}_4, \mathbf{J}, \mathbf{A}_1, \mathbf{A}_2, \mathbf{A}_3, \mathbf{A}_4, \Lambda) \\ &= \frac{1}{2}\|\mathbf{Y}_h - \mathbf{MU}_1\mathbf{D}\|_F^2 + \frac{\mu}{2}\|\mathbf{PB} - \mathbf{U}_1 - \mathbf{A}_1\|_F^2 \\ &+ \frac{\lambda_m}{2}\|\mathbf{Y}_m - \mathbf{RMU}_2\|_F^2 + \frac{\mu}{2}\|\mathbf{P} - \mathbf{U}_2 - \mathbf{A}_2\|_F^2 \\ &+ \lambda_\varphi\varphi(\mathbf{U}_3, \mathbf{U}_4) + \frac{\mu}{2}\|\nabla_x\mathbf{P} - \mathbf{U}_3 - \mathbf{A}_3\|_F^2 + \frac{\mu}{2}\|\nabla_y\mathbf{P} - \mathbf{U}_4 - \mathbf{A}_4\|_F^2 \\ &+ \gamma\|\mathbf{J}\|_* + \frac{\sigma}{2}\|\mathbf{J} - \mathbf{M}\|_F^2 + \Lambda^T(\mathbf{J} - \mathbf{M}) + l_R^+(\mathbf{J})\end{aligned} \tag{5.14}$$

where $\mathbf{A}_1 \sim \mathbf{A}_4$ and Λ denote the Lagrangian multiplier, $\|\|_*$ represents the kernel norm of the matrix. $l_R^+\,()$ indicates the positive operator of elements, realizing the truncation of positive elements in the matrix.

$$\begin{aligned}\mathbf{P}^{(k+1)} &= \arg\min_{\mathbf{P}} \frac{\mu}{2}\left\|\mathbf{PB}-\mathbf{U}_1^{(k)}-\mathbf{A}_1^{(k)}\right\|_F^2 \\ &+ \frac{\mu}{2}\left\|\mathbf{P}-\mathbf{U}_2^{(k)}-\mathbf{A}_2^{(k)}\right\|_F^2 \nabla_x\mathbf{P} \\ &+ \frac{\mu}{2}\left\|\nabla_x\mathbf{P}-\mathbf{U}_3^{(k)}-\mathbf{A}_2^{(k)}\right\|_F^2 + \frac{\mu}{2}\left\|\nabla_y\mathbf{P}-\mathbf{U}_4^{(k)}-\mathbf{A}_3^{(k)}\right\|_F^2\end{aligned} \tag{5.15}$$

Let the derivative of the function be zero, we can get the solution:

$$\begin{aligned}\mathbf{P}^{(k+1)} &= \left[\mathbf{BB}^T + \mathbf{I} + \nabla_x\nabla_x^T + \nabla_y\nabla_y^T\right]^{-1} \\ &\cdot\left[\left(\mathbf{U}_1^{(k)}+\mathbf{A}_1^{(k)}\right)\mathbf{B}^T + \left(\mathbf{U}_2^{(k)}+\mathbf{A}_2^{(k)}\right)\right. \\ &\left.+\left(\mathbf{U}_3^{(k)}+\mathbf{A}_3^{(k)}\right)\nabla_x^T + \left(\mathbf{U}_4^{(k)}+\mathbf{A}_4^{(k)}\right)\nabla_y^T\right]\end{aligned} \tag{5.16}$$

Within formula (5.16), the computation of image gradients necessitates the manipulation of extensive matrices. Considering the operational memory, processing velocity, and the periodically blocked cyclic characteristic of the gradient calculation matrix, the employment of the fast Fourier transform (FFT) serves as an effective tool in addressing the calculation, thereby mitigating the computational complexity to $O(p \times v\log(v))$.

Get the optimization function about the sub-pixel dictionary by separating variable $\mathbf{M}$:

$$\begin{aligned}\mathbf{M}^{(k+1)} &= \arg\min_{\mathbf{M}} \frac{1}{2}\left\|\mathbf{Y}_h-\mathbf{MU}_1^{(k)}\mathbf{D}\right\|_F^2 + \frac{\lambda_m}{2}\left\|\mathbf{Y}_m-\mathbf{RMU}_2^{(k)}\right\|_F^2 \\ &+ \frac{\sigma}{2}\left\|\mathbf{J}^{(k)}-\mathbf{M}\right\|_F^2 + \Lambda^T\left(\mathbf{J}^{(k)}-\mathbf{M}\right)\end{aligned} \tag{5.17}$$

The minimization function of $\mathbf{U}_1$ is a quadratic problem:

$$\mathbf{U}_1^{(k+1)} = \arg\min_{\mathbf{U}_1} \frac{1}{2}\|\mathbf{Y}_h-\mathbf{MU}_1\mathbf{D}\|_F^2 + \frac{\mu}{2}\left\|\mathbf{P}^{(k+1)}\mathbf{B}-\mathbf{U}_1-\mathbf{A}_1^{(k)}\right\|_F^2 \tag{5.18}$$

For the down-sampling operation in the process, a mask matrix can be adopted to avoid the large memory occupied by the down-sampling matrix. A mask matrix $\mathbf{D}$ is used to decompose $\mathbf{U}_1$ into $\mathbf{U}_1\mathbf{D}$ and $\mathbf{U}_1\overline{\mathbf{D}}$, where $\overline{\mathbf{D}}$ indicates the pixel location not selected by $\mathbf{D}$ in the image.

$$\mathbf{U}_1^{(k+1)}\mathbf{D} = \left[\mathbf{M}^T\mathbf{M}+\mu\mathbf{I}\right]^{-1}\left[\mathbf{M}^T\mathbf{Y}_h + \mu\left(\mathbf{P}^{(k+1)}\mathbf{B}-\mathbf{A}_1^{(k)}\right)\right]\mathbf{D} \tag{5.19}$$

$$\mathbf{U}_1^{(k+1)}\overline{\mathbf{D}} = \left(\mathbf{P}^{(k+1)}\mathbf{B}-\mathbf{A}_1^{(k)}\right)\overline{\mathbf{D}} \tag{5.20}$$

Moreover, the optimization of variable $\mathbf{U}_2$ is also a minimized quadratic problem. By taking the derivative of the objective function and keeping the derivative zero, the solution of the variable can be shown in the formula (5.21). The computational complexity is $O(p \times v)$.

$$\begin{aligned}\mathbf{U}_2^{(k+1)} &= \arg\min_{\mathbf{U}_2} \frac{\lambda_m}{2}\|\mathbf{Y}_m-\mathbf{RMU}_2\|_F^2 + \frac{\mu}{2}\left\|\mathbf{P}^{(k+1)}-\mathbf{U}_2-\mathbf{A}_2^{(k)}\right\|_F^2 \\ &= \left[\lambda_m\mathbf{M}^T\mathbf{R}^T\mathbf{RM}+\mu\mathbf{I}\right]^{-1}\left[\lambda_m\mathbf{M}^T\mathbf{R}^T\mathbf{Y}_m + \mu\left(\mathbf{P}^{(k+1)}-\mathbf{A}_2^{(k)}\right)\right]\end{aligned} \tag{5.21}$$

Formula (5.22) represents the optimization function of $\mathbf{U}_3$, $\mathbf{U}_4$. Since the formula contains the constraint terms representing the spatial prior information, the variables can be jointly solved using the pixel-by-pixel soft threshold function. The computational complexity is $O(p \times v \log(v))$.

$$\mathbf{U}_3^{(k+1)}, \quad \mathbf{U}_4^{(k+1)} = \arg\min_{\mathbf{U}_3, \mathbf{U}_4} \lambda_\varphi \varphi(\mathbf{U}_3, \mathbf{U}_4) + \frac{\mu}{2}\left\|\nabla_x \mathbf{P}^{(k+1)} - \mathbf{U}_3 - \mathbf{A}_3^{(k)}\right\|_F^2 + \frac{\mu}{2}\left\|\nabla_y \mathbf{P}^{(k+1)} - \mathbf{U}_4 - \mathbf{A}_4^{(k)}\right\|_F^2 \tag{5.22}$$

The introduction of variable $\mathbf{J}$ ensures a low-rank constraint on the sub-pixel dictionary. Similarly, $\|\|_*$ represents the kernel norm of a matrix, and $l_R^+()$ represents the positive operator of the matrix elements, which realizes the truncation of the positive elements in the matrix. What's more, the optimization of $\mathbf{J}$ can be effectively solved by using Singular Value Thresholding (SVT).

$$\mathbf{J}^{(k+1)} = \arg\min_{\mathbf{J}} \gamma\|\mathbf{J}\|_* + \frac{\sigma}{2}\|\mathbf{J} - \mathbf{M}\|_F^2 + \Lambda^T(\mathbf{J} - \mathbf{M}) + l_R^+(\mathbf{J}) \tag{5.23}$$

In the singular value threshold operator, firstly, singular value decomposition is performed on the input low-rank matrix, assuming the rank of the input matrix $\mathbf{G}$ is r, there is:

$$SVD(\mathbf{G}) \approx \mathbf{USV}, \quad \mathbf{S} = diag\left(\{s_k\}_{1 \le k \le r}\right) \tag{5.24}$$

For the arbitrary $\tau \ge 0$, introducing the soft threshold operator D_r:

$$D(\mathbf{G}) = \mathbf{U}D_r(\mathbf{S})\mathbf{V}, D_r(\mathbf{S}) = diag\left(\{s_k - \tau\}^+\right) \tag{5.25}$$

Then, $\|\mathbf{G}\|_*$ can be expressed as $\|D_r(\mathbf{S})\|_{1,1}$; hence, the update mode of the auxiliary variable $\mathbf{J}$ can be expressed as:

$$\mathbf{J}^{k+1} = \max\{\mathbf{0}, D_r(\mathbf{M} - \Lambda/\sigma)\} \tag{5.26}$$

The Lagrange multipliers are updated as follows:

$$\mathbf{A}_1^{(k+1)} = \mathbf{A}_1^{(k)} - \left(\mathbf{P}^{(k+1)}\mathbf{B} - \mathbf{U}_1^{(k+1)}\right) \tag{5.27}$$

$$\mathbf{A}_2^{(k+1)} = \mathbf{A}_2^{(k)} - \left(\mathbf{P}^{(k+1)} - \mathbf{U}_2^{(k+1)}\right) \tag{5.28}$$

$$\mathbf{A}_3^{(k+1)} = \mathbf{A}_3^{(k)} - \left(\nabla_x \mathbf{P}^{(k+1)} - \mathbf{U}_3^{(k+1)}\right) \tag{5.29}$$

$$\mathbf{A}_4^{(k+1)} = \mathbf{A}_4^{(k)} - \left(\nabla_y \mathbf{P}^{(k+1)} - \mathbf{U}_4^{(k+1)}\right) \tag{5.30}$$

$$\Lambda^{(k+1)} = \Lambda + \sigma\left(\mathbf{J}^{(k+1)} - \mathbf{M}\right) \tag{5.31}$$

5.3.1.4 The Reconstruction of HR-HSI in a Large Scene

For the optimized sub pixel dictionary, the large scene HR-MSI can be sparsely represented by the model in formula (5.32):

$$\min_{\mathbf{X}} \frac{1}{2}\|\mathbf{Y}_{in} - \mathbf{RMX}\|_F^2 + \eta\|\mathbf{X}\|_{1,1}, \quad \text{s.t. } \mathbf{1}^T\mathbf{X} = 1 \tag{5.32}$$

where $\mathbf{Y}_{in}$ represents the input large-scene MSI, $\mathbf{X}$ indicates the sparse representation coefficients encoded on MSI by using the sub-pixel dictionary. $\|\mathbf{X}\|_{1,1}$ represents a sparse constraint on representation coefficients. The sum of sparse representation coefficients is constrained to be 1 in $\mathbf{1}^T\mathbf{X} = 1$.

$\mathbf{R} \in \mathbb{R}^{b_m \times b_h}$ is a spectral down-sampling matrix, which can be calculated from the SRF of the HSI sensor.

Based on the optimization model, auxiliary variables are introduced to obtain the following augmented Lagrangian function:

$$\begin{aligned} &\mathcal{L}(\mathbf{X}, \mathbf{O}, \mathbf{\Delta}) = \frac{1}{2}\|\mathbf{Y}_{in} - \mathbf{RMX}\|_F^2 + \eta\|\mathbf{O}\|_{1,1} \\ &+ \mathbf{\Delta}^T(\mathbf{O} - \mathbf{X}) + \frac{\rho}{2}\|\mathbf{O} - \mathbf{X}\|_F^2 \\ &\text{s.t. } \mathbf{1}^T\mathbf{X} = \mathbf{1} \end{aligned} \tag{5.33}$$

where $\mathbf{\Delta}$ and ρ represent the Lagrange multiplier and Lagrangian penalty parameters, respectively.

After applying ADMM and fixing other variables, the sparse coefficient $\mathbf{X}$ can be optimized by solving the constrained ordinary least squares regression.

$$\begin{aligned} &\min_{\mathbf{X}} \frac{1}{2}\|\mathbf{Y}_{in} - \mathbf{RMX}\|_F^2 + \mathbf{\Delta}^T(\mathbf{O} - \mathbf{X}) + \frac{\rho}{2}\|\mathbf{O} - \mathbf{X}\|_F^2 \\ &\text{s.t. } \mathbf{1}^T\mathbf{X} = \mathbf{1} \end{aligned} \tag{5.34}$$

Solving formula (5.35) yields an analytical solution:

$$\mathbf{X} \leftarrow \mathbf{A}^{-1}\mathbf{B} - \mathbf{C}\left(\mathbf{I}_{1 \times L}\mathbf{A}^{-1}\mathbf{B} - 1\right) \tag{5.35}$$

where $\mathbf{I}_{1 \times L}$ represents a column vector of all 1s with a length of L. The remaining intermediate variables are expressed as follows:

$$\mathbf{A} = \left(\mathbf{RM}^T\right)\mathbf{RM} + \rho\mathbf{I}_{L \times L} \tag{5.36}$$

$$\mathbf{B} = \mathbf{RM}^T\mathbf{Y}_{in} + \rho\mathbf{O} + \mathbf{\Delta} \tag{5.37}$$

$$\mathbf{C} = \mathbf{A}^{-1}\mathbf{I}_{L \times 1}\left(\mathbf{I}_{1 \times L}\mathbf{A}^{-1}\mathbf{I}_{L \times 1}\right)^{-1} \tag{5.38}$$

The solution for the auxiliary variable $\mathbf{O}$ can be obtained through variable separation, leading to the following minimization problem:

$$\min_{\mathbf{O}} \eta\|\mathbf{O}\|_{1,1} + \mathbf{\Delta}^T(\mathbf{O} - \mathbf{X}) + \frac{\rho}{2}\|\mathbf{O} - \mathbf{X}\|_F^2 \tag{5.39}$$

The l_1 norm of variable $\mathbf{O}$ is involved in the optimization problem, which can be solved by the soft threshold operator:

$$\mathbf{O} \leftarrow sign\left(\mathbf{X} - \frac{\mathbf{\Delta}}{\rho}\right) \odot \max\left\{\mathbf{0}, \left|\mathbf{X} - \frac{\Delta}{\rho}\right| - \frac{\eta}{\rho}\right\} \tag{5.40}$$

where $\odot$ represents a Hadamard product of the matrix and *sign*() is a symbolic function.

The Lagrange multiplier is updated as follows:

$$\mathbf{\Delta} \leftarrow \mathbf{\Delta} + \rho(\mathbf{O} - \mathbf{X}) \tag{5.41}$$

Under the assumption that the overlapped HS–MS images share the same set of representation coefficients, the reconstructed HR-HSI can be generated by formula (5.42) via sparse representation coefficients obtained based on MS images:

$$\mathbf{Y}_{out} = \mathbf{MX} \tag{5.42}$$

5.3.2 Results and Analysis

As shown in Figure 5.5, in Chikusei data, the influence of the atomic number of coupled dictionaries on the evaluation index of reconstructed HSI is displayed, and with the increase of the atomic number, the quality of the reconstructed image initially improves, and then decreases. Subsequently, the optimal result is achieved when the dictionary atomic number is 300.

In the experiment, HR-HSI is reconstructed using the optimal dictionary atom number previously mentioned. Additionally, it is shown schematically for several bands of reconstructed HR-HSI and the comparison with original HSI is represented in Figure 5.6. Excellent spatial and

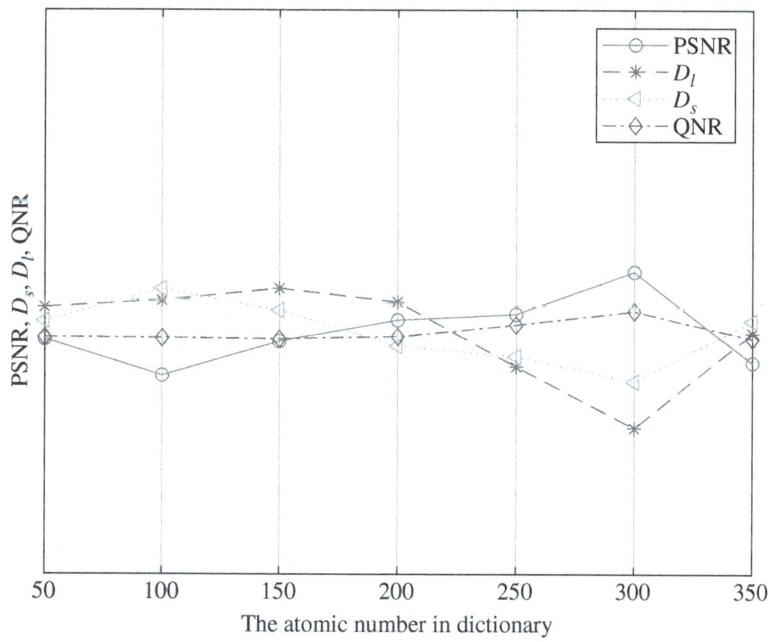

Figure 5.5 The variation of evaluation metrics with the change of atomic numbers in the dictionary in Chikusei data.

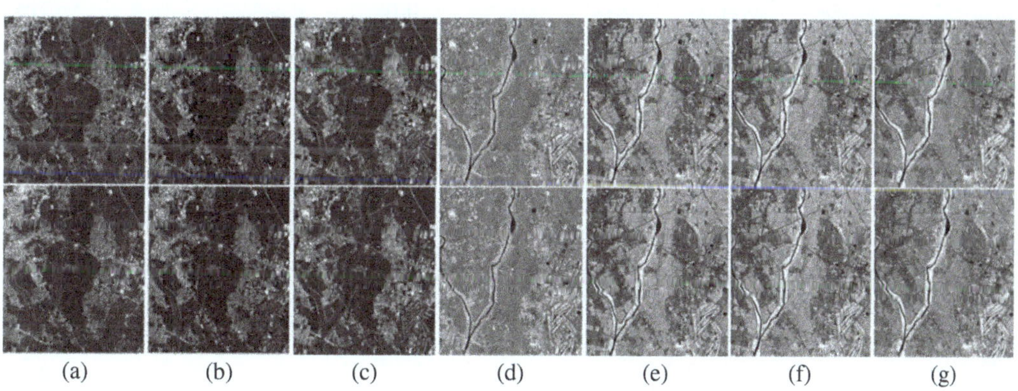

Figure 5.6 The recovery of each band (reconstructed HSI above and original HSI below), selecting 4 (a), 27 (b), 46 (c), 68 (d), 79 (e), 94 (f), and 126 (g) bands to display, respectively.

spectral reconstruction is evident across all chosen bands. SVM classifier is used to classify and evaluate the reconstruction of Chikusei data. By randomly selecting 0.5% labeling data in GF-YR for training data, the KNN classifier is used to obtain a classification image of the whole data.

For comparison, specifically, we utilize J-SLoL [31], MPRNet [45], and MSSNet [46]. Among these methods, J-SLoL belongs to the approach of dictionary learning, whereas MPRNet and MSSNet represent the method of deep learning. In order to ensure a fair comparison and highlight the effectiveness of the proposed method, in J-SLoL, we explored various atomic numbers within the dictionary and ultimately chose the image exhibiting the optimal reconstruction effect for index calculation. Additionally, in the training process of MPRNet and MSSNet, for Chikusei data, crop the overlapping area into several 64×64 blocks by randomly selecting a starting point, keeping a 50% repetition rate to ensure the coverage of the entire training area, and keep the number of blocks is 800. During the testing process, considering data volume and memory usage, the data is cropped to 32 image blocks with a size of 336×336. There occurs a certain overlapping area in the cropped image blocks, which leads to a total image size of 1290×1508. The pixel values within the overlapping regions are ascertained by computing the average. Similarly, in GF-YR data, with the overlapping area of 500×500, the area is cropped into images of 256×256, maintaining a 50% repetition rate to ensure comprehensive coverage of the training area, we randomly select a starting point to designate the training field. Ultimately, the total of training blocks is 500. As for the testing process, the data is cropped into 256×256 with the number of 64, which leads to a total size of 1468×1526.

Tables 5.5 and 5.6 compare evaluation metrics for reconstructed HR-HSI using various methods in Chikusei data and GF-YR data, respectively. The proposed Sub-CDL excels on Chikusei data, achieving optimal results in PSNR, SAM, OA, KAPPA, SSIM, D_S, D_λ, and QNR metrics. Specifically, PSNR has improved by 0.7789, OA has risen by 0.13%, and SSIM has improved by 0.0043. Notably, D_s and D_λ have reached the experimental minimal, reflecting reduced spatial–spectral distortion and higher image quality.

Table 5.5 Comparison of evaluation indicators of reconstruction HSIs on Chikusei data.

Methods	PSNR	SSIM	SAM	D_λ	D_s	QNR	OA	KAPPA
Sub-CDL	**38.5630**	**0.9739**	**1.8112**	**0.0192**	**0.0372**	**0.9443**	**0.7607**	**0.7185**
MPRNet	37.7841	0.9514	3.8679	0.0545	0.0404	0.9073	0.7495	0.7059
J-SLoL	37.7805	0.9696	1.8396	0.0370	0.0449	0.9198	0.7597	0.7173
MSSNet	36.0318	0.9472	3.1497	0.0729	0.1061	0.8287	0.7153	0.6710

Bold numerical values indicates the situation where the metric achieves the best performance among all the experimental methods.

Table 5.6 Comparison of evaluation indicators of reconstruction HSIs on GF-YR data.

Methods	D_λ	D_s	QNR	OA
Sub-CDL	**0.0872**	0.1586	**0.7679**	**0.7916**
MPRNet	0.1238	0.1496	0.7451	0.7726
J-SLoL	0.1667	0.1218	0.7317	0.7815
MSSNet	0.1614	**0.1121**	0.7444	0.7842

Bold data in each column of the table denotes the best experimental result among the methods for that particular metric.

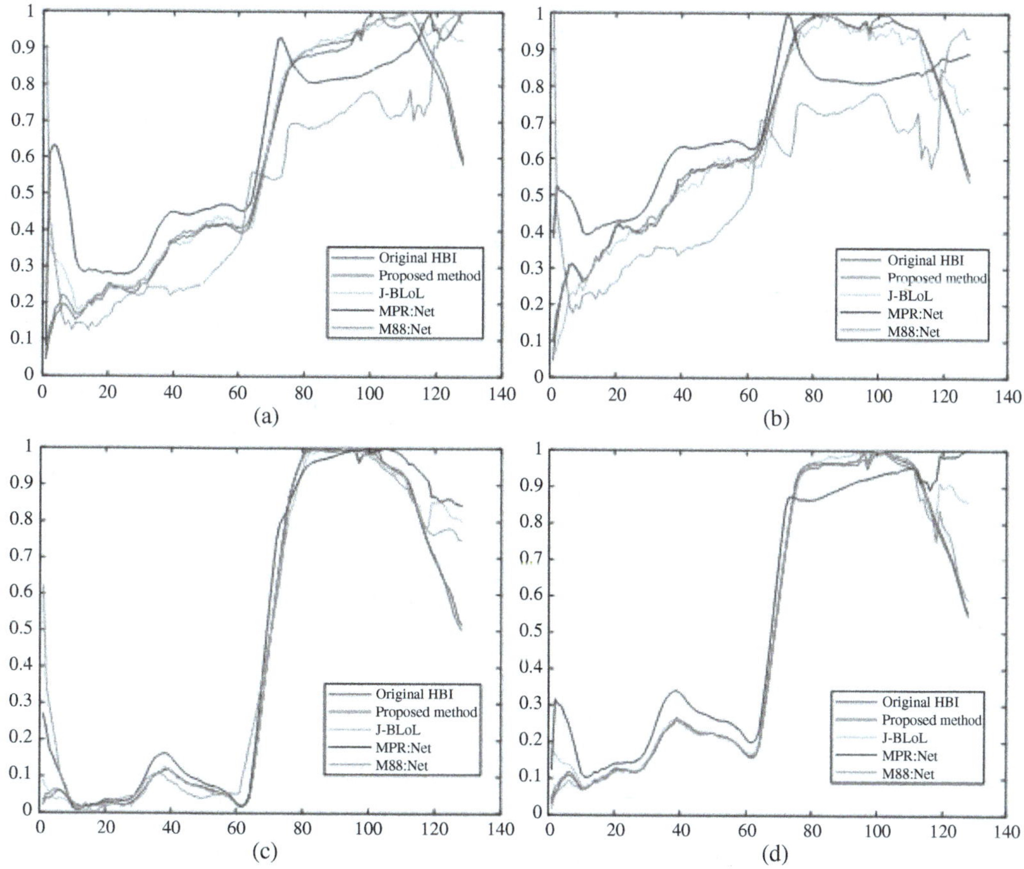

Figure 5.7 Schematic illustration of the spectral profile of a fixed-position pixel in reconstructed HR-HSI. (a) (194,73), (b) (538,946), (c) (1291,174), and (d) (1143,1041).

Meanwhile, the unsupervised evaluation indexes in each method are consistent with supervised evaluation, indicating the effectiveness of unsupervised indexes. As for GF-YR data, proposed Sub-CDL has effective improvement on D_λ, QNR, and OA. Specifically, $D_\lambda$has decreased by 0.0366, and QNR and OA have archived the maximum of the experimental methods.

To demonstrate the reconstructed HSIs clearly, as shown in Figure 5.7, spectral curves of pixels at fixed spatial locations in various reconstruction HSIs in Chikusei data are plotted for comparison. The lighter curve represents the original HR-HSI, while different curves indicate different methods. Specifically, specific coordinates are chosen to demonstrate the results, including (194,73), (538,946), (1291,174), (1143,1041). Notably, both J-SLoL and the proposed Sub-CDL closely approximate the original HSI on Chikusei data. However, MPRNet and MSSNet exhibit offsets at certain coordinates, indicating imperfect spectral restoration in the selected range, possibly due to specific ground features. In the four regions, spectral curves of comparison methods exhibit shifts in several initial and final bands, whereas the proposed method consistently demonstrates excellent recovery in the range of 363∼1018 nm.

Figures 5.8 and 5.9 demonstrate the classification effect of each method in Chikusei and GF-YR data, respectively. Table 5.7 compares reconstruction results in the test set of the Chikusei dataset

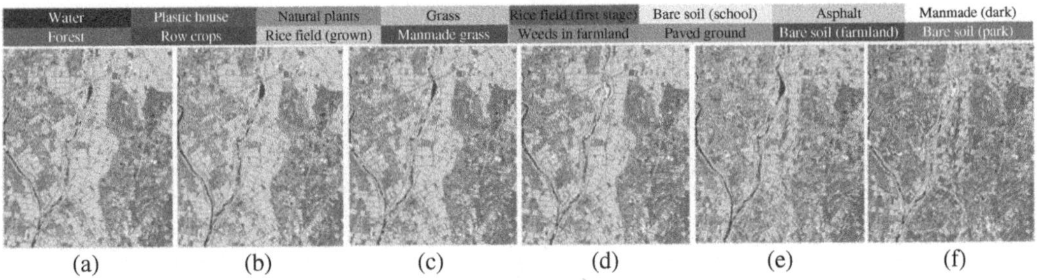

Figure 5.8 Comparison of subpixel classification results of Chikusei data. (a) Original HR-HSI, (b) proposed Sub-CDL, (c) MPRNet, (d) J-SLoL, (e) MSSNet, and (f) HR-MSI.

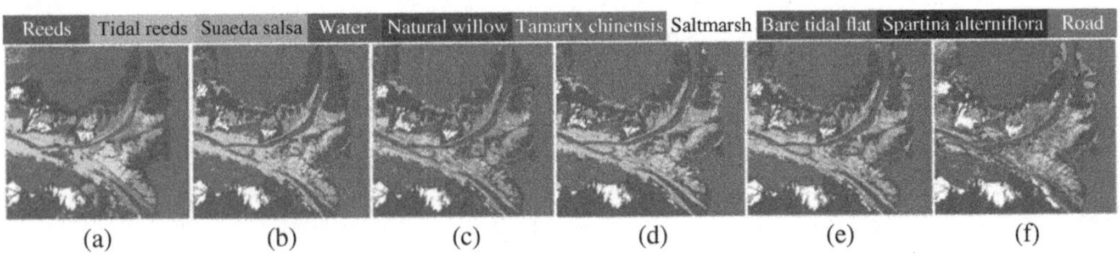

Figure 5.9 Comparison of subpixel classification results of GF-YR data. (a) Labels, (b) proposed Sub-CDL, (c) MPRNet, (d) J-SLoL, (e) MSSNet, and (f) HR-MSI.

Table 5.7 Comparison of classification accuracy of reconstruction Chikusei HR-HSIs by different methods.

Labels	Categories	HR-HSI	Sub-CDL	J-SLoL	MPRNet	MSSNet	HR-MSI
1	Rice field (first stage)	0.6437	0.6468	0.6409	0.6334	0.6488	**0.6720**
2	Rice field (grown)	**0.9285**	0.9127	0.8912	0.9048	0.7432	0.5300
3	Natural plant	**0.8683**	0.8572	0.8542	0.8430	0.8678	0.8432
4	Row crops	0.8388	0.8309	0.8281	0.8437	0.8347	**0.8452**
5	Asphalt	0.7119	0.7059	0.7043	0.6952	**0.7317**	0.7113
6	Forest	0.8711	**0.9156**	0.8826	0.8562	0.8877	0.8423
7	Water	0.3897	0.4489	0.2733	**0.4979**	0.4380	0.2543
8	Plastic house	**0.7795**	0.7517	0.7514	0.7764	0.7475	0.7565
9	Bare soil (school)	0.6136	0.5858	0.5782	**0.6215**	0.6098	0.6056
10	Bare soil (farmland)	0.9310	**0.9581**	0.9497	0.9473	0.9506	0.9439
11	Manmade grass	0.2452	0.2304	0.2429	0.2604	**0.3004**	0.2210
12	Paved ground	0.9666	**0.9759**	0.9710	0.8868	0.9499	0.9733
13	Manmade (dark)	0.1503	0.1547	0.1275	0.1643	**0.1739**	0.1282
14	Weeds in farm	0.7255	0.7225	**0.7429**	0.6988	0.7295	0.7284
15	Bare soil (park)	0.3459	0.2633	0.2627	**0.3708**	0.3151	0.2640
16	grass	0.8463	0.8565	**0.8619**	0.8393	0.8588	0.8439
Evaluation indicators	OA	**0.7692**	0.7607	0.7495	0.7597	0.7153	0.6241
	KAPPA	**0.7279**	0.7185	0.7059	0.7173	0.6710	0.5737

Bold numerical values in each row denote the classification method achieving the highest accuracy for that specific category.

Table 5.8 Comparison of classification accuracy of reconstruction GF-YR HR-HSIs by different methods.

Labels	Categories	MSI	Sub-CDL	J-SLoL	MPRNet	MSSnet
1	Reeds	0.3606	**0.5850**	0.5221	0.5030	0.5786
2	Tamarix chinensis	0.4891	**0.5965**	0.4631	0.4588	0.4674
3	Tidal reeds	0.2802	**0.4996**	0.4300	0.4369	0.4478
4	Saltmarsh	**0.9416**	0.8402	0.8372	0.8217	0.8311
5	Suaeda salsa	0.4214	**0.4999**	0.4059	0.4701	0.4357
6	Naked tidal flat	0.6147	0.6801	0.6466	**0.7306**	0.6755
7	Water	0.8633	**0.9577**	0.9565	0.8745	0.9510
8	Spartina alterniflora	0.7344	0.8684	0.8818	0.8035	**0.8876**
9	Nature willow	**0.4252**	0.3001	0.3693	0.1235	0.4229
10	Road	0.0413	0.0350	0.0309	0.0150	**0.0451**
Evaluation indicators	OA	0.6970	**0.7916**	0.7815	0.7726	0.7842

Bold data in each row indicates the method with the highest classification accuracy for the current category.

for both single-class and overall classification accuracy. In Chikusei data, the original HR-HSI achieves 76.92% classification accuracy, while the original HR-MSI reaches 62.41%. The proposed Sub-CDL outperforms other reconstruction methods, achieving an overall classification accuracy of 76.07% on the test set, closely matching the HR-HSI, and achieves a significant improvement compared to HR-MSI. Other reconstruction methods scored 74.95%, 75.97%, and 71.53%, respectively. Notably, Sub-CDL exhibits superior reconstruction results in classes Forest, Bare soil (farmland), and Paved ground, and remains consistently stable classification accuracy across various other categories, indicating the effectiveness in preserving the image quality of the proposed method.

Similarly, in GF-YR data, as shown in Table 5.8, Sub-CDL archives the highest classification accuracy among the four methods in classes Reeds, Tamarix chinensis, Tidal Reeds, Suaeda salsa, and Water, which scored the highest OA to 79.16%, much higher than MSI's categorization. Accordingly, the proposed Sub-CDL has a universal categorization advantage across diverse feature types in Chikusei and GF-YR data.

5.3.3 Conclusion

In Chapter 3, a sub-pixel coupled dictionary method called Sub-CDL is proposed, leveraging sub-pixel representation for reconstructing large-scene and HR-HSI using overlapping regions of LR-HSI and HR-MSI. Minimizing spatial and spectral reconstruction distortions, Sub-CDL enhanced the image authenticity and classification accuracy of reconstructed HR-HSIs. Innovatively, sub-pixel representation coefficients are combined to construct a coupled dictionary to address the differences in spatial resolution. By incorporating a spatial down-sampling matrix and a spatial blur matrix into the sub-pixel dictionary learning model, the accuracy of spatial recovery is further enhanced and SRF is applied to resolve spectral disparities in input images. Furthermore, spatial regularization constraints and sub-pixel coupled dictionary low-rank constraints are utilized to enhance the precision of learned coupled dictionaries. Experimental results demonstrate that the reconstructed HR-HSIs exhibit superior image authenticity and classification accuracy at a range of 363∼2500 nm, while the distortions of reconstructed images are minimized. Yet, the method requires selecting parameters manually, which may complicate the calculations in the method. Consequently, the multi-objective optimization method can be considered to avoid the manual selection of complex parameters.

5.4 A Collaborative Spectral-super-resolution Model Based on Adaptive Learning

5.4.1 The Proposed Method

In this section, an adaptive learning-based mapping model is proposed for precise reconstruction and fine classification of HSIs. We innovatively design an adaptive learning module and a self-attention block and felicitously combine them with the image fusion and spectral resolution module, to enhance model generalization capabilities and significantly achieve high quality and reconstruction precision. A self-attention block is innovatively constructed in a spectral super-resolution network to allow the network's attention to focus on the parts related to the current task, thereby capturing non-local self-similarity and spectral correlation. Moreover, we innovatively design a self-learning network into image reconstruction to increase the a priori SRF and learn the unknown spatial degradation function. Thus adjust the network structure and parameters dynamically and improve the performance of the model in processing spectral super-resolution tasks and eventually enhance the reconstructed image quality.

5.4.1.1 Network Structure

The overall structure of the proposed method is shown in Figure 5.10. Both low-resolution hyperspectral images (LR-HSI) and high-resolution multispectral images (HR-MSI) covering the same area were required as training data for the network. The network was trained unsupervised to reconstruct high-spatial-resolution hyperspectral images for large scenes (HR-HSI) with the LR-HSI and the HR-MSI reference images. Thus, completing the collaborative mapping of the original hyperspectral image at the spatial scale.

Firstly, multispectral and hyperspectral images were used as inputs, and the image fusion module was used in the network to generate pseudo labels. Secondly, the spectral super-resolution network was supervised and trained based on the pseudo labels to learn the general image prior information of the mapping from MSIs to HSIs. Then, the output of the spectral super-resolution network was used to calculate the loss with the pseudo labels generated by the fusion module and, thus, guide the update of network parameters. The dotted line from the preliminary resconstruction module to the spectral super-resolution module in Figure 5.10.

Then, an adaptive learning module was designed for the preliminary reconstructed images generated by the spectral super-resolution network, to learn the residuals between the preliminary reconstructed images and the real HSI to correct the influence of pseudo labels on the reconstruction results. Finally, the output of the adaptive learning module was HR-HSIs. They were reconstructed from the original input data of LR-HSIs and HR-MSIs using a special degradation network and a given SRF. Then the loss was calculated to guide the spatial degradation process of the network learning image and update the parameters of the adaptive learning module. The remaining dotted lines in Figure 5.10 represents the direction of gradient backpropagation in the adaptive learning network. It should be noted that the image fusion module in the model requires the GLP fusion scheme [33], which completes image fusion in an unsupervised manner.

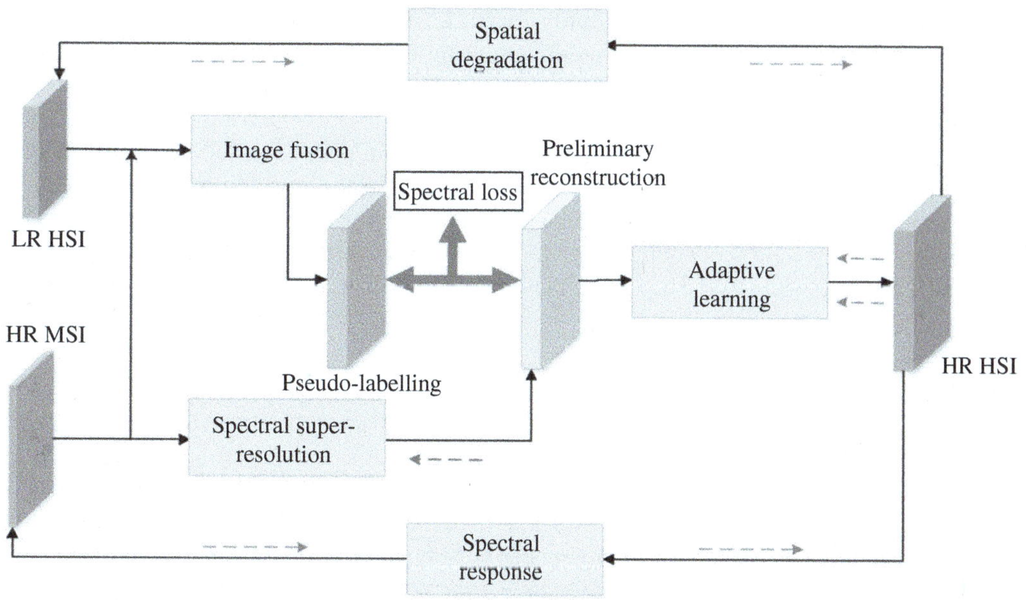

Figure 5.10 The structure of the collaborative mapping model based on adaptive learning.

5.4.1.2 Attention Mechanism

The attention mechanism originated from the phenomenon that humans can naturally and effectively find salient areas in complex scenes. More specifically, the human visual system filters out less important ones as it processes information, and the system only focuses on the information of interest. The information processing mechanism mentioned above is called the attention mechanism.

The attention mechanism in the network can be seen as a process of dynamically adjusting the weights of input image features based on the task, allowing the network's attention to focus on key parts of the data, thereby the model can pay more attention to the parts related to the current task and can process the input data more accurately. And ultimately, better results are obtained. From this perspective, traditional neural networks use convolutional operations to feature map the input image, allowing the network to focus on features that are more closely related to the task. The process above is also a simple attention mechanism.

The characteristics of the attention mechanism can be expressed as:

$$Attention = f(g(x), x) \tag{5.43}$$

in which $g(x)$ represents the process of the network paying attention to key areas by entering information. And $f(g(x), x)$ represents the procedure of processing input data based on $g(x)$. Particularly, for the self-attention mechanism, the specific process in formula (5.43) can be expressed as:

$$Q, K, V = Linear(x) \tag{5.44}$$

$$g(x) = \text{Softmax}(QK) \tag{5.45}$$

$$f(g(x), x) = g(x)V \tag{5.46}$$

According to the different domains that the attention module focuses on, attention mechanisms can be divided into channel attention, spatial attention, temporal attention, self-attention, mixed attention, etc.

The channel attention mechanism can automatically learn the weights of each channel based on the task. Apparently, in neural networks, different channels often represent different image features. Therefore, the process of channel attention can be seen as a feature selection process that enables the network to focus on key features.

The core of the basic channel attention mechanism is compression–excitation module, which learns the relationships between different channels by using global average pooling layers, fully connected layers, and nonlinear layers. And, ultimately, output attention vectors. Accordingly, the corresponding elements are multiplied in the vectors to change the input features of each channel. In this case, if X is used as the input and Y is used as the output, the process can be expressed as follows:

$$g(x) = \sigma(W_2\delta(W_1 GAP(X))) \tag{5.47}$$

$$Y = g(x)X \tag{5.48}$$

where W_1 and W_2 represent the fully connected layers, and $GAP(\,)$ represents the function of global pooling. Moreover, $\delta$and σ represent the activation functions ReLU( ) and *Sigmoid*( ), respectively. The channel attention module not only suppresses noise but, in particular, emphasizes the important characteristic channels. Moreover, it requires lower computational resources. Accordingly, a channel attention module can be added after each residual unit.

The spatial attention mechanism is an adaptive region selection mechanism based on targets, which focuses attention on the target region while suppressing feature activation in irrelevant regions. In reality, the attention gate is a representative spatial attention module, in which, given the input feature map X, the process can be represented as:

$$g(x) = \sigma\left(\varphi\left(\delta\left(\phi_x(X) + \phi_g(G)\right)\right)\right) \tag{5.49}$$

$$Y = g(x)X \tag{5.50}$$

where $G \in \mathbb{R}^{C' \times H \times W}$ represents the gating signal, which is collected at a coarser scale. We can use additive attention to obtain the gating coefficients. Particularly, the gating signal provides activation and contextual information for image regions, and the spatial regions of interest are selected by analyzing this signal. Then, $\varphi(\,)$, $\phi_x(\,)$, and $\phi_g(\,)$ represent 1×1 convolution operation. Similarly, δ and σ represent the activation functions named ReLU( ) and *Sigmoid*( ), respectively. Furthermore, Y represents the output of the module. Undeniably, attention gates guide the model's attention to the desired spatial regions while suppressing feature activation in irrelevant regions. Due to the lightweight design, the representational capacity of the model is greatly enhanced without significantly increasing computational costs. Moreover, the model is universal and modular, which makes it easy to use in various neural network models.

The temporal attention mechanism is an adaptive mechanism for dynamically selecting temporal regions, which determines the periods requiring attention, and the mechanism is commonly used for video processing. The time-adaptive module efficiently and flexibly captures complex time relationships in low complexity. The module mainly includes two branches: the localized branch and the global branch, respectively. Let $X \in \mathbb{R}^{C \times T \times H \times W}$ represent the input feature, which contains the time dimension, and thus the localized branch can be expressed as:

$$g(x) = \sigma(Conv1D(\delta(Conv1D(GAPGAP(X))))) \tag{5.51}$$

$$X_1 = g(x)X \tag{5.52}$$

The global features focus on generating a channel-based adaptive kernel, which relies on the global temporal information of each channel. And for the Cth channel, the kernel can be written as:

$$\Theta_c = \mathrm{Softmax}\left(FC_2\left(\delta\left(FC_1\left(GAP(X)_c\right)\right)\right)\right) \tag{5.53}$$

where $FC(\ )$ represents the fully connected layer, and $\mathrm{Conv}1D(\ )$ represents the convolution operation of 1D. The final output of the module can be expressed as:

$$Y = \Theta \otimes X_1 \tag{5.54}$$

5.4.1.3 Spectral-super-resolution Network Based on Self-attention Mechanism

The attention mechanism in the network can be seen as a process of dynamically adjusting the weights of input image features based on the task, allowing the network's attention to focus on key parts of the data, thereby the model can pay more attention to the parts related to the current task and can process the input data more accurately. And, ultimately, better results can be obtained. For the task of spectral super-resolution, compared to traditional convolutional neural networks, the self-attention-based model has certain advantages in capturing non-local self-similarity and remote correlation. The structure of the spectral super-resolution model adopted in Figure 5.10 is shown in Figure 5.11.

Firstly, the network performs a feature mapping against the input MSI, where the mapping part of Conv1 includes two progressive 3 × 3 convolution operations, which can raise the dimensions of

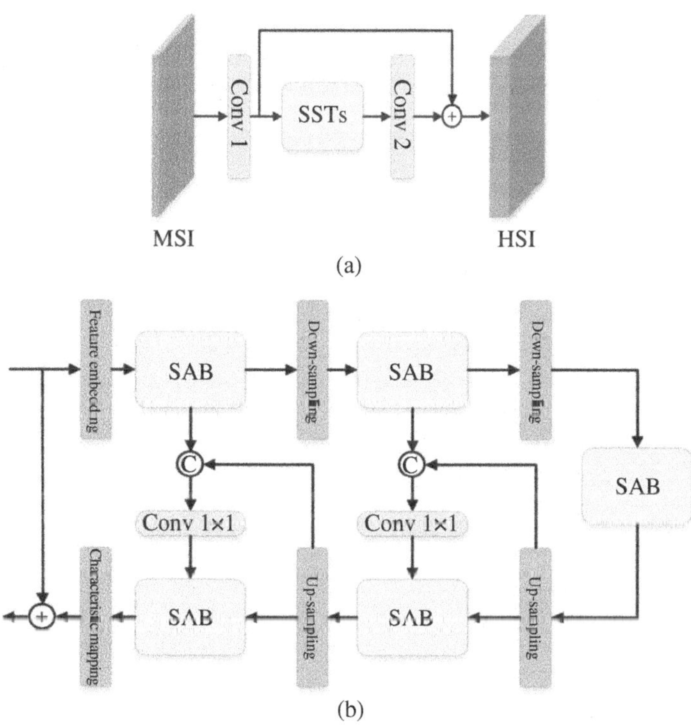

Figure 5.11 The structure of spectral super-resolution network based on self-attention mechanism. (a) Spectral super-resolution network and (b) single-stage spectral transformation module (SST).

the feature. Furthermore, the mapping part of Conv2 contains a 3×3 convolution operation that keeps the feature dimension unchanged. Particularly, the network has residual connections between the output of Conv1 and Conv2.

The main part of the network is composed of multiple cascaded single-stage spectral transformation modules (SST). And the structure of SST is shown in Figure 5.11b. Specifically, the main part of the module is symmetrically connected as a U-shaped structure. And three blocks are included in SST: the up-sampling block, the down-sampling block, and the spectral attention block (SAB), ensuring that the network can generate features of different levels. At the same time, jump connections between the corresponding levels of the encoder and the decoder are designed to accomplish feature aggregation, where the feature embedding and the feature mapping modules are both composed of 3×3 convolutional operations with constant input and output feature dimensions. Moreover, the down-sampling block is a stepwise 4×4 convolution, which increases the number of channels in the feature map while decreasing the size of the feature map. Furthermore, the up-sampling block is a stepwise 2×2 transposed convolution. With the aim of avoiding information loss during up-sampling, a hopping connection is maintained between the decoder and the encoder while undergoing a 1×1 convolution block for feature aggregation. Ultimately, the residual connection is established between the output and the input of the module.

The specific structure of the spectral attention module (SAB) is shown in Figure 5.12, which is mainly composed of three kinds of blocks for serial connections: the batch normalization, the feed-forward network, and the spectral multi-headed self-attention module (S-MSA), with residual connections between the inputs and outputs of the module. Moreover, the batch normalization makes the forward propagation of the network more stable, and at the same time makes the process of gradient backpropagation more stable, which avoids the overfitting of the network to some degree. And, as shown in Figure 5.12b, the feed-forward network consists of three blocks serially connected: the 1×1 convolution, the 3×3 depth-wise convolution, and the GELU activation function.

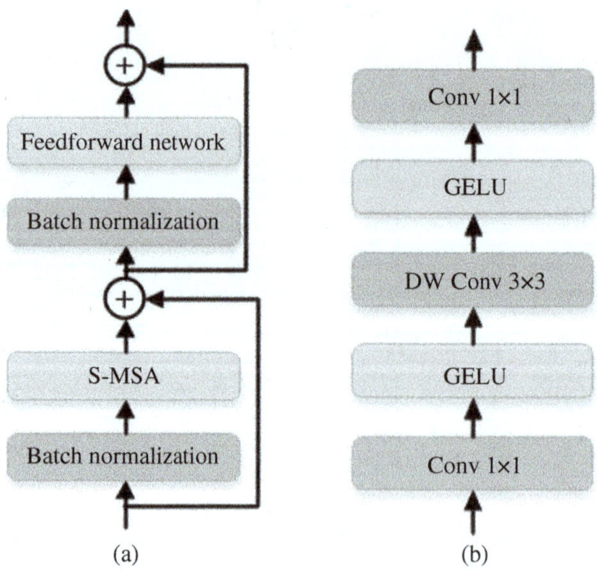

Figure 5.12 The spectral self-attention module (SAB). (a) The specific structure of SAB and (b) the structure of the feedforward network in SAB.

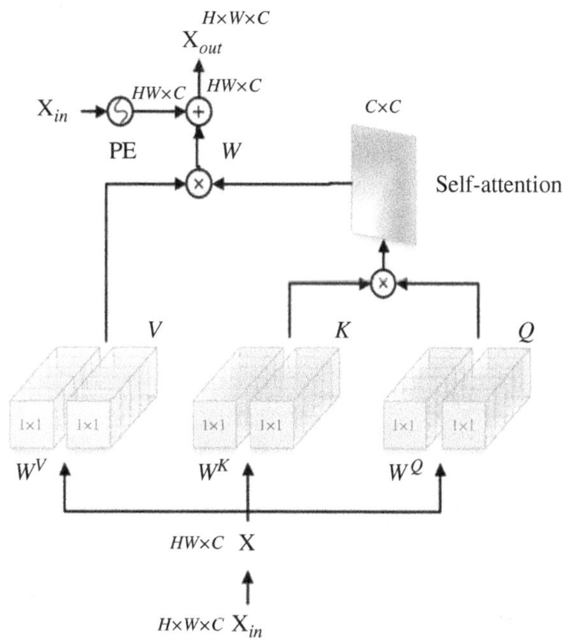

Figure 5.13 The spectral multi-headed self-attention module (S-MSA).

Specifically, the structure of the spectral multi-headed self-attention module (S-MSA) is shown in Figure 5.13. The module considers each spectral feature map as a unit and calculates the autocorrelation along the spectral dimension to capture non-local correlations.

In the S-MSA, firstly, recombine the input feature maps $\mathbf{X}_{in} \in \mathbb{R}^{H\times W\times C}$ as $\mathbf{X} \in \mathbb{R}^{HW\times C}$, and thus perform three linear feature maps to obtain Q, K, and V, respectively.

$$Q = XW^Q, \quad K = XW^K, \quad V = XW^V \tag{5.55}$$

where Q, K, and V are the learnable parameters. Then, the three features are divided into heads along the spectral channel dimension: $Q = [Q, \ldots, Q_N]$, $K = [K, \ldots, K_N]$, and $V = [V, \ldots, V_N]$. And the size of each head is $d_h = C/N$. As shown in Figure 4.4, we have $N = 1$ at this point. And then, self-attention is calculated according to the obtained Q, K and formula (5.56):

$$A_j = \text{softmax}\left(\sigma_j K_j^T Q_j\right), \quad \text{head} = V_j A_j \tag{5.56}$$

where K_j^T represents the transpose of the matrix K^T. σ_j is a learnable parameter. In the network, $K_j^T Q_j$ is re-weighted by σ_j to accommodate the self-attention named A_j. And then, the output features of divided heads are aggregated and undergo linear mapping. Finally, the positional information about the spectral features is embedded, and we can obtain the final output of the module $X_{out} \subset \mathbb{R}^{H\times W\times C}$.

$$X_{out} = \left(\underset{j=1}{\overset{N}{\text{concat}}}(\text{head}_j)\right) W + f_p(V) \tag{5.57}$$

where $W \in \mathbb{R}^{C\times C}$ is a learnable parameter and $f_p(\cdot)$ is a function that generates position information, which includes two 3×3 depth-wise convolutions, a GELU nonlinear activation function, and the recombination process. In reality, the purpose is to ensure that the position information of different spectral units can be saved in advance when the module operates on the input through the network.

5.4.1.4 Adaptive Learning Network

Based on the pseudo labels obtained by the fused multispectral and hyperspectral training data, the spectral super-resolution network can generate preliminary reconstructed images with high spatial spectral resolution. Specifically, in order to introduce the SRF priors into the model and learn the specific spatial degradation function of the image, an adaptive learning module is required in the network for the preliminary reconstructed images. Through the spatial degradation network and the given SRF, the preliminary reconstructed image is mapped to the original HSI and MSI, respectively, as shown in Figure 5.12, by adjusting the residual pixel by pixel and refining the specific details of the image to complete unsupervised adaptive learning.

The training process of the adaptive learning module can be represented by formula (5.58):

$$\min_{\theta, \vartheta} \|Y_m - RZ\|^2 + \|Y_m - ZH\|^2, \quad \text{s.t. } Z = \mathcal{G}(Z'; \theta), \quad ZH = \mathcal{H}(Z'; \vartheta) \tag{5.58}$$

where Z' is the preliminary reconstructed images generated for the spectral super-resolution network, and Z represents a reconstructed image of the final output in the network. Moreover, $\mathcal{G}(Z'; \theta)$ represents the feature mapping process of adaptive learning modules, and $\mathcal{H}(\cdot; \vartheta)$ represents the process of image space degradation. And specifically, θ and ϑ are the learnable parameters in the adaptive learning module and the spatial degradation networks, respectively.

The main structure of the adaptive learning network is shown in Figure 5.14. To recover specific details of the image, a residual architecture is introduced in the module, which mainly includes a feature mapping block, self-guided block, and output convolutional layer. For the input image Z', firstly, the module performs three layers of 3×3 convolution operations, which keeps the input and output feature dimensions invariant and performs the ReLU activation function. This is followed by self-guided modules and single-layer convolution operations to ensure that the main part of the module can recover the residual between the real HS image and the initially reconstructed image of the spectral super-resolution network. Then, eventually, the output image, named Z, is obtained by making a residual connection with the input image.

The structure of the self-guided module in the network is shown in Figure 5.15. Specifically, the input feature guides the output feature of the network through two branches, assuming that F and F' are the input and output features of the self-guided module, respectively. Therefore, the feature mapping process of the module can be represented as follows:

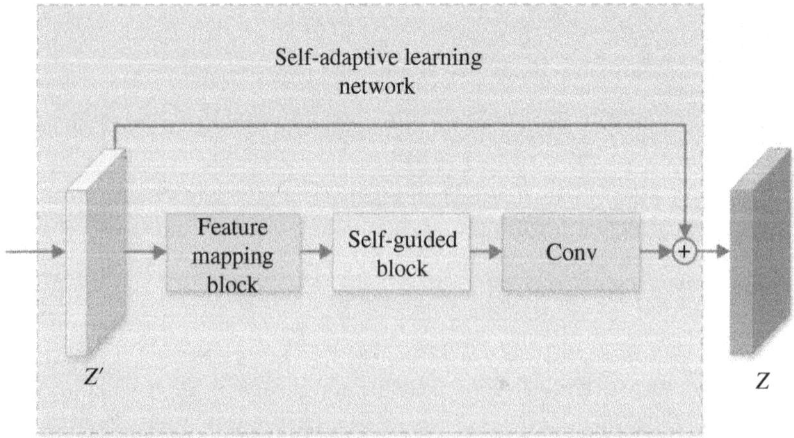

Figure 5.14 Self-adaptive learning network.

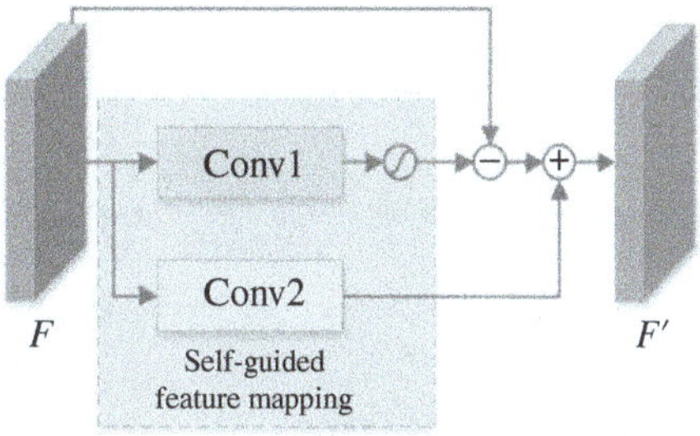

Figure 5.15 The structure of the self-guided block.

$$A = P_1(F; \upsilon_1); \quad B = P_2(F; \upsilon_2) \tag{5.59}$$

$$F' = A \cdot F + B \tag{5.60}$$

where $P_1(\cdot)$ represents the process of convolution Conv1 and the activation functionSigmoid$(\cdot)$, and then $P_2(\cdot)$ represents the operation of convolution named Conv2. Moreover, A and B are the output of the middle layer.

For the spatial degradation network in the adaptive learning process, and considering the limited amount of data in the MSI and HSI, the structure of the network should be designed to minimize the computational complexity in the unsupervised learning process to avoid the overfitting of the network. Therefore, the model adopts a simple structure to implement the degradation network to greatly reduce the number of parameters in the learning process. In reality, it often involves spatial down-sampling, spatial blurring, and noise destruction in the image spatial degradation process, where the process of spatial down-sampling and spatial blurring can be expressed as the convolution of the image and a specific kernel, and, specifically, the impact of the noise is close to the addictive zero-mean stochastic noise. Therefore, the process of spatial degradation can be expressed as:

$$ZH = (Z*k)\downarrow_s + N \tag{5.61}$$

where k represents a two-dimensional spatial convolution kernel, and $*$ represents the convolution of the same kernel k and each band of the image, respectively. S represents the scaling factor for spatial down-sampling, and N represents the additive noise. To design the structure of the network, a single two-dimensional convolutional layer with a step size S is used to achieve spatial down-sampling and blur. Particularly, the main learnable parameter is the convolutional kernel named k. Seeing that the loss function designed in formula (5.58) has the function of absorbing additive noise, there is no need to design a specific structure for N.

5.4.2 Experiment Results and Analysis

5.4.2.1 Data Preprocessing

The datasets used in the experiment are Houston and GF-YR, which need to be preprocessed before the experiment. The size of the overlapping area between HSI and MSI in the Houston data is 70×1902. During the training process, the data preprocessing was performed as follows. Firstly, crop the overlapping regions to multiple 64×64 image blocks, which keeps the 50% repetition rate to ensure the coverage of the entire training area. Then, crop the original training image by randomly selecting a starting point. And finally, keep the number of training blocks to 800. The partially cropped training data are shown in Figure 5.16.

Furthermore, for GF-YR data, the size of the overlapping area is 500×500, and the regions are cropped to multiple 128×128 image blocks. Similarly, the GF-YR data also needs to keep a 50%

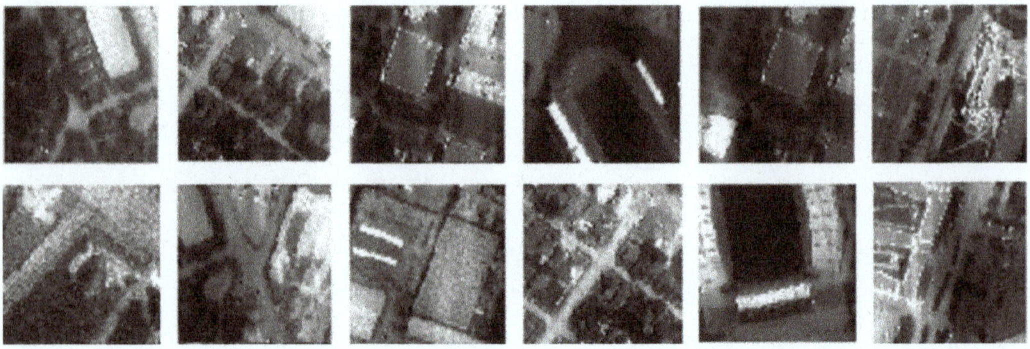

Figure 5.16 A portion of the Houston training data.

repetition rate to ensure the coverage of the training area, and then we also need to randomly select a starting point to choose the training field. And eventually, keep the number of training blocks to 500.

During the image testing process, considering the amount of data in the image and the memory usage during program operation, the original test image also needs to be cropped. Specifically, the Houston data were cropped to 10 image blocks with a size of 336×336. This requires certain areas of overlap between different image blocks, which results in a total image size of 336×1902. Similarly, the GF-YR data were cropped to 256×256 image blocks with a data volume of 64 and, after splicing, the full image size was 1468×1562. During the splicing process, the pixel values of the overlapping regions were determined by taking the average.

5.4.2.2 Analysis of the Training Process

The training and testing of the spectral super-resolution network use the Pytorch framework. During the training process, the batch size of the training data was set to eight, the parameter optimization algorithm was selected as Adam, and the parameter selection was optimized to $\beta_1 = 0.9$, $\beta_2 = 0.999$. Moreover, the learning rate was initialized to 4×10^{-4} and was adjusted by using the cosine annealing scheme based on 200 cycles. The target of the network was the MRAE loss function between the output image and the pseudo labels generated by the fusion module. As shown in formula (5.62), Y and $\hat{Y}$ represent the test image and the reference image, respectively.

$$\mathrm{MRAE}(Y, \hat{Y}) = \frac{1}{N}\sum_{i=1}^{N}\frac{|Y[i] - \hat{Y}[i]|}{Y[i]} \tag{5.62}$$

Similarly, the training and testing of the adaptive learning network also use the Pytorch framework. During the training process, adaptive learning was performed on individual training data based on the given SRF. The average absolute error as a loss function to output was set, which calculates the average error of each pixel between the HSI and MSI image. Moreover, the number of iterations for network training was set to 1500. In the adaptive module, the initial network parameters were randomly initialized, and the parameter optimization algorithm was selected as Adam. Furthermore, the learning rate was initialized to 9×10^{-5}, and the learning rate weight setting was adjusted to 1×10^{-5}. The size of the convolution kernel in the spatial degenerate network was 32×32. The parameters were initialized using a Gaussian template, and similarly, the parameter optimization algorithm was also selected as Adam, and the learning rate was initialized to 1×10^{-4}, adjusting the weight to 1×10^{-3}.

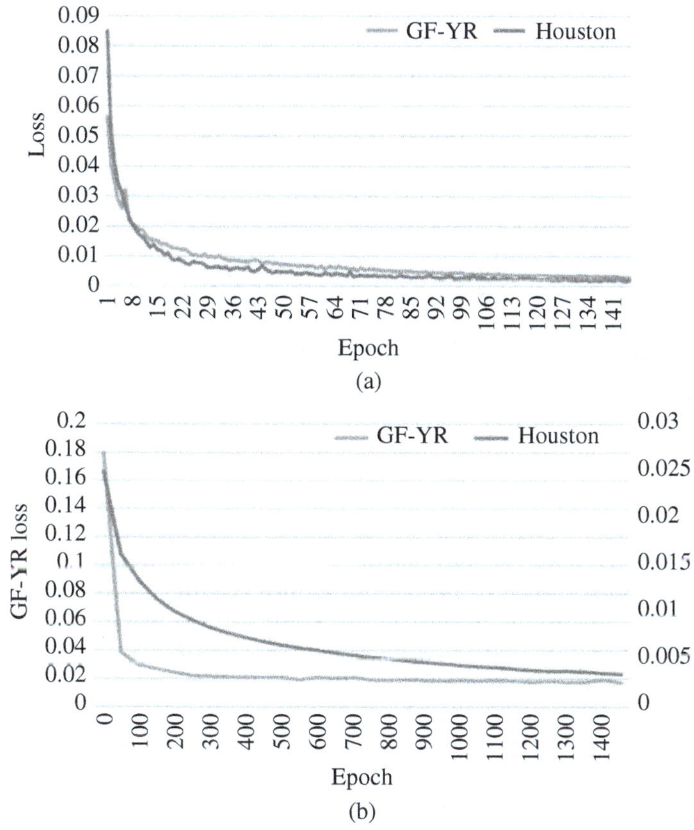

Figure 5.17 The training process of the network. (a) The training process of the spectral super-resolution network and (b) the training process of the self-adaptive learning network.

Figure 5.17a shows the variation in the loss of the spectral super-resolution network with the number of iterations. In the first 50 iterations, the loss of the network rapidly decreased to zero, and with the increase in iterations, the loss stabilized and became closer to zero. Similarly, Figure 5.17b shows the loss of the adaptive learning network varies with the number of iterations. During the training process, the number of iterations was set to 1500. As the number of iterations increases, although the loss of the network still decreases to a certain extent, the efficiency of network improvement decreases, and the loss of the network gradually tends to stabilize.

Figure 5.18 represents the time required for training the spectral super-resolution network on different datasets. The network was trained on the TITAN Xp GPU, and the figure calculates the time required for each iteration in the first 50 iterations of the network. For Houston data, the average time taken for 50 iterations resulted in 122.95 seconds for each iteration. And, for GF-YR data, similarly, the average time was 190.22 seconds. During the training process of the adaptive learning network, the Houston data were cropped with 10 image blocks and the network had 1500 iterations. Moreover, the average training time for each image block was 335.06 seconds. And, for GF-YR, the training data were a single sheet size of 500 × 500. We also set the number of iterations to 1500, and the network training took 4339 seconds.

As shown in Figure 5.19, the spectral curves of a fixed pixel on Houston data achieve a comparative analysis between the reconstructed image and the real HS image during the training iteration

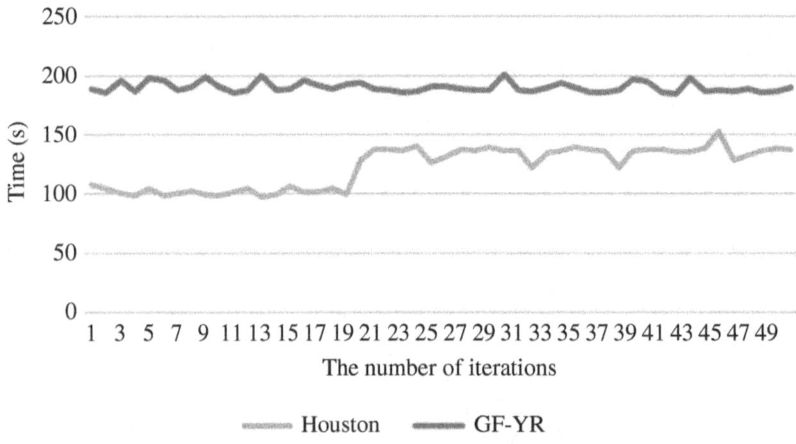

Figure 5.18 The time required for the training process of spectral super-resolution network.

process of the adaptive learning network, where the light curve shows the pixels from the reconstructed image, and the dark curve shows the pixels on the real HSI. At the initial iteration, there is a significant deviation between the output of the network and the real HSI. However, due to learning from the training data in the spectral super-resolution network, the reconstructed data curve is roughly similar to the true curve, where there is a lot of noise.

With the iteration of the adaptive learning network, the residual learning between the reconstructed image and the real HSI is achieved, and the output spectral curve of the network gradually approaches the real HS image. In particular, in the first 10 iterations of the network, there is a significant improvement in the output image; when the number of iterations is 100, the network output reaches a high degree of overlap with the real HSI; and when the number of iterations is 1000, the output of the network coincides with the spectral curve of the real HSI, and has fine reconstruction results in the spectral range of 364–1046 nm.

5.4.2.3 Comparative Experiment and Analysis

In the experiment, reconstruction tests were conducted on the cropped image blocks. Owing to the overlapping areas between different image blocks, the output image needed to be concatenated. At the same time, the pixel values of the overlapping areas were determined by taking the average value.

Figure 5.20 shows the reconstruction and classification results of the Houston data, where (a) is the Houston original HS image, and (b) is the reconstructed image. The model introduced spectral response priors through adaptive learning, and consequently, the reconstructed image was given a function of spectral preservation. Moreover, Figure 5.20c shows the results of using the SVM classifier to classify the reconstructed data, and the number of labels for the training sets and test sets of the various classes during the classification process is shown in Table 5.3.

As shown in Figure 5.21, we compare the spectral curves of various categories between the reconstructed data and the real HS data. Figure 5.21a–f depicts the spectral curves of six cover categories: Grass healthy, Synthetic Grass, Soil, Water, Tennis Court, and Running Track, respectively. And, specifically, the dark gray curve represents the spectral curve of the corresponding pixel in the real HS image, and the gray curve represents the spectral curve of the reconstruction results in the same

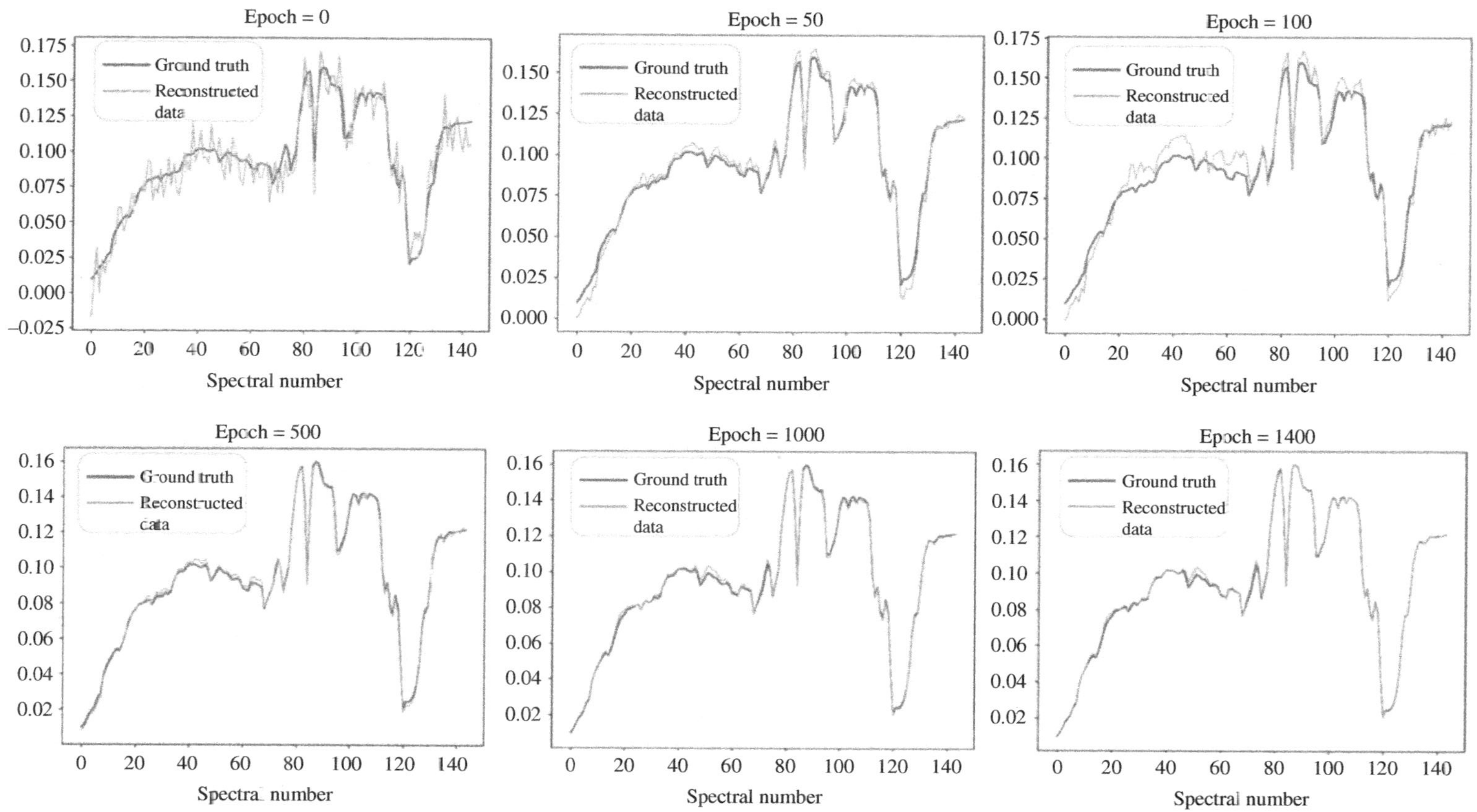

Figure 5.19 The variation in spectral curve with the number of iterations in the adaptive learning network.

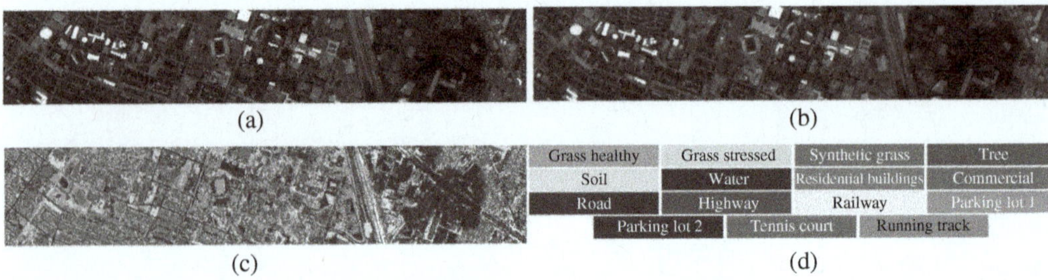

Figure 5.20 The reconstruction and classification image of Houston data. (a) The real HS image of Houston data, (b) the reconstruction image of Houston data, (c) the results of using the SVM classifier, and (d) all feature categories.

pixel. In particular, it can be seen that although some deviation occurs, the spectral curve fits, and the evaluation index of the spectral loss (SAM) is 1.2894.

For the reconstruction image of the Houston data, an SVM classifier was used for classification. The number of labels used in the training and testing sets for each category is shown in Table 5.3. And, eventually, we can obtain the confusion matrix shown in Figure 5.22, and the OA of classification is 76.53%. The highest accuracy for a single category is 99%, which is the sixth category, and the land feature is water.

In the confusion matrix, the row coordinates represent the category of the input image, and the column coordinates represent the category of network prediction. Moreover, the values in the grid show the proportion of the situation represented by the coordinates in the total number of data in this category, and the depth of the color in the grid represents the size of the grid value.

For the GF-YR data, the reconstructed hyperspectral data includes 295 bands. As shown in Figure 5.23b, selecting bands 56, 39, and 25 for a false-color display can obtain the reconstructed image, which has a certain degree of spectral preservation on the selected three bands, and the color presented is basically consistent with the real HSI. Moreover, Figure 5.23c shows the result of classifying reconstructed images by using the KNN classifier, and the overall classification accuracy is 82.51%.

Tables 5.9 and 5.10 represent the evaluation index of the reconstruction results in different methods of the Houston and GF-YR data, respectively, and the highlighted data are the best indicator among the various methods. Specifically, J-SLoL [31], MPRNet [45], CGCDL [33], and MSSNet [46] are used as comparison methods, where J-SLoL and CGCDL are dictionary learning methods, and MPRNet and MSSNet are deep learning methods. To ensure a fair comparison and highlight the effectiveness of the proposed method, we opted for the same training and testing dataset to conduct a comparison test. In J-SLoL and CGCDL, we traversed the different atomic numbers of the dictionary, and finally selected the image with the best reconstruction effect for index calculation; and, in MPRNet and MSSNet, where the network ran on TITAN Xp GPU, the parameter optimization algorithm was also selected as Adam, and the initial learning rate was 2×10^{-4}, which steadily decreased to 1×10^{-6} using the cosine annealing strategy.

In Tables 5.9 and 5.10, the various indexes of the proposed method were significantly improved compared with the comparison methods. For the Houston data, the proposed method improved PSNR by 6.4482, and classification accuracy increased by 2.78%. For the GF-YR, the classification accuracy of the reconstructed model improved by 2.59%, and the global image quality evaluation index QNR improved by 0.1661.

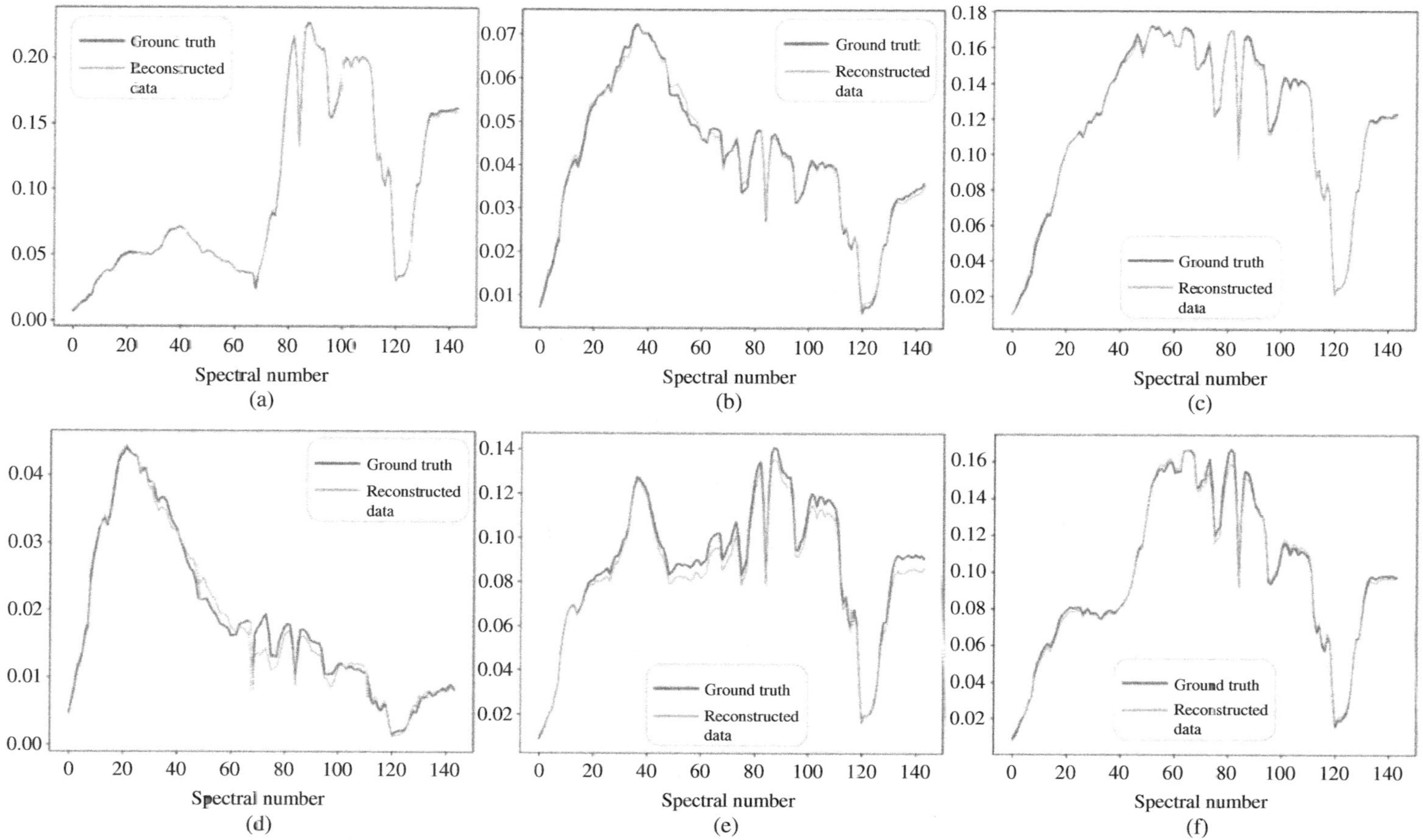

Figure 5.21 The spectral curves of various categories between the Houston reconstruction data and the truth data. (a) Grass healthy, (b) synthetic grass, (c) soil, (d) water, (e) tennis court, and (f) running track.

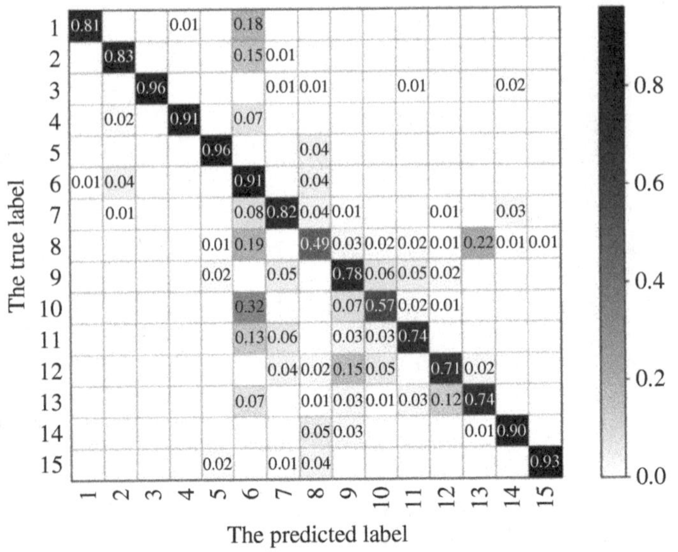

Figure 5.22 The confusion matrix of the Houston classification results.

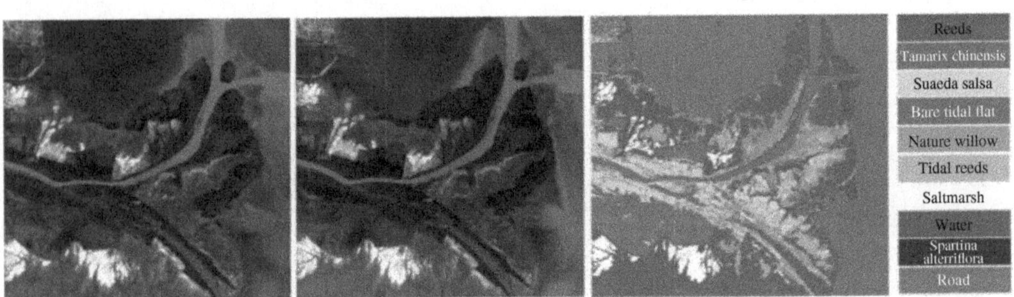

(a) (b) (c) (d)

Figure 5.23 The reconstruction and classification results of GF-YR data. (a) The real HS image of GF-YR, (b) the reconstruction HSI of GF-YR, (c) the classification results of GF-YR, and (d) all feature categories.

Table 5.9 Evaluation indicators for reconstruction results in the Houston dataset.

	PSNR	SAM (°)	SSIM	OA	D_S	D_λ	QNR
Proposed	**43.5576**	**1.2894**	**0.9996**	**0.7653**	**0.0170**	**0.0074**	**0.9756**
J-SLoL	35.0719	5.5209	0.9699	0.6764	0.0374	0.0622	0.9027
MPRNet	34.6842	4.2354	0.9541	0.6896	0.0694	0.0781	0.8579
CGCDL	35.5778	4.7765	0.9977	0.6907	0.0364	0.1106	0.8570
MSSNet	31.2342	3.0510	0.9367	0.6975	0.0518	0.1174	0.8367

Bold values indicate the best performance metrics among various methods (the proposed method along with the comparison methods) for each evaluation criterion.

Table 5.10 Evaluation indicators for reconstruction results in the GF-YR dataset.

	OA	D_S	D_λ	QNR
Proposed	0.8251	**0.0471**	**0.0549**	**0.9004**
J-SLoL	0.7815	0.1218	0.1667	0.7317
MPRNet	0.7726	0.1496	0.1238	0.7451
CGCDL	**0.8636**	0.1803	0.1772	0.6744
MSSNet	0.7842	0.1121	0.1614	0.7451

Bold values represent the best performing values corresponding to each evaluation criterion.

However, for the GF data, the OA in classification is slightly lower than CGCDL, which could be due to CGCDL's focus on classifying reconstructed images, neglecting spectral super-resolution. Consequently, while CGCDL achieves high classification accuracy, its spectral and spatial authenticity is slightly compromised. In contrast, our proposed method effectively balances the similarity of image reconstruction with high classification accuracy, delivering impressive results on both Houston and GF datasets.

5.4.2.4 Ablation Experiments on Partial Network Structures

In the multispectral–hyperspectral collaborative mapping model based on adaptive learning, the adaptive learning network introduces spectral response priors and learns the specific spatial degradation functions of the image. And, then, through the spatial degradation network and the given SRF, the preliminarily reconstructed image is mapped to the original HSI and MSI, respectively. The residual is adjusted pixel by pixel and, thus, the details of the image are refined to complete the unsupervised adaptive learning. The image fusion module provides pseudo labels for the training of spectral super-resolution networks based on training HSI and MSI, enabling the network to learn the mapping between HSI and MSI in a supervised manner. In order to verify the performance of some modules in the network, this section conducted ablation experiments on the following two network structures: the adaptive learning module and the image fusion module. Particularly, in the ablation experiment of the image fusion module, the module is replaced by a bilinear interpolation operation.

As shown in Figure 5.24, the reconstructed spectral curves of some categories before and after adaptive learning for GF-YR data are represented, where (a–f) depict the spectral curves of six categories: Reed, Tidal Reed, Saltmarsh, Bare Tidal Flats, Water, and Spartina Alterniflora, respectively. Specifically, the darkest curve in the figure represents the spectra of corresponding pixels in the real HS image. Moreover, the lightest curve represents the output of the network before adaptive learning, and the yellow curve represents the spectra of the same pixels in the reconstruction results of the network after adaptive learning. It can be seen that before the adaptive learning, although the output of the network's spectral curve roughly follows the curve of the real HSI, there is still a certain offset. And noise is generated in some bands, causing the network to produce more spikes. Whereas, after the adaptive learning, the fitting of spectral curves further improves, and finally, has fine reconstruction results in the 295 spectral bands with the spectral range of 400–2500 nm.

As shown in Tables 5.11 and 5.12, the comparison of the evaluation indicators for the adaptive learning network and the ablation experiment of the image fusion module is represented, where w/o adaptation represents the reconstruction results of the model after removing the adaptive learning network, and w/o fusion represents the reconstruction results of the model after removing

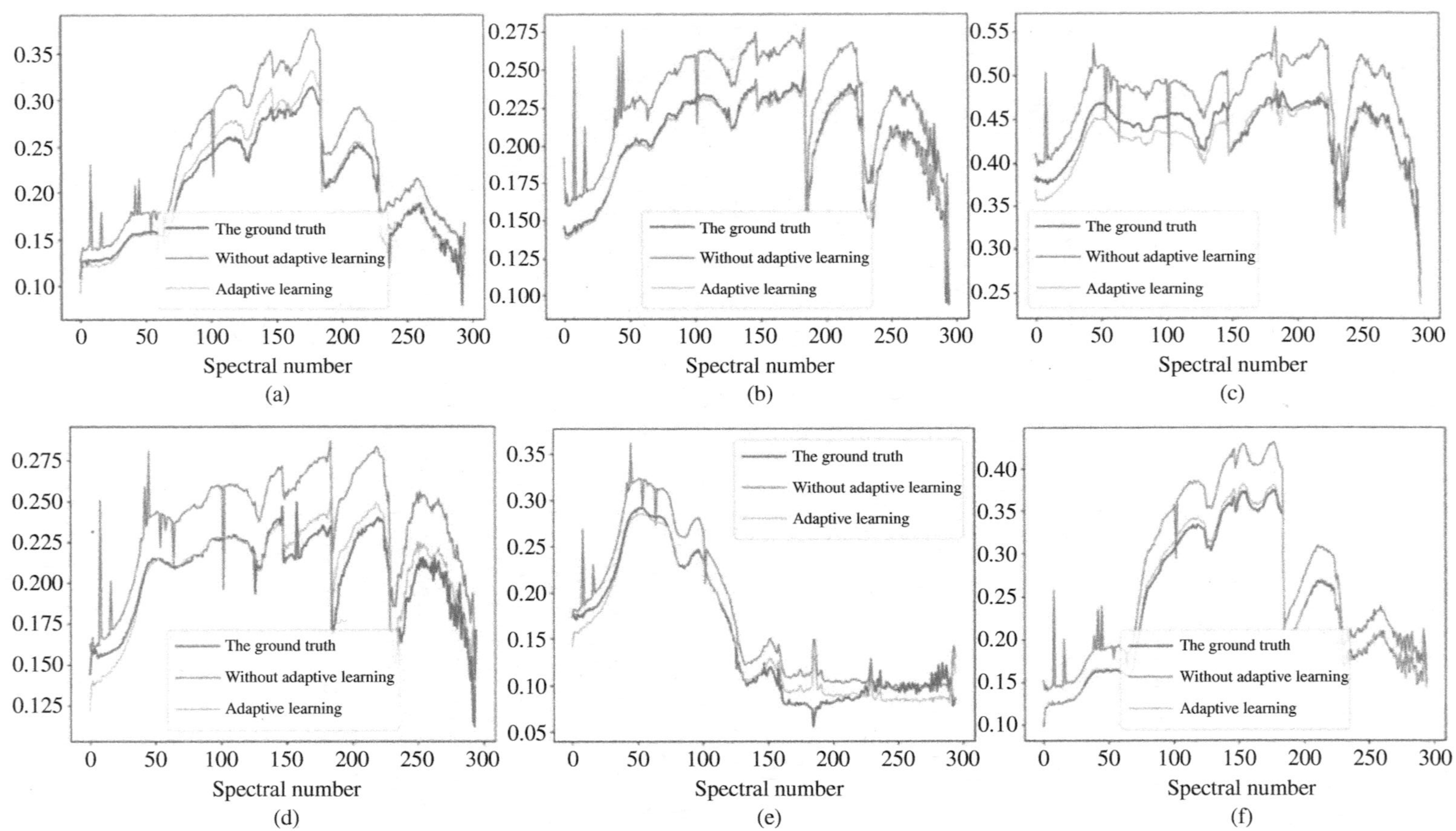

Figure 5.24 The reconstructed spectral curves of some categories before and after adaptive learning for GF-YR data. (a) Reed, (b) tidal reed, (c) saltmarsh, (d) bare tidal flats, (e) water, and (f) Spartina alterniflora.

Table 5.11 Comparison of evaluation indicators for reconstruction results of ablation experiments on the Houston dataset.

Methods	PSNR	SAM (°)	SSIM	OA	D_S	D_λ	QNR
w/o adaptation	40.9896	1.3752	**0.9997**	0.7480	**0.0164**	0.0094	0.9741
w/o fusion	36.6576	3.2535	0.9538	0.7644	0.0331	0.0345	0.9315
Proposed	**43.5576**	**1.2894**	0.9996	**0.7653**	0.0170	**0.0074**	**0.9756**

Bold values indicate which method achieves the optimal value under the current metric.

Table 5.12 Comparison of evaluation indicators for reconstruction results of ablation experiments on the GF-YR dataset.

Methods	OA	D_S	D_λ	QNR
w/o adaptation	0.8150	0.0736	0.0552	0.8752
w/o fusion	0.8077	0.1726	0.1259	0.7232
Proposed	**0.8251**	**0.0471**	**0.0549**	**0.9004**

Bold values represent the optimal values for each evaluation criterion in the GF-YR dataset.

the image fusion module. Specifically, in the Houston data, the adaptive learning network improves the SNR, spectral loss, and classification accuracy of the reconstruction image by using spectral response priors. Although the spatial evaluation index is slightly reduced, the overall reconstruction effect is better. Moreover, the fusion module obviously improves the SNR by 6.9, and the spectral loss evaluation index SAM is improved by 2.9641, which improves the reconstruction quality of the network. Similarly, for the GF-YR data, both modules can improve classification accuracy and the unsupervised spatial and spectral evaluation indexes.

5.4.3 Conclusion

For multispectral–hyperspectral collaborative mapping and refined classification tasks, to avoid the complex parameter selection based on dictionary learning, a collaborative mapping model based on adaptive learning is constructed in Chapter 4, which provides the required pseudo labels through a fusion module. We innovatively proposed an adaptive learning-based multi-hyperspectral collaborative mapping model. A physical model embedding is realized by designing an adaptive learning network to introduce the SRF, which further guides the high precision of spectral reconstruction. Specifically, using the adaptive learning module to incorporate spectral response priors that adjust the output of the super-resolution network to preserve spectral information in reconstructed data and the attention-based model, has advantages in capturing the characteristics conducive to spectral super-resolution. The image fusion module leverages spatial and spectral consistency in training data, providing pseudo labels for spectral super-resolution training. The implementation of these modules can significantly enhance the quality and precision of reconstruction. Moreover, an adaptive learning network is designed to increase the spectral response prior and learn the unknown spatial degradation function, so as to further improve the quality of the reconstructed image. Then, ablation experiments are designed to verify the effectiveness of the relevant network structures. Finally, we obtain the conclusion that the classification accuracy of reconstruction results in the mapping model based on adaptive learning has been greatly improved. In addition, there are still some issues worth considering and researching: in the mapping model based on adaptive learning, adding an image fusion block to the training process of the model should be considered to further improve the learning ability.

5.5 Conclusion

The topic innovatively proposes two image super-resolution methods for acquiring HSIs with high spatial resolution and large scenes, which are:

1) A sub-pixel coupled dictionary learning method: which harnesses sub-pixel representation to reconstruct HR-HSIs with large scenes and high spatial resolution using overlapping regions of LR-HSI and HR-MSI. By minimizing spatial and spectral distortions, Sub-CDL enhances image authenticity and classification accuracy. The innovation lies in combining sub-pixel representation coefficients into a coupled dictionary to bridge spatial resolution gaps. Incorporating spatial down-sampling and blur matrices into the model improves spatial recovery, while SRF addresses spectral disparities. Spatial regularization and low-rank constraints refine the optimization equations.
2) An adaptive learning spectral super-resolution method: in order to avoid the manual setting of a priori information and the complex parameter selection in multispectral–hyperspectral image collaborative mapping based on dictionary learning, and in order to adjust the network parameters automatically, a mapping model based on adaptive learning is proposed. Specifically, based on the self-attention spectral super-resolution network, an image fusion module is introduced to provide pseudo-labeling for the training of the network, while a self-adaptive learning network is designed to increase the a priori SRF and learn the unknown spatial degradation function.

However, there are still some aspects that we should continue to study:

1) In dictionary learning method, how to select parameters manually. The multi-objective optimization method can be considered to avoid the manual selection of complex parameters
2) In deep learning method, how to further improve the learning ability. An image fusion block could be added to the training process.
3) A new method that combines the advantages of both dictionary learning and deep learning should be designed.

References

1 Wang, Q., Huang, J., Shen, T., and Gu, Y. (2024). EHGNN: enhanced hypergraph neural network for hyperspectral image classification. *IEEE Geosci. Remote Sens. Lett.* 21: 1–5.

2 Bai, Y., Wang, J., Zhou, K. et al. (2024). Mapping lithium-bearing pegmatite with short-wave infrared (SWIR) hyperspectral imaging of Jingerquan Li–Be–Nb–Ta pegmatite deposit, Eastern Tianshan, NW China. *IEEE Trans. Geosci. Remote Sens.* 62: 1–15.

3 Oudijk, Adriënne E., Hasler, O., Øveraas, Henning, Marty, Sabine, Williamson, David R., Svendsen, Thea, Berg, Simen, et al. (2022). Campaign for hyperspectral data validation in North Atlantic Coastal Waters. *2022 12th Workshop on Hyperspectral Imaging and Signal Processing: Evolution in Remote Sensing (WHISPERS)*, 1–5, Rome, Italy (13–16 September 2022). IEEE.

4 Rocha, A.D., Groen, T.A., Skidmore, A.K., and Willemen, L. (2021). Role of sampling design when predicting spatially dependent ecological data with remote sensing. *IEEE Trans. Geosci. Remote Sens.* 59 (1): 663–674.

5 Kallel, A., Mura, M.D., Fakhfakh, S., and Romdhane, N.B. (2023). Physics-based fusion of Sentinel-2 and Sentinel-3 for higher resolution vegetation monitoring. *IEEE Trans. Geosci. Remote Sens.* 61: 1–17.

6 Duarte, M.M. and Azevedo, L. (2023). Automatic detection and identification of floating marine debris using multispectral satellite imagery. *IEEE Trans. Geosci. Remote Sens.* 61: 1–15.

7 Bai, W., Zhang, P., Liu, H. et al. (2023). A fast piecewise-defined neural network method to retrieve temperature and humidity profile for the vertical atmospheric sounding system of FengYun-3E satellite. *IEEE Trans. Geosci. Remote Sens.* 61: 1–10.

8 Fiscante, N., Addabbo, P., Biondi, F. et al. (2022). Unsupervised sparse unmixing of atmospheric trace gases from hyperspectral satellite data. *IEEE Geosci. Remote Sens. Lett.* 19: 1–5.

9 Wang, J. and Li, C. (2021). Development and prospect of hyperspectral imager and its application. *Chin. Space Sci. Technol.* 41: 22–33.

10 Zhao, D., Wang, Q., Zhang, J., and Bai, C. (2023). Mine diversified contents of multispectral cloud images along with geographical information for multilabel classification. *IEEE Trans. Geosci. Remote Sens.* 61: 1–15.

11 Li, M., Luo, Q., and Liu, S. (2022). Application of hyperspectral imaging technology in quality inspection of agricultural products. *2022 International Conference on Computers, Information Processing and Advanced Education (CIPAE)*, 369–372, Ottawa, ON, Canada (26–28 August 2022). IEEE.

12 Rayhana, R., Ma, Z., Liu, Z. et al. (2023). A review on plant disease detection using hyperspectral imaging. *IEEE Trans. AgriFood Electron.* 1: 108–134.

13 Tang, X., Liu, X., Yan, P. et al. (2022). An MLP network based on residual learning for rice hyperspectral data classification. *IEEE Geosci. Remote Sens. Lett.* 19: 1–5.

14 Zhou, Q., Wang, S., andGuan, K. (2023). Advancing airborne hyperspectral data processing and applications for sustainable agriculture using RTM-based machine learning. *IGARSS 2023 – 2023 IEEE International Geoscience and Remote Sensing Symposium*, 1269–1272, Pasadena, CA, USA (16–21 July 2023). IEEE.

15 Li, N., Jiang, S., Xue, J. et al. (2024). Texture-aware self-attention model for hyperspectral tree species classification. *IEEE Trans. Geosci. Remote Sens.* 62: 1–5.

16 Seo, J., Yu, J., and Wang, L. (2023). Indicator spectral bands and logistic models for detecting diesel and gasoline polluted soils based on close-range hyperspectral image data. *IEEE Trans. Geosci. Remote Sens.* 61: 1–13.

17 Guo, T., Luo, F., Guo, J. et al. (2024). Hyperspectral target detection with target prior augmentation and background suppression-based multidetector fusion. *IEEE J. Sel. Top. Appl. Earth Obs. Remote Sens.* 17: 1765–1780.

18 Gi, J., Gong, Z., Xue, W. et al. (2021). An unmixing-based network for underwater target detection from hyperspectral imagery. *IEEE J. Sel. Top. Appl. Earth Obs. Remote Sens.* 14: 5470–5487.

19 Sun, L., Ma, Z., and Zhang, Y. (2024). ABLAL: adaptive background latent space adversarial learning algorithm for hyperspectral target detection. *IEEE J. Sel. Top. Appl. Earth Obs. Remote Sens.* 17: 411–427.

20 Wang, S., Feng, W., Quan, Y. et al. (2022). Subfeature ensemble-based hyperspectral anomaly detection algorithm. *IEEE J. Sel. Top. Appl. Earth Obs. Remote Sens.* 15: 5943–5952.

21 Zhang X, Huang W, Wang Q, Li X. SSR-NET: spatial–spectral reconstruction network for hyperspectral and multispectral image fusion. *IEEE Trans. Geosci. Remote Sens.* 2021;59:5953–5965

22 Dong, W., Fu, F., Shi, G. et al. (2016). Hyperspectral image super-resolution via non-negative structured sparse representation. *IEEE Trans. Image Process.* 25 (5): 2337–2352.

23 Liu, T. and Li, X. (2024). Multi-sensor multispectral reconstruction framework based on projection and reconstruction. *Sci. China Inf. Sci.* 67: 132303.

24 Li, T. and Gu, Y. (2022). Progressive spatial–spectral joint network for hyperspectral image reconstruction. *IEEE Trans. Geosci. Remote Sens.* 60: 1–14.

25 Du, D., Gu, Y., Liu, T., and Li, X. (2023). Spectral reconstruction from satellite multispectral imagery using convolution and transformer joint network. *IEEE Trans. Geosci. Remote Sens.* 61: 1–15.

26 Li, T., Liu, T., Wang, Y. et al. (2022). Spectral reconstruction network from multispectral images to hyperspectral images: a multitemporal case. *IEEE Trans. Geosci. Remote Sens.* 60: 1–16.

27 Arad, B. and Ben-Shahar, O. (2016). Sparse recovery of hyperspectral signal from natural RGB images. *Lect. Notes Comput. Sci* 9911: 19–34.

28 Wu, J., Aeschbacher, J., and Timofte, R. (2017). In defense of shallow learned spectral reconstruction from RGB images. *2017 IEEE International Conference on Computer Vision Workshops (ICCVW)*, 471–479, Venice, Italy (22–29 October 2017). IEEE.

29 Yokoya, N., Heiden, U., and Bachmann, N. (2018). Spectral enhancement of multispectral imagery using partially overlapped hyperspectral data and sparse signal representation. *Proceedings of the Whispers*, Amsterdam, The Netherlands (23–26 September 2018).

30 Fotiadou, K., Tsagkatakis, G., and Tsakalides, P. (2019). Spectral super resolution of hyperspectral images via coupled dictionary learning. *IEEE Trans. Geosci. Remote Sens.* 57 (5): 2777–2797.

31 Gao, L., Hong, D., Yao, J. et al. (2021). Spectral superresolution of multispectral imagery with joint sparse and low-rank learning. *IEEE Trans. Geosci. Remote Sens.* 59 (3): 2269–2280.

32 Han, X., Yu, J., Luo, J., and Sun, W. (2019). Reconstruction from multispectral to hyperspectral image using spectral library-based dictionary learning. *IEEE Trans. Geosci. Remote Sens.* 57 (3): 1325–1335.

33 Liu, T., Gu, Y., and Jia, X. (2022). Class-guided coupled dictionary learning for multispectral-hyperspectral remote sensing image collaborative classification. *Sci. China Technol. Sci.* 65: 744–758.

34 Liu, T., Gu, Y., Yu, W. et al. (2022). Separable coupled dictionary learning for large-scene precise classification of multispectral images. *IEEE Trans. Geosci. Remote Sens.* 60: 1–14.

35 Rostami, M. and Beheshti Shirazi, A.A. (2023). Hyperspectral image super-resolution via learning an undercomplete dictionary and intra-algorithmic postprocessing. *IEEE Trans. Geosci. Remote Sens.* 61: 1–15.

36 Yan, H., Zhao, Y., Chan, J.C., and Kong, S.G. (2023). Spectral super-resolution based on dictionary optimization learning via spectral library. *IEEE Trans. Geosci. Remote Sens.* 61: 1–16.

37 Nie, X., Xue, Z., Lin, C. et al. (2024). Structure-prior-constrained low-rank and sparse representation with discriminative incremental dictionary for hyperspectral image classification. *IEEE Trans. Geosci. Remote Sens.* 62: 1–19.

38 Yan, Y., Zhang, L., and Li, J. (2018). Accurate spectral super-resolution from single RGB image using multi-scale CNN. *Pattern Recognition and Computer Vision: First Chinese Conference, PRCV 2018*, 206–217, Guangzhou, China (23–26 November 2018).

39 Han, X., Zhang, H., Xue, J., and Sun, W. (2022). A spectral–spatial jointed spectral super-resolution and its application to HJ-1A satellite images. *IEEE Geosci. Remote Sens. Lett.* 19: 5505905.

40 Hu, X., Cai, Y., and Lin, J. (2022). HDNet: high-resolution dual-domain learning for spectral compressive imaging. *Proceedings of the Proceedings of the IEEE/CVF Conference on Computer Vision and Pattern Recognition*, New Orleans, LA, USA, 19–24 June 2022, pp. 17542–17551.

41 Li, J., Du, S., Song, R. et al. (2022). HASIC-Net: hybrid attentional convolutional neural network with structure information consistency for spectral super-resolution of RGB images. *IEEE Trans. Geosci. Remote Sens.* 60: 5522515.

42 Zamir, S.W., Arora, A., Khan, S., Hayat, M., Khan, F.S., Yang, M.H., and Shao, L. (2021). Multi-stage progressive image restoration. *2021 IEEE/CVF Conference on Computer Vision and Pattern Recognition (CVPR)*, 14816–14826, Nashville, TN, USA (20–25 June 2021). IEEE.

43 Li, J., Du, S., Wu, C., Leng, Y., Song, R., and Li, Y. (2022). DRCR net: dense residual channel re-calibration network with non-local purification for spectral super resolution. *Proceedings of the 2022 IEEE/CVF Conference on Computer Vision and Pattern Recognition Workshops (CVPRW)*, 1258–1267, New Orleans, LA, USA (19–20 June 2022). IEEE.

44 He, J., Yuan, Q., Li, J. et al. (2022). DsTer: a dense spectral transformer for remote sensing spectral super-resolution. *Int. J. Appl. Earth Obs. Geoinf.* 109: 102773.

45 Zamir, S.W., Arora, A., Khan, S., Hayat, M., Khan, F.S., Yang, M.-H., et al. (2021). Multi-stage progressive image restoration. *2021 IEEE/CVF Conference on Computer Vision and Pattern Recognition (CVPR)*, 14816–14826, Nashville, TN, USA (20–25 June 2021). IEEE.

46 Yan, Y., Zhang, L., Li, J., Wei, W., and Zhang, Y. (2018). Accurate spectral super-resolution from single RGB image using multi-scale CNN. *Proceedings of the Chinese Conference on Pattern Recognition and Computer Vision (PRCV)*, 206–217, Guangzhou, China (23–26 November 2018). Berlin/Heidelberg, Germany: Springer.

6

Hyperspectral Image Reconstruction From Supervision to Blindness

Jie Xie[1], Jie Wu[2], Zhicheng Wang[3], Lina Zhuang[4], and Leyuan Fang[2]

[1] *School of Rail Transportation, Soochow University, Suzhou, China*
[2] *College of Electrical and Information Engineering, Hunan University, Changsha, China*
[3] *Department of Earth Sciences and the Laboratory for Space Research, The University of Hong Kong, Hong Kong, China*
[4] *Aerospace Information Research Institute, Chinese Academy of Sciences, Beijing, China*

Mathematical Symbols Used in This Chapter

$\boldsymbol{Z} \in \mathbb{R}^{L \times N}$: HR HSI.
$\boldsymbol{Y}_h \in \mathbb{R}^{L \times n}$: LR HSI.
$\boldsymbol{Y}_m \in \mathbb{R}^{l \times N}$: HR MSI.
$\boldsymbol{\Gamma} \in \mathbb{R}^{l \times L} : \mathbb{R}^{L \times N} \rightarrow \mathbb{R}^{l \times N}$: Spectral dimensionality reduction operator.
$\boldsymbol{D}$: Spectral vector of materials.
$\boldsymbol{W}_i$: Window centered on pixel i.
h_j: Weighting coefficients.
L_{cyc}: Cycle consistency loss.
$\mathbf{S} \in \mathbb{R}^{N_{row}N_{col} \times n_{row}n_{col}}$: Spatial sub-sampler.
$\mathbf{N}_h \in \mathbb{R}^{L \times n_{row}n_{col}}$: Additive Gaussian noise.
$\mathbf{M} \in \mathbb{R}^{l \times L}$: Spectral response function.
$\mathbf{N}_m \in \mathbb{R}^{l \times N_{row}N_{col}}$: White Gaussian noise, respectively.
$\boldsymbol{G}$: Lagrange multiplier.
$\psi_{\lambda\phi_{E2E}}(\cdot)$: Moreau proximity operator or denoising operator of ϕ_{E2E}.
$\boldsymbol{R}_{hr} \in \mathbb{R}^{L \times F}$: Spectral response matrix of the hyperspectral imaging sensor.
$\boldsymbol{R}_{lr} \in \mathbb{R}^{l \times F}$: Spectral response matrix of the multispectral imaging sensor.
$\boldsymbol{R}(\boldsymbol{G})$: All regularization terms for the generator.

6.1 Introduction

Hyperspectral images (HSIs) have drawn increasing attention from researchers across many remote-sensing applications, including weather forecasting [1], military reconnaissance [2, 3], and precision agriculture [4, 5]. However, the spatial resolution of HSIs is often constrained by the capabilities of imaging sensors. For instance, the hyperspectral imaging sensors of Gaofen-5 have a spatial resolution of 30 meters per pixel, limiting its ability to observe fine details on the

Machine-Learning-Based Hyperspectral Image Processing, First Edition. Edited by Bing Zhang.

Earth's surface [6]. Additionally, the mixing of different objects within a single pixel of an HSI can lead to endmember spectral mixtures, rendering them unsuitable for accurate land cover classification. Therefore, enhancing the spatial resolution of HSIs is crucial for their effective application. While enhancing hardware capabilities to improve photon sensing can indeed enhance the spatial resolution of HSIs, this process requires significant time and resources to update hardware. Hence, the development of HSI super-resolution (SR) methods becomes essential.

Directly super-resolving low-spatial-resolution HSIs (LR HSIs) to high-spatial-resolution HSIs (HR HSIs) is indeed an intuitive approach. Many SR methods developed for natural images can be directly applied to HSI SR. However, these methods may introduce spectral distortion in their SR results due to different SR errors across different spectral bands. Moreover, the spatial degradation of each pixel in HSIs varies, making it challenging to describe with a general HSI SR model. In contrast, multispectral images (MSIs) typically comprise a limited number of spectral bands with reduced spectral information but boast finer spatial resolution, capturing more detailed spatial structures of land covers. Thus, fusing LR HSIs and MSIs is a promising approach to obtain HR HSIs. These HR HSIs would retain the same spectral resolution as LR HSIs while benefiting from the enhanced spatial resolution of MSIs. Although this method can yield satisfactory results, it requires registered LR HSIs and MSIs covering the same land covers at the same time, which can be difficult to achieve. Given the challenges associated with acquiring HSIs, with more than 90% of remote-sensing images being MSIs [7–9], researchers have increasingly focused on MSI spectral super-resolution (SpeSR). This unique strategy enriches MSIs with spectral information to acquire HR HSIs effectively.

The traditional strategy employed in the aforementioned methods [10–16] involves modeling the degradation process from HR images to LR images and subsequently deducing the inverse process from low resolution to high resolution. When the point spread function (PSF) of a hyperspectral imaging sensor is known, the real HSI can be conceptualized as a linear spatial degradation of HR HSI. For instance, in [10], a coupled non-negative matrix factorization scheme is proposed to fuse HSIs and MSIs by alternately estimating two factors of the HR HSI. In [11], spectral unmixing is integrated with the fusion of HSIs and MSIs, where the spectral basis and abundances of original HSIs and HR HSIs are iteratively estimated. Sparse coding, dictionary learning, and tensor representation are effective strategies for addressing the HSI SR inverse problem. For example, in [12], dictionary learning is employed to construct a non-negative structured sparse representation model based on nonlocal HSI spatial similarities for HSI SR. In [13], sparse tensor factorization is performed for HSIs and MSIs separately, estimating dictionaries of three modes and sparse core tensors. In cases where the PSF is unknown but the spectral response of the camera is known, matrix factorization techniques are commonly used in HSI and MSI fusion methods. Specifically, a spectral mode HSI unfolding matrix is first computed and then factored into a spectral basis and coefficients. This transforms the problem of obtaining the HR HSI into estimating a spectral basis and coefficients. In [14, 15], dictionary learning and sparse priors are utilized to learn the spectral basis and compute coefficients from HSIs and MSIs, respectively. Additionally, in [16], these methods are extended to remote HSIs, where the spectral basis is learned using singular value decomposition (SVD).

With the great success in computer vision achieved by deep learning, it has emerged as a powerful tool in the HSI SR task, using spatial, spatial–spectral, and spectral information. These methods can be categorized into three classes: (i) Direct SR from LR HSIs to HR HSIs: These methods extend research on natural image SR to the domain of HSIs. For example, in [17], Li et al. introduce a spatial constraint to preserve spectral information while enhancing spatial details. Arun et al. [18] propose a 3D convolutional neural network (CNN)-based single-image super-resolution (SISR) method using sparse coding. Li et al. [19] design a dual-stage deep model for HSI SR, utilizing adjacent bands to enhance spatial–spectral representation in the coarse stage and refining results in the fine stage using enhanced back-projection under spectral angle constraint. (ii) Fusion of LR HSIs and MSIs for HR HSIs: These methods aim to extract spectral and spatial information from LR HSIs and MSIs, respectively, to obtain HR HSIs. For instance, Dian et al. propose a three-stage deep model in [20], where LR HSIs and MSIs are fused in the first stage, priors are learned in the second stage using a residual module, and learned priors are incorporated into the fused result in the third stage. Zheng et al. [21] utilize edge features extracted by the Sobel operator to aid in the fusion of LR HSIs and MSIs, and an ensemble loss function is designed to train this deep model. Guarino et al. [22] apply transfer learning to meet challenges, such as data scarcity and lack of ground truth, in HSI SR based on deep learning. (iii) SpeSR of MSIs to HR HSIs: These methods focus on enhancing the spectral resolution of MSIs to obtain HR HSIs. For example, Zhao et al. [23] design a hierarchical framework consisting of key modules like the PixelShuffle layer, residual dense block, and residual global block to fuse inter-level information, eliminate artifacts, and enlarge the perceptive field, respectively. Li et al. introduce an adaptive attention network in [24] to capture global information from MSIs to HSIs and discover correlations among different channels. Wu et al. [25] optimize the original deep model for lightweight inference to deploy it on portable devices for practical applications.

All the aforementioned learning-based methods necessitate supervised information to optimize the parameters of their models. Specifically, spatial information-based methods require paired LR HSIs and HR HSIs, spatial–spectral information-based methods require registered LR HSIs, MSIs, and HR HSIs, and spectral information-based methods require paired MSIs and HR HSIs. However, obtaining HR HSIs as supervised information is impractical in real-world scenarios. Typically, LR HSIs are downsampled to construct the training set, and the original LR HSIs themselves serve as the ground truth. Nevertheless, this downsampling process fails to accurately represent the real degradation process. To address this issue, several blind HSI SR methods have been proposed, particularly those focusing on estimating unknown degradation. For instance, in [26], Zhang et al. model the fusion of LR HSIs and MSIs as an energy-minimizing problem, representing spatial and spectral degradation based on imaging priors. In [27], HSI SR and degradation are alternately estimated to maintain bidirectional data consistency. In [28], a content-aware reassembly of features module and a squeeze-and-excitation block are introduced to reduce spatial distortion and feature redundancy. In [29], a nonnegative matrix factorization network using a transfer learning strategy is designed to refine a limited number of HSIs with unknown spatial degradation. In [30], subspace representation is introduced for HSI and MSI fusion, utilizing the SVD and alternating direction method of multipliers (ADMM) to estimate the spectral subspace and corresponding coefficients, respectively. For the ADMM, the final problem can be thought of as the denoising problem, which can be solved by a CNN denoiser training on synthetic data. In [31], spatial degradation is estimated from the image itself using a specific generative adversarial network (GAN). In [32], spatial and spectral degradation are considered as two independent processes, with spatial degradation of the MSI equivalent to spectral degradation of the LR HSI. In [33], the HSI SR method is extended to fuse LR HSIs and MSIs from different satellites. In [34], GAN is adopted to spectrally super-resolve MSIs using intrinsic imaging degradation models of MSIs and unpaired HSIs and MSIs. In [35], a masked transformer is constructed to unsupervisedly excavate latent hyperspectral characteristics, with a mask-guided band augment module presented to improve bandwise correlation and continuity. Moreover, a special loss function is designed to reduce spectral distortion, which is based on the intrinsic mapping from HSIs to MSIs and the inherent spectral structural similarity (SSIM).

In this chapter, we will review the advancements of HSI SR from the supervised method to the blind method. In Section 6.2, our proposed HSI SR method based on sparse representation using full supervised information is presented. In Section 6.3, a weakly supervised deep learning method is proposed for remote-sensing image SR. In Section 6.4, unsupervised HSIs and MSIs fusion for HSI SR is converted to self-supervised denoising. In Section 6.5, a blind SpeSR method using unpaired HSIs and MSIs is designed to obtain high spatial- and spectral-resolution images. In Section 6.6, some discussions and conclusions are provided.

6.2 Full Supervised HSI SR

6.2.1 Sparse Representation Based HSI SR Reconstruction

HSI SR reconstruction aims to generate a HR HSI $\mathbf{Z} \in \mathbb{R}^{L\times N}$ using the observed LR HSI $\mathbf{Y}_h \in \mathbb{R}^{L\times n}$ and HR MSI $\mathbf{Y}_m \in \mathbb{R}^{l\times N}$ of the same scene, where $N = N_{row} \times N_{col}$ and $n = n_{row} \times n_{col}$. N_{row}, n_{row}, N_{col}, and n_{col} indicate the spatial dimension, and B, b indicate the spectral dimension. Here, $N_{row} \gg N_{col}$, $N_{col} \gg n_{col}$, $L \gg l$, we assume that the LR HSI $\mathbf{Y}_h$ and the HR MSI $\mathbf{Y}_m$ can be linearly mapped from the target image $\mathbf{Z}$: preserved and the spatial dimension is ignored. The HSI is spectrally downsampled from the full-spectrum image, i.e.,

$$\mathbf{Y}_h = \mathbf{ZH}, \tag{6.1}$$

$$\mathbf{Y}_m = \mathbf{\Gamma Z}, \tag{6.2}$$

where $\mathbf{H} \in \mathbb{R}^{N\times n}: \mathbb{R}^{L\times N} \rightarrow \mathbb{R}^{L\times n}$ is a spatial dimensionality reduction operator, while $\mathbf{\Gamma} \in \mathbb{R}^{l\times L}$: $\mathbb{R}^{L\times N} \rightarrow \mathbb{R}^{l\times N}$ is a spectral dimensionality reduction operator.

The sparse representation [36] assumes that a pixel in $\mathbf{Z} \in \mathbb{R}^{L\times N}$ can be represented as linear combinations of several distinct spectral signatures:

$$\mathbf{Z} \approx \mathbf{D}\alpha_i, \tag{6.3}$$

where $\mathbf{D}$ is a spectral dictionary and α_i is the sparse coefficient. Each atom in $\mathbf{D}$ represents the spectral vector of materials in the captured area. Since the observed HSI Y_h is the low spatial resolution version of $\mathbf{Z}$, $\mathbf{y}_h^i$ can be represented as:

$$\mathbf{y}_h^i = \sum_{j\in W_i} \mathbf{h}_i \mathbf{z}_i = \mathbf{D}\sum_{j\in W_i} \mathbf{h}_i \alpha_i = \mathbf{D}\beta_i, \tag{6.4}$$

where $\mathbf{W}_i$ is a window centered on pixel i and h_j denotes the weighting coefficients. Each pixel in $\mathbf{Y}_h$ can be linearly represented by the pixels of $\mathbf{Z}$ within window $\mathbf{W}_i$. As illustrated in Eq. (6.2), pixel-wise form of MSI $\mathbf{y}_m^i$ can be represented as:

$$\mathbf{y}_m^i = \mathbf{\Gamma z}_i \approx \mathbf{\Gamma D}\alpha_i. \tag{6.5}$$

As can been seen in Eqs. (6.4) and (6.5), we can easily estimate the spectral dictionary $\mathbf{D}$ and coefficient matrix $\mathbf{A} = [\alpha_1, ..., \alpha_i, ..., \alpha_N]$ from the observed Y_h and $\mathbf{Y}_m$. Then, the target image $\mathbf{Z}$ would be reconstructed as:

$$\mathbf{Z} \approx \mathbf{DA}. \tag{6.6}$$

For the whole image, we can rewrite Eq. (6.4) as $\mathbf{Y}_h = \mathbf{DB}$, where $\mathbf{B} = [\beta_1, ..., \beta_i, ..., \beta_n]$. Generally, spectral dictionary $\mathbf{D}$ can be obtained by solving the following optimal problem:

$$\underset{D,B}{\text{argmin}} \frac{1}{2} \|\mathbf{Y}_h - \mathbf{DB}\|_F^2 + \lambda \left\|\mathbf{B}\right\|. \tag{6.7}$$

According to Eq. (6.5), we have $\mathbf{Y}_m = \mathbf{\Gamma DA}$. Therefore, once the spectral dictionary $\mathbf{D}$ is learned, fractional abundance coefficient matrix $\mathbf{A}$ can be obtained by decomposing the MSI Y_m on the transformed dictionary $\mathbf{\Gamma D}$. To pursue a compact representation $\mathbf{A}$, Song et al. introduced a pixel based sparse model [37] to solve the following problem:

$$\underset{\alpha_i}{\text{argmin}} \|\alpha_i\|_0 \text{s.t.} \left\|\mathbf{y}_m^i - \mathbf{D}\alpha_i\right\|_F \leq \eta_1. \tag{6.8}$$

The fractional abundance coefficient matrix $\mathbf{A}$ can be constructed as $\mathbf{A} = [\alpha_1, ..., \alpha_i, ..., \alpha_N]$.

In general, pixel-based sparse model in [16, 37] ignores the local spatial similarity of the MSI image and thus the spatial information cannot be sufficiently utilized. To address this issue, Akhtar et al. [36] introduces a patch-based sparse model. Specifically, the MSI is firstly divided into many non-overlapped fixed patches, and the i-th patch can be denoted as $\mathbf{Y}_i^P$, which is composed of multiple pixels. Then, a joint sparse regularization is utilized to decompose the patch $\mathbf{Y}_i^P$:

$$\underset{A_i^P}{\text{argmin}} \left\|\mathbf{A}_i^P\right\|_{row_0} \text{s.t.} \left\|\mathbf{Y}_i^P - \mathbf{\Gamma D A}_i^P\right\|_F \leq \eta_2, A_i^P \geq 0, \tag{6.9}$$

where $\mathbf{A}_i^P$ is the sparse coefficients matrix of $\mathbf{Y}_i^P$, η_2 denotes the tolerable error, and ℓ_{row_0} denotes the row sparse, which con- strains pixels within $\mathbf{Y}_i^P$ to be decomposed on the same atoms with different weights. The final fractional abundance matrix is $\mathbf{A} = \left[\mathbf{A}_1^P, ..., \mathbf{A}_i^P, ..., \mathbf{A}_{k_1}^P\right]$, where k_1 is the total number of patches. After estimating the spectral dictionary and fractional abundance vectors from the observed HSI $\mathbf{Y}_h$ and MSI $\mathbf{Y}_m$, the target image can be reconstructed by $\mathbf{Z} = \mathbf{DA}$.

6.2.2 Proposed Full Supervised HSI SR

Since HSI usually has very complex structures, different variations might be existed within a window of fixed size. Thus, the patch-based joint sparsity model cannot reflect such complex structures of HSI. In this section, we propose a superpixel based sparse representation (SSR) model for HSI SR reconstruction. The SSR can be divided into the following three parts: (i) Learning spectral dictionary from low resolution HSI to extract spectral information; (ii) Applying the joint decomposition on the observed MSI to obtain spatial information; and (iii) Fusing the spectral with spatial information to reconstruct the high resolution HSI. More descriptions of the proposed SSR method will be detailed as follows (also illustrated in Figure 6.1).

Since dictionary learning has achieved promising result on image reconstruction [39], we first train a spectral dictionary $\mathbf{D}$ from the observed HSI via an online dictionary learning (ODL) algorithm [40]. Specially, given the HSI $\mathbf{Y}_h$, the spectral dictionary can be learned by solving the following optimization problem:

$$\mathbf{D}, \mathbf{B} = \underset{\mathbf{D},\mathbf{B}}{\text{argmin}} \frac{1}{2} \| Y_h - \mathbf{DB}\|_F^2 + \lambda \| \mathbf{B}\|_1 \text{s.t.} d_k > 0, \tag{6.10}$$

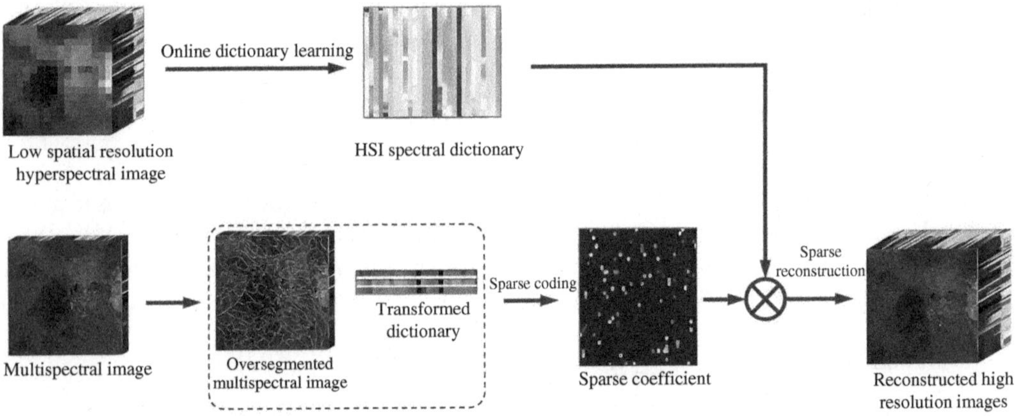

Figure 6.1 The whole procedure of the proposed SSR approach [38] / with permission of Elsevier.

where $d_k > 0$ means that the spectral vectors of HSI are positive. Once the HSI spectral dictionary $\mathbf{D}$ is obtained, the transformed dictionary corresponding to MSI would be constructed by reducing spectral dimension of HSI spectral dictionary as $\mathbf{\Gamma D}$.

Secondly, the MSI is decomposed on the transformed dictionary to obtain the sparse coefficient carrying the spatial information. To sufficiently utilize the spatial information, the joint decomposition is applied on the superpixels rather than fixed patches. The main steps of the joint decomposition on the superpixel are summarized as follows: (i) Superpixels segmentation on MSI; and (ii) Joint decomposition of superpixels.

To segment the observed MSI more efficiently, we first apply the sparse principal component analysis [41] to get the first principal component. Since the first principal component contains the most important information of the MSI, it is used as the base image to create superpixels segmentation map via entropy rate superpixel (ERS) segmentation [42]. Specially, the base image is first mapped to a graph $G = (V, E)$, where the vertices set V denote the pixels of base image and E is the edge set representing the pairwise similarity among adjacent pixels. Then, the graph image is clustered into K connected subgraphs (corresponding to the superpixels) by choosing a subset A from E. To obtain the homogeneous, compact and balanced superpixels, the entropy rate constraint $\mathcal{H}(A)$ and balance constraint $\mathcal{B}(A)$ are considered and the objective function of superpixels segmentation can be formulated as follows:

$$\max_{A} [\mathcal{H}(A) + \mu\mathcal{B}(A)] \text{s.t.} A \subseteq E, \tag{6.11}$$

where $\mu \geq 0$ is the weight controlling the contribution of entropy rate term and balance term. The problem can be effectively solved by a greedy algorithm as described in [42]. Once the map is created, the superpixels patch can be extracted from MSI following the guidance of the segmentation map. The procedure of superpixels segmentation map creation is illustrated in Figure 6.2.

After obtaining the superpixels, we can jointly decompose superpixels on the transformed dictionary to get the sparse coefficients. In general, pixels within a superpixel $\mathbf{Y}_i^{SP}$ are assumed to have very similar spectral characteristics. The SSR exploits the local similarity by imposing a joint sparse regularization on pixels of each superpixel. Specially, the pixels within each superpixel can be simultaneously decomposed on the same sets of atoms in transformed dictionary $\mathbf{\Gamma D}$ as $\mathbf{Y}_i^{SP} \approx \mathbf{\Gamma D A}_i^{SP}$, where $\mathbf{A}_i^{SP}$ is the joint coefficients for the $\mathbf{Y}_i^{SP}$. As illustrated in Eq. (6.9), the joint sparse regularization is achieved by placing a ℓ_{row_0} norm on $\mathbf{A}_i^{SP}$. The ℓ_{row_0} norm can restrict

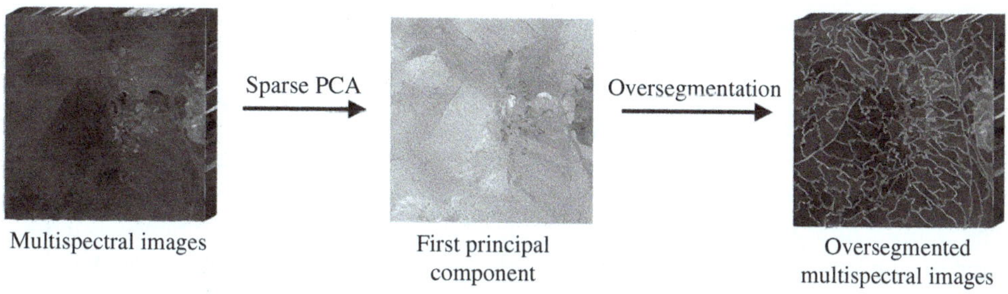

Figure 6.2 Procedure of superpixel creation [38] / with permission of Elsevier.

the sparse coefficients of pixels in each superpixel to be row sparse, with slight different values reflecting the differences among pixels. Then, the SSR pursuits the $\mathbf{A}_i^{SP}$ by solving the following optimal problem:

$$\underset{\mathbf{A}_i^{SP}}{\operatorname{argmin}} \left\| \mathbf{A}_i^{SP} \right\|_{row_0} \text{s.t.} \left\| \mathbf{Y}_i^{SP} - \mathbf{\Gamma D A}_i^{SP} \right\|_F \leq \eta_3, \mathbf{A}_i^{SP} \geq 0. \tag{6.12}$$

Equation (6.12) can be efficiently solved by a generalized simultaneous orthogonal match pursuit (G-SOMP+) [36]. The schematic diagram of the superpixel-based sparse representation is shown in Figure 6.3. Finally, we can reconstruct the high resolution HSI $\mathbf{Z}$ by multiplying the learned spectral dictionary $\mathbf{D}$ with the sparse coefficient $\mathbf{A}$ as $\mathbf{Z} = \mathbf{DA}$, where the $\mathbf{A} = \left[\mathbf{A}_1^{SP}, \ldots, \mathbf{A}_i^{SP}, \ldots, \mathbf{A}_K^{SP}\right]$ is the overall coefficient matrix, and K is the total number of superpixels.

6.2.3 Experimental Results

1) *Datasets and quantitative metrics:* We test the proposed SSR approach on three popular HSI datasets: Indian Pines [43], Cuprite Mine Nevada [44] and Pavia Center [45]. The Indian Pines image is captured by airborne visible/infrared imaging spectrometer (AVIRIS) over the agricultural

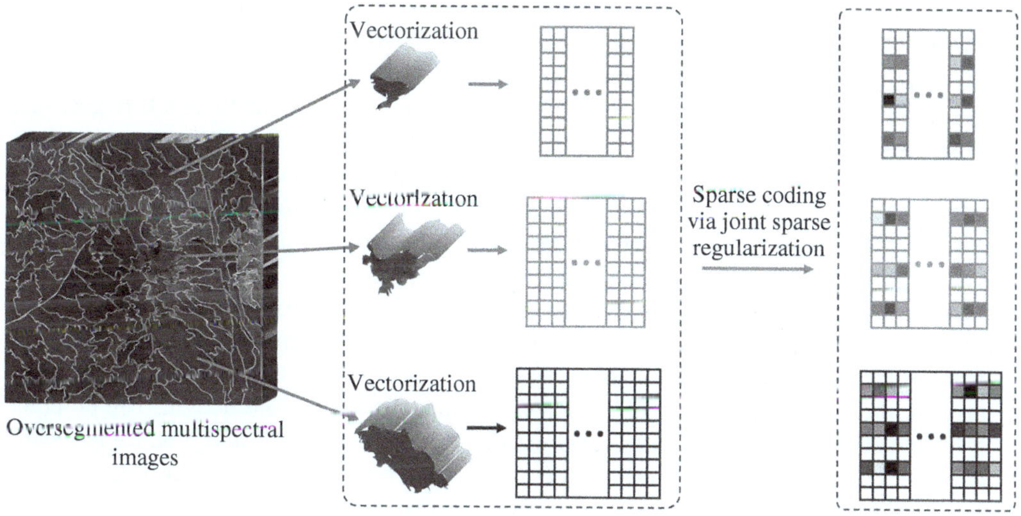

Figure 6.3 Schematic diagram of superpixel-based sparse representation [38] / with permission of Elsevier.

Indian Pines test site of northwestern Indiana and 20 water absorption bands (104–108, 150–163, and 220) are removed in our experiments. The dataset can be downloaded on the website: https://www.dynamo.ecn.purdue.edu/~biehl/MultiSpec/. We crop the bottom right corner of the data (of a size 512×512) as the ground truth image, since it has rich spatial structure. The electromagnetic wavelength of Cuprite Mine Nevada image ranges from 400 to 2500 nm with an interval of 10 nm and the spatial resolution is 20 m. This dataset is available on the following website: https://aviris.jpl.nasa.gov/data/free_data.html. In our experiments, as in [36], we crop the top left region (of size 512×512) as the ground truth image after abandoning those bands with low SNR and water absorptions. Pavia Center image is recorded by the reflective optics system imaging spectrometer (ROSIS-03) sensor over the Center of Pavia area, and its spectrum ranges from 430 to 860 nm with an interval of 4 nm. The Pavia Center dataset can be downloaded from: https://www.ehu.eus/ccwintco/index.php?title=Hyperspectral_Remote_Sensing_Scenes. After abandoning the nosiest band, the bottom right part of this dataset is cropped to the size of $512 \times 512 \times 102$, which is used as the ground truth image in the following experiment.

In our experiment, the ground truth image is downsampled 32 times to obtain the LR HSI Y_h. Specifically, each pixel $\mathbf{y}_h^i \in Y_h$ is generated by averaging pixels within a 32×32 window of ground truth image centering on location i. For MSI Y_m, we directly select several bands from the ground truth image. For Indian Pine and Cuprite Mine images, we choose the bands whose center wavelengths are the same as USGS/NASA Landsat 7 images to simulate MSI. That is, the bands whose center wavelengths are 480, 560, 660, 830, 1650, and 2220 nm would be chosen. For Pavia Center image, we choose the blue, green, red and near-infrared channel (corresponding to 480, 560, 660, and 830 nm, respectively) of ground truth to simulate MSI. Three widely used metrics: root mean square error (RMSE), relative dimensionless global error in synthesis (ERGAS) [46] and spectral angle mapper (SAM) [47] to measure performance of different methods. For the RMSE, ERGAS, and SAM metrics, the smaller value corresponds to the better performance.

2) *Results comparison:* We compare the proposed method with two well-known HSI SR approaches: SASFM[37] and G-SOMP+ [36] methods. For the proposed method, the number of atoms number L and superpixels K are two main parameters needed to be tuned. For the atoms number L, we choose it to be 30, 270, and 270 for Cuprite Mine, Indian Pine, and Pavia Center images, respectively. For the number of superpixels K, we set it to be 6000 for all the three test images. For the parameters of the two compared methods, their parameters are selected to the default values in [36, 37] to reach their best results.

Qualitative and quantitative results are shown in Figures 6.4–6.6 and Table 6.1, respectively. As can be seen in Figure 6.4, the river region in Indian Pine image is not well reconstructed, large error occurred between the SASFM reconstructed image and ground truth. The G-SOMP+ method delivered a better result, but still creating a lot of reconstructed burrs in the river. By contrast, the proposed SSR method can provide a better reconstruction with less burrs. The results on the Cuprite Mine image (see Figure 6.5) and the Pavia Center image (see Figure 6.6) also show the superiority of the proposed method over the compared methods. This is because the SASFM coded the MSI in a pixelwise way, thus ignoring local structure similarity of the image. Although G-SOMP+ [36] method considers local structure similarity within a fixed window, the fixed window may not sufficiently utilize the spatial information. The proposed SSR method can generally better reconstruct the high-resolution HSI and produce less burrs with the adopted superpixel strategy. The experiment results in Table 6.1 also demonstrate the superiority of our method over other compared methods.

3) *Effect of the selected atoms number and number of superpixels:* Here, we discuss the effects of selected atoms number L and number of superpixels K on the performance of the SSR method.

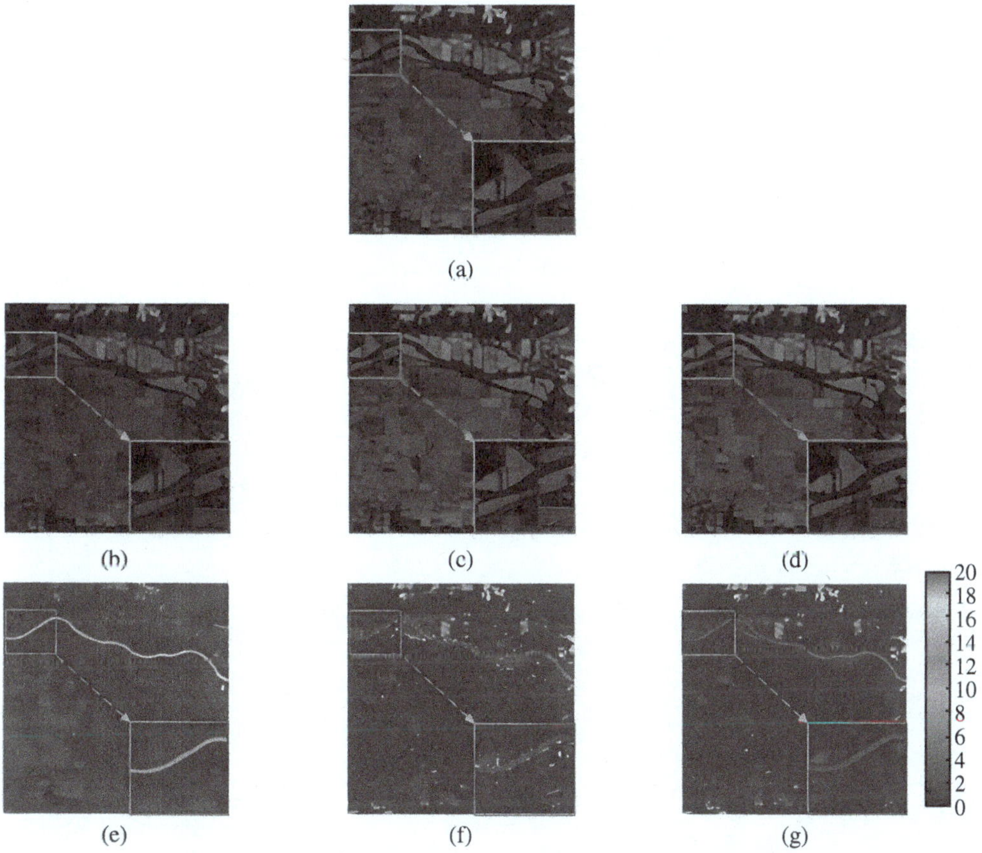

Figure 6.4 Comparisons of SASFM [37], G-SOMP+ [36] and proposed SSR methods [38] on the Indian Pines image. (a) Ground truth image, (b) SASFM reconstructed result, (c) G-SOMP+ reconstructed result, (d) SSR reconstructed result, (e) absolute error between SASFM result and ground truth, (f) absolute error between G-SOMP+ result and ground truth, and (g) absolute error between SSR result and ground truth. *Source:* [38] / with permission of Elsevier.

Table 6.2 shows the overall reconstructed performance (in RMSE) under different atoms numbers for all the three datasets. As can be observed, the RMSE value of our proposed method will first decrease and then become stable, as the atom number increases. But, when the atoms number is too large, heavy computational cost will be created on the sparse coding part.

Table 6.3 shows the influence of the number of superpixels K on the performance of the proposed SSR method (in RMSE). As can be observed, the value of RMSE is relatively high when the number of superpixels is lower than 1000. However, when the number further increases, the value of RMSE becomes comparatively stable. The reason is that when the superpixel number is large, the superpixel size will become small, and thus the pixels within superpixels will be very similar. On the other hand, further reducing superpixel size will also create an additional computational complexity for the sparse coding.

6.3 Weakly Supervised HSI SR

Remote-sensing image SR aims to recover detailed HR images from LR images. Generally, the HR images I^{HR} are degraded to LR images I^{LR} by a degradation model:

$$I^{LR} = \left(I^{HR} \otimes k\right)\downarrow_s + n, \tag{6.13}$$

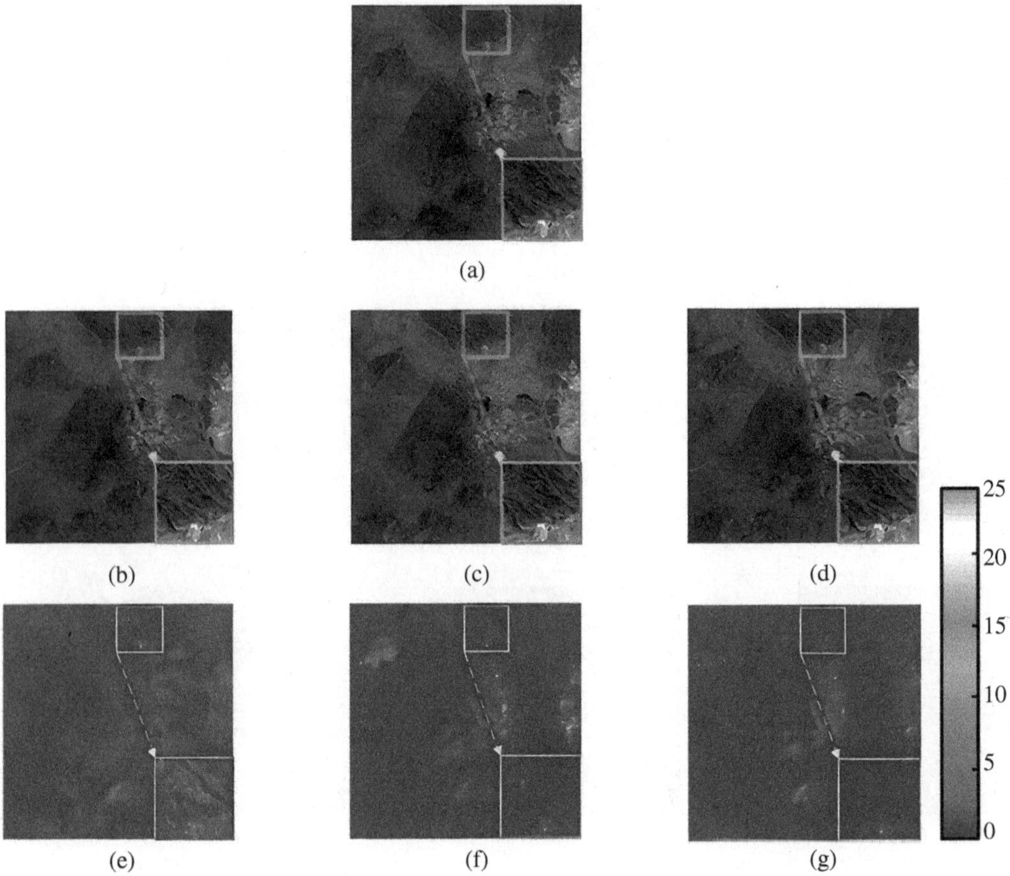

Figure 6.5 Comparisons of SASFM [37], G-SOMP+ [36] and proposed SSR methods [38] on Pavia Center image. (a) Ground truth image, (b) SASFM reconstructed result, (c) G-SOMP+ reconstructed result, (d) SSR reconstructed result, (e) absolute error between SASFM result and ground truth, (f) absolute error between G-SOMP+ result and ground truth, and (g) absolute error between SSR result and ground truth. *Source:* [38] / with permission of Elsevier.

where k is a blur kernel, and $\otimes$ is the convolution operation, and $\downarrow_s$ is downsampling operation with a scale factor of s, and n is the additional noise. For remote-sensing images, the degradation model is unknown so that the SR is an ill-posed problem with infinite solutions. The difficulty of SR is to limit the solution space to obtain better SR results.

1) *CNN-based remote-sensing image SR:* With the rapid development of deep learning methods, CNN-based remote-sensing image SR methods have achieved good performance. These methods aim to learn the mapping function $F(\cdot)$ from the paired HR and LR data sets:

$$I^{SR} = F\left(I^{LR}\right), \tag{6.14}$$

where I^{SR} represents a reconstructed SR image and I^{LR} is downsampled from HR images I^{HR} by bicubic interpolation. The loss function of CNN-based SR generally uses the mean absolute error (MAE) to measure the difference between I^{SR} and I^{HR}:

$$L_{MAE}\left(F, I^{HR}, I^{LR}\right) = \left\|F\left(I^{LR}\right) - I^{HR}\right\|_1, \tag{6.15}$$

where L_{MAE} represents the MAE loss function to optimize the CNN network parameters.

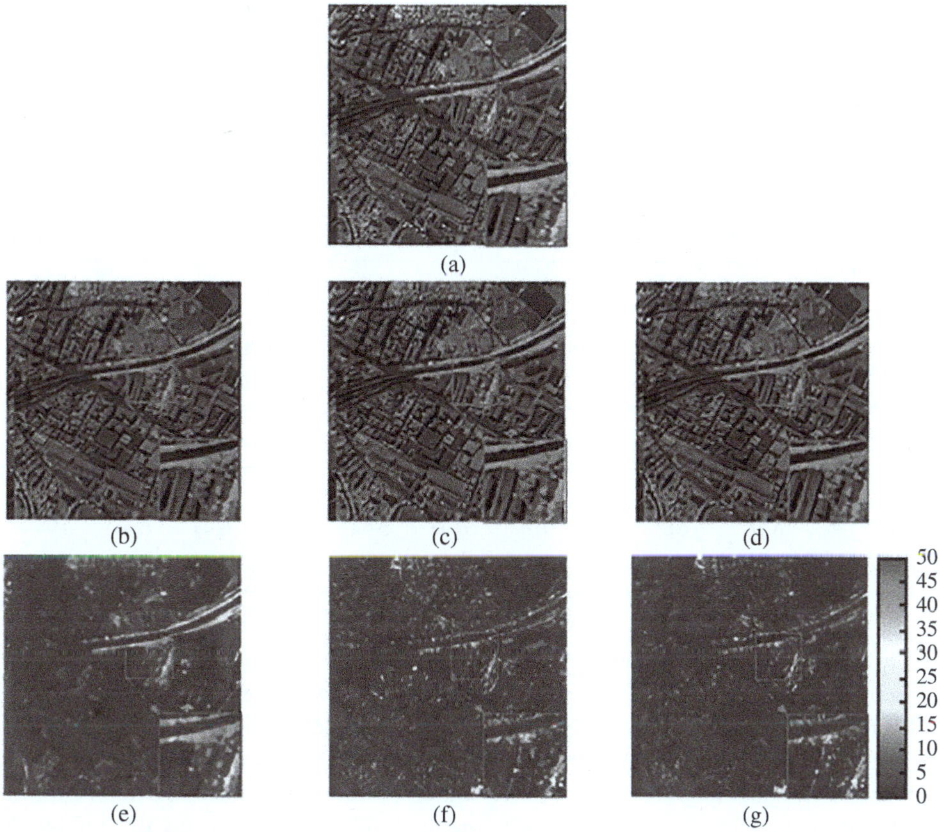

Figure 6.6 Comparisons of SASFM [37], G-SOMP+ [36], and proposed SSR methods [38] on Cuprite Mine image. (a) Ground truth image, (b) SASFM reconstructed result, (c) G-SOMP+ reconstructed result, (d) SSR reconstructed result, (e) absolute error between SASFM result and ground truth, (f) absolute error between G-SOMP+ result and ground truth, and (g) absolute error between SSR result and ground truth. *Source:* [38] / with permission of Elsevier.

Table 6.1 Comparisons among different methods: SASFM [37], G-SOMP+ [36] and the proposed SSR [38]. The best result is labeled in bold.

Methods	SASFM [37]	G-SOMP+ [36]	SSR [38]
Indian Pine			
RMSE	1.174	1.125	**1.092**
ERGAS	**0.056**	0.058	**0.056**
SAM	0.871	0.737	**0.716**
Cuprite Mine			
SE	1.331	1.016	**0.943**
ERGAS	0.051	0.040	**0.039**
SAM	0.802	0.555	**0.526**
Pavia Center			
RMSE	4.230	3.810	**3.450**
ERGAS	0.301	0.250	**0.235**
SAM	4.038	3.302	**2.981**

Table 6.2 The effect of selected atoms number $\mathcal{L}$ on the performance of SSR method (in RMSE) [38] / with permission of Elsevier.

Datasets\L	1	30	60	90	120	150	180	210	240	270	300
Indian Pine	1.22	1.11	1.10	1.10	1.10	1.10	1.09	1.09	1.09	1.09	1.09
Cuprite Mine	0.97	0.94	0.94	0.94	0.94	0.94	0.94	0.94	0.93	0.93	0.94
Pavia Center	60.57	3.92	3.77	3.66	3.60	3.67	3.61	3.54	3.49	3.45	4.30

Table 6.3 The effect of number of superpixels $\mathcal{K}$ on the performance of SSR method (in RMSE) [38] / with permission of Elsevier.

Datasets\K	1	1000	2000	3000	4000	5000	6000	7000	8000	9000	10,000
Indian Pine	1.53	1.09	1.09	1.09	1.09	1.09	1.09	1.09	1.09	1.09	1.09
Cuprite Mine	0.99	0.94	0.94	0.94	0.94	0.94	0.94	0.94	0.94	0.94	0.94
Pavia Center	4.20	3.41	3.41	3.41	3.41	3.43	3.45	3.46	3.47	3.48	3.48

Recently, CNN-based methods have been applied for the remote-sensing images SR. In [48], Lei et al. proposed a local- global-combined network (LGCNet) to learn the multi-level representations of remote-sensing images including both local details and global environmental priors. A deep distillation recursive network (DDRN) [49] was introduced for video satellite image SR with ultra-dense residual blocks and a recursive strategy to mitigate memory consumption. Lu et al. [50] presented a multi-scale residual neural network (MRNN) by adopting the multi-scale nature of satellite images to reconstruct high-frequency information. Pan et al. [51] proposed a residual dense back-projection network (RDBPN) to enhance the resolution of RGB remote-sensing images with dense back-projection blocks, which utilized residual learning in both global and local manners. In [52], Zhang et al. proposed a mixed high-order attention network improved by a high-order attention module to restore the missing details. Driven by the dense connections [53], Dong et al. developed a dense-sampling SR network [54] named DSSR to achieve the large-scale SR reconstruction by using the dense-sampling mechanism and wide feature attention block. However, these CNN-based methods need paired data sets to train the SR network. The typical way for synthesizing the paired data is the utilization of the bicubic model that is quite different from the real-world remote-sensing degradation model. Therefore, these CNN-based methods achieve poor performance when applied to real LR remote-sensing images.

2) *GAN-based remote-sensing image SR:* Recently, benefiting from the adversarial learning strategy, the GAN-based SR methods have achieved impressive results with more detailed information and visual effect in natural image SR [55–57] and remote-sensing image SR. The GAN-based methods are typically composed of a generator and a discriminator. For SR tasks, the generator is used to reconstruct SR images and the discriminator aims to distinguish SR images from HR images. The loss function of GAN-based SR methods is as follows:

$$L_{adv}\left(G, D, I^{HR}, I^{LR}\right) = \log\left(D\left(I^{HR}\right)\right) + \log\left(1 - D\left(G\left(I^{LR}\right)\right)\right), \tag{6.16}$$

where G is the generator to learn the SR mapping function and D is the discriminator. The min–max two-player game between the generator and the discriminator makes the generated data be indistinguishable from the real ones.

For remote-sensing SR, most of the researchers improve the performance from two aspects: (i) the structure of the generator; (ii) the judgment ability of the discriminator. Specifically, Jiang et al. [58] proposed a GAN-based edge-enhancement network (EEGAN), where the generator was improved by an ultra-dense subnetwork and an edge-enhancement subnetwork to increase the robustness of satellite image SR reconstruction. In [59], Lei et al. proposed a coupled-discriminated GANs (CDGAN), in which the discriminator was specifically designed to take SR and HR images as inputs to improve the discrimination ability of the discriminator. Though GAN-based methods reconstruct SR results with fine texture and details, they still need paired data sets to training, which limits the generalization ability of the model. In addition, these methods are more sensitive to noise which results in the compensated high-frequency details (e.g., image edges) of SR results may be inconsistent with the ground truth images.

3) *Image domain translation:* Image domain translation aims to transform an input image (source domain) into a specific target image (target domain), e.g., mapping aerial images to map images [60]. Inspired by the GANs, the image domain translation methods have gained fruitful progress. In [61], the CycleGAN proposed by Zhu et al. can learn the translation between two different domains X and Y. The CycleGAN has two generators $G_1 : X \to Y$ and $G_2 : Y \to X$ accompanied by two discriminators D_X and D_Y. In addition, the CycleGAN adopts the cycle consistency loss to reduce the space of possible mapping functions. For each image $x \in X$ and $y \in Y$, the cycle consistency loss can be expressed as:

$$L_{cyc}(G_1, G_2, x, y) = \|G_2(G_1(x)) - x\|_1 + \|G_1(G_2(y)) - y\|_1, \tag{6.17}$$

where L_{cyc} describes the cycle consistency loss.

6.3.1 Proposed CPWSNN for Unpaired Remote-sensing SR

As described above, domain translation can achieve image transformation between two different domains. Therefore, for unpaired real remote-sensing images, we adopt the image domain translation to synthesize the LR images from real HR images and utilize the synthetic LR and the real HR to train the SR network. However, as shown in Figure 6.7, compared with the natural images (see Figure 6.7a), the remote-sensing images (see Figure 6.7b) have a larger size and much richer contents, i.e., much more objects with different shapes and textures. Therefore, the typical domain translation cannot be applied directly to remote-sensing images, since it cannot well represent the complex content in remote-sensing image, thereby causing content distortions (e.g., fake textures, artificial objects, and other kinds of distortions) in the synthetic data (see Figure 6.7c).

To solve the above issue, we propose the CPWNN method for unpaired remote-sensing image SR. Firstly, we incorporate the perceptual loss into the image domain translation to synthesize pseudo-LR remote-sensing images from real HR images, as shown in Figure 6.8. The perceptual loss ensures that the generated pseudo-LR images and the real LR images have the same content and semantic information. Then, the generated pseudo-LR images and the real HR images compose the paired HR–LR training data to provide supervision for the SR network which utilizes a pixel-wise loss. Furthermore, we propose the degradation consistency loss and the edge retention loss to constrain the GAN-based SR network training procedure. The degradation consistency loss is proposed to constrain the solution space of the SR model to avoid the artificial objects in its results. The edge retention loss is proposed to prevent the SR network from generating fake edges and textures by constraining the edges information in its results. Finally, the results can have more realistic

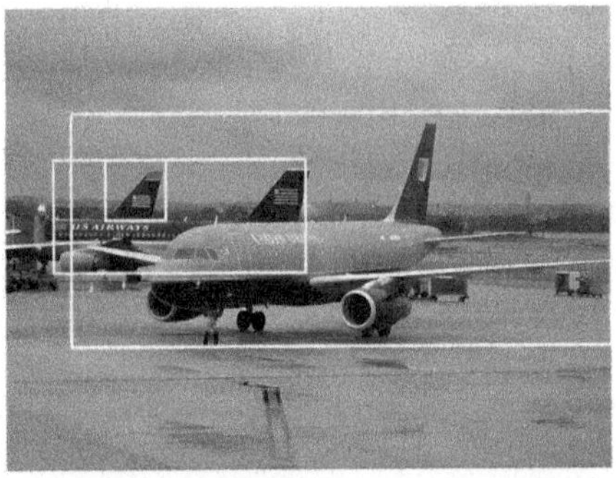

(a)

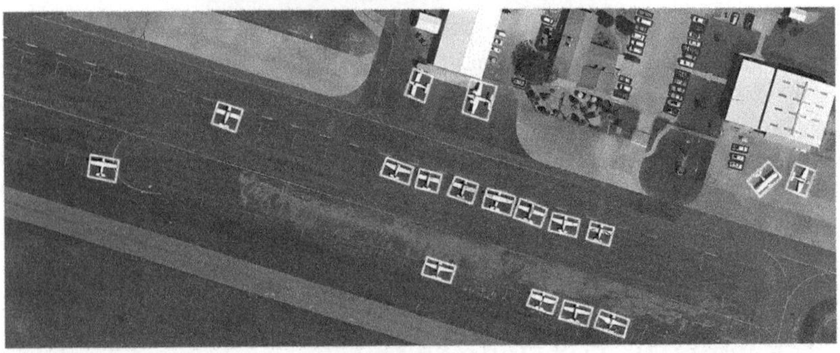

(b)

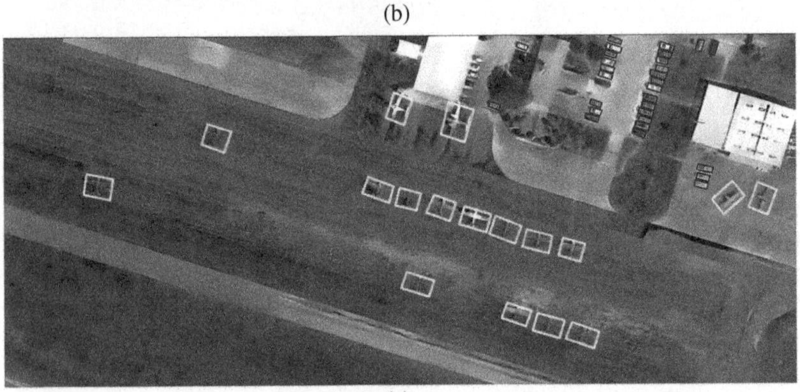

(c)

Figure 6.7 Comparison of airplanes in a natural image (a) and a remote-sensing image (b). Image (c) is the SR reconstructed remote-sensing image for (b) without content-preserving constraints. Airplanes are marked by white rectangles [62] / with permission of Springer Nature. (a) Airplanes in a natural image, (b) airplanes in a remote-sensing image, and (c) an SR reconstructed remote-sensing image without content-preserving constraints.

textures and detailed information with the object information unchanged. The SR reconstruction process is shown in Figure 6.9.

1) *Pseudo-LR remote-sensing image generation using domain translation with the perceptual loss*: Domain translation aims to generate pseudo-LR remote-sensing images that are the LR version of real HR remote-sensing images by learning a translation between the bicubic domain and the real LR domain. Then, the pseudo-LR images and real HR images compose paired data to provide supervision for the SR network. Similar to the CycleGAN [61], as described in

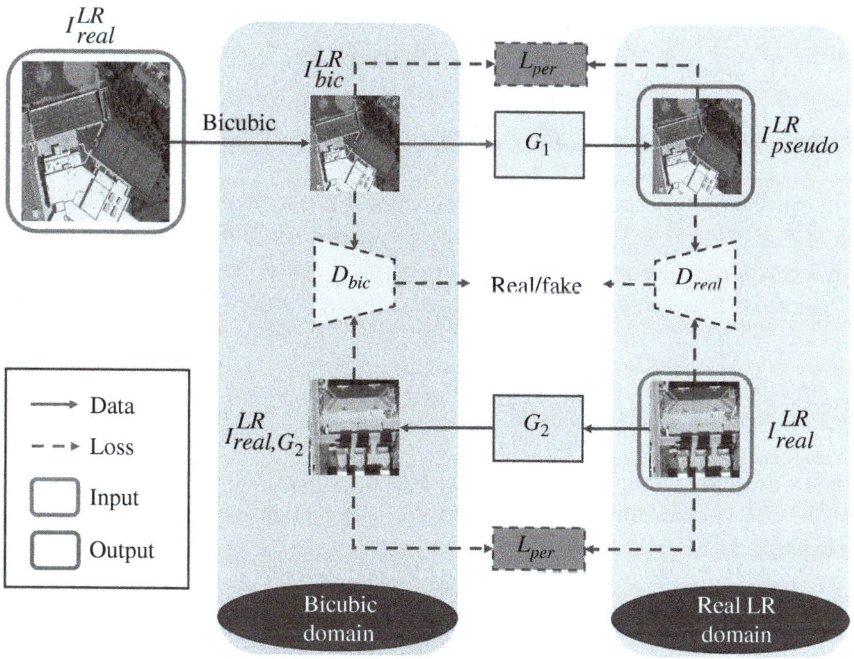

Figure 6.8 The framework for generating the pseudo-LR remote-sensing image I^{LR}_{pseudo} by domain translation with the perceptual loss L_{per}. D_{real} encourages G_1 to map the image I^{LR}_{bic} from the bicubic domain to the real LR domain, and vice versa for D_{bic} and G_2. The generated pseudo-LR image I^{LR}_{pseudo} and the real HR image I^{HR}_{real} make up the paired data for the subsequent SR network training [62] / with permission of Springer Nature.

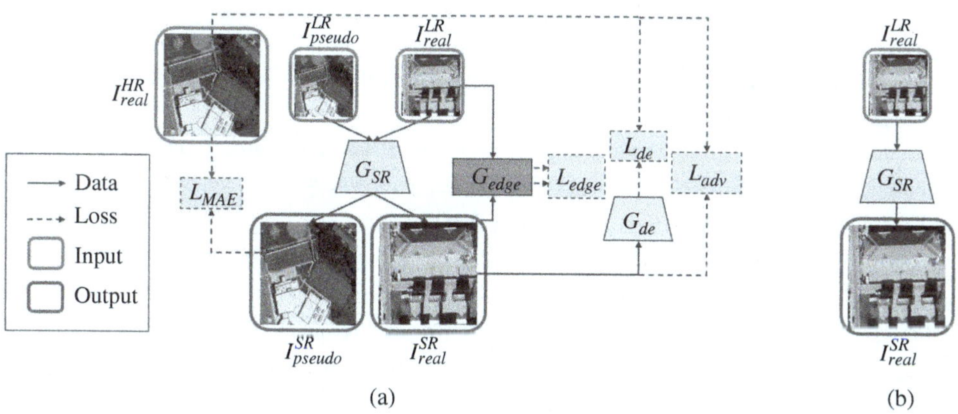

Figure 6.9 Remote-sensing images SR reconstruction by the SR network with the edge retention loss L_{edge} and the degradation consistency loss L_{de}. In (a) the training phase, the SR network G_{SR} is trained under the supervision of the pseudo paired data (pseudo-LR image I^{LR}_{pseudo} and real HR image I^{HR}_{real}) and the unpaired data (real LR image I^{LR}_{real} and real HR image I^{HR}_{real}). In (b) the testing phase, the well-trained G_{SR} reconstructs I^{LR}_{real} to I^{SR}_{real} [62] / with permission of Springer Nature.

subsection 3.0.3, our domain translation is composed of two generators (G_1, G_2) and two discriminators (D_{real}, D_{bic}). Given a real HR image I^{HR}_{real}, we downscale it by the bicubic interpolation operation to get I^{LR}_{bic}. G_1 is used to learn the mapping function from the bicubic domain to the real LR domain and generate a pseudo-LR image I^{LR}_{pseudo} from I^{LR}_{bic}. G_2 is a reverse mapping network to map the real LR image I_{real}^{LR} to its bicubic domain as I_{real,G_2}^{LR} and is used to assist the training of G_1. D_{real} is a discriminator of G_1 to distinguish I_{pseudo}^{LR} from I_{real}^{LR}. Similarly, D_{bic} is the discriminator of G_2 to distinguish I_{real,G_2}^{LR} from I_{bic}^{LR}. The architecture of G_1 and G_2 is composed of eight residual blocks [63]. The two discriminators D_{real} and D_{bic} are implemented with the structure of PatchGAN [60].

In the domain translation process, we adopt the perceptual loss to avoid object deformation and other content distortions in the pseudo-LR image. In general, since there are more objects and semantic information in the feature space than the pixel space, the perceptual loss can measure the difference of between two different images to preserve the content. The perceptual loss is described as:

$$L_{per}(G_1, G_2) = \left\|\phi_{m,n}\left(I_{pseudo}^{LR}\right) - \phi_{m,n}(I_{bic}^{LR})\right\|_1 + \left\|\phi_{m,n}\left(I_{real,G_2}^{LR}\right) - \phi_{m,n}(I_{real}^{LR})\right\|_1, \tag{6.18}$$

where $\phi_{m,n}$ denotes the feature map extracted by the n-th convolutional layer before mth max pooling layer of the VGG19 extractor. The identity loss L_{idt} is applied to avoid the color variation issue, which is expressed as:

$$L_{idt}(G_1, G_2) = \|I_{real,G_1}^{LR} - I_{real}^{LR}\|_1 + \|I_{bic,G_2}^{LR} - I_{bic}^{LR}\|_1. \tag{6.19}$$

The full loss functions of image domain translation are shown as follows:

$$\begin{aligned} L_{pseudo-LR} = {} & L_{adv}\left(G_1, D_{real}, I_{real}^{LR}, I_{bic}^{LR}\right) + L_{adv}\left(G_2, D_{bic}, I_{bic}^{LR}, I_{real}^{LR}\right) + \lambda_1 L_{cyc}\left(G_1, G_2, I_{bic}^{LR}, I_{real}^{LR}\right) \\ & + \lambda_2 L_{idt}(G_1, G_2) + \lambda_3 L_{per}(G_1, G_2), \end{aligned} \tag{6.20}$$

where λ_1, λ_2, and λ_3 are hyperparameters to weight the contributions of each loss function. L_{adv} is the adversarial loss function described in Eq. (6.16). L_{cyc} is the cycle consistency loss described in Eq. (6.17).

2) *Remote-sensing images SR reconstruction by the SR network with the degradation consistency loss and the edge retention loss:* The SR network G_{SR} aims to reconstruct a detailed SR image I_{real}^{SR} from a real LR image I_{real}^{LR}. In this section, we use the RRDBNet proposed in [56] as the SR network architecture, since it has achieved impressive performance. After obtaining the pseudo-LR image I_{pseudo}^{LR} by the domain translation, we utilize the G_{SR} to generate the pseudo-SR image I_{pseudo}^{SR}. The pseudo-LR image I_{pseudo}^{LR} and real HR image I_{real}^{HR} provide paired supervision for the training of the SR network that uses MAE loss. In addition, we adopt the GAN-based framework to train the SR network on I_{real}^{SR} and I_{real}^{HR}, which can produce more realistic results on real LR data. D_{hr} is a discriminator (utilizing the same structure as PatchGAN [60]) to distinguish I_{real}^{SR} from I_{real}^{HR}. However, the training process of GANs is unstable resulting in SR reconstructed results with fake textures, artificial objects, and other content distortions. So, we propose the edge retention loss L_{edge} and degradation consistency loss L_{de} to constrain the solution space of the SR network.

Edge retention loss: The edge retention loss is proposed to prevent the SR network from generating fake edges and textures using the edge priors. In this loss, we use the DexiNed network [64] to extract the edge information from real LR and SR images and adopt the binary cross entropy (BCE) loss to measure the difference between the edge information of real LR and SR images. The edge retention loss can be expressed as follows,

$$L_{edge}\left(G_{edge}\right) = -\left[I^{LR}_{real,BIC\circ G_{edge}} \log\left(I^{SR}_{real,G_{edge}}\right) + \left(1 - I^{LR}_{real,BIC\circ G_{edge}}\right)\log\left(1 - I^{SR}_{real,G_{edge}}\right)\right], \tag{6.21}$$

where G_{edge} is the DexiNed edge detection network and BIC represents the bicubic interpolation to upscale I^{LR}_{real} to the size of I^{SR}_{real}. $I^{LR}_{real,BIC\circ G_{edge}}$ represents the edge information extracted by the edge detection network from the bicubic upsampled I^{LR}_{real}. $I^{SR}_{real,G_{edge}}$ stands for the edge information of I^{SR}_{real}.

Degradation consistency loss: The degradation consistency loss is introduced to avoid the generation of unreal objects or other content distortions in SR results. The degradation network G_{de} (see Figure 6.10) is adopted to provide constraints for the SR network. Specifically, G_{de} degrades the SR result to I^{LR}_{de}, which is $I^{LR}_{de} = G_{de}\left(I^{SR}_{real}\right)$. The degradation consistency loss L_{de} is expressed as follows:

$$L_{de}(G_{de}, D_{de}) = \log\left(D_{de}\left(I^{LR}_{real}\right)\right) + \log\left(1 - D_{de}\left(I^{LR}_{de}\right)\right) + a \cdot \left\|I^{LR}_{real} - I^{LR}_{de}\right\|_1, \tag{6.22}$$

where D_{de} (utilizing the same structure as the PathGAN [60]) is a discriminator to distinguish I^{LR}_{de} from I^{LR}_{real}, and a is a weight hyperparameter.

Full loss function: The full loss function of the SR network is composed of the MAE loss L_{MAE}, the edge retention loss L_{edge}, the degradation consistency loss L_{de}, and the adversarial loss L_{adv}:

$$\begin{aligned} L_{SR} = {} & \omega_1 \cdot L_{MAE}\left(G_{SR}, I^{HR}_{real}, I^{LR}_{pseudo}\right) + \omega_2 \cdot L_{edge}\left(G_{edge}, D_{edge}\right) + \omega_3 \cdot L_{de}(G_{de}, D_{de}) \\ & + \omega_4 \cdot L_{adv}\left(G_{SR}, D_{hr}, I^{HR}_{real}, I^{LR}_{real}\right), \end{aligned} \tag{6.23}$$

where ω_1, ω_2, ω_3, and ω_4 are weights of each loss. L_{MAE} and L_{adv} are estimated by Eqs. (6.15) and (6.16), respectively.

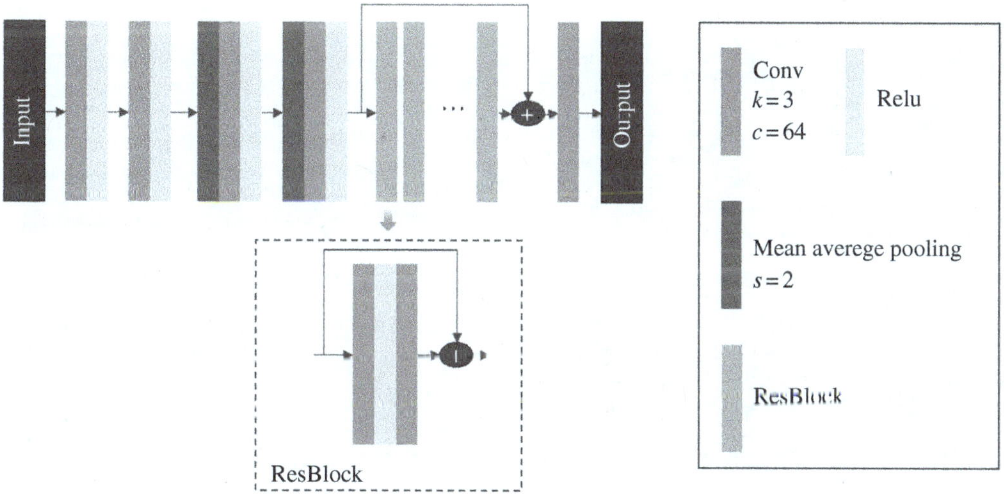

Figure 6.10 The network structure of G_{de} network [62] / with permission of Springer Nature.

6.3.2 Experiment Results

1) *Evaluation dataset:* Our method can be trained on unpaired data sets with different spatial resolutions captured by different satellites. To verify the effectiveness of the proposed method, we construct two datasets: a synthetic unpaired SR dataset and a real unpaired SR dataset. More details of these datasets are described as follows.

Synthetic unpaired SR dataset: The experiments of synthetic unpaired SR are conducted based on the RRSSRD [65] dataset. The HR images of the RRSSRD dataset are acquired from WorldView-2 and GaoFen-2, with the spatial resolution of 0.5 m/pixel and 0.8 m/pixel. In the training phase, to acquire the synthetic LR dataset, we degrade the real HR images to LR images by adding noise and downsampling. The noise degradation is the additive white gaussian noise (AWGN) with the noise level $\sigma = 7.65$ and the downsampling is the nearest interpolation with scale factor 4. To train our method in an unpaired way, we randomly select about half of the HR images (2021 images) from the RRSSRD training data set as the real HR images. The remaining half of the HR images (2022 images) are degraded to noisy LR images that are used as real LR images. In the testing phase, we conduct experiments on the RRSSRD test set. The test LR images are degraded from test HR images using the same degradation used for the training phase. We denote the test sets as synthetic test sets.

Real unpaired SR dataset: In the training phase, we train our model on the unpaired real HR data and real LR data. For real HR data, we select images with a spatial resolution of 0.1–0.2 m/pixel from the DOTA dataset [66] collected from the Google Earth, GF-2, and JL-1 satellites. For real LR data, we choose the Google Ref data with the spatial resolution of 0.6 m/pixel from the RRSSRD dataset [65] captured from Google Earth. The real HR data has 544 images of various sizes, while the real LR data has 4045 images with the size of 480 × 480. To balance the amount of training data, we randomly crop the HR image into 4500 patches with the size of 960 × 960. Examples of real HR and LR data sets can be seen in Figure 6.11. In the testing phase, we adopt the Google Ref data from the RRSSRD test set as our real LR test set. In the RRSSRD test set, the Google Ref images in #1 test set and #2 test set are the same, and the Google Ref images in #3 test set and #4 test set are the same as well. Therefore, we choose the #1 test set and #3 test set as our test data sets and denote them as Real #1 test set and Real #2 test set, respectively.

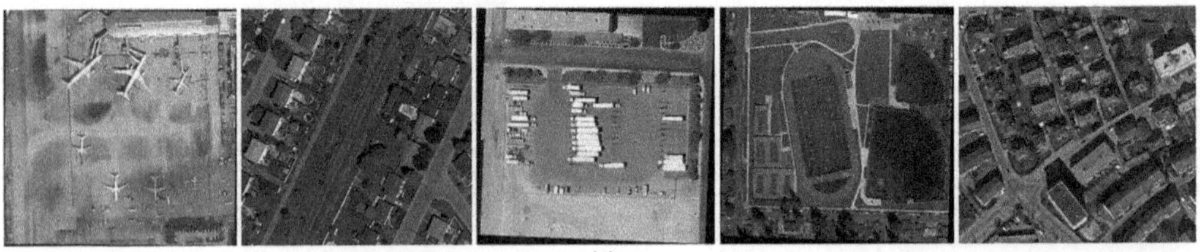
(a)

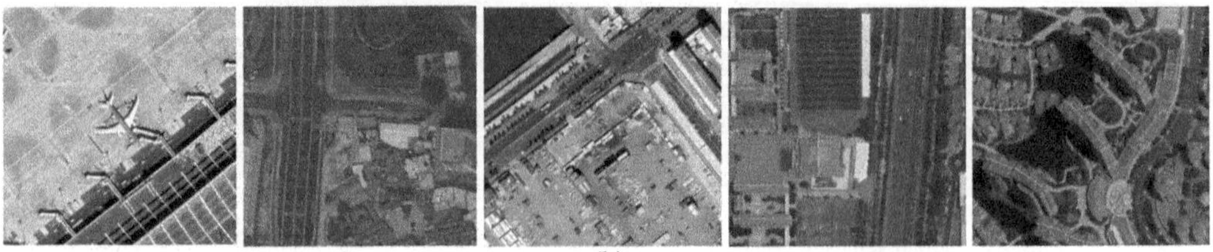
(b)

Figure 6.11 Examples of real HR and LR images. (a) Real HR images and (b) real LR images [62] / with permission of Springer Nature.

Evaluation metrics: To evaluate the proposed method, a blind image quality analyzer called as the natural image quality evaluator (NIQE) [67] is first used as the evaluation metric on both synthetic and real unpaired SR dataset. The NIQE does not require the ground truth and only calculates the measurable deviations from statistical regularities, without being trained on human-rated distorted images. The lower score of the reconstructed image represents better visual result. In the synthetic SR dataset, we adopt the peak signal-to-noise ratio (PSNR) [68], SSIM [68], learned perceptual image patch similarity (LPIPS) [69], and NIQE for evaluation. The PSNR and SSIM are the most commonly used evaluation metrics in image SR. The higher the scores of PSNR and SSIM, the better the reconstruction performance can be achieved. The reconstruction images with lower scores of LPIPS mean better image quality.

Implementation details: In our experiments, we adopt data augmentation on training samples, including the rotation of 90°, 180°, 270°, and horizontally flipping. In the training process of the domain translation, both the real LR images and bicubic downsampled images are cropped to the size of 64×64. In Eq. (6.18), the parameters m and n are set to 5 and 4, respectively. The parameters of Eq. (6.20) are set to $\lambda_1 = \lambda_2 = 10$, $\lambda_3 = 1$. For the training of SR process, the patch sizes of pseudo-LR images and real LR images are set as 48×48 and the patch size of real HR images is 192×192. We set the parameters of Eq. (6.22) as $a = 1$ and the parameters of Eq. (6.23) are set as $\omega_1 = 10$, $\omega_2 = 0.5$, $\omega_3 = 1$, $\omega_4 = 0.1$. All experiments are conducted based on Pytorch with two GTX-1080 Ti graphics processing units. For both domain translation and SR process, the training stops when the epoch is 500. The learning rate is chosen to be $1 \times 10e{-4}$ and the batch size is set as 16. The Adam optimization [70] is used to optimize the model parameters, where β_1 is 0.9 and β_2 is 0.999. Since the spatial resolution of real HR images is four times higher than that of real LR images, the SR scale factor is selected to be 4 in our experiments.

2) *Experiments on synthetic unpaired remote-sensing images:* In the synthetic unpaired remote-sensing images, we adopt the PSNR, SSIM, NIQE, and LPIPS metrics on different SR methods. The compared CNN-based methods include the SRCNN [71], EDSR [72], our baseline model RRDBNet [56], and RCAN [74]. In addition, we choose the ESRGAN [56] as the typical GAN-based method for the comparison. The CNN-based methods and the GAN-based method are all paired-based methods. Furthermore, one unpaired natural image SR method, named as the CinCGAN [75], and an unsupervised SR method, named as ZSSR [73] are also included in the comparison. The paired SR methods are all trained based on the paired RRSSRD dataset. The unpaired SR methods are optimized on the synthetic unpaired dataset as mentioned in subsection a. All methods are evaluated on the synthetic test sets.

As shown in Table 6.4, we quantitatively evaluated the SR results using four metrics, including PSNR, SSIM, NIQE, and LPIPS, where the best result is labeled in bold and the second best result is underlined. As can be seen, our CPWSNN achieves the highest scores on almost all metrics. Besides this, there are visual and quantitative comparisons in Figure 6.12. The CNN-based methods including the SRCNN, EDSR, RRDBNet, and RCAN cannot reconstruct the rich details in the images and caused many artifacts. The GAN-based method ESRGAN mistakenly treats noise as high-frequency detail information and amplifies the noise and artifacts. The results of the ZSSR method suffer from serious noise. CinCGAN has relatively good visual effects, but causes color distortion. The visual results of our CPWSNN are the closest to HR images and have the highest scores for the quantitative metrics.

3) *Experiments on real unpaired remote-sensing images:* In these experiments, to test the above paired-based methods (i.e., SRCNN [71], EDSR [72], RRDBNet [56], RCAN [74], and ESRGAN [56]), we utilize the bicubic method to degrade the real HR to the LR and construct the paired

Table 6.4 Quantitative comparison with different methods on the synthetic test sets. For PSNR and SSIM, a higher score indicates a better result. Whereas for NIQE and LPIPS, a lower score indicates a better result. In each row, the best result is labeled in bold and the second-best result is underlined.

Dataset	Metric	SRCNN [71]	EDSR [72]	RRDBNet [56]	ESRGAN [56]	ZSSR [73]	RCAN [74]	CinCGAN [75]	CPWSNN [62]
Synthetic #1 test	PSNR	24.69	26.81	26.83	24.65	26.45	25.88	26.74	**28.09**
	SSIM	0.628	0.696	0.682	0.556	0.657	0.629	0.735	**0.739**
	NIQE	9.770	8.487	8.939	5.528	9.007	8.671	6.744	**3.720**
	LPIPS	0.522	0.546	0.542	0.503	0.674	0.583	0.433	**0.254**
Synthetic #2 test	PSNR	25.56	26.19	25.70	22.88	26.05	24.94	26.62	**27.83**
	SSIM	0.624	0.661	0.636	0.504	0.629	0.573	**0.715**	0.700
	NIQE	11.85	8.671	8.728	6.364	9.354	9.204	6.801	**3.647**
	LPIPS	0.754	0.625	0.619	0.584	0.746	0.666	0.456	**0.295**
Synthetic #3 test	PSNR	23.48	25.10	24.71	23.34	25.04	24.36	25.39	**26.12**
	SSIM	0.568	0.633	0.609	0.499	0.607	0.575	0.658	**0.664**
	NIQE	9.798	9.082	9.148	5.778	8.886	9.135	6.791	**3.610**
	LPIPS	0.637	0.654	0.639	0.497	0.766	0.661	0.494	**0.274**
Synthetic #4 test	PSNR	24.96	26.62	26.18	22.75	26.36	25.26	26.15	**28.11**
	SSIM	0.593	0.652	0.631	0.487	0.623	0.562	0.689	**0.697**
	NIQE	9.820	9.492	9.470	7.129	9.720	10.218	7.055	**3.983**
	LPIPS	0.605	0.635	0.627	0.596	0.747	0.664	0.459	**0.311**

training dataset. Since the real LR images have no corresponding ground truth images, we only utilize the NIQE metric to evaluate the SR performance, where the results are shown in Table 6.5. As can be observed, our CPWSNN is superior to all the other methods on the NIQE metric. Visual comparisons of different methods are illustrated in Figure 6.13. As can be seen, the SR results of the CNN-based methods, which are SRCNN, EDSR, RRDBNet, and RCAN, cannot produce much detail and suffer from blur. The GAN-based method ESRGAN has a better visual result but amplifies blocky artifacts. The results of the unsupervised method ZSSR have certain suppression effects on blocky artifacts, while the textures and details of the SR results are not obvious. CinCGAN has similar results with the CNN-based methods both in visual effects and the NIQE metric. Compared with other methods, the proposed CPWSNN has the best visual effects. For example, the edges and textures information are richer, and the objects can be seen more clearly in CPWSNN SR results.

4) *Ablation studies:* To further verify the effects of each loss to our method, we conducted ablation studies, including the perceptual loss in domain translation, the degradation consistency loss, and edge retention loss in SR training process.

   Studies of perceptual loss in domain translation: We conduct experiments with and without perceptual loss in the domain translation training process to validate the content-preserving effectiveness of the perceptual loss. Visual results are shown in Figure 6.14. It is obvious that the objects and color information of pseudo-LR images generated by domain translation without

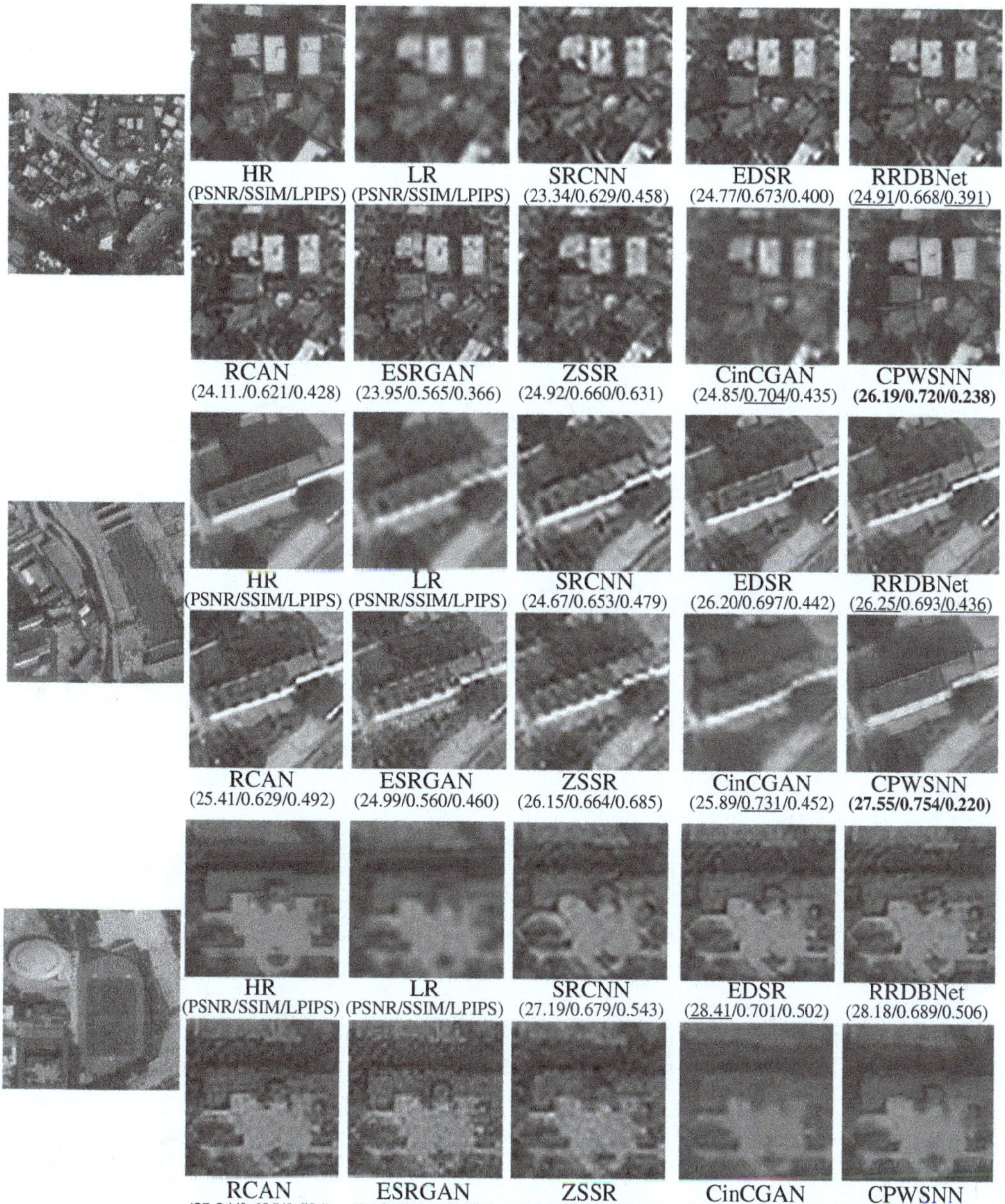

Figure 6.12 Experimental results on synthetic test sets. The results of the PSNR/SSIM/LPIPS of each SR image are presented. The best result is in bold. The second-best result is underlined [62] / with permission of Springer Nature.

perceptual loss are heavily changed. We can figure out that the perceptual loss has the strong ability to prevent objects deformation and color variation. Tables 6.6 and 6.7 show the quantitative comparison on SR results with respect to the use of the perceptual loss in domain translation based on synthetic LR images and real LR images, respectively. As can be seen in Tables 6.6 and 6.7, the performance is improved by adding the perceptual loss.

Table 6.5 NIQE metric comparison of different methods on real test sets. A lower score indicates a better result. The best results are in bold and the second-best results are underlined.

DATASET	SRCNN [71]	EDSR [72]	RRDBNet [56]	ESRGAN [56]	ZSSR [73]	RCAN [74]	CinCGAN [75]	CPWSNN [62]
Real #1 test	8.047	4.792	7.075	5.278	7.396	5.290	6.447	**3.895**
Real #2 test	9.206	5.691	7.775	5.128	7.434	6.161	6.943	**4.114**

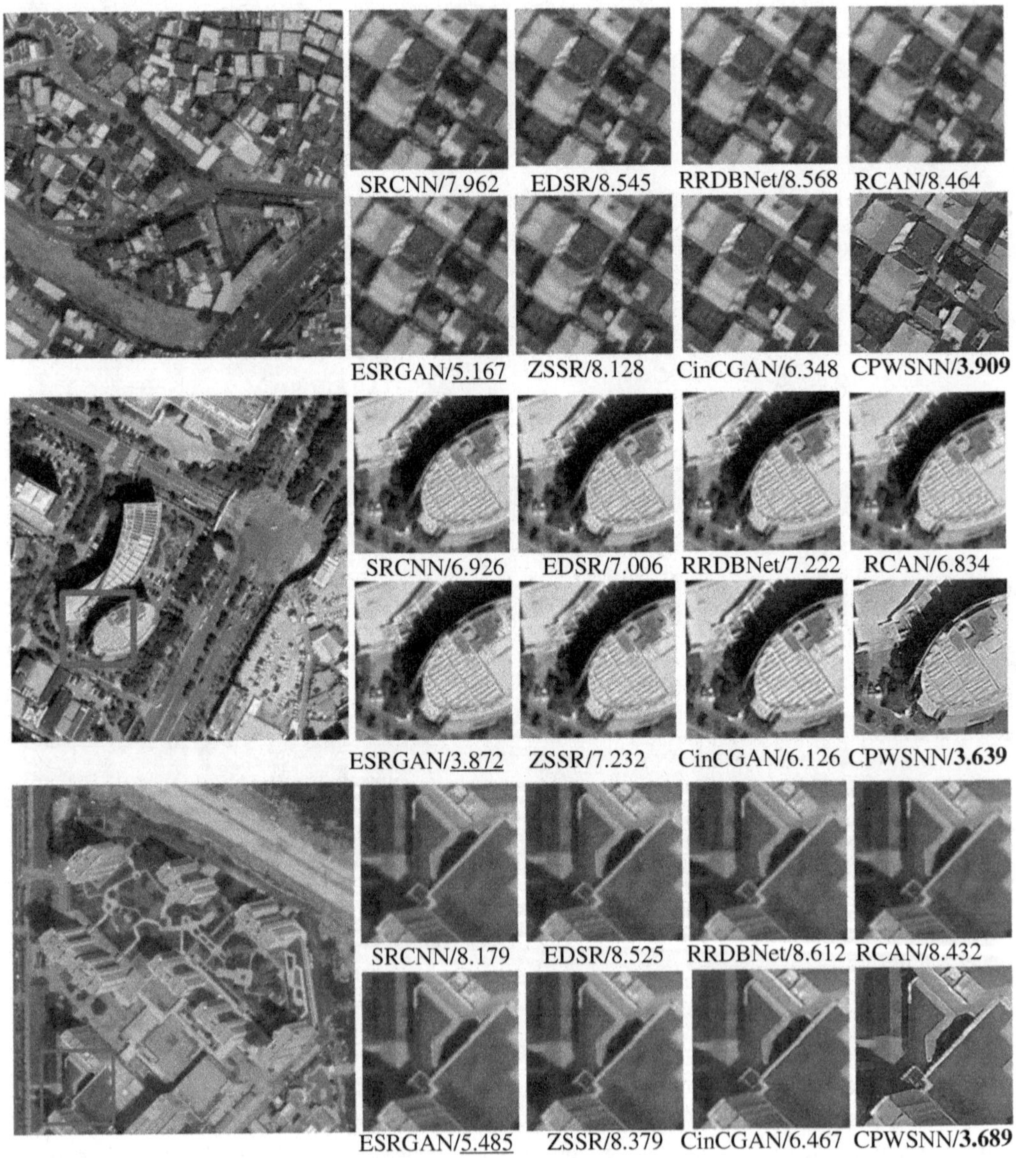

Figure 6.13 Experimental results on Real test sets consist of real LR remote-sensing images. The results of the NIQE of each SR image are presented. A lower score indicates better results [62] / with permission of Springer Nature.

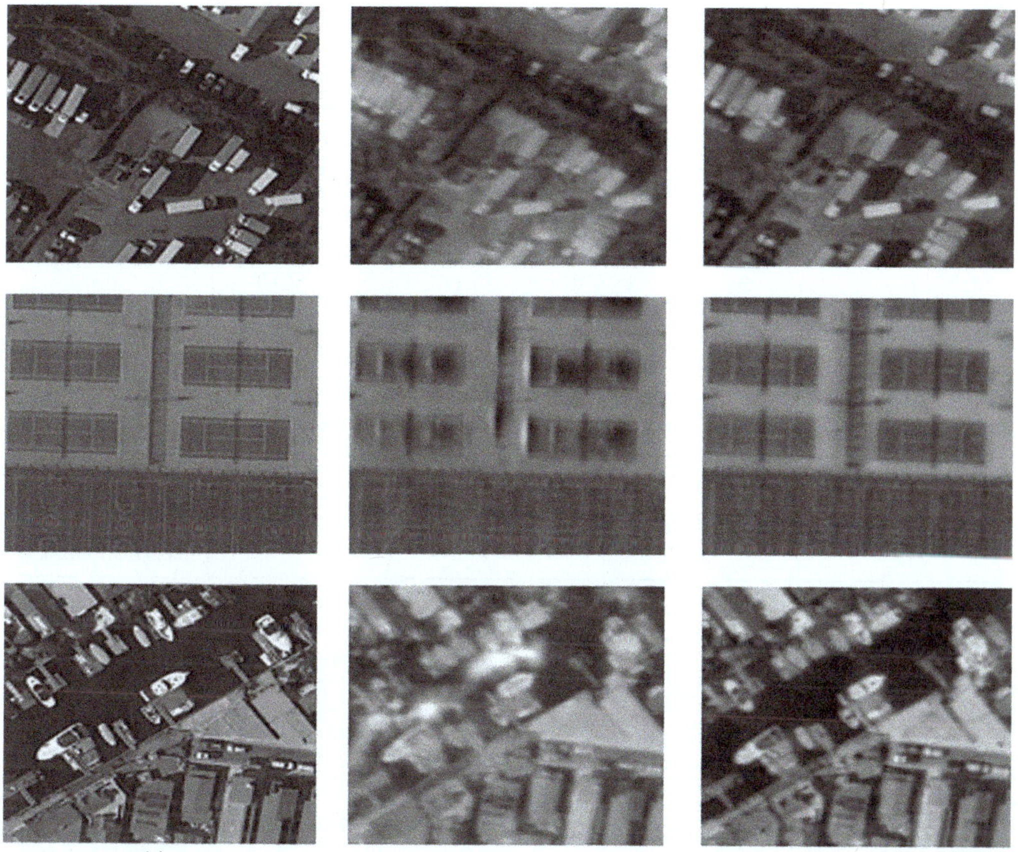

Figure 6.14 Visual effect of the perceptual loss in domain translation. (a) Real HR images (zoom in for best view), (b) pseudo-LR images generated by domain translation without perceptual loss, and (c) pseudo-LR images generated by domain translation with the perceptual loss [62] / with permission of Springer Nature.

Table 6.6 Quantitative comparison on SR results with respect to the use of the perceptual loss in domain translation based on synthetic test sets. The best results are in bold [62] / with permission of Springer Nature.

	Synthetic #1 test	Synthetic #2 test	Synthetic #3 test	Synthetic #4 test
Methods	PSNR/SSIM/LPIPS	PSNR/SSIM/LPIPS	PSNR/SSIM/LPIPS	PSNR/SSIM/LPIPS
Without perceptual loss	26.50/0.694/ 0.385	26.54/0.661/ 0.432	24.84/0.614/ 0.331	26.26/0.651/ 0.439
With perceptual loss	**28.09/0.739/ 0.247**	**27.83/0.701/ 0.295**	**26.21/0.664/ 0.266**	**28.11/0.696/ 0.313**

Studies on edge retention loss and degradation consistency loss in SR training process: We designed several experiments to study the effects of the edge retention loss and degradation consistency loss in the SR training process (without the edge retention loss and degradation consistency loss, without edge retention loss, and the full loss). Table 6.8 shows the quantitative comparisons of the SR network trained with different losses based on the synthetic #1 test set. The SR network trained with the full loss function has the best quantitative results in terms of the metrics of PSNR and LPIPS. Figure 6.15 shows the visual results on different loss functions

Table 6.7 NIQE metric comparison on SR results about the perceptual loss in the domain translation based on real test sets. The best results are in bold [62] / with permission of Springer Nature.

Method/test set	Real #1 test	Real #2 test
Without perceptual loss	4.659	4.939
With perceptual loss	**3.895**	**4.114**

Table 6.8 Quantitative comparison of SR network trained with different loss based on the real #1 test set [62] / with permission of Springer Nature.

MAE loss and adversarial loss	Edge retention loss	Degradation consistency loss	PSNR/SSIM/LPIPS
✓	×	×	21.28/0.601/0.432
✓	×	✓	23.58/0.593/0.385
✓	✓	✓	**28.09/0.739/0.254**

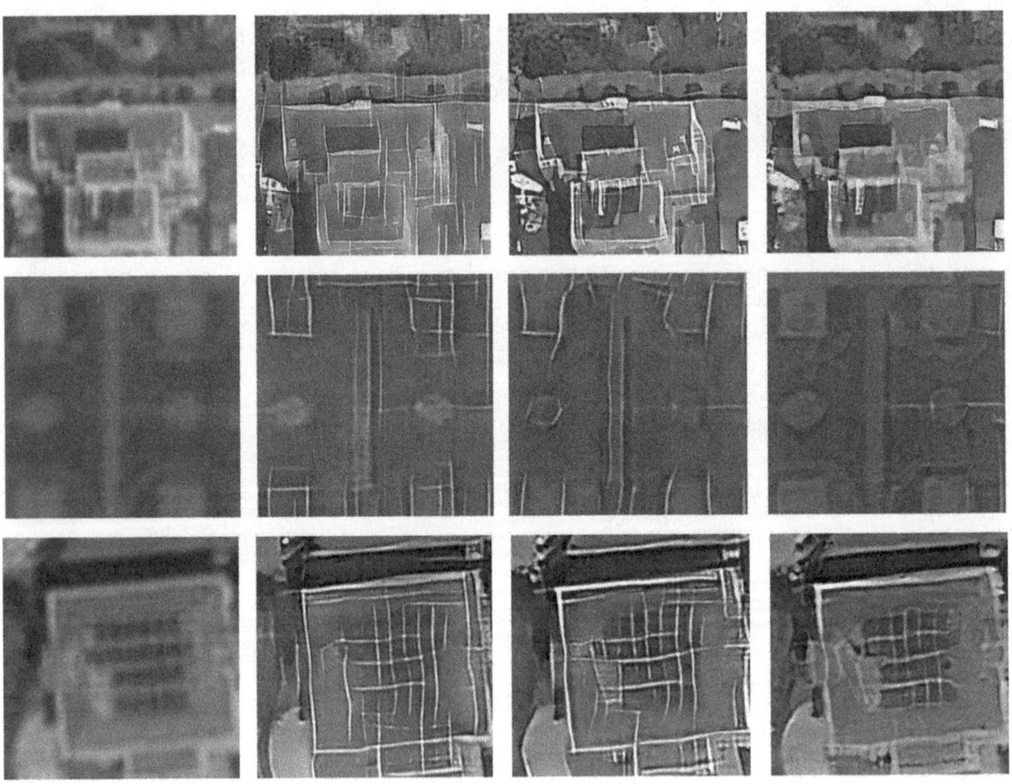

(a) (b) (c) (d)

Figure 6.15 Visual comparison on SR network trained with different loss based on real test sets. (a) LR, (b) SR result without L_{edge} and L_{de}, (c) SR result without L_{edge}, and (d) SR result full loss [62] / with permission of Springer Nature.

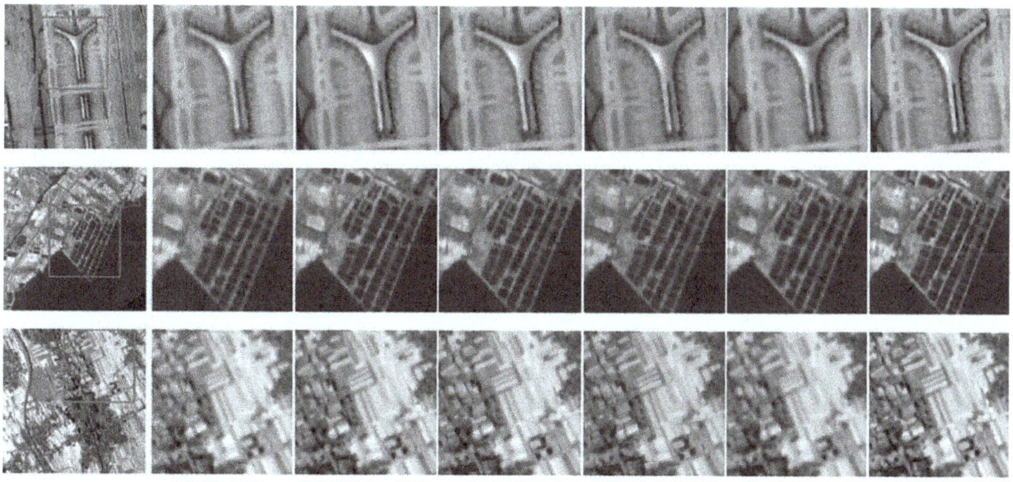

Figure 6.16 Experimental results on TG1HRS dataset. We show the third band.

on real test sets. The SR network trained without edge retention loss and degradation consistency loss generate artificial results with color variation and unreal objects. By adding the degradation consistency loss, the color variation issue can be suppressed, but the SR results still have artificial edges. When the edge retention loss is further adopted, the generation of fake edges and textures can be prevented. Figure 6.15d indicates that the degradation consistency loss and edge retention loss can provide constraints for the SR network to avoid generating unreal objects, color variation, unreal edges, and other content distortion issues.

5) *Experimental results on HSI SR:* In this section, the proposed CPWSNN is adopted for HSI SR on the Tiangong-1 hyperspectral remote-sensing (TG1HRS) dataset. The TG1HRS dataset consists of 204 HSIs, each of which contains one band of the full spectrum with a spatial resolution of 5 m, 54 bands of the visible and near-infrared spectrum with a spatial resolution of 10 m, and 52 bands of the short-wave infrared spectrum with a spatial resolution of 20 m. The visible and near-infrared bands and short-wave infrared bands are thought as HR images and LR images, respectively. Because no ground truth can be obtained for the evaluation of the experiments, only visual results can be observed. In Figure 6.16, the third band of some images in the TG1HRS dataset is shown, where images predicted by the CPWSNN have more regular and sharp transitions at the edge region compared with images predicted by other methods.

6.4 Self-supervised HSI SR

A novel user-friendly HSI and MSI fusion method is introduced, integrated with a blind deep self-supervised image prior. By leveraging two characteristics of eigenimages, the E2E-fusion framework is proposed for HSI and MSI fusion through a plug-and-play (PnP) technique with the use of deep self-supervised prior.

6.4.1 Problem Formulation

Let a third-order tensor $\mathcal{Y}_h \in \mathbb{R}^{n_{row} \times n_{col} \times L}$ denote an LR-HSI with n spectral vectors and L spectral bands, acquired by a hyperspectral sensor. Assuming that the noise in the image follows a Gaussian distribution, the observed LR-HSI can be written as follows:

$$\mathcal{Y}_h = \mathcal{X}_h + \mathcal{N}_h, \tag{6.24}$$

where $\mathcal{X}_h \in \mathbb{R}^{n_{row} \times n_{col} \times L}$, $\mathcal{N}_h \in \mathbb{R}^{n_{row} \times n_{col} \times L}$ denote the clean LR-HSI cube, and the corresponding white Gaussian noise cube, respectively.

The HR-MSI is acquired by a multispectral sensor, which can also be expressed as the third-order tensor data, i.e., $\mathcal{Y}_m \in \mathbb{R}^{N_{row} \times N_{col} \times l}$, with the size of $N_{row} \times N_{col}$ and l spectral bands. Assuming that the noise in the image follows a Gaussian distribution, the observed HR-MSI can be defined as follows:

$$\mathcal{Y}_m = \mathcal{X}_m + \mathcal{N}_m, \tag{6.25}$$

where $\mathcal{X}_m \in \mathbb{R}^{N_{row} \times N_{col} \times l}$, $\mathcal{N}_m \in \mathbb{R}^{N_{row} \times N_{col} \times l}$ denote the clean HR-MSI cube and the corresponding white Gaussian noise cube, respectively.

Our aim is to obtain an HR-HSI, $\mathbf{Z} \in \mathbb{R}^{N_{row} \times N_{col} \times L}$, by making full use of the spectral information of LR-MSI and the spatial information of HR-MSI in the same scene simultaneously. In this section, we unfold the data cubes of LR-HSI, HR-MSI, and HR-HSI into matrix format along the spectral dimension, termed $\mathbf{Y}_h \in \mathbb{R}^{L \times n}$, $\mathbf{Y}_m \in \mathbb{R}^{l \times N}$, and $\mathbf{Z} \in \mathbb{R}^{L \times N}$, respectively. LR-HSI can be regarded as a reduced quality representation of HR-HSI in the spatial dimension; hence, the LR-HSI can be expressed as follows:

$$\mathbf{Y}_h = \mathbf{ZBS} + \mathbf{N}_h, \tag{6.26}$$

where $\mathbf{B} \in \mathbb{R}^{N_{row}N_{col} \times N_{row}N_{col}}$ is a spatial blurring operator of $\mathbf{Z}$, and represents the hyperspectral sensor's PSF. Matrices $\mathbf{S} \in \mathbb{R}^{N_{row}N_{col} \times n_{row}n_{col}}$ and $\mathbf{N}_h \in \mathbb{R}^{L \times n_{row}n_{col}}$ are the spatial sub-sampler and additive Gaussian noise, respectively. The blurring operator $\mathbf{B}$ is detailed as follows:

$$\mathbf{B} = \mathbf{FKF}^{-1}, \tag{6.27}$$

where $\mathbf{F}$ and $\mathbf{F}^{-1}$ represent the fast Fourier transform (FFT) and its inverse transformation. K is a diagonal matrix that holds the eigenvalues of the matrix $\mathbf{B}$.

Accordingly, the HR-MSI can be regarded as a downsampled version of the HR-HSI in spectral dimension, which can be represented as follows:

$$\mathbf{Y}_m = \mathbf{MZ} + \mathbf{N}_m, \tag{6.28}$$

where $\mathbf{M} \in \mathbb{R}^{l \times L}$ and $\mathbf{N}_m \in \mathbb{R}^{l \times N_{row}N_{col}}$ are the spectral response function and the white Gaussian noise, respectively.

We assume that spectral vectors of LR-HSIs live in a low-dimensional subspace because of the strong correlation among the bands [76–79]. The subspace representation of HSIs has been widely used in HSI processing fields and has shown promising results [80]. Hence, HR-HSI, $\mathcal{Z} \in \mathbb{R}^{N_{row} \times N_{col} \times L}$, can be also represented into a low-dimensional subspace. Based on the subspace theory, the $\mathbf{Z}$ can be expressed as follows:

$$\mathbf{Z} = \mathbf{CA}, \tag{6.29}$$

where columns of $\mathbf{C} \in \mathbb{R}^{L \times p}(p \ll L)$ hold an orthogonal basis for the p-dimensional subspace and $\mathbf{C}^T\mathbf{C} = \mathbf{I}_k$ with $\mathbf{I}_k$ representing the identity matrix of dimension k. Matrix $\mathbf{A} \in \mathbb{R}^{p \times N_{row}N_{col}}$ holds the representation coefficients of $\mathbf{O}$ with respect to $\mathbf{C}$ and we will call the images associated with rows of

A as *eigenimages*. Furthermore, the dimension of the subspace, p, is much smaller than L. As the LR-HSI can be regarded as a downsampled version of an HR-HSI in the spatial domain, we assume that the LR-HSI and HR-HSI share the same subspace **C** [30, 81].

Hence, the spectral subspace of **C** can be estimated via eigendecomposition of the spectral correlation matrix (denoted as $\mathbf{R}_y = \mathbf{Y}_h\mathbf{Y}_h^T/(n_{row}n_{col})$) of the LR-HSI:

$$\mathbf{R}_y = \mathbf{U}\mathbf{\Sigma}^2\mathbf{U}^T, \tag{6.30}$$

where **U** and **Σ** are eigenvector and eigenvalue matrices of the correlation matrix $\mathbf{R}_y$, respectively. The eigenvalues in diagonal matrix $\mathbf{\Sigma}^2$ are ordered by non-increasing magnitude. The spectral subspace is approximately spanned by p eigenvectors associated with the p largest eigenvalues, i.e.,

$$\mathbf{C} = \mathbf{U}(:,1:p). \tag{6.31}$$

Using subspace representation of spectral vectors, observation models of LR-HSI and HS-MSI can be re-formulated as:

$$\mathbf{Y}_h = \mathbf{CABS} + \mathbf{N}_h, \tag{6.32}$$

and

$$\mathbf{Y}_m = \mathbf{MCA} + \mathbf{N}_m. \tag{6.33}$$

6.4.2 Fusion Method: E2E-fusion

Given the spectral subspace **C**, the fusion of the LR-HSI and HR-HSI can be formulated as follows:

$$\min_A \frac{1}{2}\|\mathbf{Y}_h - \mathbf{CABS}\|_F^2 + \frac{\lambda_1}{2}\|\mathbf{Y}_m - \mathbf{MCA}\|_F^2 + \lambda_2\phi_{E2E}(\mathbf{A}), \tag{6.34}$$

where first two terms are data-fidelity derived from observation models Eqs. (6.32) and (6.33), respectively. Non-negative parameter λ_1 models the noise intensity difference between two images in terms of Frobenius norm. Symbol λ_2 is non-negative regularization parameter, whose setting depends on the noise intensity of **A**. The function $\phi_{E2E}(\cdot)$ represents an image prior extracted from an Eigenimage2Eigenimage (E2E) network. The prior information of the **A** has been exploited for LR-HSI and HR-MSI images fusion. Different image priors (such as sparsity, total variation, and low-rank priors) have been used on **A** to improve the accuracy of the coefficient estimation [47, 81]. In this section, we propose a new self-supervised deep learning image prior, E2E, to estimate the coefficient **A**. The flowchart of the proposed fusion method is illustrated in Figure 6.17.

We solve the objective function Eq. (6.34) via the ADMM. By introducing a multiple auxiliary variable **V**, the augmented Lagrangian function of Eq. (6.34) is

$$L(\mathbf{A},\mathbf{V},\mathbf{G}) = \frac{1}{2}\|\mathbf{Y}_h - \mathbf{CABS}\|_F^2 + \frac{\lambda_1}{2}\|\mathbf{Y}_m - \mathbf{MCA}\|_F^2 + \lambda_2\phi_{E2E}(\mathbf{V}) + \frac{\mu}{2}\left\|\mathbf{V} - \mathbf{A} + \frac{\mathbf{G}}{\mu}\right\|_F^2, \tag{6.35}$$

where **G** is the Lagrange multiplier and μ is the penalty parameter. The variables **A**,**V**, and **G** are updated sequentially, and these steps are shown in Algorithm 6.1. The optimization details of the loss function are as given in the following.

Update **A**: The optimization problem for **A** is

$$\mathbf{A} = \arg\min_A \frac{1}{2}\|\mathbf{Y}_h - \mathbf{CABS}\|_F^2 + \frac{\lambda_1}{2}\|\mathbf{Y}_m - \mathbf{MCA}\|_F^2 + \frac{\mu}{2}\left\|\mathbf{V} - \mathbf{A} + \frac{\mathbf{G}}{\mu}\right\|_F^2, \tag{6.36}$$

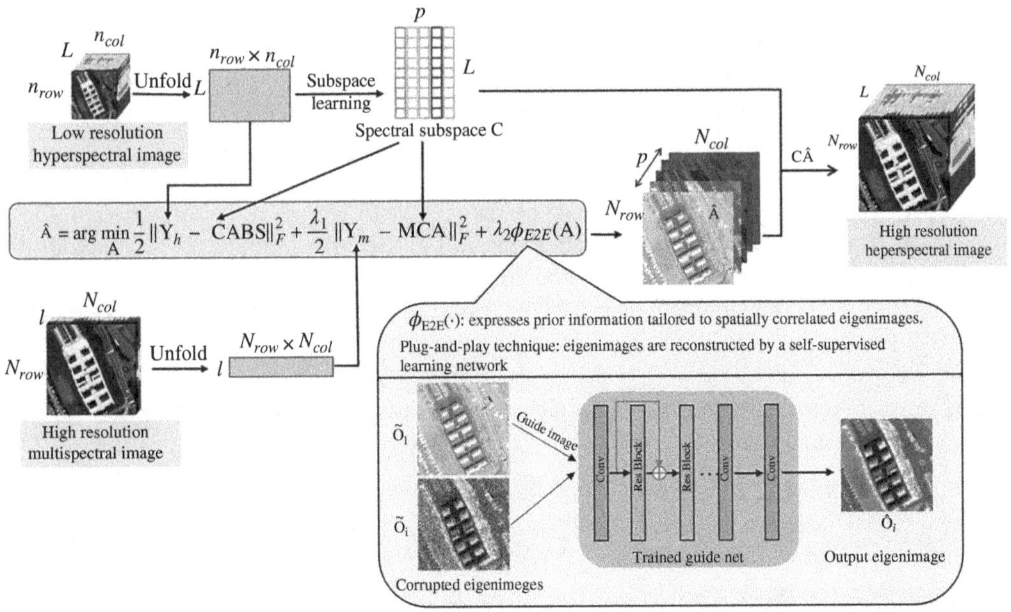

Figure 6.17 Flowchart of the proposed fusion framework, E2E-fusion [82] / with permission of IEEE.

which is strongly convex. Let the derivative of Eq. (6.36) with respect to A to be 0, then, we acquire the Sylvester equation (see [83] for more details) as follows:

$$\mathbf{H}_1\mathbf{A} + \mathbf{A}\mathbf{H}_2 = \mathbf{H}_3, \tag{6.37}$$

where

$$\mathbf{H}_1 = \mu(\mathbf{MC})^T\mathbf{MC} + \mu\mathbf{I}, \tag{6.38}$$

$$\mathbf{H}_2 = \mathbf{BS}(\mathbf{BS})^T, \tag{6.39}$$

$$\mathbf{H}_3 = \mathbf{C}^T\mathbf{Y}_h(\mathbf{BS})^T + \lambda_1(\mathbf{MC})^T\mathbf{Y}_m + \mu\left(\mathbf{V} + \frac{\mathbf{G}}{\mu}\right), \tag{6.40}$$

Update $\mathbf{V}$: The optimization problem for $\boldsymbol{V}$ is

$$\begin{aligned}\mathbf{V} &= \arg\min_{V} \frac{\mu}{2}\left\|\mathbf{V} - \mathbf{A} + \frac{\mathbf{G}}{\mu}\right\|_F^2 + \lambda_2\phi_{E2E}(\mathbf{V}) \\ &= \psi_{\lambda\phi_{\mathrm{E2E}}}\left(\mathbf{A} - \frac{\mathbf{G}}{\mu}\right),\end{aligned} \tag{6.41}$$

where $\psi_{\lambda\phi_{\mathrm{E2E}}}(\cdot)$ is the so-called Moreau proximity operator or deoising operator [84] of ϕ_{E2E}. We solve Eq. (6.41) using PnP technique. The core idea of PnP is to plug an off-the-shelf denoiser into the framework instead of investing effort in designing a new regularizer. In this section, we plug a blind self-supervised deep learning network, E2E [85], into Eq. (6.41), leading to

$$\mathbf{V} \leftarrow \mathrm{E2E}\left(\mathbf{A} - \frac{\mathbf{G}}{\mu}\right), \tag{6.42}$$

where the function E2E(·) outputs denoised eigenimages. A detailed description of the E2E network is given in Section 5.3.

Update **G**: The optimization problem for **G** is

$$\mathbf{G} = \mathbf{G} + \mu(\mathbf{V} - \mathbf{A}). \tag{6.43}$$

Algorithm 6.1 The Proposed E2E-fusion Algorithm

Input: Y_h, Y_m
1: **for** $k = 1$, $k < Iter$, k++ **do**
2: Update **A** via (37)
3: Update **V** via (42)
4: Update **G** via (43)
5: $k = k + 1$;
6: **end for**
7. **Z** - **CA**;
Output: Z

6.4.3 Plugged Self-supervised Deep Learning Prior: E2E

The PnP trick enables us to directly use eigenimage priors extracted from deep denoising neural networks. However, the performance of deep learning-based denoisers highly depends on the quantity and quality of training data. Furthermore, paired noisy–clean training eigenimages are generally unavailable in hyperspectral remote-sensing areas. To solve this problem, this work resorts to the self-supervised learning technique, meaning our network can train itself to learn one part of noisy input from another part of the noisy input.

Here, we propose a self-supervised deep image prior, termed E2E. This E2E prior explores two main characteristics of eigenimage data. First, neighboring pixels in eigenimages T are highly correlated; therefore, we can generate two noisy paired subimages from a single noisy image for network training. The highly correlated property of eigenimages can be illustrated using a toy example, and one of the interdisciplinary computational vision laboratory (ICVL) images of size 256 × 256 pixels was carried out. Figure 6.18 briefly shows the high correlation between neighboring pixels in the first band of the eigenimage. Figure 6.18a shows the first band of eigenimage. Correlation coefficients of two horizontal, vertical, and adjacent diagonal pixels in the eigenimage are 0.8912, 0.8855, and 0.8280, respectively (shown in Figure 6.18b–d). In this section, we further study the high quality of the first eigenimage. More specifically, the first band of eigenimages learned from a noisy HSI has a much higher SNR than the remaining eigenimages, which can be used as a guide image to denoise of remaining eigenimages. The high quality of the first eigenimage can be illustrated using an example. The Washington DC Mall data with the size of 304 × 304 × 191, and the Indian Pines data with the size of 144 × 144 × 191 were used to show the characteristics of the eigenimages. We first project these two data into the low dimensional subspace, and the number of subspaces, p, is set as 6. Figures 6.19a–f and 6.20a–f display the eigenimages in order. It is evident that the first eigenimage in both datasets exhibits high visual quality. What stands out in Figures 6.19g and 6.20g are the rapid decrease of the eigenimages in terms of PSNR, and the first eigenimage has a much higher PSNR than the remaining eigenimages on both of two datasets.

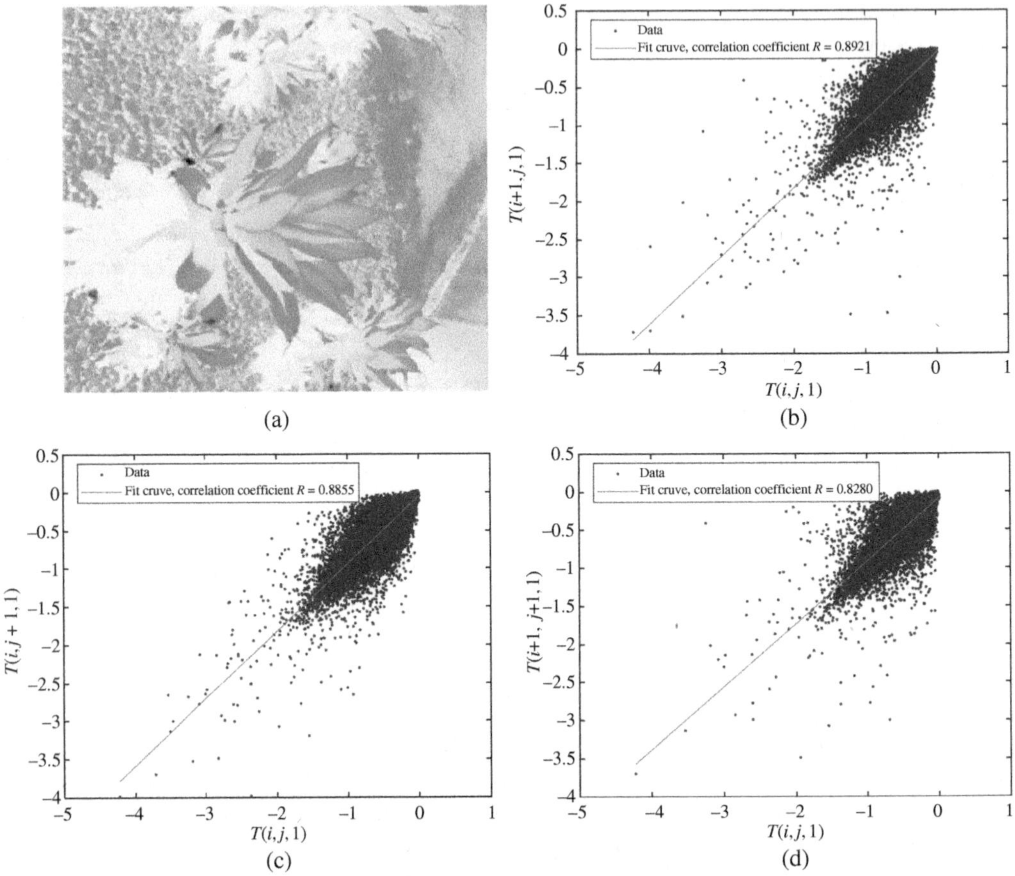

Figure 6.18 ICVL image. (a) First eigenimage and (b–d) correlation of two vertical, horizontal, and diagonal adjacent pixels in the first eigenimage [82] / with permission of IEEE.

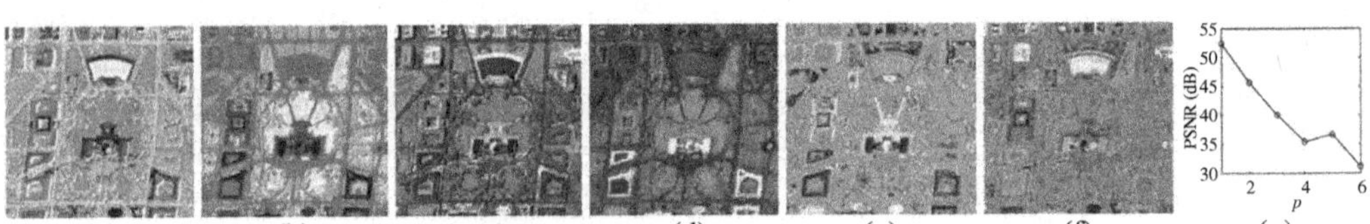

Figure 6.19 Washington DC image. (a–f) One to six eigenimages and (g) PSNR of each eigenimage [82] / with permission of IEEE.

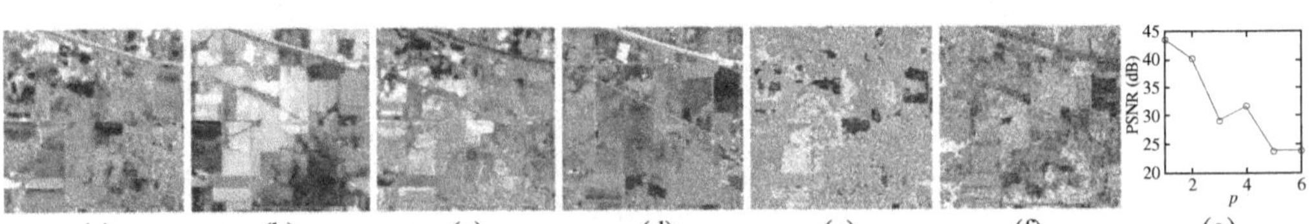

Figure 6.20 Indian Pines image. (a–f) One to six eigenimages and (g) PSNR of each eigenimage [82] with permission of IEEE.

Hence, based on the phenomenon that the first band of eigenimages has higher quality, we will use it as the guide image to assist in the denoising of other eigenimages.

To use the proposed E2E self-supervised deep prior, we reformulate the matrix $\left(\mathbf{A} - \frac{\mathbf{G}}{\mu}\right)$ into a third tensor, denoted as $\tilde{\mathcal{O}} \in \mathbb{R}^{N_{row} \times N_{col} \times p}$. For simplicity, let o_i represent the ith eigenimage, i.e., the i-th mode-3 slice of $\tilde{\mathcal{O}}$. Hence, the solution of Eq. (6.41) can be reformulated as follows:

$$\mathbf{V}(i,\ :) \leftarrow \text{reshape}(f_\theta(\text{cat}(o_1, o_i)), \quad [1, N_{row} \times N_{col}]), \quad (i = 1, \ldots, p), \tag{6.44}$$

where function reshape($\mathbf{R}$, $[1, N]$) reshapes matrix $\mathbf{R}$ into a $1 \times N$ vector. By exploiting the above two characteristics of eigenimage data, we propose a self-supervised learning eigenimage network:

$$o_i = f_\theta(\text{cat}(o_1, o_i)), \quad (i = 1, 2, \ldots, p), \tag{6.45}$$

where f_θ is the denoising network parameterized by θ, function cat($\mathbf{A}$, $\mathbf{B}$) concatenates matrix $\mathbf{B}$ to the end of matrix $\mathbf{A}$ along dimension 3, and $o_i := \tilde{O}(:\,,\ :\,, i)$ represents ith corrupted eigenimage and o_i represents an estimation of i-th eigenimage. Here, o_1 serves as a guide image in the network as it contains high-quality spatial information. We guide our network using the first eigenimage, so that the network can learn structured information from the first eigenimage. As the scene across different eigenimages is the same, the structured learned information can help to build a denoising network for other eigenimages.

The training part of our E2E framework is introduced below. Considering the fact that collecting a large amount of aligned noisy–clean training data is challenging in the hyperspectral remote-sensing areas, we generate training eigenimage pairs from single noisy eigenimages using random neighbor sub-samplers defined in [86]. Figure 6.21 gives a toy example of generating an image pair with a neighbor sub-sampler $G = (g_1, g_2)$. Basically, the neighbor sub-sampler enables us to split a single noisy eigenimage into two noisy sub-eigenimages. More specifically, the sub-sampler randomly selects two adjacent elements in a 2×2 window and assigns them to two subimages. Meanwhile, we only consider horizontal and vertical adjacent pixels because the correlation coefficients of horizontal and vertical adjacent pixels are larger than diagonal adjacent pixels (shown in Figure 6.18).

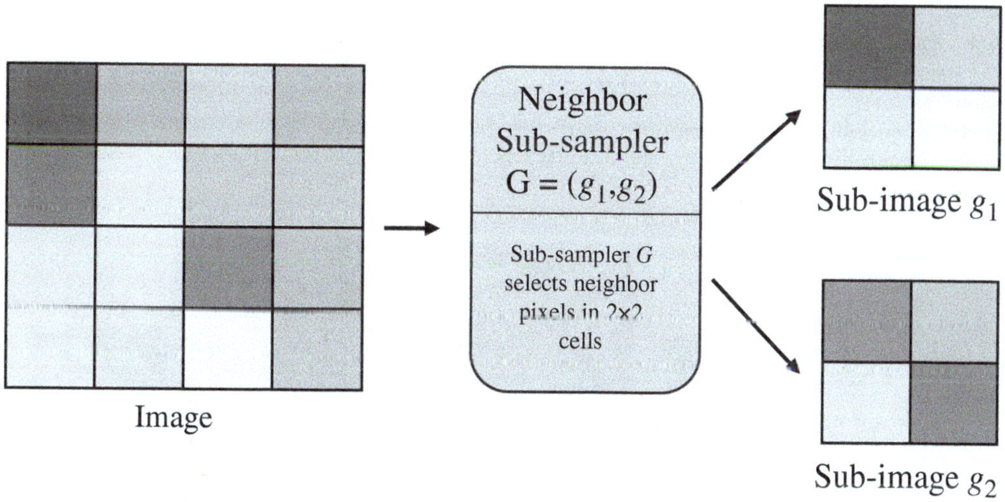

Figure 6.21 A toy example of generating an image pair with a neighbor sub-sampler $G = (g_1, g_2)$. [82] / with permission of IEEE.

After generating sampled image pairs, we can train a network with aligned pairwise noisy–noisy eigenimages:

$$\arg\min_{\theta} \sum_{i} \mathbb{E}_{(o_1,o_i)} \| f_\theta(\text{cat}(g_1(o_1), g_1(o_i))) - g_2(o_i) \|_F^2, \tag{6.46}$$

where $(g_1(o_i), g_2(o_i))$ is a training pair of noisy–noisy eigenimages.

The sampled images are closely resembled, because their pixels are adjacent in the same noisy source image. However, the underlying clean versions of two sampled images usually differ slightly, implying the denoising result of the network optimized by Eq. (6.46) may be over-smooth [86]. To mitigate this over-smoothness, the slight difference between sampled pairs is included in the loss function by adding a constraint below.

By introducing the image difference into Eq. (6.46), we consider the following constrained optimization problem for E2E framework:

$$\begin{aligned} \min_{\theta} \quad & \sum_{i} \mathbb{E}_{(o_1,o_i)} \| f_\theta(\text{cat}(g_1(o_1), g_1(o_i))) - g_2(o_i) \|_F^2 \\ & + \gamma \mathbb{E}_{(o_1,o_i)} \| f_\theta(\text{cat}(g_1(o_1), g_1(o_i))) - g_2(o_i) \\ & - (g_1(f_\theta(\text{cat}(o_1, o_i))) - g_2(f_\theta(\text{cat}(o_1, o_i)))) \|_F^2, \end{aligned} \tag{6.47}$$

where γ is a nonnegative parameter. Compared with the training loss of [86], one can see that in our training loss Eq. (6.47), our network input data is a two-band-image (instead of a single-band-image in [86]). Our eigenimage denoising network explores the characteristic of the first eigenimage data, which is high quality with high SNRs. Hence, we can use the first eigenimage (corresponding to the largest eigenvalue) as an auxiliary input and design an eigenimage-guided network. Ablation experiments demonstrate that the use of guide eigenimage does improve fusion performance significantly.

We estimate eigenimages $\hat{\mathbf{A}}$ by solving Eq. (6.34). Meanwhile, the subspace basis, $\mathbf{C}$, is obtained by implementing eigendecomposition of the spectral correlation matrix of the LR-HSI. By multiplying $\hat{\mathbf{A}}$ and $\mathbf{C}$ together, then we obtain the HR-HSI, $\hat{\mathbf{Z}}$.

$$\hat{\mathbf{Z}} = \mathbf{C}\hat{\mathbf{A}}. \tag{6.48}$$

6.4.4 Experiments

In this section, we test the effectiveness of the proposed E2E-fusion method on four simulated datasets and a real dataset, respectively (see Figure 6.22 for more details). Meanwhile, we compare with several state-of-the-art methods and analyze the fusion results of all methods visually and quantitatively.

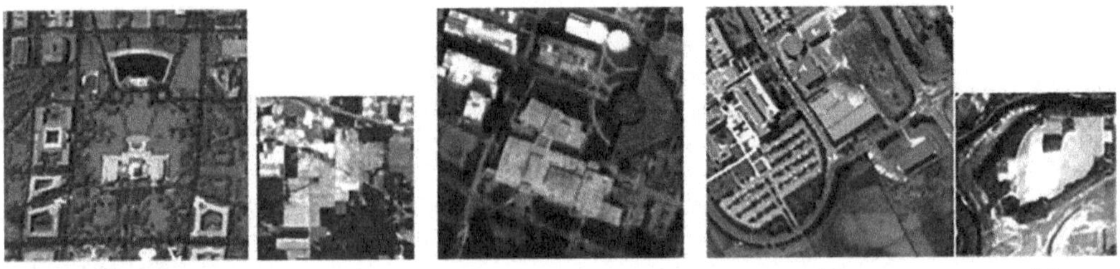

(a) (b) (c) (d) (e)

Figure 6.22 HSIs used in the experiments. (a) Subimage of Washington DC Mall data, (b) Indian Pines, (c) subregion of the University of Houston data, (d) subregion of the Pavia University, and (e) sentinel-2A data [82] / with permission of IEEE.

1) *Experimental Datasets:* In the study, all simulated datasets were synthesized via a similar method mentioned in [87, 88]. More specifically, an LR-HSI is synthesized by applying a Gaussian filter with standard deviation 2 [30] on an HR-HSI, and the size of the Gaussian kernel is kept the same with the downsampling ratio. An HR-MSI is generated by using the spectral response function from visible to shortwave infrared (SWIR) bands of Landsat 8 [89, 90]. The downsampling ratio is set to 8 for the Washington DC Mall and the University of Houston data, and 4 for the Indian Pines and Pavia data. Zero-mean Gaussian white noise was added to clean LR-HSIs and HR-MSIs, yielding a series of noisy images with signal-to-noise ratios (SNRs) 35 dB, and 30 dB, respectively.

   The first simulated dataset (i.e., Washington DC Mall) was widely used in HSI analysis [76, 78, 91]. It was acquired by the HYDICE sensor in 1995 in Washington DC, United States. This full Washington DC Mall image has a region of 1280 × 307 pixels, and the spatial resolution is 3 m. The image consists of 210 bands, and spectral wavelength is ranging from 0.4 to 2.5 μm. After removing the low SNRs and atmospheric absorption bands, 191 bands were kept. The subregion consisting of 304 × 304 × 191 pixels was clipped from the full dataset as a reference HR-HSI (see Figure 6.22a).

   The second dataset (i.e., Indian Pines) was acquired by the AVIRIS sensor over the Indian Pines test site in Northwestern Indian. The image has 224 spectral bands with the size of 145 × 145 pixels, and the spectral wavelength range is from 0.4 to 2.5 μm. After removing bands caused by water vapor absorption and low SNRs, the subregion consisting of 144 × 144 × 191 pixels was chosen from the full dataset as a reference HR-HSI (see Figure 6.22b).

   The third dataset is University of Houston data, which was used in the 2018 IEEE Geoscience and Remote Sensing Society (GRSS) Data Fusion Contest [92]. The image contains 601 × 2384 pixels and 48 bands ranging from 0.38 to 1.05 μm. The subimage consisting of 320 × 320 × 46 pixels was chosen from the whole dataset as a reference HR-HSI for our experiments (see Figure 6.22c).

   The fourth Pavia University data was collected by the ROSIS-3 optical airborne sensor. This image contains 115 bands and with the size of 610 × 340 × 115. After removing bands caused by water vapor absorption and low SNRs, the subregion consisting of 304 × 304 × 191 pixels was clipped from the full dataset as a reference HR-HSI in this study (see Figure 22d).
2) *Implementation Details of E2E-fusion:* The proposed E2E-fusion method is based on a PnP framework, and a ResNet [63] network architecture is used for training the deep PnP prior. More specifically, Figure 6.23 displays the proposed network structure in detail. In this study, the network structure includes two basic units: convolution layer and nonlinear activation layer. The $\mathcal{F}_{\theta E2E}$ is the proposed eigenimage-guided network, which contains R blocks by using two convolution layers and a rectified linear unit (Conv + ReLU + Conv), and the number of kernels

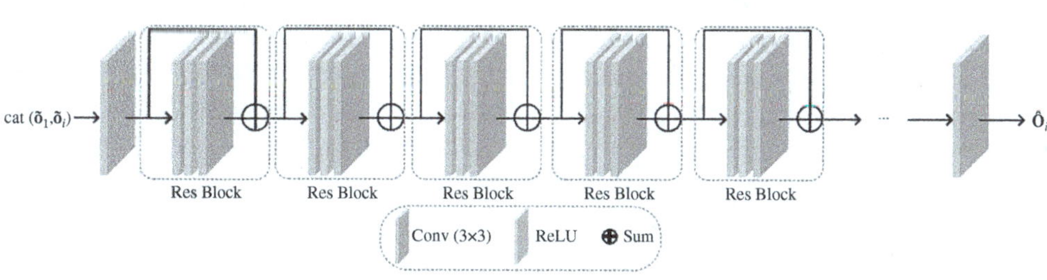

Figure 6.23 Details of the proposed guidance network prior, $\mathcal{F}_{\theta E2E}$ [82] / with permission of IEEE.

and the size were set as 64 and 3×3, respectively. Meanwhile, for each block, pixel-wise sum was used for aggregating input feature maps and output feature maps. The ICVL hyperspectral dataset [93] was used to train the ResNet network, which was acquired by ground-based cameras with high SNR. Thus, we simulated noisy HSIs by adding independent Gaussian noise into the original ICVL images. Let $n_i \in \mathbb{R}^b$ denote noise vector of the ith spectral pixel. We simulated pixelwise and bandwise independent Gaussian noise: $n_i \sim \mathcal{G}(0, \mathbf{D}^2)$, where $\mathcal{G}$ is a zero-mean Gaussian distribution and $\mathbf{D}$ is a diagonal matrix with diagonal elements $d_{ii} = \alpha\text{median}(X(:, :, i))$. We set $\alpha = 0.12$. We set the noise intensity of each band according to the median value per band, so that images with diverse noise intensities can be used to train a flexible denoising network. The network training was conducted on the framework of PyTorch. More specifically, the patch size of the image and the batch size are set to 64 and 16, respectively. The initial learning rate of the network is 0.0003 and half-decayed per 20 epochs, and the number of training epochs is 100. The Adam optimizer is chosen for training the network, and the loss function and the value of the hyperparameter in it keep the same value as in Neighbor2Neighbor [86].

3) *Compared Methods:* We compare the proposed method with several state-of-the-art fusion methods, including the generalized Laplacian pyramid hypersharpening (GLPHS) method [94], coupled nonnegative matrix factorization (CNMF) [10], Hyperspectral superresolution (HySure) method [81], and CNN-Fus [30]. It is mentioned that GLPHS, CNMF, HySure, CNN-Fus, and E2E-fusion methods were tested in MATLAB R2022a on Windows 11 with 12GB RAM. A demo of Matlab version for the proposed E2E-fusion method will be released at http://github.com/LinaZhuang. The parameters in all compared methods (GLPHS, CNMF, HySure, and CNN-Fus) were fine-turned to get the optimal results manually in all experiments. For a fair comparison, the dimension of spectral subspace, p, was set to the same value in the CNN-Fus method and E2E-fusion method.
4) *Quantitative Indexes:* We use five well-known metrics to evaluate the image fusion quality numerically when the reference image is available. They are the mean peak SNR (MPSNR) index, the mean structural similarity (MSSIM) index, the mean feature similarity (MFSIM) index, the SAM index, and the ERGAS index.
5) *Parameter analysis of proposed E2E-fusion:* The dimension of subspace, p, is a crucial parameter, which will influence the fusion results. To test the effect of p, we plot the fusion performance of our method with various of p on four simulated datasets in terms of MPSNR (shown in Figure 6.24). It is clear that the fusion results keep a relatively stable value on the Indian Pines image and University of Houston image as p changes. The performance of Pavia University decreased gradually when the p is larger than 7, and the fusion result decreased sharply on the Washington DC Mall. Therefore, the dimension of subspace, p, should be chosen carefully to obtain the best fusion results.
6) *Experimental Results on Simulated Datasets:* The fusion performance of all methods on four synthesized datasets in terms of MPSNR, MSSIM, MFSIM, SAM, and ERGAS is shown in Table 6.9, and the best results are shown in bold. The dimension of spectral subspace, p, was set to 6, 10, 5, and 6 for Washington DC Mall, Indian Pines, University of Houston, and Pavia University, respectively. It is clear that the proposed method can achieve better fusion results in most cases. The proposed E2E-fusion and CNN-Fus methods perform superior numerically compared with GLPHS, CNMF, and HySure. Both CNN-Fus and E2E-fusion are PnP-based frameworks. For the CNN-Fus method, an FFDNet with a noise level map was plugged into the fusion framework; therefore, the parameter of the noise level map needs to be fine-tuned carefully to get the optimal results. However, our E2E-fusion method is user-friendly as a blind and self-supervised learning network is plugged into our method. Furthermore, a guide image

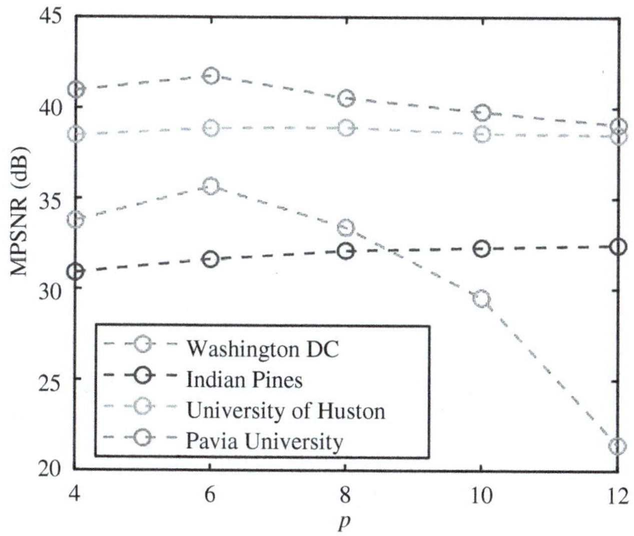

Figure 6.24 Effect of the dimension of subspace, p, on four simulated datasets [82] / with permission of IEEE.

strategy is adopted in our eigenimage denoising network, so that the high-quality information of the first eigenimage is fully exploited. Therefore, although our fusion method is blind, its performance is comparable to the unblind CNN-FUS.

The running times of all methods are reported in Table 6.9. For further comparison, we also show the PSNR, SSIM, and FSIM of per band of four simulated datasets in Figure 6.25. Meanwhile, we also display the fusion results on four simulated datasets virtually, including the 126th band of Washington DC Mall, the 116th band of Indian Pines, the 6th band of Houston University, and the 90th band of Pavia University. Meanwhile, the corresponding error maps were displayed via the absolute difference values between reference images and fusion results (shown in Figures 6.26–6.29). We can see that CNN-Fus and the proposed method perform superior over other competitors, and the proposed E2E-fusion keeps less noise.

We remark that our fusion method is user-friendly, as it plugs a blind eigenimage learning network, requiring no parameter. However, the performance of most HSI and MSI fusion techniques, in particular traditional machine-learning-based models proposed in the literature, is sensitive to the setting of regularization parameter. Both our proposed E2E-fusion and CNN-Fus can achieve a better fusion result compared with other methods. However, to achieve a promising fusion result, the parameter, λ, in CNN-Fus should be turned carefully. What can be clearly seen in Figure 6.30, the MPSNR of CNN-Fus is the dramatic decline in the suboptimal parameter range, while the proposed E2E-fusion (requiring no regularization parameter) can keep a stable fusion accuracy.

7) *Ablation Experiments:* A series of ablation studies were conducted to verify the effectiveness of our plugged E2E eigenimage prior, and the fusion results are shown in Table 6.10. We first change the objective function into $\min_{\mathbf{A}} \frac{1}{2}\|\mathbf{Y}_h - \mathbf{CABS}\|_F^2 + \frac{\lambda_1}{2}\|\mathbf{Y}_m - \mathbf{MCA}\|_F^2$, with only subspace representations, but without regularizer. The results show that only with the subspace projection cannot obtain promising fusion results. After considering the deep self-supervised-based PnP prior, Table 6.10 shows that there has been a steady increase in terms of MPSNR

Table 6.9 Numerical analysis of the proposed method and compared methods on five metrics.

Scenario	Metric	GLPHS [94]	CNMF [10]	HySure [81]	CNN-FUS [30]	E2E-fusion [82]
Washington DC	MPSNR (dB)	25.57	26.29	25.15	34.12	**35.57**
	MSSIM	0.8834	0.8754	0.9171	0.9762	**0.9789**
	MFSIM	0.9284	0.9059	0.9372	0.9763	**0.9781**
	SAM	7.8675	7.2016	7.8341	2.9973	**2.8741**
	ERGAS	2.3804	2.2357	2.4975	0.9266	**0.8343**
	Time (s)	38.04	**10.13**	19.09	173.08	328.34
Indian Pines	MPSNR (dB)	25.58	30.13	28.62	31.44	**32.21**
	MSSIM	0.8750	0.9340	0.9272	0.9413	**0.9506**
	MFSIM	0.9375	0.9639	0.9526	0.9670	**0.9692**
	SAM	3.6867	2.6756	3.2686	2.6502	**2.4473**
	ERGAS	3.2974	1.8738	2.1541	1.6736	**1.5513**
	Time (s)	9.08	4.35	**3.30**	50.46	74.65
The University of Houston	MPSNR (dB)	24.15	27.25	26.22	37.65	**38.49**
	MSSIM	0.8548	0.8174	0.8824	0.9690	**0.9782**
	MFSIM	0.9294	0.9183	0.9269	0.9828	**0.9875**
	SAM	6.3338	4.2028	6.9859	2.4635	**1.9229**
	ERGAS	2.5012	1.7542	2.0711	0.6689	**0.6036**
	Time (s)	**2.34**	7.52	17.80	48.32	39.40
Pavia University	MPSNR (dB)	31.88	33.36	32.24	41.94	**42.00**
	MSSIM	0.9178	0.9368	0.9069	0.9809	**0.9818**
	MFSIM	0.9434	0.9645	0.9410	0.9898	**0.9905**
	SAM	4.4292	3.2795	5.6945	2.2050	**2.0889**
	ERGAS	3.8889	3.3437	3.9180	1.2240	**1.2100**
	Time (s)	**10.08**	14.00	20.22	98.30	89.64

The bold values indicate the best performance for the corresponding metric.

on four simulated datasets compared with no regularizer. Consider the first eigenimage as the guide image to denoise the remaining eigenimages, which obtains a dramatic increase in terms of PSNR compared with no guide image on all datasets. These ablation experiments show that our deep eigenimage prior and our trick of using guide eigenimage do improve fusion performance significantly.

We also compare with two state-of-the-art fusion networks, namely, an interpretable deep network for MSI and HSI fusion (MHF-Net) [95] and HSI SR via deep spatiospectral attention CNN (HSR-Net) [96], which were trained on Columbia Imaging and Vision Laboratory (CAVE) dataset and tested on the same dataset. For a comparison, we retained the MHF-Net, HSR-Net, and our E2E-fusion with 20 CAVE images, and tested on 12 images, which keep the same setting in [95]. More specifically, the "E2E-fusion (trained by CAVE noisy–noisy pairs)" is trained with a self-supervised technique proposed in this section, meaning its training only uses noisy CAVE images without clean CAVE images, while the "E2E-fusion (trained by ICVL noisy–noisy

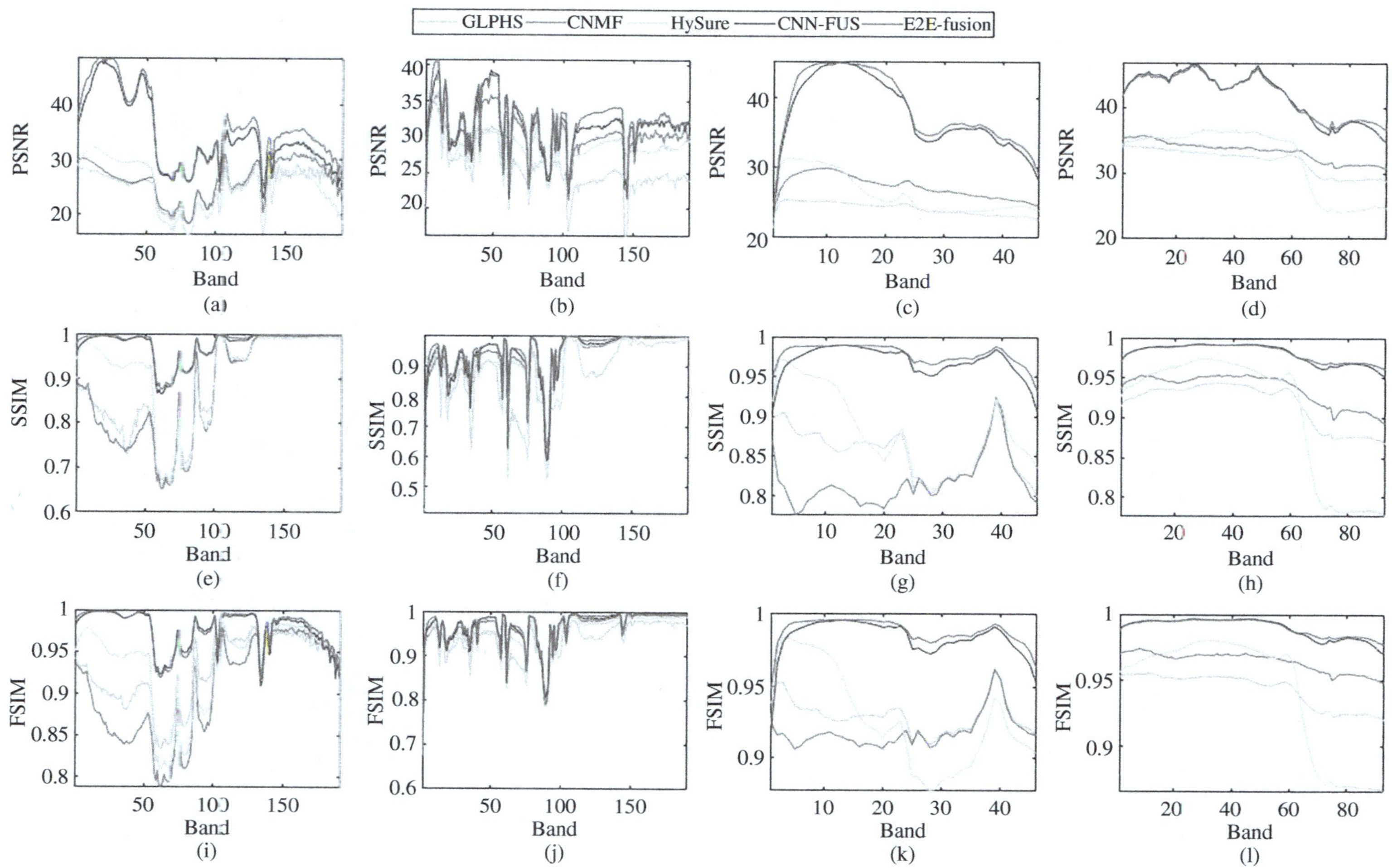

Figure 6.25 (a), (e), and (i) stand for the PSNR, SSIM, and FSIM value on Washington DC, respectively. (b), (f), and (j) stand for the PSNR, SSIM, and FSIM value on Indian Pines, respectively. (c), (g), and (k) stand for the PSNR, SSIM, and FSIM value on the University of Houston, respectively. (d), (h), and (l) stand for the PSNR, SSIM, and FSIM value on Pavia University, respectively [82] / with permission of IEEE.

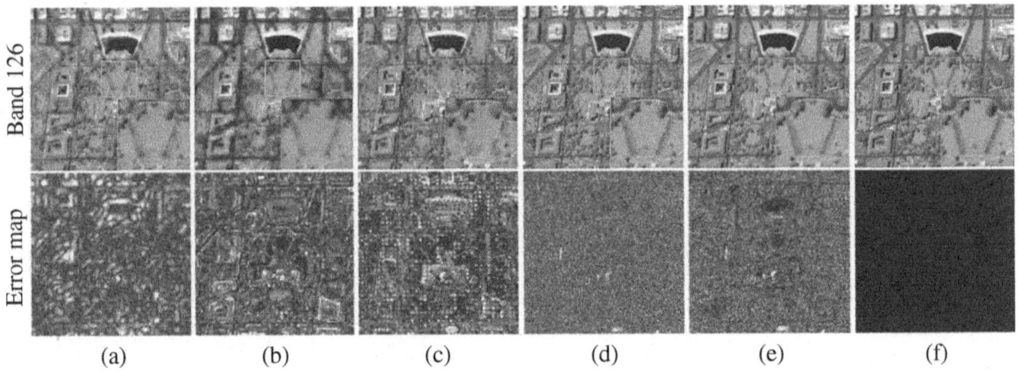

Figure 6.26 Band 126 and error map of the Washington DC Mall. (a) GLPHS [94], (b) CNMF [10], (c) HySure [81], (d) CNN-Fus [30], (e) E2E-fusion [82], and (f) reference / with permission of IEEE.

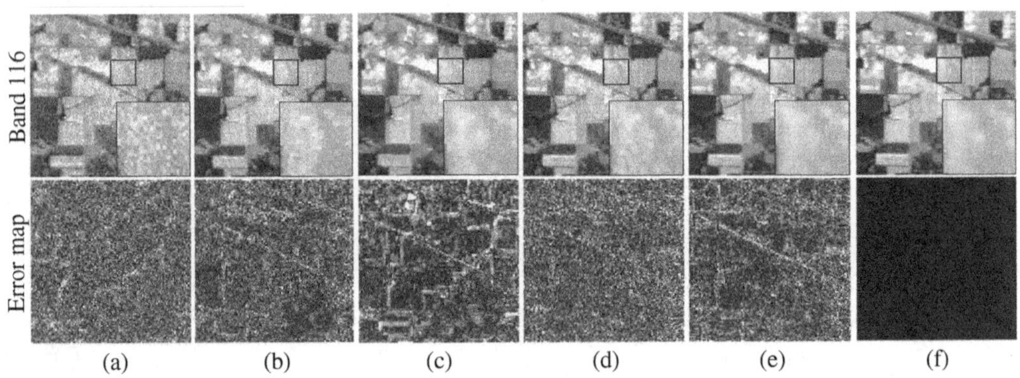

Figure 6.27 Band 116 and error map of the Indian Pines. (a) GLPHS [94], (b) CNMF [10], (c) HySure [81], (d) CNN-Fus [30], (e) E2E-fusion [82], and (f) reference / with permission of IEEE.

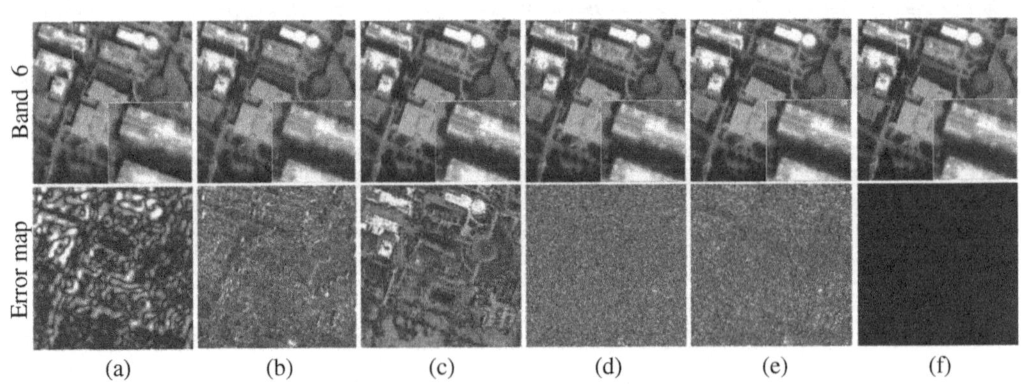

Figure 6.28 Band 6 and error map of the Houston University. (a) GLPHS [94], (b) CNMF [10], (c) HySure [81], (d) CNN-Fus [30], (e) E2E-fusion [82], and (f) reference / with permission of IEEE.

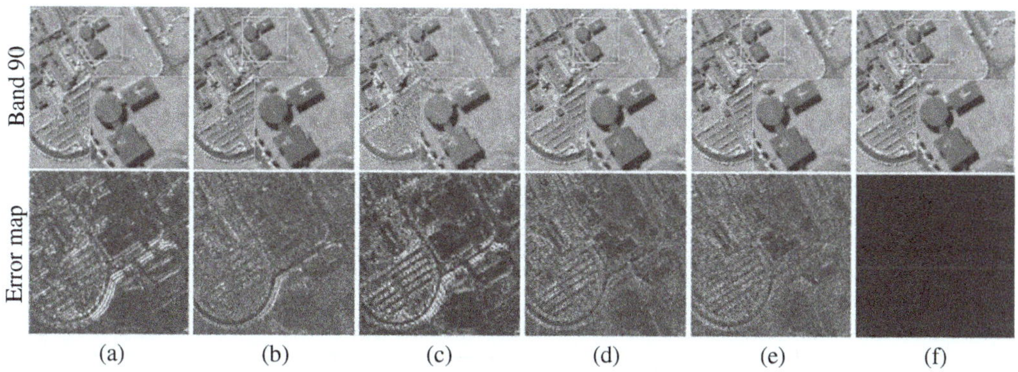

Figure 6.29 Band 90 and error map of the Pavia University. (a) GLPHS [94], (b) CNMF [10], (c) HySure [81], (d) CNN-Fus [30], (e) E2E-fusion [82], and (f) reference / with permission of IEEE.

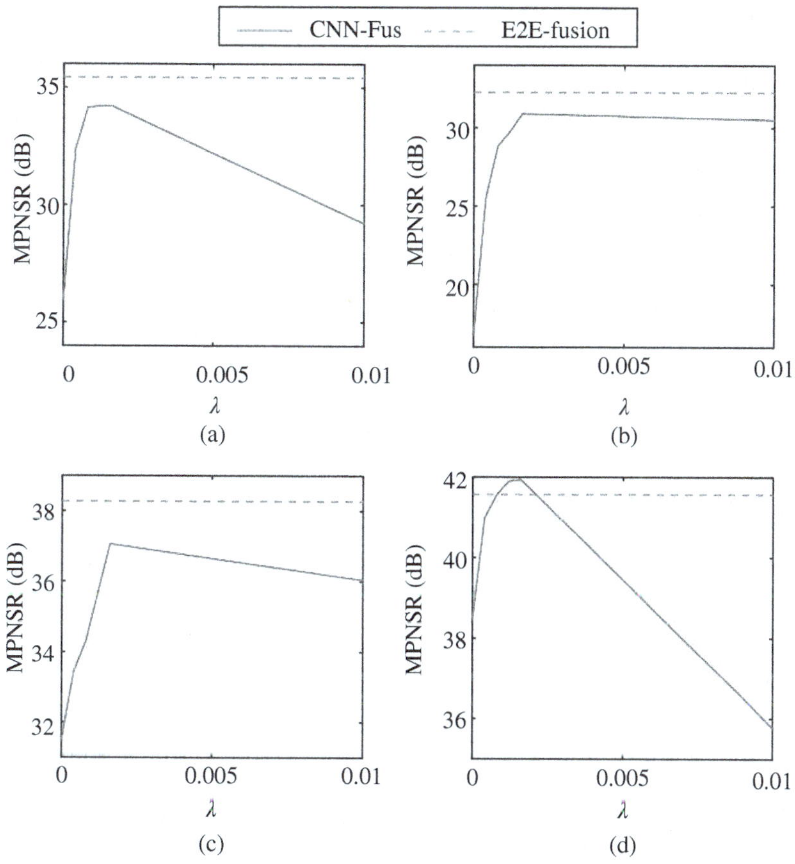

Figure 6.30 Effect of the noise level, λ, on four simulated datasets. (a) Washington DC, (b) Indian Pines, (c) the University of Houston, and (d) Pavia University [82] / with permission of IEEE.

Table 6.10 Results of ablation experiment in terms of MPSNR on four simulated datasets [82] / with permission of IEEE.

Scenario	Metric	E2E-fusion (without regularizer)	E2E-fusion (without guide image)	E2E-fusion (proposed)
Washington DC	MPSNR (dB)	28.45	33.10	35.57
Indian Pines	MPSNR (dB)	22.07	29.86	32.21
University of Houston	MPSNR (dB)	31.92	35.43	38.49
Pavia University	MPSNR (dB)	39.46	41.01	42.00

Note: The objective function of "E2E-fusion (without regularizer)" is $\min_{\mathbf{A}} \frac{1}{2}\|\mathbf{Y}_h - \mathbf{CABS}\|_F^2 + \frac{\lambda_1}{2}\|\mathbf{Y}_m - \mathbf{MCA}\|_F^2$. "E2E-fusion (without guide image)" adopts a network: $o_i = f_\theta(o_i)$, $(i = 1, 2, \ldots, p)$.

pairs)" is trained on ICVL dataset with the same way, i.e., the testing images are not the same as the training images. In Table 6.11, the proposed "E2E-fusion (trained by CAVE noisy–noisy pairs)" and "E2E-fusion (trained by ICVL noisy–noisy pairs)" methods perform better in average than CMHF-Net. However, both do not perform better than HSR-Net. One possible reason is that the E2E-fusion is a self-supervised method, and only noisy data is used, whereas the clean

Table 6.11 Quantitative assessment of MHF-Net, HSR-Net, and E2E-fusion methods.

Image name	Index	MHF-Net [95]	HSR-Net [96]	E2E-fusion trained by ICVL noisy–noisy pairs [82]	E2E-fusion trained by CAVE noisy–noisy pairs [82]	E2E-f usion trained by CAVE noisy–clean pairs [82]
balloons ms	MPSNR (dB)	43.56	47.36	45.97	46.08	47.24
clay ms	MPSNR (dB)	46.15	48.77	46.80	47.15	48.24
cloth ms	MPSNR (dB)	40.51	41.95	41.17	41.79	41.95
face ms	MPSNR (dB)	45.65	46.81	45.89	46.65	47.72
fake and real beers ms	MPSNR (dB)	41.60	43.20	43.18	43.40	45.10
fake and real food ms	MPSNR (dB)	46.95	47.99	45.47	46.10	46.98
fake and real sushi ms	MPSNR (dB)	47.24	48.55	46.85	47.55	47.38
jelly beans ms	MPSNR (dB)	43.17	43.26	40.10	40.40	41.76
paints ms	MPSNR (dB)	40.38	42.01	39.72	40.83	41.89
photo and face ms	MPSNR (dB)	43.57	45.07	45.11	46.21	47.05
real and fake apples ms	MPSNR (dB)	49.04	51.74	50.05	50.40	51.74
sponges ms	MPSNR (dB)	40.45	42.80	42.22	42.72	44.00
Acreage Value	MPSNR (dB)	44.02	45.79	44.38	44.94	**45.92**

The bold values indicate the best performance for the corresponding metric.

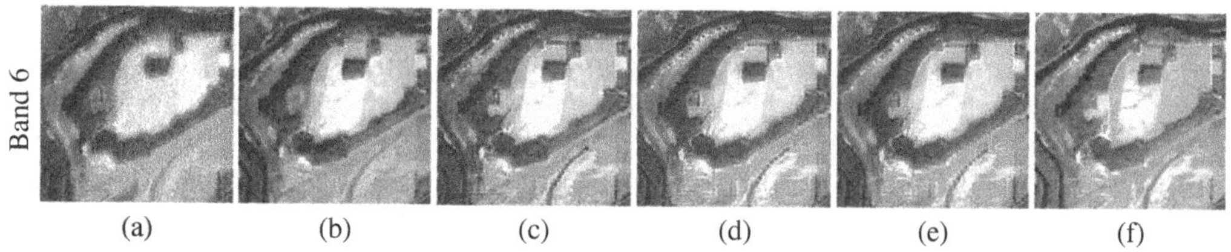

Figure 6.31 Bands 6's fusion result of the Hyperion LR-HSI, and Sentinel-2A. (a) GLPHS [94], (b) CNMF [10], (c) HySure [81], (d) CNN-Fus [30], (e) E2E-fusion [82], and (f) reference / with permission of IEEE.

data is considered and employed in HSR-Net. Therefore, we tested a counterpart of our method, "E2E-fusion (trained by CAVE noisy–clean pairs)," which means we train the same network using the clean images. Note that our proposed method is to train the prior in Eq. (6.34), which is different from HSR-Net. We see in Table 6.10 that the fusion results of "E2E-fusion (trained by CAVE noisy–clean pairs)" are comparable to that of the HSR-Net. The results show that given clean images as training data, the fusion precision of our network can achieve state-of-the-art results similar to HSR-Net. This observation implies that the framework of our fusion network is properly designed and is comparable to state-of-the-art fusion networks. Furthermore, we reiterate that we aim to propose a user-friendly fusion network for scenarios without a requirement of clean images. The E2E-fusion (trained by noisy–noisy pairs) has achieved promising and reasonable performance.

8) *Experimental Results on Real Dataset:* A real dataset is also used to verify the fusion result of the proposed E2E-fusion method. The HR-MSI is acquired by the Sentinel-2A satellite, and 4 bands with a resolution of 10 m are used in our experiments. The subregion containing 150×150 pixels was chosen from a scene for our experiments (see Figure 6.22e). The LR-HSI is collected by the Hyperion sensor by the Earth Observing-1 Satellite with a spatial resolution of 30 m. The LR-HSI has 220 bands ranging from 0.4 to 2.5 μm. After removing the low SNRs and atmospheric absorption bands, 89 bands were kept. The subregion that contains $50 \times 50 \times 89$ pixels was chosen from a scene for testing the fusion results. We estimate the **B** and **M** by using the method proposed in [81]. The fusion results of sixth band are shown in Figure 6.31. It is clear that the CNN-Fus and our proposed E2E-fusion method can enrich more information in the bottom right part compared with GLPHS, CNMF, and HySure.

6.5 Blind HSI SR

6.5.1 Imaging Model

In terms of spectral resolution, images can be divided into two classes, i.e., high- and low-spectral resolution images. In this section, HSIs and MSIs are high- and low-spectral resolution images respectively, and they are denoted as tensors. The first dimension of the tensor represents the number of spectral bands, and the second and the third dimensions stand for the spatial size of images. The LR HSI can be denoted by $\mathcal{Y}_h \in \mathbb{R}^{L \times n_{row} \times n_{col}}$. $\mathcal{Y}_m \in \mathbb{R}^{l \times N_{row} \times N_{col}}$ represents the HR MSI. Both HSI and MSI are imaged with solar light as the light source, which provides full-spectrum information [97–99]. If the effect of spatial resolution is ignored, the spectral bands of HSI and MSI can be considered as downsampling of the full-spectrum information from solar light. When the spatial size of all images is fixed to N_{row} and N_{col}, the HR HSI and the full-spectrum image are denoted by $\mathcal{Z} \in \mathbb{R}^{L \times N_{row} \times N_{col}}$ and $\mathcal{Z}_{full} \in \mathbb{R}^{F \times N_{row} \times N_{col}}$, where F represents full spectrum bands.

If $N = N_{row} \times N_{col}$, $\mathbf{Z} \in \mathbb{R}^{L \times N}$, $\mathbf{Y}_m \in \mathbb{R}^{l \times N}$, and $\mathbf{Z}_{full} \in \mathbb{R}^{F \times N}$ are reshaped from $\mathcal{Z} \in \mathbb{R}^{L \times N_{row} \times N_{col}}$, $\mathcal{Y}_m \in \mathbb{R}^{l \times N_{row} \times N_{col}}$, and $\mathcal{Z}_{full} \in \mathbb{R}^{F \times N_{row} \times N_{col}}$, where the spectral dimension is preserved and the spatial dimension is ignored. The HSI is spectrally downsampled from the the full-spectrum image, i.e.,

$$\mathbf{Z} = \mathbf{R}_{hr}\mathbf{Z}_{full}, \tag{6.49}$$

where $\mathbf{R}_{hr} \in \mathbb{R}^{L \times F}$ is the spectral response matrix of the hyperspectral imaging sensor, whose rows stand for the spectral response of each band. The MSI is spectrally downsampled from the the full-spectrum image, i.e.,

$$\mathbf{Y}_m = \mathbf{R}_{lr}\mathbf{Z}_{full}, \tag{6.50}$$

where $\mathbf{R}_{lr} \in \mathbb{R}^{l \times F}$ is the spectral response matrix of the multispectral imaging sensor, whose rows stand for the spectral response of each band. From Eqs. (6.49) and (6.50), the mapping relationship between $\mathbf{R}_{lr} \in \mathbb{R}^{l \times F}$ and $\mathbf{R}_{hr} \in \mathbb{R}^{L \times F}$ can be obtained as

$$\mathbf{Y}_m = \mathbf{R}_{lr}\mathbf{R}_{hr}^{-1}\mathbf{Z}, \tag{6.51}$$

and

$$\mathbf{Z} = \mathbf{R}_{hr}\mathbf{R}_{lr}^{-1}\mathbf{Y}_m. \tag{6.52}$$

When the $\mathbf{R}_{hl} \in \mathbb{R}^{l \times L}$ and the $\mathbf{R}_{lh} \in \mathbb{R}^{L \times l}$ are equal to the $\mathbf{R}_{lr}\mathbf{R}_{hr}^{-1}$ and the $\mathbf{R}_{lr}\mathbf{R}_{hr}^{-1}$, respectively, the Eqs. (6.51) and (6.52) can be denoted as

$$\mathbf{Y}_m = \mathbf{R}_{hl}\mathbf{Z}, \tag{6.53}$$

and

$$\mathbf{Z} = \mathbf{R}_{lh}\mathbf{Y}_m. \tag{6.54}$$

If HSIs and MSIs are paired, the $\mathbf{R}_{hl}$ can be regressed from $\mathbf{Y}_{hr}$ and $\mathbf{Y}_{lr}$, and the SpeSR is to seek the $\mathbf{R}_{lh}$.

6.5.2 Proposed BliEstGAN

Although CNN-based methods have shown powerful performance on the SpeSR task, it is very difficult to obtain paired high- and low-spectral resolution images (such as MSI and HSI pairs) for training the CNN model. It is a common condition that high- and low-spectral resolution images are not paired, for example, MSIs and HSIs are from different remote-sensing image sources with different spatial resolution and cover different areas. As shown in Figure 6.32, because the MSI and HSI are acquired from different sources, two images in two dark-colored boxes are not paired. Note that the spatial resolution of the MSI is generally higher than that of the HSI, and unpaired images cannot be used to train the CNN model for SpeSR. Thus, paired HSI and MSI are desired to be generated. To achieve this goal, in this section, the spectral degradation between the HSI and the MSI is first estimated, where the $\mathbf{R}_{ehl}$ is the estimation of the $\mathbf{R}_{hl}$, to generate the pseudo-MSI $\mathbf{Y}_{lr}$ (i.e., image in the upper left box) from the HSI, and then these images are paired to train the CNN model for SpeSR. Finally, the CNN model can spectrally super-resolve the MSI to the target

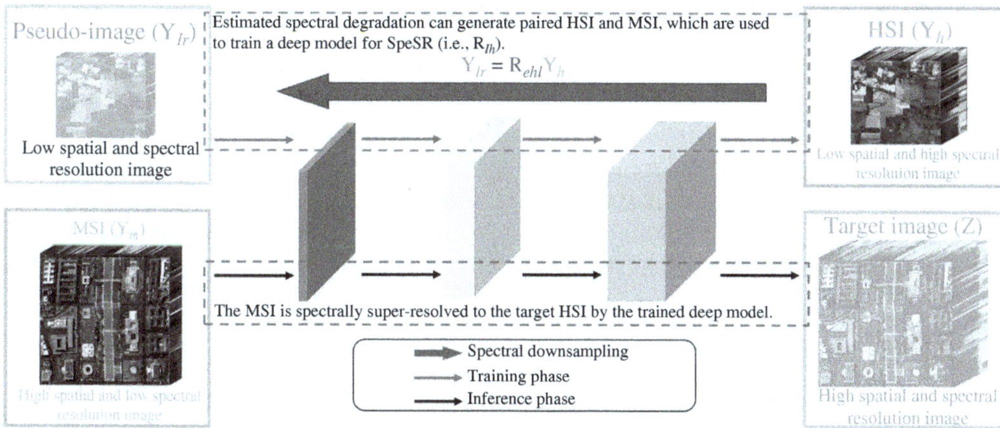

Figure 6.32 The flowchart of CNN-based methods for SpeSR [100] / with permission of IEEE.

HSI, as can be illustrated by the image in lower right box in Figure 6.32. Due to unpaired HSIs and MSIs, the spectral degradation still cannot be directly estimated by a basic CNN model that needs supervised information to train its own parameters. The GAN is appropriated for unsupervised learning by gaming strategy, which is exploited to blindly estimate the spectral degradation between unpaired HSIs and MSIs, which is shown in Figure 6.33. After finishing the training of the GAN model, the generator is equivalent to the $\mathbf{R}_{ehl}$. In addition, it is necessary to explain why the GAN model is used to estimate the spectral degradation from HSI to MSI, rather than the mapping relationship from MSI to HSI. This is because the spectral super resolution (SR) is an ill-posed problem, and the spectral degradation is unique. And the imaging mechanism of spectral degradation can be represented as some regularization to help the GAN model estimate $\mathbf{R}_{ehl}$.

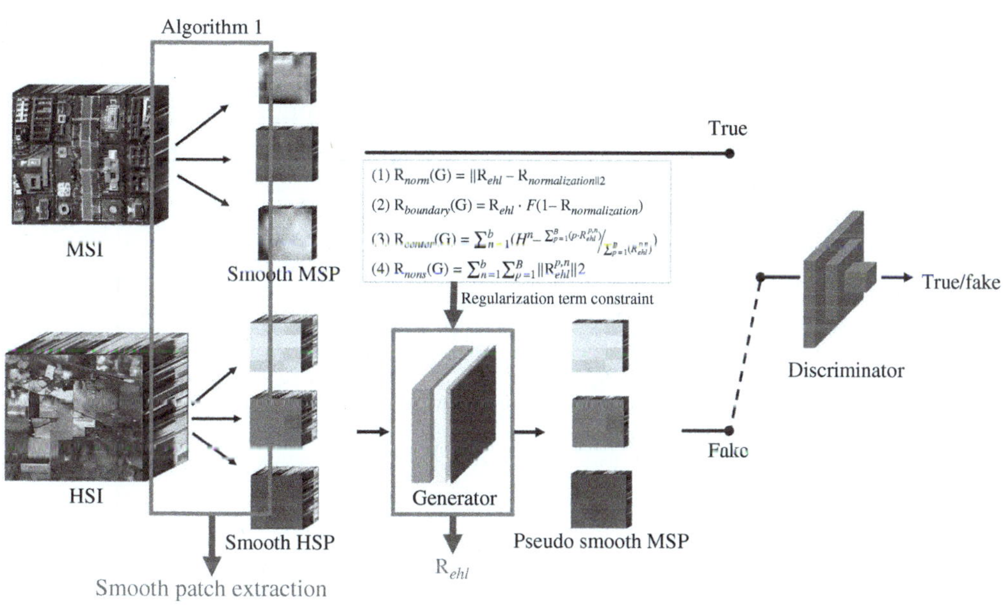

Figure 6.33 The architecture of the proposed BliEstGAN [100] / with permission of IEEE.

6.5.3 Architecture of the BliEstGAN

1) *Architecture of the BliEstGAN:* The GAN contains the generator and the discriminator, which become increasingly strong through alternate optimization. The generator is hoped to learn the spectral degradation between hyperspectral domain and multispectral domain using unpaired HSIs and MSIs. HSIs are input into the generator to generate pseudo-MSIs. The discriminator is actually a binary classifier, whose results correspond to the true and the fake, to discriminate between real MSIs and pseudo-MSIs. Because the different spatial resolutions of HSIs and MSIs are easy to distinguish by the discriminator [101], smooth hyperspectral patches (HSPs) and multispectral patches (MSPs) are cropped from HSIs and MSIs, respectively, to maintain the balance between the discriminator and the generator, which is also shown in Figure 6.33. Furthermore, since smooth patches contain little spatial detail, they are similar and can constitute paired HSIs and MSIs to some extent. To collect smooth HSPs and MSPs, a threshold method based on local variance is designed. First, HSPs and MSPs are cropped with a fixed-sized stride from HSIs and MSIs, respectively. Second, the variance of each patch is calculated. Finally, if the variance of the patch is less than the set threshold, the patch is thought as a smooth patch. The details of cropping smooth HSPs and MSPs are shown in Algorithm 6.2. From Figure 6.33, Algorithm 6.2 is the pre-process of the BliEstGAN. Assume the number of HSIs is N_{hr}, and the $\mathbf{Y}_h^n$ represents the n-th HSI. Assume the number of MSIs is N_{lr}, and the $\mathbf{Y}_m^n$ represents the n-th MSI. The Stride, ξ_{HSI}, ξ_{MSI}, W, and H represent the length of stride, the variance threshold for HSIs, the variance threshold for MSIs, the width of patch, and the height of patch. Note that the width and height of HSPs are equal to those of MSPs.

According to the imaging mechanisms, the design of the proposed GAN model is shown in Tables 6.12 and 6.13. Specifically, on the one hand, the spectral degradation is pixel-wise and is thought to be identical for each pixel, as shown in imaging model (i.e., Eq. (6.53)). Thus, first,

Algorithm 6.2 Smooth patch extraction from HSIs and MSIs

Input: Y_h^n, Y_m^n, ξ_{HSI}, ξ_{MSI}, Stride, W, H
for $n = 1$ **to** N_{hr} **do**
  Patches P_{HSI}^j with size of $W \times H$ are cropped from Y_h^n by the stride of *stride*,
  The variance of each HSP (i.e., P_{HSI}^j) is calculated to obtain σ_{HSI}^j,
  if $\sigma_{HSI}^j \leq \xi_{HSI}$ **then**
    The patch P_{HSI}^j is thought as smooth patch P_{SHSI}^j.
  end if
end for
for $n = 1$ **to** N_{lr} **do**
  Patches P_{MSI}^j with size of $W \times H$ are cropped from Y_m^n by the stride of *stride*,
  The variance of each MSP (i.e., P_{MSI}^j) is calculated to obtain σ_{MSI}^j,
  if $\sigma_{MSI}^j \leq \xi_{MSI}$ **then**
    The patch P_{MSI}^j is thought as smooth patch P_{SMSI}^j.
  end if
end for
All patches of P_{SHSI}^j and P_{SMSI}^j constitute the set of P_{SHSI} and P_{SMSI}, respectively,
Output: P_{SHSI}, P_{SLSI}.

Table 6.12 The details of the generator [100] / with permission of IEEE.

Order of the layer	Name of the layer	Input and its size	Details of the layer	Output and its size
1	Convolution layer	HSPs (i.e., P_{SHSI}): $64 \times 64 \times L$	Size of convolution kernels: $64 \times 1 \times 1 \times L$ Strides: 1, zero padding: 0	Feature maps: $64 \times 64 \times 64$
2	Convolution layer	Feature maps: $64 \times 64 \times 64$	Size of convolution kernels: $64 \times 1 \times 1 \times 64$ Strides: 1, zero padding: 0	Feature maps: $64 \times 64 \times 64$
3	Convolution layer	Feature maps: $64 \times 64 \times 64$	Size of convolution kernels: $64 \times 1 \times 1 \times 64$ Strides: 1, zero padding: 0	Feature maps: $64 \times 64 \times 64$
4	Convolution layer	Feature maps: $64 \times 64 \times 64$	Size of convolution kernels: $64 \times 1 \times 1 \times 64$ Strides: 1, zero padding: 0	Feature maps: $64 \times 64 \times 64$
5	Convolution layer	Feature maps: $64 \times 64 \times 64$	Size of convolution kernels: $64 \times 1 \times 1 \times 64$ Strides: 1, zero padding: 0	Feature maps: $64 \times 64 \times 64$
6	Convolution layer	Feature maps: $64 \times 64 \times 64$	Size of convolution kernels: $l \times 1 \times 1 \times 64$ Strides: 1, zero padding: 0	Feature maps: $64 \times 64 \times l$
7	Absolute layer	Feature maps: $64 \times 64 \times l$	Absolute function	MSPs (i.e., P_{SMSI}^{pseudo}): $64 \times 64 \times l$

the generator consists of only linear mapping units, i.e., convolution layers, and they have a spatial size of 1×1. Note that, compared with a single convolution layer, multiple convolution layers are easier to optimize [102]. Under this circumstance, all local optimal solutions are globally optimal and equal [103]. Second, all elements in the downsampling matrix are positive, so a special layer using an absolute function for all input is designed to avoid negative values. Finally, after the training phase, the identity matrix is input to obtain the equivalent mapping matrix of the generator, i.e., the estimated downsampling matrix $\mathbf{R}_{ehl}$ in Figures 6.32 and 6.33. This estimated matrix $\mathbf{R}_{ehl}$ can be used to downsample real HSIs to paired pseudo-MSIs, along with real HSIs to train CNN models for SpeSR. On the other hand, the discriminator is important for the generator to have good estimation ability by discriminating the differences between real MSIs and pseudo-MSIs. Obviously, spatial and spectral consistency are the main factors to consider, which must be reflected in the design of the discriminator. First of all, to collect spatial information, convolution kernels with a large kernel size (i.e., 7×7) are accepted in the first layer [104]. Then, to explore spectral information, seven convolution layers only containing convolution kernels with a kernel size of 1×1 are adopted. Moreover, eight spectral normalization layers [105] and seven batch normalization layers [106] are introduced to increase the stability of the discriminator and accelerate its convergence. At the end, the activation layer adopts the sigmoid function, whose results are 0 or 1 to exactly correspond to fake or true. The parameters of the generator and the discriminator are optimized in turn. While the parameters of the one are optimized, the parameters of the other are frozen, and the parameters of the discriminator are optimized first.

Table 6.13 The details of the discriminator [100] / with permission of IEEE.

Order of the layer	Name of the layer	Input and its size	Details of the layer	Output and its size
1	Convolution layer	MSPs (i.e., P_{SMSI} and P_{SMSI}^{pseudo}): $64 \times 64 \times l$	Size of convolution kernels: $64 \times 7 \times 7 \times l$ Strides: 1, zero padding: 0	Feature maps: $62 \times 62 \times 64$
2, 6, 10, 14, 18, 22, 26, 30	Spectral normalization layer	Feature maps: $62 \times 62 \times 64$	$\epsilon = 10^{(-12)}$	Feature maps: $62 \times 62 \times 64$
3, 7, 11, 15, 19, 23, 27	Batch normalization layer	Feature maps: $62 \times 62 \times 64$	$\epsilon = 10^{(-5)}$	Feature maps: $62 \times 62 \times 64$
4, 8, 12, 16, 20, 24, 28	Activation layer	Feature maps: $62 \times 62 \times 64$	ReLU function	Feature maps: $62 \times 62 \times 64$
5, 9, 13, 17, 21, 25, 29	convolution layer	Feature maps: $62 \times 62 \times 64$	Size of convolution kernels: $64 \times 1 \times 1 \times 64$ Strides: 1, zero padding: 0	Feature maps: $62 \times 62 \times 64$
31	Absolute layer	Feature maps: $62 \times 62 \times 64$	Sigmoid function	True or Fake: $62 \times 62 \times 64$

2) *Loss function:* To optimize the parameters of the BliEstGAN, a suitable loss function is required. First, the parameters and the output of the discriminator are defined as **D** and **D**(X) ($0 < \mathbf{D}(\mathbf{X}) < 1$), respectively, where X represents any input images of the discriminator. Meanwhile, the parameters and the output of the generator are defined as **G** and **G(X)**, respectively, where X represents any input images of the generator. Second, the object loss function for the discriminator is denoted as:

$$\mathbf{D} = \operatorname{argmax}\left(\|\mathbf{D}(P_{SMSI})\|_1 + \|\mathbf{D}(\mathbf{G}(P_{SHSI})) - 1\|_1\right), \tag{6.55}$$

while the **G** is frozen and the **D** is optimized by the back propagation algorithm. After optimization of the discriminator, the generator needs to be optimized. The basic object loss function for the generator is denoted as:

$$\mathbf{G} = \operatorname{argmin}\left(\|\mathbf{D}(P_{SMSI})\|_1 + \|\mathbf{D}(\mathbf{G}(P_{SHSI})) - 1\|_1\right). \tag{6.56}$$

However, due to unpaired MSIs and HSIs, the right convergence for the generator is very difficult. As shown in Figure 6.33, some regularization terms must be designed based on imaging prior information to obtain an effective generator, so the object loss function for the generator is denoted as:

$$\mathbf{G} = \operatorname{argmin}\left(\|\mathbf{D}(P_{SMSI})\|_1 + \|\mathbf{D}(\mathbf{G}(P_{SHSI})) - 1\|_1 + \mathbf{R}(\mathbf{G})\right), \tag{6.57}$$

where the **R**(**G**) represents all regularization terms for the generator. The **R**(**G**) contains four regularization terms, i.e., $\mathbf{R}_{norm}(\mathbf{G})$, $\mathbf{R}_{boundary}(\mathbf{G})$, $\mathbf{R}_{center}(\mathbf{G})$, and $\mathbf{R}_{nons}(\mathbf{G})$. The details of the proposed four regularization terms are defined below:

$$\mathbf{R}_{norm}(\mathbf{G}) = \|\mathbf{R}_{ehl} - \mathbf{R}_{normalization}\|_2, \tag{6.58}$$

$$\mathbf{R}_{boundary}(\mathbf{G}) = \boldsymbol{R}_{ehl} \cdot F(1 - \mathbf{R}_{normalization}), \tag{6.59}$$

$$\mathbf{R}_{center}(\mathbf{G}) = \sum_{n=1}^{b}\left(\mathbf{H}^n - \frac{\sum_{p=1}^{L}\left(p \cdot \mathbf{R}_{ehl}^{p,n}\right)}{\sum_{p=1}^{L}\left(\mathbf{R}_{ehl}^{p,n}\right)}\right) \tag{6.60}$$

$$\mathbf{R}_{nons}(\mathbf{G}) = \sum_{n=1}^{l}\sum_{p=1}^{L}\|\mathbf{R}_{ehl}^{p,n}\|_2, \tag{6.61}$$

where the $\mathbf{R}_{ehl}^{p,n}$ is the estimated downsampling matrix, and the p and the n represent the position of the element in the $\mathbf{R}_{ehl}^{p,n}$. Moreover, the $\mathbf{R}_{normalization}$ is the guided matrix, and it is designed based on normal distribution with mathematical expectation and variance set by imaging spectrum and experiences. The $\mathbf{R}_{boundary}(\mathbf{G})$ is used to avoid the large value in the non-center region. Assume the x is the input of the function $\mathbf{F}(x)$ in Eq. (6.59), the definition of the $\mathbf{F}(x)$ is as follows:

$$\mathbf{F}(x) = \begin{cases} 0, \text{ if } \quad x \quad \text{in} \quad \text{center} \quad \text{region} \\ x, \text{ if } \quad x \quad \text{not} \quad \text{in} \quad \text{center} \quad \text{region} \end{cases} \tag{6.62}$$

where the center region can be acquired from $\mathbf{H}^n$. The $\mathbf{R}_{center}(\mathbf{G})$ is to encourage the barycenter of each sampling vector to the expected position, which is based on the imaging spectrum and recorded in $\mathbf{H}^n$. The $\mathbf{R}_{nons}(\mathbf{G})$ is adopted to suppress the sparsity of the CNN model, which is easy to appear for the CNN model and is not consistent to the real spectral downsampling matrix. Based on above-mentioned, the $\mathbf{R}(\mathbf{G})$ is formulated as follows:

$$\mathbf{R}(\mathbf{G}) = \lambda_1\mathbf{R}_{norm}(\mathbf{G}) + \lambda_2\mathbf{R}_{boundary}(\mathbf{G}) + \lambda_3\mathbf{R}_{center}(\mathbf{G}) + \lambda_4\mathbf{R}_{nons}(\mathbf{G}), \tag{6.63}$$

where the λ_1, λ_2, λ_3, and λ_4 are coefficients of each regularization terms, and how to set these parameters is analyzed in Section 6.4 by the experimental results. Finally, the discriminator and the generator are optimized alternately to achieve a satisfactory estimated spectral downsampling matrix.

6.5.4 Experimental Results

1) *Data Sets Description:* To verify the effectiveness of the proposed method for the blind SpeSR, some experiments are performed on three data sets that are designed based on two publicly available data sets. The first and second data sets are derived from the ARAH HS data set [107]. The third data set is the Houston University data set [92].

The ARAH HS data set consists of 480 pairs of HSIs and MSIs (i.e., RGB images), which were distributed in the NTIRE 2020 Spectral Recovery Challenge [107]. All images have the same spatial size of 512 × 482 and their spectral coverage ranges from 400 to 700 nm, where all HSIs contain 31 spectral bands. In the challenge, 480 pairs of images are selected for training, and the rest are used for validation. However, unpaired HSIs and MSIs are needed to be processed effectively. To prove this, our method first randomly divide 480 pairs of images from RARAH dataset into two groups, where each group contains 240 pairs of HSIs and MSIs. Then, the RARAH data set removes all MSIs from one group and all HSIs in the other group, respectively. The examples of MSIs in a group of RARAH data are illustrated in Figure 6.34. Next, the red and blue bands of all MSI are interchanged in the RARAH data to construct the VARAH dataset. Figure 6.35 shows the examples of MSIs in the VARAH data set.

The Houston University data set was distributed in the 2018 IEEE GRSS Data Fusion Contest [92] consisting of an HSI and an MSI (i.e., RGB image). The HSI and the MSI are aligned, covering Houston University campus and its neighborhood, which can be shown in Figure 6.36. The HSI with a ground sampling distance (GSD) of 1 m has a spatial size of 1202 × 4172 and contains

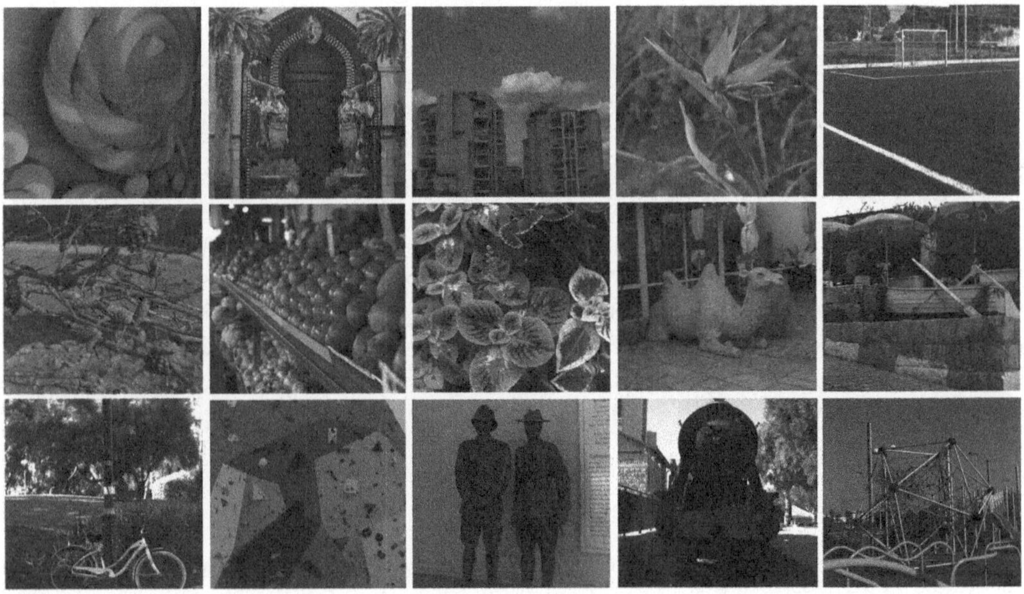

Figure 6.34 Some examples of MSIs in the RARAH data set [100] / with permission of IEEE.

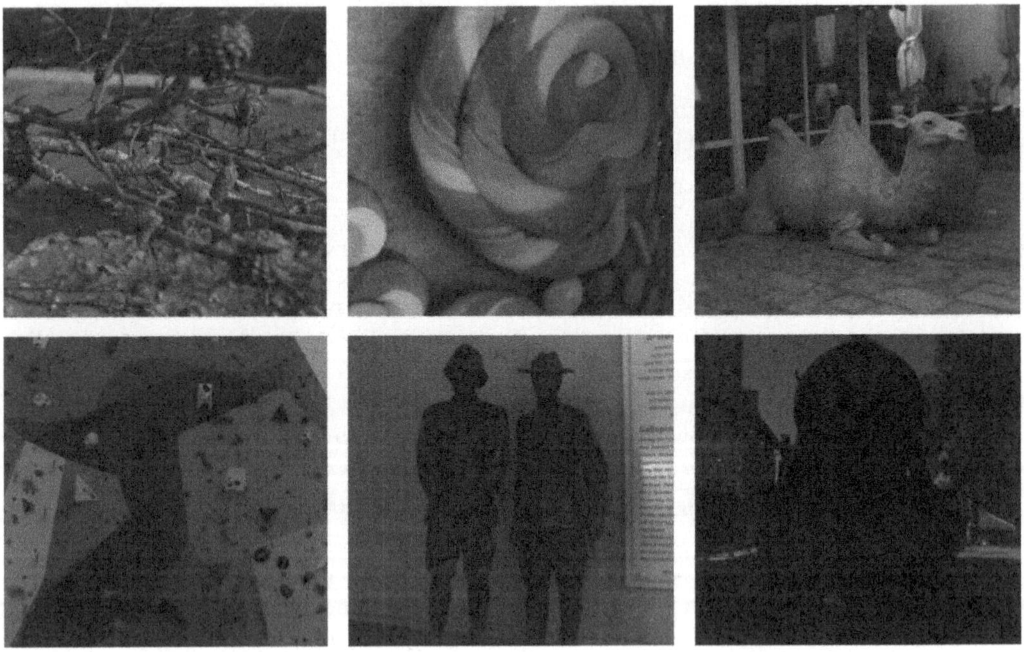

Figure 6.35 Some examples of MSIs in the VARAH data set [100] / with permission of IEEE.

50 spectral bands ranging from 380 to 1050 nm. The original MSI with a GSD of 0.05 m has a spatial size of $24{,}040 \times 83{,}440$ and is downsampled to a spatial size of 1202×4172 for matching the HSI. To prove the effectiveness of the proposed BliEstGAN, half area of the MSI are removed, and another area of the HSI are removed in the experiments. It is important to note that the MSI and the HSI are imaged under different conditions.

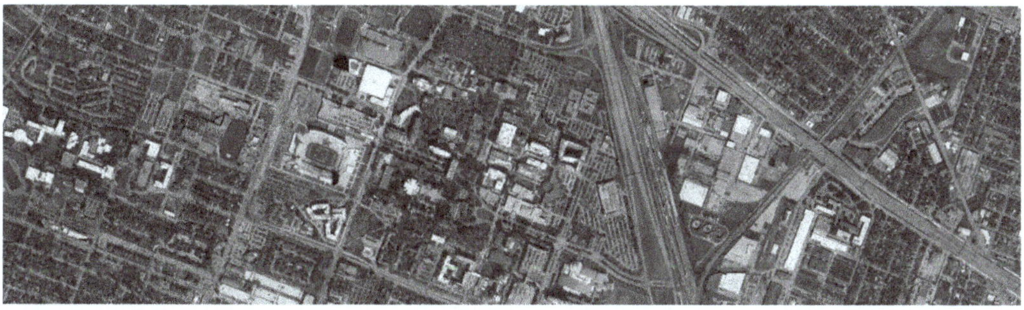

Figure 6.36 Land cover of the Houston University data set [100] / with permission of IEEE.

2) *Evaluation Metrics:* To effectively evaluate the performance of the proposed BliEstGAN. The mean square error (MSE), PSNR, and SSIM are adopted to measure all results. The hierarchical regression network (HRN) [23], the adaptive weighted attention network (AWAN) [24], the high-resolution dual-domain learning network (HDNet) [108], the multi-stage spectral-wise transformer (MST++) [109], and the masked transformer (MFormer) [35] are used to verify whether the better estimation of spectral degradation has a good impact on the SpeSR. The hyper parameters of the HRN and the AWAN are set as reported in their references, and the code for the proposed method will be released after the manuscript is accepted. All experiments are repeated 10 times to calculate the average values as the final results.
3) *Ablation Study:* In this section, the contributions of each regularization term, i.e., $\mathbf{R}_{norm}(\mathbf{G})$, $\mathbf{R}_{boundary}(\mathbf{G})$, $\mathbf{R}_{center}(\mathbf{G})$, and $\mathbf{R}_{nons}(\mathbf{G})$, are explored. In detail, the ablation experiments are performed on the ARAH HS data set. The estimation of spectral degradation and the SpeSR are used as objective tasks, where the sets of regularization terms are only related to the BliEstGAN and the AWAN is utilized as the SpeSR method. As shown in Table 6.14, all four regularization terms are helpful to improve the estimation results and the final SpeSR results. Moreover, after removing $\mathbf{R}_{norm}(\mathbf{G})$ and $\mathbf{R}_{center}(\mathbf{G})$, the experimental results are not satisfactory, which indicates that the prior imaging knowledge is still important for the estimation of spectral degradation. In real case, it is easy to obtain prior imaging knowledge, especially from HSIs, as it is also indispensable for the applications for HSIs.

Table 6.14 Contribution evaluations of each regularization term [100] / with permission of IEEE.

Tasks	$R_{norm}(G)$	$R_{center}(G)$	$R_{nons}(G)$	$R_{boundary}(G)$	**MSE**	**PSNR**	**SSIM**
Spectral degradation estimation	✓	✓	✓	✓	6.89	43.90	0.99
	✓	✓	✓	×	12.71	40.32	0.99
	✓	✓	×	×	17.94	38.81	0.99
	✓	×	×	×	193.36	28.56	0.94
	×	×	×	×	626.79	23.73	0.85
Spectral super-resolution	✓	✓	✓	✓	0.0003	35.2896	0.9793
	✓	✓	✓	×	0.0008	30.8746	0.9744
	✓	✓	×	×	0.0011	28.7937	0.9709
	✓	×	×	×	0.0094	20.0785	0.8867
	×	×	×	×	0.0127	14.4279	0.8397

4) *Parameter Analysis:* In this section, the sets of λ_1, λ_2, λ_3, and λ_4 are analyzed by experimental results. All parameters are tested on 19 different numbers, i.e., 0.1, 0.2, 0.3, 0.4, 0.5, 0.6, 0.7, 0.8, 0.9, 1, 2, 3, 4, 5, 6, 7, 8, 9, and 10. The experiment is performed on the ARAH HS data set. The estimation of spectral degradation and the SpeSR are used as objective tasks, where the sets of these coefficients are only related to the BliEstGAN and the AWAN is utilized as the SpeSR method. The PSNR is adopted to evaluate the experimental results. The results of spectral degradation estimation and the SpeSR are shown in Figures 6.37 and 6.38, respectively. The better the performance of spectral degradation estimation, the better the performance of SpeSR. According to these results, λ_1, λ_2, λ_3, and λ_4 are set to 5, 0.5, 1, and 5.
5) *Estimation of Spectral degradation:* In this section, the proposed BliEstGAN is expected to estimate the spectral degradation between unpaired HSIs and MSIs. To measure the effectiveness of the proposed method, the guided matrix $\mathbf{R}_{normalization}$ is adopted as the baseline. As

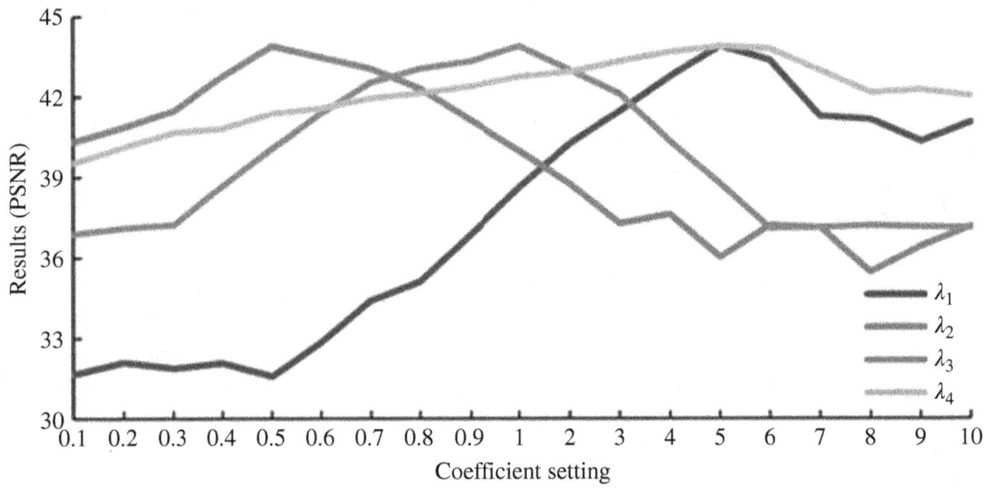

Figure 6.37 Effects of different coefficient setting on spectral degradation estimation [100] / with permission of IEEE.

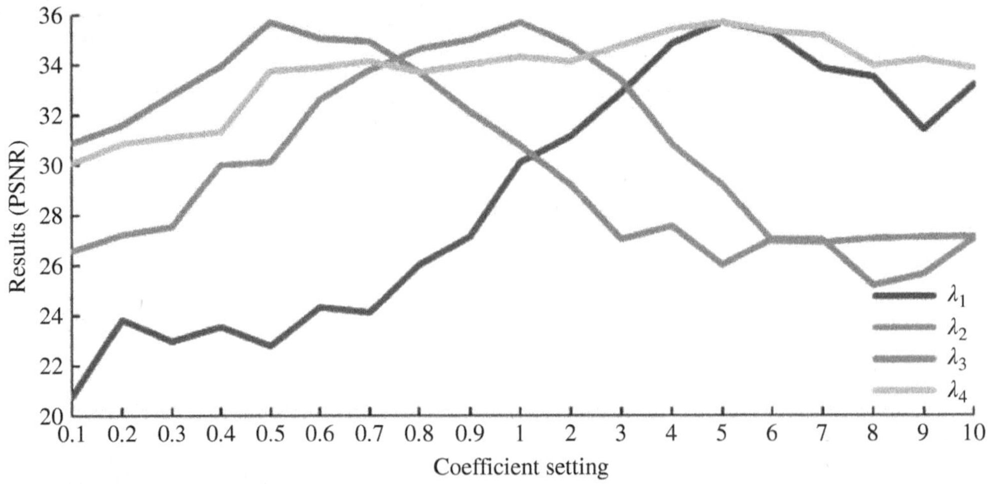

Figure 6.38 Effects of different coefficient setting on SpeSR [100] / with permission of IEEE.

Table 6.15 The estimation of spectral degradation by different methods [100] / with permission of IEEE.

Data sets	Evaluation metrics	Ground truth	Baseline	BliEstGAN	BliEstGAN (paired)
ARAH HS data set	MSE	0.00	41.98	6.89	2.84
	PSNR	$+\infty$	35.26	43.90	46.88
	SSIM	1.00	0.98	0.99	1.00
VARAH HS data set	MSE	0.00	49.35	13.32	5.36
	PSNR	$+\infty$	34.66	39.80	43.38
	SSIM	1.00	0.98	0.99	0.99
Houston data set	MSE	0.00	4138.48	752.93	109.58
	PSNR	$+\infty$	12.23	20.89	27.73
	SSIM	1.00	0.48	0.69	0.95

demonstrated in Table 6.15, compared with the baseline, the proposed method can obtain a better estimation of spectral degradation between unpaired HSIs and MSIs. Furthermore, because of the consistency of spectral degradation for an HSI, the SSIMs of both the baseline and the BliEstGAN are very good. This means that the same spectral degradation helps to maintain the structural consistency. However, due to the different imaging conditions of the HSI and the MSI in the Houston data set, the estimated results of the Houston data set are not very good. As shown in Figure 6.39, compared with the baseline, the color of the MSIs (i.e., RGB images) estimated by the proposed BliEstGAN is visually closer to the color of the ground truth, especially for the Houston data set. In addition, an experiment is designed to explore how paired or unpaired high- and low-spectral resolution images affect the spectral degradation estimation of the BliEstGAN. To conduct this experiment, high- and low-spectral resolution image pairs are selected to train the BliEstGAN, whose results are shown in the last column of Table 6.15. Obviously, paired high- and low-spectral resolution images can largely improve the performance of the BliEstGAN, since explicit spectral degradation between high- and low-spectral resolution images is provided.

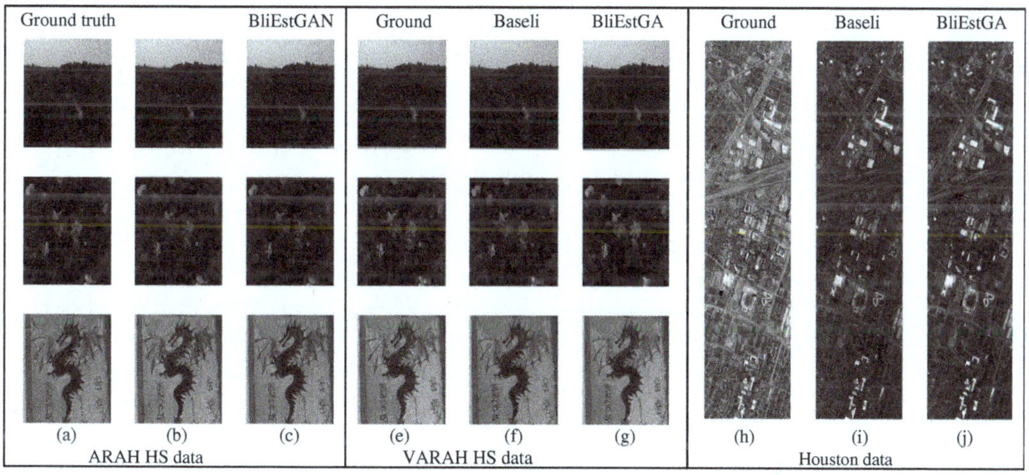

Figure 6.39 Some spectral degradation estimated examples in different data set. (a), (e), and (h) are real images, (b), (f), and (i) are images estimated by the baseline, (c), (g), and (j) are images estimated by the proposed BliEstGAN [100] / with permission of IEEE.

6) *Spectral super-resolution based on spectral degradation estimation:* In this section, five CNN-based methods (i.e., the HRN [23], the AWAN [24], the HDNet [108], the MST++ [109], and the MFormer [35]) for SpeSR are presented to prove if the BliEstGAN can improve the final SpeSR results. For each data set, the spectral degradation is estimated by the baseline and the BliEstGAN to generate paired HSIs and MSIs for training the models of five CNN-based methods. Note that the SpeSR results based on the ground truth are assumed to be the performance upper bound of five SpeSR methods. As illustrated in Table 6.16, compared with the baseline, the SpeSR results based on the proposed BliEstGAN are better than those based on the baseline in terms of all evaluation metrics (i.e., MSE, PSNR, and SSIM). For some methods performed on the ARAH HS data set, such as the HDNet and the MST++, the SpeSR performances based on the BliEstGAN approach the SpeSR performance using the ground truth. In addition, it can also be observed that the SSIMs of all methods are good, which demonstrates that the consistency of SpeSR for each pixel can maintain high SSIM of HSIs. Thus, the SpeSR results can be corrected by imposing a specific bias. In Figure 6.40, the 11th band of an HSI is reconstructed from the ARAH HS data set and the VARAH HS data set, respectively. From the absolute error heat maps, it can be observed that the performance of the MST++ based on BliEstGAN approaches the performance of the MST++ based on ground truth. Moreover, in Figure 6.41, the spectral response curse for a selected patch is presented, where the performances of the SpeSR methods based on baseline are not good.

Table 6.16 SpeSR results based on different spectral degradation methods [100] / with permission of IEEE.

Data sets	SpeSR methods	Parameter amount (millions)	GFLOPs	Inference times (s)	Evaluation metrics	Ground truth	Baseline	BliEstGAN
ARAH HS data set	HRN [23]	31.70	786.29	430.401	MSE	0.0001	0.0039	0.0004
					PSNR	39.7458	24.0781	33.6917
					SSIM	0.9861	0.9068	0.9688
	AWAN [24]	3.55	1298.93	153.892	MSE	0.0001	0.0027	0.0003
					PSNR	41.3201	25.7483	35.2896
					SSIM	0.9977	0.9176	0.9793
	HDNet [108]	2.66	834.29	396.315	MSE	0.0001	0.0006	0.0001
					PSNR	39.9148	31.2189	39.8261
					SSIM	0.9874	0.9194	0.9972
	MST++ [109]	1.62	110.64	380.775	MSE	0.0001	0.0006	0.0001
					PSNR	41.4944	32.3164	40.3639
					SSIM	0.9981	0.9283	0.9977
	MFormer [35]	1.72	231.21	966.509	MSE	0.0006	0.0416	0.0085
					PSNR	33.1558	19.2819	26.1247
					SSIM	0.9769	0.9092	0.9549
VARAH HS data set	HRN [23]	31.70	786.29	431.134	MSE	0.0004	0.0071	0.0016
					PSNR	37.2663	21.5664	27.9947
					SSIM	0.9896	0.9138	0.9667
	AWAN [24]	3.55	1298.93	153.932	MSE	0.0001	0.0041	0.0009
					PSNR	39.6877	23.9956	30.0496

Table 6.16 (Continued)

Data sets	SpeSR methods	Parameter amount (millions)	GFLOPs	Inference times (s)	Evaluation metrics	Ground truth	Baseline	BLiEstGAN
					SSIM	0.9965	0.9257	0.9780
	HDNet [108]	2.66	834.29	407.344	MSE	0.0001	0.0021	0.0003
					PSNR	39.0887	25.9462	36.2779
					SSIM	0.9858	0.9449	0.9897
	MST++ [109]	1.62	110.64	372.961	MSE	0.0001	0.0019	0.0003
					PSNR	41.7845	26.9019	37.6359
					SSIM	0.9983	0.9571	0.9903
	MFormer [35]	1.72	231.21	964.064	MSE	0.0005	0.0368	0.0071
					PSNR	33.2225	19.5138	26.3159
					SSIM	0.9812	0.9052	0.9580
Houston data set	HRN [23]	31.71	66.57	39.248	MSE	0.0010	0.0043	0.0026
					PSNR	36.1552	29.9422	32.0643
					SSIM	0.8925	0.3511	0.7069
	AWAN [24]	3.56	109.98	14.023	MSE	0.0012	0.0042	0.0027
					PSNR	35.6824	29.9083	31.8883
					SSIM	0.8855	0.3309	0.6490
	HDNet [108]	2.67	70.64	36.611	MSE	0.0007	0.0031	0.0018
					PSNR	37.4816	31.2692	33.7438
					SSIM	0.9047	0.6637	0.7359
	MST++ [109]	1.63	9.37	34.336	MSE	0.0005	0.0027	0.0012
					PSNR	38.6438	31.8412	34.3745
					SSIM	0.9172	0.6724	0.7711
	MFormer [35]	1.73	19.58	87.948	MSE	0.0035	0.0159	0.0081
					PSNR	30.6276	23.4628	26.4713
					SSIM	0.6092	0.2765	0.3036

6.6 Conclusion and Discussion

This chapter discusses various methods for HSI SR, ranging from supervised to blind methods aimed at obtaining HR HSIs. These methods are built upon the fundamental imaging model, with the objective of addressing the inherently ill-posed nature of the HR HSI task through learning-based techniques.

Based on the extent of supervised information utilized, learning-based methods can be classified into three categories: fully supervised, weakly supervised, and unsupervised methods. In addition, if HSIs and MSIs are unpaired in unsupervised methods, it can be thought of as blind HSI SR. The application of sparse representation, a crucial tool, is introduced for HSI SR under full supervision. Furthermore, employing the superpixel strategy aids in extracting spatial information effectively. Due to the resource-intensive nature of annotating images when using deep learning-based

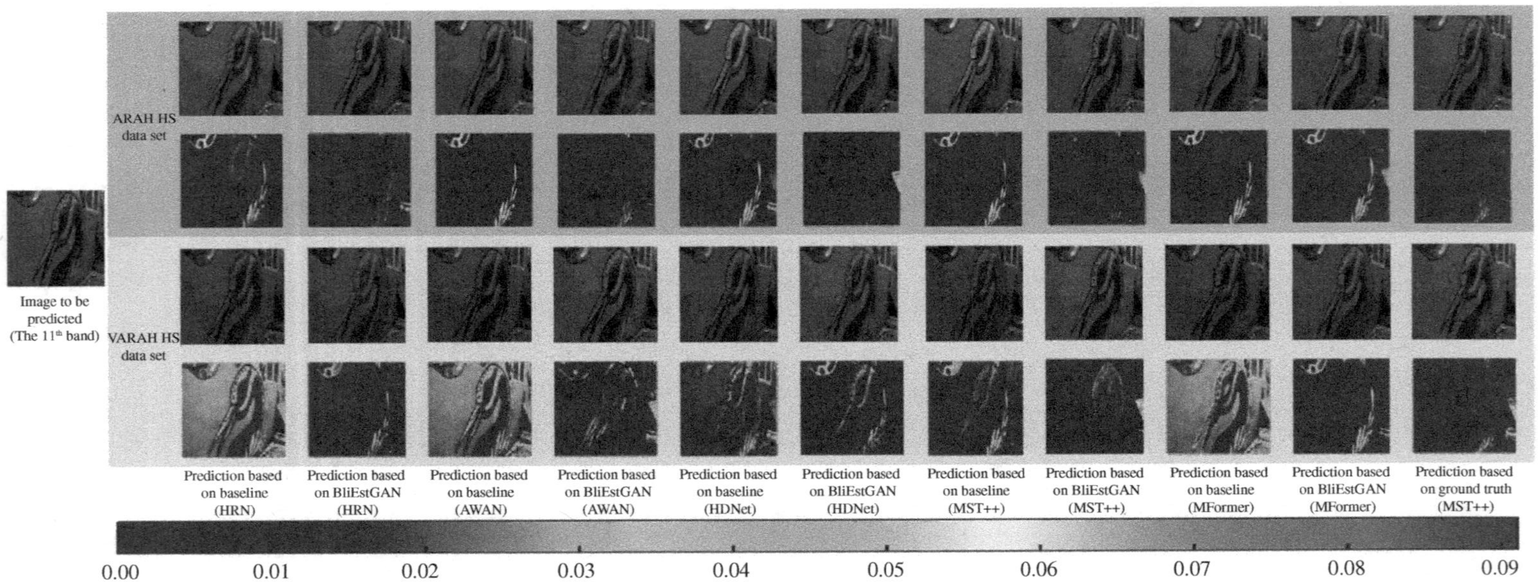

Figure 6.40 The 11th band of an HSI and the absolute error heat maps are based on different SpeSR methods and different spectral degradations [100] / with permission of IEEE.

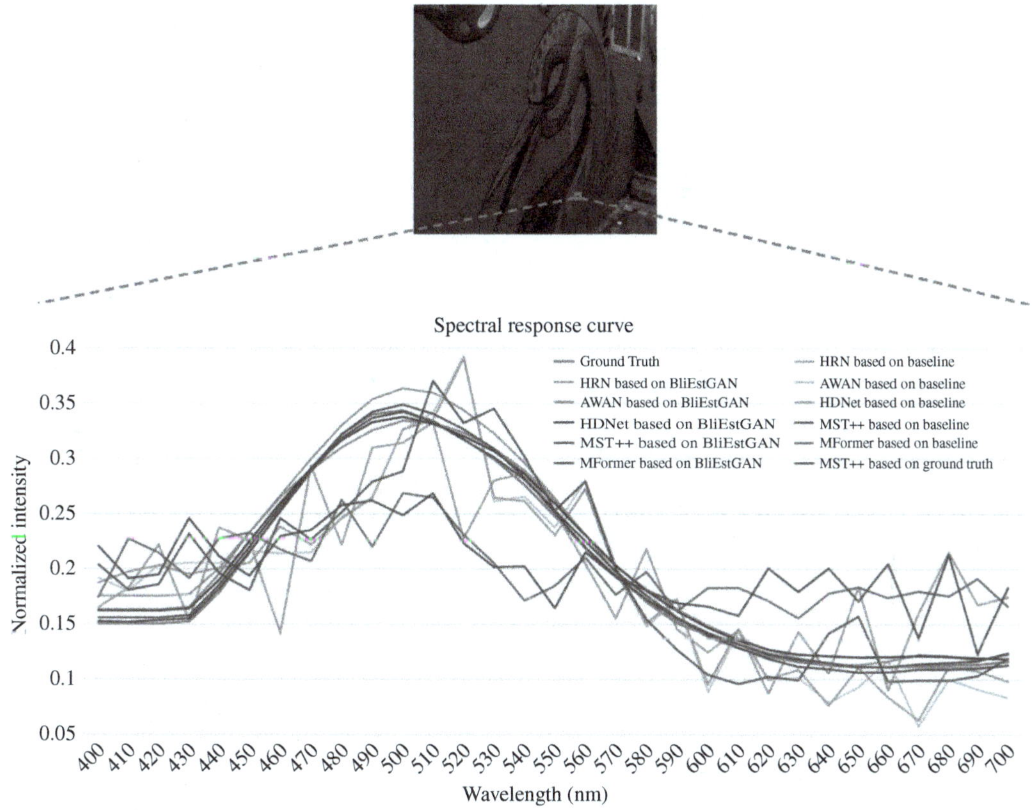

Figure 6.41 The average spectral response curve for a selected 5 × 5 field location in the box [100] / with permission of IEEE.

methods, efforts have been made to extend these techniques to HSI SR under weak or no supervision. Notably, GAN models have proven to be effective in capturing implicit relationships between unpaired HR and LR HSIs. Additionally, certain optimization frameworks enable the transformation of the HSI SR task into an alternative task, such as the denoising task, which is easy to generate synthetic datasets in self-supervised strategies.

While fully supervised methods generally yield superior results compared to weakly supervised and unsupervised methods, the collection of fully supervised data presents challenges. In practice, unsupervised learning-based methods, particularly those leveraging unpaired HSIs and MSIs for blind HSI SR, are better suited for real-world applications. Moreover, existing evaluation metrics typically require full supervision information, and synthetic data is often employed to validate the effectiveness of proposed methods. However, synthetic data may not accurately capture the genuine relationship between HR and LR HSIs. Consequently, the development of blind evaluation metrics tailored for real-world applications remains a promising avenue for future research.

References

1 Nadimpalli, R., Srivastava, A., Prasad, V.S. et al. (2020). Impact of insat-3D/3DR radiance data assimilation in predicting tropical cyclone Titli over the Bay of Bengal. *IEEE Trans. Geosci. Remote Sens.* 58 (10): 6945–6957.

2 Pontius, J., Martin, M., Plourde, L., and Hallett, R. (2008). Ash decline assessment in emerald ash borer-infested regions: a test of tree-level, hyperspectral technologies. *Remote Sens. Environ.* 112 (5): 2665–2676.
3 Li, S., Song, W., Fang, L. et al. (2019). Deep learning for hyperspectral image classification: an overview. *IEEE Trans. Geosci. Remote Sens.* 57 (9): 6690–6709.
4 Hassanzadeh, A., Zhang, F., Murphy, S.P. et al. (2022). Toward crop maturity assessment via UAS-based imaging spectroscopy—a snap bean pod size classification field study. *IEEE Trans. Geosci. Remote Sens.* 60: 1–17.
5 Wu, L., Fang, L., Yue, J. et al. (2022). Deep bilateral filtering network for point-supervised semantic segmentation in remote sensing images. *IEEE Trans. Image Process.* 31: 7419–7434.
6 Liu, Y., Zuo, Z., Tian, J. et al. (2021). Research on generic optical remote sensing products: a review of scientific exploration, technology research, and engineering application. *IEEE J. Sel. Top. Appl. Earth Obs. Remote Sens.* 14: 3937–3953.
7 Amani, M. et al. (2020). Google earth engine cloud computing platform for remote sensing big data applications: a comprehensive review. *IEEE J. Sel. Top. Appl. Earth Obs. Remote Sens.* 13: 5326–5350.
8 Zhang, B., Wu, Y., Zhao, B. et al. (2022). Progress and challenges in intelligent remote sensing satellite systems. *IEEE J. Sel. Top. Appl. Earth Obs. Remote Sens.* 15: 1814–1822.
9 Fang, L., Jiang, Y., Yan, Y. et al. (2023). Hyperspectral image instance segmentation using spectral–spatial feature pyramid network. *IEEE Trans. Geosci. Remote Sens.* 61: 1–13.
10 Yokoya, N., Yairi, T., and Iwasaki, A. (2012). Coupled nonnegative matrix factorization unmixing for hyperspectral and multispectral data fusion. *IEEE Trans. Geosci. Remote Sens.* 50 (2): 528–537.
11 Lanaras, C., Baltsavias, E., and Schindler, K. (2015). Hyperspectral super-resolution by coupled spectral unmixing. *2015 IEEE International Conference on Computer Vision (ICCV)*, 3586–3594, Santiago, Chile (7–13 December 2015). IEEE.
12 Dong, W., Fu, F., Shi, G. et al. (2016). Hyperspectral image super-resolution via non-negative structured sparse representation. *IEEE Trans. Image Process.* 25 (5): 2337–2352.
13 Li, S., Dian, R., Fang, L., and Bioucas-Dias, J.M. (2018). Fusing hyperspectral and multispectral images via coupled sparse tensor factorization. *IEEE Trans. Image Process.* 27 (8): 4118–4130.
14 Charles, A.S., Olshausen, B.A., and Rozell, C.J. (2011). Learning sparse codes for hyperspectral imagery. *IEEE J. Sel. Top. Signal Process.* 5 (5): 963–978.
15 Kawakami, R., Wright, J., Tai, Y.W., Matsushita, Y., Ben-Ezra, M., and Ikeuchi, K. (2011). High-resolution hyperspectral imaging via matrix factorization. *CVPR 2011*, 2329–2336, Colorado Springs, CO, USA (20–25 June 2011). IEEE.
16 Huang, B., Song, H., Cui, H. et al. (2014). Spatial and spectral image fusion using sparse matrix factorization. *IEEE Trans. Geosci. Remote Sens.* 52 (3): 1693–1704.
17 Li, Y., Hu, J., Zhao, X. et al. (2017). Hyperspectral image super-resolution using deep convolutional neural network. *Neurocomputing* 266: 29–41.
18 Arun, P.V., Buddhiraju, K.M., Porwal, A., and Chanussot, J. (2020). CNN-based super-resolution of hyperspectral images. *IEEE Trans. Geosci. Remote Sens.* 58 (9): 6106–6121.
19 Li, Q., Yuan, Y., Jia, X., and Wang, Q. (2022). Dual-stage approach toward hyperspectral image super-resolution. *IEEE Trans. Image Process.* 31: 7252–7263.
20 Dian, R., Li, S., Guo, A., and Fang, L. (2018). Deep hyperspectral image sharpening. *IEEE Trans. Neural Netw. Learn. Syst.* 29 (11): 5345–5355.
21 Zheng, Y., Li, J., Li, Y. et al. (2022). Edge-conditioned feature transform network for hyperspectral and multispectral image fusion. *IEEE Trans. Geosci. Remote Sens.* 60: 1–15.
22 Guarino, G., Ciotola, M., Vivone, G., and Scarpa, G. (2024). Band-wise hyperspectral image pansharpening using CNN model propagation. *IEEE Trans. Geosci. Remote Sens.* 62: 1–18.

23 Zhao, Y., Po, L.M., Yan, Q., Liu, W., and Lin, T. (2020). Hierarchical regression network for spectral reconstruction from RGB images. *2020 IEEE/CVF Conference on Computer Vision and Pattern Recognition Workshops (CVPRW)*, 1695–1704, Seattle, WA, USA (14–19 June 2020). IEEE.

24 Li, J., Wu, C., Song, R., Li, Y., and Liu, F. (2020). Adaptive weighted attention network with camera spectral sensitivity prior for spectral reconstruction from RGB images. *2020 IEEE/CVF Conference on Computer Vision and Pattern Recognition Workshops (CVPRW)*, 1894–1903, Seattle, WA, USA (14–19 June 2020). IEEE.

25 Wu, C., Li, J., Song, R. et al. (2023). RepCPSI: coordinate-preserving proximity spectral interaction network with reparameterization for lightweight spectral super-resolution. *IEEE Trans. Geosci. Remote Sens.* 61: 1–13.

26 Zhang, L., Nie, J., Wei, W. et al. (2021). Deep blind hyperspectral image super-resolution. *IEEE Trans. Neural Netw. Learn. Syst.* 32 (6): 2388–2400.

27 Wang, W., Zeng, W., Huang, Y., Ding, X., and Paisley, J. (2019). Deep blind hyperspectral image fusion. *2019 IEEE/CVF International Conference on Computer Vision (ICCV)*, 4149–4158, Seoul, Korea (South) (27 October–2 November 2019). IEEE.

28 Wang, W., Fu, X., Zeng, W. et al. (2023). Enhanced deep blind hyperspectral image fusion. *IEEE Trans. Neural Netw. Learn. Syst.* 34 (3): 1513–1523.

29 Liang, Z., Wang, S., Zhang, T., and Fu, Y. (2023). Blind super-resolution of single remotely sensed hyperspectral image. *IEEE Trans. Geosci. Remote Sens.* 61: 1–14.

30 Dian, R., Li, S., and Kang, X. (2021). Regularizing hyperspectral and multispectral image fusion by CNN denoiser. *IEEE Trans. Neural Netw. Learn. Syst.* 32 (3): 1124–1135.

31 Bell-Kligler, S., Shocher, A., and Irani, M. (2019). Blind super-resolution kernel estimation using an internal-GAN. *Proceedings of the 33rd International Conference on Neural Information Processing Systems, Vancouver, BC, Canada* (pp. 284–293). Curran Associates Inc.

32 Guo, A., Dian, R., and Li, S. (2020). Unsupervised blur kernel learning for pansharpening. *IGARSS 2020 – 2020 IEEE International Geoscience and Remote Sensing Symposium*, 633–636, Waikoloa, HI, USA (26 September–2 October 2020). IEEE.

33 Guo, A., Dian, R., and Li, S. (2023). A deep framework for hyperspectral image fusion between different satellites. *IEEE Trans. Pattern Anal. Mach. Intell.* 45 (7): 7939–7954.

34 Zhu, Z., Liu, H., Hou, J., Zeng, H., and Zhang, Q. (2021). Semantic-embedded unsupervised spectral reconstruction from single RGB images in the wild. *2021 IEEE/CVF International Conference on Computer Vision (ICCV)*, 2259–2268, Montreal, QC, Canada (10–17 October 2021). IEEE.

35 Li, J., Leng, Y., Song, R. et al. (2023). Mformer: taming masked transformer for unsupervised spectral reconstruction. *IEEE Trans. Geosci. Remote Sens.* 61: 1–12.

36 Akhtar, N., Shafait, F., and Mian, A. 2014. Sparse spatio-spectral representation for hyperspectral image super-resolution. *Event 13th European Conference on Computer Vision*, 63–78, Zurich, Switzerland (6–12 September 2014). SpringerLink.

37 Song, H., Huang, B., Zhang, K., and Zhang, H. (2014). Spatio-spectral fusion of satellite images based on dictionary-pair learning. *Inf. Fusion* 18 (1): 148–160.

38 Fang, L., Zhuo, H., and Li, S. (2018). Super-resolution of hyperspectral image via superpixel-based sparse representation. *Neurocomputing* 273: 171–177.

39 Shen, Y., Li, J., Zhu, Z. et al. (2015). Image reconstruction algorithm from compressed sensing measurements by dictionary learning. *Neurocomputing* 151: 1153–1162.

40 Mairal, J., Bach, F., Ponce, J., and Sapiro, G. (2009). Online dictionary learning for sparse coding. *ICML'09: Proceedings of the 26th Annual International Conference on Machine Learning*, 689–696, Montreal, Quebec, Canada (14–18 June 2009).

41 Zou, H., Hastie, T., and Tibshirani, R. (2006). Sparse principal component analysis. *J. Comput. Graph. Stat.* 15 (2): 265–286.

42 Liu, M.Y., Tuzel, O., Ramalingam, S., and Chellappa, R. (2011). Entropy rate superpixel segmentation. *CVPR 2011*, 2097–2104, Colorado Springs, CO, USA (20–25 June 2011). IEEE.

43 Landgrebe, D.A. and Biehl, L. 1992. 220 band hyperspectral image: Aviris image Indian Pine test site 3. School of Engineering Education, Purdue University, West Lafayette.

44 Green, R.O. et al. (1998). Imaging spectroscopy and the airborne visible/infrared imaging spectrometer (AVIRIS). *Remote Sens. Environ.* 65 (3): 227–248.

45 Dell'Acqua, F., Gamba, P., Ferrari, A. et al. (2004). Exploiting spectral and spatial information in hyperspectral urban data with high resolution. *IEEE Geosci. Remote Sens. Lett.* 1 (4): 322–326.

46 Wald, L. (2000). Quality of high resolution synthesised images: is there a simple criterion? *Fusion of Earth Data: Merging Point Measurements, Raster Maps and Remotely Sensed Images*, 99–103, Sophia Antipolis, France (January 2000).

47 Wei, Q., Bioucas-Dias, J., Dobigeon, N., and Tourneret, J.Y. (2015). Hyperspectral and multispectral image fusion based on a sparse representation. *IEEE Trans. Geosci. Remote Sens.* 53 (7): 3658–3668.

48 Lei, S., Shi, Z., and Zou, Z. (2017). Super-resolution for remote sensing images via local–global combined network. *IEEE Geosci. Remote Sens. Lett.* 14 (8): 1243–1247.

49 Jiang, K., Wang, Z., Yi, P. et al. (2018). Deep distillation recursive network for remote sensing imagery super-resolution. *Remote Sens* 10 (11): 1700.

50 Lu, T., Wang, J., Zhang, Y. et al. (2019). Satellite image super-resolution via multi-scale residual deep neural network. *Remote Sens* 11 (13): 1588.

51 Pan, Z., Ma, W., Guo, J., and Lei, B. (2019). Super-resolution of single remote sensing image based on residual dense backprojection networks. *IEEE Trans. Geosci. Remote Sens.* 57 (10): 7918–7933.

52 Zhang, D., Shao, J., Li, X., and Shen, H.T. (2021). Remote sensing image super-resolution via mixed high-order attention network. *IEEE Trans. Geosci. Remote Sens.* 59 (6): 5183–5196.

53 Huang, G., Liu, Z., Maaten, L.V.D., and Weinberger, K.Q. (2017). Densely connected convolutional networks. *2017 IEEE Conference on Computer Vision and Pattern Recognition (CVPR)*, 2261–2269, Honolulu, HI, USA (21–26 July 2017). IEEE.

54 Dong, X., Sun, X., Jia, X. et al. (2021). Remote sensing image super-resolution using novel dense-sampling networks. *IEEE Trans. Geosci. Remote Sens.* 59 (2): 1618–1633.

55 Ledig, C. et al. (2017). Photo-realistic single image super-resolution using a generative adversarial network. *2017 IEEE Conference on Computer Vision and Pattern Recognition (CVPR)*, 105–114, Honolulu, HI, USA (21–26 July 2017). IEEE.

56 Wang, X., Yu, K., Wu, S., Gu, J., Liu, Y., Dong, C., Qiao, Y., and Loy, C.C. (2018). ESRGAN: enhanced super-resolution generative adversarial networks. *Proceedings of the European Conference on Computer Vision (ECCV) Workshops*, Munich, Germany, Sep. 8–14, 2018, pp. 63–79.

57 Zhang, W., Liu, Y., Dong, C., and Qiao, Y. (2019). RankSRGAN: generative adversarial networks with ranker for image super-resolution. *2019 IEEE/CVF International Conference on Computer Vision (ICCV)*, 3096–3105, Seoul, Korea (South) (27 October–2 November 2019). IEEE.

58 Jiang, K., Wang, Z., Yi, P. et al. (2019). Edge-enhanced GAN for remote sensing image superresolution. *IEEE Trans. Geosci. Remote Sens.* 57 (8): 5799–5812.

59 Lei, S., Shi, Z., and Zou, Z. (2020). Coupled adversarial training for remote sensing image super-resolution. *IEEE Trans. Geosci. Remote Sens.* 58 (5): 3633–3643.

60 Isola, P., Zhu, J., Zhou, T., and Efros, A.A. (2017). Image-to-image translation with conditional adversarial networks. *2017 IEEE Conference on Computer Vision and Pattern Recognition (CVPR)*, 5967–5976, Honolulu, HI, USA (21–26 July 2017). IEEE.

61 Zhu, J.Y., Park, T., Isola, P., and Efros, A.A. (2017). Unpaired image-to-image translation using cycle-consistent adversarial networks. *2017 IEEE International Conference on Computer Vision (ICCV)*, 2242–2251, Venice, Italy (22–29 October 2017). IEEE.

62 Wu, J., Cong, R., Fang, L. et al. (2023). Unpaired remote sensing image super-resolution with content-preserving weak supervision neural network. *Sci. China Inf. Sci.* 66 (1): 119105.

63 He, K., Zhang, X., Ren, S., and Sun, J. (2016). Deep residual learning for image recognition. *2016 IEEE Conference on Computer Vision and Pattern Recognition (CVPR)*, 770–778, Las Vegas, NV, USA (27–30 June 2016). IEEE.

64 Soria, X., Riba, E., and Sappa, A. (2020). Dense extreme inception network: towards a robust CNN model for edge detection. *2020 IEEE Winter Conference on Applications of Computer Vision (WACV)*, 1912–1921, Snowmass, CO, USA (1–5 March 2020). IEEE.

65 Dong, R., Zhang, L., and Fu, H. (2022). RRSGAN: reference-based super-resolution for remote sensing image. *IEEE Trans. Geosci. Remote Sens.* 60: 1–17.

66 Xia, G.S. et al. (2018) DOTA: a large-scale dataset for object detection in aerial images. *2018 IEEE/CVF Conference on Computer Vision and Pattern Recognition*, 3974–3983, Salt Lake City, UT, USA (18–23 June 2018). IEEE.

67 Mittal, A., Soundararajan, R., and Bovik, A.C. (2013). Making a "completely blind" image quality analyzer. *IEEE Signal Process. Lett.* 20 (3): 209–212.

68 Wang, Z., Bovik, A.C., Sheikh, H.R., and Simoncelli, E.P. (2004). Image quality assessment: from error visibility to structural similarity. *IEEE Trans. Image Process.* 13 (4): 600–612.

69 Zhang, R., Isola, P., Efros, A.A., Shechtman, E., and Wang, O. (2018). The unreasonable effectiveness of deep features as a perceptual metric. *Proceedings – 2018 IEEE/CVF Conference on Computer Vision and Pattern Recognition, CVPR 2018*, 586–595, Salt Lake City, UT, USA (18–22 June 2018). IEEE Computer Society.

70 Kingma, D.P. and Ba, J.L. (2015). Adam: a method for stochastic optimization. *International Conference on Learning Representations*, 1–15, San Diego (7–9 May 2015).

71 Dong, C., Loy, C.C., He, K., and Tang, X. (2016). Image super-resolution using deep convolutional networks. *IEEE Trans. Pattern Anal. Mach. Intell.* 38 (2): 295–307.

72 Lim, B., Son, S., Kim, H., Nah, S., and Lee, K.M. (2017). Enhanced deep residual networks for single image super-resolution. *2017 IEEE Conference on Computer Vision and Pattern Recognition Workshops (CVPRW)*, 1132–1140, Honolulu, HI, USA (21–26 July 2017). IEEE.

73 Shocher, A., Cohen, N., and Irani, M. (2018). Zero-shot super-resolution using deep internal learning. *2018 IEEE/CVF Conference on Computer Vision and Pattern Recognition (CVPR)*, 3118–3126, Salt Lake City, UT, USA (18–23 June 2018). IEEE.

74 Zhang, Y. et al. (2018). Image super-resolution using very deep residual channel attention networks. *Computer Vision – ECCV 2018: 15th European Conference*, 294–310, Munich, Germany (8–14 September 2018).

75 Yuan, Y., Liu, S., Zhang, J., Zhang, Y., Dong, C., and Lin, L. (2018). Unsupervised image super-resolution using cycle-in-cycle generative adversarial networks. *2018 IEEE/CVF Conference on Computer Vision and Pattern Recognition Workshops (CVPRW)*, Salt Lake City, UT, USA, Jun. 18–23, 2018, pp. 701–710.

76 Zhuang, L. and Bioucas-Dias, J.M. (2018). Fast hyperspectral image denoising and inpainting based on low-rank and sparse representations. *IEEE J. Sel. Top. Appl. Earth Obs. Remote Sens.* 11 (3): 730–742.

77 Zhuang, L., Gao, L., Zhang, B. et al. (2020). Hyperspectral image denoising and anomaly detection based on low-rank and sparse representations. *IEEE Trans. Geosci. Remote Sens.* 60: 1–17.

78 Zhuang, L., Fu, X., Ng, M.K., and Bioucas-Dias, J.M. (2021). Hyperspectral image denoising based on global and nonlocal low-rank factorizations. *IEEE Trans. Geosci. Remote Sens.* 59: 10438–10454.

79 Fu, X., Guo, Y., Xu, M., and Jia, S. (2023). Hyperspectral image denoising via robust subspace estimation and group sparsity constraint. *IEEE Trans. Geosci. Remote Sens.* 61: 5512716.

80 Zhuang, L. and Ng, M.K. (2020). Hyperspectral mixed noise removal by ℓ_1-norm-based subspace representation. *IEEE J. Sel. Top. Appl. Earth Obs. Remote Sens.* 13: 1143–1157.

81 Simões, M., Bioucas-Dias, J., Almeida, L., and Chanussot, J. (2015). A convex formulation for hyperspectral image superresolution via subspace-based regularization. *IEEE Trans. Geosci. Remote Sens.* 53 (6): 3373–3388.

82 Wang, Z., Ng, M.K., Michalski, J., and Zhuang, L. (2023). A self-supervised deep denoiser for hyperspectral and multispectral image fusion. *IEEE Trans. Geosci. Remote Sens.* 61: 1–14.

83 Wei, Q., Dobigeon, N., and Tourneret, J.-Y. (2015). Fast fusion of multi-band images based on solving a Sylvester equation. *IEEE Trans. Image Process.* 24 (11): 4109–4121.

84 Combettes, P.L. and Wajs, V.R. (2005). Signal recovery by proximal forward-backward splitting. *Multiscale Model Simul.* 4 (4): 1168–1200.

85 Zhuang, L., Ng, M.K., Gao, L. et al. (2023). Eigenimage2eigenimage (E2E): a self-supervised deep learning network for hyperspectral image denoising. *IEEE Trans. Neural Netw. Learn. Syst.* 35: 16262–16276.

86 Huang, T., Li, S., Jia, X., Lu, H., and Liu, J. (2021). Neighbor2neighbor: self-supervised denoising from single noisy images. *2021 IEEE/CVF Conference on Computer Vision and Pattern Recognition (CVPR)*, 14781–14790, Nashville, TN, USA (20–25 June 2021). IEEE.

87 Wald, L., Ranchin, T., and Mangolini, M. (1997). Fusion of satellite images of different spatial resolutions: Assessing the quality of resulting images. *Photogramm. Eng. Remote Sens.* 63 (6): 691–699.

88 Fu, X., Jia, S., Xu, M. et al. (2022). Fusion of hyperspectral and multispectral images accounting for localized inter-image changes. *IEEE Trans. Geosci. Remote Sens.* 60: 1–18.

89 Barsi, J.A., Lee, K., Kvaran, G. et al. (2014). The spectral response of the Landsat-8 operational land imager. *Remote Sens* 6 (10): 10232–10251.

90 Zheng, K., Gao, L., Liao, W. et al. (2020). Coupled convolutional neural network with adaptive response function learning for unsupervised hyperspectral super resolution. *IEEE Trans. Geosci. Remote Sens.* 59 (3): 2487–2502.

91 Zhuang, L. and Ng, M.K. (2021). FastHyMix: fast and parameter-free hyperspectral image mixed noise removal. *IEEE Trans. Neural Netw. Learn. Syst.* 34: 4702–4716.

92 Le Saux, B., Yokoya, N., Hänsch, R., and Prasad, S. (2018). 2018 IEEE GRSS data fusion contest: multimodal land use classification [technical committees]. *IEEE Geosci. Remote Sens. Mag.* 6 (1): 52–54.

93 Arad, B. and Ben-Shahar, O. (2016). Sparse recovery of hyperspectral signal from natural RGB images. *European Conference on Computer Vision*, Amsterdam, The Netherlands, September 16, 2016, pp. 19–34.

94 Yokoya, N., Grohnfeldt, C., and Chanussot, J. (2017). Hyperspectral and multispectral data fusion: a comparative review of the recent literature. *IEEE Geosci. Remote Sens. Mag.* 5 (2): 29–56.

95 Xie, Q., Zhou, M., Zhao, Q. et al. (2020). MHF-Net: an interpretable deep network for multispectral and hyperspectral image fusion. *IEEE Trans. Pattern Anal. Mach. Intell.* 44: 1457–1473.

96 Hu, J.-F., Huang, T.-Z., Deng, L.-J. et al. (2022). Hyperspectral image super-resolution via deep spatiospectral attention convolutional neural networks. *IEEE Trans. Neural Netw. Learn. Syst.* 33 (12): 7251–7265.

97 Cohen, J. (1964). Dependency of the spectral reflectance curves of the Munsell color chips. *Psychon. Sci.* 1: 369–370.

98 Zhao, Y. and Berns, R.S. (2007). Image-based spectral reflectance reconstruction using the matrix R method. *Color. Res. Appl.* 32 (5): 343–351.

99 Gijsenij, A., Gevers, T., and Weijer, J.V.D. (2011). Computational color constancy: survey and experiments. *IEEE Trans. Image Process.* 20 (9): 2475–2489.

100 Xie, J., Fang, L., Wu, C. et al. (2024). Blind spectral super-resolution by estimating spectral degradation between unpaired images. *IEEE Trans. Geosci. Remote Sens.* 62: 1–14.

101 He, K., Zhang, X., Ren, S., and Sun, J. (2015). Spatial pyramid pooling in deep convolutional networks for visual recognition. *IEEE Trans. Pattern Anal. Mach. Intell.* 37 (9): 1904–1916.

102 Arora, S., Cohen, N., and Hazan, E. (2018). On the optimization of deep networks: implicit acceleration by overparameterization. *Proceedings of the 35th International Conference on Machine Learning*, Stockholm, Sweden, Jul. 10–15, 2018, vol. 80, pp. 244–253.

103 Kawaguchi, K. (2016). Deep learning without poor local minima. *Advances in Neural Information Processing Systems 29 (NIPS 2016)*, Barcelona, Spain, Dec. 5–10, 2016, pp. 586–594.

104 Simonyan, K. and Zisserman, A. (2015). Very deep convolutional networks for large-scale image recognition. *International Conference on Learning Representations (ICLR2015)*, San Diego, CA, USA, May 7–9, 2015, pp. 1–14.

105 Miyato, T., Kataoka, T., Koyama, M., and Yoshida, Y. (2018). Spectral normalization for generative adversarial networks. *International Conference on Learning Representations (ICLR 2018)*, Vancouver, BC, Canada, Apr. 30–May 3, 2018, pp. 1–26.

106 Ioffe, S. and Szegedy, C. (2015). Batch normalization: accelerating deep network training by reducing internal covariate shift. *ICML'15: Proceedings of the 32nd International Conference on International Conference on Machine Learning*, Lille, France, Jul. 6–11, 2015, pp. 448–456.

107 Arad, B. et al. (2020). NTIRE 2020 challenge on spectral reconstruction from an RGB image. *2020 IEEE/CVF Conference on Computer Vision and Pattern Recognition Workshops (CVPRW)*, Seattle, WA, USA, Jun. 14–19, 2020, pp. 1806–1822.

108 Hu, X., Cai, Y., Lin, J., Wang, H., Yuan, X., Zhang, Y., Timofte, R., and Gool, L.V. (2022). HDNet: high-resolution dual-domain learning for spectral compressive imaging. *2022 IEEE/CVF Conference on Computer Vision and Pattern Recognition (CVPR)*, 17521–17530, New Orleans, LA, USA (18–24 June 2022). IEEE.

109 Cai, Y., Lin, J., Lin, Z., Wang, H., Zhang, Y., Pfister, H., Timofte, R., and Gool, L.V. (2022). MST++: multi-stage spectral-wise transformer for efficient spectral reconstruction. *Proceedings of the IEEE conference on computer vision and pattern Recognition (CVPR), Workshops*, New Orleans, LA, USA, Jun. 18–24, 2022, pp. 744–754.

7

Hyperspectral Image Reconstruction Based on Unsupervised Learning

Ying Qu[1], Jiangsan Zhao[2], Hairong Qi[3], Chiman Kwan[4], and Liqiang Zhang[1]

[1] *State Key Laboratory of Remote Sensing and Digital Earth, Faculty of Geographical Science, Beijing Normal University, Beijing, China*
[2] *Department of Agricultural Technology, Norwegian Institute of Bioeconomy Research (NIBIO), Ås, Norway*
[3] *Department of Electrical Engineering and Computer Science, Advanced Imaging and Collaborative Information Processing Group, The University of Tennessee, Knoxville, TN, USA*
[4] *Applied Research LLC, Rockville, MD, Rockville, USA*

Mathematical Symbols Used in This Chapter

$\overline{Y_h} \in \mathbb{R}^{m \times n \times L}$:	LR HSI.
$\overline{Y_m} \in \mathbb{R}^{M \times N \times l}$:	HR MSI.
$\overline{X} \in \mathbb{R}^{M \times N \times L}$:	HHSI.
$S_h \in \mathbb{R}^{mn \times c}$, $S_m \in \mathbb{R}^{MN \times c}$:	Coefficients.
D_h, D_m:	Spectral bases of LR HSI and HR MSI.
$R \in \mathbb{R}^{L \times l}$:	Camera response function.

7.1 Introduction

It has been demonstrated that HSI improves the performance of a variety of remote-sensing tasks, including object recognition and classification [1–5], image segmentation [6], object tracking [7–9] environmental monitoring [10], and change detection [11, 12]. However, due to hardware limitations, the high spectral resolution of HSI can only be reached at the expense of its spatial resolution. This is because the finer the spectral resolution is, the less is the radiation energy that can reach the sensor within a limited wavelength range [13, 14]. On the contrary, despite having a high spatial resolution, MSI or RGB images usually have a limited spectral resolution. Very often, images with both high spectral and spatial resolution are required to produce better recognition and analysis results [4]. Fusing hyperspectral with MSI or RGB images is a natural way to generate high-resolution (HR) images in both spatial and spectral domains. This procedure is referred to as *hyperspectral image super-resolution (HSI-SR)* [14, 15].

The HSI-SR problem originates from *multispectral pan-sharpening (MSI-PAN)*, where a HR panchromatic (PAN) image is used to improve the spatial resolution of the MSI image. Traditional methods can be roughly divided into three categories: component substitution (CS) [16–18] and multiresolution analysis (MRA)-based methods [19], matrix factorization-based [4], and

Machine-Learning-Based Hyperspectral Image Processing, First Edition. Edited by Bing Zhang.

Bayesian-based approaches [20]. CS-based methods segregate the spectral and spatial information of data by projecting it onto a predetermined space. Then, the low-spatial spatial component in MSI is replaced with a high-spatial-resolution component extracted from PAN imagery. Various CS-based approaches have been developed to tackle hyper-sharpening, yielding promising outcomes according to diverse criteria [21–23]. Similarly, MRA-based approaches capture spatial details by initially applying a spatial filter to the HR images. Subsequently, these spatial details are injected into the low-resolution (LR) HSIs [19, 20, 24, 25]. These traditional methods, although extensively developed over decades [16, 26], are not readily applicable to solving hyperspectral image super-resolution (HSI-SR) problems since they usually suffer from spectral distortion [4].

Recent approaches mainly fall into two categories: Bayesian-based methods and matrix factorization-based methods [4, 20]. The Bayesian-based approaches focus on estimating the posterior distribution of the HR HSI given the LR HSI and HR multispectral imagery (MSI), which provides a flexible way to regularize the solution space of HR HSI by utilizing appropriate prior distributions [27]. However, the assumption of prior distribution may not hold for images with complex backgrounds. On the other hand, Matrix factorization-based methods, such as dictionary-based approaches, assume that HR HSI is a linear combination of a properly chosen overcomplete dictionary and sparse coefficients [28]. Simões et al. introduced HySure, which considers both spatial and spectral characteristics of the data and applies vector-based total variation regularization to solve the problem [29]. Akhtar et al. [14] presented a nonparametric Bayesian strategy for HSI-SR, which involves learning a spectral dictionary from LR HSI within the Bayesian framework and then estimating spatial coefficients. Yokoya et al. [30] employed a decomposition technique for both LR HSI and HR MSI, which determine optimal nonnegative bases and coefficients alternately to generate HR HSI. Wycoff et al. [31] and Lanaras et al. [15] further improved the fusion performance through alternating direction method of multipliers (ADMM) and sparse constraint, respectively. However, most of these approaches rely on the assumption that the down-sampling function between the spatial coefficients of HR HSI and LR HSI is known in advance, which may not hold true due to complex environmental conditions.

Recently, there have been numerous endeavors [32, 33] to tackle the HSI-SR problem using deep learning techniques, following the pioneering work of Dong et al. [34]. These efforts focus on learning the mapping function between LR HSI and HR HSI through various frameworks. For example, Huang et al. [35], Masi et al. [36], and Wei et al. [37] learn the mapping function through sparse tied-weights denoising autoencoder, supervised SRCNN, and deep residual network, respectively. Furthermore, spatial constraint strategy [38] and low-rankness prior of the spectral domain [39] are used to improve the super-resolution performance. However, these supervised deep-learning-based methods face challenges in real applications due to several reasons. First, the scale differences between LR HSI and HR MSI can be substantial, reaching up to 10 times or more [40, 41]. Most existing SR methods only handle up to eight times upscaling. Second, these methods assume that the mapping function between LR and HR imagery is the same as that in real applications, which may not hold true for images acquired with different sensors or different spectral bands, leading to spectral distortion. Third, supervised learning requires a large dataset, knowledge of the down-sampling function, and availability of HR HSI, which are often unrealistic for HSI.

To address the above challenges, in this chapter, we introduce the first unsupervised solution for HSI-SR based on deep learning, which extracts spectral and spatial information from LR HSI and HR MSI through two Dirichlet networks with sum-to-one and sparsity constraints. Moreover, the method is further improved to reduce spectral distortion and handle fusion problems without multimodality registration through a mutual information (MI) network. In the end, to relieve the camera response function (CRF) dependence between LR-HSI and HR-MSI, the loss of the Gram matrix of abundance maps is used during CRF learning.

7.2 Problem Formulation

Before describing the methods, we first describe the problem in a mathematical way. Given LR HSI $\overline{Y_h} \in \mathbb{R}^{m \times n \times L}$, where m, n, and L denote its width, height, and number of spectral bands, respectively. HR MSI is denoted by $\overline{Y_m} \in \mathbb{R}^{M \times N \times l}$, where M, N, and l denote its width, height, and number of spectral bands, respectively. The goal is to reconstruct $\overline{X} \in \mathbb{R}^{M \times N \times L}$ with both high spectral and spatial resolutions. In general, the spatial resolution of MSI is higher than that of HSI, while the spectral resolution of HSI is higher than that of MSI, i.e., $M > m$, $N > n$, $L > l$.

To facilitate the subsequent process, the 3D images are unfolded into 2D matrices, which are denoted as $Y_h \in \mathbb{R}^{mn \times L}$, $Y_m \in \mathbb{R}^{MN \times l}$, and $X \in \mathbb{R}^{MN \times L}$. Assuming that each pixel can be approximated by a linear combination of c spectral bases and their corresponding coefficients [42], the decomposition procedure can be described as

$$Y_h = S_h D_h \tag{7.1}$$

$$Y_m = S_m D_m \tag{7.2}$$

where $S_h \in \mathbb{R}^{mn \times c}$, $S_m \in \mathbb{R}^{MN \times c}$ denote the coefficients, and D_h, D_m denote the spectral bases of LR HSI and HR MSI, respectively. With S_m carrying high spatial information and D_h carrying high spectral information, the desired HS HSI is generated by

$$X = S_m D_h \tag{7.3}$$

In addition, the relationship between the HR HSI and LR MSI in the spectral domain can be expressed as

$$D_m = D_h R \tag{7.4}$$

where $R \in \mathbb{R}^{L \times l}$ is the CRF of a given sensor. It is worth noting that since both HR HSI and LR MSI are linear combinations of spectral signatures, the representation of them, S_h and S_m, should meet the non-negative and sum-to-one constraints.

The challenges to address the problem include (i) the absence of ground truth HR HSI, (ii) the registration of the LR HSI and HR MSI, and (iii) the absence of a CRF in real applications. To address these challenges, the key is to utilize shared information from multimodalities to extract proper spectral and spatial information from unregistered multimodality images to prevent spectral distortion.

7.3 Unsupervised Hyperspectral Image Super-resolution with Dirichlet Net

We start to explore this problem with a simple case, where LR HSI and HR MSI/RGB are well registered. An unsupervised network structure is proposed as the first effort to solve the HSI-SR problem with deep learning in an unsupervised manner. The proposed method is referred

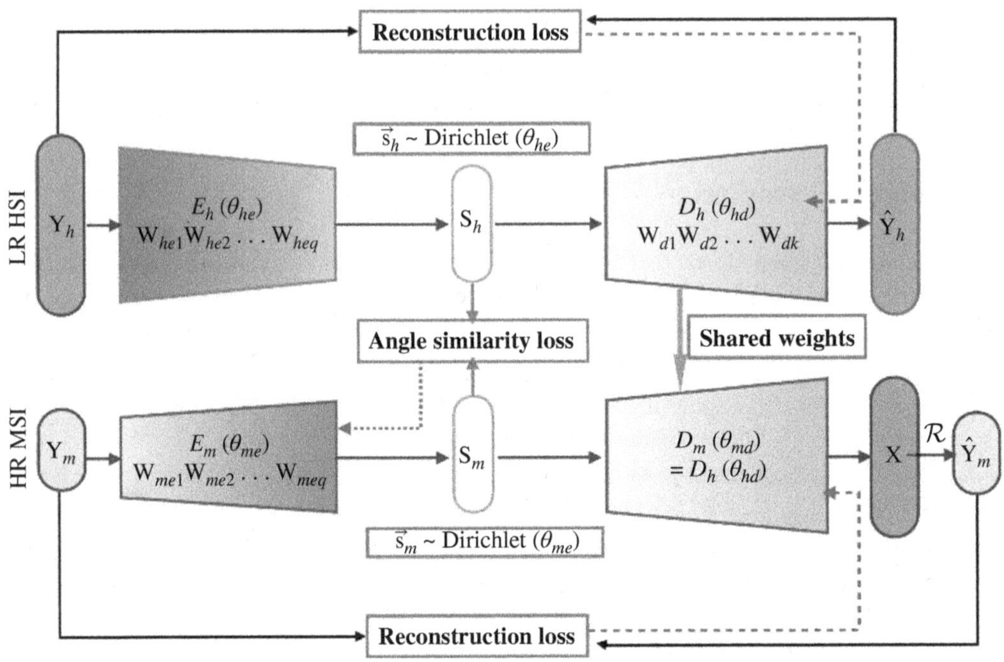

Figure 7.1 The architecture of the proposed unsupervised sparse Dirichlet Net (uSDN).

to as uSDN. The key to solving this problem is to extract high spectral information from LR HSI and high spatial information from HR MSI. The architecture of the proposed method is shown in Figure 7.1. Here, we emphasize three distinctive features of this architecture. The network consists of two encoder–decoder structures for the representation learning of both LR HSI and HR MSI. The two encoder–decoder structures share the same decoder weights to facilitate the extraction of spectral and spatial information from multiple modalities in an unsupervised manner. Both representations S_h and S_m are encouraged to follow a Dirichlet distribution, which naturally integrates the sum-to-one property into the network while imposing a sparsity constraint. To tackle the spectral distortion challenge, the angular differences of the representations from the two modalities are encouraged to have similar patterns by minimizing their angular differences.

7.3.1 Network Architecture

As shown in Figure 7.2, the top branch reconstructs the LR HSI with an encoder and a decoder structure. The encoder projects the data from the image space to a coefficient space, while the decoder reconstructs the HSI from the coefficient space. Assuming that the activation function is the identity function and there is no bias in the decoder, the decoder consists of a few fully connected layers denoted as $\theta_{he} = W_1 W_2 ... W_k$, which carries the spectral basis in Eq. (7.1). The representation layer of the network preserves the coefficient S_h. The bottom branch reconstructs the HR MSI in a similar way. According to Eqs. (7.1)–(7.4), the spectral bases of MSI/RGB can be acquired by compressing the spectral bases of HSI. Thus, in the network, LR HSI and HR MSI share the same decoder. The spectral bases of the MSI are obtained by

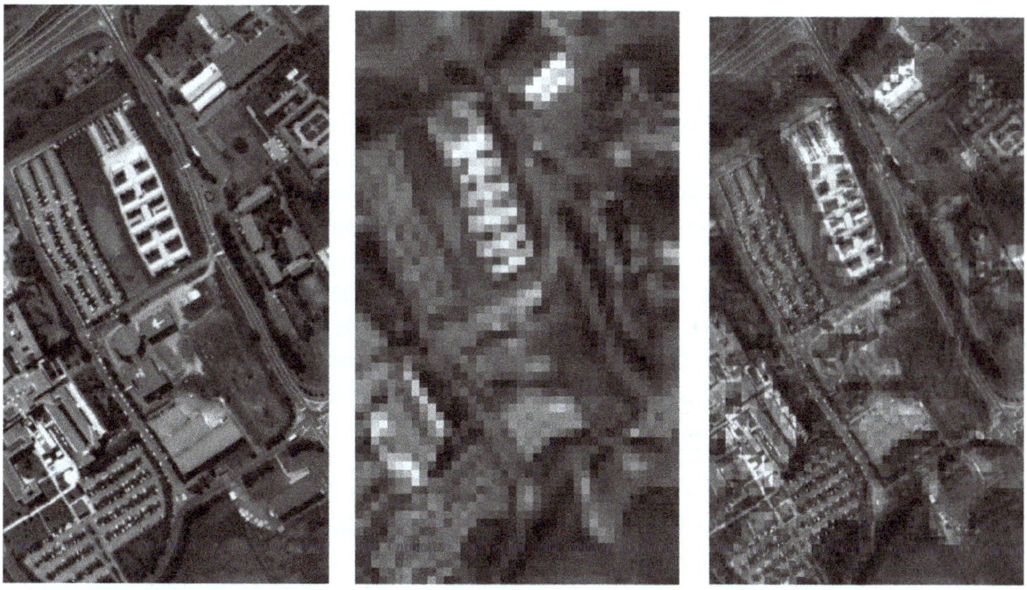

(a) (b) (c)

Figure 7.2 Unregistered hyperspectral image super-resolution with SFIM. (a) HR MSI, (b) LR HSI, and (c) fused image with SFIM [49].

compressing the spectral bases of the HSI with the CRF R. $\widehat{Y_m}$ is reconstructed by compressing the HR HSI with $\widehat{Y_m} = RX$.

7.3.2 Dirichlet Net with Sparse Constraints

Since the representation layer preserves the coefficients of the images, it should meet the non-negative and sum-to-one constraints [30, 31]. To naturally incorporate the sum-to-one property, the notes of the representation layer are enforced to follow a Dirichlet distribution which is generated with a stick-breaking process [43]. One way to illustrate the process is to break a stick of unit length into c pieces, each of whose length is generated according to a Dirichlet distribution. In the proposed network, the values of the notes in the representation layer reflect the length of the broken stick, which are learned through a couple of stacked fully connected layers.

Due to the fact that each pixel of the image only consists of a few spectral bases, an entropy function [44] is introduced to enforce the sparsity of the representations. When the data gets sparse, the entropy function approaches zero monotonically. More details can be found in Section 3.2 of [42].

7.3.3 Angle Similarity

Although the number of spectral bands in HR MSI/RGB and LR HSI and their spatial resolution are different, they capture the same scene, meaning that their representations should have similar patterns. Such similar patterns are enforced by minimizing the angular difference between the two representations. Note that since two representations have different spatial resolutions, we increase the size of the LR S_h with the nearest neighborhood. In this way, the spectral distortion is largely reduced. More details can be found in Section 3.3 of [42].

7.4 Unsupervised and Unregistered Hyperspectral Image Super-resolution

Despite numerous studies for HSI-SR, all existing approaches require at least one prerequisite to solve the problem, precise registration between the two input modalities, namely HSI and MSI/RGB. As shown in Figure 7.2, the accuracy of registration is crucial for the quality of the reconstructed HR HSI since it determines how effectively the two input modalities (HSI and MSI) are fused [2, 4, 42, 45, 46]. Recently, a few methods have introduced registration as a preliminary step prior to data fusion [45, 47, 48]. Nonetheless, these preliminary steps are limited in their ability to address large-scale discrepancies, e.g., more than eight-pixel offsets in two modalities [45]. Furthermore, since a single pixel in the LR MSI can cover hundreds of pixels in the corresponding HR HSI, HSI and MSI registration remains a difficult problem even within the registration community. Due to the significant spectral difference, multiband images and the spectral response function (SRF) must be taken into account during registration [49–52].

To solve the HSI-SR problem without multimodality registration, we have made substantial extensions. Although having different resolutions, the representations of the overlapped region of LR HSI, HR MSI, and HR HSI should ideally follow similar patterns under the assumption of linear combination, because the representations reflect how the spectral basis is constructed for each pixel. Based on the above fact, we improved the previous unsupervised network structure with MI. As illustrated in Figure 7.3, the network projects the LR HSI onto the same statistical space as the HR MSI to extract both the spectral and spatial information of the multimodalities through the same encoder–decoder structure, stabilizing the fusion process for two unregistered modalities. To naturally satisfy the nonnegative and sum-to-one physical criteria, the network representations are enforced to have a Dirichlet distribution. Moreover, to prevent spectral distortion, we employ MI to extract optimal and correlated representations from multi-modalities. Because the two modalities are unregistered, the associated representations are optimized by maximizing the MI between the representations and their own inputs. Furthermore, a collaborative $l_{2,1}$-norm is employed, which helps the network reconstruct individual pixels as precisely as possible. With the aforementioned architecture, the proposed method can operate directly on

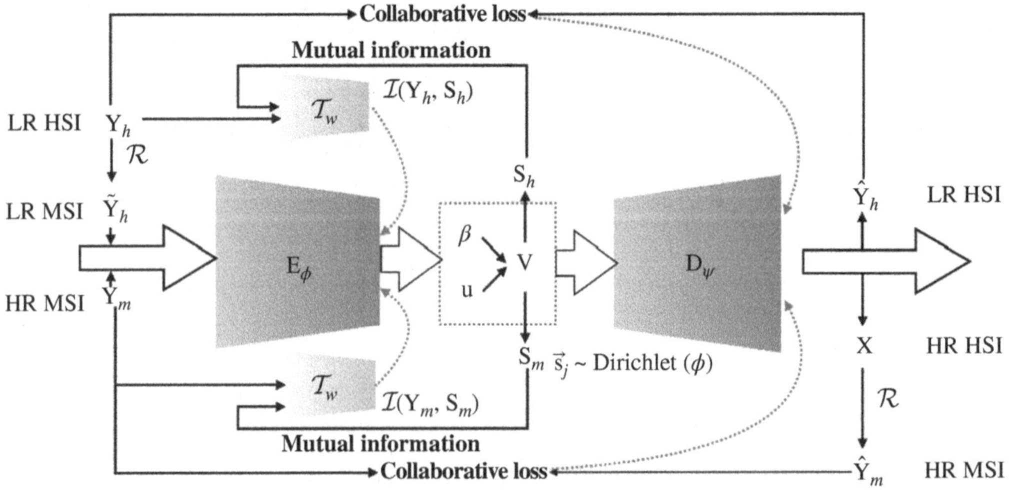

Figure 7.3 The architecture of the proposed unsupervised unregistered Mutual Dirichlet Net (u^2-MDN).

unregistered images with significantly decreased spectral distortion. The proposed method is referred to as unregistered and unsupervised mutual Dirichlet Net or u^2-MDN for short. To the best of our knowledge, this is the first attempt to solve the HSI-SR problem directly on unregistered image pairs.

7.4.1 Network Architecture

As shown in Figure 7.3, the input and output of the network are both LR HSI and HR MSI. In order to stabilize the network, we project Y_h into the same spectral space with a given CRF R, which is defined by fixed weights. In this way, without the requirement of extra settings, both modalities are connected to share the same encoder. Since it is not easy to extract spectral information D_m directly from HR MSI carrying low spectral information, it is transformed from D_h through a CRF. Therefore, in the network design, both modalities shared the same decoder structure D_h defined with network weights. Then, the output of the layer before the fixed weights carrying the CRF is the reconstructed X.

7.4.2 Mutual Dirichlet Network with Collaborative Constraint

Similar to our previous approach, the representations S are encouraged to be non-negative and sum-to-one with a stick-breaking structure. Moreover, for both modalities, the network should be able to learn the correlated and optimized representations generated by the encoder E_ϕ. That is, the two representations S_h and S_m should follow similar patterns. In the other way, the MI of the two representations should be maximized. To reinforce the similarity of LR HSI and HR MSI, we introduce MI, which captures the non-linear statistical dependencies between variables. However, since the two modalities do not register with each other, it is challenging to maximize such MI directly with neural networks. Therefore, in the network design, we can extract optimal representations by maximizing the MI between the input images and their respective representations through an MI network.

The structure of the network T_w is shown in Figure 7.4. Let's define the input domain as $\mathbb{Y} = \{Y_h, Y_m\}$, and the representation domain as $\mathbb{S} = \{S_h, S_m\}$. T_w consists of two fully connected layers, with $\mathbb{Y}$ and $\mathbb{S}$ as input images. Both the extracted representations and the raw image are stacked and fed into the network during the training procedure. To further reduce the spectral distortion, the collaborative $l_{2,1}$ loss is integrated into the network. More details can be found in Section IV.B of [50].

7.4.3 Experimental Results

7.4.3.1 Datasets

We evaluate the proposed method with Hyperspec Chikusei and Pavia datasets. In order to match a system modulation transfer function (MTF) [4], the image pairs are simulated using the Walds protocol [51], where the LR HSI is generated by applying a Gaussian filter with its full width at half maximum (FWHM) equal to the SR ratio. The MSI is produced by employing MSI spectral reflection functions (SRFs) from various sensors as filters to degrade the HR HSI in the spectral domain. Please refer to [4] for more details. Given that nonrigid deformation is typically unavoidable [46], random shifts in pixels are introduced to simulate the nonrigid distortion, following the protocol in [52, 53]. The methods are evaluated with erreur relative

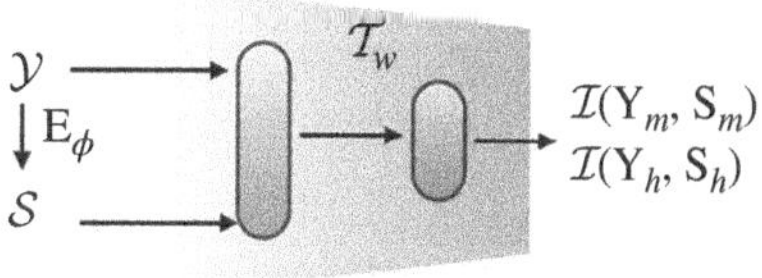

Figure 7.4 The details of the MI structure.

globale adimensionnelle de synthese (ERGAS), the peak signal-to-noise ratio (PSNR), and the spectral angle mapper (SAM) [51, 53].

7.4.3.2 Experimental Results with Unregistered Image Pairs

Table 7.1 presents the results of different methods on unregistered image pairs. It is worth noting that we only choose methods that may be applied to unregistered image pairs. Both the traditional CS-based GSA [18] and MTF-based SFIM [49] fail in this scenario. This is due to the fact that the spatial features could not be directly incorporated to increase the spatial resolution of the LR HSI when the two modalities were unregistered. Compared to the traditional methods, the sparse-coding-based NSSR and matrix-factorization-based CNMF are more reliable. However, their performance also suffers in benchmarked datasets. The rationale is that when the LR HSI and HR MSI are unregistered, the adopted predefined downsampling function will cause a considerable amount of spectral distortion. The performance of the integrated fusion method [52] is good for images with small distortion but fails with images with large distortion. This is because additional registration distortion may be introduced during optimization. Compared to the state-of-the-art, the suggested u^2-MDN can handle difficult cases substantially better. The primary factor contributing to the performance gain is that the network is able to use collaborative loss and MI to extract the optimal and most correlated spatial representations from two modalities. This effectively preserves both the spatial and, more importantly, the spectral information.

We show the reconstructed HR HSI in Figure 7.5 to visualize the reconstructed results for unregistered image pairs. It is evident that most of the methods were unable to effectively manage pairs of unregistered images with significant displacement. The reconstructed result from SFIM has some blocking artifacts. As shown in Figure 7.5e,f, the integrated fusion method and NSSR fail due to the large displacement between the two modalities. GSA and CNMF handle unregistered image pairs better than the other approaches as shown in Figure 7.5b and d. Compared to the state of the art, the proposed method has much less spectral and spatial distortion even with unregistered image pairs as shown in Figure 7.5g.

7.4.3.3 Experimental Results on Unregistered Real Image Pairs

Using real unregistered image pairs with both rigid and nonrigid distortions, we further evaluate the proposed approach and show the results in Figure 7.6. It is evident that the proposed approach, utilizing MI, can enhance the spatial resolution of the LR HSI while maintaining its spectral resolution, even with unregistered LR HSI and HR MSI with large displacement.

Table 7.1 Results of nonregistered remote-sensing image fusion.

	Chikusei			Pavia		
Methods	**ERGAS**	**PSNR**	**SAM**	**ERGAS**	**PSNR**	**SAM**
GSA [18]	4.4617	27.3028	7.6554	3.5149	27.161	12.6803
SFIM [49]	6.8057	23.8192	5.8405	5.2757	23.8248	9.2951
CNMF [30]	6.5318	25.5878	4.7582	4.4232	25.2803	7.9551
NSSR [54]	5.8158	25.8475	5.4245	5.0728	25.5778	8.2277
Integrated [52]	8.9107	21.4644	7.5126	10.2734	7.4938	20.7214
u^2-MDN	**1.5843**	**45.4919**	**1.0899**	**0.8898**	**40.4446**	**2.4371**

Bold values indicate which method achieves the optimal value under the current metric.

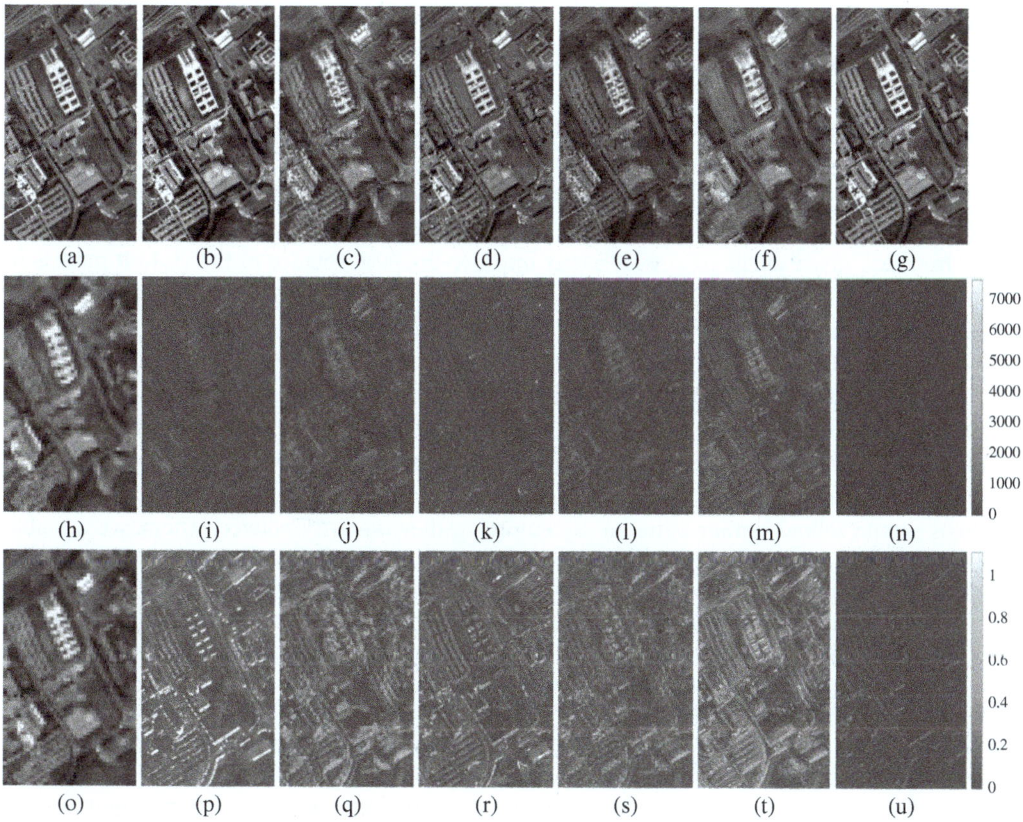

Figure 7.5 Reconstructed results given unregistered nonrigid distorted image pairs from the Pavia dataset. (a) Reference HR HSI. (h) Distorted LR HSI. (o) LR HSI. (b)–(g) Reconstructed results. (i)–(n) average absolute difference between the reconstructed HSI and reference HSI over different spectral bands, from different methods. (p)–(u) SAM of each pixel between the reconstructed HSI and reference HSI from different methods. (a) Ref HR HSI, (b) GSA, (c) SFIM, (d) CNMF, (e) NSSR, (f) integrated, (g) u^2-MDN, (h) distorted LR HSI, (i) difference of GSA, (j) difference of SFIM, (k) difference of CNMF, (l) difference of NSSR, (m) difference of integrated, (n) difference of u^2-MDN, (o) LR HSI, (p) SAM of GSA, (q) SAM of SFIM, (r) SAM of CNMF, (s) SAM of NSSR, (t) SAM of Integrated, and (u) SAM of u^2-MDN.

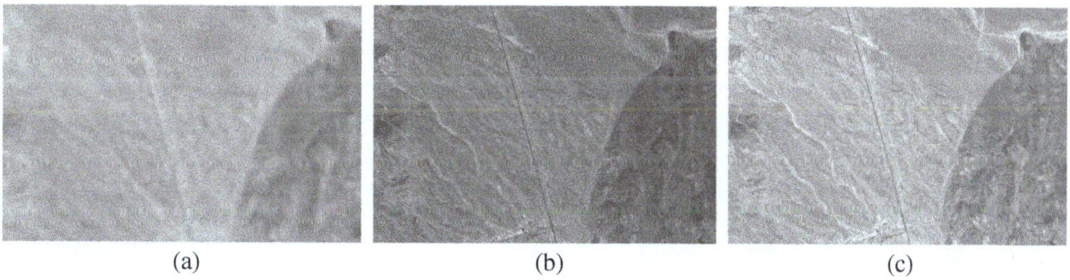

Figure 7.6 (a) Real LR HSI of the real data from Hyperion, (b) Real HR MSI of the real data from WorldView3 (images courtesy: Maxar), and (c) Reconstructed HR HSI from the proposed method.

7.5 Improving SR Performance with Endmember-assisted Camera Response Function Learning

Despite the fact that u^2MDN can generate HR-HSI based on unregistered image pairs in an unsupervised manner, its effectiveness depends heavily on the known CRF [50]. That is, the model may suffer from severe distortion if the HR MSI/RGB images are captured from a new camera with an unknown CRF in real-world applications. Therefore, it is necessary to develop an approach to learn a CRF from any given image pair, which may improve the performance of the HSI-SR models in future studies.

In this section, an unsupervised CRF learning network is proposed for any given HSI and MSI/RGB image pairs. The logic of this work is to ensure that the given HR MSI/RGB images and the LR MSI/RGB images generated by LR HSI with CRF are located in the same color space, such that the performance of the trained HSI-SR can be preserved. Let's use the RGB image as an example for simplicity. The network is trained to decompose image pairs into representations and the corresponding coefficients. If the CRF is correct, then the representations of the LR RGB and HR RGB should follow similar patterns. By enforcing the similarity between them, we are able to learn the CRF in an unsupervised manner.

7.5.1 Network Architecture

As shown in Figure 7.7, an LR-RGB is first created from the existing LR-HSI through a linear network carrying CRF, and decomposed into representations and spectral information. The proposed method consists of a share encoder–decoder structure to reconstruct both HR RGB and LR RGB generated by LR HSI with learnable CRF weights. The input data is projected into latent presentation space via three fully connected layers. The preceding layers of the encoder were closely

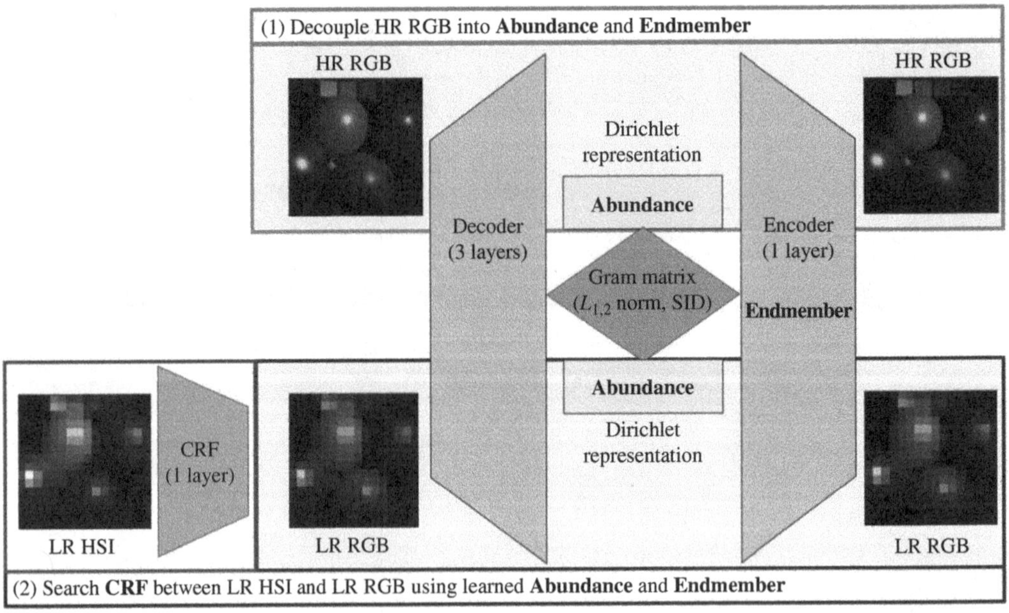

Figure 7.7 The architecture of the proposed CRF learning structure.

linked to the final layer in order to enhance the representation capacity of the network. The representation meets the non-negative and sum-to-one constraints with stick-breaking structures [50]. The decoder is a fully connected layer with nine nodes, which is used to reconstruct the input HR-RGB image from the representations.

Since the spectral information of RGB can be achieved by projecting LR-HSI with CRF, the generated LR RGB and HR RGB should share the same representations and spectral bases in a given pixel. The CRF weights consist of one fully connected layer. Since the representations of LR RGB and HR RGB have different resolutions, we use their Gram matrices to optimize the network. The product of the representation map and its transposed map is used to generate a Gram matrix, which is a square matrix with the same number of rows and columns as the number of channels, $GM^{9\times 9}$. For instance, the representation maps of HR RGB and LR RGB images can be expressed as $GM^{9\times 9}_{HR}$ and $GM^{9\times 9}_{LR}$, respectively. Then we optimize the network by reducing the distance between $GM^{9\times 9}_{HR}$ and $GM^{9\times 9}_{LR}$. More details can be found in Section IV of [55].

7.5.2 Experimental Results

Two commonly used CRFs of both Nikon 700D (Nikon) [50] and Canon 500D (Canon) [56] cameras and six datasets were employed to evaluate the proposed method. The LR HSI is generated by a Gaussian filter. We set the super-resolution scale of datasets as 8. Three methods HSCNNR [57], u^2MDN [50], and WLRTR [58] were evaluated with learnt CRF based on the six datasets CAVE [59], ICVL [60], Chikusei [4], Cuprite [4], Salinas [61], and KSC [62].

We generate synthetic images based on Nikon CRF to evaluate the u^2MDN, HSCNNR, and WLRTR models. Given the learned CRF, all three models suffer from slight-to-no-performance drop when testing on Nikon RGB images. The performance of the three methods dropped significantly when we tested the model on a dataset generated with Canon CRF. The u^2MDN model is invariant to the image rotation, while WLRTR models suffer from a large performance drop. More details can be found in Section V of [55].

7.6 Conclusions

In this chapter, to address the challenges of HSI-SR, we introduced the first unsupervised image fusion solution for HSI-SR based on deep learning, which extracts spectral and spatial information from LR HSI and HR MSI through two Dirichlet networks with sum-to-one and sparsity constraints. Moreover, the method is further improved to reduce spectral distortion and handle fusion problems without multimodality registration through an MI network. In the end, to relieve the CRF dependence between LR-HSI and HR-MSI, the loss of the Gram matrix of abundance maps is used during CRF learning. Extensive experiments on benchmark datasets demonstrated the superiority of the proposed approaches over the state of the art.

References

1 Chakrabarti, A. and Zickler, T. (2011). Statistics of real-world hyperspectral images. *CVPR 2011*, 193–200, Colorado Springs, CO, USA (20–25 June 2011). IEEE.

2 Bioucas-Dias, J.M., Plaza, A., Dobigeon, N. et al. (2012). Hyperspectral unmixing overview: geometrical, statistical, and sparse regression-based approaches. *IEEE J. Sel. Top. Appl. Earth Obs. Remote Sens.* 5 (2): 354–379.

3 Kwan, C., Ayhan, B., Chen, G. et al. (2006). A novel approach for spectral unmixing, classification, and concentration estimation of chemical and biological agents. *IEEE Trans. Geosci. Remote Sens.* 44 (2): 409–419.

4 Yokoya, N., Grohnfeldt, C., and Chanussot, J. (2017). Hyperspectral and multispectral data fusion: a comparative review of the recent literature. *IEEE Geosci. Remote Sens. Mag.* 5 (2): 29–56.

5 Su, Y., Gao, L., Jiang, M. et al. (2023). NSCKL: normalized spectral clustering with kernel-based learning for semisupervised hyperspectral image classification. *IEEE Trans. Cybern.* 53 (10): 6649–6662.

6 Gasparyan, H.A., Davtyan, T.A., and Agaian, S.S. (2024). A novel framework for solar panel segmentation from remote sensing images: utilizing Chebyshev transformer and hyperspectral decomposition. *IEEE Trans. Geosci. Remote Sens.* 62: 1–11.

7 Gao, L., Wang, D., Zhuang, L. et al. (2023). BS3LNet: a new blind-spot self-supervised learning network for hyperspectral anomaly detection. *IEEE Trans. Geosci. Remote Sens.* 61: 1–18.

8 Van Nguyen, H., Banerjee, A., Chellappa, R. (2010). Tracking via object reflectance using a hyperspectral video camera. *2010 IEEE Computer Society Conference on Computer Vision and Pattern Recognition*, 44–51, San Francisco, CA, USA (13–18 June 2010). IEEE.

9 Uzkent, B., Rangnekar, A., and Hoffman, M. (2017). Aerial vehicle tracking by adaptive fusion of hyperspectral likelihood maps. *2017 IEEE Conference on Computer Vision and Pattern Recognition Workshops (CVPRW)*, Honolulu, HI, USA (21–26 July 2017). IEEE.

10 Balsi, M., Bouchelaghem, S., Conti, L., Moroni, M., and Scalia, R.2023). Real-time plastic litter detection using hyperspectral sensing on drone. *13th Workshop on Hyperspectral Imaging and Signal Processing: Evolution in Remote Sensing (WHISPERS)* [Internet], 1–4, Athens, Greece (31 October–2 November 2023). IEEE. https://ieeexplore.ieee.org/document/10431217 (accessed 22 April 2024).

11 Kwon, H. and Nasrabadi, N.M. (2005). Kernel matched signal detectors for hyperspectral target detection. *2005 IEEE Computer Society Conference on Computer Vision and Pattern Recognition (CVPR'05)*, 6, San Diego, CA, USA (21–23 September 2005). IEEE.

12 Borengasser, M., Hungate, W.S., and Watkins, R. (2007). *Hyperspectral Remote Sensing: Principles and Applications*. 2007. CRC Press.

13 Kawakami, R., Matsushita, Y., Wright, J., Ben-Ezra, M., Tai, Y.W., and Ikeuchi, K. (2011). High-resolution hyperspectral imaging via matrix factorization. *CVPR 2011*, 2329–2336, Colorado Springs, CO, USA (20–25 June 2011). IEEE.

14 Akhtar, N., Shafait, F., and Mian, A. (2015). Bayesian sparse representation for hyperspectral image super resolution. *2015 IEEE Conference on Computer Vision and Pattern Recognition (CVPR)*, 3631–3640, Boston, MA, USA (7–12 June 2015). IEEE.

15 Lanaras, C., Baltsavias, E., and Schindler, K. (2015). Hyperspectral super-resolution by coupled spectral unmixing. *2015 IEEE International Conference on Computer Vision (ICCV)*, 3586–3594, Santiago, Chile (7–13 December 2015). IEEE.

16 Thomas, C., Ranchin, T., Wald, L., and Chanussot, J. (2008). Synthesis of multispectral images to high spatial resolution: a critical review of fusion methods based on remote sensing physics. *IEEE Trans. Geosci. Remote Sens.* 46 (5): 1301–1312.

17 Chavez, J., Sides, S.C., and Anderson, J.A. (1990). Comparison of three different methods to merge multiresolution and multispectral data: LANDSAT TM and SPOT panchromatic. *AAPG Bulletin (American Association of Petroleum Geologists), (USA)* [Internet], Honolulu, HI, USA (29 July–3 August 1990). https://www.osti.gov/biblio/6165108 (accessed 28 August 2021).

18 Aiazzi, B., Baronti, S., and Selva, M. (2007). Improving component substitution pansharpening through multivariate regression of MS $+ $ Pan data. *IEEE Trans. Geosci. Remote Sens.* 45 (10): 3230–3239.

19 Aiazzi, B., Alparone, L., Baronti, S. et al. (2006). MTF-tailored multiscale fusion of high-resolution MS and Pan imagery. *Photogramm. Eng. Remote Sens.* 72 (5): 591–596.

20 Loncan, L., de Almeida, L.B., Bioucas-Dias, J.M. et al. (2015). Hyperspectral pansharpening: a review. *IEEE Geosci. Remote Sens. Mag.* 3 (3): 27–46.

21 Schaepman, M.E., Jehle, M., Hueni, A. et al. (2015). Advanced radiometry measurements and earth science applications with the airborne prism experiment (APEX). *Remote Sens. Environ.* 158: 207–219.

22 Selva, M., Aiazzi, B., Butera, F. et al. (2015). Hyper-sharpening: a first approach on SIM-GA data. *IEEE J. Sel. Top. Appl. Earth Obs. Remote Sens.* 8 (6): 3008–3024.

23 Selva, M., Santurri, L., and Baronti, S. (2019). Improving hypersharpening for WorldView-3 data. *IEEE Geosci. Remote Sens. Lett.* 16 (6): 987–991.

24 Mallat, S.G. (1989). A theory for multiresolution signal decomposition: the wavelet representation. *IEEE Trans. Pattern Anal. Mach. Intell.* 11 (7): 674–693.

25 Burt, P. and Adelson, E. (1983). The Laplacian pyramid as a compact image code. *IEEE Trans. Commun.* 31 (4): 532–540.

26 Zhou, J., Kwan, C., and Budavari, B. (2016). Hyperspectral image super-resolution: a hybrid color mapping approach. *J. Appl. Remote. Sens.* 10 (3): 035024.

27 Wei, Q., Dobigeon, N., and Tourneret, J.Y. (2014). Bayesian fusion of hyperspectral and multispectral images. *2014 IEEE International Conference on Acoustics, Speech and Signal Processing (ICASSP)*, Florence, Italy (4–9 May 2014).

28 Wei, Q., Bioucas-Dias, J., Dobigeon, N., and Tourneret, J.Y. (2015). Hyperspectral and multispectral image fusion based on a sparse representation. *IEEE Trans. Geosci. Remote Sens.* 53 (7): 3658–3668.

29 Simões, M., Bioucas-Dias, J., Almeida, L.B., and Chanussot, J. (2015). A convex formulation for hyperspectral image superresolution via subspace-based regularization. *IEEE Trans. Geosci. Remote Sens.* 53 (6): 3373–3388.

30 Yokoya, N., Yairi, T., and Iwasaki, A. (2012). Coupled nonnegative matrix factorization unmixing for hyperspectral and multispectral data fusion. *IEEE Trans. Geosci. Remote Sens.* 50 (2): 528–537.

31 Wycoff, E., Chan, T.H., Jia, K., Ma, W.K., and Ma, Y. (2013). A non-negative sparse promoting algorithm for high resolution hyperspectral imaging. *2013 IEEE International Conference on Acoustics, Speech and Signal Processing*, 1409–1413, Vancouver, BC, Canada (26–31 May 2013). IEEE.

32 Chang, Y., Yan, L., Fang, H. et al. (2019). HSI-DeNet: hyperspectral image restoration via convolutional neural network. *IEEE Trans. Geosci. Remote Sens.* 57 (2): 667–682.

33 Arun, P., Buddhiraju, K.M., Porwal, A., and Chanussot, J. (2020). CNN-based super-resolution of hyperspectral images. *IEEE Trans. Geosci. Remote Sens.* 58: 6106–6121.

34 Dong, C., Loy, C.C., He, K., and Tang, X. (2016). Image super-resolution using deep convolutional networks. *IEEE Trans. Pattern Anal. Mach. Intell.* 38 (2): 295–307.

35 Huang, W., Xiao, L., Wei, Z. et al. (2015). A new pan-sharpening method with deep neural networks. *IEEE Geosci. Remote Sens. Lett.* 12 (5): 1037–1041.

36 Masi, G., Cozzolino, D., Verdoliva, L., and Scarpa, G. (2016). Pansharpening by convolutional neural networks. *Remote Sens.* 14 (8): 594.

37 Wei, Y., Yuan, Q., Shen, H., and Zhang, L. (2017). Boosting the accuracy of multi-spectral image pan-sharpening by learning a deep residual network. *IEEE Geosci. Remote Sens. Lett.* 14: 1795–1799.

38 Li, Y., Hu, J., Zhao, X. et al. (2017). Hyperspectral image super-resolution using deep convolutional neural network. *Neurocomputing* 266: 29–41.

39 Xie, Q., Zhou, M., Zhao, Q., Meng, D., Zuo, W., and Xu, Z.2019). Multispectral and hyperspectral image fusion by MS/HS fusion net. *2019 IEEE/CVF Conference on Computer Vision and Pattern Recognition (CVPR)*, Long Beach, CA, USA (15–20 June 2019). IEEE.

40 Kwan, C., Budavari, B., Bovik, A.C., and Marchisio, G. (2017). Blind quality assessment of fused WorldView-3 images by using the combinations of pansharpening and hypersharpening paradigms. *IEEE Geosci. Remote Sens. Lett.* 14 (10): 1835–1839.

41 Kwan, C., Haberle, C., Echavarren, A., Ayhan, B., Chou, B., Budavari, B., et al. (2018) Mars surface mineral abundance estimation using THEMIS and TES images. *2018 9th IEEE Annual Ubiquitous Computing, Electronics & Mobile Communication Conference (UEMCON)*, New York, NY, USA (8–10 November 2018). IEEE.

42 Qu, Y., Qi, H., and Kwan, C. (2018). Unsupervised sparse Dirichlet-Net for hyperspectral image super-resolution. *2018 IEEE/CVF Conference on Computer Vision and Pattern Recognition*, 2511–2520, Salt Lake City, UT, USA (18–23 June 2018). IEEE.

43 Nalisnick, E. and Smyth, P. (2017). Deep generative models with stick-breaking priors. *Proceedings of the 5th International Conference on Learning Representations*, France 24–26 April 2017.

44 Huang, S. and Tran, T.D. (2018). Sparse signal recovery via generalized entropy functions minimization. *IEEE Trans. Signal Process.* 67 (5): 1322–1337.

45 Zhou, Y., Rangarajan, A., and Gader, P.D. (2017). Nonrigid registration of hyperspectral and color images with vastly different spatial and spectral resolutions for spectral unmixing and pansharpening. *2017 IEEE Conference on Computer Vision and Pattern Recognition Workshops (CVPRW)*, 1571–1579, Honolulu, HI, USA (21–26 July 2017). IEEE.

46 Baronti, S., Aiazzi, B., Selva, M. et al. (2011). A theoretical analysis of the effects of aliasing and misregistration on pansharpened imagery. *IEEE J. Sel. Top. Signal Process.* 5 (3): 446–453.

47 Van der Meer, F.D., Van der Werff, H.M., Van Ruitenbeek, F.J. et al. (2012). Multi-and hyperspectral geologic remote sensing: a review. *Int. J. Appl. Earth Obs. Geoinf.* 14 (1): 112–128.

48 Wei, Q., Dobigeon, N., and Tourneret, J.Y. (2015). Fast fusion of multi-band images based on solving a Sylvester equation. *IEEE Trans. Image Process.* 24 (11): 4109–4121.

49 Liu, J. (2000). Smoothing filter-based intensity modulation: a spectral preserve image fusion technique for improving spatial details. *Int. J. Remote Sens.* 21 (18): 3461–3472.

50 Qu, Y., Qi, H., Kwan, C. et al. (2022). Unsupervised and unregistered hyperspectral image super-resolution with mutual Dirichlet-Net. *IEEE Trans. Geosci. Remote Sens.* 60: 1–18.

51 Wald, L., Ranchin, T., and Mangolini, M. (1997). Fusion of satellite images of different spatial resolutions: assessing the quality of resulting images. *Photogramm. Eng. Remote Sens.* 63 (6): 691–699.

52 Zhou, Y., Rangarajan, A., and Gader, P.D. (2020). An integrated approach to registration and fusion of hyperspectral and multispectral images. *IEEE Trans. Geosci. Remote Sens.* 58 (5): 3020–3033.

53 Kruse, F.A., Lefkoff, A., Boardman, J. et al. (1993). The spectral image processing system (SIPS)—interactive visualization and analysis of imaging spectrometer data. *Remote Sens. Environ.* 44 (2–3): 145–163.

54 Dong, W., Fu, F., Shi, G. et al. (2016). Hyperspectral image super-resolution via non-negative structured sparse representation. *IEEE Trans. Image Process.* 25 (5): 2337–2352.

55 Zhao, J., Qu, Y., Ninomiya, S., and Guo, W. (2022). Endmember-assisted camera response function learning, toward improving hyperspectral image super-resolution performance. *IEEE Trans. Geosci. Remote Sens.* 60: 1–14.

56 Rei, K., Zhao, H., Tan, R.T., and Ikeuchi, K. (2024). Camera Spectral Sensitivity and White Balance Estimation from Sky Images. *Int. J. Comput. Vis.* 105: https://doi.org/10.1007/s11263-013-0632-1.

57 Shi, Zhan, Chen, Chang, Xiong, Zhiwei, Liu, Dong, and Wu, Feng. (2018). HSCNN+: advanced CNN-based hyperspectral recovery from RGB images. *2018 IEEE/CVF Conference on Computer Vision and Pattern Recognition Workshops (CVPRW)*. https://ieeexplore.ieee.org/document/8575292 (accessed 8 May 2024).

58 Chang, Y., Yan, L., Zhao, X.L. et al. (2020). Weighted low-rank tensor recovery for hyperspectral image restoration. *IEEE Trans. Cybern.* 50: 4558–4572.

59 Yasuma, F., Mitsunaga, T., Iso, D., and Nayar, S.K. (2010). Generalized assorted pixel camera: postcapture control of resolution, dynamic range, and spectrum. *IEEE Trans. Image Process.* 19 (9): 2241–2253.

60 Arad, Boaz and Shahar, Ohad ben (2024). Sparse recovery of hyperspectral signal from natural RGB images. *European Conference on Computer Vision*, 19–34. https://link.springer.com/chapter/10.1007/978-3-319-46478-7_2 (accessed 8 MAy 2024).

61 Shahriyar, S., Paul, M., Murshed, M., and Ali, M. (2016). Lossless hyperspectral image compression using binary tree based decomposition. *2016 International Conference on Digital Image Computing: Techniques and Applications (DICTA)*, 1–8, Gold Coast, QLD, Australia. https://ieeexplore.ieee.org/document/7797060 (accessed 8 May 2024).

62 Adrián Alcolea, Mercedes E. Paoletti, Juan M. Haut, Javier Resano, and Antonio Plaza Inference in supervised spectral classifiers for on-board hyperspectral imaging: an overview *Remote Sens* 12 534. https://www.mdpi.com/2072-4292/12/3/534 (accessed 8 May 2024).

8

Hyperspectral Image Reconstruction Based on Adaptive Learning

Ke Zheng[1], *Jiaxin Li*[2,3], *Lianru Gao*[2], *and Bing Zhang*[2,3]

[1] *College of Geography and Environment, Liaocheng University, Liaocheng, China*
[2] *Aerospace Information Research Institute, Chinese Academy of Sciences, Beijing, China*
[3] *College of Resources and Environment, University of Chinese Academy of Sciences, Beijing, China*

Mathematical Symbols Used in This Chapter

$\mathrm{X} \in \mathbb{R}^{M \times N \times L}$	High spectral and high spatial resolution HSI.
$Y \in \mathbb{R}^{m \times n \times L}$	Low spatial resolution HSI.
$Z \in \mathbb{R}^{M \times N \times l}$	High spatial resolution MSI.
$A \in \mathbb{R}^{MN \times p}$	Abundances matrix.
$E \in \mathbb{R}^{p \times L}$	Endmembers matrix.
$\mathbf{R} \in \mathbb{R}^{L \times l}$	Spectral response function (SRF).
$\mathbf{Z}_{lr} \in \mathbb{R}^{m \times n \times l}$	Low spatial resolution MSI (LMSI).
$\tilde{\mathbf{Z}}$	Reconstructed HMSI **Z**.
$\tilde{\mathbf{X}}$	Estimated target image.
Cov	Covariance.
Var	Variance.

8.1 Introduction

The hyperspectral imaging system often has a trade-off between spectral resolution and spatial resolution, due to the need to balance between grating slit size, field of view, focal length, orbit height, and imaging plane size in order to achieve high imaging signal-to-noise ratio. This causes the spatial resolution of HSI to usually be coarser than that of multispectral imagery (MSI). The limited spatial resolution restricts further applications of HSI. To enhance the spatial resolution of HSI, a natural solution is to fuse it with higher-resolution MSI. This approach is called hyperspectral and multispectral image fusion (HSI-MSI Fusion), also known as hyperspectral image super-resolution (HSI-SR) reconstruction.

Machine-Learning-Based Hyperspectral Image Processing, First Edition. Edited by Bing Zhang.

8.2 Problem Formulation

The HSI-MSI Fusion problem requires the estimation of the HSI, which has both high spectral and high spatial resolution and is denoted as $\mathrm{X} \in \mathbb{R}^{M \times N \times L}$, where M, N, and L are the width, height, and number of spectral bands. The input images include a low spatial resolution HSI denoted as $Y \in \mathbb{R}^{m \times n \times L}$, and a high spatial resolution MSI denoted as $Z \in \mathbb{R}^{M \times N \times l}$, where m and n are the width and height of $\mathbf{Y}$, and l is the number of spectral bands in $\mathbf{Z}$. In particular, $n \leq N$, $m \leq M$ and $l \leq L$. For convenience, we call the low spatial resolution HSI, high spatial resolution MSI, and target HSI as LHSI, HMSI, and HHSI, respectively. To simplify the notation in this section, we unfold the 3D data cube to form a 2D matrix: the 2D matrices of the three types of image are denoted as $X \in \mathbb{R}^{MN \times L}$, $Y \in \mathbb{R}^{mn \times L}$, and $Z \in \mathbb{R}^{MN \times l}$, respectively.

The relationship between the three images $\mathbf{X}$, $\mathbf{Y}$, and $\mathbf{Z}$ according to the hyperspectral linear unmixing model is shown in Figure 8.1. In the linear spectral unmixing model, each pixel of the HSI is assumed to be a linear combination of a set of pure spectral bases (called endmembers) and the coefficients of each pure spectral basis (called abundances). According to the linear spectral unmixing model, the target HSI can be described as:

$$\mathbf{X} = \mathbf{A}\mathbf{E} \tag{8.1}$$

where the matrix $A \in \mathbb{R}^{MN \times p}$ is formed from the abundances, the matrix $E \in \mathbb{R}^{p \times L}$ is made up of the endmembers, and p is the number of pure spectral bases. This equation describes the degree of mixing for each pixel in the image $\mathbf{X}$.

Similarly, the input $\mathbf{Y}$ can also be expressed as a linear combination of the same endmembers, $\mathbf{E}$:

$$\mathbf{Y} = \mathbf{A}_h\mathbf{E} = \mathbf{S} * \mathbf{X} = \mathbf{S} * \mathbf{A}\mathbf{E} \tag{8.2}$$

where the matrix $\mathbf{A}_h \in \mathbb{R}^{mn \times p}$ consists of the $\mathbf{Y}$ abundances, the matrix $\mathbf{S} \in \mathbb{R}^{L_m \times L_n}$ is the point spread function (PSF), which describes the spatial degradation function, and $*$ denotes the

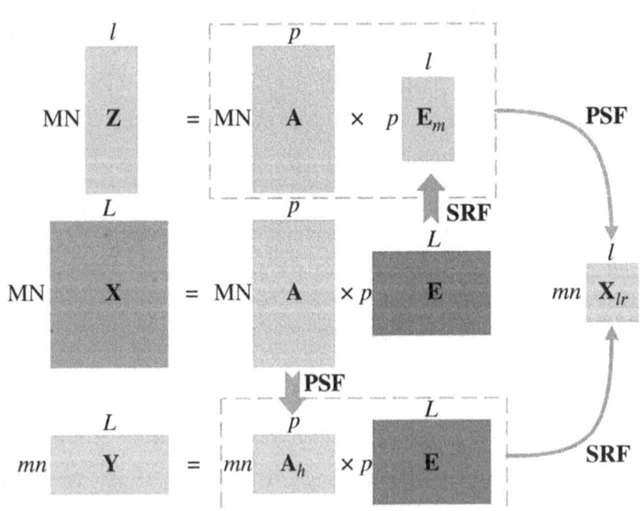

Figure 8.1 The illustration of the relationship between the HMSI, the LHSI, and the target HSI based on the linear unmixing model.

convolution operator. L_m and L_n are the spatial size of the convolution filter. **Y** also denotes the spatially degraded version of image **X**; and the input **Z** is the spectrally degraded version of **X**:

$$\mathbf{Z} = \mathbf{XR} = \mathbf{AER} \tag{8.3}$$

where the matrix $\mathbf{R} \in \mathbb{R}^{L \times l}$ is the spectral response function (SRF), which describes the spectral degradation process.

Moreover, the spectral degraded version of **Y** should approximate to the spatially degraded version of **Z**:

$$\mathbf{Z}_{lr} = \mathbf{YR} = \mathbf{S} * \mathbf{Z} \tag{8.4}$$

where the matrix $\mathbf{Z}_{lr} \in \mathbb{R}^{m \times n \times l}$ represents the low spatial resolution MSI (LMSI).

In addition, our goal is to estimate **X** using the inputs **Y** and **Z** with the following constraints also satisfied:

$$\begin{aligned} &\sum_{j=1}^{p} a_{ij} = 1 \quad \forall\ i,j \\ &a_{ij} \geq 0 \quad \forall\ i,j \\ &1 \geq e_{ij} \geq 0 \quad \forall\ i,j \end{aligned} \tag{8.5}$$

where a_{ij} is a component unit of **A** and e_{ij} is a component unit of **E**. These constraints relate to the sum-to-one property of the abundance, the non-negative property of the abundance and the bounded non-negative property of the endmembers, respectively. In addition, the abundances should be sparse, meaning that each HSI pixel is composed of only a few pure spectral bases.

8.3 Numerical Model-guided Nonlinear Spectral Unmixing

According to Eqs. (8.1)–(8.3), to solve the HSI–MSI fusion problem, the key point is to estimate the high spatial resolution abundance matrix **A** and the spectral bases matrix **E**. The HMSI provides detailed spatial contextual information that is highly correlated with **A**. Also, the LHSI preserves the spectral information, which is highly consistent with the target spectral endmembers matrix **E**. Based on this idea, we will introduce an unsupervised HSI-SR deep learning method called HyCoNet which is based on linear spectral unmixing.

8.3.1 Unsupervised HSI-SR method - HyCoNet

8.3.1.1 Coupled Autoencoder Network for Image Fusion

The HyCoNet network is composed of three autoencoder nets, as shown in Figure 8.2. The upper one is called LHSI autoencoder and the lower one HMSI autoencoder. The estimated target HSI, **X**, is embedded in the HMSI autoencoder. The LMSI autoencoder can be seen at the upper right.

Since the 2D convolution layer, which has a kernel size of 1 × 1, is equivalent to the fully connected layer when applied to a spectral vector, all the fully connected layers in the traditional autoencoder network are replaced by the convolution layers, as shown in Figure 8.2. In addition, all the convolution kernel sizes are set to be 1 × 1, except for the PSF convolution layer. Instead of using the fully connected layer, the convolution layer is used to preserve the spatial structure of the input image cube for easy implementation of the PSF operation. Further details of the PSF operation are discussed below.

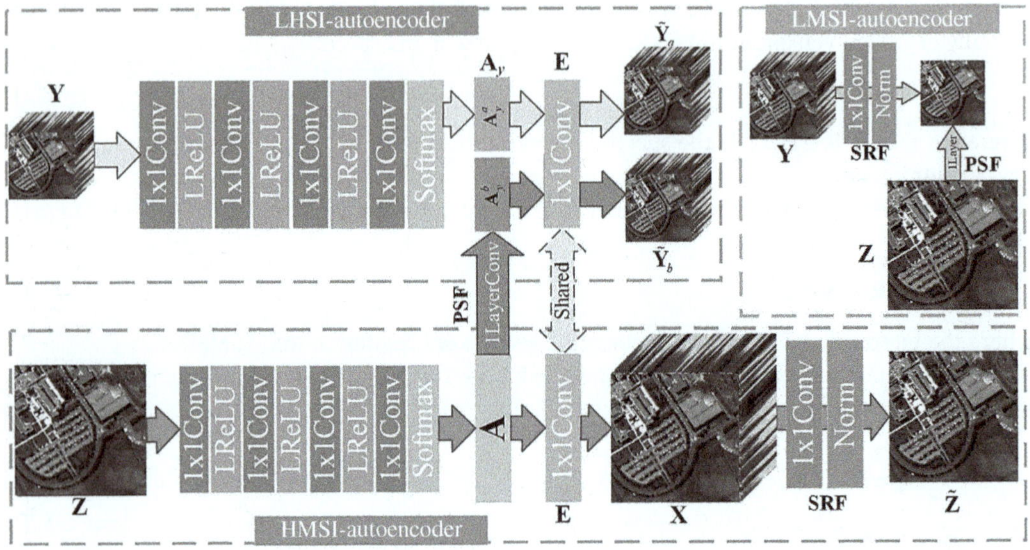

Figure 8.2 The HyCoNet network contains three coupled autoencoder nets: LHSI Autoencoder, HMSI Autoencoder, and LMSI autoencoder.

In the LHSI autoencoder, the network tries to learn an approximation to the identity function $f(\mathbf{X}_h) \approx \mathbf{X}_h$. Since the input LHSI contains sufficient spectral information, the endmembers $\mathbf{E}$ and abundances $\mathbf{A}_h$ can be extracted during the reconstruction process for this autoencoder.

The module before the latent variable $\mathbf{A}_y^a$ is the encoder:

$$\mathbf{A}_y^a = f_{en}(\mathbf{Y}) \tag{8.6}$$

where the $f_{en}()$ tries to learn a nonlinear mapping which transforms the input LHSI to its abundances $\mathbf{A}_y^a$; $\mathbf{A}_y^a \in \mathbb{R}^{m \times n \times p}$ represents the abundances of $\mathbf{X}_h$, and p is the number of endmembers.

The module after the latent variable is the decoder function:

$$\tilde{\mathbf{Y}}_a = f_{de}\left(\mathbf{A}_y^a\right) \tag{8.7}$$

where $\tilde{\mathbf{Y}}_a$ is the output of this autoencoder, which represents the reconstructed input image cube. The decoder function $f_{de}()$ is a convolution layer without bias, denoted as the shared "1x1Conv" layer labeled "E" in Figure 8.2. This layer is also used in the HMSI autoencoder, meaning that these two autoencoders share the same parameters as this convolution layer. The parameters of the shared convolution layer are denoted as the endmembers $\mathbf{E} \in \mathbb{R}^{p \times 1 \times 1 \times L}$ (1×1 represents the spatial size of this convolution kernel). The size of each convolution kernel is $p \times 1 \times 1$ and the number of kernels is L.

The reason that we call the latent variables $\mathbf{A}_y^a$ and parameters $\mathbf{E}$ the abundances and endmembers, respectively, is that they are trying to reconstruct $\mathbf{Y}$ by matrix multiplication: $\tilde{\mathbf{Y}}_a = \boldsymbol{A}_y^a\boldsymbol{E}$. This is the same idea as matrix decomposition except that the process is optimized by gradient descent in neural network. In order to satisfy the non-negativity restrictions for $\mathbf{A}_h$ and $\mathbf{E}$, several tricks are applied, as described in more detail in Part B.

The structure of the HMSI autoencoder is similar to that of the LHSI autoencoder and includes an encoder function $h_{en}()$ and a decoder function $h_{de}()$. The encoder function can be expressed as:

$$\mathbf{A} = h_{en}(\mathbf{Z}) \tag{8.8}$$

where $\mathbf{A}$ is the high-resolution abundance, $h_{en}()$ is the encoder function, and $\mathbf{Z}$ is the input HMSI.

The decoder for the HMSI autoencoder consists of two parts – a shared convolution layer and the SRF:

$$\tilde{\mathbf{Z}} = h_{de}(\mathbf{A}) = SRF(f_{de}(\mathbf{A})) \tag{8.9}$$

where $\tilde{\mathbf{Z}}$ is the reconstructed HMSI $\mathbf{Z}$, $h_{de}()$ is the decoder function, $f_{de}()$ is the shared convolution layer containing the parameters of the endmember matrix $\mathbf{E}$, and $SRF()$ is the spectral resampling operation. The high-resolution target HSI is the output of the shared convolution layer:

$$\tilde{\mathbf{X}} = f_{de}(\mathbf{A}) \tag{8.10}$$

where $\tilde{\mathbf{X}}$ is the estimated target image.

To handle the situation where the SRF parameters are unknown, a convolution layer and a normalization layer are placed after the target $\tilde{\mathbf{X}}$ to learn the unknown parameters of the SRF. The SRF consists of spectral resampling from HSI to MSI and the process can be defined as:

$$\varphi_i = \frac{\int_{\lambda_{i,L}}^{\lambda_{i,U}} R(\lambda)\varepsilon(\lambda)d\lambda}{\int_{\lambda_{i,L}}^{\lambda_{i,U}} R(\lambda)d\lambda} \tag{8.11}$$

where φ_i is the spectral radiance of band i of the HMSI, λ is the wavelength, $\lambda_{i,U}$ and $\lambda_{i,L}$ are the wavelength bounds of band i of the HMSI, $R()$ is the SRF, and ε is the spectral radiance of the HHSI. To implement the spectral resampling in the neural network, a convolution layer with kernel size 1×1 (labeled "SRF" in Figure 8.2) is added after the target image $\tilde{\mathbf{X}}$ to simulate the numerator of Eq. (7.11). A normalization layer (labeled "Norm" in Figure 8.2) follows the convolution layer and simulates the denominator of Eq. (7.11). Therefore, the SRF process within our network can be expressed as:

$$\varphi_i = SRF(\varepsilon_\lambda) = \frac{\sum_{\lambda=\lambda_{i,L}}^{\lambda_{i,U}} w_{i,\lambda}\varepsilon_\lambda}{\sum_{\lambda=\lambda_{i,L}}^{\lambda_{i,U}} w_{i,\lambda}} \tag{8.12}$$

where φ_i is the band i image in $\tilde{\mathbf{Z}}$, $w_{i,\lambda}$ is the weight of the SRF convolution layer, and ε_λ is the band with wavelength λ in $\tilde{\mathbf{X}}$. The use of this function means that the convolution layer and the normalization layer integrate the HSI $\tilde{\mathbf{X}}$ with the weights of the convolution layer between the upper and lower spectral bounds. It also means that our network assumes the spectral coverage of HMSI bands is known and that each convolution kernel of the convolution layer only covers the spectral range corresponding to the bands in $\tilde{\mathbf{X}}$. The number of convolution kernels is equal to the number of bands in $\tilde{\mathbf{Z}}$.

The PSF means that a given pixel is a weighted combination of contributions from the pixel and its neighboring pixels. In the fusion problem, this means that a pixel in the LHSI is a weighted combination of local pixels from the high-resolution HSI. Therefore, the PSF is a convolution process, and a convolution operation can easily be implemented as part of the convolutional neural network. In our network, to simulate the PSF, a convolution layer with one input channel and one output channel is implemented for every band in the HSI. According to the definition of the PSF, the relationship between $\mathbf{X}$ and $\mathbf{Y}$ can be expressed as $\mathbf{Y} = PSF(\mathbf{X})$. Also, $\tilde{\mathbf{Y}}$ and $\tilde{\mathbf{X}}$ are composed of the same linear unmixing endmembers. Therefore, another low-resolution abundance $\mathbf{A}_y^b$ can be characterized as:

$$\mathbf{A}_y^b = PSF(\mathbf{A}) \tag{8.13}$$

where $PSF()$ is the convolution layer labeled 'PSF' and denoted as '1LayerConv' in Figure 8.2. The spatial size of this PSF convolution kernel is the same as the ratio of the ground sampling distance (GSD) of the LHSI to that of the HMSI, and the stride of the convolution layer equals the kernel size. The PSF process acts as a bridge between the LHSI autoencoder and the HMSI autoencoder and forces the reconstructed image to be spectrally consistent $\tilde{\mathbf{X}}$.

In addition, the spatial degraded version of the HMSI is equivalent to the spectrally degraded version of the LHSI shown as "LMSI- Autoencoder" in Figure 8.2. This relation can be expressed as:

$$PSF(\mathbf{Z}) = \tilde{\mathbf{Z}}_{lr}^a \approx \tilde{\mathbf{Z}}_{lr}^b = SRF(\mathbf{Y}) \tag{8.14}$$

where $\tilde{\mathbf{Z}}_{lr}^a$ and $\tilde{\mathbf{Z}}_{lr}^b$ are the estimated LMSI (low spatial resolution MSI).

8.3.1.2 Joint Loss Function

Figure 8.3 shows flow charts for the method, including input images, output images, and corresponding target images. The first row of Figure 8.3 indicates the inference of the input $\mathbf{Y}$ in the LHSI-Autoencoder, corresponding to the data flow from $\mathbf{Y}$ to $\tilde{\mathbf{Y}}_a$ through the LHSI autoencoder in Figure 8.2. The inference of HMSI $\mathbf{Z}$ includes two parts. The first is shown as the second row of Figure 8.3, which includes the PSF operation to generate the LHSI – this process corresponds to the PSF operation pathway in Figure 8.2. The second part can be seen in the third row of Figure 8.3 and consists of the SRF operation; this process corresponds to the SRF operation pathway in Figure 8.2. The last row of Figure 8.3 shows the relationship between the two LMSIs. Therefore, the objective function for reconstruction can be expressed as:

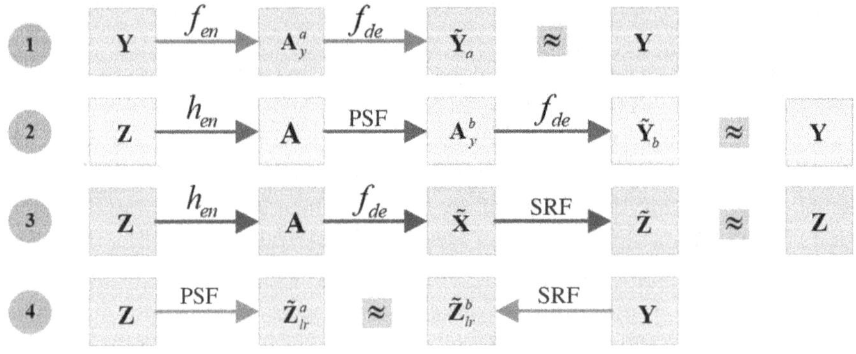

Figure 8.3 The illustration of flow charts for the inputs $\mathbf{X}_h$ and $\mathbf{X}_m$.

$$\mathcal{L}_{base}(\mathbf{Y},\mathbf{Z}) = \left\|\mathbf{Y}-\tilde{\mathbf{Y}}_y^a\right\|_1 + \alpha\left\|\mathbf{Y}-\tilde{\mathbf{Y}}_y^b\right\|_1 + \beta\left\|\mathbf{Z}-\tilde{\mathbf{Z}}_m\right\|_1 + \gamma\left\|\tilde{\mathbf{Z}}_{lr}^a-\tilde{\mathbf{Z}}_{lr}^b\right\|_1 \tag{8.15}$$

where α, β, and γ are trade-off parameters that tune the weights between these reconstruction errors.

The sum-to-one and non-negative properties given in Eq. (8.5) also need to be satisfied. First, we constrain the sum of the abundances in the channel dimension to meet the sum-to-one property:

$$\mathcal{L}_{sum2one}(\mathbf{Y},\mathbf{Z}) = \left\|1-\sum_{i=1}^{p}\mathbf{A}_i\right\|_1 + \left\|1-\sum_{i=1}^{p}\mathbf{A}_{y,i}^a\right\|_1 + \left\|1-\sum_{i=1}^{p}\mathbf{A}_{y,i}^b\right\|_1 \tag{8.16}$$

where i indicates the ith band of the abundance matrix $\mathbf{A}$. Although the softmax function can be used to strictly enforce the sum-to-one property for the abundances, the resulting convergence accuracy is lower than for the proposed method.

Secondly, to enforce the non-negative property, several tricks are applied during training. The clamp function is applied to the output of the last convolution layer of both the encoder nets and decoder nets to force all the elements of the abundances and reconstruction images into the range [0,1]. Although we tried to use the sigmoid activation layer for this purpose, we found that it was difficult to make the network converge using this function. In addition, the weights of the shared convolution layer (containing the endmember parameter matrix, $\mathbf{E}$), PSF layer, and SRF layer should also meet the non-negative property. Since the weights of these layers may be updated to a negative value after the back-propagation, we applied the clamp function to these layers after the weights were updated to force these weights into the non-negative range. The range of the clamp function was [0,1]. As a result, the weights satisfied the non-negative and bounding constraints for each forward propagation, except for the first time.

Since each pixel of the HSI is composed of a small number of pure spectral bases, the abundance matrix $\mathbf{A}$ should be sparse. To guarantee the sparsity of the abundance, the KL divergence is used to ensure that most of the elements in the abundance are close to a small number:

$$\begin{aligned}\mathcal{L}_{sparse}(\mathbf{Y},\mathbf{Z}) &= \sum_{i=1}^{s}\sum_{j=1}^{p} KL(a \parallel \tilde{a}_{i,j}) \\ &= \sum_{i=1}^{s}\sum_{j=1}^{p}\left(a\log\left(\frac{a}{\tilde{a}_{i,j}}\right) + (1-a)\log\left(\frac{1-a}{1-\tilde{a}_{i,j}}\right)\right)\end{aligned} \tag{8.17}$$

where s is the number of pixels, p is the number of convolution kernels and also the number of endmembers, a is a sparsity parameter which is set to a small value close to zero (0.0001 in our network), and $\tilde{a}_{i,j}$ is an element of the abundance matrix $\mathbf{A}$. To satisfy this constraint, the elements of $\mathbf{A}$ must mostly be near zero. The sparsity constraint is also applied to the abundance matrix $\mathbf{A}_y^a$.

Ultimately, our aim is to solve the fusion problem in accordance with the optimization problem:

$$\mathcal{L}(\mathbf{Y},\mathbf{Z}) = \mathcal{L}_{base}(\mathbf{Y},\mathbf{Z}) + \mu\mathcal{L}_{sum2one}(\mathbf{Y},\mathbf{Z}) + \nu\mathcal{L}_{sparse}(\mathbf{Y},\mathbf{Z}) \tag{8.18}$$

where μ and ν are the trade-off parameters used to balance the errors. This loss function can be directly used in the optimizer, thus providing a simple and direct solution.

8.3.2 HSI-SR with Collaborative Registration – NonRegSRNet

8.3.2.1 Motivation

The prerequisite assumption of the HyCoNet method is that HSI and MSI have been fully registered. Generally, HSI and MSI can be easily registered using rigid registration methods if both types of imagery are captured by the same satellite platform. However, in most cases, the data acquired by different platforms tend to suffer from the effects of complex noises or spectral variabilities in the imaging process. Further, the acquisition time and satellite location for the two types of imagery are different; usually, a nonrigid deformation may be comprised between the two sets of data. This requires the multimodal data to be transformed into a unified representation so that the nonrigid registration can be achieved. When trying to unify the data representation, the correlation between the HSI and MSI is particularly important. The SR process involves finding this relationship, meaning that a good SR method is of great help in image registration. Good image registration is also an important prerequisite for HSI SR, which means that these two processes can complement each other and help to achieve better registration and fusion results.

Deformable image registration is of fundamental importance to the fusion of HSI and MSI as the results of the fusion are seriously affected by the accuracy of the registration. Deformable image registration means a dense, nonlinear correspondence is established between the HSI and MSI pairs. From Figure 8.4, it can be seen that image registration is essential to help mitigate the effects of deformation and facilitate the generation of better fusion results.

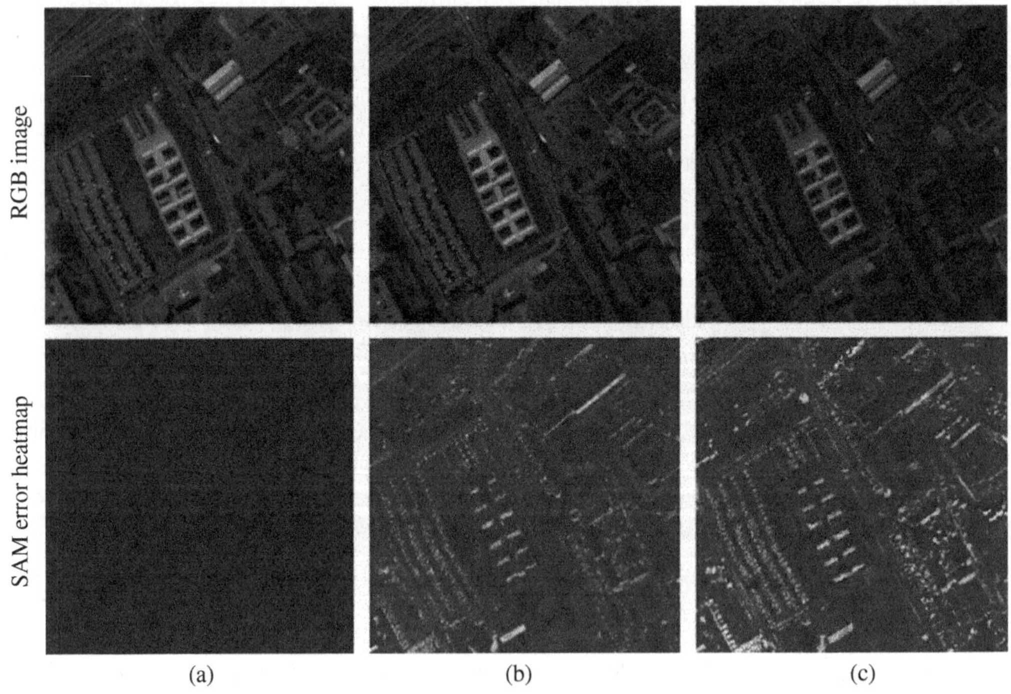

Figure 8.4 Comparison of ideal registration and nonrigid deformation showing how the registration accuracy seriously affects the results of the SR reconstruction. Here, CNMF [1] is used as the criterion for the comparison. (a) Ground truth, (b) well-registered PSNR:36.3169, and (c) unregistered PSNR:33.3875.

8.3.2.2 Overview

In this part, we will describe the benefits of the integration of nonrigid registration and HSI SR. The challenges that we faced drive us to design a network that incorporated both registration and fusion had the ability to carry out these functions successfully in a balanced way and was robust. Figure 8.5 shows the framework of the NonRegSRNet: it consists mainly of an HSI autoencoder subnetwork, an MSI autoencoder subnetwork, and a registration subnetwork. The structure of HSI autoencoder and MSI autoencoder is quite similar to that in HyCoNet. The registration network acts as a link that re-establishes the spatial relations between the abundances, whereas the spatial deformation correction is performed using displacement field prediction and the STN. The outputs of each sub-network and the corresponding self-similar component parts are fed into the loss function to drive the unsupervised learning.

In the registration formulation, the moving image (also called as source image) is warped to register with the fixed image (also called as target image). We assume the high-resolution MSI is the fixed image due to it describing more spatial detailed features about the ground objects and the low-resolution HSI is moving image, respectively. Therefore, let $\mathbf{Y}_m$, $\mathbf{Z}_f$ denote the input low-resolution HSI and high-resolution MSI defined over a 3-D domain $\mathbf{Y}_m \in \mathbb{R}^{m\times n\times L}$ and $\mathbf{Z}_f \in \mathbb{R}^{M\times N\times l}$, where m, n, and L are the width, height, and the number of spectral bands of $\mathbf{Y}_m$, and M, N, and l are the width, height, and the number of bands of $\mathbf{Z}_f$. For convenience, we call the low-resolution HSI and high-resolution MSI as LHSI and HMSI, respectively.

8.3.2.3 Registration Module

The HSI and MSI autoencoders have structures that are similar to those in HyCoNet, so we will focus on the registration module next. The registration module was used to densely match the corresponding pixels. Generally, the HSI and MSI can be overall registered easily through affine

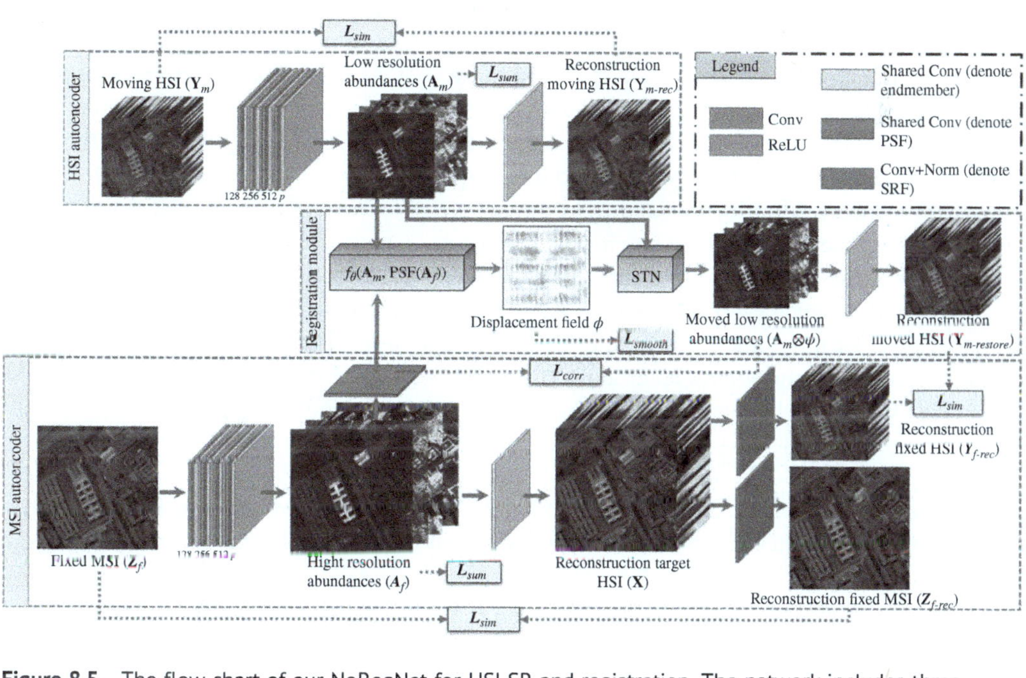

Figure 8.5 The flow chart of our NoRegNet for HSI SR and registration. The network includes three sub-modules: MSI autoencoder, HSI autoencoder, and Registration module.

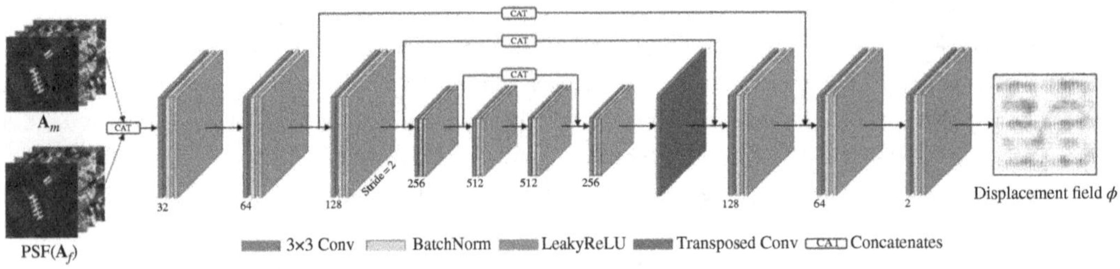

Figure 8.6 Part of the registration module to predict displacement field θ, which can be denoted as $f_\theta(\mathbf{A}_m, PSF(\mathbf{A}_f))$

alignment methods for a large-scale remote-sensing image. More difficult is the local nonlinear deformation, such as deformation of an individual object or a local area. Therefore, we assume that $\mathbf{Y}_m$ and $\mathbf{Z}_f$ are affinely aligned as a preprocessing step, and there is only nonlinear deformation for the two images.

As shown in Figure 8.6, let $f_\theta(\mathbf{A}_m, PSF(\mathbf{A}_f))$ denote the module function, where θ are the parameters of the convolutional layers and the module network which is resembled with the UNet. The concatenated $\mathbf{A}_m$ and $PSF(\mathbf{A}_f)$ are fed into $f_\theta()$, where $\mathbf{A}_m$ is the needed registration abundances coming from LrHSI autoencoder, $PSF(\mathbf{A}_f)$ is the output of PSF process from HrMSI autoencoder. The output is the displacement field $\phi \in \mathbb{R}^{m \times n \times 2}$, where each pixel of ϕ represents the deformation displacement parameters for x- and y-axes, which can be formulated as follows:

$$\phi = f_\theta(\mathbf{A}_m, PSF(\mathbf{A}_f)) \tag{8.19}$$

In this module, the convolutional layers extract hierarchical features of the input abundances pairs to generate the displacement field ϕ. Both the encoder and decoder consist of a stacked convolutional layer, batch normalization layer, and LeakReLU layer. In the encoder part, a stride of one convolutional layer was set to be 2 to reduce the size of feature maps for forming multi-scale feature representation as shown in Figure 8.6. In the decoder part, a transposed convolutional layer was implemented to increase the size of the feature maps to restore to the original size. On the other hand, to enhance feature diversity, similar to the image/feature pyramid, concatenating skip connections were applied to connect features at multiple levels.

In order to register the deformed moving abundance $\mathbf{A}_m$, a modified spatial transformer network is used to implement gradient-based interpolation, where the learned displacement field grid ϕ is used to warp $\mathbf{A}_m$, which can be denoted as $\mathbf{A}_m \otimes \phi$. For each output location, the grid ϕ specifies the input pixel locations x and y sampling positions. After processing by the shared endmember convolutional layer, the interpolated abundances can be transformed to the registered LrHSI $\mathbf{Y}_{m-restored}$, which can be formulated:

$$\mathbf{Y}_{m-restored} = \mathbf{A}_m \otimes \phi \times \mathbf{E} \tag{8.20}$$

where $\otimes$ denotes the grid sample, $\mathbf{A}_m$ is the moving abundance, ϕ is the displacement field, and $\mathbf{E}$ is the parameter of the shared convolutional layer denoted the endmembers.

8.3.2.4 Loss Function

To train the model in an unsupervised manner, we defined several loss functions to constrain the registration and SR tasks.

1) ***Unsupervised Similarity:***
An unsupervised similarity loss $\mathcal{L}_{sim}$ that measures the similarity between the input data and outputs, and we defined the L1 norm as our similarity function which can be formulated as:

$$\mathcal{L}_{sim} = \|\mathbf{Y}_m - \mathbf{Y}_{m-rec}\|_1 + \alpha\left\|\mathbf{Z}_f - \mathbf{Z}_{f-rec}\right\|_1 + \beta\left\|\mathbf{Y}_{m-restore} - \mathbf{Y}_{f-rec}\right\|_1 \tag{8.21}$$

where α and β are the trade-off parameters to balance the contributions of different losses.

2) ***Correlation Coefficient:***
The correlation coefficient is used to minimize the similarity between $\mathbf{A}_f$ and $\mathbf{A}_m \otimes \phi$:

$$Corr\left(\mathbf{A}_f, \mathbf{A}_m \otimes \phi\right) = \frac{Cov\left(\mathbf{A}_f, \mathbf{A}_m \otimes \phi\right)}{\sqrt{Var\left(\mathbf{A}_f\right)Var\left(\mathbf{A}_m \otimes \phi\right))}} \tag{8.22}$$

where Cov is the covariance and Var is the variance. A higher correlation coefficient means a higher similarity; therefore, the loss function is:

$$\mathcal{L}_{corr}\left(\mathbf{A}_f, \mathbf{A}_m \otimes \phi\right) = 1 \quad Corr\left(\mathbf{A}_f, \mathbf{A}_m \otimes \phi\right) \tag{8.23}$$

3) ***Smooth Constraint:***
Minimizing the $\mathcal{L}_{corr}$ may encourage ϕ to be non-smooth; thus, we defined a diffusion regularizer to smooth the displacement field ϕ:

$$\mathcal{L}_{smooth}(\phi) = \left\|\frac{\partial \phi}{\partial x}\right\|_2 + \left\|\frac{\partial \phi}{\partial y}\right\|_2 \tag{8.24}$$

where the differences between neighboring pixels are used to compute the approximate spatial gradients: $\frac{\partial \phi}{\partial x} \approx \phi(x+1, y) - \phi(x, y)$, $\frac{\partial \phi}{\partial y} \approx \phi(x, y+1) - \phi(x, y)$.

4) ***Summation Constraint:***
For the spectral unmixing discussed in this chapter, we would like the abundance to satisfy sum-to-one and non-negative constraint. To this end, we introduce the summation constraint on the abundance $\mathbf{A}_m$, PSF($\mathbf{A}_f$) and $\mathbf{A}_f$:

$$\mathcal{L}_{sum}\left(\mathbf{A}_m, PSF\left(\mathbf{A}_f\right), \mathbf{A}_f\right) = \left\|1 - \sum_{i=1}^{P} \mathbf{A}_m^i\right\|_1 + \left\|1 - \sum_{i=1}^{P} \mathbf{A}_f^i\right\|_1 + \left\|1 - \sum_{i=1}^{P} PSF\left(\mathbf{A}_f\right)^i\right\|_1 \tag{8.25}$$

where P denotes the number of endmembers. To satisfy the non-negative constraint, clamp function is added before the abundance $\mathbf{A}_m$ and $\mathbf{A}_f$.

Furthermore, the parameters of the PSF layer, SRF, and Endmember layers should also meet the requirements of non-negative constraint. Therefore, we impose a clamp function for these parameters after the parameters are updated for each back-propagation to force these weights be assigned to the range [0,1].

In summary, the final loss function for the proposed network can be formulated as below:

$$\mathcal{L}_{total} = \mathcal{L}_{sim} + \gamma\mathcal{L}_{corr} + \delta\mathcal{L}_{smooth} + \mu\mathcal{L}_{sum} \tag{8.26}$$

where γ, δ, and μ are the trade-off parameters.

8.4 Experiment and Results

8.4.1 Experimental Result of HyCoNet

The proposed HyCoNet was evaluated using Pavia University (PU) and Washington DC (WDC) dataset. In the experiment, simulated spatial downsampling was used to generate the LHSI using a Gaussian filter, as is widely used in remote sensing [2]. In the experiment, the width and height of the Gaussian filter was set equal to the ratio of the high-resolution GSD to the low-resolution GSD. The GSD ratio was set to 4 for PU data and 8 for WDC data. The standard deviation of the Gaussian filters was set to $\sigma = 0.5$ in visual performance and $\sigma = [0.5,1,2]$ in quantitative performance. To simulate the HMSI, the SRF for the blue to SWIR2 bands of the Landsat 8 were used [3]. The blue–green–red bands of the Landsat 8 SRF were used for PU data, and the blue to SWIR2 part of the Landsat 8 SRF was used for WDC data.

Following the work of Yokoya [4], in this study, a set of baseline methods were used for comparison. These included CNMF [1], GSOMP [5], FUSE [6], GLPHS [7], GSA [8], HySure [9], Lanaras's method (for convenience, we called it ICCV[15] because it was published in proceedings of the 2015 International Convention on Computer Vision) [10], MAPSMM [11], and SFIM-HS [12].

8.4.1.1 Visual Performance

Firstly, we used color-composite and heatmap images to visually evaluate the performance of the fusion results when $\sigma = 0.5$. In Figures 8.7 and 8.8, the first column is the RGB composite image (displayed in grayscale), the second column is the RMSE heatmap, the third column is the MRAE heatmap, which can be considered to show the pixel-wise error for the reconstructed image cube, and the fourth column is the SAM error, which represents the spectral consistency of each pixel in the reconstructed image.

From Figures 8.7 and 8.8, it can be seen that HyCoNet achieves the best visual effects among the three visualization evaluation indicators.

8.4.1.2 Quantitative Performance

We investigated the quantitative performance of all the compared methods at different deviation of the Gaussian filters, and the quality measures obtained are shown in Tables 8.1 and 8.2. The mSAM is the mean of the SAM for all pixels and is used to evaluate the spectral consistency of the reconstructed HSI. The mPSNR is the mean PSNR of all the bands and is a measure of the spatial quality. The ERGAS is a global statistical measure used to evaluate the dimensionless global error for fused data.

8.4.2 Experimental Result of NonRegSRNet

This section also uses PU and WDC as test data. The original HrHSI was used as a reference for conducting the quality assessment. The LrHSI was generated using an isotropic Gaussian PSF. The SR scale ratios were set as 4 for these two data. We used the blue–green–red Landsat-8 SRF, and the blue to SWIR2 SRF to generate the HrMSI data for the PU and HrMSI WDC datasets, respectively.

To simulate the non-rigid deformed LrHSI, we linearly combine multiple Gaussian distributions to generate the deformation field. The non-linear transformation can be formed as $\mathcal{T}(x) = x + v(x)$ (Zhou_Rangarajan_Gader_2020). $v(x)$ can be formulated as Gaussian mixture distribution $v(x) = \sum_k \mathbf{c}_k \mathcal{N}(x \mid \mu_k, \sigma^2)$, where k is the k-th Gaussian component, c_k is the k-th mixture coefficient,

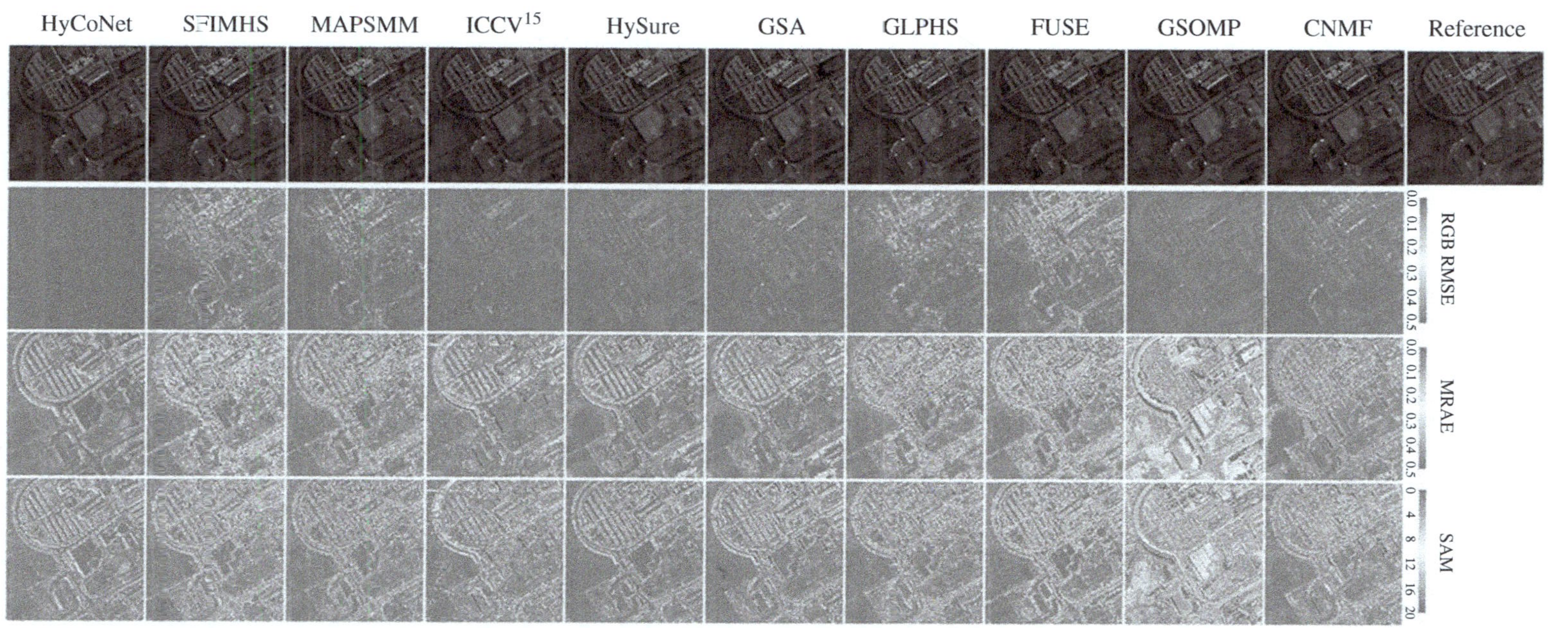

Figure 8.7 The visualization of Pavia University fusion results. The first column is the RGB composite of fusion results; the second column is the RMSE error map; the third column is the MRAE error map of the HSI cube; the fourth column is the SAM error map of the HSI cube.

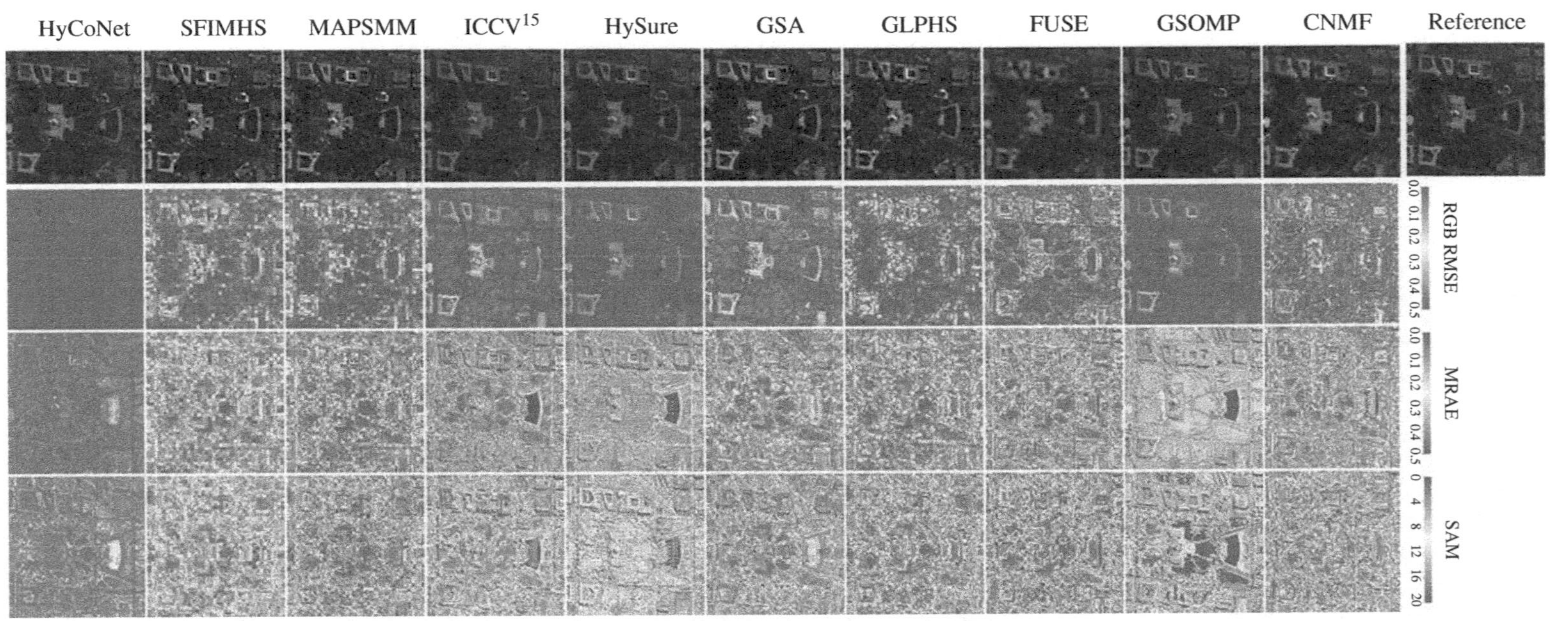

Figure 8.8 The visualization of Washington DC fusion results.

Table 8.1 Quality measures for Pavia University.

		CNMF	GSOMP	FUSE	GLPHS	GSA	HySure	ICCV15	MAPSMM	SFIMHS	HyCoNet
$\sigma = 0.5$	mSAM	4.8715	10.5319	4.7626	5.4793	4.1585	4.0756	4.4325	5.1705	5.4588	**3.4107**
	mPSNR	31.8724	29.0635	27.7470	30.4492	34.3943	34.5460	34.7154	30.8779	23.2267	**38.7647**
	ERGAS	4.3905	8.7599	6.4135	4.6189	3.1379	3.3403	3.2346	4.4652	25.2178	**2.8285**
$\sigma = 1$	mSAM	4.4029	9.0941	4.4667	4.7169	3.4810	3.5015	4.0694	4.0270	4.8534	**3.4002**
	mPSNR	34.8032	31.0354	28.1708	32.9595	37.5222	36.9652	36.2953	34.9411	24.9070	**38.9132**
	ERGAS	3.5658	9.2775	6.1141	3.7639	**2.6955**	2.8068	2.8824	3.2969	20.8983	2.7435
$\sigma = 2$	mSAM	3.7239	8.4744	4.4371	4.3608	3.4896	3.6159	4.0755	4.0317	4.5768	**3.4286**
	mPSNR	36.0128	32.0907	28.2257	34.6668	38.4449	37.5251	36.7325	37.4392	27.3538	**38.5481**
	ERGAS	3.1366	8.4769	6.0774	3.4117	**2.6507**	2.9766	2.8770	3.1937	16.5452	2.8722

Bold values indicates the optimal result for each line.

Table 8.2 Quality measures for Washington DC.

		CNMF	GSOMP	FUSE	GLPHS	GSA	HySure	ICCV15	MAPSMM	SFIMHS	HyCoNet
$\sigma = 0.5$	mSAM	8.8273	13.1330	8.6505	6.9509	7.177	9.9828	8.8196	7.3361	7.2102	**3.1984**
	mPSNR	25.8781	25.3023	24.9366	27.5713	27.3163	26.4899	27.5002	26.9298	25.2003	**34.8730**
	ERGAS	2.8031	3.4564	3.0064	2.2598	2.267	2.7298	2.6514	2.4260	3.4973	**1.4334**
$\sigma = 1$	mSAM	7.2022	10.9944	8.2811	5.8102	5.8450	7.7087	8.0205	5.9814	6.0686	**3.2828**
	mPSNR	27.8536	27.9343	25.7046	29.3968	30.0065	28.7836	29.9389	28.8842	26.9397	**34.9646**
	ERGAS	2.299	3.108	2.8820	1.874	1.7830	2.3315	2.2540	1.9589	36.0251	**1.3959**
$\sigma = 2$	mSAM	5.8034	9.6210	7.9871	4.1380	4.872	6.5962	7.3153	3.7289	4.4360	**3.4581**
	mPSNR	32.6577	28.9048	26.2474	33.4368	35.6293	29.8371	31.1686	33.7772	30.8051	**35.8561**
	ERGAS	1.6080	2.6798	2.7159	1.3183	1.3323	2.0079	1.9705	**1.2007**	2.5060	1.4778

Bold values indicates the optimal result for each line.

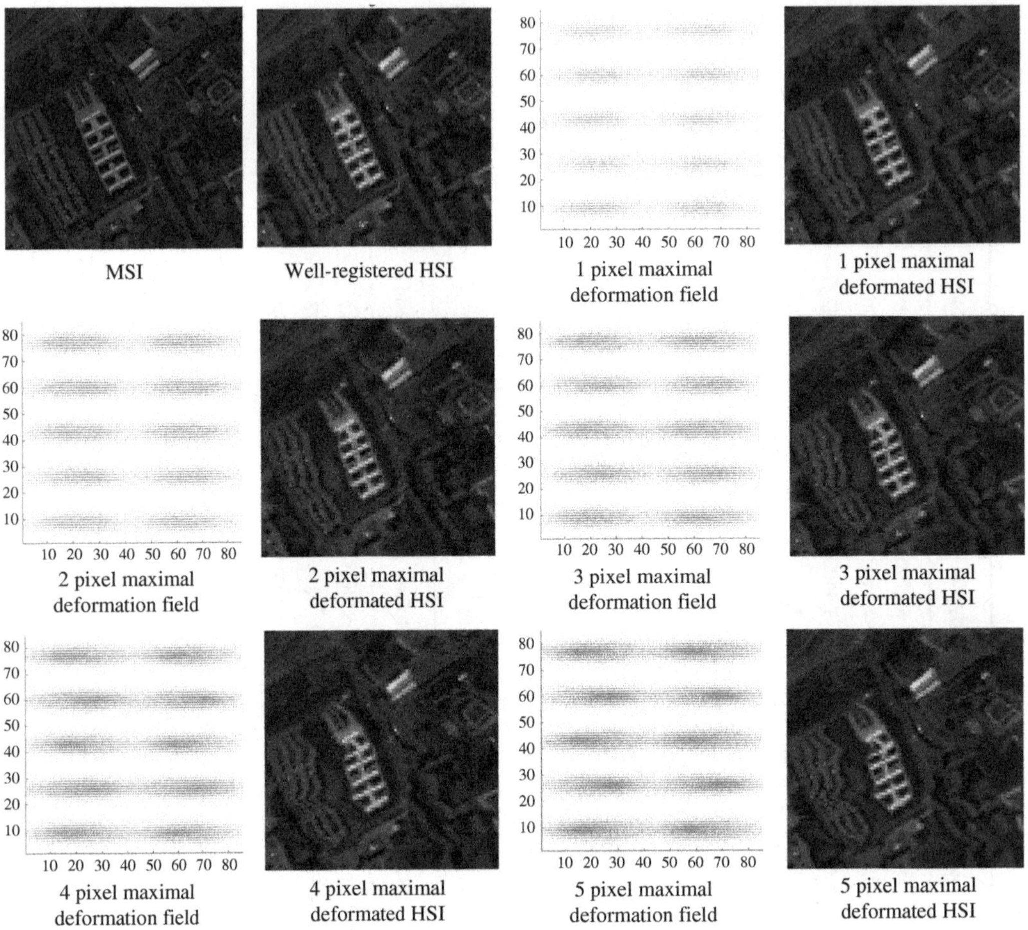

Figure 8.9 Visualization images of PU data under different deformation fields.

μ_k is the mean of the k-th component, and σ is the standard deviation. The non-linear transformation was applied to the spatially downsampled LrHSI (see Figures 8.9 and 8.10).

We first evaluate the performance on nine SR methods by using well-registered input date. Secondly, LSQ free-form non-rigid registration method [13] was used to register the deformed images and the fusion results obtained using different SR methods based on these registered images were compared.

To fully compare the different SR methods, a set of baseline methods were used for comparison: these included traditional methods, e.g., GSA [8], FUSE [6], ICCV[15] [10], CNMF [1], and HySure [9]; and deep learning methods, e.g., uSDN [14], PixAwaRefin [15], CUCaNet [16], and u2MDN [17]. The parameters of all the compared methods were tuned to their optimal values.

8.4.2.1 Washington DC Data

We first evaluated the visual quality of the fused images obtained using the WDC data. Figure 8.11 shows the errors in the fused imagery obtained using different methods under different deformation conditions. The sizes of the errors are given using the MRAE. The first row of Figure 8.11 shows

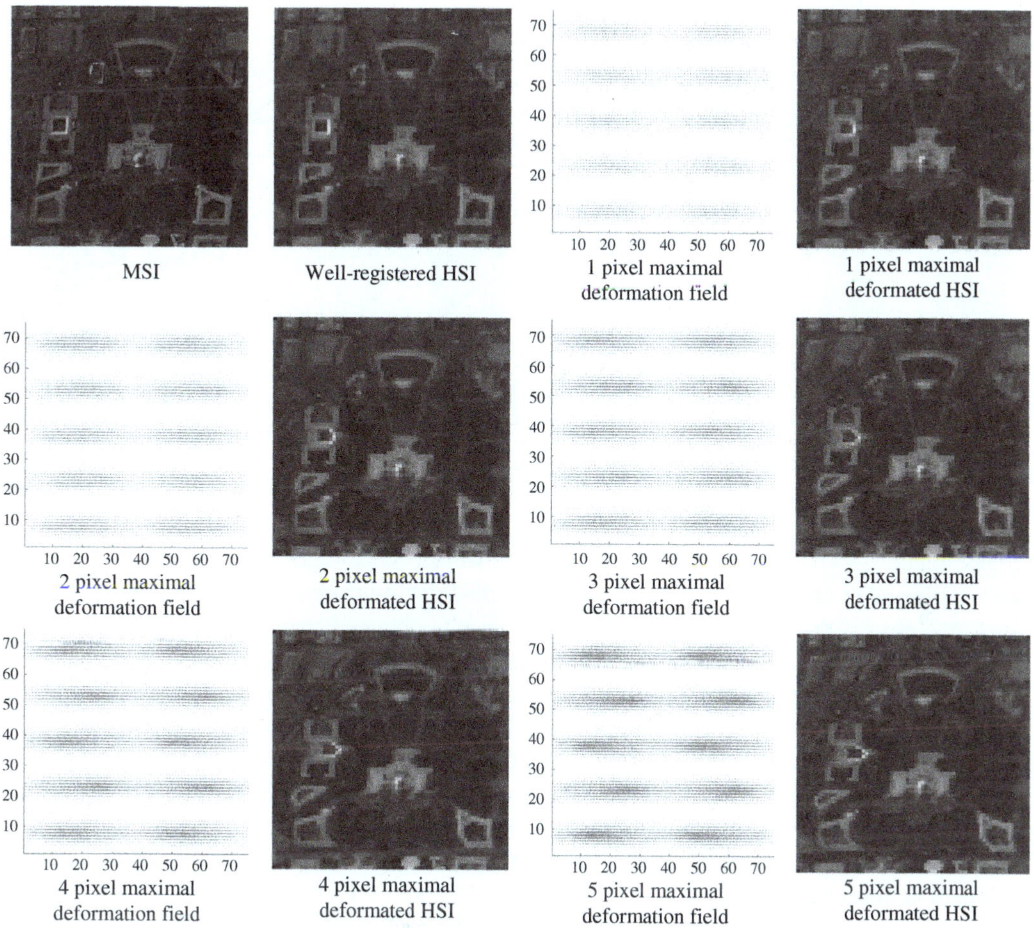

Figure 8.10 Visualization images of WDC data under different deformation fields.

the errors obtained under well-registered conditions. It can be seen that most of the compared algorithms produce good fusion results under such conditions – the exceptions are FUSE and HySure, which produce serious ground object boundary errors. Slight material-dependent errors can be seen in the results for ICCV[15], CNMF, and uSDN.

The second to fourth rows in Figure 8.11 represent the SR results after registration and fusion processing successively. The deformed images were first registered using the LSQ free-form method [13] and then processed using different SR methods. The proposed method was not included in this as it takes the deformed image as the input and outputs the SR results directly. Due to the limits of space, here, we only show the performance results obtained under three sets of deformation conditions: those with maximum deformations of 1 pixel, 3 pixels, and 5 pixels. Compared to the well-registered input, even though the input to the SR method was processed using the registration method, the fusion results obtained using the different methods are very different. The results for CUCaNet are markedly different because this method uses cross attention to transfer

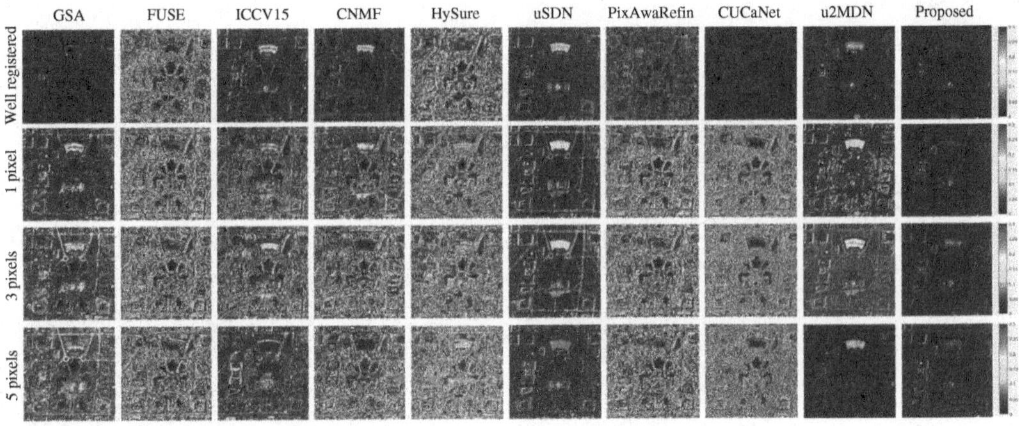

Figure 8.11 Visualization result of WDC data.

cross-domain information between two stream networks. Since there is still a certain degree of deformation after image registration, the use of cross-domain information will lead to a poor performance even if the deformation is slight. The results obtained using uSDN exhibit material-dependent errors that result in the reconstruction of some of the ground objects being poor. The GSA results gradually become poorer as the deformation magnitude increases. The results obtained using the remaining methods are relatively poor. The u2MDN shows excellent performance under the condition of 5 pixels maximum displacement benefited from adopting mutual information to capture the non-linear statistical dependencies between the input images. But the stability of this method is weak when dealing with different deformations.

Table.8.3 shows the quality measure results obtained using the WDC data under different conditions. The results for GSA, CUCaNet, uSDN, u2MDN, and the proposed method show a better reconstruction accuracy than the other methods under well-registered conditions; however, an increase in deformation leads to a sudden worsening of the performance of GSA and CUCaNet. Although the results for uSDN are inferior to those obtained using GSA and CUCaNet, the stability of uSDN is better, indicating that uSDN is less sensitive to the deformation. However, from a comparison of all of the methods, it can be seen that the proposed method is the most stable and produces the best performance under a range of deformation conditions.

8.4.2.2 Pavia University Data

To make a further evaluation of the different methods, we also carried out experiments using the PU data. The results of this are shown in Figure 8.12 and Table 8.4. The quantitative results are similar to those for the WDC data. Generally, it can be observed that, under well-registered conditions, CUCaNet reconstructs spatial information well and that the overall performance drops as soon as the amount of deformation starts to increase. Of all the methods compared, the results for uSDN and the proposed method are the most stable and accurate. The subspace-based methods (ICCV[15] and CNMF) produce reasonably good performances, but the results are not as good as those obtained using the GSA. These results indicate that the proposed method produces highly accurate and stable results under a variety of deformation conditions.

Table 8.3 Quality results of WDC data.

	Maximal deformation magnitude											
	Well-registration		1 pixel		2 pixel		3 pixel		4 pixel		5 pixel	
Quality	SAM	PSNR	SAM	PSNR	SAM	PSNR	SAM	PSNR	SAM	PSNR	SAM	PSNR
GSA	1.766	**40.649**	3.252	35.212	3.913	33.609	4.186	33.009	4.306	32.468	4.962	31.481
FUSE	5.582	28.860	7.445	26.416	8.042	25.844	8.318	25.578	8.425	25.331	8.830	24.959
ICCV15	2.264	36.943	5.350	31.046	6.244	29.928	6.523	29.632	6.505	29.443	4.202	30.108
CNMF	2.019	37.406	3.941	30.560	4.793	28.566	5.432	28.454	5.376	27.194	6.483	25.350
HySure	5.919	30.536	7.188	27.940	6.918	27.560	6.959	27.601	7.260	25.998	7.475	25.660
uSDN	2.252	36.511	2.844	35.310	2.398	35.100	3.033	35.096	2.359	35.559	3.023	34.425
PixAwaRefin	2.783	34.202	7.668	26.566	8.423	26.080	8.930	25.463	8.928	25.615	9.494	25.261
CUCaNet	1.487	40.799	7.877	26.187	9.536	24.392	10.033	24.015	11.134	23.535	11.412	23.161
u2MDN	2.057	35.739	2.935	32.291	4.466	31.291	4.362	31.325	4.714	31.380	2.035	37.160
Proposed	**1.410**	39.309	**1.467**	**38.244**	**1.668**	**38.856**	**1.738**	**38.604**	**1.764**	**38.187**	**1.695**	**39.054**

Bold values indicates the best result for each column.

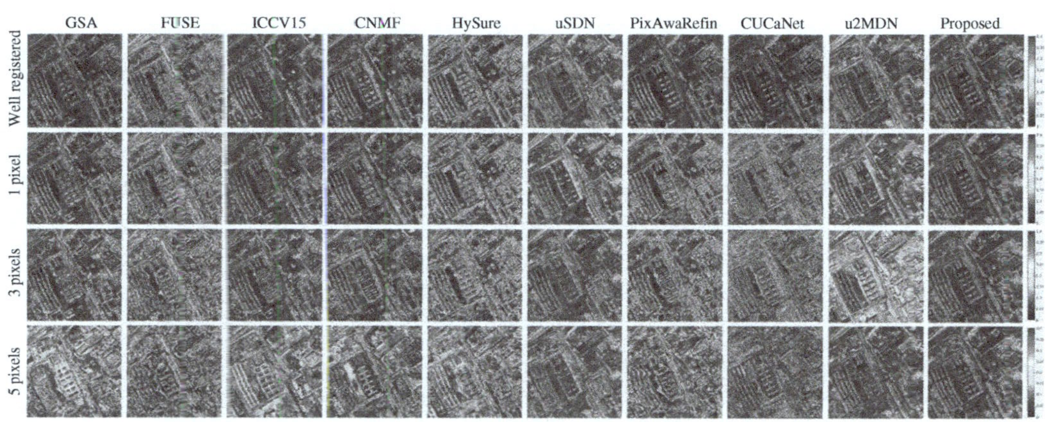

Figure 8.12 Visualization result of PU data.

Table 8.4 Quality results of PU data.

	Maximal deformation magnitude											
	Well-registration		1 pixel		2 pixel		3 pixel		4 pixel		5 pixel	
Quality	**SAM**	**PSNR**	**SAM**	**PSNR**	**SAM**	**PSNR**	**SAM**	**PSNR**	**SAM**	**PSNR**	**SAM**	**PSNR**
GSA	3.890	38.924	4.452	36.444	4.575	35.844	4.762	35.196	7.317	27.497	7.183	27.743
FUSE	5.200	28.868	6.262	27.137	6.506	26.818	6.916	26.439	9.262	23.509	9.238	23.617
ICCV15	4.151	36.711	4.593	34.856	4.527	34.220	4.778	33.733	7.324	25.995	7.296	26.047
CNMF	4.317	36.226	4.463	34.729	4.675	34.236	5.118	33.087	10.214	28.130	12.226	26.954
HySure	6.772	32.794	8.375	31.469	8.795	31.136	8.758	31.059	10.625	25.622	11.179	25.707
uSDN	5.694	36.564	5.749	35.409	5.945	35.666	5.522	36.007	6.133	34.883	5.877	35.525
PixAwaRefin	**3.474**	36.630	5.489	32.098	5.776	31.943	6.307	31.282	9.016	28.399	8.796	28.516
CUCaNet	3.827	**39.721**	6.992	26.504	7.535	25.928	8.967	24.187	12.077	20.932	13.146	20.499
u2MDN	5.804	36.189	6.615	32.504	6.394	33.904	8.604	29.893	8.048	31.269	5.333	36.472
Proposed	3.692	38.648	**4.348**	**38.321**	**4.296**	**38.541**	**4.345**	**38.549**	**4.392**	**38.452**	**4.368**	38.243

Bold values indicates the best result for each column.

8.5 Conclusion

In the part, two unsupervised deep learning methods were introduced to address the fusion problem of hyperspectral image and multispectral image: HyCoNet and NonRegSRNet. HyCoNet utilizes three coupled autoencoder networks to extract spectral information from low-resolution HSI and spatial-contextual information from high-resolution MSI. It adaptively learns the PSF based on the correlation between high- and low-resolution abundances and learns the SRF through autoencoder reconstruction. The NonRegSRNet integrates non-rigid registration and super-resolution into a unified model with a triple convolutional neural network, allowing the super-resolution and registration processes to complement each other, resulting in improved performance for both. This network is capable of adaptively learning spatial and SRFs, enabling it to adapt to various imaging conditions and produce stable reconstructed images. Extensive experiments demonstrate these methods effectiveness in producing highly accurate and stable reconstructed images under complex conditions across two simulated benchmark datasets.

References

1 Yokoya, N., Yairi, T., and Iwasaki, A. (2011). Coupled nonnegative matrix factorization unmixing for hyperspectral and multispectral data fusion. *IEEE Trans. Geosci. Remote Sens.* 50 (2): 528–537.

2 Hong, D. et al. (2019). Learnable manifold alignment (LeMA): a semi-supervised cross-modality learning framework for land cover and land use classification. *ISPRS J. Photogramm. Remote Sens.* 147: 193–205.

3 Barsi, J.A. et al. (2014). The spectral response of the Landsat-8 operational land imager. *Remote Sens* 6 (10): 10232–10251.

4 Yokoya, N., Grohnfeldt, C., and Chanussot, J. (2017). Hyperspectral and multispectral data fusion: a comparative review of the recent literature. *IEEE Geosci. Remote Sens. Mag.* 5 (2): 29–56.

5 Akhtar, Naveed, Shafait, Faisal, and Mian, Ajmal. (2014). Sparse spatio-spectral representation for hyperspectral image super-resolution. *13th European Conference on Computer Vision, Proceedings, Part VII*, Zurich, Switzerland (6–12 September 2014). Springer International Publishing.

6 Wei, Q., Dobigeon, N., and Tourneret, J.-Y. (2015). Fast fusion of multi-band images based on solving a Sylvester equation. *IEEE Trans. Image Process.* 24 (11): 4109–4121.

7 Selva, M. et al. (2015). Hyper-sharpening: a first approach on SIM-GA data. *IEEE J. Sel. Top. Appl. Earth Obs. Remote Sens.* 8 (6): 3008–3024.

8 Aiazzi, B., Baronti, S., and Selva, M. (2007). Improving component substitution pansharpening through multivariate regression of MS $+ $ Pan data. *IEEE Trans. Geosci. Remote Sens.* 45 (10): 3230–3239.

9 Simoes, M. et al. (2014). A convex formulation for hyperspectral image superresolution via subspace-based regularization. *IEEE Trans. Geosci. Remote Sens.* 53 (6): 3373–3388.

10 Lanaras, Charls, Baltsavias, Emmanuel, and Schindler, Konrad. (2015). Hyperspectral super-resolution by coupled spectral unmixing. *Proceedings of the IEEE International Conference on Computer Vision (ICCV)*, Santiago, Chile (7–13 December 2015). IEEE.

11 Eismann, M.T. and Hardie, R.C. (2005). Hyperspectral resolution enhancement using high-resolution multispectral imagery with arbitrary response functions. *IEEE Trans. Geosci. Remote Sens.* 43 (3): 455–465.

12 Liu, J.G. (2000). Smoothing filter-based intensity modulation: a spectral preserve image fusion technique for improving spatial details. *Int. J. Remote Sens.* 21 (18): 3461–3472.

13 Zhou, Y., Rangarajan, A., and Gader, P.D. (2019). An integrated approach to registration and fusion of hyperspectral and multispectral images. *IEEE Trans. Geosci. Remote Sens.* 58 (5): 3020–3033.

14 Qu, Ying, Qi, Hairong, and Kwan, Chiman. (2018). Unsupervised sparse Dirichlet-Net for hyperspectral image super-resolution. *Proceedings of the IEEE Conference on Computer Vision and Pattern Recognition*, Salt Lake City, UT, USA (18–23 June 2018). IEEE.

15 Wei, W. et al. (2020). Unsupervised recurrent hyperspectral imagery super-resolution using pixel-aware refinement. *IEEE Trans. Geosci. Remote Sens.* 60: 1–15.

16 Yao, Jing, Hong, D., Chanussot, J. et al. (2020). Cross-attention in coupled unmixing nets for unsupervised hyperspectral super-resolution. *16th European Conference on Computer Vision, Proceedings Part XXIX*, Glasgow, UK (23–28 August 2020). Springer International Publishing.

17 Qu, Y. et al. (2021). Unsupervised and unregistered hyperspectral image super-resolution with mutual Dirichlet-Net. *IEEE Trans. Geosci. Remote Sens.* 60: 1–18.

9

Hyperspectral Unmixing with Nonnegative Matrix Factorization

Jun Li[1], *Yuanchao Su*[2], *Shaoquan Zhang*[3], *and Ruoqing Xu*[2]

[1] School of Computer Science and Hubei Key Laboratory of Intelligent Geo-Information Processing, University of Geosciences, Wuhan, China
[2] College of Geomatics, Xi'an University of Science and Technology, Xi'an, China
[3] Jiangxi Province Key Laboratory of Water Information Cooperative Sensing and Intelligent Processing, School of Information Engineering, Nanchang Institute of Technology, Nanchang, China

9.1 Introduction

Over recent decades, numerous unmixing techniques have been devised under the framework of the linear mixture model (LMM), broadly categorized into two main types: endmember extraction and abundance estimation [1–8]. These techniques are further divided into two principal groups. One group includes several endmember extraction methods that operate under the assumption that the scene contains at least one pure pixel [9–11]. This group features techniques such as vertex component analysis (VCA) [12], pixel purity index (PPI) [13], N-FINDR [14], and the simplex growing algorithm (SGA) [15]. However, due to the complex nature of terrestrial environments, pure pixels are seldom found in hyperspectral imagery. Addressing this reality, alternative endmember extraction methods have shifted away from assuming the presence of pure pixels. For example, methods such as the minimum volume enclosing simplex (MVES) [17], minimum volume simplex analysis (MVSA) [18], and the simplex identification via split augmented Lagrangian (SISAL) [19], all part of the simplex growing approaches [16], typically generate virtual endmembers that may lack physical realism. The precision of endmember extraction critically impacts the effectiveness of abundance estimation.

From a signal processing standpoint, hyperspectral unmixing is often approached as a blind source separation (BSS) problem [5]. In addressing BSS, nonnegative matrix factorization (NMF) has emerged as a common solution and has recently been applied to hyperspectral unmixing [20]. NMF-based unmixing aims to simultaneously decompose hyperspectral images into two components: one representing the endmember matrix and the other the abundance matrix [21]. Furthermore, due to its inherent properties, NMF is particularly well suited for the task of scene unmixing [22].

In NMF-based unmixing strategies that apply constraints on endmembers, a common technique is to analyze the inherent structure of the entire endmember set. For instance, the minimum volume constraint (MVC) has been incorporated into the NMF framework, culminating in the development of the MVC–NMF method for hyperspectral unmixing [23]. Wang et al. [24] proposed the endmember dissimilarity constrained NMF (EDC-NMF) approach, which utilizes the distinctiveness of endmembers to extract spectrally diverse and smooth spectra from the dataset, thus enhancing hyperspectral unmixing efficacy. Furthermore, Huck et al. [25] introduced the

Machine-Learning-Based Hyperspectral Image Processing, First Edition. Edited by Bing Zhang.

minimum dispersion-constrained (MiniDisCo) NMF method, designed to unmix hyperspectral images by ensuring that the endmember spectra demonstrate minimal variation.

For the NMF-based unmixing strategies that force constraints on the abundances, since most pixels in hyperspectral images are mixed by a subset of endmembers, the abundance matrix exhibits sparsity [26]. Under this presumption, a sparse constraint was acquainted into the NMF model. From a scientific point of view, the L_0 regularizer is a direct strategy that delivers the sparsest outcomes. In any case, the L_0 regularizer is nonconvex and hard to compute, and it is typically replaced by the L_1 regularizer. At that point, the L_1 regularizer is often replaced by the L_p (for $0 \leq p < 1$) regularizer [27] to accomplish greater sparsity results. Xu et al. [28] outlined that $L_{1/2}$ was productive and could be taken as a surrogate of the $L_p(0 < p < 1)$ regularizer. Enlivened by this, the $L_{1/2}$ regularizer was brought into the NMF model for unmixing, to confine the sparsity of abundance maps [29]. The graph-regularized $L_{1/2}$-NMF (GLNMF) technique was proposed to distinguish the complex structure of the hyperspectral information [30]. Since this technique consolidates sparsity limitations into the NMF model, it gives preferred outcomes over other inadequate NMF calculations. The robust collaborative NMF (R-CoNMF) acquainted the $L_{2,1}$ regularizer to promote row sparsity [31]. To additionally improve the sparsity of abundance maps, a weighting methodology was embraced to reduce the nonzero coefficients on the sparse solution. A weighted L_1 regularizer was added to the NMF model [32], and it displays better outcomes than the nonweighted L_1 regularizer. Besides, a double-weighted sparse regularizer was proposed, in which two weights are utilized to improve the column sparsity and row sparsity of the abundance matrix, individually [33]. Hyperspectral images are rich in spatial information, and studies have demonstrated that incorporating this spatial data into NMF-based unmixing models significantly enhances the exploitation of endmember characteristics [34]. For example, the NMF model has been augmented with abundance separation and smoothness constraints (ASSNMF) to facilitate improved hyperspectral unmixing [35]. Additionally, local neighborhood weights have been incorporated into the NMF model to better utilize spatial context [36]. The structured sparse-regularized NMF (SSNMF) method was introduced, which uses a graph Laplacian to capture the complex structures within the hyperspectral manifold space, enhancing the accuracy in identifying endmembers [37]. Moreover, the total variation (TV) regularized reweighed sparse NMF (TV-RSNMF) technique was developed, employing the TV regularizer to delineate the piecewise structure of the abundance matrix [37].

In the field of sparse unmixing, which functions as a semi-supervised method reliant on an existing spectral library, spatial weighting factors are combined with sparse regularizers to accurately represent the spatial structure of the data. For instance, the local collaborative sparse unmixing (LCSU) was proposed, using spatial weighting to foster collaboration and ensure strong unmixing results [38]. Moreover, a spectral–spatial weighted sparse unmixing method was introduced, utilizing spatial weighting elements to effectively integrate both spectral and spatial information from hyperspectral images [39].

In this section, we introduce two NMF unmixing methods: (i) robust collaborative nonnegative matrix factorization (R-CoNMF), and (ii) spectral–spatial weighted sparse NMF (SSWNMF).

9.2 Methodologies

9.2.1 R-CoNMF for Hyperspectral Unmixing

Let $\mathbf{Y} \equiv [y_1, \ldots, y_n] \in R^{d \times n}$ be the matrix representation of a hyperspectral image with n spectral vectors and d spectral bands. Under the LMM, we have [40]

$$\begin{aligned} &\mathbf{Y} = \mathbf{MS} + \mathbf{N} \\ &\text{s.t.}: \quad \mathbf{S} \geq 0, \mathbf{1}_p^T\mathbf{S} = \mathbf{1}_n^T. \end{aligned} \tag{9.1}$$

where $\mathbf{M} \equiv \lfloor m_1, ..., m_p \rfloor \in R^{d \times p}$ is a so-called mixing matrix containing p endmembers; m_i denotes the i–th endmember signature; $\mathbf{S} \equiv [s_1, ..., s_n] \in R^{p \times n}$ is the abundance matrix containing the endmember fractions s_i, for pixels $i = 1, ..., n$; $\mathbf{S} \geq 0$ is the abundance non negativity constraint [41] to be understood in the component-wise sense; $1_p^T\mathbf{S} = 1_n^T$ is the sum to-one constraint that stems from a physical interpretation of the abundance vector; and $1_p = [1, 1, ..., 1]^T$ is a column vector of size p (the notation $[\bullet]^T$stands for vector or matrix transpose). Finally, $\mathbf{N}$ collects the errors that may affect the measurement process (e.g., noise).

Here, we tackle the challenge of estimating the number of endmembers, represented as "p," the mixing matrix "$\mathbf{M}$," and the abundance matrix "$\mathbf{S}$." Although the exact number "p" is not known in advance, we operate under the assumption that we have access to an overestimate, denoted as "q," such that $q \geq p$. This approach addresses a typical scenario where it is easier to compute an overestimate of the number of endmembers than to determine the exact count. Our method focuses on determining "p," "$\mathbf{M}$," and "$\mathbf{S}$" through the application of the following NMF optimization process:

$$\begin{aligned} &\min_{\mathbf{A},\mathbf{X}} \left(\frac{1}{2}\right) \|\mathbf{Y} - \mathbf{AX}\|_F^2 + \alpha\|\mathbf{X}\|_{2,1} + \frac{\beta}{2}\|\mathbf{A} - \mathbf{P}\|_F^2 \\ &\text{s.t.}: \quad \mathbf{X} \in \mathcal{S}_{q-1} \quad \mathbf{A} \in \mathcal{A}_{q-1} \end{aligned} \tag{9.2}$$

where $\|\bullet\|_2$ and $\|\bullet\|_F$ stand for the Euclidean and Frobenius norms, respectively; $\mathbf{A} \equiv [\mathbf{a}_1, ..., a_q] \in R^{d \times q}$ and $\mathbf{X} \in R^{q \times n}$ are optimization variables linked with the mixing matrix and the abundance matrix, respectively; $\| \mathbf{X}\|_{2,1} \equiv \sum_{i=1}^{q} \| \mathbf{x}^i\|_2$ denotes the $l_{2,1}$ (see, e.g., [42]) mixed norm of matrix $\mathbf{X}$ (x_i denotes the ith row of X); $\mathbf{P} \equiv [y_i, ..., y_{iq}]$ is a set of q spectrally observed vectors inferred with a pure-pixel algorithm and, thus, that are close to the extremes of the simplex; α and β are regularization parameters; S_{q-1} is the collection of $q \times n$ matrices whose columns belong to the probability simplex of dimension $q - 1$; and A_{q-1} is the collection of matrices of size $d \times q$ whose columns belong to the affine set of dimension $q - 1$ that best represents the data $\mathbf{Y}$ in the mean square error sense [17].

The objective function shown on the right-hand side of (Eq. (9.2)) has three terms: a data fidelity term $\| \mathbf{Y} - \mathbf{AX} \|_F^2$, which promotes solutions with low reconstruction error; the $l_{2,1}$ mixed norm $\|\mathbf{X}\|_{2,1}$ which promotes row sparsity on $\mathbf{X}$ [43], that is, it promotes solutions with complete rows x^i set to zero; and the term, $(\beta/2)\|\mathbf{A} - \mathbf{P}\|_F^2$ which pushes the columns of $\mathbf{A}$ toward a given solution $\mathbf{P}$. For example, $\mathbf{P}$ can be a solution provided by a pure-pixel-based algorithm, which, jointly with the constraint $\mathbf{X} \in S_{q-1}$, pushes the endmembers to the extremes of the simplex defined by the data $\mathbf{Y}$. Another choice is $\mathbf{P} = [y, ..., y]$, where $\bar{y}$ is the sample mean vector. This choice has a minimum-volume flavor.

As shown in the optimization (Eq. (9.2)), we conclude that the proposed optimization aims at finding a couple ($\mathbf{A}$, $\mathbf{X}$) yielding low reconstruction error, low number of nonzero rows of $\mathbf{X}$, and a simplex defined by the columns of $\mathbf{A}$ constrained by a given solution or minimum volume. The balance between these three terms is set by the regularization parameters α and β.

Let Λ stand for a set of naturals, $\mathbf{A}|_\Lambda \equiv [\mathbf{a}_i, i \in \Lambda]$ and $\mathbf{X}|^\Lambda = [(x^i)^T, i \in \Lambda]^T$, i.e., $\mathbf{A}_\Lambda$ is a matrix containing the columns of $\mathbf{A}$ with indexes in set Λ, and $\mathbf{X}^\Lambda$ is a matrix containing the rows of $\mathbf{X}$ with indexes in set Λ In addition, let rowsupp($\mathbf{X}$) $\equiv \{i, : x^i \neq 0\}$, i.e., rowsupp($\mathbf{X}$) denotes the row support of $\mathbf{X}$. With these definitions in place, we introduce

$$\hat{\mathbf{M}} \equiv \hat{\mathbf{A}}_{|rowsupp(\hat{\mathbf{X}})} \tag{9.3}$$

$$\hat{\mathbf{S}} \equiv \hat{\mathbf{X}}^{|rowsupp(\hat{\mathbf{X}})} \tag{9.4}$$

Provided that the mixed-norm term $\alpha \, \| \mathbf{X} \|_{2,1}$ in Eq. (9.2) drives the rows of $\mathbf{X}$ not corresponding to endmembers to zero, then it is expected that, apart from a permutation, the data fidelity and the volume terms drive $(\mathbf{A}, \mathbf{X})$ to solutions close to $(\mathbf{M}, \mathbf{S})$ in the sense that $\hat{\mathbf{M}} \simeq \mathbf{M}$ and $\hat{\mathbf{S}} \simeq \mathbf{S}$.

The nonconvex data fidelity term $(1/2) \, \| \mathbf{Y} - \mathbf{AX} \|_F^2$ present in Eq. (9.2) makes the respective optimization hard. Herein, we adopt the proximal alternating optimization (PAO) [44], which, under suitable conditions, converges to a critical point of the underlying nonconvex objective function. For notational convenience, we redefine the optimization (Eq. (9.2)) as follows:

$$\min_{\mathbf{A} \in \mathbb{R}^{d \times q}, \mathbf{X} \in \mathbb{R}^{q \times n}} L(\mathbf{A}, \mathbf{X})$$

where

$$\begin{aligned} L(\mathbf{A}, \mathbf{X}) \equiv \frac{1}{2} \|\mathbf{Y} - \mathbf{AX}\|_F^2 + \alpha \|\mathbf{X}\|_{2,1} + \frac{\beta}{2} \|\mathbf{A} - \mathbf{P}\|_F^2 \\ + \iota_{\mathcal{S}_{q-1}}(\mathbf{X}) + \iota_{\mathcal{A}_{q-1}}(\mathbf{A}) \end{aligned} \tag{9.5}$$

where $\iota_{q-1} : \mathbb{R}^{q \times n} \rightarrow \mathbb{R} \cup \{+\infty\}$ and $\iota_{\mathcal{A}_{q?1}} : \mathbb{R}^{d \times q} \rightarrow \mathbb{R} \cup \{ +\infty \}$ denote the indicator function of sets $\mathcal{S}_{q-1}$ and $\mathcal{A}_{q-1}$, respectively; that is, $\iota_{\mathcal{S}_{q-1}}(\mathbf{X}) = +\infty$ if $\mathbf{X} \notin \mathcal{S}_{q-1}$, and $\iota_{\mathcal{S}_{q-1}}(\mathbf{X}) = 0$ otherwise; $\iota_{\mathcal{A}_{q-1}}(\mathbf{A}) = +\infty$ if $\mathbf{A} \in \mathcal{A}_{q-1}$, and $\iota_{\mathcal{A}_{q-1}}(\mathbf{A}) = 0$ otherwise.

Given $(\mathbf{A}_{(0)}, \mathbf{X}_{(0)})$, PAO generates the sequence $(\mathbf{A}_{(t)}, \mathbf{X}_{(t)}) \rightarrow (\mathbf{A}_{(t+1)}, \mathbf{X}_{(t)}) \rightarrow (\mathbf{A}_{(t+1)}, \mathbf{X}_{(t+1)})$ as follows:

$$\mathbf{A}_{(t+1)} = \arg\min_{\mathbf{A}} L(\mathbf{A}, \mathbf{X}_{(t)}) + \frac{\lambda_t}{2} \|\mathbf{A} - \mathbf{A}_{(t)}\|_F^2 \tag{9.6}$$

$$\mathbf{X}_{(t+1)} = \arg\min_{\mathbf{X}} L(\mathbf{A}_{(t+1)}, \mathbf{X}) + \frac{\mu_t}{2} \|\mathbf{X} - \mathbf{X}_{(t)}\|_F^2 \tag{9.7}$$

where λ_t, μ_t, for $t = 0, 1, \dots$, are sequences of positive numbers. We remark that the above procedure can be interpreted as a regularized version of a two-block nonlinear Gauss–Seidel method [45].

Let $\mathcal{A}_{q-1} \equiv \{\mathbf{z} \in \mathbb{R}^d : \mathbf{z} = \bar{\mathbf{y}} + \mathbf{V}\boldsymbol{\alpha}, \boldsymbol{\alpha} \in \mathbb{R}^{q-1}\}$, where $\bar{\mathbf{y}}$ is the sample mean observed vector, and $\mathbf{V} \in \mathbf{R}^{d \times (q-1)}$ is a matrix holding the first $(q-1)$ principal components of the data $\mathbf{Y}$. We remark that the columns of $\mathbf{V}$ are orthonormal, i.e., $\mathbf{V}^T\mathbf{V} = \mathbf{I}_{q-1}$, where $\mathbf{I}_{q-1}$ denotes the identity matrix of dimension $q - 1$. In addition, we also define $\mathbf{Y} \equiv [\bar{\mathbf{y}}, \dots, \bar{\mathbf{y}}] \in \mathbb{R}^{d \times q}$ and write $\mathbf{A} = \mathbf{Y} + \mathbf{V}\boldsymbol{\Delta}$. We remark that any $\mathbf{A} \in \mathcal{A}_{q-1}$ admits a unique representation in the form $= \overline{\mathbf{Y}} + \mathbf{V}\boldsymbol{\Delta}$, where $\boldsymbol{\Delta} = \mathbf{V}^T(\mathbf{A} - \overline{\mathbf{Y}})$.

With the above definitions in place, the solution to the quadratic optimization is

$$\mathbf{A}_{(t+1)} = \overline{\mathbf{Y}} + \mathbf{V}\boldsymbol{\Delta}_{(t+1)} \tag{9.8}$$

$$\begin{aligned} \boldsymbol{\Delta}_{(t+1)} = \mathbf{V}^T \left((\mathbf{Y} - \overline{\mathbf{Y}})\mathbf{X}_{(t)}^T + \beta(\mathbf{P} - \overline{\mathbf{Y}}) + \lambda_t \boldsymbol{\Delta}_{(t)} \right) \\ \cdot \left(\mathbf{X}_{(t)}\mathbf{X}_{(t)}^T + (\beta + \lambda_t)\mathbf{I} \right)^{-1} \end{aligned} \tag{9.9}$$

where $\mathbf{I}$ denotes the identity matrix of suitable size and $(\bullet)^T$ denotes the transpose operator. By defining $\mathbf{Y}'_{(t)} \equiv [\mathbf{Y}^T \sqrt{\mu_t} \, \mathbf{X}_t^T]^T$ and $\mathbf{A}'_{(t+1)} \equiv \left[\mathbf{A}_{(t+1)}^T \sqrt{\mu_t}\mathbf{I}\right]^T$, the optimization Eq. (9.7) can be written as

$$\min_{\mathbf{X}} \frac{1}{2} \left\|\mathbf{Y}'_{(t)} - \mathbf{A}'_{(t+1)}\mathbf{X}\right\|_F^2 + \alpha \|\mathbf{X}\|_{2,1} + \iota_{\mathcal{S}_{q-1}}(\mathbf{X}) \tag{9.10}$$

where $t_2 - t_{2.1}$ is the optimization solved by CLSUnSAL [46], being a generalization of the sparse unmixing by variable splitting and augmented Lagrangian (SUnSAL) [47].

9.2.2 SSWNMF for Hyperspectral Unmixing

Motivated by the accomplishment of weighted L_1 minimization in improving signal sparsity [48], and furthermore by the achievement of the double reweighted sparse unmixing with TV (DRSU-TV) [33], in this work we fuse the spectral and spatial weighting factors into the L_1-NMF model, and the objective function is characterized as follows:

$$\begin{aligned}&\min_{\mathbf{M},\mathbf{S}} \frac{1}{2}\|\mathbf{Y}-\mathbf{MS}\|_F^2 + \lambda\left\|\left(\mathbf{H}_{spe}\mathbf{H}_{spa}\right)\odot\mathbf{S}\right\|_{1,1}\\ &\text{s.t.}:\quad \mathbf{M}\geq 0,\quad \mathbf{S}\geq 0,\quad \mathbf{1}_m^{\mathrm{T}}\mathbf{S}=\mathbf{1}_N^{\mathrm{T}}\end{aligned} \tag{9.11}$$

where $\|\mathbf{S}\|_{1,1} = \sum_{i=1}^{N}\left\|\mathbf{s}_j\right\|_1$ with s_j being the jth column of endmember abundance matrix $\mathbf{S}$. The operator $\odot$ is the element-wise multiplication of two factors, and $\lambda \geq 0$ means the regularization parameter. Let $\mathbf{H}_{spe} \in \mathbb{R}^{m\times m}$ be the spectral weighting factor, which expects to advance the sparsity of the rows in the abundance matrix, as demonstrated as follows:

$$\mathbf{H}_{spe}^{t+1} = \text{diag}\left[\frac{1}{\|\mathbf{S}^t(1,:)\|_2+\varepsilon},\ldots,\frac{1}{\|\mathbf{S}^t(m,:)\|_2+\varepsilon}\right] \tag{9.12}$$

where $\mathbf{S}^t(i,:)$ means the ith row in the evaluated matrix at the tth iteration and $\varepsilon > 0$. It is noted that, as appeared in Eq. (9.12), it is recommended that huge estimations of $\mathbf{H}_{spe}$ dishearten nonzero entries in the assessed abundance matrix, while small weights can be utilized to support nonzero entries [33].

Additionally, taking into account the significance of considering spatial data for NMF unmixing, we consider the way that hyperspectral images ordinarily show high spatial correlation among adjoining pixels, which implies that the abundance map can be viewed as piecewise smooth. With this in mind, similar to the S^2WSU calculation in [39], for the spatial weighting factor $\mathbf{H}_{spa} \in \mathbb{R}^{m\times N}$, we let $h_{spa,ij}^{t+1}$ be the component of the ith line and jth row in $\mathbf{H}_{spa}$ at iteration $t+1$. We consider the spatial neighbors as follows:

$$h_{spa,ij}^{t+1} = \frac{1}{f_{\mathcal{N}(s_{ij})}\left(s_{ij}^t\right)+\varepsilon} \tag{9.13}$$

where $\mathcal{N}(s_{ij})$ represents the adjacent set for element $s_{ij}(i = 1, \ldots, m, j = 1, \ldots, N)$. In other words, it represents the neighborhood of the jth pixel (i.e., s_{ij}) in the ith row of the abundance matrix. $f(\cdot)$ is a function that explicitly exploits the spatial correlations through the neighborhood system. Here, both neighbor coverage and importance are used to incorporate the spatial correlation as follows:

$$f_{\mathcal{N}(s_{ij})}(s_{ij}) = \frac{\sum_{s_b\in\mathcal{N}_8(s_{ij})}\theta_b s_b}{\sum_{s_b\in\mathcal{N}_8(s_{ij})}\theta_b} \tag{9.14}$$

where θ represents the neighborhood significance. Here, an eight-connected (3×3 window) is utilized for analysis. It is noted that, for the center pixels s_{ij} and its neighboring pixels s_b we have $\theta_b = (1/im(s_b, s_{ij}))$, where the function $im(\cdot)$ indicates the significance of the two components s_b and

s_{ij}. Let (e, g) and (k, m) be the spatial coordinates of s_b and s_{ij}. We consider the Euclidean distance, that is, $\theta_b = 1/((e-k)^2 + (g-m)^2)^{1/2}$.

Compared to other sparse NMF hyperspectral unmixing techniques, our SSWNMF introduces two significant innovations. The first is the integration of a spectral weighting factor into the sparse NMF model, which proves more effective than L_1 (or potentially $L_{2,1}$) regularizers in enhancing the row sparsity of the abundance matrix. The second key advancement is the inclusion of a spatial weighting factor in the NMF model. This method embeds spatial relationships via a weighting factor, avoiding the use of spatial prior regularization techniques like those found in TV-based sparse NMF strategies. This approach results in fewer regularization parameters and reduces computational complexity. To address this issue, the optimization of Eq. (9.11) is split into two convex subproblems and the procedure is solved by a multiplicative iterative calculation [49]. The two split subproblems are given in Eqs. (9.15) and (9.16), separately

$$\begin{cases} \mathbf{M} = \arg\min\limits_{\mathbf{M}} J(\mathbf{M}, \mathbf{S}) \\ \mathbf{S} = \arg\min\limits_{\mathbf{S}} J(\mathbf{M}, \mathbf{S}). \end{cases} \tag{9.15}$$

The proposed approach consists of two phases: endmember estimation and abundance estimation. In each phase, one variable is conditionally updated based on the current values of other variables, thereby iteratively reducing the value of the objective function. A detailed description of this process is provided below.

9.2.2.1 Endmember Estimation Step

The objective minimization function is as follows:

$$J(\mathbf{M}) = \arg\min_{\mathbf{M}} \frac{1}{2}\|\mathbf{Y} - \mathbf{MS}\|_F^2 + \mathbf{Tr}(\Psi\mathbf{M}) \tag{9.16}$$

where $\mathbf{Tr}(\cdot)$ means the trace of a matrix. It ought to be noticed that the nonnegative constraints are added to the objective function (Eq. (9.17)). Let $\Psi \in \mathbb{R}^{d\times m}$ be the Lagrange multiplier in matrix format. At that point, we take the derivative with respect to $\mathbf{M}$ as follows:

$$\nabla_{\mathbf{M}} J(\mathbf{M}) = \mathbf{MSS}^T - \mathbf{YS}^T + \Psi. \tag{9.17}$$

Based on the Karush–Kuhn–Tucker condition $\Psi_{dm}\mathbf{M}_{dm} = 0$, it follows that:

$$\left(\mathbf{MSS}^T - \mathbf{YS}^T\right).*\mathbf{M} = 0 \tag{9.18}$$

By applying transposition and division, the update rule for endmember estimation can be derived as follows:

$$\mathbf{M} \leftarrow \mathbf{M}.*\left(\mathbf{YS}^T\right)./\left(\mathbf{MSS}^T\right). \tag{9.19}$$

9.2.2.2 Abundance Estimation Step

The objective minimization function is formulated as

$$J(\mathbf{S}) = \arg\min_{\mathbf{S}} \frac{1}{2}\left\|\mathbf{Y}_f - \mathbf{M}_f\mathbf{S}\right\|_F^2 + \lambda\left\|\left(\mathbf{H}_{spe}\mathbf{H}_{spa}\right) \odot \mathbf{S}\right\|_{1,1} + \mathbf{Tr}(\Phi\mathbf{S}) \tag{9.20}$$

where $\mathbf{Y}_f$ and $\mathbf{M}_f$ represent the augmented matrices: $\mathbf{Y}_f = \begin{bmatrix} \mathbf{Y} \\ \delta\mathbf{1}_N^T \end{bmatrix}$, $\mathbf{M}_f = \begin{bmatrix} \mathbf{M} \\ \delta\mathbf{1}_m^T \end{bmatrix}$, $\Phi \in \mathbb{R}^{m\times N}$ denote the Lagrange multiplier in matrix format, and the spectral weighted matrix $\mathbf{H}_{spe}$ and the spatial weighted matrix $\mathbf{H}_{spa}$ are estimated as shown in Eqs. (9.18) and (9.19), respectively. Then, taking the derivative with respect to **S**, we have

$$\nabla_{\mathbf{S}} J(\mathbf{S}) = \mathbf{M}_f^T \mathbf{M}_f \mathbf{S} - \mathbf{M}_f^T \mathbf{Y}_f + \lambda\left(\mathbf{H}_{spe}\mathbf{H}_{spa}\right) + \Phi. \tag{9.21}$$

Mathematically, based on the Karush–Kuhn–Tucker condition $\Phi_{mN}\mathbf{S}_{mN} = 0$, it follows that:

$$\left(\mathbf{M}_f^T \mathbf{M}_f \mathbf{S} - \mathbf{M}_f^T \mathbf{Y}_f + \lambda\left(\mathbf{H}_{spe}\mathbf{H}_{spa}\right)\right).*\mathrm{S} = 0. \tag{9.22}$$

Similarly, by applying transposition and division, the update rule of **S** is as follows:

$$\mathbf{S} \leftarrow \mathbf{S}.*\left(\mathbf{M}_f^T \mathbf{Y}_f\right)./\left(\mathbf{M}_f^T \mathbf{M}_f \mathbf{S} + \lambda\left(\mathbf{H}_{spe}\mathbf{H}_{spa}\right)\right). \tag{9.23}$$

9.3 Experiments

9.3.1 Experiments for Testing R-CoNMF

9.3.1.1 Experiments with Simulated Data

The advantage of using synthetic scenes is that they offer a fully controlled analysis scenario in which the properties of our algorithm can be precisely investigated. The synthetic scenes have been generated using the LMM in Eq. (9.1). The scenes comprise $n = 4000$ pixels, and the spectral signatures used for their generation were randomly selected from the USGS digital spectral library. To ensure the difference among the endmembers used for simulation purposes, the spectral angle distance (SAD) between any two spectral signatures is bigger than 10°.

Table 9.1 displays the results obtained by MVC–NMF and our proposed R-CoNMF algorithm for all considered performance discriminators for different values of $q = p = \{4,6,8,10,15\}$. In all cases, we considered an SNR of 30 dB and reported the results obtained from averaging the results of 30 Monte Carlo runs.

We evaluate the performance of R-CoNMF in the case that the number of estimated endmembers coincides with the number of real endmembers. From the results reported in Table 9.1, we can make the following observations. First and foremost, when there are only a few endmembers in the image (e.g., $q = p = 4$), all algorithms obtained very good results. This is expected, since in this case, it is relatively easy to solve the optimization problem. It is interesting to observe that as the number of endmembers increases, R-CoNMF obtained very good performance (note the good performance obtained for the case $q = p = 10$). Even in a very difficult scenario such as $q = p = 15$, the

Table 9.1 Evaluation of the performance of R-CoNMF in the unmixing of a synthetic hyperspectral data set, simulated with SNR = 30 db, for different numbers of endmembers and $q = p$.

$q = p$	$\left\Vert\hat{\mathrm{M}}-\mathrm{M}\right\Vert_F$	$\frac{1}{\sqrt{n \times p}}\left\Vert\hat{\mathrm{M}}-\mathrm{M}\right\Vert_F$	SAD	RRE
4	0.17	0.01	0.64	0.03
6	0.20	0.01	0.54	0.03
8	0.76	0.02	1.89	0.03
10	1.28	0.03	2.77	0.03
15	3.13	0.05	5.25	0.04

Table 9.2 Unmixing results obtained by conmf in a simulated scenario with $p = 5$, $q = 5$, and different noise levels, with SNR values of 20, 40, 60, and 80 dB.

SNR	$\|\hat{\mathbf{M}}-\mathbf{M}\|_F$	$\frac{1}{\sqrt{n \times p}}\|\hat{\mathbf{M}}-\mathbf{M}\|_F$	SAD	RRE
20	0.91	0.03	3.68	0.10
40	0.21	0.01	0.58	0.01
60	0.22	0.01	0.70	1e–3
80	0.21	0.01	0.66	4e–4

solution provided by R-CoNMF is still useful. It should be noted that in cases with a relatively high number of endmembers (i.e., $q = p \geq 8$), the other algorithms yield useless results. This is because when the number of endmembers increases, most pixels are likely to fluctuate around the facets, which is a situation in which minimum-volume-based algorithms are likely to fail [40]. Even in this difficult scenario, in which MVC–NMF, MVSA, and SISAL could not provide feasible results, the proposed R-CoNMF was able to provide a reasonable solution. Based on this experiment, we can conclude that R-CoNMF is quite robust and has no strong constraints related with the quality of the analyzed data set.

We demonstrate the efficacy of the proposed R-CoNMF under varying noise conditions using a simulated scenario where $q = p = 5$. The primary objective of this experiment is to evaluate the algorithm's performance across different noise levels. Table 9.2 presents the unmixing results of R-CoNMF at signal-to-noise ratio (SNR) values of 20, 40, 60, and 80 dB. As illustrated in Table 9.2, at moderately low noise levels (i.e., SNR below 40 dB), R-CoNMF achieves impressive unmixing outcomes. Conversely, as the noise level significantly increases (i.e., SNR at 20 dB), the quality of the unmixing results deteriorates, particularly in terms of the spectral angle distortion (SAD) metric. It is important to note, however, that an SNR of 20 dB is generally unrealistic given the SNR capabilities of current imaging spectrometers. Therefore, the results documented in Table 9.2 attest to the high noise robustness of the proposed R-CoNMF.

9.3.1.2 Experiments with Real Hyperspectral Data

In the real-data experiments, we utilized the well-known airborne visible/infrared imaging spectrometer (AVIRIS) Cuprite dataset, which is publicly available online in reflectance units [50]. This dataset has been extensively employed to validate the performance of endmember extraction algorithms. Specifically, our experiments focused on a 250 × 191 pixels subset. The scene includes 224 spectral bands ranging from 0.4 to 2.5 μm, with a nominal spectral resolution of 10 nm. Before proceeding with the analysis, bands 1–2, 105–115, 150–170, and 223–224 were excluded due to water absorption and low SNR, leaving a total of 188 spectral bands. The cuprite site is mineralogically significant and features several exposed minerals of interest, all of which are included in the USGS library used in our experiments, specifically the splib064 released in September 2007. In our experiments, we utilized spectra from this library (convolved and downsampled to match AVIRIS wavelengths) to verify the quality of the endmembers identified by R-CoNMF. Given the extensive use of these data as a benchmark in previous spectral unmixing research, and to conserve space, we limit our comparisons to MVC–NMF in this chapter. For a more comprehensive comparison with other methods, we refer readers to the review detailed in [40].

Figure 9.1 shows the abundance maps corresponding to the three endmembers with lower ζ. It can be observed that (i) corresponds to mineral Buddingtonite, (ii) is Muscovite, and (iii) is a noisy map due to the impact of spectral variability and data complexity. However, as shown by its

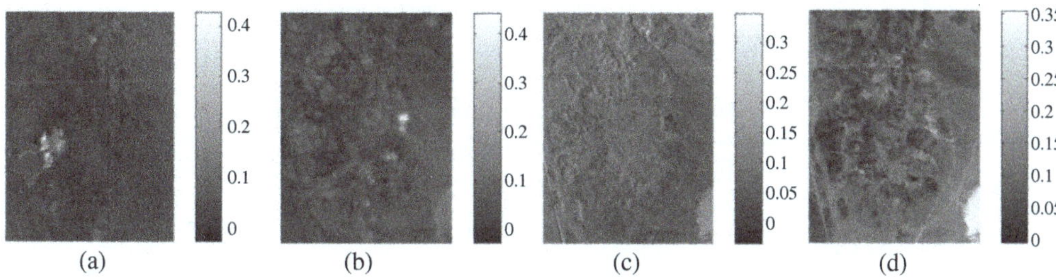

Figure 9.1 Abundance maps obtained by R-CoNMF. (a) Buddingtonite, (b) Muscovite, (c) Noisy, and (d) Montmorillonite.

corresponding abundance map (see Figure 9.1c), the map is noisy in comparison with the other abundance maps. For further analysis, Figure 9.1d shows the abundance map of Montmorillonite. It is clear that when $q > p$, some of the endmembers are duplicates (alterations) of the real ones, i.e., Figure 9.1c is a duplicate of Figure 9.1d.

9.3.2 Experiments for Testing SSWNMF

9.3.2.1 Experiments with Simulated Data

Here, nine spectral signatures were selected from the United States Geological Survey (USGS) library for our experiments. The USGS library comprises 224 spectral bands distributed uniformly across the wavelength range of 0.4–2.5 μm. The simulated images, as described in [51], consist of 100×100 pixels, with each pixel containing 224 bands. The abundance maps adhere to the abundance nonnegativity constraint (ANC) and the abundance sum constraint (ASC), and exhibit piecewise smoothness, meaning they are generally smooth with sharp transitions. These spatial characteristics of the data are crucial for evaluating the performance of various unmixing algorithms. After the data cube was generated, the scene was subjected to independent and identically distributed Gaussian noise at four different SNR levels: 20, 30, 40, and 50 dB.

In this experiment, simulated data corrupted by varying SNRs were used to evaluate the effectiveness of the proposed SSWNMF unmixing technique. We considered four different SNR levels, ranging from 20 to 50 dB, with increments of 10 dB. Table 9.3 presents the SAD results obtained by various methods under different SNR conditions and also includes the root mean square error (RMSE) results. It is important to note that all results are averaged over 10 independent Monte Carlo simulations. Table 9.4 reveals that SSWNMF generally achieves lower or comparable RMSE results relative to other tested methods. In conclusion, the spectral and spatial weighted approach employed by SSWNMF enhances NMF unmixing performance in this scenario, demonstrating its potential to improve results in hyperspectral unmixing tasks.

To further demonstrate the performance of various algorithms, Figure 9.2 (left) displays the abundance maps for endmember 1 at an SNR of 30 dB. It is important to note that only the

Table 9.3 Average sad scores (along with their standard deviations) obtained after 10 MC runs by different methods with simulated data.

	SNR = 20 dB	SNR = 30 dB	SNR = 40 dB	SNR = 50 dB
VCA	0.1358	0.0350	0.0125	0.0049
SSWNMF	0.0636	0.0122	0.0029	0.0012

Table 9.4 Average RMSE scores (along with their standard deviations) obtained after 10 runs by different methods with simulated data.

	SNR = 20 dB	SNR = 30 dB	SNR = 40 dB	SNR = 50 dB
VCA	0.1704	0.0548	0.0164	0.0087
SSWNMF	0.1339	0.0386	0.0122	0.0041

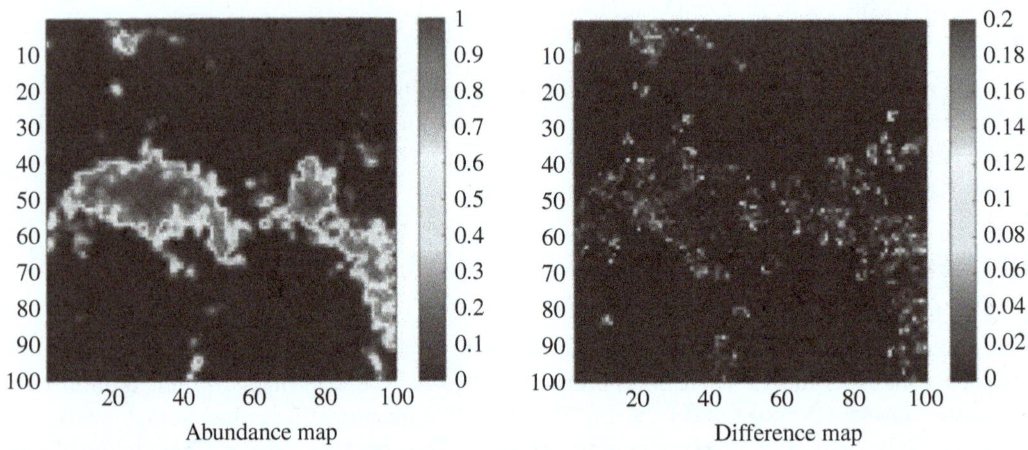

Figure 9.2 Abundance obtained by SSWNMF. Abundance map is from synthetic data under SNR = 30 dB. Difference map compares the ground-truth abundance and the outcome.

abundance map of endmember 1 was selected for display, as all endmembers exhibited similar patterns in their abundance maps. Figure 9.2 (right) also shows the difference maps between the estimated abundances and the original ones.

9.3.2.2 Experiments with Real Data

The Urban dataset comprises 307 × 307 pixels and initially included 210 spectral bands. Due to significant interference from water vapor and environmental factors, several bands – specifically 1–4, 76, 87, and 101–111, along with 136–153 and 198–210 – have been excluded, leaving 162 bands available for analysis. This scene boasts a spatial resolution of 2 × 2 m and a spectral resolution of 10 nm, spanning wavelengths from 0.4 to 2.5 μm. The Scenario has the six endmembers: asphalt road, grass, tree, roof, metal, and dirt.

Table 9.5 shows the SAD and ARE scores obtained by the seven considered unmixing methods for the Urban scene, including the SAD scores for each ground class and their average value. We can see from Table 9.5 that the proposed SSWNMF method achieves very good performance in terms of SAD and can well recognize most endmembers. For illustration, Figure 9.3 displays a comparison of the endmember signatures derived from the SSWNMF method against the reference signatures obtained from the spectral library. It is clear that the endmember signatures correlate well spectrally with their respective reference counterparts. Furthermore, Figure 9.3 also showcases the abundance maps produced by our proposed SSWNMF method, where the grayscale values indicate

Table 9.5 SADs and AREs along with their standard deviations obtained after 10 MC runs by different tested methods for the urban data set.

	SAD							
	Road	Grass	Tree	Roof	Metal	Dirt	Mean SAD	ARE
VCA	0.2246	0.1981	0.2137	0.2673	0.1848	0.1992	0.2146	0.0119
SSWNMF	0.0782	0.1490	0.1173	0.0713	0.1241	0.0802	0.1034	0.0048

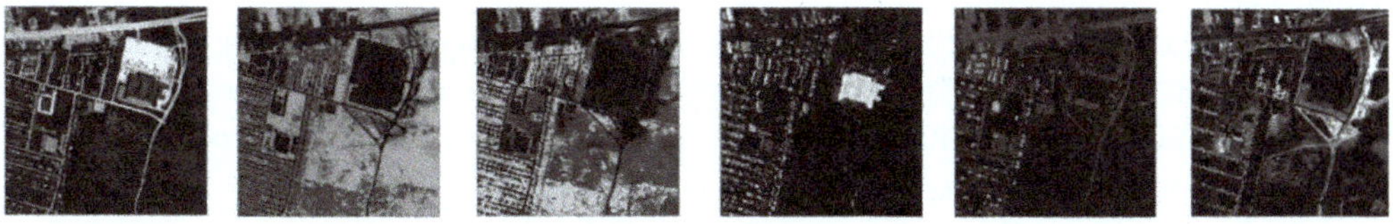

(a) (b) (c) (d) (e) (f)

Figure 9.3 Unmixing results obtained by the SSWNMF method. (Top) Endmembers. (Bottom) Abundance maps. (a) Asphalt road, (b) grass, (c) tree, (d) roof, (e) metal, and (f) dirt.

abundance levels. These maps also clearly display detailed spatial and textural characteristics for each land cover type.

9.4 Conclusion

Hyperspectral unmixing is a crucial process in analyzing hyperspectral remote sensing images, which are captured across a broad range of the electromagnetic spectrum. Each pixel in a hyperspectral image contains a spectrum that is a detailed fingerprint of all the materials present within the area covered by that pixel. The goal of hyperspectral unmixing is to determine the abundance proportion of each endmember in every pixel. The evolution of hyperspectral unmixing reflects a growing sophistication in handling the complexities of real-world data, shifting from simple linear assumptions to advanced models that account for spatial, spectral, and non-linear complexities [52]. The continuing development of these techniques is vital for improving the accuracy and applicability of hyperspectral imaging in fields such as environmental monitoring, agriculture, mineralogy, and military applications [53].

References

1 Bioucas-Dias, J.M., Plaza, A., Camps-Valls, G. et al. (2013). Hyperspectral remote sensing data analysis and future challenges. *IEEE Geosci. Remote Sens. Mag.* 1 (2): 6–36.

2 Chen, J., Zhao, M., Wang, X. et al. (2023). Integration of physics-based and data-driven models for hyperspectral image unmixing: a summary of current methods. *IEEE Signal Process. Mag.* 40 (2): 61–74.

3 Thorp, K.R., French, A.N., and Rango, A. (2013). Effect of image spatial and spectral characteristics on mapping semi-arid rangeland vegetation using multiple endmember spectral mixture analysis (MESMA). *Remote Sens. Environ.* 132: 120–130.

4 Borsoi, R.A., Imbiriba, T., Bermudez, J.C.M., and Richard, C. (2020). A blind multiscale spatial regularization framework for kernel-based spectral unmixing. *IEEE Trans. Image Process.* 29: 4965–4979.

5 Ma, W.-K. et al. (2014). A signal processing perspective on hyperspectral unmixing: insights from remote sensing. *IEEE Signal Process. Mag.* 31 (1): 67–81.

6 Hong, D., Gao, L., Yao, J. et al. (2022). Endmember-guided unmixing network (EGU-Net): a general deep learning framework for self-supervised hyperspectral unmixing. *IEEE Trans. on Neural Netw. Learn. Syst.* 33 (11): 6518–6531.

7 Yao, J., Hong, D., Xu, L. et al. (2022). Sparsity enhanced convolutional decomposition: a novel tensor-based paradigm for blind hyperspectral unmixing. *IEEE Trans. Geosci. Remote Sens.* 60: 1–14.

8 Zouaoui, A., Muhawenayo, G., Rasti, B. et al. (2023). Entropic descent archetypal analysis for blind hyperspectral unmixing. *IEEE Trans. Image Process.* 32: 4649–4663.

9 Qian, Y., Xiong, F., Qian, Q., and Zhou, J. (2020). Spectral mixture model inspired network architectures for hyperspectral unmixing. *IEEE Trans. Geosci. Remote Sens.* 58 (10): 7418–7434.

10 Ammanouil, R., Ferrari, A., Richard, C., and Mathieu, S. (2017). Nonlinear unmixing of hyperspectral data with vector-valued kernel functions. *IEEE Trans. Image Process.* 26 (1): 340–354.

11 Su, Y., Xu, X., Li, J. et al. (2021). Deep autoencoders with multitask learning for bilinear hyperspectral unmixing. *IEEE Trans. Geosci. Remote Sens.* 59 (10): 8615–8629.

12 Nascimento, J.M.P. and Dias, J.M.B. (2005). Vertex component analysis: a fast algorithm to unmix hyperspectral data. *IEEE Trans. Geosci. Remote Sens.* 43 (4): 898–910.

13 Boardman, J., Kruse, F., and Green, R. (1995). Mapping target signatures via partial unmixing of AVIRIS data. *Proceedings of the Fifth JPL Airborne Earth Science Workshop*, 95–101, Pasadena (23–26 January 1995).

14 Winter, M.E. (1999). N-FINDR: an algorithm for fast autonomous spectral end-member determination in hyperspectral data. *Proc. SPIE* 3753: 266–275.

15 Chang, C.-I., Wu, C.-C., Liu, W., and Ouyang, Y.-C. (2006). A new growing method for simplex-based endmember extraction algorithm. *IEEE Trans. Geosci. Remote Sens.* 44 (10): 2804–2819.

16 Craig, M.D. (1994). Minimum-volume transforms for remotely sensed data. *IEEE Trans. Geosci. Remote Sens.* 32 (3): 542–552.

17 Chan, T.-H., Chi, C.-Y., Huang, Y.-M., and Ma, W.-K. (2009). A convex analysisbased minimum-volume enclosing simplex algorithm for hyperspectral unmixing. *IEEE Trans. Signal Process.* 57 (11): 4418–4432.

18 Li, J., Agathos, A., Zaharie, D. et al. (2015). Minimum volume simplex analysis: a fast algorithm for linear hyperspectral unmixing. *IEEE Trans. Geosci. Remote Sens.* 53 (9): 5067–5082.

19 Bioucas-Dias, J.M. (2009). A variable splitting augmented Lagrangian approach to linear spectral unmixing. *2009 First Workshop on Hyperspectral Image and Signal Processing: Evolution in Remote Sensing*, 1–4, Grenoble, France (26–28 August 2009). IEEE.

20 Wang, X., Zhong, Y., Zhang, L., and Xu, Y. (2017). Spatial group sparsity regularized nonnegative matrix factorization for hyperspectral unmixing. *IEEE Trans. Geosci. Remote Sens.* 55 (11): 6287–6304.

21 Xu, X., Li, J., Li, S., and Plaza, A. (2020). Generalized morphological component analysis for hyperspectral unmixing. *IEEE Trans. Geosci. Remote Sens.* 58 (4): 2817–2832.

22 Heslop, D., von Dobeneck, T., and Höcker, M. (2007). Using non-negative matrix factorization in the 'unmixing' of diffuse reflectance spectra. *Mar. Geol.* 241 (1–4): 63–78.

23 Miao, L. and Qi, H. (2007). Endmember extraction from highly mixed data using minimum volume constrained nonnegative matrix factorization. *IEEE Trans. Geosci. Remote Sens.* 45 (3): 765–777.

24 Wang, N., Du, B., and Zhang, L. (2013). An endmember dissimilarity constrained non-negative matrix factorization method for hyperspectral unmixing. *IEEE J. Sel. Top. Appl. Earth Obs. Remote Sens.* 6 (2): 554–569.

25 Huck, A., Guillaume, M., and Blanc-Talon, J. (2010). Minimum dispersion constrained nonnegative matrix factorization to unmix hyperspectral data. *IEEE Trans. Geosci. Remote Sens.* 48 (6): 2590–2602.

26 Wu, Z., Ye, S., Liu, J. et al. (2014). Sparse non-negative matrix factorization on GPUs for hyperspectral unmixing. *IEEE J. Sel. Top. Appl. Earth Obs. Remote Sens.* 7 (8): 3640–3649.

27 Chen, F. and Zhang, Y. (2013). Sparse hyperspectral unmixing based on constrained l_p–l_2 optimization. *IEEE Geosci. Remote Sens. Lett.* 10 (5): 1142–1146.

28 Xu, Z., Chang, X., Xu, F., and Zhang, H. (2012). $L_{1/2}$ regularization: a thresholding representation theory and a fast solver. *IEEE Trans. Image Process.* 23 (7): 1013–1027.

29 Qian, Y., Jia, S., Zhou, J., and Robles-Kelly, A. (2011). Hyperspectral unmixing via $l_{1/2}$ sparsity-constrained nonnegative matrix factorization. *IEEE Trans. Geosci. Remote Sens.* 49 (11): 4282–4297.

30 Lu, X., Wu, H., Yuan, Y. et al. (2013). Manifold regularized sparse NMF for hyperspectral unmixing. *IEEE Trans. Geosci. Remote Sens.* 51 (5): 2815–2826.

31 Li, J., Bioucas-Dias, J.M., Plaza, A., and Liu, L. (2016). Robust collaborative nonnegative matrix factorization for hyperspectral unmixing. *IEEE Trans. Geosci. Remote Sens.* 54 (10): 6076–6090.

32 He, W., Zhang, H., and Zhang, L. (2017). Total variation regularized reweighted sparse nonnegative matrix factorization for hyperspectral unmixing. *IEEE Trans. Geosci. Remote Sens.* 55 (7): 3909–3921.

33 Wang, R., Li, H.-C., Pizurica, A. et al. (2017). Hyperspectral unmixing using double reweighted sparse regression and total variation. *IEEE Geosci. Remote Sens. Lett.* 14 (7): 1146–1150.

34 Shi, C. and Wang, L. (2014). Incorporating spatial information in spectral unmixing: a review. *Remote Sens. Environ.* 149: 70–87.

35 Liu, X., Xia, W., Wang, B., and Zhang, L. (2011). An approach based on constrained nonnegative matrix factorization to unmix hyperspectral data. *IEEE Trans. Geosci. Remote Sens.* 49 (2): 757–772.

36 Liu, J., Zhang, J., Gao, Y. et al. (2012). Enhancing spectral unmixing by local neighborhood weights. *IEEE J. Sel. Top. Appl. Earth Obs. Remote Sens.* 5 (5): 1545–1552.

37 Zhu, F., Wang, Y., Xiang, S. et al. (2014). Structured sparse method for hyperspectral unmixing. *ISPRS J. Photogramm. Remote Sens.* 88: 101–118.

38 Zhang, S., Li, J., Liu, K. et al. (2016). Hyperspectral unmixing based on local collaborative sparse regression. *IEEE Geosci. Remote Sens. Lett.* 13 (5): 631–635.

39 Zhang, S., Li, J., Li, H.-C. et al. (2018). Spectral–spatial weighted sparse regression for hyperspectral image unmixing. *IEEE Trans. Geosci. Remote Sens.* 56 (6): 3265–3276.

40 Bioucas-Dias, J. et al. (2012). Hyperspectral unmixing overview: geometrical, statistical, and sparse regression-based approaches. *IEEE J. Sel. Top. Appl. Earth Obs. Remote Sens.* 5 (2): 354–379.

41 Keshava, N. and Mustard, J.F. (2002). Spectral unmixing. *IEEE Signal Process. Mag.* 19 (1): 44–57.

42 Eldar, Y. and Rauhut, H. (2010). Average case analysis of multichannel sparse recovery using convex relaxation. *IEEE Trans. Image Process.* 56 (1): 505–519.

43 Fornasier, M. and Rauhut, H. (2008). Recovery algorithms for vector-valued data with joint sparsity constraints. *SIAM J. Numer. Anal.* 46 (2): 577–613.

44 Attouch, H., Bolte, J., Redont, P., and Soubeyran, A. (2010). Proximal alternating minimization and projection methods for nonconvex problems: an approach based on the Kurdyka–Lojasiewicz inequality. *Math. Oper. Res.* 35 (2): 438–457.

45 Grippof, L. and Sciandrone, M. (1999). Globally convergent block-coordinate techniques for unconstrained optimization. *Optim. Methods Softw.* 10 (4): 587–637.

46 Iordache, M.-D., Bioucas-Dias, J., and Plaza, A. (2013). Collaborative sparse regression for hyperspectral unmixing. *IEEE Trans. Geosci. Remote Sens.* 52 (1): 341–354.

47 Bioucas-Dias, J. and Figueiredo, M. (2010). Alternating direction algorithms for constrained sparse regression: application to hyperspectral unmixing. *2010 2nd Workshop on Hyperspectral Image and Signal Processing: Evolution in Remote Sensing*, 1–4, Reykjavik, Iceland (14–16 June 2010). IEEE.

48 Candès, E.J., Wakin, M.B., and Boyd, S.P. (2008). Enhancing sparsity by reweighted l_1 minimization. *J. Fourier Anal. Appl.* 14 (5): 877–905.

49 Lee, D.D. and Seung, H.S. (2000). Algorithms for non-negative matrix factorization. *Proceedings of the 14th International Conference on Neural Information Processing Systems*, Denver, CO, USA, Nov 27–Dec. 2, 2000, pp. 556–562.

50 Swayze, G., Clark, R., Sutley, S., and Gallagher, A. (1992). AVIRIS mineral mapping at Cuprite, Nevada. *Summaries of the Third Annual JPL Airborne Geoscience Workshop*, Pasadena, California, USA, June 1–5, pp. 47–49.

51 Iordache, M.-D., Bioucas-Dias, J.M., and Plaza, A. (2012). Total variation spatial regularization for sparse hyperspectral unmixing. *IEEE Trans. Geosci. Remote Sens.* 50 (11): 4484–4502.

52 Zhang, S., Zhang, G., Li, F. et al. (2022). Spectral-spatial hyperspectral unmixing using nonnegative matrix factorization. *IEEE Trans. Geosci. Remote Sens.* 60: 1, 5505713–13.

53 Su, Y., Zhu, Z., Gao, L. et al. (2024). DAAN: a deep autoencoder-based augmented network for blind multilinear hyperspectral unmixing. *IEEE Trans. Geosci. Remote Sens.* 62: 1, 5512715–15.

10

Hyperspectral Unmixing Based on Low-rank Representation and Sparse Constraint

Xiangrong Zhang, Jingyan Zhang, Guanchun Wang, and Licheng Jiao

School of Artificial Intelligence, Xidian University, Xi'an, China

10.1 Introduction

Hyperspectral remote sensing has been widely applied in many fields due to three unique characteristics, namely, space, radiation, and spectrum. The research on hyperspectral image analysis includes feature extraction, dimensionality reduction, classification, and unmixing [1–6]. Due to the complexity of objects and low spatial resolution of remote sensors, it is common to observe mixed pixels in a remote-sensing image, especially a hyperspectral image, thereby hyperspectral unmixing (HU) is becoming more and more important in the research community [5]. HU refers to a process that separates each pixel of hyperspectral images into a collection of constituent spectral signatures, known as endmembers, and a set of fractional abundances [6]. Due to the low spatial resolution of a hyperspectral spectrometer and the complexity of natural surface features, the spectrum of a single pixel cannot necessarily reflect the characteristics of a single material, and it may be a mixture of several different spectra of materials [7]. Unmixing is an ill-posed inverse problem for various environmental conditions and data sets, and it is a challenging problem to solve [6, 8].

Unmixing algorithms depend on the types of mixing. Standard spectral unmixing models can be divided into two categories, linear and nonlinear mixing models [9]. Linear mixing models (LMMs) hold when the mixing scale is macroscopic [10–13]. The explanation of the linear analysis is straightforward. LMMs have been widely studied and applied in recent years [14]. Traditional linear spectral unmixing algorithms usually consist of two steps: endmember extraction [15, 16] and abundance estimation [17–19]. For the first step, referred to as endmember extraction, a preliminary understanding of the study area should be made beforehand. Then, endmembers are extracted after the number of endmembers is estimated and determined.

However, the LMM is not a suitable approximation in some situations. Due to the complicated relationship between the actual terrain and the influence of atmospheric scattering, the spectral mixture demonstrates severe nonlinearity in many real-world scenarios. Thus, a series of nonlinear models have been widely investigated. The generalized bilinear model (GBM) [9] is one of the most commonly used methods based on a nonlinear model. In addition, gradient descent algorithms [20] and semi-nonnegative matrix factorization (semi-NMF) [21] are typical methods to solve the endmember problem, while the latter outperforms the former. However, the sparsity of the data has not been considered for most of the existing nonlinear unmixing algorithms. Zhang et al. [22] extended the GBM incorporating the sparsity constraint of the abundance matrix with the semi-NMF by

Machine-Learning-Based Hyperspectral Image Processing, First Edition. Edited by Bing Zhang.

dividing the GBM into the linear and the second-order parts, which can be optimized by using an alternating optimization algorithm. By using the tensor-based framework, a GBM- and tensor-based method [24] addresses the nonlinear unmixing task as a nonnegative tensor factorization (NTF) problem and exploits the spatial correlation of abundance maps [23].

Single sparse unmixing (SU) assumes that pixels in the image consist of a relatively small set of spectral features in the available spectral library. However, it is NP-difficult to solve the SU problem directly. The collaborative sparse HU using l_0 norm (CSUnL0) [24] algorithm developed collaborative sparse HU using the l_0 norm by introducing a row-hard-threshold function. The joint-sparse-blocks and low-rank unmixing (JSpBLRU) [25] algorithm combines single and joint sparsity. A reweighted low-rank and joint-sparse unmixing approach with an effective library pruning strategy (RLSU-LP) [26] is designed by using a confidence index. The superpixel-based collaborative sparse and low-rank regularization for spectral unmixing (SCLRSU) [27] method improves the performance of traditional spatial regularization-based SU methods. To further impose sparsity on the solution, a spectral-spatial weighted sparse unmixing (S2WSU) [28] framework uses both spectral and spatial weighting factors.

Third-order tensors maintain the 3D structure of hyperspectral images, but these decomposition processes may be inconsistent with the physical mechanism of unmixing. By incorporating the sparsity regularization into the matrix-vector nonnegative tensor factorization (MV-NTF) [29] during the abundance estimation process, the obtained abundance is closer to the true one. Through the use of weighted nonlocal low-rank tensor decomposition regularization [29] effectively preserves spatial details and unmixing results. A new sparsity-constrained low-rank tensor factorization model (SCLT) [30] proposes to maintain the low-rank spatial structure of the raw data and the sparsity of the abundance tensor throughout the iterative process. A multidimensional low-rank (MdLRR) HU method [31] maximizes the utilization of spatial–spectral information by considering the low-rank attributes of 3D abundance tensors across various modes. The high mutual coherence of large standard spectral libraries consistently affects SU performance. To cope with this challenge, some research established Spectral–Spatial Low-Rank Sparse Unmixing (SSLRSU) [32], which uses double weighting factors to improve the row sparsity of the abundance matrix and the sparsity of each abundance map.

In this chapter, we will first provide a review of single LMM algorithms, which are mainly divided into dictionary-based algorithms and those algorithms without dictionary. Then, two hybrid unmixing model algorithms based on sparse constraints will be summarized and introduced, namely, hybrid unmixing based on adaptive region segmentation for hyperspectral imagery [34], and sketch-based region adaptive SU applied to hyperspectral image [35].

10.2 Linear Unmixing Algorithms

The traditional spectral unmixing algorithms with LMM focus on the study of the endmember extraction [15, 16] and the abundance estimation [17]. A variety of endmember identification algorithms based on geometrical and statistical approaches have been exploited [8]. In many cases, the identification of the endmembers in the original hyperspectral data becomes a challenge due to the lack of pure pixels in the scenes and the difficulty in estimating the number of endmembers in a given scene. To deal with these problems, the unmixing algorithms which regard a large standard spectral library as endmembers, have been proposed [33]. Here, two algorithms with dictionary and without dictionary for HU are introduced in the part.

10.2.1 Hyperspectral Unmixing via Low-rank Representation

Recently, to avoid identifying the endmembers in the original hyperspectral data, some researchers use the spectral library as the endmembers and utilize some models based on low-rank representation (LRR) to estimate the abundance at the same time [36, 37]. However, the high mutual coherence of the library signatures makes this model perform badly. It does not distinguish well between the true endmembers and the others. To mitigate the drawback, a new unmixing algorithm via LRR based on space consistency constraint and spectral library pruning has been proposed.

The HU via LRR with space consistency constraint and spectral library pruning (SLP-SCC-LRR) algorithm can be described as an iterative process. First, we use the model of the LRR with the space consistency constraint to estimate the abundance while the whole spectral library acts as the endmembers dictionary. Because the number of the real endmembers is much smaller than the whole spectral library, there exist several endmembers whose abundance values are very low. Secondly, we prune the spectral library based on the abundance matrix obtained in the previous step. The pruning strategy follows such an assumption that if the abundance map of one material does not contain any large values, it is not a real endmember and will be removed from the spectral library. After this step, we can get a pruned spectral library which is a subset of the original one. Then, the pruned spectral library is the new endmembers dictionary and the same process in the first step is performed again, and so on. When meeting the stop conditions, the algorithm terminates. Based on the dictionary pruning strategy, the proposed algorithm can use the spectral library as endmembers and avoid extracting them from the hyperspectral image, compared with the algorithm in [38]. In addition, the algorithm can also better capture the spatial structure of data than the sparsity-based unmixing algorithms. The whole process is summarized in Figure 10.1.

10.2.1.1 Space Consistency Constraint

The spatial information is used in the process of unmixing, whose core idea is shown in Figure 10.2. If the current pixel is the i-th observation signal (y_i), we select its n nearest neighborhoods ($n = 3$). Typically, the current pixel is similar to its spatial neighbor, but this requires a prerequisite, that is, the uniform region. If the current pixel lies at the border, the pixels in the box of Figure 10.2 may belong to multiple substances. Thus, in addition to the spatial neighbor as the prior information, we also measure the distance between the current pixel and its nearest neighbor to distinguish the pixels that are adjacent to each other but belong to different kinds. As shown, the 3∗3 neighborhood of the current pixel contains 8 pixels, the pixel i is at the boundary, and only the j-th, k-th, and m-th endmembers are the same kind of the pixel i. At this point, it is needed to judge by the distance measure to avoid misidentifying the boundary as a homogeneous region. The detail of measurement process is: first, calculate the Euclidean distance between the current pixel and its neighbors, and then, select the nearest p pixels as the true neighbors.

In summary, the so-called spatial consistency constraint reflects the following facts:

1) The pixels of the near neighborhood in the image have similar endmembers and their corresponding abundance.
2) The pixels of the near spectral distance have similar endmembers and their corresponding abundance.
3) By considering both of the above points, selecting p pixels with the nearest distance to the current pixels from the n neighborhood as the true neighbors constrains their abundances to be similar.

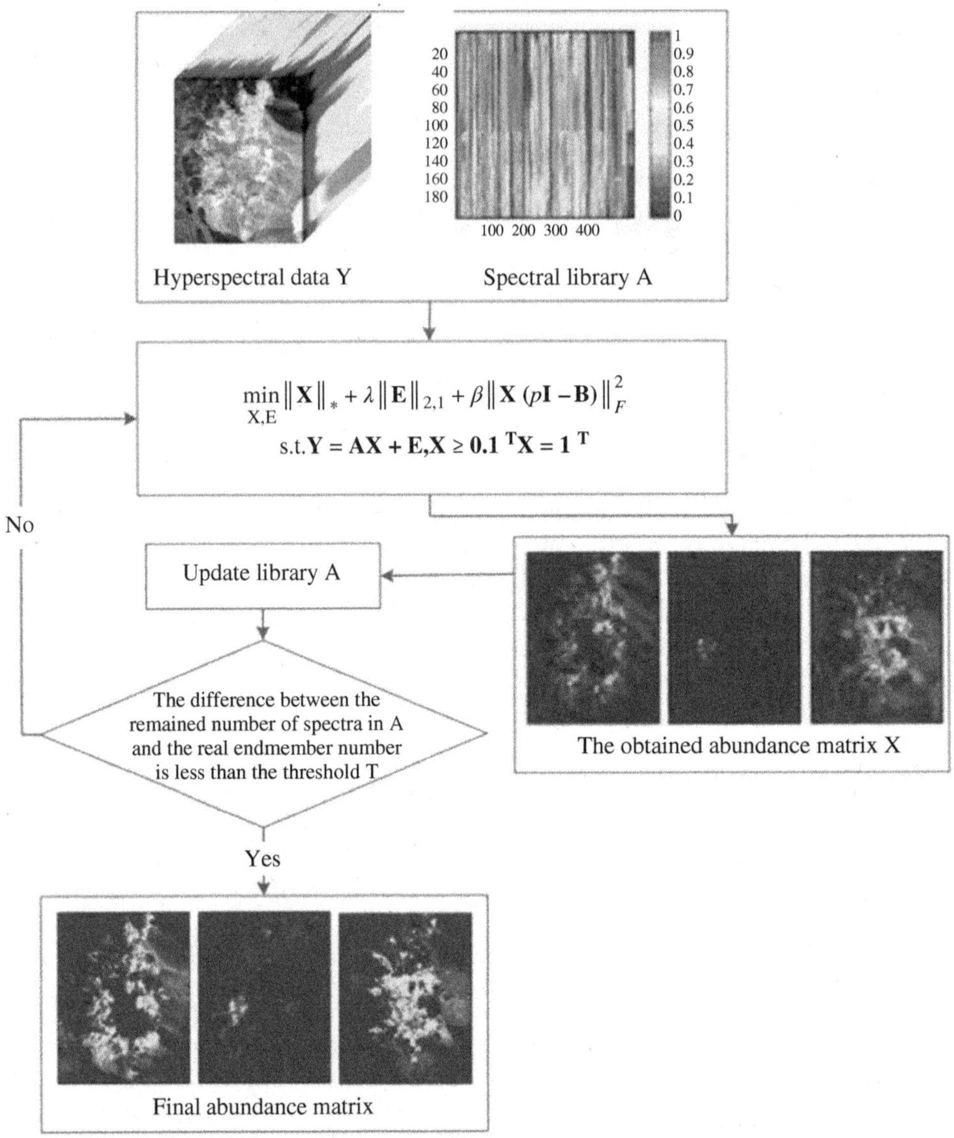

Figure 10.1 The flow chart of SLP-SCC-LRR method.

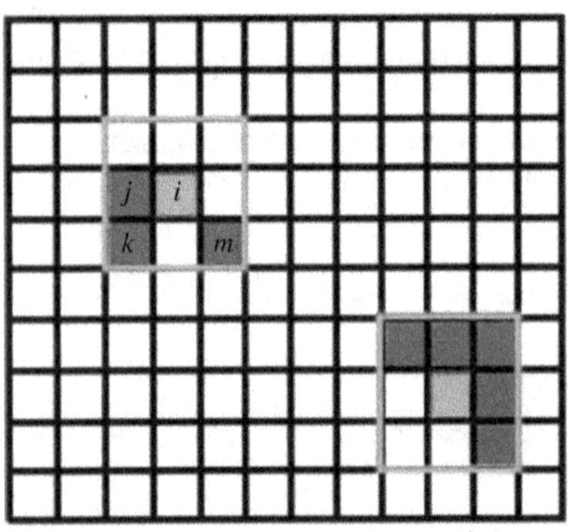

Figure 10.2 The schematic for space consistency of hyperspectral image.

Then, an optimization model based on the LRR with the spatial consistency constraint for the estimation of the abundance as follows:

$$\begin{aligned} &\min_{\mathbf{X},\mathbf{E}} \|\mathbf{X}\|_* + \lambda\|\mathbf{E}\|_{2,1} + \beta\|\mathbf{X}(p\mathbf{I}-\mathbf{B})\|_F^2 \\ &\text{s.t. } \mathbf{Y} = \mathbf{AX} + \mathbf{E}, \quad \mathbf{X} \geq 0, \quad \mathbf{1}^T\mathbf{X} = \mathbf{1}^T \end{aligned} \tag{10.1}$$

where $\mathbf{Y} \in \mathcal{R}^{L\times N}$ is the hyperspectral data, $\mathbf{A} \in \mathcal{R}^{L\times K}$ is the spectral library, $\mathbf{X} \in \mathcal{R}^{K\times N}$ is the abundance matrix, $\mathbf{E} \in \mathcal{R}^{L\times N}$ is the noise matrix, and $\mathbf{I} \in \mathcal{R}^{N\times N}$ is the unit matrix. The λ and β are coordinate parameters, m is the number of the endmember, and p refers to the p true neighbors. The size of matrix $\mathbf{B}$ is $n*n$, and it can be calculated by the method that if $\mathbf{y}_j$ is similar to $\mathbf{y}_i$, then the matrix $\mathbf{B}$ equals to $\boldsymbol{\omega}_{ij}$, or equals to zero, where $\boldsymbol{\omega}_{ij}$ is the similarity of the observation vectors $\mathbf{y}_i$ and $\mathbf{y}_j$. We set $\boldsymbol{\omega}_{ij}$ to be 1. In addition, two constraints need to be satisfied for proper unmixing: (i) the endmember and the abundance matrices are nonnegative (abundance nonnegative constraint, ANC) and (ii) the sum of each column of the abundance matrix is one (abundance sum constraint, ASC). That is, $\mathbf{X} \geq 0$, $\mathbf{1}^T\mathbf{X} = \mathbf{1}^T$.

The optimization problem can be solved by the method of augmented Lagrange multiplier (ALM) [39]. The ANC is added in each step of the iterative process, while the ASC is embodied in the normalization process of the last step of the iteration. Because the ANC has obvious physical meaning, that is, the value of abundance cannot be negative, so the general solution is to add it. The ASC needs to choose to add or not based on the actual situation.

10.2.1.2 Spectral Library Pruning

After solving optimization (Eq. (10.1)), we can obtain the fractional abundances matrix $\mathbf{X}$ corresponding to the spectral library $\mathbf{A}$. Compared with the size of the spectral library, the number of endmembers in a given scene is usually much smaller. Thus, sparsity exists among the lines of the obtained abundances matrix $\mathbf{X}$, and each line of $\mathbf{X}$ denotes the abundance map corresponding to one endmember. To utilize the sparsity, we propose a dictionary pruning strategy to prune the abundance matrix $\mathbf{X}$ and its corresponding spectral signatures in $\mathbf{A}$.

This strategy can be described as two steps:

1) Compute the number of the pixels whose abundance value corresponding to one endmember is smaller than a preset threshold ε.
2) If the number is equal to the total number of pixels in the scene, remove the spectral corresponding signature from the endmember matrix.

It means that if one endmember is rarely distributed over the scene, it is not a real endmember. That is our motivation of using the strategy to prune the spectral library $\mathbf{A}$. In the experiments on simulated data, we set ε to be 0.02 and then if one endmember is distributed under 2% over the scene, it will be removed from the library. And we set ε to 0.01 in the experiments of real data because real data are more complex than simulated data. In each iteration, the size of spectral library will decrease and the abundance of the retained endmembers will increase. Thus, in each iteration, the value of ε will be updated by ε*iterations.

Then, we can get a pruned spectral library $\mathbf{A}$ as the endmember matrix in which the number of spectral signatures is smaller than the original one. By using this pruned spectral library $\mathbf{A}$, we solve the optimization (Eq. (10.1)) again and obtain a new fractional abundances matrix $\mathbf{Y}$. According to the dictionary pruning strategy, we can prune the spectral library $\mathbf{A}$ repeatedly until the number of spectral signatures retained meets the stopping condition.

A threshold T acting as the stop condition is defined to control this iterative process. The stop condition can be described like that when the difference between the number of spectral signatures retained and the estimated number of endmembers in a scene is less than T, the algorithm stops. Thus, a higher value of T means that it retains more endmembers from the spectral library. Here, the hyperspectral subspace identification by minimum error (HySime) algorithm [40] is used to estimate the number of endmembers. In the experiments with simulated data, the range of values for T is 1 to 10 and in the experiments with real data, we set T to be 25. We retain more endmembers for real data because they are more complex than simulated data. When the situation is complex (e.g., low SNR, big endmember number, or a very large library), we set ε to be a small value and T to be a large value to avoid removing the true endmembers from the library. After several iterations, we can get a good result for the optimization problem. The whole process of this method has been summarized in Figure 10.1.

10.2.2 Hyperspectral Unmixing via Sparse Nonnegative Matrix Factorization

The NMF-based unmixing approach has gained attention in HSI due to its successful applications in various fields. The main task of NMF [41] is decomposing a non-negative matrix into the product of two nonnegative matrices to reduce the dimension of high-dimensional data. Since its goal is similar to that of spectral unmixing, the NMF model has been widely employed in unmixing. However, the NMF model has an ill-conditioned problem, which tends to fall into a local optimal solution. Therefore, it is necessary to add some specific constraints of endmembers and abundances to the NMF model based on the characteristic of HU.

Inspired by the advantage of NMF model, a sparse NMF unmixing algorithm based on endmember independence and spatial weighted abundance for HSI is developed. Its purpose is to extract independent endmembers and obtain smooth abundances. For the endmembers, it is considered that the more independent the endmembers are, the better they can characterize the HSI. Thus, the constraint of endmembers via autocorrelation matrix is added to the NMF model. In addition, only a subset of endmembers participates in the mixing of pixels, which leads to the sparsity of abundances. Therefore, the sparse constraint for abundances is adopted, and a weight in view of spatial information is introduced to make the abundances smoother. Furthermore, in order to exploit the latent manifold structure of the HSI data, manifold regularization is also employed in our model. In general, the sparse nonnegative matrix factorization for HU based on endmember independence and spatial weighted abundance (EASNMF) algorithm not only puts forward the appropriate constraints based on the characteristics of endmembers and abundance, but also fully integrates the spatial–spectral information for HU. The flow chart of EASNMF algorithm is shown in Figure 10.3.

10.2.2.1 Endmember Independence Constraint

The HSI data is formed by different endmembers with a certain proportion, and it is easy to find that the endmembers should be independent of each other. For independence, the autocorrelation matrix can be adapted to constrain the endmembers. If the endmembers are independent of each other, their autocorrelation matrix should be a diagonal. That is, the off-diagonal elements of its autocorrelation matrix should be as close to 0 as possible. Therefore, the NMF model with endmember independence constraint is as follows:

$$\begin{aligned}&\min_{\mathbf{A},\mathbf{X}} \frac{1}{2}\|\mathbf{Y}-\mathbf{A}\mathbf{X}\|_F^2 + \alpha\left(\left\|\mathbf{A}^T\mathbf{A}\right\|_1 - \|\mathbf{A}\|_F^2\right)\\&\text{s.t. } \mathbf{X}\geq 0,\quad \mathbf{1}^T\mathbf{X}=\mathbf{1}^T\end{aligned} \tag{10.2}$$

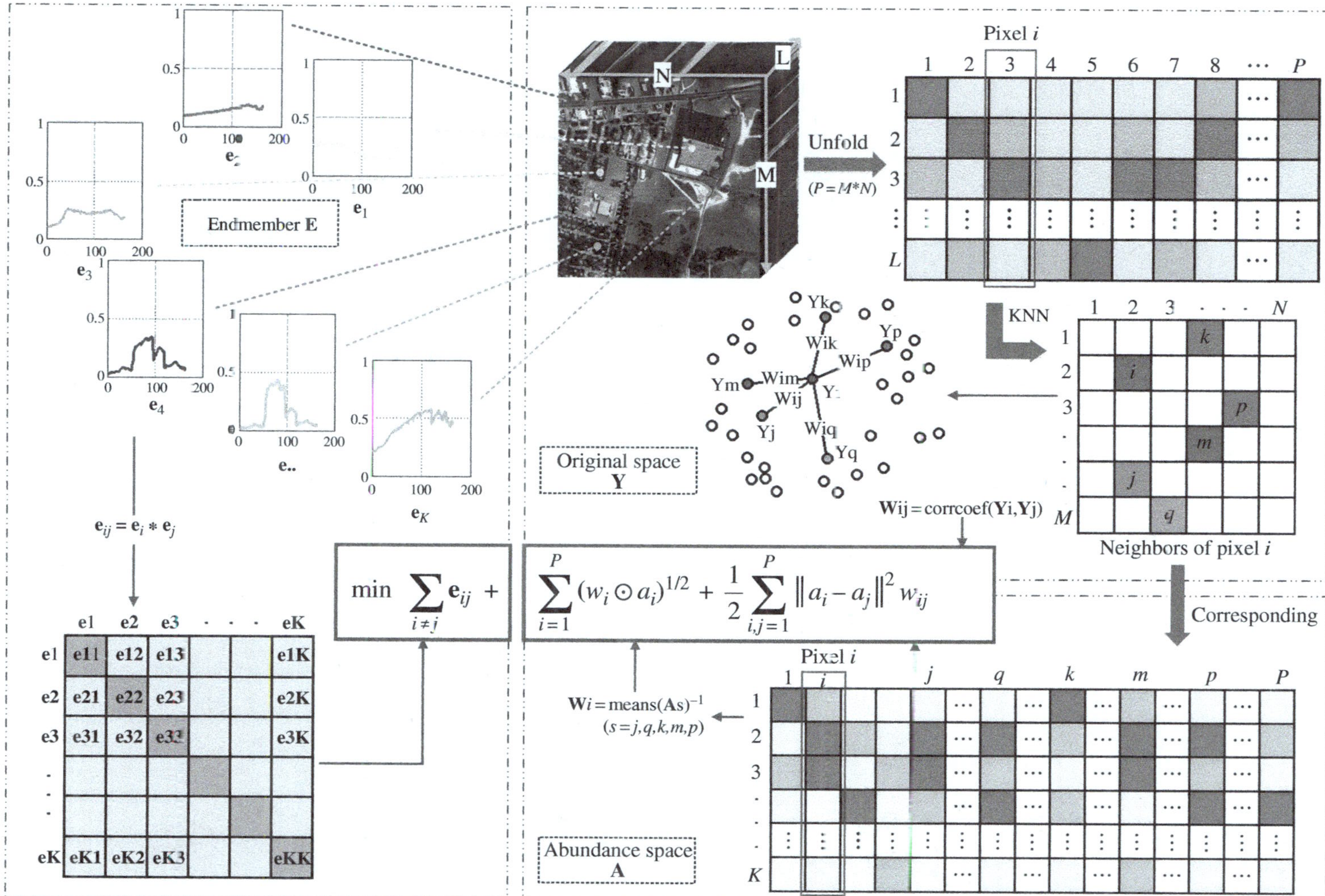

Figure 10.3 The flow chart of EASNMF method.

where $\mathbf{A} \in \mathcal{R}^{L \times K}$ is the endmember matrix and α is the parameter to balance the data fidelity and endmember independence term. The second term refers to the sum of the off-diagonal elements of the autocorrelation matrix for endmembers, i.e., the difference between the sum of all the elements (the first sub-term) and the sum of the diagonal elements (the second sub-term). The purpose of the second term in Eq. (10.2) is to make the endmembers independent of each other as much as possible; that is, the correlation between different endmembers should be as small as possible.

10.2.2.2 Abundance Sparse and Spatial Weighted Constraint

Studies have shown that most of the mixed pixels are mixtures with only a few endmembers on the scene [42]. Thus, the corresponding abundance is sparsity, which can be considered an intrinsic property of HU. Therefore, the sparsity constraint as an effective tool has been introduced to HU. As mentioned before, the $L_{1/2}$ regularizer proposed by [43] is proved to provide a sparse and accurate result. Taking the sparsity of abundance into consideration, the sparse constraint of abundance is added into the model, which is formed as follows:

$$\begin{aligned} &\min_{\mathbf{A},\mathbf{X}} \frac{1}{2}\|\mathbf{Y}-\mathbf{AX}\|_F^2 + \alpha\left(\left\|\mathbf{A}^T\mathbf{A}\right\|_1 - \|\mathbf{A}\|_F^2\right) + \beta\|\mathbf{X}\|_{1/2} \\ &\text{s.t. } \mathbf{X} \geq 0, \quad \mathbf{1}^T\mathbf{X} = \mathbf{1}^T \end{aligned} \tag{10.3}$$

where β is the weight parameter to adjust the effect of the last term in Eq. (10.3), and $\|\mathbf{X}\|_{1/2} = \sum_{i,j}^{K,P} \left(\mathbf{x}_{ij}\right)^{1/2}$.

Moreover, the neighboring pixels are more likely to have similar fractional abundance values, which are considered spatial structure information. This information can be constructed as a weight matrix for abundances to make full use of. Suppose the pixel $\mathbf{y}_j$, whose corresponding abundance value is $\mathbf{x}_j$, is one neighbor of the pixel $\mathbf{y}_i$, and there are m neighbors for pixel $\mathbf{y}_i$. For each iteration of abundance, the abundance average of the neighborhood for each pixel is calculated to construct a weight matrix $\mathbf{W} = \left[w_1, w_2, \ldots, w_p\right] \in \mathcal{R}^{K \times P}$ for the next iteration. The element in weight matrix $\mathbf{W}$ is computed as follows:

$$w_i^{(k+1)} = 1/\left(\frac{1}{m}\sum_{j=1}^{m} \mathbf{x}_j\right)^k + eps \tag{10.4}$$

where *eps* is a predetermined positive constant. Here the Euclidean distance is adopted to calculate the similarity of pixels in the image, and then m pixels with the smallest values are chosen as the neighbors to obtain the element of weight matrix $\mathbf{W}$ in Eq. (10.4). It is hoped that if the spectral signatures of pixels are similar, their abundance values should be similar. The model with the weight matrix $\mathbf{W}$ is expressed as below:

$$\begin{aligned} &\min_{\mathbf{A},\mathbf{X}} \frac{1}{2}\|\mathbf{Y}-\mathbf{AX}\|_F^2 + \alpha\left(\left\|\mathbf{A}^T\mathbf{A}\right\|_1 - \|\mathbf{A}\|_F^2\right) + \beta\|\mathbf{W}\odot\mathbf{X}\|_{1/2} \\ &\text{s.t. } \mathbf{X} \geq 0, \quad \mathbf{1}^T\mathbf{X} = \mathbf{1}^T \end{aligned} \tag{10.5}$$

where $\odot$ is the term-by-term Hadamard product.

In this part, the priors of sparseness and spatial information are integrated into the NMF model to shrink the solution space and further promote the unmixing performance. However, it just considers the sparse characteristic for unmixing and neglects the intrinsic geometrical structure of HSI. Therefore, it is necessary to further explore the potential characteristics of HSI data for unmixing.

10.2.2.3 Manifold Regularization Constraint

As is well known, HSI is a kind of high-dimensional data. Moreover, manifold learning finds the representation in low-dimensional manifold space for high-dimensional space data. It can dig into the essence of data and discover its inherent laws. In Eq. (10.5), only the sparse characteristic and the Euclidean structure of hyperspectral data are taken into consideration. It is necessary to introduce the intrinsic manifold structure into the proposed model to render better performance of HU.

There are P pixels in HSI and each pixel can be considered a data point. Thus, the nearest-neighbor graph is constructed by each pixel as its vertices and its weight matrix is denoted as $\mathbf{W}_g$. The weight between two pixels $\mathbf{y}_i$ and $\mathbf{y}_j$ is defined as follows.

$$w_{g_{ij}} = \begin{cases} corrcoef\left(\mathbf{y}_i, \mathbf{y}_j\right) & \mathbf{y}_j \in \mathbb{N}(\mathbf{y}_i) \\ 0 & otherwise \end{cases} \tag{10.6}$$

Here $corrcoef(\cdot)$ means the correlation coefficient and it is calculated by $\frac{cov\left(y_i, y_j\right)}{\sqrt{var(y_i)var\left(y_j\right)}}$, where cov(·) and $var(\cdot)$ separately mean the covariance and variance. That is, if the pixel $\mathbf{y}_j$ is a neighbor of pixel $\mathbf{y}_i$, the weight between these two pixels is obtained by computing their correlation coefficient. The correlation coefficient is usually used to describe the degree of correlation between two variables in statistics, whose absolute value is between 0 and 1. Generally speaking, the closer its absolute value is to 1, the greater the correlation between two variables is.

Furthermore, based on the analysis before, if two pixels $\mathbf{y}_i$ and $\mathbf{y}_j$ are close in the original space, their representations $\mathbf{x}_i$ and $\mathbf{x}_j$ in the new space should also be close [44]. For this purpose, the manifold constraint is proposed as below:

$$\begin{aligned} \frac{1}{2}\sum_{i,j=1}^{N} \|\mathbf{x}_i - \mathbf{x}_j\|^2 \mathbf{W}_{g_{ij}} &= \sum_{i=1}^{N} \mathbf{x}_i^T \mathbf{x}_i \mathbf{D}_{ii} - \sum_{i,j=1}^{N} \mathbf{x}_i^T \mathbf{x}_j \mathbf{W}_{g_{ij}} \\ &= Tr\left(\mathbf{X}\mathbf{D}\mathbf{X}^T\right) - Tr\left(\mathbf{X}\mathbf{W}_g\mathbf{X}^T\right) = Tr\left(\mathbf{X}\mathbf{L}\mathbf{X}^T\right) \end{aligned} \tag{10.7}$$

where Tr(·) indicates the trace of the matrix, $\mathbf{D}_{ii} = \sum_{i=1}^{P} \mathbf{W}_{g_{ij}}$ and $\mathbf{L} = \mathbf{D} - \mathbf{W}_g$. Then, incorporating the manifold regularization into the model, the final objective function is exhibited as follows

$$\begin{aligned} &\min_{\mathbf{A},\mathbf{X}} \frac{1}{2}\|\mathbf{Y} - \mathbf{A}\mathbf{X}\|_F^2 + \alpha\left(\left\|\mathbf{A}^T\mathbf{A}\right\|_1 - \|\mathbf{A}\|_F^2\right) + \beta\|\mathbf{W} \odot \mathbf{X}\|_{1/2} + \frac{\gamma}{2} Tr\left(\mathbf{X}\mathbf{L}\mathbf{X}^T\right) \\ &\text{s.t.} \quad \mathbf{X} \geq 0, \quad \mathbf{1}^T\mathbf{X} = \mathbf{1}^T \end{aligned} \tag{10.8}$$

where γ acts as the penalty parameter to control the manifold regularization term.

10.3 Hybrid Unmixing Algorithms

The linear spectral mixture model (LMM) assumes no interactions between ground objects, while the non-linear model (non-LMM) considers the scattering of incident radiation within the scene and interactions among various ground objects. Due to the complexity of surface features, a single mixture model can hardly describe all mixing cases accurately. Thus, a hybrid unmixing algorithm with sparse constraints is introduced in this section [34]. Moreover, aiming at the problem that most

SU methods only consider a single sparse constraint, another improved method is also explored in this section.

10.3.1 Hybrid Unmixing via Region Adaptive Segmentation

Unmixing is an important issue of hyperspectral images. Most unmixing methods adopt LMMs for simplicity. However, multiple scattering usually occurs between vegetation and soil in a bilinear scene. Thus, nonlinear mixing problems which are difficult to be solved should be taken into consideration under this circumstance. In practice, both linear and nonlinear spectral mixtures exist in hyperspectral scenes. Considering the characteristics of different regions in images, a hybrid unmixing algorithm for hyperspectral images based on region adaptive segmentation has been proposed.

The method first uses a standard *K*-means clustering algorithm to obtain different regions, including homogeneous regions and detailed regions. The model of the homogeneous regions is assumed to be linear, which will be pursued using the method of sparse-constrained nonnegative matrix factorization (SNMF), and the mixing in the detailed regions is assumed to be based on a nonlinear model. A new nonlinear unmixing method, called graph-regularized semi-NMF (GSNMF), which considers the manifold structure of hyperspectral data is considered as the unmixing method to deal with the detailed regions [34]. Finally, by combining the unmixing results of the two regions, the accuracy of abundance estimation is improved, and the edge information of the bilinear abundance is well preserved, and the flowchart is shown in Figure 10.4.

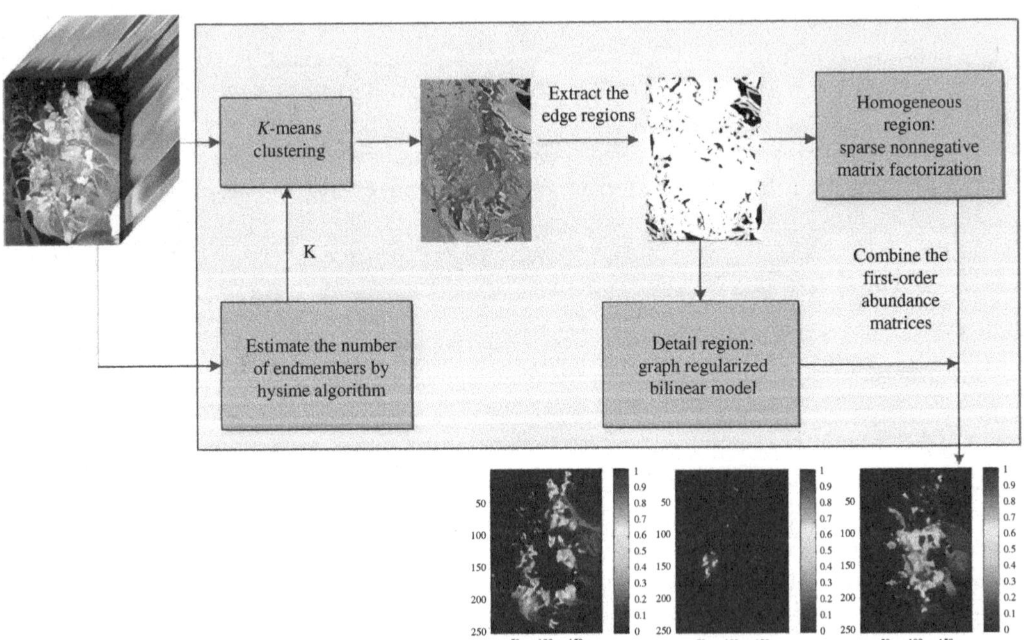

Figure 10.4 The flow chart of RASU method.

10.3.1.1 Adaptive Region Segmentation

First, the hyperspectral image is segmented to extract edge information. Three segmentation methods, namely K-means clustering, super-pixel segmentation, and thresholding segmentation, are adopted. Among them, the number of clusters k in K-means clustering is determined by estimating the number of endmembers using the Hysime algorithm. Then, the segmented image is labeled.

Next, the entire image is scanned with a 2×2 pixel window: If there are different labels within the window, it is determined to be a detailed region; otherwise, it is classified as a homogeneous region. For example, if the labels of the pixels in the window are (1,1,1,2) or (1,1,2,3), it is a detailed region; if the labels are all the same (such as 1,1,1,1), it is a homogeneous region. Finally, the image is divided into a detailed region and a homogeneous region, which will enter the subsequent processing.

10.3.1.2 Unmixing Model for a Homogeneous Region

The homogeneous region is unmixed by the linear model, SNMF. Then, an NMF algorithm, based on the Euclidean distance, is used to construct the new objective function as follows:

$$\begin{aligned} &\min_{\mathbf{A},\mathbf{X}_1} \frac{1}{2}\|\mathbf{Y}_1 - \mathbf{A}\mathbf{X}_1\|_F^2 + \lambda\|\mathbf{X}_1\|_{1/2} \\ &\text{s.t. } \mathbf{X}_1 \geq 0, \quad \mathbf{1}^T\mathbf{X}_1 = \mathbf{1}^T \end{aligned} \tag{10.9}$$

where the first term of the objective function is the reconstruction error (RE) based on the linear model, and the second term is a sparse constraint. $\mathbf{X}_1 \in \mathcal{R}^{K \times P_1}$ is the abundance matrix of the homogeneous regions, λ is the parameter of the sparse regularization whose range is generally from 0.001 to 0.5.

10.3.1.3 Unmixing Model for a Detailed Region

The detailed regions use the GSNMF algorithm for unmixing, which is based on GBM. GBM has been widely used for hyperspectral image unmixing. The second-order photon interactions between different endmembers are considered as the additional terms to the LMM, assuming that the third-order or higher-order interactions are negligible [45]. The GBM can be written as:

$$\mathbf{Y}_2 = \mathbf{A}\mathbf{X}_2 + \mathbf{B}\mathbf{E}_2 + \mathbf{N} \tag{10.10}$$

where $\mathbf{A} \in \mathcal{R}^{L \times K}$ is the endmember matrix of K endmembers, $\mathbf{X}_2 \in \mathcal{R}^{K \times P_2}$ is the first-order abundance matrix, $\mathbf{B} \in \mathcal{R}^{L \times K(K-1)/2}$ is the bilinear endmember matrix, $\mathbf{E}_2 \in \mathcal{R}^{K(K-1)/2 \times P_2}$ is the second-order abundance matrix, and $\mathbf{N} \in \mathcal{R}^{L \times P_2}$ is the noise matrix. The proposed GSNMF considers the graph constraint of HU based on GBM. Its objective function composed of errors and graph constraints is as follows:

$$\begin{aligned} &\min_{\mathbf{A},\mathbf{X}} \frac{1}{2}\|\mathbf{Y}_2 - \mathbf{A}\mathbf{X}_2 - \mathbf{B}\mathbf{E}_2\|_F^2 + \frac{\mu}{2} Tr\left(\mathbf{X}_2\mathbf{L}\mathbf{X}_2^T\right) \\ &\text{s.t. } \mathbf{X}_2 \geq 0, \quad \sum_{i=1}^{K} (\mathbf{X}_2)_{\mathbf{il}} = \mathbf{1}, \quad 0 \leq \mathbf{E}_2 \leq \mathbf{X}_2^* \end{aligned} \tag{10.11}$$

where $\mathbf{X}_2^* \in \mathcal{R}^{K(K-1)/2 \times P_2}$ with each element is calculated by $\left(\mathbf{X}_2^*\right)_{(i,j)p} = (\mathbf{X}_2)_{ip}(\mathbf{X}_2)_{jp}, p \in \{1, 2, \ldots, P\}$, and $(\bullet)_{ij}$ denotes the value for the i-th row and j-th column of the matrix. It should be noted that in this chapter, we adopt the updated $\mathbf{A}$ of the homogeneous regions as the endmember of the detailed regions to keep the endmember matrix of the whole image identical.

10.3.1.4 Unmixing Model for a Detailed Region

The first-order abundance matrix $\mathbf{X}_1 \in \mathcal{R}^{K \times P_1}$ of the homogeneous region $\mathbf{Y}_1$ and the first-order abundance matrix $\mathbf{X}_2 \in \mathcal{R}^{K \times P_2}$ of the detailed region $\mathbf{Y}_2$ are combined as $\mathbf{X} \in \mathcal{R}^{K \times P}$ in order to derive the first-order abundance of the whole image. The second-order abundance of the detailed region is selected as the nonlinear abundance of the whole image. Overall, this chapter uses the GSNMF model considering second-order photon interactions between different materials.

10.3.2 Sketch-based Region Adaptive Sparse Hybrid Unmixing

In fact, the pixels in detail regions are more likely to be severely mixed with more endmembers participating, and the sparsity degree of its corresponding abundances is relatively low. The assumption in this study is that most pixels in the image are mixed [46, 47], and the pixels in the detail regions are more likely to be heavily mixed with more endmembers participating than in the homogeneous regions. Therefore, it is inferred that the sparsity degree of the abundances for these two regions is obviously different, and the sparsity degree of abundances in homogeneous regions is relatively high.

The sketch-based region adaptive sparse unmixing (SRASU) method first extracts endmembers from the whole image as the initial set. Then, a sketch-based region generation method is used to identify two distinct regions. The $L_{1/2}$ sparse regularizer is applied to constrain the abundances in homogeneous regions. After that, the abundances of homogeneous regions and updated endmembers are obtained. For detailed regions, a classical sparse model with the L_1 regularizer and the updated endmembers are utilized. Finally, the final abundances are acquired by merging the two abundance matrices. The SRASU algorithm is shown in Figure 10.5.

10.3.2.1 Region Generation Based on Sketch Map

Human vision is essentially a process of information processing. Accordingly, Marr [6] proposed a theoretical framework for visual computing, in which the extraction of the initial sketch map is a key step to analyze and understand the scene information contained in the image. Then, Guo et al. [48] presented the mathematical theoretical model and the extraction algorithm of sketch map. The sketch map extraction algorithm proposed by Guo et al. [48] is applied to the HSI analysis in this article. Then, the rectangular window with direction is designed for the obtained sketch map that is used to distinguish the homogeneous regions $\mathbf{Y}_1 \in \mathcal{R}^{L \times P_1}$ and detail regions $\mathbf{Y}_2 \in \mathcal{R}^{L \times P_2}$.

The algorithm for obtaining two kinds of regions includes sketch map extraction and region generation. For sketch map extraction, the steps are as follows: (i) construct the basic dictionary of the image; (ii) generate brightness change map; (iii) obtain initial sketch map by non-maximum suppression operation; (iv) get the sketch map by greedy tracking operation; and (v) extract the final sketch map using a set of graph operators. The sketch map composed of sketch lines with directional characteristics can reflect the structure information of the original image. In addition, the areas that the sketch lines are located indicate regions with high spectral variance, containing a lot of details, such as edges and textures. More details can be found in these articles [48, 49].

For the task of region generation, we use the rectangular window with the direction to divide the image into two different regions. The specific operations are as follows. The center of the rectangular window is aligned with one end of each sketch line. The long side of the rectangular window is parallel to the sketch line. The rectangular window slides along the direction of the sketch line until the center is aligned with the other end. The area that window slides contains detailed information corresponding to the detail regions. The remaining area of an image is considered as the homogeneous regions.

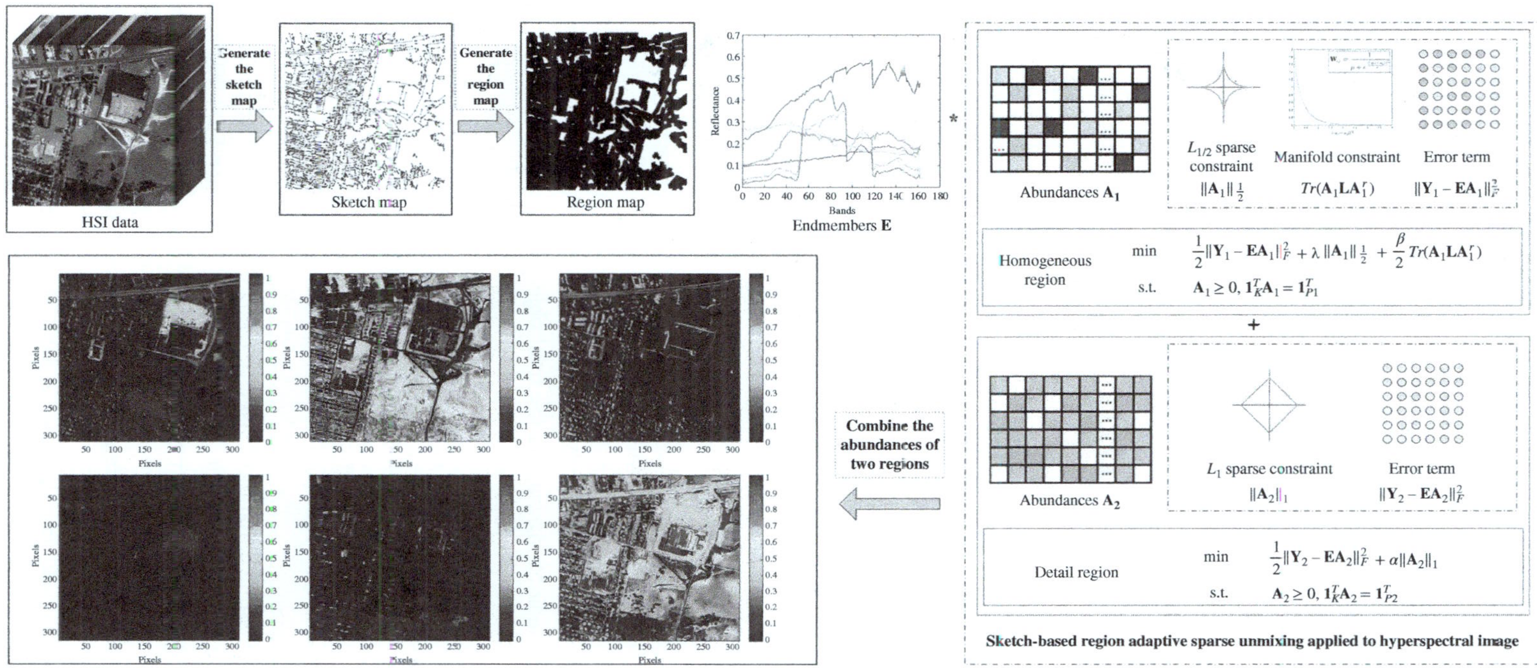

Figure 10.5 The flow chart of SRASU method.

10.3.2.2 Sparse Unmixing for Homogeneous Regions

In homogeneous regions $\mathbf{Y}_1$, due to the fewer mixtures, the corresponding abundance is relatively sparser compared with other regions, which means that higher sparsity degree is preferred in these regions. Therefore, we use the $L_{1/2}$ regularizer to constrain the abundance of homogeneous regions to enhance its sparsity. Due to the $L_{1/2}$ regularizer, the $L_{1/2}$-NMF method can enforce the sparsity of abundances. Inspired by $L_{1/2}$-NMF, the sparse constraint with the $L_{1/2}$ regularizer is also adopted in our model. Moreover, in order to exploit the latent manifold structure of hyperspectral data in the feature space, a sparsity-constrained NMF with manifold regularization (MSNMF) for HU is proposed.

For the homogeneous regions $\mathbf{Y}_1 \in \mathcal{R}^{L\times P_1}$ with P_1 pixels, a weighted graph is constructed where each pixel is considered as a node. The main idea is that when the pixels are closer, their corresponding abundances are more similar. Thus, the weight between notes $\mathbf{y}_i$ and $\mathbf{y}_j$ is defined as follows:

$$\mathbf{W}_{ij} = 1/\left(\mu + \exp\left(\left\|\mathbf{y}_i - \mathbf{y}_j\right\|^2/\sigma\right)\right) \tag{10.12}$$

where $\mu \in (-1, +\infty)$ is the parameter for controlling the maximum and σ is the scaling parameter for $\mathbf{W}_{ij}$. By the constraints of manifold and sparsity with $L_{1/2}$ regularizer, the whole objective function, consisting of the error reconstruction term, is as follows:

$$\begin{aligned}&\min_{\mathbf{A},\mathbf{X}_1} \frac{1}{2}\|\mathbf{Y}_1 - \mathbf{A}\mathbf{X}_1\|_F^2 + \lambda\|\mathbf{X}_1\|_{1/2} + \frac{\beta}{2}Tr(\mathbf{X}_1\mathbf{L}\mathbf{X}_1^T)\\ &\text{s.t. } \mathbf{X}_1 \geq 0, \quad \mathbf{1}^T\mathbf{X}_1 = \mathbf{1}^T\end{aligned} \tag{10.13}$$

where λ and β are the parameters.

10.3.2.3 Sparse Unmixing for Detail Regions

In detail regions $\mathbf{Y}_2$, most pixels are generated by various endmembers. Therefore, the sparsity degree of abundance matrix is lower. By adopting the L_1 regularizer to constrain the abundance $\mathbf{X}_2 \in \mathcal{R}^{K\times P_2}$ of detail regions, we can get the final objective function as follows:

$$\begin{aligned}&\min_{\mathbf{A},\mathbf{X}_1} \frac{1}{2}\|\mathbf{Y}_2 - \mathbf{A}\mathbf{X}_2\|_F^2 + \alpha\|\mathbf{X}_2\|_1\\ &\text{s.t. } \mathbf{X}_2 \geq 0, \quad \mathbf{1}^T\mathbf{X}_2 = \mathbf{1}^T\end{aligned} \tag{10.14}$$

where the last term is the sparse constraint on the abundance in detail regions and α is a weight parameter. The algorithm fully considers the spatial difference of data through different abundance constraints on two regions.

In this chapter, it is assumed that most pixels in the HSI are mixed. The pure signatures are more likely to be present in spatially homogeneous regions [46, 47]. Therefore, the initial endmembers are extracted by the VCA algorithm from the whole image, which includes all possible endmembers. Then, the endmembers are optimized in homogeneous regions for more finely extraction. In order to unify the endmembers of two regions, the obtained endmembers are used for detail regions unmixing. In addition, the function (Eq. (10.14)) is the same as the objective function of the SUnSAL algorithm. Therefore, the update criterion for $\mathbf{X}_2$ is achieved according to the SUnSAL algorithm. Finally, the abundance matrix $\mathbf{X}$ is obtained by combining $\mathbf{X}_1$ and $\mathbf{X}_2$.

10.4 Experiments

10.4.1 Datasets Description

1) **Synthetic dataset 1**: Data provided by Dr. M. D. Iordache and Prof. J. M. Bioucas-Dias were used. The data is 100×100 pixels in size and contains 224 bands. By randomly selecting nine spectra from the USGS spectral library as endmembers, the abundance of this synthetic data obeys the Dirichlet distribution. The true abundance maps corresponding to the nine endmembers are presented in Figure 10.6. In addition, Gaussian noise with a signal-to-noise ratio (SNR) of 30 dB was added to the synthesized data1, and the *SNR* was defined as follows.

$$SNR = 10\log_{10}\frac{E[\mathbf{y}^T\mathbf{y}]}{E[\mathbf{n}^T\mathbf{n}]} \tag{10.15}$$

where $\mathbf{y}$ and $\mathbf{n}$ denote the image pixels and noise, respectively, and $E[\cdot]$ denotes the expectation operation.

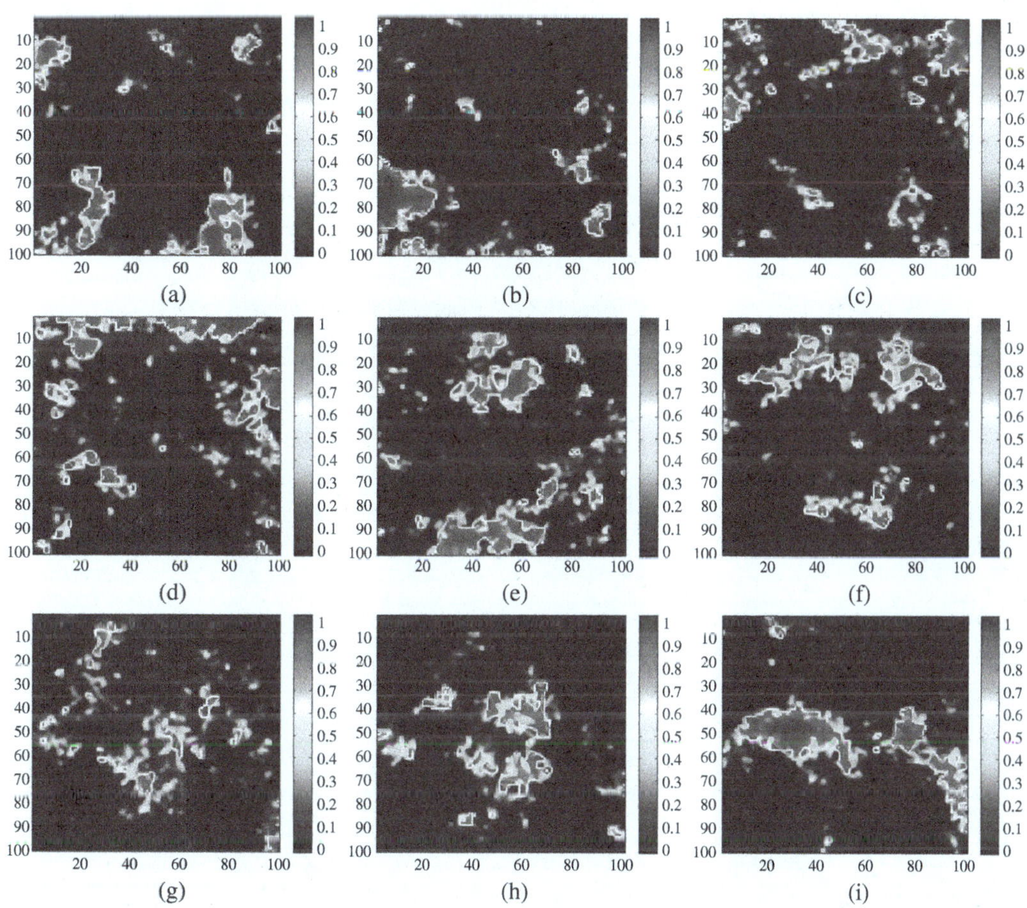

Figure 10.6 True abundance maps corresponding to endmembers in synthetic dataset 1. (a) Endmember 1, (b) endmember 2, (c) endmember 3, (d) endmember 4, (e) endmember 5, (f) endmember 6, (g) endmember 7, (h) endmember 8, and (i) endmember 9.

2) **Synthetic dataset 2:** The dataset is 100×100 pixels in size and contains nine endmembers. According to the calculation in the GBM, the second-order endmembers and second-order abundances are obtained from the endmembers and abundances. Then, according to the GBM using the endmembers and abundances and the second-order endmembers and second-order abundances, the corresponding data are synthesized, i.e., the product of the endmembers and abundances, the product of the second-order endmembers and the second-order abundances, and the two are added together for summation. Finally, 20 dB of noise is added to complete the synthesis of this data.
3) **Cuprite dataset:** This dataset covers the Cuprite mine in Las Vegas, Nevada, United States, and is 250×190 pixels in size, with spatial and spectral resolutions up to 20 m and 10 nm. It contains 224 bands between 400 and 2500 nm, of which bands 1–2, 105–115, 150–170, and 223–224 are excluded due to water vapor and atmospheric contamination, leaving 188 bands. Figure 10.7 illustrates this dataset and its reference map. The dataset contains various mineral species and the true number of endmembers is unknown. Due to the subtle differences between some of the minerals, most studies consider the dataset to have twelve telomorphs, namely alunite, sodium feldspar, aqueous ammonium feldspar, blueschist, kaolinite 1, kaolinite 2, montmorillonite, albite, chlorite, magnesia-aluminum garnet, sphene, and chalcedony.

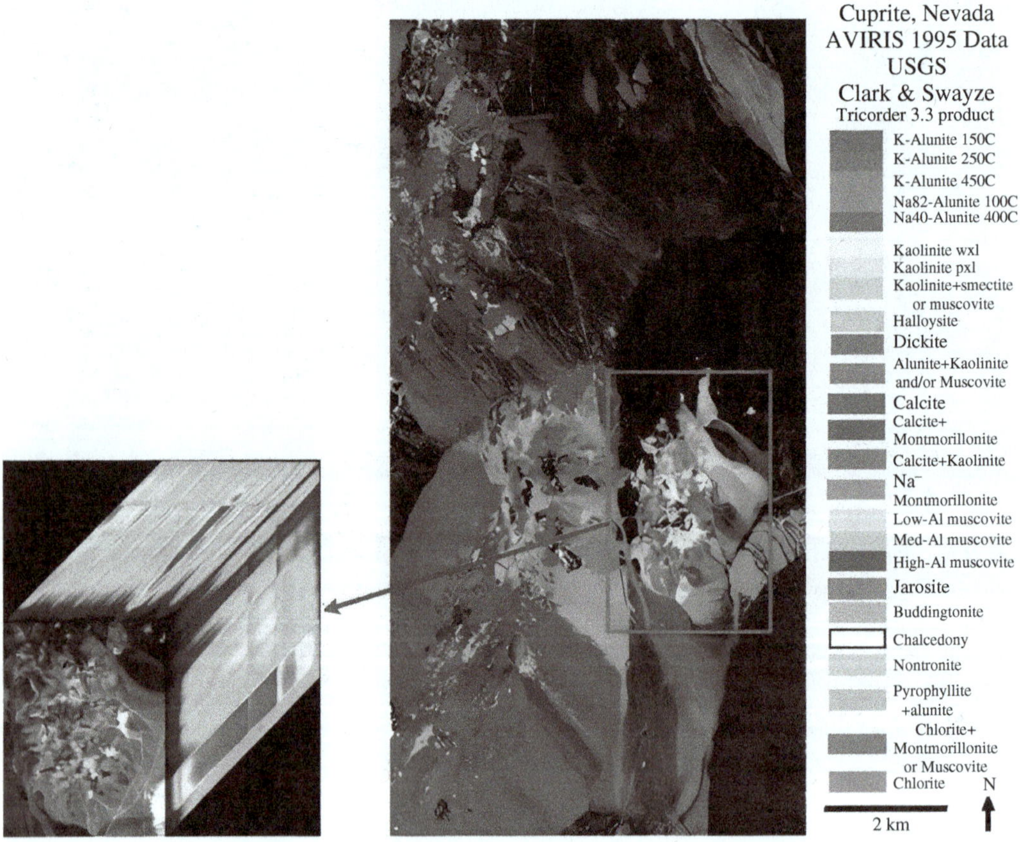

Figure 10.7 Cuprite dataset and its reference map.

10.4.2 Evaluation Metrics

1) **SAD:** Spectral angle distance (SAD) measures the similarity between two spectra by calculating the angle between them, and when two spectra are more similar, their SAD values are smaller. Assuming that the extracted spectrum of an endmember is $\tilde{\mathbf{E}}_q$ and its true spectrum is $\mathbf{E}_q$, the SAD value between the two is calculated as follows:

$$SAD(\mathbf{E}_q, \tilde{\mathbf{E}}_q) = \arccos\left(\frac{\mathbf{E}_q^T \tilde{\mathbf{E}}_q}{\|\mathbf{E}_q\| \|\tilde{\mathbf{E}}_q\|}\right) \tag{10.16}$$

2) **RMSE:** Root mean square error (RMSE) is used to measure the error between the estimated abundance matrix and its true value. The smaller the RMSE value, the smaller the difference between the estimated abundance and the true value, i.e., the better the abundance estimation. The *RMSE* value between the estimated and true values of abundance is calculated as follows:

$$RMSE(\mathbf{A}, \tilde{\mathbf{A}}) = \left(\frac{1}{P}\|\mathbf{A} - \tilde{\mathbf{A}}\|^2\right)^{\frac{1}{2}} \tag{10.17}$$

3) **RE:** *RE* is used to measure the difference between the reconstructed data and the original data. The smaller this error is, the better the reconstruction of the algorithm is. Its calculation formula is as follows:

$$RE = \left(\frac{1}{P}\|\Upsilon - \tilde{\Upsilon}\|^2\right)^{\frac{1}{2}} \tag{10.18}$$

where Υ is the original data and $\tilde{\Upsilon}$ is the reconstructed data.

10.4.3 Comparison Results

The abundance maps of the SLP-SCC-LRR algorithm were compared with those of comparison algorithms, including $L_{1/2}$-NMF [50], GLNM [47], MVCNMF [51], and CoNMF [52]. Figure 10.8 illustrates the abundance maps estimated by the different algorithms, and due to paper constraints, only the abundance maps corresponding to three representative endmembers are placed, i.e., endmembers 2, 6, and 9. Comparison with Figure 10.6 reveals that the abundance maps obtained by SLP-SCC-LRR are smoother than that of $L_{1/2}$-NMF. In addition, GLNMF produces superior results, but it is absent from the spatially detailed parts of the image, such as the texture details in the homogeneous region in Figure 10.8a. Since there is no specific limit on the abundance, the background region of the multiple abundance maps estimated by MVCNMF is more blurred compared to the other methods. Although CoNMF can simultaneously handle the tasks of estimating the number of endmembers, endmember extraction, and abundance estimation in the unmixing task, no specific constraints are performed and the results are not satisfactory. Overall, the endmembers and abundances obtained by SLP-SCC-LRR are closer to the real values, indicating that the algorithm is effective for the unmixing task.

To quantitatively evaluate the algorithm, the average SAD and RMSE values of the unmixing results of SLP-SCC-LRR and the comparison algorithms, as well as the corresponding SAD and RMSE values for the nine endmembers are presented in Table 10.1. It can be seen that the best and second-best experimental results are mostly obtained by the SLP-SCC-LRR algorithm

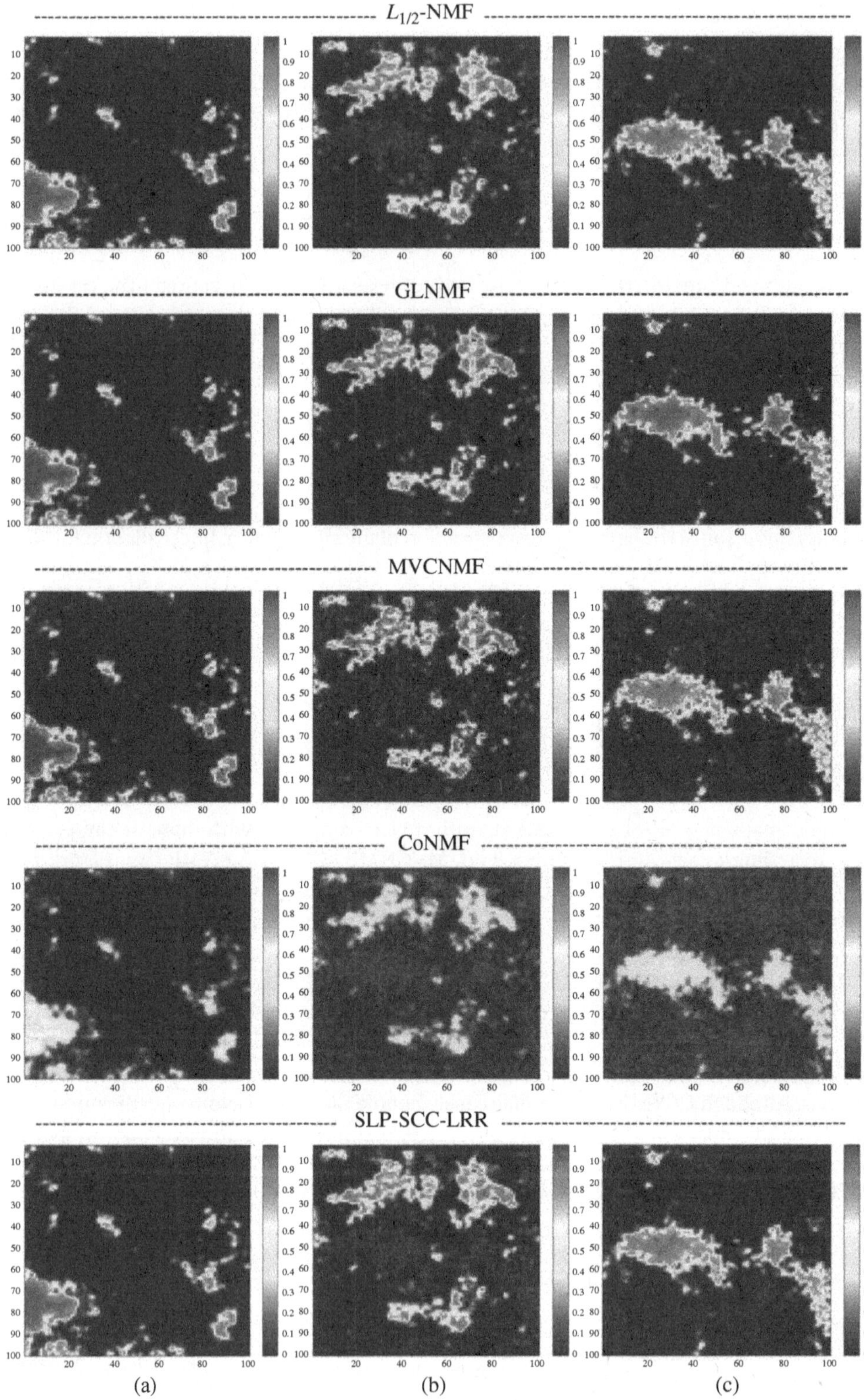

Figure 10.8 Abundance maps of the SLP-SCC-LRR algorithm and the comparison algorithms on synthetic dataset 1. (a) Endmember 2, (b) endmember 6, and (c) endmember 9.

Table 10.1 SAD and RMSE values of SLP-SCC-LRR and the comparison algorithms on synthetic dataset 1.

Method		$L_{1/2}$-NMF	GLNMF	MVCNMF	CoNMF	SLP-SCC-LRR
SAD	Average value	0.0218	0.0318	0.0444	0.2215	**0.0188**
	Endmember 1	0.0141	0.0346	0.0203	0.2233	**0.0138**
	Endmember 2	0.0083	0.0151	0.0200	0.1250	**0.0076**
	Endmember 3	0.0396	**0.0319**	0.0974	0.3549	0.0333
	Endmember 4	0.0060	0.0101	0.0096	0.0821	**0.0054**
	Endmember 5	0.0151	0.0190	0.0192	0.1102	**0.0132**
	Endmember 6	0.0540	0.1077	0.0713	1.4470	**0.0411**
	Endmember 7	0.0099	**0.0074**	0.0240	0.0661	0.0100
	Endmember 8	**0.0075**	0.0153	0.0235	0.0476	**0.0075**
	Endmember 9	0.0415	0.0454	0.1141	0.8180	**0.0378**
RMSE	Average value	0.0257	0.0264	0.0391	0.0973	**0.0252**
	Abundance 1	0.0173	0.0183	0.0273	0.0883	**0.0168**
	Abundance 2	0.0165	0.0174	0.0255	0.0839	**0.0163**
	Abundance 3	**0.0335**	0.0368	0.0527	0.1104	0.0341
	Abundance 4	0.0203	0.0248	0.0299	0.0945	**0.0199**
	Abundance 5	**0.0202**	0.0257	0.0259	0.0934	0.0204
	Abundance 6	0.0382	**0.0357**	0.0598	0.1124	0.0368
	Abundance 7	**0.0129**	0.0191	0.0301	0.0631	0.0137
	Abundance 8	0.0195	0.0210	0.0371	0.0837	**0.0189**
	Abundance 9	0.0527	**0.0385**	0.0638	0.1459	0.0500

The bold values indicate the best performance for the corresponding metric.

compared to the listed comparison algorithms. Due to the consideration of endmember independence and spatial similarity, the SLP-SCC-LRR algorithm outperforms the other unmixing algorithms listed.

The experimental results of the proposed EASNMF algorithm on synthetic dataset 2 are presented in Figure 10.9. The abundance maps corresponding to endmembers 1, 2, and 7 are shown in the figure. To compare the unmixing results with the comparison algorithms, including $L_{1/2}$-semi-NMF [22], Gr-semi-NMF [45], and LR-semi-NMF, the abundance maps estimated by the different algorithms are also shown in Figure 10.9. $L_{1/2}$-semi-NMF processes the abundance map by introducing sparse constraints, which suppresses the noise to a certain extent. Gr-semi-NMF enhances the capture of the local structure of the data by streaming constraints, so that the abundance map retains the details while suppressing the background noise to a certain extent. However, there are still some irregular noises in the background part of their abundance maps. LR-semi-NMF only considers the low-rank property of the image and acquires abundance maps with more noises in the background. Through the comparative analysis, it can be found that EASNMF obtains a cleaner background of the abundance maps due to the LRR of the model and the self-representation manifold canonical while retaining some detailed information. Furthermore, our algorithm's

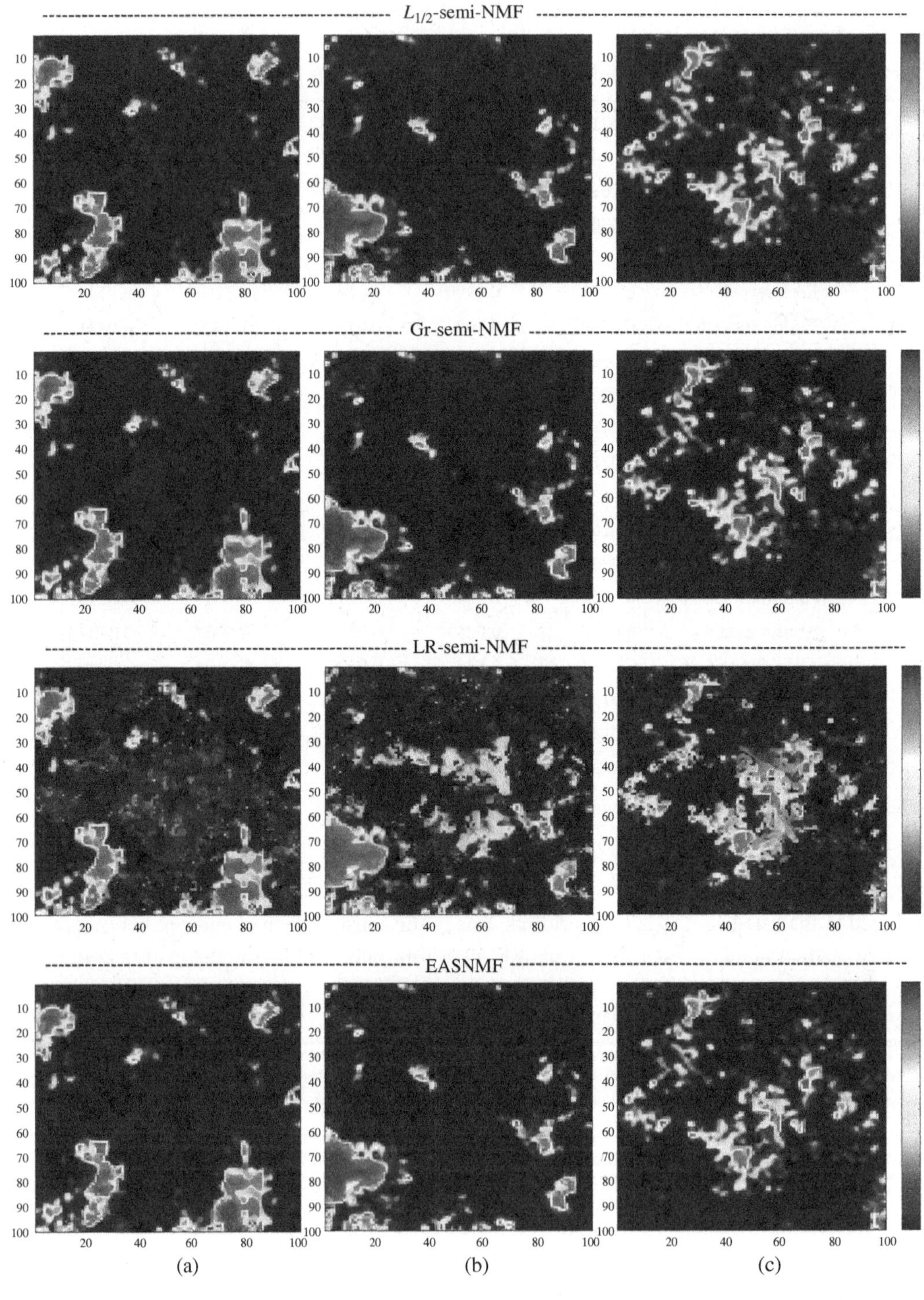

Figure 10.9 Abundance maps of EASNMF and the comparison algorithms on synthetic dataset 2. (a) Endmember 1, (b) endmember 2, and (c) endmember 7.

Table 10.2 RE and RMSE values of EASNMF and the comparison algorithms on synthetic dataset 2.

	$L_{1/2}$-semi-NMF	Gr-semi-NMF	LR-semi-NMF	EASNMF
RE ($\times 10^{-4}$)	317	315	469	**315**
RMSE ($\times 10^{-4}$)	284	283	1417	**279**

estimated abundance is closer to the real abundance, which indicates that it has a better unmixing performance.

In addition, in order to analyze the experimental results of different algorithms more comprehensively, the RE and RMSE values corresponding to the experimental results of EASNMF and the comparison algorithms are listed in Table 10.2. It can be seen that EASNMF has a smaller error compared to the comparison algorithm. In summary, EASNMF outperforms the comparison algorithms in terms of unmixing results.

The unmixing results were obtained after experiments on the Cuprite dataset using the RASU algorithm as well as the comparison algorithms, including VCA-FCLS [59], $L_{1/2}$-NMF, and Gr-semi-NMF. The abundance maps of this algorithm against other comparison algorithms are presented in Figure 10.10. In addition, Table 10.3 lists the SAD values of the endmembers extracted by the proposed and compared algorithms. As can be seen from the figure, the abundance maps obtained by using only the VCA-FCLS algorithm have rougher boundaries and the detailed parts are not clear enough. Since the VCA-FCLS algorithm relies on the assumption of linearity, its adaptability to nonlinear data is poor, resulting in difficulty in accurately distinguishing the abundance of different minerals. In contrast, the abundance map obtained by the $L_{1/2}$-NMF algorithm has a cleaner background, but its SAD value is higher in the unmixing results of multiple end-elements, which indicates that there is a deficiency in the end-element extraction ability. The Gr-semi-NMF algorithm exhibits a lower SAD value on most of the end-elements, which shows a higher unmixing accuracy; however, there are still some noise interferences in its abundance maps. It can be seen that the endmembers extracted by RASU are closer to their real spectral curves, and its endmember extraction results are better than the other algorithms. The experimental results show that the RASU algorithm is effective for the task of unmixing hyperspectral images.

The abundance maps obtained by SRASU are presented in Figure 10.11 and the SAD values corresponding to the unmixing results of SRASU and the comparison algorithms are presented in Table 10.4, including the mean values and the values of each endmember. Since the Cuprite dataset is real data, it lacks real endmembers and abundances. Therefore, to calculate the SAD values of the extracted endmembers, the spectra corresponding to 12 endmembers were selected from the spectral library in the experiment as the endmember reference values of this dataset. Through analysis and comparison, it can be found that the extracted endmembers of SRASU are closer to the reference values than other existing algorithms. In conclusion, the SRASU algorithm has a better unmixing effect.

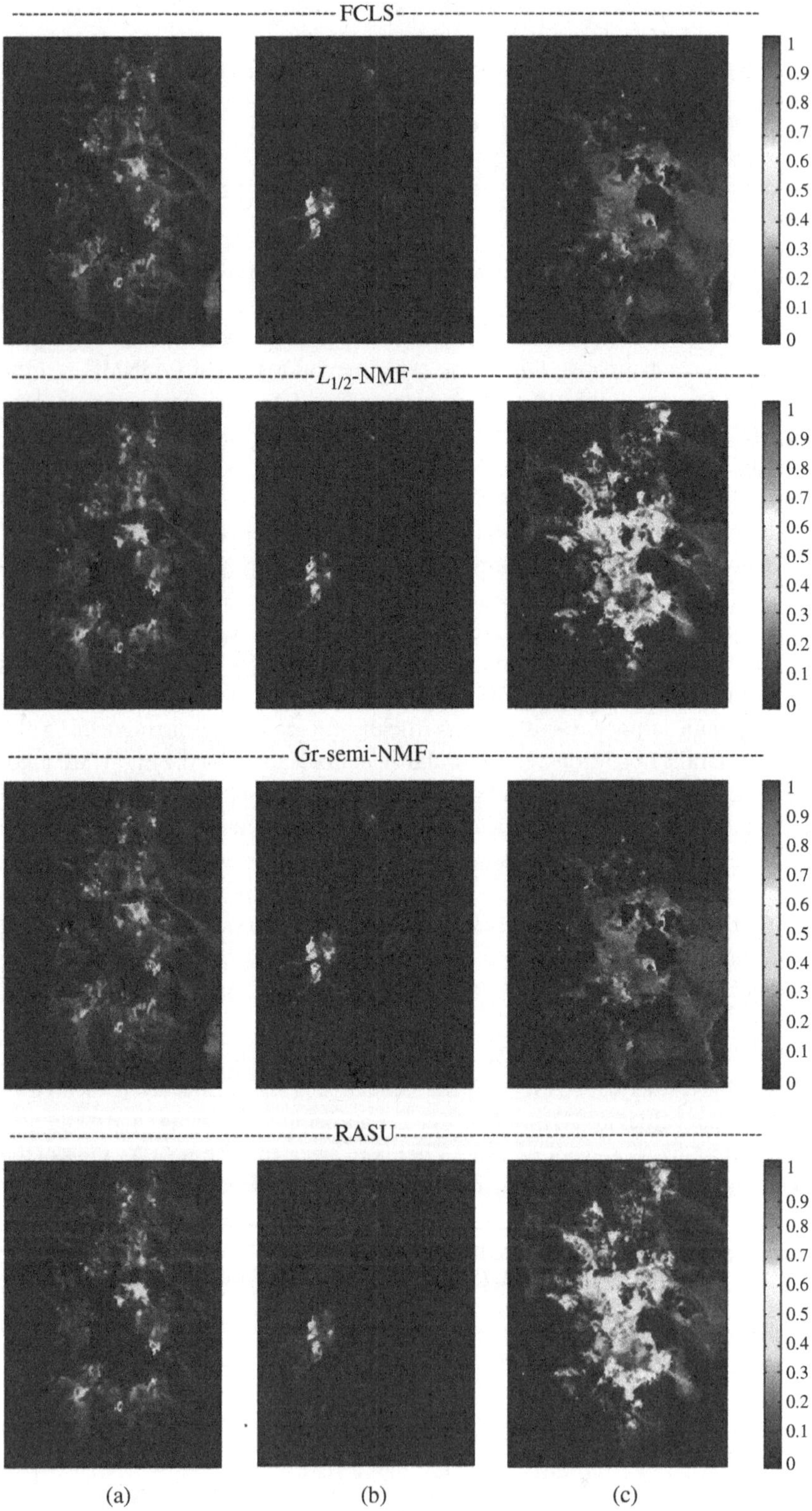

Figure 10.10 Abundance maps obtained by different algorithms on Cuprite dataset. (a) Alunite, (b) aqueous ammonium feldspar, and (c) chalcedony.

Table 10.3 SAD values of RASU and the comparison algorithms on Cuprite dataset.

Method		$L_{1/2}$-NMF	Gr-semi-NMF (VCA)	RASU
SAD	Average value	0.0784	0.0825	**0.0773**
	Alunite	0.1033	**0.0952**	0.1033
	Sodium feldspar	**0.0592**	0.0685	0.0599
	Aqueous ammonium feldspar	**0.0676**	0.1215	0.0697
	Bluestone	0.1120	**0.0736**	0.1106
	Kaolinite 1	0.0808	0.0881	**0.0758**
	Kaolinite 2	0.0926	**0.0732**	0.0900
	Montmorillonite	0.0928	0.0942	**0.0895**
	Muscovite	0.0636	0.0636	**0.0629**
	Chlorodacrylonitrile	0.0969	**0.0884**	0.0951
	Magnesium-aluminum garnet	0.0877	**0.0823**	0.0856
	Titanite	0.0622	0.0629	**0.0608**
	Chalcedony	0.1583	**0.1301**	0.1595

The bold values indicate the best performance for the corresponding metric.

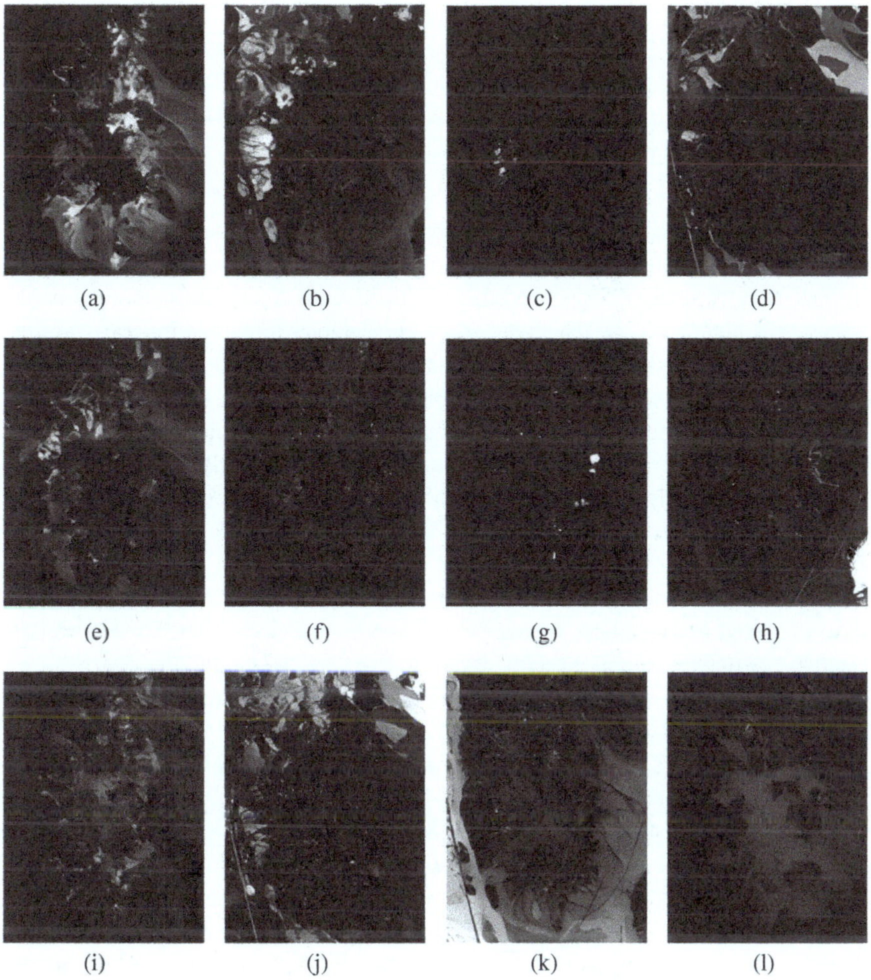

Figure 10.11 Abundance maps estimated by the SRASU algorithm on Cuprite dataset. (a) Alunite, (b) sodium feldspar, (c) aqueous ammonium feldspar, (d) blueschist, (e) kaolinite 1, (f) kaolinite 2, (g) montmorillonite, (h) leucomalachite, (i) chrysocolla, (j) magnesium-aluminum garnet, (k) titanite, and (l) chalcedony.

Table 10.4 SAD values of SRASU algorithm and comparison algorithm on Cuprite dataset.

Method		SUnSAL	$L_{1/2}$-NMF	GLNMF	MVCNMF	SRASU
SAD	Average value	0.0833	0.0808	0.0804	0.0838	**0.0799**
	Alunite	**0.0971**	0.1045	0.1087	0.1052	0.1191
	Sodium feldspar	0.1701	0.1718	0.1634	0.1738	**0.1433**
	Aqueous ammonium Feldspar	0.1215	0.1128	**0.1117**	0.1229	0.1138
	Bluestone	0.2030	0.2005	0.1984	0.2031	**0.1891**
	Kaolinite 1	0.0896	0.0852	0.0842	0.0864	**0.0787**
	Kaolinite 2	**0.0914**	0.1073	0.1160	0.1076	0.1511
	Montmorillonite	0.0942	0.0862	**0.0847**	0.0952	0.0850
	Muscovite	0.0625	0.0632	0.0630	0.0651	**0.0616**
	Chlorodacrylonitrile	**0.1052**	0.1101	0.1103	0.1124	0.1204
	Magnesium-aluminum garnet	0.1207	0.0835	0.0719	0.0903	**0.0719**
	Titanite	0.1758	0.1740	0.1725	0.1737	**0.1687**
	Chalcedony	**0.1789**	0.1799	0.1839	0.1831	0.1953

The bold values indicate the best performance for the corresponding metric.

10.5 Conclusions

In this chapter, we mainly introduce some algorithms based on LRR and sparse constraints. To improve the accuracy of spectral unmixing, the LRR algorithm based on the space consistency constraint and spectral dictionary pruning is proposed. Compared with the existing sparsity-based unmixing algorithms, this algorithm, which takes space consistency into account, can capture the global structure. Moreover, the algorithm contains dictionary pruning steps, which can identify a subset of the spectral library. The size of the subset, which contains the true endmembers in the spectral library, is much smaller than the original one. Thus, this strategy can not only mitigate the aforementioned effect but also improve the accuracy of unmixing significantly.

In addition, a sparse NMF algorithm based on endmember independence and spatially weighted abundance for HU is presented. This method not only considers the characteristics of endmembers and their abundances at the same time but also makes full use of the spatial–spectral information in the image. First, the endmember independence constraint is added to the NMF model based on the assumption that the extracted endmembers should be independent of each other. Then, a weight matrix is constructed by the neighborhood pixel for abundance to make it smooth. Besides, inspired by the manifold learning, the connection weight between two pixels by the correlation coefficient is constructed to further explore the structure of HSI data.

Then, due to the complexity of the actual surface features, HSIs not only contain the linear spectral mixtures, but also the nonlinear spectral mixture. However, most of the unmixing methods for hyperspectral images only consider the existence of an LMM or a non-LMM. Considering the coexistence of the linear spectral mixture model and the nonlinear spectral mixture model, a hyperspectral image unmixing method based on adaptive region segmentation has been introduced.

Finally, inspired by the sparsity difference in spatial of HSIs, a novel method called SRASU applied to HSI has been proposed. The assumption of this study is that most pixels in the image are mixed, and the pixels in detail regions are more likely to be heavily mixed with more endmembers participating than in homogeneous regions. Therefore, the sparsity degrees of the abundances for these two regions are obviously different, and the sparsity degree of abundance in homogeneous regions is relatively high.

In the future, considering different interpretation tasks requires different unmixing degrees, future research will focus on jointly optimizing the HSI unmixing with downstream tasks, further improving hyperspectral interpretation performance.

References

1 Brown, A. (2006). Spectral curve fitting for automatic hyperspectral data analysis. *IEEE Trans. Geosci. Remote Sens.* 44 (6): 1601–1608.

2 Li, S., Lu, T., Fang, L. et al. (2016). Probabilistic fusion of pixel-level and superpixel-level hyperspectral image classification. *IEEE Trans. Geosci. Remote Sens.* 54 (12): 7416–7430.

3 Jia, X., Kuo, B., and Crawford, M. (2013). Feature mining for hyperspectral image classification. *Proc. IEEE* 101 (3): 676–697.

4 Zhang, X., Song, Q., Liu, R. et al. (2014). Modified co-training with spectral and spatial views for semisupervised hyperspectral image classification. *IEEE J. Sel. Top. Appl. Earth Obs. Remote Sens.* 7 (6): 2044–2055.

5 Plaza, A., Du, Q., Bioucas-Dias, J. et al. (2011). Foreword to the special issue on spectral unmixing of remotely sensed data. *IEEE T. Geosci. Remote Sens.* 49: 4104–4111.

6 Bioucas-Dias, J., Plaza, A., Dobigeon, N. et al. (2012). Hyperspectral unmixing overview: geometrical, statistical, and sparse regression-based approaches. *IEEE J. Sel. Top. Appl. Earth Obs. Remote Sens.* 5 (2): 354–379.

7 Keshava, N. (2003). A survey of spectral unmixing algorithms. *Lincoln Lab. J.* 14 (1): 55–78.

8 Keshava, N. and Mustard, J. (2002). Spectral unmixing. *IEEE Signal Process. Mag.* 19 (1): 44–57.

9 Dobigeon, N., Tourneret, J., Richard, C. et al. (2014). Nonlinear unmixing of hyperspectral images: models and algorithms. *IEEE Signal Process. Mag.* 31 (1): 82–94.

10 Adams, J., Smith, M., and Johnson, P. (1986). Spectral mixture modeling: a new analysis of rock and soil types at the Viking Lander 1 site. *J. Geophys. Res. Solid Earth* 91 (B8): 8098–8112.

11 Settle, J. and Drake, N. (1993). Linear mixing and the estimation of ground cover proportions. *Int. J. Remote Sens.* 14 (6): 1159–1177.

12 Petrou, M. and Foschi, P. (1999). Confidence in linear spectral unmixing of single pixels. *IEEE Trans. Geosci. Remote Sens.* 37 (1): 624–626.

13 Settle, J. (2006). On the effect of variable endmember spectra in the linear mixture model. *IEEE Trans. Geosci. Remote Sens.* 44 (2): 389–396.

14 Li, J., Agathos, A., Zaharie, D. et al. (2015). Minimum volume simplex analysis: a fast algorithm for linear hyperspectral unmixing. *IEEE Trans. Geosci. Remote Sens.* 53 (9): 5067–5082.

15 Plaza, A., Martinez, P., Perez, R. et al. (2004). A quantitative and comparative analysis of endmember extraction algorithms from hyperspectral data. *IEEE Trans. Geosci. Remote Sens.* 42 (3): 650–663.

16 Du, Q., Raksuntorn, N., Younan, N. et al. (2008). End-member extraction for hyperspectral image analysis. *Appl. Opt.* 47 (28): 77–84.

17 Heinz, D. and Chang, C.-I. (2001). Fully constrained least squares linear spectral mixture analysis method for material quantification in hyperspectral imagery. *IEEE Trans. Geosci. Remote Sens.* 39 (3): 529–545.

18 Brown, A., Hook, S., Baldridge, A. et al. (2010). Hydrothermal formation of clay-carbonate alteration assemblages in the Nili Fossae region of Mars. *Earth Planet. Sci. Lett.* 297 (1–2): 174–182.

19 Brown, A., Sutter, B., and Dunagan, S. (2008). The MARTE VNIR imaging spectrometer experiment: design and analysis. *Astrobiology* 8 (5): 1001–1011.

20 Halimi, A., Altmann, Y., Dobigeon, N. et al. (2011). Unmixing hyperspectral images using the generalized bilinear model. *2011 IEEE International Geoscience and Remote Sensing Symposium*, 1886–1889, Vancouver, BC, Canada (24–29 July 2011). IEEE.

21 Yokoya, N., Chanussot, J., and Iwasaki, A. (2014). Nonlinear unmixing of hyperspectral data using semi-nonnegative matrix factorization. *IEEE Trans. Geosci. Remote Sens.* 52 (2): 1430–1437.

22 Zhang, X., Cheng, C., An, J. et al. (2015). Sparsity-constrained generalized bilinear model for hyperspectral unmixing. *2015 IEEE International Geoscience and Remote Sensing Symposium (IGARSS)*, 5055–5058, Milan, Italy (26–31 July 2015). IEEE.

23 Gao, L., Wang, Z., Zhuang, L. et al. (2022). Using low-rank representation of abundance maps and nonnegative tensor factorization for hyperspectral nonlinear unmixing. *IEEE Trans. Geosci. Remote Sens.* 60: 1–17.

24 Shi, Z., Shi, T., Zhou, M. et al. (2018). Collaborative sparse hyperspectral unmixing using l_0 norm. *IEEE Trans. Geosci. Remote Sens.* 56 (9): 5495–5508.

25 Huang, J., Huang, T., Deng, L. et al. (2019). Joint-sparse-blocks and low-rank representation for hyperspectral unmixing. *IEEE Trans. Geosci. Remote Sens.* 57 (4): 2419–2438.

26 Zhang, X., Yuan, Y., and Li, X. (2022). Reweighted low-rank and joint-sparse unmixing with library pruning. *IEEE Trans. Geosci. Remote Sens.* 60: 1–16.

27 Chen, T., Liu, Y., Zhang, Y. et al. (2022). Superpixel-based collaborative and low-rank regularization for sparse hyperspectral unmixing. *IEEE Trans. Geosci. Remote Sens.* 60: 1–16.

28 Zhang, S., Li, J., Li, H. et al. (2018). Spectral–spatial weighted sparse regression for hyperspectral image unmixing. *IEEE Trans. Geosci. Remote Sens.* 56 (6): 3265–3276.

29 Sun, L., Wu, F., Zhan, T. et al. (2020). Weighted nonlocal low-rank tensor decomposition method for sparse unmixing of hyperspectral images. *IEEE J. Sel. Top. Appl. Earth Obs. Remote Sens.* 13: 1174–1188.

30 Dong, L. and Yuan, Y. (2021). Sparse constrained low tensor rank representation framework for hyperspectral unmixing. *Remote Sens.* 13 (8): 1473.

31 Wu, L., Huang, J., and Guo, M. (2023). Multidimensional low-rank representation for sparse hyperspectral unmixing. *IEEE Geosci. Remote Sens. Lett.* 20: 1–5.

32 Ren, L., Hong, D., Gao, L. et al. (2023). Hyperspectral sparse unmixing via nonconvex shrinkage penalties. *IEEE Trans. Geosci. Remote Sens.* 61: 1–15.

33 Zhang, X., Li, C., Zhang, J. et al. (2018). Hyperspectral unmixing via low-rank representation with space consistency constraint and spectral library pruning. *Remote Sens.* 10 (2): 1–21.

34 Zhang, J., Zhang, X., Tang, X. et al. (2020). Sketch-based region adaptive sparse unmixing applied to hyperspectral image. *IEEE Trans. Geosci. Remote Sens.* 58 (12): 8840–8856.

35 Ertürk, A., Iordache, M., and Plaza, A. (2016). Sparse unmixing-based change detection for multitemporal hyperspectral images. *IEEE J. Sel. Top. Appl. Earth Obs. Remote Sens.* 9 (2): 708–719.

36 Erturk, A., Iordache, M., and Plaza, A. (2017). Sparse unmixing with dictionary pruning for hyperspectral change detection. *IEEE J. Sel. Top. Appl. Earth Obs. Remote Sens.* 10 (1): 321–330.

37 Rogge, D., Rivard, B., and Zhang, J. (2007). Integration of spatial-spectral information for the improved extraction of endmembers. *Remote Sens. Environ.* 110: 287–303.

38 Lin, Z., Chen, M., and Ma, Y. (2013). The augmented lagrange multiplier method for exact recovery of corrupted low-rank matrices. *J. Struct. Biol.* 181 (2): 116–127.

39 Fazel, M. 2002. Matrix rank minimization with applications. Ph.D. Thesis. Department of Electrical Engineering, Stanford University, Stanford.

40 Lee, D. and Seung, H. (2000). Algorithms for non-negative matrix factorization. *Proceedings of the 14th Annual Neural Information Processing Systems Conference, (NIPS)*, Denver, CO, Nov 27 – Dec 2, 2000, 535–541.

41 He, W., Zhang, H., and Zhang, L. (2017). Total variation regularized reweighted sparse nonnegative matrix factorization for hyperspectral unmixing. *IEEE Trans. Geosci. Remote Sens.* 55 (7): 3909–3921.

42 Xu, Z., Zhang, H., Wang, Y. et al. (2010). $L_{1/2}$ regularization. *Sci. China Inf. Sci.* 53 (6): 1159–1169.

43 Lu, X., Wu, H., Yuan, Y. et al. (2013). Manifold regularized sparse NMF for hyperspectral unmixing. *IEEE Trans. Geosci. Remote Sens.* 51 (5): 2815–2826.

44 Chen, X. and Vierling, L. (2006). Spectral mixture analyses of hyperspectral data acquired using a tethered balloon. *Remote Sens. Environ.* 103 (3): 338–350.

45 Martin, G. and Plaza, A. (2011). Region-based spatial preprocessing for endmember extraction and spectral unmixing. *IEEE Geosci. Remote Sens. Lett.* 8 (4): 745–749.

46 Zhao, C., Zhao, G., and Jia, X. (2017). Hyperspectral image unmixing based on fast kernel archetypal analysis. *IEEE J. Sel. Top. Appl. Earth Obs. Remote Sens.* 10 (1): 331–346.

47 Marr, D. and Ullman, S. (2010). *Vision: A Computational Investigation into the Human Representation and Processing of Visual Information*. Cambridge, MA: MIT Press.

48 Guo, C., Zhu, S., and Wu, Y. (2007). Primal sketch: integrating structure and texture. *Comput. Vis. Image Underst.* 106 (1): 5–19.

49 Bioucas, J. and Figueiredo, M. (2010). Alternating direction algorithms for constrained sparse regression: application to hyperspectral unmixing. *2nd Workshop on Hyperspectral Image and Signal Processing: Evolution in Remote Sensing*, 1–4, Reykjavik, Iceland (14–16 June 2010). IEEE.

50 Qian, Y., Jia, S., Zhou, J. et al. (2011). Hyperspectral unmixing via $L_{1/2}$ sparsity-constrained nonnegative matrix factorization. *IEEE Trans. Geosci. Remote Sens.* 49 (11): 4282–4297.

51 Li, J., Bioucas-Dias, J., Plaza, A. et al. (2016). Robust collaborative nonnegative matrix factorization for hyperspectral unmixing. *IEEE Trans. Geosci. Remote Sens.* 54 (10): 6076–6090.

52 Chen, C. (2015). *Hyperspectral Unmixing Based on Generalized Bilinear Model*. Shaanxi: Xidian University.

11

Endmember Purification and Geographical Knowledge Graph-guided Endmember Selection

Wenfei Luo and Rui Wu

School of Geographical Science, South China Normal University, Guangzhou, China

11.1 Introduction

Spectral unmixing is a useful tool for exploring hyperspectral remote-sensing image. Indeed, it is a fundamental technique that provides valuable low-rank and sub-pixel information for hyperspectral image compression, restoration, target detection, classification, recognition, and so on. And it also has a wide range of potential applications in many fields. Endmember plays an important role in spectral unmixing. Therefore, this chapter presents two stories about endmembers, namely endmember recovery and endmember selection. Endmember recovery aims to restore the endmember's pure signatures from an image consisting of mixed pixels. These recovered endmembers are essential for improving unmixing performance. And most importantly, they have much clearer features, making them easier to identify. This will be helpful for material identification. Once we have representative endmembers, we need to identify which ones are contained in a given pixel. This process is referred to as *endmember selection*.

The technique related to endmember recovery can be traced back to [1, 2] in 1993. It was regarded as a problem of blind source separation (BSS) [3]. For the past two decades, non-negative matrix factorization (NMF) has been the most widely used method for this problem. Unfortunately, it has not received universal attention in many application areas. Indeed, most research focuses on the use of abundances and ignores the valuable information provided by endmembers. As we mentioned above, these recovered endmembers have clearer features without the interference of mixed pixels, noise, and artifacts. So, they can improve our ability to recognize what's in the area. Another problem is that whether we can believe these endmembers. In fact, it is difficult to satisfy the assumption of sufficiently scattered condition [4] in a natural scene, as the information on some endmembers may be limited. Under this circumstance, it is impossible to accurately recover all endmembers using the NMF model, even for those endmembers that have rich information. However, can we still recover some endmembers of interest (EOIs)? For this purpose, we proposed an affine simplicial cone (ASC) model [5]. This model uses a subset of pixels to recover EOI rather than an entire image. And we also presented a method for recovering a single endmember based on the ASC model. To differentiate, we refer to this method as *endmember purification* (EP).

As a supplement to our previous work, we will present further discussions of EP in this chapter. Firstly, we will discuss the performance improvement in the view of robust learning. The goal is to

Machine-Learning-Based Hyperspectral Image Processing, First Edition. Edited by Bing Zhang.

select the best subset that satisfies the sufficiently sparse condition and to remove the interferences. We will present a low boundary of the fraction of good pixels remaining. The second consideration is the framework of the EP algorithm. Since the parameters are divided into three groups, block coordinate descent (BCD) is naturally the most appropriate method to solve the problem. It has been used for the affine NMF problem [6] which is a problem with three sets of parameters. However, in our experience, this method is not satisfactory. Therefore, this chapter will present a better framework to solve the NMF problem with three sets of parameters. The code for this work can be available from the website (https://github.com/spdelphi/Endmember-Purification).

Endmember selection is a model selection problem. It can be initially pursued by a technique of multiple endmember spectral mixture analysis (MESMA) in 1998 [7]. However, the number of endmembers would be enormous. It caused the computational complexity of MESMA to increase exponentially. In this situation, sparseness constraints was first introduced into the NMF model [8]. In 2011, sparse unmixing with L1 norm was proposed [9, 10] and became the most popular endmember selection method. However, the resulting abundance values may not be reliable, as many combinations of abundance values can reconstruct the pixel well in the presence of noise [11]. Introducing additional prior knowledge could help alleviate this dilemma. For example, a house is rarely built on a steep slope. So, we tend to avoid selecting the building (house) endmember in this area. In this chapter, we will create a geographical knowledge graph (Geo-KG) to aid in endmember selection. For additional information on this method, the reader may also refer to our recent work [12].

11.2 Endmember Purification

11.2.1 Problem of Endmember Purification

Let's briefly review the traditional linear mixing model (LMM) in the following

$$\mathbf{y}[n] = \sum_{i=0}^{d} a_i[n]\mathbf{e}_i + \mathbf{x}[n], \tag{11.1}$$

where $\mathbf{y}[n]$ is the n-th pixel of the image, $\mathbf{e}_i$ is the i-th endmember in a scene, $a_i[n]$ is the corresponding abundance of the n-th pixel in terms of $\mathbf{e}_i$, and $\mathbf{x}[n]$ is the noise. For brevity, we omit the index n when necessary. Furthermore, the abundances should satisfy the following physical constraints

$$\sum_{i=0}^{d} a_i = 1, \quad a_i \geq 0 \tag{11.2}$$

Therefore, the unmixing problem based on LMM can be written by

$$\begin{aligned} &\min_{\mathbf{M},\mathbf{A}} \|\mathbf{Y} - \mathbf{E}\mathbf{A}\|_F^2 \\ &\text{s.t.} \mathbf{A} \geq 0, 1_{1\times(m+1)}\mathbf{A} = 1_{1\times N}, \end{aligned} \tag{11.3}$$

where $\mathbf{E} = [\mathbf{e}_0, \ldots, \mathbf{e}_m] \in \mathbb{R}^{L\times(m+1)}$, $\mathbf{A} = [\mathbf{a}[1], \ldots, \mathbf{a}[N]] \in \mathbb{R}^{(m+1)\times N}$, and $\mathbf{a}[\cdot]$ is a column vector of abundances for the pixel.

According to Eq. (11.1), the LMM can be rewritten as

$$\text{y} = \text{e0} + \text{a1}(\text{e1} - \text{e0}) + \text{a2}(\text{e2} - \text{e0}) + \ldots + \text{ad}(\text{ed} - \text{e0}) + \text{x} \tag{11.4}$$

By defining scaling factors $\omega_i > 0$, $i = 1,..., m$, replacing $\omega_i(\mathbf{e}_i - \mathbf{e}_0)$ by $\mathbf{r}_i$, and releasing "sum to one" constraint, we have

$$y = e0 + b1r1 + b2r2 + ... + bdrd + x \tag{11.5}$$

This model is called ASC. Although the ASC model derives from LMM, it has several advantages which LMM cannot provide. The number of faces of ASC is nearly a half of LMM such that the ASC model needs less geometrical information than LMM. Consequently, the ASC model can capture locally geometrical structure of data. This capability is very important since most scenes of remote-sensing image are complex such that it is very hard to find a general and accurate model to theoretically describe the whole scene. Benefitting from ASC, we can still recover many endmembers based on the locally geometrical structure of image.

Without loss of generality, suppose that $\mathbf{e}_0$ is the endmember expected to recover, the EP problem can be interpreted to find an $ASC\{\mathbf{e}_0,\mathbf{R}\}$ such that

$$\min_{\mathbf{e}_0 \in \mathbb{R}^L, \mathbf{R} \in \mathbb{R}^{L \times m}, \mathbf{B} \geq 0} \left\| \mathbf{Y} - \mathbf{e}_0 \mathbf{1}^{1 \times N} - \mathbf{RB} \right\|_F^2, \tag{11.6}$$

where $\mathbf{Y}$ represents an image, $\mathbf{R} = [\mathbf{r}_1, \mathbf{r}_2, ..., \mathbf{r}_m]$ is the matrix of rays, and $\mathbf{B}$ is a matrix in which the element $b_{i,j}$ is the corresponding scaling coefficient of the i-th ray for the j-th pixel.

11.2.2 Endmember Purification and Robust Learning

Denote the feasible space of Eq. (11.3) by

$$F_{LMM} = \left\{ \mathbf{E} \middle| \arg\min_{\mathbf{E}} \|\mathbf{Y} - \mathbf{EA}\|_F^2, \mathbf{E} = [\mathbf{e}_0, ..., \mathbf{e}_m] \in \mathbb{R}^{L \times (m+1)} \right\}. \tag{11.7}$$

We omit the coefficient $\mathbf{A}$ because we can always find the best estimate under a given $\mathbf{E}$. The residual is denoted by

$$\mathbf{X} = \mathbf{Y} - \mathbf{EA}. \tag{11.8}$$

Thus, the objective function can be replaced by

$$\|\mathbf{X}\|_F^2 = [vec(\mathbf{X})]^T vec(\mathbf{X}) = \sum_{n=1}^{N} (\mathbf{x}[n])^T \mathbf{x}[n]. \tag{11.9}$$

Proposition 1: Let $\mathbf{E}^*$ and $\mathbf{A}^*$ be ground truth. If the estimate $\hat{\mathbf{E}} \in F_{LMM}$ and $\mu(\hat{\mathbf{X}}) = \mu(\mathbf{X}^*)$, then

$$\mu(\mathbf{X}^*) = \mathbf{0}_{L \times 1}, \tag{11.10}$$

where $\mathbf{X}^* = \mathbf{Y} - \mathbf{E}^*\mathbf{A}^*$, $\hat{\mathbf{X}}$ is the corresponding estimate given by $\hat{\mathbf{E}}$, and $\mu(\cdot)$ is the mean of columns of a matrix. Otherwise, we can find another better solution $\mathbf{X}'$ such that $\|\mathbf{X}'\|_F^2 < \|\hat{\mathbf{X}}\|_F^2$.

Proof: Obviously, Eq. (11.9) is the energy of residual and

$$\|\mathbf{X}\|_F^2 = \left(\sigma^2(\mathbf{X}) + \mu(\mathbf{X})^T \mu(\mathbf{X})\right) N, \tag{11.11}$$

where $\sigma^2(\cdot)$ is the variance of columns of a matrix.

If $\mu(\mathbf{X}^*) \neq \mathbf{0}_{L \times 1}$, we can easily find another solution

$$\mathbf{X}' = \hat{\mathbf{X}} - \mu(\mathbf{X}^*) \mathbf{1}_{1 \times N} \tag{11.12}$$

such that

$$\|\mathbf{X}'\|_F^2 = N\sigma^2(\mathbf{X}') = N\sigma^2(\hat{\mathbf{X}}). \tag{11.13}$$

Thus, $\|\mathbf{X}'\|_F^2 < \|\hat{\mathbf{X}}\|_F^2$. Meanwhile,

$$\mathbf{X}' = \hat{\mathbf{X}} - \mu(\mathbf{X}^*)\mathbf{1}_{1\times N} = \mathbf{Y} - \hat{\mathbf{E}}\hat{\mathbf{A}} - \mu(\mathbf{X}^*)\mathbf{1}_{1\times N} \tag{11.14}$$

$$= \mathbf{Y} - \left(\hat{\mathbf{E}} + \mu(\mathbf{X}^*)\mathbf{1}_{1\times(m+1)}\right)\hat{\mathbf{A}}, \tag{11.15}$$

since the sum-to-one constraint in Eq. (11.3) holds, namely $\mathbf{1}_{1\times(m+1)}\hat{\mathbf{A}} = \mathbf{1}_{1\times N}$. We can see that $\mathbf{E}' = \left(\hat{\mathbf{E}} + \mu(\mathbf{X}^*)\mathbf{1}_{L\times(m+1)}\right)$ is a better solution which contradicts Eq. (11.7).

It should be noted that Eq. (11.10) is merely a sufficient but not necessary condition of $\hat{\mathbf{M}} \in F_{LMM}$. However, the contrapositive proposition provides us a useful tool to identify the feasible solution. That is $\mu(\hat{\mathbf{X}}) = \mu(\mathbf{X}^*) \neq \mathbf{0}_{L\times 1}$ implying $\hat{\mathbf{E}} \notin F_{LMM}$. This helps us introduce the information theory of robust learning into our analysis. Before our discussion, we briefly review some important definitions and their propositions. The readers can be referred to the dissertation [13] for more details.

Definition 1
A set of points $\{\mathbf{x}_i\}_{i\in S}$ lying in $\mathbb{R}^L$ is (σ,ε)-resilient in a norm $\|\cdot\|$ if, for all subsets $T \subseteq S$ of size at least $(1-\epsilon)|S|$,

$$\left\|\frac{1}{|T|}\sum_{i\in T}(\mathbf{x}_i - \mu(\mathbf{X}_S))\right\| \le \sigma, \tag{11.16}$$

where $\mathbf{X}_s$ is a matrix whose columns are the points belonging to S. A key fact is that even in high dimensions, distributions can be resilient with a parameter σ that does not grow with the dimension. For example, the isotropic Gaussian distribution $(\boldsymbol{\mu},\mathbf{I})$ is $\left(O\left(\varepsilon\sqrt{\log(2/\varepsilon)}\right),\varepsilon\right)$-resilient in ℓ_2-norm.

By resilience, we can separate a set of pixels S into two groups, i.e., a set of good pixels S_g and a set of corrupted pixels S_c for the rest. When S_g is resilient, we can find a strategy for approximately recovering the mean of S_g by the following proposition.

Proposition 2: Suppose that S contains an unknown set S_g of size $(1-\varepsilon)N$ that is resilient with an unknown mean $\boldsymbol{\mu}_{Sg}$. Then if $\varepsilon < 1/2$, it is possible to recover a $\hat{\mu}$ such that

$$\|\hat{\boldsymbol{\mu}} - \boldsymbol{\mu}_{Sg}\| \le 2\sigma^*\left(\frac{\varepsilon}{1-\varepsilon}\right), \tag{11.17}$$

where $\sigma^*(\cdot)$ denotes the smallest σ such that S_g is $(\sigma,\cdot)$-resilient.

This proposition states that if we have ε fraction of corrupted pixels, we can remove $\frac{\varepsilon}{1-\varepsilon}$ fraction of pixels to estimate $\boldsymbol{\mu}_{Sg}$ without losing resilience when $\sigma^*\left(\frac{\varepsilon}{1-\varepsilon}\right)$ is small. Figure 11.1 shows the relationship between ε and $\frac{\varepsilon}{1-\varepsilon}$. We can see that ε cannot be too large. Otherwise, $\frac{\varepsilon}{1-\varepsilon}$ would increase rapidly such that this proposition cannot be adopted anymore.

In practice, we find a maximally overlapped subset with S_g and guess the mean of this subset. Robust learning uses a weighted method such that pixels in S_g have larger weight, while corrupted

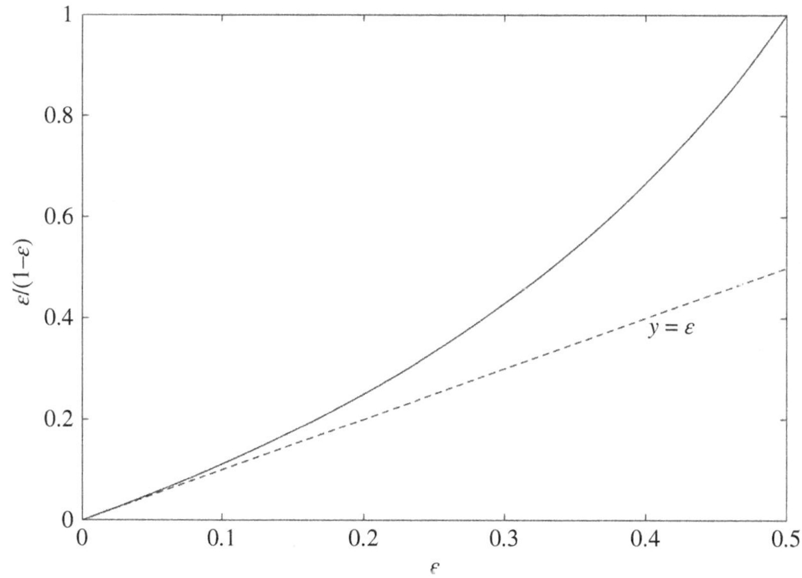

Figure 11.1 The relationship of ε and $\frac{\varepsilon}{1-\varepsilon}$.

pixels have smaller weight. In this way, we can select a maximally overlapped subset with S_g. For unmixing problem, however, several problems remain as follows.

The unmixing model has a strong geometric structure. Hence, some pixels located on the boundary are crucial. However, they can be easily removed and considered to be outliers. Figure 11.2 illustrates an example. Many important pixels, located outside the simplex, are constructed by the initial endmembers. Therefore, they have large residuals and are assigned extremely small weights from start to finish. Consequently, the algorithm becomes insensitive to these crucial pixels.

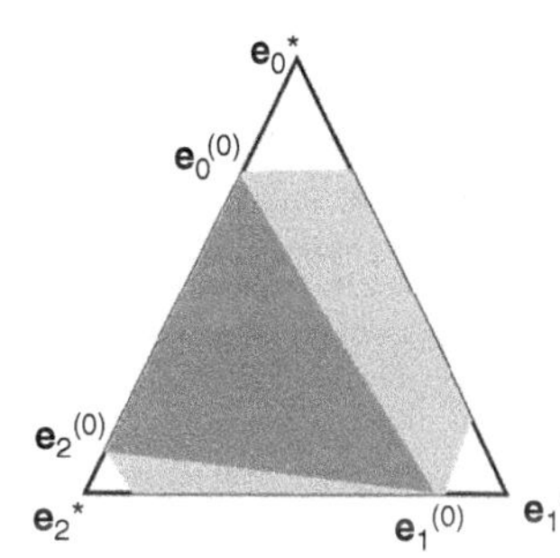

Figure 11.2 The initial endmembers $\mathbf{e}_i^{(0)}$ and the true endmembers $\mathbf{e}_i^*$.

Secondly, although the model error makes significant contribution to residual, the corrupted pixels have high correlation to specific endmembers. Hence, they are different from outliers which are random and entirely isolated from good pixels. Consequently, the corrupted pixels are not easy to detect. What's worse, model mismatch can lead to a majority of corrupted pixels ($\varepsilon > 1/2$), compared to a small number of outliers.

Thirdly, model uniqueness is another important problem. The remaining pixels must satisfy a sufficiently scattered condition to ensure model uniqueness of LMM. As we mentioned above, the corrupted pixels may not be easy to detect. So, when we remove corrupted pixels, we may also remove a lot of good pixels, especially some crucial pixels. Therefore, the remaining pixels may not satisfy the sufficiently scattered condition.

To mitigate this dilemma, we split the unmixing problem into several subproblems such that we merely consider one single endmember each time rather than all endmembers together. This leads to our Eq. (11.6). At this time, we only preserve crucial pixels related to a specific endmember rather than all good pixels. As a result, the task can be simplified. Specifically, suppose that we now recover the endmember $\mathbf{e}_0$, we categorize the good pixels into three groups, i.e., a set of critical pixels S_F, a set of interior pixels S_I, and a set of unrelated pixels S_0 as follows:

$$\begin{aligned} S_F &= \left\{ i \middle| \mathbf{y}[i] \in \bigcup_{j=1}^{m} F_j \right\}, \\ S_0 &= \{ i | \mathbf{y}[i] \in F_0 \}, \\ S_I &= \{1, \ldots, N\} \setminus (S_F \cup S_0 \cup S_c), \end{aligned} \tag{11.18}$$

where F_i is the i-th facets of the ground-truth simplex, i.e.,

$$F_i = \left\{ \mathbf{y} \in \mathbb{R}^L \middle| \begin{array}{l} \mathbf{y} = a_0\mathbf{e}_0^* + \ldots + a_m\mathbf{e}_m^*, \\ a_i = 0, \quad a_j \geq 0, \quad \sum_{k=0}^{m} a_k = 1, \quad j = 0, \ldots, m, \quad j \neq i \end{array} \right\}. \tag{11.19}$$

We can see that the pixels in S_0 do not provide any valuable information for recovering $\mathbf{e}_0$. Therefore, we can remove them safely. Compared to the number of faces of LMM, we have $n_{faces}(LMM) = 2 \times n_{faces}(ASC) - m \approx 2 \times n_{faces}(ASC)$, where $n_{faces}(\cdot)$ represents the number of faces of a model. We can see that the number of crucial pixels we need can be reduced almost by half.

Let $S_{g0} = S_F \cup S_I$, $S_g = S_{g0} \cup S_0$. Figure 11.3 illustrates the difference of overlapping subsets of S_g and S_{g0}. In Figure 11.3a, there are a set of good pixels S_g and a set of corrupted pixels S_c. Note that the corrupted pixels are usually not easy to detect. Robust learning finds a subset $\hat{S}$ that overlaps both S_g and S_c, see Figure 11.3b. This subset is quite different from S_g. It leads to significant errors in endmembers. If we consider only $\mathbf{e}_0$, we can separate the related subset S_{g0} from S_g by removing the unrelated pixels. Most importantly, many corrupted pixels can also be removed, see Figure 11.3c. As a result, we can find a subset that overlaps S_{g0} with less corrupted pixels, see Figure 11.3d. The result may be better than Figure 11.3b since the number of corrupted pixels is reduced.

Theoretically, assume $|S_{g0}| > 0$, $|S_0| > 0$, and $|S_C| > 0$. Obviously,

$$\frac{|S_{g0}| + |S_0|}{|S_C| + |S_{g0}| + |S_0|} > \frac{|S_{g0}|}{|S_C| + |S_{g0}|}. \tag{11.20}$$

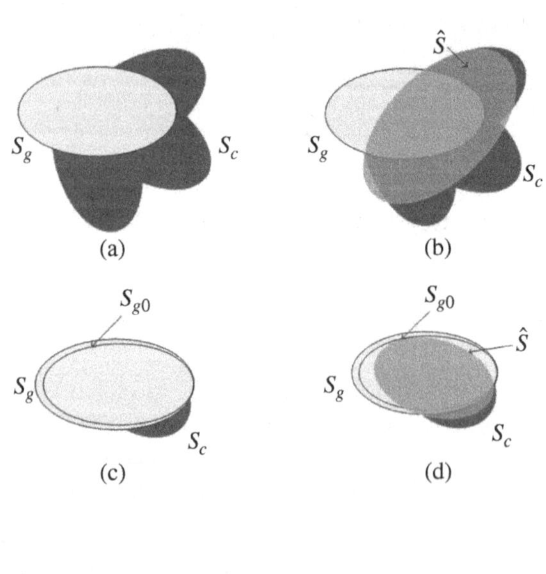

Figure 11.3 The comparison of the overlapping subsets between the removal of unrelated pixels or not. (a) Good pixels in S_g and corrupted pixels. (b) overlapping subset of S_{g0}, (c) good pixels in S_{g0} and the corrupted pixels, and (d) overlapping subset of S_{g0}.

It implies that if there are a lot of corrupted pixels, the performance will degrade if we remove only S_0.

However, if there is a $(1 - \varepsilon_C)$-fraction of corrupted pixels unrelated to $\mathbf{e}_0$, we can also remove them when we remove all unrelated pixels. Hence, we have fewer corrupted pixels such that the number of corrupted pixels remains to be

$$|S_{C0}| = \varepsilon_C |S_C|. \tag{11.21}$$

Let

$$\frac{|S_{g0}|}{|S_{C0}| + |S_{g0}|} - \frac{|S_{g0}| + |S_0|}{|S_C| + |S_{g0}| + |S_0|} \geq 0, \tag{11.22}$$

we have

$$\frac{|S_{g0}|}{|S_{g0}| + |S_0|} \geq \varepsilon_C \quad and \quad \frac{|S_0|}{|S_{g0}| + |S_0|} \leq 1 - \varepsilon_C \tag{11.23}$$

It means that if the fraction of unrelated good pixels in S_g is not greater than the fraction of unrelated corrupted pixels in S_C, the performance can be improved. For a complicated scene where it is impossible to handle corrupted pixels, this result gives us a hope to recover some endmembers if their related pixels are not corrupted or are slightly corrupted.

We further assume that a $(1-\varepsilon)$-fraction of good pixels in S_{g0} are removed, the resulting fraction of good pixels is

$$\frac{\varepsilon |S_{g0}|}{|S_{C0}| + \varepsilon |S_{g0}|}. \tag{11.24}$$

Let

$$\frac{\varepsilon |S_{g0}|}{|S_{C0}| + \varepsilon |S_{g0}|} - \frac{|S_{g0}| + |S_0|}{|S_C| + |S_{g0}| + |S_0|} \geq 0, \tag{11.25}$$

we have

$$\varepsilon \geq \varepsilon_C + \varepsilon_C \frac{|S_0|}{|S_{g0}|}. \tag{11.26}$$

This inequality provides a low boundary of the fraction of good pixels remaining.

11.2.3 Unrelated-pixel-removal Algorithm

To remove those unrelated pixels, one simple way is to utilize geometry structure of image. Let $\mathbf{E}^{(0)} = [\mathbf{e}_0{}^{(0)}, \ldots, \mathbf{e}_m{}^{(0)}]$ and $\mathbf{e}_i{}^{(0)}$ denote the i-th initialized endmember. Thus,

$$\mathbf{E}^{(0)} = \mathbf{E}^* \mathbf{K}, \tag{11.27}$$

where $\mathbf{K} = [\boldsymbol{\kappa}_0, \ldots, \boldsymbol{\kappa}_m] \in \mathbb{R}^{(m+1) \times (m+1)}$ and $\boldsymbol{\kappa}_i = [\kappa_{i,0}, \ldots, \kappa_{i,m}]^{\mathrm{T}}$ is the ground truth of the i-th abundances. If $\mathbf{K}$ satisfies

$$\boldsymbol{\kappa}_i = \underset{\mathbf{a}^*[n],\, n = 1, \ldots, N}{\arg\max} \left(a_i^*[n]\right), \tag{11.28}$$

$$\kappa_{i,i} > \sum_{j=0, j \neq i}^{m} \kappa_{i,j}, \tag{11.29}$$

where $\mathbf{a}^*[n] = [a_0{}^*[n],\ldots, a_m{}^*[n]]^{\mathrm{T}}$ is the ground-truth abundances for the n-th pixels, we can remove the pixels whose $a_0{}^{(0)}[n] < t_a$, where $t_a > 0$ is a threshold and $a_0{}^{(0)}[n]$ is the initialized abundance of $\mathbf{e}_i{}^{(0)}$ by using non-negative constrained LS (NCLS) [14] or fully constrained LS (FCLS) [15]. Equations (11.28) and (11.29) are easily satisfied by using any classical endmember extraction algorithm, e.g., vertex component analysis (VCA) [16]. More discussion can be seen in our work [5] Section III.A. This method can remove a small number of good pixels while it preserves enough information of geometrical structure such that it can guarantee model uniqueness. In addition, this method can easily satisfy the Eq. (11.26) in practice, as long as not all corrupted pixels are related to $\mathbf{e}_0$.

11.2.4 Endmember Purification Algorithm with Three Blocks

To guarantee model uniqueness, we introduce l_1-norm and consider the following problem

$$\begin{aligned}&\min_{\mathbf{e}_0,\mathbf{R},\mathbf{B}} \frac{1}{2}\|\mathbf{Y}-\mathbf{R}\mathbf{B}-\mathbf{e}_0\mathbf{1}_{1\times N}\|_F^2 + \lambda\|\mathbf{B}\|_{1,1}\\ &+ \frac{\lambda_B}{2}\|\mathbf{B}-\mathbf{B}^{(i)}\|_F^2 + \frac{\lambda_R}{2}\|\mathbf{R}-\mathbf{R}^{(i)}\|_F^2 + \frac{\lambda_e}{2}\|\mathbf{e}_0-\mathbf{e}_0{}^{(i)}\|_F^2.\\ &\text{s.t. } \mathbf{1}_{1\times L}(\mathbf{R}\odot\mathbf{R}) = \mathbf{1}_{1\times m},\quad \mathbf{B}\geq\mathbf{0}\end{aligned} \tag{11.30}$$

There are three groups of parameters involved in this problem, i.e., $\mathbf{e}_0$, $\mathbf{R}$, and $\mathbf{B}$. Similar to the rule of BCD method, we can update these parameters alternatingly.

To update $\mathbf{B}$, consider the following subproblem in the $i+1$ step

$$\begin{aligned}&\min \frac{1}{2}\|\mathbf{Z}-\mathbf{R}\mathbf{B}\|_F^2 + \lambda\|\mathbf{B}\|_1 + \frac{\lambda_B}{2}\|\mathbf{B}-\mathbf{B}^{(i)}\|_F^2,\\ &\text{s.t. } \mathbf{B}\geq\mathbf{0}\end{aligned} \tag{11.31}$$

where $\mathbf{Z} = \mathbf{Y} - \mathbf{e}_0\mathbf{1}_{1\times n}$. Let

$$\mathbf{Z}' = \begin{bmatrix}\mathbf{Z}\\ \sqrt{\lambda_B}\mathbf{B}^{(i)}\end{bmatrix} \textit{and } \mathbf{R}' = \begin{bmatrix}\mathbf{R}\\ \sqrt{\lambda_B}\mathbf{I}_{m\times m}\end{bmatrix} \tag{11.32}$$

Then the problem can be rewritten by

$$\begin{aligned}&\min \frac{1}{2}\|\mathbf{Z}'-\mathbf{R}'\mathbf{B}\|_F^2 + \lambda\|\mathbf{B}\|_1.\\ &\text{s.t. } \mathbf{B}\geq\mathbf{0}\end{aligned} \tag{11.33}$$

This problem can be solved by sparse unmixing by variable splitting and augmented Lagrangian (SUnSAL) algorithm [10].

To update $\mathbf{R}$, let

$$I_R(\mathbf{R})\begin{cases} 0, & \mathbf{1}_{1\times L}(\mathbf{R}\odot\mathbf{R}) = \mathbf{1}_{1\times m}\\ +\infty & \mathbf{1}_{1\times L}(\mathbf{R}\odot\mathbf{R}) \neq \mathbf{1}_{1\times m}\end{cases}. \tag{11.34}$$

Thus, the problem can be rewritten by

$$\min \frac{1}{2}\|\mathbf{Z}-\mathbf{R}\mathbf{B}\|_F^2 + \frac{\lambda_R}{2}\|\mathbf{R}-\mathbf{R}^{(i)}\|_F^2 + I_R(\mathbf{R}). \tag{11.35}$$

It can be solved by proximal gradient descent method. The first two terms can be rewritten by

$$\begin{aligned}&\frac{1}{2}\mathrm{tr}\left(\mathbf{Z}\mathbf{Z}^{\mathrm{T}}\right)-\mathrm{tr}\left(\mathbf{B}\mathbf{Z}^{\mathrm{T}}\mathbf{R}\right)+\frac{1}{2}\mathrm{tr}\left(\mathbf{R}\mathbf{B}\mathbf{B}^{\mathrm{T}}\mathbf{R}^{\mathrm{T}}\right)\\&+\frac{\lambda_R}{2}\mathrm{tr}\left(\mathbf{R}\mathbf{R}^{\mathrm{T}}\right)-\lambda_R\mathrm{tr}\left(\left(\mathbf{R}^{(i)}\right)^{\mathrm{T}}\mathbf{R}\right)+\frac{\lambda_R}{2}\mathrm{tr}\left(\left(\mathbf{R}^{(i)}\right)^{\mathrm{T}}\mathbf{R}^{(i)}\right).\end{aligned} \tag{11.36}$$

We have the following Jacobian matrix and let it be zeros, i.e.,

$$\left(\mathbf{B}\mathbf{B}^{\mathrm{T}}+\lambda_R\mathbf{I}\right)\mathbf{R}^{\mathrm{T}}-\mathbf{B}\mathbf{Z}^{\mathrm{T}}-\lambda_R\left(\mathbf{R}^{(i)}\right)^{\mathrm{T}}=0. \tag{11.37}$$

Thus, we obtain the following solution

$$\mathbf{R}^*=\left(\mathbf{Z}\mathbf{B}^{\mathrm{T}}+\lambda_R\mathbf{R}^{(i)}\right)\left(\mathbf{B}\mathbf{B}^{\mathrm{T}}+\lambda_R\mathbf{I}\right)^{-\mathrm{T}}. \tag{11.38}$$

Consider the following proximal operator

$$prox_{I_R}(\mathbf{R}^*)=\arg\min_{\mathbf{R}}\left\{I_R(\mathbf{R})+\frac{1}{2}\|\mathbf{R}-\mathbf{R}^*\|_F^2\right\}=P_{C_{\mathbf{R}}}(\mathbf{R}^*), \tag{11.39}$$

where $P_{C_{\mathbf{R}}}(\cdot)$ is the projection from $\cdot$ onto $C_{\mathbf{R}}$, and $C_{\mathbf{R}}$ represents the feasible region of $\mathbf{R}$. We have the update rule of R as follows

$$\mathbf{R}^{(i+1)}=\mathbf{R}^*/\left(sqrt\left(\left(\mathbf{1}^{L\times L}(\mathbf{R}^*\odot\mathbf{R}^*)\right)\right)\right), \tag{11.40}$$

where $\odot$ is the Hadamard product, / represents the element-wise division, and $sqrt(\cdot)$ represents the element-wise operation of square root.

To update $\mathbf{e}_0$, we consider the following problem

$$\min_{\mathbf{e}_0}\frac{1}{2}\|\mathbf{Y}-\mathbf{R}\mathbf{B}-\mathbf{e}_0\mathbf{1}_{1\times N}\|_F^2+\frac{\lambda_e}{2}\left\|\mathbf{e}_0-\mathbf{e}_0{}^{(i)}\right\|_F^2. \tag{11.41}$$

We can easily obtain the solution as follows:

$$\mathbf{e}_0{}^{(i+1)}=\frac{(\mathbf{Y}-\mathbf{R}\mathbf{B})\mathbf{1}_{1\times N}+\lambda_e\mathbf{e}_0{}^{(i)}}{N+\lambda_e}. \tag{11.42}$$

This solution is approximately the mean of residual of **RB**. It was proposed by [6] which was used to solve the affine NMF problem. Unfortunately, this is not a good solution. The reason will be discussed in the following section. Instead, consider

$$\mathbf{Y}-\mathbf{R}\mathbf{B}-\mathbf{e}_0\mathbf{1}_{1\times N}=\mathbf{0}. \tag{11.43}$$

From Eq. (11.42), we know that the least square solution of $\mathbf{e}_0$ is

$$\mathbf{e}_0=\frac{(\mathbf{Y}-\mathbf{R}\mathbf{B})\mathbf{1}_{1\times N}}{N}. \tag{11.44}$$

Thus,

$$\mathbf{Y}-\frac{\mathbf{Y}\mathbf{1}_{N\times N}}{N}=\mathbf{R}\mathbf{B}\left(\mathbf{I}_N-\frac{\mathbf{1}_{N\times N}}{N}\right). \tag{11.45}$$

Let

$$\mathbf{C} = \mathbf{B}\left(\mathbf{I}_N - \frac{\mathbf{1}_{N\times N}}{N}\right)\mathbf{B}^{\mathrm{T}}. \tag{11.46}$$

As a result,

$$\mathbf{R} = \left(\mathbf{Y} - \frac{\mathbf{Y}\mathbf{1}_{N\times N}}{N}\right)\mathbf{B}^{\mathrm{T}}\mathbf{C}^{-1}. \tag{11.47}$$

Interestingly, the matrix $\mathbf{C}$ is exactly the covariance matrix of the rows of $\mathbf{B}$. Replacing Eq. (11.47) into Eq. (11.41), the sub-problem can be rewritten by

$$\min_{\mathbf{e}_0} \frac{1}{2}\|\mathbf{W} - \mathbf{e}_0\mathbf{1}_{1\times N}\|_F^2 + \frac{\lambda_e}{2}\|\mathbf{e}_0 - \mathbf{e}_0{}^{(i)}\|_F^2, \tag{11.48}$$

where

$$\mathbf{W} = \mathbf{Y} - \left(\mathbf{Y} - \frac{\mathbf{Y}\mathbf{1}_{N\times N}}{N}\right)\mathbf{B}^{\mathrm{T}}\mathbf{C}^{-1}\mathbf{B}. \tag{11.49}$$

Let

$$\frac{\partial\left(\frac{1}{2}\|\mathbf{W} - \mathbf{e}_0\mathbf{1}_{1\times N}\|_F^2 + \frac{\lambda_e}{2}\|\mathbf{e}_0 - \mathbf{e}_0{}^{(i)}\|_F^2\right)}{\partial \mathbf{e}_0} = \mathbf{W}\mathbf{1}_{N\times 1} + N\mathbf{e}_0 + \lambda_e\mathbf{e}_0 - \lambda_e\mathbf{e}_0{}^{(i)} = 0, \tag{11.50}$$

we can obtain the final solution as follows:

$$\mathbf{e}_0{}^{(i+1)} = \frac{\mathbf{W}\mathbf{1}_{N\times 1} + \lambda_e\mathbf{e}_0{}^{(i)}}{N + \lambda_e}. \tag{11.51}$$

The only difference with Eq. (11.42) is the calculation of the residuals. However, the performance can be very different, as will be shown in the experimental section. The Algorithm 11.1 is summarized as follows.

Algorithm 11.1 Endmember Purifying Algorithm with Three Blocks

Input: Input image $\mathbf{Y}$, an initial endmember matrix $\mathbf{E}^{(0)}$ with EOI in the first column, the parameters λ_B, λ, λ_R, and λ_{e0} in Eqs. (11.31), (11.35), and (11.41) respectively, a maximum number of iterations $i_{\max}$, a convergence tolerance threshold σ.
1 Initialize $\mathbf{e}_0$ with the first column of $\mathbf{E}^{(0)}$.
2 Initialize each ray by $\mathbf{r}_i^{(0)} := \mathbf{e}_i^{(0)} - \mathbf{e}_0^{(0)}$.
3 Obtain $\mathbf{B}^{(0)}$ by using SUnSAL with $\mathbf{Y}$, $\mathbf{e}_0^{(0)}$, and $\mathbf{R}^{(0)}$.
4 Set i:=0.
Repeat
5 Solve the Eq. (11.33) by using SUnSAL to obtain $\mathbf{B}^{(i+1)}$.
6 Update $\mathbf{R}^{(i+1)}$ by Eq. (11.40).
7 Update $\mathbf{e}_0^{(i+1)}$ by Eq. (11.51).
8 Set i:=i+1.
Until $i > i_{\max}$ or $\left\|\mathbf{Y} - \mathbf{R}^{(i)}\mathbf{B}^{(i)} - \mathbf{e}_0^{(i)}\mathbf{1}_{1\times N}\right\|_F^2 < \sigma$
Output: $\mathbf{e}_0^{(i)}$.

11.2.5 Endmember Purification Algorithm with Two Blocks

In this section, we develop another EP algorithm in the framework of alternating proximal minimization algorithm with two blocks [17]. Then we reveal the reason why the Eq. (11.51) is better than Eq. (11.42).

Let

$$\mathrm{M} \equiv [\mathrm{e0}, \mathrm{R}] \tag{11.52}$$

The problem is rewritten by

$$\begin{aligned}&\min_{\mathbf{e}_0, \mathbf{M}} \frac{1}{2}\|\mathbf{Y}-\mathbf{M}\tilde{\mathbf{B}}\|_F^2 + \lambda\|\mathbf{B}\|_{1,1}\\ &\text{s.t. } \mathbf{1}_{1\times L}(\mathbf{R}\odot\mathbf{R}) = \mathbf{1}_{1\times m}, \mathbf{B}\geq 0,\end{aligned} \tag{11.53}$$

where

$$\tilde{\mathbf{B}} = \begin{bmatrix}\mathbf{1}^{1\times N}\\ \mathbf{B}^{m\times N}\end{bmatrix}. \tag{11.54}$$

Similar to the method used to obtain the update rule of **R**, let

$$\frac{\partial\left(\left\|\mathbf{Y}-\mathbf{M}\tilde{\mathbf{B}}^{(i)}\right\|_F^2 + \lambda_M\left\|\mathbf{M}-\mathbf{M}^{(i)}\right\|_F^2\right)}{\partial\mathbf{M}} = 0, \tag{11.55}$$

yield

$$\mathbf{M}^* = \left(\mathbf{Y}\left(\tilde{\mathbf{B}}^{(i)}\right)^{\mathrm{T}} + \lambda_M\mathbf{M}^{(i)}\right)\left(\tilde{\mathbf{B}}^{(i)}\left(\tilde{\mathbf{B}}^{(i)}\right)^{\mathrm{T}} + \lambda_M\mathbf{I}^{m\times m}\right)^{-1}. \tag{11.56}$$

Thus, the update rule of $\mathbf{M}^{(i+1)}$ is

$$\mathbf{M}^{(i+1)} = \mathbf{M}^*/\left(sqrt\left(\left[\mathbf{0}^{L\times 1}, \mathbf{1}^{L\times m}\right]\odot\left(\mathbf{1}^{L\times L}(\mathbf{M}^*\odot\mathbf{M}^*)\right)\right) + \left[\mathbf{1}^{L\times 1}, \mathbf{0}^{L\times m}\right]\right). \tag{11.57}$$

where $\odot$ is the Hadamard product, / represents the element-wise division, and $sqrt(\cdot)$ represents the element-wise operation of square root. The algorithm is showed in Algorithm 11.2 as follows.

Algorithm 11.2 Endmember Purifying Algorithm with Two Blocks

Input: Input image **Y**, an initial endmember matrix $\mathbf{E}^{(0)}$ with EOI in the first column, the parameters λ_B, λ, λ_R, and λ_{e0} in Eqs. (11.31), (11.35), and (11.41) respectively, a maximum number of iterations $i_{\max}$, a convergence tolerance threshold σ.

1 Initialize $\mathbf{e}_0$ with the first column of $\mathbf{E}^{(0)}$.

2 Initialize each ray by $\mathbf{r}_i^{(0)} := \mathbf{e}_i^{(0)} - \mathbf{e}_0^{(0)}$, obtain $\mathbf{R}^{(0)} = [\mathbf{r}_1^{(0)},\ldots,\mathbf{r}_m^{(0)}]$, and $\mathbf{M}^{(0)} = [\mathbf{e}_0, \mathbf{R}^{(0)}]$.

3 Obtain $\mathbf{B}^{(0)}$ by using SUnSAL with **Y**, $\mathbf{e}_0^{(0)}$, and $\mathbf{R}^{(0)}$.

4 Set i:=0.

Repeat

5 Solve the Eq. (11.33) by using SUnSAL to obtain $\mathbf{B}^{(i+1)}$,

6 Update $\mathbf{M}^{(i+1)}$ by Eq. (11.57).

7 Set i:=i + 1.

Until $i > i_{\max}$ or $\left\|\mathbf{Y}-\mathbf{M}^{(i)}\tilde{\mathbf{B}}^{(i)}\right\|_F^2 < \sigma$

Output: $\mathbf{e}_0 = \mathbf{M}_{:,0}^{(i)}$.

Now let us further compare the Eqs. (11.42) and (11.51). For simplicity, we ignore the regularized items. From Eq. (11.56), we know

$$\mathbf{M}^* = \left(\mathbf{Y}\left[\mathbf{1}^{N\times 1} \quad \mathbf{B}^{\mathrm{T}}\right]\right)\left(\tilde{\mathbf{B}}^{(i)}\left(\tilde{\mathbf{B}}^{(i)}\right)^{\mathrm{T}}\right)^{-1}. \tag{11.58}$$

And

$$\tilde{\mathbf{B}}^{(i)}\left(\tilde{\mathbf{B}}^{(i)}\right)^{\mathrm{T}} = \begin{bmatrix}\mathbf{1}^{1\times N}\\ \mathbf{B}\end{bmatrix}\left[\mathbf{1}^{N\times 1} \quad \mathbf{B}^{\mathrm{T}}\right] = \begin{bmatrix} N & \mathbf{1}^{1\times N}\mathbf{B}^{\mathrm{T}} \\ \mathbf{B}\mathbf{1}^{N\times 1} & \mathbf{B}\mathbf{B}^{\mathrm{T}}\end{bmatrix}. \tag{11.59}$$

According to the first form of inverse matrix of block matrix [18], the first column of the inverse matrix can be written by

$$\begin{bmatrix} N & \mathbf{1}^{1\times N}\mathbf{B}^{\mathrm{T}} \\ \mathbf{B}\mathbf{1}^{N\times 1} & \mathbf{B}\mathbf{B}^{\mathrm{T}}\end{bmatrix}^{-1} = \begin{bmatrix} \left(N - \mathbf{1}^{1\times N}\mathbf{B}^{\mathrm{T}}\left(\mathbf{B}\mathbf{B}^{\mathrm{T}}\right)^{-1}\mathbf{B}\mathbf{1}^{N\times 1}\right)^{-1} & \cdots \\ -\left(\mathbf{B}\mathbf{B}^{\mathrm{T}}\right)^{-1}\mathbf{B}\mathbf{1}^{N\times 1}\left(N - \mathbf{1}^{1\times N}\mathbf{B}^{\mathrm{T}}\left(\mathbf{B}\mathbf{B}^{\mathrm{T}}\right)^{-1}\mathbf{B}\mathbf{1}^{N\times 1}\right)^{-1} & \cdots \end{bmatrix}. \tag{11.60}$$

Thus,

$$\mathbf{e}_0 = \mathbf{Y}\left[\mathbf{1}^{N\times 1} \quad \mathbf{B}^{\mathrm{T}}\right]\begin{bmatrix} 1 \\ -\left(\mathbf{B}\mathbf{B}^{\mathrm{T}}\right)^{-1}\mathbf{B}\mathbf{1}^{N\times 1}\end{bmatrix}\left(N - \mathbf{1}^{1\times N}\mathbf{B}^{\mathrm{T}}\left(\mathbf{B}\mathbf{B}^{\mathrm{T}}\right)^{-1}\mathbf{B}\mathbf{1}^{N\times 1}\right)^{-1}. \tag{11.61}$$

And

$$\mathbf{Y}\left[\mathbf{1}_{N\times 1} \quad \mathbf{B}^{\mathrm{T}}\right]\begin{bmatrix} 1 \\ -\left(\mathbf{B}\mathbf{B}^{\mathrm{T}}\right)^{-1}\mathbf{B}\mathbf{1}_{N\times 1}\end{bmatrix} = (\mathbf{Y} - \mathbf{R}_{LS}\mathbf{B})\mathbf{1}_{N\times 1}. \tag{11.62}$$

Compare to the Eq. (11.42), we can see that Eq. (11.42) ignores the term $\mathbf{1}^{1\times N}\mathbf{B}^{\mathrm{T}}(\mathbf{B}\mathbf{B}^{\mathrm{T}})^{-1}\mathbf{B}\mathbf{1}^{N\times 1}$. Hence, Eq. (11.42) is not consistent with the two-block solution.

Let us look at the second form of inverse matrix as follows [19]

$$\begin{bmatrix} N & \mathbf{1}_{1\times N}\mathbf{B}^{\mathrm{T}} \\ \mathbf{B}\mathbf{1}_{N\times 1} & \mathbf{B}\mathbf{B}^{\mathrm{T}}\end{bmatrix}^{-1} = \begin{bmatrix} \frac{1}{N} + \frac{1}{N}\mathbf{1}_{1\times N}\mathbf{B}^{\mathrm{T}}\left(\mathbf{B}\mathbf{B}^{\mathrm{T}} - \mathbf{B}\mathbf{1}_{N\times 1}\mathbf{1}_{1\times N}\mathbf{B}^{\mathrm{T}}/N\right)^{-1}\mathbf{B}\mathbf{1}_{N\times 1}\frac{1}{N} & \cdots \\ -\frac{1}{N}\left(\mathbf{B}\mathbf{B}^{\mathrm{T}} - \mathbf{B}\mathbf{1}_{N\times 1}\mathbf{1}_{1\times N}\mathbf{B}^{\mathrm{T}}/N\right)^{-1}\mathbf{B}\mathbf{1}_{N\times 1} & \cdots \end{bmatrix}. \tag{11.63}$$

We have

$$\begin{aligned} \mathbf{e}_0 &= \mathbf{Y}\left[\mathbf{1}_{N\times 1} \quad \mathbf{B}^{\mathrm{T}}\right]\begin{bmatrix} 1 + \frac{1}{N}\mathbf{1}_{1\times N}\mathbf{B}^{\mathrm{T}}\mathbf{C}^{-1}\mathbf{B}\mathbf{1}_{N\times 1} \\ -\mathbf{C}^{-1}\mathbf{B}\mathbf{1}_{N\times 1}\end{bmatrix}\frac{1}{N} \\ &= \mathbf{Y}\mathbf{1}_{N\times 1} + \frac{1}{N}\mathbf{Y}\mathbf{1}_{N\times N}\mathbf{B}^{\mathrm{T}}\mathbf{C}^{-1} - \mathbf{Y}\mathbf{B}^{\mathrm{T}}\mathbf{C}^{-1}\mathbf{B}\mathbf{1}_{N\times 1}. \end{aligned} \tag{11.64}$$

We can see that Eq. (11.64) is equivalent to the Eq. (11.51). It implies that Eq. (11.51) includes the relationship between $\mathbf{e}_0$ and $\mathbf{R}$, which will be better than Eq. (11.42).

11.2.6 Overall Algorithm

We integrate all processes into an overall algorithm, see Algorithm 11.3. It includes three sub-algorithms, namely unrelated pixel removal (UPR), dimensional reduction (RD), and EP. For EP, we can choose one of the aforementioned algorithms. The step of RD is optional. We can also use any algorithm of DR before EP. In practice, we recommend the RD method proposed in [20, 21]. The step of unrelated pixels' removal is also optional. However, we prefer to remove unrelated pixels for robustness, as we mentioned in the previous section.

Algorithm 11.3 Overall Algorithm

Input: A hyperspectral image $\mathbf{Y}$, an initial endmember matrix $\mathbf{E}^{(0)}$ with EOI in the first column, a threshold t_a to remove the pixels in S_0, the parameters in each EP algorithm.

Unrelated pixels' removal (Optional):

Obtain $\mathbf{A}^{(0)}$ by LS algorithm. NNLS or FCLS is recommended.

Remove all pixels whose $a_0 < t_a$, obtain a subset $\mathbf{Y}_0$.

Dimensional Reduction (Optional):

$\mathbf{Y}_0 := \mathbf{Y}_0 - (\mathbf{Y}_0 \mathbf{1}_{N\times N})/N$

Obtain $\mathbf{UDV}^T = \mathbf{Y}_0 \mathbf{Y}_0^T/N$ by using Singular Value Decomposition (SVD).

Let $\mathbf{U}_m := \mathbf{U}_{:,1:m}$

$\mathbf{Y}_0 := \mathbf{D}^{-1}\mathbf{U}_m^T \mathbf{Y}_0$

$\mathbf{E}^{(0)} := \mathbf{D}^{-1}\mathbf{U}_m^T(\mathbf{E}^{(0)} - (\mathbf{Y}_0 \mathbf{1}_{N\times m+1})/N$

Endmember purification:

Choose Algorithm 11.1 or 11.2 with the new $\mathbf{Y}_0$ and $\mathbf{E}^{(0)}$ as input to obtain $\mathbf{e}_0$.

Output: $\mathbf{e}_0 := \mathbf{U}_m \mathbf{D} \mathbf{e}_0 + \mathbf{Y}_0 \mathbf{1}_{N\times 1}$

11.3 Unmixing with Geographic Knowledge Graph

In the section, we discuss endmember selection by the aid of Geo-KG. From the definition of endmember [22], we know that endmembers are the distinct substances having relatively constant spectral properties that dominate the surface within a given scene. Hence, endmember can be regarded as geographic entity. Each geographic entity is closely linked to its geographic environment and presents unique properties. These relationships can be modeled by GeoKG. Figure 11.4 illustrates an example of GeoKG on land cover types at the conceptual level. The nodes of GeoKG represent concepts, i.e., land cover types in this example. The edges demonstrate the relationships among the concepts or among the concepts and their properties. Obviously, this GeoKG provides valuable knowledge to tell whether an endmember is in that area. For this reason, endmembers can be chosen by the aid of Geo-KG.

Figure 11.5 presents a technical workflow of unmixing with GeoKG. The first question is how to acquire the knowledge necessary to construct a GeoKG. Fortunately, we have plenty of data acquiring from remote sensing and other resources such as digital elevation model (DEM). We can extract knowledge from those data. Section 11.3.1 discusses a method for extracting knowledge from multiple remote-sensing sources. The second challenge is how to integrate GeoKG into the unmixing process. Section 11.3.2 considers a technique of GeoKG embedding such that the GeoKG can be presented in a vector space. Then, the knowledge about endmember can be reasoned according to the vector space. Finally, a spectral unmixing algorithm by the aid of GeoKG is presented in

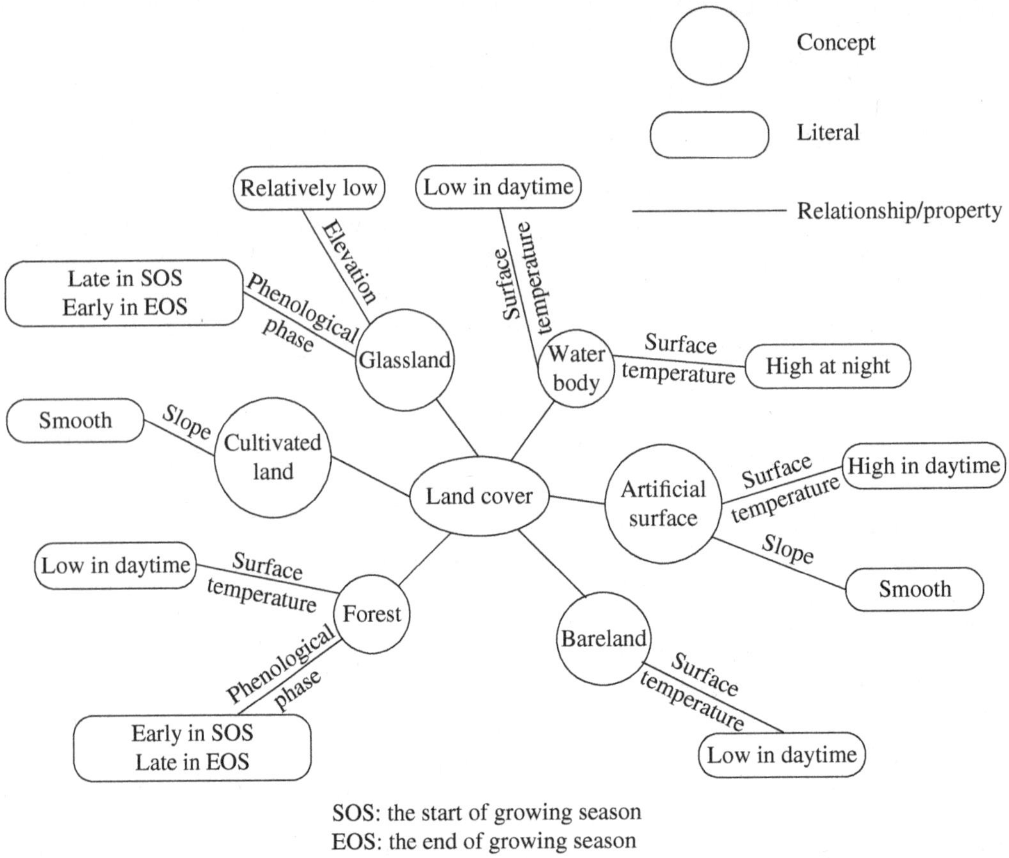

Figure 11.4 A GeoKG on land cover types at the conceptual level.

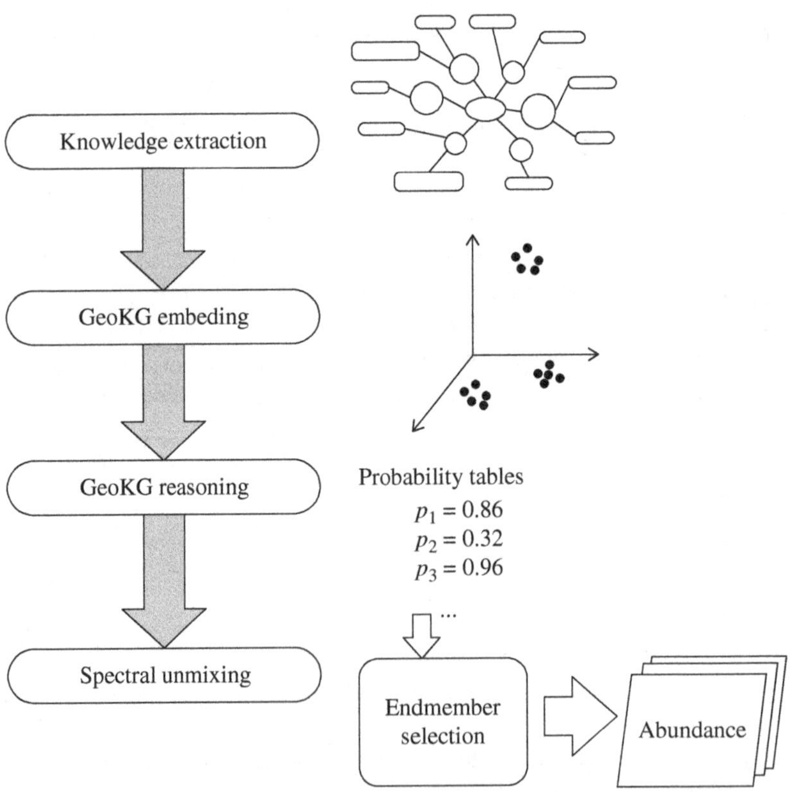

Figure 11.5 A technical workflow of unmixing with GeoKG.

Section 11.3.3. It is important to mention that the purpose of this book is to present a framework of GeoKG for unmixing. While there are various methods and techniques such as deep learning that can be employed to enhance this framework, they will not be covered in this book.

11.3.1 Knowledge Extraction

There should be a relationship between the endmember and its geographic environment. Each endmember has its own unique properties. To discover these relationships, we can employ some auxiliary data. As an example, three properties of the endmember, namely the phenological phase of vegetation, spectral features, and surface temperature, as well as three terrain factors, namely altitude, slope, and aspect, are considered. The corresponding data can be found in Table 11.1.

According to the data, a method of supervised learning can be used to extract knowledge. Specifically, a number of samples are labeled from the data by expert. In order to augment more reliable samples, a classification and regression trees (CART) [23] is employed and trained by these samples. We then use the pure nodes of the tree, i.e., the Gini index and deviance are zero, as the rules to generate more reliable samples from the data. The expert confirms these samples again. Therefore, the resulted samples present expert knowledge that can be used to make a GeoKG. For example, Figure 11.6 clearly shows that the forest is distributed at higher altitudes than other types.

Table 11.1 The usage of data.

Data source	Data product	Usage
Landsat-8 OLI	Normalized difference water index (NDWI)	Spectral features
Landsat-8 OLI	Multi-temporal normalized difference vegetation indexes (mNDVIs)	Phenological phase
Landsat-8 TIRS	Surface temperature	Surface temperature
GDEMV2	Altitude, slope, and aspect	Terrain factors

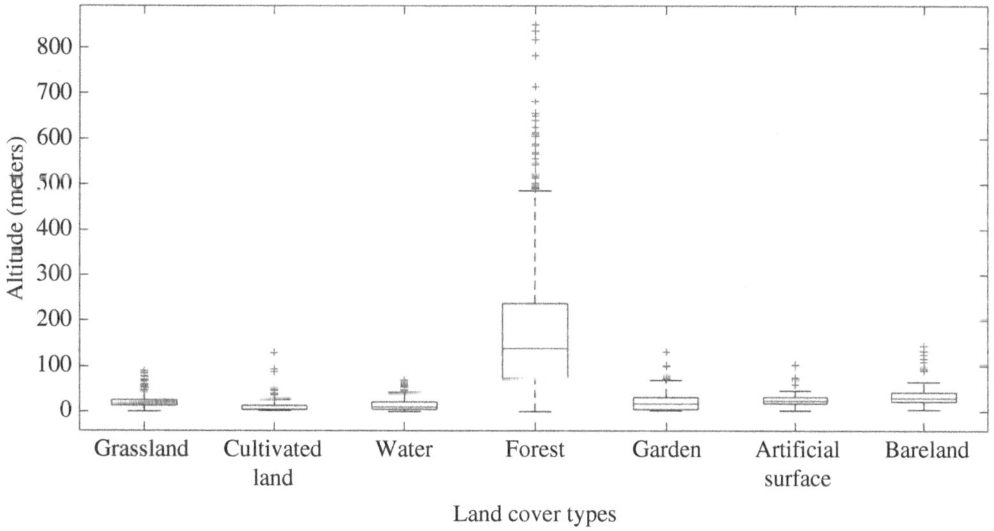

Figure 11.6 The distributions of altitude of different cover types.

Finally, these samples are stored in triples in the form of (head, relation, tail), e.g., ("a forest object," "has properties," "<15,18,300,0.28,0.38,0.43,0.33>") where the tail represents the values of <surface temperature, slope, altitude, mNDVIs>; aspect and NDWI are omitted in this example.

11.3.2 GeoKG Embedding and Reasoning

Knowledge representation has experienced a long period history of development [24]. Knowledge graph embedding (KGE) aims to learn a low-dimensional vector space to represent the entities and relations so that a scoring function can be used to measure the plausibility of triples. It implies that the reasoning result can be measured in numerical terms. Therefore, embedding can naturally be a suitable method for the unmixing task, since the unmixing problem belongs to the field of numerical optimization.

The transE model [25] is one of the most classical KGE models. In this model, the elements of a triple (h,r,t) are mapped into a vector space. Boldface characters **h**, **r**, and **t** denote these vectors, respectively. The relation vector **r** can be expressed by using **h** and **t** as follows

$$\mathbf{h}+\mathbf{r}\approx\mathbf{t}. \tag{11.65}$$

Obviously, a negative sample (h′,r,t′) satisfies

$$\mathbf{h}'+\mathbf{r}\neq\mathbf{t}'. \tag{11.66}$$

Hence, the scoring function can be easily calculated by the distance, i.e.,

$$f(\mathbf{h},\mathbf{r},\mathbf{t})=\|\mathbf{h}-\mathbf{r}-\mathbf{t}\|_{\ell_1/\ell_2}, \tag{11.67}$$

where l_1/l_2 represents l_1-norm or l_2-norm. Therefore, the embedding problem becomes

$$\min_{\mathbf{h},\mathbf{r},\mathbf{t}}\sum_{(h,r,t)\in S}\sum_{(h',r,t')\in S'}[\lambda+f(\mathbf{h},\mathbf{r},\mathbf{t})-f(\mathbf{h}',\mathbf{r},\mathbf{t}')]_+, \tag{11.68}$$

where S is the set of positive samples, S' is the set of negative samples, and $\lambda>0$ is a margin hyperparameter.

However, some issues still remain. Most KGE models aim to embed word into vector, which requires that the elements of a triple are discrete. However, the properties of the endmember are measured in numerical form. Furthermore, the scale of each property may vary widely. Some properties may be easily ignored when we calculate the scoring function. For these reasons, the transE model cannot be trained by using the triples obtained in the previous section.

To solve these issues, we first map the properties into a vector space by using probability measure. Specifically, for a given endmember $\mathbf{e}_i$, we have a probability density function of the j-th property v_j, denoted by $p_{i,j}(v_j)$. Assume

$$p_{i,j}(\cdot)\sim N\left(\mu_{i,j},\sigma_{i,j}\right), \tag{11.69}$$

where $\mu_{i,j}$, $\sigma_{i,j}$ represent the mean and variance of the j-th property of $\mathbf{e}_i$ respectively. In this way, the tail of the triple ("$\mathbf{e}_i$," "has properties," "$<v_1,v_2,\ldots,v_q>$") can be embedded into a vector space with the value of $<p_{i,1}(v_1),p_{i,2}(v_2),\ldots,p_{i,q}(v_q)>$. Then, we can train the transE model in the same vector space by fixing the tail of the triples, which satisfies

$$\min_{\mathbf{h},\mathbf{r}}\sum_{(h,r,t)\in S}\sum_{(h',r,t')\in S'}[\lambda+f(\mathbf{h},\mathbf{r},\mathbf{t})-f(\mathbf{h}',\mathbf{r},\mathbf{t}')]_+. \tag{11.70}$$

Then obtain the embedding vectors $\hat{\mathbf{h}}$ and $\hat{\mathbf{r}}$ for each endmember.

Once we have $\hat{\mathbf{h}}_1,...,\hat{\mathbf{h}}_m$ and $\hat{\mathbf{r}}_1,...,\hat{\mathbf{r}}_m$, we can reason about the existence of endmembers by using the transE model. From Eq. (11.65), we know that if the value of $f(\mathbf{h},\mathbf{r},\mathbf{t})$ is small enough, then we can assert that h (the endmember) and t (the pixel with the properties) have the relationship r. This gives us a mechanism to determine the existence of endmembers.

For a given pixel, we firstly obtain its q properties $<v_1,v_2,..., v_q>$ from the data sources. Then calculate m vectors by Eq. (11.69), denoted by $\mathbf{t}_i = <p_{i,1}(v_1),p_{i,2}(v_2),..., p_{i,q}(v_q)>$, $i = 1,..., m$. Thus, we can calculate the relation vector in the following

$$\mathbf{r}_i = \mathbf{t}_i - \hat{\mathbf{h}}_i. \tag{11.71}$$

Then we can compare the relation $\mathbf{r}_i$ and $\hat{\mathbf{r}}_i$. Obviously, if the pixel has similar relation, the pixel is inclined to contain this endmember. Therefore, we calculate the distance between $\mathbf{r}_i$ and $\hat{\mathbf{r}}_i$ as follows

$$\|\mathbf{r}_i - \hat{\mathbf{r}}_i\|_{\ell_1/\ell_2} = \left\|\mathbf{t}_i - \hat{\mathbf{h}}_i - \hat{\mathbf{r}}_i\right\|_{\ell_1/\ell_2} = f\left(\hat{\mathbf{h}}_i, -\hat{\mathbf{r}}_i, \mathbf{t}_i\right). \tag{11.72}$$

Let

$$pr_i(n) = f\left(\hat{\mathbf{h}}_i, -\hat{\mathbf{r}}_i, \mathbf{t}_i(n)\right), \tag{11.73}$$

where $\mathbf{t}_i(n)$ represents the embedding vector of tail for the n-th mixed pixel of a hyperspectral image. Hence, $pr_i(n)$ is the prior knowledge obtained by GeoKG.

11.3.3 Unmixing Algorithm

To take advantage of the prior knowledge provided by GeoKG, a weighted sparse unmixing algorithm is developed. Consider the following objective function

$$\min_{\mathbf{x}} \frac{1}{2}\|\mathbf{y} - \mathbf{E}\mathbf{x}\|_2^2 + \lambda\|\boldsymbol{\omega} \odot \mathbf{x}\|_1 \quad \text{s.t.}\mathbf{x} \geq 0, \tag{11.74}$$

where $\mathbf{x}$ is the estimated abundance vector and ω is a weight vector that controls the sparseness for the corresponding element of $\mathbf{x}$. Obviously, small ω_i (lower than 1) increases the sparseness of x_i, and vice versa. To introduce the prior knowledge Eq. (11.73), we calculate the weight as follows

$$w_i = \frac{(c+1)*\max(pr_i)}{pr_i + c*\max(pr_i) + \varepsilon}, \tag{11.75}$$

where $c \geq 0$ is an adjusting factor, $\varepsilon > 0$ is small enough, and $\max(pr_i)$ represents the maximum value of pr_i for all pixels. Obviously, $c \to +\infty$ implies $\mathbf{w} = \mathbf{1}$ and Eq. (11.74) becomes the traditional sparse unmixing problem. When $c = 0$, w_i represents the inverse of the normalized pr_i, implying that the weight is completely determined by the prior knowledge.

Equation (11.74) can be solved by alternating direction method of multipliers (ADMM). Consider the problem as follows:

$$\min_{\mathbf{x}} \frac{1}{2}\|\mathbf{y} - \mathbf{u}_1\|_2^2 + \lambda\|\boldsymbol{\omega} \odot \mathbf{u}_2\|_1 + \frac{\mu}{2}\|\mathbf{E}\mathbf{x} - \mathbf{u}_1 - \mathbf{d}_1\|_2^2 + \frac{\mu}{2}\|\mathbf{x} - \mathbf{u}_2 - \mathbf{d}_2\|_2^2.$$
$$\text{s.t. } \mathbf{u}_1 = \mathbf{E}\mathbf{x}, \quad \mathbf{u}_2 = \mathbf{x}, \quad \mathbf{x} \geq 0 \tag{11.76}$$

We can separate it into the following subproblems

$$\arg\min_{\mathbf{x}} \frac{\mu}{2}\|\mathbf{Ex}-\mathbf{u}_1-\mathbf{d}_1\|_2^2 + \frac{\mu}{2}\|\mathbf{x}-\mathbf{u}_2-\mathbf{d}_2\|_2^2, \tag{11.77}$$

$$\arg\min_{\mathbf{u}_1} \frac{1}{2}\|\mathbf{y}-\mathbf{u}_1\|_2^2 + \frac{\mu}{2}\|\mathbf{Ex}-\mathbf{u}_1-\mathbf{d}_1\|_2^2, \tag{11.78}$$

$$\arg\min_{\mathbf{u}_2} \lambda\|\boldsymbol{\omega}\odot\mathbf{u}_2\|_1 + \frac{\mu}{2}\|\mathbf{x}-\mathbf{u}_2-\mathbf{d}_2\|_2^2, \tag{11.79}$$

$$\arg\min_{\mathbf{d}_1} \frac{\mu}{2}\|\mathbf{Ex}-\mathbf{u}_1-\mathbf{d}_1\|_2^2, \tag{11.80}$$

$$\arg\min_{\mathbf{d}_2} \frac{\mu}{2}\|\mathbf{x}-\mathbf{u}_2-\mathbf{d}_2\|_2^2. \tag{11.81}$$

By solving these subproblems, we obtain the following update rules

$$\mathbf{x}^{(i+1)} \leftarrow \left(\mathbf{E}^T\mathbf{E}+\mathbf{I}\right)^{-1}\left(\mathbf{E}^T\left(\mathbf{u}_1^{(i)}+\mathbf{d}_1^{(i)}\right)+\left(\mathbf{u}_2^{(i)}+\mathbf{d}_2^{(i)}\right)\right), \tag{11.82}$$

$$\mathbf{u}_1^{(i+1)} \leftarrow \frac{1}{\mu+1}\left[\mathbf{y}+\mu\left(\mathbf{Ex}^{(i+1)}-\mathbf{d}_1^{(i)}\right)\right], \tag{11.83}$$

$$\mathbf{u}_2^{(i+1)} \leftarrow soft\left(\mathbf{x}^{(i+1)}-\mathbf{d}_2^{(i)}, \frac{\lambda}{\mu}\boldsymbol{\omega}\right), \tag{11.84}$$

$$\mathbf{d}_1^{(i+1)} \leftarrow \mathbf{d}_1^{(i)}-\mathbf{Ex}^{(i+1)}+\mathbf{u}_1^{(i+1)}, \tag{11.85}$$

$$\mathbf{d}_2^{(i+1)} \leftarrow \mathbf{d}_2^{(i)}-\mathbf{x}^{(i+1)}+\mathbf{u}_2^{(i+1)}. \tag{11.86}$$

where

$$soft(a,b) = sign(a)*\max\{|a|-b,0\}. \tag{11.87}$$

Therefore, the unmixing algorithm (Algorithm 11.4) can be summarized as follows.

Algorithm 11.4 Knowledge Graph Embedding Spectral Unmixing (KGESU) algorithm

, a hyper-
parameter μ, a maximum number of iterations $i_{\max}$, a convergence tolerance threshold σ.
1 Let $\mathbf{x}^{(0)}:=(\mathbf{E}^T\mathbf{E}+\mu\mathbf{I})^{-1}\mathbf{E}^T\mathbf{y}$.
2 Let $\mathbf{u}_1:=\mathbf{Ex}^{(0)}$, $\mathbf{u}_2:=\mathbf{x}^{(0)}$.
3 Let $\mathbf{d}_1:=\mathbf{0}$, $\mathbf{d}_2:=\mathbf{0}$.
4 Let $i:=0$.
5 Calculate w by using Eq. (11.75).
Repeat
6 Set $i:=i+1$
7 Update $\mathbf{x}$ by using Eq. (11.82).
8 Update $\mathbf{u}_1$ and $\mathbf{u}_2$ by Eqs. (11.83) and (11.84), respectively.
9 Update $\mathbf{d}_1$ and $\mathbf{d}_2$ by Eqs. (11.85) and (11.86), respectively.
Until $i > i_{\max}$ or $\left\|\mathbf{x}^{(i)}-\mathbf{x}^{(i-1)}\right\|_2^2 < \sigma$
Output: $\mathbf{x}^{(i)}$.

11.4 Experimental Results and Analysis

We evaluate the EP algorithms and KGESU algorithm in this section. Section 11.4.1 compares three versions of EP algorithms, i.e., the EP algorithm with two blocks (EP_2B), the EP algorithm with three blocks (EP_3B) by using Eq. (11.51), and the EP algorithm with three blocks by using Eq. (11.42) the similar updating rule of $\mathbf{e}_0$ as affine NMF (EP_A). It should be noted that EP_A is not an affine NMF algorithm since it uses a different model. Section 11.4.2 compares the proposed KGESU algorithm with four classical unmixing algorithms that use endmember selection different strategies, including FCLS [26], sparse unmixing by variable splitting and augmented Lagrangian (SUnSAL) [10], multiple endmember spectral mixture analysis (MESMA) [7], and spectral–spatial weighted sparse regression (S2WSR) [27].

11.4.1 Experiments for EP algorithms

Two groups of data are used to evaluate the EP algorithms, namely synthetic datasets and real hyperspectral remote-sensing datasets. The score of spectral angle distance (SAD) in degree between the estimated endmembers and true endmembers is used to evaluate the performance of these algorithms.

11.4.1.1 Synthetic Data Experiments

The synthetic datasets with the size of 5000 pixels were generated by seven endmembers selected from the USGS spectral library [28]. The maximum endmember purity level (MEPL) was used to control the maximum abundance occurring in the datasets, i.e., $a_i^*[n] \le MEPL$, for $i = 1, \ldots, m + 1$, and $n = 1, \ldots, N$. Zero-mean Gaussian noise in different levels of signal-to-noise ratio (SNR) was added to the datasets. These synthetic datasets were varied by controlling MEPLs ranging from 0.6 to 0.9 and SNRs ranging from 10 to 50 dB.

Regarding the hyperparameters, we set $\lambda_M = \lambda_B = 10^{-4}$, and $t_a = 0.01$, following our previous work. The value of λ is sensitive to the noise level and its setting follows

$$\lambda = \begin{cases} 10^{-3}, & SNR \ge 40 \ dB \\ 10^{-2}, & 20 \ dB < SNR < 40 \ dB \\ 10^{-1}, & SNR \le 20 \ dB \end{cases}. \tag{11.88}$$

All endmembers were initialized by running the VCA algorithm [16]. All the algorithms performed the DR step before the EP operation.

The SAD scores are reported in Tables 11.2 and 11.3. We can see that the performance of EP_2B and EP_3B is almost the same. Although EP_A slightly improves the qualities of the endmembers compared to the initialization, its performance is much worse than the other two algorithms. It implies that the algorithm easily gets trapped in a local solution when it uses a simple way of residual calculation involved in the updating rule Eq. (11.42). However, calculating the residuals in Eq. (11.51) significantly improves the performance, as shown by the results of EP_3B. Figure 11.7 also compares the results in the case of $MELP = 0.7$. EP_2B and EP_3B estimated six endmembers accurately when $SNR = 20$ dB. Even if at very low SNR (10 dB), some results obtained by these two algorithms are still close to the references. However, the endmembers obtained by EP_A are not satisfactory, which is consistent with the SAD scores.

We further compare the execution time of these algorithms in Table 11.4. The time of other cases is similar. We can see that the EP algorithms with three blocks are faster than two blocks. EP_3P achieves the best trade-off between execution time and performance among these algorithms.

Table 11.2 SAD scores of endmembers (in radians, ×10^{-3}) with *MELP* = 0.6, 0.7, and different SNRs (in dB).

MELP = 0.6					*MELP* = 0.7				
SNR	**Init**	**EP_2B**	**EP_3B**	**EP_A**	**SNR**	**Init**	**EP_2B**	**EP_3B**	**EP_A**
Inf	59.80	8.970	8.970	50.17	Inf	41.79	1.010	1.010	21.28
50	57.73	21.73	21.73	51.84	50	42.35	0.640	0.640	26.04
40	57.11	6.830	6.830	45.59	40	46.92	3.470	3.470	21.62
30	49.81	9.300	9.300	56.61	30	34.65	5.400	5.400	24.65
20	46.76	23.61	23.61	62.18	20	38.16	15.66	15.66	43.92
10	81.39	72.46	72.46	75.38	10	75.65	49.10	49.10	77.50

Table 11.3 SAD scores of endmembers (in radians, ×10^{-3}) with *MELP* = 0.8, 0.9, and different SNRs (in dB).

MELP = 0.8					*MELP* = 0.9				
SNR	**Init**	**EP_2B**	**EP_3B**	**EP_A**	**SNR**	**Init**	**EP_2B**	**EP_3B**	**EP_A**
Inf	31.41	0.560	0.560	8.120	Inf	14.41	0.410	0.410	1.990
50	31.02	0.410	0.410	7.800	50	15.07	0.470	0.470	1.810
40	30.06	2.780	2.780	8.110	40	12.34	5.200	5.200	1.150
30	22.04	6.170	6.170	13.61	30	10.19	9.430	9.430	6.710
20	24.20	9.380	9.380	33.34	20	20.89	8.840	8.840	29.54
10	76.57	49.60	49.60	71.87	10	75.03	47.86	47.86	72.22

11.4.1.2 HYDICE Dataset Experiment

The second group of datasets was the image collected by the hyperspectral sensor HYDICE in an urban area, which is a widely used image. The image is of size 307 × 307, with 210 bands in 10 nm spectral resolution, ranging from 400 to 2500 nm. After removing low SNR bands, namely 1–4, 76, 87, 101–111, 136–153, and 198–210, 162 bands were used. The initial endmembers followed our previous work [5]. In addition, we provided two more initial endmembers, i.e., unknown building materials, since their spectra demonstrate different features than other materials, see Figure 11.8 (the endmembers #10 and #11). These two endmembers are slightly similar to the endmembers #4 and #5, respectively. But they have different absorb feature and slope. It became a challenge for the algorithms to differentiate between these endmembers.

Due to the complexity of a scene, it is advisable to vary the thresholds t_a with different endmembers according to the practical distribution of the data. In our experience, if the spectra of two endmember are similar, a high threshold value should be set in case the endmembers interferent each other. Furthermore, if there are only a small number of pixels containing a particular endmember, a high threshold value should be set for that endmember in order to increase the proportion of good pixels. The thresholds we used for this image are listed in Table 11.5.

Figure 11.8 compares the endmembers obtained by the compared algorithms. We further calculated the abundance maps by using SUnSAL [10], see Figure 11.9. We can see that EP_2B failed to recover the endmember of grass. Furthermore, it cannot differentiate the endmembers #4, #5, #10, and #11. The results obtained by EP_2B and EP_3B are similar. For the endmember #4 and #10, EP_3B is slight better. We have to admit that the materials in a scene can be very complex and some potential endmember may not be easy to find. Therefore, it is not possible to conclude which algorithm is better until we know everything about the scene.

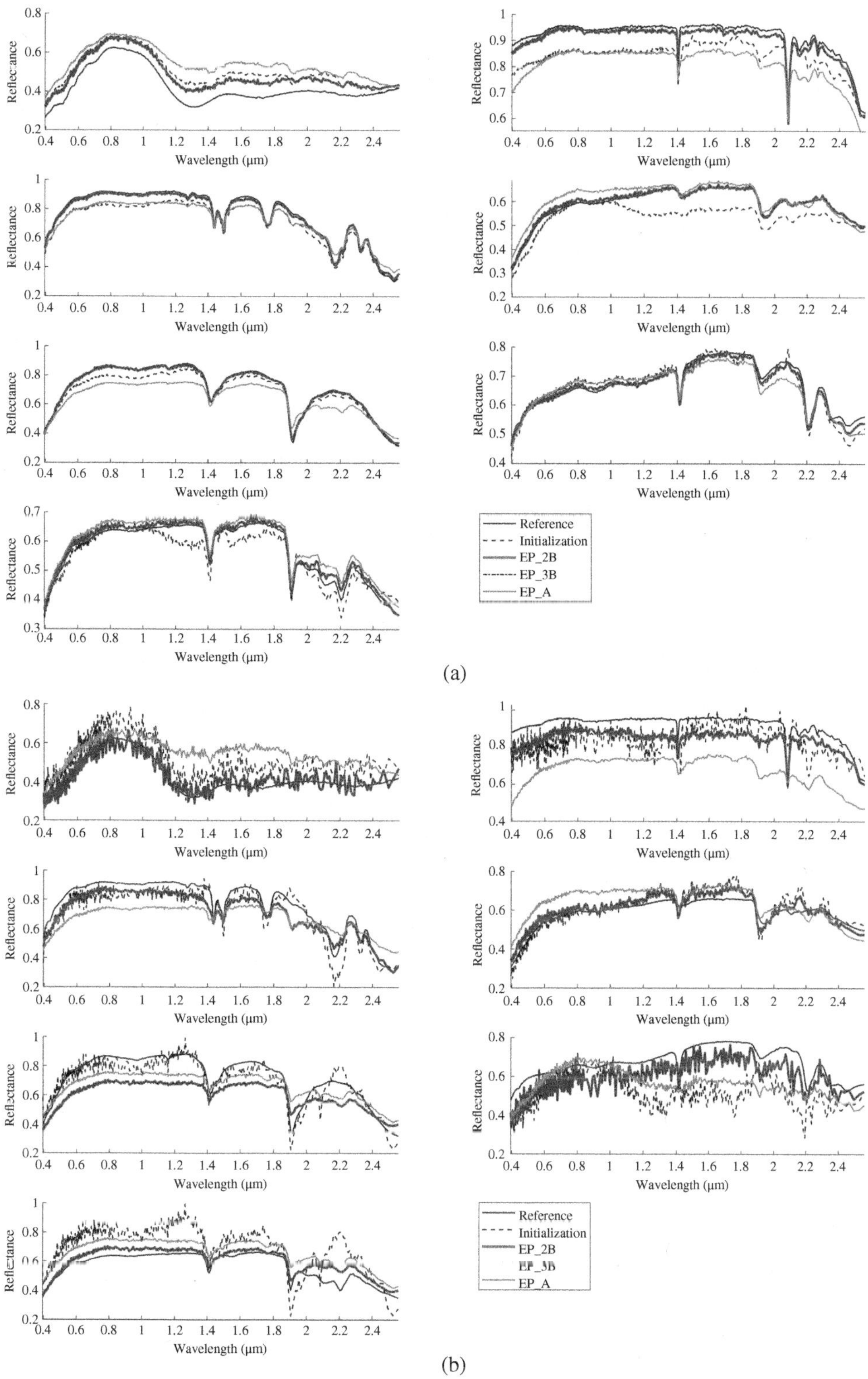

Figure 11.7 The endmembers obtained by the compared algorithms in the case of $MELP = 0.7$. (a) $SNR = 20$ dB and (b) $SNR = 10$ dB.

Table 11.4 The execution time (in milliseconds) with $m = 7$, $MELP = 0.7$ and different SNRs (in dB).

SNR	EP_2B	EP_3B	EP_A
Inf	36,921	27,765	29,906
50	35,554	28,781	32,094
40	36,000	29,094	30,093
30	31,847	23,953	28,547
20	30,959	24,031	26,187
10	35,978	30,422	29,906
Mean	34,543	27,341	29,456
Standard deviation	2489	2730	1964

11.4.2 Experiments for KGESU algorithm

The image used for unmixing was collected by the Chinese satellite GaoFen-5 (GF-5). The sensor has 330 bands covered visible/near-infrared (VNIR) and shortwave infrared (SWIR) with spectral resolution 10 nm. We selected 106 VNIR bands for the experiment according to the quality of these bands. We then performed the unmixing algorithms with this image.

To evaluate the unmixing results, the most common method is to use a high spatial resolution image as a reference. Specifically, we can classify the high spatial resolution image and calculate the percentage of pixels that are classified into a given class in the region corresponding to a mixed pixel of the hyperspectral image. This percentage can be used as a measure of abundance. Unfortunately, this method is very sensitive to the registration error. Hence, accurate registration at the subpixel level becomes a major obstacle.

To solve this issue, we evaluated the unmixing accuracy using a window instead of a single pixel. Although there may be a shift between two images, the overlap region occupies most area of the window. Hence, the contribution of the invalid region can be small enough to be ignored.

For clarity, let $a_{i,c}$ denote the abundance of the endmember corresponding to the cover type c for the i-th pixel in the window, N_c denote the number of pixels classified into c in the window, and N_{hps} denote the total number of pixels of the hyperspectral image in the window. We have

$$A_c = N_c S_{pan} = \sum_{i=1}^{N_{hps}} a_{i,c} S_{hps}, \tag{11.89}$$

where A_c is the total area of the cover type c in the window, S_{pan} is the spatial resolution of the high spatial resolution image, and S_{hps} is the spatial resolution of the hyperspectral image. Therefore,

$$\frac{A_c}{A} = \frac{N_c S_{pan}}{N_{pan} S_{pan}} = \frac{\sum_{i=1}^{N_{hps}} a_{i,c} S_{hps}}{N_{hps} S_{hps}}, \tag{11.90}$$

where A is the area of the window and N_{pan} is the total number of pixels in the window. Thus,

$$p_c = \frac{N_c}{N_{pan}} = \frac{\sum_{i=1}^{N_{hps}} a_{i,c}}{N_{hps}} = \overline{a}_c. \tag{11.91}$$

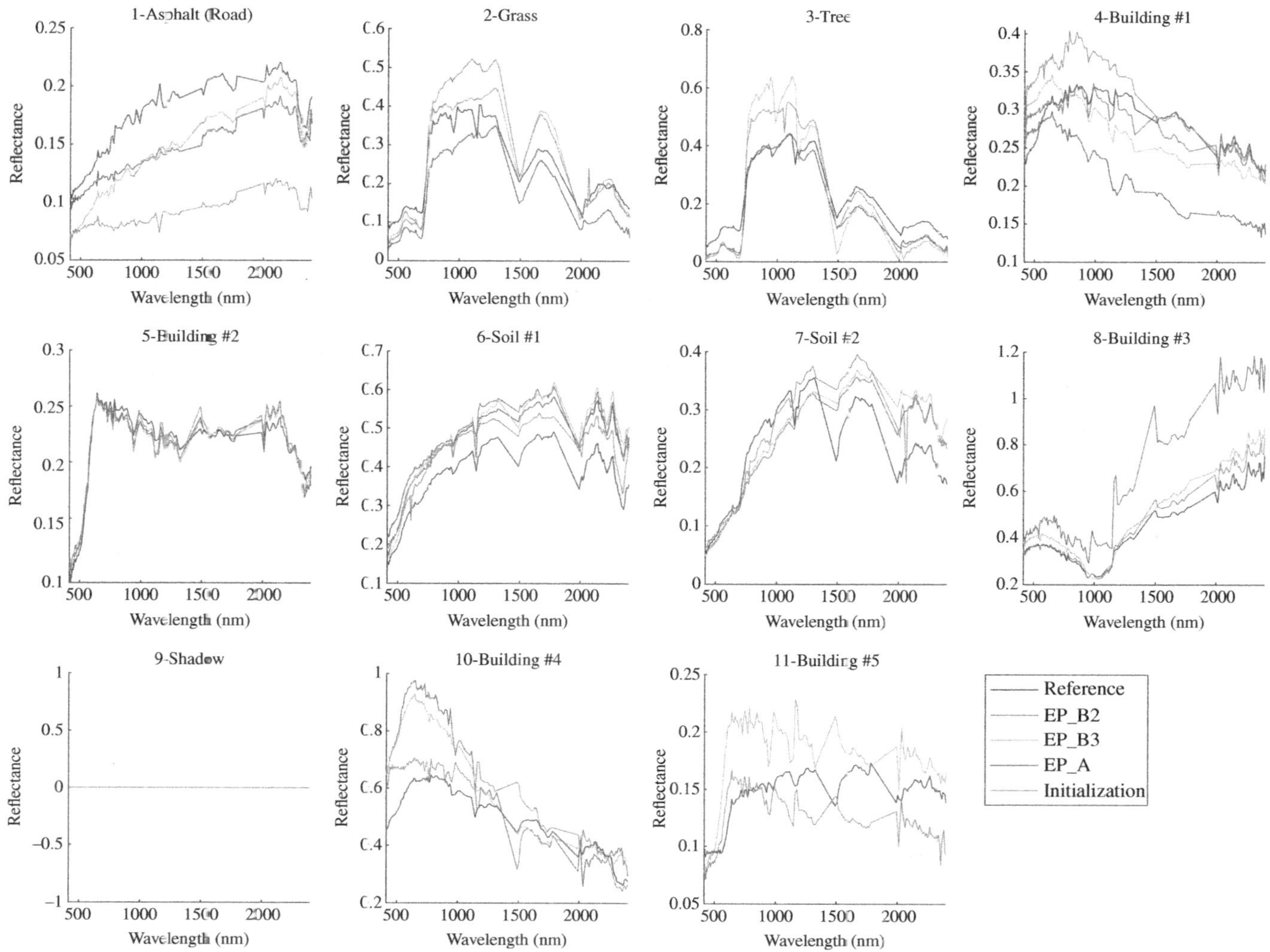

Figure 11.8 The endmembers obtained by the compared algorithms with the HYDICE image.

Table 11.5 The thresholds for different endmembers.

ID	1	2	3	4	5	6	7	8	9	10	11
name	Asphalt	Grass	Tree	Building #1	Building #2	Soil #1	Soil #2	Building #3	Shadow	Building #4	Building #5
t_a	0.3	0.2	0.1	0.2	0.5	0.4	0.3	0.1	—	0.1	0.3

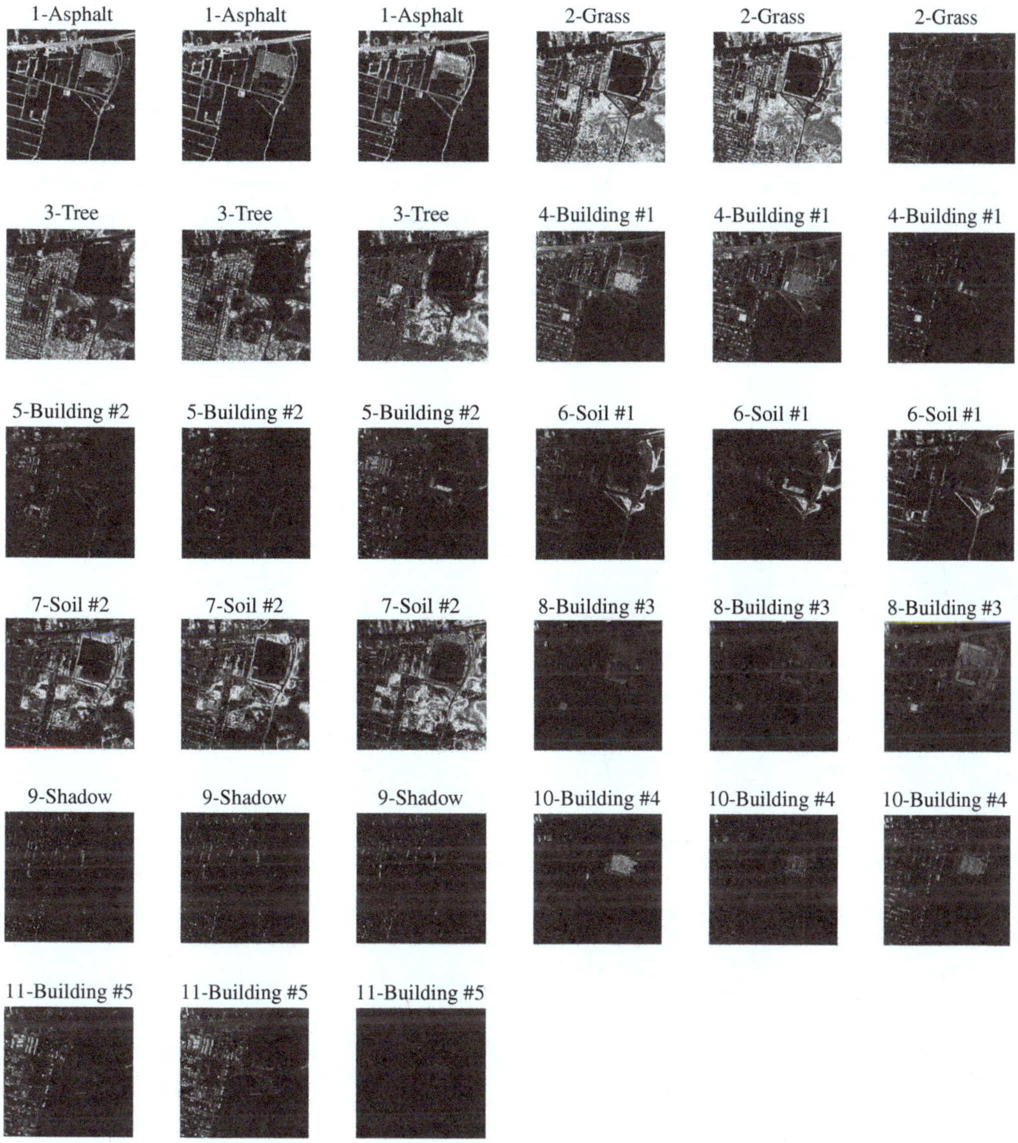

Figure 11.9 The abundance corresponding maps, where the order of the columns is EP_2B, EP_3B, and EP_A.

This means that the percentage of N_c in the window is equal to the mean of the abundance of cover type c in the same window. Considering the registration error, we can calculate the fraction of overlapping region by [29]

$$a_{overlap} = \left(1 - \frac{s_x}{p \times q}\right) \times \left(1 - \frac{s_y}{p \times q}\right) \times 100\%. \tag{11.92}$$

where p is the window size, s_x and s_y are the shift in two directions, and q is the ratio of S_{hps} to S_{pan}. Obviously, $a_{overlap}$ increases as the window size p increases. However, it also leads to coarse comparison. For example, switching the positions of any pair of pixels does not change the value of p_c or $\overline{a}_c$. For this reason, we should have at least 75% proportion of overlap area for the requirement.

We selected five subimages with the size of 50 × 50 to evaluate the quality of the unmixing results. To create the references, we used the high spatial resolution images collected by another Chinese satellite GaoFen-2 (GF-2). The pan band (1 m) and the other bands (4 m) were fused into a 1-m spatial resolution multispectral image. We then generated the classification maps by using active learning and support vector machine (SVM) classifier. These maps were used as the references, see Figure 11.10.

Consider the window size p, we have $S_{hps} = 30$ m and $S_{pan} = 10$ m. Assume that there is at most 0.6 m shift in two directions. Thus, we have 77.44% overlapped area when the window size is 5. Signal to reconstruction error (SRE) [30] and root mean square error (RMSE) scores were used for the evaluation. Table 11.6 lists the scores of the unmixing results.

KGESU received the best scores for these subimages. Figure 11.11 also compares the abundance maps obtained from the first sub-image. We can see that the results of SUnSAL and KGESU are

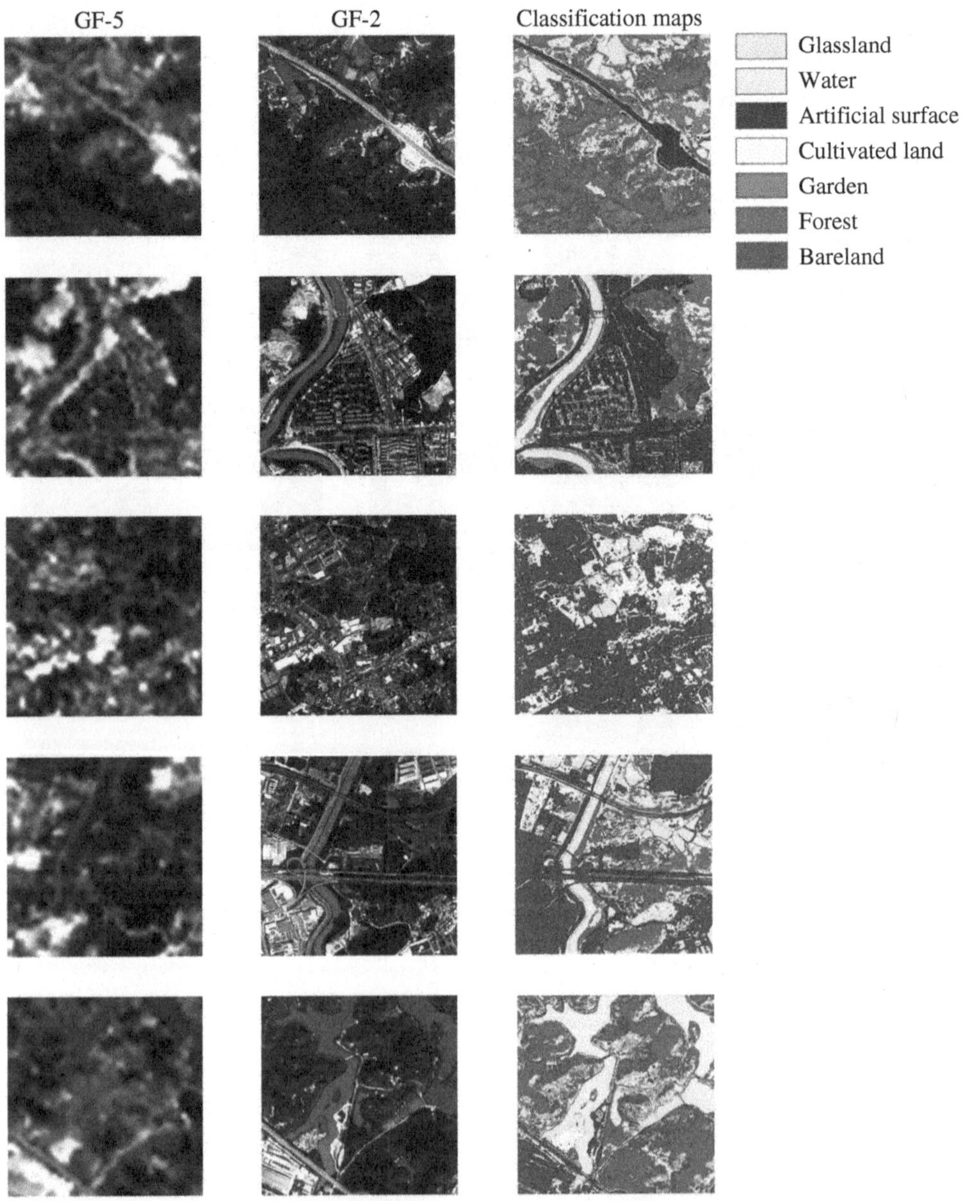

Figure 11.10 The sub-images of GF-5 used for unmixing and the references.

Table 11.6 The SRE and RMSE scores of the compared algorithms.

Sub-image	Scores	Algorithms				
		FCLS	**MEMSA**	**SUnSAL**	**S2WSU**	**KGESU**
1	SRE	1.7491	1.1571	3.0610	1.3550	3.3136
	RMSE	0.1685	0.1876	0.1242	0.1620	0.1083
2	SRE	1.1682	0.1408	3.1512	1.0695	3.2012
	RMSE	0.1749	0.1791	0.1138	0.1999	0.1100
3	SRE	2.7802	3.0059	3.6308	2.2533	3.6865
	RMSE	0.1430	0.1222	0.1052	0.1624	0.1039
4	SRE	1.8147	1.4608	2.3049	1.5017	2.2453
	RMSE	0.1428	0.1492	0.1274	0.1555	0.1236
5	SRE	1.9311	1.8253	2.7193	1.6747	3.0529
	RMSE	0.1674	0.1748	0.1384	0.1440	0.1235

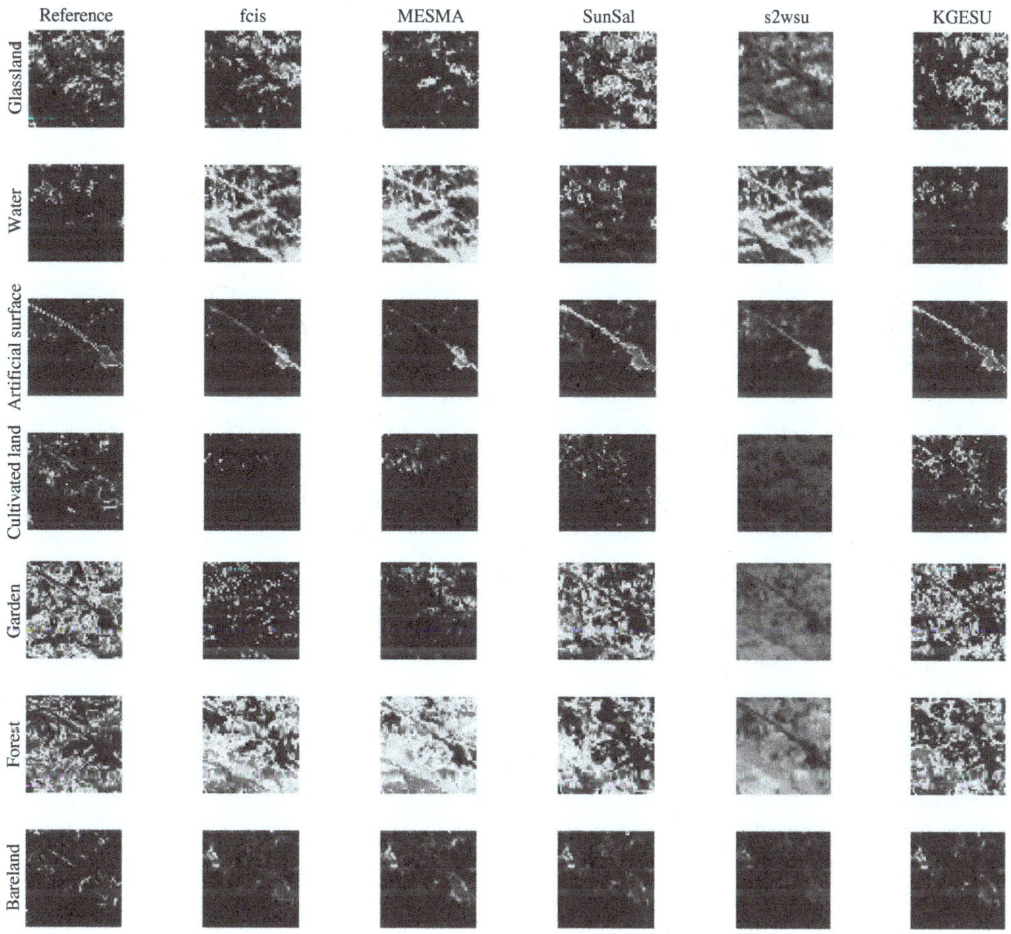

Figure 11.11 The abundance maps obtained by the compared algorithms with the GF-5 image.

closer to the references than others. And KGESU is better than SUnSAL. This means that additional geographic knowledge can help improve the unmixing performance.

11.5 Conclusion

Endmember recovery is a challenging task due to the complexity of the scene. Instead of recovering all endmembers together with the whole image, we present an EP method to recover a single endmember from a subset of the image. Since a lot of unrelated pixels have been removed, the task can be simplified. This chapter also proposes a new framework with three blocks. The performance of the EP algorithm in this framework is better than the traditional BCD algorithm with the same number of blocks. Furthermore, we also introduce geographic knowledge into the spectral unmixing process. From the experiments, we can conclude that the additional knowledge improves the unmixing performance. The combination of KGE and spectral unmixing highlights the future of unmixing with knowledge reasoning. Not only does it improve the performance of unmixing, but it also provides valuable knowledge about the endmembers.

Acknowledgment

This work was supported by the National Natural Science Foundation of China under Grant 40901232.

References

1 Craig, M.D. (1994). Minimum-volume transforms for remotely sensed data. *IEEE Trans. Geosci. Remote Sens.* 32 (3): 542–552. https://doi.org/10.1109/36.297973.

2 Boardman, J.W. (1993). Automated spectral unmixing of AVIRIS data using convex geometry concepts. *Summaries of the 4th Annual JPL Air-borne Geosciences Workshop*, 11–14, Pasadena, October 25–29, 1993.

3 Ma, W. et al. (2014). A signal processing perspective on hyperspectral unmixing: insights from remote sensing. *IEEE Signal Process. Mag.* 31 (1): 67–81. https://doi.org/10.1109/MSP.2013.2279731.

4 Fu, X., Huang, K., Sidiropoulos, N.D., and Ma, W. (2019). Nonnegative matrix factorization for signal and data analytics: identifiability, algorithms, and applications. *IEEE Signal Process. Mag.* 36 (2): 59–80. https://doi.org/10.1109/MSP.2018.2877582.

5 Luo, W.F., Gao, L.R., Hong, D.F. et al. (2022). *IEEE Trans. Geosci. Remote Sens.* 60: 23, 5545423. https://doi.org/10.1109/tgrs.2022.3228231.

6 Laurberg, H. and Hansen, L. K. (2007). On affine non-negative matrix factorization. *32nd IEEE International Conference on Acoustics, Speech and Signal Processing*, 653pp., Honolulu, HI (15–20 April 2007). IEEE.

7 Roberts, D.A., Gardner, M., Church, R. et al. (1998). Mapping chaparral in the Santa Monica Mountains using multiple endmember spectral mixture models. *Remote Sens. Environ.* 65 (3): 267–279. https://doi.org/10.1016/S0034-4257(98)00037-6.

8 Hoyer, P.O. (2004). Non-negative matrix factorization with sparseness constraints (in English). *J. Mach. Learn. Res.* 5: 1457–1469. [Online]. <Go to ISI>://WOS:000236328400003.

9 Iordache, M.-D., Bioucas-Dias, J.M., and Plaza, A. (2011). Sparse unmixing of hyperspectral data. *IEEE Trans. Geosci. Remote Sens.* 49 (6): 2014–2039. https://doi.org/10.1109/tgrs.2010.2098413.

10 Bioucas-Dias, J.M. and Figueiredo, M.A.T. (2010). Alternating direction algorithms for constrained sparse regression: application to hyperspectral unmixing. *2010 2nd Workshop on Hyperspectral Image and Signal Processing: Evolution in Remote Sensing*, 1–4, Reykjavik, Iceland (14–16 June 2010). IEEE. 10.1109/WHISPERS.2010.5594963.

11 Lapotre, M.G.A., Ehlmann, B.L., and Minson, S.E. (2017). A probabilistic approach to remote compositional analysis of planetary surfaces. *J. Geophys. Res. Planets.* 122 (5): 983–1009. https://doi.org/10.1002/2016je005248.

12 Rui, W., Wenfei, L., and Jianghao, C. Knowledge graph embedding spectral unmixing. *Nat. Remote Sens. Bull.* 28: 2073–2088.

13 Steinhardt, J. (2018). Robust learning: information theory and algorithms. Doctor of Philosophy. Department of Computer Science, Stanford University.

14 C. L. Lawson and R. J. Hanson, Solving least squares problems *Classics in Applied Mathematics*, Vol. 15, 350. Society for Industrial and Applied Mathematics, 1995.

15 Heinz, D., Chang, C., and Althouse, M.L.G. (1999). Fully constrained least-squares based linear unmixing [hyperspectral image classification]. *IEEE 1999 International Geoscience and Remote Sensing Symposium. IGARSS'99 (Cat. No.99CH36293)*, vol. 2, 1401–1403, Hamburg, Germany (28 June–2 July 1999). 10.1109/IGARSS.1999.774644.

16 Nascimento, J.M.P. and Dias, J.M.B. (2005). Vertex component analysis: a fast algorithm to unmix hyperspectral data. *IEEE Trans. Geosci. Remote Sens.* 43 (4): 898–910. https://doi.org/10.1109/TGRS.2005.844293.

17 Attouch, H., Bolte, J., Redont, P., and Soubeyran, A. (2010). Proximal alternating minimization and projection methods for nonconvex problems: an approach based on the Kurdyka-Lojasiewicz inequality. *Math. Oper. Res.* 35 (2): 438–457. https://doi.org/10.1287/moor.1100.0449.

18 Hotelling, H. (1943). Further points on matrix calculation and simultaneous equations. *Ann. Math. Stat.* 14 (4): 440–441.

19 Banachiewicz, T. (1937). Zur Berechnung der Determinanten, wie auch der Inversen, und zur daruaf basierten Auflösung der Systeme linearer Gleichungen. *Acta Astron.* 3: 41.

20 Bioucas-Dias, J.M. (2009). A variable splitting augmented Lagrangian approach to linear spectral unmixing. *2009 First Workshop on Hyperspectral Image and Signal Processing: Evolution in Remote Sensing*, 1–4, Grenoble, France (26–28 August 2009). 10.1109/WHISPERS.2009.5289072.

21 Li, J., Bioucas-Dias, J.M., Plaza, A., and Liu, L. (2016). Robust collaborative nonnegative matrix factorization for hyperspectral unmixing. *IEEE Trans. Geosci. Remote Sens.* 54 (10): 6076–6090. https://doi.org/10.1109/TGRS.2016.2580702.

22 Keshava, N. and Mustard, J.F. (2002). Spectral unmixing (in English). *IEEE Signal Process. Mag.* 19 (1): 44–57. https://doi.org/10.1109/79.974727.

23 De'ath, G. and Fabricius, K.E. (2000). Classification and regression trees: a powerful yet simple technique for ecological data analysis (in English). *Ecology* 81 (11): 3178–3192. https://doi.org/10.1890/0012-9658(2000)081[3178:Cartap]2.0.Co;2.

24 Ji, S.X., Pan, S.R., Cambria, E. et al. (2022). A survey on knowledge graphs: representation, acquisition, and applications (in English). *IEEE Trans. Neural Netw. Learn. Syst.* 33 (2): 494–514. https://doi.org/10.1109/tnnls.2021.3070843.

25 Bordes, A., Usunier, N., Garcia-Duran, A. et al. (2013). Translating embeddings for modeling multi-relational data. *Adv. Neural Inf. Proces. Syst.* 26: 2787–2795.

26 Heinz, D.C. and Chein, I.C. (2001). Fully constrained least squares linear spectral mixture analysis method for material quantification in hyperspectral imagery. *IEEE Trans. Geosci. Remote Sens.* 39 (3): 529–545. https://doi.org/10.1109/36.911111.

27 Zhang, S.Q., Li, J., Li, H.C. et al. (2018). Spectral-spatial weighted sparse regression for hyperspectral image unmixing (in English). *IEEE Trans. Geosci. Remote Sens.* 56 (6): 3265–3276. https://doi.org/10.1109/tgrs.2018.2797200.

28 Clark, R.N., Swayze, Gregg A., Wise, Richard A. et al. (2007). USGS digital spectral library splib06a. Data Series. Reston, VA. Report 231. http://pubs.er.usgs.gov/publication/ds231. Accessed date: October 4, 2007.

29 Hou, S.W. et al. (2022). RFSDAF: a new spatiotemporal fusion method robust to registration errors (in English). *IEEE Trans. Geosci. Remote Sens.* 60: 18, 5616018. https://doi.org/10.1109/tgrs.2021.3138078.

30 Bioucas-Dias, J.M. et al. (2012). Hyperspectral unmixing overview: geometrical, statistical, and sparse regression-based approaches. *IEEE J. Sel. Top. Appl. Earth Obs. Remote Sens.* 5 (2): 354–379. https://doi.org/10.1109/JSTARS.2012.2194696.

12

Hyperspectral Unmixing Based on Deep Autoencoder Networks

Yuanchao Su[1], Jun Li[2], Lianru Gao[3], Ruoqing Xu[1], Zhiqing Zhu[1], and Paolo Gamba[4]

[1] *College of Geomatics, Xi'an University of Science and Technology, Xi'an, China*
[2] *School of Computer Science and Hubei Key Laboratory of Intelligent Geo-Information Processing University of Geosciences, Wuhan, China*
[3] *Aerospace Information Research Institute, Chinese Academy of Sciences, Beijing, China*
[4] *Laboratory of Telecommunications and Remote Sensing, Department of Electrical, Computer and Biomedical Engineering, University of Pavia, Pavia, Italy*

12.1 Introduction

The spectral mixing model is the basis for the design of unmixing methods and also serves as a bridge between physical imaging and spectral interpretation [1–4]. Currently, spectral mixing models can be divided into two categories: linear spectral mixture model (LMM) and nonlinear spectral mixture model (NLMM) [5]. The LMM assumes that the signal received by the imaging spectrometer is the direct reflection of the light incident on the object and that a mixed pixel is equivalent to a linear weighted sum of endmember spectra, where the weights correspond to the respective abundances [6–9]. The NLMM is a generic term for a class of models that typically consider complex natural phenomena such as photon–matter interactions and atmospheric scattering in their modeling process [10]. The results obtained are theoretically closer to reality but more complex to model and invert [4]. Therefore, due to its simple structure and good universality, most existing unmixing methods are based on the LSMM [11].

In recent years, deep learning (DL) has substantially impacted the advancement of hyperspectral imaging (HSI) processing, and unmixing is no exception [12–14]. Nowadays, DL techniques have emerged as the dominant approach for processing mixed pixels in hyperspectral remote sensing [15–18]. Among various DL models, autoencoders are particularly popular for developing unmixing methods [19–21]. An autoencoder includes an encoder and a decoder, and it uses its hidden layers to extract high-level features from the data [22–28]. This capability makes autoencoders especially effective for hyperspectral unmixing, where the goal is to derive a low-dimensional representation for abundance estimation [29–32]. However, a common limitation of autoencoder-based unmixing methods is their focus solely on spectral information, often overlooking the spatial relationships between pixels [33–36].

Machine-Learning-Based Hyperspectral Image Processing, First Edition. Edited by Bing Zhang.

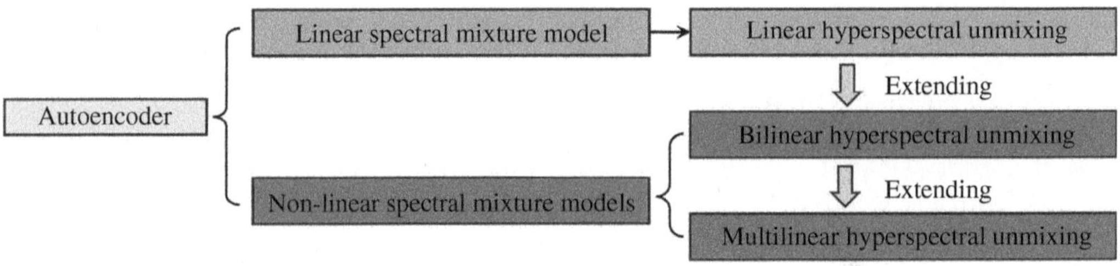

Figure 12.1 Unmixing using autoencoders is different according to the spectral mixture model that is considered.

Recently, convolutional neural networks (CNNs) have been utilized to effectively combine spatial and spectral information in hyperspectral images (HSIs), capitalizing on their ability to capture local pixel correlations [37]. This advantage has led to the development of numerous unmixing methods, some of them jointly considering CNN and autoencoders, such as the CNN-based autoencoder unmixing (CNNAEU), [33] and the 3D CNN Autoencoder network [34]. Other approaches are instead based on CNNs only, such as the minimum simplex convolutional network (MiSiCNet) [38], deep interpretable fully CNN (DIFCNN) [39], Bayesian fully CNN (BCUN) [40], and 3D CNN autoencoder network [34]. Among these, the CNNAEU, MiSiCNet, DIFCNN, and BCUN are built on the LSMM and are unable to address the scattering interactions during unmixing. Most CNN-based methods use 2D convolution kernels, focusing only on spatial information and failing to fully integrate spatial and spectral correlations [34]. For instance, while the 3D CNN Autoencoder Network employs a 3D convolution kernel to better address the spatial–spectral structures of HSIs, it still does not tackle the issues arising from multiple scattering [41].

In this section, we introduce three DL-based unmixing methods that are based on the LSMM, the bilinear mixture model (BMM), and the multilinear mixture model (MLMM). The BMM is an expansion of LSMM, modeling the second-order scattering of photons [42]. The MLMM extends the BMM to include all orders of interactions [43]. Note that these three methods can implement unsupervised unmixing that does not require prior knowledge. Figure 12.1 lists the specific contents for this section, where we classify the different methods and provide their relationships.

12.2 Methodologies

12.2.1 Deep Autoencoder Network for Linear Unmixing

I would include in the following text – in the right position – references to the paper(s) where this approach has been proposed. The DAEN operates in two primary phases. Initially, spectral signatures are extracted using stacked autoencoders (SAEs), which serve to provide optimal initial conditions for the network. Subsequently, a variational autoencoder (VAE) is utilized to estimate the endmembers and their abundances. The VAE framework, which incorporates variational inference with traditional autoencoder structures, allows for unsupervised learning and is compatible with gradient descent (GD) training. Unlike standard autoencoders, VAEs integrate a reparameterization technique that rigorously maintains the constraint that abundance estimates sum to one.

12.2.1.1 Blind Signal Separation (BSS) for Unmixing

Let $\mathbf{Y} = [\mathbf{y}_1, \mathbf{y}_2, ..., \mathbf{y}_n] \in \mathbb{R}^{c\times n}$ be matrix representation of a hyperspectral dataset with n spectral vectors and c spectral bands. Under the LSMM, we have

$$\begin{aligned} &\mathbf{Y} = \mathbf{EA} + \Upsilon \\ &\text{s.t.} \quad \mathbf{A} \geq 0, \quad \mathbf{1}_m^T\mathbf{A} = \mathbf{1}_n^T \end{aligned} \tag{12.1}$$

where $\mathbf{E} = [\mathbf{e}_1, \mathbf{e}_2, ..., \mathbf{e}_m] \in \mathbb{R}^{c\times m}$ is the mixing matrix containing m endmembers, and $\mathbf{A} = [\mathbf{a}_1, \mathbf{a}_2, ..., \mathbf{a}_n] \in \mathbb{R}^{m\times n}$ is the abundance matrix, and $\mathbf{A} \geq 0, 1_m^T\mathbf{A} = 1_n^T$ are the so-called abundance non-negativity and sum to-one constraints, which stem from a physical interpretation of the abundance vectors, and $1_m = [1, 1, ..., 1]^T$ is a column vector of size m. Finally, Υ is the error matrix that may affect the measurement process (e.g., noise).

For a given observation $\mathbf{Y}$, unmixing aims at obtaining the mixing matrix $\mathbf{E}$ and the abundance matrix $\mathbf{A}$. In this study, we tackle the simultaneous estimation of $\mathbf{E}$ and $\mathbf{A}$ by seeking a solution with the following NMF-based optimization:

$$(\mathbf{E}, \mathbf{A}) = \arg\min_{\mathbf{E},\mathbf{A}} \frac{1}{2}\|\mathbf{Y} - \mathbf{EA}\|_F^2 + \mu\, f_1(\mathbf{E}) + \lambda f_2(\mathbf{A}) \tag{12.2}$$

where $\|\cdot\|_F^2$ denotes the Frobenius norm, $f_1(\mathbf{E})$ and $f_2(\mathbf{A})$ are two regularizers on the mixing matrix $\mathbf{E}$ and the abundance fractions $\mathbf{A}$, respectively, with μ and λ being the regularization parameters.

12.2.1.2 SAEs for Initialization

Based on the geometry assumption that endmembers are generally located around the vertices of the data simplex, we use a pure pixel-based method to extract a set of candidate pixels as the training set for the SAEs. Specifically, we adopt VCA to obtain a set of k candidates, with $k > m$. As VCA considers random directions in the subspace projection, we run it for θ times, resulting in ω candidates, with $\omega \cdot = \theta\, k$. These ω candidates are then grouped into m training sets $\{\mathbf{C}_i\}_{i=1}^m$ based on the spectral angle distance (SAD) and clustering, with $\mathbf{L}_i = [\mathbf{I}_1, \mathbf{I}_2, ..., \mathbf{I}_{i_n}] \in \mathbb{R}^{c\times i_n}$ and i_n is the number of samples in $\mathbf{L}_i$. Let $\mathbf{I}_{i_o}$ and $\mathbf{I}_{j_o}$ be the cluster centers of $\mathbf{L}_i$ and $\mathbf{L}_j$, respectively. For any candidate $\mathbf{I}_{i_o}$ in $\mathbf{L}_i$, for $i_s = 1, ..., i_n$, we have $SAD(\mathbf{I}_{i_o}, \mathbf{I}_{i_s}) \leq SAD(\mathbf{I}_{j_o}, \mathbf{I}_{j_s})$, for any $j = 1, ..., m$ and $j \neq i$, where

$$SAD(\mathbf{I}_{i_o}, \mathbf{I}_{i_s}) = arc\cos\left(\frac{[\mathbf{I}_{i_o}, \mathbf{I}_{i_s}]}{\|\mathbf{I}_{i_o}\|\cdot\|\mathbf{I}_{i_s}\|}\right) \tag{12.3}$$

In terms of θ and k, we empirically set $\theta = 30$ and $k = 3$ m, respectively. By enforcing nonnegativity, the training of SAEs minimizes the reconstruction error (RE) as follows:

$$\min \sum_{s=1}^{i_n} \|\mathbf{I}_s - \hat{\mathbf{e}}_i\|_2^2 \tag{12.4}$$

where $\hat{\mathbf{e}}_i$ is the reconstructed signature of the ith endmember, the reconstructed signature is denoted as

$$\hat{\mathbf{e}}_i = \mathbf{M}_i\mathbf{f}\left(\mathbf{M}_i^T\mathbf{L}_i\right) \tag{12.5}$$

where $\mathbf{M}_i$ is the matrix of weights between the input and hidden neurons or those from hidden to output neurons, and $\mathbf{f}(\cdot)$ is activation function given by

$$\mathbf{f}(\mathbf{g}_i) = \frac{1}{1 + \exp(-\boldsymbol{\rho}_i . * \mathbf{g}_i - \boldsymbol{\xi}_i)} \tag{12.6}$$

where $\mathbf{g}_i = \mathbf{M}_i^T \mathbf{L}_i$, ρ_i and ξ_i are the parameters aimed at controlling the information transmission between neurons, and $.^*$ is the dot product, i.e., elementwise operator. Note that the number of input neurons and output neurons is the same as the hidden neurons, while the number of hidden neurons here is set as the number of bands. Then, we can use a gradient rule to update ρ_i and ξ_i as follows:

$$\begin{cases} \Delta\boldsymbol{\rho}_i = \gamma\left(1 - \left(2 + \frac{1}{\tau}\right)\mathbf{f}_i + \frac{1}{\tau}\mathbf{f}_i^2\right) \\ \Delta\boldsymbol{\xi}_i = \gamma\frac{1}{\boldsymbol{\xi}_i} + \mathbf{g}_i\Delta\boldsymbol{\rho}_i \end{cases} \tag{12.7}$$

where γ and τ are hyperparameters in the learning process controlling the mean activity level of the desired output distribution. We set $\gamma = 0.001$ and $\tau = 0.2$. With the aforementioned definition in hand, the learning reduces to the following update rule:

$$\Delta\mathbf{M}_i \Leftarrow \eta\Delta\hat{\mathbf{e}}_i\mathbf{f}_i^T + |\mathbf{M}_i| \tag{12.8}$$

where $\Delta\,\hat{\mathbf{e}}_i$ is the gradient of candidate i for update, $|\mathbf{M}_i|$ enforces the weight matrix to be nonnegative, and η is an adaptive learning rate. We set $\eta = \hat{\eta}\left(\|\mathbf{f}_i\|^2 + \epsilon\right)^{-1}$ with $\hat{\eta} = 0.002$, where $\varepsilon = 0.001$ is a small parameter to ensure the positivity of η.

Let $\hat{\mathbf{e}}_i^t$, $\hat{\mathbf{e}}_i^{t+1}$ be the reconstructions from the tth and $(t+1)$th autoencoders, respectively. The SAEs ends when $\|\hat{\mathbf{e}}_i^{t+1} - \hat{\mathbf{e}}_i^t\|_2^2$ converges. After the endmember matrix $\hat{\mathbf{E}}$ is reconstructed, based on the linear mixing model, the abundances $\hat{\mathbf{A}}$ can be obtained via the fully constrained least square (FCLS). In the learning of the VAE, $\hat{\mathbf{E}}$ and $\hat{\mathbf{A}}$ are used as initializations of $\mathbf{E}$ and $\mathbf{A}$, respectively.

12.2.1.3 VAE for Unmixing

For the first regularizer $f_1(\mathbf{E})$ on the mixing matrix, following, we have

$$f_1(\mathbf{E}) = \text{MinVol}(\mathbf{E}) \tag{12.9}$$

where MinVol($\cdot$) is a function aiming at enclosing all the pixels into the simplex constructed by the endmembers. Specifically, we set $\text{MinVol}(\mathbf{E}) = \|\det(\mathbf{E})\|$, with $\|\det(\mathbf{E})\|$ being the volume defined by the origin and the columns of $\mathbf{E}$.

With respect to regularizer $f_2(\mathbf{A})$ on the abundance matrix, in order to ensure the nonnegativity and sum-to-one constraints, we employ the VAE to penalize the solution of $\mathbf{A}$, denoted as

$$f_2(\mathbf{A}) = VAE(\mathbf{A}) \tag{12.10}$$

where the neurons of all hidden layers are set as the number of endmembers, while the number of inputs and outputs corresponds to the number of pixels.

With these definitions in mind, we obtain the following objective function:

$$(\mathbf{E}, \mathbf{A}) = \arg\min_{\mathbf{E},\mathbf{A}} \frac{1}{2}\|\mathbf{Y} - \mathbf{E}\mathbf{A}\|_F^2 + \mu\ \text{MinVol}(\mathbf{E}) + \lambda VAE(\mathbf{A}) \tag{12.11}$$

In the following, we present the VAE-based regularizer in detail. Let **U** and **V** be the **LV**, we define $f_2(\mathbf{A})$ as

$$f_2(\mathbf{A}(\mathbf{U},\mathbf{V})) = \left\| \frac{1}{2n}\left(\mathbf{1}_{m\times n} + \ln \mathbf{V}^2 - \mathbf{U}^2 - \mathbf{V}^2\right)\mathbf{1}_n \right\|_2^2 \tag{12.12}$$

where $1_{m\times n} \in \mathbb{R}^{m\times n}$ with all elements being 1, and vector $1_n = [1, \dots, 1]^T \in \mathbb{R}^n$, $\mathbf{U} = [\mathbf{u_1}, \dots, \mathbf{u_n}] \in \mathbb{R}^{m\times n}$, $\mathbf{V} = [\mathbf{v_1}, \dots, \mathbf{v_n}] \in \mathbb{R}^{m\times n}$. Let $\mathbf{u_j} = [\mathrm{u}_{1,\,j}, \dots, \mathrm{u}_{m,\,j}]^{\mathrm{T}} \in \mathbb{R}^m$and $\mathbf{v_j} = [\mathrm{v}_{1,\,j}, \dots, \mathrm{v}_{m,\,j}]^{\mathrm{T}} \in \mathbb{R}^m$ be the reparameters of **LV**, we define $h_{i,j} = Cons(u_{i,j}, v_{i,j})$, where $Cons(\cdot)$ represents adecay function as follows:

$$Cons(u_{i,j}, v_{i,j}) = \begin{cases} u_{i,j} + \sigma v_{i,j}, & 0 < (u_{i,j} + \sigma v_{i,j}) < 1 \\ 0, & \text{otherwise,} \end{cases} \tag{12.13}$$

where σ is a parameter can be obtained via Monte Carlo (MC) sampling. In order to meet the abundance sum-to-one constraint, we have

$$h_{m,j} = 1 - \sum_{i=1}^{m-1} a_{i,j} \tag{12.14}$$

We propose an iterative scheme to optimize **E** and **A**, respectively, both of which are solved by a GD method. The first-order derivatives of the objective function are computed as follows:

$$\begin{cases} \nabla_{\mathbf{U}}(\mathbf{E},\mathbf{A}) = d(\mathbf{U}) - \dfrac{2\lambda}{n}\mathbf{z}(\mathbf{1}_n)^T .* \mathbf{U} \\ \nabla_{\mathbf{V}}(\mathbf{E},\mathbf{A}) = d(\mathbf{V}) + \dfrac{2\lambda}{n}\mathbf{z}(\mathbf{1}_n)^T .* (\ln \mathbf{V}./\mathbf{V} - \mathbf{V}) \end{cases} \tag{12.15}$$

where ./ is the dot division, $\mathbf{z} = \dfrac{1}{2n}\left(1_{m\times n} + \ln \mathbf{V}^2 - \mathbf{U}^2 - \mathbf{V}^2\right)1_n$. $d(\mathbf{U})$and $d(\mathbf{V})$ are the gradients of reconstructed errors.

With respect to the updates of **E** and **A**, we employ the GD method for the solutions as follows:

$$\begin{aligned} \mathbf{E} &\Leftarrow \mathbf{E} + \Delta\mathbf{E} \\ \mathbf{A} &\Leftarrow \mathbf{A} + \Delta\mathbf{A} \end{aligned} \tag{12.16}$$

where $\Delta\mathbf{E}$ and $\Delta\mathbf{A}$ are the gradients for **E** and **A**, respectively. Specifically:

1) for **A**,we have

$$\Delta\mathbf{A} = -\varphi(\nabla_{\mathbf{U}}(\mathbf{E},\mathbf{A}) + \sigma\nabla_{\mathbf{V}}(\mathbf{E},\mathbf{A})) \tag{12.17}$$

where φ is the learning rates that can be estimated by the Armijo rule;

2) for **E** we obtain $\Delta\mathbf{E}$ via Adadelta as follows:

$$\Delta\mathbf{E} = -\frac{RMS[\Delta\mathbf{E}]}{RMS[\nabla\mathbf{E}(\mathbf{E},\mathbf{A})]}\nabla_{\mathbf{E}}(\mathbf{E},\mathbf{A}) \tag{12.18}$$

where RMS[·] is the root mean square. The first-order derivatives of the objective function are calculated as

$$\nabla_{\mathbf{E}}(\mathbf{E},\mathbf{A}) = (\mathbf{EA}-\mathbf{Y})\mathbf{A}^T + \mu d(\text{MinVol}(\mathbf{E})) \tag{12.19}$$

where $d(\text{MinVol}(\mathbf{E}))$ is the gradient for the volume function.

12.2.2 Deep Autoencoder Network for Bilinear Unmixing

In this second methodology, autoencoders are collaboratively trained to minimize the discrepancy between original data and their reconstructions. The training process involves two phases: pretraining and fine-tuning. Initially, each autoencoder independently pretrains its layers layer-by-layer. Following this, all factors undergo a fine-tuning phase to optimize performance. Within the multi-task learning (MTL) framework, these autoencoders are assigned to two distinct tasks, each featuring $2\sigma - 1$ hidden layers, mirroring the symmetrical structure of the encoder and decoder. In Task 1, the endmembers are derived from the weight matrices of the decoder, and the central hidden layer, denoted as $\mathbf{A}_o$, represents the abundance matrix. Conversely, Task 2 focuses on estimating interaction outliers from the decoder's final layer, with interaction abundances represented by $\mathbf{B}_o$ in the central hidden layer. For the autoencoder addressing the linear term, the number of nodes in each hidden layer matches the number of endmembers. For the autoencoder that handles the bilinear term, the nodes in each hidden layer equal the number of virtual endmembers. Both autoencoders are designed with input and output nodes corresponding to the total number of pixels in the scene.

12.2.2.1 BMM

Let $\mathbf{Y} \equiv [y_1, y_2, ..., y_n] \in \mathbb{R}^{c\times n}$ be an HSI with n spectral pixels and c spectral bands. In this work, the constraints of the BMM are derived from the Fan model. For an HSI, the matrix form of the BMM is denoted as

$$\begin{aligned} &\mathbf{Y} = \mathbf{EA} + \mathbf{DB} + \Upsilon \\ &\text{s.t. } \mathbf{A} \geq \mathbf{0}, \quad \mathbf{B} \geq \mathbf{0}, \quad \mathbf{1}_m^T\mathbf{A} = \mathbf{1}_n^T \end{aligned} \tag{12.20}$$

where $\mathbf{D} \equiv [\mathbf{d}_1, \mathbf{d}_2, ..., \mathbf{d}_t] \in \mathbb{R}^{c\times t}$ contains t virtual endmembers, and $\mathbf{D} \equiv [\mathbf{b}_1, \mathbf{b}_2, ..., \mathbf{b}_t] \in \mathbb{R}^{t\times n}$ denotes an interaction abundance matrix, with $t = m(m-1)/2$. We assume that a virtual endmember $\mathbf{d}_{(i,j)}$ is initialized by the corresponding endmembers. With these assumptions in mind, we have

$$\mathbf{d}_{(i,j)} = \mathbf{e}_i \odot \mathbf{e}_j \tag{12.21}$$

where $\odot$ is the Hadamard product, $\mathbf{e}_i$ is the i-th endmember signature in $\mathbf{E}$, $\forall i \in \{1, ..., m-1\}$, $j \in \{i+1, ..., m\}$. Let $b_{(i,j),q}$ be an interaction abundance, initialized by

$$b_{(i,j),q} = a_{i,q}a_{j,q} \tag{12.22}$$

where $b_{(i,j),q}$ is an element of $\mathbf{b}_q$ at the q-th column of $\mathbf{B}$, and $a_{i,q}$ and $a_{j,q}$ are the i-th element and the j-th element of the q-th column of $\mathbf{A}$, respectively.

12.2.2.2 Hierarchical BMM

Let $\mathbf{Y}_L \in \mathbb{R}^{c\times n}$ be the linear term with

$$\begin{cases} \mathbf{Y}_L = \mathbf{EA} \\ \mathbf{Y}_N = \mathbf{DB} \end{cases} \tag{12.23}$$

where $\mathbf{Y}_N \in \mathbb{R}^{c\times n}$ be the bilinear term with

Then, we have

$$\begin{cases} \mathbf{Y}_L = \mathbf{E}_1\mathbf{E}_2 \cdots \mathbf{E}_o\mathbf{A}_o \\ \mathbf{Y}_N = \mathbf{D}_1\mathbf{D}_2 \cdots \mathbf{D}_o\mathbf{B}_o \end{cases} \tag{12.24}$$

where o is the number of hidden layers of the encoder or decoder. For the autoencoders used, the structure of the encoder is the same as that of the decoder. In the hierarchy, $\mathbf{E}_1, ..., \mathbf{E}_o$ denote weight matrices between adjacent layers, and $\mathbf{A}_1, ..., \mathbf{A}_o$ represent hidden layers. Similarly, $\mathbf{D}_1, ..., \mathbf{D}_o$ are weight matrices, and $\mathbf{B}_1, ..., \mathbf{B}_o$ represent hidden layers. The hierarchies for the multiple hidden representations are given as:

$$\begin{aligned} &\mathbf{A}_{o-1} \approx \mathbf{E}_o\mathbf{A}_o \\ &\mathbf{A}_2 \approx \mathbf{E}_3 \cdots \mathbf{E}_o\mathbf{A}_o \\ &\mathbf{A}_1 \approx \mathbf{E}_2 \cdots \mathbf{E}_o\mathbf{A}_o \end{aligned} \tag{12.25}$$

and

$$\begin{aligned} &\mathbf{B}_{o-1} \approx \mathbf{D}_o\mathbf{B}_o \\ &\mathbf{B}_2 \approx \mathbf{D}_3 \cdots \mathbf{D}_o\mathbf{B}_o \\ &\mathbf{B}_1 \approx \mathbf{D}_2 \cdots \mathbf{D}_o\mathbf{B}_o \end{aligned} \tag{12.26}$$

For the linear term, $\mathbf{Y}_L$ is first decomposed into $\mathbf{E}_1$ and $\mathbf{A}_1, \mathbf{Y}_L \approx \mathbf{E}_1\mathbf{A}_1$, and the hidden layers are then decomposed one-by-one, $\mathbf{A}_q \approx \mathbf{E}_{q+1}\mathbf{A}_{q+1}$, $\mathbf{A}_q \in \mathbb{R}^{m \times n}$, $q = 2, ..., o-1$. In the same way, the bilinear term is expressed as $\mathbf{Y}_N \approx \mathbf{D}_1\mathbf{B}_1$, $\mathbf{B}_q \approx \mathbf{D}_{q+1}\mathbf{B}_{q+1}$, $\mathbf{B}_q \in \mathbb{R}^{t \times n}$. For the linear components, **E** and **A** are given by the following mathematical formulations:

$$\begin{aligned} &\mathbf{E} = \mathbf{E}_1 \cdots \mathbf{E}_{o-1}\mathbf{E}_o, \\ &\mathbf{A} = \mathbf{A}_o \end{aligned} \tag{12.27}$$

In the same way as the bilinear components, **D** and **B** are given as follows:

$$\begin{aligned} &\mathbf{D} = \mathbf{D}_1 \cdots \mathbf{D}_{o-1}\mathbf{D}_o, \\ &\mathbf{B} = \mathbf{B}_o \end{aligned} \tag{12.28}$$

shows the structure of the MTL. In the framework, the two autoencoders correspond to two tasks, and each autoencoder has 2_{o-1} hidden layers, because the encoder and the decoder have the same structure, as illustrated in Figure 12.2. In Task 1, the endmembers are obtained from weight matrices of the decoder, and the abundance matrix corresponds to $\mathbf{A}_o$ in the middle hidden layer. While in Task 2, interaction outliers are estimated from the last layer of the decoder, and the interaction abundances correspond to $\mathbf{B}_o$ in the middle hidden layer. For the autoencoder of the corresponding linear term, the number of nodes in each hidden layer is set to the number of endmembers. For the autoencoder of the corresponding bilinear term, the number of nodes in each hidden layer amounts to the number of virtual endmembers. The number of input and output nodes of the two autoencoders is equal to the number of pixels in the scene.

12.2.2.3 Task 1 for Estimating Linear Components

Task 1 is used for estimating the endmember signatures and the abundance fractions, and the objective function of the subproblem is written as

$$\mathcal{C}_{Task1} = \frac{1}{2}\left(\|\mathbf{Y} - \mathbf{E}_1\mathbf{E}_2 \cdots \mathbf{E}_o\mathbf{A}_o - \mathbf{DB}\|_F^2 + \mu\Re(\mathbf{A}_k)\right), \tag{12.29}$$

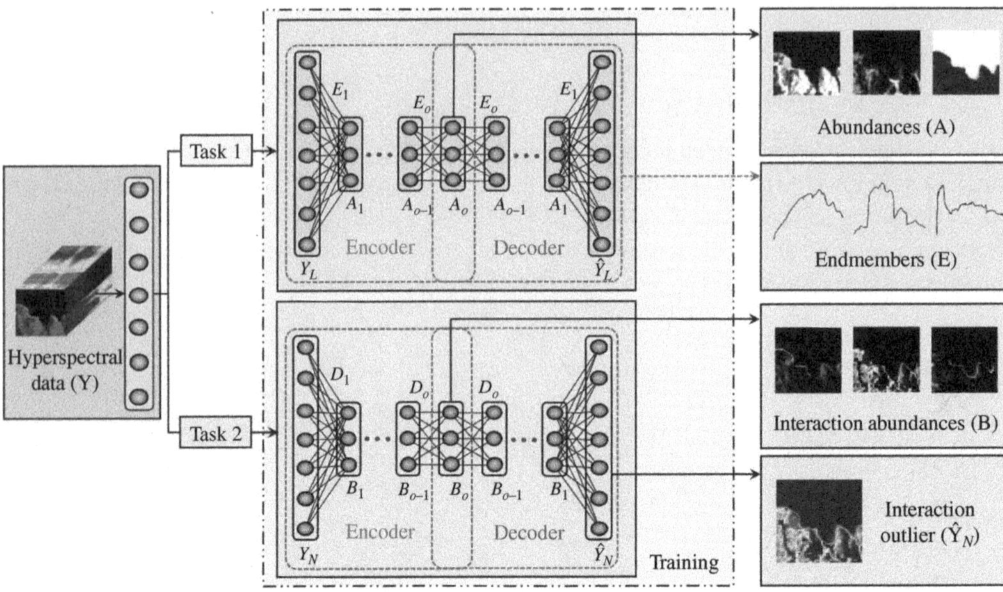

Figure 12.2 Flowchart of the proposed method. Task 1 is used for updating the linear components, estimating the endmember signatures **E** and abundance fractions **A**. Task 2 responds to the bilinear components, obtaining the interaction abundances **B** and the interaction outliers $\hat{Y}_N$.

where μ is the regularization coefficient of Task 1. For this task, **D** and **B** are regarded as the constant matrices. With respect to $\mathbf{A}_k$, each of its rows corresponds to a node of the k-th hidden layer. Note that, although $\mathbf{A}_k$ is related to abundances, it is not directly equivalent to abundance fractions. Where $\Re(\mathbf{A}_k) = Tr\left(\mathbf{A}_k\mathbf{L}\mathbf{A}_k^{\mathrm{T}}\right)$ controls the smoothness of $\mathbf{A}_k$, where $\mathrm{Tr}(\cdot)$ denotes the trace norm. Here, $\mathbf{L} = \mathbf{X} - \mathbf{W}$ is a diagonal matrix, in which each diagonal element is the column sum of $\mathbf{W}$. In this autoencoder, all hidden layers share $\mathbf{L}$ and the nodes associated with the abundances. The graph connection is denoted as:

$$w_{ph} = \begin{cases} \exp\left(-\dfrac{\left\|\mathbf{y}_p - \mathbf{y}_h\right\|^2}{2\sigma^2}\right), & \text{if } p \neq h \\ 0, & \text{otherwise} \end{cases} \tag{12.30}$$

where $\mathbf{y}_p$ and $\mathbf{y}_h$ are vectors of $\mathbf{Y}$, $\forall p \in \{1, ..., n-1\}$, $h \in \{p+1, ..., n\}$. The parameter σ can be estimated from a conjugate inverse Gamma distribution. The generation of $\mathbf{W}$ is defined as follows:

$$\mathbf{W} = \begin{bmatrix} 0 & w_{12} & \cdots & w_{1n} \\ w_{21} & 0 & \cdots & w_{2n} \\ \vdots & \vdots & \ddots & \vdots \\ w_{n1} & w_{n2} & \cdots & 0 \end{bmatrix} \tag{12.31}$$

Summing up w_{ph} in each row of $\mathbf{W}$, the diagonal matrix $\mathbf{X}$ is obtained as

$$\mathbf{X} = \begin{bmatrix} w_{12} + \cdots w_{1n} & 0 & \cdots & 0 \\ 0 & w_{21} + \cdots w_{2n} & \cdots & 0 \\ \vdots & \vdots & \ddots & \vdots \\ 0 & 0 & \cdots & w_{n1} + \cdots w_{n(n-1)} \end{bmatrix} \tag{12.32}$$

To meet the ASC and accelerate convergence, we use the multiplicative update rule (MUR) to obtain $\mathbf{E}_1$ and $\mathbf{A}_1$.

$$\begin{aligned} \mathbf{E}_1 &\leftarrow \mathbf{E}_1 \odot \left(\mathbf{Y}\mathbf{A}_1^T\right) \cdot / \left(\mathbf{E}_1\mathbf{A}_1\mathbf{A}_1^T\right) \\ \mathbf{A}_1 &\leftarrow \mathbf{A}_1 \odot \left(\widetilde{\mathbf{A}}_1^{\;T}\widetilde{\mathbf{Y}}\right) \cdot / \left(\widetilde{\mathbf{E}}^T\widetilde{\mathbf{E}}\mathbf{A}_1\right) \end{aligned} \tag{12.33}$$

where $\tilde{\mathbf{Y}}$ and $\widetilde{\mathbf{A}}_1$ are the augmented matrices for satisfying the ASC constraint. As a result, we have

$$\tilde{\mathbf{Y}} = \begin{bmatrix} \mathbf{Y} \\ \delta\mathbf{1} \end{bmatrix}, \quad \tilde{\mathbf{A}}_1 = \begin{bmatrix} \mathbf{A}_1 \\ \delta\mathbf{1} \end{bmatrix} \tag{12.34}$$

where δ is able to control the impact of the ASC constraint. For the deep autoencoder, δ can affect $\mathbf{A}_1$, and then it can also affect $\mathbf{A}_k$, because $\mathbf{A}_1$ is associated with $\mathbf{A}_k$. After evaluating the performance of our algorithm with different values of δ, with respect to other weights and hidden layers, GD is employed to implement the optimization. The first-order partial derivatives of $\mathcal{C}_{Task1}$ with respect to $\mathbf{A}_k$ are defined as

$$\nabla_{\mathbf{A}_k}\mathcal{C}_{Task\,1} = \mathbf{E}_k^T\mathbf{\Psi}^T(\mathbf{\Psi}\mathbf{E}_k\mathbf{A}_k - \mathbf{Y}) + \mu\mathbf{A}_k\mathbf{L} \tag{12.35}$$

where Ψ is defined as $\Psi = \mathbf{E}_1\mathbf{E}_2 \ldots \mathbf{E}_{k-1}$. Similarly, we have the partial derivative of $\mathcal{C}_{Task1}$ for $\mathbf{E}_k$

$$\nabla_{\mathbf{E}_k}\mathcal{C}_{Task\,1} = \mathbf{\Psi}^T\left(\mathbf{\Psi}\mathbf{E}_k\tilde{\mathbf{A}}_k - \mathbf{Y}\right)\tilde{\mathbf{A}}_k^T \tag{12.36}$$

where $\tilde{\mathbf{A}}_k$ is a reconstruction, $\tilde{\mathbf{A}}_k = \mathbf{E}_{k+1} \ldots \mathbf{E}_o$. Afterward, $\mathbf{E}_k$ and $\mathbf{A}_k$ are updated via the GD. Considering the ANC, we add the rectified linear unit ReLU activation to the k-th hidden layer

$$\begin{aligned} \mathbf{A}_k &\leftarrow \mathrm{ReLU}(\mathbf{A}_k - \eta_A\nabla_{\mathbf{A}_k}\mathcal{C}_{Task1}) \\ \mathbf{E}_k &\leftarrow \mathbf{E}_k - \eta_E\nabla_{\mathbf{E}_k}\mathcal{C}_{Task1} \end{aligned} \tag{12.37}$$

where $\mathrm{ReLU}(\cdot) = \max(\cdot, 0)$, the corresponding learning rates η_E and η_A are estimated by Armijo rule [44]. Finally, we obtain the abundances $\mathbf{A}$ and endmembers $\mathbf{E}$ as follows:

$$\begin{aligned} \mathbf{A} &= \mathbf{A}_o \\ \mathbf{E} &= \mathbf{E}_1 \cdots \mathbf{E}_{o-1}\mathbf{E}_o \end{aligned} \tag{12.38}$$

12.2.2.4 Task 2 for Estimating Bilinear Components

Task 2 is focused on estimating the bilinear components, specifically the interactions between abundance fractions and outliers. In HSI, scattering interactions primarily occur at the boundaries and mixing regions between materials. Consequently, compared to material distributions, these scattering interactions typically exhibit a low-rank property. The objective function for this subproblem is defined as follows:

$$\mathcal{C}_{Task\,2} = \frac{1}{2}\left(\|\mathbf{Y} - \mathbf{E}\mathbf{A} - \mathbf{D}_1\mathbf{D}_2 \cdots \mathbf{D}_o\mathbf{B}_o\|_F^2 + \upsilon\|\mathbf{B}_o\|_*\right) \tag{12.39}$$

where $\|\mathbf{B}_o\|_* = Tr\left(\sqrt{\mathbf{B}_o^T\mathbf{B}_o}\right)$ is used to impose low rank, $\|\cdot\|_*$denotes the nuclear norm, and v is the regularization coefficient. We adopt it to update $\mathbf{B}_r \in \mathbb{R}^{t\times n}$:

$$\mathbf{B}_r \leftarrow \mathbf{B}_r \odot \sqrt{\frac{[\mathbf{\Phi}^T(\mathbf{Y}-\mathbf{EA})]^+ + [\mathbf{\Phi}^T\mathbf{\Phi}]^-\mathbf{B}_r}{[\mathbf{\Phi}^T(\mathbf{Y}-\mathbf{EA})]^- + [\mathbf{\Phi}^T\mathbf{\Phi}]^+\mathbf{B}_r}} \tag{12.40}$$

where $\mathbf{\Phi} = \mathbf{D}_1\mathbf{D}_2...\mathbf{D}_{r-1}$, $r = 1, ..., o-1$, $[\cdot]^+$ and $[\cdot]^-$are the positive and negative parts of the matrix, respectively. The update rule of $\mathbf{D}_r \in \mathbb{R}^{t\times t}$ is denoted as:

$$\mathbf{D}_r \leftarrow \mathbf{D}_r \odot (\mathbf{\Phi}^T(\mathbf{Y}-\mathbf{EA})\mathbf{B}_r^T)./(\mathbf{\Phi}^T\mathbf{\Phi}\mathbf{D}_r\mathbf{B}_r\mathbf{B}_r^T) \tag{12.41}$$

In Task 2, the m-th hidden layer needs a constraint to ensure a low rank and nonnegative attribute on interaction abundances,; thus, we first set $\mathbf{D}_o = \mathbf{D}_{o-1}$ and $\mathbf{B}_o = \mathbf{B}_{o-1}$ to provide the initial values for $\mathbf{D}_o$ and $\mathbf{B}_o$. We adopt the following rule to update $\mathbf{B}_o$:

$$\mathbf{B}_o \leftarrow sgn(\tilde{\mathbf{B}}_o) \odot \text{ReLU}\left(\tilde{\mathbf{B}}_o - \Lambda_{\tilde{B}}\right) \tag{12.42}$$

where $sgn(\cdot)$ represents the sign function, and the threshold is given as $\Lambda_{\tilde{B}} = \lambda./\left(|\tilde{\mathbf{B}}_o| + \lambda\right)$ with $\lambda = 0.001$. The hyperparameter λ avoids that the denominator is a zero matrix.

$$\tilde{\mathbf{B}}_o = \mathbf{U}\ \ diag(\tilde{\mathbf{S}})\ \ \mathbf{V}^T \tag{12.43}$$

where $\mathbf{U},\mathbf{S},\mathbf{V}$ are obtained by a singular value decomposition (SVD) of $\mathbf{B}_o$, i.e., $[\mathbf{U}, \mathbf{S}, \mathbf{V}] = SVD(\mathbf{B}_o)$ and $\hat{\mathbf{S}} = \max(|diag(\mathbf{S})| - \Lambda_S, \mathbf{0})$, with$\Lambda_S = \lambda./(|diag(\mathbf{S})| + \lambda)$. Let $\mathbf{D} = \mathbf{D}_1...\mathbf{D}_{o-1}\mathbf{D}_o$. Then, we obtain the interaction abundances and interaction outliers as follows:

$$\begin{aligned} &\mathbf{B} = \mathbf{B}_o \\ &\hat{\mathbf{Y}}_N = \mathbf{DB} \end{aligned} \tag{12.44}$$

12.2.2.5 Implementation Details

We provide the implementation details for our algorithm. First and foremost, we emphasize that we assume the number of endmembers to be known in advance. In Task 1, $\mathbf{E}_1$ is obtained by running a pure pixel-based unmixing algorithm (e.g., VCA). Meanwhile, $\mathbf{A}_1$ is obtained by using the FCLS. Afterward, $\mathbf{E}_k$ and $\mathbf{A}_k$ are initialized by using the same strategy. With respect to Task 2, the weights and hidden layers are initialized by using the corresponding factors resulting from Task 1. More specifically, the initialization of $\mathbf{d}_{(i,j),\,1}$ is calculated by $\mathbf{d}_{(i,j),\,1} = \mathbf{e}_{i,\,1} \odot \mathbf{e}_{j,1}$, where $\mathbf{e}_{i,1}$ and $\mathbf{e}_{j,1}$ are two column vectors in $\mathbf{E}_1$, $\forall i \in \{1, ..., m-1\}$, $\quad j \in \{i+1, ..., m\}$. Then, $\mathbf{D}_1$ is composed of $\mathbf{d}_{(i,j),\,1}$. Here, we assume that $b_{(i,\,j),q,1}$ is an element of the q-th column of $\mathbf{B}_1$, $b_{(i,\,j),\,q,1} = a_{i,q,\,1}a_{j,q,1}$, where $a_{i,q,1}$ and $a_{j,q,1}$ are the i-th element and the j-th element of the q-th column of $\mathbf{A}_1$, respectively. Afterward, $\mathbf{B}_1$ is composed by $b_{(i,\,j),q,1}$. The weights and nodes of other layers are then initialized using this same strategy. Finally, the fine-tuning of each layer is performed until the RE achieves convergence.

12.2.3 Deep Autoencoder Network for Multilinear Unmixing

In the DAAN (deep autoencoder analysis network) framework, we deploy two encoders to specifically address linear mixtures and multiple scattering phenomena, respectively. Encoder 1 targets the linear components, utilizing 3-D convolutional layers to harness the spatial–spectral structure of HSI and capture local correlations. Additionally, a Gaussian constraint is applied within Encoder

1 to smooth the estimated abundances, particularly for homogeneous pixels. Encoder 2 is dedicated to assessing the effects of multiple scattering through a hierarchical representation. In the DAAN's decoder, a Softmax layer is incorporated to ensure adherence to abundance non-negativity constraint (ANC) and abundance sum constraint (ASC). We further enhance the network's resilience to noise and robustness in low-quality scenarios by integrating $L_{1/2}$ regularization. The network parameters are refined through backward gradient propagation during the learning process. Ultimately, the resulting endmembers and abundances, free from the influence of scattering interactions, are the final products of the unmixing process.

12.2.3.1 Multilinear Mixture Model

The multilinear mixture model (MLMM) is enriched by bilateral mixing models (BMMs) and broadens the interaction framework to encompass all orders, effectively modeling multiple scattering phenomena in imaging. This model operates on the principles of a discrete Markov chain, representing the reflection process and positing that incoming light rays from a source will invariably interact with at least one material. Subsequent to each interaction with an endmember, there is a transition probability p that the photon will undergo further interactions, and a complementary probability $(1-p)$ that it will escape the scenario and be captured by the sensors. The likelihood of a photon interacting with the m-th endmember is proportional to its abundance fraction. As the photon scatters, the light intensity is modified according to the albedo of the material encountered. When the distinctions between the albedo and the endmember spectrum are minimal, the albedo is approximated to be equivalent to the endmember spectrum. The MLMM is formulated as follows:

$$\begin{aligned}\mathbf{y} &= (1-p)\sum_{k=1}^{m} \mathbf{e}_k a_k + (1-p)p\sum_{k=1}^{m}\sum_{j=1}^{m}(\mathbf{e}_k \odot \mathbf{e}_j)a_k a_j \\ &+ (1-p)p^2\sum_{k=1}^{m}\sum_{j=1}^{m}\sum_{i=1}^{m}(\mathbf{e}_k \odot \mathbf{e}_j \odot \mathbf{e}_i)a_k a_j a_i + \ldots\end{aligned} \tag{12.45}$$

where p is regarded as the scattering parameter. If we neglect noise, the above formula can be simplified as

$$\mathbf{y} = \frac{(1-p)\sum_{k=1}^{m} a_k \mathbf{e}_k}{1-p\sum_{k=1}^{m} a_k \mathbf{e}_k} \tag{12.46}$$

where a_k represents the proportion of the endmember $\mathbf{e}_k$ in the pixel.

12.2.3.2 Encoder 1 for Linear Mixture Component

Encoder 1 stacks three 3-D convolutional layers. The first layer adopts a $3 \times 3 \times 6$ convolutional kernel. The second and third layers use the same $3 \times 3 \times 4$ convolutional kernel, while the fourth layer adopts a $1 \times 1 \times 3$ convolutional kernel. The first three 3-D convolutional layers are employed to explore local correlations from spatial–spectral information in an HSI, while the last convolutional layer is utilized to reduce information redundantly and reshape the size of abundances. Moreover, we adopt the ReLU as the activation to avoid negative values in training. Moreover, we adopt the Gaussian constraint to ensure the smoothness of abundances, considering that homogeneous pixels tend to be distributed in adjacent regions in an HSI. Let $\mathbf{g}^{(r)}$ be the Gaussian weights between the central pixel and the adjacent pixels, which can be expressed as

$$\mathbf{g} \Leftarrow g_r = e^{-\frac{\left\|\mathbf{a}_{ce} - \mathbf{a}_{ad}^{(r)}\right\|^2}{2\sigma^2}}, \quad \forall\left\{\mathbf{a}_{ce}, \mathbf{a}_{ad}^{(r)}\right\} \in \mathbf{K}^{(4)} \tag{12.47}$$

where $r = 1, 2, \ldots q$ is the number of adjacent pixels, $\mathbf{a}_{ce}$ is the central pixel, $\mathbf{a}_{ad}^{(r)}$ is the r-th adjacent pixel, and $\mathbf{K}^{(4)} \in \mathbb{R}^{c\times n}$ denotes the spatial–spectral features by the fourth 3-D convolutional layer. We assume that $\mathbf{d}$ is the weight of adjacent pixels, and it can be written as

$$\mathbf{d} = \sum_{r=0}^{q} \mathbf{g}^{(r)}\mathbf{a}_{ad}^{(r)} \tag{12.48}$$

Let $s^{(t)}$ denote the difference weight between the central and the adjacent pixels, which can be expressed as

$$s^{(t)} = \left\|\mathbf{a}_{ce}^{(t)} - \mathbf{d}^{(t)}\right\|_F^2 \tag{12.49}$$

where $\mathbf{a}_{ce}^{(t)}$ is the abundance of the t-th central pixel, $\mathbf{d}^{(t)}$ is the t-th weighted adjacent pixels, $t = 1, 2, \ldots, n$. The difference weight $s^{(t)}$ will be updated with the implementation of DAAN. A diagonal matrix $\mathbf{S} \in \mathbb{R}^{n\times n}$ is composed of $s^{(t)}$, which can enhance the smoothness of abundances, and the regularization can be written as

$$\mathbf{B} = \mathbf{K}^{(4)}\mathbf{S} \tag{12.50}$$

where $\mathbf{B} \in \mathbb{R}^{m\times n}$ is a latent feature matrix, and $\mathbf{K}^{(4)}$ is the feature matrix output from the fourth 3-D convolutional layer. The matrix $\mathbf{S}$ is then multiplied by the feature matrix output from the fourth 3-D convolutional layer to obtain smooth latent features for the subsequent process.

12.2.3.3 Encoder 2 for Multilinear Interaction Component

Encoder 2 hierarchically implements the MLMM to handle elaborate scattering interactions. The matrix expression of the MLMM can be written as

$$\mathbf{Y} = \left((\mathbf{I}-\mathbf{P})(\mathbf{EA})^T\right)^T \Big/ \left(\mathbf{\Phi} - \left(\mathbf{P}(\mathbf{EA})^T\right)^T\right) \tag{12.51}$$

where $\mathbf{I} \in \mathbb{R}^{n\times n}$ is an identity matrix, $\mathbf{P} \in \mathbb{R}^{n\times n}$ represents a diagonal matrix that contains n scattering parameters, and $\mathbf{\Phi} \in \mathbb{R}^{c\times n}$ represents a matrix of all ones. Since $\mathbf{P}$ is a diagonal matrix, the above formula can be rewritten as

$$\begin{aligned}\mathbf{Y} &= \mathbf{EA}(\mathbf{I}-\mathbf{P})/(\mathbf{\Phi} - \mathbf{EAP}) \\ &= \frac{\mathbf{EA} - \mathbf{EAP}}{\mathbf{\Phi} - \mathbf{EAP}}\end{aligned} \tag{12.52}$$

The hierarchical expression of Eq. (12.52) can be written as

$$\mathbf{Y} = \frac{\mathbf{EA}_1\mathbf{A}_2\cdots\mathbf{A}_h - \mathbf{EA}_1\mathbf{A}_2\cdots\mathbf{A}_h\mathbf{P}_h}{\mathbf{\Phi} - \mathbf{EA}_1\mathbf{A}_2\cdots\mathbf{A}_h\mathbf{P}_h} \tag{12.53}$$

where $\mathbf{A}_1\mathbf{A}_2...\mathbf{A}_h$ are hierarchical expressions of abundances, $\mathbf{A}_1 \in \mathbb{R}^{m\times n}$, and $\mathbf{A}_2\mathbf{A}_3, ..., \mathbf{A}_h \in \mathbb{R}^{n\times n}$. In Encoder 2, scattering parameters can be hierarchically estimated by hidden layers, and the procedure can be approximated as

$$\begin{aligned} &\mathbf{P}_{h-1} \approx \mathbf{A}_h\mathbf{P}_h \\ &\quad\vdots \\ &\mathbf{P}_2 \approx \mathbf{A}_3\cdots\mathbf{A}_h\mathbf{P}_h \\ &\mathbf{P}_1 \approx \mathbf{A}_2\cdots\mathbf{A}_h\mathbf{P}_h \end{aligned} \tag{12.54}$$

where $\mathbf{P}_1\mathbf{P}_2\cdots\mathbf{P}_h$ are the hidden layers in the block. The abundance and the scattering parameter matrices can be obtained by the following scheme:

$$\begin{aligned} &\mathbf{A} = \mathbf{A}_1\mathbf{A}_2\cdots\mathbf{A}_h \\ &\mathbf{P} = \mathbf{P}_h \end{aligned} \tag{12.55}$$

12.2.3.4 Loss Function

The proposed DAAN considers the smoothness of abundances and the impact of multiple scattering. Therefore, the optimization can be formalized as

$$\begin{aligned} \psi_{\mathbf{A},\mathbf{P}} &= \alpha_1 \\ &\left(\arg\min_{\mathbf{A}} \frac{1}{2}\left(\left\|\mathbf{Y} - \frac{\mathbf{E}\mathbf{A}_1\mathbf{A}_2\cdots\mathbf{A}_h - \mathbf{E}\mathbf{A}_1\mathbf{A}_2\cdots\mathbf{A}_h\mathbf{P}_h}{\mathbf{\Phi} - \mathbf{E}\mathbf{A}_1\mathbf{A}_2\cdots\mathbf{A}_h\mathbf{P}_h}\right\|\right)\right) \\ &+ \lambda f(\mathbf{A}) + \alpha_2\left(\arg\min_{\mathbf{P}} \frac{1}{2}\left(\left\|\mathbf{Y} - \frac{\mathbf{E}\mathbf{A} - \mathbf{E}\mathbf{A}\mathbf{P}_h}{\mathbf{\Phi} - \mathbf{E}\mathbf{A}\mathbf{P}_h}\right\|\right)\right) \end{aligned} \tag{12.56}$$

where α_1, α_2, and λ are regularization coefficients, and $f(\mathbf{A})$ is the $L_{1/2}$ regularization. In Eq. (12.56), α_1 and α_2 are associated with two sub-optimizations concerning the linear mixture component and multilinear interaction component, respectively. The $L_{1/2}$ regularization is adopted to enhance the performance of abundance estimation

$$f(\mathbf{A}) = \left(\sum_{k=1}^{m}\sum_{u=1}^{n} |a_{ku}|^{1/2}\right)^2 \tag{12.57}$$

where a_{ku} is an abundance fraction. We adopt the SAD as a complement to measure information loss in the training

$$\Gamma_{SAD} = \frac{1}{n}\sum_{u=1}^{n} \arccos\left(\frac{\mathbf{y}_u\hat{\mathbf{y}}_u}{\|\mathbf{y}_u\|_2\|\hat{\mathbf{y}}_u\|_2}\right) \tag{12.58}$$

The loss function of DAAN is expressed as

$$\Gamma = \psi_{\mathbf{A},\mathbf{P}} + \Gamma_{SAD} \tag{12.59}$$

12.2.4 Decoder for BSS

In the decoder, we employ the Softmax function to ensure ANC and ASC.

$$\mathbf{A}_1 \Leftarrow \text{Softmax}(\mathbf{B}) \tag{12.60}$$

where **B** is obtained from the fourth convolutional layer. The decoder adopts Adam as the optimizer to implement GD to update endmembers, hierarchical expressions, and scattering parameters. Let $\mathbf{G}_{(\varphi)}$ be the gradient of **E**. Following [31], the biased first and second moments in φ-th iteration can be updated as

$$\begin{cases} \boldsymbol{\Theta}_{(\varphi)} = \boldsymbol{\beta}_1 \boldsymbol{\Theta}_{(\varphi-1)} + (1-\beta_1)\mathbf{G}_{(\varphi)} \\ \boldsymbol{\Psi}_{(\varphi)} = \boldsymbol{\beta}_2 \boldsymbol{\Psi}_{(\varphi-1)} + (1-\beta_2)\mathbf{G}_{(\varphi)} \odot \mathbf{G}_{(\varphi)} \end{cases} \tag{12.61}$$

where $\boldsymbol{\Theta}_{(\varphi)}$ and $\boldsymbol{\Psi}_{(\varphi)}$ are the biased first and second moments, respectively. In (2.3.17), β_1 and β_2 are the exponential decay rates.

The bias corrections can be expressed as

$$\begin{cases} \hat{\boldsymbol{\Theta}}_{(\varphi)} = \dfrac{\boldsymbol{\Theta}_{(\varphi)}}{1-\beta_1^{\varphi}} \\ \hat{\boldsymbol{\Psi}}_{(\varphi)} = \dfrac{\boldsymbol{\Psi}_{(\varphi)}}{1-\beta_2^{\varphi}} \end{cases} \tag{12.62}$$

where β_1^{φ} and β_2^{φ} denote β_1 and β_2 to the power φ. The update of **E** can be expressed as

$$\mathbf{E}_{(\varphi+1)} \Leftarrow \mathbf{E}_{(\varphi)} - \frac{\eta}{\sqrt{\hat{\boldsymbol{\Psi}}_{(\varphi)}} + \boldsymbol{\Omega}} \odot \widehat{\boldsymbol{\Theta}}_{(\varphi)} \tag{12.63}$$

where η is the learning rate, and Ω consists of small constants to avoid division by zero. For **E**, $\mathbf{A}_l$, and **P**, the optimization can be expressed simply as

$$\mathbf{E}, \mathbf{A}_l, \mathbf{P} \Leftarrow \text{Adam}(\mathbf{E}, \mathbf{A}_l, \mathbf{P}) \tag{12.64}$$

where $\mathbf{A}_l \in \mathbb{R}^{n\times n}$, $l = 2, 3, \ldots, h$. Note that the settings of β_1, β_2, η and Ω follow the recommendations in [31]. Moreover, we use normalization to avoid outliers when estimating **P**, and the process can be written as

$$p = \frac{p - p_{min}}{p_{max} - p_{min}} \tag{12.65}$$

where $p_{\min}$ and $p_{\max}$ are the minimum and maximum in **P**. Afterward, we can obtain abundance matrix **A**. Finally, the proposed DAAN can output endmembers, abundances, and scattering parameters.

The proposed DAAN represents a model-driven unmixing approach grounded in the MLMM and utilizes a hierarchical strategy to address this physical model. Additionally, as an unsupervised nonlinear unmixing method, DAAN does not depend on prior knowledge, which enhances its universality and usability compared to many data-driven and supervised alternatives.

12.3 Experimental Results

In a first experiment, we utilize the Samson dataset, which comprises 156 spectral bands spanning wavelengths from 0.401 to 0.889 μm and includes an image resolution of 95 × 95 pixels. The dataset serves as a validation tool and features three distinct endmembers in the ground truth image: soil, trees, and water. Table 12.1 demonstrates the obtained quantitative results for the considered

Table 12.1 SADS (in radians) and RES along with their standard deviations obtained by DAEN for the Samson data.

	SAD					
	Soil	**Tree**	**Water**	**Mean SAD**	**RMSE**	**RE**
DAEN	0.0405	0.0196	0.0279	0.0293	0.6097	0.0062

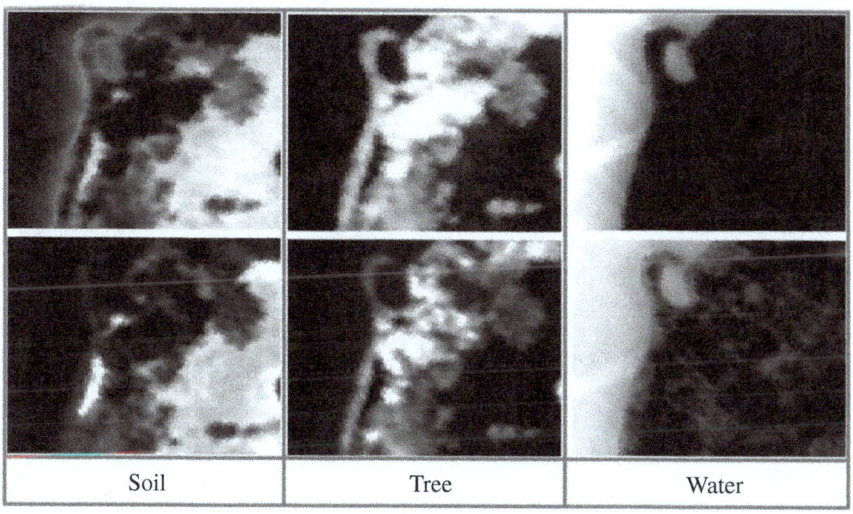

Figure 12.3 Results obtained by the proposed DAEN on the Samson data set. (Top) Ground truth abundance maps on Samson data. (Bottom) Estimated abundance maps from the proposed DAEN.

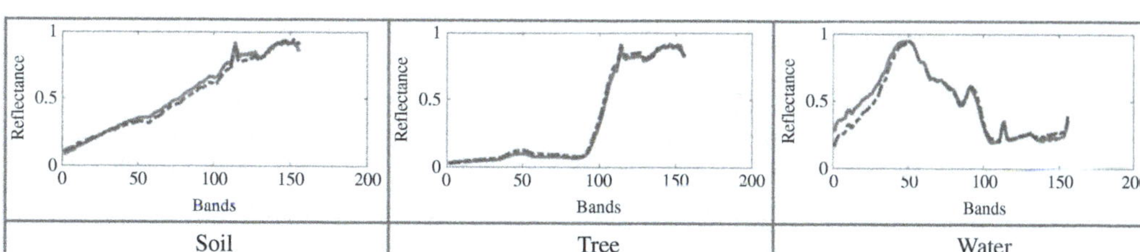

Figure 12.4 Estimated endmember signatures (solid lines) along with their corresponding reference signatures dashed lines.

methods. The abundance maps obtained by DAEN are shown in Figure 12.3, and the estimated endmembers are provided in Figure 12.4.

A second free test set is the Jasper Ridge dataset, consisting of 512 × 614 pixels, was collected by the airborne visible/infrared imaging spectrometer (AVIRIS) over Jasper Ridge in California. The dataset originally included 224 spectral bands covering wavelengths from 0.38 to 2.5 μm. To account for water vapor and atmospheric effects, bands 1–3, 108–112, 154–166, and 220–224 were excluded, resulting in a refined selection of 198 spectral bands used for second experiments. To streamline the

Table 12.2 SADS (in radians) RMSEs, and res obtained by DMBU in the Jasper Ridge data.

	SAD						
	Road	**Soil**	**Tree**	**Water**	**Mean SAD**	**RMSE**	**RE**
DMBU	0.0991	0.1920	0.1752	0.1319	0.1496	0.2474	0.0162

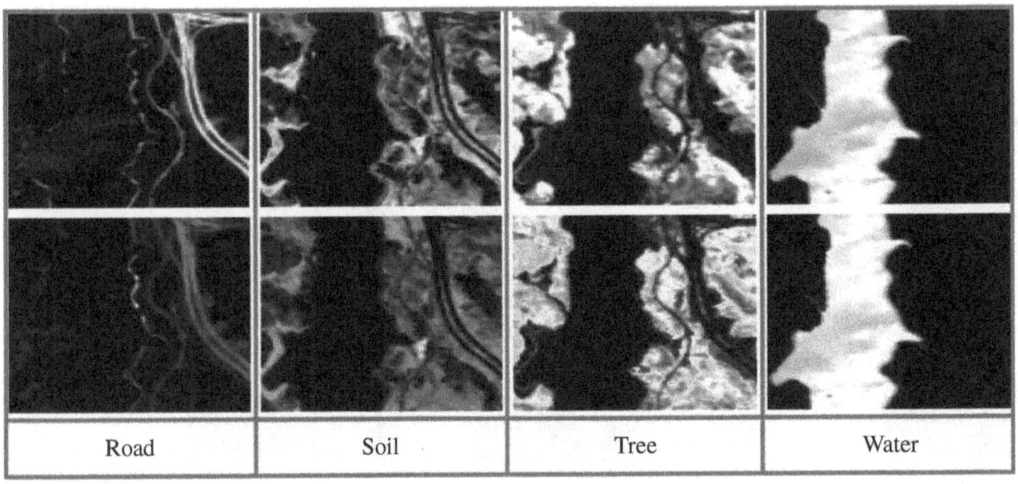

Figure 12.5 Results obtained by DMBU on the Jasper Ridge data. (Top) Reference abundance maps. (Bottom) Estimated abundance maps.

complexity of the dataset, a 100 × 100 pixel subimage was extracted from the original dataset. This subimage is commonly employed for testing unmixing algorithms and encompasses four distinct endmembers: road, soil, tree, and water. Table 12.2 indicates that the proposed DMBU obtained the best RMSE and RE scores in this experiment. Figure 12.5 shows the abundances estimated via DMBU, and it can be seen that these abundances match well with the corresponding references. Figure 12.6 reveals that the endmembers estimated via DMBU also exhibit a good match with the corresponding library signatures. Figure 12.7 illustrates the interaction abundance maps estimated by DMBU in the Jasper Ridge data.

The third test set is the Moffett Field dataset is a prominent choice for testing nonlinear unmixing methods. Collected by the AVIRIS sensor in the Moffett area at the southern tip of San Francisco, California, United States, this dataset spans wavelengths from 0.4 to 2.5 μm and includes 224 bands per pixel. It features a 50 × 50 pixel area, which encapsulates three key objects: soil, vegetation, and water. After the exclusion of noisy bands, 189 bands were used for the experiments. The selected region comprises three endmembers typical of the coastal areas represented in the image—vegetation, water, and soil. This subset is extensively used in remote sensing to assess nonlinear unmixing methods and boasts broad applicational scope. Figure 12.8 displays unmixing results obtained by DAAN. Since there are no attached ground truths with the Moffett Field data, we only provide unmixing results without the qualitative and quantitative comparisons.

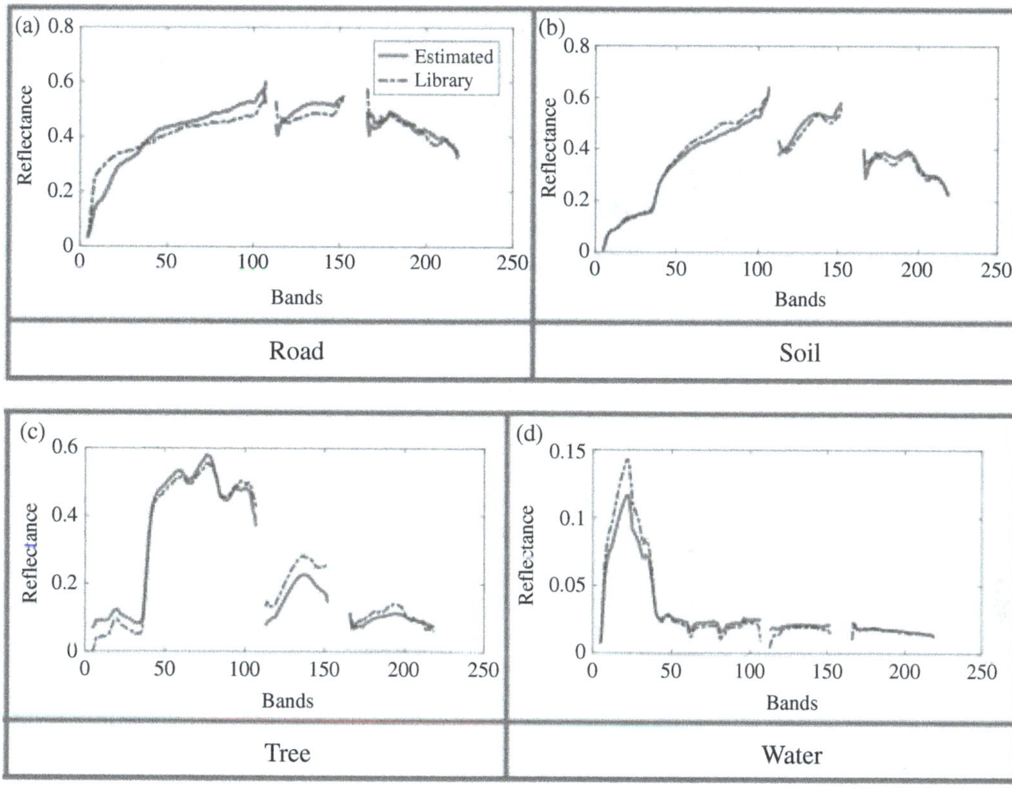

Figure 12.6 Comparison of the estimated endmembers (solid lines) with the reference signatures (dashed lines). (a) Road, (b) soil, (c) tree, and (d) water.

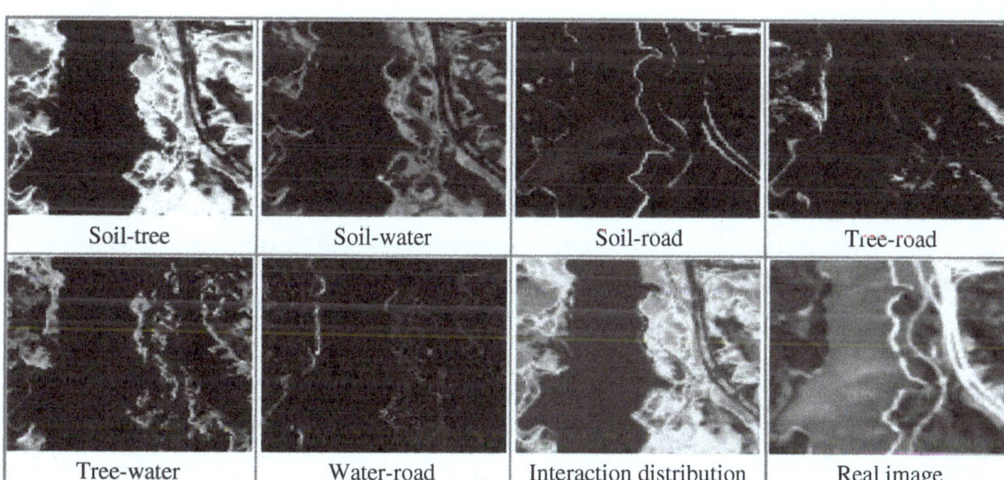

Figure 12.7 Interaction abundance maps and interaction distribution map estimated by DMBU in the Jasper Ridge subimage.

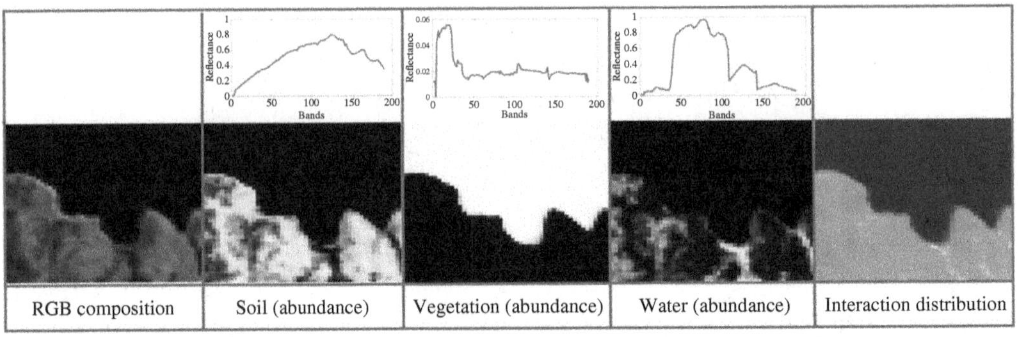

Figure 12.8 Results obtained by DAAN on the Moffett field data.

12.4 Conclusion

In recent years, the field of HSI processing has been profoundly transformed by advancements in DL, particularly in the area of unmixing. DL techniques have now become the leading approach for addressing mixed pixels in hyperspectral remote-sensing applications. Among the diverse range of DL models, autoencoders are especially noteworthy for their effectiveness in unmixing methods. Comprising an encoder and a decoder, autoencoders utilize their hidden layers to extract high-level features from data. This capability renders them exceptionally adept at hyperspectral unmixing, where the objective is to derive a compact, low-dimensional representation that facilitates accurate abundance estimation. However, a significant limitation of autoencoder-based unmixing methods is their tendency to concentrate solely on spectral information, often at the expense of capturing spatial relationships between pixels.

12.5 Discussion

Hyperspectral datasets with large-scale dimensions continue to face significant computational bottlenecks, highlighting the need for optimization strategies. Future research could explore model compression, distributed training, or lightweight architectures to reduce computational overhead. Additionally, current nonlinear mixture models frameworks rely on prior assumptions about scattering parameters, limiting their ability to address unknown nonlinear effects such as terrain shadows and atmospheric artifacts. Integrating physics-based models with deep networks may enhance generalization in complex nonlinear scenarios.

References

1 Bioucas-Dias, J.M., Plaza, A., Camps-Valls, G. et al. (2013). Hyperspectral remote sensing data analysis and future challenges. *IEEE Geosci. Remote Sens. Mag.* 1 (2): 6–36.

2 Chen, J., Zhao, M., Wang, X. et al. (2023). Integration of physics-based and data-driven models for hyperspectral image unmixing: a summary of current methods. *IEEE Signal Process. Mag.* 40 (2): 61–74.

3 Thorp, K.R., French, A.N., and Rango, A. (2013). Effect of image spatial and spectral characteristics on mapping semi-arid rangeland vegetation using multiple endmember spectral mixture analysis (MESMA). *Remote Sens. Environ.* 132: 120–130.

4 Borsoi, R.A., Imbiriba, T., Bermudez, J.C.M., and Richard, C. (2020). A blind multiscale spatial regularization framework for kernel-based spectral unmixing. *IEEE Trans. Image Process.* 29: 4965–4979.

5 Ma, W.-K. et al. (2014). A signal processing perspective on hyperspectral unmixing: insights from remote sensing. *IEEE Signal Process. Mag.* 31 (1): 67–81.

6 Hong, D., Gao, L., Yao, J. et al. (2022). Endmember-guided unmixing network (EGU-Net): a general deep learning framework for self-supervised hyperspectral unmixing. *IEEE Trans. Neural Netw. Learn. Syst.* 33 (11): 6518–6531.

7 Yao, J., Hong, D., Xu, L. et al. (2022). Sparsity enhanced convolutional decomposition: a novel tensor-based paradigm for blind hyperspectral unmixing. *IEEE Trans. Geosci. Remote Sens.* 60: 1–14.

8 Zouaoui, A., Muhawenayo, G., Rasti, B. et al. (2023). Entropic descent archetypal analysis for blind hyperspectral unmixing. *IEEE Trans. Image Process.* 32: 4649–4663.

9 Qian, Y., Xiong, F., Qian, Q., and Zhou, J. (2020). Spectral mixture model inspired network architectures for hyperspectral unmixing. *IEEE Trans. Geosci. Remote Sens.* 58 (10): 7418–7434.

10 Ammanouil, R., Ferrari, A., Richard, C., and Mathieu, S. (2017). Nonlinear unmixing of hyperspectral data with vector-valued kernel functions. *IEEE Trans. Image Process.* 26 (1): 340–354.

11 Su, Y., Xu, X., Li, J. et al. (2021). Deep autoencoders with multitask learning for bilinear hyperspectral unmixing. *IEEE Trans. Geosci. Remote Sens.* 59 (10): 8615–8629.

12 Zhang, X., Sun, Y., Zhang, J. et al. (2018). Hyperspectral unmixing via deep convolutional neural networks. *IEEE Geosci. Remote Sens. Lett.* 15 (11): 1755–1759.

13 Su, Y., Marinoni, A., Li, J. et al. (2018). Stacked nonnegative sparse autoencoders for robust hyperspectral unmixing. *IEEE Geosci. Remote Sens. Lett.* 15 (9): 1427–1431.

14 Borsoi, R.A., Imbiriba, T., and Closas, P. (2023). Dynamical hyperspectral unmixing with variational recurrent neural networks. *IEEE Trans. Image Process.* 32: 2279–2294.

15 Gao, L., Han, Z., Hong, D. et al. (2022). CyCU-Net: cycle-consistency unmixing network by learning cascaded autoencoders. *IEEE Trans. Geosci. Remote Sens.* 60: 1–14.

16 Han, Z., Hong, D., Gao, L. et al. (2021). Deep half-siamese networks for hyperspectral unmixing. *IEEE Geosci. Remote Sens. Lett.* 18 (11): 1996–2000.

17 Min, A., Guo, Z., Li, H., and Peng, J. (2022). JMnet: joint metric neural network for hyperspectral unmixing. *IEEE Trans. Geosci. Remote Sens.* 60: 1–12.

18 Rasti, B., Koirala, B., Scheunders, P., and Ghamisi, P. (2022). UnDIP: hyperspectral unmixing using deep image prior. *IEEE Trans. Geosci. Remote Sens.* 60: 1–15.

19 Rasti, B. and Koirala, B. (2022). SUnCNN: sparse unmixing using unsupervised convolutional neural network. *IEEE Geosci. Remote Sens. Lett.* 19: 1–5.

20 Han, Z., Hong, D., Gao, L. et al. (2022). Multimodal hyperspectral unmixing: insights from attention networks. *IEEE Trans. Geosci. Remote Sens.* 60: 1–13.

21 Han, Z., Hong, D., Gao, L. et al. (2022). AutoNAS: automatic neural architecture search for hyperspectral unmixing. *IEEE Trans. Geosci. Remote Sens.* 60: 1–14.

22 Su, Y., Li, J., Plaza, A. et al. (2019). DAEN: deep autoencoder networks for hyperspectral unmixing. *IEEE Trans. Geosci. Remote Sens.* 57 (7): 4309–4321.

23 Qu, Y. and Qi, H. (2019). UDAS: an untied denoising autoencoder with sparsity for spectral unmixing. *IEEE Trans. Geosci. Remote Sens.* 57 (3): 1698–1712.

24 Ozkan, S., Kaya, B., and Akar, G.B. (2019). EndNet: sparse autoencoder network for endmember extraction and hyperspectral unmixing. *IEEE Trans. Geosci. Remote Sens.* 57 (1): 482–496.

25 Xu, X., Song, X., Li, T. et al. (2022). Deep autoencoder for hyperspectral unmixing via global-local smoothing. *IEEE Trans. Geosci. Remote Sens.* 60: 1–16.

26 Wang, M., Zhao, M., Chen, J., and Rahardja, S. (2019). Nonlinear unmixing of hyperspectral data via deep autoencoder networks. *IEEE Geosci. Remote Sens. Lett.* 16 (9): 1467–1471.

27 Zhao, M., Yan, L., and Chen, J. (2021). LSTM-DNN based autoencoder network for nonlinear hyperspectral image unmixing. *IEEE J. Sel. Top. Signal Process.* 15 (2): 295–309.

28 Zhao, M., Chen, J., and Dobigeon, N. (2024). AE-RED: a hyperspectral unmixing framework powered by deep autoencoder and regularization by denoising. *IEEE Trans. Geosci. Remote Sens.* 62: 1–15.

29 Ghosh, P., Roy, S.K., Koirala, B. et al. (2022). Hyperspectral unmixing using transformer network. *IEEE Trans. Geosci. Remote Sens.* 60: 1–16.

30 Palsson, B., Sveinsson, J.R., and Ulfarsson, M.O. (2022). Blind hyperspectral unmixing using autoencoders: a critical comparison. *IEEE J. Sel. Top. Appl. Earth Obs. Remote Sens.* 15: 1340–1372.

31 Zhou, C. and Rodrigues, M.R.D. (2022). ADMM-based hyperspectral unmixing networks for abundance and endmember estimation. *IEEE Trans. Geosci. Remote Sens.* 60: 1–18.

32 Jin, Q., Ma, Y., Mei, X., and Ma, J. (2022). TANet: an unsupervised two-stream autoencoder network for hyperspectral unmixing. *IEEE Trans. Geosci. Remote Sens.* 60: 1–15.

33 Palsson, B., Ulfarsson, M.O., and Sveinsson, J.R. (2021). Convolutional autoencoder for spectral-spatial hyperspectral unmixing. *IEEE Trans. Geosci. Remote Sens.* 59 (1): 535–549.

34 Zhao, M., Wang, M., Chen, J., and Rahardja, S. (2022). Hyperspectral unmixing for additive nonlinear models with a 3-D-CNN autoencoder network. *IEEE Trans. Geosci. Remote Sens.* 60: 1–15.

35 Su, Y., Zhu, Z., Gao, L. et al. (2024). DAAN: a deep autoencoder-based augmented network for blind multilinear hyperspectral unmixing. *IEEE Trans. Geosci. Remote Sens.* 62: 1–15.

36 Xiong, F., Zhou, J., Tao, S. et al. (2022). SNMF-Net: learning a deep alternating neural network for hyperspectral unmixing. *IEEE Trans. Geosci. Remote Sens.* 60: 1–16.

37 He, D., Zhong, Y., Wang, X., and Zhang, L. (2021). Deep convolutional neural network framework for subpixel mapping. *IEEE Trans. Geosci. Remote Sens.* 59 (11): 9518–9539.

38 Rasti, B., Koirala, B., Scheunders, P., and Chanussot, J. (2022). MiSiCNet: minimum simplex convolutional network for deep hyperspectral unmixing. *IEEE Trans. Geosci. Remote Sens.* 60: 1–15.

39 Borsoi, R.A., Erdogmuş, D., and Imbiriba, T. (2023). Learning interpretable deep disentangled neural networks for hyperspectral unmixing. *IEEE Trans. Comput. Imaging* 9: 977–991.

40 Fang, Y., Wang, Y., Xu, L. et al. (2022). BCUN: Bayesian fully convolutional neural network for hyperspectral spectral unmixing. *IEEE Trans. Geosci. Remote Sens.* 60: 1–14.

41 Qi, L., Gao, F., Dong, J. et al. (2022). SSCU-Net: spatial–spectral collaborative unmixing network for hyperspectral images. *IEEE Trans. Geosci. Remote Sens.* 60: 1–15.

42 Heylen, R. and Scheunders, P. (2016). A multilinear mixing model for nonlinear spectral unmixing. *IEEE Trans. Geosci. Remote Sens.* 54 (1): 240–251.

43 Heylen, R., Andrejchenko, V., Zahiri, Z. et al. (2019). Nonlinear hyperspectral unmixing with graphical models. *IEEE Trans. Geosci. Remote Sens.* 57 (7): 4844–4856.

44 Nocedal, J. and Wright, S.J. (2006). *Numerical Optimization*, 33–36. New York, NY: Springer.

13

Numerical-model-guided Nonlinear Spectral Unmixing

Bin Yang[1] *and Bin Wang*[2,3]

[1] *School of Computer Science and Technology, Donghua University, Shanghai, China*
[2] *Key Laboratory for Information Science of Electromagnetic Waves (MoE), Fudan University, Shanghai, China*
[3] *Image and Intelligence Laboratory, School of Information Science and Technology, Fudan University, Shanghai, China*

13.1 Introduction

Hyperspectral remote-sensing sensors record radiance responses of land covers at hundreds of continuous bands from the visible to the near-infrared (NIR) spectral domain. The high spectral resolution gives every observed object a characteristic spectral fingerprint which makes different types of land covers easier to recognize. However, the spatial resolution of hyperspectral remote-sensing images is usually limited, and the significant increase of spectral information cannot avoid the severe decrease in the performance of object recognition induced by mixed pixels [1]. Spectral unmixing decomposes pixels into a set of pure material endmember spectra and their proportional abundance coefficients [2], providing a remarkable technical solution to the problem of mixed pixels. But the ill-posed procedures for solving inverse problems inevitably deteriorate the unmixing results for complex and diverse hyperspectral data. In the presence of mixing model errors, nonconvexity of optimization problems, noise and anomaly perturbation, etc. numerical models and data-driven learning approaches have been extensively exploited by combining with the inherent spatial–spectral features of hyperspectral data [3] and improved for spectral unmixing in years [4–6]. According to the specific assumption of the physical spectral mixing process, a large number of linear and nonlinear spectral unmixing methods are proposed.

13.1.1 Linear and Nonlinear Spectral Unmixing

Linear unmixing methods are developed based on the famous linear mixture model (LMM) assuming that the incident light is directly received after it interacts with only one material [1]. Pixels are mathematically represented as the linear combination of endmembers and abundances, and they are located geometrically on the simplex spanning the set of endmembers. The simplified physical interpretation of the mixing process has greatly facilitated the study of linear unmixing [2]. Convex geometry [7–9], linear regression [10], nonnegative matrix/tensor factorization (NMF/NTF) [11–16], and statistical approaches, etc. being compatible with the LMM, can be easily leveraged to construct effective linear unmixing frameworks. Although a lot of improvements have been

Machine-Learning-Based Hyperspectral Image Processing, First Edition. Edited by Bing Zhang.

made for linear unmixing, nonlinear mixing effects in real scenarios are inevitably uninterpretable in linear unmixing, resulting in an increase in unmixing errors and a decrease in unmixing reproducibility and applicability [5, 6].

Due to the differences of observed scenarios, nonlinear unmixing methods are usually proposed based on different nonlinear mixing assumptions. Typical radiative transfer processes in multilayer mixtures of large 3D scenarios such as vegetated areas and urban regions [17], and in intimate mixtures such as sand and turbid estuarine and coastal water lead pixels to be nonlinearly mixed following different modes. Typically, the classical Hapke model can be used for intimate mixtures, but the heavy dependence on physical scene parameters has restricted its applications [6]. Nonlinear mixture models with simplified numerical forms are more popular in the study of nonlinear unmixing. Bilinear mixture models (BMMs) only introduce second-order scatterings into the LMM and are suitable to address the multilayer nonlinear mixing effects. Representative BMMs include the Fan model (FM) [18], generalized bilinear model (GBM) [19], and polynomial post-nonlinear model (PPNM) [20]. In addition, the kernel-based representation of second-order scatterings improves the BMMs to be suitable for more general unmixing situations [21–23]. Different from the BMMs, the p-order polynomial model [24] and the multilinear mixing (MLM) model [25] take higher orders of scatterings into account to explain more complex nonlinearity.

Compared to linear unmixing, nonlinear unmixing is commonly more complex, e.g., more constraints and parameters are required to be handled, and more intractable modeling, calculating, and learning problems must be addressed. Firstly, the introduction of mathematical terms of multiple scatterings into mixture models increases the negative effect of collinearity on the regression of nonlinear unmixing [26, 27] and makes the calculation of unmixing variables sensitive to noise. Secondly, due to the nonconvexity of nonlinear unmixing problems, unmixing results are often nonunique and sensitive to the initializations, and the issue of overfitting is more likely to occur and severely decreases the unmixing accuracy and reliability [23, 28]. Finally, the nonlinear manifold of hyperspectral data is far more complex than a linear simplex, which raises the difficulty level of learning hidden features for unmixing [4, 29].

13.1.2 Numerical Models Versus Data-driven Learning for Nonlinear Spectral Unmixing

A straightforward idea to implement nonlinear unmixing is the optimization of unknown variables in the numerical mixture models such as the BMMs by minimizing the discrepancy between the model-based reconstructed pixels and their corresponding real observed pixels. With the integration of augmented constraints [3] (e.g., sparsity, spatial–spectral similarity, and low rankness of abundances) into the evaluation of data reconstruction, numerical-model-guided constrained optimization problems for nonlinear unmixing are formulated. Taylor-approximation-based least squares, gradient descent algorithm (GDA), alternating direction method of multipliers (ADMM), etc. are employed to optimize the unknown variables iteratively [20, 30–33]. Compared to the gradient-based methods, swarm intelligence methods and multiple objective optimization technologies have not only been proven to be superior in solving nonconvex linear unmixing problems [34–39] but also are adopted in complex nonlinear unmixing tasks to obtain better unmixing results [40–43]. Notably, although nonlinear unmixing can be improved by introducing the structural features of hyperspectral data into the optimization of numerical models, the accuracy, reliability, and stability of nonlinear unmixing are far from the high requirements of quantitative remote-sensing applications. Therefore, a lot of recent improvements have been explored to mitigate the collinearity [26, 27], increase the generalization and spatial–spectral representation of nonlinear unmixing [23, 41, 42], and interpret the wavelength-dependent nonlinearity in unmixing [44–46], etc.

Compared to numerical-model-guided nonlinear unmixing, nonlinear unmixing based on data-driven learning is usually achieved by resorting to traditional machine learning methods (e.g., kernel tricks [21, 28] and manifold learning [29, 47]) and advanced deep neural networks (DNNs) [48]. Classical kernel-based methods target at using kernel functions (e.g., Gaussian radial basis kernel function) in the original hyperspectral data space to implicitly map the data into a high-dimensional Hilbert feature space and formulating a simpler linear processing task [21, 23]. In this sense, nonlinear unmixing can be easily implemented in kernel-transformed linear spaces [28]. However, kernel-based methods are sensitive to the selection of kernel functions and their hyperparameters, and the issue of overfitting is significant. In terms of manifold learning-based nonlinear unmixing, to capture the structures of complex data manifolds, graph models [29] are commonly employed to represent the nearest-neighbor relationships between pixels. Based on the geodesic distance [47], a new coordinate system can be built in a low-dimensional feature space that enables linear unmixing to solve the original nonlinear unmixing problem. However, the heavy computational burden and the drawback of idealizing data to be flat manifolds often limit the development of such nonlinear unmixing methods.

As a representative technology of artificial intelligence, deep learning has recently gained tremendous development and is being widely applied in various tasks of hyperspectral data processing due to its powerful capabilities of feature extraction and learning [49]. In a DNN for unmixing, a group of carefully designed network modules are connected where the input hyperspectral data are nonlinearly mapped multiple times to produce the inherent latent features, which effectively facilitates the learning of endmembers and abundances. Deep autoencoder (AE) networks are popularly exploited to build the backbone unmixing networks due to their consistency to the unmixing process, i.e., hyperspectral data are reduced to the dimension of abundances in an encoder and the low-dimensional abundances are then reconstructed to the original dimension of data in a decoder. The fine learning of hyperspectral data's structural features in the encoder (e.g., sparse, denoising, variational, and attention convolutional AEs) [50–56] to generate robust abundances and the reformulation of AEs' loss functions using different constraints of endmembers and abundances to enhance the convergence and accuracy of training are two feasible approaches to improve the effectiveness of AE-based unmixing. The intrinsic advantages of DNN in extracting complex features through a nonlinear transformation not only achieve the successful applications of DNN-based linear unmixing but also make the potential of DNN for nonlinear unmixing have been extensively explored [57–65]. However, the lack of theoretical grounding of DNN for the radiation transfer mechanism always requires the integration of mixture models (e.g., the BMMs, MLM, and Hapke model) [4, 62, 64, 65] into the design of the decoder to promote the physical meaning of unmixing results.

Generally, research on data-driven learning-based nonlinear unmixing is far from mature compared to numerical-model-guided nonlinear unmixing. Although data-driven learning methods have shown their unique and attractive potential for nonlinear unmixing, efficient solutions to the essential problems in nonlinear unmixing including overfitting, sensitivity to hyperparameters, and weak interpretability need to be carefully explored. Deep unrolling has recently been employed to transform the iterative update steps of numerical-model-guided nonlinear unmixing optimization problems into multiple connected network modules [65], which is considered to improve the accuracy and interpretability of nonlinear unmixing. However, numerical-model-guided methods can provide more explicit mathematical representations of models and optimization, which is critical to understanding the match between nonlinear unmixing and real situations, and to establish a solid theoretical foundation to promote the development of nonlinear unmixing frontier, e.g., to reveal the inherent mechanisms of the physical nonlinear mixing coupled with spectral variability. Moreover, different from the physical radiation transfer differential equations such as the Hapke model and the DNNs, numerical-model-guided nonlinear unmixing usually has lower computational costs of parameters and relies on no prior information of observed scenes. This enables newly proposed nonlinear unmixing assumptions to be validated and improved efficiently.

In this chapter, three representative numerical-model-guided nonlinear unmixing methods are introduced which conducted different improvements to the existing BMMs and MLM to achieve better unmixing accuracies and generalization for nonlinear unmixing. The first method [26, 27] exploited the geometric characteristics of BMMs to construct geometric projection mechanisms to produce the approximate linearly mixed components of pixels. After the BMMs-based nonlinear unmixing problem is transformed into a traditional linear unmixing problem, the influence of collinearity caused by the terms of second-order scatterings can be effectively reduced. The second method [23] designed novel kernel functions to transform the GBM and PPNM into their equivalent kernel forms to derive a flexible nonparametric representation of the nonlinearity and retain the physical meaning of second-order scatterings. The third method [44] extended the MLM to provide vectorized nonlinear probability parameters for each pixel. Then, a novel band-wise nonlinear unmixing mode is constructed that can distinguish different levels of nonlinearity and reduce the unmixing error simultaneously in every band.

In the remainder of this chapter, the BMMs, MLM, and their extensions are briefly introduced in Section 13.2. Then, Section 13.3 presents the technical details of the three numerical-model-guided nonlinear unmixing methods, and experimental results for simulated data and real hyperspectral images are accordingly discussed. Finally, Section 13.4 concludes the whole chapter, and Section 13.5 discusses challenges and future directions.

13.2 Nonlinear Mixture Models and Extensions

13.2.1 Linear, Bilinear, and Multilinear Mixture Models

Given a matrix $\mathbf{X} \in \mathbb{R}^{n \times m}$ representing a hyperspectral image with m pixels and n bands, the endmember matrix and the abundance matrix can be denoted as $\mathbf{A} = (\mathbf{a}_1, \mathbf{a}_2, \ldots, \mathbf{a}_r) \in \mathbb{R}^{n \times r}$ and $\mathbf{S} = (\mathbf{s}_1, \mathbf{s}_2, \ldots, \mathbf{s}_m) \in \mathbb{R}^{r \times m}$, respectively. r is the number of endmembers. In the mixture models, endmembers and abundances should be nonnegative, and the sum-to-one constraint of abundances is usually required to be satisfied, i.e., $\sum_{i=1}^{r} s_{i,j} = 1, j = 1, 2, \ldots, m$. Then, an LMM-based pixel $\mathbf{x}_j \in \mathbb{R}^{n \times 1}$ that is linearly combined by $\mathbf{A}$ and $\mathbf{s}_j$ can be written as

$$\mathbf{x}_j = \sum_{i=1}^{r} \mathbf{a}_i s_{i,j} + \boldsymbol{\varepsilon}_j = \mathbf{A}\mathbf{s}_j + \boldsymbol{\varepsilon}_j, \tag{13.1}$$

where $\boldsymbol{\varepsilon}_j$ is the noise and model error. The BMMs further introduce second-order scatterings presented by the Hadamard product $\mathbf{a}_i \odot \mathbf{a}_k = (a_{i,1}a_{k,1}, a_{i,2}a_{k,2}, \ldots, a_{i,n}a_{k,n})^T$ between every two endmembers into Eq. (13.1). The specific definition of nonlinear parameters and the consideration of self-interactions between the same endmembers make typical BMMs such as the GBM [19] and PPNM [20] different. A general numerical form of BMMs can be derived as

$$\mathbf{x}_j = \sum_{i=1}^{r} \mathbf{a}_i s_{i,j} + \sum_{i=1}^{t_1} \sum_{k=t_2}^{r} b_{i,k,j} (\mathbf{a}_i \odot \mathbf{a}_k) s_{i,j} s_{k,j} + \boldsymbol{\varepsilon}_j, \tag{13.2}$$

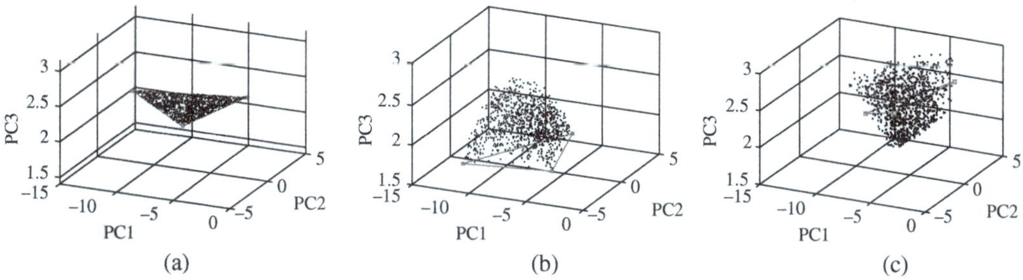

Figure 13.1 Geometric distribution of the LMM-based and BMMs-based simulated data. (a) LMM, (b) GBM, and (c) PPNM. *Source:* [26] / with permission of IEEE.

where $b_{i,k,j}$ represents a nonlinear parameter to measure the contribution of second-order scatterings. Equation (13.2) is the GBM, if $t_1 = r - 1$, $t_2 = i + 1$, $0 \leq b_{i,k,j} \leq 1$, and it becomes the PPNM, if $t_1 = r$, $t_2 = 1$ and $b_{i,k,j}$ is transformed to $b_j \in \mathbb{R}$. The PPNM is usually considered to be more general due to the addition of self-interactions and simple parameters. The BMMs reduce to the LMM when $b_{i,k,j} = 0$. As shown in Figure 13.1, the geometric manifold of the BMMs-based data is more complex than the simplex of the LMM-based data in the feature space.

The MLM [25] further introduces high-order scatterings into the PPNM. With the use of a scalar probability parameter P to measure any orders of light interactions, the MLM is able to interpret flexibly different degrees of multiple scatterings. Notably, the MLM is built following four assumptions. First, the incident light interacts with at least one material. Second, after the light interacts with a material, it is reflected to other materials with a probability P for further interactions, while leaving the scene with a probability $1 - P$ to reach the remote-sensing sensors. Third, the light is more likely to interact with materials having larger abundances. Finally, the material's single scattering albedo (SSA) decides the intensity of light being scattered. In practical applications, SSA may be assumed to be similar to reflectance, and the mathematical form of the MLM is as follows

$$\begin{aligned} \mathbf{x}_j &= (1-P_j)\sum_{i=1}^{r}\mathbf{a}_i s_{i,j} + (1-P_j)P_j\sum_{i=1}^{r}\sum_{k=1}^{r}(\mathbf{a}_i \odot \mathbf{a}_k)s_{i,j}s_{k,j} \\ &\quad + (1-P_j)P_j^2\sum_{i=1}^{r}\sum_{k=1}^{r}\sum_{l=1}^{r}(\mathbf{a}_i \odot \mathbf{a}_k \odot \mathbf{a}_l)s_{i,j}s_{k,j}s_{l,j} + \cdots + \boldsymbol{\varepsilon}_j, \qquad \mathbf{x}_j = \frac{(1-P)\mathbf{y}_j}{1-P\mathbf{y}_j} + \boldsymbol{\varepsilon}_j \\ &= (1-P_j)\mathbf{y}_j + P_j\mathbf{y}_j \odot \mathbf{x}_j + \boldsymbol{\varepsilon}_j \end{aligned} \tag{13.3}$$

where $\mathbf{y}_j = \sum_{i=1}^{r}\mathbf{a}_i s_{i,j}$ denotes the linear mixing component based on the LMM. The nonlinear probability parameter $P_j < 1$ can quantify the influence of various multiple scatterings, which enables the MLM to integrate the single scatterings, second-order scatterings, high-order scatterings, etc. If $P_j = 0$, the MLM is equivalent to the LMM. On contrary, a pixel $\mathbf{x}_j$ is considered to be dominated by nonlinear mixing effects when P_j approaches close to 1. $P_j < 0$ is allowed considering factors such as the extra illumination of a 3D structure outside the pixel's instantaneous field of view.

13.2.2 Kernel-transformed BMMs

In light of the complex nonlinear mixing mechanism in real scenarios, the specific prior form in Eq. (13.2) is often considered to be strict. Kernel trick has a promising potential to provide a model-free and flexible representation of the nonlinearity. However, the purely data-driven kernel approaches inevitably result in overfitting that seriously reduces the unmixing accuracy. To reduce the influence of overfitting and match the physical meaning of second-order scatterings, equivalent kernel forms of the classical BMMs have been derived [23]. Two novel kernels designed for the GBM and the PPNM transform the BMMs to their kernel-based nonparametric representations in Eq. (13.4).

$$\mathbf{x}_j = \mathbf{A}\mathbf{s}_j + \mathbf{K}\boldsymbol{\beta}_j, \quad \begin{cases} \mathbf{K}_{GBM} = \left(\mathbf{A}\mathbf{A}^T\right)^2 - \left(\mathbf{A}^2\right)^T\mathbf{A}^2 \\ \mathbf{K}_{PPNM} = \left(\mathbf{A}\mathbf{A}^T\right)^2 \end{cases} \tag{13.4}$$

where $\boldsymbol{K} \in \mathbb{R}^{n\times n}$ is a Gram matrix for kernel transformation. For the GBM, $[\mathbf{K}_{GBM}]_{i,j} = \kappa_{GBM}(\tilde{\mathbf{a}}_i, \tilde{\mathbf{a}}_j) = \left(\tilde{\mathbf{a}}_i\tilde{\mathbf{a}}_j^T\right)^2 - \tilde{\mathbf{a}}_i^2\left(\tilde{\mathbf{a}}_j^2\right)^T$, and $[\mathbf{K}_{PPNM}]_{i,j} = \kappa_{PPNM}(\tilde{\mathbf{a}}_i, \tilde{\mathbf{a}}_j) = \left(\tilde{\mathbf{a}}_i\tilde{\mathbf{a}}_j^T\right)^2$ corresponds to the PPNM where $\tilde{\mathbf{a}}_i$ is the ith row vector of $\mathbf{A}$. $\boldsymbol{\beta}_j \in \mathbb{R}^{n\times 1}$ is a nonlinear parameter vector concerning the pixel $\mathbf{x}_j$. Compared to the popular Gaussian kernel, the implicit nonlinear mapping of $\kappa(\tilde{\mathbf{a}}_i, \tilde{\mathbf{a}}_j) = \phi(\tilde{\mathbf{a}}_i)\phi(\tilde{\mathbf{a}}_j)^T$ in Eqs. (13.5) and (13.6) is theoretically suitable for expressing the second-order scatterings. For instance, Eq. (13.7) proves that the kernel-transformed GBM in Eq. (13.4) can be equivalent to the GBM. Similarly, the case of the PPNM can be easily proved. Notably, abundances are integrated into the nonlinear part $\mathbf{K}\boldsymbol{\beta}_j$, which eases the optimization. The kernel-transformed BMMs (KBMMs) effectively retain the physical meaning of second-order scatterings using a flexible nonparametric representation.

$$\begin{cases} (\mathbf{K}_{GBM}\boldsymbol{\beta})_l = \phi(\tilde{\mathbf{a}}_l)\left(\sum_{i=1}^{n}\phi(\tilde{\mathbf{a}}_i)\beta_i\right)^T = \sum_{i=1}^{r-1}\sum_{j=i+1}^{r} b_{i,j}a_{l,i}a_{l,j} \\ \phi(\tilde{\mathbf{a}}_i) = \sqrt{2}(a_{i,1}a_{i,2}, a_{i,1}a_{i,3}, \ldots, a_{i,r-1}a_{i,r}). \end{cases} \tag{13.5}$$

$$\begin{cases} (\mathbf{K}_{PPNM}\boldsymbol{\beta})_l = \phi(\tilde{\mathbf{a}}_l)\left(\sum_{i=1}^{n}\phi(\tilde{\mathbf{a}}_i)\beta_i\right)^T = \sum_{i=1}^{r}\sum_{j=1}^{r} b_{i,j}a_{l,i}a_{l,j} \\ \phi(\tilde{\mathbf{a}}_i) = \left(a_{i,1}a_{i,1}, \ldots, a_{i,r}a_{i,r}, \sqrt{2}a_{i,1}a_{i,2}, \ldots, \sqrt{2}a_{i,r-1}a_{i,r}\right) \end{cases} \tag{13.6}$$

$$\begin{aligned} \mathbf{x}_j &= \sum_{i=1}^{r}\mathbf{a}_i s_{i,j} + \sum_{i=1}^{r-1}\sum_{k=i+1}^{r}\zeta_{i,k,j}(\mathbf{a}_i \odot \mathbf{a}_k)s_{i,j}s_{k,j} \\ &= \sum_{i=1}^{r}\mathbf{a}_i s_{i,j} + \sum_{i=1}^{r-1}\sum_{k=i+1}^{r}\left(2\sum_{l=1}^{n}\beta_{l,j}a_{l,i}a_{l,k}\right)(\mathbf{a}_i \odot \mathbf{a}_k) \\ &= \sum_{i=1}^{r}\mathbf{a}_i s_{i,j} + \begin{bmatrix} \phi(\tilde{\mathbf{a}}_1)\left(\sum_{i=1}^{n}\phi(\tilde{\mathbf{a}}_i)\beta_{i,j}\right)^T \\ \phi(\tilde{\mathbf{a}}_2)\left(\sum_{i=1}^{n}\phi(\tilde{\mathbf{a}}_i)\beta_{i,j}\right)^T \\ \vdots \\ \phi(\tilde{\mathbf{a}}_n)\left(\sum_{i=1}^{n}\phi(\tilde{\mathbf{a}}_i)\beta_{i,j}\right)^T \end{bmatrix} = \mathbf{A}\mathbf{s}_j + \begin{bmatrix} \left(\mathbf{K}_{GBM}\boldsymbol{\beta}_j\right)_1 \\ \left(\mathbf{K}_{GBM}\boldsymbol{\beta}_j\right)_2 \\ \vdots \\ \left(\mathbf{K}_{GBM}\boldsymbol{\beta}_j\right)_n \end{bmatrix}, \quad \zeta_{i,k,j} = \frac{2\sum_{l=1}^{n}\beta_{l,j}a_{l,i}a_{l,k}}{s_{i,j}s_{k,j}} \\ &= \mathbf{A}\mathbf{s}_j + \mathbf{K}_{GBM}\boldsymbol{\beta}_j \end{aligned} \tag{13.7}$$

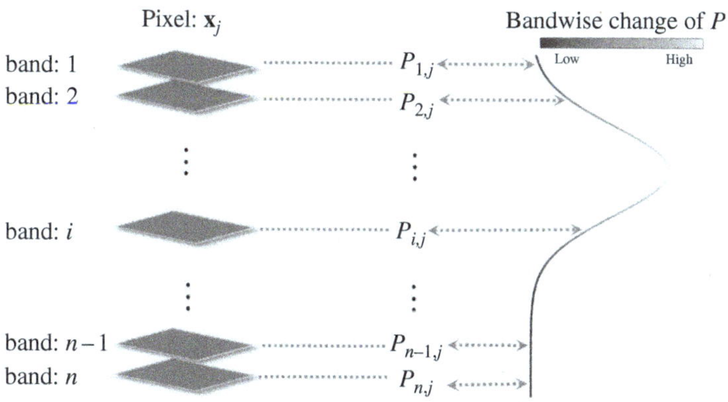

Figure 13.2 Schematic diagram of the EMLM model. *Source:* [44] / with permission of IEEE.

13.2.3 Band-wise Extended MLM

The radiative transfer of light is always a function of wavelength, and electromagnetic waves on different bands interact with ground objects in different ways. Therefore, the degrees of multiple scatterings are likely to change at different wavelengths of the observed pixels, resulting in the presence of wavelength-dependent nonlinear mixing intensities. For instance, the special structures and scattering properties of vegetation lead to the significant reflection and transmission of light in the NIR region. As a result, a higher intensity of nonlinear mixing can be often recognized in the NIR bands of pixels in the vegetated regions.

However, although numerical mixture models in literature have nonlinear parameters to account for the pixel-dependent nonlinear intensity, they assume implicitly that all bands of a pixel follow the same mixing mode, i.e., the degrees of multiple scatterings at each band are the same. The discrepancy between this assumption and the real situations inevitably produces prominent errors in the unmixing process and reduces the accuracies of quantitative remote-sensing applications. A straightforward solution to this problem is to construct a reasonable numerical model to interpret the nonlinear mixing effect in each band as accurately as possible. Typically, the scalar probability parameter P of the MLM can be vectorized for every pixel to explain the band-wise nonlinearity [44]. As shown in Figure 13.2, the ith band of an MLM-based pixel $\mathbf{x}_j$ is assigned $P_{i,j}$, and thus a probability parameter vector $\mathbf{P}_j = (P_{1,j}, P_{2,j}, \ldots, P_{n,j})^T \in \mathbb{R}^{n\times 1}$ can be derived for $\mathbf{x}_j$. In this sense, the MLM in Eq. (13.3) can be extended to be the following form

$$\mathbf{x}_j = (\mathbf{1}_n - \mathbf{P}_j) \odot \mathbf{y}_j + \mathbf{P}_j \odot \mathbf{y}_j \odot \mathbf{x}_j + \boldsymbol{\varepsilon}_j \tag{13.8}$$

where $\mathbf{y}_j = \sum_{i=1}^{r} \mathbf{a}_i s_{i,j}$ and $\mathbf{1}_n$ denotes a column vector of all 1s. $\mathbf{P}_j$ quantifies the change of nonlinear intensity in each band due to its inherent physical meaning. Nonlinear unmixing based on the band-wise extended MLM (EMLM) in Eq. (13.8) has a markable advantage in explaining the wavelength-dependent nonlinear mixing effects, leading to the synchronous reduction of unmixing residuals in all bands and the improvement of nonlinear unmixing performance.

13.3 Numerical-model-guided Nonlinear Spectral Unmixing

Three numerical-model-guided nonlinear unmixing methods, named GCBAE (Geometric Characteristics of the BMMs-based Abundance Estimation) [26], KBU (Kernel-based Bilinear Unmixing) [23], and BNLSU (Band-wise Nonlinear Spectral Unmixing) [44] are presented in this section.

In brief, the first method exploits the geometric characteristics of the BMMs for abundance estimation. The second method implements supervised nonlinear unmixing based on the KBMMs. The third method conducts band-wise nonlinear unmixing based on the EMLM to estimate abundances. After their algorithm principles are elaborated, their nonlinear unmixing performances are validated in experiments conducted on simulated datasets and real hyperspectral remote-sensing images.

13.3.1 Geometric Characteristics of BMMs-guided Nonlinear Spectral Unmixing

In the BMMs, $\mathbf{a}_i \odot \mathbf{a}_k$ $(i, k = 1, 2, ..., r)$ are considered to be virtual endmembers that represent second-order scatterings. They are commonly highly correlated to true endmembers, inducing a significant increase in the collinearity. As a result, the BMMs-based unmixing can be seriously deteriorated and is sensitive to noises. A critical approach to improve the nonlinear unmixing accuracy lies in the reduction of the negative influence of the collinearity.

According to Eq. (13.2) and the geometric characteristics of GBM and PPNM in Figure 13.1, it can be concluded that a BMM-based pixel $\mathbf{x}_j$ consists of a linear part $\mathbf{x}^{LMM} = \sum_{i=1}^{r} \mathbf{a}_i s_i$ and a nonlinear part $\mathbf{x}_j^{NL} = \sum_{i=1}^{t_1} \sum_{k=t_2}^{r} b_{i,k,j}(\mathbf{a}_i \odot \mathbf{a}_k) s_{i,j} s_{k,j}$, and the position of $\mathbf{x}_j$ in the r-dimensional feature space is identified by pulling $\mathbf{x}^{LMM}$ out from the $(r-1)$-dimensional simplex Δ^{r-1} spanned by true endmembers $(\mathbf{a}_1, \mathbf{a}_2, ..., \mathbf{a}_r)$ along the direction given by the force of all $\mathbf{a}_i \odot \mathbf{a}_k$. In this sense, a straightforward idea is that a nonlinear vertex $\mathbf{p}$ can be generated to span an r-dimensional convex hull $C^r = \left\{ \mathbf{x} = \sum_{i=1}^{r} \mathbf{a}_i h_i + \mathbf{p} h_{r+1} \middle| \sum_{i=1}^{r+1} h_i = 1 \right\}$ with true endmembers to include and approximately represent all the BMM-based pixels. Such a vertex $\mathbf{p}$ can be regarded as an extra endmember to concentrate the contribution of all the virtual endmembers. The normalized barycentric coordinates $(h_{1,j}, h_{2,j}, ..., h_{r,j})$ of $\mathbf{x}_j$ with respect to $(\mathbf{a}_1, \mathbf{a}_2, ..., \mathbf{a}_r)$ in C^r can be easily calculated by traditional linear unmixing methods such as the least squares satisfying the sum-to-one constraint. The contribution of $\mathbf{p}$ in $\mathbf{x}_j$, i.e., $\mathbf{p}h_{r+1,j}$ corresponds to the second-order scatterings defined nonlinear part of $\mathbf{x}_j$. Moreover, based on the normalization of $(h_{1,j}, h_{2,j}, ..., h_{r,j})$, $\mathbf{x}_j$ is projected to its approximate linear mixing component $\mathbf{y} \approx \sum_{i=1}^{r} \mathbf{a}_i s_i$. Since C^r should enclose all the pixels as tightly as possible, the nonlinear vertex $\mathbf{p}$ can be determined as the intersection of r $(r-1)$-dimensional hyperplanes $H_1, H_2, ..., H_r$ spanned by every $(r-1)$ true endmember and the BMMs-based pixels constructed by them as shown in Figure 13.3a. It can be proved that such a vertex $\mathbf{p}$ is unique [26].

Firstly, to determine $H_1, H_2, ..., H_r$ and obtain $\mathbf{p}$, nonlinear mixing midpoints $\boldsymbol{\omega}_1, ..., \boldsymbol{\omega}_{r-1}, \boldsymbol{\omega}_r$ are first calculated in Eq. (13.9) according to the GBM and PPNM. Then, after the hyperspectral data is reduced to be r-dimensional by principal component analysis (PCA), $H_1, H_2, ..., H_r$ can be achieved by using the sets of $\{\boldsymbol{\omega}_1, \mathbf{a}_2, ..., \mathbf{a}_r\}$,$\{\mathbf{a}_1, \boldsymbol{\omega}_2, ..., \mathbf{a}_r\}$, $\cdots$, $\{\mathbf{a}_1, \mathbf{a}_2, ..., \boldsymbol{\omega}_r\}$, respectively. It should be noted that $\mathbf{p} \in \mathbb{R}^{r \times 1}$ must be located on $H_1^{r-1}, H_2^{r-1}, ..., H_r^{r-1}$ simultaneously, and if $\mathbf{p}$ lies on H_q^{r-1}, the volume of the simplex spanned by $\mathbf{p}$ and $\{\mathbf{a}_1, ..., \mathbf{a}_{q-1}, \boldsymbol{\omega}_q, \mathbf{a}_{q+1}, ..., \mathbf{a}_r\}$ should be zero in Eq. (13.10). Therefore, $\mathbf{p}$ can be calculated by Eq. (13.11).

$$\boldsymbol{\omega}_q = \begin{cases} \dfrac{1}{r-1}\sum_{i=1}^{r} \mathbf{a}_i + \dfrac{1}{(r-1)^2}\sum_{i=1}^{r-1}\sum_{k=i+1}^{r} (\mathbf{a}_i \odot \mathbf{a}_k), \quad (i \neq q, k \neq q, q = 1, ..., r), & GBM \\ \dfrac{1}{r-1}\sum_{i=1}^{r} \mathbf{a}_i + \dfrac{1}{(r-1)^2}\sum_{i=1}^{r}\sum_{k=1}^{r} (\mathbf{a}_i \odot \mathbf{a}_k), \quad (i \neq q, k \neq q, q = 1, ..., r), & PPNM \end{cases} \tag{13.9}$$

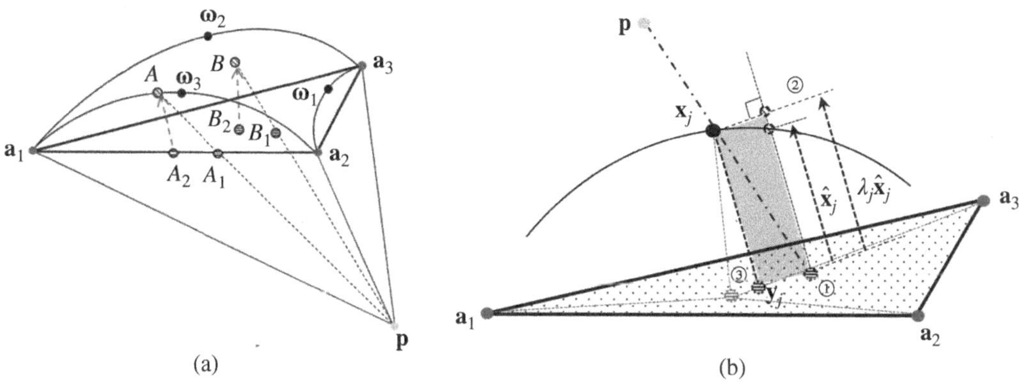

Figure 13.3 The principle of geometric-projection-based abundance estimation. (a) Nonlinear vertex and projection bias and (b) correction of projection bias. *Source:* [26] / with permission of IEEE.

$$\det(\mathbf{M}_q) = \det\begin{pmatrix} 1 & \cdots & 1 & 1 & 1 & \cdots & 1 & 1 \\ \mathbf{U}^T\mathbf{a}_1 & \cdots & \mathbf{U}^T\mathbf{a}_{q-1} & \mathbf{U}^T\boldsymbol{\omega}_q & \mathbf{U}^T\mathbf{a}_{q+1} & \cdots & \mathbf{U}^T\mathbf{a}_r & \mathbf{p} \end{pmatrix}$$
$$= (-1)^{r+2}\det(\mathbf{M}_{q1}) + (-1)^{r+3}\det(\mathbf{M}_{q2})p_1 + \cdots + (-1)^{2r+2}\det(\mathbf{M}_{q(r+1)})p_r = 0 \tag{13.10}$$

$$\begin{pmatrix} (-1)^{r+3}\det(\mathbf{M}_{12}) & \cdots & (-1)^{2r+2}\det(\mathbf{M}_{1(r+1)}) \\ \vdots & \vdots & \vdots \\ (-1)^{r+3}\det(\mathbf{M}_{q2}) & \cdots & (-1)^{2r+2}\det(\mathbf{M}_{q(r+1)}) \\ \vdots & \vdots & \vdots \\ (-1)^{r+3}\det(\mathbf{M}_{r2}) & \cdots & (-1)^{2r+2}\det(\mathbf{M}_{r(r+1)}) \end{pmatrix} \begin{pmatrix} p_1 \\ p_2 \\ \vdots \\ p_r \end{pmatrix} = \begin{pmatrix} (-1)^{r+3}\det(\mathbf{M}_{11}) \\ (-1)^{r+3}\det(\mathbf{M}_{21}) \\ \vdots \\ (-1)^{r+3}\det(\mathbf{M}_{r1}) \end{pmatrix} \tag{13.11}$$

In Eqs. (13.10) and (13.11), $\mathbf{M}_{qi} \in \mathbb{R}^{r\times r}$ is a known sub-matrix obtained by deleting row i and column $r+1$ of $\mathbf{M}_q$, and $\mathbf{U} \in \mathbb{R}^{n\times r}$ is the matrix of the first r principal component vectors of data. Based on the use of $\mathbf{p}$ and $(\mathbf{a}_1, \mathbf{a}_2, ..., \mathbf{a}_r)$, projection coordinates $\hat{\mathbf{s}}_j$ $(j = 1, 2, \cdots, m)$ of every pixel can be easily generated using Eqs. (13.12) and (13.13), where δ is a small positive parameter. Thus, a BMM-based pixel $\mathbf{x}_j$ can be effectively projected to its approximate linear mixing component $\mathbf{y}_j = \sum_{i=1}^{r} \mathbf{a}_i\hat{s}_{i,j}$. As depicted in Figure 13.3a, a small projection bias exists between $\mathbf{y}_j$ and the true linear mixing component $\mathbf{x}_j^{LMM}$ because of noises and the construction of the nonlinear vertex $\mathbf{p}$.

$$\hat{\mathbf{s}}_j = \left(h_1/\sum_{i=1}^{r} h_i,\ \ h_2/\sum_{i=1}^{r} h_i,\ \ \cdots\ ,\ \ h_r/\sum_{i=1}^{r} h_i\right)^T \tag{13.12}$$

$$\mathbf{h}_j = \left(\tilde{\mathbf{M}}^T\tilde{\mathbf{M}}\right)^{-1}\tilde{\mathbf{M}}^T\begin{pmatrix} \delta\mathbf{U}^T\mathbf{x}_j \\ 1 \end{pmatrix},\quad \tilde{\mathbf{M}} = \begin{pmatrix} \delta\mathbf{U}^T\mathbf{a}_1 & \cdots & \delta\mathbf{U}^T\mathbf{a}_r & \delta\mathbf{p} \\ 1 & \cdots & 1 & 1 \end{pmatrix} \tag{13.13}$$

In the above process, the use of a nonlinear vertex $\mathbf{p}$ with low correlation to $(\mathbf{a}_1, \mathbf{a}_2, ..., \mathbf{a}_r)$ replaces the direct participation of virtual endmembers in unmixing, leading to a significant reduction of the collinearity.

Secondly, the projection coordinate $\hat{\mathbf{s}}_j$ may deviate slightly from the true abundance $\mathbf{s}_j$, but an asymptotically identical relationship between $\hat{\mathbf{s}}_j$ and $\mathbf{s}_j$ in geometry can be exploited to approach $\hat{\mathbf{s}}_j$ to $\mathbf{s}_j$ [26]. First, without considering the nonlinear parameters $b_{i,k,j}$, the initial nonlinear component $\hat{\mathbf{x}}_j^{(0)} = \sum_{i=1}^{t_1}\sum_{k=t_2}^{r}(\mathbf{a}_i \odot \mathbf{a}_k)\hat{s}_{i,j}\hat{s}_{k,j}$ of each pixel based on the GBM and PPNM can be directly obtained using the projection coordinate $\hat{\mathbf{s}}_j^{(0)}$ in Eq. (13.12) and $\hat{\mathbf{x}}_j^{(0)}$ is linearly dependent on the true $\sum_{i=1}^{t_1}\sum_{k=t_2}^{r}(\mathbf{a}_i \odot \mathbf{a}_k)s_{i,j}s_{k,j}$. Then, as shown in Figure 13.3b, in each iteration, $\lambda_j^{(t)}\hat{\mathbf{x}}_j^{(t)}$ is used to approach $\mathbf{x}_j^{NL}$ based on the simplified linear regression in Eq. (13.14). The pixels' projected points can be further corrected as $\mathbf{y}_j^{(t+1)}$ $(j = 1, 2, \ldots, m)$ according to Eq. (13.15).

Algorithm 13.1 GCBAE

The corrected $\mathbf{y}_j^{(t+1)}$ becomes closer to $\mathbf{x}_j^{LMM}$ (e.g., the bottom dashed circle on the simplex spanned by $\mathbf{a}_1$, $\mathbf{a}_2$, $\mathbf{a}_3$ in Figure 13.3b), and the projection bias is reduced. Moreover, to remove the projection bias and produce more accurate abundances, the traditional fully constrained least squares (FCLS) method [10] is employed to estimate each pixel's new projection coordinate $\hat{\mathbf{s}}_j^{(t+1)}$ using $\mathbf{y}_j^{(t+1)}$ that will be updated again by Eq. (13.15) in the next iteration. Finally, when $\hat{\mathbf{s}}_j$ with satisfactory accuracy is obtained, the nonlinear parameters $b_{i,k,j}$ in the BMMs can be easily obtained using methods such as quadratic programming. The whole procedure of GCBAE is summarized in Algorithm 13.1.

$$\min_{\lambda} \frac{1}{2}\left\| \mathbf{x}_j - \left(\sum_{i=1}^{r}\mathbf{a}_i\hat{s}_{i,j}^{(t)} + \lambda_j^{(t)}\hat{\mathbf{x}}_j^{(t)}\right)\right\|_F^2 \tag{13.14}$$

$$\begin{cases} \mathbf{y}_j^{(t+1)} = \mathbf{x}_j - \lambda_j^{(t)}\hat{\mathbf{x}}_j^{(t)} \\ \lambda_j^{(t)} = \left(\mathbf{x}_j - \sum_{i=1}^{r}\mathbf{a}_i\hat{s}_{i,j}^{(t)}\right)^T\hat{\mathbf{x}}_j^{(t)} / \left(\hat{\mathbf{x}}_j^{(t)T}\hat{\mathbf{x}}_j^{(t)}\right) \end{cases} \tag{13.15}$$

13.3.2 KBMM-guided Nonlinear Spectral Unmixing

The KBMM in Eq. (13.4) provides the kernel-based nonparametric transformation for the GBM and PPNM to represent the nonlinearity flexibly. The numerical fitting of the KBMM's nonlinear part is only dependent on the kernel-based representation, removing the direct participation of abundances. This advantage greatly facilitates the optimization of unknown unmixing variables in the KBMM. In this sense, the optimization subproblem for updating the abundances **S** can be simplified to a linear unmixing problem, which can significantly reduce the computational complexity even though some regularizers may be introduced into the nonlinear unmixing task. Since the spatial information of hyperspectral data plays a critical role in unmixing, KBU formulates a compact constrained optimization problem in Eq. (13.16) for nonlinear unmixing based on the KBMM and the total variation (TV) regularizer for abundances. As a representative of many prior constraints, the TV regularizer in Eq. (13.17) is regarded as a paradigm to integrate the spatial smoothness of abundances into the KBMM-based nonlinear unmixing to produce more accurate unmixing results. Finally, the ADMM is employed to solve the problem in Eq. (13.16).

$$\begin{aligned}&\min_{\mathbf{S},\mathbf{B}} \sum_{j=1}^{m}\left(\frac{1}{2}\|\mathbf{e}_j\|^2 + \frac{\lambda_1}{2}\boldsymbol{\beta}_j{}^T\mathbf{K}\boldsymbol{\beta}_j\right) + \lambda_2 J_{sp}(\mathbf{S})\\ &\text{s.t. } \mathbf{S}^T\mathbf{1}_r = \mathbf{1}_m, \quad \mathbf{S}\geq 0, \quad \mathbf{x}_j = \mathbf{A}\mathbf{s}_j + \mathbf{K}\boldsymbol{\beta}_j + \mathbf{e}_j\end{aligned} \tag{13.16}$$

$$J_{sp}(\mathbf{S}) = \sum_{j=1}^{m}\sum_{i\in\mathcal{N}(j)}\|\mathbf{s}_j - \mathbf{s}_i\|_1 = \|\mathbf{SH}\|_{1,1} \tag{13.17}$$

In Eq. (13.16), **K** is determined according to the GBM or the PPNM. λ_1 and λ_2 are two small positive parameters that balance the influences of nonlinear parameters and abundance smoothness on unmixing, respectively. $\mathbf{H}\in\mathbb{R}^{m\times 4m}$ is a constant matrix and $\|\cdot\|_{1,1}$ is the sum of the ℓ_1-norms of the columns of a matrix. In the framework of ADMM, an augmented Lagrangian function can be derived in Eq. (13.18) after two auxiliary variables **G** and **V** satisfying constraints $\mathbf{V}=\mathbf{S}$ and $\mathbf{G}=\mathbf{VH}$are introduced to Eq. (13.16). In iterations, subproblems with respect to **B**, **S**, **G**, **V** and two Lagrange multipliers $\mathbf{D}_1$ and $\mathbf{D}_2$ are optimized in sequence. Until the convergence conditions are met, the variables **B**, **G**, **V**, $\mathbf{D}_1$, and $\mathbf{D}_2$ are accordingly updated by Eq. (13.19) and **S** is updated by solving the subproblem in Eq. (13.20) resorting to quadratic programming. Notably, the TV regularizer enables the estimated abundances to be similar for four local neighboring pixels, and it only functions on **S**, which retains a regularized linear subproblem for updating abundances.

$$\begin{aligned}L(\mathbf{S},\mathbf{B},\mathbf{G},\mathbf{V},\mathbf{D}_1,\mathbf{D}_2) = &\sum_{i=1}^{m}\left(\frac{1}{2}\|\mathbf{x}_j - \mathbf{A}\mathbf{s}_j - \mathbf{K}\boldsymbol{\beta}_j\|^2 + \frac{\lambda_1}{2}\boldsymbol{\beta}_j{}^T\mathbf{K}\boldsymbol{\beta}_j\right) + \lambda_2\|\mathbf{G}\|_{1,1}\\ &+ \frac{\rho}{2}\|\mathbf{S}-\mathbf{V}-\mathbf{D}_1\|_F^2 + \frac{\rho}{2}\|\mathbf{G}-\mathbf{VH}-\mathbf{D}_2\|_F^2\end{aligned} \tag{13.18}$$

$$\text{s.t. } \mathbf{S}^T\mathbf{1}_r = \mathbf{1}_m, \quad \mathbf{S}\geq \mathbf{0}$$

$$\begin{cases}\boldsymbol{\beta}_j{}^{(t+1)} = (\mathbf{K}+\lambda_1\mathbf{I})^{-1}\left(x_j - \mathbf{A}\mathbf{s}_j{}^{(t)}\right)\\ \mathbf{V}^{(t+1)} = \left(\mathbf{S}^{(t+1)} - \mathbf{D}_1{}^{(t)} + \left(\mathbf{G}^{(t)} - \mathbf{D}_2{}^{(t)}\right)\mathbf{H}^T\right)\left(I + \mathbf{H}\mathbf{H}^T\right)^{-1}\\ \mathbf{G}^{(t+1)} = soft\left(\mathbf{V}^{(t+1)}\mathbf{H} + \mathbf{D}_2{}^{(t)}, \lambda_2/\rho\right)\\ \mathbf{D}_1{}^{(t+1)} = \mathbf{D}_1{}^{(t)} + \left(\mathbf{V}^{(t+1)} - \mathbf{S}^{(t+1)}\right)\\ \mathbf{D}_2{}^{(t+1)} = \mathbf{D}_2{}^{(t)} + \left(\mathbf{V}^{(t+1)}\mathbf{H} - \mathbf{G}^{(t+1)}\right)\end{cases} \tag{13.19}$$

$$
\begin{aligned}
\mathbf{s}_j^{(t+1)} &= \arg\min_{\mathbf{s}_j} \frac{1}{2}\left\|\mathbf{x}_j - \mathbf{A}\mathbf{s}_j - \mathbf{K}\boldsymbol{\beta}_j^{(t)}\right\|^2 + \frac{\rho}{2}\left\|\mathbf{s}_j - \mathbf{v}_j^{(t)} - \mathbf{d}_{1,j}^{(t)}\right\|^2 \\
&\text{s.t. } \mathbf{1}^T\mathbf{s}_j = \mathbf{1}, \quad \mathbf{s}_j \geq \mathbf{0}
\end{aligned} \tag{13.20}
$$

In Eq. (13.18), $\|\cdot\|_F$ is the Frobenius norm and ρ is a small positive parameter. $soft(\cdot)$ in Eq. (13.19) denotes a soft threshold operator. In Eq. (13.20), $\mathbf{v}_j$ and $\mathbf{d}_{1,j}$ represent the jth column of $\mathbf{V}$ and $\mathbf{D}_1$, respectively. The stop criteria include the maximum number of iterations $T_{\max}$ and $\|\mathbf{S}^{(t)} - \mathbf{S}^{(t-1)}\|_F < \eta$. $\mathbf{S}$ and $\mathbf{V}$ can be initialized by FCLS, and $\mathbf{B}$, $\mathbf{D}_1$, $\mathbf{D}_2$ are initialized by zeros. The whole procedure of KBU is summarized in Algorithm 13.2.

Algorithm 13.2 KBU

13.3.3 EMLM-guided Band-wise Nonlinear Spectral Unmixing

Based on the EMLM in Eq. (13.8), nonlinear unmixing can be conducted to interpret the wavelength-dependent nonlinearity. The increase of matching degree to real scenarios in the EMLM can effectively reduce the residual at each band, leading to the estimation of more accurate abundances. Moreover, due to the sparsity of abundances and the smooth change of the nonlinear intensity among neighboring bands, two physical constraints, i.e., the ℓ_1-norm-based sparseness constraint for $\mathbf{S}$ and the Laplacian-matrix-based smoothness constraint for $\mathbf{P}$ can be adopted to formulate a constrained optimization problem for nonlinear unmixing in Eq. (13.21).

$$
\begin{aligned}
&\min_{\mathbf{S},\tilde{\mathbf{P}}} \frac{1}{2}\sum_{j=1}^{m}\left\|\left(\mathbf{A}\odot\left((\mathbf{1}_n - \mathbf{P}_j + \mathbf{P}_j\odot\mathbf{x}_j)\mathbf{1}_r^T\right)\right)\mathbf{s}_j - \mathbf{x}_j\right\|_F^2 + \lambda_1\|\mathbf{S}\|_{1,1} + \frac{\lambda_2}{2}trace\left(\tilde{\mathbf{P}}^T\mathbf{L}\tilde{\mathbf{P}}\right) \\
&\text{s.t. } s_{i,j} \geq 0, \quad \sum_{i=1}^{r} s_{i,j} = 1, \quad P_{i,j} < 1
\end{aligned} \tag{13.21}
$$

$$
\begin{cases}
\frac{1}{2}trace\left(\tilde{\mathbf{P}}^T\mathbf{L}\tilde{\mathbf{P}}\right) = \frac{1}{2}\sum_{j=1}^{m}\sum_{i=1}^{n}\sum_{k=1}^{n}\left(P_{i,j} - P_{k,j}\right)^2 W_{i,k} \\
W_{i,k} = \begin{cases} e^{-\frac{\|\mathbf{X}(i,:) - \mathbf{X}(k,:)\|_F^2}{\theta^2}}, & i\text{th band and } k\text{th band are neighbors} \\ 0, & \text{others} \end{cases}
\end{cases} \tag{13.22}
$$

In Eq. (13.21), $\|\cdot\|_{1,1}$ is the ℓ_1 norm for a matrix, *trace*(·) denotes the trace operation on a matrix, and λ_1 and λ_2 are two small positive regularization parameters. $\tilde{\mathbf{P}} = (\mathbf{P}_1, \mathbf{P}_2, ..., \mathbf{P}_m) \in \mathbb{R}^{n \times m}$ represents a nonlinear probability parameter matrix of the same size as the input hyperspectral data **X**. **L** is a Laplacian matrix defined in Eq. (13.22) based on the weight coefficients $W_{i,k}$ $(i, k = 1, 2, ..., n)$ between every two data vectors $\mathbf{X}(i,:)$ and $\mathbf{X}(k,:)$at the ith band and the kth band, respectively, i.e., $\mathbf{L} = \mathbf{D} - \mathbf{W}$, where **D** is a diagonal matrix satisfying $D_{i,i} = \sum_{k=1}^{n} W_{i,k}$. Notably, if the weight $W_{i,k}$ is large, the nonlinear probability parameters $P_{i,j}$ and $P_{k,j}$ of two corresponding bands should be similar. Since neighboring bands are often highly correlated, $trace\left(\tilde{\mathbf{P}}^T\mathbf{L}\tilde{\mathbf{P}}\right)$ makes the probability parameters $\tilde{\mathbf{P}}$ describe the smooth change of nonlinear intensities among different bands in every pixel. The parameter θ in Eq. (13.22) can be set as 1. It is considered that the introduction of $trace\left(\tilde{\mathbf{P}}^T\mathbf{L}\tilde{\mathbf{P}}\right)$ and $\|\mathbf{S}\|_{1,1}$ into the EMLM-based nonconvex numerical optimization problem can mitigate the influence of bad local minima and obtain accurate unmixing results in line with ground truth.

Then, ADMM is employed to optimize the unmixing variables in Eq. (13.21). After two new variables **G** and **V** satisfying constraints $\mathbf{G} = \mathbf{S}$ and $\mathbf{V} = \tilde{\mathbf{P}}$ are added, the augmented Lagrangian for Eq. (13.21) can be derived in Eq. (13.23) using two Lagrange multipliers $\mathbf{D}_1$ and $\mathbf{D}_2$. The variables $\mathbf{S}, \tilde{\mathbf{P}}, \mathbf{G}, \mathbf{V}$ and dual variables $\mathbf{D}_1, \mathbf{D}_2$ are alternately minimized in the sequential optimization with respect to their corresponding subproblems in Eq. (13.23) when other related variables are fixed. Eqs. (13.24) to (13.27) provide the technical details of updating $\mathbf{S}$, $\mathbf{G}$, $\tilde{\mathbf{P}}$, $\mathbf{V}$, $\mathbf{D}_1$, and $\mathbf{D}_2$ in each step.

$$\begin{aligned} L\left(\mathbf{S}, \tilde{\mathbf{P}}, \mathbf{G}, \mathbf{V}, \mathbf{D}_1, \mathbf{D}_2\right) = & \frac{1}{2}\sum_{j=1}^{m} \|(\mathbf{A} \odot ((\mathbf{1}_n - \mathbf{P}_j + \mathbf{P}_j \odot \mathbf{x}_j)\mathbf{1}_r^T))\mathbf{s}_j - \mathbf{x}_j\|_F^2 \\ & + \lambda_1\|\mathbf{G}\|_{1,1} + \frac{\lambda_2}{2} trace\left(\mathbf{V}^T\mathbf{L}\mathbf{V}\right) + \tau_B(\mathbf{S}) + \tau_C(\tilde{\mathbf{P}}) \\ & + \frac{\rho}{2}\left(\|\mathbf{S} - \mathbf{G} + \mathbf{D}_1\|_F^2 + \|\tilde{\mathbf{P}} - \mathbf{V} + \mathbf{D}_2\|_F^2\right) \end{aligned} \tag{13.23}$$

$$\begin{cases} \mathbf{s}_j^{(t+1)} = \left(\left(\tilde{\mathbf{A}}^{(t)}\right)^T\tilde{\mathbf{A}}^{(t)} + \rho\mathbf{I}_{r\times r}\right)^{-1}\left(\tilde{\mathbf{A}}^{(t)}\mathbf{x}_j + \rho\left(\mathbf{g}_j^{(t)} - \mathbf{d}_{1,j}^{(t)}\right)\right) \\ \tilde{\mathbf{A}}^{(t)} = \mathbf{A} \odot \left(\left(\mathbf{1}_n - \mathbf{P}_j^{(t)} + \mathbf{P}_j^{(t)} \odot \mathbf{x}_j\right)\mathbf{1}_r^T\right) \\ \mathbf{S}^{(t+1)} = \max\left(\mathbf{S}^{(t+1)}, 0\right), \quad \mathbf{S}^{(t+1)} = \mathbf{S}^{(t+1)}./\left(\mathbf{1}_{r\times r}\mathbf{S}^{(t+1)}\right) \end{cases} \tag{13.24}$$

$$\begin{aligned} \mathbf{G}^{(t+1)} &= soft\left(\mathbf{S}^{(t+1)} + \mathbf{D}_1^{(t)}, \lambda_1/\rho\right) \\ &= \max\left(\left|\mathbf{S}^{(t+1)} + \mathbf{D}_1^{(t)}\right| - (\lambda_1/\rho)\mathbf{1}_{r\times m}, 0\right) \odot sign\left(\mathbf{S}^{(t+1)} + \mathbf{D}_1^{(t)}\right) \end{aligned} \tag{13.25}$$

$$\begin{cases} \tilde{\mathbf{P}}^{(t+1)} = \min\left(\begin{array}{c} \left(\rho\left(\mathbf{V}^{(t)} - \mathbf{D}_2^{(t)}\right) - \mathbf{Y}^{(t+1)} \odot (\mathbf{1}_{r\times m} - \mathbf{X}) \odot \left(\mathbf{X} - \mathbf{Y}^{(t+1)}\right)\right) \\ ./\left(\left(\mathbf{Y}^{(t+1)}\right)^2 \odot (\mathbf{1}_{r\times m} - \mathbf{X})^2 + \rho\mathbf{1}_{n\times m}\right), \quad 1 \end{array}\right) \\ \mathbf{V}^{(t+1)} = (\lambda_2\mathbf{L} + \rho\mathbf{I}_{n\times n})^{-1}\left(\rho\left(\tilde{\mathbf{P}}^{(t+1)} + \mathbf{D}_2^{(t)}\right)\right) \end{cases} \tag{13.26}$$

$$\begin{cases} \mathbf{D}_1^{(t+1)} = \mathbf{D}_1^{(t)} + \mathbf{S}^{(t+1)} - \mathbf{G}^{(t+1)} \\ \mathbf{D}_2^{(t+1)} = \mathbf{D}_2^{(t)} + \tilde{\mathbf{P}}^{(t+1)} - \mathbf{V}^{(t+1)} \end{cases} \tag{13.27}$$

In Eq. (13.23), $\tau_B(\mathbf{S}), \tau_C(\tilde{\mathbf{P}})$ enforce $\mathbf{S}, \tilde{\mathbf{P}}$ to satisfy their corresponding constraints in Eq. (13.21), respectively. ρ is a small positive penalty parameter. In Eq. (13.24), $\mathbf{g}_j^{(t)}$ and $\mathbf{d}_{1,j}^{(t)}$ represent the jth column of $\mathbf{G}^{(t)}$ and $\mathbf{D}_1^{(t)}$, respectively. Until the stopping criteria (i.e., the maximum number of iterations and the primal residual value) are satisfied, $\mathbf{S}, \mathbf{G}, \tilde{\mathbf{P}}, \mathbf{V}, \mathbf{D}_1,$ and $\mathbf{D}_2$ will be updated alternately in iterations. In the initialization, $\mathbf{D}_1^{(0)}$ and $\mathbf{D}_2^{(0)}$ are set as zeros, abundances estimated by FCLS are used to obtain $\mathbf{S}^{(0)}$ and $\tilde{\mathbf{P}}^{(0)}$ which are further used to initialize $\mathbf{G}^{(0)}$ and $\mathbf{V}^{(0)}$, respectively. It is considered that BNLSU provides an explicit form for band-wise nonlinear unmixing and its mathematical optimization is simple. Algorithm 13.3 summarizes the whole procedure of BNLSU.

Algorithm 13.3 BNLSU

13.3.4 Experimental Results

13.3.4.1 Simulated Data and Real Hyperspectral Data for Experiments

In the generation of simulated datasets, endmembers' spectra (224 bands covering wavelengths from 0.38 to 2.5 μm) were selected from the United States Geological Survey (USGS) digital spectral library, and abundances were randomly generated according to the Dirichlet distribution or by the Gaussian fields method, satisfying the nonnegative and sum-to-one constraint. A series of datasets containing 2000 pixels were produced according to the GBM, PPNM, and EMLM. The nonlinear parameters of the GBM and the PPNM were uniformly drawn in the sets [0,1] and (−0.3,0.3), respectively. The nonlinear probability parameters $\mathbf{P}$ of each EMLM-based pixel were generated to change smoothly in the range of (0,1) according to the shape of Gaussian functions [44]. Finally, to study the robustness of nonlinear unmixing, additive zero-mean white Gaussian noises were added to produce simulated datasets with different signal-to-noise ratios (SNR), and different numbers of endmembers were adopted to change the mixing complexity. As an important supplement to the numerically generated simulated data, physical-based simulated data of virtual citrus orchards and forests in [66–69] were further exploited to give a more reasonable validation for nonlinear unmixing results. The virtual observation scenes were rendered by multiple sub-models of an extended physically based ray-tracing (PBRT) model. Two types of orchard sub-datasets named Orc_2 (constituted by trees and soil) and Orc_3 (constituted by trees, weeds, and soil), and four types of forest sub-datasets constructed by different proportions of beech and poplar (named Frst_b20p80, Frst_b40p60, Frst_b60p40, and Frst_b80p20) were used for experiments.

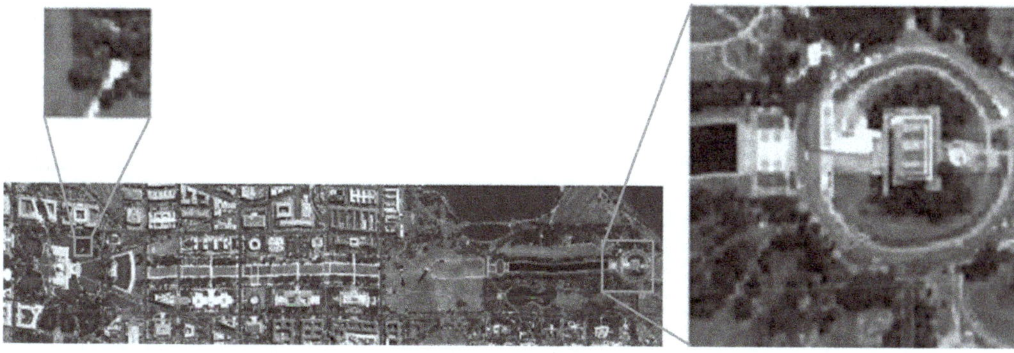

Figure 13.4 HYDICE Washington DC Mall dataset and its selected subregions for experiments.

In terms of experiments with real hyperspectral data, two subregions selected from the HYDICE Washington DC Mall dataset shown in Figure 13.4 and a subregion of the dataset acquired over Moffett Field by the airborne visible infrared imaging spectrometer (AVIRIS) shown in Figure 13.5 were used for unmixing evaluation. The spatial resolution of the HYDICE data and the AVIRIS data is 2 and 20 m, respectively. The HYDICE data have 210 bands and the AVIRIS data have 224 bands. After the bands seriously affected by water-vapor absorption and noises were removed, 165 bands of the HYDICE data (serial numbers of the removed bands are 16–101, 108–136, 153–202) and 188 bands of the AVIRIS data (serial numbers of the removed bands 5–104, 116–149, 171–221) remained. The two subregions of the HYDICE data in Figure 13.4 contain 30×30 and 100×100 pixels, respectively, where typical land covers include trees, grass, roads, roofs, water, and shadows. The size of the selected subregion of the AVIRIS data in Figure 13.5 is 50×50-pixel, and three types of land covers, i.e., water, soil, and vegetation exist in this area.

According to the characteristics of the numerical-model-guided nonlinear unmixing methods, in the experiments, GCBAE and KBU were compared with four methods (i.e., FCLS [10], K-Hype [21], GBM-GDA [19], and PPNM-GDA [20]), and BNLSU was further compared with PPNM-GDA [20], p(4) linear [24] (i.e., the order of multiple scatterings is set as 4), MLM [25], and NDU(Sp.+P) [22] using separable kernels constructed by a second-order polynomial kernel. To compare the methods

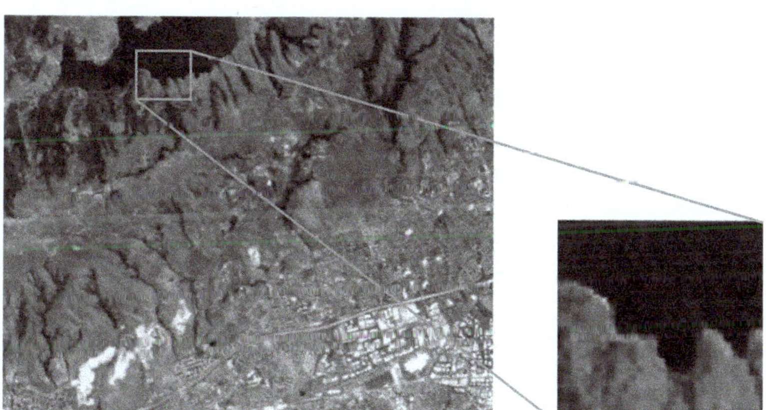

Figure 13.5 AVIRIS Moffett Field dataset and its selected subregion for experiments.

quantitively, the root mean square error (RMSE) between the estimated abundance $\tilde{\mathbf{s}}_j$ and the real abundance $\mathbf{s}_j$ in Eq. (13.28) and the reconstruction error (RE) between the model-based reconstructed pixel $\tilde{\mathbf{x}}_j$ and the original pixel $\mathbf{x}_j$ in Eq. (13.29) were calculated.

$$RMSE = \sqrt{\frac{1}{mr}\sum_{j=1}^{m} \|\mathbf{s}_j - \tilde{\mathbf{s}}_j\|_2^2} \tag{13.28}$$

$$RE = \sqrt{\frac{1}{mn}\sum_{j=1}^{m} \|\mathbf{x}_j - \tilde{\mathbf{x}}_j\|_2^2} \tag{13.29}$$

13.3.4.2 Experimental Results for GCBAE

Firstly, the simulated datasets based on the GBM and the PPNM were used to validate the unmixing performance of GCBAE. Figure 13.6 indicates that the construction of a nonlinear vertex $\mathbf{p}$ to replace all the virtual endmembers (i.e., $\mathbf{a}_i \odot \mathbf{a}_k$ $(i, k = 1, 2, \ldots, r)$) greatly increases the average distance of explanatory variables to be consistent with the average distance of true endmembers. It can be concluded that the correlation between true endmembers and $\mathbf{p}$ becomes weak, leading to the reduction of the influence of the collinearity on unmixing. Moreover, the unmixing accuracy of GCBAE was compared with other methods in the experiments for analyzing the influences of noise intensity (i.e., SNR was set as 40, 30, and 20 dB, respectively) and the number of endmembers (i.e., r was 3, 5, and 8, respectively). Tables 13.1 and 13.2 have listed the RMSEs and REs of the corresponding experimental results. It can be observed that as the noise intensity or the number of endmembers increases, the unmixing accuracies of most methods decrease. GCBAE can provide more accurate abundances in all cases and its RE is the best for both the GBM-based and the PPNM-based datasets. It can be concluded that the reduction of the collinearity based on the use of a nonlinear vertex $\mathbf{p}$ enables GCBAE to have remarkable advantages in solving the numerical model-based nonlinear unmixing problems.

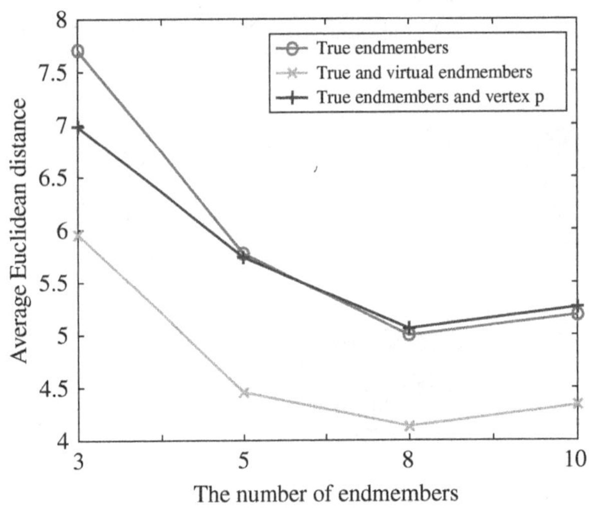

Figure 13.6 Average distances of different sets of explanatory variables. *Source:* [26] / with permission of IEEE.

Table 13.1 Comparison of unmixing accuracy for simulated datasets with different SNRs.

		RMSE					RE				
Model	**SNR (dB)**	**FCLS**	**K-Hype**	**GBM-GDA**	**PPNM-GDA**	**GCBAE**	**FCLS**	**K-Hype**	**GBM-GDA**	**PPNM-GDA**	**GCBAE**
GBM	40	0.0658 ± 0.0000	0.0171 ± 0.0001	0.0640 ± 0.0001	0.0134 ± 0.0001	**0.0091 ± 0.0001**	0.0120 ± 0.0000	0.0476 ± 0.0001	0.0120 ± 0.0000	0.0054 ± 0.0000	**0.0053 ± 0.0000**
	30	0.0667 ± 0.0001	0.0244 ± 0.0002	0.0646 ± 0.0001	0.0206 ± 0.0001	**0.0171 ± 0.0002**	0.0200 ± 0.0000	0.0511 ± 0.0002	0.0200 ± 0.0000	0.0169 ± 0.0000	**0.0168 ± 0.0000**
	20	0.0730 ± 0.0005	0.0577 ± 0.0007	0.0696 ± 0.0005	0.0481 ± 0.0007	**0.0449 ± 0.0007**	0.0545 ± 0.0001	0.0794 ± 0.0006	0.0544 ± 0.0001	**0.0532 ± 0.0000**	**0.0532 ± 0.0001**
PPNM	40	0.0764 ± 0.0001	0.0129 ± 0.0001	0.0784 ± 0.0001	0.0081 ± 0.0006	**0.0057 ± 0.0001**	0.0114 ± 0.0000	0.0512 ± 0.0001	0.0116 ± 0.0000	**0.0050 ± 0.0000**	**0.0050 ± 0.0000**
	30	0.0773 ± 0.0001	0.0231 ± 0.0003	0.0791 ± 0.0001	0.0188 ± 0.0002	**0.0174 ± 0.0003**	0.0189 ± 0.0000	0.0542 ± 0.0002	0.0190 ± 0.0000	0.0159 ± 0.0000	**0.0158 ± 0.0000**
	20	0.0835 ± 0.0005	0.0618 ± 0.0009	0.0842 ± 0.0005	0.0512 ± 0.0007	**0.0498 ± 0.0007**	0.0513 ± 0.0000	0.0796 ± 0.0004	0.0514 ± 0.0001	0.0502 ± 0.0000	**0.0501 ± 0.0000**

Source: Adapted from [26]. Bold values represent the best results in this table.

Table 13.2 Comparison of unmixing accuracy for simulated datasets with different numbers of endmembers.

		RMSE					RE				
Model	***r***	**FCLS**	**K-Hype**	**GBM-GDA**	**PPNM-GDA**	**GCBAE**	**FCLS**	**K-Hype**	**GBM-GDA**	**PPNM-GDA**	**GCBAE**
GBM	3	0.0342 ± 0.0000	0.0230 ± 0.0000	0.0134 ± 0.0000	0.0187 ± 0.0000	**0.0085 ± 0.0000**	0.0152 ± 0.0000	0.0457 ± 0.0000	0.0048 ± 0.0000	0.0029 ± 0.0000	**0.0019 ± 0.0000**
	5	0.0656 ± 0.0000	0.0161 ± 0.0000	0.0639 ± 0.0000	0.0124 ± 0.0001	**0.0077 ± 0.0000**	0.0108 ± 0.0000	0.0473 ± 0.0000	0.0109 ± 0.0000	0.0020 ± 0.0000	**0.0017 ± 0.0000**
	8	0.0765 ± 0.0000	0.0185 ± 0.0000	0.0699 ± 0.0001	0.0127 ± 0.0005	**0.0067 ± 0.0000**	0.0126 ± 0.0000	0.0657 ± 0.0000	0.0113 ± 0.0000	0.0022 ± 0.0001	**0.0019 ± 0.0000**
PPNM	3	0.0606 ± 0.0000	0.0092 ± 0.0000	0.0616 ± 0.0000	0.0022 ± 0.0022	**0.0005 ± 0.0000**	0.0193 ± 0.0000	0.0621 ± 0.0000	0.0186 ± 0.0000	0.0020 ± 0.0004	**0.0017 ± 0.0000**
	5	0.0762 ± 0.0000	0.0113 ± 0.0000	0.0784 ± 0.0000	0.0054 ± 0.0009	**0.0019 ± 0.0000**	0.0103 ± 0.0000	0.0509 ± 0.0000	0.0106 ± 0.0000	0.0017 ± 0.0001	**0.0016 ± 0.0000**
	8	0.0738 ± 0.0000	0.0160 ± 0.0001	0.0725 ± 0.0000	0.0113 ± 0.0007	**0.0031 ± 0.0001**	0.0096 ± 0.0000	0.0598 ± 0.0001	0.0092 ± 0.0000	0.0019 ± 0.0001	**0.0017 ± 0.0000**

Source: Adapted from [26]. Bold values represent the best results in this table.

Secondly, two subregions of the HYDICE Washington DC Mall dataset in Figure 13.4 were used for experiments. Endmembers extracted by VCA were used by every compared method to estimate the abundances. Due to the inaccessible real abundances, as a qualitative comparison, the estimated abundance maps for the subregion containing 30 × 30 pixels are displayed in Figure 13.7. Moreover, the REs of the unmixing results are provided in Table 13.3. Like most of the compared

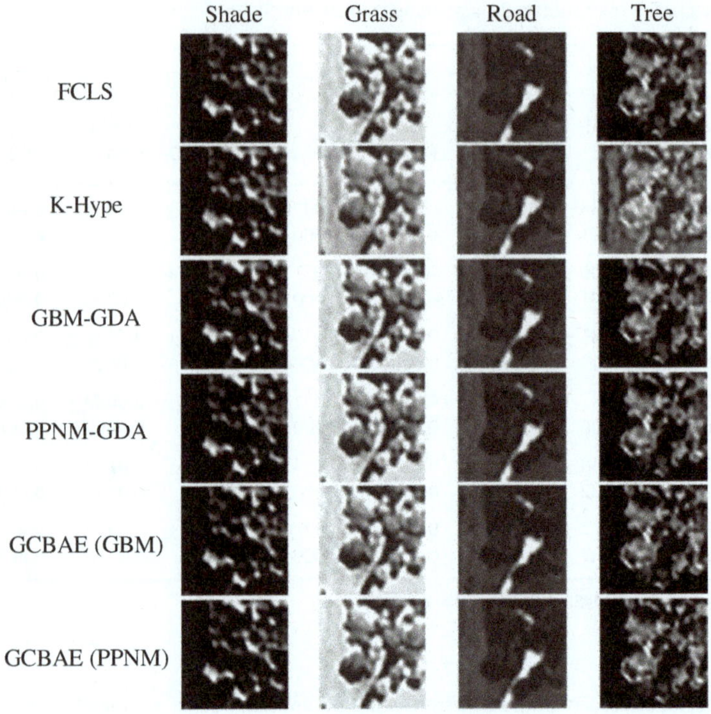

Figure 13.7 Abundance maps estimated by the compared methods for the HYDICE data's subregion containing 30 × 30 pixels. *Source:* [26] / with permission of IEEE.

Table 13.3 Comparison of REs for the HYDICE datasets.

Method	Subregion with 30 × 30 pixels	Subregion with 100 × 100 pixels
FCLS	0.0194	0.0305
K-Hype	0.0823	0.0622
GBM-GDA	0.0192	0.0281
PPNM-GDA	0.0093	0.0107
GCBAE (GBM)	**0.0159**	**0.0277**
GCBAE (PPNM)	**0.0092**	**0.0101**

Source: Adapted from [26]. Bold values represent the best results in this table.

methods, GCBAE clearly revealed the spatial distributions of four types of land covers based on the GBM and the PPNM. Nonlinear unmixing methods have smaller REs than FCLS. If the model assumption is the same (i.e., GBM or PPNM), GCBAE performs better in data reconstruction. It indicates that GCBAE has stable unmixing performances for different BMM-based assumptions. Experimental results in Figure 13.8 further prove that GCBAE performs well in processing real hyperspectral images of different sizes, and it provides similar abundances in line with the practical situation whether the GBM or the PPNM is used.

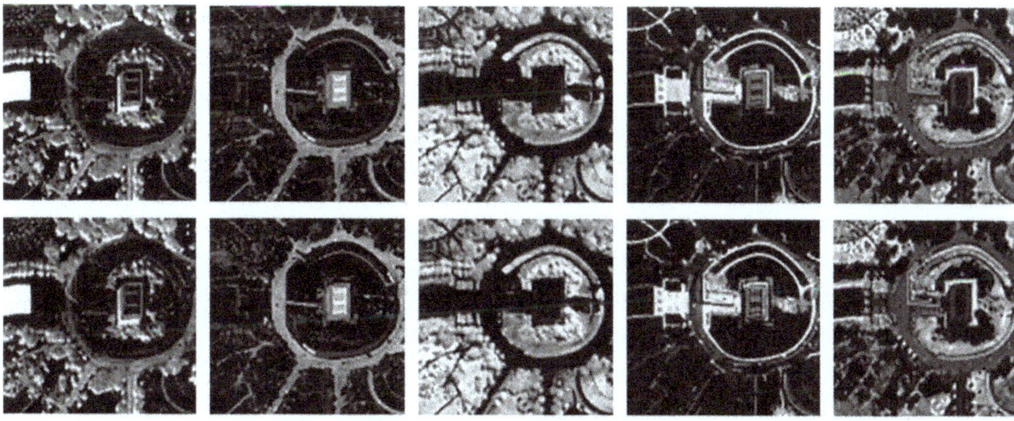

(a) (b) (c) (d) (e)

Figure 13.8 Abundance maps estimated by GCBAE based on the GBM (i.e., top row) and the PPNM (i.e., bottom row) for the HYDICE data's subregion containing 100 × 100 pixels. Each column displays the abundance map of one of the land covers. (a) Water, (b) roofs, (c) trees, (d) roads, and (e) grass. *Source:* [26] / with permission of IEEE.

13.3.4.3 Experimental Results for KBU

Firstly, two kinds of simulated datasets constructed based on the GBM and PPNM with SNR being set as 20 and 30 dB, respectively, were used for experiments. To study the function of kernel transformation on the BMMs, RE for the data reconstruction was replaced by RE* to represent the RE of the pixels' nonlinear parts. According to Table 13.4, in terms of the GBM-based datasets, KBU using the kernel transformation for the GBM (i.e., KBU(GBM)) has achieved the best unmixing results.

Table 13.4 Comparison of unmixing accuracy for simulated datasets with different SNRs.

		SNR (dB)	FCLS	GBM-GDA	PPNM-GDA	K-Hype	KBU(GBM)	KBU (PPNM)
GBM	RMSE	30	0.0760 ± 0.0000	0.0468 ± 0.0000	0.0270 ± 0.0000	0.0386 ± 0.0002	**0.0166 ± 0.0000**	0.0190 ± 0.0000
		20	0.0779 ± 0.0001	0.0501 ± 0.0001	0.0337 ± 0.0001	0.0669 ± 0.0004	**0.0225 ± 0.0000**	0.0247 ± 0.0000
	RE*	30	0.0387 ± 0.0000	0.0207 ± 0.0000	0.0089 ± 0.0000	0.0180 ± 0.0001	**0.0048 ± 0.0000**	0.0069 ± 0.0000
		20	0.0390 ± 0.0000	0.0210 ± 0.0000	0.0103 ± 0.0000	0.0320 ± 0.0001	**0.0078 ± 0.0000**	0.0082 ± 0.0000
PPNM	RMSE	30	0.0893 ± 0.0000	0.0815 ± 0.0000	0.0489 ± 0.0000	0.0568 ± 0.0002	0.0307 ± 0.0000	**0.0277 ± 0.0000**
		20	0.0912 ± 0.0001	0.0833 ± 0.0001	0.0541 ± 0.0001	0.0771 ± 0.0005	0.0326 ± 0.0000	**0.0309 ± 0.0000**
	RE*	30	0.0478 ± 0.0000	0.0414 ± 0.0000	0.008 ± 0.0000	0.0264 ± 0.0001	0.0132 ± 0.0000	**0.0116 ± 0.0000**
		20	0.0484 ± 0.0000	0.0413 ± 0.0001	0.0106 ± 0.0000	0.0367 ± 0.0001	0.0141 ± 0.0000	**0.0129 ± 0.0000**

Source: Adapted from [23]. Bold values represent the best results in this table.

Table 13.5 Comparison of unmixing accuracy for the physical-based virtual forest datasets.

	Frst_b20p80		Frst_b40p60		Frst_b60p40		Frst_b80p20	
Method	**RMSE**	**RE***	**RMSE**	**RE***	**RMSE**	**RE***	**RMSE**	**RE***
FCLS	0.0462	0.0084	0.0608	0.0116	0.0605	0.0129	0.0568	0.0082
GBM-GDA	0.0457	0.0081	0.061	0.011	0.0606	0.0131	0.0558	0.0074
PPNM-GDA	0.0449	0.0069	0.0568	0.0095	0.0546	0.0101	0.0554	0.0074
K-Hype	0.0775	0.0106	0.0652	0.0109	0.0532	0.0098	0.0727	0.0094
KBU(GBM)	0.0419	0.0057	0.0526	0.0085	0.0555	0.0096	0.0534	0.0076
KBU(PPNM)	**0.0366**	**0.0052**	**0.0465**	**0.0071**	**0.049**	**0.0082**	**0.0474**	**0.0071**

Source: Adapted from [23]. Bold values represent the best results in this table.

Moreover, KBU(GBM) can also provide accurate abundances for the PPNM-based simulated datasets. Similarly, KBU(PPNM) performs better than the other compared methods in unmixing PPNM-based simulated datasets. It implies that the performance of KBU may be affected simultaneously by the forms of kernel transformation and data. However, the kernel transformation does not affect the superiority of KBU compared to the traditional GBM-GDA and PPNM-GDA owing to its flexible representation of different forms of nonlinearity.

Secondly, the physical-based virtual forest datasets were further employed to verify the nonlinear unmixing performance of KBU in processing complex datasets where nonlinear mixing effects and spectral variability exist. As shown in Table 13.5, based on the kernel transformation for the PPNM, KBU(PPNM) outperforms all the methods due to the inherent generalization of the PPNM. Although KBU(GBM) is worse than KBU(PPNM), it can provide more accurate unmixing results for most forest datasets compared to the other traditional unmixing methods. The experimental results have validated that KBU can deal with different nonlinear mixing data accurately.

Finally, the AVIRIS Moffett Field dataset in Figure 13.5 was used to carry out the experiments. Figure 13.9 shows the abundance maps and the spatial distributions of nonlinear intensity provided

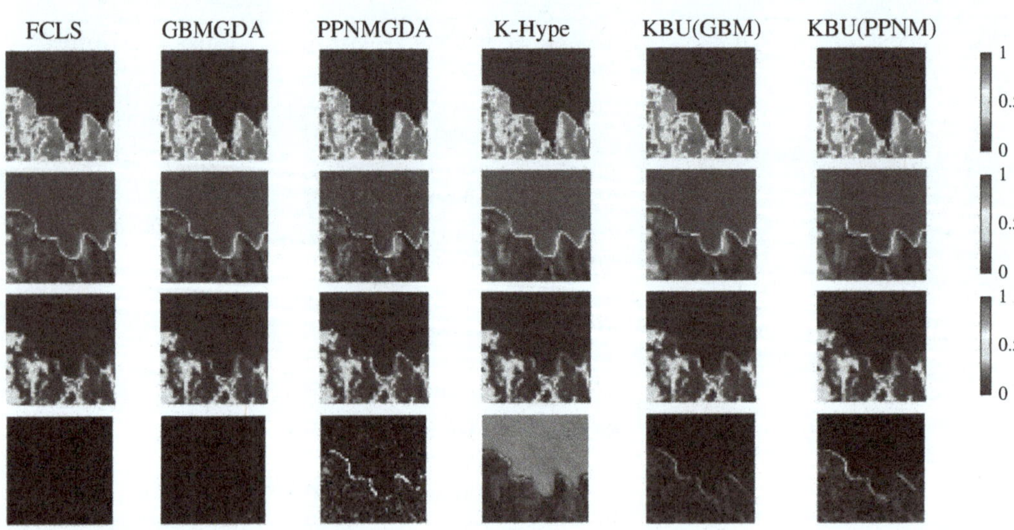

Figure 13.9 Abundance maps and nonlinear intensity maps of AVIRIS Moffett Field data estimated by different methods. From top to bottom: soil, water, vegetation, and nonlinear intensity. *Source:* [23] / with permission of IEEE.

Table 13.6 REs of the compared methods for the AVIRIS Moffett dataset.

FCLS	GBM-GDA	PPNM-GDA	K-Hype	KBU(GBM)	KBU(PPNM)
0.0065	0.0064	0.0061	**0.0055**	0.0064	0.0063

Source: Adapted from [23]. Bold values represent the best results in this table.

by the compared methods, and Table 13.6 compares the REs. It is clear that most of the methods can reasonably reveal the spatial distributions of three typical land covers except that the abundances of water estimated by PPNMGDA have large errors. Although K-Hyper has the best RE, its nonlinear intensity map of water may not be in line with the ground truth, indicating that the issue of overfitting may occur. Due to the integration of the kernel transformation and the TV smoothness regularizer into the numerical-model-guided nonlinear unmixing framework, KBU can successfully detect the strong nonlinear mixing effects on the boundaries of different land covers and obtain acceptable abundances for real hyperspectral data.

13.3.4.4 Experimental Results for BNLSU

To evaluate the nonlinear unmixing performance of BNLSU, simulated datasets were generated based on the EMLM for experiments. The number of endmembers was set as 3, 4, and 5, and the SNR was set as 20, 40, and 60 dB. In Table 13.7, RMSE and RE of five unmixing methods

Table 13.7 Comparison of unmixing accuracy for simulated datasets with different numbers of endmembers and different SNRs.

		RMSE					RE				
r	SNR (dB)	PPNMGDA	p(4)-linear	MLM	NDU (Sp.+P)	BNLSU	PPNMGDA	p(4)-linear	MLM	NDU (Sp.+P)	BNLSU
3	20	0.1462 ± 0.0005	0.2509 ± 0.0017	0.1357 ± 0.0003	**0.1046 ± 0.0001**	0.1257 ± 0.0025	0.0716 ± 0.0001	0.0607 ± 0.0002	0.0706 ± 0.0001	0.0298 ± 0.0000	**0.0189 ± 0.0001**
	40	0.1418 ± 0.0001	0.2380 ± 0.0003	0.1320 ± 0.0000	0.1018 ± 0.0000	**0.0278 ± 0.0001**	0.0494 ± 0.0000	0.0264 ± 0.0000	0.0480 ± 0.0000	0.0112 ± 0.0000	**0.0041 ± 0.0000**
	60	0.1479 ± 0.0001	0.2481 ± 0.0000	0.1400 ± 0.0000	0.1053 ± 0.0000	**0.0281 ± 0.0000**	0.0511 ± 0.0000	0.0271 ± 0.0000	0.0497 ± 0.0000	0.0106 ± 0.0000	**0.0019 ± 0.0000**
4	20	0.1858 ± 0.0004	0.2853 ± 0.0007	0.1836 ± 0.0004	**0.1415 ± 0.0007**	0.1567 ± 0.0022	0.0693 ± 0.0001	0.0545 ± 0.0002	0.0686 ± 0.0001	0.0292 ± 0.0000	**0.0236 ± 0.0003**
	40	0.1866 ± 0.0002	0.2716 ± 0.0009	0.1832 ± 0.0000	0.1431 ± 0.0000	**0.0797 ± 0.0004**	0.0478 ± 0.0000	0.0166 ± 0.0000	0.0469 ± 0.0000	0.0102 ± 0.0000	**0.0066 ± 0.0001**
	60	0.1810 ± 0.0001	0.2671 ± 0.0002	0.1775 ± 0.0000	0.1391 ± 0.0000	**0.0771 ± 0.0001**	0.0473 ± 0.0000	0.0158 ± 0.0000	0.0465 ± 0.0000	0.0092 ± 0.0000	**0.0072 ± 0.0000**
5	20	0.1699 ± 0.0006	0.2692 ± 0.0007	0.1671 ± 0.0004	**0.1264 ± 0.0000**	0.1779 ± 0.0017	0.0651 ± 0.0001	0.0486 ± 0.0001	0.0642 ± 0.0001	0.0266 ± 0.0000	**0.0183 ± 0.0003**
	40	0.1710 ± 0.0005	0.2605 ± 0.0005	0.1678 ± 0.0000	0.1248 ± 0.0000	**0.0706 ± 0.0005**	0.0463 ± 0.0000	0.0146 ± 0.0001	0.0449 ± 0.0000	0.0094 ± 0.0000	**0.0062 ± 0.0001**
	60	0.1709 ± 0.0006	0.2572 ± 0.0001	0.1667 ± 0.0000	0.1287 ± 0.0000	**0.0690 ± 0.0001**	0.0471 ± 0.0000	0.0147 ± 0.0000	0.0457 ± 0.0000	0.0089 ± 0.0000	**0.0036 ± 0.0001**

Source: Adapted from [44]. Bold values represent the best results in this table.

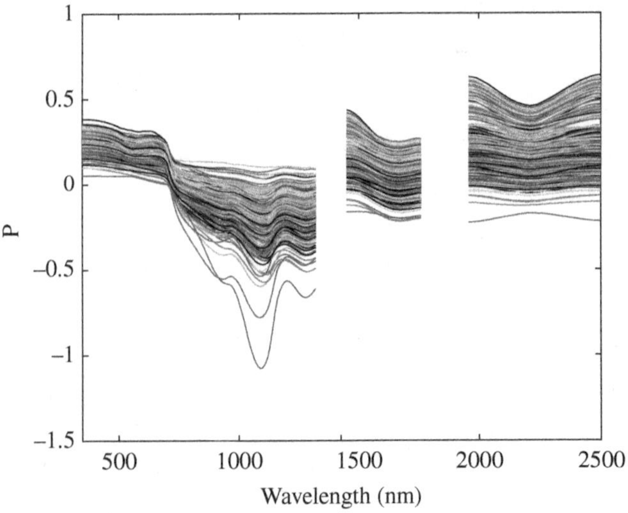

Figure 13.10 The probability parameters estimated by BNLSU for each pixel's different bands in the Orc_2 dataset of the virtual orchard scene. *Source:* [44] / with permission of IEEE.

are compared. It can be observed that BNLSU can produce more accurate abundances than the others when the noise intensity is not strong, and its RE is the best in all situations. As a kernel-based band-wise nonlinear unmixing method, NDU(Sp.+P) also has competitive unmixing accuracies, indicating that it is important to consider band-dependent nonlinearity for unmixing such data. The RMSE of BNLSU is worse than that of NDU(Sp.+P) when the SNR is 20 dB. It implies that the band-dependent calculation of nonlinear probability parameters in the EMLM may be sensitive to large noises, resulting in the propagation of related errors to the estimation of abundances (Figure 13.10).

To carry out quantitative analysis on the BNLSU's advantages in dealing with band-dependent nonlinearity for unmixing, the physical-based virtual orchard and forest datasets were further employed for experiments. Figure 13.11 shows the probability parameters *P* estimated by BNLSU for each pixel's different bands in the Orc_2 dataset. It can be observed that the nonlinear intensity represented by the value of *P* changes at different wavelengths, implying that significant band-dependent nonlinear mixing effects exist in this dataset. BNLSU has obtained the most accurate abundances for six different datasets in Table 13.8. It can be concluded that the band-wise extension of MLM to explain the nonlinearity in the EMLM enables BNLSU to capture the characteristics of the simulated radiative transfer process in the virtual scenes. Moreover, large RMSEs of abundances and low REs for four forest datasets provided by NDU(Sp.+P) indicate that this kernel-based band-wise unmixing method may suffer from the influence of overfitting.

Finally, two real hyperspectral datasets, i.e., the AVIRIS Moffett Field dataset and the HYDICE Washington DC Mall datasets, were used to compare the methods. Figures 13.11 and 13.12 display the land covers' abundance maps estimated by different methods. It can be clearly observed that the spatial distribution of water identified by BNLSU in Figure 13.11 is in line with the ground truth, i.e., water only is present in the upper area of the whole image. Compared to the other methods, BNLSU performs much better in abundance estimation for the real hyperspectral data. In Figure 13.13, the band-wise REs and the nonlinear intensity maps of different methods are provided. BNLSU is able to reduce the unmixing residuals at different bands simultaneously and highlight the area with stronger nonlinear intensity located on the boundary between water and

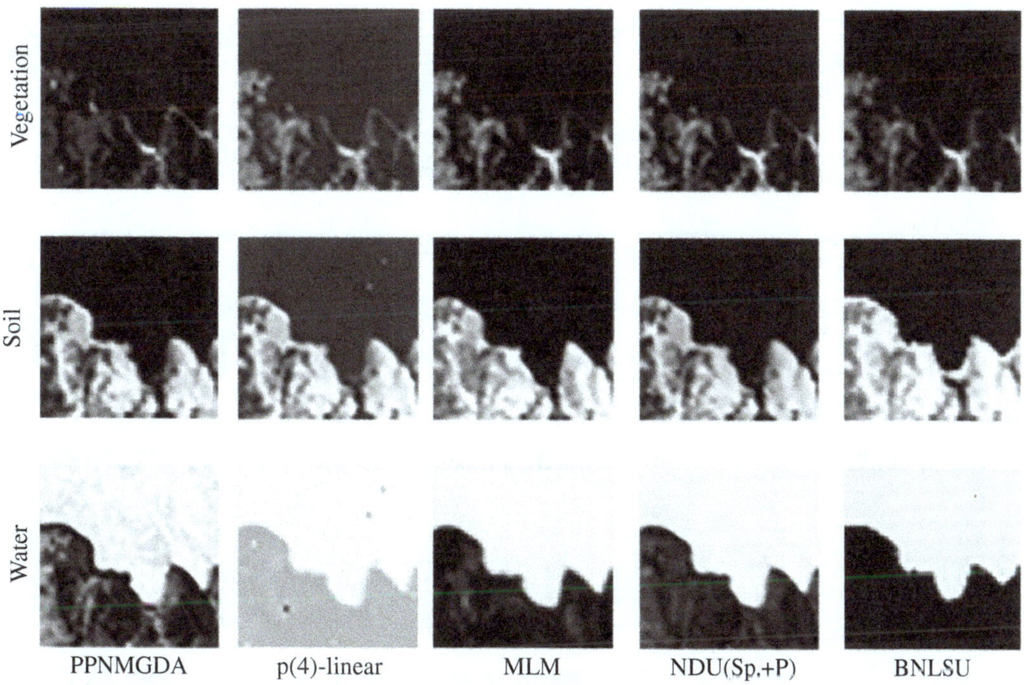

Figure 13.11 Abundance maps estimated by different methods for the HYDICE Washington DC Mall data. *Source:* [44] / with permission of IEEE.

Table 13.8 Comparison of unmixing accuracy for the simulated datasets of virtual orchards and forests.

Virtual scenes datasets		PPNMGDA	p(4)-linear	MLM	NDU(Sp.+P)	BNLSU
RMSE	Orc_2	0.1105	0.0601	0.1245	0.0952	**0.0497**
	Orc_3	0.1615	0.1574	0.1902	0.1636	**0.1216**
	Frst_b20p80	0.0636	0.0422	0.0494	0.0841	**0.0385**
	Frst_b40p60	0.0897	0.0546	0.0631	0.1532	**0.0424**
	Frst_b60p40	0.0975	0.0563	0.0620	0.2110	**0.0348**
	Frst_b80p20	0.0792	0.0518	0.0543	0.1696	**0.0356**
RE	Orc_2	0.0115	0.0077	0.0148	0.0040	**0.0026**
	Orc_3	0.0121	0.0061	0.0182	0.0029	**0.0011**
	Frst_b20p80	0.0036	0.0045	0.0042	**0.0001**	0.0043
	Frst_b40p60	0.0039	0.0026	0.0031	**0.0001**	0.0017
	Frst_b60p40	0.0037	0.0018	0.0025	**0.0001**	0.0007
	Frst_b80p20	0.0034	0.0020	0.0025	**0.0001**	0.0007

Source: Adapted from [44]. Bold values represent the best results in this table.

soil (or vegetation). Moreover, it can be inferred that the strong multiple scatterings commonly in the shadow-covered regions can be explained in the unmixing results of BNLSU by comparing the abundance map of shade in Figure 13.12 with the nonlinear intensity map recognized by BNLSU in Figure 13.13. Table 13.9 proves that BNLSU has smaller REs and a good data fitting ability for

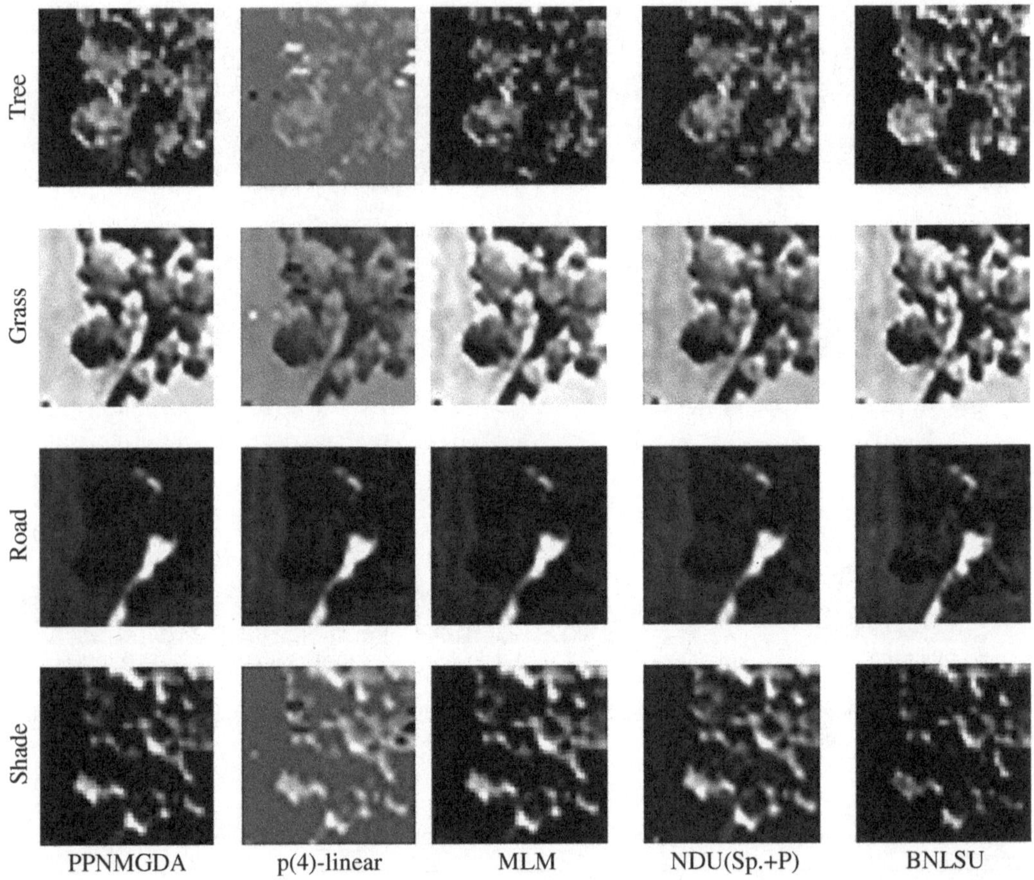

Figure 13.12 Abundance maps estimated by different methods for the AVIRIS Moffett Field data. *Source:* [44] / with permission of IEEE.

unmixing two real hyperspectral images. The above experimental results indicate that BNLSU can unmix complex hyperspectral data effectively, and the abundance estimation is significantly improved by considering the inherent band-dependent nonlinear mixing effects in real scenarios.

13.4 Conclusions

This chapter presents three numerical-model-guided nonlinear unmixing methods. GCBAE exploited the geometric characteristics to construct a nonlinear vertex and projected the BMMs-based pixels to their approximate linear components. The combination of transforming nonlinear unmixing to linear unmixing and projection bias correction in GCBAE has significantly reduced the influence of the collinearity and improved the unmixing accuracy. KBU developed two new kernel functions without extra parameters to transform the GBM and PPNM to their equivalent forms. Kernel-based transformation can effectively retain the physical meaning of second-order scatterings and improve the generalization to different nonlinear mixing situations. Using a TV regularizer as a paradigm to build a nonlinear unmixing framework, KBU can adopt the spatial information of hyperspectral data to produce more accurate abundances. BNLSU interpreted the wavelength-dependent nonlinear mixing effects by extending the MLM to have vectorized nonlinear probability parameters for every pixel. The sparsity of abundances and the smoothness of

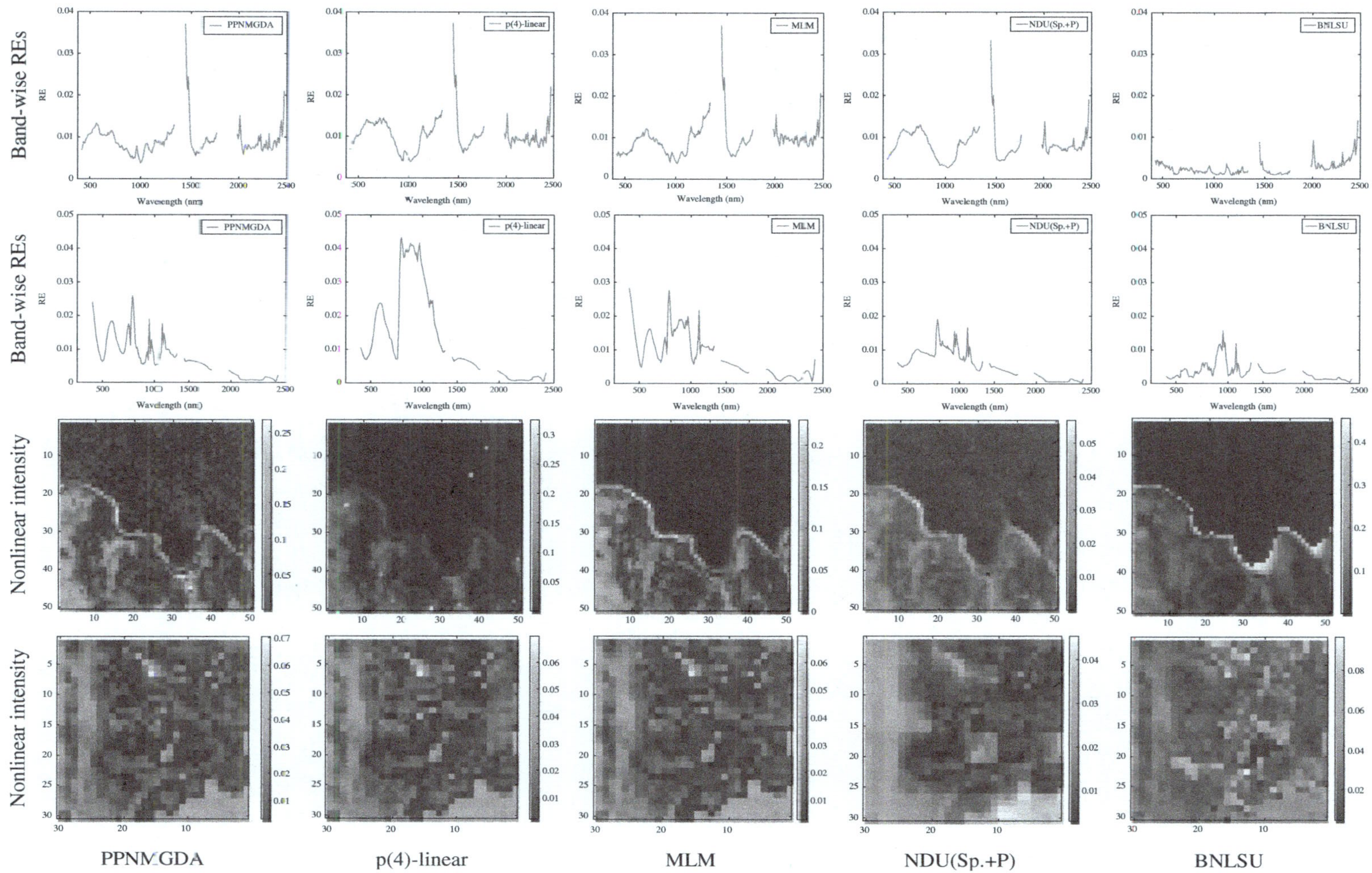

Figure 13.13 Band-wise REs and the spatial distributions of the nonlinear intensity of different methods for the AVIRIS Moffett data and the HYDICE Washington DC Mall data. *Source:* [44] / with permission of IEEE.

Table 13.9 Comparison of REs for two real hyperspectral remote-sensing images.

Datasets	PPNMGDA	p(4)-linear	MLM	NDU(Sp.+P)	BNLSU
AVIRIS Moffett Field	0.0098	0.0111	0.0102	0.0090	**0.0032**
HYDICE Washington DC Mall	0.0093	0.0185	0.0107	0.0069	**0.0042**

Source: Adapted from [44]. Bold values represent the best results in this table.

nonlinear intensity along with bands were further employed to formulate a band-wise nonlinear unmixing framework based on the EMLM. Experiments with simulated data and real hyperspectral remote-sensing images have validated that the three numerical-model-guided nonlinear unmixing methods can address the issue of the influence of the collinearity, the physically meaningful generalization for different types of nonlinearities, and the wavelength-dependent nonlinearity and provide more accurate and robust unmixing results.

Although the numerical-model-guided nonlinear unmixing is usually physically meaningful and the corresponding optimization problems can be accurately solved with low computational complexity, some improvements could be made in the future studies. First, the nonlinear mixing effects and spectral variability are commonly coupled in real scenarios. It is necessary to reduce the influence of spectral variability on nonlinear unmixing. Second, transforming the optimization processes of the numerical-model-guided nonlinear unmixing into neural network modules using deep unrolling technologies is very promising for constructing deep nonlinear unmixing networks with powerful feature extraction abilities and unmixing interpretability.

13.5 Challenges and Future Directions

Numerical model-guided nonlinear unmixing methods provide a straightforward and effective way to physically interpret the nonlinear mixing effects, revealing the land covers' spectral constituents and spatial distributions in hyperspectral remote sensing images. However, considerable challenges are present in processing hyperspectral data with the increasing amount and complexity, and meeting the requirements for more refined real quantitative applications. In-depth research must be explored to develop nonlinear unmixing methods with higher computational efficiency and accuracy, richer interpretation capabilities, and generalization ability for a wider range of application scenarios.

Firstly, given the high computational complexity of nonlinear unmixing, real-time processing data with higher resolutions and larger scenarios is intractable. Specifically, GCBAE transforms the complex nonlinear unmixing problem into a simple linear one, and its computational complexity is affected by the number of endmembers. The computational burden of KBU mainly comes from the kernel-based operations highly dependent on the data size. The computational complexity of updating major variables in BNLSU is $O(mn^3)$ where m and n are the numbers of pixels and bands, respectively. Therefore, to satisfy the requirement of real-time unmixing hyperspectral data on board or edge devices, it is important to develop faster nonlinear unmixing methods by employing parallel computing architecture and high-performance hardware in the future.

Secondly, integrating high-dimensional multi-source multi-modal data, domain knowledge, and advanced deep learning techniques to build an intelligent and universal nonlinear unmixing framework can be very challenging. A highly promising research domain could be the investigation of large artificial intelligent models for multi-source remote sensing image unmixing. The advantages of numerical model-guided physical interpretation and deep neural networks-driven data learning integrated into such models can promote intelligent and reliable applications for precise unmixing and effectively generalize unmixing to different remote sensing datasets.

Finally, nonlinear unmixing theories and methods for complex nature scenarios such as estuarine and coastal water bodies and related applications are rarely studied, and reliable ground truth of real hyperspectral remote sensing data for validating unmixing performance is usually inaccessible. Consequently, in light of specific application tasks, it is of significance to develop advanced unmixing techniques for interpreting the intricate radiative transfer processes in various natural scenarios. Moreover, combined with real hyperspectral remote sensing images labeled with in-situ collected data, simulated hyperspectral data generated by deep generative models considering nonlinear unmixing and spectral variability have a great potential to provide reliable datasets for quantitative unmixing research.

References

1 Keshava, N. and Mustard, J.F. (2002). Spectral unmixing. *IEEE Signal Process. Mag.* 19 (1): 44–57.

2 Bioucas-Dias, J.M., Plaza, A., Dobigeon, N. et al. (2012). Hyperspectral unmixing overview: geometrical, statistical, and sparse regression-based approaches. *IEEE J. Sel. Top. Appl. Earth Obs. Remote Sens.* 5 (2): 354–379.

3 Peng, J., Sun, W., Li, H.-C. et al. (2021). Low-rank and sparse representation for hyperspectral image processing: a review. *IEEE Geosci Remote Sens. Mag.* 2–35.

4 Chen, J., Zhao, M., Wang, X. et al. (2023). Integration of physics-based and data-driven models for hyperspectral image unmixing: a summary of current methods. *IEEE Signal Process. Mag.* 40 (2): 61–74.

5 Dobigeon, N., Tourneret, J.-Y., Richard, C. et al. (2014 Jan). Nonlinear unmixing of hyperspectral images: models and algorithms. *IEEE Signal Process. Mag.* 31 (1): 82–94.

6 Heylen, R., Parente, M., and Gader, P. (2014). A review of nonlinear hyperspectral unmixing methods. *IEEE J. Sel. Top. Appl. Earth Obs. Remote Sens.* 7 (6): 1844–1868.

7 Nascimento, J.M.P. and Dias, J.M.B. (2005). Vertex component analysis: a fast algorithm to unmix hyperspectral data. *IEEE Trans. Geosci. Remote Sens.* 43 (4): 898–910.

8 Tao, X., Wang, B., and Zhang, L. (2009). Orthogonal bases approach for the decomposition of mixed pixels in hyperspectral imagery. *IEEE Geosci. Remote Sens. Lett.* 6 (2): 219–223.

9 Li, J., Agathos, A., Zaharie, D. et al. (2015). Minimum volume simplex analysis: a fast algorithm for linear hyperspectral unmixing. *IEEE Trans. Geosci. Remote Sens.* 53 (9): 5067–5082.

10 Heinz, D.C. and Chang, C.I. (2001). Fully constrained least squares linear spectral mixture analysis method for material quantification in hyperspectral imagery. *IEEE Trans. Geosci. Remote Sens.* 39 (3): 529–545.

11 Miao, L. and Qi, H. (2007). Endmember extraction from highly mixed data using minimum volume constrained nonnegative matrix factorization. *IEEE Trans. Geosci. Remote Sens.* 45 (3): 765–777.

12 Liu, X., Xia, W., Wang, B., and Zhang, L. (2011). An approach based on constrained nonnegative matrix factorization to unmix hyperspectral data. *IEEE Trans. Geosci. Remote Sens.* 49 (2): 757–772.

13 Qian, Y., Jia, S., Zhou, J., and Robles-Kelly, A. (2011). Hyperspectral unmixing via l1/2 sparsity-constrained nonnegative matrix factorization. *IEEE Trans. Geosci. Remote Sens.* 49 (11): 4282–4297.

14 Lu, X., Wu, H., Yuan, Y. et al. (2013). Manifold regularized sparse NMF for hyperspectral unmixing. *IEEE Trans. Geosci. Remote Sens.* 51 (5): 2815–2826.

15 Qian, Y., Xiong, F., Zeng, S. et al. (2017). Matrix-vector nonnegative tensor factorization for blind unmixing of hyperspectral imagery. *IEEE Trans. Geosci. Remote Sens.* 55 (3): 1776–1792.

16 Zheng, P., Su, H., Lu, H., and Du, Q. (2023). Adaptive hypergraph regularized multilayer sparse tensor factorization for hyperspectral unmixing. *IEEE Trans. Geosci. Remote Sens.* 61: 1–18.

17 Somers, B., Cools, K., Delalieux, S. et al. (2009). Nonlinear hyperspectral mixture analysis for tree cover estimates in orchards. *Remote Sens. Environ.* 113 (6): 1183–1193.

18 Fan, W., Hu, B., Miller, J., and Li, M. (2009). Comparative study between a new nonlinear model and common linear model for analysing laboratory simulated-forest hyperspectral data. *Int. J. Remote Sens.* 30 (11): 2951–2962.

19 Halimi, A., Altmann, Y., Dobigeon, N., and Tourneret, J.-Y. (2011). Nonlinear unmixing of hyperspectral images using a generalized bilinear model. *IEEE Trans. Geosci. Remote Sens.* 49 (11): 4153–4162.

20 Altmann, Y., Halimi, A., Dobigeon, N., and Tourneret, J.Y. (2012). Supervised nonlinear spectral unmixing using a postnonlinear mixing model for hyperspectral imagery. *IEEE Trans. Image Process.* 21 (6): 3017–3025.

21 Chen, J., Richard, C., and Honeine, P. (2013). Nonlinear unmixing of hyperspectral data based on a linear-mixture/nonlinear-fluctuation model. *IEEE Trans. Signal Process.* 61 (2): 480–492.

22 Ammanouil, R., Ferrari, A., Richard, C., and Mathieu, S. (2017). Nonlinear unmixing of hyperspectral data with vector-valued kernel functions. *IEEE Trans. Image Process.* 26 (1): 340–354.

23 Gu, J., Yang, B., and Wang, B. (2022). Nonlinear unmixing for hyperspectral images via kernel-transformed bilinear mixing models. *IEEE Trans. Geosci. Remote Sens.* 60: 1–13.

24 Marinoni, A. and Gamba, P. (2015). A novel approach for efficient p-linear hyperspectral unmixing. *IEEE J. Sel. Top. Signal Process.* 9 (6): 1156–1168.

25 Heylen, R. and Scheunders, P. (2016). A multilinear mixing model for nonlinear spectral unmixing. *IEEE Trans. Geosci. Remote Sens.* 54 (1): 240–251.

26 Yang, B., Wang, B., and Wu, Z. (2018). Nonlinear hyperspectral unmixing based on geometric characteristics of bilinear mixture models. *IEEE Trans. Geosci. Remote Sens.* 56 (2): 694–714.

27 Yang, B., Wang, B., and Wu, Z. (2018). Unsupervised nonlinear hyperspectral unmixing based on bilinear mixture models via geometric projection and constrained nonnegative matrix factorization. *Remote Sens.* 10 (5): 801.

28 Zhu, F. and Honeine, P. (2016). Biobjective nonnegative matrix factorization: linear versus kernel-based models. *IEEE Trans. Geosci. Remote Sens.* 54 (7): 4012–4022.

29 Yang, B., Chen, Z., and Wang, B. (2020). Nonlinear endmember identification for hyperspectral imagery via hyperpath-based simplex growing and fuzzy assessment. *IEEE J. Sel. Top. Appl. Earth Obs. Remote Sens.* 13: 351–366.

30 Pu, H., Chen, Z., Wang, B., and Xia, W. (2015). Constrained least squares algorithms for nonlinear unmixing of hyperspectral imagery. *IEEE Trans. Geosci. Remote Sens.* 53 (3): 1287–1303.

31 Yokoya, N., Chanussot, J., and Iwasaki, A. (2014). Nonlinear unmixing of hyperspectral data using semi-nonnegative matrix factorization. *IEEE Trans. Geosci. Remote Sens.* 52 (2): 1430–1447.

32 Fevotte, C. and Dobigeon, N. (2015). Nonlinear hyperspectral unmixing with robust nonnegative matrix factorization. *IEEE Trans. Image Process.* 24 (12): 4810–4819.

33 Gao, L., Wang, Z., Zhuang, L. et al. (2022). Using low-rank representation of abundance maps and nonnegative tensor factorization for hyperspectral nonlinear unmixing. *IEEE Trans. Geosci. Remote Sens.* 60: 1–17.

34 Zhang, B., Sun, X., Gao, L., and Yang, L. (2011). Endmember extraction of hyperspectral remote sensing images based on the discrete particle swarm optimization algorithm. *IEEE Trans. Geosci. Remote Sens.* 49 (11): 4173–4186.

35 Yang, B., Luo, W., and Wang, B. (2017). Constrained nonnegative matrix factorization based on particle swarm optimization for hyperspectral unmixing. *IEEE J. Sel. Top. Appl. Earth Obs. Remote Sens.* 10 (8): 3693–3710.

36 Miao, Y. and Yang, B. (2021). Sparse unmixing for hyperspectral imagery via comprehensive-learning-based particle swarm optimization. *IEEE J. Sel. Top. Appl. Earth Obs. Remote Sens.* 14: 9727–9742.

37 Miao, Y. and Yang, B. (2022). Multilevel reweighted sparse hyperspectral unmixing using superpixel segmentation and particle swarm optimization. *IEEE Geosci. Remote Sens. Lett.* 19.

38 Gong, M., Li, H., Luo, E. et al. (2017). A multiobjective cooperative coevolutionary algorithm for hyperspectral sparse unmixing. *IEEE Trans. Evol. Comput.* 21 (2): 234–248.

39 Xu, X., Pan, B., Chen, Z. et al. (2020). Simultaneously multiobjective sparse unmixing and library pruning for hyperspectral imagery. *IEEE Trans. Geosci. Remote Sens.* 59: 3383–3395.

40 Luo, W., Gao, L., Plaza, A. et al. (2016). A new algorithm for bilinear spectral unmixing of hyperspectral images using particle swarm optimization. *IEEE J. Sel. Top. Appl. Earth Obs. Remote Sens.* 9 (12): 5776–5790.

41 Yang, B. (2022). Supervised nonlinear hyperspectral unmixing with automatic shadow compensation using multiswarm particle swarm optimization. *IEEE Trans. Geosci. Remote Sens.* 60: 1–18.

42 Yin, Z. and Yang, B. (2023). Unsupervised nonlinear hyperspectral unmixing with reduced spectral variability via superpixel-based Fisher transformation. *Remote Sens.* 15 (20): 5028.

43 Zhang, H. and Yang, B. (2024). Geometrical projection improved multi-objective particle swarm optimization for unsupervised nonlinear hyperspectral unmixing. *Int. J. Remote Sens.* 45 (6): 1849–1882.

44 Yang, B. and Wang, B. (2018). Band-wise nonlinear unmixing for hyperspectral imagery using an extended multilinear mixing model. *IEEE Trans. Geosci. Remote Sens.* 56 (11): 6747–6762.

45 Li, M., Yang, B., and Wang, B. (2022). Spectral–spatial reweighted robust nonlinear unmixing for hyperspectral images based on an extended multilinear mixing model. *IEEE Trans. Geosci. Remote Sens.* 60: 1–17.

46 Li, M., Yang, B., and Wang, B. (2023). A coarse-to-fine scheme for unsupervised nonlinear hyperspectral unmixing based on an extended multilinear mixing model. *IEEE Trans. Geosci. Remote Sens.* 61: 1–15.

47 Koirala, B., Zahiri, Z., Lamberti, A., and Scheunders, P. (2020). Robust supervised method for nonlinear spectral unmixing accounting for endmember variability. *IEEE Trans. Geosci. Remote Sens.* 59: 7434–7448.

48 Palsson, B., Sveinsson, J.R., and Ulfarsson, M.O. (2022). Blind hyperspectral unmixing using autoencoders: a critical comparison. *IEEE J. Sel. Top. Appl. Earth Obs. Remote Sens.* 15: 1340–1372.

49 Zhang, L. and Zhang, L. (2022). Artificial intelligence for remote sensing data analysis: a review of challenges and opportunities. *IEEE Geosci Remote Sens. Mag.* 10 (2): 270–294.

50 Ozkan, S., Kaya, B., and Akar, G.B. (2019). EndNet: sparse autoencoder network for endmember extraction and hyperspectral unmixing. *IEEE Trans. Geosci. Remote Sens.* 57 (1): 482–496.

51 Qu, Y. and Qi, H. (2019). uDAS: an untied denoising autoencoder with sparsity for spectral unmixing. *IEEE Trans. Geosci. Remote Sens.* 57 (3): 1698–1712.

52 Su, Y., Li, J., Plaza, A. et al. (2019). DAEN: deep autoencoder networks for hyperspectral unmixing. *IEEE Trans. Geosci. Remote Sens.* 57 (7): 4309–4321.

53 Palsson, B., Ulfarsson, M.O., and Sveinsson, J.R. (2021). Convolutional autoencoder for spectral–spatial hyperspectral unmixing. *IEEE Trans. Geosci. Remote Sens.* 59 (1): 535–549.

54 Gao, L., Han, Z., Hong, D. et al. (2022). CyCU-Net: cycle-consistency unmixing network by learning cascaded autoencoders. *IEEE Trans. Geosci. Remote Sens.* 60: 1–14.

55 Ghosh, P., Roy, S.K., Koirala, B. et al. (2022). Hyperspectral unmixing using transformer network. *IEEE Trans. Geosci. Remote Sens.* 60: 1–16.

56 Han, Z., Hong, D., Gao, L. et al. (2022). Multimodal hyperspectral unmixing: insights from attention networks. *IEEE Trans. Geosci. Remote Sens.* 60: 1–13.

57 Su, Y., Xu, X., Li, J. et al. (2021). Deep autoencoders with multitask learning for bilinear hyperspectral unmixing. *IEEE Trans. Geosci. Remote Sens.* 59 (10): 8615–8629.

58 Li, H., Borsoi, R.A., Imbiriba, T. et al. (2021). Model-based deep autoencoder networks for nonlinear hyperspectral unmixing. *IEEE Geosci. Remote Sens. Lett.* 19: 5506105.

59 Yang, X., Chen, J., and Chen, Z. (2023). Spectral-spatial adversarial network for nonlinear hyperspectral unmixing of imbalanced datasets. *Int. J. Appl. Earth Obs. Geoinf.* 123: 103478.

60 Zhao, M., Yan, L., and Chen, J. (2021). LSTM-DNN based autoencoder network for nonlinear hyperspectral image unmixing. *IEEE J. Sel. Top. Signal Process.* 15 (2): 295–309.

61 Zhao, M., Wang, M., Chen, J., and Rahardja, S. (2022). Hyperspectral unmixing for additive nonlinear models with a 3-D-CNN autoencoder network. *IEEE Trans. Geosci. Remote Sens.* 60: 1–15.

62 Jin, D. and Yang, B. (2023). Graph attention convolutional autoencoder-based unsupervised nonlinear unmixing for hyperspectral images. *IEEE J. Sel. Top. Appl. Earth Obs. Remote Sens.* 16: 7896–7906.

63 Chen, J., Gamba, P., and Li, J. (2023). MAHUM: a multitasks autoencoder hyperspectral unmixing model. *IEEE Trans. Geosci. Remote Sens.* 61: 1–16.

64 Rasti, B., Koirala, B., and Scheunders, P. (2022). HapkeCNN: blind nonlinear unmixing for intimate mixtures using Hapke model and convolutional neural network. *IEEE Trans. Geosci. Remote Sens.* 60: 1–15.

65 Li, M., Yang, B., and Wang, B. (2024). EMLM-Net: an extended multilinear mixing model-inspired dual-stream network for unsupervised nonlinear hyperspectral unmixing. *IEEE Trans. Geosci. Remote Sens.* 62: 1–16.

66 Stuckens, J., Somers, B., Delalieux, S. et al. (2009). The impact of common assumptions on canopy radiative transfer simulations: a case study in citrus orchards. *J. Quant. Spectrosc. Radiat. Transf.* 110 (1–2): 1–21.

67 Somers, B., Tits, L., and Coppin, P. (2014). Quantifying nonlinear spectral mixing in vegetated areas: computer simulation model validation and first results. *IEEE J. Sel. Top. Appl. Earth Obs. Remote Sens.* 7 (6): 1956–1965.

68 Dobigeon, N., Tits, L., Somers, B. et al. (2014). A comparison of nonlinear mixing models for vegetated areas using simulated and real hyperspectral data. *IEEE J. Sel. Top. Appl. Earth Obs. Remote Sens.* 7 (6): 1869–1878.

69 Tits, L., Somers, B., Stuckens, J. et al. (2014). Validating nonlinear mixing models: benchmark datasets from vegetated areas. *6th Workshop on Image and Signal Processing: Evolution in Remote Sensing (WHISPERS)*, Lausanne, Switzerland (24–27 June 2014). IEEE.

14

Spatial–Spectral Gabor-based Hyperspectral Image Classification

Sen Jia, Shuyu Zhang, Qi Ren, Wangquan He, Meng Xu, and Jiasong Zhu

College of Computer Science and Software Engineering, Shenzhen University, Shenzhen, China

14.1 Spatial–Spectral Gabor Feature Extraction

14.1.1 2-D Gabor Wavelets

14.1.1.1 Introduction

Considering the regularity and local continuity of surface material distribution in hyperspectral images (HSIs), the comprehensive application of spectral and spatial information for classification is of paramount importance. This section proposes a novel spectral–spatial Gabor surface feature extraction method designed for the 3-D structure of HSIs [1]. It utilizes a combination of filters across varying orientations and frequencies to seize the local textures and edge details in HSIs, integrating these with spectral data to enhance the classification performance. First, Gabor magnitude pictures (GMPs) are extracted by applying a set of predefined 2-D Gabor filters to HSIs. Second, the GSF has been extended to the spectral–spatial domains to comply with the 3-D structure of hyperspectral imagery, called 3-DGSF, which utilizes the first-order derivative of GMPs. Meanwhile, simple linear iterative clustering (SLIC) segmentation method is adopted to divide the original HSI into disjoint superpixels. Third, principal component analysis (PCA) is employed to reduce the dimensionality of each extracted 3-DGSF feature cube. Next, a support vector machine (SVM) classifier is applied to each reduced 3-DGSF feature, and the majority voting strategy is used to obtain the classification results. Finally, the superpixel map obtained by SLIC is used to regularize the classification map.

14.1.1.2 2-D Gabor Surface Feature

GSF is a Gabor feature-based texture analysis method in the spatial domain, which uses the first-order and second-order derivative information of GMPs [2, 3] to represent an image. First, GMPs are obtained by using a series of 2-D Gabor filters with multiple scales and orientations as follows:

$$\Psi_{f_u,\theta_v}(x,y) = \exp\left(-\pi\left(a^2x'^2 + b^2y'^2\right)\right) \cdot \exp\left(j2\pi f_u x'^2\right) \tag{14.1}$$

$$x' = x\cos\theta_v + y\sin\theta_v, y' = -x\sin\theta_v + y\cos\theta_v \tag{14.2}$$

Machine-Learning-Based Hyperspectral Image Processing, First Edition. Edited by Bing Zhang.

where f_u and θ_v denote the central frequency and orientation of the Gabor filter, respectively, and a and b scale the two axes of the Gaussian envelope. Since the spatial structure of land covers is usually unknown, the frequency and orientation of Gabor filters should vary in a range to cover the whole 2-D domain, obtaining sufficient discriminative features for subsequent processing [4]. Thus, the parameters of Gabor filters are set as follows:

$$a = 0.9589f_u, b = 1.1866f_u \tag{14.3}$$

$$f_u \in [0.03589,\ 0.09473, 0.25, 0.6577], \quad \theta_v \in [0°, 40°, 80°, 120°, 160°, 180°] \tag{14.4}$$

After denoting the Gabor filters as $\{\Phi_t, t = 1, 2, ..., T\}$, GMPs are extracted by convoluting each spectral band of HSI with every Gabor filter, i.e.,

$$\mathbf{G}^t(x, y, b) = |(\mathcal{R}_b \otimes \Phi_t)(x, y)| \tag{14.5}$$

where $\mathcal{R}_b \in \mathbb{R}^{X \times Y}$ is the bth band, and $\otimes$ and $|\cdot|$ are convolution and absolute operators, respectively. $\mathbf{G}^t(x, y) = [\mathbf{G}^t(x, y, 1); \mathbf{G}^t(x, y, 2); ...; \mathbf{G}^t(x, y, B)] \in \mathbb{R}^B$ is the response of the tth Gabor filter at all bands. A GMP $\mathbf{G}^t \in \mathbb{R}^{X \times Y \times B}$ which has the same size as the original HSI can be obtained by applying Φ_t on all pixels of the HSI. Further, a total of T GMPs $\mathbf{G}^t$, $t = 1, 2, ..., T$ are extracted after each Gabor filter Φ_t, $t = 1, 2, ..., T$ is convolved with the HSI. Secondly, $\mathbf{G}^t$ is filtered by symmetric gradient operator $[-1, 0, 1]$ along the two spatial dimensions x and y, and the gradient pictures $\mathbf{G}^t_x$, $\mathbf{G}^t_y$, $\mathbf{G}^t_{xx}$, and $\mathbf{G}^t_{yy}$ can be obtained. Then, they are thresholded by the median value to get the binary pictures $\mathbf{S}^t_x$, $\mathbf{S}^t_y$, $\mathbf{S}^t_{xx}$, and $\mathbf{S}^t_{yy}$, respectively, which are jointly encoded by the way similar to local binary pattern (LBP). The weights of $\mathbf{S}^t_x$, $\mathbf{S}^t_y$, $\mathbf{S}^t_{xx}$, and $\mathbf{S}^t_{yy}$ are assigned as 2^3, 2^2, 2^1, and 2^0, respectively, and the GSF code $\mathbf{E}^t$ can be represented as follows:

$$\mathbf{E}^t = 2^3\mathbf{S}^t_x + 2^2\mathbf{S}^t_y + 2^1\mathbf{S}^t_{xx} + 2^0\mathbf{S}^t_{yy} \tag{14.6}$$

Finally, the features employed in the classification task are GSF cooccurrence histograms accumulated over a small region in GSF code $\mathbf{E}^t$. Obviously, $\mathbf{E}^t$ has only 16 kinds of values, so the GSF histogram feature to be constructed is 16-D. Let $\mathbf{h}^t_{GSF} \in \mathbb{R}^{16}$ denote the cooccurrence of GSF code $\mathbf{E}^t$ at spatial location (x, y), which can be computed as:

$$\mathbf{h}^t_{\mathrm{GSF}}(i) = \sum_{j=-\lfloor \frac{V_x}{2} \rfloor}^{\lfloor \frac{V_x}{2} \rfloor} \sum_{k=-\lfloor \frac{V_y}{2} \rfloor}^{\lfloor \frac{V_y}{2} \rfloor} I(\mathbf{E}^t(m+j, n+k), i), i \in \{0, ..., 15\} \tag{14.7}$$

$$I(\mathbf{E}^t(m+j, n+k), i) = \begin{cases} 1, & \mathbf{E}^t(m+j, n+k) = i \\ 0, & \text{otherwise} \end{cases} \tag{14.8}$$

where V_x and V_y are the size of local small patch, and $\lfloor \cdot \rfloor$ is the round down operator.

14.1.1.3 Gabor Surface Feature Method for Hyperspectral Image Classification

Gabor Surface Feature Extraction

GSF is primarily utilized for processing grayscale and color images. However, it inadequately captures the spectral–spatial context within 3-D HSIs, extracting only spatial features. Moreover, this method overlooks raw images' discerning details, which are critical for comprehensive analysis. For HSI, both the original image and the information derived from GMPs are utilized as the representation. After obtaining a GMP $\mathbf{G}^t$, its gradient images $\mathbf{G}_x^t$, $\mathbf{G}_y^t$, and $\mathbf{G}_b^t$ are derived from the spatial domain (x, y) and the spectral dimension b, respectively, through the application of the template $[-1, 0, 1]$. Then, $\mathbf{G}^t$, $\mathbf{G}_x^t$, $\mathbf{G}_y^t$, and $\mathbf{G}_b^t$ are thresholded by their median values to obtain the binary values $\mathbf{M}^t$, $\mathbf{M}_x^t$, $\mathbf{M}_y^t$, and $\mathbf{M}_b^t$, respectively. Next, $\mathbf{M}^t$, $\mathbf{M}_x^t$, $\mathbf{M}_y^t$, and $\mathbf{M}_b^t$ are jointly encoded by the way similar to LBP coding strategy. Here, the weights of $\mathbf{M}^t$, $\mathbf{M}_x^t$, $\mathbf{M}_y^t$, and $\mathbf{M}_b^t$ are assigned as 2^3, 2^2, 2^1, and 2^0, respectively. The 3-DGSF code can be represented as follows:

$$\mathbf{F}^t = 2^3\mathbf{M}^t + 2^2\mathbf{M}_x^t + 2^1\mathbf{M}_y^t + 2^0\mathbf{M}_b^t, \quad t = 1, 2, \ldots, T \tag{14.9}$$

where $\mathbf{F}^t$ is the 3-DGSF map, which can well fuse the first derivative information of GMPs.

After generating the 3-DGSF map, histogram features are extracted. Obviously, 3-DGSF map $\mathbf{F}^t$ has 16 different values, and thus the dimension of 3-DGSF histogram feature is also 16. If 3-DGSF histogram at any position (x, y, b) is represented as $\mathbf{h}_{3\text{DGSF}}^t \in \mathbb{R}^{16}$:

$$\mathbf{h}_{3\text{DGSF}}^t(i) = \sum_{j=-\lfloor \frac{W_x}{2} \rfloor}^{\lfloor \frac{W_x}{2} \rfloor} \sum_{k=-\lfloor \frac{W_y}{2} \rfloor}^{\lfloor \frac{W_y}{2} \rfloor} \sum_{l=-\lfloor \frac{W_b}{2} \rfloor}^{\lfloor \frac{W_b}{2} \rfloor} I(\mathbf{F}^t(x+j, y+k, b+l), i) \quad i \in \{0, \ldots, 15\} \tag{14.10}$$

$$I(\mathbf{F}^t(x+j, y+k, b+l), i) = \begin{cases} 1, & \mathbf{F}^t(x+j, y+k, b+l) = i \\ 0, & \text{otherwise} \end{cases} \tag{14.11}$$

where $\mathbf{h}_{3\text{DGSF}}^t(i)$ records the cooccurrence of the 3-DGSF code i within a small 3-DGSF cube, and W_x, W_y, and W_b are the size of the small 3-DGSF cube. For the whole HSI, the surface feature cube $\mathbf{H}_{3\text{DGSF}}^t \in \mathbb{R}^{X \times Y \times (16 \times B)}$ can be thus obtained. To improve the time efficiency, PCA is applied to reduce the dimensionality of GSF $\mathbf{H}_{3\text{DGSF}}^t$, and the reduced feature cube $\mathbf{H}_{3\text{DGSF}'}^t$ is thus obtained, which can be used for the subsequent fusion method to accomplish the classification task.

SVM-based Fusion for Classification

For supervised HSI classification, it is presupposed that the scene encompasses P distinct classes, with a cumulative total of L training samples available across all such classes. For each feature $\mathbf{H}_{3\text{DGSF}}^t, t = 1, \ldots, T$, the training set of the p-th class is represented by $\mathbf{A}_p^t = \left[\boldsymbol{a}_{p,1}^t, \boldsymbol{a}_{p,2}^t, \ldots, \boldsymbol{a}_{p,L_c}^t\right] \in \mathbb{R}^{B \times L_p}$, where each column $\boldsymbol{a}_{p,j} (j = 1, 2, \ldots, L_p)$ is a B-dimensional feature vector. It is worth mentioning that the location axes of both the training and test sequences are the same for all the feature cubes. In addition, let $\mathbf{A}^t = \left[\mathbf{A}_1^t, \mathbf{A}_2^t, \ldots, \mathbf{A}_P^t\right] \in \mathbb{R}^{B \times L}$ represent the corresponding training samples in $\mathbf{H}_{3\text{DGSF}}^t$, which is the concatenation of L training samples from all classes, where $L = L_1 + L_2 + \ldots + L_P$. For the SVM-based fusion method, we can obtain a total of T predicted labels of each pixel by using SVM to classify each 3-DGSF. Finally, the class label of test sample $\boldsymbol{y}$ is associated with the class having the highest frequency over all the T tasks, that is,

$$\text{Class}(\boldsymbol{y}) = \arg\max_p \sum_{t=1}^{T} \delta(\chi_t, p), \quad p = 1, \ldots, P \tag{14.12}$$

$$\delta(\chi_t, p) = \begin{cases} 1, & \text{if } \chi_t = p \\ 0, & \text{if } \chi_t \neq p \end{cases} \tag{14.13}$$

where χ_t is the predicted label of test sample obtained from the t-th 3-DGSF and δ is an indicator function. Then, the SLIC-based superpixel map enhances the accuracy of the predicted label.

Classification with Superpixel Guidance

To better utilize the HSI's spatial context of surface materials, an initial SLIC-based superpixel map is required. Suppose there are K superpixels generated by the SLIC segmentation algorithm. Since the superpixel map is directly achieved from the original HSI, the location information for each pixel is the same for all the GSFs. Let $\mathbf{P}_k = [\mathbf{P}_k(:,1), \ldots, \mathbf{P}_k(:,N_k)] \in \mathbb{R}^{2\times N_k}$ represent the location information for the kth superpixel, where N_k is the number of pixels in the kth superpixel. Therefore, the labels of all the pixels in the kth superpixel are identified by majority voting strategy, which can be mathematically calculated by the following formula:

$$\text{Class}(\mathbf{P}_k) = \arg\max_{p} \sum_{\mathbf{y}\in\mathbf{P}_k} \delta(\text{Class}(\mathbf{y}), p), \quad p = 1, \ldots, P. \tag{14.14}$$

14.1.2 3-D Gabor Wavelets

14.1.2.1 Introduction

2-D Gabor filters excel at extracting spatial textures and structural information from HSIs. However, the inherent noise present can diminish their capacity for feature discrimination. In contrast, 3-D Gabor filters more effectively extract the spatial–spectral information. By predefining a set of 3-D Gabor filters across various scales and orientations, the convolution with HSIs thoroughly exploits the spatial–spectral interplay. Due to the unknown structure of surface materials, an extensive array of 3-D Gabor filters must be preemptively designed, inevitably leading to a proliferation of Gabor features. While these extracted 3-D Gabor features encapsulate vital material discrimination information, they also introduce a significant level of redundancy and demand increased computational and storage resources. Consequently, to boost the efficiency of HSI classification, it is imperative to integrate the feature selection process with Gabor feature extraction. To better accommodate the spatial–spectral structure of HSIs, this section expands the 2-D Gaussian filter, commonly employed for scale-invariant feature transformations, into the third dimension, proposing an innovative 3-D Gaussian–Gabor feature extraction and selection framework (abbreviated as GG-IFDPC) [5]. First, a group of 3-D Gaussian–Gabor filters are convolved with the concatenated data of both extended multi-attribute profile (EMAP) features and raw hyperspectral data. Second, an improved fast-density peak clustering (IFDPC) method is introduced to select the most representative features from each extracted 3-D Gaussian–Gabor feature cube. Finally, the retained features are combined to accomplish the classification task.

14.1.2.2 3-D Gabor Wavelet

The basic Gabor function is a Gaussian kernel function modulated by a sinusoidal plane wave. A circular 3-D Gabor wavelet can be defined as follows [6]:

$$\Psi_{f,\theta,\varphi}(x,y,b) = \frac{1}{s} \times \exp(j2\pi(ux+vy+wb)) \times \exp\left(\frac{x^2+y^2+b^2}{2\sigma^2}\right) \tag{14.15}$$

where $s = (2\pi)^{3/2}\sigma^3$, $u = f\sin\varphi\cos\theta$, $v = f\sin\varphi\cos\theta$, $w = f\cos\varphi$, and (x, y, b) represents a spatial location (x, y) in spectral band b. s is a normalization value and σ is the width of Gaussian envelop in the spatial–spectral domain. Besides, f is the central frequency of the sinusoidal plane wave, while ϕ and θ are the angles of the wave vector in frequency domain. In most cases, the structural information of surface materials cannot be well modeled in advance, so a set of 3-D Gabor filters with different frequencies f and orientations (ϕ, θ) should be provided to extract sufficient discriminative features from HSI cube. Usually, the values of parameters (f, ϕ, θ) are selected from the following ranges:

$$f \in \left[\frac{1}{2}, \frac{1}{4}, \frac{1}{8}, \frac{1}{16}\right], (\theta, \varphi) \in \left[0, \frac{\pi}{4}, \frac{\pi}{2}, \frac{3\pi}{4}\right]. \tag{14.16}$$

It can be derived that $\varphi = 0$ and different values of θ correspond to the same Gabor wavelet, and thus, 52 Gabor wavelets can be finally obtained, which are denoted as $\{\Psi_m, m = 1, 2, \ldots, 52\}$.

14.1.2.3 3-D Gaussian–Gabor Feature Extraction and Selection

3-D Gaussian–Gabor Filter

3-D Gaussian–Gabor filters Υ_m are defined as:

$$\Upsilon_m = \Psi_m \otimes g, \quad m = 1, \ldots, 52 \tag{14.17}$$

where $\otimes$ is the convolution operation and Ψ_m are the aforementioned 3-D Gabor filters. g denotes the 3-D Gaussian filter that is expressed as:

$$g(x, y, b) = \frac{1}{(2\pi)^{3/2}\sigma^3} \cdot \exp\left(-\frac{x^2 + y^2 + b^2}{2\sigma^2}\right) \quad x, y, b \subseteq [-r, r] \tag{14.18}$$

where r is the radius of template and σ is the standard deviation of Gaussian function. It is worth pointing out that although the Gabor filter contains a Gaussian function, the main idea of Gaussian filter and Gabor one is totally different, which concerns the noise reduction and feature discriminability of HSI, respectively. Since the Gaussian filter is isotropic, the number of 3-D Gaussian–Gabor filters is the same as that of 3-D Gabor ones.

Let $\mathbf{R} \in \mathbb{R}^{X \times Y \times B}$ denote the HSI that contains B spectral bands and $X \times Y$ spatial pixels. In order to incorporate more discriminative information, the EMAP feature is also considered. The EMAP feature is denoted as $\mathbf{E} \in \mathbb{R}^{X \times Y \times Z}$, where Z is the number of extracted EMAP features. Specifically, the EMAP feature cube $\mathbf{E}$ and the original HSI $\mathbf{R}$ are directly concatenated, $\mathbf{C} = \text{cat}(\mathbf{E}, \mathbf{R})$, where $\mathbf{C} \in \mathbb{R}^{X \times Y \times P}$ $(P = B + Z)$ and operator *cat* means the concatenation of two feature cubes along the spectral dimension. Therefore, the corresponding 3-D Gaussian–Gabor features $\mathbf{G}^m \in \mathbb{R}^{X \times Y \times P}$ are computed by:

$$\mathbf{G}^m = |\Upsilon_m \otimes \mathbf{C}|, \quad m = 1, \ldots, 52 \tag{14.19}$$

where $|\cdot|$ calculates the magnitude of the convolution results. Meanwhile, there are 52 3-D Gabor–Gaussian filters in total, and thus the dimension of extracted features is as large as $52 \times P$. The plethora of features risks inducing the Hughes phenomenon and introduces redundancy that may degrade classification performance. Consequently, a feature selection approach utilizing the fast-density peak-based clustering (FDPC) algorithm is implemented.

Improved FDPC Algorithm

The FDPC algorithm has been improved from two aspects and applied to pick out the most discriminative features from the extracted 3-D Gaussian–Gabor features. Specifically, the $\ell_{2,1}$-norm is introduced to measure the feature similarity, which could increase the robustness of similarity computation. Alternatively, the selection manner of cluster centers concentrates on the features that are away from the ones with higher densities (whereas the FDPC algorithm tends to choose the features with high local density), which is more suitable for the feature selection task of 3-D Gaussian–Gabor feature cube. Furthermore, instead of taking the 3-D Gaussian–Gabor features $\mathbf{G}^m$ as a whole, the IFDPC algorithm deals with $\mathbf{G}^m$ individually to make the feature selection procedure more stable.

In the following, the IFDPC is presented in detail. Each 3-D Gaussian–Gabor feature $\mathbf{G}^m$ contains P feature maps, which can be considered as P data points from the clustering viewpoint. First, a distance matrix $\mathbf{S}^m \in \mathbb{R}^{P\times P}$ is constructed for each 3-D Gaussian–Gabor feature to measure the feature similarity, and any entry $\mathbf{S}_{ij}^m$ represents the similarity between the i-th and j-th feature maps of $\mathbf{G}^m$. Traditionally, the Euclidean distance is calculated with the Frobenius norm as follows:

$$\| \mathbf{S}_{ij}^m \|_F = \| \mathbf{G}_i^m - \mathbf{G}_j^m \|_F = \sqrt{\sum_{x,y=1}^{X,Y} \left(\mathbf{G}_{ixy}^m - \mathbf{G}_{jxy}^m\right)^2} \tag{14.20}$$

where $\mathbf{G}_i^m$ and $\mathbf{G}_j^m$ represent the i-th and j-th feature maps of $\mathbf{G}^m$, respectively, in which $\mathbf{G}_{ixy}^m$ and $\mathbf{G}_{jxy}^m$ correspond to the value at spatial location (x, y), respectively. However, the squaring in the Frobenius norm calculation can greatly affect the distance values, rendering the norm sensitive to minor variations in feature maps and potentially reducing the measure's robustness [7]. To alleviate the negative impact of the squared operation, in the IFDPC algorithm, the $\ell_{2,1}$-norm is introduced to compute $\mathbf{S}_{ij}^m$ as follows:

$$\| \mathbf{S}_{ij}^m \|_{2,1} = \| \mathbf{G}_i^m - \mathbf{G}_j^m \|_{2,1} = \frac{1}{2}\left(\sum_{x=1}^{X}\sqrt{\sum_{y=1}^{Y}\left(\mathbf{G}_{ixy}^m - \mathbf{G}_{jxy}^m\right)^2} + \sum_{y=1}^{Y}\sqrt{\sum_{x=1}^{X}\left(\mathbf{G}_{ixy}^m - \mathbf{G}_{xy}^m\right)^2}\right) \tag{14.21}$$

It is worth pointing out that since the feature selection procedure with each $\mathbf{G}^m$ is carried out in the same way, the superscript m of $\mathbf{S}^m$ is omitted hereafter for simplicity, and $\mathbf{S}$ denotes the $\ell_{2,1}$-norm distance matrix of any 3-D Gaussian–Gabor feature cube. Besides, since the two spatial dimensions should be handled in no particular order, the summation of two $\ell_{2,1}$-norms based distance in Eq. (14.21) guarantees the rotational invariance of feature maps.

Second, two important quantities of ρ_i and $\delta_i (i = 1, \dots, P)$ are computed to characterize the representativeness of each feature map based on the $\ell_{2,1}$-norm distance matrix $\mathbf{S}$. On the one hand, a Gaussian kernel is adopted to estimate the local density ρ_i, which can avoid the interference of large statistical errors caused by a small set of points, and ρ_i is defined as:

$$\rho_i = \sum_{i=1, i\neq j}^{P} \exp\left(-\left(\| \mathbf{S}_{ij}\|_{2,1}/d_c\right)^2\right). \tag{14.22}$$

According to the chosen rule of d_c in FDPC [8], d_c is practically set as the $5\% \times P \times (P-1)$-th smallest value in $\mathbf{S}$. On the other hand, the computation of parameter δ_i, which measures the intra-class distance, is the same as that of FDPC. After the two parameters ρ_i and δ_i have been calculated, they are normalized to make the following processing more stable.

Third, different from the FDPC algorithm that directly utilizes the multiplication of both parameters to achieve the ranking-based clustering, the IFDPC concentrates on the feature selection task of hyperspectral imagery, which needs the selected features to be as low correlation as possible, that is, the point chosen by FDPC should have a large value of ρ_i and a small value of δ_i. Therefore, the points with the value of δ_i higher than a predefined threshold can be considered as a possible cluster center; otherwise, it is just a trivial point. In the IFDPC algorithm, the median value of δ_i (denoted as δ_{me}) is regarded as the predefined threshold, and the feature score $\omega_i (i = 1, \ldots, P)$ of each point is computed by:

$$\omega_i = \begin{cases} \rho_i * \delta_i, & \text{if } \delta_i > \delta_{\text{me}} \\ 0, & \text{otherwise.} \end{cases} \tag{14.23}$$

The feature maps are ordered according to the obtained feature scores ω_i. After the largest values of feature scores are chosen as the cluster centers, the remaining points are distributed into the cluster of its nearest neighbor with higher density:

$$\mathcal{J}_i = \begin{cases} \min\limits_{j \in \mathcal{C}} \| \mathbf{S}_{ij} \|_{2,1}, & \text{if } i \notin \mathcal{C} \\ \mathcal{C}_j, & \text{if } i \in \mathcal{C}_j \end{cases} \tag{14.24}$$

where $\mathcal{C}$ means the index of cluster center and $\mathcal{J}_i$ is the label, which means that the i-th feature map belongs to the j th cluster. Meanwhile, it is worth pointing out that the isolated cluster stopping criterion [9] is adopted to automatically determine the number of selected features in each 3-D Gaussian–Gabor feature cube. The number of cluster centers gradually increases, and the partition process continues until an isolated cluster has been found. Thus, the selected features can be obtained in a totally unsupervised manner. Through applying the IFDPC algorithm on all 3-D Gaussian–Gabor feature cubes $\mathbf{G}^m$, the most discriminative and representative features can be achieved.

The distribution of two parameters (ρ and δ) and PCA-based mapping of the Indian Pines dataset within IFDPC results are depicted in Figure 14.1c, d. Similarly, the results of FDPC are shown in Figure 14.1a, b. Meanwhile, Table 14.1 lists the selected feature maps in order of the feature scores ω, and the correlation coefficient is also utilized to quantify two compared methods. Here, the Pearson correlation coefficient is adopted and defined as [10]:

$$Cor_{ij} = \frac{cov\left(\mathbf{G}_i^m, \mathbf{G}_j^m\right)}{std\left(\mathbf{G}_i^m\right) std\left(\mathbf{G}_j^m\right)} \tag{14.25}$$

where *cov* and *std* denote covariance and standard deviation, respectively.

It can be observed that the first three selected features, i.e., the 534th, 426th, and 379th feature maps, are the same for both the approaches, which is reasonable since the feature scores of the three feature maps are very high, while the intra-class distance δ is larger than the median value δ_{me}. Furthermore, for the rest of selected feature maps, the FDPC tends to pick out feature maps with large values of ρ (as shown in Figure 14.1a), while the IFDPC is prone to select feature maps with large values of δ (as shown in Figure 14.1c). Feature maps with larger δ, suggesting lower correlation, are prioritized in feature selection. Moreover, the feature maps selected by FDPC basically concentrate together (as shown in Figure 14.1b), while those obtained by IFDPC are more scattered in Figure 14.1d. Meanwhile, in Table 14.1, the mean correlation coefficient of IFDPC is much smaller than that of FDPC. In summary, Figure 14.1 and Table 14.1 confirm the IFDPC algorithm's efficacy in selecting Gaussian–Gabor features, both visually and quantitatively.

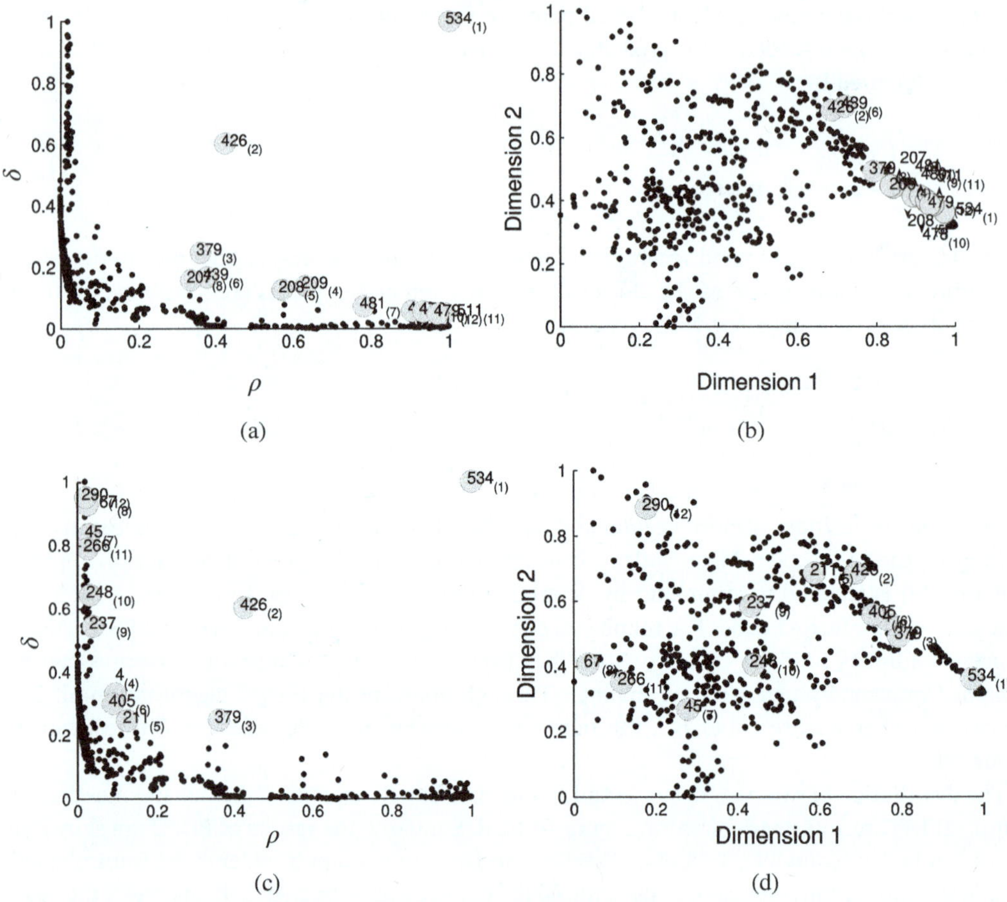

Figure 14.1 Feature selection analysis of the 7-th Gaussian–Gabor features. Large circles indicate selected features, with numbers denoting their order. (a–d) Visualize the selected features in both the distribution diagram of ρ-δ and the 2-D space using the FDPC and IFDPC algorithms.

Table 14.1 Correlation coefficients for 7-th Gaussian–Gabor features via FDPC and IFDPC.

Methods	Select features	*Cor*
FDPC	534/426/379/209/439/481/207/480/478/511/479	0.624
IFDPC	534/426/379/4/211/405/45/67/237/248/266/290	0.261

Applying the IFDPC algorithm to each 3-D Gaussian–Gabor feature cube retains key feature maps for subsequent classification. After the selected feature maps $\mathbf{\Upsilon}$ have been achieved by the GG-IFDPC algorithm, the SVM classifier is employed to accomplish the classification task.

14.2 Pixel-wise Gabor Features for Hyperspectral Image Classification

14.2.1 Prior Optimization-based Gabor Wavelets

14.2.1.1 Introduction

While the previous sections have detailed methods based on Gabor features, they did not incorporate the prior knowledge, which could impede the effective extraction of information. Moreover, processing a large quantity of Gabor features poses a significant challenge to airborne computing systems, limiting the efficiency of method. To address this issue, some studies have already been conducted based on prior information. For instance, the sparse-representation-based classification (SRC) method, which represents test samples as a sparse linear combination of all training samples and assigns them to the category with the least representation error, has been successfully applied in the field of pattern recognition. Building on this, a collaborative representation method based on 3-D Gabor features (3GCR) has been proposed [11]. Considering the non-uniform spatial distribution of materials and the varying characteristics of Gabor filters, some Gabor features may negatively impact the representation of materials. To tackle this issue, a multi-task joint sparse representation method based on Gabor cube selection (GS-MTJSRC) has been proposed [12]. Additionally, given the difficulty and time-consuming nature of manual annotation, there are usually limited labeled samples available for training supervised classifiers. Therefore, this section introduces a method based on 3-D Gabor wavelet phase encoding and Hamming distance matching (abbreviated as 3DGPC-HDM) [13]. The proposed method, instead of considering the large volume of Gabor magnitude features, exploits the Gabor phase features with certain orientations (i.e., the direction parallel to the spectral axis), which are then encoded by a quadrant bit coding (QBC) scheme. After that, a normalized Hamming distance matching (HDM) method is adopted to determine the similarity of two samples, and the nearest-neighbor classifier is routinely utilized for pixel-wise recognition.

14.2.1.2 3-D Gabor-wavelet-based Phase Coding

Gabor Phase with Particular Orientation

For a certain Gabor wavelet $\Psi_{i,j,k}$, the coefficient $\mathbf{G}_{i,j,k}(x, y, b) = (\mathbf{R} \otimes \Psi_{i,j,k})(x, y, b)$ represents the local signal change information around location (x, y, b). Since Gabor wavelet $\Psi_{i,j,k}$ is complex, the convolution coefficient at (x, y, b) can be described by magnitude $\mathbf{M}_{i,j,k}(x, y, b)$ and phase $\mathbf{P}_{i,j,k}(x, y, b)$ as follows:

$$\mathbf{M}_{i,j,k}(x, y, b) = \sqrt{\mathrm{Re}\left(\mathbf{G}_{i,j,k}(x, y, b)\right)^2 + \mathrm{Im}\left(\mathbf{G}_{i,j,k}(x, y, b)\right)^2} \tag{14.26}$$

$$\mathbf{P}_{i,j,k}(x, y, b) = \arg\tan \frac{Im\left(\mathbf{G}_{i,j,k}(x, y, b)\right)}{Re\left(\mathbf{G}_{i,j,k}(x, y, b)\right)} \tag{14.27}$$

where Im and Re operations get the imaginary and real parts of the complex coefficient, respectively.

According to the definition of Gabor magnitude $\mathbf{M}_{i,j,k}(x, y, b)$and phase $\mathbf{P}_{i,j,k}(x, y, b)$, it can be found that Gabor magnitude computes the distance between origin point and complex convolving result, while Gabor phase represents the angle between real part and imaginary part. Adjacent spatial pixels have similar magnitudes but varied phases, indicating greater stability in Gabor magnitude than phase. Thus, Gabor filter orientation significantly affects the discriminability of phase features [14, 15].

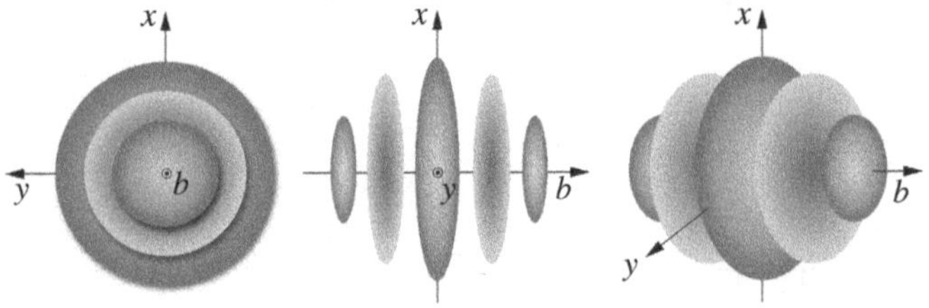

Figure 14.2 Gabor filter with orientation (0, 0, 1) viewed from three directions.

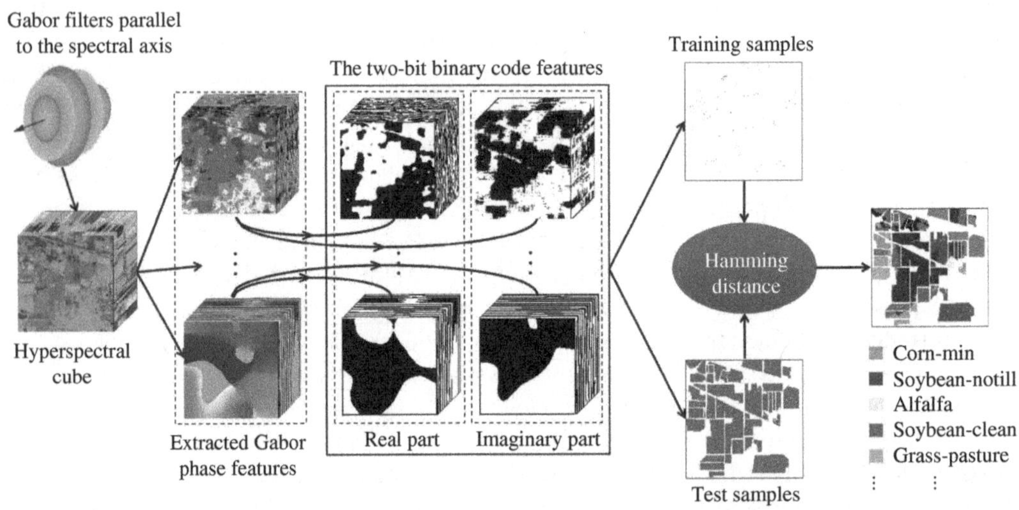

Figure 14.3 System block diagram of the 3DGPC-HDM framework for HSI classification.

In this section, we have observed that the Gabor phase features with the direction parallel to the spectral axis, that is, the Gabor filter with orientation (0, 0, 1) (as shown in Figure 14.2), contain more discriminative information than the others. This is expected since the Gabor filters that are parallel to the spectral axis are in accordance with the data structure of HSI, as displayed in Figure 14.3. In contrast, when the orientation of the Gabor filters is arranged at some angle (or even perpendicular) to the spectral axis, the discriminative power of phase responses in the convolved data cube can be affected substantially by the instability of phase and incompatibility between the Gabor filter and HSI. Therefore, only one Gabor filter in each scale is applied for feature extraction of Gabor phase. As aforementioned, the phase features obtained by other Gabor filters are excluded. The features of the designed subcubes from the Gabor filter can significantly improve the efficiency of the feature extraction procedure as the number of features is much smaller than the full number. At the same time, it can significantly increase the classification performance as it avoids dealing with the redundancy in the other features.

Quadrant Bit Feature Coding

Due to the sensitivity of Gabor phase features to position variation, it is unrealistic to directly utilize the Gabor phase information for feature matching. Thus, to increase the stability and discriminative ability of Gabor phase features, QBC [16] is applied to the Gabor phase feature set, which encodes phase information according to the quadrant that it belongs to. Concretely, it is worth pointing that the Gabor filters with orientation (0, 0, 1) correspond to the circumstance that both the parameters θ and φ in are $\pi/2$, that is, j and k are equal to 2. Each pixel in the resultant Gabor feature cube $\mathbf{G}_{i,2,2}(x, y, b)$, $i = 0, \ldots, I-1$ has been encoded into two bits, $(\mathbf{F}_i^{\mathrm{Re}}(x, y, b), \mathbf{F}_i^{\mathrm{Im}}(x, y, b))$, by the following rules:

$$\mathbf{F}_i^{\mathrm{Re}}(x,y,b) = \begin{cases} 1 & \text{if} \quad \mathbf{P}_{i,2,2}(x,y,b) \in \{\mathrm{I}, \mathrm{IV}\} \\ 0 & \text{if} \quad \mathbf{P}_{i,2,2}(x,y,b) \in \{\mathrm{II}, \mathrm{III}\} \end{cases} \tag{14.28}$$

$$\mathbf{F}_i^{\mathrm{Im}}(x,y,b) = \begin{cases} 1 & \text{if} \quad \mathbf{P}_{i,2,2}(x,y,b) \in \{\mathrm{I}, \mathrm{II}\} \\ 0 & \text{if} \quad \mathbf{P}_{i,2,2}(x,y,b) \in \{\mathrm{III}, \mathrm{IV}\}. \end{cases} \tag{14.29}$$

From Eqs. (14.28) and (14.29), it can be easily observed that the QBC method assigns two bits for each pixel based on the quadrant of the Gabor phase. That is, the coding values should be the same (either 0 or 1) within every 90° ((0°, 90°], (90°, 180°], (180°, 270°], (270°, 360°]). Hence the Gabor phase features are simplified and quantified by the QBC procedure. Furthermore, to compute the QBC values more directly, the encoding methods given in Eqs. (14.28) and (14.29) can be reformulated as follows [17]:

$$\mathbf{F}_i^{\mathrm{Re}}(x,y,b) = \begin{cases} 1 & \text{if } \mathrm{Re}(\mathbf{G}_{i,2,2}(x,y,b)) > 0 \\ 0 & \text{otherwise} \end{cases} \tag{14.30}$$

$$\mathbf{F}_i^{\mathrm{Im}}(x,y,b) = \begin{cases} 1 & \text{if } \mathrm{Im}(\mathbf{G}_{i,2,2}(x,y,b)) > 0 \\ 0 & \text{otherwise} \end{cases} \tag{14.31}$$

where $\mathrm{Re}(\mathbf{G}_{i,2,2}(x, y, b))$ and $\mathrm{Im}(\mathbf{G}_{i,2,2}(x, y, b))$ are the real and imaginary parts of the Gabor convolution result, respectively. Transforming the Gabor phase (the range is 0–2π) into binary code (0 or 1) by the QBC strategy not only increases the stability of Gabor phase features, but also accelerates the following feature matching procedure, eventually improving the efficiency of the proposed classification framework. In each subfigure of Figure 14.4, the first image represents the real part, and the second denotes the imaginary part. The QBC procedure notably enhances the Gabor phase stability, allowing the derived QBC features to be directly applied in classification.

14.2.1.3 Hamming Distance-based Matching and Classification

After the Gabor phase features of HSI have been encoded by the QBC strategy (4 scales are considered), 8 binary feature cubes, $\mathbf{F}_i^{\mathrm{Re}}$ and $\mathbf{F}_i^{\mathrm{Im}}$, $i = 0, \ldots, 3$, have been obtained. For any given test sample $\mathbf{t}$ located at the spatial position (x_{tr}, y_{tr}), the normalized Hamming distance, as detailed in [16], is employed to quantify the material similarity in the context of pixelwise classification. Concretely, assuming the spatial axes of any training sample $\mathbf{s}$ in the training set $\mathbf{A}$ are (x_{tr}, y_{tr}), the normalized Hamming distance between the test sample $\mathbf{t}$ and the training sample $\mathbf{s}$ is computed by:

$$D_0 = \frac{\sum_{i=0}^{3}\sum_{b=1}^{B}(\mathrm{bit}_i^{\mathrm{Re}} + \mathrm{bit}_i^{\mathrm{Im}})}{8 \times B} \tag{14.32}$$

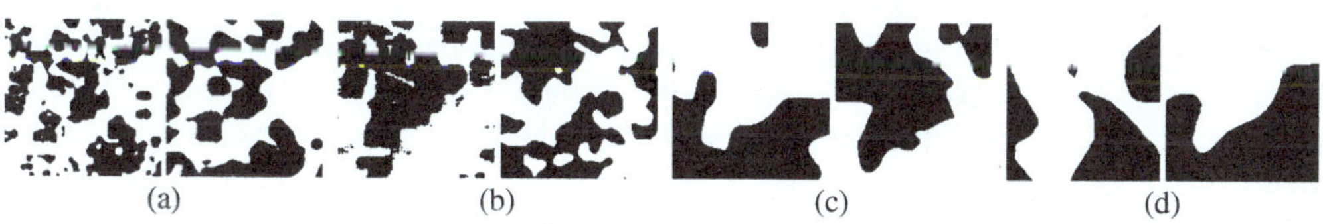

Figure 14.4 QBC of the 10-th band image in the Indian Pines data set with four different scales. (a) First quadrant, (b) Second quadrant, (c) Third quadrant, and (d) Fourth quadrant. The first image in each subfigure represents the real part, while the second represents the imaginary part.

$$\begin{aligned} \text{bit}_i^{\text{Re}} &= \mathbf{F}_i^{\text{Re}}(x_{tt}, y_{tt}, b) \oplus \mathbf{F}_i^{\text{Re}}(x_{tr}, y_{tr}, b) \\ \text{bit}_i^{\text{Im}} &= \mathbf{F}_i^{\text{Im}}(x_{tt}, y_{tt}, b) \oplus \mathbf{F}_i^{\text{Im}}(x_{tr}, y_{tr}, b) \end{aligned} \tag{14.33}$$

where $\oplus$ is the bit XOR operator, i.e., the result is equal to 0 if and only if the 2 bits, $\mathbf{F}_i^{\text{Re}}(x_{tt}, y_{tt}, b)$ and $\mathbf{F}_i^{\text{Re}}(x_{tr}, y_{tr}, b)$, are equal to each other. Otherwise, the result is equal to 1. The smaller the Hamming distance, the more similar between the test sample and the training sample. At last, the nearest-neighbor classifier is used for recognition.

14.2.1.4 Experimental Results

Experimental Data

The hyperspectral data set is the commonly used Indian Pines data acquired by the AVIRIS instrument over the agricultural area of Northwestern Indiana in 1992, which has a spatial dimension of 145×145 and 224 spectral bands. The spatial resolution of the data is 20 m per pixel. Due to atmospheric absorption, 4 zero bands and 35 lower signal-to-noise ratio bands are discarded, and 185 channels are preserved. The ground truth contains 10, 366 labeled pixels and 16 ground-truth classes.

Each experiment is repeated 10 times with different training sets to make the comparison fair, and both mean accuracies and standard deviation are reported. Concerning the evaluation metrics, overall accuracy (OA) and Kappa coefficient are adopted to quantify the classification performance. Specifically, OA is computed by dividing the sum of the correctly classified samples by the total number of test samples, while Kappa coefficient is calculated by accounting for all elements in the confusion matrix. Higher values of the two metrics correspond to better classification performance.

The classification results are compared visually and quantitatively with seven methods, i.e., three 3-D Gabor magnitude-based methods and four state-of-the-art spectral–spatial-integrated classification techniques, including generalized composite kernel (GCK) machines [18], subspace multinomial logistic regression classifier with Markov random fields-based multilevel logistic prior (MLR*sub*MLL) [19], multiple feature (extracted from linear and nonlinear transformations) learning-based classification (MFL) [20, 21], and local binary patterns-based extreme learning machine (LBP-ELM) [22]. As depicted in [23], after all Gabor magnitude feature cubes have been extracted, a feature selection and fusion process is applied to reduce the redundancy among the large number of Gabor features. Further, 3 representative multiclass classifiers, including *K*-nearest neighbors (KNN)[24, 25], SVM with radial basis function (RBF) kernel (RBFSVM) [26], and SRC [27], are used to finish the classification with fused magnitude (FM), respectively, which are abbreviated as FM-KNN, FM-RBFSVM, and FM-SRC, respectively.

Module Ablation Analysis

In order to verify the validity of choosing only 4 Gabor phase feature cubes for the subsequent encoding and matching procedure, Figure 14.5a–c shows the results of KNN, RBFSVM, and SRC on each Gabor magnitude feature cube, while Figure 14.5d shows the results of HDM on the encoded feature of each Gabor phase cube, respectively. Here 4 situations are considered, that is, fixed number samples, 3, 5, 10, and 15, of the labeled samples are selected from each class to form the training sets, respectively. Meanwhile, the results on all Gabor magnitude features and encoded phase cubes with different sizes of training sets are represented by distinct dotted lines. From Figure 14.5, it can be observed that the accuracy difference between the 4 Gabor features with orientation (0, 0, 1), i.e., numbered 8, 21, 34, and 47, and the rest are more distinct in Figure 14.5d than the other 3 figures. The performance of HDM on the 4 encoded feature cubes of Gabor phase is significantly higher than the other. Moreover, the results on all encoded Gabor phase cubes are much lower than those on all Gabor magnitude cubes. This is mainly because the stability of Gabor

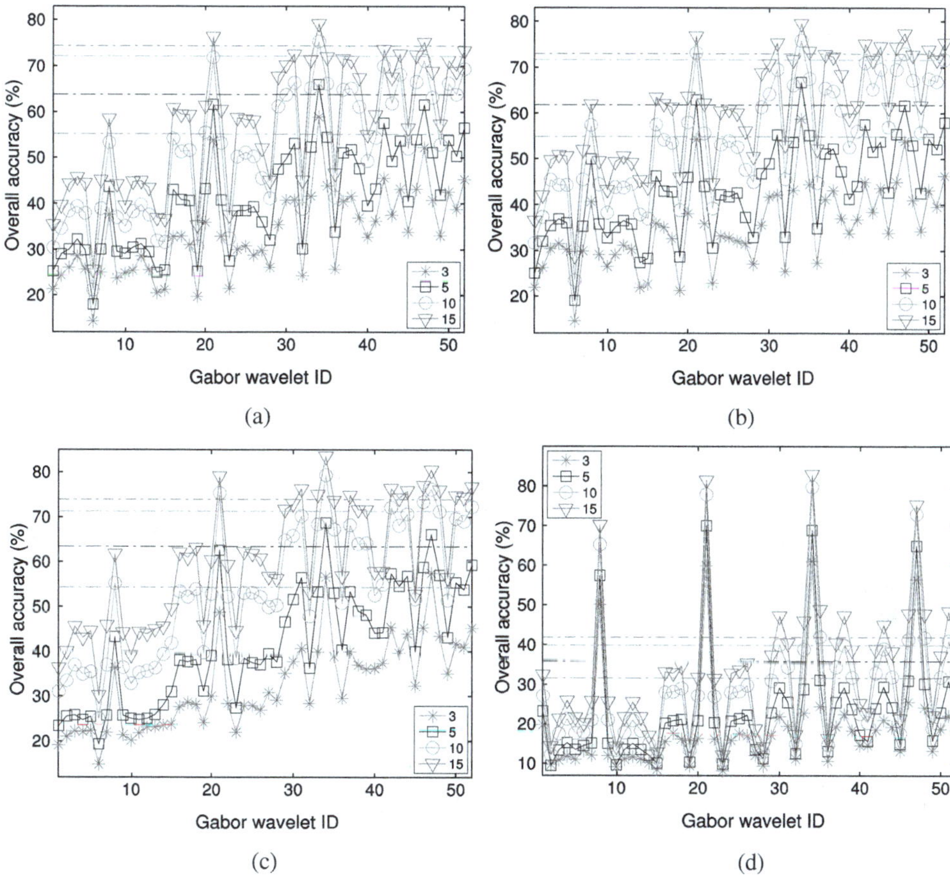

Figure 14.5 OA versus 52 Gabor feature cubes using different number of training samples per class. (a) KNN on the Gabor magnitude feature. (b) RBFSVM on the Gabor magnitude feature. (c) SRC on Gabor magnitude feature. (d) HDM on the encoded Gabor phase feature. The dotted lines represent the OA of the corresponding training size on all 52 Gabor magnitude cubes (the first three figures) and all 52 encoded Gabor phase cubes (the last figure).

magnitude features is considerably higher than that of Gabor phase, and less informative Gabor phase feature cubes can severely deteriorate the classification performance. Therefore, the orientations of Gabor filters can have a crucial impact on the representability of the Gabor phase features, as displayed in Figure 14.5d, and it would be desirable and practicable to choose the 4 Gabor phase feature cubes with orientation (0, 0, 1) for encoding, rather than taking all the 52 Gabor phase feature cubes into consideration.

Experimental Results Analysis

With respect to the 8 compared techniques, the OA and Kappa coefficient measure as functions of the number of training samples per class are displayed in Figure 14.6a, b. Besides, the experiments with different percentages of labeled samples per class as training samples are also carried out, as illustrated in Figure 14.6c, d. The performance of 3 Gabor magnitude-based methods (FM-KNN, FM-RBFSVM, and FM-SRC) and LBP-ELM is comparable, while 3DGPC-HDM provides the best results, demonstrating the effectiveness of the proposed approach. In particular, when the training size is extremely small, the differences between the algorithms are apparent. It is worth mentioning that since the feature fusion procedure of Gabor magnitude is carried out on the training set, the

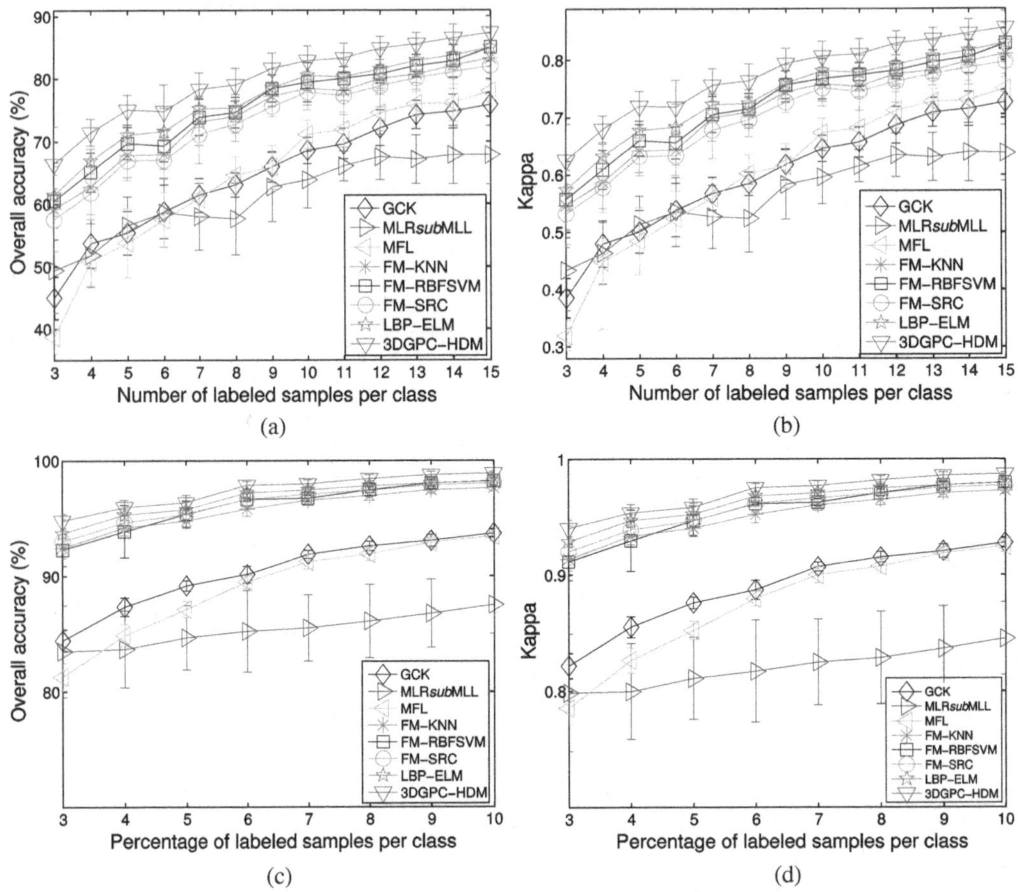

Figure 14.6 Indian Pines data. (a) OA. (b) Kappa as functions of the number of labeled samples per class. (c) OA. (d) Kappa as functions of the percentage of labeled samples per class.

most discriminative feature set may not be picked out due to the limited training samples, and the classification accuracy can be decreased. Contrarily, only 4 typical Gabor phase feature cubes have been taken into account in 3DGPC-HDM; thus, the feature fusion procedure is not necessary.

Concerning the case that the training size is only 3 labeled samples per class, the classification accuracy for each class, the OA and Kappa coefficient using various techniques are shown in Table 14.2. From the table, it can be seen that the results yielded by 3DGPC-HDM are better than those obtained by other methods in most cases. Figure 14.7 illustrates the training set, test set, and classification maps of the 8 techniques in a single experiment. It can be visually observed that the map of 3DGPC-HDM (Figure 14.7j) is in better accordance with the real map (Figure 14.7b) than the others.

14.2.2 Deep-learning-based Gabor Wavelets

14.2.2.1 Introduction

Unlike traditional methods that require detailed engineering and deep domain expertise, convolutional neural networks (CNNs) are dedicated to automatically learning high-level hierarchical features from original data. The features learned by CNNs are more distinctive, abstract, and robust

Table 14.2 Performance of 8 methods classified with 3 labeled samples per class.

Class	GCK	MLR *sub*MLL	MFL	FM-KNN	FM-RBFSVM	FM-SRC	LBP-ELM	3DGPC-HDM
C1	74.89	94.23	71.08	92.06	87.28	94.02	96.08	**97.39**
C2	52.18	67.67	42.09	89.90	88.21	96.81	**98.06**	97.65
C3	31.66	32.73	26.94	44.53	**49.17**	39.84	43.77	42.72
C4	35.57	43.74	34.79	51.50	50.07	49.59	**61.78**	59.68
C5	58.82	86.27	38.23	98.82	94.90	98.63	**99.41**	97.65
C6	27.88	25.84	22.19	44.97	46.58	46.51	53.50	**58.22**
C7	66.35	53.96	54.67	65.36	65.73	62.83	61.11	**72.19**
C8	67.17	82.97	51.79	75.20	78.35	76.64	83.14	**83.36**
C9	28.67	8.70	34.58	60.92	57.11	58.28	77.00	**78.94**
C10	91.73	95.21	85.65	98.70	98.70	**99.13**	98.56	98.26
C11	38.31	60.51	26.75	80.00	78.66	83.59	87.96	**88.14**
C12	83.52	**100.00**	71.17	**100.00**	94.71	**100.00**	98.23	99.41
C13	28.68	29.17	21.29	38.44	38.77	36.47	39.13	**51.33**
C14	38.98	39.85	36.81	56.92	58.68	51.18	48.48	**63.09**
C15	70.65	**78.38**	63.56	69.03	74.13	68.41	68.18	67.55
C16	89.61	90.65	78.18	88.52	87.94	90.00	89.04	**90.86**
OA	44.98	49.41	38.73	59.24	60.51	57.51	61.42	**66.45**
Kappa	0.386	0.434	0.320	0.547	0.558	0.532	0.574	**0.626**

Bold values represent the best results in this table.

compared to those obtained by traditional methods. However, CNN models involve numerous free parameters, and to avoid overfitting, they require a large number of training samples. This challenge is particularly pronounced for high-dimensional HSI data with a scarcity of labeled data. Additionally, CNNs usually face non-convex optimization issues during the parameter learning process, which are typically addressed by stochastic gradient descent methods. This could result in the loss of key information, such as features across different scales and orientations. Despite these challenges, CNNs have achieved significant success in HSI classification tasks. Nevertheless, the efficiency of CNN models is compromised by the traditional stochastic gradient descent method used for parameter updates, and the high-dimensional nature of HSI data, combined with limited training samples, further increases the risk of overfitting. To address the issue, the section integrates prior knowledge into the original CNN architecture. The goal is to combine the scale and orientation analysis capabilities of 3-D Gabor filters with the powerful learning mechanism of CNNs, guiding the CNN model to produce more robust features that can handle variations in direction and scale, thus simplifying the complexity of traditional CNN training.

A novel deep network with multilayer and multibranch architecture is proposed, named 3-D Gabor CNN (3DG CNN) [28]. More precisely, since the predefined 3-D Gabor filters in multiple scales and orientations could well characterize the internal spatial–spectral structure of HSI data from various perspectives, the 3-D Gabor-modulated kernels (3-D GMKs) are employed to replace the random initialization kernels. Moreover, the specially designed multibranch architecture enables the network to better integrate the scalable property of 3-D Gabor filters; thus, the representative ability and robustness of the extracted features can be greatly improved. Alternatively, the

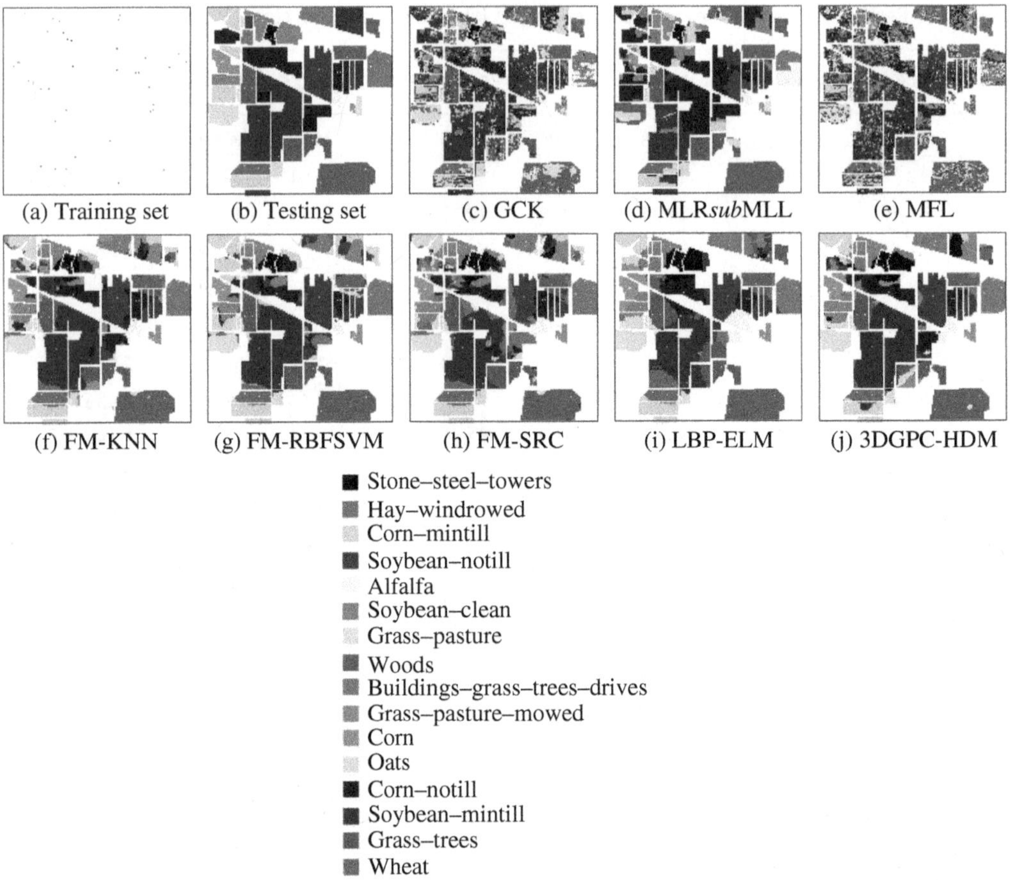

Figure 14.7 Performance comparison of different classification methods on the Indian Pines dataset. (a) Training set, (b) Test set, and classification maps on Indian Pines dataset obtained by (c) GCK, (d) MLRsubMLL, (e) MFL, (f) FM-KNN, (g) FM-RBFSVM, (h) FMSRC, (i) LBP-ELM, (j) 3DGPC-HDM.

number of network parameters is substantially reduced due to the incorporation of 3-D Gabor modulation, relieving the training complexity and alleviating the training process from overfitting.

14.2.2.2 Convolutional Neural Network

Due to the large flexibility of CNNs and their ability to make strong assumptions about the input images, CNNs have also been applied to the HSI data and become one of the most successful tools for classification [29]. Typically, the computation process of a CNN can be divided into two parts: forward computation and backward computation.

1) *Forward Computation Process:* In the convolutional layers, each convolution neuron processes data only for its receptive field to obtain the feature map for the next layer. The forward computation process of convolutional layers is to convolve the input feature maps with convolutional kernels channel by channel and perform an accumulation operation to obtain the output feature maps. The input feature maps F and the output feature maps $\hat{F}$ of a convolutional layer can be denoted as:

$$F = \{F_i \mid i = 1, 2, \ldots, I\} \tag{14.34}$$

$$\hat{F} = \{\hat{F}_o \mid o = 1, 2, ..., O\} \tag{14.35}$$

where I and O are the numbers of the input and output feature maps; F_i and $\hat{F}_o$ represent the i-th input feature map and the o-th output feature map, respectively. Then, $\hat{F}_o$ can be obtained by the following convolution:

$$\hat{F}_o = \sum_{i=1}^{I} F_i \otimes C_{i,o} \tag{14.36}$$

where $C_{i,o}$ refers to the channel of convolutional kernel corresponding to $\hat{F}_o$ and F_i.

2) *Backward Computation Process:* CNNs learn model parameters by minimizing the loss function with the gradient descent method and the backpropagation (BP) algorithm. After the forward computation of all the layers, the gradients of the loss function for each parameter are computed with BP algorithm, and parameters are then updated in the opposite direction of gradients, which can be formulated as follows:

$$\delta = \frac{\partial L}{\partial C_{i,o}} \tag{14.37}$$

$$C_{i,o} = C_{i,o} - \eta\delta \tag{14.38}$$

where L is the loss function, δ is the gradient of the loss function computed by chain rule, and η is the learning rate.

14.2.2.3 3-D Gabor Convolutional Neural Network for Classification

Different from 2-D Gabor filters that extract only spatial signal correlations, 3-D Gabor filters can effectively characterize signal variation in joint spatial–spectral domains. To harness the synergistic benefits of both the CNN model and Gabor filtering, the 3-D GMKs are herein introduced, constituting the inaugural endeavor in the literature to seamlessly integrate 3-D Gabor filters and standard convolution kernels (SCKs) within CNN architectures. Then, a specially designed multibranch 3DG-CNN using 3-D GMKs is proposed for the HSI classification tasks.

Subsequently, the following steps are outlined: the methodological details regarding the derivation of 3-D GMKs via 3-D Gabor filters are initially furnished. Next, the forward and backward propagation processes of deep CNN models are elucidated, incorporating 3-D GMKs with augmented scale and orientation resilience. Third, we illustrate the designed architecture of 3DG-CNN.

3-D Gabor-Modulated Kernels

As mentioned before, 3-D Gabor filters are steerable and manipulable with adjustable orientations and scales. To incorporate the attributes into the Gabor CNN, a set of 3-D Gabor filters with different orientations and scales are predefined, denoted as:

$$\Psi = \{ \Psi_{u,v} \mid u = 1, 2, ..., U, v = 1, 2, ..., V \} \tag{14.39}$$

where U and V are the number of scales and orientations, respectively. To cover the entire 3-D space as much as possible and obtain the features in all directions, 3-D Gabor filters with different orientations can be designed by changing the value of parameter θ and φ. Here, with $\pi/4$ as the step size, parameters θ and φ are respectively selected as:

$$\{\theta, \varphi\} \in \left\{0, \frac{\pi}{4}, \frac{\pi}{2}, \frac{3\pi}{4}\right\}. \tag{14.40}$$

It is easy to notice that the frequency vector points to the same direction with different θ when $\varphi = 0$. There are in total 13 different orientations, i.e., $V = 13$. Moreover, to enhance multiscale feature representation, 4 different scales are selected in this place, i.e., scale factors f are selected as:

$$f \in \{0.5, 0.25, 0.125, 0.0625\} \tag{14.41}$$

where it varies from coarse to fine and could well characterize the texture features of surface materials (i.e., $U = 4$).

For the modulation procedure, 3-D GMKs are created by manipulating 3-D Gabor kernels on the SCKs to produce the scale- and orientation-enhanced feature maps. Before being modulated by 3-D Gabor kernels, SCKs are first learned by the BP algorithm. The SCKs in 3DG-CNN encode the orientation channel of 3-D Gabor filters. Suppose that the size of an SCK in 3DG-CNN can be expressed as $N \times W \times W$, where $W \times W$ refers to the size of the kernel and N represents the channel. Furthermore, the dimensions of the weight per layer in 3DG-CNN can be represented as $O \times I \times N \times W \times W$, where O and I refer to the channel of output and input feature map, respectively. For implementation convenience and to keep the consistency and continuity of the channel quantity, N is set to be the same as V, which is the orientation number of the 3-D Gabor filters. A GMK is obtained based on a modulation procedure by manipulating an SCK via a 3-D Gabor filter bank with V 3-D Gabor filters for the u-th scale. Equation (14.42) and Figure 14.8a show the details

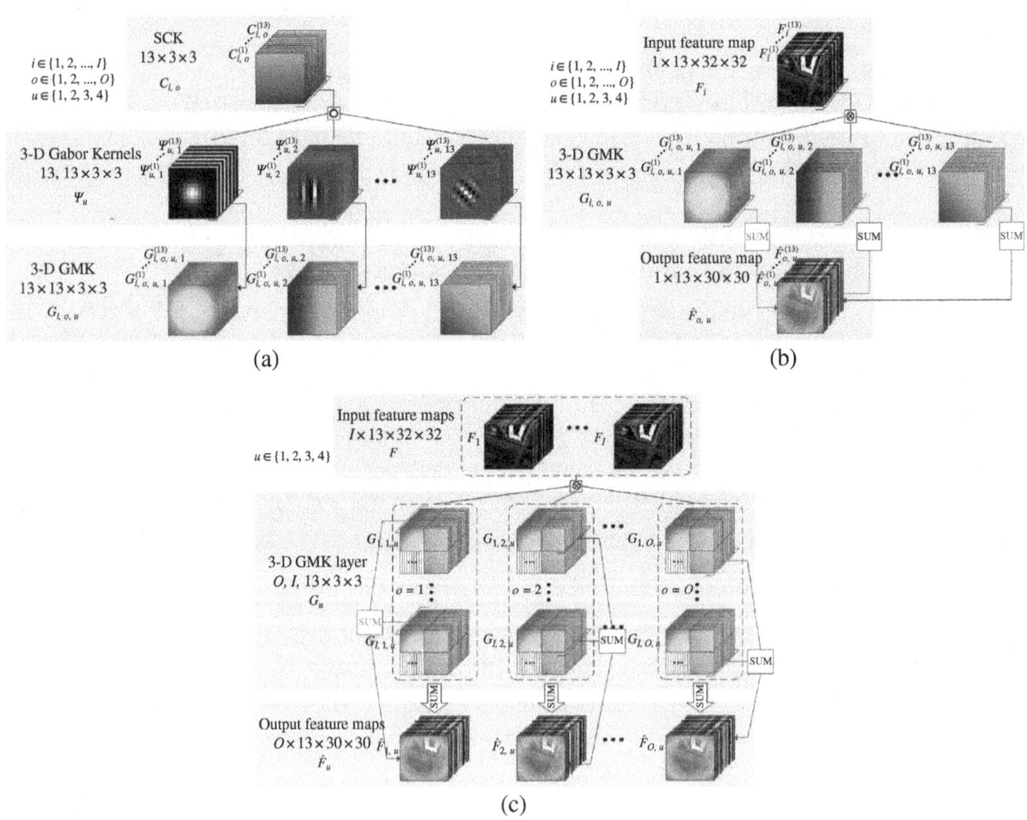

Figure 14.8 (a) Modulation process of 3-D GMK. (b) Illustration of 3-D GMK convolution. (c) Forward convolution process of 3-D GMK convolutional layer.

of the kernel modulation process. With respect to the v-th orientation and the u-th scale 3-D Gabor filter $\Psi_{u,v}$, the modulated subkernel $G_{i,o,u,v}$ of an SCK $C_{i,o}$ can be calculated by:

$$G_{i,o,u,v}^{(n)} = C_{i,o}^{(n)} \circ \Psi_{u,v}^{(n)} \tag{14.42}$$

where i and o refer to the i-th input feature map and the o-th output feature map, (n) represent the n-th channel, and $\circ$ is an element-by-element multiplication operation. Then, a 3-D GMK for a given scale u can be defined as:

$$G_{i,o,u} = \{G_{i,o,u,v} \mid v = 1, 2, \ldots, V\}. \tag{14.43}$$

It can be seen from Figure 14.8a that a 3-D GMK consists of V 3-D subkernels ($V = 13$), and the size of a 3-D GMK is $V \times N \times W \times W$. Yet, under actual circumstances, only $N \times W \times W$ parameters of SCKs will be saved, as the 3-D Gabor filters are already predefined. In essence, this implies that the employment of GMKs enables the extraction of enriched feature maps without increasing the parameter count. The capability of multiple 3-D Gabor kernels is integrated by learning a single 3-D SCK, which reduces the training parameters while maintaining superior classification ability. Given that CNNs typically employ real-valued convolutions, only the real components of 3-D Gabor filters are utilized in the modulation.

Forward Computation Process

In the forward computation procedure of deep models, 3-D GMK convolution is performed on the input feature maps to produce output feature maps with scale and orientation robustness enhanced. Moreover, the notation used to denote the i-th input feature map and the o-th output feature map of a 3-D GMK convolutional layer is as follows:

$$F_i = \left\{F_i^{(n)} \mid n = 1, 2, \ldots, N\right\} \tag{14.44}$$

$$\hat{F}_{o,u} = \left\{\hat{F}_{o,u}^{(n)} \mid n = 1, 2, \ldots, N\right\} \tag{14.45}$$

where each input and output feature map of 3DG-CNN are of N channels, corresponding to V orientations of 3-D Gabor filters, respectively (i.e., $N = V = 13$). u demonstrates that the output feature map is generated by the 3-D GMK at the u-th scale. Then, for all I input feature maps F that each has N channels, the convolution procedure to obtain each channel of $\hat{F}_o$ can be formulated as:

$$\hat{F}_{o,u}^{(v)} = \sum_{i=1}^{I} \sum_{n=1}^{N} F_i^{(n)} \otimes G_{i,o,u,v}^{(n)} \tag{14.46}$$

where (v) represents the v-th channel of output feature map $\hat{F}_{o,u}$, and (n) represents the n-th channel of input feature map F_i and subkernel $G_{i,o,u,v}$. Intuitively, Figure 14.8b illustrates an example of the convolution process of a 3-D GMK on a single input feature map with $N = 13$ channels, whereas Figure 14.8c presents the forward convolution process of a 3-D GMK convolutional layer with multiple input and output feature maps.

Backward Computation Process

As mentioned above, in 3DG-CNN, only the weights of SCKs need to be learned by the BP algorithm and saved after the forward calculation process. Employing the chain rule, the gradients of the loss function with respect to each parameter within each SCK are computed, effectively aggregating the gradients of all constituent subkernels in each 3-D GMK. This procedure can be mathematically expressed as:

$$\delta = \frac{\partial L}{\partial C_{i,o}} = \sum_{v=1}^{V} \frac{\partial L}{\partial G_{i,o,u,v}} \circ \Psi_{u,v} \tag{14.47}$$

where L is the loss function and δ refers to the gradient. After that, the weights of SCKs are updated on the contrary direction of the gradients according to Eq. (14.38). During the backward computation, only the partial derivative of SCKs is calculated, which is easy to implement and is the same as standard CNNs.

Network Architecture

The details of the architecture are illustrated in Figure 14.9. Empirically, the patch size of the input feature map is set to 5×5. The kernel size of 3-D GMK is $13 \times 3 \times 3$, and the step size of 3-D GMK is set to 1. The layer width of each 3-D GMK layer is set to 64, and no padding is adopted in the convolution. After each layer of the 3-D GMK+ batch normalization (BN)+ReLU structure, the spatial size of the output feature map is reduced by 2. Therefore, a two-layer structure is used to make the size of the output feature map of convolutional layers be 1×1. To adapt to the dimensionality of the filter size and maintain the coupling of the input feature maps and the 3-D GMKs, the input of 3DG-CNN is normalized as independent patches of 13 bands. Through dividing the whole HSI cube into separated subsets, 3DG-CNN reduces not only the number of parameters to be learned but also the sliding operations of SCKs in the spectral dimension ($\lfloor B/13 \rfloor$ versus $B - 13$, where B is the number of spectral bands). Thus, the complexity of training procedure can be further alleviated. Besides, a four-branch architecture of 3-D GMK convolutional layers is adopted, which corresponds to the 4 scales of 3-D Gabor filters. This multibranch architecture design can make use of the scalable property of 3-D Gabor filters in the learning procedure and extract features with multiscale robustness enhancement. In each 3-D GMK, all $V = 13$ orientations of 3-D Gabor filters are involved; hence, the extracted features are also enhanced for multiorientation representation. The loss function employed is cross entropy, a commonly utilized metric in deep learning networks for addressing multiclassification problems. Formally, it can be defined as:

$$L = -\sum_{x \in \mathcal{X}} \mathbb{P}_{\text{label}}(x) \log \mathbb{P}_{\text{pred}}(x) \tag{14.48}$$

where $x \in \mathcal{X}$ refers to the training samples. $\mathbb{P}_{\text{label}}$ and $\mathbb{P}_{\text{pred}}$ indicate real sample distribution and predicted probability distribution computed by a softmax layer, respectively. Additionally, BN

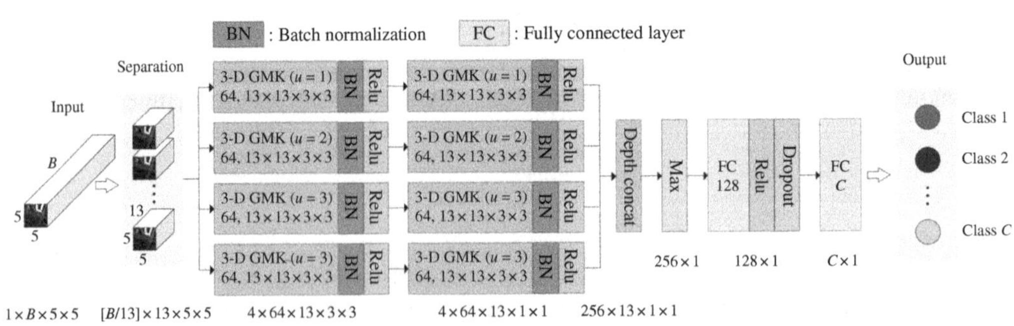

Figure 14.9 The detailed architecture of the proposed 3DG-CNN.

and ReLU activation functions are incorporated after each 3-D GMK convolutional layer, as well as following the initial fully connected (FC) layer. A dropout layer [30] is also adopted after the first FC layer to avoid overfitting.

14.2.2.4 Experimental Results

Experimental Data

The Pavia University dataset was acquired by the reflective optics spectrometer (ROSIS) sensor in 2003 over Northern Italy. Typically, 12 noisy bands are discarded, leaving 103 channels for experimental use. It is of size 610×340 with a ground-sampling distance of 1.3 m per pixel, including 42,776 labeled samples across 9 land cover classes.

Module Ablation Analysis

To verify the rationality of the multibranch structure ($U = 4$), it is compared with the single-/double-/triple-branch ($U = 1/2/3$) version of 3DG-CNN. For a fair comparison, all branches of the compared networks are consistent with the branches of 3DG-CNN, in which the two 3-D GMK convolutional layers of a single branch have the same scale of 3 D Gabor kernels. The scale factors used in the compared network with U branches are all the U-combinations of $f \in \{0.5, 0.25, 0.125, 0.0625\}$. As listed in each column of Table 14.3, the values of classification accuracy are averaged by U runs of the U branch network with different combinations of f. Experimental results consistently show that the multibranch structure of 3DG-CNN ($U = 4$) can extract more discriminative features by involving various scales from large to small.

Due to the significant differences among the structures of compared DL-based methods, to facilitate a fair comparison, the computation cost of a single 2-D SCK layer, 3-D SCK layer, 2-D GMK layer, and 3-D GMK layer with the same layer width (setting to be 64) is calculated on all datasets. Quantitatively, the parameter size, memory burden, and computation time of these single layers are reported in Table 14.4. It is clearly shown that the 3-D GMK layer is more parameter saving than the others, which is of less training complexity. As for computation time, the 3-D GMK layer is second

Table 14.3 Ablation study results toward the multibranch structure of 3DG-CNN.

Data set	Accuracy	$U = 1$	$U = 2$	$U = 3$	$U = 4$
Pavia University	OA(%)	92.12	93.35	93.86	**94.78**
	AA(%)	93.56	94.76	95.10	**96.42**
	Kappa	0.89	0.91	0.92	**0.93**

Bold values represent the best results in this table.

Table 14.4 Comparison of the computation consumption on Pavia University dataset.

Data set	Layers	Parameter size	Memory (MB)	Time (s)
Pavia University	2-D SCK	59,328	0.23	**0.03**
	3-D SCK	177,984	0.68	0.19
	2-D GMK	237,312	0.91	0.40
	3-D GMK	**52,416**	**0.20**	0.05

Bold values represent the best results in this table.

Table 14.5 Classification accuracy (%) and Kappa measure for the Pavia University dataset.

Class	RAW-SVM	CGDA-SVM	LDA-SVM	2DG-SVM	3DG-SVM	2DCNN	3DCNN	MB-CNN	MS-CNN	2DG-CNN	3DG-CNN
C1	64.65	56.71	79.13	77.82	86.84	91.81	92.65	96.52	94.32	94.74	**96.52**
C2	64.31	74.77	81.26	83.76	87.97	91.44	92.44	87.82	88.62	92.32	**93.52**
C3	67.82	71.07	73.28	84.16	81.75	92.79	92.50	90.10	90.51	92.99	**94.49**
C4	93.98	92.71	95.08	87.27	91.10	96.89	95.35	**98.87**	97.93	96.74	96.92
C5	99.58	99.39	99.93	99.90	**100.0**	99.98	99.93	**100.0**	**100.0**	**100.0**	99.94
C6	70.44	75.60	86.51	80.78	**97.78**	90.63	85.14	89.76	90.52	92.42	92.39
C7	87.39	70.17	79.93	88.22	95.90	98.56	97.20	98.04	98.32	**99.05**	98.73
C8	75.23	64.65	72.61	78.06	70.66	93.69	89.99	91.80	93.97	95.56	**95.70**
C9	**99.88**	61.96	99.61	97.52	97.00	99.65	99.21	99.57	99.40	99.64	99.60
OA	70.62	72.60	82.26	83.12	88.15	92.65	92.10	91.50	91.75	93.88	**94.78**
AA	80.36	74.11	85.26	86.39	89.89	95.05	93.83	94.72	94.84	95.94	**96.42**
Kappa	0.63	0.63	0.77	0.78	0.85	0.91	0.90	0.89	0.90	0.92	**0.93**

Bold values represent the best results in this table.

only to the 2-D SCK layer even though what are learned in the training procedure of the 3-D GMK layer are actually 3-D SCKs.

Experimental Results Analysis

To purposefully illustrate the performance and verify the validity of our proposed 3DG-CNN, 5 ML-based classifiers and 5 advanced DL-based methods are utilized in comparison, including SVM with raw HSI data (RAW-SVM), SVM with collaborative graph-embedding-based discriminant analysis (CGDA-SVM) [31], SVM with linear discriminant analysis (LDA-SVM) [32], SVM with 2-D Gabor features (2DG-SVM), SVM with 3-D Gabor features (3DG-SVM), 2DCNN [33], 3DCNN [34], multi-branch CNN (MB-CNN) [35], multiscale CNN (MS-CNN) [36], 2-D Gabor CNN (2DG-CNN) [37].

It can be seen from Table 14.5 that RAW-SVM provides the worst result. Besides, all the DL-based models perform better classification results than the ML-based methods, and 2DG-CNN and 3DG-CNN achieve higher accuracy than 2DCNN and 3DCNN with scale and orientation information enhanced by Gabor filtering. Classification maps of the 9 compared methods are presented in Figure 14.10. It can be easily observed from Figure 14.10 that our 3DG-CNN obtains not only the smoothest but also the most accurate map in regard to the ground truth, which again proves the effectiveness of the proposed 3DG-CNN approach.

14.3 Superpixel-wise Gabor Features for HSI Classification

14.3.1 Superpixel Segmentation-based Gabor Wavelets

14.3.1.1 Introduction

As introduced in the previous subsection, combining the priors and deep-learning-based methods with Gabor can effectively achieve intelligent interpretation of HSIs. These methods extract the spatial texture features of HSIs through the Gabor operator and combine them with spectral

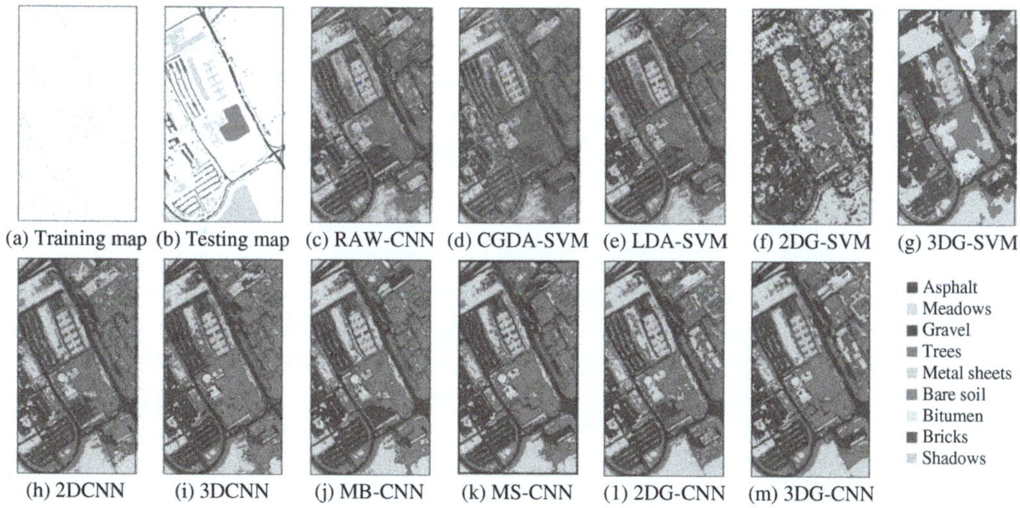

Figure 14.10 (a) Training map. (b) Testing map. (c–m) Classification maps.

information to classify each pixel. However, pixel-level Gabor classification methods need to classify each pixel in the image, which leads to data redundancy and increases computation since features between neighboring pixels are often highly similar. In addition, pixel-level analyses are susceptible to noise interference. Superpixel-level Gabor-based classification methods provide an improved solution to these problems. By composing neighboring pixels with similar features into superpixels and using Gabor filters to extract spatial texture features on these superpixels, this approach is more conducive to capturing the characteristics of land cover more accurately.

From the perspective of local spatial–spectral coherence of HSI, a flexible Gabor (FG)-based superpixel-level unsupervised linear discriminant analysis (abbreviated as FG-*Su*ULDA) framework is introduced for HSI classification [38]. Firstly, through extending the sinusoidal plane wave in the 3-D Gabor filter into a more general form, a set of 3-D FG wavelets are established to sufficiently examine the diverse spatial–spectral distribution characteristics of materials. Concretely, 5 types of sinusoidal waves, including the circular 3-D Gabor filter, are carefully selected for feature extraction. Secondly, the linear discriminant analysis (LDA) algorithm is employed to remove the redundancy and retain the most discriminative content from the obtained large number of 3-D FG features. Specifically, an unsupervised LDA strategy with the guidance of entropy rate superpixel (ERS) segmentation, named *Su*ULDA, is elaborated to eliminate the dependence of the traditional LDA algorithm on training samples, and the robustness of *Su*ULDA can be promoted. Since it is reasonable to regard the pixels in a single superpixel as the same class with a high probability, the within-superpixel scatter matrix and between-superpixel scatter matrix of *Su*ULDA are computed and combined, respectively, to complete the feature reduction task in an unsupervised manner. Finally, the obtained features are concatenated as input to the SVM classifier.

14.3.1.2 ERS Segmentation

ERS is a superpixel segmentation method that divides an HSI into K perceptually uniform regions, where K is the number of superpixels [39]. This method initializes an undirected graph $U = (P, D)$ to describe the HSI, where P represents the pixel set and D denotes the edge set. It aims to search a subset of the edge set $A \subseteq D$ so that $U_E = (P, A)$ divides the image into K superpixels which are compact, homogeneous, and balanced. Specifically, entropy rate of a random walk on the graph $\mathcal{H}(A)$ and a balancing term on the cluster distribution $\mathcal{B}(A)$ are utilized. The objective function is defined as:

$$\underset{\text{A}}{\arg\max}\, \mathcal{H}(A) + \alpha\mathcal{B}(A) \text{ s.t.} A \subseteq D \tag{14.49}$$

where $\alpha > 0$ is the balance coefficient between two terms and their definitions are explained in [39].

The process extracts K non-overlapping superpixels from hyperspectral data, grouping pixels likely of the same material into uniform clusters. The ERS method guarantees spatial homogeneity and uniform distribution of superpixels, where each superpixel has approximate number of pixels. The value of K is computed by a heuristic function as follows [40]:

$$K = \text{floor}\left(\frac{X \times Y}{1000 \times \delta^{\sqrt{\text{Res}}}}\right) \tag{14.50}$$

where floor $(\cdot)$ means the rounding down operation to the nearest integer. $X \times Y$ is the spatial coverage of the HSI, and Res is the spatial resolution. The parameter δ should be less than 1 and set to 0.7 in [40]. Since the values of all parameters in Eq. (14.50), including X, Y, δ, and Res, can be preset or known in advance, the computation of K can be automatically assigned, which is the most important parameter in superpixel segmentation method.

14.3.1.3 Flexible Gabor-based Superpixel-level Unsupervised LDA Classification

3-D Flexible Gabor Filter

Circular 3-D Gabor features uniformly capture adjacent spectral and spatial information due to their isotropic nature. However, this could lead to oversmoothing the inhomogeneous spatial–spectral structures and edges in HSI, reducing discriminative capacity. Fortunately, in order to explore different structural characteristics of materials and increase the expressivity of complex spatial–spectral correlations, a 3-D flexible sinusoidal wave $v_\lambda(x, y, b)$ is designed as follows:

$$v_\lambda(x,y,b) = \exp\left(j2\pi\left(F_x x^{\lambda_1} + F_y y^{\lambda_2} + F_b b^{\lambda_3}\right)^{\frac{1}{\lambda_4}}\right) \tag{14.51}$$

where $\boldsymbol{\lambda} = (\lambda_1, \lambda_2, \lambda_3, \lambda_4)$ is a set of parameters that control the grating degree of the oriented complex sinusoidal wave. Concretely, the parameters (λ_1, λ_2) describe the response intensity in the spatial domain, while λ_3 depicts the intensity in the spectral domain. The last parameter λ_4 adjusts the response intensity of the whole structure and is calculated as:

$$\lambda_4 = \frac{\lambda_1 + \lambda_2 + \lambda_3}{3} \tag{14.52}$$

By importing the set of parameters $\boldsymbol{\lambda}$ and referring to Eq. (14.16), the 3-D flexible Gabor wavelet can be calculated as follows:

$$\Psi_\lambda(x,y,b) = u(x,y,b) \times v_\lambda(x,y,b) \tag{14.53}$$

Similarly, by taking different scales f and orientations (θ, φ), Ψ_λ also produces $Z = 52$ 3-D flexible Gabor wavelets, which are expressed as $\Psi_{(\lambda,\, z)}$, $z = 1, \ldots, Z$. Altering the $\boldsymbol{\lambda}$ parameter in 3-D Gabor filters enhances the spatial–spectral extraction, yet for a balance between representation and complexity, only 5 specific $\boldsymbol{\lambda}$ settings are employed, including the circular form.

Concerning the HSI cube $\mathbf{R} \in \mathbb{R}^{X \times Y \times B}$ that contains $X \times Y$ spatial pixels and B spectral bands, the 3-D flexible Gabor (FG) features can be computed by

$$\mathbf{G}_{(\lambda,z)} = |\Psi_{(\lambda,z)} \otimes \mathbf{R}|, \lambda \in \Omega, z = 1, \dots, Z \tag{14.54}$$

where $\otimes$ is the convolutional operator and $|\cdot|$ denotes the magnitude of the convolutional results. Several critical issues can be observed from Eq. (14.54). First, the convolutional computation is directly applied to $\mathbf{R}$ without data stretching; hence, the internal spatial–spectral correlation can be fully characterized, and the dimensions of each achieved 3-D FG feature cube are the same as the raw HSI, i.e., $\mathbf{G}_{(\lambda, z)} \in \mathbb{R}^{X \times Y \times B}$. Second, through varying parameter $\boldsymbol{\lambda}$ with each circumstance of z, $z = 1, \dots, Z$ ($Z = 52$), 260 modules in total that adequately capture the discriminative representation of materials from different aspects can be thus collected. Third, the achieved large number of 3-D FG feature cubes indicates a massive computation requirement and may also cause an unstable classification due to the aforementioned Hughes phenomenon. Therefore, an unsupervised LDA-based feature reduction procedure with the aid of superpixel segmentation is applied. For the convenience of the following description, the obtained 3-D FG feature cubes are denoted as $\mathbf{G}_{m,z}$, $m = 1, \dots, 5$; $z = 1, \dots, 52$.

Superpixel-Level Unsupervised LDA

To provide pseudo-labels for the proposed *Su*ULDA algorithm to accomplish the feature reduction task, the simple but effective ERS algorithm is introduced. First, a 2-D superpixel map $\mathbf{E} = \{\mathbf{E}_1, \mathbf{E}_2, \dots, \mathbf{E}_K\} \in \mathbb{R}^{X \times Y}$ using the ERS method from the HSI $\mathbf{R}$ is obtained, where K can be automatically computed by Eq. (14.50), and $\mathbf{E}_k$ represents the k-th superpixel (assuming that N_k pixels are contained within the superpixel), i.e.,

$$\mathbf{E}_k = \{\mathbf{E}_{(x,y)} \mid \mathbf{E}_{(x,y)} = k\}, k = 1, \dots, K \tag{14.55}$$

Second, concerning any one of those FG feature cubes, which is denoted as $\mathbf{G}'$, let $g_k \in \mathbb{R}^{N_k \times B}$ be the feature matrix of the k-th superpixel $\mathbf{E}_k$ ($k = 1, \dots, K$), where $g_k^i \in \mathbb{R}^B$ is the i-th pixel ($i = 1, \dots, N_k$). Namely, g_k^i is a feature vector from $\mathbf{G}'$. The mean vector $\boldsymbol{\mu}_k$ of superpixel $\mathbf{E}_k$ is computed as:

$$\boldsymbol{\mu}_k = \frac{1}{N_k}\sum_{i=1}^{N_k} \mathbf{g}_k^i \tag{14.56}$$

Alternatively, let $\boldsymbol{\mu}_k \in \mathbb{R}^B$ denote the spatial average vector of the whole FG feature cube $\mathbf{G}'$, which is defined as:

$$\boldsymbol{\mu} = \frac{1}{X \times Y}\sum_{k=1}^{K}\sum_{i=1}^{N_k} \mathbf{g}_k^i \tag{14.57}$$

Thereby, 2 superpixel-level scatter matrices (i.e., $\boldsymbol{S}_w$ and $\boldsymbol{S}_b$) can be derived. More precisely, the within-superpixel scatter matrix $\boldsymbol{S}_w \in \mathbb{R}^{B \times B}$ depicts the distance between pixels in the same superpixel and the related mean vector, which is calculated by:

$$\boldsymbol{S}_w = \sum_{k=1}^{K}\left(\sum_{i=1}^{N_k}(\mathbf{g}_k^i - \boldsymbol{\mu}_k)(\mathbf{g}_k^i - \boldsymbol{\mu}_k)^T\right) \tag{14.58}$$

Likewise, the between-superpixel scatter matrix $\boldsymbol{S}_b \in \mathbb{R}^{B\times B}$ describes the distance between mean vectors of different superpixels, and it can be computed by:

$$\boldsymbol{S}_b = \sum_{k=1}^{K} (\boldsymbol{\mu}_k - \boldsymbol{\mu})(\boldsymbol{\mu}_k - \boldsymbol{\mu})^T \tag{14.59}$$

In order to preserve the information of superpixel for classification, the optimization function of the proposed *Su*ULDA in the project direction $\boldsymbol{a}$ can be defined as follows:

$$\arg\max_{\boldsymbol{a}} \frac{\boldsymbol{a}^T \boldsymbol{S}_b \boldsymbol{a}}{\boldsymbol{a}^T \boldsymbol{S}_w \boldsymbol{a}} \tag{14.60}$$

where $\boldsymbol{a}^T\boldsymbol{S}_b\boldsymbol{a}$ describes the distance between centers (the center is the mean vector of features after reduction in the same superpixel) of different superpixels in subspace. Meanwhile, $\boldsymbol{a}^T\boldsymbol{S}_w\boldsymbol{a}$ represents the covariance of each superpixel in subspace and describes the distance between the pixels in the same superpixel. For optimal discriminative ability, the value of $\boldsymbol{a}^T\boldsymbol{S}_b\boldsymbol{a}$ should be maximized while the value of $\boldsymbol{a}^T\boldsymbol{S}_w\boldsymbol{a}$ should be minimized.

Similar to the traditional LDA method, the objective function of *Su*ULDA can be solved by:

$$[\gamma, \mathbf{A}] = SVD\left(\mathbf{S}_w^{-1}\mathbf{S}_b\right) \tag{14.61}$$

where SVD and $(\cdot)^{-1}$ denote the singular value decomposition and matrix inversion operators, respectively. $\gamma \in \mathbb{R}^B$ is the eigenvalue vector sorted from high to low, and $\mathbf{A} \in \mathbb{R}^{B\times B}$ is the corresponding eigenvector matrix. By picking out the d largest eigenvalues from γ, the reduced eigenvector matrix $A_d \in \mathbb{R}^{B\times d}$ is utilized for dimensionality reduction of $\mathbf{G}'$. It is worth pointing out that the value of d is constraint by that the sum of d largest eigenvalues is larger than 90% of the sum of all eigenvalues, and thus more than 90% of the energy in the 3-D FG feature cube is preserved by d eigenvectors. The compressed feature cube $\mathbf{H}' \in \mathbb{R}^{X\times Y\times d}$ is computed as:

$$\mathbf{H}' = \mathbf{G}' \times \mathbf{A_d} \tag{14.62}$$

At last, by employing the *Su*ULDA algorithm on each 3-D FG feature cube $G_{m,z}$, $m = 1, \ldots, 5$; $z = 1, \ldots, 52$, the corresponding FG-*Su*ULDA feature cubes $\mathbf{H}_{m,z}$, $m = 1, \ldots, 5$; $z = 1, \ldots, 52$, can be achieved.

SVM-based Classification

After all the FG-*Su*ULDA feature cubes $\mathbf{H}_{m,z}$, $m = 1, \ldots, 5$; $z = 1, \ldots, 52$, have been extracted by the proposed FG-*Su*ULDA framework, they are concatenated for classification. Since the dimension of each $\mathbf{H}_{m,z}$ is much smaller than that of $\mathbf{G}_{m,z}$, *i. e.*, $d \ll B$, the efficiency of the following classification procedure can be promoted. Here, the SVM method is applied. To implement classification, the one-against-all scheme is utilized for multi-class manipulation, and 10-fold cross-validation is used for the definition of SVM parameters. Besides, the linear kernel is adopted to achieve an efficient and accurate classification result. Figure 14.11 shows the schematic diagram of the proposed FG-*Su*ULDA approach to make the method more easily to be understood.

With respect to the parameters contained in the proposed FG-*Su*ULDA approach, they can be either preset (such as the convolutional coefficients in the FG model) or determined during algorithm execution (such as the number of superpixels K and compressed feature number d). Therefore, the robustness and generalization of FG-*Su*ULDA can be ensured, since the parameters of SVM classifier can be learned by cross-validation.

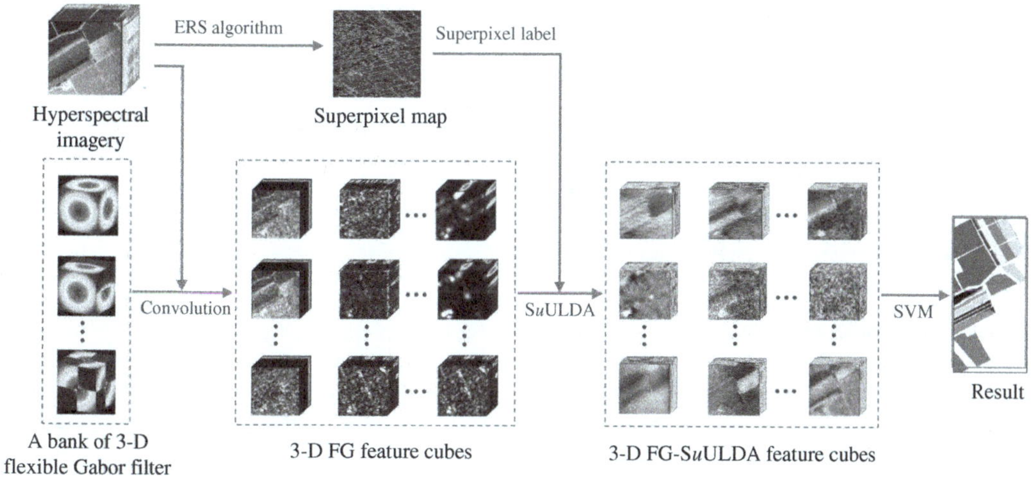

Figure 14.11 System block diagram of the proposed FG-SuULDA framework.

14.3.1.4 Experimental Results

Experimental Data

The hyperspectral dataset Botswana was acquired by the NASA EO-1 satellite over the Okavango Delta, Botswana, in 2001–2004. The spatial resolution of the data is 30 m per pixel. The spatial and spectral dimensions are 1476 × 256 and 242. After removing the uncalibrated and noisy bands associated with water absorption features, the remaining 145 bands are reserved for analysis. The dataset contains 14 ground-truth classes and 3248 labeled samples.

The classification performance is quantitatively assessed by the OA, AA, and Kappa coefficient. Besides, due to the aforementioned small sample size problem, the training samples are randomly selected in numbers ranging from 3 to 15 for each class, and the retained labeled samples form a testing set. Each experiment is repeated 10 times with different training samples to ensure reliable results, and the mean values of 3 quantitative metrics are reported.

Module Ablation Analysis

To evaluate the effectiveness of FG and *Su*ULDA, 3 methods are taken into consideration. Specifically, 3-D circular Gabor magnitude (CGabor) uses concatenated circular Gabor features without feature reduction, while the so-called CG-*Su*ULDA combines these features with *Su*ULDA. Meanwhile, the CGabor feature is combined with the designed *Su*ULDA to form the CG-*Su*ULDA. FG features without *Su*ULDA are excluded due to high computational costs, and FG-PCA is tested to highlight the importance of *Su*ULDA. All methods employ the SVM classifier with the same settings.

Table 14.6 shows classification performance on the Botswana datasets using 4 methods, with 3 training samples per class. CGabor ranks lowest in accuracy due to redundancy and negative impacts of combining circular Gabor features, which exacerbates the Hughes phenomenon and in turn justifies the need for feature dimensionality reduction. Generally, the FG-based methods, FG-PCA and FG-*Su*ULDA, outperform CGabor, highlighting the importance of FG module. Moreover, the two *Su*ULDA-based techniques excel over CGabor and FG-PCA, showing the efficiency of the *Su*ULDA module in discarding redundant features and enhancing the discriminative ability of Gabor features through superpixel-level structural information.

Table 14.6 Classification performance of 4 ablation methods on Botswana dataset.

Metric	CGabor	CG-*Su*ULDA	FG-PCA	FG-*Su*ULDA
OA	72.98	80.93	78.76	**88.16**
AA	72.95	81.10	79.97	**88.53**
Kappa	0.70	0.79	0.77	**0.87**

Bold values represent the best results in this table.

Experimental Results Analysis

Experiments are designed to assess the superiority and rationality of FG-*Su*ULDA framework. First, 4 state-of-the-art spatial–spectral feature extraction frameworks, including nonlinear multiple feature learning-based classification (NMFL) [20], local binary patterns and extreme learning machine (LBP-ELM) [22], 3-D convolutional neural network (3-D CNN) [34], and a graph convolutional network-based method (miniGCN) [41], are chosen for comparison. Second, 3 different kinds of features, i.e., raw HSI (RAW), kernel principal component analysis (KPCA), and orthogonal total variation component analysis (OTVCA) [33], are compared with the FG-*Su*ULDA-extracted feature.

The classification results by 8 compared methods are illustrated in Figure 14.12, with varying sizes of training samples. Likewise, the FG-*Su*ULDA provides the best accuracies in all circumstances, indicating the importance of the flexible Gabor extension. Again, when the training set is only 3 samples per class, the class accuracy and classification maps of 8 methods in comparison are provided in Table 14.7 and Figure 14.13, respectively. All these results constantly demonstrate the superiority and effectiveness of the FG-*Su*ULDA approach, even though the spatial distribution of materials in the data is indistinct.

14.3.2 Multiscale Superpixel-based Gabor Wavelets

14.3.2.1 Introduction

Superpixel Gabor classification method uses the superpixel segmentation map as a preprocessing step to enhance the relationships between pixels within superpixels and utilizes the Gabor filters to

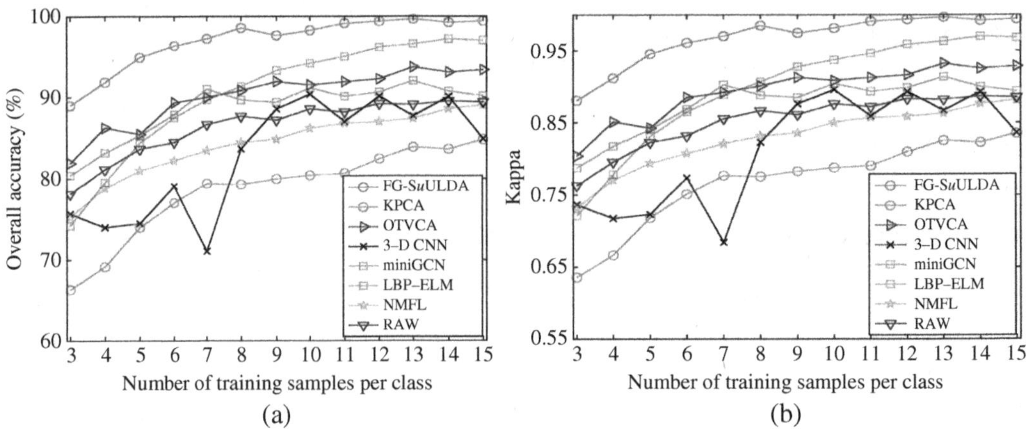

Figure 14.12 (a) OA and (b) Kappa versus the number of training samples per class.

Table 14.7 Classification performance of 8 compared methods on Botswana dataset.

Class	RAW	KPCA	OTVCA	NMFL	LBP-ELM	3-DCNN	miniGCN	FG-*Su*ULDA
C1	99.25	99.25	**100.00**	97.38	74.83	99.89	**100.00**	80.34
C2	82.45	82.14	94.13	89.29	79.08	69.90	**98.98**	97.65
C3	85.65	82.26	67.84	85.28	61.77	**92.18**	73.39	92.14
C4	81.27	65.80	81.96	**91.75**	62.22	91.65	66.51	85.61
C5	71.58	58.93	63.16	67.07	65.79	45.75	**80.08**	79.92
C6	53.42	30.36	50.56	67.63	62.37	60.41	47.74	**78.42**
C7	87.54	75.68	**98.54**	88.52	86.29	96.09	98.05	96.60
C8	84.30	72.25	80.50	**88.70**	74.55	72.60	81.50	80.90
C9	69.71	47.99	59.65	82.86	66.85	68.33	93.25	**98.33**
C10	73.51	57.55	**100.00**	46.90	86.04	70.49	71.02	86.04
C11	72.52	71.52	88.74	62.68	79.27	68.71	**96.36**	83.64
C12	94.27	81.18	**100.00**	52.02	75.28	86.52	98.31	91.24
C13	65.58	45.00	91.89	66.87	96.08	69.13	48.30	**100.00**
C14	**99.35**	98.91	96.74	71.74	63.48	69.78	85.87	86.09
OA	78.12	66.31	81.91	75.28	74.19	75.66	80.41	**88.16**
AA	78.54	69.20	83.84	75.92	74.65	75.82	81.38	**88.53**
Kappa	0.76	0.64	0.80	0.75	0.74	0.74	0.79	**0.87**

Bold values represent the best results in this table.

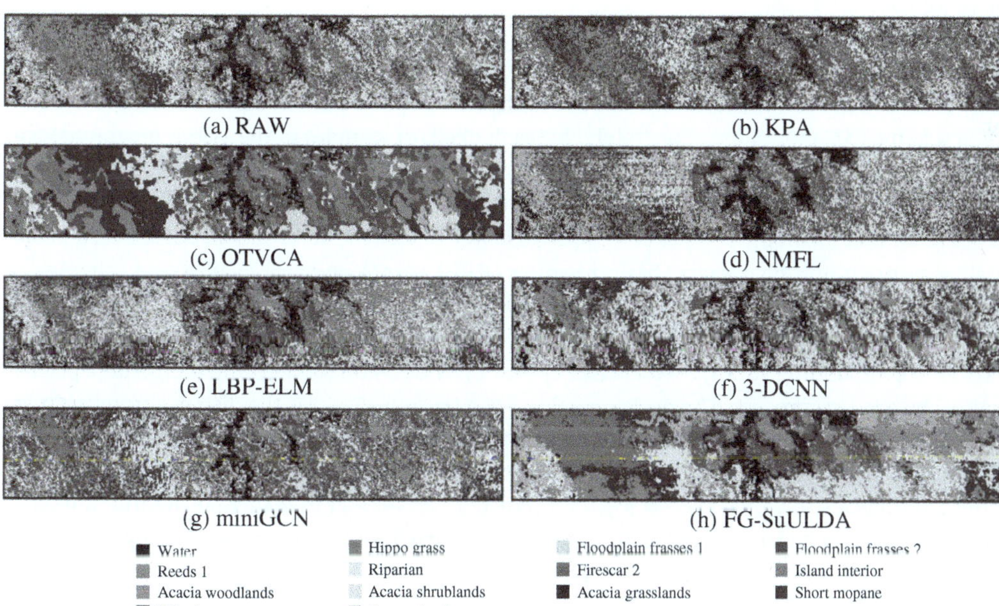

Figure 14.13 Classification maps on Botswana dataset obtained by (a) RAW, (b) KPCA, (c) OTVCA, (d) NMFL, (e) LBP-ELM, (f) 3-D CNN, (g) miniGCN, and (h) FG-SuULDA.

extract the spatial texture features on these units, combined with spectral information to achieve fine recognition of land cover types. These methods reduce data redundancy and noise interference while improving the accuracy and robustness of land cover classification. However, it is not a trivial task to precisely estimate the number of extracted superpixels, which controls the segmentation scale of the scene and has a crucial impact on HSI analysis. Specifically, if the number of superpixels is too large (corresponding to over-segmentation), the number of pixels in each superpixel is relatively small and the same material may be partitioned into several superpixels, which could decrease the classification performance with small training samples. Most existing methods use a fixed scale to obtain image segmentation results. In practical scenes, the spatial properties of land covers may exhibit considerable diversity due to variations in type, size, and shape. Therefore, superpixels with a single fixed scale are often difficult to adapt to all classes of land covers, thus affecting the acquisition of texture features by the Gabor operator. To address these challenges, constructing multi-scale methods becomes a solution.

From the perspective of superpixel regularization, a cascade superpixel regularized Gabor feature fusion (CSRGFF) method is introduced for HSI classification [42]. The model employs Gabor filters that are consistent with the internal features of the HSI and have varying scales, to directly convolve with the original HSI to obtain amplitude and phase features. Moreover, instead of directly estimating the number of superpixels, a series of superpixel graphs is extracted from the raw HSI with different numbers of superpixels, which are employed to regularize the weighting cube in a cascade mode from over-segmentation to under-segmentation. The regularized results are summed to get the final weighting cube, and the classification map can thus be achieved by taking the maximal weight of each pixel.

14.3.2.2 Cascade Superpixel Regularized Gabor Feature Fusion for Classification

Confidence Cube Computation

The confidence cubes are calculated based on the Gabor magnitude feature cubes M_i, $(i = 1, \ldots, 4)$, which are acquired by Eq. (14.26). Since the characteristic of Gabor magnitude and phase features is totally different, the computed confidence cubes should be specifically designed to comply with the coding scheme of Gabor phase. Concretely, for each pixel (or sample) in the Gabor magnitude feature cube M_i, the goal is to get the confidence scores of pixel belonging to each class, and then the corresponding confidence cube $\mathbf{C}_i$ can be achieved. For a certain pixel in M_i, C_i^c denotes the confidence score that it belongs to class c. In order to better represent the confidence score C_i^c, an SVM classifier is used, in which radial basic function (RBF) kernel and one-against-one scheme are employed for multi-class classification [25]. Suppose there are C significant materials existing in the scene, $C \times (C-1)$ classifiers can be thus constructed by SVMs with training samples. For each classifier corresponding to any two classes c_1 and c_2, a decision value δ for the certain pixel is obtained by a voting process. The decision value δ can be considered as the distance from the pixel to the optimal hyperplane [43], and therefore, this value can be used to construct confidence score to different classes. Mathematically, in the proposed method, a decision matrix $D \in \mathbb{R}^{C \times C}$ is built for the certain pixel, in which $\mathrm{D}_{c^1c^2} = \delta \; if \; \delta > 0, else \; \mathrm{D}_{c^2c^1} = -\delta$, and the other entries in D are set as 0. After the decision matrix D is built, the confidence score of the certain pixel belonging to class c in M_i is computed by:

$$C_i^c = \frac{\sum_{j=1}^{C} \mathbf{D}_{cj}}{2 \times n_c} + \frac{\sqrt{n_c}}{2 \times \sqrt{C}}, c = 1, \ldots, C \tag{14.63}$$

where n_c is the number of non-zero entries in the c-th row of the matrix D. It can be evidently observed from Eq. (14.65) that the range of the obtained SVM-based probability output is [0, 1]. Meanwhile, the larger the confidence score C_i^c, the higher probability that the certain pixel belongs to the c-th class. After all the pixels in the Gabor Magnitude feature cube M_i have been processed by the carefully designed confidence score representation, the confidence cube $\mathbf{C}_i \in \mathbb{R}^{X \times Y \times C}$ can be thus achieved. So finally, 4 different confidence cubes $\mathbf{C}_i$, $i = 1, \ldots, 4$ can be obtained based on 4 different Gabor magnitude feature cubes M_i, $i = 1, \ldots, 4$.

Hamming Cube Computation

In order to further improve classification performance as well as effectively fuse the Gabor magnitude and phase features, QBC [16] and Hamming distance-based matching are conducted to generate the Hamming cubes. QBC is a coding method that encodes phase information according to the quadrant to which it belongs. Concretely, for each value $\mathbf{P}_i(x, y, z)$ in the i-th Gabor phase feature cube, it is encoded into two bits, $\left(Q_i^{\mathrm{Re}}(x,y,z), Q_i^{\mathrm{Im}}(x,y,z)\right)$, by the following rules:

$$\mathbf{Q}_i^{\mathrm{Re}}(x,y,z) = \begin{cases} 1 & \text{if} \quad \mathbf{P}_i(x,y,z) \in \{\mathrm{I}, \mathrm{IV}\} \\ 0 & \text{if} \quad \mathbf{P}_i(x,y,z) \in \{\mathrm{II}, \mathrm{III}\} \end{cases} \tag{14.64}$$

$$\mathbf{Q}_i^{\mathrm{Im}}(x,y,z) = \begin{cases} 1 & \text{if} \quad \mathbf{P}_i(x,y,z) \in \{\mathrm{I}, \mathrm{II}\} \\ 0 & \text{if} \quad \mathbf{P}_i(x,y,z) \in \{\mathrm{III}, \mathrm{IV}\} \end{cases} \tag{14.65}$$

From Eqs. (14.64) and (14.65), it can be easily seen that the QBC codes of phase value are encoded based on the quadrant that it lies. That is, any two phase values are encoded into two same bits both in $\mathbf{Q}^{\mathrm{Re}}$ and $\mathbf{Q}^{\mathrm{Im}}$ if they lie in the same quadrant, while the coding bits are completely different in the opposite quadrant (i.e., quadrant 14.3.2.1 and 14.3.2.3 or quadrant 14.3.2.2 and 14.3.2.4). After 4 Gabor phase feature cubes have been encoded from the QBC coding method, 8 binary feature cubes, $\mathbf{Q}^{\mathrm{Re}}$ and $\mathbf{Q}^{\mathrm{Im}}$, $i = 1, \ldots, 4$, are obtained. For any two certain pixels p and q with spatial positions (x_p, y_p) and (x_q, y_q), in order to measure their similarity based on the QBC codes, the Hamming distance [16] is adopted. Concretely, the Hamming distance between the pixels p and q in the i-th QBC feature cube is computed by:

$$h_i(p,q) = \frac{\sum_{z=1}^{Z} \left(bit_i^{Re} + bit_i^{Im}\right)}{2 \times Z} \tag{14.66}$$

$$\begin{aligned} \mathrm{bit}_i^{\mathrm{Re}} &= Q_i^{\mathrm{Re}}\left(x_p, y_p, z\right) \oplus Q_i^{\mathrm{Re}}\left(x_q, y_q, z\right) \\ \mathrm{bit}_i^{\mathrm{Im}} &= Q_i^{\mathrm{Im}}\left(x_p, y_p, z\right) \oplus Q_i^{\mathrm{Im}}\left(x_q, y_q, z\right) \end{aligned} \tag{14.67}$$

where $\oplus$ is the bit XOR operator, i.e., the result is equal to 0 if and only if two bits, $\mathbf{Q}_i(x_p, x_p, z)$ and $\mathbf{Q}_i(x_q, y_q, z)$, are equal. From that, it can be easily found that the value of Hamming distance is between 0 and 1. The smaller the value, the more similar between the pixels p and q. Based on the Hamming distance calculation between two pixels, the Hamming distance of a pixel-to-class is defined. Precisely, the Hamming distance between the pixel p and the c-th class is computed by:

$$Hcal_i^c = \min_{\mathrm{label}\left(A_j\right) = c} h_i\left(p, A_j\right) \tag{14.68}$$

where **A** is the training set composed of labeled pixels, and $\mathbf{A}_j$ is the j-th sample (or pixel) in **A**. The number i represents that such calculation is computed based on the i-th QBC feature cube. Same as the confidence score achieved from the Gabor magnitude features, the range of Hamming distance is also between 0 and 1. The pixel-to-category Hamming distance of all the pixels can be calculated in this way, and finally 4 Hamming cubes, $\mathbf{H}_i \in \mathbb{R}^{X\times Y\times C}$, $i = 1, \ldots, 4$, can be generated.

Cascade Superpixel Regularization

The confidence score reflects the similarity between the pixel and the class, and similarity is higher if the score is larger. By contrast, the Hamming distance measures the distance between the pixel and the class, and therefore, larger value means smaller similarity between them. Based on the analysis, the confidence cubes $\mathbf{C}_i$, $i = 1, \ldots, 4$ and Hamming cubes $\mathbf{H}_i$, $i = 1, \ldots, 4$ obtained from the Gabor magnitude and phase features, respectively, are combined to construct the weighting cube:

$$W = \sum_{i=1}^{4}(C_i - H_i) \tag{14.69}$$

For illustrative purposes, Figure 14.14 shows the system block diagram of the proposed framework. In practice, it is commonly accepted that introducing more parameters can increase the flexibility of the algorithm, but the complexity and usability of the algorithm can also be degraded. Since the ranges of $\mathbf{C}_i$, $i = 1, \ldots, 4$ and $\mathbf{H}_i$, $i = 1, \ldots, 4$ are the same, i.e., they both take values from 0 to 1, they can be directly combined without balancing the two terms, and the practicability of the proposed method can be ensured. The weighting cube **W** integrates two types of similar features, increasing decision accuracy. Though directly classifying pixels by their highest weight yields decent results, it overlooks spatial information. In order to reflect the spatial regularity of surface materials in the scene and further boost the classification performance, an effective method has been adopted to regularize the weighting cube, i.e., the weight of each pixel in the same superpixel is regularized to be equal. Specifically, ERS is applied to obtain the superpixel graph (it is worth pointing out that the first 3 PCA bands are used for the ERS method), and then the regularization

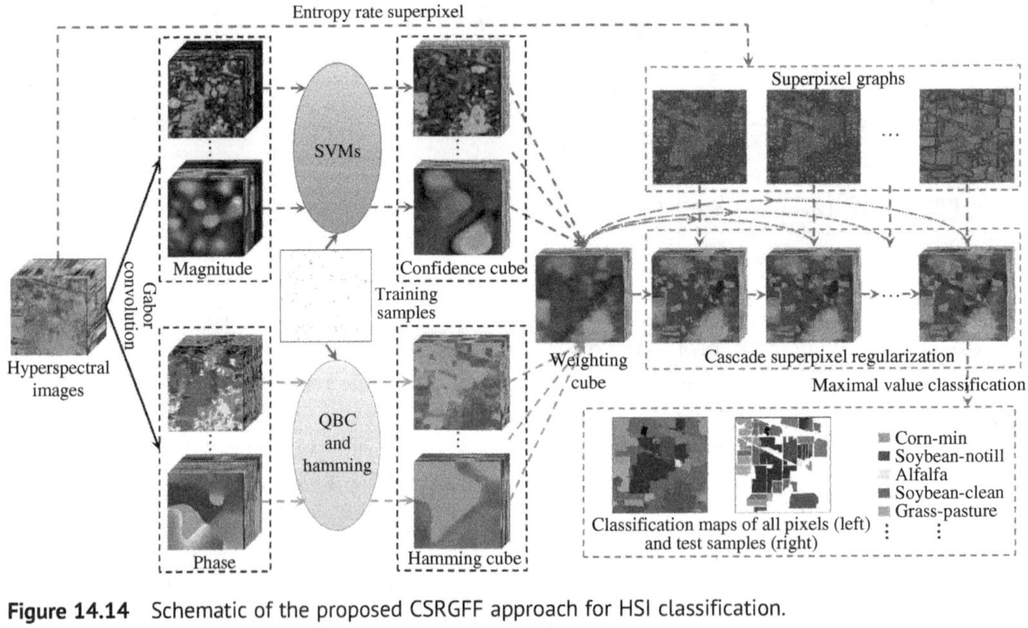

Figure 14.14 Schematic of the proposed CSRGFF approach for HSI classification.

is carried out in each superpixel one by one. Since each superpixel is homogeneous as much as possible, the weight of this class is set to 1 and others to 0 for each pixel in this superpixel. Otherwise, the weights of all these pixels for each class are replaced by the mean value of them. Through regularizing the weighting cube in this way, the spatial information of surface materials contained in superpixels can be integrated into the weighting cube.

14.3.2.3 Experimental Results

Experimental Data

The experiments use the Indian Pines dataset described previously to validate the effectiveness of the proposed CSRGFF model. In terms of comparative analysis, the proposed method is compared with 7 algorithms, including two deep-learning-based methods (3D-CNN [44] and LSTM-CNN [45]), two state-of-the-art spatial–spectral-integrated methods (GCK machine [18] and local binary pattern-based extreme learning machine (LBP-ELM) [22]), and two 3D Gabor-based methods. Moreover, in order to illustrate the effectiveness of the designed cascade superpixel regularization, the last Gabor-based comparing method is implemented by conducting the weighting cube **W**, which is called 3DG-MP. Ten labeled samples per class are selected for training, and the rest for testing, with experiments repeated ten times to minimize the bias. Results are measured using OA and the Kappa coefficient.

Parameter Analysis

1) The initial (B) and terminal (E) number of superpixels

The quality of superpixels generated by the ERS method significantly impacts their regularization performance. The proposed cascade superpixel regularization addresses this by processing from over-segmentation to under-segmentation, making parameter selection for initial (B) and terminal (E) number of superpixels straightforward and the classification accuracy robust to their changes. Specifically, concerning different initial numbers of superpixels B, which varies from 500 to 1000 with a step size of 100 (here the terminal number of superpixels E is set as 50), and parameter terminal E, which varies from 10 to 50 with B set to 500, the OA with different sizes of training set is shown in Figure 14.15a, b, respectively. All these observations imply that the classification performance is insensitive and robust to the variation of parameters B and E.

Since a series of superpixel sizes from over-segmentation to under-segmentation in cascade superpixel regularization procedure have been fixed in advance and can adapt to Indian Pines dataset, the estimation of the number of extracted superpixels is avoided.

2) Cascade Superpixel Regularization

In order to demonstrate the superiority of the proposed cascade superpixel regularization procedure, it is compared with single superpixel regularization on the Gabor fused weighting cube **W**, abbreviated as SSRGFF, which regularizes the weighting cube only one time. Figure 14.15c displays the compared results of both methods on Indian Pines, where the number of superpixels ranges from 500 to 50. It should be noted that for CSRGFF, the initial number of superpixels (B) is set to 500, while the values on the X-axis in Figure 14.15c represent the terminal number of superpixels (E). For example, when E equals to 500, which is equal to the value of B, CSRGFF is just the same as SSRGFF. In addition, if E equals to 300, the superpixel regularization process of CSRGFF is cascaded from 500 to 300. As expected, the performance of SSRGFF relies on the number of superpixels, and it is unrealistic to accurately estimate the number of superpixels in practice. Alternatively, the classification accuracy of the proposed CSRGFF approach improves continuously as parameter E decreases, verifying the effectiveness of the proposed technique. Since superpixel maps at different scales reveal material spatial structures, that is, over-segmentation ensures superpixel

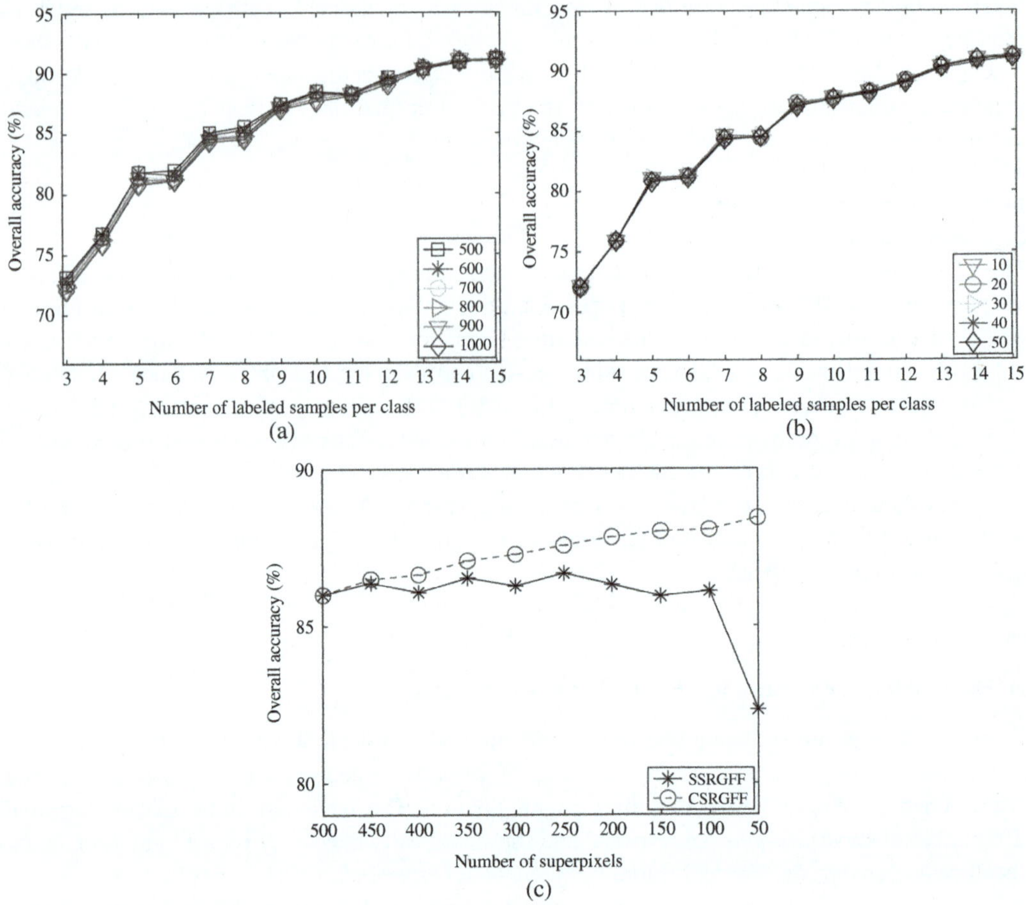

Figure 14.15 Parameter analysis of (a) the initial (*B*) and (b) the terminals (*E*) number of superpixels. (c) Comparison of SSRGFF and CSRGFF with different number of superpixels.

homogeneity, while under-segmentation captures object shapes and boundaries. The CSRGFF approach effectively fuses these maps by regularizing weights from over-segmentation to under-segmentation in cascade mode.

Experimental Results Analysis

The proposed CSRGFF approach is quantitatively and visually compared with 6 alternatives, including LSTM-CNN, 3D-CNN, GCK, LBP-ELM, 3DGPC-HDM, and 3DG-MP. Each experiment is repeated 10 times, and both the mean and standard variation are reported. It is worth pointing out that the excellent performance of deep-learning-based methods usually depends on a large amount of training samples, which are used to optimize the huge number of parameters. For HSI classification, small sample size is a general problem in practice, which is the main concern of this approach, so the deep-learning-based methods can be less efficient. When only 10 labeled samples per class are used for training, the detailed classification performance on Indian Pines dataset, including the class accuracy, OA, and Kappa, is listed in Table 14.8. Likewise, the classification performance of CSRGFF is higher than the rest methods in most cases. Further, Figure 14.16

Table 14.8 Classification performance of seven compared methods on Indian Pines dataset.

Class	LSTM-CNN	3D-CNN	GCK	LBP-ELM	3DGPC-HDM	3DG-MP	CSRGFF
C1	97.26	95.47	94.94	98.00	**98.59**	96.24	97.29
C2	87.30	93.11	93.70	99.77	**99.98**	99.83	99.52
C3	48.32	57.90	61.75	70.12	71.53	76.58	**83.45**
C4	71.85	67.08	63.57	86.68	82.18	77.01	**88.41**
C5	82.04	96.85	84.55	99.77	98.64	97.27	**100.00**
C6	54.89	53.71	52.45	71.27	77.50	83.03	**91.57**
C7	69.42	83.32	78.99	83.72	81.40	84.21	**85.26**
C8	78.10	85.16	79.40	**91.39**	89.45	90.48	91.29
C9	50.84	74.29	74.19	93.57	94.08	**94.24**	90.78
C10	95.77	99.62	94.38	**100.00**	**100.00**	**100.00**	96.25
C11	79.66	71.54	64.46	96.52	96.74	97.72	**97.99**
C12	98.00	**100.00**	98.00	**100.00**	**100.00**	**100.00**	**100.00**
C13	55.17	52.54	47.21	69.92	74.00	73.92	**78.55**
C14	55.07	55.75	65.50	71.59	80.05	80.95	**87.26**
C15	84.08	91.95	90.00	88.49	88.78	92.40	**95.14**
C16	97.55	98.73	98.66	97.43	97.72	97.43	**100.00**
OA	65.25	68.47	68.53	80.52	82.89	83.86	**88.44**
	(2.26)	(2.74)	(2.11)	(2.35)	(2.33)	(2.16)	(2.57)
Kappa	0.61	0.65	0.65	0.78	0.81	0.82	**0.87**
	(0.02)	(0.03)	(0.02)	(0.03)	(0.03)	(0.02)	(0.03)

Bold values represent the best results in this table.

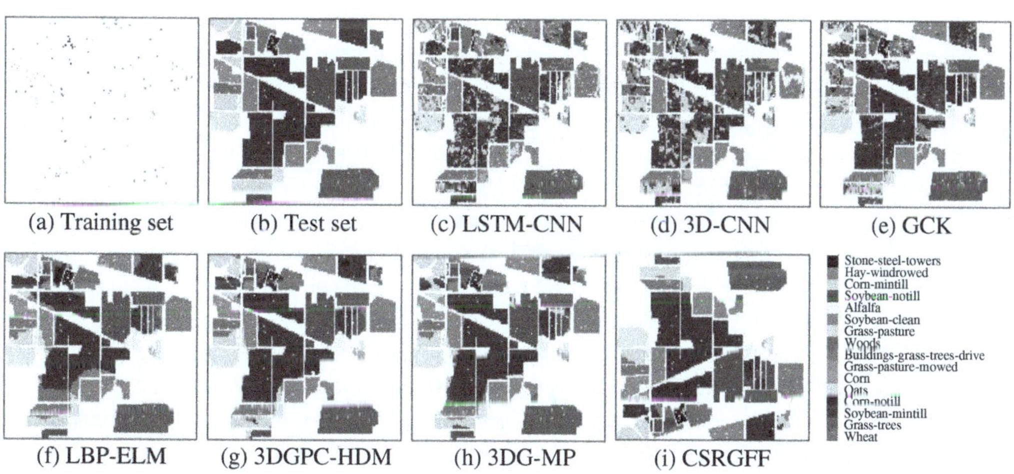

Figure 14.16 Classification maps obtained by different comparison methods on Indian Pines dataset. (a) Training set, (b) Test set, and classification maps on Indian Pines dataset obtained by (c) LSTM-CNN (d) 3D-CNN (e) GCK (f) LBPELM (g) 3DGPC-HDM (h) 3DG-MP (i) CSRGFF.

displays the training set, the testing set, and the classification maps obtained by various methods in one experiment. Obviously, the classification map achieved by CSRGFF is more consistent with the ground truth (Figure 14.16(b)). All these observations have demonstrated the superiority of the proposed CSRGFF approach.

References

1 Jia, S., Wu, K., Zhu, J., and Jia, X. (2019). Spectral-spatial Gabor surface feature fusion approach for hyperspectral imagery classification. *IEEE Trans. Geosci. Remote Sens.* 57 (2): 1142–1154.

2 Shen, L. and Bai, L. (2006). A review on Gabor wavelets for face recognition. *Pattern. Anal. Applic.* 9 (2–3): 273–292.

3 Weldon, T.P., Higgins, W.E., and Dunn, D.F. (1996). Efficient Gabor filter design for texture segmentation. *Pattern Recogn.* 29 (12): 2005–2015.

4 Jia, S., Deng, B., Zhu, J. et al. (2017). Superpixel-based multitask learning framework for hyperspectral image classification. *IEEE Trans. Geosci. Remote Sens.* 55 (5): 2575–2588.

5 Jia, S., Zhuang, J., Zhu, J. et al. (2019). 3-D gaussian-gabor feature extraction and selection for hyperspectral imagery classification. *IEEE Trans. Geosci. Remote Sens.* 57 (11): 8813–8826.

6 Shen, L. and Bai, L. (2008). 3D Gabor wavelets for evaluating SPM normalization algorithm. *Med. Image Anal.* 12 (3): 375–383.

7 Lai, Z., Xu, Y., Yang, J. et al. (2017). Rotational invariant dimensionality reduction algorithms. *IEEE Trans. Cybern.* 47 (11): 3733–3746.

8 Rodriguez, A. and Laio, A. (2014). Clustering by fast search and find of density peaks. *Science* 344 (6191): 1492–1496.

9 Jia, S., Tang, G., Zhu, J., and Li, Q. (2016). A novel ranking-based clustering approach for hyperspectral band selection. *IEEE Trans. Geosci. Remote Sens.* 54 (1): 88–102.

10 Adler, J. and Parmryd, I. (2010). Quantifying colocalization by correlation: the pearson correlation coefficient is superior to the mander's overlap coefficient. *Cytometry Part A* 77: 733–742.

11 Jia, S., Shen, L., and Li, Q. (2015). Gabor feature-based collaborative representation for hyperspectral imagery classification. *IEEE Trans. Geosci. Remote Sens.* 53 (2): 1118–1129.

12 Jia, S., Hu, J., Xie, Y. et al. (2016). Gabor cube selection based multitask joint sparse representation for hyperspectral image classification. *IEEE Trans. Geosci. Remote Sens.* 54 (6): 3174–3187.

13 Jia, S., Shen, L., Zhu, J., and Li, Q. (2017). A 3-d Gabor phase-based coding and matching framework for hyperspectral imagery classification. *IEEE Trans. Cybern.* 48 (4): 1176–1188.

14 Dong, Y., Tao, D., Li, X. et al. (2015). Texture classification and retrieval using shearlets and linear regression. *IEEE Trans. Cybern.* 45 (3): 358–369.

15 Guo, Z., Wang, X., Zhou, J., and You, J. (2016). Robust texture image representation by scale selective local binary patterns. *IEEE Trans. Image Process.* 25 (2): 687–699.

16 Daugman, J.G. (1993). High confidence visual recognition of persons by a test of statistical independence. *IEEE Trans. Pattern Anal. Mach. Intell.* 15 (11): 1148–1161.

17 Zhang, B., Shan, S., Chen, X., and Gao, W. (2007). Histogram of Gabor Phase Patterns (HGPP): a novel object representation approach for face recognition. *IEEE Trans. Image Process.* 16 (1): 57–68.

18 Li, J., Marpu, P.R., Plaza, A. et al. (2013). Generalized composite kernel framework for hyperspectral image classification. *IEEE Trans. Geosci. Remote Sens.* 51 (9): 4816–4829.

19 Li, J., Bioucas-Dias, J.M., and Plaza, A. (2012). Spectral-spatial hyperspectral image segmentation using subspace multinomial logistic regression and markov random fields. *IEEE Trans. Geosci. Remote Sens.* 50 (3): 809–823.

20 Li, J., Huang, X., Gamba, P. et al. (2015). Multiple feature learning for hyperspectral image classification. *IEEE Trans. Geosci. Remote Sens.* 53 (3): 1592–1606.

21 Zhong, Z., Fan, B., Ding, K. et al. (2016). Efficient multiple feature fusion with hashing for hyperspectral imagery classification: a comparative study. *IEEE Trans. Geosci. Remote Sens.* 54 (8): 4461–4478.

22 Li, W., Chen, C., Su, H., and Du, Q. (2015). Local binary patterns and extreme learning machine for hyperspectral imagery classification. *IEEE Trans. Geosci. Remote Sens.* 53 (7): 3681–3693.

23 Shen, L.L. and Jia, S. (2011). Three-dimensional gabor wavelets for pixel-based hyperspectral imagery classification. *IEEE Trans. Geosci. Remote Sens.* 49 (12): 5039–5046.

24 Hart, P.E., Stork, D.G., and Duda, R.O. (2000). *Pattern Classification*. Wiley Hoboken.

25 Chen, Y., Lin, Z., and Zhao, X. (2013). Riemannian manifold learning based k-nearest-neighbor for hyperspectral image classification. *IEEE Trans. Geosci. Remote Sens. Symp.* 1975–1978. Available from: http://ieeexplore.ieee.org/document/6723195/.

26 Chang, C.C. and Lin, C.J. (2011). LIBSVM: a library for support vector machines. *ACM Trans. Intell. Syst. Technol.* 2 (3): 1–27.

27 Wright, J., Yang, A.Y., Ganesh, A. et al. (2009). Robust face recognition via sparse representation. *IEEE Trans. Pattern Anal. Mach. Intell.* 31 (2): 210–227.

28 Jia, S., Liao, J., Xu, M. et al. (2021). 3-D Gabor convolutional neural network for hyperspectral image classification. *IEEE Trans. Geosci. Remote Sens.* 60: 1–16.

29 Cheng, G., Han, J., and Lu, X. (2017). Remote sensing image scene classification: benchmark and state of the art. *Proc. IEEE* 105 (10): 1865–1883.

30 Hinton, G.E, Srivastava, N., Krizhevsky, A. et al. (2012). Improving neural networks by preventing co-adaptation of feature detectors. arXiv. http://arxiv.org/abs/1207.0580. (accessed 11 May 2025).

31 Ly, N.H., Du, Q., and Fowler, J.E. (2014). Collaborative graph-based discriminant analysis for hyperspectral imagery. *IEEE J. Sel. Top. Appl. Earth Obs. Remote Sens.* 7 (6): 2688–2696.

32 Bruce, L.M., Koger, C.H., and Li, J. (2002). Dimensionality reduction of hyperspectral data using discrete wavelet transform feature extraction. *IEEE Trans. Geosci. Remote Sens.* 40 (10): 2331–2338.

33 Rasti, B., Hong, D., Hang, R. et al. (2020). Feature extraction for hyperspectral imagery: the evolution from shallow to deep: overview and toolbox. *IEEE Geosci. Remote Sens. Mag.* 8: 60–88.

34 Ben Hamida, A., Benoit, A., Lambert, P., and Ben, A.C. (2018). 3-D deep learning approach for remote sensing image classification. *IEEE Trans. Geosci. Remote Sens.* 56 (8): 4420–4434.

35 Gao, H., Yang, Y., Lei, S. et al. (2019). Multi-branch fusion network for hyperspectral image classification. *Knowl.-Based Syst.* 167: 11–25.

36 He, M., Li, B., and Chen, H. (2017). Multi-scale 3D deep convolutional neural network for hyperspectral image classification. *IEEE International Conference on Image Processing,* 3904–3908. http://ieeexplore.ieee.org/document/8297014/ (accessed 11 May 2025).

37 Kingma, D.P. and Ba, J. (2014). Adam: a method for stochastic optimization. arXiv. https://arxiv.org/abs/1412.6980. (accessed 11 May 2025).

38 Jia, S., Zhao, Q., Zhuang, J. et al. (2021). Flexible Gabor-based superpixel-level unsupervised LDA for hyperspectral image classification. *IEEE Trans. Geosci. Remote Sens.* 59 (12): 10394–10409.

39 Liu, M.Y., Tuzel, O., Ramalingam, S., and Chellappa, R. (2011). Entropy rate superpixel segmentation. CVPR 2011. pp. 2097–2104. https://ieeexplore.ieee.org/abstract/document/5995323 (accessed 11 May 2024).

40 Jia, S., Deng, X., Zhu, J. et al. (2019). Collaborative representation-based multiscale superpixel fusion for hyperspectral image classification. *IEEE Trans. Geosci. Remote Sens.* 57 (10): 7770–7784.

41 Hong, D., Gao, L., Yao, J. et al. (2021). Graph convolutional networks for hyperspectral image classification. *IEEE Trans. Geosci. Remote Sens.* 59 (7): 5966–5978.

42 Jia, S., Lin, Z., Deng, B. et al. (2020). Cascade superpixel regularized Gabor feature fusion for hyperspectral image classification. *IEEE Trans. Neural Networks Learn. Syst.* 31 (5): 1638–1652.

43 Cortes, C. and Vapnik, V. (1995). Support-vector networks. *Mach. Learn.* 20 (3): 273–297.

44 Li, Y., Zhang, H., and Shen, Q. (2017). Spectral-spatial classification of hyperspectral imagery with 3D convolutional neural network. *Remote Sens* 9 (1): 67.

45 Xu, Y., Zhang, L., Du, B., and Zhang, F. (2018). Spectral-spatial unified networks for hyperspectral image classification. *IEEE Trans. Geosci. Remote Sens.* 56 (10): 5893–5909.

15

Domain Adaptation for Hyperspectral Image Classification

Chong Li[1], *Weiwei Sun*[2], *Jiangtao Peng*[3], *and Kai Ren*[4]

[1] *Faculty of Mathematics and Statistics, Ningbo University, Ningbo, China*
[2] *Department of Geography and Spatial Information Techniques, Ningbo University, Ningbo, China*
[3] *Faculty of Mathematics and Statistics, Hubei University, Wuhan, China*
[4] *Faculty of Electrical Engineering and Computer Science, Ningbo University, Ningbo, China*

15.1 Basic Concepts of Domain Adaptation

Hyperspectral images (HSI) typically capture the reflectance signals of objects in the range of 400–2500 nm with >100 bands (1, 2). Thanks to the fine spectral resolution, HSI is widely used for agricultural monitoring, resource exploration, environmental protection and other fields [3–7]. Therefore, how to obtain effective information from HSI is an important research direction. Classification aims to obtain distribution information of ground cover from HSI data and provide data support for environmental monitoring and resource exploration. However, the classification of HSI poses significant challenges due to factors such as the large amount of data, high dimensionality, and limited availability of labeled data. In practical applications, the HSI used for training the classification model

Definition 15.1

A domain $D = \{\chi, P(X)\}$ is composed of a feature space χ and a marginal probability distribution of inputs $P(X)$, where $X = \{x_1, \cdots, x_n\} \in \chi$ is a set of learning samples.

Definition 15.2

A task $T = \{Y, f(x)\}$ consists of classification results Y and a classifier $f(x)$, where $f(x) = Q(y \mid x)$ can be interpreted as the conditional probability distribution [12].

For DA, there are two domains, i.e., source domain D_s and target domain D_t. In general, source domain has labels, and target domain has limited or no labeled samples. Given a labeled data set from the source domain, $\left\{\left(x_1^s, y_1^s\right), \left(x_2^s, y_2^s\right), \cdots, \left(x_{n_s}^s, y_{n_s}^s\right)\right\}$ with $x_i^s \in R^D$ and $y_i^s \in \{1, 2, \cdots, C\}$. The sample and label set of source domain are $X_s - \left\{x_1^s, x_2^s, \cdots, x_{n_s}^s\right\}$ and $Y_s = \left\{y_1, y_2, \cdots, y_{n_s}\right\}$, respectively. Let $X_t = \left\{x_1^t, \cdots, x_{n_t}^t\right\}$ denote the unlabeled data set from the target domain. DA considers the following situation: the class space of source and target

Machine-Learning-Based Hyperspectral Image Processing, First Edition. Edited by Bing Zhang.

domains are the same: $\gamma_s = \gamma_t$, but the marginal distribution and conditional probability distribution between the domains are inconsistent: $P_s(X_s) \neq P_t(X_t)$ and $Q_s(y_s \mid X_s) \neq Q_t(y_t \mid X_t)$. The aim of DA is to predict the target label using the model trained on the source samples.

(called source domain, SD) and the HSI to be classified (called target domain, TD) are obtained from different scenes. The problem of inconsistent distribution arises from variations in acquisition environmental conditions or sensors, significantly complicating the HSI classification process [8, 9]. Domain adaptation (DA) is a machine learning technique aimed at addressing distributional differences between the source domain and the target domain [10, 11]. In machine learning tasks, the source domain typically represents the training data, while the target domain denotes the new dataset on which the model is intended to be applied. Owing to potential disparities in data distributions between the source and target domains, models trained solely on the source domain might exhibit suboptimal performance when applied to the target domain. The overarching objective of DA is to mitigate these distributional discrepancies by appropriately adjusting either the model or the data, thereby facilitating the model to generalize effectively on the target domain.

15.2 Domain Adaptation for Hyperspectral Image Classification

Traditional DA methods include those based on distribution alignment, feature selection, and subspace learning [13–15]. Distribution-alignment-based methods address the distinct probability distributions between source data and target data by minimizing the distribution discrepancy through linear or non-linear transformations. This includes aligning the marginal distribution, conditional distribution, and joint distribution [16–18]. Feature-selection-based methods assume the existence of shared features between SD and TD, extracting these shared features to align the distributions for DA classification [19–21]. Subspace-learning-based methods posit the existence of a subspace with similar distributions for source and target data, enabling DA classification within this shared subspace. These methods employ statistical feature alignment and manifold learning techniques for subspace extraction [22, 23]. In contrast to traditional DA methods, deep DA methods employ deep neural networks (DNNs) to automatically learn features [24]. These methods include discrepancy-based, adversarial-based, and so on [25]. Discrepancy-based deep DA methods emphasize the alignment of marginal or conditional distributions between different domains, and these methods commonly employ adaptation layers that utilize metrics like the maximum mean discrepancy (MMD). Adversarial-based deep DA methods employ adversarial learning to minimize discrepancies between the source and target domains, producing transferable and domain-invariant features.

Deep DA methods utilize the power of deep learning to automatically extract discriminative features, enabling effective DA. Long et al. [26] proposed a method called deep adaptation network (DAN) in their study. DAN utilizes DNNs to learn transferable cross-domain features. By incorporating adaptation layers based on multi-kernel variants of maximum mean discrepancy (MK-MMD) [27], DAN effectively adjusts the marginal distribution between domains. Li et al. [28] proposed a method called two-stage deep DA (TDDA). Firstly, TDDA utilizes MMD to learn a deep embedding space, thereby minimizing the distribution discrepancy between different domains. Secondly, a spatial–spectral coupled network is employed to further minimize distribution shift and enhance the discriminative power of the deep embedding space. Sun et al. [29] proposed D-CORAL, an extension of correlation alignment (CORAL) [30] tailored for deep architectures. D-CORAL employs a nonlinear transformation to align the marginal distribution between domains, leading to enhanced performance in DA. However, the existing deep DA methods usually focus on aligning the marginal distribution and often overlook the influence of each sample in the SD and TD on the network weights. Long et al. [31] proposed a joint adaptation network (JAN), which uses labeled SD and pseudo-labeled TD to construct MMD and conditional MMD, and achieves alignment of joint distributions by means of adversarial training. Wang et al. [32] introduced a DA method specifically designed for multi-temporal HSI using graph neural network (GNN). They employed GNN for feature extraction and integrated both domain-wise CORAL and class-wise CORAL into the GNN network, enabling comprehensive adaptation performance for joint distribution alignment. In summary, the studied deep DA methods have provided compelling evidence for the advanced and effective utilization of deep learning in DA.

15.3 Deep Domain-adaptation-based Hyperspectral Image Classification

This section provides a comprehensive overview of deep domain-adaptation-based algorithms for hyperspectral image classification. We discuss the principles and implementation details of these algorithms, including DA networks and domain-invariant feature representations. Through experimental results and case studies, we demonstrate the effectiveness of these algorithms in real-world scenarios.

15.3.1 Deep Domain Adaptation Framework

The deep DA framework deep dynamic adaptation network based on joint correlation alignment (DDAN-JCA) consists of the dual-channel residual network (DCRN), the attention mechanism module (AMM), and the dynamic joint CORAL algorithm. Figure 15.1 shows the methodology of the proposed DDAN-JCA, where the source data $X_s \in R^{n_s \times d}$ with labels $Y_s \in R^{n_s \times 1}$ and the target data $X_t \in R^{n_t \times d}$ without labels, d is feature dimensionality, n_s, n_t represent the number of samples of source data and target data, respectively. First, the feature extractor G_d (DCRN) receives multiple 3D cubes (select the 3D HSI cube with spatial dimension of 9×9), which are samples taken from the HSI of both SD and TD. To adjust the marginal distribution between domains in our method, we employ the marginal distribution CORAL strategy. Then, we utilize the G_a (AMM) to capture local information effectively. And we address the adaptation of conditional distribution between domains by incorporating the conditional distribution CORAL strategy. After that, we train a classifier (D_c) using the source labeled data and employ two feature extractors

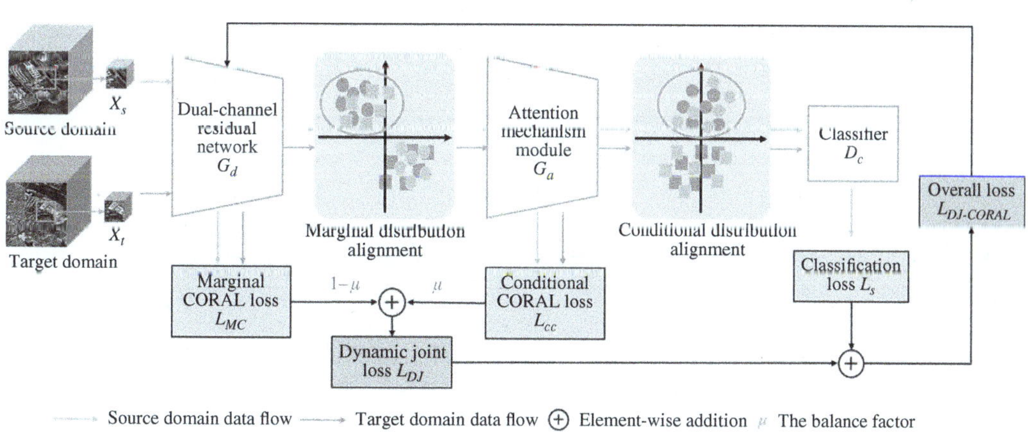

Figure 15.1 Deep dynamic adaptation network based on joint correlation alignment (DDAN-JCA).

(G_d and G_a) with shared weights to process source and target data. Finally, we dynamically adjust the losses associated with marginal and conditional distributions using the dynamic distribution adaptation strategy.

15.3.1.1 Network

Traditional CNNs suffer from vanishing gradients with increasing depth, while residual networks address this issue by enabling effective gradient flow. For HSI classification, conventional CNN-based methods may overlook vital spectral and spatial features. To address this, we employ the DCRN [33], which integrates spectral and spatial features effectively. DCRN comprises spectral feature extraction, spatial feature extraction, and spatial–spectral fusion modules (see Figure 15.2). Spectral feature extraction involves two convolutional layers and a residual block, followed by subsampling and convolution operations, enabling the extraction of discriminative spectral features. Spatial feature extraction includes convolution and a residual block to capture spatial correlations

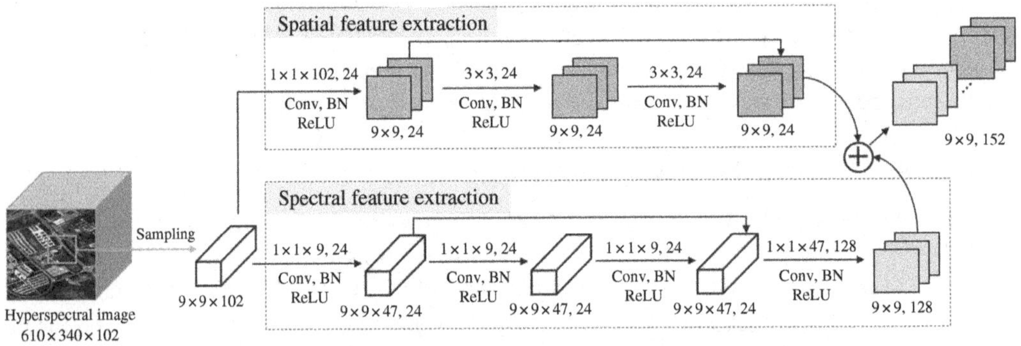

Figure 15.2 The dual-channel residual network (DCRN).

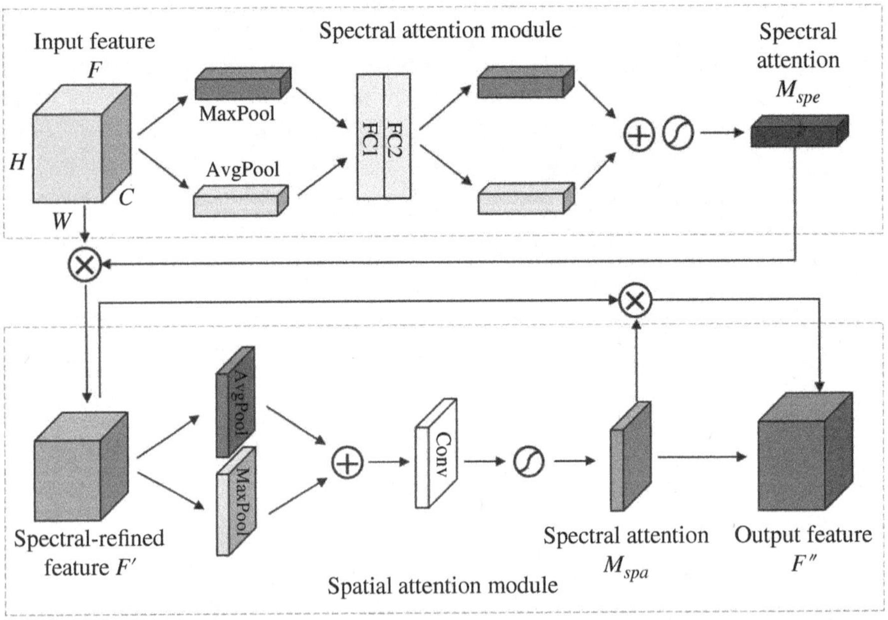

Figure 15.3 The attention mechanism module (AMM).

and preserve important spatial information. Spatial–spectral fusion combines spectral and spatial features, resulting in a more comprehensive representation. This fusion facilitates improved performance in HSI classification tasks by leveraging both spectral and spatial information effectively.

To strengthen effective features and accelerate network convergence, Woo et al. [34] introduced an AMM combining spectral and spatial attention mechanisms within DDAN-JCA to enhance feature effectiveness and accelerate network convergence. Figure 15.3 displays the architecture of AMM employed in this chapter. The spectral attention module diminishes channel redundancy and captures inter-channel relationships in the feature map F with dimensions $\mathrm{H} \times \mathrm{W} \times \mathrm{C}$. It generates a 1-D attention vector M_{spe} of size $1 \times 1 \times \mathrm{C}$ to signify the importance of each channel. This vector is then applied to F through element-wise multiplication, resulting in the refined feature map F'. By integrating the spectral attention module, the method emphasizes discriminative spectral information while minimizing redundant channels, thereby enhancing feature representation and classification performance. Subsequent to the spectral attention module, the spatial attention module further enhances informative regions within the feature map. It produces a 2D spatial attention map M_{spa} highlighting relevant spatial regions, achieved via convolution operations with a 9×9 kernel. The output feature map F'' is obtained by applying attention mechanisms and convolutions from both spectral and spatial attention modules. This integration effectively captures and emphasizes informative spectral and spatial features, resulting in improved discriminative power and performance in HSI classification tasks. F'' represents the final feature map of F.

15.3.1.2 Algorithms

In the DDAN-JCA framework, we utilize the dynamic joint CORAL algorithm to align marginal and conditional distributions, respectively. Additionally, to address the challenges of both global domain shifts and shifts within relevant subdomains, we introduce a dynamic joint CORAL algorithm. This algorithm dynamically adjusts the alignment strategy to effectively reduce distribution shifts in both the overall domain and specific subdomains. By combining these strategies, DDAN-JCA achieves comprehensive distribution adaptation, leading to improved HSI classification performance.

We employ CORAL to align the marginal distributions in cross-scene HSI classification tasks. We aim to reduce the distribution discrepancy and enhance the transferability of the learned features in different scenes. We design the marginal CORAL loss as L_{MC}

$$L_{MC} = \frac{1}{4d^2} \|C_s - C_t\|_F^2, \tag{15.1}$$

where $\|\cdot\|_F$ represents the matrix Frobenius norm, d is feature dimensionality, C_s and C_t refer to the covariance matrices of transformed features.

$$C_s = \frac{1}{n_s - 1}\left(Z_s'Z_s - \frac{1}{n_s}(1'Z_s)'(1'Z_s)\right), \tag{15.2}$$

$$C_t = \frac{1}{n_t - 1}\left(Z_t'Z_t - \frac{1}{n_t}(1'Z_t)'(1'Z_t)\right), \tag{15.3}$$

where 1 represents a column vector with all elements being ones. n_s and n_t represent the total number of source and target data samples, respectively. Z_s and Z_t indicate the feature matrices of the source and target data. Z_s' and Z_t' are the transpose matrices of Z_s and Z_t respectively.

Referring to L_{MC}, we introduce the conditional CORAL loss (L_{CC}) in our method.

$$L_{CC} = \frac{1}{4d^2 C} \sum_{i=1}^{C} \|C_s^i - C_t^i\|_F^2, \tag{15.4}$$

$$C_s^i = \frac{1}{n_s^i - 1}\left((Z_s^i)'Z_s^i - \frac{1}{n_s^i}(1'Z_s^i)'(1'Z_s^i)\right), \tag{15.5}$$

$$C_t^i = \frac{1}{n_t^i - 1}\left((Z_t^i)'Z_t^i - \frac{1}{n_t^i}(1'Z_t^i)'(1'Z_t^i)\right), \tag{15.6}$$

where C represents the number of classes, C_s^i and C_t^i represent the covariance matrices of the ith class in the SD and TD, respectively. n_s^i and n_t^i are the corresponding numbers of data samples for each class. $Z_s = \left[Z_s^1, Z_s^2, \cdots, Z_s^C\right] \in R^{n_s \times C}$ represents the feature matrix of the source data, where Z_s^i denotes the data of the ith class in the feature space. Similarly, the target data can be divided into C classes based on their pseudo labels. $Z_t = \left[Z_t^1, Z_t^2, \cdots, Z_t^C\right] \in R^{n_t \times C}$ represents the target data that is predicted to belong to each class.

By jointly considering L_{MC} and L_{CC} with the balance factor $\mu \in [0, 1]$, we formulate the dynamic joint loss (L_{DJ}) as a weighted combination of the two loss terms. This dynamic joint loss allows us to effectively balance the contributions of marginal and conditional distributions alignments, enabling adaptive distribution adaptation for improved performance in cross-scene HSI classification tasks.

$$L_{DJ} = (1 - \mu)L_{MC} + \mu L_{CC}, \tag{15.7}$$

where the parameter μ is employed to assign a relative weight to L_{MC} and L_{CC}. Taking inspiration from [35], we adopt an adaptive approach to dynamically estimate the value of μ for weight assignment.

$$\mu = \frac{\sum_{i=1}^{C} d_A\left(Z_s^i, Z_t^i\right)}{d_A(Z_s, Z_t) + \sum_{i=1}^{C} d_A\left(Z_s^i, Z_t^i\right)}, \tag{15.8}$$

where $d_A(\cdot,\cdot)$ means the A-distance [36].

For DDAN-JCA, our training procedure includes two stages. Firstly, we train a marginal distribution CORAL based on DCRN, and define a loss function $\hat{L}$ that aims to minimize the discrepancy in second-order statistics between SD and TD. We can effective alignment of the marginal distribution between domains, facilitating better feature extraction and transferability.

$$\hat{L} = L_s + \alpha L_{MC}, \tag{15.9}$$

where α is a hyperparameter, L_s is defined as the SD classification loss.

$$L_s = \frac{1}{n_s} L_{ce}(f(Z_s), Y_s), \tag{15.10}$$

where $L_{ce}(\cdot, \cdot)$ represents the cross-entropy loss, and $f(\cdot)$ represents the domain-shared softmax classifier.

Secondly, we utilize the trained DCRN and AMM to predict pseudo labels for the target data. These pseudo labels are then used in conjunction with the conditional distribution CORAL algorithm to further enhance the alignment between SD and TD. The overall loss function $L_{DJ-\text{CORAL}}$ consists of the dynamic joint loss and the classification loss, which enables the model to simultaneously optimize the domain alignment and classification accuracy, leading to improved cross-scene classification performance.

$$L_{DJ-\text{CORAL}} = L_s + \alpha((1 - \mu)L_{MC} + \mu L_{CC}) \tag{15.11}$$

where α is used to balance the importance between classifier adaptation and distribution adjustment. And μ is used to balance the contribution of L_{MC} and L_{CC}. By minimizing these losses, the model adapts to the TD while maintaining discriminative features and accurate classification.

15.3.2 Experimental Data

15.3.2.1 Pavia Dataset

The Pavia datasets consist of two subsets: the University of Pavia (UP, called SD) includes 610 × 610 pixels and 103 spectral bands, and the Pavia Center (PC, called TD) includes 1096 × 1096 pixels and 102 spectral bands. These datasets were captured using ROSIS sensors, Pavia, northern Italy [37]. It should be noted that both datasets contain some invalid samples, which were excluded from the experiment. Consequently, the final UP and PC datasets consist of 610 × 315 and 1096 × 715 pixels, respectively. To ensure an equal number of spectral bands between UP and PC and to have seven common categories, the last band in UP was removed, and their specific details can be found in Table 15.1 and Figure 15.4.

15.3.2.2 Houston Dataset

The Houston dataset consist of Houston 2013 [38] (called SD) and Houston 2018 [39] (called TD). The former includes 349 × 1905 pixels and 144 spectral bands. The latter includes 209 × 955 pixels and 48 spectral bands. These datasets were captured using different sensors and at different

Table 15.1 The Pavia dataset.

Class		Number of samples	
ID	**Name**	**Source (UP)**	**Target (PC)**
1	Tree	3064	7598
2	Asphalt	6631	9248
3	Brick	3682	2685
4	Bitumen	1330	7287
5	Shadow	947	2863
6	Meadow	18649	3090
7	Bare soil	5029	6584
Total		39332	39335

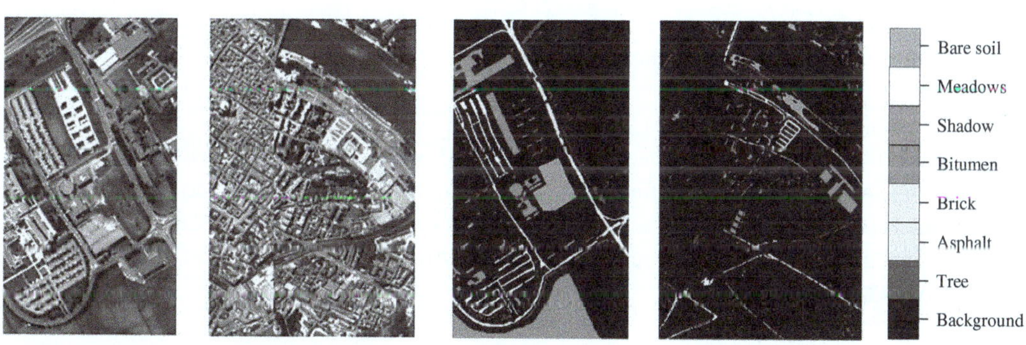

Hyperspectral image of UP | Hyperspectral image of PC | Ground-truth map of UP | Ground-truth map of PC

Figure 15.4 The Pavia dataset.

Table 15.2 The Houston dataset.

Class		Number of samples	
ID	**Name**	**Source (Houston 2013)**	**Target (Houston 2018)**
1	Grass healthy	345	1353
2	Grass stressed	365	4888
3	Trees	365	2766
4	Water	285	22
5	Residential buildings	319	5347
6	Non-residential buildings	408	32459
7	Road	443	6365
Total		2530	53200

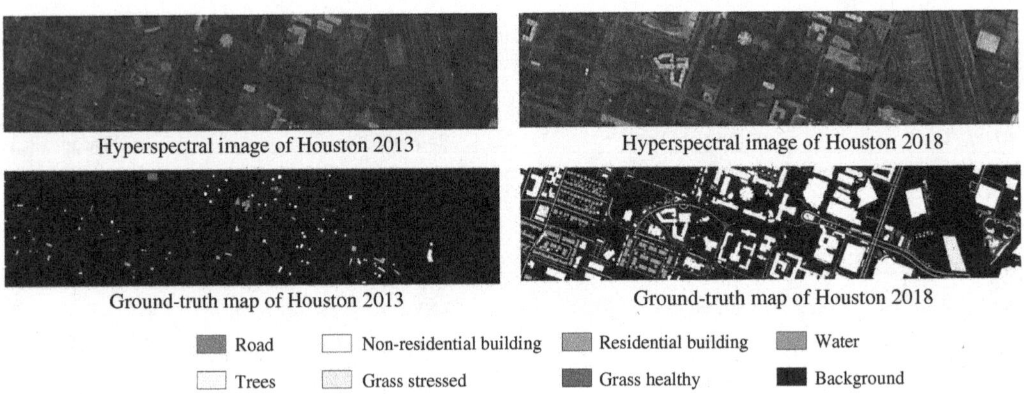

Figure 15.5 The Houston dataset.

acquisition times in Houston, TX, United States. To align with the Houston 2018 dataset, we selected an overlapping region of 209 × 955 pixels from the Houston 2013 dataset and extracted 48 spectral bands from it. Both datasets include seven land cover classes, and their specific details can be found in Table 15.2 and Figure 15.5.

15.3.2.3 Indiana Pines Dataset

The Indiana Pines dataset was collected using AVIRIS in Northwest Tippecanoe Country, IN, United States. According to the method described in [40], the dataset was divided into two disjoint subsets, referred to as SD and TD. Each domain includes 400 × 300 pixels and 220 spectral bands. Both domains include seven land cover classes, and their specific details can be found in Table 15.3 and Figure 15.6.

15.3.3 Experimental Results

We compared the proposed DDAN-JCA method with machine learning method (SVM [41]) and deep learning methods, including DAN [23], DANN [42], D-CORAL [29], CDA [43], and J-CORAL

Table 15.3 The Indiana pines dataset.

Class		Number of samples	
ID	Name	Source scene	Target scene
1	Concrete/asphalt	4867	2942
2	Corn clean Till	9822	6029
3	Corn cleanTill EW	11414	7999
4	Orchard	5106	1562
5	Soybeans cleanTill	4731	4792
6	Soybeans cleanTill EW	2996	1638
7	Wheat	3223	10739
Total		42159	35701

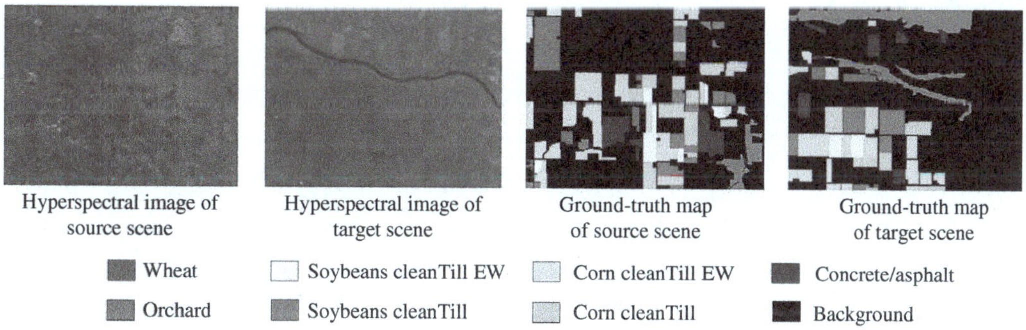

Figure 15.6 The Indiana Pines dataset.

(DCRN and AMM with the joint CORAL algorithm). In all the experiments, a fair sampling strategy is employed, where 10% of the samples are randomly selected from each class in the SD. This method ensures equal representation and fairness in the experimental setup. The methods in this chapter are implemented by pytorch. For the deep DA algorithms DAN, DANN, D-CORAL, CDA, J-CORAL, and DDAN-JCA, the patch_size is chosen from a set of options {5, 7, 9, 11}, while the batch_size is uniformly set to 64. The learning rate lr is selected from {0.001, 0.0001}. To assess the classification performance of each method, the evaluation metrics used are the overall accuracy (OA) and kappa coefficient (κ) [44] on the TD. These metrics provide a comprehensive measure of the accuracy and agreement between predicted and ground-truth labels.

Tables 15.4–15.6 present the OA and κ of different methods on three datasets, and its classification accuracy for land cover classes. Considering the potential effects of random sampling, all experiments were conducted 10 times. The final classification results are obtained by calculating the mean value from these ten runs, ensuring a reliable and robust evaluation of the methods' performance.

Deep learning algorithms outperform traditional SVM methods in classification, with the DAN algorithm achieving significantly higher OAs on the Pavia, Houston, and Indiana datasets by

Table 15.4 Classification accuracies of PC in different methods.

Class	SVM	DAN	DANN	D-CORAL	CDA	J-CORAL	Ours
1	93.57	96.72	96.49	92.83	93.29	91.29	**96.98**
2	88.76	73.76	89.91	85.70	93.18	93.44	**96.63**
3	67.87	70.74	75.55	**76.56**	76.07	74.02	73.57
4	28.35	77.05	57.59	59.99	65.72	67.34	**78.65**
5	99.68	**100.00**	**100.00**	99.79	99.93	99.93	**100.00**
6	46.10	54.57	71.79	72.09	**78.92**	75.42	78.56
7	79.18	67.26	68.03	76.54	69.41	78.86	**81.85**
OA (%)	64.14	77.91	79.87	80.12	82.35	83.49	**87.93**
κ	0.5488	0.7353	0.7578	0.7612	0.7880	0.8012	**0.8547**

Table 15.5 Classification accuracies of Houston 2018 in different methods.

Class	SVM	DAN	DANN	D-CORAL	CDA	J-CORAL	Ours
1	60.47	89.28	88.30	61.79	83.37	**91.06**	78.49
2	70.83	63.54	72.09	80.76	72.65	**84.78**	68.02
3	65.98	69.96	**73.07**	56.29	71.22	61.97	67.68
4	77.43	94.48	95.17	81.82	96.82	95.54	**100.00**
5	58.37	60.15	65.59	**94.69**	51.46	65.08	54.68
6	54.62	57.90	58.43	60.98	67.67	65.63	**81.71**
7	61.20	69.35	**70.84**	59.84	66.64	68.74	46.94
OA (%)	52.99	61.46	63.42	65.83	66.99	68.18	**72.78**
κ	0.4133	0.4610	0.4882	0.5125	0.5194	0.5384	**0.5656**

Table 15.6 Classification accuracies of Indiana (TD) in different methods.

Class	SVM	DAN	DANN	D-CORAL	CDA	J-CORAL	Ours
1	9.18	12.47	**15.64**	3.13	4.83	4.01	2.89
2	21.65	2.44	25.91	0.78	7.15	0.81	**32.86**
3	16.41	55.56	43.24	76.89	77.60	89.01	**92.23**
4	91.17	**95.26**	79.83	87.90	85.66	84.07	92.51
5	**2.46**	0.35	0.27	0.06	0.35	0.08	0.88
6	22.16	2.56	0.24	0	0.49	0	**45.60**
7	92.81	97.19	**98.90**	97.97	98.03	98.39	97.09
OA (%)	41.34	50.45	51.64	52.08	52.60	53.72	**56.07**
κ	0.2939	0.3428	0.3497	0.3931	0.3829	0.3969	**0.4171**

13.77%, 8.47%, and 9.11%, respectively. This improvement is attributed to the deep learning methods' ability to extract discriminative features through hierarchical structured networks, capturing intricate patterns effectively. However, solely relying on methods like MMD (DAN), discriminant methods (DANN), or CORAL (D-CORAL) for domain or class alignment yields lower results compared to pseudo-labeling (CDA). CDA outperforms DAN by 4.44%, DANN by 2.48%, and D-CORAL by 2.23% on the Pavia dataset. Similarly, on the Houston dataset, CDA achieves improvements of 5.53%, 3.57%, and 1.16% over DAN, DANN, and D-CORAL, respectively. On the Indiana dataset, CDA surpasses DAN by 2.15%, DANN by 0.96%, and D-CORAL by 0.52%. This emphasizes CDA's advantage in considering both transferability and discriminability. Considering both domain and class alignment, J-CORAL outperforms CDA, focusing solely on class alignment. J-CORAL achieves higher accuracies of 1.14%, 1.19%, and 1.12% compared to CDA on the Pavia, Houston, and Indiana datasets, respectively. Incorporating a dynamic distribution adaptation strategy further enhances performance over J-CORAL. Our method exhibits higher accuracies of 4.44%, 4.60%, and 2.35% compared to J-CORAL on the Pavia, Houston, and Indiana datasets, respectively. This dynamic strategy allows adjusting the relative importance between marginal and conditional distributions, leading to effective distribution adaptation and superior classification results.

Furthermore, Figures 15.7–15.9 depict the classification maps of PC, Houston 2018, and Indiana (TD). Our proposed DDAN-JCA method can accurately classify a larger number of samples. As a result, the generated mapping maps exhibit a higher level of consistency with ground-truth maps.

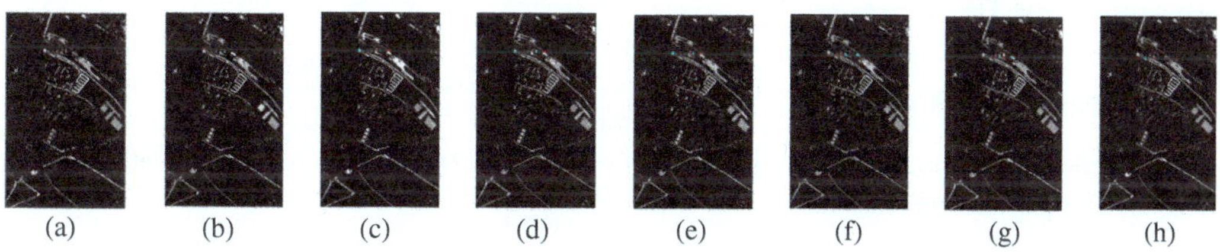

Figure 15.7 Classification map of PC in different methods: (a) Ground truth, (b) SVM, (c) DAN, (d) DANN, (e) D-CORAL, (f) CDA, (g) J-CORAL, and (h) DDAN-JCA (our method).

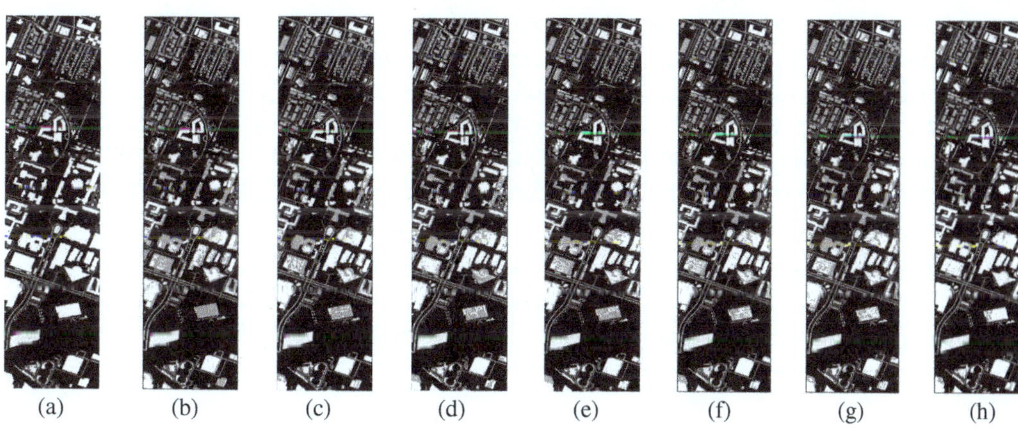

Figure 15.8 Classification map of Houston 2018 in different methods: (a) Ground truth, (b) SVM, (c) DAN, (d) DANN, (e) D-CORAL, (f) CDA, (g) J-CORAL, and (h) DDAN-JCA (our method).

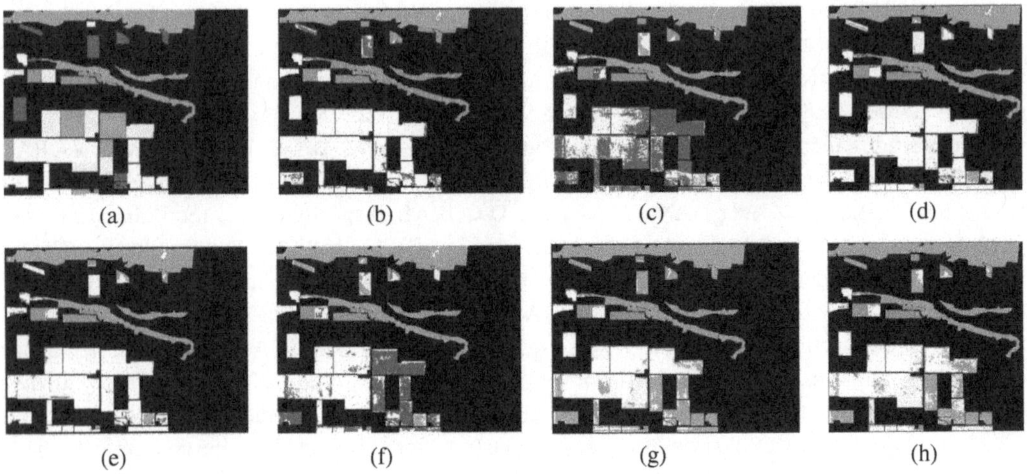

Figure 15.9 Classification map of Indiana (TD) in different methods: (a) Ground truth, (b) SVM, (c) DAN, (d) DANN, (e) D-CORAL, (f) CDA, (g) J-CORAL, and (h) DDAN-JCA (our method).

The improved classification accuracy achieved by DDAN-JCA is visually evident in the prediction maps, indicating its effectiveness in capturing and preserving the underlying patterns and structures in the TD.

15.3.4 Experimental Analysis

In the discussion section, we will evaluate the effectiveness of DDAN-JCA in terms of both ablation analysis and parameters analysis.

15.3.4.1 Ablation Analysis

To validate the effectiveness of each component in DDAN-JCA, we trained and evaluated different model variants using the same experimental parameters defined previously. As depicted in Table 15.7, these ablation experiments explore three different cases. Case 1: Combination of DCRN and marginal CORAL algorithm to implement marginal distribution alignment of SD and TD. Case 2: Combination of DCRN and AMM with the joint CORAL algorithm to implement marginal distribution alignment and conditional distribution alignment of SD and TD. Case 3: Our method employs DCRN and AMM with the dynamic joint CORAL algorithm. The proposed DDAN-JCA method simultaneously aligns the marginal distribution of overall features extracted by DCRN and the conditional distribution of the local information extracted using AMM. At the same time,

Table 15.7 Classification results (OA%) on three different settings.

Task	Pavia	Houston	Indiana
Case 1	80.12	65.83	52.18
Case 2	83.49	68.18	53.72
Case 3	87.93	72.78	56.07

the dynamic joint CORAL algorithm can dynamically adjust the importance of marginal distribution and conditional distribution by using a balance factor. The experimental results substantiate the effectiveness of the proposed DDAN-JCA method.

15.3.4.2 Parameters Analysis

In the proposed DDAN-JCA method, the adjustment of several parameters, including the balance factor μ, the parameter α, and the parameter patch_size, is crucial for achieving optimal performance. The balance factor μ determines the relative contributions of L_{MC} and L_{CC}, balancing overall distribution alignment and classifier adaptation. Parameter α controls the balance between classifier adaptation and distribution alignment, while patch_size influences the performance by determining the size of input 3D HSI cubes.

To calculate μ adaptively, we utilize Eq. (15.8) instead of exhaustive searching. Table 15.8 consistently shows $\mu > 0.5$ in all classification tasks, affirming the effectiveness of our adaptive estimation method. It suggests assigning more weight to the conditional distribution loss, enhancing classification performance by dynamically adjusting μ. Parameter α plays a critical role in determining the weight assigned to the dynamic joint loss. Sensitivity analysis using five values {0.1, 0.5, 1.0, 1.5, 2.0} reveals optimal α values for each dataset, maximizing classification accuracy: 0.5 for the PC dataset, 1 for the Houston 2018 dataset, and 0.5 for the Indiana dataset, shown in Figure 15.10 Selecting appropriate α significantly influences classification performance across datasets. Conducting sensitivity analysis on patch sizes ($5 \times 5, 7 \times 7, 9 \times 9$, and 11×11) highlights the importance of patch_size selection. Figure 15.11 demonstrates that using a 9×9 patch_size consistently yields the highest OA on the Pavia, Houston, and Indiana datasets. This underscores the necessity of careful patch_size consideration during preprocessing for optimal classification outcomes.

Table 15.8 Classification results (OA %) for L_{MC} and L_{CC} of different weight values.

Task	Pavia	Houston	Indiana
$\mu L_{MC} + (1-\mu)L_{CC}$	85.50	70.90	54.18
$(1-\mu)L_{MC} + \mu L_{CC}$	87.93	72.78	56.07

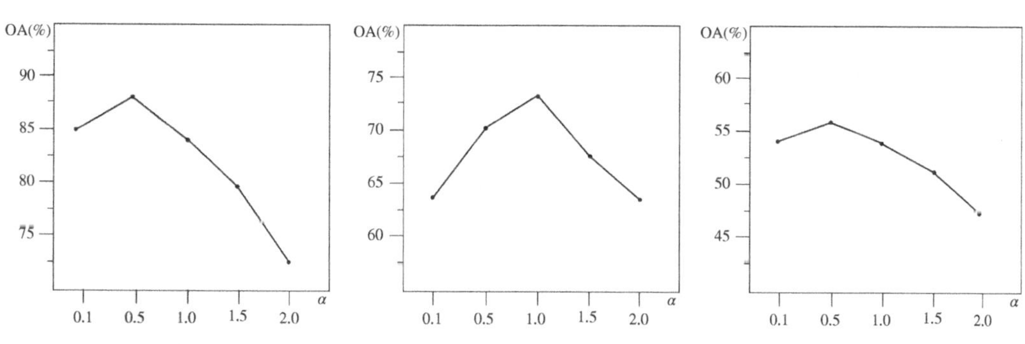

Figure 15.10 Sensitivity analysis of α on three datasets: (a) PC, (b) Houston 2018, (c) Indiana (target domain).

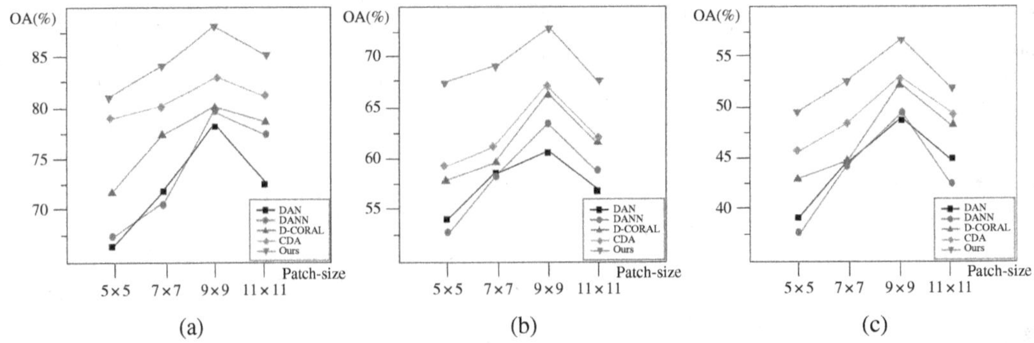

Figure 15.11 Sensitivity analysis of patch_size on three datasets: (a) PC, (b) Houston 2018, (c) Indiana (target domain).

15.4 Conclusion

In conclusion, DA presents a promising approach to addressing the challenges encountered in hyperspectral image classification. By effectively transferring knowledge across different domains, domain adaptation techniques enable classifiers to adapt to novel environments with limited labeled data. Future research directions include exploring more robust adaptation techniques, addressing domain shifts in heterogeneous environments, and developing scalable algorithms suitable for large-scale hyperspectral datasets.

References

1 Ghamisi, P., Yokoya, N., Li, J. et al. (2018). Advances in hyperspectral image and signal processing: a comprehensive overview of the state of the art. *IEEE Geosci. Remote Sens. Mag.* 5 (4): 37–78.

2 Qian, S.E. (2021). Hyperspectral satellites, evolution and development history. *IEEE J. Sel. Top. Appl. Earth Obs. Remote Sens.* 14: 7032–7056.

3 Liu, J., Feng, Q., Liang, T. et al. (2022). Estimating the forage neutral detergent fiber content of alpine grassland in the Tibetan plateau using hyperspectral data and machine learning algorithms. *IEEE Trans. Geosci. Remote Sens.* 60: 1–17.

4 Luo, B., Yang, C., Chanussot, J., and Zhang, L. (2013). Crop yield estimation based on unsupervised linear unmixing of multidate hyperspectral imagery. *IEEE Trans. Geosci. Remote Sens.* 51 (1): 162–173.

5 Ghamisi, P., Plaza, J., Chen, Y. et al. (2017). Advanced spectral classifiers for hyperspectral images: a review. *IEEE Geosci. Remote Sens. Mag.* 5 (1): 8–32.

6 Deng, B., Jia, S., and Shi, D. (2019). Deep metric learning-based feature embedding for hyperspectral image classification. *IEEE Trans. Geosci. Remote Sens.* 58 (2): 1422–1435.

7 Chang, C. (2007). Hyperspectral data exploitation: theory and applications.

8 Zhang, Y., Li, W., Zhang, M. et al. (2021). Topological structure and semantic information transfer network for cross-scene hyperspectral image classification. *IEEE Trans. Neural Networks Learn. Syst.* 1–14.

9 Zhu, W., Zhao, C., Feng, S., and Qin, B. (2022). Multiscale short and long range graph convolutional network for hyperspectral image classification. *IEEE Trans. Geosci. Remote Sens.* 60: 1–15.

10 Zhang, Y., Li, W., Tao, R. et al. (2021). Cross-Scene Hyperspectral Image Classification With Discriminative Cooperative Alignment. *IEEE Trans. Geosci. Remote Sens.* 59 (11): 9646–9660.

11 Wang, J., Lan, C., Liu, C. et al. (2021). Generalizing to unseen domains: a survey on domain generalization. *IEEE Trans. Knowl. Data Eng.* 4627–4635.

12 Peng, J., Huang, Y., Sun, W. et al. (2022). Domain adaptation in remote sensing image classification: a survey. *IEEE J. Sel. Top. Appl. Earth Obs. Remote Sens.* 15: 9842–9859.

13 Peng, J., Sun, W., Ma, L. et al. (2019). Discriminative transfer joint matching for domain adaptation in hyperspectral image classification. *IEEE Geosci. Remote Sens. Lett.* 16 (6): 972–976.

14 Huang, Y., Peng, J., Ning, Y. et al. (2021). Graph embedding and distribution alignment for domain adaptation in hyperspectral image classification. *IEEE J. Sel. Top. Appl. Earth Obs. Remote Sens.* 14: 7654–7666.

15 Huang, Y., Peng, J., Ning, Y. et al. (2021). Distribution alignment and discriminative feature learning for domain adaptation in hyperspectral image classification. *IEEE Geosci. Remote Sens. Lett.* 19: 1–5.

16 Pan, S.J., Tsang, I.W., Kwok, J.T., and Yang, Q. (2011). Domain adaptation via transfer component analysis. *IEEE Trans. Neural Netw.* 22 (2): 199–210.

17 Long, M., Wang, J., Ding, G. et al. (2014). Transfer joint matching for unsupervised domain adaptation. *IEEE Conference on Computer Vision & Pattern Recognition (CVPR)*, Columbus, OH, USA, June 23–28, 2014, pp. 1410–1417.

18 Wang, J., Chen, Y., Hu, L. (2018). Stratified transfer learning for cross-domain activity recognition. *IEEE International Conference on Pervasia Computing and Communications (PerCom)*, Athens, Greece, March 19–23, 2018, pp. 1–10.

19 Blitzer, J., McDonald, R., Pereira, F. (2006). Domain adaptation with structural correspondence learning. *Proceedings of the 2006 Conference on Empirical Methods in Natural Language Processing (EMNLP)*, Sydney, Australia, July 22–27, 2006, pp. 120–128.

20 Gu, Q., Li, Z., Han, J. (2011). Joint feature selection and subspace learning. *IJCAI 2011, Proceedings of the 22nd International Joint Conference on Artificial Intelligence*, Barcelona, Catalonia, Spain (16–22 July 2011).

21 Li, J., Zhao, J., Ke, L. (2016). Joint feature selection and structure preservation for domain adaptation.

22 Fernando, B., Habrard, A., Sebban, M., Tuytelaars, T. (2013). Unsupervised visual domain adaptation using subspace alignment. *IEEE International Conference on Computer Vision (ICCV)*, Sydney, Australia, December 1–8, 2013, pp. 2960–2967.

23 Baktashmotlagh, M., Harandi, M.T., Lovell, B.C. et al. (2014). *Domain Adaptation on the Statistical Manifold*. CVPR.

24 Ball, J.E., Anderson, D.T., and Chan, C.S. (2017). Comprehensive survey of deep learning in remote sensing: theories, tools, and challenges for the community. *J. Appl. Remote. Sens.* 11 (4): 042609.

25 Farahani, A., Voghoei, S., Rasheed, K., Arabnia, H.R. (2021). A brief review of domain adaptation.

26 Long, M. and Wang, J. (2015). Learning transferable features with deep adaptation networks. *Int. Conf. Mach. Learn.* 37: 97–105.

27 Gretton, A., Borgwardt, K.M., Rasch, M. et al. (2012). A kernel two-sample test. *J. Mach. Learn. Res.* 13: 723–773.

28 Li, Z., Tang, X., Li, W. et al. (2020). A two-stage deep domain adaptation method for hyperspectral image classification. *Remote Sens.* 12 (7): 1054.

29 Sun, B. and Saenko, K. (2016). Deep CORAL. correlation alignment for deep domain adaptation.

30 Sun, B., Feng, J., Saenko, K. (2015). Return of frustratingly easy domain adaptation.

31 Long, M., Zhu, H., Wang, J., and Jordan, M.I. (2016). Deep transfer learning with joint adaptation networks.

32 Wang, W., Ma, L., Chen, M., and Du, Q. (2021). Joint correlation alignment-based graph neural network for domain adaptation of multitemporal hyperspectral remote sensing images. *IEEE J. Sel. Top. Appl. Earth Obs. Remote Sens.* 14: 3170–3184.

33 Xu, Y., Li, Z., Li, W. et al. (2022). Dual-channel residual network for hyperspectral image classification with noisy labels. *IEEE Trans. Geosci. Remote Sens.* 60: 1–11.

34 Woo, S., Park, J., Lee, J.-Y., and Kweon, I.S. (2018). CBAM: convolutional block attention module.

35 Wang, J., Feng, W., Chen, Y. et al. (2018). Visual domain adaptation with manifold embedded distribution alignment.

36 Schölkopf, B., Platt, J., and Hofmann, T. (2007). Analysis of representations for domain adaptation. *Nips* 19: 137–144.

37 Licciardi, G., Pacifici, F., Tuia, D. et al. (2009). Decision fusion for the classification of hyperspectral data: outcome of the 2008 GRS-S data fusion contest. *IEEE Trans. Geosci. Remote Sens.* 47 (11): 3857–3865.

38 Debes, C., Merentitis, A., Heremans, R. et al. (2014). Hyperspectral and LiDAR data fusion: outcome of the 2013 GRSS data fusion contest. *IEEE J. Sel. Top. Appl. Earth Obs. Remote Sens.* 7 (6): 2405–2418.

39 Saux, B.L., Yokoya, N., Hansch, R., and Prasad, S. (2018). 2018 IEEE GRSS data fusion contest: multimodal land use classification [technical committees]. *IEEE Trans. Geosci. Remote Sens.* 6 (1): 52–54.

40 Ye, M., Qian, Y., Zhou, J., and Yuan, Y.T. (2017). Dictionary learning-based feature-level domain adaptation for cross-scene hyperspectral image classification. *IEEE Trans. Geosci. Remote Sens.* 55 (3): 1544–1562.

41 Melgani, F. and Bruzzone, L. (2004). Classification of hyperspectral remote sensing images with support vector machines. *IEEE Trans. Geosci. Remote Sens.* 42 (8): 1778–1790.

42 Ganin, Y., Ustinova, E., Ajakan, H. et al. (2016). Domain-adversarial training of neural networks. *J. Mach. Learn. Res.* 17 (1): 2030–2096.

43 Liu, Z., Ma, L., and Du, Q. (2021). Class-wise distribution adaptation for unsupervised classification of hyperspectral remote sensing images. *IEEE Trans. Geosci. Remote Sens.* 59 (1): 508–521.

44 Ding, Y., Chong, Y., Pan, S., Zheng, C. (2023). Sensing R. Diversity-connected graph convolutional network for hyperspectral image classification.

16

Unsupervised Domain Adaptation for Classification of Hyperspectral Images

Li Ma[1] *and Qian Du*[2]

[1] *School of Mechanical Engineering and Electronic Information, China University of Geosciences, Wuhan, China*
[2] *Department of Electrical and Computer Engineering, Mississippi State University, Mississippi State, MS, USA*

16.1 Introduction

For classification of hyperspectral remote-sensing images, it is often costly, difficult, and time consuming to acquire labeled samples. Suppose we have abundant labeled data from a previous hyperspectral remote-sensing image. It may be beneficial to reuse these labeled data to classify a new image that is temporally or spatially disjoint to the previous one. However, it would be typically problematic if the labeled samples are directly used to train a classifier, since the spectral features may vary significantly in the new image because of the changed soil moisture, vegetation composition, topography, and the angle of the sun [1, 2]. Domain adaptation is capable of addressing this problem since it attempts to learn an adaptive classifier for the new image by transferring knowledge from the original image [3, 4]. The initial image with abundant labeled information is known as source domain, and the subsequent image with few or no labeled data is referred to as the target domain.

Domain adaptation approaches can be categorized as semi-supervised technique and unsupervised technique, according to the availability of the target labeled data. When there are abundant source labeled data, but limited target labeled data is accessible, a method is typically referred to as a semi-supervised domain adaptation approach [5, 6]; in contrast, when there is no target labeled data, the method is referred to as an unsupervised domain adaptation approach. Since unsupervised approach has no requirement for the labeled information of target domain, it is able to achieve automatic classification of target image and have wider applications. We focus on unsupervised domain adaptation methods in this chapter.

In unsupervised domain adaptation scenario, the source domain and target domain are usually acquired by the same sensor, and the two domains share the same label space. The target data points are classified as one of the source class.

16.1.1 Traditional Unsupervised Domain Adaptation Methods for Hyperspectral Image Classification

Traditional unsupervised domain adaptation algorithms for classification of hyperspectral images are generally categorized as classifier-based methods and feature-based methods. Classifier-based approaches aim to learn an adaptive classifier for target data by leveraging knowledge from the

Machine-Learning-Based Hyperspectral Image Processing, First Edition. Edited by Bing Zhang.

source data [7–13]. Bruzzone et al. proposed multiple domain adaptive classifiers, including the adaptive maximum likelihood classifier [7], the adaptive support vector machine (SVM) [8], and the adaptive Bayesian classifier [9]. Crawford et al. proposed binary hierarchical classifier [10] and Laplacian SVM classifier [11] for cross-domain classification of hyperspectral. Sun et al. introduced maximum mean discrepancy (MMD)-based feature alignment strategy to multi-kernel SVM classifier [12]. Zhong et al. proposed an iterative training sample updating approach to obtain an adaptive target classifier for hyperspectral image classification [13].

Feature-based approaches seek a shared feature space where the data distributions between domains become similar. In the common feature space, the labeled data from the source domain can be used to classify the target data. There are multiple feature alignment strategies. (i) MMD-based feature alignment strategy [14] constrains the means of two domains to be close in a reproducing kernel Hilbert space. Matasci et al. applied transfer component analysis to learn a common subspace by using MMD for classification of hyperspectral images [15]. Peng et al. combined MMD and manifold regularization in the KPCA-embedding space [16]. (ii) Subspace alignment (SA) that aligns the subspace eigenvectors of two domains is widely used for domain adaptation [17]. Wei et al. utilized subspace-alignment-based adaptation and low-rank-representation-based classifier to improve the robustness of domain adaptation to label noise [18]. Yang et al. employed kernel SA for classification of hyperspectral remote-sensing data [19]. (iii) Similar to MMD, minimizing the means of two domains in a dimensionality reduced feature space can obtain feature alignment [20]. Zhu et al. proposed a class centroid alignment approach by moving the target domain samples toward source domain, with the moving direction equaling to the difference of the associated class centroids between domains [21]. Luo et al. combined the joint distribution adaptation (JDA) [20] and manifold regularization for a better adaptation performance [22]. (iv) Covariance alignment that minimizes the covariance difference between domains can obtain domain adaptation [23]. Wei et al. performed domain adaptation by employing correlation alignment (CORAL) between the two hyperspectral data [24]. Ma et al. proposed centroid and covariance alignment approach that utilizes both the first-order and second-order statistics [25]. (v) Manifold alignment uses the corresponding points as bridges to match manifolds of two domains [26]. Tuia et al., Yang et al., and Ma et al. utilized manifold alignment approaches for cross-domain hyperspectral image classification [27–30], and they employed different strategies to obtain the corresponding points in unsupervised manner. (vi) Maximizing the correlation coefficient can lead to feature alignment between domains. Both Qin et al. and Li et al. applied canonical correlation analysis for unsupervised domain adaptation [31, 32]. (vii) Reconstruction-based method is able to achieve feature alignment, since the two domain data sets will have similar distributions if one domain can be reconstructed from the other one [33]. In [34], low-rank-representation-based approach that utilizes the reconstruction strategy was proposed to reduce the differences in the new representation. In [35], SA, MMD alignment, and data reconstruction are combined to achieve domain adaptation. In addition, Gross et al. proposed a nonlinear feature normalization method to align the spectral characteristics of multiple domains [36]. Zhang et al. presented a locality robust domain adaptation method, which combines the row-sparsity constraint, discriminant regularization, and manifold regularization [37]. Wei et al. proposed to fuse different domain adaptation methods by calculating weights of these methods for each target point, where the adaptive weights are obtained by the neighborhood consistency criterion [38]. Persello and Bruzzone proposed a kernel-based domain-invariant feature selection approach for knowledge transfer [39].

Most of these traditional methods utilized linear transformation or required the calculation of a kernel matrix or Laplacian matrix. Therefore, they cannot explore the nonlinear property of hyperspectral remote-sensing data or are not capable of processing large-scale data. In addition, they generally perform the feature alignment and classification sequentially and thus cannot obtain the domain-invariant feature and adaptive classifier simultaneously.

16.1.2 Deep-learning-based Unsupervised Domain Adaptation Methods for Hyperspectral Image Classification

In recent years, deep neural networks have been exploited for domain adaptation due to its powerful feature representation ability [40, 41]. It is able to obtain both the aligned features and adaptive classifier, and is suitable for large-scale data.

For classification of hyperspectral remote-sensing images, there are two types of deep-learning-based unsupervised domain adaptation networks. One is discrepancy-based domain adaptation, which applies feature alignment strategies to constrain the network extracted features to be domain invariant. It is often composed of a feature extraction module and a classifier module, where the feature extraction module is used to extract domain-invariant features by cooperating with feature alignment strategies, and the classifier module performs classification. The other one utilizes the adversarial learning between a feature extractor and a discriminator to make the source and target features indistinguishable.

For the discrepancy-based unsupervised domain adaptation, Ma and Song achieved unsupervised domain adaptation by aligning class centroid in a deep neural network [42]. Song et al. introduced SA strategy in a convolutional neural network to realize domain adaptation [43]. Garea et al. proposed TCANet with MMD strategy for domain adaptation [44]. Wang et al. proposed a domain adaptation method by using MMD and manifold regularization with a deep network [45]. Chen et al. applied an augmented associative learning (AAL) network, which employs the criterion of cycle consistency to achieve features that are both domain-invariant and discriminative [46]. Wang et al. combined graph neural network and covariance alignment strategy for classification of multi-temporal hyperspectral remote-sensing images [47]. Zhang et al. also utilized graph neural network, where the graph optimal-transmission-based topological relationship alignment and MMD-based distribution alignment are applied [48]. Li et al. employed confident learning method [49] and contrastive learning method [50] for domain adaptation. In [49], a classifier consistency criterion is applied to reduce the domain discrepancy and generate pseudo-labels, and then the confident learning is used to select high confident target samples. In [50], one-class classification and local MMD were introduced to obtain aligned features and contrastive learning is used to enhance the feature separability.

Generative adversarial network (GAN) has achieved outstanding performance in various fields. It is highly useful for transforming images to another specific domain [51], and thus it is suitable for domain adaptation that aims to match two domains. Applying adversarial learning for domain adaptation results in adversarial adaptation network, where the discriminator performs a binary domain classification while the feature extractor generates domain-invariant features such that they cannot be separated by the discriminator [52, 53]. In the field of hyperspectral image classification, Elshamli et al. applied the domain-adversarial neural networks (DANN) [54] to obtain domain-invariant features [55]. Bejiga and Melgani applied a variant of DANN that uses the Wasserstein-1 metric to measure the distance between the domains [56]. Liu et al. employed a class-wise adversarial adaptation strategy with MMD for cross-domain classification of hyperspectral images [57]. Deng et al. utilized adversarial discriminative domain adaptation [52] and introduced a metric learning method to minimize the distance between target samples and the nearest source cluster centers [58]. Ma et al. employed multiple classifiers as discriminators and variational autoencoder as the generator [59]. Huang et al. proposed a spatial–spectral weighted adversarial domain adaptation method for wetland mapping with hyperspectral images [60]. Yu et al. introduced a content-wise alignment strategy through an adversarial framework, where the content-wise scheme is integrated with a class-wise alignment and a style-perceive regularization [61]. Yu et al. also utilized adversarial adaptation in conjunction with a dense-based compaction network to extract discriminative spectral–spatial feature [62].

In this chapter, we present two traditional unsupervised domain adaptation methods as well as recent advances in hyperspectral classification with two deep learning methods. The traditional methods include manifold alignment method [30], and centroid and covariance alignment method [25]. The deep-learning-based methods contain the class-wise adversarial adaptation method [57] and the augmented associative-learning-based method [46].

16.2 Unsupervised Domain Adaptation Problem

Unsupervised domain adaptation method attempts to make use of the prior knowledge of the source domain to learn an adaptive classifier for the target domain where the labeled information is not available. Generally, a common feature space between domains is learned in unsupervised domain adaptation methods, where the classifier trained on source data becomes suitable for classification of target data.

Let $\mathbf{X}^s \in \mathrm{R}^{D \times Ns}$ represent the source domain data with class labels $\mathbf{Y}^s \in \mathrm{R}^{1 \times Ns}$, $\mathbf{X}^t \in \mathrm{R}^{D \times Nt}$ denote the target domain data without labeled information, where D is the feature dimensionality, N_s is the number of labeled instances in the source domain, N_t is the number of unlabeled instances in the target domain, $\mathbf{X}^s$ and $\mathbf{X}^t$ are distributed differently but related. There are C classes in both domains denoted as $\mathbf{\Omega} = [\Omega_1, ..., \Omega_C]$. In the following, we present two traditional unsupervised domain adaptation methods and two deep-learning-based unsupervised domain adaptation methods.

16.3 Traditional Unsupervised Domain Adaptation Methods

We present two traditional unsupervised domain adaptation methods, manifold alignment method [30] and centroid and covariance alignment method [25]. Both apply feature alignment strategy to obtain domain-invariant features and then employ SVM on the aligned features. For better feature alignment performance, two preprocessing strategies are used. Firstly, we utilize a spatial filtering to process the hyperspectral remote-sensing image. Since the spatially neighboring points are likely from the same class, we represent each pixel as the mean spectra of all the pixels in its spatial 3×3 neighborhood. Secondly, we make the overall sample mean of each domain equals to zero, which can remove the overall mean difference between domains and reduce the distribution drift between domains.

16.3.1 Unsupervised Manifold Alignment Method

Manifold alignment approach not only aligns the two manifolds but also preserves the local geometry of each manifold. The objective of manifold alignment is to learn a global transformation matrix $\mathbf{F} \in R^{d \times p}$ that the transformed source data $\mathbf{F}^T\mathbf{X}^s$ and target data $\mathbf{F}^T\mathbf{X}^t$ are well aligned, where p $(p < d)$ is the dimensionality of the common feature space. The objective function of manifold alignment is expressed as:

$$\min \sum_{i,j=1}^{Ns} \left\|\mathbf{F}^T\mathbf{x}_i^s - \mathbf{F}^T\mathbf{x}_j^s\right\|^2 \mathbf{W}_{ij}^s + \sum_{i,j=1}^{Nt} \left\|\mathbf{F}^T\mathbf{x}_i^t - \mathbf{F}^T\mathbf{x}_j^t\right\|^2 \mathbf{W}_{ij}^t + \sum_{i=1}^{Ns}\sum_{j=1}^{Nt} \left\|\mathbf{F}^T\mathbf{x}_i^s - \mathbf{F}^T\mathbf{x}_j^t\right\|^2 \mathbf{W}_{ij}^{st} \tag{16.1}$$

where $\mathbf{x}^s_i$ denotes the i-th source data point, $\mathbf{x}^t_j$ denotes the j-th target data point, $\mathbf{W}^s$ and $\mathbf{W}^t$ are the graph adjacency matrix that summarize the neighborhood relations of the source and target data, respectively, and $\mathbf{W}^{st}$ represents the similarity matrix across domains. The first two terms preserve the local properties of each neighborhood within each domain, and the third term achieves the feature alignment across domains.

The original manifold alignment methods are semi-supervised, which require prior knowledge to build relation matrix $\mathbf{W}^{st}$ between domains. In unsupervised domain adaptation scenario, we investigate unsupervised manifold alignment (UMA) method. The most crucial issue in UMA approach is how to obtain the cross-domain relationships in an unsupervised manner. We propose to use the probabilistic prediction results of target data to build the relations with source data. The similarity between a target point $\mathbf{x}^t_j$ and a source point $\mathbf{x}^s_i$ is expressed as:

$$\mathbf{W}_{ij}^{st} = \sum_{k=1}^{C} \mathbf{P}\left(\mathbf{x}_j^t, \Omega_k\right) \delta\left(\mathbf{x}_i^s, \Omega_k\right) \tag{16.2}$$

where $\mathbf{P} \in R^{Nt \times C}$ denotes the probabilistic classification results of target data, and $\mathbf{P}(\mathbf{x}^t_j, \Omega_k)$ represents the probability of $\mathbf{x}^t_j$ belonging to the k-th class. If the $\mathbf{x}^s_i$ belongs to Ω_k, the similarity W_{ij}^{st} equals to $\mathbf{P}(\mathbf{x}^t_j, \Omega_k)$.

16.3.2 Class Centroid and Covariance Alignment (CCCA) Method

Class centroid and covariance alignment (CCCA) utilizes the centroid and covariance matrix to describe the distribution of the spectral data, and performs distribution alignment on a per-class basis. It is implemented in the original spectral space, such that the target domain data remain unchanged, and the source domain data are transformed to be aligned to that of the target domain. The flowchart of the CCCA method is shown in Figure 16.1. Covariance alignment is first achieved by transforming each source class, and centroid alignment is then performed by translating each source class. After the adaptation, an SVM classifier is trained on the aligned source data and is used to predict the target data. The CCCA adaptation can refine the predictions, and the improved predictions can also facilitate the estimation of statistics and thus improve CCCA result. Therefore, CCCA is iterated until the prediction is stable.

In source domain, the data, the centroid, and the covariance matrix of class-j are denoted as $\mathbf{X}^s_j$, $\mathbf{u}^s_j$, and $\sum^s_j$, respectively. For the predicted class-j in target domain, they are expressed as $\mathbf{X}^t_j$, $\mathbf{u}^t_j$, and $\sum^t_j$, respectively. The class covariance alignment is performed by transforming each source class. Suppose the transformation matrix for class-j is denoted as $\mathbf{P}_j \in R^{D \times D}$, and the transformed source class-j is obtained by:

$$\mathbf{X}_{j\,(\mathrm{cov})}^s = \mathbf{P}_j \mathbf{X}_j^s, j = 1, \ldots, C \tag{16.3}$$

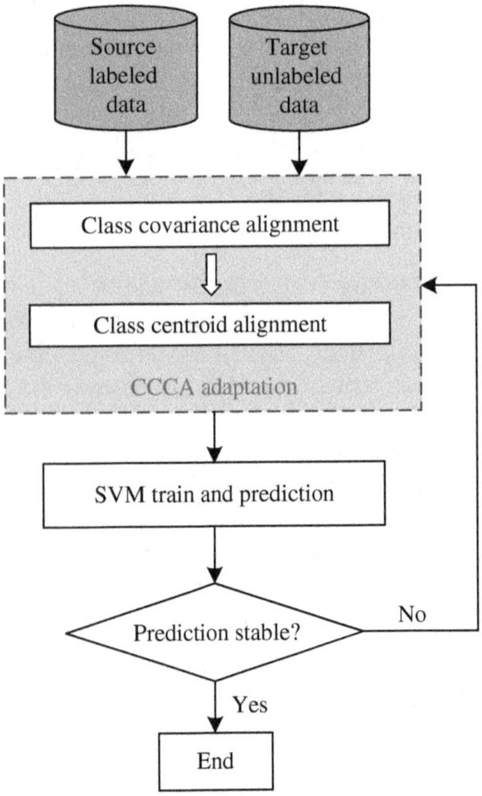

Figure 16.1 The flowchart of the CCCA algorithm.

Then the covariance matrix of $\mathbf{X}^s_{j\,(\mathrm{cov})}$ is expressed as:

$$\boldsymbol{\Sigma}^s_{j\,(\mathrm{cov})} = \left(\mathbf{X}^s_{j\,(\mathrm{cov})} - \mathbf{u}^s_{j\,(\mathrm{cov})}\right)\left(\mathbf{X}^s_{j\,(\mathrm{cov})} - \mathbf{u}^s_{j\,(\mathrm{cov})}\right)^T = \left(\mathbf{P}_j\mathbf{X}^s_j - \mathbf{P}_j\mathbf{u}^s_j\right)\left(\mathbf{P}_j\mathbf{X}^s_j - \mathbf{P}_j\mathbf{u}^s_j\right)^T = \mathbf{P}_j\boldsymbol{\Sigma}^s_j\mathbf{P}_j{}^T \tag{16.4}$$

where $\mathbf{u}^s{}_{j(\mathrm{cov})}$ denotes the centroid of source class-j after covariance alignment. The objective of covariance alignment requires that the covariance matrix of the new transformed source data equals to that of the target data, which is expressed by $\sum^s{}_{j(\mathrm{cov})} = \sum^t{}_j$, $j = 1,\ldots,C$. Then we obtain an analytical solution of the transformation matrix, which is calculated by:

$$\mathbf{P}_j = \boldsymbol{\Sigma}_j^{t\frac{1}{2}}\boldsymbol{\Sigma}^s_{j\,(OCA)}{}^{\frac{-1}{2}} \tag{16.5}$$

After covariance alignment, the variance of each band and correlation between bands of source data have been well aligned to those of target data. Although the covariance matrix is aligned, the centroids of the two data sets are quite different, indicating the need for centroid alignment. The centroid difference of class-j between domains is denoted as: $\mathbf{d}_j = \mathbf{u}^s{}_{j(\mathrm{cov})} - \mathbf{u}^t{}_j$, $j = 1,\ldots,C$. For each source data point, we move it toward target domain with the direction equaling to the centroid difference of its respective class. Let $\mathbf{X}^s{}_{ij(\mathrm{cov})}$ denote the i-th point from class-j of source data after covariance alignment. Since it belongs to class-j, we move this point with the direction equaling to $\mathbf{d}_j$, and the new spectral signature becomes:

$$\mathbf{X}^s_{ij\,(\mathrm{CCCA})} = \mathbf{X}^s_{ij\,(\mathrm{cov})} - \mathbf{d}_j \tag{16.6}$$

Moving all the source data points toward target domain, we can achieve $\mathbf{u}^s_{j(\text{CCCA})} = \mathbf{u}^t_j, j = 1,\ldots,C$, the coincidence of the cross-domain centroids. It is worth noting that the class centroid alignment is achieved by a translation operation. Therefore, the covariance matrix of each source class is preserved, and the previous covariance alignment is not influenced. Both the centroid alignment and covariance alignment can be achieved.

16.4 Deep-learning-based Unsupervised Domain Adaptation Methods

We present two deep-learning-based unsupervised domain adaptation networks, which are class-wise distribution adaptation (CDA) network [57] and AAL network [46].

16.4.1 Class-wise Distribution Adaptation Network

For hyperspectral remote-sensing images, different classes may have different spectral shift. Therefore, we conduct the domain adaptation on a per-class basis. CDA network is a conjunction of class-wise adversarial adaptation and class-wise probability MMD. The flowchart of CDA is shown in Figure 16.2, which contains three parts: a feature extractor G_f, a classifier G_c, and C discriminators $G_d^c|_{c=1}^C$. The feature extractor G_f generates domain-invariant features $G_f(\mathbf{X}_s)$ and $G_f(\mathbf{X}_t)$ for source data and target data, respectively, the classifier G_c outputs the probability prediction results $\mathbf{P}_s \in R^{C \times Ns}$ and $\mathbf{P}_t \in R^{C \times Nt}$, and the domain discriminator G_d^c yields the domain predictions for data from the c-th class. In addition, the probability MMD (PMMD) constraint is included to contribute to the training of the feature extractor. The loss function of CDA is defined as:

$$\begin{aligned} L\left(\mathbf{X}_s, \mathbf{Y}_s, \mathbf{X}_t, \mathbf{D}_s, \mathbf{D}_t; \boldsymbol{\theta}_f, \boldsymbol{\theta}_d^c|_{c=1}^C, \boldsymbol{\theta}_c\right) &= L_{src_{cls}}(\mathbf{X}_s, \mathbf{Y}_s; \boldsymbol{\theta}_f, \boldsymbol{\theta}_c) \\ -\lambda_1 L_{\text{domain}}\left(\mathbf{X}_s, \mathbf{D}_s, \mathbf{X}_t, \mathbf{D}_t; \boldsymbol{\theta}_f, \boldsymbol{\theta}_d^c|_{c=1}^C\right) &+ \lambda_2 L_{\text{PMMD}}(\mathbf{X}_s, \mathbf{X}_t; \boldsymbol{\theta}_f) + \beta L_{\text{entropy}}(\mathbf{X}_t; \boldsymbol{\theta}_f, \boldsymbol{\theta}_c) \end{aligned} \tag{16.7}$$

where the first term denotes the cross-entropy classification loss on source labeled data, the second term represents the domain classification loss of the discriminators, the third term expresses the

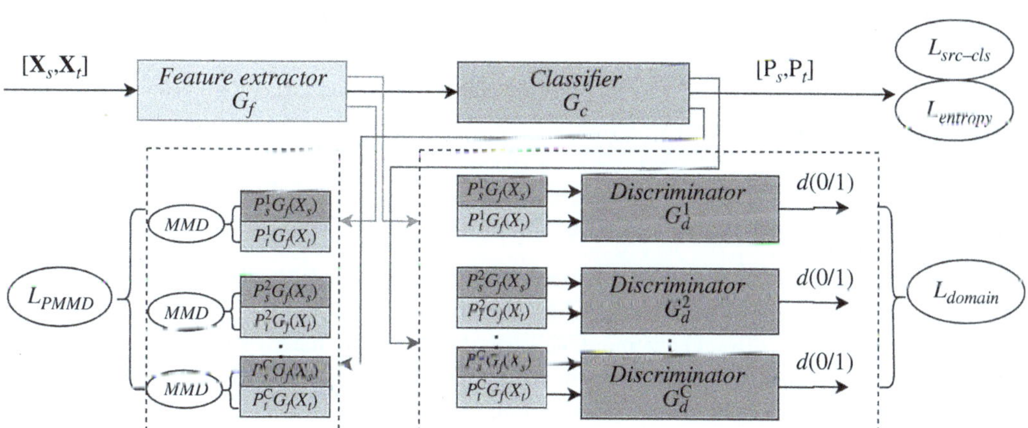

Figure 16.2 The flowchart of the class-wise distribution adaptation algorithm.

PMMD loss, and the fourth term denotes the entropy constraint on the classification results of the target data. The $\mathbf{D}_s \in R^{1 \times N_s}$ and $\mathbf{D}_t \in R^{1 \times N_t}$ denote the domain labels of source data and target data, respectively, with the elements of $\mathbf{D}_s$ equaling to 0 and the elements of $\mathbf{D}_t$ equaling to 1. The notations $\lambda_1, \lambda_2, \beta$ are the trade-off hyper-parameters, $\boldsymbol{\theta}_f$ represents the parameter of the feature extractor, $\boldsymbol{\theta}_c$ denotes the parameter of the classifier, and $\boldsymbol{\theta}_d^c|_{c=1}^C$ is the parameter of the c-th domain discriminator. We describe the class-wise adversarial adaptation-based loss and class-wise PMMD-based loss in the following part.

The learning of the feature extractor and the discriminator is adversarial, since the discriminator aims to distinguish the source domain and target domain while the feature extractor attempts to make confusion across domains. C domain discriminators $G_d^c|_{c=1}^C$ are designed to align data distributions of each class, resulting in class-wise adversarial adaptation. The domain classification loss is defined as:

$$L_{\text{domain}}\left(\mathbf{X}_s, \mathbf{D}_s, \mathbf{X}_t, \mathbf{D}_t; \boldsymbol{\theta}_f, \boldsymbol{\theta}_d^c|_{c=1}^C\right) = \frac{1}{N_s + N_t} \sum_{c=1}^{C} \sum_{(\mathbf{x}_i, d_i) \in (\mathbf{X}_s \cup \mathbf{X}_t, \mathbf{D}_s \cup \mathbf{D}_s)} L_d\left(G_d^c\left(p_i^c G_f(\mathbf{x}_i)\right), d_i\right) \tag{16.8}$$

$$L_d\left(h_i^c, d_i\right) = -d_i \log h_i^c - (1 - d_i) \log\left(1 - h_i^c\right) \tag{16.9}$$

where d_i is the domain label of the data $\mathbf{x}_i$, p_i^c denotes the probability of assigning $\mathbf{x}_i$ to the c-th class, $p_i^c G_f(\mathbf{x}_i)$ represents the probability-weighted feature of $\mathbf{x}_i$, and $h_i^c = G_d^c(p_i^c G_f(\mathbf{x}_i))$ denotes the domain prediction of the c-th discriminator. If p_i^c is large, which means $\mathbf{x}_i$ has a high probability to be from the c-th class, $G_f(\mathbf{x}_i)$ will go to the c-th discriminator G_d^c and contribute to the domain confusion of the c-th class with a high probability. L_d is the domain classification loss function on a data point $\mathbf{x}_i$. The feature extractor is trained by maximizing the domain classification loss, while the discriminators are trained by minimizing the domain classification loss.

The class-wise PMMD achieves domain adaptation by drawing the cross-domain centroids of each class to be close in the common feature space. We utilize the predicted probability outputs of target data to estimate the centroid of each class, and thus it is called probability MMD method. The loss function of the class-wise PMMD is defined as:

$$L_{\text{PMMD}}\left(\mathbf{X}_s, \mathbf{X}_t; \boldsymbol{\theta}_f\right) = \sum_{c=1}^{C} \left\| \frac{1}{N_s} \sum_{x_i \in \mathbf{X}_s} p_i^c G_f(\mathbf{x}_i) - \frac{1}{N_t} \sum_{x_j \in \mathbf{X}_t} p_j^c G_f(\mathbf{x}_j) \right\|_2^2 \tag{16.10}$$

where p_i^c and p_j^c are the prediction results of source data point $\mathbf{x}_i$ and target data point $\mathbf{x}_j$ belonging to the c-th class, respectively.

16.4.2 Augmented Associative Learning Network

Association means the similarity relationships between two embeddings. The cross-domain similarity matrix summarizes the relationships between source and target data, and thus an accurate similarity matrix indicates the achievement of distribution adaptation between domains. Therefore, associative learning can be applied to domain adaptation. We present an AAL network and apply it to cross-domain hyperspectral image classification.

The flowchart of the proposed approach is shown in Figure 16.3. The network contains a feature extractor G_f and a classifier G_c, where G_f aims to generate domain-invariant features, and G_c conducts classification and outputs the probability prediction results of the two domains. Two loss

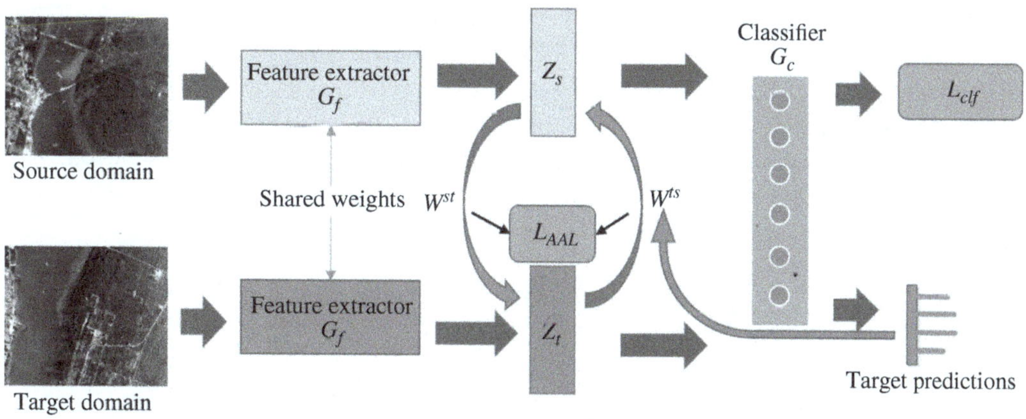

Figure 16.3 The flowchart of the augmented associative learning algorithm.

functions are utilized, which are cross-entropy loss on source data and AAL loss to obtain feature alignment.

Associative learning is conducted by employing the cycle consistency criterion in a two-step transition procedure. The first-step transition indicates the departure walk from source data to target data with the first transition probability matrix. The second-step transition denotes the return walk from target data back to source data with the second transition probability matrix. The two-step transitions produce a cycle that starts from source data and ends up getting back to source data. Since the source data are labeled, the labeled information of the starting and ending source data can be used to determine if a circle is consistent. If a starting source sample belongs to the same class as the ending source sample, the cycle is consistent. Otherwise, the cycle is inconsistent. Since the inconsistent cycles may be produced by the spectral drift or the overlapping spectra between source classes, with a walking loss that is defined to penalize the inconsistent cycles, domain-invariant and discriminative features can be achieved.

We need to calculate the first and second transition matrices. Using the network-generated features, the cross-domain $\mathbf{W}^{st}$ is expressed as:

$$\mathrm{W}_{ij}^{st} = G_f\left(\mathbf{x}_i^s\right)^{\mathrm{T}}\left(G_f\left(\mathbf{x}_j^t\right)\right) \tag{16.11}$$

Then the first-step transition probability matrix $\mathbf{P}^{st}$ is defined by softmaxing $\mathbf{W}^{st}$ over rows. The second cross-domain similarity matrix $\mathbf{W}^{ts}$ is obtained from the source labels and the target probability prediction results. Let $\mathbf{Y}_j^t \in \mathrm{R}^{1\times C}$ denote the probabilistic prediction result of target data $\mathbf{x}_j^t$, and $\mathbf{Y}_j^{tc}$ represents the probability of $\mathbf{x}_j^t$ belonging to the c-th class. The similarity between $\mathbf{x}_i^s$ and $\mathbf{x}_j^t$ is expressed as:

$$\mathrm{W}_{ji}^{ts} = \sum_{k=1}^{C} \mathbf{Y}_j^{tk}\,\delta\left(\mathbf{y}_i^s, \Omega_k\right) \tag{16.12}$$

The second-step transition probability matrix $\mathbf{P}^{ts}$ is obtained by softmaxing $\mathbf{W}^{ts}$ over rows. With these two different similarity matrices, the cycle consistency criterion is augmented to be more robust.

Let $G_f(\mathbf{x}_i^s)$ and $G_f(\mathbf{x}_j^s)$ denote two source sample features in the common feature space, respectively. The round-trip probability of starting at $G_f(\mathbf{x}_i^s)$ and ending up at $G_f(\mathbf{x}_j^s)$ is defined as:

$$\mathrm{P}_{ij}^{sts} = \sum_{k=1}^{N_t} \mathrm{P}_{ik}^{st}\mathrm{P}_{kj}^{ts} \tag{16.13}$$

where the superscript "*sts*" in $\mathbf{P}_{ij}^{sts}$ denotes the round trip from source to target and back to source, $\mathbf{P}_{ik}^{st}$ represents the transition probability from source data $G_f(\mathbf{x}_i^s)$ to target data $G_f(\mathbf{x}_k^t)$, and $\mathbf{P}_{kj}^{ts}$ represents the transition probability from the target data $G_f(\mathbf{x}_k^t)$ to source data $G_f(\mathbf{x}_j^s)$. The similarity of $G_f(\mathbf{x}_i^s)$ and $G_f(\mathbf{x}_j^s)$ is expressed by summing their relations to all the target data points. If the two source points are from the same class, there should exist walking paths and the $\mathbf{P}_{ij}^{sts}$ should be large. Otherwise, they should not be connected via target data and the $\mathbf{P}_{ij}^{sts}$ should equal to zero. An indicator matrix $\mathbf{T}$ is defined as:

$$\mathrm{T}_{ij} = \begin{cases} 1/N_s^c & \mathbf{x}_i^s, \mathbf{x}_j^s \in \Omega_c \\ 0 & \text{else} \end{cases} \tag{16.14}$$

where N_s^c denotes the number of points in class Ω_c. T_{ij} equals to $1/N_s^c$ when the two source data points $\mathbf{x}^s_i$ and $\mathbf{x}^s_j$ are from the same class Ω_c, and is equal to zero if they belong to different class. Therefore, the matrix $\mathbf{T}$ is an indicator matrix that accurately characterizes the category relationships between source data points. Then the matrix $\mathbf{T}$ is used to evaluate the accuracy of matrix $\mathbf{P}^{sts}$. The walking loss of all the source data pairs is then defined as:

$$L_{\text{walk}}\left(\mathbf{X}^s, \mathbf{X}^t; \boldsymbol{\theta}_f, \boldsymbol{\theta}_c\right) = \sum_{\mathbf{x}_i^s, \mathbf{x}_j^s \in \mathbf{X}^s} \sum_{\mathbf{x}^t \in \mathbf{X}^t} L_c\left(\mathrm{P}_{ij}^{sts}, \mathrm{T}_{ij}\right) = \sum_{\mathbf{x}_i^s, \mathbf{x}_j^s \in \mathbf{X}^s} \sum_{\mathbf{x}^t \in \mathbf{X}^t} -\mathrm{T}_{ij} \log \mathrm{P}_{ij}^{sts} \tag{16.15}$$

where L_c is the standard cross-entropy loss function. If the starting and ending source samples are from different classes ($\mathrm{T}_{ij} = 0$) but there is a walk between them ($\mathrm{P}_{ij}^{sts} > 0$), then the cross-entropy loss will be very large.

The walking loss promotes the correct associations between domains, but it cannot guarantee that every target sample have connections with source data. If some target samples are not associated with source data, these samples will not participate the network training. Therefore, the visiting loss is thus introduced to enforce every target sample to be "visited" by source samples, which is defined as:

$$L_{\text{visit}} = L_c\left(\mathbf{p}^{\text{visit}}, \mathbf{v}\right) \tag{16.16}$$

where L_c denotes the cross-entropy loss function, $\mathbf{v} \in \mathrm{R}^{Ntb \times 1}$ is a vector with element equaling to $1/N_{tb}$, N_t^b is the numbers of the target samples in one batch. $\mathbf{p}^{\text{visit}} \in \mathrm{R}^{Ntb \times 1}$ denotes the associations of all the target samples to source domain by column summing of transition probability matrix $\mathbf{P}^{st}$. By using the visiting loss function, all the target samples are constrained to be associated with source samples.

16.5 Experimental Results and Analysis

16.5.1 Results of the Traditional Unsupervised Domain Adaptation Methods

16.5.1.1 Data Description

Hyperspectral remote-sensing images from two sensors were utilized for experiments. One was acquired by NASA EO-1 Hyperion instrument, which collected 242-band data at a 30-m spatial resolution, covering 357–2576-nm range of the spectrum in 10-nm spectral resolution. Removing noisy and uncalibrated bands, we have 145 bands left for experiments. Hyperion collected three multi-temporal images over the Okavango Delta, Botswana (BOT), in May, June, and July 2001, where June and July images have the same field-of-view, and the May image was acquired over an adjacent overlapping area. The three images with 1476×256 pixels include nine identified classes.

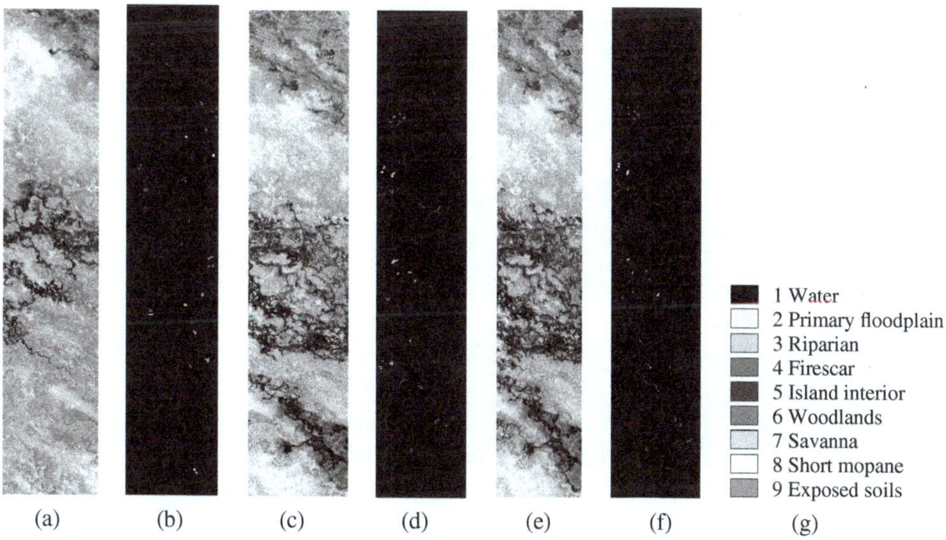

Figure 16.4 BOT data in May, June, and July. (a) BOT image in May. (b) Labeled information of image in May. (c) BOT image in June. (d) Labeled information of image in June. (e) BOT image in July. (f) Labeled information of image in July. (g) Class legend.

These Hyperion images are available from the U.S. Geological Survey, and the reference data were collected by Prof. Crawford in conjunction with the University of Botswana. Any two of the three images can be selected as source and target data. Thus, we have six data pairs that were used for domain adaptation experiments. The grayscale image and labeled information in May, June, and July are shown in Figure 16.4.

The other data set was collected by ITRES-CASI-1500, which acquired 144-band data at a 2.5-m spatial resolution, covering 380–1050 nm portion of the spectrum. An image collected over the University of Houston campus and its neighboring area in 23 June, 2012, was released by the 2013 IEEE GRSS Data Fusion Contest. The data is named "grss_dfc_2013" [63]. The image contains a large shadow region, where four land cover types are located. We used the four classes inside and outside the shadow region in experiments, since the spectra change significantly under shadow. Figure 16.5 displays the grayscale image and the labeled information of the two domain images (shadow area and bright area).

16.5.1.2 Comparison of the UMA and CCCA with Other Traditional Domain Adaptation Methods

We compared UMA [30] and CCCA [25] with five traditional domain adaptation approaches, including semi-supervised transfer component analysis (SSTCA) [15], SA [17], neighborhood-based class centroid alignment (NCCA) [21], CORAL [23], and JDA [20]. In addition, SVM that is trained by the original source data was also employed for comparison, which is named as the dir_SVM. The proposed CCCA is parameter free. For SSTCA, SA, NCCA, and JDA, we chose the best parameters that can achieve the highest accuracies. CORAL is also parameter free.

The overall accuracy (OA) of the eight algorithms on the six data sets is listed in Table 16.1. Several observations can be drawn from comparing these methods. (i) dir_SVM used the source data to classify the target data without domain adaptation strategy. If the data pair (for example BOT "June–July" and "July–June") has small spectral drift, it can obtain satisfactory performance. Otherwise, the classification accuracies are low (such as BOT "June–May" and "July–May"). (ii) All domain adaptation methods obtained higher accuracies than dir_SVM,

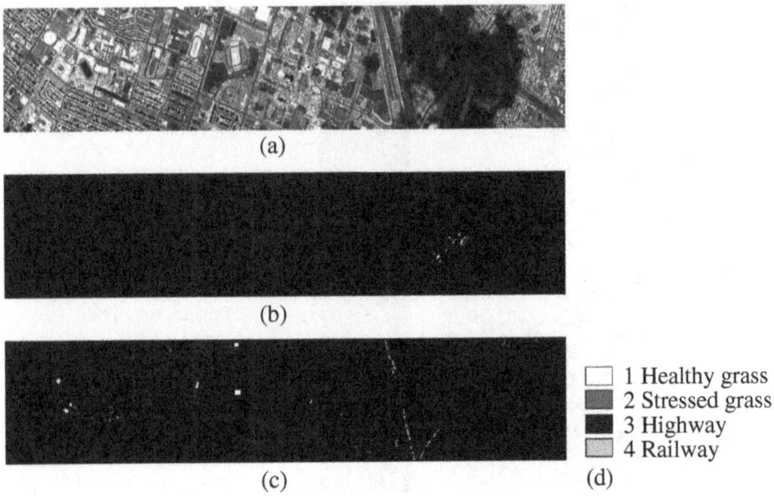

Figure 16.5 Grss_dfc_2013 data. (a) Grayscale image. (b) Labeled information inside the shadow area. (c) Labeled information in the bright area. (d) Class legend.

Table 16.1 The overall accuracy (OA%) of different traditional domain adaptation methods.

Data name	Data Pair: Source image	Data Pair: Target Image	dir_SVM	SSTCA	SA	NCCA	CORAL	JDA	UMA	CCCA
BOT	May	June	62.97	76.91	88.45	93.31	87.38	87.14	92.14	**95.38**
	June	May	48.80	77.27	79.18	65.70	80.44	80.38	86.71	**93.48**
	May	July	73.26	88.81	88.52	91.78	88.30	85.41	92.37	**93.63**
	July	May	56.58	68.48	76.52	71.08	76.96	81.85	86.52	**93.67**
	June	July	87.04	91.63	93.48	95.33	94.22	90.37	96.30	**97.19**
	July	June	87.44	87.53	92.54	94.55	92.89	89.63	96.43	**97.57**
grss_dfc_2013	Shadow	Bright	49.50	70.8	79.78	76.13	81.32	67.86	**89.13**	83.30
	Bright	Shadow	65.16	77.55	90.19	77.21	73.94	76.26	92.39	**92.90**

indicating their positive transfer learning ability. (iii) Compared with the other five domain adaptation methods, UMA and CCCA yielded better performances. For the "difficult" data pairs like BOT "July–May," CCCA obtained more than 35% improvement with respect to dir_SVM and more than 7%~24% to other domain adaptation methods. (iv) Compared with UMA, CCCA obtained higher accuracies on most of the data pairs.

16.5.1.3 Alignment Performance of UMA and CCCA

This experiment is used to show the alignment performance of UMA and CCCA. Figure 16.6 shows scatter plot before and after UMA using data BOT May–June. Different classes were plotted with different colors, and the points in the same class from different domains were plotted with the same color but different shapes. In Figure 16.6a, we can see the spectra of target class 8 is similar to that of source classes 5 and 7, so many pixels were misclassified as class 5 or 7. After UMA domain

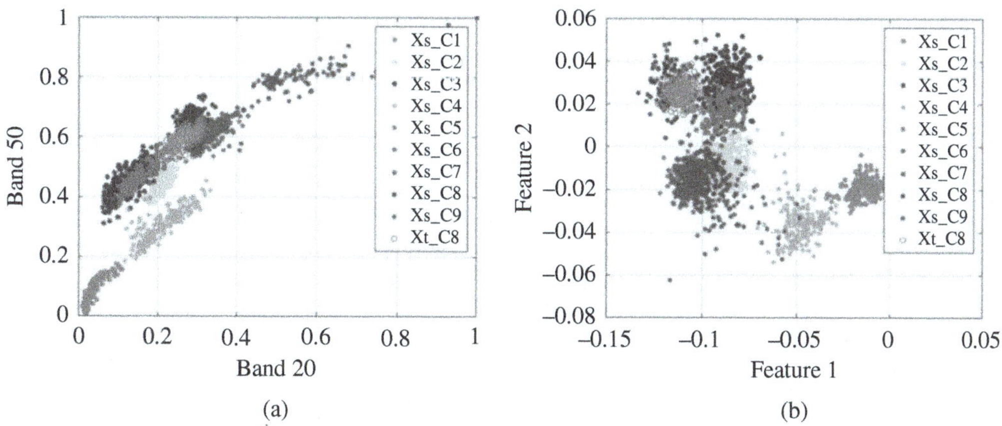

Figure 16.6 Alignment performance of UMA for BOT May–June data. (a) Class 8 before alignment. (b) Class 8 after alignment.

adaptation, as shown in Figure 16.6b, target class 8 has well matched to source class 8 and separated from source classes 5 and 7. Figure 16.7 illustrates the alignment performance of CCCA, where (a) and (b) show the feature alignment of target class 8 using BOT May–June data, (c) and (d) plot all the source and target classes in the same figure using BOT July–May data. Figure 16.7a shows that target class 8 is closer to source class 5 and class 7. In Figure 16.7b, by employing CCCA, target class 8 is not only aligned to source class 8, but also distinguished from source classes 5 and 7. In Figure 16.7c, d, black dots denote the centroids of the source data, and the black stars represent the centroids of target data. Before alignment, noticeable spectral drift can be observed. By applying CCCA, the data distribution of each source class becomes similar to that of the corresponding target class. As shown in Figure 16.7d, both the centroids and variations of each class are well aligned, demonstrating the good alignment performance of the CCCA approach.

16.5.2 Results of Deep-learning-based Unsupervised Domain Adaptation Methods

16.5.2.1 Data Description

Images from two remote-sensing sensors were used for experiments. The first one was multi-temporal BOT hyperspectral images which was described in Section 16.5.1.1. The second data was collected by NASA airborne visible/infrared imaging spectrometer (AVIRIS) instrument on 23 March, 1996, at an 18-m spatial resolution over the area of Kennedy Space Center (KSC) in Florida. It acquires 224-band data that covers 400–2500-nm portion of the spectrum. After removing water absorption and noisy bands, 176 bands were remained. Two spatially disjoint images (KSC1 and KSC2) contain ten common land cover types. The grayscale images and labeled information are shown in Figure 16.8.

16.5.2.2 Comparison of CDA and AAL with Other Deep-learning-based Unsupervised Domain Adaptation Networks

We compared CDA [57] and AAL [46] with four popular domain adaptation networks, including DAN [40], D-CORAL [41], DANN [54], and MADA [53]. In addition, deep neural network with

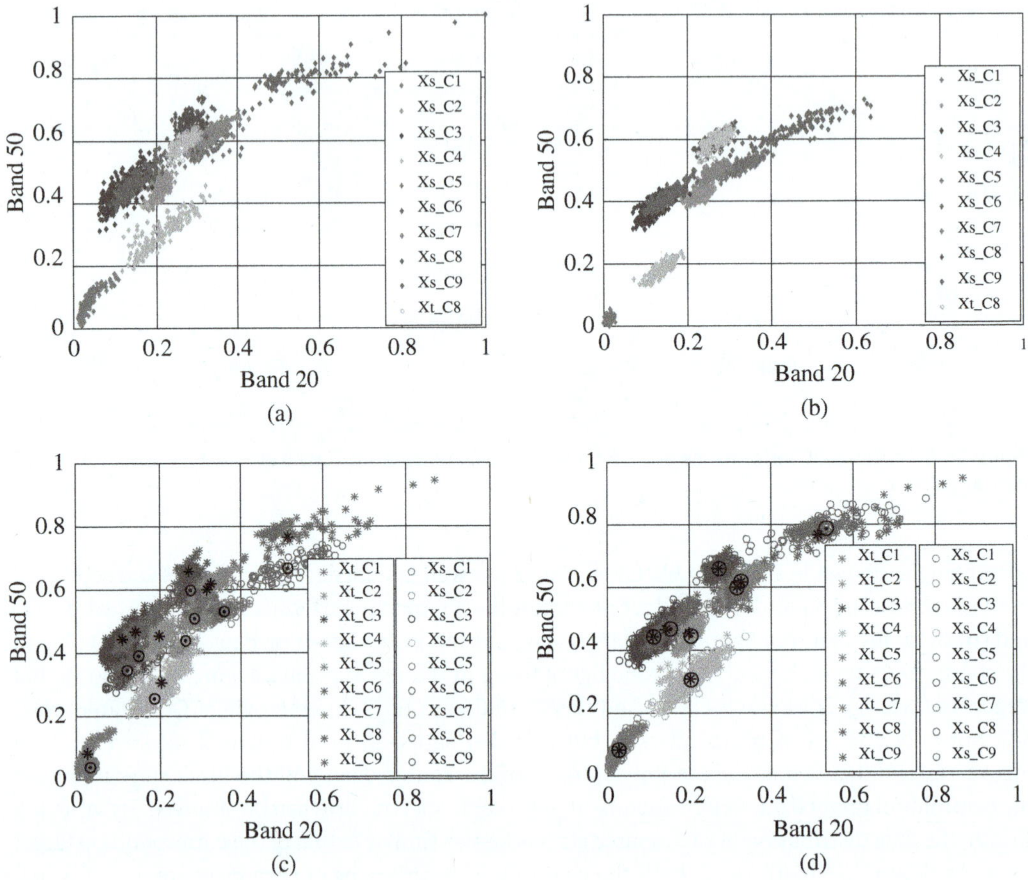

Figure 16.7 Alignment performance of CCCA. (a) BOT May–June Class 8 before alignment. (b) BOT May–June Class 8 after alignment. (c) BOT July–May 9 classes before alignment. (d) BOT July–May 9 classes after alignment.

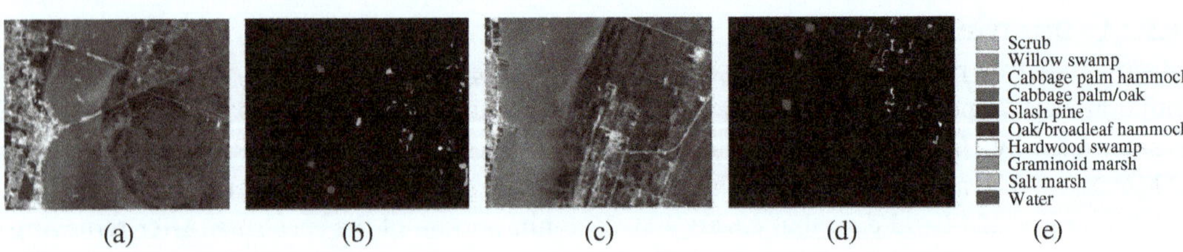

Figure 16.8 KSC1 and KSC2 data. (a) KSC1 image. (b) Labeled information of KSC1 image. (c) KSC2 image. (d) Labeled information of KSC2 image. (e) Class legend.

ReLU activation function (RDNN) that directly uses source data to classify target data was also employed for comparison.

Before the network training, each spectral band was normalized to have standard normal distribution $N(0, 1)$ for both source and target data. Since both domains have the same mean values, this preprocessing method is useful to reduce the overall distribution shift across domains. For a fair

Table 16.2 The overall accuracy (OA%) of different domain adaptation methods.

Data sets		RDNN(NA)	RDNN	DAN	D-CORAL	DANN	MADA	CDA	AAL
BOT	May–June	72.30	89.38	89.80	90.44	87.83	91.51	92.62	**93.79**
	June–May	62.84	80.11	83.57	84.53	78.30	82.12	87.85	**91.14**
	May–July	66.53	86.00	87.52	87.87	86.52	90.29	**91.27**	91.25
	July–May	57.07	68.47	72.97	74.97	69.04	73.10	79.78	**83.59**
	June–July	88.72	92.86	91.79	92.14	92.90	94.76	95.05	**95.30**
	July–June	84.20	89.63	90.26	89.97	89.84	91.54	93.14	**94.50**
KSC	KSC1-KSC3	61.32	67.57	68.11	67.10	70.32	72.99	**74.21**	73.53
	KSC3-KSC1	64.42	62.70	62.52	67.08	65.03	74.69	**76.20**	75.03

comparison, such data processing method was applied to all the compared methods. It is worth noting that we also conducted RDNN with another preprocessing method, which scales the whole data set to $[-1, 1]$. Since this normalization does not have domain adaptation effect like performing $N(0, 1)$ on each spectral band, the RDNN with this processing method was named as RDNN(NA).

The OA of these algorithms on the six data sets is listed in Table 16.2. It can be seen that RDNN outperformed RDNN (NA) for most of the datasets, which demonstrates that performing normal initialization $N(0, 1)$ on each spectral band is useful for domain adaptation. If the spectral shift across domains is small (for example BOT June–July), RDNN can achieve a satisfactory performance. However, for the data pairs that have big spectral drift (such as BOT July–May, KSC1-KSC3, KSC3-KSC1), the accuracies of RDNN are low. Almost all the domain adaptation methods obtained higher accuracies than RDNN, demonstrating their positive transfer learning ability. The DANN can obtain higher accuracies than RDNN for most of the data sets. The MADA outperformed RDNN and DANN, because MADA considers the alignment of each specific class. The CDA and AAL yielded a superior performance than other methods. AAL performed the best on BOT data and CDA obtained the highest accuracies on KSC data.

16.5.2.3 Alignment Performance of CDA and AAL Method

This experiment was used to show the alignment performance of CDA and AAL methods. Figure 16.9 plots the t-SNE embeddings, which were used to visualize the features of the RDNN(NA), CDA, and AAL networks. We used BOT May–June and June–May data pairs for illustration. Figure 16.9a–c plots the features extracted by the three networks on BOT May–June data, and (d–f) plots the features extracted on BOT June–May data. In each figure, different classes were displayed in different grayscales, and the points in the same class from different domains were plotted with the same grayscale but different shapes. From Figure 16.9a, d, it can be observed that some classes have large within-class variances, indicating the feature differences across domains. In addition, different classes may have overlapping features, which produces difficulty of classification. As shown in Figure 16.9b–f, the features of the same class between domains were well aligned after applying CDA and AAL approaches. The two domain adaptation networks also provided good separation of different classes.

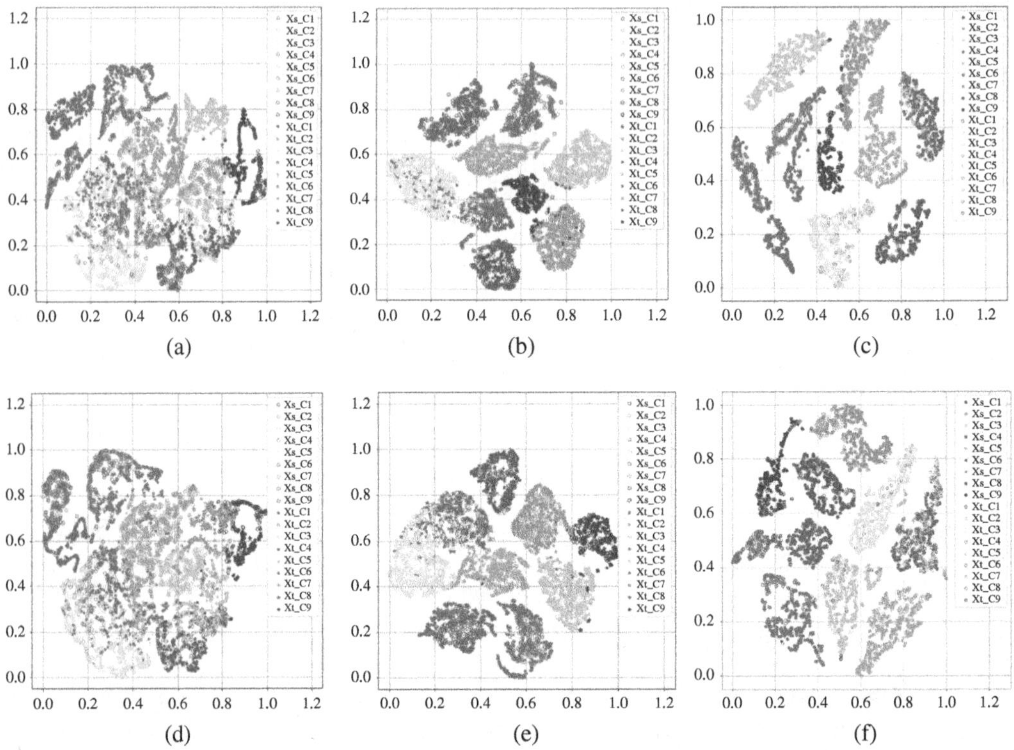

Figure 16.9 The t-SNE visualization of features extracted by RDNN(NA), CDA, and AAL. (a) RDNN(NA) for BOT May–June. (b) CDA for BOT May–June. (c) AAL for BOT May–June. (d) RDNN(NA) for BOT June–May. (e) CDA for BOT June–May. (f) AAL for BOT June–May.

16.6 Conclusions

This chapter presents a review of the unsupervised domain adaptation for classification of hyperspectral images and describes two traditional UDA methods and two deep-learning-based UDA networks. Both traditional and deep-learning-based methods usually employ some feature alignment strategies to obtain domain-invariant features. For the four presented methods, UMA employs the manifold alignment strategy, CCCA utilizes the centroid and covariance alignment strategy, CDA applies adversarial learning and MMD strategies, and AAL exploits associative learning strategy. In the experiments with hyperspectral remote-sensing images, all the four UDA methods perform well on classification of cross-domain hyperspectral images. UMA and CCCA outperform several popular traditional UDA methods, and alignment visualization demonstrates that both methods can obtain aligned features between domains. Comparing CDA and AAL with some other deep-learning-based UDA networks, their superior classification accuracies are demonstrated. The alignment experiment also show that CDA and AAL obtain both domain-invariant and discriminative feature representations.

References

1 Tuia, D., Persello, C., and Bruzzone, L. (2016). Domain adaptation for the classification of remote sensing data: an overview of recent advances. *IEEE Geosci. Remote Sens. Mag.* 4 (2): 41–57.

2 Peng, J., Huang, Y., Sun, W. et al. (2022). Domain adaptation in remote sensing image classification: a survey. *IEEE J. Sel. Top. Appl. Earth Obs. Remote Sens.* 15: 9842–9859.

3 Zhuang, F., Qi, Z., Duan, K. et al. (2021). A comprehensive survey on transfer learning. *Proc. IEEE* 109 (1): 43–76.

4 Niu, S., Liu, Y., Wang, J., and Song, H. (2020). A decade survey of transfer learning (2010–2020). *IEEE Trans. Artif. Intell.* 1 (2): 151–166.

5 Zhou, X. and Prasad, S. (2018). Deep feature alignment neural networks for domain adaptation of hyperspectral data. *IEEE Trans. Geosci. Remote Sens.* 56 (10): 5863–5872.

6 Zhou, L. and Ma, L. (2019). Extreme learning machine-based heterogeneous domain adaptation for classification of hyperspectral images. *IEEE Geosci. Remote Sens. Lett.* 16 (11): 1781–1785.

7 Bruzzone, L. and Prieto, D. (2001). Unsupervised retraining of a maximum likelihood classifier for the analysis of multi-temporal remote sensing images. *IEEE Trans. Geosci. Remote Sens.* 39 (2): 456–460.

8 Bruzzone, L. and Marconcini, M. (2010). Domain adaptation problems: a DASVM classification technique and a circular validation strategy. *IEEE Trans. Pattern Anal. Mach. Intell.* 32 (5): 770–787.

9 Bahirat, K., Bovolo, F., Bruzzone, L., and Chaudhuri, S. (2012). A novel domain adaptation Bayesian classifier for updating land-cover maps with class differences in source and target domains. *IEEE Trans. Geosci. Remote Sens.* 50 (7): 2810–2826.

10 Rajan, S., Ghosh, J., and Crawford, M. (2006). Exploiting class hierarchy for knowledge transfer in hyperspectral data. *IEEE Trans. Geosci. Remote Sens.* 44 (11): 3408–3417.

11 Kim, W. and Crawford, M. (2010). Adaptive classification for hyperspectral image data using manifold regularization kernel machines. *IEEE Trans. Geosci. Remote Sens.* 48 (11): 4110–4121.

12 Sun, Z., Wang, C., Wang, H., and Li, J. (2013). Learn multiple-kernel SVMs for domain adaptation in hyperspectral data. *IEEE Geosci. Remote Sens. Lett.* 10 (5): 1224–1228.

13 Zhong, S. and Zhang, Y. (2020). An iterative training sample updating approach for domain adaptation in hyperspectral image classification. *IEEE Geosci. Remote Sens. Lett.* 18 (10): 1821–1825.

14 Pan, S., Tsang, I., Kwok, J., and Yang, Q. (2011). Domain adaptation via transfer component analysis. *IEEE Trans. Neural Netw.* 22 (2): 199–210.

15 Matasci, G., Volpi, M., Kanevski, M. et al. (2015). Semisupervised transfer component analysis for domain adaptation in remote sensing image classification. *IEEE Trans. Geosci. Remote Sens.* 53 (7): 3550–3564.

16 Peng, J., Sun, W., Ma, L., and Du, Q. (2019). Discriminative transfer joint matching for domain adaptation in hyperspectral image classification. *IEEE Geosci. Remote Sens. Lett.* 16 (6): 972–976.

17 Frenando, B, Habrad, A., and Sebban, M. (December 2013). Unsupervised visual domain adaptation using subspace alignment. *IEEE International Conference on Computer Vision*. Sydney, Australia, Dec. 1–8, 2013, pp. 2960–2967.

18 Wei, W., Li, W., Zhang, L. et al. (2019). Robust hyperspectral image domain adaptation with noisy labels. *IEEE Geosci. Remote Sens. Lett.* 16 (7): 1135–1139.

19 Yang, W., Peng, J., and Sun, W. (2020). Ideal regularized discriminative multiple kernel subspace alignment for domain adaptation in hyperspectral image classification. *IEEE J. Sel. Top. Appl. Earth Obs. Remote Sens.* 13: 5833–5846.

20 Long, M., Wang, J., Ding, G. et al. (December 2013). Transfer feature learning with joint distribution adaptation. *IEEE International Conference on Computer Vision*. Sydney, Australia, Dec. 1–8, 2013, pp. 2200–2207.

21 Zhu, L. and Ma, L. (2016). Class centroid alignment based domain adaptation for classification of remote sensing images. *Pattern Recogn. Lett.* 83: 124–132.

22 Luo, C. and Ma, L. (2018). Manifold regularized distribution adaptation for classification of remote sensing images. *IEEE Access* 6 (1): 4697–4708.

23 Sun, B., Feng, J., and Saenko, K. (2016). Correlation alignment for unsupervised domain adaptation. arXiv preprint. arXiv:1612.01939.

24 Wei, T., Fan, W., Peng, J., Sur, W.2019). Correlation alignment based on sparse matrix transform for unsupervised domain adaptation in hyperspectral image classification. *IEEE International Geoscience and Remote Sensing Symposium*. Yokohama, Japan, Jul. 28–Aug. 2, 2019, pp. 2698–2701.

25 Ma, L., Crawford, M., Zhu, L., and Liu, Y. (2019). Centroid and covariance alignment-based domain adaptation for unsupervised classification of remote sensing images. *IEEE Trans. Geosci. Remote Sens.* 57 (4): 2305–2323.

26 Ham, J., Lee, D., and Saul, L. (January 2005). Semisupervised alignment of manifolds. *International Workshop on Artificial Intelligence and Statistics*. Bridgetown, Barbados, Jan. 6–8, 2005. pp. 120–127.

27 Yang, H. and Crawford, M. (2015). Spectral and spatial proximity-based manifold alignment for multitemporal hyperspectral image classification. *IEEE Trans. Geosci. Remote Sens.* 53 (11): 1–14.

28 Yang, H. and Crawford, M. (2016). Domain adaptation with preservation of manifold geometry for hyperspectral image classification. *IEEE J. Sel. Top. Appl. Earth Obs. Remote Sens.* 9 (2): 543–555.

29 Tuia, D., Volpi, M., Trolliet, M., and Camps-Valls, G. (2014). Semisupervised manifold alignment of multimodal remote sensing images. *IEEE Trans. Geosci. Remote Sens.* 52 (12): 7708–7720.

30 Ma, L., Luo, C., Peng, J., and Du, Q. (2019). Unsupervised manifold alignment for cross-domain classification of remote sensing images. *IEEE Geosci. Remote Sens. Lett.* 16 (10): 1650–1654.

31 Qin, Y., Bruzzone, L., Li, B., and Ye, Y. (2019). Cross-domain collaborative learning via cluster canonical correlation analysis and random walker for hyperspectral image classification. *IEEE Trans. Geosci. Remote Sens.* 57 (6): 3952–3966.

32 Li, X., Zhang, L., Du, B., and Zhang, L. (2019). On gleaning knowledge from cross domains by sparse subspace correlation analysis for hyperspectral image classification. *IEEE Trans. Geosci. Remote Sens.* 57 (6): 3204–3220.

33 Zhang, L., Zuo, W., and Zhang, D. (2016). Latent sparse domain transfer learning for visual adaptation. *IEEE Trans. Image Process.* 25 (3): 1177–1191.

34 Shi, Q., Du, B., and Zhang, L. (2015). Domain adaptation for remote sensing image classification: a low-rank reconstruction and instance weighting label propagation inspired algorithm. *IEEE Trans. Geosci. Remote Sens.* 53 (10): 5677–5689.

35 Zhang, Y., Li, W., Tao, R. et al. (2021). Cross-Scene hyperspectral image classification with discriminative cooperative alignment. *IEEE Trans. Geosci. Remote Sens.* 59 (11): 9646–9660.

36 Gross, W., Tuia, D., Soergel, U., and Middelmann, W. (2019). Nonlinear feature normalization for hyperspectral domain adaptation and mitigation of nonlinear effects. *IEEE Trans. Geosci. Remote Sens.* 57 (8): 5975–5990.

37 Zhang, J., Li, W., Sun, W. et al. (2024). Locality robust domain adaptation for cross-scene hyperspectral image classification. *Expert Syst. Appl.* 238: 121822.

38 Wei, H., Ma, L., Liu, Y., and Du, Q. (2021). Combining multiple classifiers for domain adaptation of remote sensing image classification. *IEEE J. Sel. Top. Appl. Earth Obs. Remote Sens.* 14: 1832–1847.

39 Persello, C. and Bruzzone, L. (2016). Kernel-based domain-invariant feature selection in hyperspectral images for transfer learning. *IEEE Trans. Geosci. Remote Sens.* 54 (5): 2615–2626.

40 Long, M., Cao, Y., Wang, J., and Jordan, M. (2015). Learning transferable features with deep adaptation networks. https://arxiv.org/abs/1502.02791. Accessed date: May 27, 2015.

41 Sun, B., Saenko, K. (2016). Deep CORAL: correlation alignment for deep domain adaptation. http://arxiv.org/abs/1607.01719v1. Accessed date: July 6, 2016.

42 Ma, L. and Song, J. (2017). Deep neural network-based domain adaptation for classification of remote sensing images. *J. Appl. Remote. Sens.* 11 (1): 042612.

43 Song, S., Yu, H., Miao, Z. et al. (2019). Domain adaptation for convolutional neural networks-based remote sensing scene classification. *IEEE Geosci. Remote Sens. Lett.* 16 (8): 1324–1328.

44 Garea, A., Heras, D., and F. Argüello F. (2019). TCANet for domain adaptation of hyperspectral images. *Remote Sens* 11 (19): 2289.

45 Wang, Z., Du, B., Shi, Q., and Tu, W. (2019). Domain adaptation with discriminative distribution and manifold embedding for hyperspectral image classification. *IEEE Geosci. Remote Sens. Lett.* 16 (7): 1155–1159.

46 Chen, M., Ma, L., Wang, W., and Du, Q. (2020). Augmented associative learning-based domain adaptation for classification of hyperspectral remote sensing images. *IEEE J. Sel. Top. Appl. Earth Obs. Remote Sens.* 13: 6236–6248.

47 Wang, W., Ma, L., Chen, M., and Du, Q. (2021). Joint correlation alignment based graph neural network for domain adaptation of multitemporal hyperspectral remote sensing images. *IEEE J. Sel. Top. Appl. Earth Obs. Remote Sens.* 14: 3170–3184.

48 Zhang, Y., Li, W., Zhang, M. et al. (2023). Topological structure and semantic information transfer network for cross-scene hyperspectral image classification. *IEEE J. Sel. Top. Appl. Earth Obs. Remote Sens.* 34 (6): 2817–2830

49 Li, Z., Xu, Q., Ma, L. et al. (2023). Supervised contrastive learning-based unsupervised domain adaptation for hyperspectral image classification. *IEEE Trans. Geosci. Remote Sens.* 61: 5524017.

50 Fang, Z., Yang, Y., Li, Z. et al. (2022). Confident learning-based domain adaptation for hyperspectral image classification. *IEEE Trans. Geosci. Remote Sens.* 60: 5527116.

51 Pan, Z., Yu, W., Yi, X. et al. (2019). Recent progress on generative adversarial networks (GANs): a survey. *IEEE Access* 7: 36322–36333.

52 Tzeng, E., Hoffman, J., Saenko, K., Darrell, T. (2017). Adversarial discriminative domain adaptation. *IEEE Conference on Computer Vision and Pattern Recognition*. Hawaii, USA, July 21–26, 2017. pp. 2962–2971.

53 Pei, Z., Cao, Z., Long, M., and Wang, J. (2018). Multi-adversarial domain adaptation. http://arxiv.org/abs/1809.02176. Accessed date: Sept. 4, 2018.

54 Ganin, Y., Ustinova, E., Ajakan, H. et al. (2016). Domain-adversarial training of neural networks. *J. Mach. Learn. Res.* 17 (59): 1–35.

55 Elshamli, A., Taylor, G., Berg, A., and Areibi, S. (2017). Domain adaptation using representation learning for the classification of remote sensing images. *IEEE J. Sel. Top. Appl. Earth Obs. Remote Sens.* 10 (9): 4198–4209.

56 Bejiga, M. and Melgani, F. (2018). An adversarial approach to cross-sensor hyperspectral data classification. *IEEE International Geoscience and Remote Sensing Symposium*. Valencia, Spain, July 22–27, 2018, pp. 3575–3578.

57 Liu, Z., Ma, L., and Du, Q. (2021). Class-wise distribution adaptation for unsupervised classification of hyperspectral remote sensing images. *IEEE Trans. Geosci. Remote Sens.* 59 (1): 508–521.

58 Deng, B., Jia, S., and Shi, D. (2020). Deep metric learning-based feature embedding for hyperspectral image classification. *IEEE Trans. Geosci. Remote Sens.* 58 (2): 1422–1435.

59 Ma, X., Mou, X., Wang, J. et al. (2021). Cross-dataset hyperspectral image classification based on adversarial domain adaptation. *IEEE Trans. Geosci. Remote Sens.* 59 (5): 4179–4190.

60 Huang, Y., Peng, J., Chen, N. et al. (2023). Cross-scene wetland mapping on hyperspectral remote sensing images using adversarial domain adaptation network. *ISPRS J. Photogramm. Remote Sens.* 203: 37–54.

61 Yu, C., Liu, C., Song, M., and Chang, C. (2022). Unsupervised domain adaptation with content-wise alignment for hyperspectral imagery classification. *IEEE Geosci. Remote Sens. Lett.* 19: 1–5.

62 Yu, C., Liu, C., Yu, H. et al. (2021). Unsupervised domain adaptation with dense-Based compaction for hyperspectral imagery. *IEEE J. Sel. Top. Appl. Earth Obs. Remote Sens.* 14: 12287–12299.

63 Debes, C., Merentitis, A., Heremans, R. et al. (2014). Hyperspectral and LiDAR data fusion: outcome of the 2013 GRSS data fusion contest. *IEEE J. Sel. Top. Appl. Earth Obs. Remote Sens.* 7 (6): 2405–2418.

17

Lightweight Models for Hyperspectral Image Classification

Hongmin Gao[1], *Shufang Xu*[2], *Zhonghao Chen*[3], *and Yiyan Zhang*[3]

[1] *School of Computer Application Technology, Hohai University, Nanjing, China*
[2] *School of Applied Electronic Technology, Anhui Normal University, Wuhu, China*
[3] *School of Computer and Information, Hohai University, Nanjing, China*

17.1 Introduction

HSI has hundreds of continuous narrow-band spectral information (high spectral resolution), which reflects the absorption and reflection of solar reflection light in different wavelength bands (i.e., visible light, infrared, or near-infrared) by the imaged ground object [1, 2]. These rich features, like fingerprint information of imaged objects, can realize an accurate detection (pixel level) of objects. Therefore, HSI has been widely used in many fields and achieved promising results, such as agricultural application [3], water quality monitoring [4], mineral distribution and composition analysis [5, 6], natural disaster prediction [7], and military field [8]. Among them, HSI classification (HSIC) is an extremely important research direction in HSI analysis [9–12].

In the early research of HSIC, due to different ground objects that can reflect corresponding spectral differences in the HSI, a large number of researchers put forward plenty of classification methods based on the spectral characteristics of a single pixel and achieved good classification results [12–14]. However, the high-dimensional data characteristics of HSI not only bring rich features but also lead to the Hughes phenomenon [15], which significantly limited the performance of HSIC [16]. Therefore, the extreme learning machine (ELM) [17] and support vector machine (SVM) [18] were put forward, which solved this problem to a certain extent. However, the spectral features contained in single pixel are easily blurred by environmental factors (i.e., salt–pepper noise) and the consequent problem of intraclass variability (and interclass similarity), which seriously hinders the classification performance of the above methods [19]. In addition, a single pixel independently will inevitably lose the spatial correlation information in the image, so the spatial features of hyperspectral images (HSIs) have been paid more and more attention by researchers. Considering that adjacent pixels in HSIs generally have similar spectral characteristics and prone to be in the same category, a series of classifiers with neighborhood blocks centered by labeled pixels as input have been proposed [20, 21]. Experiments show that the complementary information of spatial features makes the classifiers achieve better classification performance. Although these traditional machine learning methods have achieved good classification performance, the shallow handcrafted features utilized by machine learning are seriously lacking in representation capacity.

Machine-Learning-Based Hyperspectral Image Processing, First Edition. Edited by Bing Zhang.

In recent years, the excellent performance of deep learning (DL) has made it widely studied in many fields. For instance, natural language processing (NLP), computer vision (CV), and emotion analysis. In the preliminary exploration of applying DL-based methods to HSIC, the deep belief network (DBN) [22], the stacked autoencoder (SAE) [23], and their derivative models [24, 25] were introduced for HSIC. However, these methods only use the spectral information of the HSI, which is based on the premise that each pixel of the HSI is pure. In comparison, the convolutional neural network (CNN) is the most widely studied and applied structure. Its translational invariance, when extracting image features (linear and non-linear features), has the parameters sharing characteristics that make it powerful in image feature excavation. In the literature, there is a massive amount of work that applied CNN to HSI feature extraction to enhance the performance of HSIC [26–28]. On the one hand, due to the powerful extraction capabilities of the CNN for the features of complex hyperspectral data, the HSI classifier based on the CNN achieves excellent classification performance. On the other hand, the CNN-based classification models have an immensely flexible structure, which makes them well adapted to the data input of different structures and the flexible extraction of different dimensional features (spatial and spectral domains) [29–31].

Therefore, considering the spatial texture information of HSIs, the 2D-CNN model is widely introduced to HSIC [32, 33]. For example, Li et al. [32] proposed a deep 2D-CNN model, where a large number of parameters are trained by pixel pairs, and, the final classification results were obtained by voting strategy. Paoletti et al. [33] designed a deep pyramidal residual network, which not only gets more feature maps by increasing the dimension of the feature maps gradually but also reduces the computational burden of the model. Then, Pan et al. [28] used 1D and 2D CNN to extract spectral and spatial features, respectively, and fused the extracted features for classification. In addition, Chen et al. [26] and Ben et al. [34] introduced 3D-CNN based model for HSIC, which uses the 3D convolution kernel to extract spectral–spatial joint features robustly. However, although the 3D-CNN model achieved good classification performance, 3D convolution operations will greatly increase the computational complexity and consume a lot of computing resources. For this reason, 3D and 2D hierarchical extraction strategies of spectral–spatial features were proposed [35–37]. These 3D/2D hybrid models can extract spectral and spatial features in turn, which can alleviate the computational burden caused by only using full 3D convolution to some extent. With the deepening of the network model, simply deepening the network cannot further improve the classification performance, but will lead to the gradient vanishing problem [38]. Moreover, due to the scarcity of HIS-annotated samples, a large number of learnable parameters of the depth model cannot be fully trained, which results in an overfitting phenomenon [39]. To solve these problems, residual structure [40] is widely used in deep CNN to alleviate the gradient vanishing problem. For instance, in [41], a spectral–spatial residual network (SSRN) was proposed with two consecutive residual blocks (RBs) in the spectral and spatial extraction module which can perform well under the condition of small samples especially. In the meantime, Song et al. [42] constructed a deep feature fusion network (DFFN) with three different stages of residual modules to achieve complementary feature extraction, and finally fused the three levels of features before the classification. Inspired by the residual structure, a dense network [43] based on more sufficient bridging is proposed, which can not only effectively alleviate the problems such as the disappearance of the gradient, but also make use of the front layer information of the network repeatedly. Then, in [44], a dual-channel dense network was proposed to extract spectral and spatial features consecutively with several dense modules.

Although the models described above have achieved promising classification performance, they tend to consume a large number of model parameters, which limits the further improvement of classification accuracy, especially under the condition of small samples. In order to achieve high-performance detection with limited model parameters, a series of lightweight detection methods have been proposed. [45–49]. For example, Ahmad et al. [45] introduced an efficient 3-D CNN architecture characterized by reduced parameters and faster convergence time, while maintaining outstanding performance. Jia et al. [46] suggested a novel lightweight CNN (LWCNN) tailored for HSI classification. By employing spatial–spectral Schroedinger eigenmaps (SSSEs) and dual-scale convolution modules, they managed to trim down model parameters while capturing essential features, thereby enhancing efficiency and robustness. In a similar vein, Meng et al. [47] devised a lightweight spectral–spatial convolution module (LS2CM) as an alternative to conventional convolutional layers. This LS2CM substantially diminishes network parameters and computational complexity in terms of multiply accumulate operations (MACs), all while maintaining or even enhancing classification performance. Cui et al. [48] devised a lightweight spectral–spatial attention network (LSSAN) leveraging MobileNetV3 architecture, which effectively cuts down computational overhead and parameters while upholding exceptional accuracy. Wang et al. [49] introduced a hybrid convolutional model that integrates a single-layer 3-D CNN and 2-D CNN to streamline model complexity. They innovatively designed the SS-GloRe-Unit to capture global features, resulting in outstanding classification outcomes.

Furthermore, classification models based on lightweight convolutional operations have been extensively explored. These encompass models utilizing small convolutional kernels to accomplish lightweight HSIC tasks [50], substituting depth-separable convolution for regular convolution to diminish model complexity [51], and adopting inflated convolution for lightweight multi-scale spatial feature extraction [52]. Subsequently, we will illustrate an example showcasing the application of the aforementioned three lightweight convolutional kernel operations to the task of HSIC.

17.2 Lightweight Feature Extraction-based Hyperspectral Image Classification

17.2.1 Small Convolution and Feature Reuse for Spectral-Spatial Classification of Hyperspectral Images

We propose a small convolution and feature reuse (SC-FR) module for HSIs classification. The framework of the proposed method is shown in Figure 17.1. As can be seen, the principal component analysis (PCA) is first adopted on the spectral domain to reduce the dimensionality and extract the most informative N components of spectral information, which can eliminate some redundant

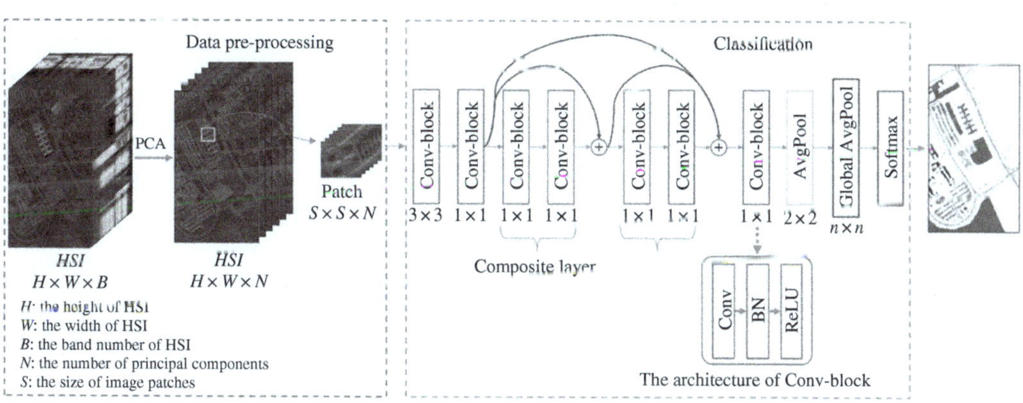

Figure 17.1 Framework of the proposed HSI classification method.

information at the same time. Then, to utilize both spectral and spatial information, $S \times S \times N$ image patches centered on labeled pixels are extracted as the inputs of the CNN, where $S \times S$ is the spatial size of image patches. In order to better achieve the HSIC, He initialization method, ReLU activation function, Softmax classifier, and BN algorithm are adopted in the proposed network. In the following, the aforementioned materials and network architecture of the proposed method will be introduced in detail.

17.2.1.1 Materials of Method

It is a key step for optimizing network model to initialize network parameters reasonably. Improper initialization of parameters will deteriorate the convergence effect of the model and even lead to the gradient dispersion. He et al. [53] proposed the He initialization method, which made the weights obey the Gaussian distribution with zero mean and $2/n_i$ variance, as below:

$$W \sim G\left[0, \sqrt{\frac{2}{n_i}}\right], \quad n_i = k_i^2 d_{i-1} \tag{17.1}$$

where k_i is the size of convolution kernels in the i-th convolution layer and d_{i-1} is the number of convolution kernels in the $i-1$ convolution layer. This method can solve the gradient explosion problem in forward propagation and the gradient vanishing problem in back propagation effectively by making the variance of output of each layer in the network equal as far as possible, so that the signal can be transmitted deeper in the network and the convergence speed of the network is accelerated.

ReLU activation function. The activation function can obviously improve the representation ability of the model, and complex multi-classification problems can be better solved by using it. In 2010, Hinton et al. [54] proposed a rectified linear unit (ReLU), which is currently one of the most commonly used activation functions in CNN and other DL models. ReLU is defined as below:

$$\mathrm{Re}\,LU(x) = \max\{0, x\} = \begin{cases} x & \text{if } x \geq 0 \\ 0 & \text{if } x < 0 \end{cases} \tag{17.2}$$

where x is the input of ReLU function.

Softmax classifier. The classifier of CNN is usually Softmax function. The principle of Softmax classifier (17.3) is to take the exponent of the linear prediction results to make it non-negative, then normalize the exponential value to the [0, 1] interval, get the corresponding probability of each class, and finally take the class with the highest probability as the output of the model. For example, the prediction is that the probability of the fourth class is 90% and the sixth class is 5% in the prediction results, so the output of the model is the label corresponding to the fourth class.

$$p_i = \frac{\exp(z_i)}{\sum_{j=1}^{m} \exp(z_j)}, \quad i = 1, \ldots, m \tag{17.3}$$

where m is the total of labeled classes, z_i represents the linear prediction result of the ith class, p_i indicates the probability that the input sample belongs to the ith class.

BN algorithm. Ioffe et al. proposed batch normalization (BN) in 2015, that is, BN algorithm. It is usually used before activation function to make the inputs of activation function with zero mean and unit variance, thus making the distribution of the input signal remain stable and speed up the training process. BN algorithm is used to process mini-batch data:

$$BN(x) = \frac{x - \mu_B}{\sqrt{\sigma_B^2 + \varepsilon}} \cdot \gamma + \beta \tag{17.4}$$

where μ_B and σ_B^2 are the mean and variance of the mini-batch, respectively, γ and β are learnable parameters. The ε represents a very small number, usually 10^{-3}, so as to prevent the variance to zero.

17.2.1.2 Small Convolution

Many recent CNN-based HSIC models extensively adopted small convolution kernels (1×1 and 3×3) in their CNN. Small convolution has become the mainstream at the research of CNN-based HSIC. Large convolution kernels can generate large receptive field, but it also means that a large number of parameters needed to be learned. As a result, traditional convolution layers have large number of learned parameters, which may cause high computation cost. In general, compared with large convolution kernels, the smaller ones have two advantages. The one is that small convolution kernels can enhance the representation ability of CNN model in the case of the same size of receptive field. Small convolution kernels can achieve the same size receptive field as large ones through multi-layer stacking, thereby increasing the network depth. Accordingly, to some extent, it makes the CNN model extract discriminative features more effectively and strengthen the generalization performance of the model.

The other advantage is that the number of network parameters will be greatly reduced by using small convolution kernels. For the lth convolution layer, assume that the size of convolution kernels is $k \times k$. And the number of input and output channels is C_{in} and C_{out}, respectively. The height and the width of output feature maps are H and W, respectively. The number of parameters P and floating-point operations (FLOPs) F (without regard to bias) in the lth convolution layer can be defined as follows:

$$P = k \times k \times C_{in} \times C_{out} \tag{17.5}$$

$$F = H \times W \times P \tag{17.6}$$

Assume $C_{in} = C_{out} = C$, according to formula (5), the number of parameters ($25C^2$) in a 5×5 convolution layer is about 2.8 times of that ($9C^2$) in a 3×3 convolution layer and 25 times of that (C^2) in a 1×1 convolution layer. Furthermore, the number of parameters of two stacked 3×3 convolution layers is $18C^2$, which is fewer than that of a 5×5 convolution layer. It should be noted that two stacked 3×3 convolution kernels can achieve the same size of receptive field as a 5×5 convolution kernel. And two stacked 3×3 convolution layers can extract more discriminative features than a 5×5 convolution layer due to the output of each convolution layer which will be typically processed by activation function. In a word, the small convolution kernels deserve to be favored when designing a CNN model.

17.2.1.3 Network Architecture

The architecture of the proposed CNN is shown in Figure 17.1. As can be seen, all convolution layers are filled with small convolution kernels, and all convolution layers are 1×1 convolution layer except the first one. First, a 3×3 convolution layer is adopted to extract both spatial contextual features and spectral features of image patches. Then, the extracted features are integrated by a 1×1 convolution layer. After that, the integrated features are fed into an SC-FR module and passed on to a 1×1 convolution layer which is followed by an average pooling layer. In the SC-FR module, through cross-layer connection (the cross line in Figure 17.2), the input and output feature maps of the first composite layer are concatenated and used as the input of the next composite layer. Similarly, the input and output feature maps of the second composite layer are concatenated and input to the following 1×1 convolution layer which is followed by an average pooling layer

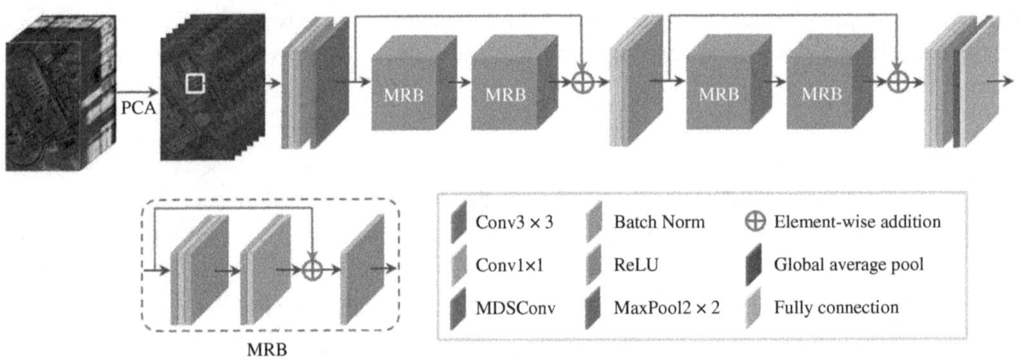

Figure 17.2 Framework of the proposed MSRN-based HSI classification method.

with kernel 2 × 2, stride 2 × 2. Finally, a global average pool layer is to summarize all the high-level features and the predicted results are output by the Softmax layer. What is more, the outputs of each convolution layer are processed by BN algorithm and ReLU, that is, Conv → BN → ReLU. For all the convolution layers, stride is set to 1 × 1 and padding is not applied, which means the size of feature maps will remain unchanged after processing by a convolution layer. Referring to the network in [35], the channel number of the first convolution layer is set to g, and that of all the other convolution layers is set to 2g. With the increase of g value, the channel number of each convolution layer is also increasing gradually, so g is called growth rate. Different growth rate (g value) means different number of new features received by each layer. As a result, we can enhance the generalization performance of the network by adjusting the growth rate.

17.2.2 Mixed Depthwise Convolution for Hyperspectral Image Classification

Some previous studies [55–59] have demonstrated that taking full advantage of different-scale information is helpful for HSIC. However, those methods using single-scale inputs usually only execute multi-scale feature extraction once, which is hard to comprehensively learn spectral–spatial feature representations at different scales, while those methods using multi-scale inputs always cause extra computation cost and longer training time. Furthermore, many state-of-the-art HSIC methods have a great number of training parameters, which will cause high computation cost.

To address the above-mentioned two issues, we design a novel multi-scale residual network (MSRN) model for HSIC, which is able to carry out multi-scale feature extraction at different levels of the network. Figure 17.1 shows the framework of the proposed classification methods. There exist some redundant bands and they can only provide very little useful information, which means they make little contribution on classification task. They may even cause negative impact on final classification because of noise existing in them. Therefore, first of all, the PCA is adopted to remove some noise and those unimportant dimensions from the original HSI. In this way, most of the useful information is retained. With that retained information, CNNs are able to extract enough discriminative features for correct classification of ground objects. Moreover, because many dimensions are removed, PCA reduces the computation cost of deep network to a certain extent. Then, image patches centered on labeled pixels are obtained and fed into the MSRN, where some patches are used for training the network and the rest of the patches are used for evaluating the performance of the trained network. Finally, the labels of test pixels can be predicted by the trained MSRN. As can be seen from Figure 17.2, the MRB is the main part of our proposed MSRN. And the MDSConv layer is the main part of the MRB, which can greatly reduce parameter number of the network. The architectures of MDSConv and MRB are detailed as follows.

17.2.2.1 MDSConv

Depthwise separable convolution is attracting increasing attention to modern CNN architecture design studies because it can not only greatly reduce the number of network parameters, but also can almost not lose the accuracy, or even increase the accuracy. Figure 17.3 shows ordinary convolution, depthwise separable convolution, and MDSConv operation. As we can see, the depthwise separable convolution divides the ordinary convolution into two parts. One is the depthwise convolution, the other is pointwise convolution, which is the 1 × 1 convolution in essence. The former

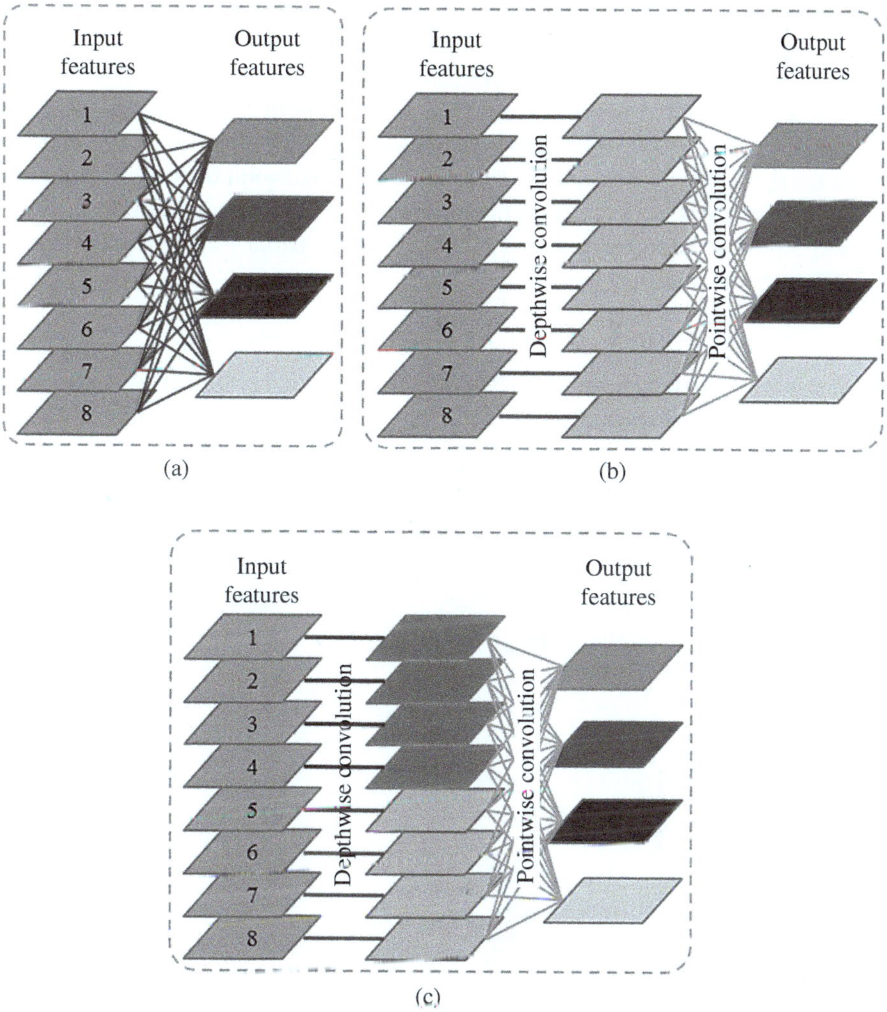

Figure 17.3 Three kinds of convolution operation: (a) Ordinary convolution, (b) Depthwise separable convolution, (c) Proposed MDSConv. Each parallelogram means one certain channel of the feature map.

convolves each channel of the input feature map separately, thus capturing the spatial features of each channel. The latter integrates all the extracted spatial features and learns the channel correlation information of input feature map. The ordinary 2-D convolution operation takes all the channels of the corresponding region into account simultaneously. In order to achieve multi-scale feature extraction, we mix up the 1×1 filter and 3×3 filter into a depthwise convolution operation and the number of two types of filters is equal, which is half of the channel number of input feature map. In other words, for each feature map, half of its channels are convolved with 1×1 filter and the rest of the channels are convolved with 3×3 filter. As shown in Figure 17.3c, the MDSConv is developed by incorporating the mixed depthwise convolution into the depthwise separable convolution. In this way, the spatial correction can be learned at different scales.

Let C_{in}, C_{out} denote the number of input channels and output channels of an ordinary 3×3 convolutional layer, respectively. Without considering bias, the parameter number P1 of this layer is $C_{in} \times C_{out} \times 3 \times 3$. Assume a depthwise separable convolution layer with 3×3 depthwise convolution has the same input and output channel number as the ordinary 3×3 convolutional layer. Then the number of parameters P2 in this layer can be calculated as $C_{in} \times 3 \times 3 + C_{in} \times C_{out}$. And the parameter number P3 of a proposed MDSConv layer can be calculated as $C_{in}/2 \times 3 \times 3 + C_{in}/2 \times 1 \times 1 + C_{in} \times C_{out}$. For example, as shown in Figure 17.4, we assume that both C_{in} and C_{out} are 64, then the P1, P2, and P3 are 36864, 4672, and 4416, respectively. Therefore, the parameters of a MDSConv layer are fewer than 1/8 of that of an ordinary 3×3 convolutional layer. It means the proposed MDSConv can speed up the training and test process. In addition, the MDSConv allows the proposed MSRN to learn more discriminative spectral–spatial feature representation for better accuracy.

17.2.2.2 MRB

The residual learning is introduced in our study to construct the deep hierarchical architecture with good generalization performance. Figure 17.5a gives the architecture of the ordinary RB. As can be

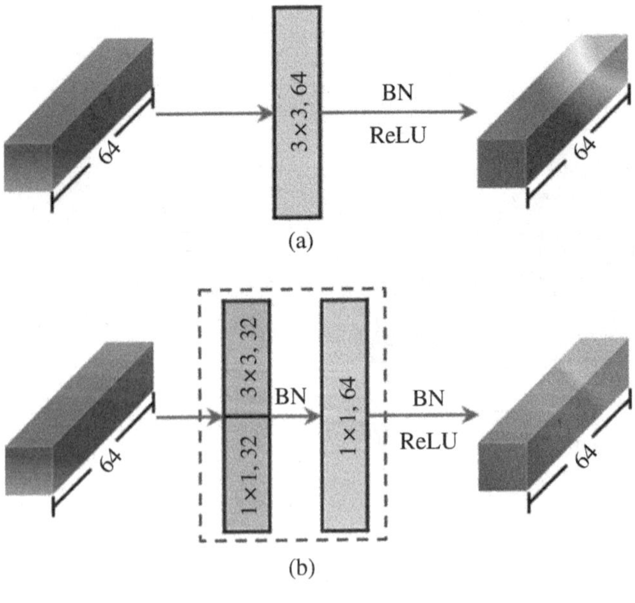

Figure 17.4 Example for comparing the parameter number between an ordinary 3 × 3 convolutional layer and an MDSConv layer. (a) Ordinary convolutional layer. (b) MDSConv layer.

observed, the ordinary RB contains two 3 × 3 convolutional layers and a shortcut connection (also known as skip connection). In addition, the BN (Batch Norm) is usually applied after the convolutional layer and before activation function, so as to accelerate convergence of the network. Each RB can be expressed as:

$$F(X) = f(G(X) + H(X)) \tag{17.7}$$

where X and $F(X)$ denote the input and output of the RB, respectively, $f(\cdot)$ denotes the activation function. $G(\cdot)$ denotes a residual learning function, which performs a nonlinear transformation with a series of operations including convolution, Batch Norm, and ReLUs. Therefore, $G(X)$ denotes the output of the Batch Norm before summation operation. The $H(X) = X$ is an identity mapping function, which is achieved by using the shortcut connection. The shortcut connection enables the gradient to propagate directly from later to earlier layers, thus mitigating the gradient vanishing which usually exists in deep network. By stacking multiple RBs, one can develop a deeper network and effectively alleviate overfitting of the network.

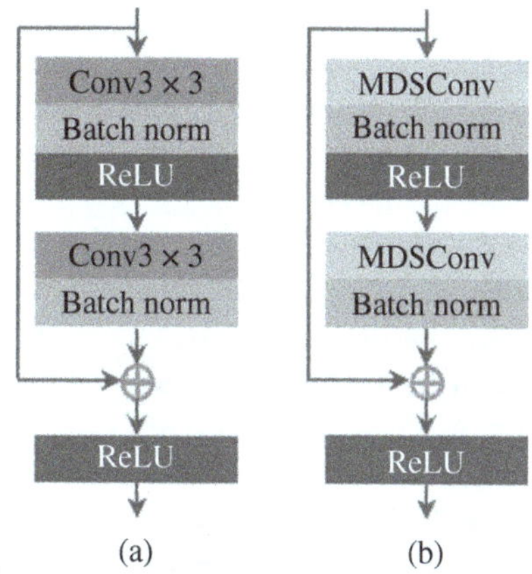

Figure 17.5 Architectures of the ordinary residual block and the proposed MRB. (a) Ordinary residual block. (b) Proposed MRB.

As shown in Figure 17.5b, this work designs the MRB by replacing the convolutional layers in ordinary RB with the MDSConv. The MRB is capable of extracting multi-scale spatial features and spectral–spatial correlated information, and it has much fewer parameters than the ordinary RB. Therefore, by staking multiple MRBs, our proposed MSRN can perform multi-scale feature extraction at different levels of network and learn more careful and comprehensive spectral–spatial feature representations of HSIs for classification. Besides, the network will converge faster and spend less time for HSIC.

17.2.2.3 Multi-scale Residual Networks

Based on the MRB, this work designs two networks, including MSRN-A and MSRN-B. As shown in Figure 17.6, the difference between these two networks is that the MSRN-B adds extra high-level shortcut connection (HSC) on two cascaded MRBs without increasing any parameters. By using the HSC, the MSRN-B can aggregate lower-level features and higher-level multi-scale features by summation. For all convolutional layers in both two networks, the stride is 1 and the padding is used, which means the spatial size of each feature map will remain unchanged after feeding into any convolutional layer. The number of filters in each convolutional layer is given in Figure 17.5. Here,

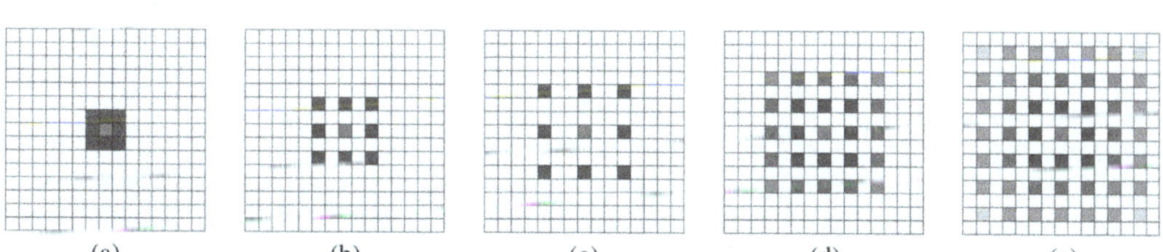

Figure 17.6 Illustration of dilated convolution and gridding phenomenon. (a) Traditional 3′3 convolution, Dilation rate = 1. (b) Dilation rate = 2. (c) Dilation rate = 3. (d–e) Gridding problem caused by dilated convolution.

we take the Pavia University dataset as an example to explain the implementation details of the designed two networks. First, 3-D image patches with the size of 15 × 15 × 10 are fed into an ordinary 3 × 3 convolutional layer which has 64 filters, and the 15 × 15 × 64 feature maps are generated. Then, the generated feature maps are subsampled by a max pooling layer with 2 × 2 kernel and stride 2, so as to reduce the computation cost of network. The size of each feature map becomes 8 × 8 × 64. Next, two MRBs are staked to extract hierarchical multi-scale features. After that, an ordinary 1 × 1 convolutional layer increases the channels of each feature map from 64 to 128, which makes multi-scale features more abundantly and fully represented. Then, feature maps with the size of 8 × 8 × 128 are transmitted two cascaded MRBs, where each convolutional layer has 128 filters. Again, another ordinary 1 × 1 convolutional layer is employed to enhance feature representation, and change the channels of feature map from 128 to 256. Finally, a global average pooling (GAP) layer is adopted to extract discriminative features for final classification, which transforms the 8 × 8 × 256 feature map to a 1 × 1 × 256 feature tensor. The full connection (FC) layer can adaptively generate 1 × L feature vector, and L is equal to the number of land cover classes in the HSI. Different from MSRN-A, in the MSRN-B, the multi-scale features extracted by the second MRB are not directly passed on to the next layer, but aggregated with the output features of the pooling layer. Similarly, the features extracted by the fourth MRB are first aggregated with the input features of the third MRB and then processed by the following layer.

17.2.3 Hierarchical Shrinkage Multiscale Network for Hyperspectral Image Classification

17.2.3.1 Receptive Fields and Dilated Convolution

It is universally known that the size of the receptive field is significant for feature extraction of CNN, mainly because the size of the receptive field determines the amount of neighbor information. Especially, in HSIC, many methods have proved that a large receptive field can improve the ability of global spatial feature extraction. However, the general method to increase the receptive field is usually realized by using a larger convolution filter, which will greatly increase the computational complexity of the model. Assuming that the number of input and output channels is the same, i.e., $C_{\text{in}} = C_{\text{out}} = C$, the convolution kernel size is $k \times k$ and the output characteristic graph size is $W \times H$. According to equations (1) and (2), the training parameter P and the number of FLOPs consumed by 5 × 5 convolution operation are 2.8 times that of 3 × 3 convolution operation.

$$P = k \times k \times C_{in} \times C_{out} \tag{17.8}$$

$$\text{FLOPs} = W \times H \times P \tag{17.9}$$

To alleviate the problem of parameter explosion with the improvement of the receptive field, the dilated convolution was first proposed by Chen et al. [53]. As shown in Figure 17.6b, c, a 3 × 3 convolution operation has a larger receptive field when the dilation rate is 2/3, but the generated training parameters do not change more than the original 3 × 3 convolution. In addition, the dilated convolution will not lead to the decline of the output resolution. Therefore, a series of HSI classification methods based on dilated convolution are proposed [54, 55]. However, it can be seen from Figure 17.6d, e that the dilated convolution extracts features by sparsely sampling the feature maps, which will lead to the damage of information continuity and the loss of local feature information (gridding problem). Therefore, when implementing pixel-level classification of HSIs with poor spatial resolution, the reduction of information continuity caused by the dilated convolution seriously limits the performance of the classification.

17.2.3.2 Framework for Proposed Hierarchical Shrinkage Multiscale Network

Figure 17.7 shows the framework of the proposed HSIC model, which takes the Pavia of University (PU) data set as an example. Firstly, PCA is applied to the original HSI to reduce its spectral dimension to avoid the Hughes phenomenon. In addition, PCA can effectively retain the main features of the HSI spectral dimension, which can not only reduce the redundant spectral bands but also decrease the burden of model training. Then, in order to fully utilize the spatial features of the HSI, the PCA-processed image is segmented into 3-D image cubes centered on labeled pixels. Subsequently, some of these cubes are used to train the parameters of the proposed hierarchical shrinkage multiscale network (HSMSN). Then, in the HSMSN, the feature maps with a high representative are obtained by novel feature extraction and fusion mechanism. In the first step of HSMSN, multi-scale features of the HSI are extracted by a hierarchical shrinkage multi-scale feature extraction network at different stages of the network. With the deepening of the network, the feature scale and diversity are decreasing, so four gradual shrinkage-scale MDMSRBs are used in different stages of HSMSN for multi-scale feature extraction. In the second step, an hierarchical feature fusion (HFF) mechanism is used to take full advantage of the features extracted in different stages of the neural network, especially the complementary fusion of high-level semantic features and low-level margin features. In the HFF, after the low-level features and high-level features are fused step by step, respectively, the two different levels of features are fused to get a feature map with more comprehensive information. Then, a GAP is used to transform the feature map into the feature vector. Finally, the classification prediction result is obtained by the feature vector via the Softmax function. In addition, as shown in Figure 17.3, MDMSRB, HSMSN, and HFF are three key components of our proposed model, which will be described in detail as follows.

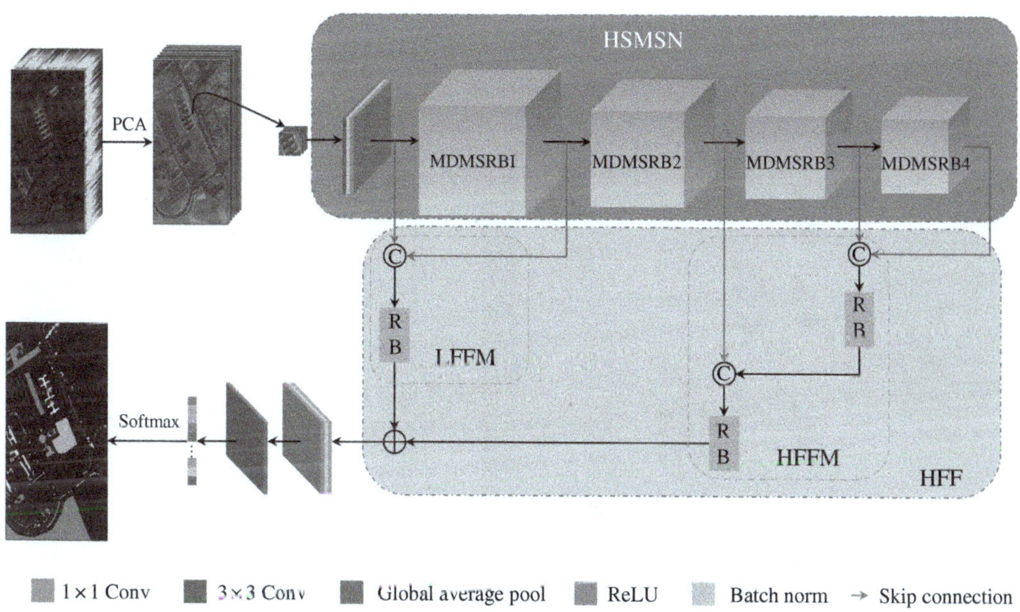

Figure 17.7 Schematic of the proposed HSMSN-HFF. © denotes feature concatenation, and ⊕ denotes feature addition. "RB" means "residual block." "LFFM" and "HFFM" represent the low-level feature fusion module and high-level feature fusion module. "HSMSN" denotes multi-depth multi-scale residual network.

17.2.3.3 Structure of MDMSRB

Studies have demonstrated that the size of the receptive field is of great help to improve the performance of HSIC. Significantly, the fusion of multi-scale spatial information and the mining of spatial relationships of different distance pixels in the receptive field can effectively enhance the utilization of spatial information. In this study, we propose MDMSRB as the backbone of the network to achieve HSI multi-scale feature extraction. The structure of MDMSRB is shown in Figure 17.8.

As can be seen from Figure 17.8, it is different from the aforementioned traditional multi-scale feature extraction fusion network, which is composed of four dilated convolution chains with diverse depths (D_1, D_2, D_3, D_4) in parallel, so as to realize multi-scale feature extraction. Specifically, the dilated convolutions with gradually rising dilation rates are stacked in every chain so that the receptive field is expanded. Therefore, multi-scale feature fusion is implemented by fusing the features excavated from four different depth-dilated convolution chains. In addition, compared with using a large convolution kernel to expand the receptive field, under the premise of the same receptive field, the dilated convolution with increasing dilation rate consumes fewer training parameters. The formula for calculating the receptive field F of superposition dilated convolution is as follows:

$$S = K + (K - 1) \times (r - 1) \tag{17.10}$$

$$F = \sum_{n=1}^{N} (S_n - 1) + 1 \tag{17.11}$$

where K and r denote convolution kernel size and dilation rate, respectively, S is the receptive field size of dilated convolution, and S_n is the receptive field size of the nth convolution kernel in one dilated convolution chain. With D_ 3 branch in Figure 17.4 as an example, one can obtain a 13×13 receptive field. According to Formulae (17.3) and (17.4), however, using the traditional 13×13 convolution kernel needs 5.26 times more training parameters and FLOPs. Therefore, MDMSRB can achieve a larger receptive field and multi-scale feature fusion with fewer parameters and FLOPs. It

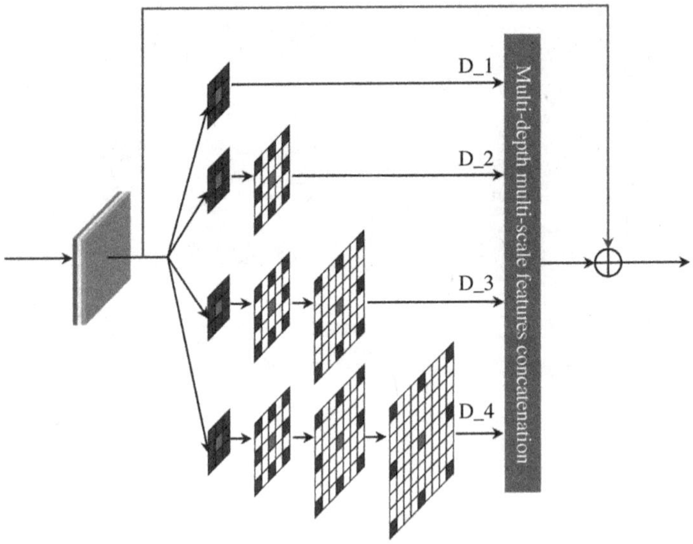

Figure 17.8 Architecture of the proposed MDMSRB.

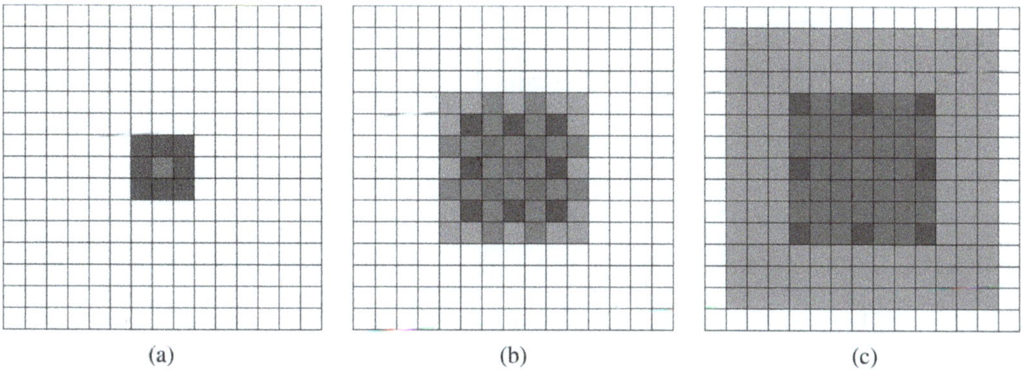

Figure 17.9 Illustration of the receptive field of superposition dilated convolution with gradually rising dilation rates. (a) Receptive field of D_1 branch. (b) Receptive field of D_2 branch. (c) Receptive field of D_3 branch.

is worth mentioning that according to the receptive field state obtained by different depth branches given in Figure 17.9, compared with Figure 17.1, this dilated convolution superposition method with different dilation rates can effectively solve the gridding problem caused by dilated convolution. Furthermore, considering the problem of gradient vanishing caused by network deepening, we use skip connection to fuse the feature maps before and after multi-scale feature extraction, and an ordinary 1×1 convolution is used to keep the scale of the feature maps consistent.

17.2.3.4 Structure of HSMSN

In the process of image feature extraction by the CNN, the state of feature extracted at different depths of the network is gradually changing from concrete to abstract, and the scale of the feature is gradually decreasing. In this process, therefore, the adaptation of the receptive field to feature scale at different depths of the network should be considered. In this work, the HSMSN is proposed to adapt to the changing feature scale in the process of feature extraction.

Similar to the standard procedure of parallelizing receptive fields of different scales in multiscale feature extraction methods, we implement four parallel branches with varying depths to realize multiscale feature extraction. Therefore, we can adjust the scale of feature extraction by using the combination of branches with different depths in different stages of the network. Specifically, in the shallow stage of feature extraction, MDMSRB1 with four scale feature extraction branches (D_1-D_4) is used for feature extraction. Then, the combinations of feature extraction branches owned by MDMSRB2-MDMSRB4 are: D_1-D_3, D_1-D_2, and D_1. As shown in Figure 17.3, the number and scale of feature extraction gradually decrease from MDMSRB1 to MDMSRB4. In this way, on the one hand, the adaptability of the model to changing features is improved; on the other hand, the model-pruning strategy effectively improves the efficiency of model feature extraction and reduces redundant parameters.

17.2.3.5 Structure of HFF

As discussed in section C, in the process of feature extraction by CNN, the change of feature state will inevitably lead to the loss of low-level boundary texture features extracted in the shallow layers of the network. These low-level features have higher resolution than high-level semantic features, which is of great significance to the extraction of spatial structure features of HSIs. Therefore, in order to improve the classification performance through the fusion of different level features, an

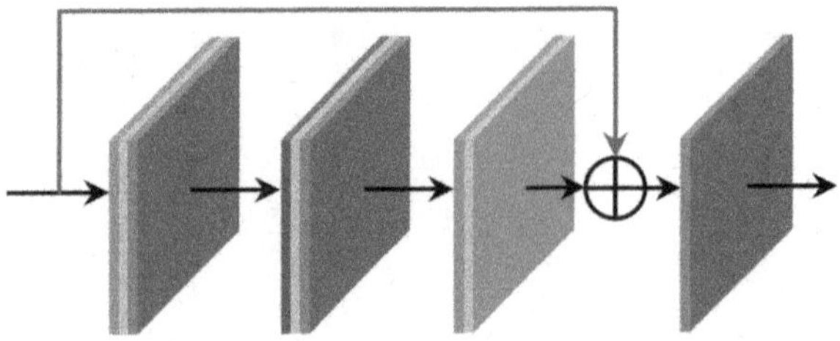

Figure 17.10 Illustration of the residual block (RB).

HHF module is applied to HSMSN to fuse the features of different stages, especially the fusion of high- and low-level features. The structure of HFF is shown in Figure 17.10, which is composed of a low-level feature fusion module (LFFM) and a high-level feature fusion module (HFFM).

As can be seen from Figure 17.10, HFF is divided into two steps: first, the low-level and high-level features are fused separately, and then the two features are fused. Specifically, the output feature $\mathbf{F}_0$ from the first convolution layer of HSMSN is directly connected with the output feature characteristic $\mathbf{F}_1$ from MDMSRB1 through concatenating. Subsequently, an RB is used to fuse the low-level features to get low-level fusion feature, i.e., $\mathbf{F}_{01}$. The structure diagram of the RB is shown in Figure 17.6, and the $\mathbf{F}_{01}$ can be represented as:

$$\mathbf{F}_{01} = g(\text{Concat}(\mathbf{F}_0 + \mathbf{F}_1) + f(\text{Concat}(\mathbf{F}_0 + \mathbf{F}_1) + \boldsymbol{\omega})) \tag{17.12}$$

where Concat(·) represents the channel connection, $f(\cdot)$ represents the residual function, $g(\cdot)$represents the ReLU function, and $\boldsymbol{\omega}$ represents the weight and bias coefficient of the residual correlation block. As a result, low-level features are effectively preserved. For high-level features, similar to low-level features fusion, we fused the output features $\mathbf{F}_3$ and $\mathbf{F}_4$ of MDMSRB3 and MDMSRB4 to obtain $\mathbf{F}_{34}$, which can be expressed as:

$$\mathbf{F}_{34} = g(\text{Concat}(\mathbf{F}_3 + \mathbf{F}_4) + f(\text{Concat}(\mathbf{F}_3 + \mathbf{F}_4) + \boldsymbol{\omega})) \tag{17.13}$$

Then, the output feature $\mathbf{F}_2$ of MDMSRB2 is fused with $\mathbf{F}_{34}$ to obtain the final high-level semantic feature, which can be expressed as:

$$\mathbf{F}_{234} = g(\text{Concat}(\mathbf{F}_2 + \mathbf{F}_{34}) + f(\text{Concat}(\mathbf{F}_2 + \mathbf{F}_{34}) + \boldsymbol{\omega})) \tag{17.14}$$

Finally, the low-level features and high-level features are directly added to obtain high-level and low-level complementary features with a high representative. Therefore, the high-resolution feature of low-level features and the strong semantic feature of high-level features are hierarchically fused for HSIC. The effectiveness of the HFF mechanism proposed in this chapter will be demonstrated by ablation experiments.

17.3 Experimental Results and Analysis

17.3.1 Data Description

In order to demonstrate the effectiveness of the proposed aforementioned three light-weight CNN-based HSIC method, three real benchmark HSI data sets are used in experiments: University of Pavia (PU), Center of Pavia (PU), and Salinas (SA). Figures 17.11–17.13 show the composite and corresponding ground-truth maps of these three HSI data sets.

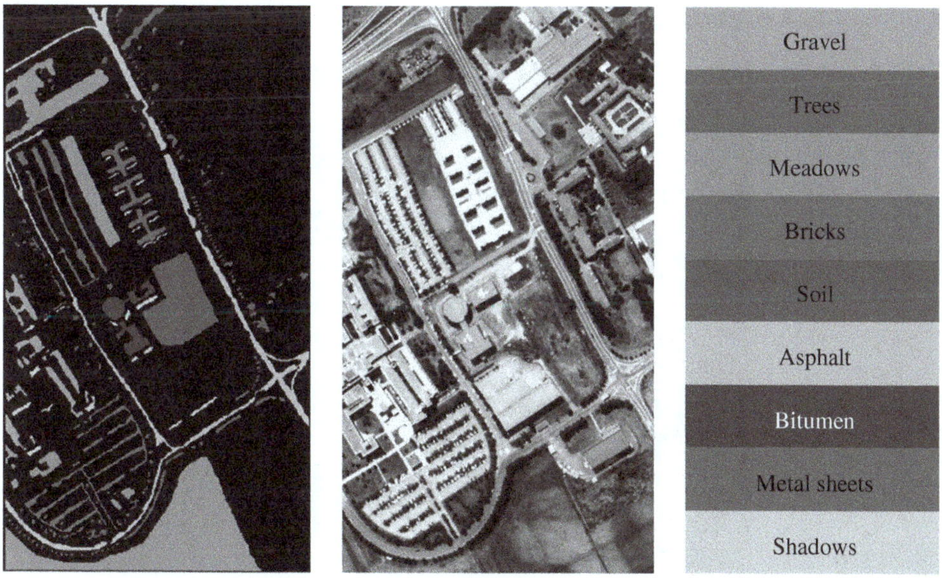

(a) (b) (c)

Figure 17.11 University of Pavia data set. (a) Ground-truth map. (b) Composite image. (c) Class legend.

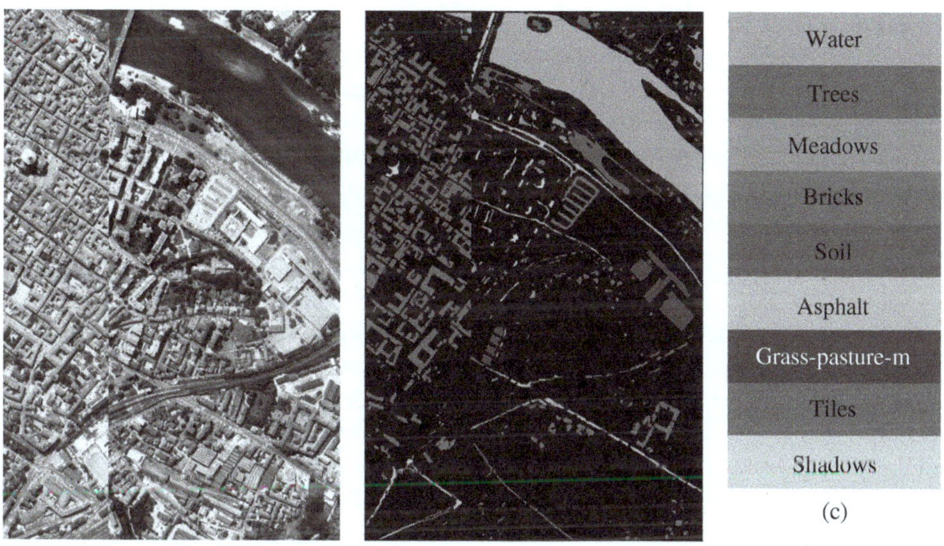

(a) (b)

Figure 17.12 Center of Pavia data set. (a) Composite image. (b) Ground-truth map. (c) Class legend.

17.3.1.1 University of Pavia Data Set

The PU image was acquired by ROSIS sensor over the University of Pavia in northwestern Italy. It has 610 × 340 pixels with spatial resolution of 1.3 m and 115 bands covering the spectral wavelength range from 0.43 to 0.86. After removing the 12 noisy bands, the other 103 high signal-to-noise ratio bands were retained for experiments. Furthermore, it contains 42,776 labeled pixels and can be divided into nine ground-truth classes.

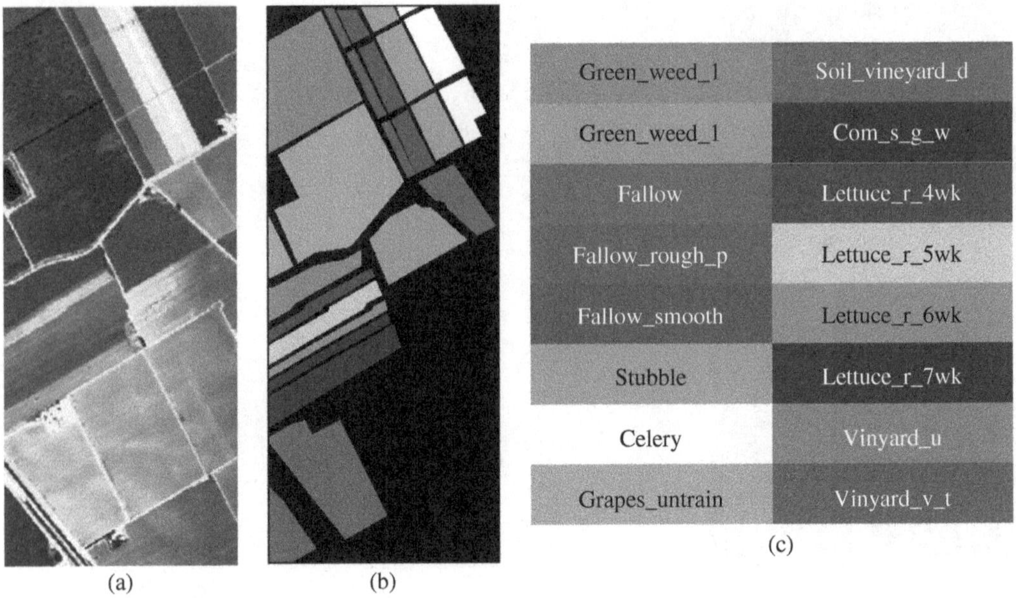

Figure 17.13 Salinas data set. (a) Composite image. (b) Ground-truth map. (c) Class legend.

17.3.1.2 Center of Pavia Data Set

The PC image was captured by the ROSIS sensor over Pavia City in northern Italy. It has 1096 × 1096 pixels with a spatial resolution of 1.3 m and 115 spectral bands covering from 400 to 1000 nm. After removing a black region of 1096 × 381 pixels and 13 noise-affected bands, the remaining region becomes a two-part image with 102 spectral bands, and the right part of 1096 × 492 pixels is used for our experiments. There are nine land-cover classes and 103,539 labeled pixels within this image.

17.3.1.3 Salinas Data Set

The third data set is SA, which was captured by the AVIRIS spectral sensor at SA Valley in California. It contains 224 bands and 512 × 217 pixels with spatial resolution of 3.7 m. Similar to the IP data set, 20 water absorption attenuation bands were removed, and the remaining 204 spectral bands with wavelength coverage range from 0.36 to 2.5 μm. In addition, 16 land cover types with 54,129 annotated pixels are available in the SA data set.

For each data set, 20 samples per class are randomly selected (from all the labeled samples) as training samples, and the rest of the labeled samples are used for testing. Tables 17.1–17.3 report the number of training samples and test samples for all data sets. Note that all input data of three data sets are standardized to zero mean and unit variance before fed into the network.

17.3.2 Parameter Analysis

Different window sizes and the number of bands for PCA have important effects on the results of the classification; therefore, we conducted the corresponding parameter-sensitive experiments. Specifically, we use five different window sizes 3 × 3, 5 × 5, 7 × 7, 9 × 9, and 11 × 11, and the number of bands for PCA dimensionality reduction is 5, 10, 15, 20, and 25, respectively. The performance of

Table 17.1 Overall and class-specific accuracies obtained by the different tested methods for the Pavia center.

Class	RF	SVM	LtCNN	S3EResBoF	LMFN	CLOLN	GhoMR	Lite-HCNet	SC-FR	MSRN	HSMSN
1	73.09	68.58	53.41	100	99.91	99.87	100	98.84	98.99	98.99	100
2	45.18	67.68	97.90	96.86	92.33	85.64	94.01	94.19	95.63	95.63	96.08
3	55.94	53.29	41.80	97.72	86.09	99.12	91.53	89.41	96.71	96.71	90.52
4	96.58	87.84	88.34	97.67	96.69	99.39	99.89	90.06	96.14	96.14	98.8
5	98.79	99.02	100.00	94.21	87.36	91.24	90.10	83.61	89.23	89.23	82.91
6	83.29	83.75	68.22	97.39	90.44	98.1	99.54	85.21	99.21	99.21	99
7	85.34	89.77	80.92	90.05	87.63	88.23	86.57	86.98	97.30	97.30	85.56
8	75.78	69.33	54.26	99.8	97.96	94.87	96.6	93.34	99.24	99.24	98.79
9	100.00	100.00	99.89	92.23	97.23	97.43	96.56	98.73	99.93	99.93	98.381
OA(%)	64.92	72.99	79.92	98.63	96.81	96.56	97.34	91.15	98.31	98.31	97.67
AA(%)	79.33	79.97	76.08	96.21	92.85	94.88	94.98	94.55	96.93	96.93	94.45
Kappa∗100(%)	57.71	66.07	73.29	98.06	95.50	95.15	96.24	92.35	97.61	97.61	96.7
Parameters(K)	—	—	2625.182	4.024	13.421	3.51	29.037	17.721	51.291	140.745	159.321
Flops(M)	—	—	368.990	23.44	47.093	0.611	433.594	6.412	100.374	370.364	2,295

Table 17.2 Overall and class-specific accuracies obtained by the different tested methods for the University of Pavia.

Class	RF	SVM	LtCNN	S3EResBoF	LMFN	CLOLN	GhoMR	Lite-HCNet	SC-FR	MSRN	HSMSN
1	98.82	99.83	99.56	90.00	80.47	50.44	80.88	85.99	95.20	95.20	90.56
2	89.68	90.86	74.33	88.08	80.69	80.7	91.24	86.89	93.83	93.83	94.48
3	76.71	91.79	95.80	94.23	85.86	93.21	97.74	86.05	86.44	86.44	90.33
4	86.34	88.11	87.92	92.41	92.71	82.45	95.6	85.32	93.59	93.59	93.63
5	60.79	85.21	85.68	100.00	100.00	99.92	99.4	100.00	99.70	99.70	98.04
6	88.85	90.40	62.44	98.28	78.94	98.54	99.98	82.89	98.00	98.00	93.61
7	78.95	88.32	88.41	99.01	89.08	99.61	97.02	77.94	100.00	100.00	95.34
8	92.82	97.71	96.62	88.59	65.57	81.81	84.05	73.89	97.98	97.98	95.14
9	98.98	99.96	87.90	93.53	97.52	96.76	95.04	94.5	97.73	97.73	99.14
OA(%)	92.65	96.58	93.43	91.05	81.48	80.46	91.18	85.94	94.97	94.97	93.79
AA(%)	85.77	92.46	86.52	93.79	85.64	87.05	93.43	85.31	95.83	95.83	94.47
Kappa*100(%)	89.67	95.17	90.70	88.41	76.15	75.19	88.54	80.9	93.40	93.40	91.86

Table 17.3 Overall and class-specific accuracies obtained by the different tested methods for the Salinas.

Class	RF	SVM	LtCNN	S3EResBoF	LMFN	CLOLN	GhoMR	Lite-HCNet	SC-FR	MSRN	HSMSN
1	97.49	97.54	100	99.9	99.95	83.05	100	98.79	100	100	100
2	99.51	97.31	98.97	99.57	100	99.97	100	99.68	99.97	99.97	100
3	87.17	89.01	85.12	98.72	99.97	67.79	99.85	98.16	99.95	99.95	100
4	98.91	98.98	97.09	96.58	99.74	100	99.85	96.29	100	100	100
5	97.67	90.22	99.1	97.78	93.88	76.78	93.23	95.3	95.22	95.22	96.12
6	98.5	97.69	99.64	100	99.83	100	99.85	100	99.75	99.75	98.3
7	97.7	99.33	87.24	98.71	99.46	96.45	99.92	98.68	99.94	99.94	100
8	48.37	59.67	57.2	75.98	79.62	88.34	91.51	83.24	85.82	85.82	92.26
9	97.51	96.13	89.58	96.3	97.935	99.9	100	92.58	100	100	100
10	81.09	87.38	94.11	92.82	96.05	84.62	95.09	89.44	94.81	94.81	95.73
11	95.52	94.75	83.4	99.81	97.56	94.08	100	90.36	100	100	100
12	98.69	99.79	99.74	99.21	99.08	94.28	99.9	99.16	98.58	98.58	99.95
13	96.54	97.32	98.21	100	99.27	97.43	99.67	94.64	99.78	99.78	100
14	94.29	91.43	99.52	97.71	99.42	83.8	100	97.05	99.81	99.81	99.43
15	65.81	67.49	85	95.71	82.89	4.41	92.23	56.51	89.98	89.98	91.43
16	93.12	97.43	98.71	98.71	96.785	90.65	93.82	97.03	98.77	98.77	99.72
OA(%)	81.64	84.21	85.46	93.05	92.39	79.57	96.47	92.93	95.01	95.01	96.63
AA(%)	90.49	91.37	92.04	96.71	96.34	85.1	98.11	88.13	97.65	97.65	98.3
Kappa∗100(%)	79.67	82.5	83.93	92.3	91.54	77.07	96.07	86.79	94.45	94.45	96.24

the three methods on the three datasets is shown in Figures 17.14–17.16. Overall, the classification accuracies of the three methods improved with increasing window size, with too small a window size not being able to contain enough features, thus leading to poorer classification performance. At the same time, if the number of PCA bands is more, the classification performance is better; to a certain extent, the classification performance improves with the increase of the number of PCA bands, but when the number of PCA bands rises to 25, the classification performance of some of the methods improves instead of declining.

In this section, in order to better validate the reliability of the three classification methods, we select some of the remaining lightweighting methods for comparison, specifically RF, SVM, LtCNN, S3EResRoF, LMFN, CLOLN, GhoMR, Lite-HCNet, and so on. The specific classification

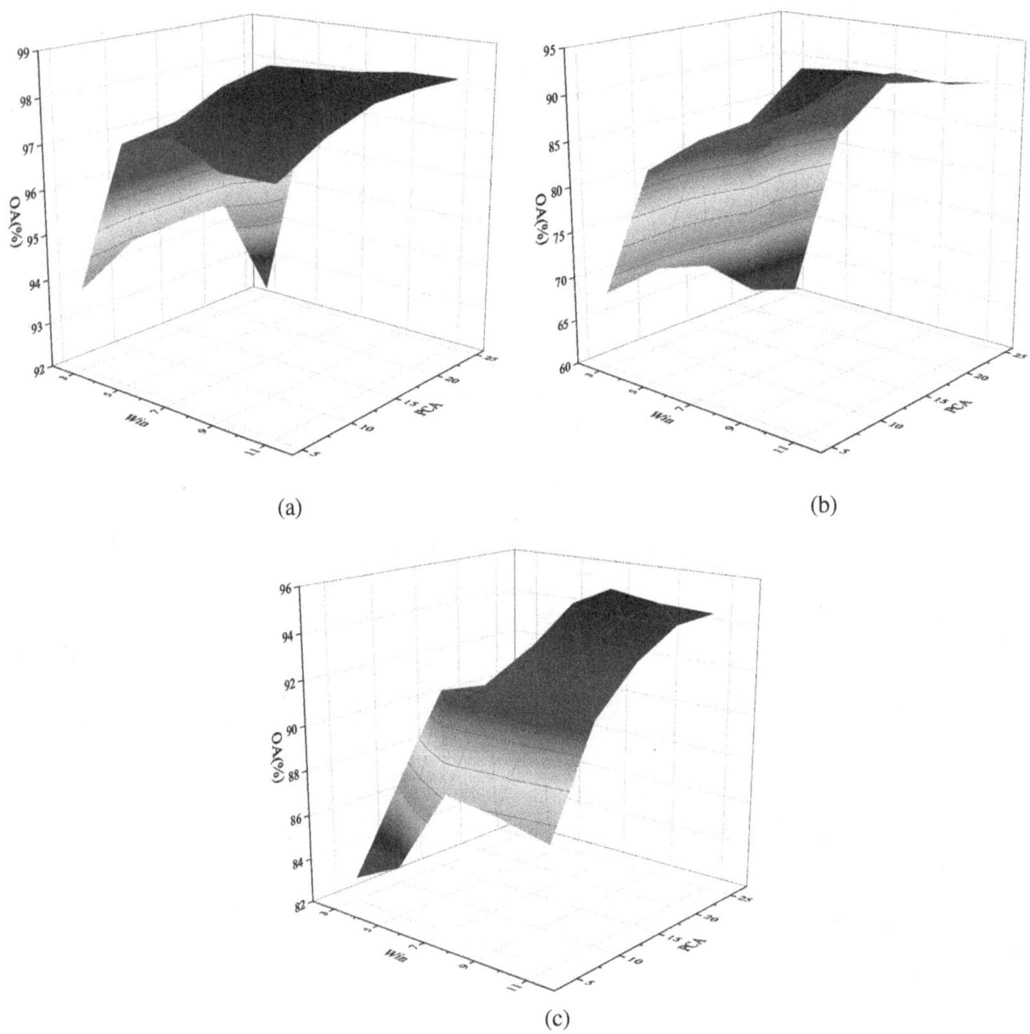

Figure 17.14 The effect of the window size and PCA on Center of Pavia for three methods. (a) SC-FR, (b) MSRN, (c) HSMASN.

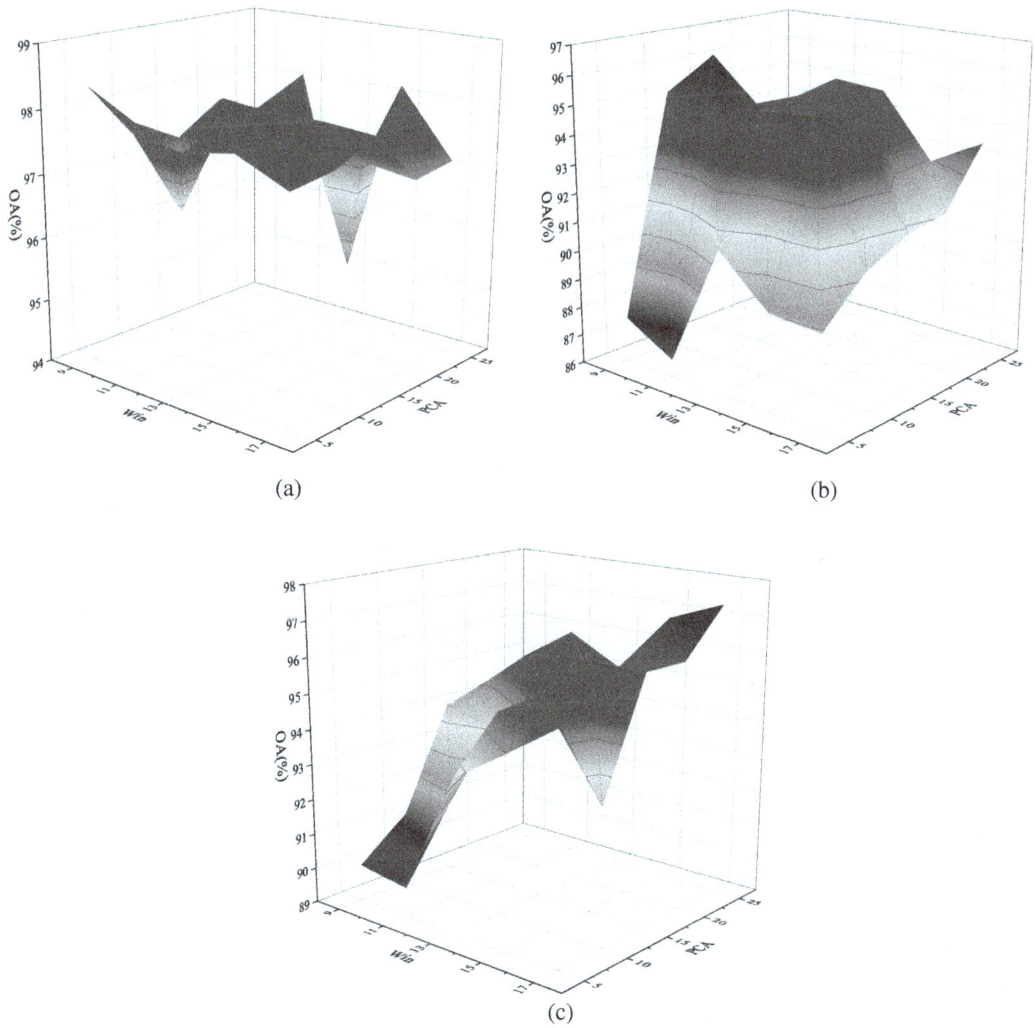

Figure 17.15 The effect of the window size and PCA on University of Pavia for three methods. (a) SC-FR, (b) MSRN, (c) HSMASN.

results of different methods are shown in Tables 17.1–17.3. Our three proposed methods achieve excellent classification results on all three datasets and have better classification performance while keeping the network structure lightweight. Although our classification methods are not the best in terms of model parameters and flops among the comparative methods, the three methods are still competitive in terms of both the combined classification performance and the number of models. For example, our method HSMSN achieves 100% classification accuracy for all eight categories on the Salinas dataset, which also demonstrates the excellent performance of our proposed method for obtaining discriminative feature features.

We also visualized the classification plots of all methods on the three datasets as shown in Figures 17.17–17.19. We can clearly see from the figure that our proposed classification method has less pretzel noise, and the classification graph has clearer boundaries of different categories and smoother lines; on the contrary, the classification graphs of different comparison experiments,

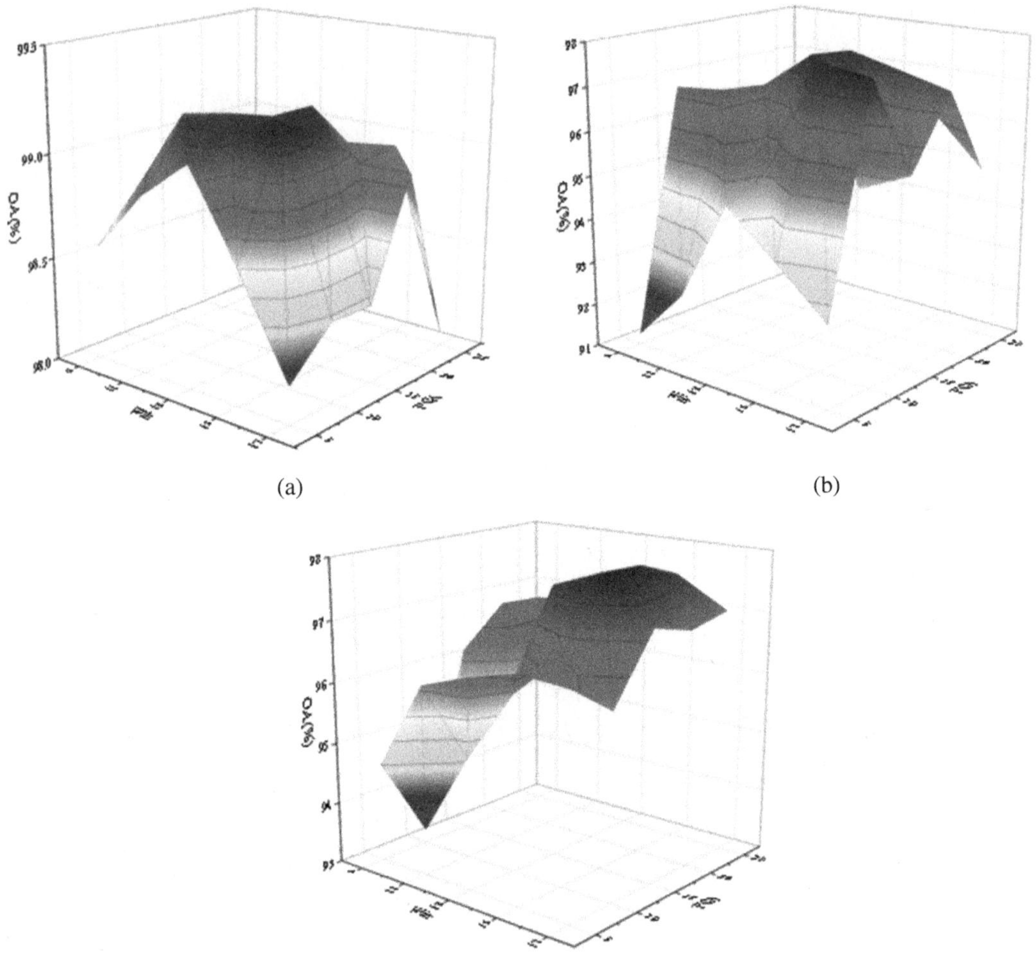

(a) (b) (c)

Figure 17.16 The effect of the window size and PCA on Salinas for three methods. (a) SC-FR, (b) MSRN, (c) HSMASN.

especially the traditional methods RF and SVM, have more pretzel noise and are more serious in granularity, because these two methods cannot obtain discriminative feature of features, and the classification effect is poorer than other methods such as S3EResBoF and LMFN. Although the classification maps have been greatly improved relative to the traditional methods, there is still inter-class intrusion present. Overall, in line with the quantitative results, our three methods show excellent classification results on all three datasets.

17.4 Conclusion

Lightweight modeling for hyperspectral remote sensing image classification is an ongoing problem, and it is a common pursuit to ensure lightweighting while taking into account classification performance. To address this problem, we propose three different models for lightweighting, while

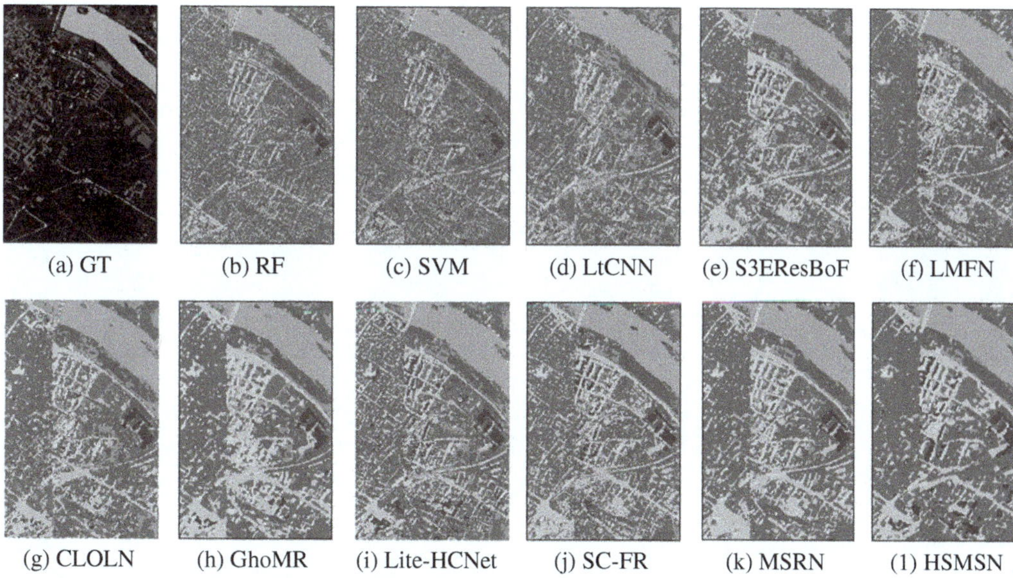

Figure 17.17 Classification maps obtained by the different tested methods for the Pavia Center data set. (a) Ground Truth. (b) Classification map of RF. (c) Classification map of SVM. (d) Classification map of LtCNN. (e) Classification map of S3EResBoF. (f) Classification map of LMFN. (g) Classification map of CLOLN. (h) Classification map of GhoMR. (i) Classification map of Lite-HCNet. (j) Classification map of SC-FR. (k) Classification map of MSRN. (l) Classification map of HSMSN.

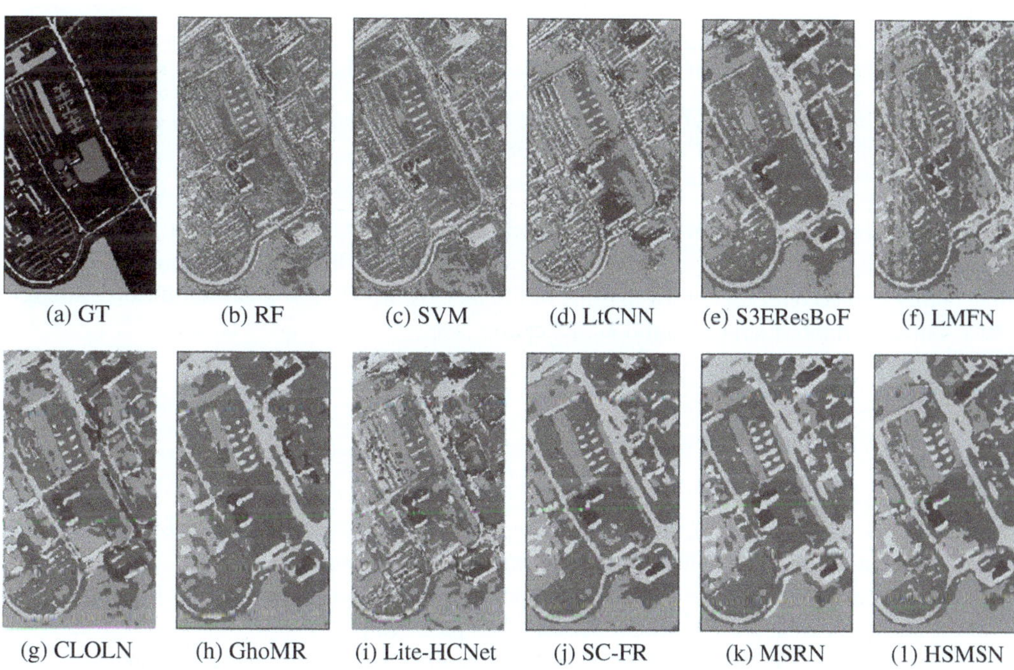

Figure 17.18 Classification maps obtained by the different tested methods for the Pavia University data set. (a) Ground Truth. (b) Classification map of RF. (c) Classification map of SVM. (d) Classification map of LtCNN. (e) Classification map of S3EResBoF. (f) Classification map of LMFN. (g) Classification map of CLOLN. (h) Classification map of GhoMR. (i) Classification map of Lite-HCNet. (j) Classification map of SC-FR. (k) Classification map of MSRN. (l) Classification map of HSMSN.

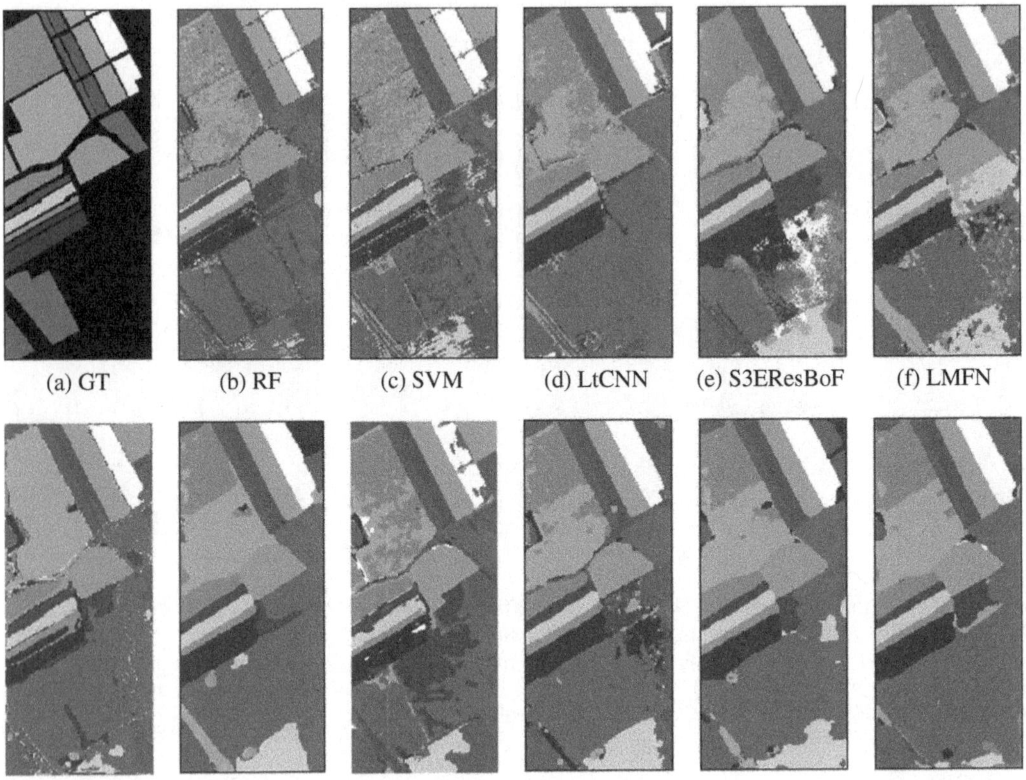

(a) GT (b) RF (c) SVM (d) LtCNN (e) S3EResBoF (f) LMFN

(g) CLOLN (h) GhoMR (i) Lite-HCNet (j) SC-FR (k) MSRN (1) HSMSN

Figure 17.19 Classification maps obtained by the different tested methods for the Salinas data set. (a) Ground Truth. (b) Classification map of RF. (c) Classification map of SVM. (d) Classification map of LtCNN. (e) Classification map of S3EResBoF. (f) Classification map of LMFN. (g) Classification map of CLOLN. (h) Classification map of GhoMR. (i) Classification map of Lite-HCNet. (j) Classification map of SC-FR. (k) Classification map of MSRN. (l) Classification map of HSMSN.

conducting extensive experiments on three datasets and using a number of different lightweighting methods for comparison. The results show that our methods have better classification performance while taking into account the lightweighting of the models, which is of great significance and reference value for the fast hyperspectral classification task.

References

1 Chen, Z., Lu, Z., Gao, H. et al. (2022). Global to local: a hierarchical detection algorithm for hyperspectral image target detection. *IEEE Trans. Geosci. Remote Sens.* 60: 1–15.

2 Chen, Z., Wang, Y., Gao, H. et al. (2023). Temporal difference-guided network for hyperspectral image change detection. *Int. J. Remote Sens.* 44 (19): 6033–6059.

3 Teke, M., Deveci, H.S., Halilolu, O. et al. (2013). A short survey of hyperspectral remote sensing applications in agriculture. *2013 6th International Conference on Recent Advances in Space Technologies (RAST)* (27–29 June 2013). Istanbul, Turkey. Piscataway, NJ: IEEE, pp. 171–176.

4 Olmanson, L., Brezonik, P.L., and Bauer, M.E. (2013). Airborne hyperspectral remote sensing to assess spatial distribution of water quality characteristics in large rivers. *Remote Sens. Environ.* 130: 254–265.

5 Acosta, I.C.C., Khodadadzadeh, M., Tusa, L. et al. (2019). A machine learning framework for drill-core mineral mapping using hyperspectral and high-resolution mineralogical data fusion. *IEEE J. Sel. Top. Appl. Earth Obs. Remote Sens.* 12 (12): 4829–4842.

6 Shi, X.Z., Aspandiar, M., and Oldmeadow, D. (2014). Using hyperspectral data and PLSR modelling to assess acid sulphate soil in subsurface. *J. Soils Sediments* 14 (5): 904–916.

7 Veraverbeke, S. et al. (2018). Hyperspectral remote sensing of fire: State-of-the-art and future perspectives. *Remote Sens. Environ.* 216: 105–121.

8 Ardouin, J., Levesque, J., Rea, T.A. (2007). A demonstration of hyperspectral image exploitation for military applications. *2007 10th International Conference on Information Fusion*, Quebec City, Canada (9–12 July 2007). Piscataway, NJ: IEEE, pp. 1–8.

9 Rasti, B. et al. (2020). Feature extraction for hyperspectral imagery: the evolution from shallow to deep (overview and toolbox). *IEEE Geosci. Remote Sens. Mag.* 8: 60.

10 Chen, Z., Wu, G., Gao, H. et al. (2023). Local aggregation and global attention network for hyperspectral image classification with spectral-induced aligned superpixel segmentation. *Expert Syst. Appl.* 232: 120828.

11 Chen, Z., Hong, D., and Gao, H. (2023). Grid network: feature extraction in anisotropic perspective for hyperspectral image classification. *IEEE Geosci. Remote Sens. Lett.* 20: 1.

12 Gao, L. et al. (2015). Subspace-based support vector machines for hyperspectral image classification. *IEEE Geosci. Remote Sens. Lett.* 12 (2): 349–353.

13 Bazi, Y. and Melgani, F. (2010). Gaussian process approach to remote sensing image classification. *IEEE Trans. Geosci. Remote Sens.* 48 (1): 186–197.

14 Chen, Y., Lin, Z., and Zhao, X. (2013). Riemannian manifold learning based k-nearest-neighbor for hyperspectral image classification. *2013 IEEE International Geoscience and Remote Sensing Symposium – IGARSS*, Melbourne, Australia (21–26 July 2013). Piscataway, NJ: IEEE, pp. 1975–1978.

15 Hughes, G. (1968). On the mean accuracy of statistical pattern recognizers. *IEEE Trans. Inf. Theory* IT-14 (1): 55–63.

16 Hong, D., Yokoya, N., Chanussot, J. et al. (2019). Learning to propagate labels on graphs: An iterative multitask regression framework for semi-supervised hyperspectral dimensionality reduction. *ISPRS J. Photogramm. Remote Sens.* 158: 35–49.

17 Cao, F., Yang, Z., Ren, J. et al. (2019). Local block multilayer sparse extreme learning machine for effective feature extraction and classification of hyperspectral images. *IEEE Trans. Geosci. Remote Sens.* 57 (8): 5580–5594.

18 Melgani, F. and Bruzzone, L. (2004). Classification of hyperspectral remote sensing images with support vector machines. *IEEE Trans. Geosci. Remote Sens.* 42 (8): 1778–1790.

19 Hong, D., Yokoya, N., Chanussot, J., and Zhu, X.X. (2019). CoSpace: common subspace learning from hyperspectral-multispectral correspondences. *IEEE Trans. Geosci. Remote Sens.* 57 (7): 4349–4359.

20 Fauvel, M., Tarabalka, Y., Benediktsson, J.A. et al. (2013). Advances in spectral–spatial classification of hyperspectral images. *Proc. IEEE* 101 (3): 652–675.

21 Fang, L., Li, S., Duan, W. et al. (2015). Classification of hyperspectral images by exploiting spectral–spatial information of superpixel via multiple kernels. *IEEE Trans. Geosci. Remote Sens.* 53 (12): 6663–6674.

22 Li, T., Zhang, J., and Zhang, Y. (2014). Classification of hyperspectral image based on deep belief networks. *2014 IEEE International Conference on Image Processing (ICIP)*. Paris, France (27–30 October 2014). Piscataway, NJ: IEEE, pp. 5132–5136.

23 Chen, Y., Lin, Z., Zhao, X. et al. (2014). Deep learning-based classification of hyperspectral data. *IEEE J. Sel. Top. Appl. Earth Obs. Remote Sens.* 7 (6): 2094–2107.

24 Zhong, P., Gong, Z., Li, S., and Schönlieb, C.B. (2017). Learning to diversify deep belief networks for hyperspectral image classification. *IEEE Trans. Geosci. Remote Sens.* 55 (6): 3516–3530.

25 Zhao, C., Wan, X., Zhao, G. et al. (2017). Spectral–spatial classification of hyperspectral imagery based on stacked sparse autoencoder and random forest. *Eur. J. Remote Sens.* 50 (1): 47–63.

26 Chen, Y., Jiang, H., Li, C. et al. (2016). Deep feature extraction and classification of hyperspectral images based on convolutional neural networks. *IEEE Trans. Geosci. Remote Sens.* 54 (10): 6232–6251.

27 Yu, H. et al. (2020). Global spatial and local spectral similarity-based manifold learning group sparse representation for hyperspectral imagery classification. *IEEE Trans. Geosci. Remote Sens.* 58 (5): 3043–3056.

28 Pan, B., Shi, Z., and Xu, X. (2018). MugNet: deep learning for hyperspectral image classification using limited samples. *ISPRS J. Photogramm. Remote Sens.* 145: 108–119.

29 Wang, J., Song, X., Sun, L. et al. (2020). A novel cubic convolutional neural network for hyperspectral image classification. *IEEE J. Sel. Top. Appl. Earth Obs. Remote Sens.* 13: 4133–4148.

30 Hong, D. et al. (2020). More diverse means better: multimodal deep learning meets remote-sensing imagery classification. *IEEE Trans. Geosci. Remote Sens.* 59: 4340.

31 Hong, D., Yokoya, N., Xia, G. et al. (2020). X-ModalNet: a semi-supervised deep cross-modal network for classification of remote sensing data. *ISPRS J. Photogramm. Remote Sens.* 167: 12–23.

32 Li, W., Wu, G., Zhang, F., and Du, Q. (2017). Hyperspectral image classification using deep pixel-pair features. *IEEE Trans. Geosci. Remote Sens.* 55 (2): 844–853.

33 Paoletti, M.E., Haut, J.M., Fernández-Beltrán, R. et al. (2019). Deep pyramidal residual networks for spectral–spatial hyperspectral image classification. *IEEE Trans. Geosci. Remote Sens.* 57 (2): 740–754.

34 Hamida, A.B., Benoit, A., Lambert, P., and Amar, C.B. (2018). 3-D deep learning approach for remote sensing image classification. *IEEE Trans. Geosci. Remote Sens.* 56 (8): 4420–4434.

35 Roy, S.K., Krishna, G., Dubey, S.R., and Chaudhuri, B.B. (2020). HybridSN: exploring 3-D–2-D CNN feature hierarchy for hyperspectral image classification. *IEEE Geosci. Remote Sens. Lett.* 17 (2): 277–281.

36 Yang, X. et al. (2020). Synergistic 2D/3D convolutional neural network for hyperspectral image classification. *Remote Sens.* 12 (12): 2033.

37 Srivastava, R.K., Greff, K., and Schmidhuber, J. (2015). Training very deep networks. *Advances in Neural Information Processing Systems* 28, pp. 2377–2385.

38 Licciardi, G., Del Frate, F., and Duca, R. (2009). Feature reduction of hyperspectral data using autoassociative neural networks algorithms. *Proceedings of the IEEE International Geosci.Remote Sens. Symp.* Cape Town, South Africa (12–17 July 2009). Piscataway, NJ: IEEE, vol. 1.pp. 176–179.

39 He, K., Zhang, X., Ren, S., Sun, J. (2016). Deep residual learning for image recognition. *2016 IEEE Conference on Computer Vision and Pattern Recognition (CVPR)* Las Vegas, NV (27–30 June 2016). Piscataway, NJ: IEEE, pp. 770–778.

40 Zhong, Z., Li, J., Luo, Z., and Chapman, M. (2018). Spectral–spatial residual network for hyperspectral image classification: a 3-D deep learning framework. *IEEE Trans. Geosci. Remote Sens.* 56 (2): 847–858.

41 Song, W., Li, S., Fang, L., and Lu, T. (2018). Hyperspectral image classification with deep feature fusion network. *IEEE Trans. Geosci. Remote Sens.* 56 (6): 3173–3184.

42 Huang, G., Liu, Z., Van Der Maaten, L., and Weinberger, K.Q. (2017). Densely connected convolutional networks. *2017 IEEE Conference on Computer Vision and Pattern Recognition (CVPR)* Honolulu, HI, USA (21–26 July 2017). Piscataway, NJ: IEEE, pp. 2261–2269.

43 Li, Z. et al. (2020). Deep multilayer fusion dense network for hyperspectral image classification. *IEEE J. Sel. Top. Appl. Earth Obs. Remote Sens.* 13: 1258–1270.

44 Ahmad, A., Khan, A.M., Mazzara, M.M. et al. (2022). A fast and compact 3-D CNN for hyperspectral image classification. *IEEE Geosci. Remote Sens. Lett.* 19: 5502205.

45 Jia, S. et al. (2021). A lightweight convolutional neural network for hyperspectral image classification. *IEEE Trans. Geosci. Remote Sens.* 59 (5): 4150–4163.

46 Meng, Z., Jiao, L., Liang, M., and Zhao, F. (2022). A lightweight spectral-spatial convolution module for hyperspectral image classification. *IEEE Geosci. Remote Sens. Lett.* 19: 5505105.

47 Cui, Y., Xia, J., Wang, Z. et al. (2022). Lightweight spectra-spatial attention network for hyperspectral image classification. *IEEE Trans. Geosci. Remote Sens.* 60: 5510114.

48 Wang, W., Ma, X., Leng, L. et al. (2022). A hybrid CNN based on global reasoning for hyperspectral image classification. *IEEE Geosci. Remote Sens. Lett.* 19: 6012605.

49 Gao, H., Yang, Y., Li, C. et al. (2019). Convolutional neural network for spectral-spatial classification of hyperspectral images. *Neural Comput. & Applic.* 31 (12): 8997–9012.

50 Gao, H., Yang, Y., Li, C. et al. (2021). Multiscale residual network with mixed depthwise convolution for hyperspectral image classification. *IEEE Trans. Geosci. Remote Sens.* 59 (4): 3396–3408.

51 Gao, H., Chen, Z., and Li, C. (2021). Hierarchical shrinkage multiscale network for hyperspectral image classification with hierarchical feature fusion. *IEEE J. Sel. Top. Appl. Earth Obs. Remote Sens.* 14: 5760–5772.

52 He, K.M., Zhang, X.Y., Ren, S.Q., Sun, J. (2015). Delving deep into rectifiers: Surpassing human-level performance on ImageNet classification.

53 Nair, V. and Hinton, G.E. (2010). Rectified linear units improve restricted Boltzmann machines. *Int. Conf. Mach. Learn.* 807–814.

54 Lee, H. and Kwon, H. (2017). Going deeper with contextual CNN for hyperspectral image classification. *IEEE Trans. Image Process.* 26 (10): 4843–4855.

55 Gong, Z., Zhong, P., Yu, Y. et al. (2019). A CNN with multiscale convolution and diversified metric for hyperspectral image classification. *IEEE Trans. Geosci. Remote Sens.* 57 (6): 3599–3618.

56 Liang, M., Jiao, L., Yang, S. et al. (2018). Deep multiscale spectral-spatial feature fusion for hyperspectral images classification. *IEEE J. Sel. Top. Appl. Earth Obs. Remote Sens.* 11 (8): 2911–2924.

57 Li, Z., Huang, L., and He, J. (2019). A multiscale deep middle-level feature fusion network for hyperspectral classification. *Remote Sens.* 11 (6): 695.

58 Li, S., Zhu, X., and Bao, J. (2019). Hierarchical multi-scale convolutional neural networks for hyperspectral image classification. *Sensors* 19 (7): 1714.

59 Zhao, W. and Du, S. (2016). Learning multiscale and deep representations for classifying remotely sensed imagery. *ISPRS J. Photogramm. Remote Sens.* 113: 155–165.

18

Ensemble Method Based Hyperspectral Image Classification

Wei Feng[1] *and Mengdao Xing*[2]

[1] *Department of Remote Sensing Science and Technology, School of Electronic Engineering, Xi'an, Shaanxi, China*
[2] *Academy of Advanced Interdisciplinary Research, Xidian University, Xi'an, Shaanxi, China*

18.1 Background

Hyperspectral image (HSI) classification has captured a lot of attention and interest in the remote sensing community. It starts with the blossom of increasing satellite launching, which ensures access to massive hyperspectral data. HSI features hundreds of narrow spectral bands on the surface of the earth [1]. HSI covers a large range of areas, in which each pixel represents a certain scene and is assigned a label. Bioucas-Dias et al. [2] have also pointed out that HSI data is of high spatial resolution, which can help assume that *the data mostly contains pure pixels*. Therefore, this makes pixel-wise analysis reasonable and feasible. Moreover, morphological profiles (MPs) can efficiently extract the spatial features and the combination of an MP and a traditional machine learning method formulates an accurate spectral-spatial classifier [3]. It is no wonder that HSI plays an important role in large-scale observation, especially for precision farming [4, 5], mineral exploration [6, 7], military surveillance [8, 9], and urban investigation [10]. For example, HSI can have an obviously positive impact on monitoring plant diseases and host–pathogen interaction. This is because (i) hyperspectral sensors can be directly applied in greenhouses and *avoid the step of extracting and transporting samples for analysis into a laboratory;* (ii) hyperspectral imaging can reveal plants' reflectance profile, for which HSI allows automatic detection of metabolic changes in plants during pathogen attack [11]. However, to efficiently and effectively explore the potential of HSI in classification tasks is challenging and worth research interest.

There are several important challenges in HSI classification tasks. According to Bioucas-Dias et al. [2], there is a detrimental unbalance between high dimensionality and limited availability of training samples. This can cause Curse of Dimensionality (i.e., Hughes phenomenon) [12] when training a classifier, especially for traditional machine learning methods. This is because when the dimension mounts, the complexity of a model will dramatically increase. Without sufficient training samples, such a phenomenon can lead to a high potential of overfitting and decreased classification performance for a model. Moreover, HSI exhibits a *nonlinear relation among the captured spectral information and the corresponding object of HSI data* [13], which poses a big challenge for traditional methods of analysis. Thus, it is needed to think up a better feature extractor (i.e., classifier) to deal with such a tough thing. Besides, HSI classification is also confronted with noisy data. As labeled HSI data is handcrafted, there is of very high possibility that some samples are labeled to

Machine-Learning-Based Hyperspectral Image Processing, First Edition. Edited by Bing Zhang.

the wrong category, which can confuse classifiers [14]. While manually correcting labels is cost-expensive and impractical, intelligently handling mislabeling problems for HSI classification seems significant.

In this chapter, we introduce how ensemble methods can boost HSI classification and deal with the aforementioned challenges.

18.2 Introduction to Ensemble Learning

The process of generating models from data is called learning or training. Usually, such a process (for example, generating a classification model) can be formulated as follows:

$$\mathrm{err}(h) = \mathbb{E}_{x \sim \mathcal{D}}[\mathbb{I}(h(x) \neq f(x))] \tag{18.1}$$

where x is defined as the instance space; $\mathcal{D}$ represents a distribution over x, and f is denoted as the ground-truth target function. The instances in training set $D = \{(x_1, y_1), (x_2, y_2), \ldots, (x_m, y_m)\}$ are sampled ***i.i.d.*** and h is the learner anticipated to construct. The learning process is intended to minimize the generalization error, err(h). According to Zhou [15], a good learner should generalize well, in other words, it should have a small generalization error.

Different from the ordinary learning process, ensemble learning is not to build a learner with minimal prediction error. Instead, it even welcomes weak learners. Figure 18.1 is the basic architecture of ensemble learning. It can be seen that ensemble learning is per se a collective decision of a series of base classifiers. And these base classifiers are generated from the training data [15]. Usually, these classifiers can be decision trees, neural networks or other learning algorithms. It is believed that *the* generalization ability of an ensemble is often much stronger than that of base classifiers [15]. Base classifiers are also referred to as weak classifiers, based on which an ensemble can boost them by extending their decision boundaries from a linear one to a nonlinear one. Figure 18.2 shows the power of integrating an ensemble in classification. Figure 18.2.a–c are base classifiers with distinct decision boundaries. Their boundaries cannot well divide the instance space into pure positive and negative regions. This is because the instances are not linearly separable. Nevertheless, with an ensemble, these boundaries can be integrated to yield a more precise boundary, which can be seen in Figure 18.2d.

There are two core steps to establish a good ensemble: (i) generating as diverse and accurate base classifiers as possible; (ii) choosing an appropriate strategy for combination, in other words, a voting scheme.

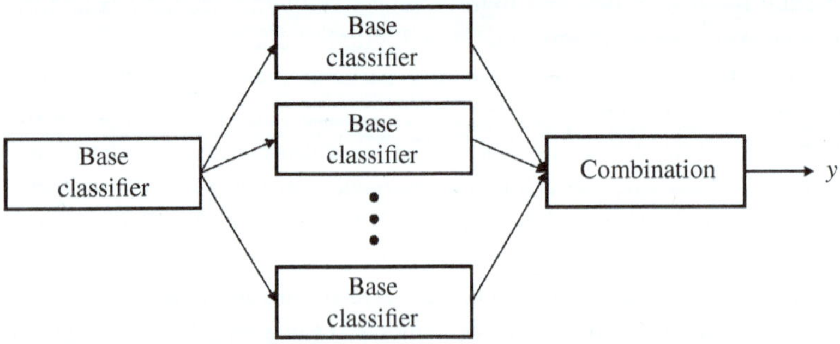

Figure 18.1 The basic architecture of the ensemble learning.

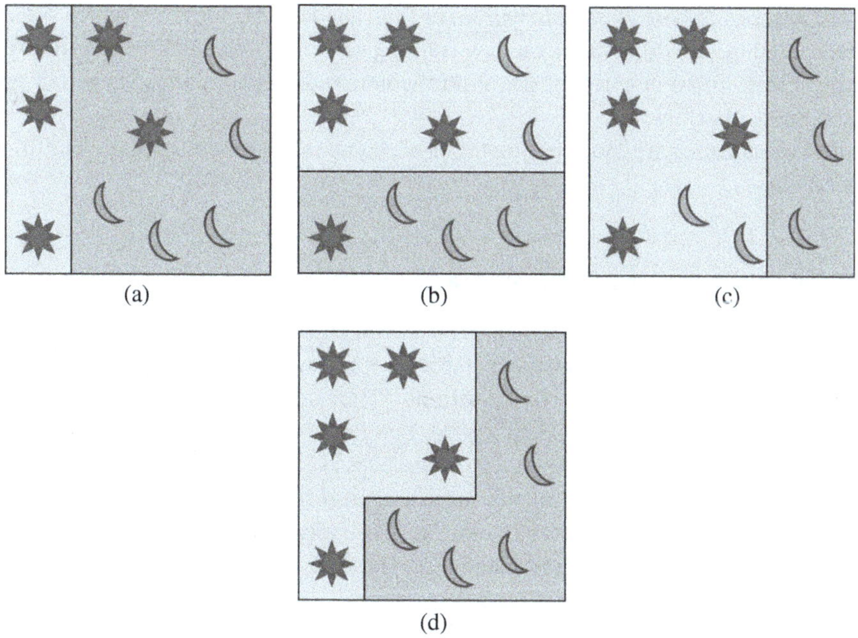

Figure 18.2 An exhibition of how an ensemble method plays its role in binary classification. The subfigures (a)–(c) are different linear base classifiers for the binary classification, and the subfigure (d) is an ensemble of these three classifiers. *Source:* [16] / with permission of Elsevier.

It can be easily understood that if base classifiers are identical when one classifier wrongly classifies an instance x, the other classifiers will also misclassify x. However, *if the errors made by the classifiers are unrelated* [17], even though a few classifiers make a wrong prediction on x, the most of classifiers can still correctly predict x. Thus, the majority vote will still yield a correct result. Obviously, if an individual classifier's error rate is high (exceeding 0.5), the error rate of an ensemble will also increase [17]. This is in accordance with the viewpoint of Hansen and Salamon that *a necessary and sufficient condition for an ensemble* is whether the base classifiers are accurate and diverse [18].

After training diverse and accurate base classifiers, a voting scheme is used to aggregate their output, which is a common procedure for a bagging-based ensemble. Among many voting schemes, majority voting is the most frequently-applied method. As its name implies, majority voting embraces each voter, and the winning result should be the one with the maximum total number of voters [19]. However, majority voting is not always a cure-all. In some cases, some other methods (for example, single transferable vote) can be a better choice. It is worth noting that compared to the simple vote count, the other methods can have difficulty in computing the preference order, which is time-consuming [19].

Ensemble learning can have four categories: Bagging, Boosting, Stacking, and Blending. Bagging is referred to as bootstrapped aggregating, a resampling technique to produce slightly different training subsets for generating diverse base classifiers. Boosting is to train a series of classifiers on one training set, during which each classifier will learn a weight-adapted training set based on the result of the previous classifiers. By doing so, the classifier will pay more attention to the easily-misclassified samples, and finally end up more powerful. Stacking is to train heterogeneous classifiers (based on different learning paradigms) and use a meta classifier to translate their outputs into a final predictive result. Blending firstly divides the dataset into a training set, a validation set and a testing set. A series of base classifiers will learn from the training set, after which their predictions on the validation set will construct a new training set, and predictions on the testing set will also be transformed into a new testing set. Both the new training set and the new testing set will be input to a meta classifier.

Since the former two categories are more frequently-used, some related methods will be introduced in detail as follows.

18.2.1 Bagging: Random Forest and Rotation Forest

Random Forest (RF) is an ensemble of decision trees and allows them to vote for the most frequently-picked class, which has been proven beneficial for land cover situations [20]. Decision Tree (DT) can gradually classify data by tree split algorithms. RF creates a large number of decision trees. The learning process of DT is a rule-based binary tree building. DT, in the realm of supervised learning, is a model that systematically partitions a data space into subsets corresponding to a certain rule. It iteratively divides the data space into two branches, ensuring that each subsequent split enhances the information gain compared to its parent node. The optimization objective in decision tree-based supervised learning revolves around identifying the split that maximizes information gain, thereby facilitating classification [21]. ID3 and C4.5 are two common tree-split methods.

Breiman's random forest technique employs randomization to generate numerous decision trees [22], which are then aggregated to yield a final output through either voting for classification tasks or averaging for regression challenges. Randomization can be executed through bootstrap sampling, where the dataset is randomly sampled with replacement, termed "bootstrap aggregation" or "bagging." This process does not ensure the inclusion of every subject and some may appear multiple times. In larger datasets with n subjects, the likelihood of being omitted from a bootstrap sample of size n approaches approximately $1/e$. These omitted subjects, known as "out-of-bag" subjects, form a valuable dataset for testing the decision tree constructed from the in-sample subjects. Figure 18.3 introduces the workflow of RF.

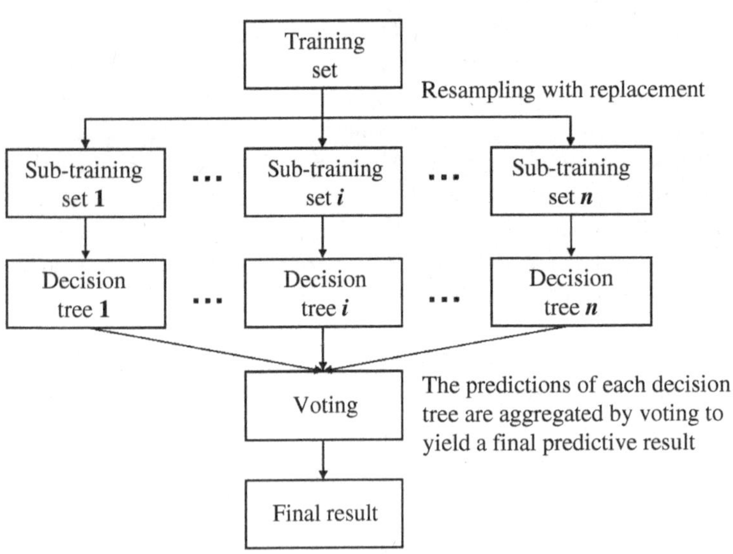

Figure 18.3 RF resamples the training set with replacement to yield different subsets and thus generate distinct decision trees. And aggregates these decision trees' predictions are aggregated by a certain voting scheme to provide the final result.

The Rotation Forest (RoF) method [23] draws upon the idea of RF. It has more diversity by combining several randomization techniques to build a sub-problem dataset which is projected into a new feature space. A RoF model of T size is built by carrying out the following steps:

1) RoF uses bootstrap technology to get several diverse training sets.
2) The feature space $\mathbb{F}$ of a training set is split randomly into G subspaces which are disjoint.
3) Then the principal component analysis (PCA) is applied separately on each subspace $\mathbb{F}_{t,g}$ $(g \leq G, t \leq T)$ to obtain the coefficients $c_{t,g}(g \leq G,\ t \leq T)$. The obtained vectors with coefficients are organized in a sparse "rotation" matrix R_t $(t \leq T)$.

$$R_t = \begin{bmatrix} c_{t,1}^{(1)} \cdots c_{t,1}^{(M_1)} & 0 & \cdots & 0 \\ 0 & c_{t,2}^{(1)} \cdots c_{t,2}^{(M_2)} & \cdots & 0 \\ \vdots & \vdots & \ddots & \vdots \\ 0 & 0 & \cdots & c_{t,q}^{(1)} \cdots c_{t,q}^{(M_G)} \end{bmatrix} \tag{18.2}$$

where $M = \lfloor D/G \rfloor$ is the feature number in each subset.
4) A rotation matrix R'_t $(t \leq T)$ is constructed by rearranging the columns of the matrix R_t to match the order of original features $\mathbb{F}$.
5) A new training dataset $S'_t = [S_t \cdot R'_t, Y_t]$ is produced, and then used to train an individual classifier $h_t(t \leq T)$.
6) The results of a series of individual classifiers, generated by repeating the aforementioned process on all diverse training sets, are fused by majority vote rule.

18.2.2 Boosting: AdaBoost, GBDT, and XGBoost

Adaboost (Adaptive Boosting) is one of the most frequently-used boosting methods. The AdaBoost algorithm is trained through a series of iterations. In each iteration, sample weights are dynamically adjusted based on the performance of the current weak learner, and a new weak learner is trained. From Figure 18.4, it can be seen that the working mechanism of the Adaboost algorithm is to first train a weak learner 1 with initial weights from the training set, and update the weights of the training samples based on the performance of the learning error rate e_1 of weak classifier 1, so that the weights of the training sample points with high learning error rate in weak learner 1 are increased, and these points with high error rate are given more attention in weak learner 2 later on. Then,

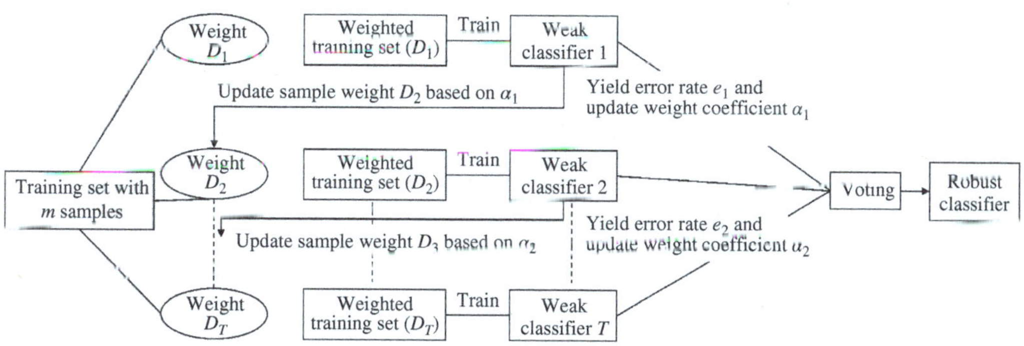

Figure 18.4 The workflow of boosting.

based on the adjusted weights of the training set, train weak learner 2. Repeat this process until the number of weak learners reaches the predetermined number T. Finally, these T weak learners are integrated through a set strategy to obtain the final strong learner.

The AdaBoost algorithm has a relatively simple structure and is easy to implement through coding. It does not require tedious parameter tuning and usually achieves good results with default settings. Moreover, compared to other integration methods, AdaBoost algorithm is less prone to overfitting, especially when the dataset is large. However, the computational load can become significant when dealing with large-scale datasets or high-dimensional features since AdaBoost is an iterative algorithm that requires multiple rounds of training weak learners. Furthermore, due to AdaBoost increasing the weight of misclassified samples, it is highly sensitive to noise and outliers.

The another boosting paradigm is GBDT (Gradient Boosting Decision Tree), which is an additive model. GBDT uses Classification And Regression Tree (CART tree) as the base learner, and through iteration, each time it fits the negative gradient to construct a new CART tree. By constructing multiple CART trees, it reduces the bias of the model and achieves better classification/regression performance. The core idea of GBDT is to minimize the loss function by fitting the negative gradient of the current model loss function each time a new CART tree is created. GBDT uses CART trees for both classification and regression. For classification, it uses exponential loss or log loss, while for regression, it uses squared error loss function, absolute value loss function, etc. When GBDT uses squared error as the loss function, the negative gradient is exactly the residual. GBDT uses CART trees as the base classifier. When constructing a new tree, the residuals of the current model are used as sample labels to train the next tree, which improves the classification performance of the model through multiple iterations. Algorithm 18.1 exhibits the procedure of conducting GBDT.

Algorithm 18.1 Gradient Boosting Decision Trees (GBDT)

1) Input: Training dataset $D = \{(x_1, y_1), (x_2, y_2), \dots, (x_n, y_n)\}$, where x_i is the feature vector and y_i is the corresponding label number of trees T; Loss function $L(y, F(x))$ for regression or classification.
2) Initialization: Initialize the model with a constant value: $f_0(x) = \arg\min_c \sum_{i=1}^{N} L(y_i, c)$.
3) For $t = 1$ to T:
   |For $i = 1$ to n:
4) |Compute the negative gradient of the loss function with respect to the current model:

$$r_{ti} = -\left[\frac{\partial L(y, f(x_i))}{\partial f(x_i)}\right]_{f(x) = f_{t-1}(x)}$$

5) |Fit a regression tree for r_{ti} to the negative gradients: obtain the leaf node regions of the t-th tree, denoted as R_{tj}, where $j = 1, 2, \dots, J$. (Get the structure of the tree).
6) |For $j = 1, 2, \dots, J$, compute:
   $|c_{tj} = \arg\min_c \sum_{x_i \in R_{mj}} L(r_{ti}, f_{t-1}(x_i + c))$
7) |Update the model by adding a tree to it: $f_t(x) = f_{t-1}(x) + \sum_{j=1}^{J} c_{tj} I(x \in R_j)$

Output: Ensemble of regression trees $F(x) = \{f_1(x), f_2(x), \dots, f_T(x)\}$

XGBoost is a specialized boosting algorithm, which is essentially an accelerated implementation of GBDT. XGBoost applies Newton's method (second-order Taylor expansion) and incorporates regularization terms to penalize the complexity of each tree, thus preventing overfitting:

$$\text{Obj} = \sum_{i=1}^{n} l(\hat{y}_i, y_i) + \sum_{t=1}^{k} \Omega(f_t) \tag{18.3}$$

The loss function can be represented as the predicted value $\hat{y}_i$ and the true value y_i. Ω represents the regularization term of the model. At the t-th step of model fitting, for example, in this step, the model's prediction for the i-th sample is:

$$\hat{y}_i^t = \hat{y}_i^{t-1} + f_t(x_i) \tag{18.4}$$

where $f_t(x_i)$ represents the new model we are adding in this iteration, i.e., the model to be fitted. At this point, the objective function can be written as:

$$\begin{aligned} \text{Obj}^{(t)} &= \sum_{i=1}^{n} l(y_i, \hat{y}_i^t) + \sum_{i=i}^{t} \Omega(f_i) \\ &= \sum_{i-1}^{n} l(y_i, \hat{y}_i^{t-1} + f_t(x_i)) + \Omega(f_t) + \text{constant} \end{aligned} \tag{18.5}$$

Then, the objective function is expanded using a second-order Taylor expansion to obtain the new objective function:

$$\text{Obj}^{(t)} = \sum_{i=1}^{n} \left[l(y_i, \hat{y}_i^{t-1}) + g_i f_t(x_i) + \frac{1}{2} h_i f_t^2(x_i) \right] + \Omega(f_t) + \text{constant} \tag{18.6}$$

Since at the t-th step $\hat{y}_i^{t-1}$ is actually a known value, $l(y_i, \hat{y}_i^{t-1})$ is a constant, which does not affect the optimization of the function. Therefore, the objective function can be written as:

$$\text{Obj}^{(t)} \approx \sum_{i=1}^{n} \left[g_i f_t(x_i) + \frac{1}{2} h_i f_t^2(x_i) \right] + \Omega(f_t) \tag{18.7}$$

Therefore, by calculating the first and second derivatives of the loss function at each step and substituting them into the above optimized equation, we can optimize the objective function to obtain $f_t(x)$ at each step. Finally, by combining these models according to the additive model, we can obtain an overall model.

18.3 Ensemble Learning in HSI Classification

Ensemble learning is usually combined with other techniques to deal with more specific problems in HSI classification.

18.3.1 Dealing with High Dimension

Recently, researchers have shown an increased interest in RF classifiers to handle HSI classification tasks. According to Xia et al., RF is insensitive to high dimensional features, which, therefore, fits in with HSI classification [24]. Different from tradition RF merely using spectral information, Xia et al. introduce a module, named Extended Multi-Extinction Profiles (EMEP), to extract spatial-spectral features to enhance performance of RF. EMEP is produced by applying extrema-oriented connected filtering to the images associated with the first informative components extracted by the independent component analysis (ICA) [24]. Besides, to better respond to the high dimensional space of HSI, Dong et al. proposed an ensemble discriminative local metric learning (EDLML) algorithm for HSI analysis [25]. It first learns robust local metrics from both the training samples and their relative neighborhoods and considers the different local discriminative distance metrics by dealing with the data region by region. By doing so, it learns a subspace to keep all the samples in the same class as near as possible, while those from different classes are separated. The learned local metrics are then used to build an ensemble metric.

Suppose that a local sample set for each training sample x_i and its KNNs as $\mathbf{X}_i = \left[\mathbf{x}_i, \mathbf{x}_{i_1}, \ldots, \mathbf{x}_{i_{k_1}}, \mathbf{x}_{i_1}, \ldots, \mathbf{x}_{i_{k_2}}\right] \in R^{d \times (k+1)}$, in which $k_1 + k_2 = k$, to capture local geometry. For each center x_i, k_1 represents the number of the nearest neighbors in the same class (NN) for x_i and k_2 is the number of NN in different classes. Specifically, the learned local metrics can be formulated as follows:

$$d_{\mathbf{M}_i}(\mathbf{x}_i, \mathbf{x}_{ij}) = \sqrt{(\mathbf{x}_i - \mathbf{x}_{ij})^T \mathbf{M}_i (\mathbf{x}_i - \mathbf{x}_{ij})} \tag{18.8}$$

where $1 \leq i \leq n, 1 \leq j \leq k^i$. Similarly, the above equation can be rewritten in a low-dimensional form

$$d_{\mathbf{M}_i}(\mathbf{x}_i, \mathbf{x}_{ij}) = \sqrt{(\mathbf{x}_i - \mathbf{x}_{ij})^T \mathbf{W}_i \mathbf{W}_i^T (\mathbf{x}_i - \mathbf{x}_{ij})} \tag{18.9}$$

where $\mathbf{W}_i \in R^{d \times m}$ is a non-squared matrix and $m \ll d$. Thus, an objective function can be formulated as:

$$\arg\min_{\mathbf{M}_i} \left(\sum_{p=1}^{k_1} d^2_{\mathbf{M}_i}(\mathbf{x}_i, \mathbf{x}_{ip}) - \sum_{q=1}^{k_2} d^2_{\mathbf{M}_i}(\mathbf{x}_i, \mathbf{x}_{iq}) \right) \tag{18.10}$$

Zhang et al. maintained that simply employing bagging or boosting on high dimensional HSI data has limited effect on improving accuracy [26]. Therefore, they proposed a new ensemble framework, called multi-view-based random rotation ensemble pruning (MVRR-EP), to effectively generate both accurate and diverse classifiers for ensemble learning. In the first place, it utilized correlation analysis to split spectral bands into multi-view. In order to generate diverse classifiers, this approach transforms each view into multiple coordinate spaces by random rotation. Then, an accuracy-guided ensemble pruning strategy is designed for pruning the component classifiers with low complementarity, and consequently, the remaining component classifiers with high complementarity are combined to construct an ensemble classifier. Figure 18.5 exhibits how MVRR-EP works for HSI classification.

In brief, this sort of ensemble method integrates a data-engineering scheme to better explore the potential of the chosen classifiers.

18.3.2 Dealing with Limited Samples

It is worth noting that there exists imbalance between limited training samples and extremely high spectral dimensions for HSI, which can make HSI classification much more challenging.

Dong et al. provide a new ensemble-based approach to handle small-sized HSI datasets [27]. It incorporates CNN into the ensemble framework, which makes small-size HSI data classification much more challenging. Therefore, Dong et al. introduce Pixel Pair Features (PPF) to assemble data, which can generate a large volume of data. PPF is related to the idea that neighboring pixels

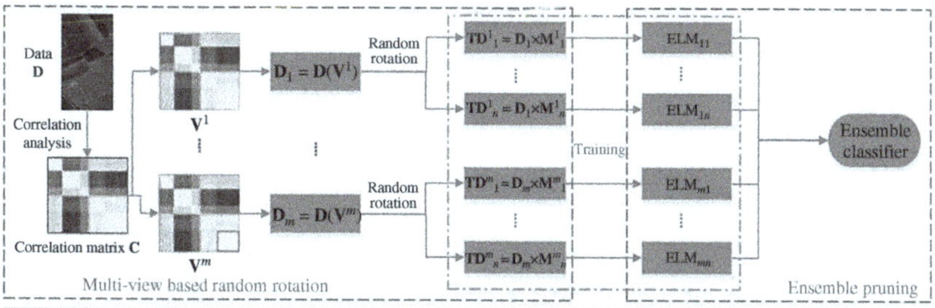

D: hyperspectral image data	V^i: the ith view (i = 1, ..., m)	M^i_j: the jth random rotation matrix (j = 1..., n) to rotate D^i
C: the correlation coefficient matrix	D^i: data D under the view V^i	TD^i_j: transformed data generated by matrix M^i_j

Figure 18.5 Flowchart of MVRR-EP. *Source:* [26] / with permission of IEEE.

have a similar spectrum as the centered pixel does and pixels within the same class share identical spectral features. Suppose that x_i and x_j are two pixels in the training set, a pixel pair $S_{ij} = [x_i, x_j]$ is produced by concatenating these two pixels. And the label for such a pixel pair is decided by:

$$\text{Label}(\mathbf{S}_{ij}) = \begin{Bmatrix} \text{if Label}(\mathbf{x}_i) = \text{Label}(\mathbf{x}_j) = c \\ 0 \text{ else} \end{Bmatrix} \tag{18.11}$$

where $c \in [1, C]$ with C is the number of categories in the HSI. Class 0 is a newly-generated class representing the inconsistency between x_i and x_j, which will not be considered in the prediction stage. Besides, this method utilizes spatial information by introducing Gray-Level Co-occurrence Matrix (GLCM). Figure 18.6 displays the workflow of Dong's approach.

As manually labeling HSI data can be time-consuming and expensive, there exists many unlabeled data in real HSI classification scenes. To deal with limited training samples, Feng et al. [28] put forward a semi-supervised rotation forest based on ensemble margin theory for HSI classification. This method iteratively increases the number of training samples with high-quality unlabeled samples chosen by ensemble margin. The applied ensemble margin is related to selecting and labeling samples under an unsupervised context. The higher the margin is, the more reliable the sample is. The ensemble margin is defined as follows:

$$\text{margin}_{\underline{\mathcal{M}}}(\mathbf{x}) = \frac{1}{V}\left(V_{\underline{\mathcal{M}}}(\mathbf{x}, \mathcal{M}_a(\mathbf{x})) - V_{\underline{\mathcal{M}}}(\mathbf{x}, \mathcal{M}_b(\mathbf{x}))\right) \tag{18.12}$$

where $\mathcal{M}$ is an ensemble classifier, $V_{\underline{\mathcal{M}}}$ is the number of decision trees in $\mathcal{M}$, $V_{\underline{\mathcal{M}}}(\mathbf{x}, c)$ represents the number of trees believing the sample $\mathbf{x}$ belongs to class c, $\mathcal{M}_a(\mathbf{x})$ is the most predicted class for $\mathbf{x}$ while $\mathcal{M}_b(\mathbf{x})$ is the second predicted class for $\mathbf{x}$.

Similarly, Fang et al. attempted to augment data by a multiscale CNN ensemble based self-Learning method [29]. This algorithm goes through two stages. Firstly, the spatial information of different scales from limited labeled training samples is extracted to train several CNN models (different base classifiers). Then, the trained multiscale CNNs are used to classify the unlabeled samples. Before classifying unlabeled samples, Fang also added an error correction module to facilitate the following classification procedure. Finally, the unlabeled samples with pseudo labels will be transferred to the labeled dataset in the next training stage. Figure 18.7 is the flowchart of Fang's approach.

Different from data-engineering methods, Cui et al. integrate semantic filtering into ensemble learning to enhance the performance of the classifier when facing limited training samples under

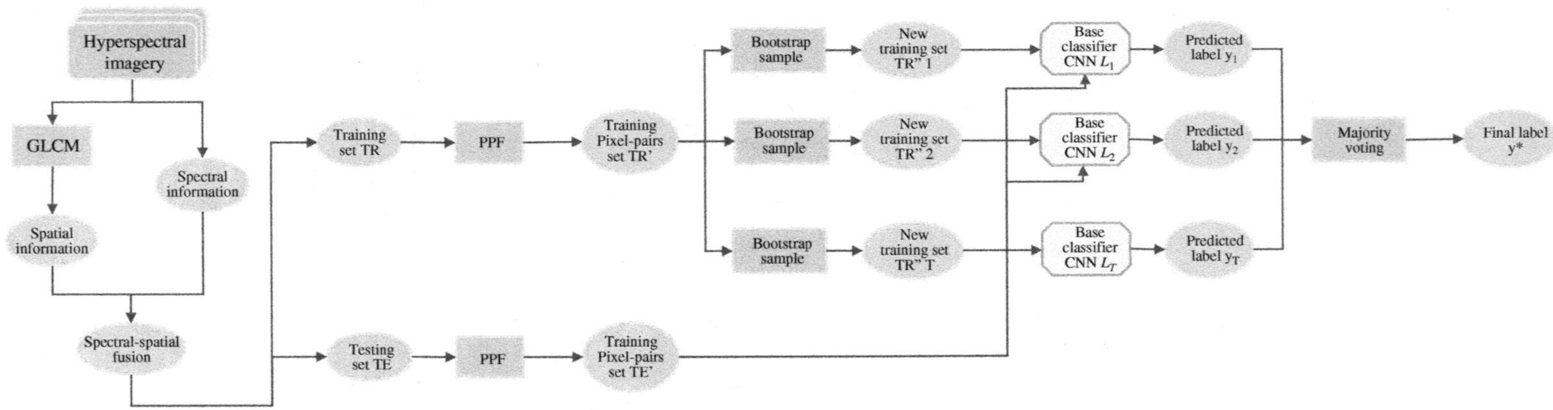

Figure 18.6 Flowchart of Ensemble CNN with PPF and GLCM. *Source:* [27] / with permission of IEEE.

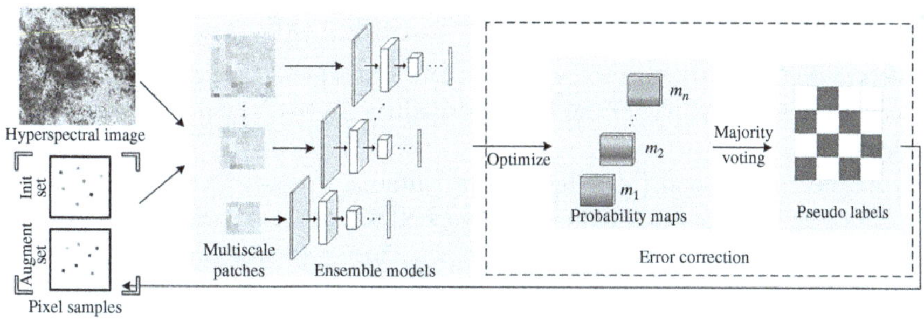

Figure 18.7 Framework of the proposed select strategy. Multiscale patches with the same centering pixel sample are used as the input of ensemble models to get the probability maps. An error correct mechanism is utilized to alleviate the label partially incorrect problem and select the pseudo samples. *Source:* [29].

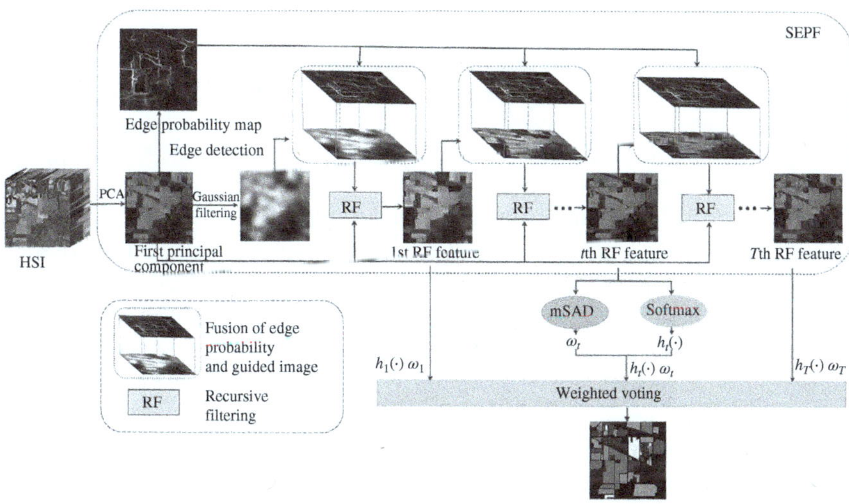

Figure 18.8 Flowchart of Cui et al.'s proposed method. *Source:* [30].

extreme high spectral dimension [30]. Figure 18.8 showcases the flowchart of Cui et al.'s proposed method in dealing with limited samples. Specifically, this method first employs Principle Component Analysis (PCA) to reduce dimensions, after which a structured edge detector is used to yield an edge probability map, indicating the probability of whether a pixel is located at an edge. Then, the guide image (dimensional-reduced and filtered feature map) and edge probability map will be fused and go through Recursive Filtering (RF) with a dimensional-reduced map to yield a new feature map. The feature map will replace the former guide image to fuse with an edge probability map. Repeat this process for T times. Each time the i-th RF feature map will go through the mSAD module and the softmax module, which will be aggregated by weighted voting, yielding the final result map. mSAD is the matrix of the spectral angle distance, expressed by:

$$\text{mSAD}(\mathbf{X}_i, \mathbf{X}_j) = \arccos\left(\frac{{x_i}^T x_j}{\|x_i\|_2 \|x_j\|_2}\right) \tag{18.13}$$

where $\mathbf{X}_c = [\mathbf{X}_1, \mathbf{X}_2, ..., \mathbf{X}_n]$ denotes a group of the training samples in class c, $\mathbf{X}_i \in \mathbb{R}^{L\times 1}$ is a pixel spectrum with L bands, n is the number of training samples in class c.

18.3.3 Dealing with Class Imbalance

Class imbalance refers to that in the training set, some classes have a significantly higher number of examples than other classes. Such imbalance can lead to a significantly biased model, especially for deep learning model.

To address such a problem, Quan et al. [31] integrate the Synthetic Minority Oversampling Technique (SMOTE) into a weighted deep rotation forest to respond to class-imbalanced HSI. SMOTE generates new synthetic samples by interpolating between neighboring minority class samples. The procedure can be operated as below:

Let X be the set of minority class instances in the feature space, and let N be the number of minority class instances. Each instance is represented as a feature vector x_i, where $i = 1, 2, \dots, N$.

1) Selecting a minority instance: Randomly choose an instance x_i from the minority class.
2) Finding nearest neighbors: Compute the distances between x_i and all other minority class instances in the feature space, using a distance metric such as Euclidean distance. Then, select the k nearest neighbors of x_i.
3) Generating synthetic instances: For each selected neighbor x_j, where $j = 1, 2, \dots, k$, compute the difference vector $\Delta x = x_j - x_i$. Multiply Δx by a random value λ between 0 and 1, and add it to x_i to generate a new synthetic instance:

$$x_{new} = x_i + \lambda \cdot \Delta x \tag{18.14}$$

Besides, Quan et al. innovatively combine extracting spatial information and SMOTE in an ensemble framework. Different from bootstrapping the training set, Quan's method employs a sliding 3 × 3 window, pixels in the same position constructing a sub training set (see Figure 18.9). Thus, SMOTE is conducted on each subset to yield distinct class-balanced subsets to train base classifiers.

SMOTE is a simple yet effective method when confronted with class imbalance problem. It is no wonder that there is much recent research utilizing SMOTE or its extension to tackle the imbalance problem [32–34].

In [16], Feng et al. proposed an ensemble framework, named ensemble synthetic pixel pair oversampling, for HSI classification. The HSI data is both class-imbalanced and small-sized, which makes classification more challenging. Therefore, Feng introduces Pixel Pair Features (PPF) to deal with small sizes. While PPF can effectively augment data, it lead to a much bigger imbalance ratio for original data. Accordingly, SMOTE is also integrated into the mentioned ensemble framework to deal with class imbalance. The workflow of [16] can be seen in Figure 18.10.

PPF is designed by [35], which assembles pixels to augment data. For training data, it selects two pixels, P_i and P_j, and concatenates them to make a pixel pair. The label for such a pair can be decided by:

$$\text{label}\left(P_i, P_j\right) = \begin{cases} c, \text{label}\left(P_i\right) = \text{label}\left(P_j\right) \\ 0, \text{label}\left(P_i\right) \neq \text{label}\left(P_j\right) \end{cases} \tag{18.15}$$

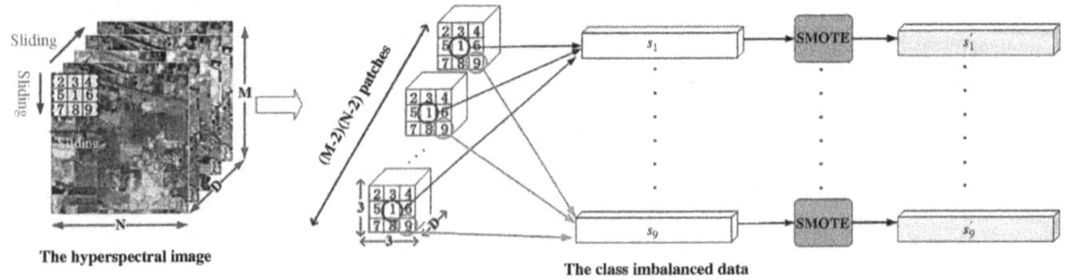

Figure 18.9 Spatial Information Extraction in Quan's proposed method.

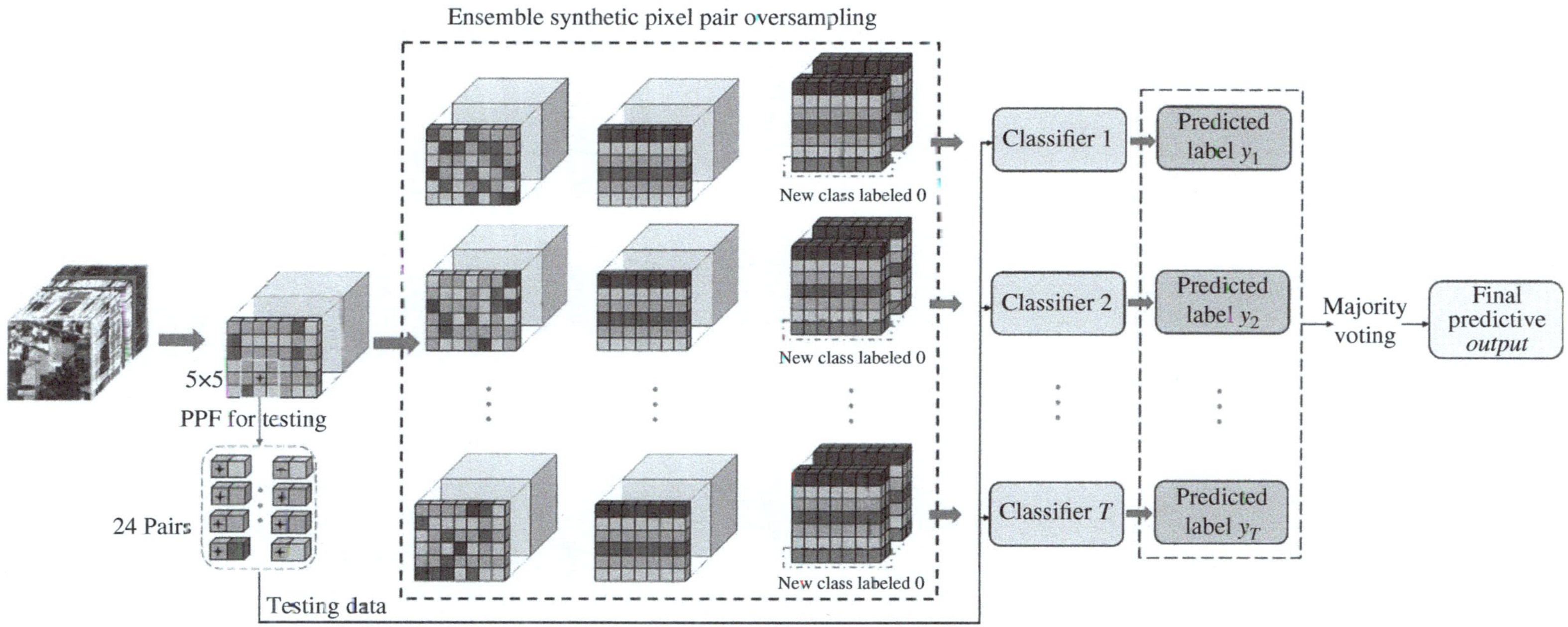

Figure 18.10 The architecture of Feng's proposed method. *Source:* [16] / with permission of Elsevier.

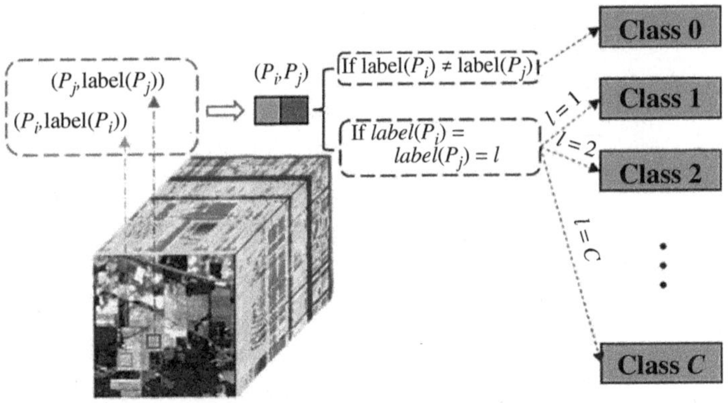

Figure 18.11 The procedure for generating PPF training data in the Feng's proposed method. *Source:* [16] / with permission of Elsevier.

Figure 18.11 exhibit how PPF augments training data. It is worth noting that in order to keep structural consistency, testing data is also transformed into PPF-like data. This can be seen in Figure 18.10.

18.3.4 Dealing with Class Noise

Real-world data is not perfect and often suffers from noise [36], for example, class noise. It is well-known that training a model needs labeled data while it is of high likelihood of inducing labeling errors [36]. It is no wonder that class noise is an inevitable issue in HSI classification. To deal with class noise, recent research has been proposed as follows:

One category of handling class noise is to detect and remove class noise. For example, the Density-Based Spatial Clustering of Application with Noise (DBSCAN) employs two parameters, the radius of the cluster and the minimum number of points, to partition all the instances. When an instance's circle encloses the least number of points, the instance can be regarded as a normal sample. Otherwise, it would be distinguished – a noise point [37]. Figure 18.12 exhibits that DBSCAN can effectively denoise HSI. After cleaning, the cleaned data can be divided into different subsets to input into base classifiers, enhancing the performance of ensemble learning.

The other category is to identify and correct class noise. In [14], hypothesis margin is incorporated into the random forest. Hypothesis margin is related to evaluating ensemble learning's performance on an instance $\mathbf{x}$, based on which $\mathbf{x}$ can be regarded correctly or incorrectly classified. Specifically, the hypothesis margin can be defined as follows:

$$\text{margin}(\mathbf{x}, y) = \frac{1}{J}\left(v(\mathbf{x}, y) - \sum_{c \neq y} v(\mathbf{x}, c)\right) \tag{18.16}$$

where y is the label of the instance, $v(\mathbf{x}, c)$ represents the number of classifiers predicting the label c for the instance $\mathbf{x}$ and J is the number of base classifiers.

And therefore, the probability that a sample $(\mathbf{x}, y)$ is mislabeling can be written as:

$$W(\mathbf{x}, y) = \frac{1}{J}\left|v(\mathbf{x}, \tilde{h}_1(\mathbf{x})) - \sum_{\tilde{h}_2 \neq y} v(\mathbf{x}, \tilde{h}_2(\mathbf{x}))\right| = \frac{1}{J}\left[\sum_{\tilde{h}_2 \neq y} v(\mathbf{x}, \tilde{h}_2(\mathbf{x})) - v(\mathbf{x}, \tilde{h}_1(\mathbf{x}))\right] \tag{18.17}$$

where $\tilde{h}_1(\mathbf{x})$ is the true label for $\mathbf{x}$ and $\tilde{h}_2(\mathbf{x})$ is the other labels.

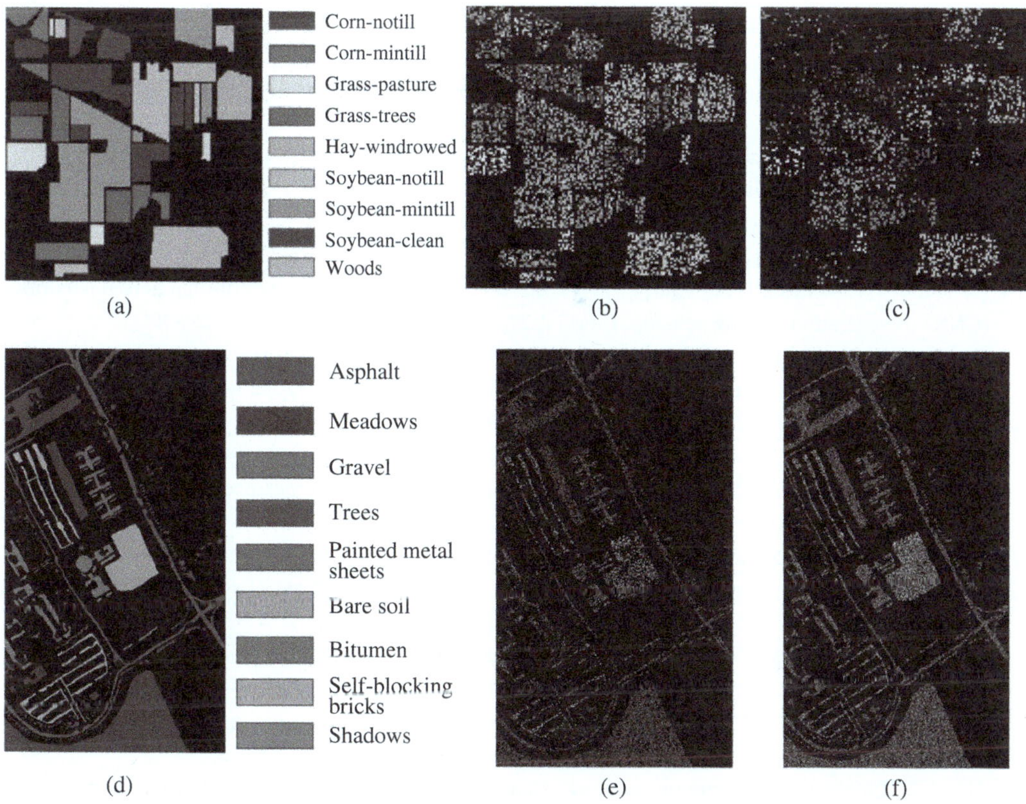

Figure 18.12 (a)–(c) originate from the Indian Pines dataset and (d)–(f) are from the Pavia University dataset. (a) Ground truth. (b) Noisy data. (c) Data after removal. (d) Ground truth. (e) Noisy data. (f) Data after removal.

After calculating the likelihood of mislabeling for each sample, order all instances in a descending order and select a certain percentage of samples to correct label. The newly constructed training set is then input into the ensemble framework and its performance on the validation set will be recorded. After several iterations, the needed filtered training set will be decided based on the best model performance on the validation set.

18.4 Conclusion

In summary, we initially explored the background of HSI classification, highlighting its complexity. Among various methods, ensemble learning emerged as a vital and effective approach. Subsequently, we introduced ensemble learning, elucidating its fundamental concept. We outlined four primary categories: bagging, boosting, stacking, and blending. Given their prevalence, we delved into bagging and boosting in greater detail, discussing notable methods such as RF, RoF, Adaboost, GBDT, and XGBoost. Additionally, we introduced the current research landscape of ensemble learning in addressing challenges in HSI classification, including high dimensionality, limited samples, class imbalance, and class noise.

References

1 Li, S., Song, W., Fang, L. et al. (2019). A deep learning for hyperspectral image classification: an overview. *IEEE Trans. Geosci. Remote Sens.* 57 (9): 6690–6709.

2 Bioucas-Dias, J.M., Plaza, A., Camps-Valls, G. et al. (2013). Hyperspectral remote sensing data analysis and future challenges. *IEEE Geosci. Remote Sens. Mag.* 1 (2): 6–36.

3 Chen, Y., Wang, Y., Gu, Y. et al. (2019). Deep learning ensemble for hyperspectral image classification. *IEEE J. Sel. Top. Appl. Earth Obs. Remote Sens.* 12 (6): 1882–1897.

4 Kattenborn, T., Leitloff, J., Schiefer, F., and Hinz, S. (2021). Review on convolutional neural networks (CNN) in vegetation remote sensing. *ISPRS J. Photogramm. Remote Sens.* 173: 24–49.

5 Galodha, A., Vashisht, R., Nidamanuri, R.R., and Ramiya, A.M. (2022). Deep convolution neural networks with resnet architecture for spectral-spatial classification of drone borne and ground based high resolution hyperspectral imagery. *Int. Arch. Photogramm. Remote Sens. Spat. Inf. Sci.* 43: 577–584.

6 Jackisch, R., Madriz, Y., Zimmermann, R. et al. (2019). Drone-borne hyperspectral and magnetic data integration: Otanmäki Fe-Ti-V deposit in Finland. *Remote Sens.* 11 (18): 2084.

7 Jackisch, R., Lorenz, S., Kirsch, M. et al. (2020). Integrated geological and geophysical mapping of a carbonatite-hosting outcrop in Siilinjärvi, Finland, using unmanned aerial systems. *Remote Sens.* 12 (18): 2998.

8 Lorenzo, P.R., Tulczyjew, L., Marcinkiewicz, M., and Nalepa, J. (2020). Hyperspectral band selection using attention-based convolutional neural networks. *IEEE Access* 8: 42384–42403.

9 Yin, J., Li, S., Zhu, H., and Luo, X. (2019). Hyperspectral image classification using CapsNet with well-initialized shallow layers. *IEEE Geosci. Remote Sens. Lett.* 16 (7): 1095–1099.

10 Bidari, I., Chickerur, S., Ranmale, H. et al. 2020. Hyperspectral imagery classification using deep learning. *2020 Fourth World Conference on Smart Trends in Systems, Security and Sustainability (WorldS4)*, 672–676. London, UK (27–28 July 2020). IEEE.

11 Thomas, S., Kuska, M.T., Bohnenkamp, D. et al. (2018). Benefits of hyperspectral imaging for plant disease detection and plant protection: a technical perspective. *J. Plant Dis. Prot.* 125: 5–20.

12 Shahshahani, B.M. and Landgrebe, D.A. (1994). The effect of unlabeled samples in reducing the small sample size problem and mitigating the Hughes phenomenon. *IEEE Trans. Geosci. Remote Sens.* 32 (5): 1087–1095.

13 Ahmad, M., Shabbir, S., Roy, S.K. et al. (2021). Hyperspectral image classification – traditional to deep models: a survey for future prospects. *IEEE J. Sel. Top. Appl. Earth Obs. Remote Sens.* 15: 968–999.

14 Feng, W., Gao, X., Boukir, S. et al. (2023). Hypothesis margin based ensemble method for the classification of noisy remote sensing data. *IEEE Trans. Geosci. Remote Sens.* 61: 5408321.

15 Zhou, Z.H. (2012). *Ensemble Methods: Foundations and Algorithms*. CRC press.

16 Feng, W., Long, Y., Dauphin, G. et al. (2024). Ensemble synthetic oversampling with pixel pair for class-imbalanced and small-sized hyperspectral data classification. *Int. J. Appl. Earth Obs. Geoinf.* 128: 103697.

17 Dietterich, T.G. (2000). Ensemble methods in machine learning. *International Workshop on Multiple Classifier Systems. MCS 2000.* (Vol. 1857, pp. 1–15). Springer, Berlin, Heidelberg.

18 Hansen, L.K. and Salamon, P. (1990). Neural network ensembles. *IEEE Trans. Pattern Anal. Mach. Intell.* 12 (10): 993–1001.

19 Leon, F., Floria, S.A., and Bădică, C. (2017). Evaluating the effect of voting methods on ensemble-based classification. *2017 IEEE international conference on innovations in intelligent Systems and applications (INISTA)*, 1–6, Gdynia, Poland (03–05 July 2017). IEEE.

20 Pal, M. (2005). Random forest classifier for remote sensing classification. *Int. J. Remote Sens.* 26 (1): 217–222.

21 Suthaharan, S. (2016). Decision tree learning. In: *Machine Learning Models and Algorithms for Big Data Classification: Thinking with Examples for Effective Learning* (pp. 237–269). Springer, Boston, MA.

22 Breiman, L. (2001). Random forests. *Mach. Learn.* 45: 5–32.

23 Rodriguez, J.J., Kuncheva, L.I., and Alonso, C.J. (2006). Rotation forest: a new classifier ensemble method. *IEEE Trans. Pattern Anal. Mach. Intell.* 28 (10): 1619–1630.

24 Xia, J., Ghamisi, P., Yokoya, N., and Iwasaki, A. (2017). Random forest ensembles and extended multiextinction profiles for hyperspectral image classification. *IEEE Trans. Geosci. Remote Sens.* 56 (1): 202–216.

25 Dong, Y., Du, B., Zhang, L., and Zhang, L. (2017). Dimensionality reduction and classification of hyperspectral images using ensemble discriminative local metric learning. *IEEE Trans. Geosci. Remote Sens.* 55 (5): 2509–2524.

26 Zhang, Y., Cao, G., and Li, X. (2020). Multiview-based random rotation ensemble pruning for hyperspectral image classification. *IEEE Trans. Instrum. Meas.* 70: 1–14.

27 Dong, S., Feng, W., Quan, Y. et al. (2022). Deep ensemble CNN method based on sample expansion for hyperspectral image classification. *IEEE Trans. Geosci. Remote Sens.* 60: 1–15.

28 Feng, W., Quan, Y., Dauphin, G. et al. (2021). Semi-supervised rotation forest based on ensemble margin theory for the classification of hyperspectral image with limited training data. *Inf. Sci.* 575: 611–638.

29 Fang, L., Zhao, W., He, N., and Zhu, J. (2020). Multiscale CNNs ensemble based self-learning for hyperspectral image classification. *IEEE Geosci. Remote Sens. Lett.* 17 (9): 1593–1597.

30 Cui, B., Dong, W., Yin, B. et al. (2023). Hyperspectral image classification method based on semantic filtering and ensemble learning. *Infrared Phys. Technol.* 135: 104949.

31 Quan, Y., Zhong, X., Feng, W. et al. (2021). SMOTE-based weighted deep rotation forest for the imbalanced hyperspectral data classification. *Remote Sens.* 13 (3): 464.

32 Lv, Q., Feng, W., Quan, Y. et al. (2021). Enhanced-random-feature-subspace-based ensemble CNN for the imbalanced hyperspectral image classification. *IEEE J. Sel. Top. Appl. Earth Obs. Remote Sens.* 14: 3988–3999.

33 Feng, W., Huang, W., and Bao, W. (2019). Imbalanced hyperspectral image classification with an adaptive ensemble method based on SMOTE and rotation forest with differentiated sampling rates. *IEEE Geosci. Remote Sens. Lett.* 16 (12): 1879–1883.

34 Feng, W., Dauphin, G., Huang, W. et al. (2019). Dynamic synthetic minority over-sampling technique-based rotation forest for the classification of imbalanced hyperspectral data. *IEEE J. Sel. Top. Appl. Earth Obs. Remote Sens.* 12 (7): 2159–2169.

35 Li, W., Wu, G., Zhang, F., and Du, Q. (2016). Hyperspectral image classification using deep pixel-pair features. *IEEE Trans. Geosci. Remote Sens.* 55 (2): 844–853.

36 Feng, W., Long, Y., Wang, S., and Quan, Y. (2023). A review of addressing class noise problems of remote sensing classification. *J. Syst. Eng. Electron.* 34 (1): 36–46.

37 Arafa, A., El-Fishawy, N., Badawy, M., and Radad, M. (2022). RN-SMOTE: reduced noise SMOTE based on DBSCAN for enhancing imbalanced data classification. *J. King Saud Univ. – Comput. Inf. Sci* 34 (8): 5059–5074.

19

Spectral-Spatial Hyperspectral Image Classification Based on Sparse Representation

Haoyang Yu[1], Jia Jia[1], Chuhan Shen[1], Jiaochan Hu[1], Chein-I Chang[1,2], and Lianru Gao[1,3]

[1] *Center of Hyperspectral Imaging in Remote Sensing, Information Science and Technology College, Dalian Maritime University, Dalian, China*
[2] *Department of Computer Science and Electrical Engineering, University of Maryland, Baltimore, MD, USA*
[3] *Aerospace Information Research Institute, Chinese Academy of Sciences, Beijing, China*

19.1 Introduction

The syncretic form of image and spectrum brings hyperspectral image (HSI) more details of terrestrial objects, and benefits the precision land-use and land-cover mapping [1, 2]. HSI classification (HSIC) is to use classifier to determine the class of each pixel based on its spectral and spatial features. Like remote sensing image classification, HSIC can be divided into supervised and unsupervised models [3, 4]. Compared to unsupervised classification, supervised models have been widely studied and applied due to their advantages in accuracy and stability [5, 6]. Under the supervision mode, a series of classic classification methods have emerged in the field.

The early classic classification approach is based on the spectral curves of ground objects for recognition. These methods mainly utilize spectrum in the spectral library and use matching algorithms to identify the type of ground coverage. Classic models include matching algorithms based on the minimum distance between spectrum, spectral waveform matching, spectral encoding matching, envelope analysis and spectral angle mapping (SAM) [7–9]. Some of these methods are sensitive to noise, while others have high requirements for spectral calibration and reflectance conversion. Some methods may even lose spectral information, so most are only suitable for rough and fast classification.

In subsequent research, another classic classification approach was gradually developed, which is based on the feature space [10]. It mainly utilizes the statistical characteristics of data to establish models. One of the classic methods is the maximum likelihood classification (MLC), which is a Bayesian statistical model estimated based on the probability distribution of samples [11]. Another classic method is the random forest classification, which is a machine learning model with tree structure developed from the decision tree algorithm [12, 13]. In addition, the support vector machine (SVM) is also a classic model. Its main principle is to find the optimal hyperplane that can maximize the margin between boundary samples [14]. And it is suitable for classifying the high-dimensional limited samples like HSI [15, 16]. With the deepening of research, based on the classic models that mainly deal with spectral features mentioned above, the spatial features

Machine-Learning-Based Hyperspectral Image Processing, First Edition. Edited by Bing Zhang.

and their combination have gradually become the key to improving classification. The representative one is the Markov random field (MRF) framework, which combines spectral and spatial features through the form of probability transformation to effectively improve the misclassification caused by complex spectral character [17]. However, due to the relatively independent processing of spatial and spectral features, there is still an imbalance in feature utilization in this post-processing framework.

For the purpose of classification, hyperspectral data actually contains high correlation between adjacent bands, and redundancy in both the spectral and spatial domains. Therefore, it has been demonstrated that HSI is essentially low-rank and can be represented sparsely [18, 19]. In this context, the sparse representation (SR)-based models have been introduced and rapidly promoted [20–22]. The main principle is that the sample to be classified should be determined as a class with less error when using linear representation of training samples [23, 24]. Under the constraints of different weight coefficients, classical models for processing spectral features can be divided into SR-based classification (SRC) and collaborative representation-based classification (CRC) [25, 26]. And in terms of combining and processing spatial and spectral features, such frameworks also have good scalability. Second generations of SRC have appeared in the literatures [27–29]. These models are basically under a common sparsity shared framework, with spatial consistency in consideration [30, 31]. Based on the inherent group-structured property, Group SRC (GSRC) is designed to reconstruct the dictionary composed of several class-dependent sub-dictionaries such that a testing sample is represented by group atoms rather than individual ones [32, 33]. In addition to the expansion of sparsity constraints, the representation model framework is constantly evolving around three main aspects. Firstly, at the level of spectral features, a series of research work focusing on feature and sample transformation has been carried out [34–37]. Secondly, at the level of spatial features, research work is oriented towards expanding by combining different levels of spatial information, such as nonlocal spatial similarity [36, 38, 39]. Thirdly, at the mining level of the model mechanism, a more simplified judgment mechanism and a multi-level feature integration framework have emerged [40, 41].

The reminder of this chapter is organized as follows: Section 19.2 reviews the classic SR-based and JR-based models. Section 19.3 introduces the proposed sparse representation-based hyperspectral image classification models from three aspects. The first one details the SR based on the feature extraction towards samples, highlighting how this technique can effectively capture the distinct characteristics of hyperspectral images. The second one discusses the integration of spatial similarity with sparse representation, which aims to improve the classification accuracy by considering the spatial relationships between pixels. And the last one presents the mechanism optimization towards sparse representation, describing the strategies employed to refine the classification process and achieve better performance. Section 19.4 evaluates the proposed methods with three widely used real hyperspectral data sets from different sensors. Section 19.5 concludes this paper with some remarks.

19.2 Related Models Description

19.2.1 SR-based Classifier

As a generation of the nearest neighbor classifier as well as the nearest subspace classifier, SRC is a simple but effective classifier which codes a tested sample $\mathbf{x}$ over a dictionary $\mathbf{D}$ such that $\mathbf{x}$ can be nearly represented by $\mathbf{x} \approx \mathbf{D}\boldsymbol{\alpha}$. SRC adopts the l_0-norm to measure the sparsity of $\boldsymbol{\alpha}$ which determines the number of non-zero values in $\boldsymbol{\alpha}$. Because the combinatorial l_0-norm minimization turns to be a non-convex NP-hard problem, the l_1-norm minimization as the closest convex function is utilized to replace it in SR formulation. Then, the class label of the tested pixel (i.e., check class by class) is determined by representing it using all training samples in $\mathbf{D}$. Therefore, SRC can be formulated as a Lagrange formulation as follows:

$$\hat{\boldsymbol{\alpha}} = \arg\min_{\boldsymbol{\alpha}} \left\{ \|\mathbf{x} - \mathbf{D}\boldsymbol{\alpha}\|_2^2 + \lambda\|\boldsymbol{\alpha}\|_1 \right\} \tag{19.1}$$

where $\|\boldsymbol{\alpha}\|_1 = \sum_{m=1}^{n} |\alpha_m|$ denotes the l_1-norm, and λ is defined as a regularization parameter that measures the relative importance of minimizing the vector α. Then, the residual of $\mathbf{x}$ is calculated. Then, the sparse representation of $\mathbf{x}$ using $\mathbf{D}$ and the optimal solution of coefficient $\hat{\boldsymbol{\alpha}}$ is given by:

$$\mathbf{r}_m(\mathbf{x}) = \|\mathbf{x} - \mathbf{D}_m\hat{\boldsymbol{\alpha}}_m\|_2^2 \tag{19.2}$$

where $\hat{\boldsymbol{\alpha}}_m$ is defined as the corresponding coefficient vector related to the class m in $\hat{\boldsymbol{\alpha}}$. Then, the final class label of $\mathbf{x}$ which is determined based on the minimum residual error between $\mathbf{x}$ and its approximation $\mathbf{D}_m\hat{\boldsymbol{\alpha}}_m$ is assigned by:

$$\text{class}(\mathbf{x}) = \arg\min_{m} \mathbf{r}_m(\mathbf{x}) \tag{19.3}$$

In this case, if $\mathbf{x}$ belongs to class m, $\mathbf{D}_m\hat{\boldsymbol{\alpha}}_m$ may represent $\mathbf{x}$ well while the most coefficients in $\hat{\boldsymbol{\alpha}}$ with $m \neq n$ are zeros, and only $\hat{\boldsymbol{\alpha}}_m$ has a value. That is, the non-zero value in $\hat{\boldsymbol{\alpha}}$ will ultimately determine the class label of $\mathbf{x}$.

19.2.2 CR-based Classifier

Compared to the competitive mechanism imposed by sparseness constraints in SRC, the collaborative mechanism is more suitable for HSIC. Therefore, the concept of CR and the CR-based classifier are introduced in this section. As shown in Figure 19.1, if considering the classification criterion of SRC from the perspective of geometric projection with letting $\hat{\mathbf{x}} = \mathbf{D}\hat{\boldsymbol{\alpha}}$ as the perpendicular projection of $\mathbf{x}$ onto the space spanned by $\mathbf{D}$, the reconstruction residual $\mathbf{r}_m(\mathbf{x})$ of m-th class in Eq. (19.2) in SRC can be further derived as:

$$\mathbf{r}_m(\mathbf{x}) = \|\mathbf{x} - \hat{\mathbf{x}}\|_2^2 + \|\hat{\mathbf{x}} - \mathbf{D}_m\hat{\boldsymbol{\alpha}}_m\|_2^2 \tag{19.4}$$

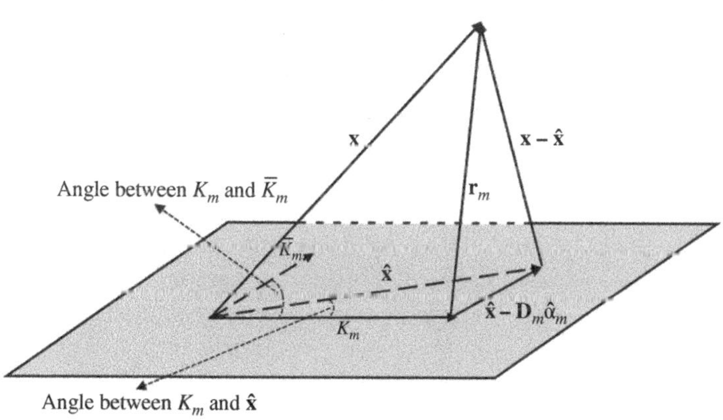

Figure 19.1 Geometric illustration of the representation of **x** over **D**.

Since $||\mathbf{x}-\hat{\mathbf{x}}||_2^2$ is a constant, $\mathbf{r}_m^*(\mathbf{x}) = ||\hat{\mathbf{x}} - \mathbf{D}_m\hat{\boldsymbol{\alpha}}_m||_2^2$ named as CR error plays a conclusive role in classification. For simplicity, via donating the parallel vectors $\kappa_m = \mathbf{D}_m\hat{\boldsymbol{\alpha}}_m$ and $\overline{\kappa}_m = \sum_{n\neq m}\mathbf{D}_n\hat{\boldsymbol{\alpha}}_n$, $\mathbf{r}_m^*(\mathbf{x})$ can be expressed as:

$$\mathbf{r}_m^*(\mathbf{x}) = \frac{\sin^2(\hat{\mathbf{x}}, \kappa_m)||\hat{\mathbf{x}}||^2}{\sin^2(\kappa_m, \overline{\kappa}_m)} \tag{19.5}$$

where $(\hat{\mathbf{x}}, \kappa_m)$ represents the angle between $\hat{\mathbf{x}}$ and κ_m. Similarly, $(\kappa_m, \overline{\kappa}_m)$ is the angle between κ_m and $\overline{\kappa}_m$. It can be concluded from Eq. (19.5) that, CR considers not only whether the angle between $\hat{\mathbf{x}}$ and κ_m is small, but also whether the angle between κ_m and $\overline{\kappa}_m$ is large. Due to eliminating the l_1-norm constraint, such a mechanism of "double checking" in CR can make HSIC more effective and robust.

Differing from SRC with l_1-norm that is time-consuming and cannot exploit the sparsity of $\boldsymbol{\alpha}$ with insufficient data samples, CRC believes that a tested sample can be collaboratively represented by the l_2-norm via all the training samples in $\mathbf{D}$. The regularized least square is utilized in CRC such that its closed-form solution can be easily achieved. Therefore, the CRC can be modeled as:

$$\hat{\boldsymbol{\alpha}} = \arg\min_{\boldsymbol{\alpha}} \left\{||\mathbf{x} - \mathbf{D}\boldsymbol{\alpha}||_2^2 + \lambda||\boldsymbol{\alpha}||_2^2\right\} \tag{19.6}$$

where $||\boldsymbol{\alpha}||_2 = \left(\sum_{m=1}^{n}|\alpha_m|^2\right)^{1/2}$ is defined as an l_2-norm constraint and λ is a regularization parameter which makes the solution stable and controls the sparsity of $\hat{\boldsymbol{\alpha}}$. Eventually, the sparsity by l_2-norm is weaker than that by l_1-norm. Then, the optimal solution of CRC can be expressed as:

$$\hat{\boldsymbol{\alpha}} = \left(\mathbf{D}^T\mathbf{D} + \lambda\mathbf{I}\right)^{-1}\mathbf{D}^T\mathbf{x} \tag{19.7}$$

Once the representation coefficient $\hat{\boldsymbol{\alpha}}$ is obtained, the combination of the dictionary and the weight vector is further considered to represent the tested pixel $\mathbf{x}$. Furthermore, we can compute residuals and obtain the final class label of the tested pixel as the same way did by Eqs. (19.2) and (19.3).

19.2.3 Joint SRC/Group SRC

19.2.3.1 Joint SRC

The classic SR-based models (i.e., SRC and CRC) take advantage of the potential sparsity of HSI to deal with the spectral characteristic for the classification. However, they do not consider the local spatial consistency among the signals, which can be further exploited for determination. In this context, the second generations of SR-based models have been designed under the JR-based framework. The Joint SRC (JSRC), as the most typical JR-based model, adopts the dictionary and the sparse coefficient to represent the testing pixel and its neighboring pixels together. With the consideration of the spatial consistency, the basic assumption of JSRC is that the sparse weight vectors associated with the neighborhood centered on the testing pixel could share a common sparsity support. Therefore, the general weight matrix is optimized towards the direction of row sparsity under a mixed norm constraint which can be solved upon the Lasso problem as follows:

$$\arg\min_{\mathbf{A}} ||\mathbf{X} - \mathbf{D}\mathbf{A}||_F^2 + \lambda||\mathbf{A}||_{1,2} \tag{19.8}$$

where $\mathbf{A}$ is a weight matrix whose columns are t weight vectors correspond to pixels in $\mathbf{X}$. Here, $||\mathbf{A}||_{1,2} = \sum_{i=1}^{n}\mathbf{a}^i$ is a $l_{1,2}$-norm regularization, where $\mathbf{a}^i$ represents the i-th row of $\mathbf{A}$, and n is the number of labeled samples in **D**, and can be solved by the simultaneously orthogonal matching pursuit (SOMP). After obtaining **A**, the class label of **X** is determined by the minimum total residual error under the Frobenius-norm constraint.

$$\text{class}(\mathbf{x}) = \arg\min_{m} \|\mathbf{X} - \mathbf{D}\delta_m(\mathbf{A})\|_F^2 \tag{19.9}$$

where $m \in [1, M]$ denotes the class index, and $\delta_m(A)$ defines an indicator operation zeroing out the elements in **A** that are not corresponding to the labeled samples of class m in **D**.

19.2.3.2 Group SRC

In SRC, the testing pixel is classified by evaluating the class-specific residual errors, which is calculated by certain group of atoms in weight vector and dictionary. Inspired by this property, group SRC model is designed to exploit the inherent structure-based priors of coefficients and dictionary, and incorporated with the spatial dependencies of pixels in neighborhood. The main idea of GSRC is to encourage sparse coefficients of only certain groups to be active and the remaining groups inactive, so that the pixels are represented by group of atoms instead of the individual ones. In GSRC, if we group atoms belonging to the same class, the matrix representing dictionary may be re-arranged as $\mathbf{D} = (\mathbf{D}_1, \ldots, \mathbf{D}_M)$ where $\mathbf{D}_m$ denotes a sub-dictionary with each column vector representing a labeled sample from class m. Therefore, the objective function of GSRC can be expressed as:

$$\arg\min_{\mathbf{A}} \|\mathbf{X} - \mathbf{D}\mathbf{A}\|_F^2 + \lambda \sum_{g \in G} \omega_g \left\|\mathbf{A}_g\right\|_2 \tag{19.10}$$

where $g \in \{G_1, \ldots, G_M\}$ indexes the M groups corresponding to the sub-dictionaries **D**, $\mathbf{A}_g$ represents the weight matrix of each group, and ω_g defines a compensation parameter for different sizes of groups. Here $\sum_{g \in G} \left\|\mathbf{A}_g\right\|_2$ defines a group-level $l_{1,2}$-norm regularization, and can be optimized by the Group Lasso algorithm. After obtaining the coefficient matrix **A**, the class label of **X** can be determined similar to Eq. (19.9). It should be noted from Eqs. (19.8) and (19.10) that GSRC would degenerate to a JSRC model if the group size reduces to one.

19.3 Hyperspectral Image Classification Based on Sparse Representation

19.3.1 Feature Extraction Based on Sparse Representation

Inspired by aforementioned work, we propose a new approach for hyperspectral imagery classification which integrates Locality Sensitive Discriminant Analysis (LSDA) with group sparse representation (GSR). The algorithm adopts LSDA to project the input data to a lower dimensional subspace which preserves the local neighborhood information and the discriminant information. Then, the projected data can be linearly represented by group-structured training samples to classify the testing set by measuring the class approximation error. The proposed approach, abbreviated as LSDA-GSR-Based Classification (LSDA-GSRC), takes advantage of both the local manifold structure and group sparse representation for better characterization and classification for hyperspectral data set.

19.3.1.1 Locality Sensitive Discriminant Analysis

Let $\mathbf{X} = \{\mathbf{x}_1, \mathbf{x}_2, ..., \mathbf{x}_n\}$ be a hyperspectral image, where $\mathbf{x}_i = [x_{i1}, x_{i2}, ..., x_{id}]^T$ denotes a spectral vector associated with an image pixel $i \in S$, n and d represent the total number of pixels and spectral bands, respectively. The principle of a subspace-based projection is to find a transformation matrix $\mathbf{A} = \{\mathbf{a}_1, \mathbf{a}_2, ..., \mathbf{a}_k\}$ that maps $\mathbf{X}$ to $\mathbf{Z} = \{\mathbf{z}_1, \mathbf{z}_2, ..., \mathbf{z}_n\} \in \mathbb{R}^{k\times n}$ ($k << d$) via $\mathbf{Z} = \mathbf{A}^T\mathbf{X}$. Under assumption that $\mathbf{x}_i \in \mathcal{M}$ ($\mathcal{M}$ denotes the underlying manifold), one can build a graph G by searching its t nearest neighbors (i.e., $N(\mathbf{x}_i) = \{\mathbf{x}_i^1, ..., \mathbf{x}_i^t\}$) and putting an edge between $\mathbf{x}_i$ and $N(\mathbf{x}_i)$. The local geometry of data manifold is then characterized by graph G with weight matrix $\mathbf{W}$ which can be defined as:

$$\mathbf{W}_{ij} = \begin{cases} 1, & \text{if } \mathbf{x}_i \in N(\mathbf{x}_j) \text{ or } \mathbf{x}_j \in N(\mathbf{x}_i) \\ 0, & \text{otherwise} \end{cases} \tag{19.11}$$

In order to develop both geometrical and discriminant structure of data manifold, LSDA is adopted to construct within-class graph G_w and between-class graph G_b by splitting $N(\mathbf{x}_i)$ into two subsets, $N_w(\mathbf{x}_i)$ and $N_b(\mathbf{x}_i)$, which can be expressed as:

$$\begin{cases} N_w(\mathbf{x}_i) = \left\{x_i^j \mid l\left(x_i^j\right) = l(x_i), 1 \le j \le t\right\} \\ N_b(\mathbf{x}_i) = \left\{x_i^j \mid l\left(x_i^j\right) \neq l(x_i), 1 \le j \le t\right\} \end{cases} \tag{19.12}$$

where $l(\mathbf{x}_i)$ is the class label of $\mathbf{x}_i$. Therefore, the weight matrices $\mathbf{W}_w$ and $\mathbf{W}_b$ of G_w and G_b can be defined as:

$$\begin{aligned} \mathbf{W}_{w,ij} &= \begin{cases} 1, & \text{if } \mathbf{x}_i \in N_w(\mathbf{x}_j) \text{ or } \mathbf{x}_j \in N_w(\mathbf{x}_i) \\ 0, & \text{otherwise} \end{cases} \\ \mathbf{W}_{b,ij} &= \begin{cases} 1, & \text{if } \mathbf{x}_i \in N_b(\mathbf{x}_j) \text{ or } \mathbf{x}_j \in N_b(\mathbf{x}_i) \\ 0, & \text{otherwise} \end{cases} \end{aligned} \tag{19.13}$$

To satisfy the criterion that connected pointes in G_w are close enough and the ones in G_b stay as distant as possible, the following two objective functions are defined for $\mathbf{Z}$.

$$\min \sum_{ij} (\mathbf{z}_i - \mathbf{z}_j)^2 \mathbf{W}_{w,ij} \tag{19.14}$$

$$\max \sum_{ij} (\mathbf{z}_i - \mathbf{z}_j)^2 \mathbf{W}_{b,ij} \tag{19.15}$$

Since $\mathbf{Z} = \mathbf{A}^T\mathbf{X}$, the objective function Eq. (19.14) can be reduced to $(\mathbf{A}^T\mathbf{X}\mathbf{D}_w\mathbf{X}^T\mathbf{A} - \mathbf{A}^T\mathbf{X}\mathbf{W}_w\mathbf{X}^T\mathbf{A})$, where $\mathbf{D}_w$is a diagonal matrix with $D_{w,ii} = \sum_j \mathbf{W}_{w,ij}$. Similarly, the objective function Eq. (19.15) can be reduced to$\mathbf{A}^T\mathbf{X}\mathbf{L}_b\mathbf{X}^T\mathbf{A}$, where $\mathbf{L}_b = \mathbf{D}_b - \mathbf{W}_b$ is the Laplacian matrix of G_b, and $\mathbf{D}_b$ is a diagonal matrix with $D_{b,ii} = \sum_j \mathbf{W}_{b,ij}$. Considering the influence of $D_{w,ii}$ to $\mathbf{x}_i$, it is suggested to impose a constraint $\mathbf{Z}^T\mathbf{D}_w\mathbf{Z} = 1$ to the objective function. Then the entire optimization problem can be represented as:

$$\begin{aligned} &\arg \max_{\mathbf{A}} \mathbf{A}^T\mathbf{X}[\alpha\mathbf{L}_b + (1-\alpha)\mathbf{W}_w]\mathbf{X}^T\mathbf{A} \\ &\quad s.t.\ \mathbf{A}^T\mathbf{X}\mathbf{D}_w\mathbf{X}^T\mathbf{A} = 1 \end{aligned} \tag{19.16}$$

where $\alpha \in [0, 1]$ is a suitable constant. The solution to Eq. (19.16) can be found by solving the following generalized eigenvalue problem.

$$\mathbf{X}[\alpha \mathbf{L}_b + (1-\alpha)\mathbf{W}_w]\mathbf{X}^T\mathbf{A} = \lambda \mathbf{X}\mathbf{D}_w\mathbf{X}^T\mathbf{A} \tag{19.17}$$

Let **A** be the solution to Eq. (19.17) with the decreasing eigenvalues and the result of LSDA can be obtained by $\mathbf{Z} = \mathbf{A}^T\mathbf{X}$, where $\mathbf{A} = \{\mathbf{a}_1, \mathbf{a}_2, \ldots, \mathbf{a}_k\}$ is a $d \times k$ matrix.

19.3.1.2 LSDA-GSR-based Classification

Considering that the main principle of sparse representation based classifiers is the representation of samples which is related to the training size, it is reasonable to implement a manifold subspace projection process for better characterization of features. Derived from the aforementioned algorithms, LSDA-GSRC for hyperspectral imagery is a two-step process: (i) local manifold subspace-based projection, where LSDA is adopted to project the training and testing sets to a lower-dimensional subspace. (ii) representation-based classification, where the projected testing set is linearly represented by group-structured training samples via GSRC. Therefore, the final objective function of LSDA-GSRC can be represented as:

$$\min_{\mathbf{B}} \frac{1}{2}\left\|L(\mathbf{Y}) - L(\mathbf{D})\mathbf{B}^L\right\|_F^2 + \lambda \sum_{g \in G} \omega_g \left\|\mathbf{B}_g^L\right\|_2 \tag{19.18}$$

where $L(\mathbf{Y})$ and $L(\mathbf{D})$ are projected by LSDA with **Y** and **D**, $\mathbf{B}^L$ is a group sparse matrix and $\mathbf{B}_g^L$ refers to the coefficients of each group corresponding to $L(\mathbf{D})$. Finally, the class label of the center testing pixel **y** in **Y** is determined by the minimum total residual error.

$$\text{class}(\mathbf{y}) = \arg\min_c \left\|L(\mathbf{Y}) - L(\mathbf{D})\delta_c(\mathbf{B}^L)\right\|_F^2 \tag{19.19}$$

where $\delta_c(\mathbf{B}^L)$ is the indicator operation which can zero out all the elements in $\mathbf{B}^L$ that do not belong to class c (Algorithm 19.1).

19.3.2 Spatial Similarity Integration with Sparse Representation

In comparison to SRC, GSRC incorporates structure priors with spatial dependencies in the local area. In order to satisfy the homogeneity assumption, GSRC usually considers a small neighborhood around the testing pixel. If the neighborhood locates at a complex scenario, such as the boundary of classes, the current spatial correlation will not be sufficient to provide an appropriate

Algorithm 19.1 LSDA-GSRC

constraint of spatial consistency, which may lead to an error of response in the representation. Therefore, under this case, the nonlocal spatial information is particularly important, due to its supplement of spatial coherence from a nonlocal distribution. In our framework, we first consider a larger patch contains the current neighborhood, and find its nonlocal spatial similar patches in defined scopes. Then, we further locate the most spectrally similar pixels to the one under investigation in the found patches. After that, a fusion pattern is designed to incorporate the found nonlocal similar pixels and the pixels in the local neighborhood. Finally, the GSR-based architecture is applied to process the fused data characterized by the manifold learning algorithm.

19.3.2.1 Local Spectral Similarity Through Nonlocal Spatial Similarity

As illustrated in Figure 19.2, let $\mathbf{P}_{i,j}$ defines a $w \times w$ pixel-sized patch with the center pixel located at $\mathbf{x}_{i,j}$. In order to satisfy the searching purpose, $\mathbf{X}$ is expanded to a $(r + w - 1) \times (c + w - 1)$ pixel-sized image, where r and c are the length of the original rows and columns. Then, we collect $w \times w$ pixel-sized patches centered on the pixels within a $v \times v$ pixel-sized search window around $\mathbf{x}_{i,j}$ $(v \leq \min(r, c))$. Here, the definition of v is mainly for the balance between the efficiency and computation time. Besides, the collection process follows a principle that the nonlocal patches should be non-overlapped with $\mathbf{P}_{i,j}$, thereby to guarantee that the contribution of the found information is apart from the ones in the local area. In order to satisfy this principle, we design a simple way to avoid the tedious process of judgment.

As illustrated in Figure 19.3, we apply a morphological operator of dilation to generate two masks centered on the location of $\mathbf{x}_{i,j}$ with size of $(2w - 1) \times (2w - 1)$ and $v \times v$, respectively. The areas between two masks (colored in white in Figure 19.2) are the locations, on which the patches centered satisfy the non-overlapped principle in defined region.

Let $\mathbf{P}$ denotes the set of collected patches, the next process is to find the subset ${}^{S}\mathbf{P} = \{{}^{s}\mathbf{P}_{a,\,b} \mid s \in [1, S]\}$ from $\mathbf{P}$, where s indexes the similar patches. The similarity between $\mathbf{P}_{i,j}$ and $\mathbf{P}$ is measured by calculating the sum of Euclidian distances between pixels in the corresponding locations as follows:

$$\underset{\mathbf{x}_p \in \mathbf{P}_{i,j},\, \mathbf{x}'_p \in {}^{s}\mathbf{P}_{a,b}}{dist}\left(\mathbf{P}_{i,j}, {}^{s}\mathbf{P}_{a,b}\right) = \sum_{p=1}^{w^2} \left\| \mathbf{x}_p, \mathbf{x}'_p \right\|_2 \tag{19.20}$$

where $\mathbf{x}_p$ and $\mathbf{x}'_p$ are the pth pixel vector in $\mathbf{P}_{i,j}$ and ${}^{s}\mathbf{P}_{a,b}$, and $\left\| \mathbf{x}_p, \mathbf{x}'_p \right\|_2$ calculates the Euclidian distance between them. With consideration of the computational cost, the calculation is suggested to perform on the first q components of singular value decomposition (SVD), which maintains the relative distance of the original space under the orthogonal projection transformation. The determination of similarity is based on judgment of the difference and its cause between the compared patches. Theoretically, two patches are considered to be similar, if the difference between them is caused only by noise. Otherwise, they are judged to be dissimilar. Assumed that the noise of each component of $\mathbf{X}$ obeys the Gaussian distribution, following, it can be transformed to a standardized normal distribution, such that calculation in Eq. (19.20) would yield variation of noise in Chi square distribution under the similar condition. In this context, we can obtain a reference value of threshold T to evaluate the $dist(\mathbf{P}_{i,j}, {}^{s}\mathbf{P}_{a,b})$ in Eq. (19.20). Here we remark that, in practice, T still needs to be fine-tuned due to the uncertainty of noise distribution and subtle spectral difference. Besides, some patches should be allowed to have no similar objects under the limitation of the threshold, which can be considered that their texture features are unique in the image.

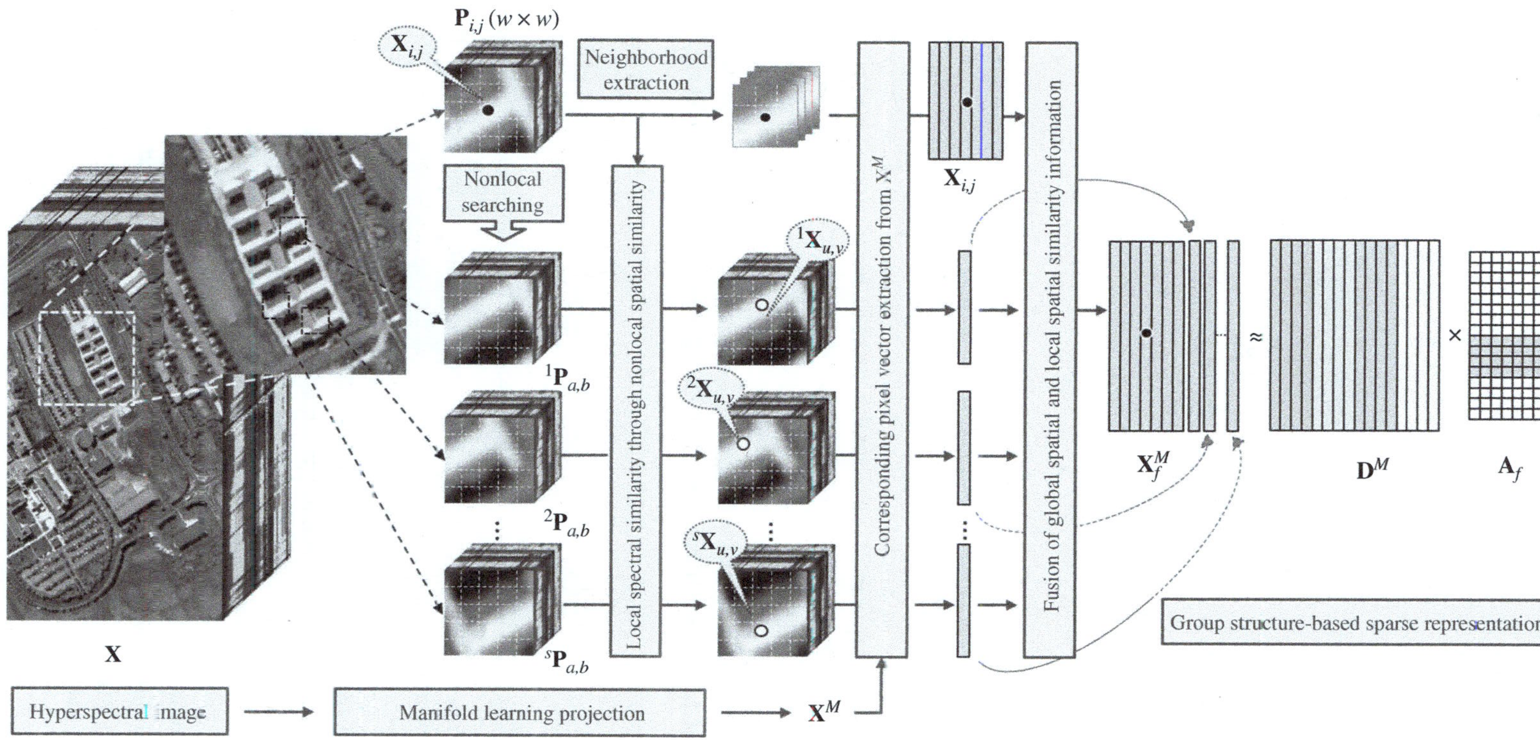

Figure 19.2 General framework for the proposed global spatial and local spectral similarity-based GSRC.

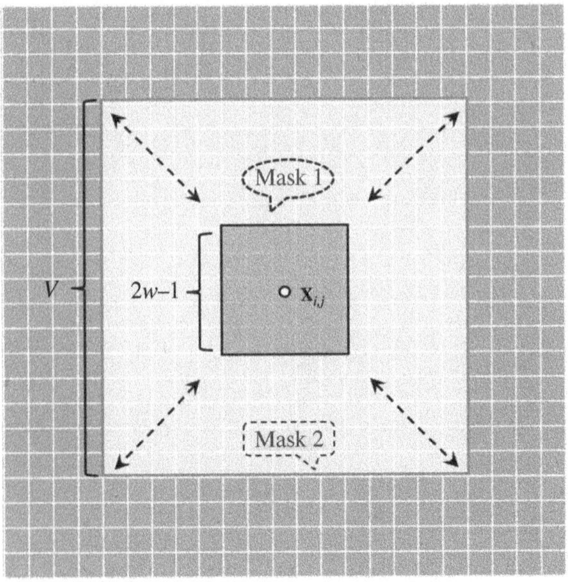

Figure 19.3 Schematic diagram of searching window.

In our experiments, the above processes do find similar patches, for instance, as shown in Figure 19.2. However, the found patches usually have a slight deviation towards the one under investigation, which may lead to inaccuracies by the direct use of their information. Therefore, we propose to perform a further local search for spectra within the found nonlocal similar patches, finding the most spectrally similar pixels to the testing pixel $\mathbf{x}_{i,j}$. Therefore, after ${}^{S}\mathbf{P}$ is obtained, the set of most spectrally similar pixels ${}^{S}\mathbf{x} = \{{}^{s}\mathbf{x}_{u,v} \in {}^{s}\mathbf{P}_{a,b} \mid s \in [1, S]\}$ towards $\mathbf{x}_{i,j}$ can be located as follows:

$$\min_{{}^{s}\mathbf{x}_{u,v}} \operatorname{dist}\left(\mathbf{x}_{i,j}, {}^{s}\mathbf{x}_{u,v}\right)_{{}^{s}\mathbf{x}_{u,v} \in {}^{s}\mathbf{P}_{a,b}} = \sum_{b=1}^{B} \left\| x_{i,j}^{b}, {}^{s}x_{u,v}^{b} \right\|_2 \tag{19.21}$$

where $x_{i,j}^{b}$ and ${}^{s}x_{u,v}^{b}$ are the values of $\mathbf{x}_{i,j}$ and ${}^{s}\mathbf{x}_{u,v}$ in b_{th} band, and $\left\| x_{i,j}^{b}, {}^{s}x_{u,v}^{b} \right\|_2$ calculates their Euclidian distance. As illustrated in Figure 19.2, ${}^{s}\mathbf{x}_{u,v}$ might not be located at the center of ${}^{s}\mathbf{P}_{a,b}$ which denotes a precise extraction of information.

19.3.2.2 Global Spatial and Local Spectral Similarity-based GSRC

In practical application, it should be noted that many patches have similar structures or have similar objects. Therefore, our proposed the following method for specific situation.

For a testing pixel, when its similar pixels exist under the conditions of aforementioned process, we first remember their locations, and then extract the corresponding vectors from $\mathbf{X}$. Let ${}^{S}\mathbf{x} = \{{}^{s}\mathbf{x}_{u,v} \mid s \in [1, S]\}$ denotes the set of the most spectrally similar pixels to $\mathbf{x}_{i,j}$ in nonlocal areas, and $\mathbf{X}_{i,j}$ represents the neighboring pixels in local area. The proposed method, named global spatial and local spectral similarity (GSLS) is actually a fusion of nonlocal and local information, which refer to ${}^{S}\mathbf{x}$ and $\mathbf{X}_{i,j}$ under this case. As illustrated in Figure 19.2, in our designed fusion framework, ${}^{S}\mathbf{x} \in \mathbb{R}^{d \times S}$ and $\mathbf{X}_{i,j}$ are combined together with their rows aligned, such that the fused data can be

Algorithm 19.2 GSLS-GSRC

represented as $\mathbf{X}_f \in \mathbb{R}^{d\times(t+S)}$. The proposed global spatial and local spectral similarity-based GSRC (GSLS-GSRC) is in fact the group structure-based representation based on GSLS, of which the objective function can be expressed as follows:

$$\arg\min_{\mathbf{A}_f} \|\mathbf{X}_f - \mathbf{D}\mathbf{A}_f\|_F^2 + \lambda \sum_{g\in G} \omega_g \|\mathbf{A}_{fg}\|_2 \tag{19.22}$$

where $\boldsymbol{A}_f \in \mathbb{R}^{n\times(t+s)}$ is the coefficient matrix, including $\mathbf{A}_{fg}$ defines the group-form weight matrix. The class label of the testing pixel $\mathbf{x}_{i,j}$ can finally be determined by the class that provides the minimum residual error as follows:

$$\text{class}(\mathbf{x}_{i,j}) = \arg\min_k \|\mathbf{X}_f - \mathbf{D}\delta_k(\mathbf{A}_f)\|_F^2 \tag{19.23}$$

The pseudo code of the proposed GSLS-GSRC approach is summarized in Algorithm 19.2.

19.3.3 Mechanism Optimization Towards Sparse Representation

No matter in the classic SR-based models or in the JR-based frameworks, the sparse coefficient is generally considered with the dictionary together. As introduced before, the sparse coefficient is processed in conjunction with the dictionary to calculate the approximate value of testing signal, such that the classification is determined according to the class-dependent minimum residual error between the approximation and the represented signal. However, the residual-based determination mechanism ignores the role of sparse coefficient to a certain extent. Specifically, traditional SR-based models mainly focus on the sparsity of coefficients, i.e., whether they are zero or not. But there is less attention on the exact value of coefficient and exploitation of hidden discriminate information under these values. Therefore, this section dissects representation-response process from the perspective of initial principle of SR, focuses on the analysis of the function of coefficients, and deduces a simplified and effective decision mechanism to form new models in the spectral and spectral-spatial domain.

19.3.3.1 AD-driven Representation-based Classifier

According to the definition of representation-based model, it can be understood as representing the testing pixel with a sparse linear combination of the labeled samples. For the sake of understanding, a simple case can be assumed as Eq. (19.24). The testing pixel is represented by a single element with non- zero coefficient from some certain classes as follows:

$$\mathbf{x}_{i,j} \approx \alpha_p \mathbf{x}_t^k + \alpha_q \mathbf{x}_{t_1}^{k\prime} + \alpha_m \mathbf{x}_{t_2}^{k\prime\prime} + \dots + \alpha_n \mathbf{x}_{t_n}^{k^*} \tag{19.24}$$

where $\|\alpha_p\|_d \geq \|\alpha_q\|_d \geq \|\alpha_m\|_d \geq \dots \geq \|\alpha_n\|_d$ denotes the weight atoms with decreasing order of measurement l_d-norm in $\hat{\boldsymbol{\alpha}}_{i,j}$. Since $\hat{\boldsymbol{\alpha}}_{i,j}$ is sparsely constrained, most atoms in it are zero. It means that the samples participated in the representation of current testing pixel are actually the ones whose weight values are not zero. In other words, the labeled samples with nonzero coefficients are active in current representation process and contribute their own feature information to the approximate representation, while the other samples with zero coefficients are essentially not involved in the subsequent calculations. Moreover, the samples with larger values of measurement play decisive roles to the representation, which means that the attribution of these samples with higher degree of activity can largely determine the class of the testing pixel.

Based on the above analysis, here a new concept is defined from the sparse coefficient to sub-dictionary, which is called activity degree (AD). The AD is calculated through the specific values of the class-dependent coefficients, which accounts the contribution of the labeled samples from different classes in the dictionary to the representation of testing pixel. The AD of a certain class k is calculated by the measurement of l_d-norm ($d = 1$ or 2) to its corresponding weight vector $\boldsymbol{\alpha}_{i,j}^k$ as the expression in Eq. (19.25). Here should be noted that some other appropriate forms of norm can also be used for measurement.

$$\mathrm{AD}_k = \left\| \boldsymbol{\alpha}_{i,j}^k \right\|_d \tag{19.25}$$

With the consideration of AD, a classifier named AD-driven representation-based classifier (ADRC) is established, of which the main principle is to divide the testing pixel into the class with the maximum AD. Specifically, Figure 19.4 shows a schematic diagram of the ADRC in a simplified situation. Assuming that only three atoms, i.e., α_p, α_q, α_m ($\|\alpha_p\|_d > \|\alpha_q\|_d > \|\alpha_m\|_d$), that are not zero after the optimization of $\hat{\boldsymbol{\alpha}}_{i,j}$, and the samples in $\mathbf{D}$ corresponding to these three atoms belong to

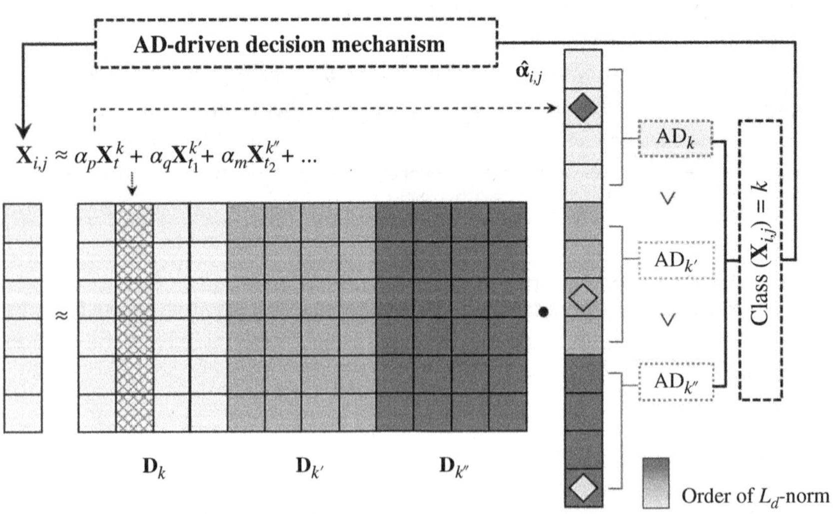

Figure 19.4 The schematic diagram of ADRC.

Algorithm 19.3 ADRC

class k, k' and k'', respectively. According to Eqs. (19.24) and (19.25), the class label of $\mathbf{x}_{i,j}$can be identified as class k, since$\mathrm{AD}_k > \mathrm{AD}_{k'} > \mathrm{AD}_{k''}$, The pseudo code is summarized in Algorithm 19.3.

The established ADRC achieves a simplified classification towards the traditional SR-based models. Since the higher AD of a certain class, the higher contribution of its samples to the representation, and subsequently results to the smaller residual error in the approximation. As long as the coefficient is nonzero, its corresponding samples is regarded as activation. Through the transformation of AD, it can effectively contribute to the determination. To a certain extent, the AD-driven decision mechanism can be considered as adopting the sparse idea to suppress the elements with lower AD as a kind of noise. Instead of the additional class-dependent residual error-based analysis, ADRC brings a simplified and effective classification.

19.3.3.2 NAD-driven Representation-based Classifier

ADRC changes the perspective of analysis and decision mechanism of the SR-based models, while the acquisition of coefficient still depends on the mutual response of spectral feature. In this case, the spectral information of the testing pixel has an important influence on the determination of its class. However, some issues, such as the same object with different spectrums, existed in HSI may produce spectral variation, which may lead to misclassification under the framework that only uses the spectral information.

In order to address these issues, most approaches focus on the utilization of spatial information in HSI. The basic assumption is that adjacent pixels in spatial position have a high probability to belonging to the same class. Thereby, such "noise pixels" in the homogeneous area can be constrained and corrected based on the spatial consistency. Inspired by this point, a novel spectral-spatial framework is established, called neighborhood ADRC (NADRC), with an extension of the aforementioned AD-driven model.

Specifically, Figure 19.5 illustrates the schematic diagram of the proposed NADRC. Following some basic conditions in ADRC, $\mathbf{A}$ represents the image of AD, where the dimensional information of each pixel is updated by its class-dependent AD. For a testing pixel $\mathbf{x}_{i,j}$, a $\widehat{w} \times \widehat{w}$pixel-sized neighborhood centered on its position is extracted from $\mathbf{A}$, and denoted as$\mathbf{A}_{i,j}$. In the case shown in Figure 19.5, it is very likely to lead to a misclassification via the AD-based decision, if there is a spectral variation of $\mathbf{x}_{i,j}$ resulting in an inaccurate response of $\hat{\boldsymbol{\alpha}}_{i,j}$. But at the same time, it can be noticed that most of its surrounding active atoms mainly concentrated in another class, which indicates that $\mathbf{x}_{i,j}$ has a high probability to locate in a homogeneous area. Therefore, it is available to take advantage of this spatial coherence to adjust the determination.

In this context, another concept is defined towards the image of AD, called neighborhood AD (NAD). The NAD evaluates the contribution of different class-dependent sub-dictionaries to the

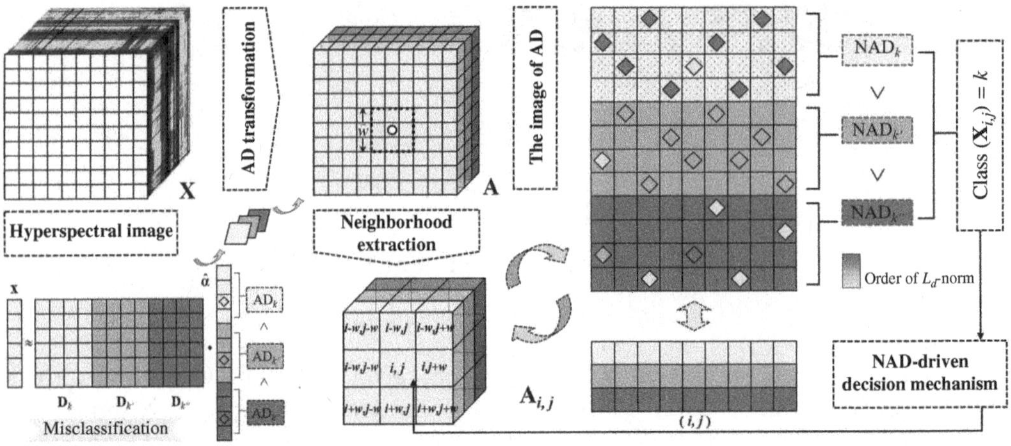

Figure 19.5 The schematic diagram of the proposed NADRC model.

representation of the testing neighborhood. The NAD of a certain class is calculated by the sum of AD as follows:

$$\mathrm{NAD}_k = \sum_{v=1}^{\widehat{w}^2} \mathrm{AD}_k^{(v)} \tag{19.26}$$

where v denotes the index of vector in the neighborhood. In this case of Figure 19.5, it is obvious that $\mathrm{NAD}_k > \mathrm{NAD}_{k'} > \mathrm{NAD}_{k''}$ in spite of $\mathrm{AD}_k < \mathrm{AD}_{k'} < \mathrm{AD}_{k''}$, such that the class label of $\mathbf{x}_{i,j}$ can be corrected as class k. The pseudo code of NADRC is summarized in Algorithm 19.4.

In general, the basis of NADRC remains spatial coherence, but its processing is more direct. Compared with the strong sparsity constraint towards neighboring signals of JR-based framework, the proposed method relaxes this condition, and takes advantage of spatial information in terms of the overall activity of each class. Instead of the high computational cost with optimization of mixed-norm constraint, and residual error-dependent discussion, NADRC implements a more effective and practical classification mode, which is demonstrated in the following experimental results of this paper.

Algorithm 19.4 NADRC

Input: $\mathbf{X}$, $\mathbf{D}$, $\mathbf{x}_{i,j}$, $\widehat{w}$

Step 1: Obtain the class-dependent AD of each pixel in **X** according to Eq. (19.25).

Step 2: Form the activity image A based on **Step 1**.

Step 3: Extract $\widehat{w} \times \widehat{w}$ pixel-sized neighborhood $A_{i,j}$ centered on the location of current testing pixel $\mathbf{x}_{i,j}$.

Step 4: Calculate the NAD of each class from $A_{i,j}$ according to Eq. (19.26).

Step 5: Identify the class with the maximum NAD.

$\kappa = \max_k \{\mathrm{NAD}_k \mid k \in [1, K]\}$

Output: class($\mathbf{x}_{i,j}$) = κ

19.4 Experimental Results and Analysis

19.4.1 Data Description

19.4.1.1 University of Pavia Data Set

The image consists of 610 × 340 pixels, with a spatial resolution of 1.3 m per pixel. The image contains 103 spectral bands, with the spectral coverage ranging from 0.43 to 0.86 μm, after 12 bands are removed due to the high noise. The reference of this image includes nine mutually exclusive classes, with a total of 42,776 labeled samples. The composite representation of this image is shown in Figure 19.6a, and Figure 19.6b provides the corresponding reference data.

19.4.1.2 Washington DC Mall Data Set

The image totally consists of 280 × 307 pixels, with a spatial resolution of 3 m per pixel. The original image contains 210 spectral bands, with the spectral coverage ranging from 0.4 to 2.5 μm. In practice, 191 bands are preserved, while the spectral bands ranging from 0.9 to 1.4 μm are removed due to the atmospheric absorption. The reference of this image includes six classes of interests, with a total of 10,190 labeled samples. Figure 19.7a shows the composite image, and the corresponding reference data is provided in Figure 19.7b.

19.4.1.3 Salinas Data Set

The image totally consists of 512 × 217 pixels, with a geometric resolution of 3.7 m per pixel. The image contains 224 spectral bands, with the spectral coverage ranging from 0.2 to 2.4 μm, after 20 bands are removed due to the water absorption. The reference data includes sixteen ground-truth classes, with a total of 54,129 labeled samples. Figure 19.8a–b show the composite image and the corresponding reference data, respectively.

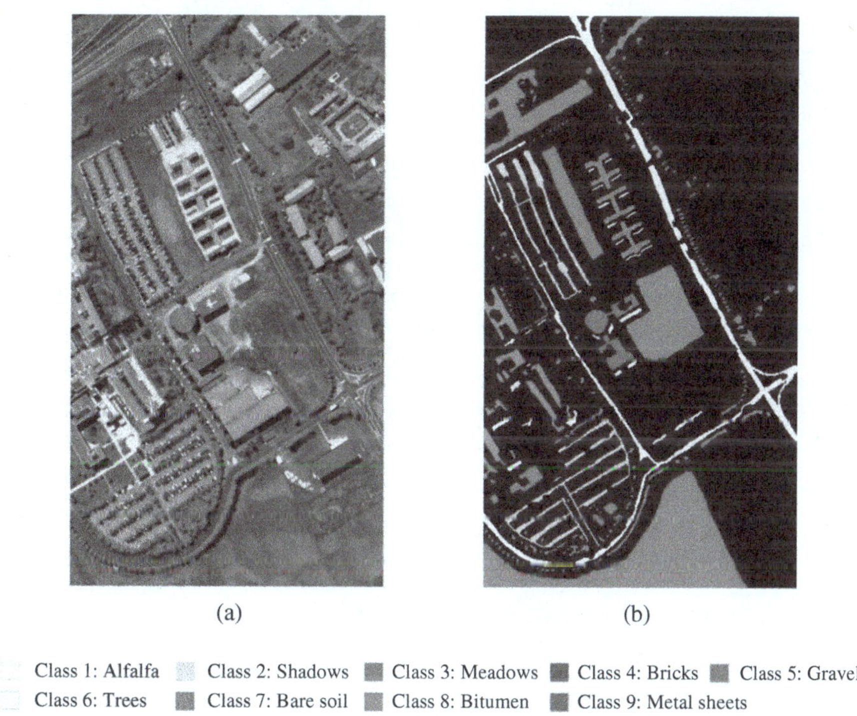

Figure 19.6 The ROSIS University of Pavia scene. (a) Composite image and (b) reference map.

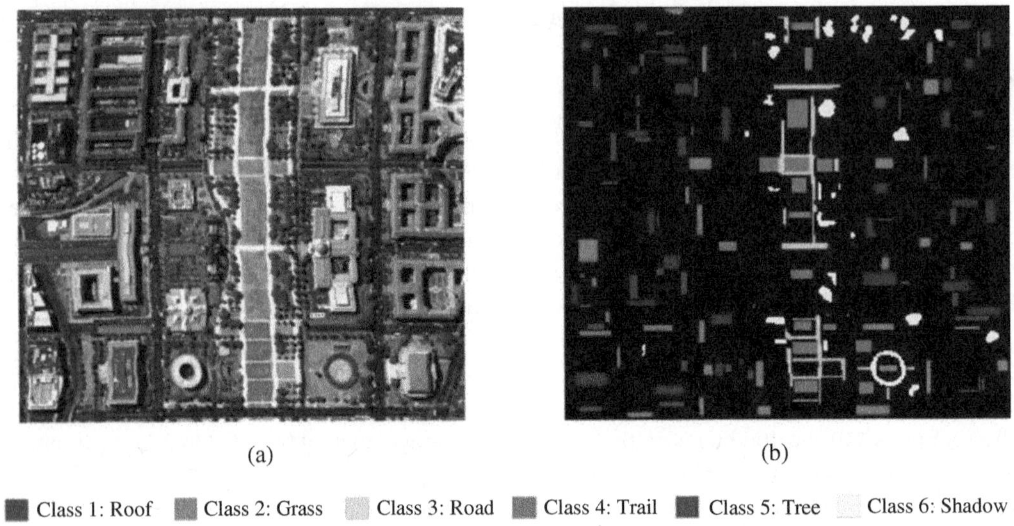

Figure 19.7 The HYDICE Washington DC Mall scene. (a) Composite image and (b) reference map.

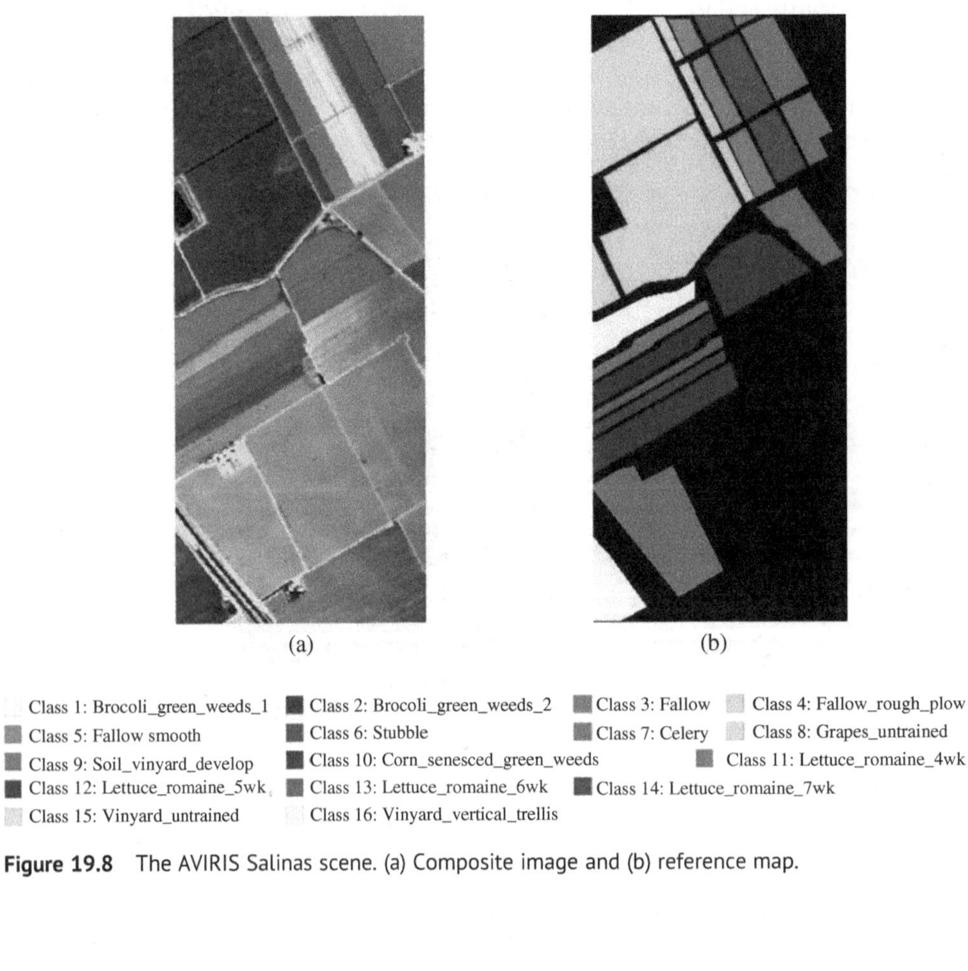

Figure 19.8 The AVIRIS Salinas scene. (a) Composite image and (b) reference map.

19.4.2 Parameter Setting

19.4.2.1 Dimensionality in NPE

The manifold learning dimensionality *d* in NPE for the proposed framework is briefly investigated. Figure 19.9a–c show the overall accuracy (OA) results as a function of *d* and the total number of labeled samples *n* selected for the GSR-based classification with different data set. According to Figure 19.9, *d* is basically set to the value which is generally optimal or suboptimal for most cases of each data set. Therefore, *d* is set to 20, 20 and 30 for the University of Pavia scene, the Washington DC Mall scene and the Salinas scene, respectively.

19.4.2.2 Searching Window Size

The relationships between the OA results, searching window size *v* and computational cost of different data sets are shown in Figure 19.10a–c. As illustrated in Figure 19.10, when *v* is extended to a certain size, OA tends to be stable, but the computation time has a relatively obvious increase. Therefore, according to Figure 19.10, with a consideration of the balance between the OA results and the computational cost, *v* is finally set to 150, 100 and 100 for the University of Pavia scene, the Washington DC Mall scene and the Salinas scene, respectively.

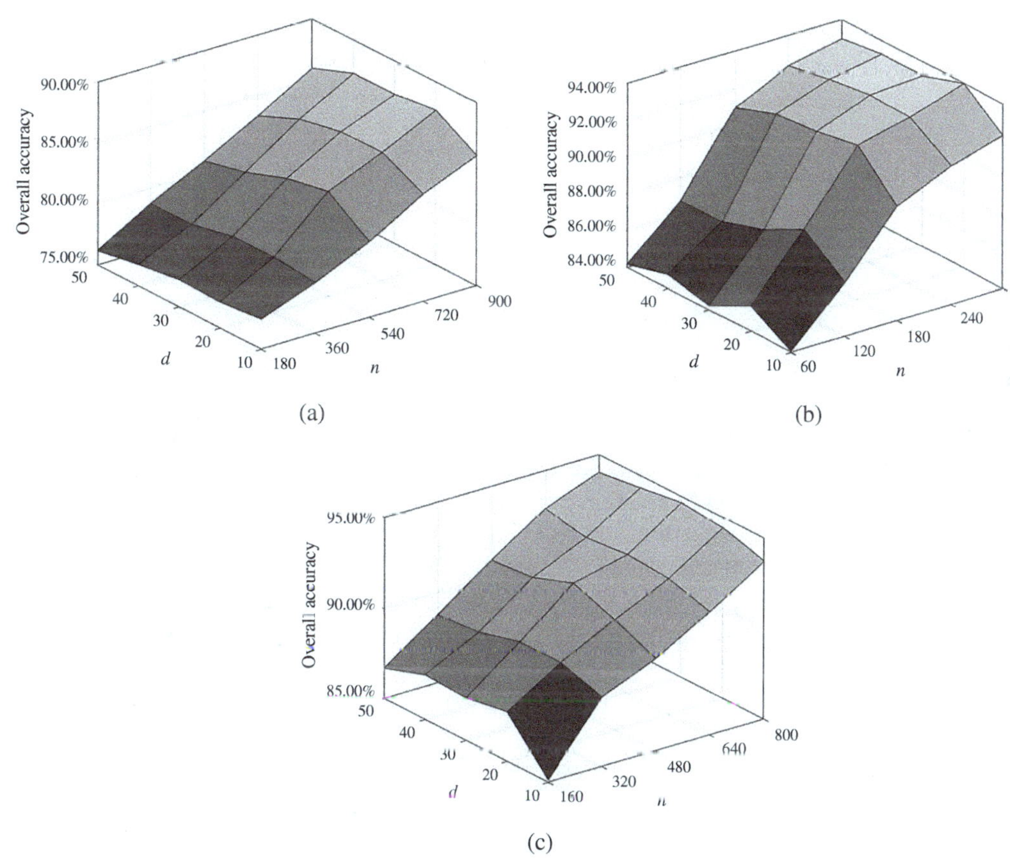

Figure 19.9 Dimensionality *d* in NPE versus the total number *n* of labeled samples selected for GSR-based representation using (a) the University of Pavia data set, (b) the Washington DC Mall data, set and (c) the Salinas data set.

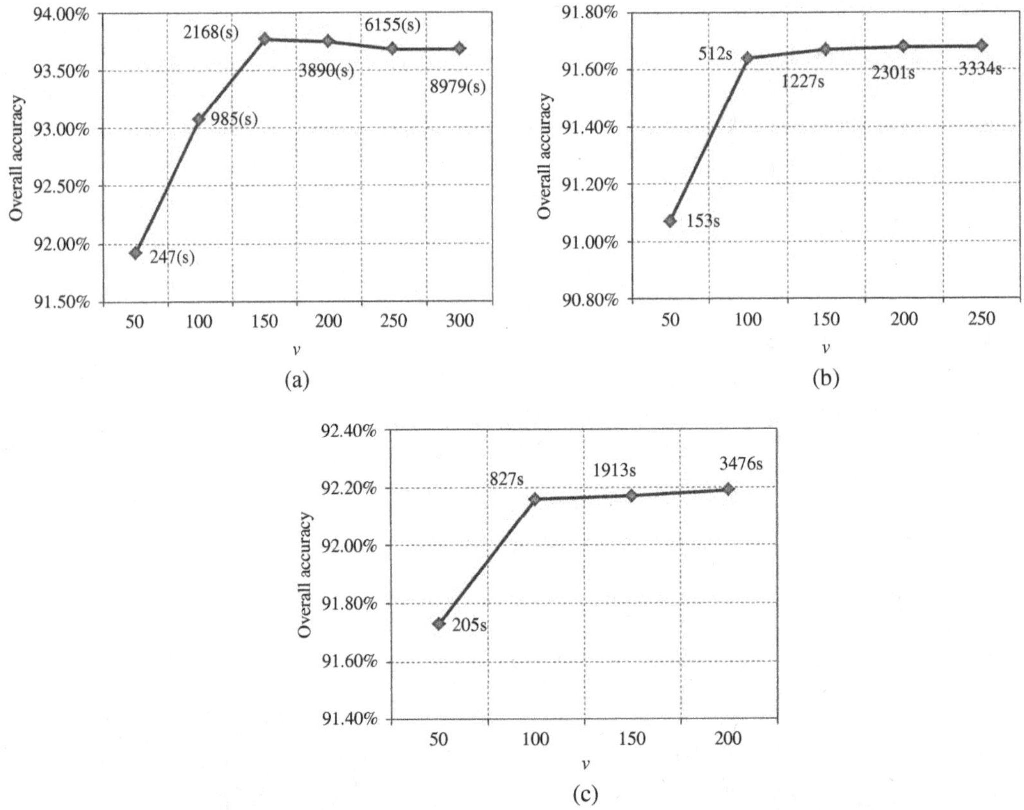

Figure 19.10 Searching window size v and the computation time (in seconds) in GSLS versus the OA results using (a) the University of Pavia data set, (b) the Washington DC Mall data set, and (c) the Salinas data set.

19.4.3 Measurement of Similarity

It is suggested to first apply SVD to preserve the first q components with consideration of the computational cost, which has been proved to be able to maintain the accuracy of the measurement of similarity. As illustrated in Figure 19.11, in our experiment, q is selected as 4, 4 and 3 with most concentrated power of signals for the University of Pavia scene, the Washington DC Mall scene and the Salinas scene, respectively. After q is settled, the degree of freedom of the variation of noise can be determined according to the size w of the current assessed patch, such that the threshold T can be further obtained by look-up table of Chi square distribution. But this just provides a reference value, which still needs to be fine-tuned in practice. Figure 19.12 briefly shows the relationship between w and the best OA results in their cases. When w reaches a certain level, the similarity information at this level is relatively reduced, such that leads to a decrease of the OA results. Therefore, w is finally select as, 12, 10 and 12 for the University of Pavia scene, the Washington DC Mall scene and the Salinas scene, respectively.

19.4.3.1 Group Structure-based Representation

The basic assumption of GSRC is that the neighboring pixels have a high probability to belong to the same class. In this context, GSRC needs to consider a small neighborhood around the testing pixel

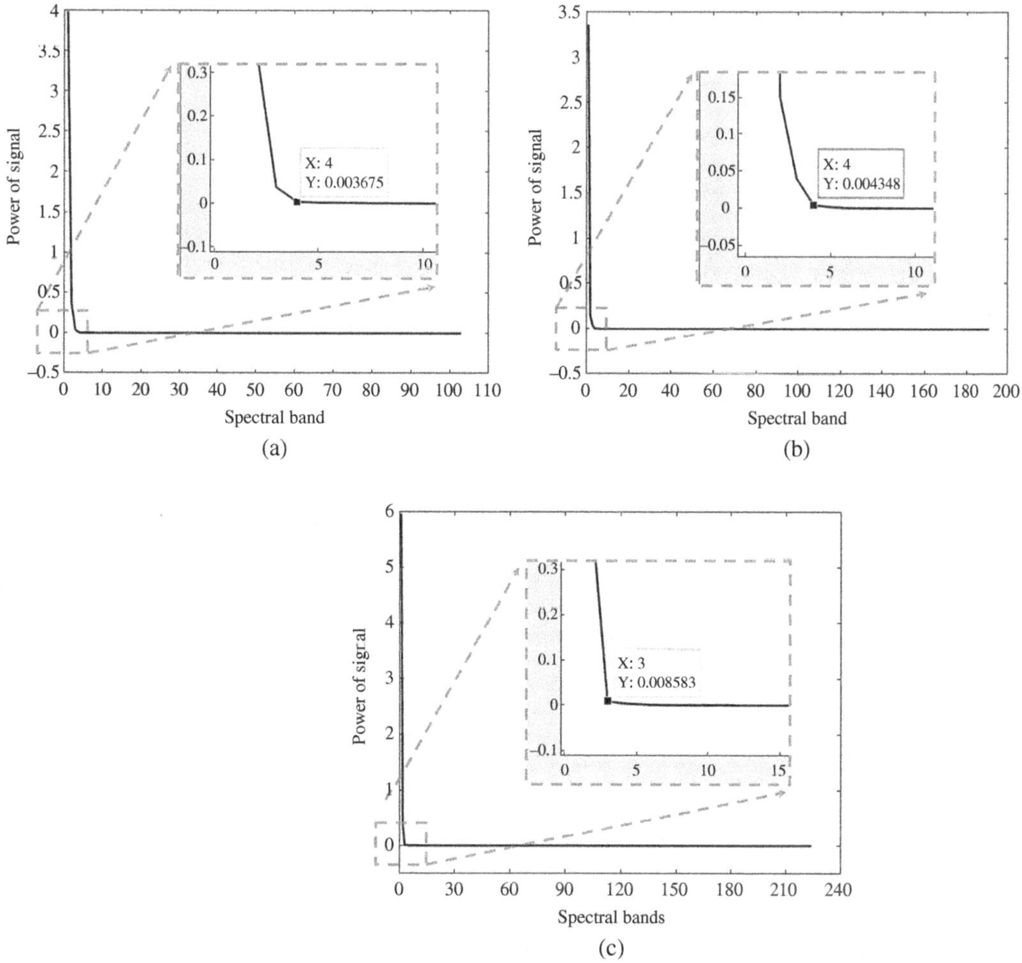

Figure 19.11 Spectral band versus the power of signal in SVD using (a) the University of Pavia data set, (b) the Washington DC Mall data set, and (c) the Salinas data set.

in order to satisfy the homogeneity assumption. Therefore, we generally consider a 3×3 pixel-sized, i.e., $t = 9$, testing neighborhood in GSRC for all three data sets. Following, the regularization parameter λ of the representation-based methods is basically set to the values ranging from 10-3 to 10-1. In the experiments of this paper, all the tested methods are performed with respect to the same number of randomly selected labeled samples per class, which means that ω_g in GSRC equals to one.

19.4.4 Results Analysis

19.4.4.1 University of Pavia Scene

In the first test with the ROSIS University of Pavia Scene, we randomly select 80 labeled samples per class with a total of 720 labeled samples (which constitutes approximately 1.68% of the available labeled samples) for the construction of the dictionary in the SR-based methods and model training in the compared SVM-based methods, where the remaining samples are used for validation. Meanwhile, we also perform SVM-based Markov Random Filed (SVM-MRF) as comparisons to evaluate

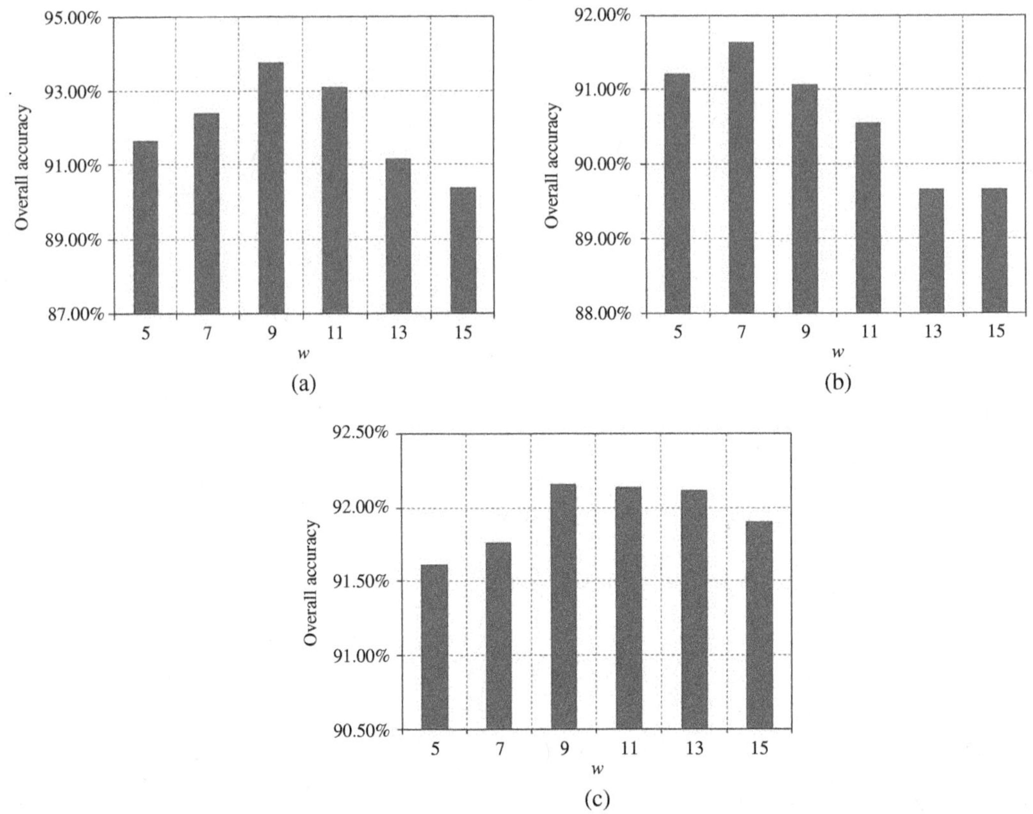

Figure 19.12 Patch size w in GSLS versus the OA results using (a) the University of Pavia data set, (b) the Washington DC Mall data set, and (c) the Salinas data set.

the proposed method. Table 19.1 reports the OA and CA results obtained by different tested methods, and their corresponding classification maps are shown in Figure 19.13. Based on these results, several preliminary conclusions can be drawn as follows:

1) SR-based models generally provide rather plausible results. Specifically, both SRC and CRC perform better than SVM whose performance is worst, which verifies the effectiveness of the representation-based framework in HSIC. In addition, it is worth noting that CRC do not have an advantage over SRC.
2) ADRC brings competitive results, which takes in to account the classification performance. Specifically, the overall accuracies of ADRC towards SRC in terms of the University of Pavia scene are constantly increasing. Based on the above analysis, it can be proved that the established AD-driven processing and decision mechanism is effective for the HSIC task.
3) SVM-MRF obtains better results in terms of the University of Pavia scene, which verifies the improvement brought by the integration of spatial coherence. This can also be confirmed by the increasing overall accuracies of JSRC towards SRC.
4) JSRC and GSRC bring better classification performances towards SVM and SRC, which further confirms the effectiveness of combining the local spatial information. Moreover, GSRC outperforms JSRC, which demonstrates the improvement of the group structure-based priors.
5) LSDA-GSRC obtains better result than SRC and GSRC, which indicates the effectiveness of both the local manifold structure and group sparse representation for better characterization and classification for hyperspectral data set. In general, LSDA-GSRC obtains better classification

Table 19.1 Overall and class-specific accuracies (in percent) obtained by the different tested methods for the ROSIS University of Pavia Scene. In all cases, 720 labeled samples in total (80 per class) were used. The best results are highlighted in bold typeface.

Class	SVM (%)	CRC (%)	SRC (%)	ADRC (%)	SVM-MRF (%)	JSRC (%)	GSRC (%)	LSDA-GSRC (%)	GSLS-GSRC (%)	NADRC (%)
1	71.50	79.98	72.67	73.17	81.51	62.14	68.66	68.53	72.04	**86.24**
2	70.23	75.85	77.16	76.90	84.72	85.69	87.36	92.34	**99.69**	89.56
3	75.92	54.57	75.18	75.44	85.41	83.71	89.14	92.25	**98.33**	92.92
4	89.82	90.77	91.06	92.17	92.29	94.16	95.99	96.23	92.62	**96.97**
5	99.26	98.43	93.75	96.82	95.97	**100.00**	**100.00**	**100.00**	**100.00**	**100.00**
6	78.18	74.40	78.03	76.44	91.80	71.96	82.10	82.80	95.74	**97.80**
7	90.75	60.53	85.04	86.90	92.03	96.17	99.25	**99.92**	99.62	97.67
8	76.22	67.81	68.77	68.49	88.81	80.72	82.40	86.41	90.22	**95.54**
9	99.83	82.24	89.02	95.28	96.17	97.89	97.36	**97.71**	93.45	97.58
OA	76.30	76.93	77.77	77.91	86.39	82.24	85.11	90.56	93.42	**93.62**

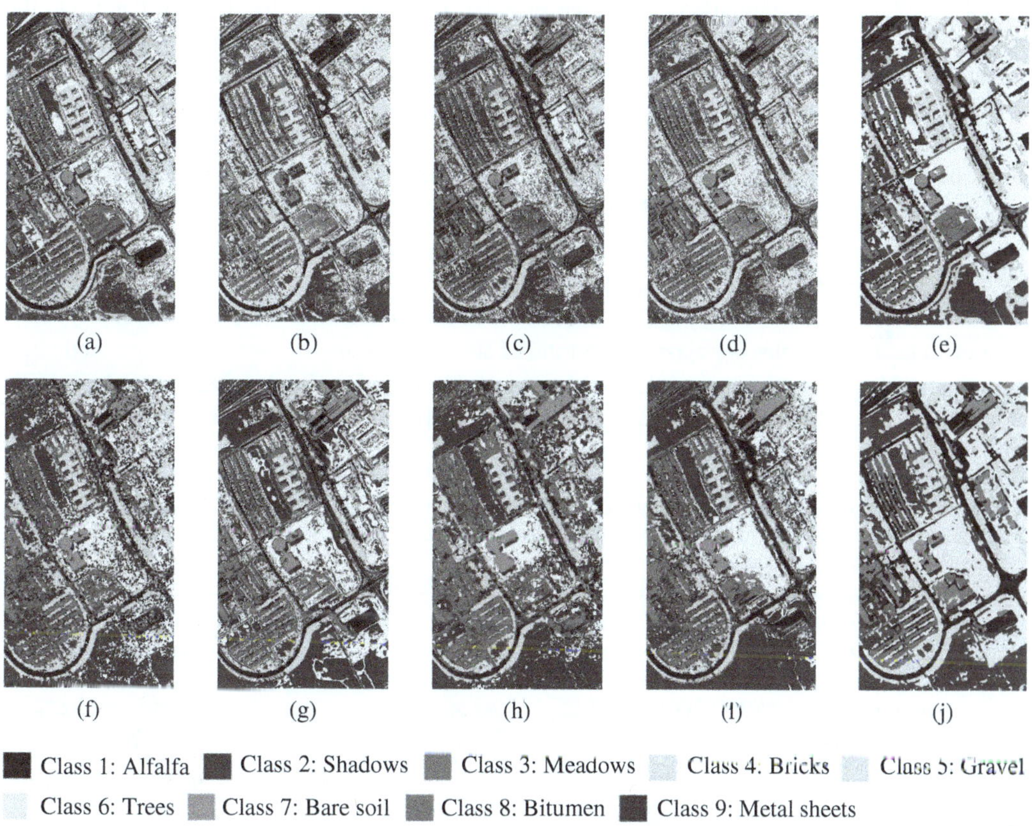

Figure 19.13 Classification maps obtained by the different tested methods for the ROSIS University of Pavia data set. In all cases, 720 labeled samples in total (80 per class) were used. The overall classification accuracies are given in the parentheses. (a) SVM (76.30%), (b) CRC (76.93%), (c) SRC (77.77%), (d) ADRC (77.91%), (e) SVM-MRF (86.39%), (f) JSRC (82.24%), (g) GSRC (85.11%), (h) LSDA-GSRC (90.56%), (i) GSLS-GSRC (93.42%), and (j) NADRC (93.62%).

result, with an overall accuracy of 90.56%, which is 12.79% and 5.45% higher than SRC and GSRC, respectively.

6) GSLS-GSRC yields better classification result, which indicates the improvement of exploration of local spectral similarity through nonlocal spatial similarity, and the effectiveness of the designed fusion pattern for cooperative representation of the global prior information. In general, GSLS-GSRC obtains better classification result, with an OA of 93.42%, which is 8.31% higher than GSRC.
7) The proposed NADRC brings stable and significant improvements, which not only supports that the spatial extension from AD to NAD-driven framework is effective, but also confirms that the composed overall constraint and decision mechanism is reliable for the HSIC task, with respect to the innovative exploration of the sparse coefficient. In these cases, NADRC obtains the best classification results in comparison with the other related tested methods for the data sets, with the overall accuracies of 93.62%, which is 8.51% higher than the best one in JR-based models, i.e., GSRC, and 15.85% higher than the original SRC, respectively.

In the second test with the ROSIS University of Pavia Scene, we also evaluate the proposed method with a varying size of training samples (from 20 to 100). As shown in Figure 19.16a, we can consolidate our pervious conclusions. On the one hand, both local and nonlocal spatial information bring improvements to the classification tasks, which can be seen from the results obtained by JSRC and GSRC in comparison with their original counterpart, i.e., SVM, respectively. On the other hand, local manifold subspace-based methods generally perform better than the original counterparts and the proposed LSDA-GSRC obtained better results in all cases. GSLS-GSRC brings a better expression of details within the classification map, which proves the effectiveness of the proposed method. Most importantly, NADRC brings stable and significant improvements in all the experimental data sets. In these cases, NADRC obtains the best classification results in comparison with the other related tested methods.

19.4.4.2 Washington DC Mall Scene and Salinas Scene

In the first tests with the Washington DC Mall scene and the Salinas scene, we randomly select 10 and 20 labeled samples per class with a total of 60 and 320 samples for training and dictionary construction (which both represent approximately 0.59% of the available labeled samples), while the remaining labeled samples are used for validation. Table 19.2 and Table 19.3 report the OA and CA results of different tested methods, where Figure 19.14 and Figure 19.15 show the

Table 19.2 Overall and class-specific accuracies (in percent) obtained by the different tested methods for the HYDICE Washington DC mall scene. In all cases, 60 labeled samples in total (10 per class) were used. The best results are highlighted in bold typeface.

Class	SVM (%)	CRC (%)	SRC (%)	ADRC (%)	SVM-MRF (%)	JSRC (%)	GSRC (%)	LSDA-GSRC (%)	GSLS-GSRC (%)	NADRC (%)
1	74.80	80.33	72.33	82.40	81.22	73.01	77.33	76.10	82.03	**82.70**
2	83.43	79.75	89.33	82.46	90.53	93.02	93.90	93.13	95.11	**95.63**
3	87.28	89.95	94.07	90.28	89.13	95.97	94.15	**99.49**	98.42	90.46
4	91.87	90.63	93.85	90.79	95.95	93.91	93.30	97.15	94.36	**98.70**
5	98.10	90.19	88.75	91.28	95.58	90.09	94.38	92.07	**94.82**	91.05
6	91.31	88.80	94.22	88.84	94.77	94.85	95.32	96.22	95.32	**98.36**
OA	85.51	85.38	86.40	86.66	89.30	87.72	89.31	90.02	91.64	**91.67**

Table 19.3 Overall and class-specific accuracies (in percent) obtained by the different tested methods for the AVIRIS Salinas scene. In all cases, 320 labeled samples in total (20 per class) were used. The best results are highlighted in bold typeface.

Class	SVM (%)	CRC (%)	SRC (%)	ADRC (%)	SVM-MRF (%)	JSRC (%)	GSRC (%)	LSDA-GSRC (%)	GSLS-GSRC (%)	NADRC (%)
1	94.49	100.00	99.35	97.96	96.45	99.85	**100.00**	**100.00**	**100.00**	**100.00**
2	96.18	87.22	91.47	97.05	97.09	97.05	99.17	**99.54**	99.33	98.47
3	90.20	51.16	84.36	53.90	93.90	83.15	**97.42**	80.56	78.24	77.35
4	95.38	87.30	97.20	99.07	94.77	99.21	99.21	**99.75**	99.64	99.54
5	94.87	98.28	96.38	94.17	95.10	99.03	98.62	99.50	**99.74**	99.47
6	95.85	99.87	98.81	99.47	92.88	**100.00**	**100.00**	**100.00**	99.92	99.26
7	94.56	99.86	98.35	99.44	95.28	99.80	99.83	**99.84**	99.75	99.18
8	55.18	90.82	55.99	74.31	65.41	59.12	63.85	71.98	**86.82**	80.88
9	91.03	99.95	96.03	96.26	95.87	98.90	99.31	99.67	**99.98**	99.18
10	76.16	84.90	80.63	62.87	81.78	88.13	**94.69**	91.14	90.42	90.90
11	87.79	93.91	95.79	92.98	90.38	99.53	**99.91**	98.34	95.88	96.66
12	96.81	31.66	98.29	100.00	98.98	**100.00**	99.84	**100.00**	**100.00**	**100.00**
13	94.52	5.46	93.78	97.05	95.56	**99.56**	98.69	99.67	**99.56**	98.50
14	88.20	97.29	90.00	94.11	91.02	95.33	**96.73**	95.89	95.42	95.37
15	55.82	32.00	61.60	46.60	51.81	63.68	69.37	77.01	86.81	**91.99**
16	91.07	93.30	96.35	86.33	95.22	98.51	98.51	97.62	**98.56**	97.97
OA	81.63	80.52	81.85	81.96	85.27	84.70	87.56	89.89	93.79	**93.88**

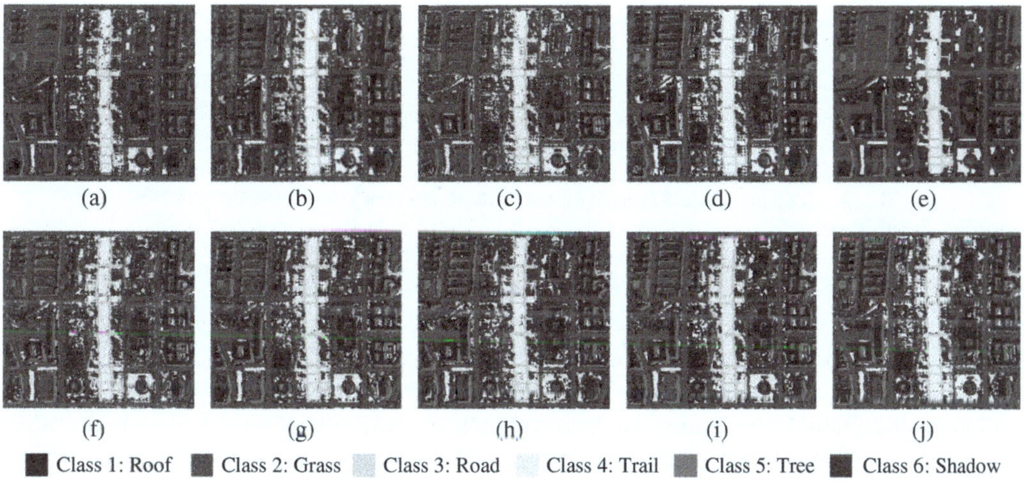

Figure 19.14 Classification maps obtained by the different tested methods for the HYDICE Washington DC Mall data set. In all cases, 60 labeled samples in total (10 per class) were used. The overall classification accuracies are given in the parentheses. (a) SVM (85.51%), (b) CRC (85.38%), (c) SRC (86.40%), (d) ADRC (86.66%), (e) SVM-MRF (89.30%), (f) JSRC (87.72%), (g) GSRC (89.31%), (h) LSDA-GSRC (90.02%), (i) GSLS-GSRC (91.64%), and (j) NADRC (91.67%).

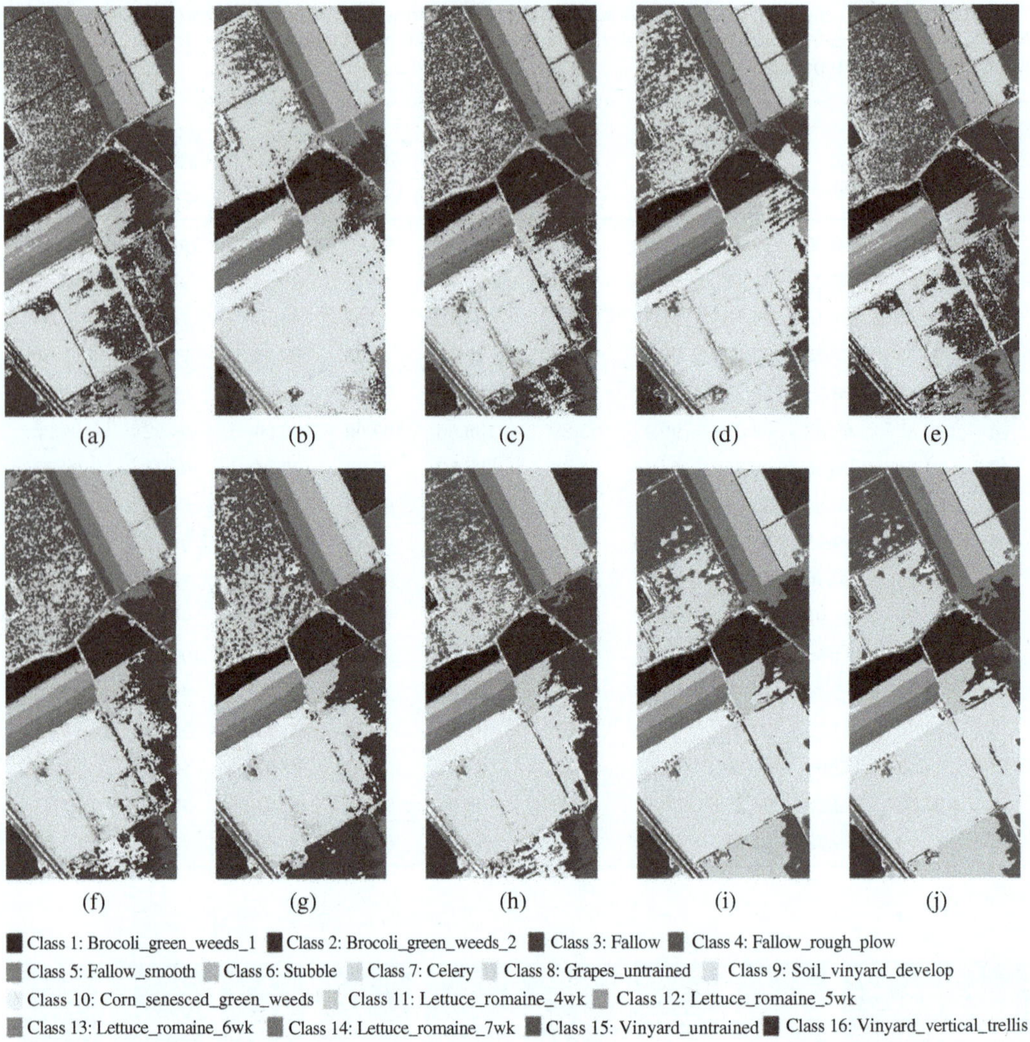

Figure 19.15 Classification maps obtained by the different tested methods for the AVIRIS Salinas data set. In all cases, 320 labeled samples in total (20 per class) were used. The overall classification accuracies are given in the parentheses. (a) SVM (81.63%), (b) CRC (80.52%), (c) SRC (81.85%), (d) ADRC (81.96%), (e) SVM-MRF (85.27%), (f) JSRC (84.70%), (g) GSRC (87.56%), (h) LSDA-GSRC (89.89%), (i) GSLS-GSRC (93.79%), and (j) NADRC (93.88%).

corresponding classification maps for Washington DC Mall scene and Salinas scene, respectively. As shown in Table 19.2 and Table 19.3, similar conclusions can be conducted with the University of Pavia's experiment. On one hand, GSRC, JSRC, ADRC and SVM-MRF achieve increases of classification results relative to SRC and SVM by integrating the local spatial consistency. On the other hand, LSDA-GSRC implements a manifold subspace projection process for better characterization of features. GSLS-GSRC also bring improvements to their original counterparts with consideration of nonlocal spatial similarity. Most importantly, the proposed NADRC obtains the best classification result with OA results of 91.67% and 93.88%, which is 5.27% and 12.03% higher than SRC for two data sets, respectively. In addition, it also provides better performances for individual classes, which can be seen from the classification maps illustrated in Figure 19.14 and Figure 19.15.

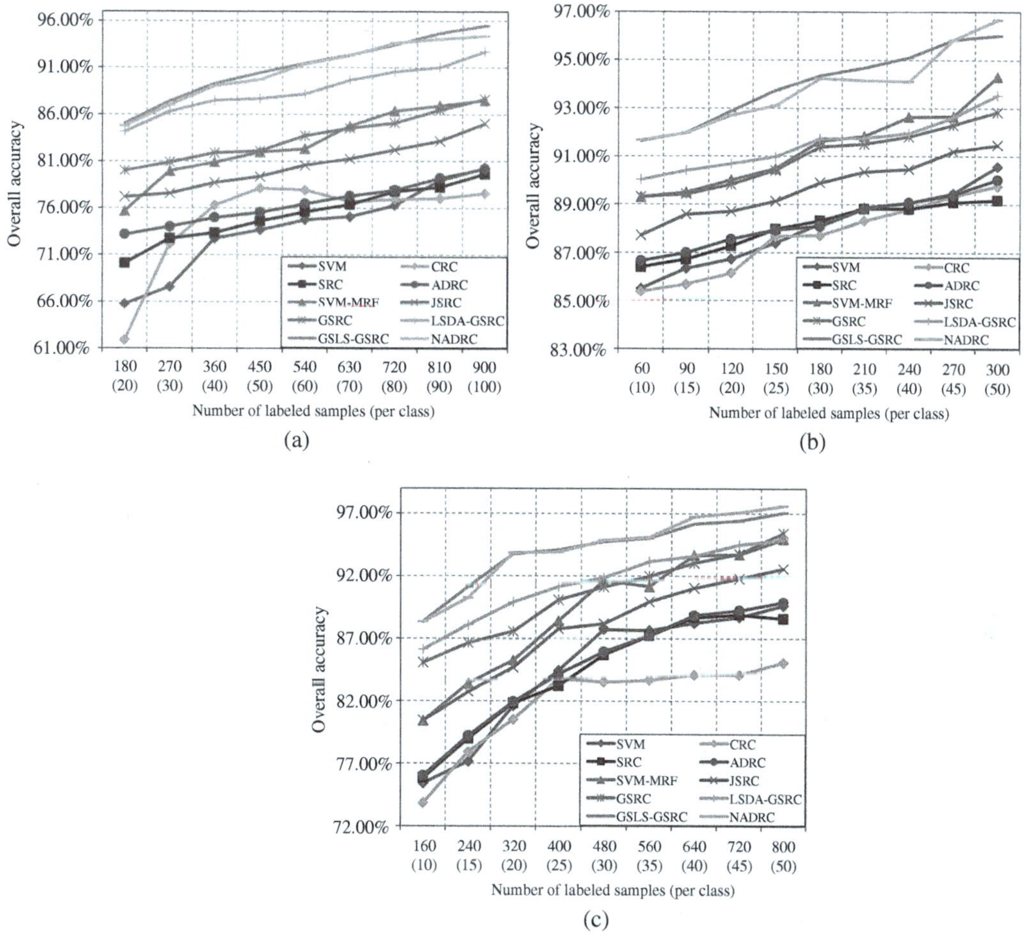

Figure 19.16 Overall classification results obtained by the different tested methods as a function of the number of labeled samples (per class) for (a) University of Pavia data set, (b) HYDICE Washington DC Mall data set, and (c) AVIRIS Salinas scene.

The second tests with Washington DC Mall scene and the Salinas scene evaluate the proposed NADRC method with a varying size of labeled samples (from 10 to 50 samples per class). Figure 19.16b and Figure 19.16c show the OA results provided by different tested methods, as a function of the number of labeled samples used for training and dictionary construction for two data sets, respectively. As shown in Figure 19.16b and Figure 19.16c, the superiority of the proposed method is confirmed by the best classification results obtained by NADRC in all cases.

19.5 Conclusion

From the perspective of potential sparse characteristic of HSI, this chapter conducts studies and proposes three new classification methods for the in-depth coordinate of spatial and spectral information, called LSDA-GSRC, GSLS-GSRC and NADRC. The LSDA-GSRC model combines the manifold learning LSDA with the GSRC model. Applying LSDA to project the input data to a local subspace, solving the problem of band redundancy under limited conditions, and representing the projected testing set by GSR for classification. The GSLS-GSRC explores the local spectral similarity through nonlocal spatial similarity, optimizes the searching mode, and designs a pattern to fuse the nonlocal and local spatial information for better representation. The ADRC is an equivalent and simplified model to the SRC model, which uses the AD-driven decision mechanism. Deeply understand and explore the sparse coefficient for concise and simplified mechanism. The NADRC model put forward a NAD of the matrix-formed coefficient, which takes advantage of spatial coherence in terms of the overall activity of each class based on the extension of AD. This chapter uses three sets of real hyperspectral data sets to analyze and verify the effectiveness and stability of the proposed methods by designing comparative experiment under different condition.

Acknowledgment

This work was supported in part by the National Natural Science Foundation of China under Grant 42101350 and Grant 42371353, in part by the China Postdoctoral Science Foundation under Grant 2022T150080 and Grant 2023T160073.

References

1 Plaza, A., Benediktsson, J.A., Boardman, J.W. et al. (2009). Recent advances in techniques for hyperspectral image processing. *Remote Sens. Environ.* 113: S110–S122.

2 Bioucas-Dias, J.M., Plaza, A., Dobigeon, N. et al. (2012). Hyperspectral unmixing overview: geometrical, statistical, and sparse regression-based approaches. *IEEE J. Sel. Top. Appl. Earth Observ. Remote Sens.* 5 (2): 354–379.

3 Hong, D., Yokoya, N., Xia, G.-S. et al. (2020). X-ModalNet: a semi-supervised deep cross-modal network for classification of remote sensing data, ISPRS-J. *Photogramm. Remote Sens.* 167: 12–23.

4 Yu, C., Liu, C., Song, M. et al. (2021). Unsupervised domain adaptation with content-wise alignment for hyperspectral imagery classification. *IEEE Geosci. Remote Sens. Lett.* 19: 1–5.

5 Li, J., Bioucas-Dias, J.M., and Plaza, A. (2013). Semisupervised hyperspectral image classification using soft sparse multinomial logistic regression. *IEEE Geosci. Remote Sens. Lett.* 10 (2): 318–322.

6 Ghamisi, P., Plaza, J., Chen, Y. et al. (2017). Advanced spectral classifiers for hyperspectral images: a review. *IEEE Geosc. Rem. Sen. M* 5 (1): 8–32.

7 Goetz, A.F.H. (1990). Hyperspectral imaging: advances in a spectrum of applications, *Proceedings Fifth Australasian Remote Sensing Conference* (8–12 October 1990). Perth, Australia.

8 Clark, C. and Clark, A.F. (1998). Spectral identification by singular value decomposition. *Int. J. Remote Sens.* 19 (12): 2317–2329.

9 Liu, Y., Lu, S., Lu, X. et al. (2019). Classification of urban hyperspectral remote sensing imagery based on optimized spectral angle map. *J Indian Soc. Remote Sens.* 47 (2): 289–294.

10 Fauvel, M., Tarabalka, Y., Benediktsson, J.A. et al. (2013). Advances in spectral-spatial classification of hyperspectral images. *Proc. IEEE* 101 (3): 652–675.

11 McIver, D. and Friedl, M. (2002). Using prior probabilities in decision-tree classification of remotely sensed data. *Remote Sens. Environ.* 81 (2–3): 253–261.

12 Tong, F. and Zhang, Y. (2022). Spectral-spatial and cascaded multilayer random forests for tree species classification in airborne hyperspectral images. *IEEE Trans. Geosci. Remote Sens.* 60: 1–11.

13 Belgiu, M. and Drăguţ, L. (2016). Random forest in remote sensing: a review of applications and future directions, ISPRS-J. *Photogramm. Remote Sens.* 114: 24–31.

14 Melgani, F. and Bruzzone, L. (2004). Classification of hyperspectral remote sensing images with support vector machines. *IEEE Trans. Geosci. Remote Sens.* 42 (8): 1778–1790.

15 Gao, L., Zhao, B., Jia, X. et al. (2017). Optimized kernel minimum noise fraction transformation for hyperspectral image classification. *Remote Sens* 9 (6): 548–568.

16 Yu, H., Gao, L., Liao, W. et al. (2017). Multiscale superpixel-level subspace-based support vector machines for hyperspectral image classification. *IEEE Geosci. Remote Sens. Lett.* 14 (11): 2142–2146.

17 Yu, H., Gao, L., Li, J. et al. (2016). Spectral-spatial hyperspectral image classification using subspace-based support vector machines and adaptive Markov random fields. *Remote Sens* 8 (4): 355–376.

18 Gao, L., Yao, D., Li, Q. et al. (2017). A new low-rank representation based hyperspectral image denoising method for mineral mapping. *Remote Sens* 9 (11): 1145–1165.

19 Zhuang, L. and Bioucas-Dias, J.M. (2018). Fast hyperspectral image denoising and inpainting based on low-rank and sparse representations. *IEEE J. Sel. Top. Appl. Earth Observ. Remote Sens.* 11 (3): 730–742.

20 Chen, Y., Nasrabadi, N.M., and Tran, T.D. (2013). Hyperspectral image classification via kernel sparse representation. *IEEE Trans. Geosci. Remote Sens.* 51 (1): 217–231.

21 Fang, L., Li, S., Kang, X. et al. (2014). Spectral-spatial hyperspectral image classification via multiscale adaptive sparse representation. *IEEE Trans. Geosci. Remote Sens.* 52 (12): 7738–7749.

22 Li, W., Liu, J., and Du, Q. (2016). Sparse and low rank graph-based discriminant analysis of hyperspectral image classification. *IEEE Trans. Geosci. Remote Sens.* 54 (7): 4094–4105.

23 Li, W., Du, Q., Zhang, F. et al. (2016). Hyperspectral image classification by fusing collaborative and sparse representations. *IEEE J. Sel. Top. Appl. Earth Obs. Remote Sens.* 9 (9): 4178–4187.

24 Li, W. and Du, Q. (2015). Collaborative representation for hyperspectral anomaly detection. *IEEE Trans. Geosci. Remote Sens.* 53 (3): 1463–1474.

25 Dundar, T. and Ince, T. (2019). Sparse representation-based hyperspectral image classification using multiscale superpixels and guided filter. *IEEE Geosci. Remote Sens. Lett.* 16 (2): 246–250.

26 Su, H., Yu, Y., Du, Q. et al. (2020). Ensemble learning for hyperspectral image classification using tangent collaborative representation. *IEEE Trans. Geosci. Remote Sens.* 58 (6): 3778–3790.

27 Jia, S., Xie, Y., Tang, G. et al. (2016). Spatial-spectral-combined sparse representation-based classification for hyperspectral imagery. *Soft Comput.* 20 (12): 4659–4668.

28 Zou, J., Li, W., Chen, C. et al. (2016). Scene classification using local and global features with collaborative representation fusion. *Inf. Sci.* 348: 209–226.

29 Yu, H., Gao, L., Liao, W. et al. (2018). Group sparse representation based on nonlocal spatial and local spectral similarity for hyperspectral imagery classification. *Sensors* 18 (6): 1695–1714.

30 Chen, Y., Nasrabadi, N.M., and Tran, T.D. (2011). Hyperspectral image classification using dictionary-based sparse representation. *IEEE Trans. Geosci. Remote Sens.* 49 (10): 3973–3985.

31 Zhang, H., Zhang, Y., Nasrabadi, N.M. et al. (2012). Joint-structured-sparsity-based classification for multiple-measurement transient acoustic signals. *IEEE Trans. Syst. Man Cybern. B* 42 (6): 1586–1598.

32 Sun, X., Qu, Q., Nasrabadi, N.M. et al. (2014). Structured priors for sparse-representation-based hyperspectral image classification. *IEEE Geosci. Remote Sens. Lett.* 11 (7): 1235–1239.

33 Li, W. and Du, Q. (2016). A survey on representation-based classification and detection in hyperspectral remote sensing imagery. *Pattern Recogn. Lett.* 83 (2): 115–123.

34 Gao, L., Yu, H., Zhang, B. et al. (2016). Locality-preserving sparse representation-based classification in hyperspectral imagery. *J. Appl. Remote. Sens.* 10 (4): 42004–42019.

35 Yu, H., Gao, L., Li, W. et al. (2017). Locality sensitive discriminant analysis for group sparse representation-based hyperspectral imagery classification. *IEEE Geosci. Remote Sens. Lett.* 14 (8): 1358–1362.

36 Yu, H., Gao, L., Liao, W. et al. (2020). Global spatial and local spectral similarity-based manifold learning group sparse representation for hyperspectral imagery classification. *IEEE Trans. Geosci. Remote Sens.* 58 (5): 3043–3056.

37 Li, J., Zhang, H., and Zhang, L. (2014). Column-generation kernel nonlocal joint collaborative representation for hyperspectral image classification, ISPRS-J. *Photogramm. Remote Sens.* 94: 25–36.

38 Yu, H., Zhang, X., Song, M. et al. (2020). Hyperspectral imagery classification based on multiscale superpixel-level constraint representation. *Remote Sens* 12 (20): 3342–3363.

39 Hu, J., Shen, X., Yu, H. et al. (2021). Extended subspace projection upon sample augmentation based on global spatial and local spectral similarity for hyperspectral imagery classification. *IEEE J. Sel. Top. Appl. Earth Observ. Remote Sens.* 14: 8653–8664.

40 Yu, H., Shang, X., Zhang, X. et al. (2021). Hyperspectral image classification based on adjacent constraint representation. *IEEE Geosci. Remote Sens. Lett.* 18 (4): 707–711.

41 Yu, H., Zhang, X., Yu, C. et al. (2020). Neighborhood activity-driven representation for hyperspectral imagery classification. *IEEE J. Sel. Top. Appl. Earth Observ. Remote Sens.* 13: 4506–4517.

20

Hyperspectral Image Classification with Limited Samples

Yuebin Wang[1], Liqiang Zhang[2], Bing Zhang[3], Antonio Plaza[4], and Xiao Xiang Zhu[5]

[1] *School of Land Science and Technology, China University of Geosciences, Beijing, China*
[2] *State Key Laboratory of Remote Sensing and Digital Earth, Faculty of Geographical Science, Beijing Normal University, Beijing, China*
[3] *Aerospace Information Research Institute, Chinese Academy of Sciences, Beijing, China*
[4] *Department of Technology of Computers and Communications, Escuela Politécnica, University of Extremadura, Cáceres, Spain*
[5] *Chair of Data Science in Earth Observation, Technical University of Munich, Munich, Germany*

20.1 Introduction

20.1.1 Introduction to Hyperspectral Imaging and Its Applications

HSI technology utilizes sensors to capture images across hundreds of narrow, contiguous spectral bands, extending from the visible to the infrared spectrum [1]. This advanced imaging method produces a comprehensive spectral profile for each pixel, which significantly enhances the ability to identify and analyze various materials and objects on the Earth's surface. HSI's detailed spectral information is invaluable in a myriad of practical applications. For instance, in agriculture, it helps in monitoring crop health and optimizing water usage, while in environmental science, it is essential for tracking pollution levels and studying vegetation [2]. Additionally, its role in city planning and land use management involves the detailed assessment of urban layouts and the monitoring of infrastructure development [3]. Hyperspectral imaging also plays a crucial role in resource exploration, aiding in the identification of minerals and other natural resources. The technology's ability to detect subtle differences in the Earth's surface makes it a powerful tool in remote sensing and geographic information systems (GIS), providing critical data for decision-makers in a wide range of sectors.

20.1.2 Challenges in HSI Classification

Despite the advanced capabilities of HSI, the classification of its data presents significant challenges primarily due to the high dimensionality of the spectral data. This phenomenon, known as the "curse of dimensionality," complicates data analysis as the increased number of dimensions can make classification models overly complex and inefficient [4]. Another major hurdle is the scarcity of labeled samples, which are essential for training supervised learning models. This lack of labeled data often necessitates the use of semi-supervised or unsupervised learning techniques that can exploit unlabeled data effectively. To address these issues, various dimensionality reduction

Machine-Learning-Based Hyperspectral Image Processing, First Edition. Edited by Bing Zhang.

strategies have been employed. Techniques like principal component analysis (PCA) [5] and independent component analysis work to reduce the number of variables under consideration, transforming high-dimensional data into a more manageable form while retaining essential information. More sophisticated methods, including manifold learning techniques such as ISOMAP [6] and locally linear embedding, are used to uncover non-linear relationships within the data, which are crucial for improving feature representation and classification accuracy. Additionally, deep learning methods are increasingly utilized to learn complex patterns and features from hyperspectral images, enhancing the overall effectiveness of classification systems. Despite these advancements, the integration of these techniques into practical applications remains challenging, requiring ongoing research and development to optimize HSI data processing and utilization.

20.1.3 Multiple Models to Address Hyperspectral Images

20.1.3.1 Deep Representative Feature Learning with Virtual Adversarial Training

Traditional classification methods like maximum likelihood and SVMs have significantly evolved with the integration of spatial-spectral CNNs and unsupervised techniques such as stacked autoencoders (SAEs), which help in feature extraction without requiring labels. These developments underscore a shift from purely supervised methods, which depend heavily on labeled data, to more flexible unsupervised and semisupervised techniques that utilize both labeled and unlabeled data for more effective classification. Addressing the shortcomings of these methods, we introduce a novel semisupervised learning framework named Deep Representative Feature Learning with Virtual Adversarial Training (DRFL-VAT) [7].

This framework (Figure 20.1) enhances feature smoothness through Local Manifold Learning (LML) and uses VAT regularization to prevent overfitting, optimizing the model parameters jointly to improve performance in HSI classification. DRFL-VAT not only offers more accurate feature representation and greater model robustness but also performs competitively against other advanced methods on widely used HSI datasets. Its key innovations include superior feature representativeness, improved local smoothness of sample features, and a bespoke optimization algorithm tailored to the specific needs of HSI classification.

20.1.3.2 DS^{4}L: Deep Semisupervised Shared Subspace Learning

HSI classification confronts issues of dimensionality and limited labeled samples. PCA and SL methods are used to address information redundancy. SL algorithms and deep learning methods like autoencoders, CNNs, and graph convolution are employed to extract representative subspaces. However, generalization enhancement and spatial information incorporation pose challenges. Our model adopts the multiview concept with multiscale input to develop shared subspaces for higher classification accuracy. Techniques such as self-supervised learning, semisupervised CNNs, and subspace clustering are used to tackle HSI classification challenges, removing redundant data or incorporating unlabeled samples for improved feature learning.

The DS^{4}L model uses nearby pixels and unlabeled samples to optimize the learned subspace, achieving superior performance with CE loss [8]. As an end-to-end semisupervised model, DS^{4}L integrates constraints for optimization, yielding high AA, thereby validating its reliability. As shown in Figure 20.2, the details of the DS^{4}L can be composed of two parts, including basic feature extraction (BFE) and deep shared SL (DSSL).

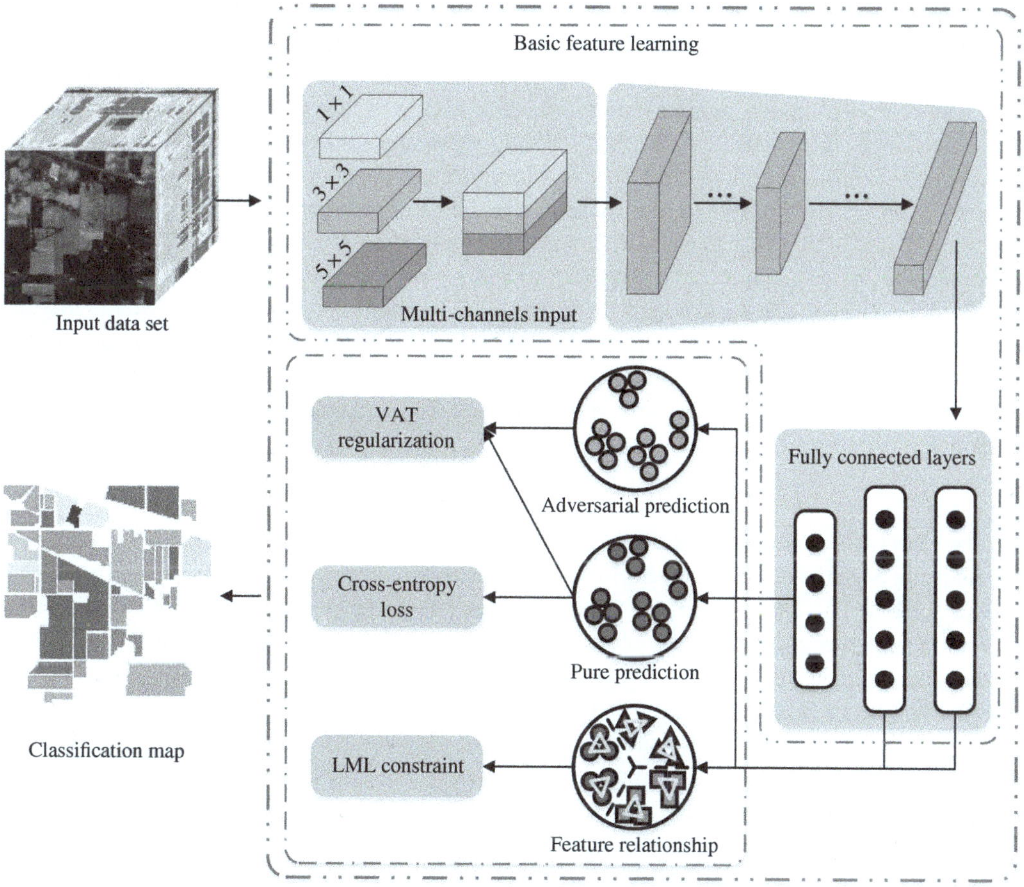

Figure 20.1 Graphical illustration of our new DRFL-VAT framework for HSI classification. VAT regularization and LML constraint are utilized to extract features of both labeled and unlabeled samples. The objective function of DRFL-VAT, including the cross-entropy loss, VAT regularization, and LML constraint, optimizes the model parameters in a semi-supervised manner.

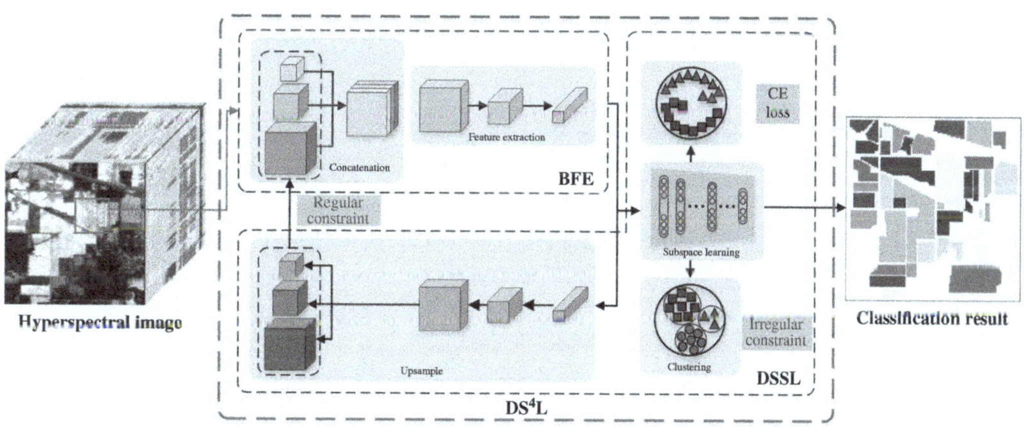

Figure 20.2 Flowchart of the DS[4]L model for HSI classification. The BFE and the DSSL are two main parts of the DS[4]L model. Furthermore, the regular and irregular constraints and CE loss are integrated into the model to obtain representative subspace features for HSI classification.

20.1.3.3 SLCRF: Subspace Learning with Conditional Random Field

Subspace learning (SL) crucially reduces redundant pixel information and compresses data using techniques like PCA and manifold learning, revealing complex data's nonlinear structures. While these methods are used in computer vision for tasks like facial recognition, their direct application in remote sensing is less effective due to HSIs' unique features. Tailored SL algorithms are developed for better class separation and feature geometry retention.

Recent innovations like the PSASL method enhance spectral-spatial correlation, minimizing common classification errors. Despite these advancements, the reliance on extensive labeled datasets limits supervised methods, shifting focus to self-supervised learning that leverages intrinsic data features. The Subspace learning with Conditional Random Field (SLCRF) approach merges semi-supervised learning with 3D Convolutional Autoencoder (3DCAE) and CRFs, enhancing subspace representations and classification accuracy [9]. As shown in Figure 20.3, SLCRF optimizes an integrated objective function, demonstrating superior performance across various public HSI datasets.

20.1.3.4 SDFL-FC: Semisupervised Deep Feature Learning with Feature Consistency

The Semisupervised Deep Feature Learning with Feature Consistency (SDFL-FC) is a method developed to enhance HSI classification by reducing reliance on large labeled datasets [10]. Utilizing a CNN to extract spectral-spatial features from 3D patches, SDFL-FC models feature consistency through fully connected layers. As shown in Figure 20.4, it incorporates two main constraints – Feature Consistency in Superpixels (FCS) and Feature Consistency in Groups (FCG) – to ensure features are representative and discriminative. This approach integrates cross-entropy loss with FCS and FCG into a unified function, optimized via a custom algorithm, significantly outperforming traditional methods on various datasets.

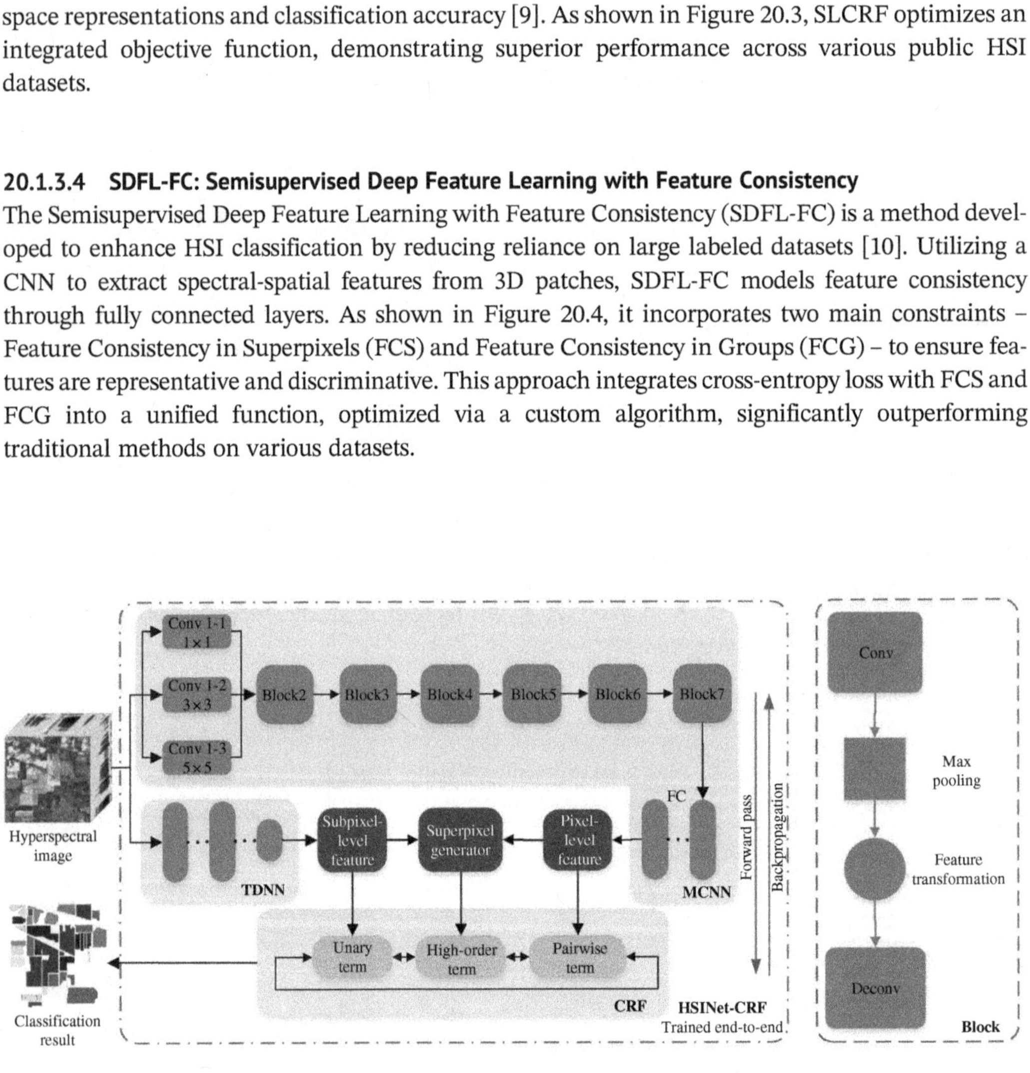

Figure 20.3 Overview of HSINet. Three contrastive losses are formulated in the subspace by incorporating subpixel, pixel, and superpixel-level features, to achieve multi-granularity feature consistency.

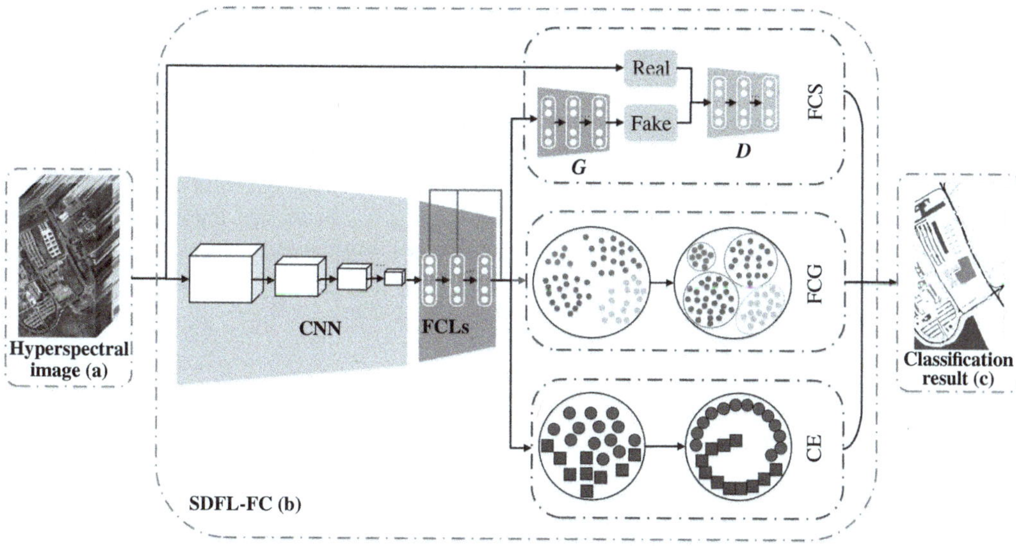

Figure 20.4 Workflow of the SDFL-FC method. (a) HSI. (b) Learning process of SDFL-FC method. (c) Classification results. In (b), the CNN extracts the spectral-spatial features, whereas the final layer feature of CNN is transmitted to FCLs. Each FCL is constrained by the FCG, whereas the final feature of FCL is transmitted to FCS, FCG, and CE loss. SDFL-FC integrates the FCS, FCG, and CEloss into a unified objective function.

20.2 Method

20.2.1 DRFL-VAT

20.2.1.1 Motivation

Supervised HSI classification methods are limited by their need for extensive labeled data, which is labor-intensive. To address this, the article proposes a semisupervised method using a CNN architecture that simultaneously extracts spatial and spectral features. This method, named DRFL-VAT, incorporates LML in CNN layers to enhance feature representativeness by exploiting the sample manifold's geometrical structure. Additionally, Virtual Adversarial Training (VAT) is included to mitigate overfitting and improve generalization, optimized through a custom algorithm. This integrated approach reduces reliance on labeled data while maintaining high classification accuracy.

20.2.1.2 Core Elements of the Model

The core elements of the DRFL-VAT model are designed to optimize HSI classification by leveraging the strengths of CNNs, LML, and VAT.

The DRFL-VAT model employs a CNN architecture to extract both spatial and spectral features from HSIs. It utilizes convolutional layers equipped with multi-scale filter banks to process various patch sizes, capturing detailed local spatial features and spectral information. These convolutional layers are followed by pooling and nonlinear layers (using Leaky ReLU activation functions) which compile a comprehensive feature map. This map is then processed through FCLs for classification.

The model integrates LML within its FCLs. LML enhances feature representativeness by constructing graphs that reflect the geometrical structure of the data manifold, thus capturing the local geometric relationships and ensuring smoother and more meaningful feature learning. VAT is incorporated to tackle the challenges posed by limited labeled data and to enhance model robustness. VAT aims to make the prediction label distribution for both pure and adversarially perturbed input data consistent, which helps in improving generalization across different data samples.

We optimize the objective function of DRFL-VAT using a customized algorithm, balancing supervised learning loss and VAT regularization. This ensures representative feature learning while minimizing overfitting.

$$\mathbf{V}_{mn}^{(u)} = \exp\left(-\frac{\mathbf{Z}_{\cdot m}^{(u)} - \mathbf{Z}_{\cdot n}^{(u)}{}_2^2}{2\omega^2}\right) \tag{20.1}$$

where ω is the heat kernel.

$$\begin{cases} D\left[q(\mathbf{Y}_{\cdot i} \mid \mathbf{X}_{\cdot i}), p\left(\mathbf{Y}_{\cdot i} \mid \mathbf{X}_{\cdot i} + \mathbf{T}_{\cdot i}^{\text{adv}}, \theta\right)\right] \\ \mathbf{T}_{\cdot i}^{\text{adv}} = \arg \max\limits_{\mathbf{T};\, \|\mathbf{T}\|_2 \le \varepsilon} D\left[q(\mathbf{Y}_{\cdot i} \mid \mathbf{X}_{\cdot i}), p(\mathbf{Y}_{\cdot i} \mid \mathbf{X}_{\cdot i} + \mathbf{T}, \theta)\right] \end{cases} \tag{20.2}$$

where $D(\cdot)$ is the Kullback–Leibler divergence, $\mathbf{T}_{i}^{\text{adv}}$ is the adversarial perturbation of $\mathbf{X}_{\cdot i}$ and ε is used to limit the size of the adversarial perturbation. $p\left(\mathbf{Y}_{\cdot i} \mid \mathbf{X}_{\cdot i} + \mathbf{T}_{\cdot i}^{\text{adv}}, \theta\right)$ is the prediction label distribution of and θ is the set of model parameters, including the weight matrix and the bias matrix. $q(\mathbf{Y}_{\cdot i} \mid \mathbf{X}_{\cdot i})$ is the true label distribution and it is unknown for unlabeled samples. Therefore, the current estimate $p\left(\mathbf{Y}_{\cdot i} \mid \mathbf{X}_{\cdot i}, \hat{\theta}\right)$ is calculated to replace the label distribution of unlabeled samples. The loss function of the VAT is given by

$$\begin{cases} D\left[p\left(\mathbf{Y}_{\cdot i} \mid \mathbf{X}_{\cdot i}, \hat{\theta}\right), p\left(\mathbf{Y}_{\cdot i} \mid \mathbf{X}_{\cdot i} + \mathbf{T}_{\cdot i}^{\text{adv}}, \theta\right)\right] \\ \mathbf{T}_{\cdot i}^{\text{adv}} = \arg \max\limits_{\mathbf{T};\, \|\mathbf{T}\|_2 \le \varepsilon} D\left[p\left(\mathbf{Y}_{\cdot i} \mid \mathbf{X}_{\cdot i}, \hat{\theta}\right), p\left(\mathbf{Y}_{\cdot i} \mid \mathbf{X}_{\cdot i} + \mathbf{T}, \theta\right)\right] \end{cases} \tag{20.3}$$

where $p\left(\mathbf{Y}_{\cdot i} \mid \mathbf{X}_{\cdot i}, \hat{\theta}\right)$ is the prediction label distribution of $\mathbf{X}_{\cdot i}$, while $\hat{\theta}$ is the set of model parameters at a specific iteration step of the training process. For semisupervised learning, $p\left(\mathbf{Y}_{\cdot i} \mid \mathbf{X}_{\cdot i}, \hat{\theta}\right)$ the true label distribution $q(\mathbf{Y}_{\cdot i} \mid \mathbf{X}_{\cdot i})$ becomes close when the training process is sufficiently iterated.

$$\begin{aligned} &\min_{g} \Theta(\theta) \\ &= \min \Phi_{\text{cel}} + \lambda_1 \Phi_{\text{LML}} + \lambda_2 \Phi_{\text{VAT}} \\ &= -\frac{1}{M_0} \sum_{j=1}^{M_0} \sum_{k=1}^{c} 1\left\{k = \mathbf{Y}_{kj}\right\} \ln\left(\mathbf{O}_{kj}\right) \\ &\quad + \lambda_1 \sum_{u=1}^{3} \operatorname{tr}\left(\mathbf{Z}^{(u)} \mathbf{L}^{(u)} \left(\mathbf{Z}^{(u)}\right)^T\right) \\ &\quad + \lambda_2 \frac{1}{M} \sum_{i=1}^{M} D\left[p\left(\mathbf{Y}_{\cdot i} \mid \mathbf{X}_{\cdot i}, \hat{\theta}\right), p\left(\mathbf{Y}_{\cdot i} \mid \mathbf{X}_{\cdot i} + \mathbf{T}_{\cdot i}^{\text{adv}}, \theta\right)\right] \end{aligned} \tag{20.4}$$

where λ_1 and λ_2 are tradeoff parameters.

In every training iteration, labeled and unlabeled samples are jointly employed to train the model parameters in order to ensure that the parameter optimization process is always performed in a semisupervised manner. The gradient calculation and parameter update in our model are accomplished by the existing open-source framework.

20.2.1.3 Optimization

The objective function of DRFL-VAT is a combination of Cross-Entropy (CE) LML loss, and VAT loss. These are balanced by trade-off parameters to form a comprehensive loss function that is aimed at minimizing errors across both labeled and unlabeled data. The model employs a gradient descent algorithm to optimize the CNN's parameters. This approach is designed to effectively reduce the overall loss function, thereby enhancing the learning process and ensuring optimal performance across the diverse conditions presented by HSI data. DRFL-VAT uses a mini-batch update strategy which includes both labeled and unlabeled samples in each batch. This semisupervised learning strategy allows for efficient training of the network and continual refinement of the model parameters, enabling it to better generalize from the available data and perform robustly in HSI classification tasks.

20.2.2 DS^{4}L

20.2.2.1 Motivation

The DS^{4}L model addresses the challenges of dimensionality and limited labeled samples in HSI classification. It utilizes a feature extraction network and a SL network. The approach starts with extracting multiscale feature maps to leverage spatial information and similarities between neighboring pixels, using the BFE network for initial processing. The DSSL network then reduces redundancy, incorporating both regular and irregular constraints to refine the representative subspace. Training utilizes labeled samples and a softmax layer to validate the subspace quality, optimizing an objective function that includes constraints and CE loss through an iterative algorithm.

20.2.2.2 Core Elements of the Model

This network processes multiscale HSI patches to create a unified feature space, enhancing both spectral and spatial information. It employs convolutional layers to scale and concatenate these patches, which improves feature richness and the model's ability to generalize across diverse data inputs. This approach effectively reduces the dimensionality of data while capturing essential details.

Following feature extraction, the DSSL Network uses FCLs integrated with regular and irregular constraints to transform high-dimensional data into a low-dimensional, discriminative subspace. The regular constraint maintains critical spectral and spatial connections, supporting robust dimensionality reduction. Conversely, the irregular constraint utilizes superpixel clustering to reduce reliance on extensive labeled datasets, facilitating semi-supervised learning.

Together, these networks refine the feature space into a manageable and representative subspace, which is then classified using a softmax layer linked to the output of the DSSL Network. This setup not only ensures precise classification but also adapts to new data through semi-supervised learning. The overall objective function of the model, combining constraints and CE loss, is optimized iteratively to balance feature integrity and classification accuracy. The DS^{4}L objective function is the following:

$$
\begin{aligned}
\Theta = \lambda_1 \Theta_R + \lambda_2 \Theta_1 + \lambda_3 \Theta_{\mathrm{CE}} + \lambda_1 \left[\frac{1}{m} \sum_{j}^{m} \left(X_i' - X_{M_j} \right)^2 \right] + \lambda_2 \left[-\frac{1}{n} \sum_{i}^{n} \exp\left(\frac{\| f_{S_i}^{L_S} - \overline{f}_{S_i} \|_2^2}{\sigma} \right) \right] \\
+ \lambda_3 \left[-\frac{1}{n} \sum_{i}^{n} \sum_{j=1}^{C} N(j) \log\left(p_i \left(\left(\hat{y}_i = j \mid f_S{}^{L_S} \right) \right) \right] \qquad (20.5)
\end{aligned}
$$

where λ_1, λ_2, and λ_3 are the parameters to balance the weight of the regular constraint, irregular constraint, and CE loss, respectively, M_j is the scale of the input data, and n is the number of predicted pixels.

20.2.2.3 Optimization

The optimization of the DS^{4}L framework uses Adam optimization and backpropagation to update the weights and biases in each layer, refining these parameters based on experimental outcomes to enhance model accuracy. It incorporates mathematical expressions to compute derivatives efficiently for different network layers, including fully connected and deconvolution layers. These derivatives help adjust the weights (W) and biases (b) directly influencing the layer outputs and overall network performance. Each layer's parameters are systematically updated by calculating the gradient of the loss function concerning those parameters, ensuring optimal adjustments for improved classification accuracy.

The optimization for the BFE Network is the following:

$$\begin{aligned} W_C^l &= W_C^l - r\left(\frac{\partial \Theta_R}{\partial W_C^l} + \frac{\partial \Theta_I}{\partial W_C^l} + \frac{\partial \Theta_{\mathrm{CE}}}{\partial W_C^l}\right) \\ b_C^l &= b_C^l - r\left(\frac{\partial \Theta_R}{\partial b_C^l} + \frac{\partial \Theta_I}{\partial b_C^l} + \frac{\partial \Theta_{\mathrm{CE}}}{\partial b_C^l}\right) \end{aligned} \tag{20.6}$$

where r is the learning rate.

The optimization for the DSSL Network is the following:

$$\begin{aligned} W_S^l &= W_S^l - r\left(\frac{\partial \Theta_I}{\partial W_S^l} + \frac{\partial \Theta_{\mathrm{CE}}}{\partial W_S^l}\right) \\ b_C^l &= b_C^l - r\left(\frac{\partial \Theta_I}{\partial b_S^l} + \frac{\partial \Theta_{\mathrm{CE}}}{\partial b_S^l}\right) \end{aligned} \tag{20.7}$$

This rigorous approach allows for precise optimization of both the BFE and DSSL networks within the system.

20.2.3 SLCRF

20.2.3.1 Motivation

The motivation behind SLCRF lies in harnessing self-supervised learning insights to improve HSI classification without extensive manual labeling. Recent studies have highlighted the potential of using inherent data characteristics as self-supervision sources, enabling enhanced feature extraction from HSI pixels. SLCRF integrates CRF to exploit spatial and categorical relationships between pixels, effectively embedding these relationships into a learning model that combines semi-supervised constraints and relationship construction. This integration aims to optimize feature representation and classification accuracy, reducing the reliance on labeled data and improving the efficiency of learning complex HSI data structures.

20.2.3.2 Core Elements of the Model

The core elements of the SLCRF model, aimed at enhancing HSI classification, revolve around the integration of SL and CRF within a semi-supervised framework. At its foundation, the model employs a 3DCAE to delineate a latent subspace from high-dimensional HSI data. This subspace is captured through an encoder-decoder mechanism where the encoder reduces the original data dimensions and the decoder attempts to reconstruct the data, minimizing reconstruction errors and controlling overfitting through weight decay.

The objective function of 3DCAE can be formulated as follows:

$$\Theta(\theta) = \frac{1}{b \times b \times d} \sum_{x=0}^{b-1} \sum_{y=0}^{b-1} \sum_{z=0}^{d-1} X_{x,y,z} - X_{x,y,z}^{(M)^2} + \frac{\alpha}{2} \|\mathrm{W}\|_F^2 \tag{20.8}$$

where α is the balancing term between the reconstruction error and the weight decay term. θ represents the set of all parameters in 3DCAE, and W consists of the weights in all layers. $X_{x,y,z}$ represents the value at position (x, y, z) of the input $X \in \mathbb{R}^{b \times b \times d}$, while $X_{x,y,z}^{(M)}$ represents the reconstructed value at position (x, y, z). The weight decay term helps to decrease the magnitude of the weights and prevent over-fitting.

By combining the relationships of the latent space and the spatial distance, we can formulate the relationship matrix S to denote the relationships in subspace:

$$S = S_1 + \gamma S_2 \tag{20.9}$$

where γ is a constant.

To leverage the spatial and spectral relationships inherent in HSIs, a relationship matrix is constructed that blends the proximities within the latent subspace and the spatial distances among pixels. This matrix is vital for defining the interaction terms in the CRF model, which uses these relationships to enforce spatial and spectral consistency in the classification outputs.

The CRF component is then seamlessly integrated, utilizing a graph-based structure where nodes represent pixel subspace embeddings and edges depict the learned relationships. This setup facilitates the application of unary and pairwise potentials, which are crucial for labeling consistency and accuracy across the HSI.

Collectively, these elements form a robust model that not only aims to reduce the dependency on labeled data but also enhances classification precision through effective subspace representation and meticulous relationship modeling.

20.2.3.3 Optimization

To optimize the Subspace Learning Conditional Random Fields (SLCRF) model for hyperspectral imaging, the Linearized Alternating Direction Method with Augmented Lagrangian and Adaptive Penalty (LADMAP) is employed. This method optimizes a complex augmented Lagrangian function, meticulously balancing reconstruction accuracy and computational efficiency.

The optimization involves iteratively updating variables – Z (representing latent subspace relationships), M (auxiliary matrix to mitigate direct dependency issues), and h (CRF weights) – under fixed conditions for the others, which is a classic approach in alternating direction methods. Specifically, when M and h are held constant, Z is optimized to minimize discrepancies between actual and predicted subspace representations, adjusted for the relationships encoded in matrix S.

Similarly, when Z and h are fixed, M is optimized to ensure the updated values properly reflect changes in Z, enhancing the model's responsiveness to new data. The optimization of h, crucial for determining the influence of unary and pairwise terms in the CRF, adjusts based on the current states of Z and M, aiming to maximize label consistency across the HSI.

Throughout this process, the Lagrangian multiplier T is adjusted to maintain constraint satisfaction, ensuring that each iterative update moves towards reducing the overall objective function. This comprehensive approach allows the SLCRF model to efficiently handle high-dimensional data, providing a robust framework for SL and spatial relationship modeling in hyperspectral imagery.

20.2.4 SDFL-FC

20.2.4.1 Motivation

To address the scarcity of labeled samples in HSI classification, we introduce the SDFL-FC method. This approach uses a CNN to extract spectral-spatial features from both labeled and unlabeled data, thereby reducing reliance on large labeled datasets. SDFL-FC ensures feature quality through FCLs that model feature consistency via two mechanisms: FCS and FCG. Integrated with CE loss, these ensure robust, homogeneous feature representation, enabling superior HSI classification performance.

20.2.4.2 Core Elements of the Model

The SDFL-FC model comprises several core elements tailored to optimize HSI classification. The CNN feature extractor plays a pivotal role by leveraging stride convolutional layers to capture spectral-spatial features from 3-D HSI data patches. This process not only emphasizes the local spatial structures but also the spectral correlations, providing a comprehensive feature set.

At the heart of SDFL-FC, FCLs transform these features into a format suitable for classification while ensuring their consistency and quality. This is achieved through mechanisms such as FCS and FCG, which ensure the homogeneity of features within superpixels and across similar groups respectively. These consistencies are crucial for maintaining the integrity of feature representation throughout the learning process.

To complement these structural features, SDFL-FC incorporates a GAN-based reconstruction approach. This element of the model minimizes the disparity between the original and reconstructed data, enhancing the representational fidelity of the extracted features. Additionally, the model's architecture facilitates robust classification through the integration of CE loss, calculated with labeled samples to fine-tune the feature extraction and classification accuracy.

$$
\begin{aligned}
\Theta &= \Theta_{\mathrm{FCS}} + \lambda_1 \Theta_{\mathrm{FCG}} + \lambda_2 \Theta_{\mathrm{CE}} \\
&= E_{X \sim p(X)}[D(X)] - E_{h_G^{(M_1)} \sim p\left(h_G^{(M_1)}\right)}\left[D\left(h_G^{(M_1)}\right)\right] \\
&\quad + \lambda_1 \left[\sum_{l_2 = 1}^{L_2} \left[\eta_{l_2} \sum_{i=1}^{n} \left\| f_i^{(l_2)} - u_i^{(l_2)} \right\|_2^2 \right] \right] \\
&\quad + \lambda_2 \left[-\frac{1}{s} \sum_{i=1}^{s} \sum_{j=1}^{C} I(j) \log\left(p\left(\hat{y}_i = j \mid f^{(L_2)}\right)\right) \right]
\end{aligned}
\tag{20.10}
$$

where λ_1 and λ_2 are used to balance the importance of the corresponding terms.

20.2.4.3 Optimization

The optimization of the SDFL-FC utilizes a customized iterative algorithm to fine-tune its components. Central to this process is the alternating minimization of the FCS alongside simultaneous optimization of the FCG and CE loss. This method employs the Adam stochastic gradient descent approach and backpropagation to ensure precise adjustments.

Specifically, optimization of the FCS involves sequential updates to the discriminator (D) and generator (G) parameters, using derivatives of the objective function to guide parameter adjustments based on respective learning rates. Conversely, the FCG and CE components are optimized through gradient descent, impacting multiple layers and ensuring that updates to weights and biases are coordinated across the network. This structured approach promotes the robustness and accuracy of the model by systematically refining the feature consistencies and classification outputs.

$$W_D^{(m_2)} = W_D^{(m_2)} - \alpha_1 \frac{\partial \Theta}{\partial W_D^{(m_2)}}, \quad b_D^{(m_2)} = b_D^{(m_2)} - \alpha_1 \frac{\partial \Theta}{\partial b_D^{(m_2)}} \tag{20.11}$$

where a_1 is the learning rate of D.

$$W_G^{(m_1)} = W_G^{(m_1)} - \alpha_2 \frac{\partial \Theta}{\partial W_G^{(m_1)}}, \quad b_G^{(m_1)} = b_G^{(m_1)} - \alpha_2 \frac{\partial \Theta}{\partial b_G^{(m_1)}} \tag{20.12}$$

where a_2 is the learning rate of D.

$$\begin{aligned} w(L_3) &= W^{(L_3)} - \alpha_3 \frac{\partial \Theta}{\partial W^{(L_3)}}, \quad b^{(L_3)} = b^{(L_3)} - \alpha_3 \frac{\partial \Theta}{\partial b^{(L_3)}} \\ w(l_2) &= W^{(l_2)} - \alpha_3 \frac{\partial \Theta}{\partial W^{(l_2)}}, \quad b^{(l_2)} = b^{(l_2)} - \alpha_3 \frac{\partial \Theta}{\partial b^{(l_2)}} \\ w(l_1) &= W^{(l_1)} - \alpha_3 \frac{\partial \Theta}{\partial W^{(l_1)}}, \quad b^{(l_1)} = b^{(l_1)} - \alpha_3 \frac{\partial \Theta}{\partial b^{(l_1)}} \end{aligned} \tag{20.13}$$

where a_3 is the learning rate of FCG and CE.

20.3 Experimental Results

20.3.1 Experimental Datasets

The classification performance of the DRFL-VAT, DS^{4}L, SLCRF, and SDFL-FC models was assessed using various HSI datasets, including Indian Pines, Salinas, Pavia University (PaviaU), and Houston. The DRFL-VAT method was tested on the Indian Pines, Salinas, and PaviaU datasets, highlighting features such as spectral band count, pixel resolution, and class diversity. For example, the Indian Pines dataset was evaluated after discarding certain bands to focus on 200 effective spectral channels. DS^{4}L's effectiveness was compared against semi-supervised methods using the same datasets, emphasizing improvements in classification accuracy through detailed dataset characteristics.

The SLCRF and SDFL-FC models expanded their evaluations to include the Houston dataset, which features a substantial number of pixels and spectral bands, thus providing a broader context for assessing model performance across different environments. This comprehensive approach across models and datasets underscores the nuanced preprocessing and analytic strategies employed to enhance the accuracy and applicability of hyperspectral classification algorithms in varied settings.

20.3.2 Experimental Results

20.3.2.1 DRFL-VAT

The DRFL-VAT model demonstrated superior classification performance compared to other methods, as shown in the comparative analysis in Figures 20.5–20.9. This success indicates that DRFL-VAT effectively leverages the local properties of samples to extract representative features for HSI

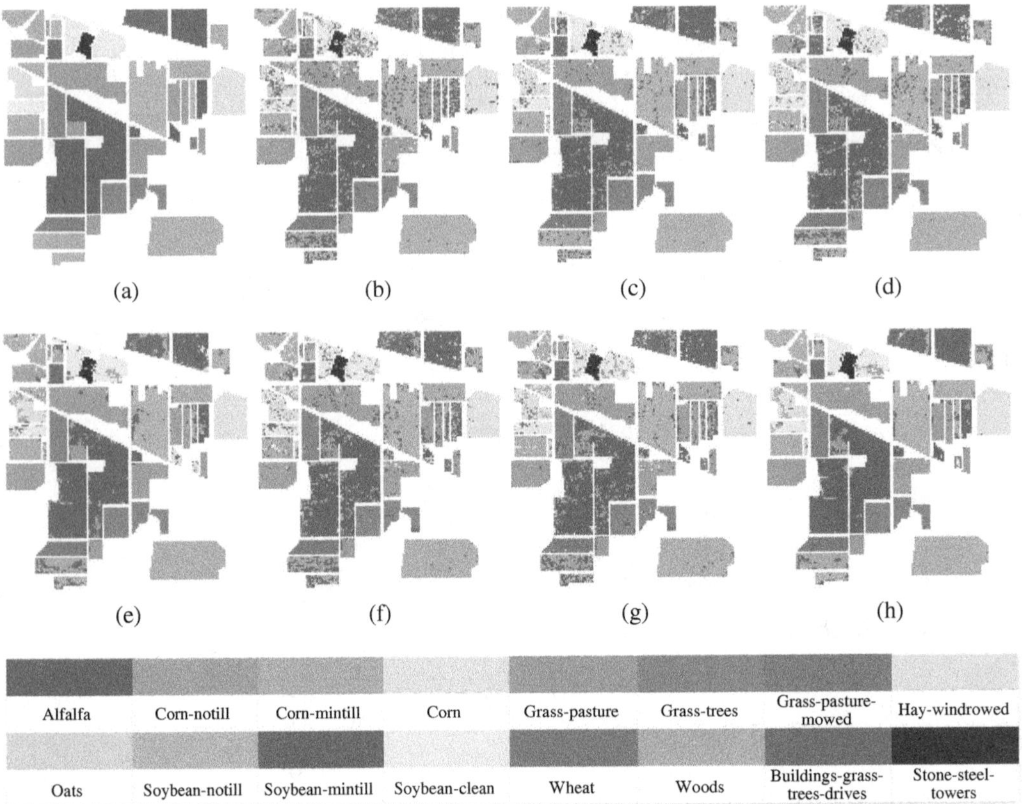

Figure 20.5 Classification maps obtained for the Indian Pines dataset by using 10% of the available labeled samples for each class. Ground truth (a) and classification maps obtained by (b) LS+SVM, (c) FC-LN, (d) GCN, (e) SSCNN, (f) SAE, (g) SGAN, and (h) DRFL-VAT.

classification. The method's use of additional loss constraints also contributed significantly to these results. However, across all methods, classification outcomes on the Indian Pines dataset were generally less favorable than those on the other datasets, likely due to its lower spatial resolution and issues with class imbalance.

20.3.2.2 DS^{4}L

The newly proposed DS^{4}L model has undergone comprehensive testing on three standard datasets, Salinas Scene, Indian Pines, and PaviaU Scene, delivering remarkable results in HSI classification. By seamlessly integrating regular and irregular constraints, DS^{4}L not only mitigates the common issues of pixel-level misclassification and the "salt and pepper" effect but also significantly enhances the classification accuracy (Figures 20.10–20.13). The AA scores achieved by DS^{4}L are particularly noteworthy, reaching 97.88% on Salinas Scene, 95.56% on Indian Pines, and 95.73% on PaviaU Scene. These results not only confirm the model's effectiveness in capturing representative subspaces but also underscore its reliability and generalizability across different HSI datasets. In conclusion, the DS^{4}L model offers a robust and accurate approach to HSI classification, setting a new benchmark in the field.

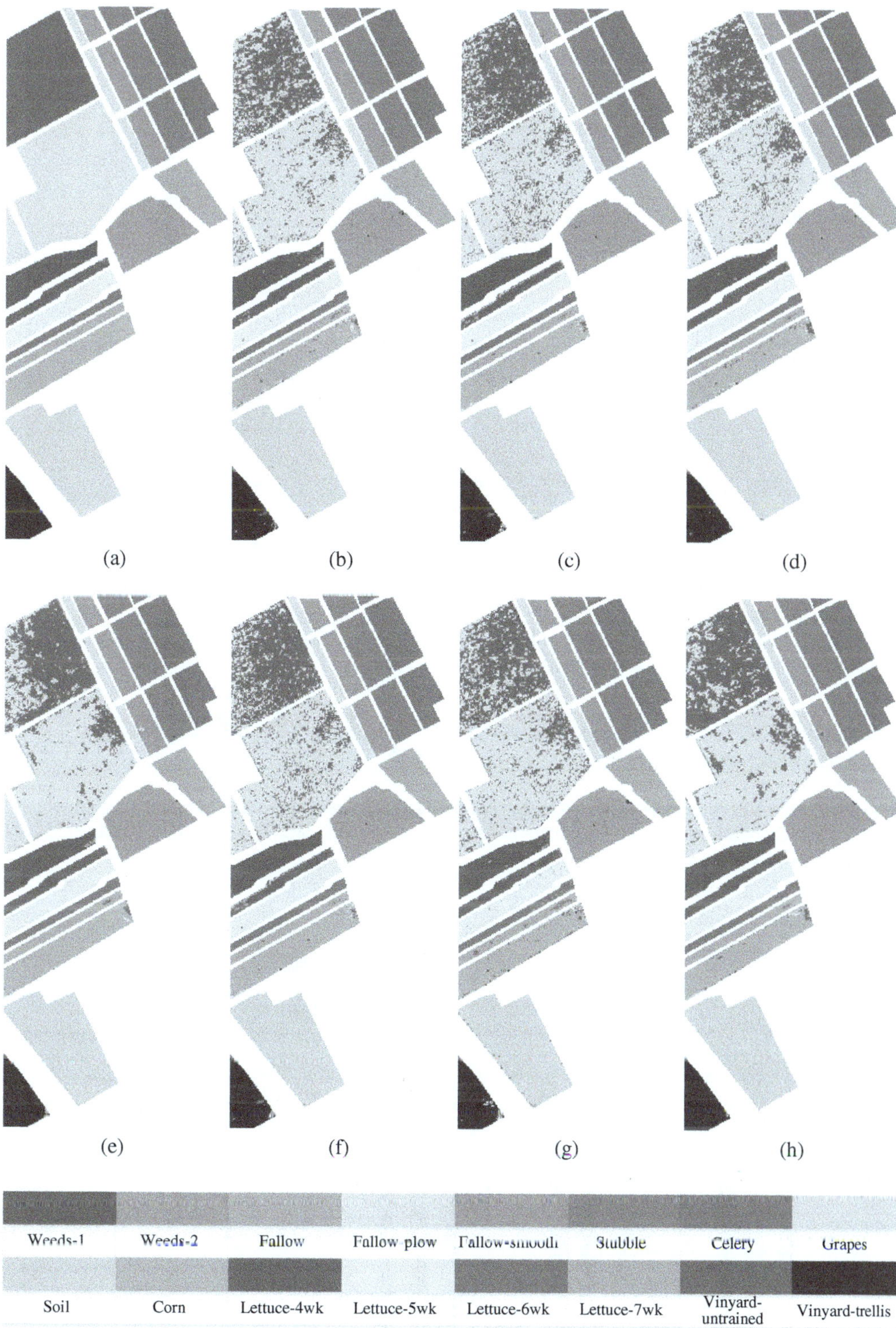

Figure 20.6 Classification maps obtained for the Salinas dataset by using 2% of the available labeled samples for each class. Ground truth (a) and classification maps obtained by (b) LS+SVM, (c) FC-LN, (d) GCN, (e) SSCNN, (f) SAE, (g) SGAN, and (h) DRFL-VAT.

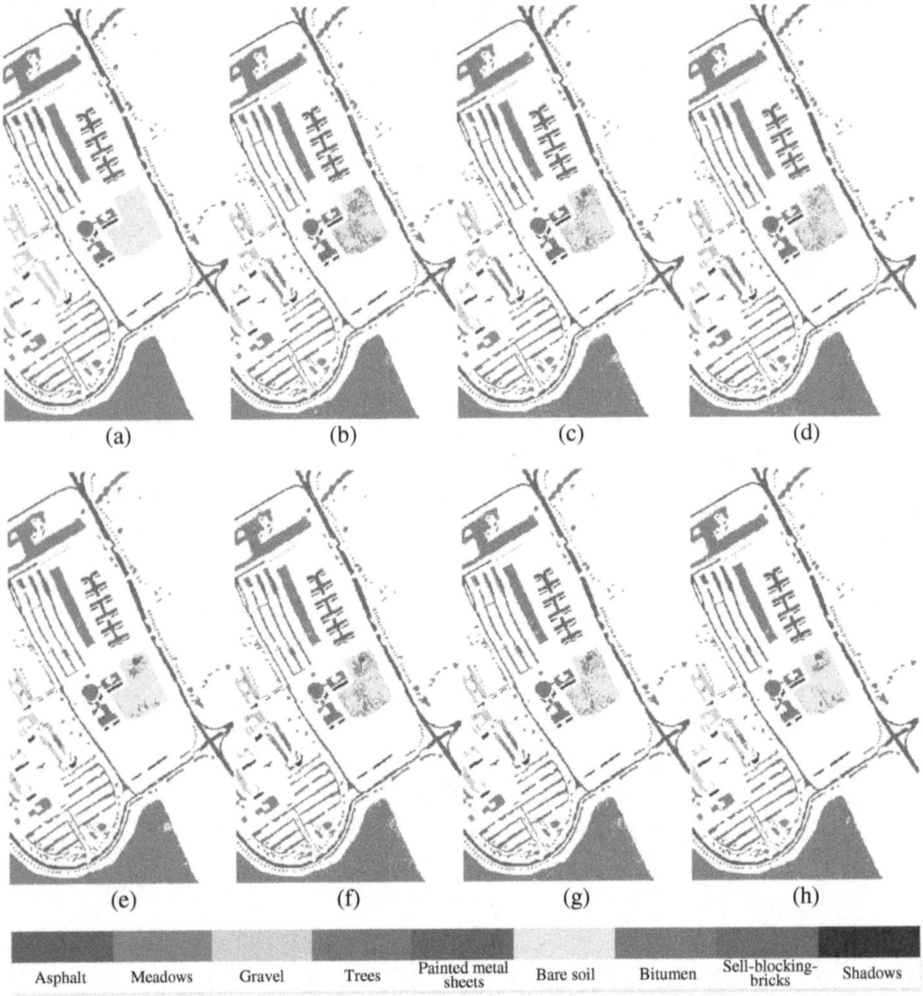

Figure 20.7 Classification maps obtained for the PaviaU dataset by using 2% of the available labeled samples for each class. Ground truth (a) and classification maps obtained by (b) LS+SVM, (c) FC-LN, (d) GCN, (e) SSCNN, (f) SAE, (g) SGAN, and (h) DRFL-VAT.

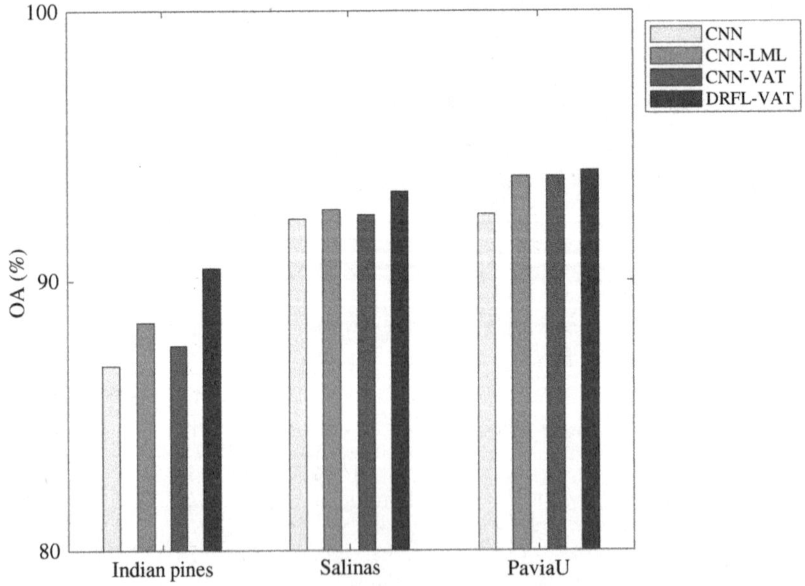

Figure 20.8 Analyzing the importance of the LML and VAT constraint.

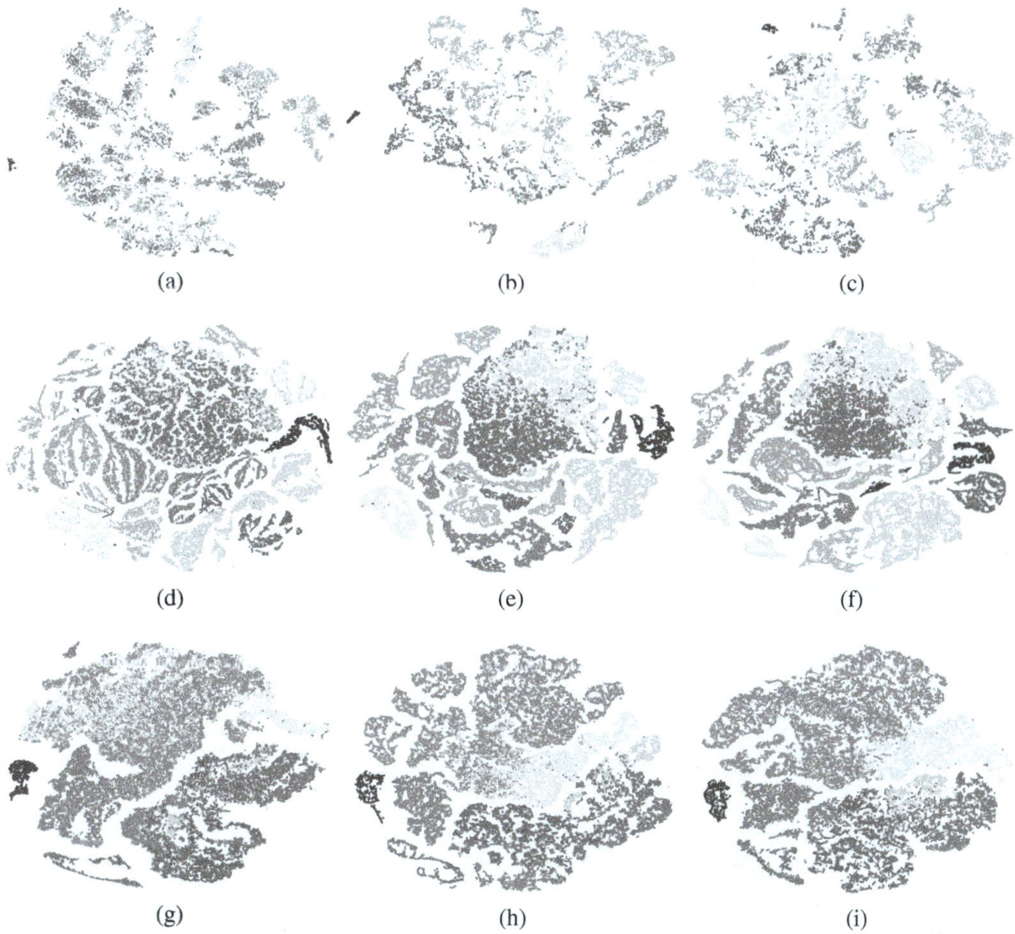

Figure 20.9 Analysis for separability of feature representation. Two-dimensional embedding visualizations on the Indian Pines dataset for (a) original data, (b) features extracted by the basic CNN, and (c) features extracted by the DRFL-VAT. The visualizations on the Salinas dataset for (d) original data, (e) features extracted by the basic CNN, and (f) features extracted by the DRFL-VAT. The visualizations on the PaviaU dataset for (g) original data, (h) features extracted by the basic CNN, and (i) features extracted by the DRFL-VAT.

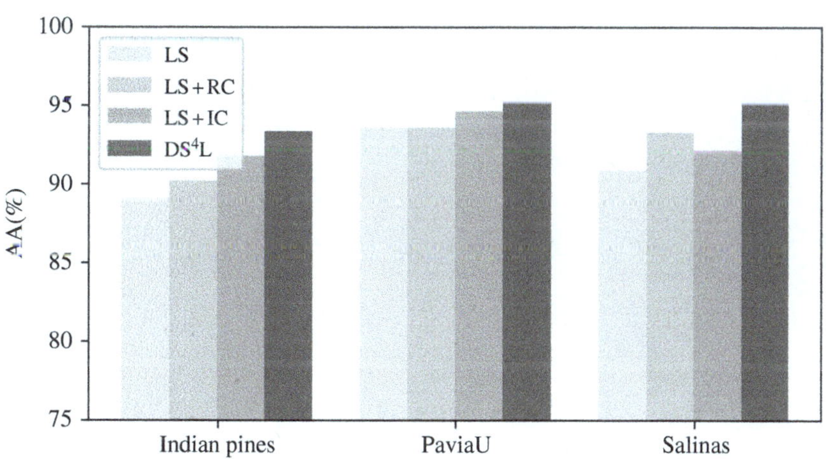

Figure 20.10 Analyzing the importance of regular constraint and irregular constraint.

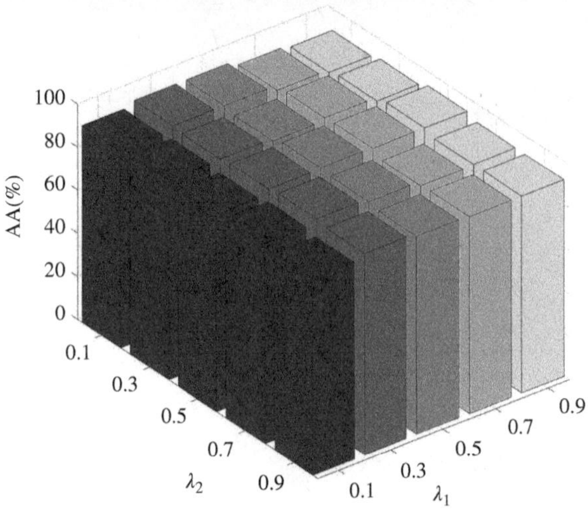

Figure 20.11 Effect of the loss function's weight parameters. Influences of λ_1 and λ_2 on the classification results for the Salinas dataset.

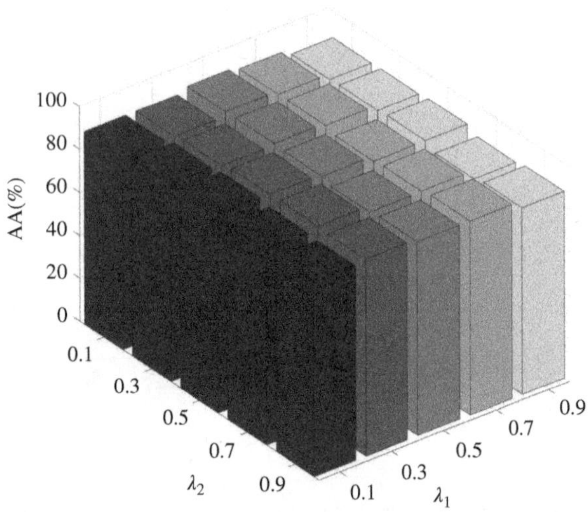

Figure 20.12 Effect of the loss function's weight parameters. Influences of λ_1 and λ_2 on the classification results for the Indian Pines dataset.

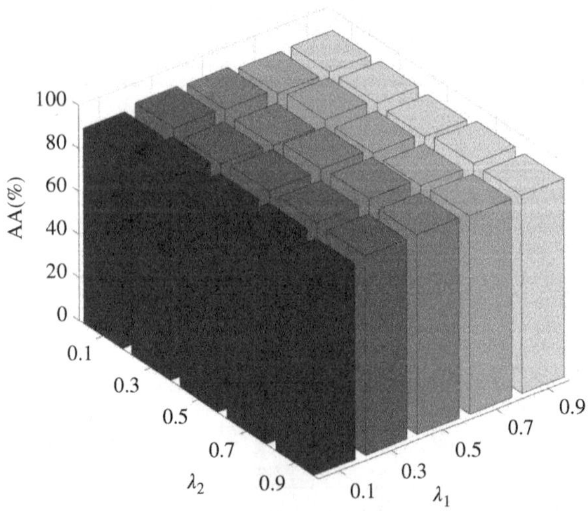

Figure 20.13 Effect of the loss function's weight parameters. Influences of λ_1 and λ_2 on the classification results for the PaviaU dataset.

20.3.2.3 SLCRF

The SLCRF method employs a spatial graph construction and tuning of balancing parameters to optimize classification. The number of feature dimensions and batch size is carefully selected alongside the learning rate to accommodate the spectral bands of each dataset.

Results indicate that SLCRF consistently outperforms related methods, yielding more compact and accurate classification results. The improvements are attributed to the effective pixel relationship modeling by the SLCRF and the integration of SL, relationship construction, and semi-supervised constraints within the CRF framework (Figures 20.14–20.17). This unified approach allows the SLCRF to excel in HSI classification, especially as the number of labeled samples increases, demonstrating robustness across different training sample sizes and outpacing the CAE-SC method in accuracy.

20.3.2.4 SDFL-FC

The SDFL-FC method demonstrates excellent performance in hyperspectral image classification tasks. By integrating FCS, FCG, and CE, the SDFL-FC method effectively enhances classification performance. Experimental comparisons with current advanced HSI classification methods

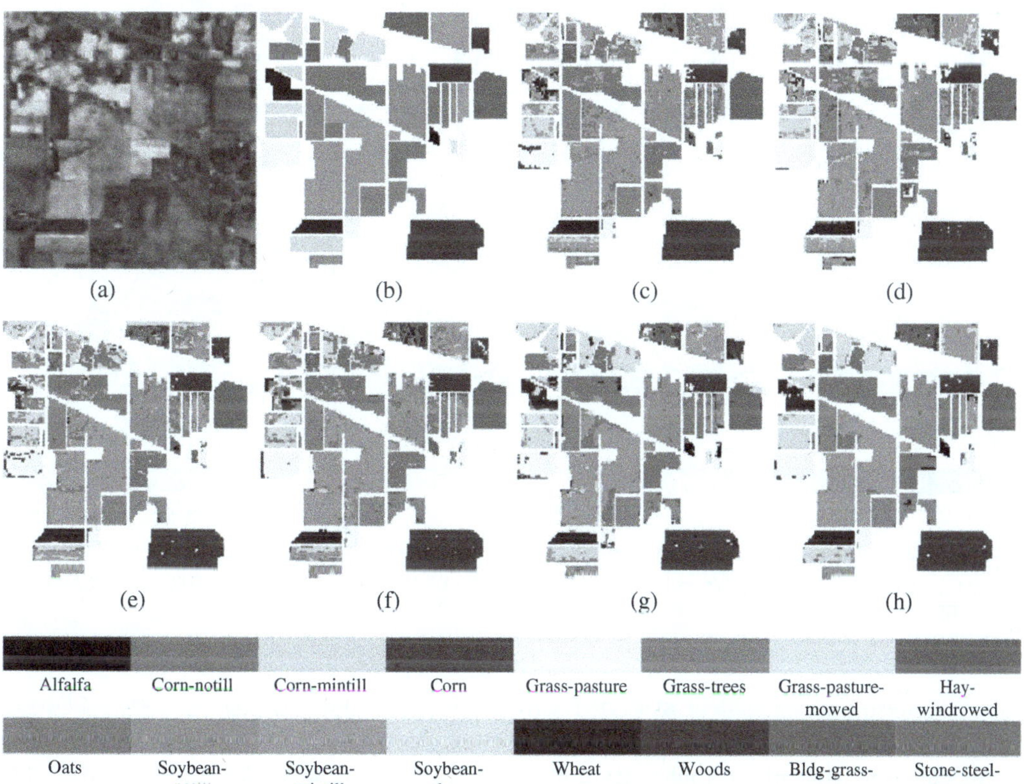

Figure 20.14 Classification maps of the different methods with 5% labeled samples for the Indian pines dataset. (a) Original image. (b) Ground truth. (c) PCA-SC. (d) LPP-SC. (e) CAE-SC. (f) SCAE-SC. (g) 3DCAE-CRF. (h) SLCRF.

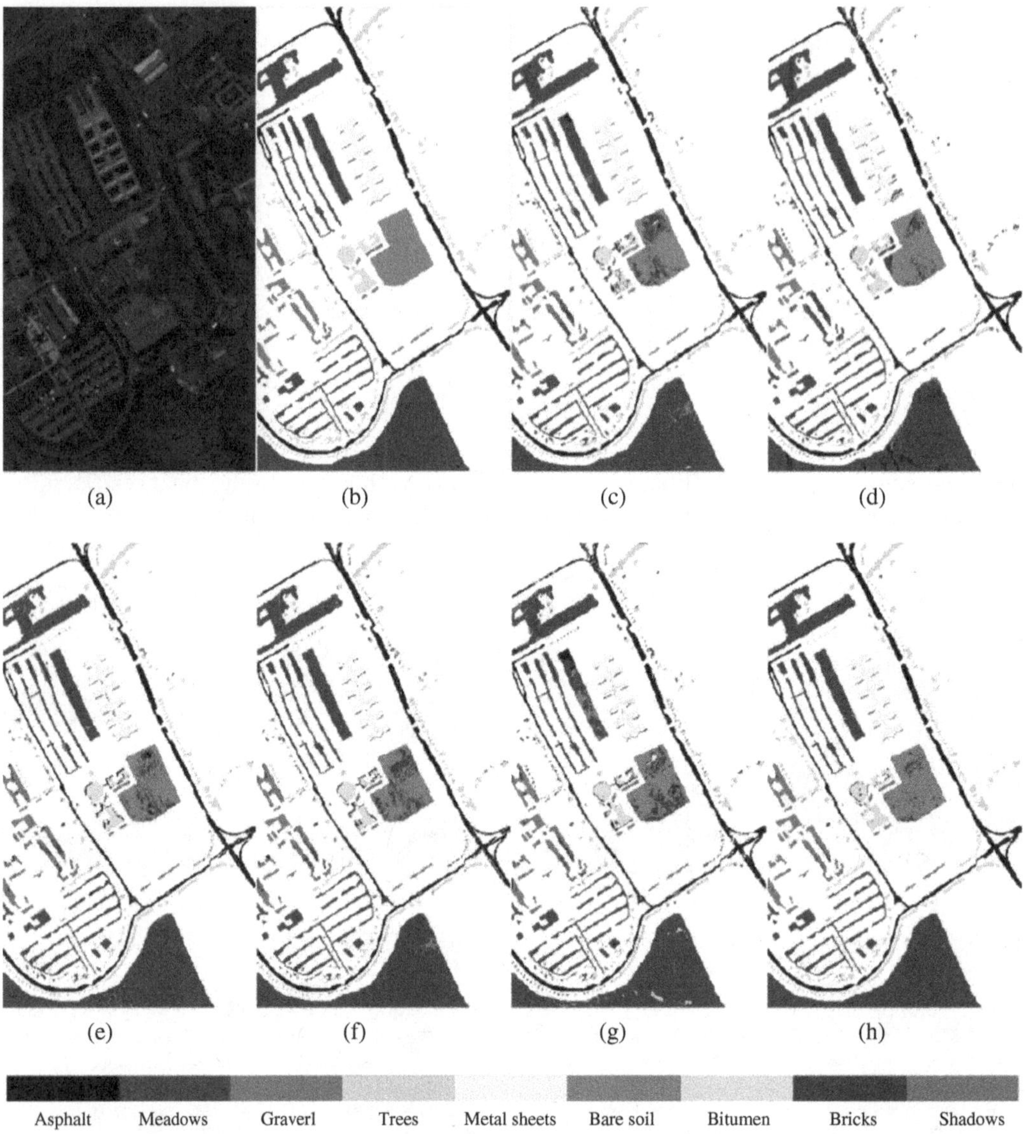

Figure 20.15 Classification maps of the different methods with 1% labeled samples for the PaviaU dataset. (a) Original image. (b) Ground truth. (c) PCA-SC. (d) LPP-SC. (e) CAE-SC. (f) SCAE-SC. (g) 3DCAE-CRF. (h) SLCRF.

show significant advantages of SDFL-FC across multiple evaluation metrics. This advantage stems from the effective utilization of unlabeled samples by SDFL-FC and the enhancement of model generalization through feature consistency constraints. Additionally, SDFL-FC employs a customized iterative optimization algorithm to further optimize model performance (Figures 20.18–20.20). Overall, the SDFL-FC method holds promising applications in the field of hyperspectral image classification, providing new insights and methodologies for related research areas.

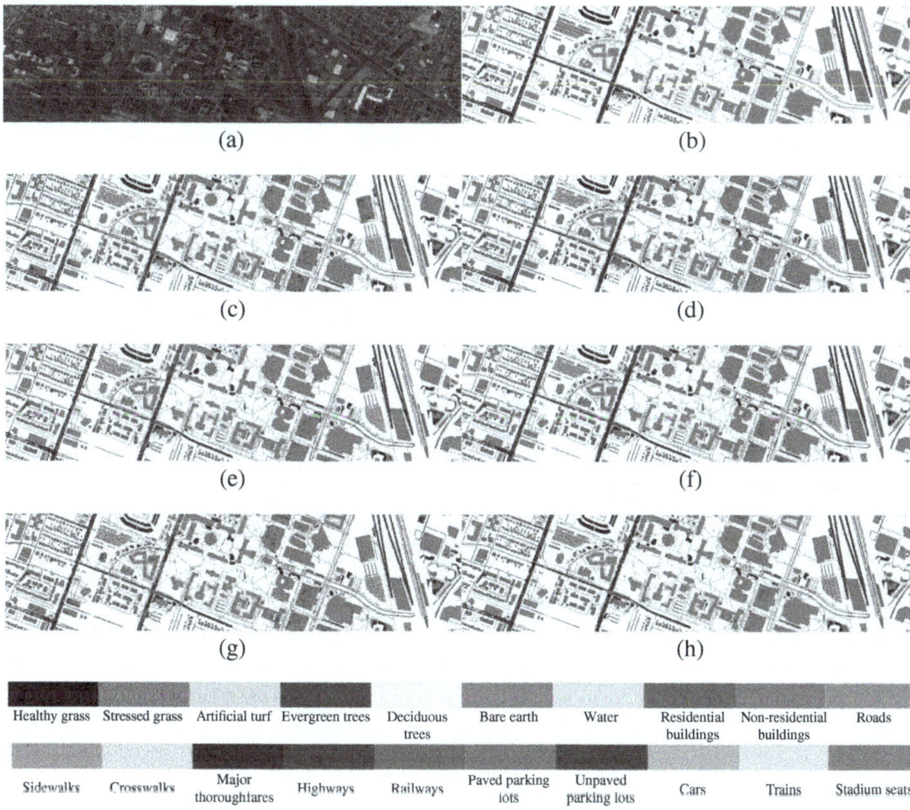

Figure 20.16 Classification maps of the different methods with 1% labeled samples for the Houston dataset. (a) Original image. (b) Ground truth. (c) PCA-SC. (d) LPP-SC. (e) CAE-SC. (f) SCAE-SC. (g) 3DCAE-CRF. (h) SLCRF.

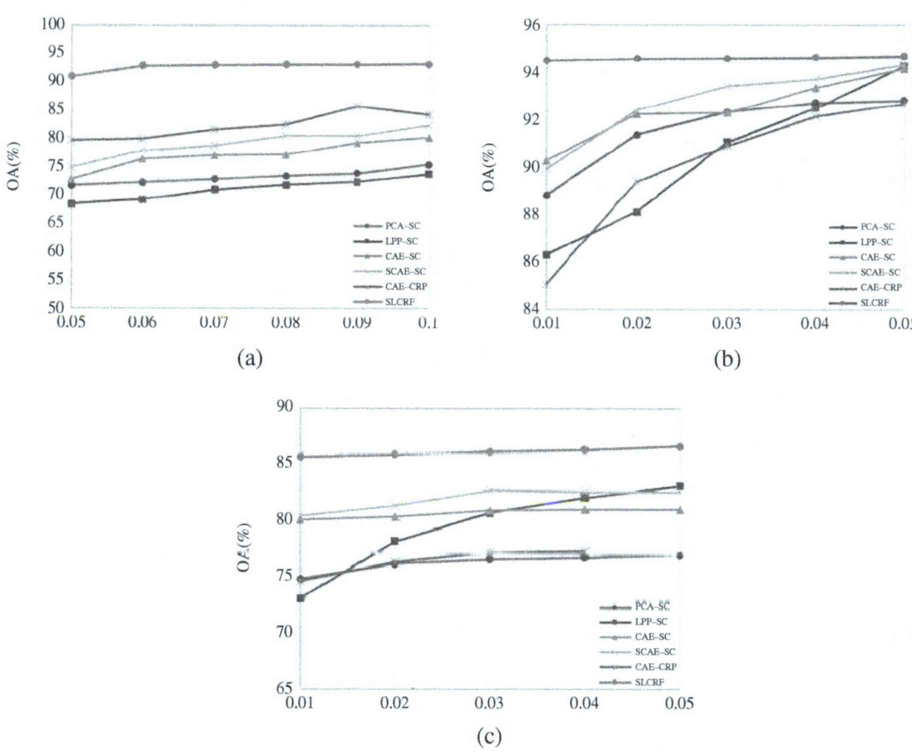

Figure 20.17 Classification results of the PCA-SC, LPP-SC, CAE-SC, SCAE-SC,3DCAE-CRF and SLCRF with different percentages of labeled image samples. (a) The Indian pines dataset. (b) The PaviaU dataset. (c) The Houston dataset.

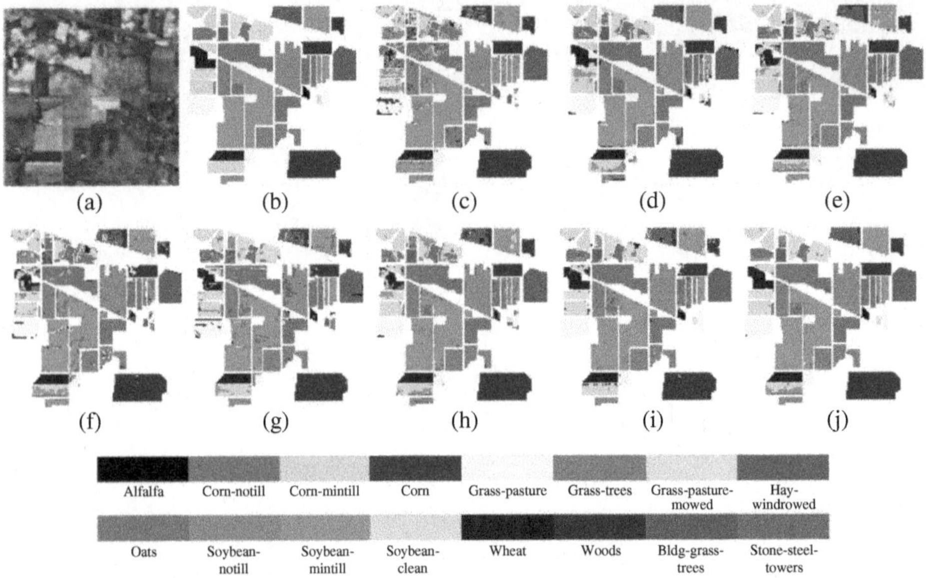

Figure 20.18 Classification maps of the different methods with 10% training samples for the Indian Pines dataset. (a) Original image. (b) Ground truth. (c) SVM-RBF. (d) ALDL. (e) PCA + CE. (f) WGAN + CE. (g) CAE + LGC. (h) SSCNN. (i) SESEMI. (j) SDFL-FC.

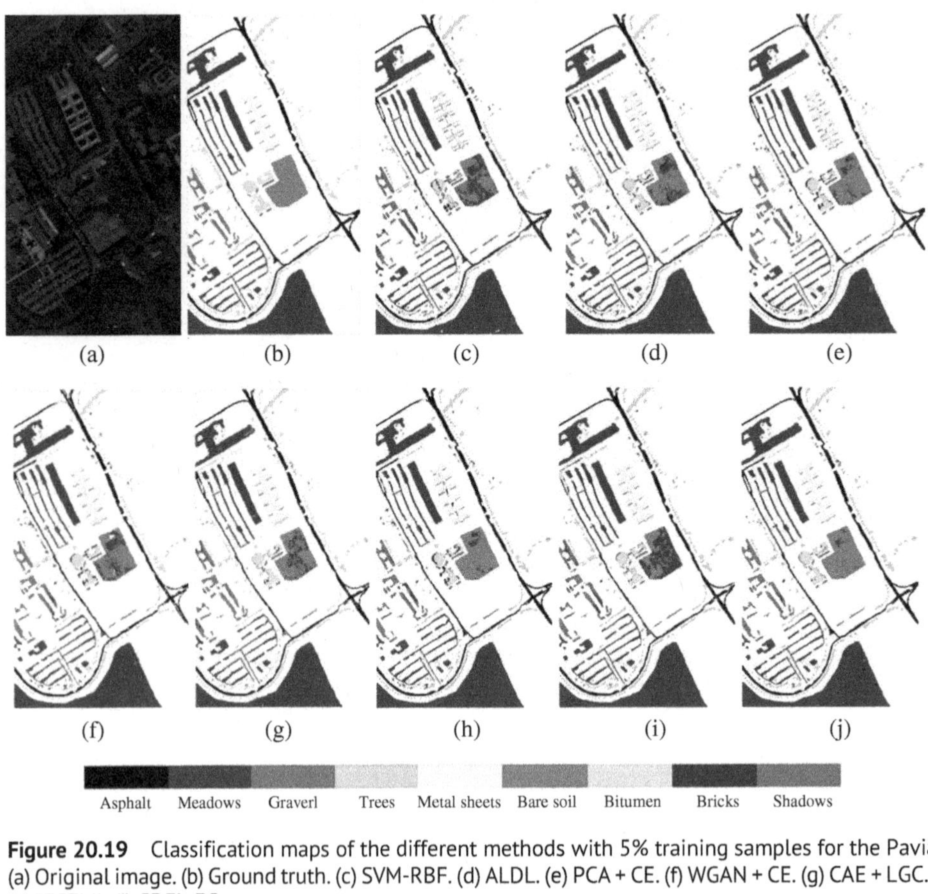

Figure 20.19 Classification maps of the different methods with 5% training samples for the PaviaU dataset. (a) Original image. (b) Ground truth. (c) SVM-RBF. (d) ALDL. (e) PCA + CE. (f) WGAN + CE. (g) CAE + LGC. (h) SSCNN. (i) SESEMI. (j) SDFL-FC.

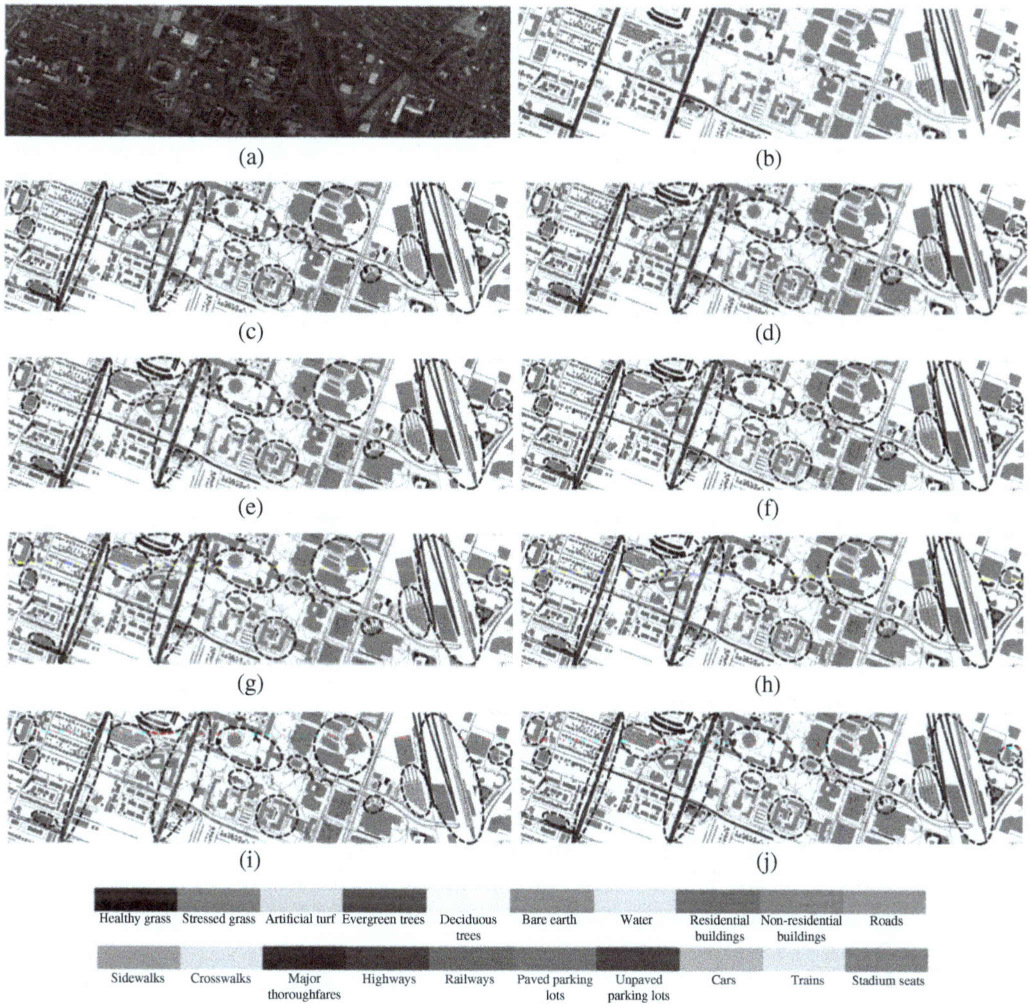

Figure 20.20 Classification maps of the different methods with 5% training samples for the Houston dataset. The regions are circled in dotted line to show the differences. (a) Original image. (b) Ground truth. (c) SVM-RBF. (d) ALDL. (e) PCA + CE. (f) WGAN + CE. (g) CAE + LGC. (h) SSCNN. (i) SESEMI. (j) SDFL-FC.

20.4 Conclusions

In the realm of HSI classification, our study presents a collection of innovative semisupervised frameworks designed to enhance classification while reducing the dependency on labeled samples. We introduce the DRFL-VAT model, which integrates deep learning with LML and VAT, effectively addressing challenges of limited sample availability and overfitting. Our DS^{4}L model employs BFE and DSSL networks, multiscale inputs, and superpixel clustering for robust feature representation and accurate classification. Similarly, the SLCRF model offers a novel SL method that leverages pixel probabilities and neighborhood relationships via a CRF.

Complementing these, our approach utilizing generative adversarial networks alongside CNNs focuses on learning both spectral and spatial features, reconstructing original data from features to honor the inherent similarities within superpixels. We also present the HSINet-CRF, which learns three complementary features at different levels through self-supervision, incorporating TDNN and MCNN, and is enhanced by a CRF framework for improved learning.

The empirical results on various HSI datasets, such as Salinas Scene, Indian Pines, and PaviaU Scene, validate the superiority of our methods over current state-of-the-art techniques. Moving forward, we aim to extend these methodologies to other remote sensing tasks and domains, investigate additional regularization strategies, and continually optimize the architectures. By integrating our models with more remote sensing data, we anticipate developing impactful applications and contributing valuable insights to the field. Future endeavors will also explore the application of these frameworks in 3-D point cloud parsing, image denoising, and other labeling and regression tasks.

References

1 Liu, S., Cao, Y., Wang, Y. et al. (2021). DFL-LC: deep feature learning with label consistencies for hyperspectral image classification. *IEEE J. Sel. Top. Appl. Earth Obs. Remote Sens.* 14: 3669–3681.

2 He, L., Li, J., Liu, C., and Li, S. (2017). Recent advances on spectral–spatial hyperspectral image classification: an overview and new guidelines. *IEEE Trans. Geosci. Remote Sens.* 56 (3): 1579–1597.

3 Zang, N., Cao, Y., Wang, Y. et al. (2021). Land-use mapping for high-spatial resolution remote sensing image via deep learning: a review. *IEEE J. Sel. Top. Appl. Earth Obs. Remote Sens.* 14: 5372–5391.

4 Zhang, H., Meng, L., Xian, W. et al. (2019). 1D-convolutional capsule network for hyperspectral image classification. *arXiv* arXiv:1903.09834.

5 Kang, X., Xiang, X., Li, S., and Benediktsson, J.A. (2017). PCA-based edge-preserving features for hyperspectral image classification. *IEEE Trans. Geosci. Remote Sens.* 55 (12): 7140–7151.

6 Teenbaum, J., Silva, D.D., and Langford, J.A. (2000). Global geometric framework for nonlinear dimensionality reduction. *Science* 290 (5500): 2319–2323.

7 Chen, J., Wang, Y., Zhang, L. et al. (2022). DRFL-VAT: deep representative feature learning with virtual adversarial training for semisupervised classification of hyperspectral image. *IEEE Trans. Geosci. Remote Sens.* 60: 1–14.

8 Zhao, X., Liu, L., Wang, Y. et al. (2022). DS^4L: deep semisupervised shared subspace learning for hyperspectral image classification. *IEEE Trans. Geosci. Remote Sens.* 60: 1–14.

9 Cao, Y., Mei, J., Wang, Y. et al. (2020). SLCRF: subspace learning with conditional random field for hyperspectral image classification. *IEEE Trans. Geosci. Remote Sens.* 59 (5): 4203–4217.

10 Cao, Y., Wang, Y., Peng, J. et al. (2020). SDFL-FC: semisupervised deep feature learning with feature consistency for hyperspectral image classification. *IEEE Trans. Geosci. Remote Sens.* 59 (12): 10488–10502.

21

Constrained Energy Minimization Based Hyperspectral Image Target Detection

Zhenwei Shi[1], Zhengxia Zou[2], Bowen Chen[1], and Liqin Liu[1]

[1] *Image Processing Centre, School of Astronautics, Beihang University, Beijing, China*
[2] *Department of Guidance, Navigation and Control, School of Astronautics, Beihang University, Beijing, China*

21.1 Introduction

Hyperspectral image Target Detection (HTD) is the task of finding and localizing the target in HSIs given the reference spectrum of the target. The reference spectrum is usually derived from a spectral library or identified target pixels in the scene. Typically, there are only one or a few target reference spectra are available.

The overall pipeline of HTD is shown in Figure 21.1. The target detection algorithm discriminates the spectra of each pixel in the HSI with the help of a priori information of the target reference spectrum and a specific detection criterion to obtain a pixel-by-pixel detection map and then distinguishes between the target and the background by setting an appropriate threshold value to obtain the final detection result.

Classic HTD algorithms can be divided into four main categories. The first category is the algorithm based on spectral similarity, which uses spectral angle or relative entropy, etc. to measure the difference between the spectrum to be detected and the reference spectrum. The second category is algorithms based on hypothesis testing. These algorithms assume that the background and target spectra obey different probability distributions, respectively, and then construct the likelihood ratio test by treating the HTD as a binary hypothesis testing problem. The third category is signal decomposition-based algorithms, which consider the spectrum of each pixel as a combination of different signal components and separate the target from the interference information by means of signal decomposition. The fourth category is Constrained Energy Minimization (CEM) [1] based algorithms. This class of algorithms designs Finite Impulse Response (FIR) filters that allow only the desired target features to pass while minimizing the energy output of other features [2].

Among the four categories of methods mentioned above, CEM-based methods are widely used due to their advantages of concise form, ease of use, and high reliability. Therefore, this chapter focuses on the introduction of a series of HTD methods based on CEM, including its original form and a series of variant algorithms, as well as summarizing and outlook.

Machine-Learning-Based Hyperspectral Image Processing, First Edition. Edited by Bing Zhang.

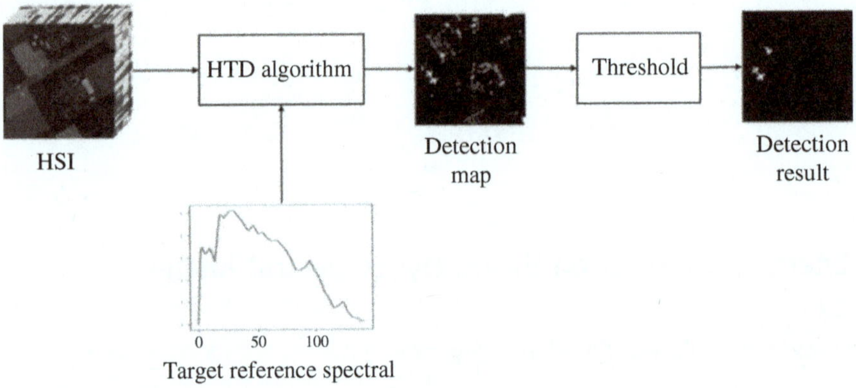

Figure 21.1 The pipeline of HTD.

21.2 Overview of CEM

To solve the problem of target detection with a single target reference spectrum, Harsanyi proposed the CEM algorithm in 1993. The basic principle of the CEM algorithm is to design an FIR linear filter that allows only the desired target feature to pass and minimizes the energy output of other features to accomplish target detection. The algorithm is also included in the remote sensing processing software ENVI and is widely used in tasks such as mineral exploration and mapping.

Suppose A hyperspectral image with a total of N pixels and D bands is represented as $\mathbf{S} = [\mathbf{r}_1, \mathbf{r}_2, ..., \mathbf{r}_N] \in \mathbb{R}^{D\times N}$, where each column vector $\mathbf{r}_i \in \mathbb{R}^{D\times 1}$ representing the spectrum of the ith pixel, while the target reference spectrum is represented by a column vector $\mathbf{d} \in \mathbb{R}^{D\times 1}$.

For the input spectrum $\mathbf{r}_i$, let the parameter vector of the CEM detector be $\mathbf{w} \in \mathbb{R}^{D\times 1}$. The detection result y_i of this pixel can be denoted as:

$$y_i = \mathbf{w}^T\mathbf{r}_i \tag{21.1}$$

The CEM detector needs to emphasize the target spectral output while suppressing the energy of the background spectra and therefore needs to minimize the output energy of the filter while obeying the constraint $\mathbf{w}^T\mathbf{d} = 1$. The average energy of the filter output can be obtained by calculating the square of the output values of all pixels after detection, i.e.:

$$\frac{1}{N}\sum_{i=1}^{N} {y_i}^2 = \frac{1}{N}\sum_{i=1}^{N}\left(\mathbf{w}^T\mathbf{r}_i\right)^2 = \mathbf{w}^T\left[\frac{1}{N}\sum_{i=1}^{N}\left(\mathbf{r}_i{\mathbf{r}_i}^T\right)\right]\mathbf{w} = \mathbf{w}^{\mathrm{T}}\mathbf{R}\mathbf{w} \tag{21.2}$$

where $\mathbf{R} = \frac{1}{N}\sum_{i=1}^{N}\left(\mathbf{r}_i{\mathbf{r}_i}^T\right) = \frac{1}{N}\mathbf{S}\mathbf{S}^T$, is the correlation matrix of $\mathbf{S}$ to be measured. At this point, solving the parameter vector ω of the CEM detector becomes solving the following optimization problem:

$$\begin{aligned} &\min_{\mathbf{w}} \quad \mathbf{w}^T\mathbf{R}\mathbf{w} \\ &\text{s.t.} \quad \mathbf{w}^T\mathbf{d} = 1 \end{aligned} \tag{21.3}$$

The Lagrange multiplier method is used to solve the above optimization problem. Let λ be a Lagrange multiplier and define the Lagrange objective function as follows:

$$J(\mathbf{w}) = \mathbf{w}^T\mathbf{R}\mathbf{w} + \lambda\left(\mathbf{w}^T\mathbf{d} - 1\right) \tag{21.4}$$

Let the derivative of the objective function be equal to 0, we get

$$\frac{\partial J(\mathbf{w})}{\partial \mathbf{w}}|_{\mathbf{w}^*} = 2\mathbf{R}\mathbf{w}^* + \lambda\mathbf{d} = 0 \Rightarrow \mathbf{w}^* = 2\lambda\mathbf{R}^{-1}\mathbf{d} \tag{21.5}$$

Using the constraints, it is obtained that

$$\mathbf{w}^T\mathbf{d} = 2\lambda\mathbf{d}^T\mathbf{R}\mathbf{d} = 1 \Rightarrow 2\lambda = \mathbf{d}^T\mathbf{R}\mathbf{d} \tag{21.6}$$

Substituting Eq. (21.6) into Eq. (21.5), the closed-form solution for the CEM detector parameter vector is given by

$$\mathbf{w}^* = \frac{\mathbf{R}^{-1}\mathbf{d}}{\mathbf{d}^T\mathbf{R}^{-1}\mathbf{d}} \tag{21.7}$$

Thus the CEM detector can then be written as

$$\delta^{\text{CEM}}(\mathbf{r}_i) = \mathbf{w}^*\mathbf{r}_i = \frac{\mathbf{R}^{-1}\mathbf{d}\mathbf{r}_i}{\mathbf{d}^T\mathbf{R}^{-1}\mathbf{d}} \tag{21.8}$$

The geometric meaning of the CEM algorithm can be represented through the whitening transformation. First, let $\mathbf{r}_0$ and $\mathbf{d}_0$ denote the mean-subtracted test spectrum and the mean-subtracted target reference spectrum. The CEM detection output for the given test spectrum $\mathbf{r}_0$ is:

$$y_{\text{CEM}}(\mathbf{r_0}) = \frac{\mathbf{d}_0^T\boldsymbol{\Gamma}^{-1}\mathbf{r}_0}{\mathbf{d}_0^T\boldsymbol{\Gamma}^{-1}\mathbf{d}_0}. \tag{21.9}$$

where $\boldsymbol{\Gamma} = (1/N)\sum_{n=1}^{N}\left[\mathbf{r}_0(n)\mathbf{r}_0^T(n)\right]$ denotes the estimated covariance matrix. Then use the following whitening transformation to it.

$$\begin{aligned}\tilde{\mathbf{r}} &= \boldsymbol{\Gamma}^{-\frac{1}{2}}\mathbf{r}_0\\ \tilde{\mathbf{d}} &= \boldsymbol{\Gamma}^{-\frac{1}{2}}\mathbf{d}_0\end{aligned} \tag{21.10}$$

At this time, $\boldsymbol{\Gamma}$ is an eye matrix. The output of CEM is

$$y_{\text{CEM}}(\mathbf{r}) = \frac{\tilde{\mathbf{d}}^T\tilde{\boldsymbol{r}}}{\|\tilde{\mathbf{d}}\|^2}. \tag{21.11}$$

Here, we consider the optimization problem:

$$\min_{\mathbf{w}} \mathbf{w}^{\mathrm{T}}\mathbf{w};\text{s.t.}\mathbf{w}^T\tilde{\mathbf{d}} = 1. \tag{21.12}$$

The solution to the above problem is $\mathbf{w}^* = \tilde{\mathbf{d}}/\|\tilde{\mathbf{d}}\|^2$ After obtaining the solution to the above optimization problem, the CEM output can be obtained by the following formula, which is consistent with the derivation result after whitening.

$$y_{\text{CEM}}(\mathbf{r}) = \mathbf{w}^{*T}\tilde{\mathbf{r}} = \frac{\tilde{\mathbf{d}}^T\tilde{\mathbf{r}}}{\|\tilde{\mathbf{d}}\|^2} \tag{21.13}$$

In practice, to enhance the numerical stability of the CEM detector during the solution process and to ensure that the correlation matrix $\mathbf{R}$ is invertible, a positive diagonal matrix $\lambda\mathbf{I}$ is often added after the correlation matrix $\mathbf{R}$. The value on the diagonal of this diagonal matrix is a very small positive value, i.e., $\mathbf{R} : \mathbf{R} + \lambda\mathbf{I}$ where $\lambda > 0$. At this time, the closed-form solution of the CEM detector becomes:

$$\mathbf{w}(\lambda)^* = \frac{(\mathbf{R} + \lambda\mathbf{I})^{-1}\mathbf{d}}{\mathbf{d}^{\mathrm{T}}(\mathbf{R} + \lambda\mathbf{I})^{-1}\mathbf{d}} \tag{21.14}$$

The above improvement is also equivalent to adding an L2 paradigm penalty term $\lambda\|\mathbf{w}\|^2$ to the original optimization objective, and the optimization problem shown in (21.3) becomes

$$\min_{\mathbf{w}} \quad \mathbf{w}^T\mathbf{R}\mathbf{w} + \lambda\|\mathbf{w}\|^2$$

$$\text{s.t.} \quad \mathbf{w}^T\mathbf{d} = 1 \tag{21.15}$$

Therefore, the CEM improved in this way is called regularized CEM (rCEM). Compared to the original CEM algorithm, rCEM has better stability.

The detection result of CEM is shown in Figure 21.2, where the Cuprite data set with a spatial resolution of 250×191 is demonstrated. The target to be detected is buddingtonite, which occupies 39 pixels as shown in Figure 21.2c.

The CEM algorithm requires only a single target reference spectrum and has a simple form and high reliability, especially in suppressing background noise compared to other classical methods. Therefore, many researchers have improved the original CEM algorithm and proposed a series of variants. Therefore, in the next section, we will focus on these variant methods and introduce them in detail.

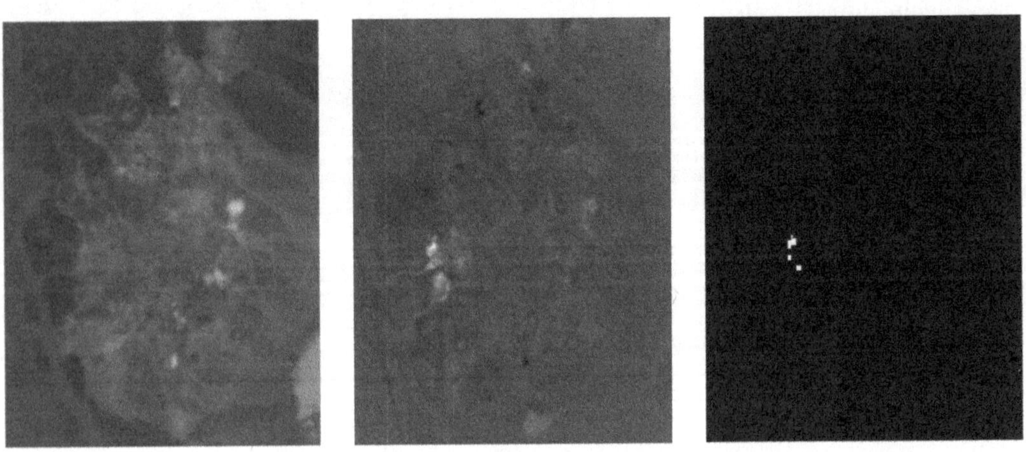

(a) (b) (c)

Figure 21.2 Detection result of CEM on Cuprite data set. (a) Original image. (b) Detection result of CEM. (c) Gtound-truth.

21.3 CEM-based Methods

HSIs acquired in the real world often have a large number of complex nonlinear features due to sensor errors, uncompensated atmospheric and environmental effects, and imaging noise. The original CEM algorithm is a linear filtering process, which cannot accurately deal with real HSI. In the past decade, thanks to advances in statistics and optimization theory, researchers have also been exploring how the CEM algorithm can be improved to better fit the target detection for real HSIs.

This section presents five improved CEM-based algorithms, namely SparseCEM [3], IC-CEM [4], TVHTD [5], hCEM [6], E-CEM [7], IKCEM [8], and SRA-CEM [9]. SparseCEM takes advantage of the small number of target pixels in hyperspectral images and adds sparsity constraint to the original CEM optimization problem to better detect targets. In order to cope with spectral changes, IC-CEM uses inequality constraint to achieve target detection, ensuring that pixels similar to the target spectrum have a greater probability of being detected as targets, and improving the detection rate with the same false alarm rate of CEM. TVHTD utilizes the spatial consistency and continuity of hyperspectral images, and based on CEM, uses the total variation term to constrain adjacent pixels to tend to belong to the same category, so that target pixels are highlighted and background pixels are further suppressed. The hCEM method utilizes the nonlinear and non-Gaussian properties of hyperspectral images to suppress background pixels layer by layer, making the target gradually stand out. ECEM introduces ensemble learning ideas on the basis of HCEM to obtain more comprehensive detection results. The details of the five methods are shown in Table 21.1.

21.3.1 SparseCEM

21.3.1.1 Method Description

CEM minimizes the output energy under the constraint that the output of a priori target spectrum is 1. Therefore, the essence of the CEM algorithm is to suppress the output of background pixels and limit the output of them to be close to zero while maintaining a high output of the target pixels. Since the number of target pixels is generally small, SparseCEM proposes adding a regularization term to CEM to make the output of a hyperspectral image is sparse [3].

Table 21.1 Comparison of the five CEM-based methods.

Method	Motivation	Basic idea
SparseCEM	Sparsity of target pixels.	Adding sparsity regularization term to CEM optimization problem.
IC-CEM	Imaging spectral changes.	Use inequality constraint to CEM optimization problem.
TVHTD	Spatial continuity of image.	Adding TV regularization term to CEM optimization problem.
hCEM	Non-Gaussian and nonlinear.	Hierarchical suppression of background.
ECEM	Boosting.	Ensemble learning.
IKCEM	Kernelization and iteration.	Extension of KCEM to IKCEM by adding spatial information to an iterative process.
SRA-CEM	The spectral uncertainty of the target.	Improve the CEM method by utilizing background spectra as prior information.

Therefore, the output of the background can be further suppressed. At the same time, the constraint $\mathbf{w}^T\mathbf{d} = 1$ the same as CEM is used to ensure that the target pixels have high output. The sparsity is constrained by the L1 norm, and thus the SparseCEM can be expressed as the following optimization problem:

$$\min_{\mathbf{w}} \mathbf{w}^T\mathbf{R}\mathbf{w} + \lambda\|\mathbf{w}^T\boldsymbol{S}\|_1; \text{s.t.}\mathbf{w}^\mathbf{T}\boldsymbol{d} = 1. \tag{21.16}$$

where $\|\cdot\|_1$ denotes the L1 norm, $\|\mathbf{w}^T\boldsymbol{S}\|_1 = \sum_{i=1}^{N} | \mathbf{w}^T\mathbf{r}_i |$ and λ is a constant. Suppose $\mathbf{w}_{\text{SpareCEM}}$ is the solution of Eq. 21.16, the output of SparseCEM is

$$y_{\text{SparseCEM}}(\mathbf{r}) = \mathbf{w}_{\text{SpareCEM}}{}^T\mathbf{r}. \tag{21.17}$$

We can set a threshold η. If $y_{\text{SparseCEM}}(\mathbf{r}) > \eta$, it is considered that there is a target in the pixel, otherwise it is considered that there is no target in the pixel.

The optimization problem in Eq. 21.16 is a second-order cone program (SOCP), which is a type of nonlinear convex optimization problem with the following standard form.

$$\min \mathbf{f}^T\mathbf{y}; \text{s.t.}\|\boldsymbol{A}_i\boldsymbol{y} + \boldsymbol{b}_i\| \leq \boldsymbol{c}_i^T\boldsymbol{y} + g_i, i = 1, \ldots, M \tag{21.18}$$

where $\mathbf{y} \in \mathbb{R}^m$ denotes the optimization variable, $\mathbf{f} \in \mathbb{R}^m, \boldsymbol{A}_i \in \mathbb{R}^{(m_i-1)\times m}, \boldsymbol{b}_i \in \mathbb{R}^{(m_i-1)}, \boldsymbol{c}_i \in \mathbb{R}^m, g_i \in \mathbb{R}$, and $\|\boldsymbol{A}_i\boldsymbol{y} + \boldsymbol{b}_i\|$ is the second-order cone program.

SparseCEM is equivalent to the following SOCP optimization problem:

$$\min_{\mathbf{w}} \mathbf{w}^T\mathbf{R}\mathbf{w} + \lambda\|\mathbf{w}^T\boldsymbol{S}\|_1; \text{s.t.}\mathbf{w}^\mathbf{T}\boldsymbol{d} \geq 1, \tag{21.19}$$

and the solution is obtained when $\mathbf{w}^\mathbf{T}\boldsymbol{d} = 1$. For real hyperspectral image, the estimated correlation matrix $\mathbf{R}$ is positive, and $\mathbf{w}^T\mathbf{R}\mathbf{w}$ and $\lambda\|\mathbf{w}^T\boldsymbol{S}\|_1$ are all positive. If $\mathbf{w}^\mathbf{T}\boldsymbol{d} = \boldsymbol{a} > \mathbf{1}$, we can replace $\mathbf{w}$ with $\mathbf{w}/a$ to reduce the value of the objective function. Meanwhile, $\left(\frac{\mathbf{w}}{a}\right)^T\mathbf{d} = 1$, thus the solution satisfies $\mathbf{w}^\mathbf{T}\boldsymbol{d} = 1$. Since $\left\|\mathbf{R}^{\frac{1}{2}}\boldsymbol{w}\right\|^2 = \mathbf{w}^T\mathbf{R}\mathbf{w}$, $\|\mathbf{w}^T\boldsymbol{S}\|_1 = \sum_{i=1}^{N} | \mathbf{r}_i{}^T\mathbf{w} |$, Eq. (21.18) is equivalent to:

$$\begin{aligned} &\min t_1 + \cdots + t_{N+1}; \\ &\text{s.t.}\lambda\left|\mathbf{r}_i{}^T\mathbf{w}\right| \leq t_n \; n = 1, \ldots, N \\ &\quad \left\|\mathbf{R}^{\frac{1}{2}}\boldsymbol{w}\right\| \leq t_{N+1} \\ &\quad 1 \leq \mathbf{d}^T\mathbf{w} \end{aligned} \tag{21.20}$$

Therefore, the SparseCEM is a SOCP problem, and can be solved use optimization tools such as CVX.

21.3.1.2 Experimental Results

The detection experiment of SparseCEM is conducted on the Hyperspectral Mapper (HyMap) data. The three target pixels have three priori spectra as shown in Figure 21.3.

The number of false alarm pixels when the target pixel is detected and the false alarm rate are shown in Table 21.2. We can find that SparseCEM significantly reduces the false alarm rate while further suppressing the output of background pixels.

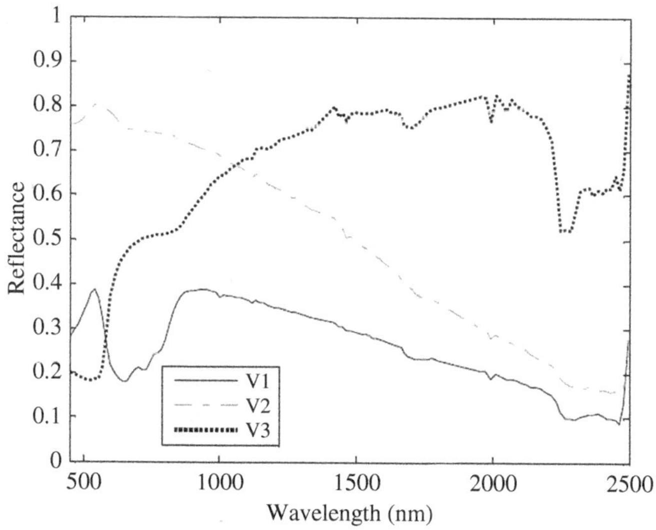

Figure 21.3 The three priori spectrum of the targets.

Table 21.2 False alarm rate of SparseCEM.

	SparseCEM		CEM	
Priori target spectrum	**False alarm pixels**	**False alarm rate**	**False alarm pixels**	**False alarm rate**
1	1424	0.00635	4415	0.01971
2	8461	0.03777	55,372	0.24719
3	2471	0.01103	2862	0.01277
Mean	4119	0.01838	20,883	0.09322

21.3.2 IC-CEM

21.3.2.1 Method Description

One of the main difficulties faced in target detection in hyperspectral remote sensing images is spectral changes. Even under laboratory conditions, the same substance may have different spectra due to changes in the surface material of the substance. In real hyperspectral images, the spectra of the same substance may be different, and the spectra of different substances may also be similar. Changes in atmospheric conditions, sensor noise, composition of substances, and the influence of surrounding substances may all cause spectral changes. In target detection in hyperspectral images, spectral changes are an important reason for false alarms and missed alarms. Therefore, it is very meaningful to develop a hyperspectral remote sensing image target detection algorithm that is robust to spectral changes.

In the field of beamforming, a robust adaptive beamforming method is proposed to solve the signal mismatching problem by optimizing the worst case scenario. CEM with Inequality Constraint (IC-CEM) method [4] applying this robust method and use an inequality constraint to ensure that when the target spectrum changes within a certain range, its output is greater than 1. In this way, even if there are certain changes in the spectrum of the target, it can still be detected, so it has a certain degree of robustness to spectral changes.

Assuming that the target spectrum changes within a spherical range of radius $\epsilon > 0$, then the spectrum of the target pixel belongs to the following set:

$$\mathcal{A}(\epsilon) = \{\mathbf{c} \mid \mathbf{c} = \mathbf{s} + \mathbf{e}, \|\mathbf{e}\| \leq \epsilon\} \tag{21.21}$$

where $\mathbf{c}$ denotes the real spectrum, $\mathbf{e}$ denotes the spectral change. IC-CEM method constructs a Finite Impulse Response (FIR) filter the same as CEM, the filter is with coefficient $\mathbf{w} = [w_1, w_2, \cdots, w_L]^T$. The target of the optimization is to minimize the output energy subject to the output of all the spectrum in $\mathcal{A}$ is greater than 1, as shown in the following equation:

$$\min_{\mathbf{w}} \mathbf{w}^T\mathbf{R}\mathbf{w}; \text{s.t.} \mathbf{w}^T\mathbf{c} \geq 1 \text{ for all } \mathbf{c} \in \mathcal{A} \tag{21.22}$$

The set $\mathcal{A}$may contain some background spectra that are similar to the target spectrum, the model may increase the output of them. However, the spectrum in $\mathcal{A}(\epsilon)$ is more likely to be a target one since ϵ is usually small. CEM uses the constraint $\mathbf{w}^T\mathbf{d} = 1$, so when minimizing the output energy, those targets that are similar to $\mathbf{d}$ will also be suppressed. IC-CEM uses inequality constraints to ensure that the output energy $\mathbf{w}^T\mathbf{R}\mathbf{w}$ is minimized while all the spectra in $\mathcal{A}(\epsilon)$ have large output. The spectra in $\mathcal{A}(\epsilon)$ are more likely to belong to the target, the inequality constraint can ensure that spectrum in $\mathcal{A}(\epsilon)$ has a large output, then minimizing the output energy $\mathbf{w}^T\mathbf{R}\mathbf{w}$ will suppress the background to a greater extent. Therefore, the output of the target spectra and background ones will be more separable, thereby obtaining better detection results. Compared with CEM, IC-CEM can achieve a higher detection rate with the same false alarm rate. When we need to ensure that all the target spectra that change within a certain change are detected without considering the false alarm rate, we can set the corresponding ϵ and the threshold as 1 to obtain the detection result.

The Eq. 21.22 is equivalent to:

$$\min_{\mathbf{w}} \mathbf{w}^T\mathbf{R}\mathbf{w}; \text{s.t.} \mathbf{w}^T\mathbf{d} + \mathbf{w}^T\mathbf{e} \geq 1 \text{ for all } \|\mathbf{e}\| \leq \epsilon. \tag{21.23}$$

For all $\|\mathbf{e}\| \leq \epsilon$, we have $\mathbf{w}^T\mathbf{e} \geq -\|\mathbf{w}\|\|\mathbf{e}\| \geq -\epsilon\|\mathbf{w}\|$, and the equations holds when $\mathbf{e}$ and $\mathbf{w}$ are in opposite directions and $\|\mathbf{e}\| = \epsilon$. Therefore, for all $\|\mathbf{e}\| \leq \epsilon$, the minimize of $\mathbf{w}^T\mathbf{d} + \mathbf{w}^T\mathbf{e}$ is $\mathbf{w}^T\mathbf{d} - \epsilon\|\mathbf{w}\|$. The optimization problem equals

$$\min_{\mathbf{w}} f_0(w) = \mathbf{w}^T\mathbf{R}\mathbf{w}; \text{s.t.} 1 + \epsilon\|\mathbf{w}\| - \mathbf{w}^T\mathbf{d} \leq 0. \tag{21.24}$$

There is no closed form solution to the optimization problem, IC-CEM uses an obstacle method, which is an interior point method, for iterative solution. The equation can be written as:

$$\min_{\mathbf{w}} f_0(w) = \mathbf{w}^T\mathbf{R}\mathbf{w} + I_u\left(1 + \epsilon\|\mathbf{w}\| - \mathbf{w}^T\mathbf{d}\right). \tag{21.25}$$

where $I_u : \mathbb{R} \rightarrow \mathbb{R}$ is an indicator function for nonnegative real numbers:

$$I_u = \begin{cases} 0 & u \leq 0 \\ \infty & u > 0 \end{cases}. \tag{21.26}$$

The indicator function I_u can be approximately expressed by the following function:

$$\hat{I}_u = -\left(\frac{1}{t}\right) \log(-u). \tag{21.27}$$

where $t > 0$ denotes the accuracy of the approximate. $\hat{I}_u$ is differentiable while I_u is non-derivable. Replace I_u with $\hat{I}_u$, the Eq. (21.25) can be approximate to:

$$\min_{\mathbf{w}} \mathbf{w}^T\mathbf{R}\mathbf{w} - \frac{1}{t}\log\left(\mathbf{w}^T\mathbf{d} - 1 - \epsilon\|\mathbf{w}\|\right). \tag{21.28}$$

The equation differentiable and convex, and equals to the following problem:

$$\min_{\mathbf{w}} f_1(\mathbf{w}) = t\mathbf{w}^T\mathbf{R}\mathbf{w} - \log\left(\mathbf{w}^T\mathbf{d} - 1 - \epsilon\|\mathbf{w}\|\right). \tag{21.29}$$

where $\phi(\mathbf{w}) = -\log(\mathbf{w}^T\mathbf{d} - 1 - \epsilon\|\mathbf{w}\|)$ denotes the barrier function, and $f_1(\mathbf{w})$ is convex. The optimization problem (21.29) can be solved by Newton method. Assume that the solution of problem (21.29) is $\mathbf{w}^*(t)$ and p^* denotes the solution of problem 21.24. It can be improved that $\mathrm{f}_0(\mathbf{w}^*(t)) - p^* \leq 1/t$. Therefore, when $t \to \infty$, $\mathbf{w}^*(t)$ converges to the solution of problem 21.24.

After obtaining the optimal solution $\mathbf{w}^*$, we project the spectra $\mathbf{r}_\mathrm{i}(i = 1, \cdots, N)$ to $\mathbf{w}^*$ and get the output of IC-CEM.

$$y(\mathbf{r}_\mathrm{i}) = \mathbf{w}^{*\mathrm{T}}\mathbf{r}_\mathrm{i}; i = 1, \cdots, N \tag{21.30}$$

We can set a threshold η. If $y(\mathbf{r}_\mathrm{i}) > \eta$, it is considered that there is a target in the pixel, otherwise it is considered that there is no target in the pixel.

21.3.2.2 Experimental Results

We conduct experiments for IC-CEM on the Cuprite data set the same as it for CEM, the change of the target spectra in this image is shown in Figure 21.4.

The detection result of IC-CEM is shown in Figure 21.5, where we can find that IC-CEM generally reduces the output of background pixels compared with CEM, and the target pixel detection results are more obvious.

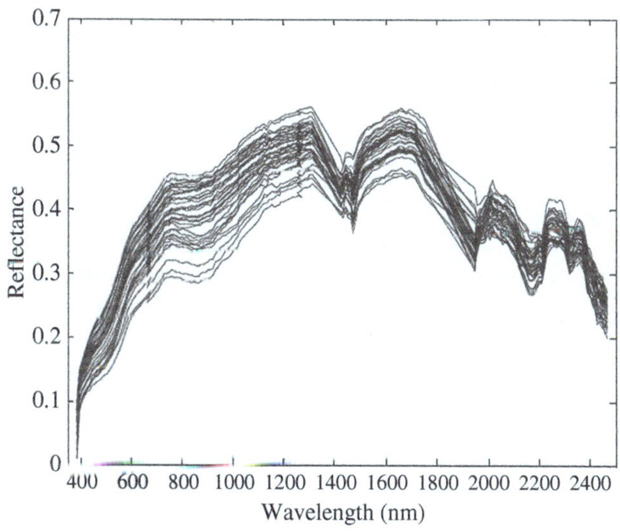

Figure 21.4 The spectral change of the target pixels in the Cuprite data set.

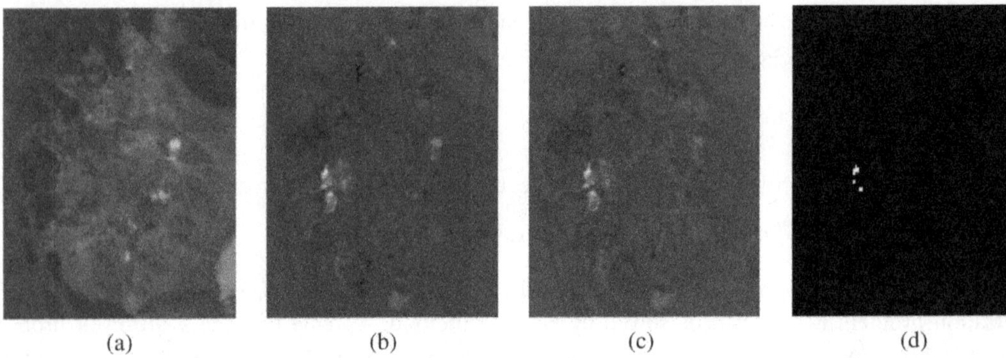

Figure 21.5 Detection result of IC-CEM on Cuprite data set. (a) Original image. (b) Detection result of IC-CEM. (c) Detection result of CEM. (d) Ground-truth.

21.3.3 TVHTD

21.3.3.1 Method Description

For hyperspectral image target detection, the spatial information between adjacent pixels can improve the detection accuracy. The Total Variation based Hyperspectral Target Detector (TVHTD) method[5] makes full use of the spatial information of hyperspectral images through total variation. The TVHTD method constructs the objective function use total variation, minimizing it under the constraint that the output of a priori target spectrum is 1 to find the best projection vector. For hyperspectral image target detection, the neighbor pixels of a target pixel are likely to be the target, while a background pixel's neighbor is likely to be the background. TVHTD uses total variation to constrain the spatial consistency and smoothness of adjacent pixels. The detection model can be represented as an optimization problem of L1 norm.

Assume that a hyperspectral image $\mathbf{S}$ with K columns and M rows and $\mathbf{r}(i, j) \in \mathbb{R}^D (i = 1, \cdots, K, j = 1, \cdots, M)$ denotes the spectrum at i-th column and j-th row. A target spectrum $\mathbf{d}$ is given as priori information, $\mathbf{r}_0$ and $\mathbf{d}_0$ denotes the spectra after removing the mean of them. CEM finds a projection vector $\mathbf{w} \in \mathbb{R}^D$ that maps $\mathbf{r}(i, j)$ to $\mathbf{w}$ to get detection output. The detection result $\mathbf{y}$ is an image with the same size as $\mathbf{S}$, where $\mathbf{y}(i, j) = \mathbf{w}^T\mathbf{r}_0(i, j)$. Minimizing the total variation of $\mathbf{y}$ ensures the spatial consistency of the detection results. The constraint $\mathbf{w}^T\mathbf{d}_0 = 1$ guarantees that the target pixel has a larger input while suppressing the output of the background pixels.

Let $\mathbf{r}_b$ denote the spectra of background pixels and $\mathbf{r}_s$ denote the spectra of target pixels, TVHTD expects the output $\mathbf{w}^T\mathbf{r}_b$ is small and $\mathbf{w}^T\mathbf{r}_s$ is large. Minimizing the total variation of $\mathbf{y}$ suppresses the output of all pixels, so TVHTD adds the constraint $\mathbf{w}^T\mathbf{d}_0 = c$ to avoid suppressing output $\mathbf{w}^T\mathbf{r}_s$ of target pixels, where c is a constant. Therefore, the result of target and background in $\mathbf{y}$ can be separated effectively. In TVHTD, c = 1 since it does not affect the direction of the optimal vector $\mathbf{w}$ and the final projection result. In addition, the constraint $\mathbf{w}^T\mathbf{d}_0 = 1$ makes the background pixels and the target pixels have different outputs, so minimizing the total variation of $\mathbf{y}$ will not make the output of the background pixels and the output of the target pixels have spatial consistency between them.

The TVHTD model:

$$\min_{\mathbf{w}} |\mathbf{y}|_{TV} \quad \text{s.t.} \mathbf{w}^T\mathbf{d}_0 = 1. \tag{21.31}$$

$|\mathbf{y}|_{TV}$ denotes the total variation of $\mathbf{y}$, it is an anisotropic total variation in TVHTD.

$$|\mathbf{y}|_{TV} = |\nabla_x \mathbf{y}|_1 + |\nabla_y \mathbf{y}|_1 \tag{21.32}$$

where $|\cdot|_1$denotes L1 norm, $\nabla_x \mathbf{y}$ and $\nabla_y \mathbf{y}$ denote the gradient of $\mathbf{y}$ in the horizontal and vertical directions. For image processing, we adopt the discrete form:

$$\begin{aligned} |\mathbf{y}|_{TV} &= |\nabla_x \mathbf{y}|_1 + |\nabla_y \mathbf{y}|_1 \\ &= \sum_{i=1}^{K}\sum_{j=1}^{M} |\mathbf{y}(i,j) - \mathbf{y}(i-1,j)| + \sum_{i=1}^{K}\sum_{j=1}^{M} |\mathbf{y}(i,j) - \mathbf{y}(i,j-1)| \\ &= \sum_{i=1}^{K}\sum_{j=1}^{M} |\mathbf{w}^T\mathbf{r}_0(i,j) - \mathbf{w}^T\mathbf{r}_0(i-1,j)| + \sum_{i=1}^{K}\sum_{j=1}^{M} |\mathbf{w}^T\mathbf{r}_0(i,j) - \mathbf{w}^T\mathbf{r}_0(i,j-1)| \end{aligned} \tag{21.33}$$

TVHTD assumes that the image $\mathbf{y}$ is periodic, using $|\mathbf{y}(1,j) - \mathbf{y}(M,j)|$ to calculate $|\mathbf{y}(1,j) - \mathbf{y}(0,j)|$ and $|\mathbf{y}(i,1) - \mathbf{y}(i,N)|$ to calculate $|\mathbf{y}(i,1) - \mathbf{y}(i,0)|$. Two matrices $\mathbf{H} \in \mathbb{R}^{D\times MK}$ and $\mathbf{V} \in \mathbb{R}^{D\times MK}$ are defined as follows:

$$\begin{aligned} \mathbf{H} = [&\mathbf{r}_0(1,1) - \mathbf{r}_0(M,1), \mathbf{r}_0(2,1) - \mathbf{r}_0(1,1), \cdots, \mathbf{r}_0(M,1) - \mathbf{r}_0(M-1,1), \\ &\mathbf{r}_0(1,2) - \mathbf{r}_0(M,2), \mathbf{r}_0(2,2) - \mathbf{r}_0(1,2), \cdots, \mathbf{r}_0(M,2) - \mathbf{r}_0(M-1,2), \cdots, \\ &\mathbf{r}_0(1,N) - \mathbf{r}_0(M,N), \mathbf{r}_0(2,N) - \mathbf{r}_0(1,N), \cdots, \mathbf{r}_0(M,N) - \mathbf{r}_0(M-1,N)] \end{aligned} \tag{21.34}$$

$$\begin{aligned} \mathbf{V} = [&\mathbf{r}_0(1,1) - \mathbf{r}_0(1,N), \mathbf{r}_0(2,1) - \mathbf{r}_0(2,N), \cdots, \mathbf{r}_0(M,1) - \mathbf{r}_0(M,N), \\ &\mathbf{r}_0(1,2) - \mathbf{r}_0(1,1), \mathbf{r}_0(2,2) - \mathbf{r}_0(2,1), \cdots, \mathbf{r}_0(M,2) - \mathbf{r}_0(M,1), \cdots, \\ &\mathbf{r}_0(1,N) - \mathbf{r}_0(1,N-1), \mathbf{r}_0(2,N) - \mathbf{r}_0(2,N-1), \cdots, \mathbf{r}_0(M,N) - \mathbf{r}_0(M,N-1)] \end{aligned} \tag{21.35}$$

Therefore, Eq. (21.31) equals to:

$$\min_{\mathbf{w}} |\mathbf{H}^T\mathbf{w}|_1 + |\mathbf{V}^T\mathbf{w}|_1; \text{s.t.} \mathbf{w}^T\mathbf{d}_0 = 1. \tag{21.36}$$

The problem is a convex optimization one and is difficult to solve due to the non-smoothness of the L1 norm. The TVHTD method uses the Split Bregman method to solve it.

Assume that the solution of Eq. (21.36) is $\mathbf{w}^*$, the detection output of pixel $\mathbf{r}_0(i, j)$ is $\mathbf{y}(i,j) = \mathbf{w}^T\mathbf{r}_0(i,j)$. We can set a threshold η. If $\mathbf{y}(i,j) > \eta$, it is considered that there is a target in the pixel, otherwise it is considered that there is no target in the pixel.

21.3.3.2 Experimental Results

We conduct experiments for TVHTD on the Cuprite data set since it has 39 pixels of targets which are spatially clustering distributed. The detection result of TVHTD is shown in Figure 21.6. We can find that the detection output of TVHTD is more spatially focused. Meanwhile, the output of all background pixels are obviously lower and smoother than that of CEM, which shows that the output has greater spatial consistency and continuity.

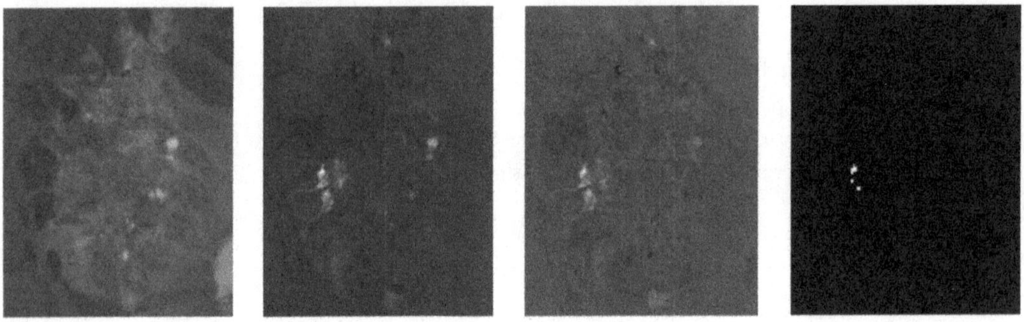

(a) (b) (c) (d)

Figure 21.6 Detection result of TVHTD on Cuprite data set. (a) Original image. (b) Detection result of TVHTD. (c) Detection result of CEM. (d) Ground-truth.

21.3.4 hCEM

21.3.4.1 Method Description

The classical CEM detector has difficulty in accurately emphasizing the target and suppressing the background in a complex real-world scene with a single round of filtering. Therefore, the CEM detector can be used to continuously enhance the detection results by applying multiple filters to the HSI to achieve the desired effect.

Zou et al. proposed the hierarchical CEM (hCEM) algorithm [6] based on this idea. hCEM connects multiple CEM detectors in series in layers and suppresses the background spectra after the detection of each layer using a nonlinear function based on the detector output. Afterward, the transformed spectra are forwarded to the next layer of detectors until the outputs of the CEM detectors converge to a constant. In this way, the unwanted background can be suppressed, allowing the CEM detector to better focus on hard-to-detect targets.

Specifically, let the output of the k-th layer detection $\mathbf{y}^k = [y_1^k, y_2^k, \ldots, y_N^k] \in \mathbb{R}^{1\times N}$ be:

$$\mathbf{y}^k = \frac{\mathbf{R}_k^{-1}\mathbf{d}\mathbf{S}^k}{\mathbf{d}^T\mathbf{R}_k^{-1}\mathbf{d}} \tag{21.37}$$

where $\mathbf{S}^k$ represents the input of the k-th layer and $\mathbf{R}_k$ represents the correlation matrix of the k-th layer. $\mathbf{S}^k$ is obtained by computing the output of the previous layer after transforming it to get the weights and then multiplying that weight by the input of the previous layer, denoted as:

$$\mathbf{r}_i^{k+1} = q(y_i^k)\mathbf{r}_i^k. \tag{21.38}$$

The nonlinear function $q(t): \mathbb{R}^1 \to \mathbb{R}^1$ acts on the spectral vector $\mathbf{r}_i^k$, which can be thought of as a "soft-threshold" operation: spectra with large output scores are retained, and spectra with small output scores are suppressed. In this way, after each layer of detection, the undesired background spectrum is gradually suppressed while the target spectra remain unchanged. hCEM defines the nonlinear suppression function as follows:

$$q(t) = \begin{cases} 1 - e^{\lambda t}, & t \geq 0 \\ 0, & t < 0 \end{cases} \tag{21.39}$$

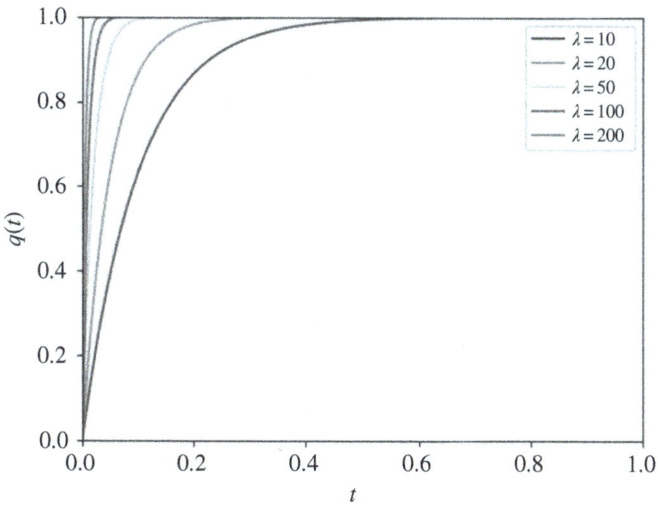

Figure 21.7 Shape of the nonlinear suppression function $q(t) = 1 - e^{\lambda t}$, $t > 0$, with different choices of λ.

where $\lambda > 0$ is employed to modulate the shape of $q(t)$, as illustrated in Figure 21.7, $q(t)$ ranges between 0 and 1 and behaves as an ascending function. This implies that as the output of a layer increases, so does the weight it applies to the input of the subsequent layer. Conversely, as the output decreases, the weight diminishes accordingly. In essence, resemblances to the target are amplified while resemblances to the background are subdued, progressively enhancing the detection effectiveness layer by layer.

The correlation matrix $\mathbf{R}_k$ of this layer is then written as

$$\mathbf{R}_k = \frac{1}{N}\mathbf{S}_k\mathbf{S}_k^T. \tag{21.40}$$

Afterwards, a new CEM detector is constructed in the $(k + 1)$ layer. The above steps will be repeated until the output y^k converges to a constant. The error δ_k between the average output energy of the current layer and the previous layer is calculated as follows

$$\delta_k = \frac{1}{N} \parallel \mathbf{y}^k \parallel_2^2 - \frac{1}{N} \parallel \mathbf{y}^{k-1} \parallel_2^2. \tag{21.41}$$

If $\delta_k < \varepsilon$ (ε is a very small positive number), the iteration is stopped.

The hCEM algorithm is summarized in Figure 21.8.

21.3.4.2 Experimental Results

Figure 21.9 shows the spectral suppression process under different layers on Cuprite data set. We selected some background pixels and all target pixels as observation points and plotted the spectral curves of these pixels in the first to third layers after hCEM. It can be found that after the third layer of the filtering process, most of the background spectra are suppressed, while almost all of the target spectra remain unchanged. That is, the target and background spectra are better separated, and the discriminative ability of the model is greatly improved.

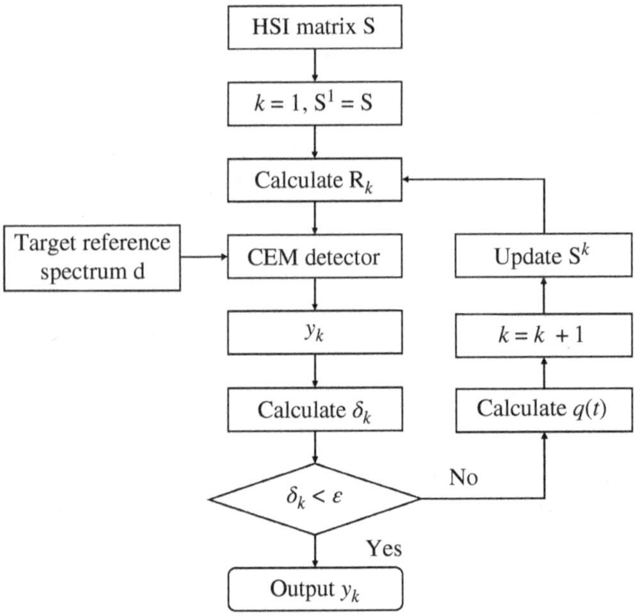

Figure 21.8 The overall of hCEM.

The detection result of hCEM is shown in Figure 21.10 and Figure 21.11. The data set used in Figure 21.10 is San Diego. It can be seen that as the number of layers increases, the background is gradually suppressed and the target is gradually highlighted.

21.3.5 E-CEM

21.3.5.1 Method Description

Although algorithms based on hierarchical detection perform well in fitting the nonlinear properties of the data, they usually introduce instability. This is because the inherent variability of the target spectral features can lead to overfitting problems when constructing a nonlinear or layered detector based on biased spectral data, resulting in a degradation of the generalization performance of the detector.

In this regard, Zhao et al. proposed Ensemble-based Constrained Energy Minimization (E-CEM) [7], which combines the idea of integrated learning to design HTD algorithms that take into account both nonlinear discriminative ability and generalization ability.

Ensemble learning stands as a crucial subset in the field of machine learning techniques, devised to augment the nonlinearity and generalization capabilities of learning systems by aggregating multiple learners. These methods can be broadly categorized into two main groups: boosting-based methods, which construct interconnected cascaded learners during both training and prediction phases, and bagging-based methods, which create independent parallel learners.

E-CEM incorporates the boosting-based approach and the bagging-based approach in ensemble learning. On the one hand, E-CEM adopts a cascaded detection architecture and uses a Sigmoid nonlinear function to convert the outputs of each layer between different layers to improve the nonlinear performance of the detectors. On the other hand, E-CEM employs a random averaging strategy to construct multiple CEM detectors randomly in each layer of the cascade and combines their

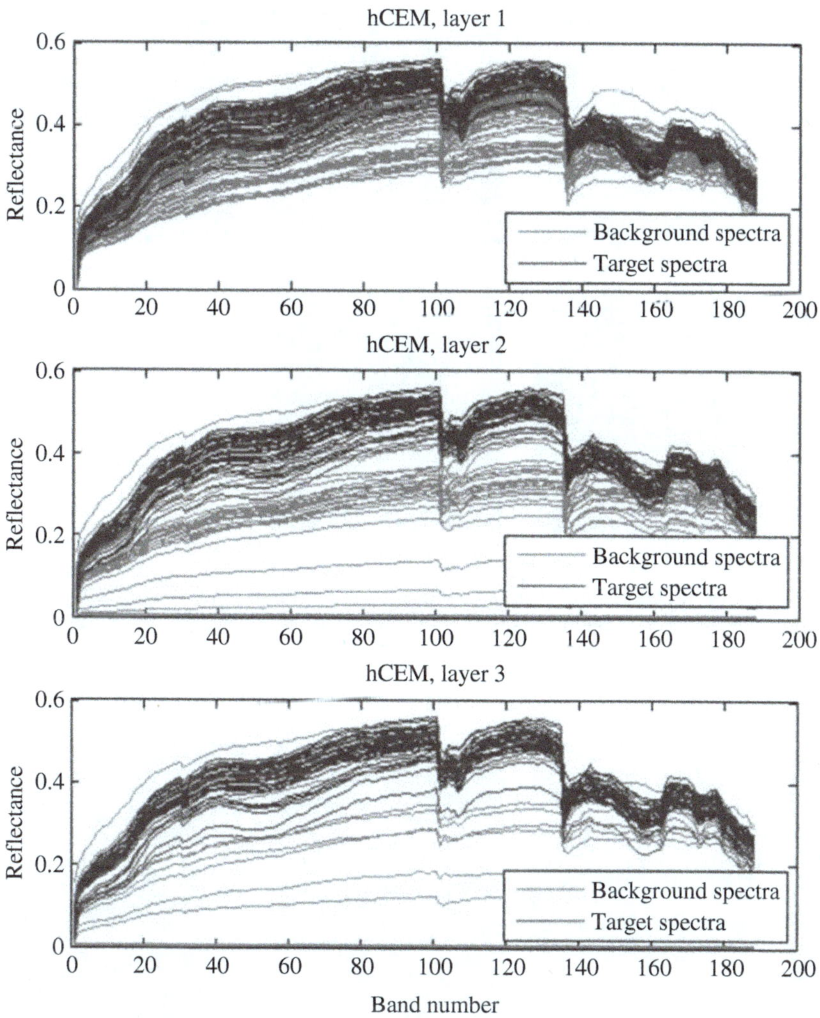

Figure 21.9 Spectral suppression process under different layers on Cuprite data set.

outputs to improve the stability of the detectors. In addition, E-CEM uses a multi-scale scanning strategy for spectral feature extraction to generate spectral features that contain information on different spectral resolutions to improve the robustness of the detector to spectral variations.

The pipeline of E-CEM is shown in Figure 21.12. E-CEM consists of two stages: multi-scale scanning and cascaded detection. The first stage inputs spectral vectors and outputs feature vectors containing multi-scale spectral information. The input to the second stage is the feature vector generated from the multi-scale scanning stage and the output is the final detection map.

(1) Multi-scale scanning

Multi-scale scanning consists of multiple parallel units. Each unit defines a sliding window of different lengths as an extractor of spectral features at different scales, and slides over the original spectral features to select spectral fragments in a certain step size. Afterwards, a series of fragments selected by the sliding window of the unit are fed into the CEM detector for detection, and the

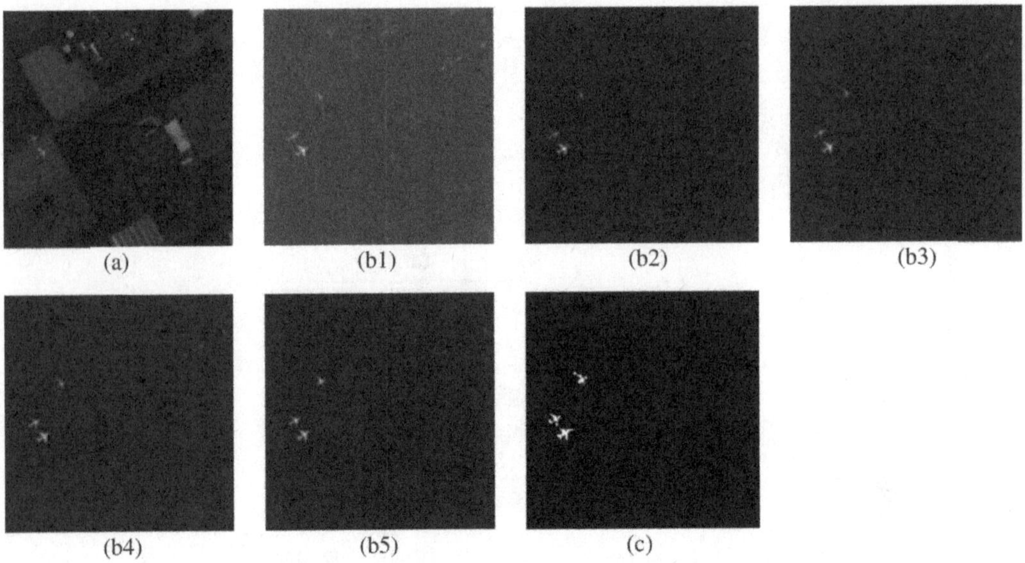

Figure 21.10 Detection result of hCEM on San Diego data set. (a) First band of HSI. (b1) Detection result of hCEM: layer 1. (b2) Detection result of hCEM: layer 2. (b3) Detection result of hCEM: layer 3. (b4) Detection result of hCEM: layer 4. (b5) Detection result of hCEM: layer 5. (c) Ground-truth.

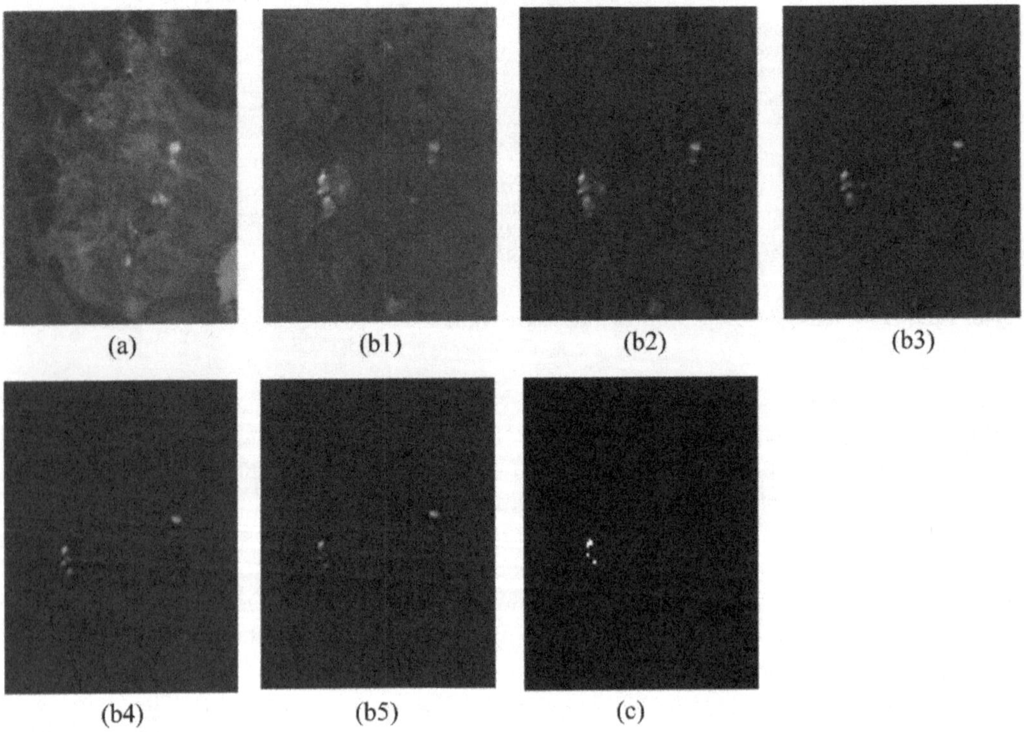

Figure 21.11 Detection result of hCEM on Cuprite data set. (a) First band of HSI. (b1) Detection result of hCEM: layer 1. (b2) Detection result of hCEM: layer 2. (b3) Detection result of hCEM: layer 3. (b4) Detection result of hCEM: layer 4. (b5) Detection result of hCEM: layer 5. (c) Ground-truth.

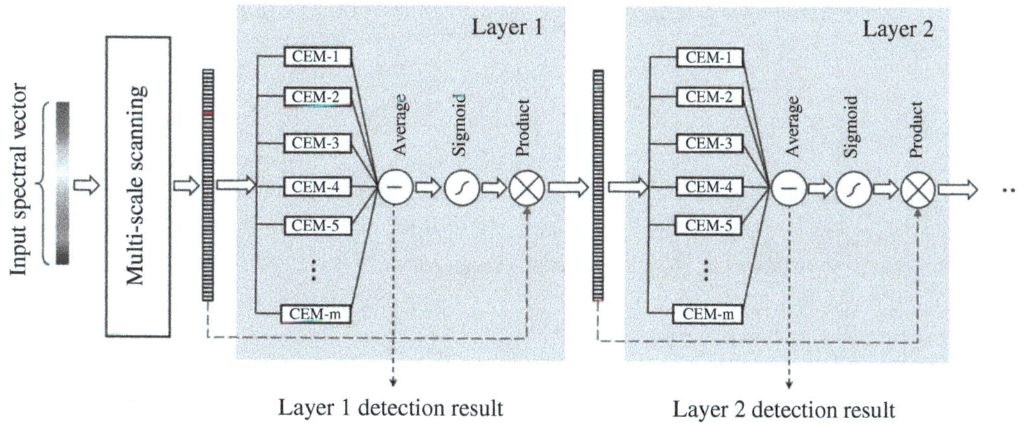

Figure 21.12 The overall of E-CEM.

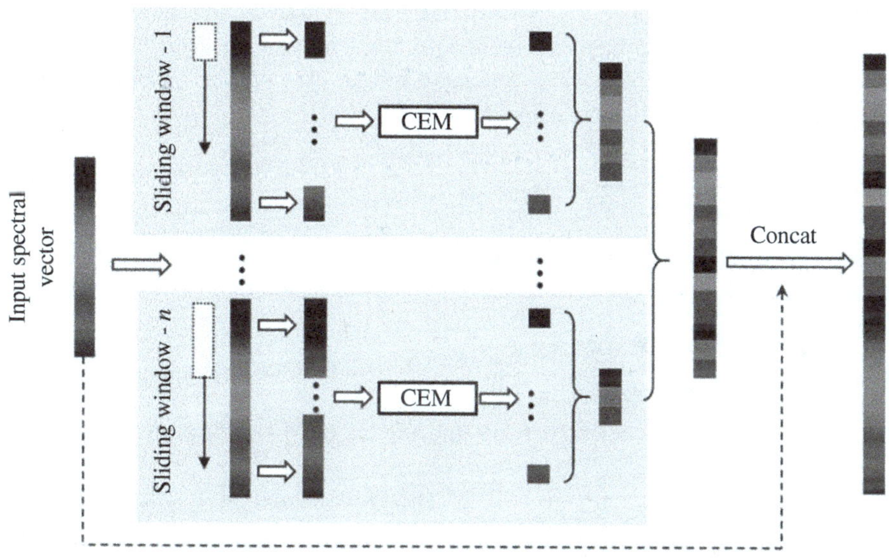

Figure 21.13 An illustration of the multi-scale scanning stage.

results are collapsed into a segment of spectral features representing such scales. Finally, the features of different scales are concatenated together with the original spectral features, which constructs a set of spectral features containing multi-scale information. Figure 21.13 shows the process of multi-scale scanning.

Specifically, suppose that the size of the sliding window of the current unit is l, the stride is s, and the input to the unit is the spectral vector $\mathbf{r}_i = [r_1, r_2, ..., r_D] \in \mathbb{R}^{D\times 1}$, which is first cropped into K fragments:

$$
\begin{aligned}
\hat{\mathbf{r}}_i^1 &= [r_1, r_2, ..., r_l]^T \\
\hat{\mathbf{r}}_i^2 &= [r_{1+s}, r_{2+s}, ..., r_{l+s}]^T \qquad (21.42) \\
&\;\;...
\end{aligned}
$$

After that the CEM detector is used to process each fragment and give the corresponding output $v_i^j, j = 1, ...K$, i.e.

$$v_i^j = \delta^{\text{CEM}}\left(\hat{\mathbf{r}}_i^j\right). \tag{21.43}$$

By joining them together, the feature vector of the input spectral vector at the current unit is obtained as $\mathbf{v}_i^l = \left[v_i^1, v_i^2, ..., v_i^K\right] \in \mathbb{R}^{K \times 1}$. Finally, the output of each unit is concatenated with the original spectral vector $\mathbf{r}_i$ to obtain the output eigenvector of the multiscale scanning stage as

$$\tilde{\mathbf{r}}_i = \left[\mathbf{v}_i^{l_1}; \mathbf{v}_i^{l_2}, ...; \mathbf{v}_i^{l_n}; \mathbf{r}_i\right] \in \mathbb{R}^{(nK + D) \times 1}, \tag{21.44}$$

where $l_1, ..., l_n$ represents the window size of each unit and n represents the total number of scanning units.

(2) Cascaded detection

The cascade detection consists of multiple detection layers. At each layer, the E-CEM is designed with m different rCEM detectors as shown in Eq. (21.14) and the regularization coefficients are set to $\lambda_1, ..., \lambda_m$ by random sampling to enhance the generalization ability of the detector.

Consider the two extreme cases of λ, one where λ equals 0 and the other where λ is infinite. When $\lambda = 0$, the rCEM will degenerate to the original CEM:

$$\lim_{\lambda \to +0} \mathbf{w}(\lambda) = \lim_{\lambda \to +0} \frac{(\mathbf{R} + \lambda\mathbf{I})^{-1}\mathbf{d}}{\mathbf{d}^T(\mathbf{R} + \lambda\mathbf{I})^{-1}\mathbf{d}} = \frac{\mathbf{R}^{-1}\mathbf{d}}{\mathbf{d}^T\mathbf{R}^{-1}\mathbf{d}}. \tag{21.45}$$

In the case where λ is infinite, rCEM is then equivalent to the projection of the spectral vector in the **d** direction, which can also be considered as a simple spectral matching:

$$\lim_{\lambda \to +\infty} \boldsymbol{\omega}(\lambda) = \lim_{\lambda \to +\infty} \frac{(\mathbf{R} + \lambda\mathbf{I})^{-1}\mathbf{d}}{\mathbf{d}^T(\mathbf{R} + \lambda\mathbf{I})^{-1}\mathbf{d}} = \frac{\mathbf{d}}{\mathbf{d}^T\mathbf{d}}. \tag{21.46}$$

Therefore, λ can be considered as a trade-off between the original CEM and the projection in the **d** direction.

Let the input multiscale spectral vector at layer s be $\tilde{\mathbf{r}}_i^s$, and the detection result scores of the outputs of m rCEM detectors be $u_1, ..., u_m$, then the average score of these detectors can be written as

$$\overline{u}^s = \frac{1}{m}\sum_{t=1}^{m} \mathbf{w}(\lambda_t)^T \tilde{\mathbf{r}}_i^s = \frac{1}{m}\sum_{t=1}^{m} \frac{(\mathbf{R} + \lambda_t\mathbf{I})^{-1}\mathbf{d}\tilde{\mathbf{r}}_i^s}{\mathbf{d}^T(\mathbf{R} + \lambda_t\mathbf{I})^{-1}\mathbf{d}}. \tag{21.47}$$

Then the input obtained at layer $s + 1$ needs to be transformed as follows:

$$\tilde{\mathbf{r}}_i^{s+1} = \tilde{\mathbf{r}}_i^s h(\overline{u}^s). \tag{21.48}$$

The transformation function is chosen as a sigmoid function, denoted as

$$h(x) = \frac{1}{1 + e^{-x}}. \tag{21.49}$$

This function indicates that features with small outputs will be suppressed, while features with large outputs will remain unchanged. This transformation process can be considered as an integration of attention mechanism. Because the target pixel will receive more attention in the subsequent layers, resulting in better detection results.

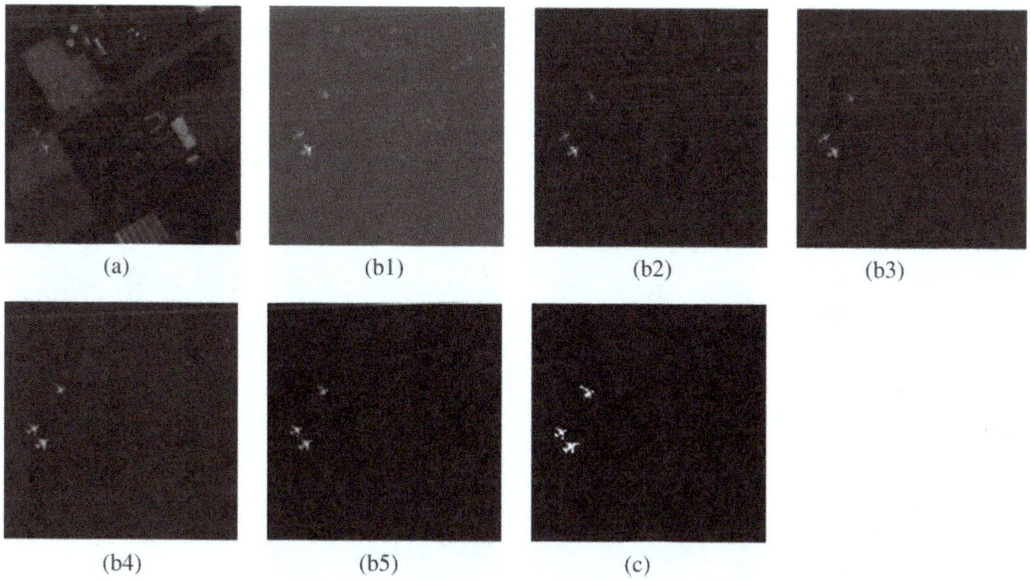

Figure 21.14 Detection result of E-CEM on San Diego data set. (a) First band of HSI. (b1) Detection result of E-CEM: layer 1. (b2) Detection result of E-CEM: layer 2. (b3) Detection result of E-CEM: layer 3. (b4) Detection result of E-CEM: layer 4. (b5) Detection result of E-CEM: layer 5. (c) Ground truth.

There are also some similarities between the architecture of E-CEM and the structure of convolutional neural networks (CNNs). For example, the rCEM detector in E-CEM functions similarly to the convolutional layer in CNN, and the same nonlinear activation function as in CNN is used in E-CEM. However, the difference is that the parameters of the convolutional layer in CNN are learnable, whereas the parameters of the rCEM detector in E-CEM are sampled from an artificially set distribution. In addition, the output of the rCEM detector is just a detection map and does not contain spectral information, so it is also necessary to multiply the spectral vectors with the output in subsequent processing.

21.3.5.2 Experimental Results

The detection result of E-CEM is shown in Figure 21.14 and Figure 21.15. It can be seen that as the number of layers increases, the background is gradually suppressed and the target is gradually highlighted.

21.4 Conclusions

The CEM-based methods we introduced in the previous section can be divided into two categories, optimization-based improvements and statistical-based improvements. The former improves from the optimization problem of the original CEM detector to adapt it to complex HSI data. The latter takes the original CEM detector as the basic unit and draws on the idea of machine learning to obtain a stronger discriminative capability by integrating multiple CEM detectors.

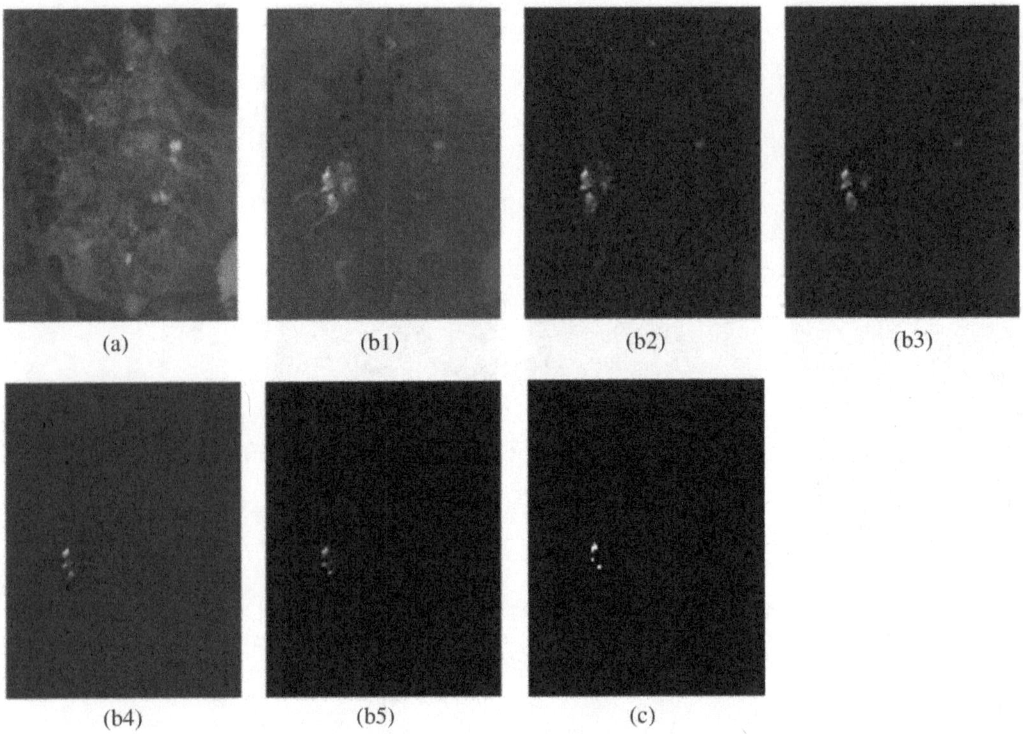

Figure 21.15 Detection result of E-CEM on Cuprite data set. (a) First band of HSI. (b1) Detection result of E-CEM: layer 1. (b2) Detection result of E-CEM: layer 2. (b3) Detection result of E-CEM: layer 3. (b4) Detection result of E-CEM: layer 4. (b5) Detection result of E-CEM: layer 5. (c) Ground-truth.

Among the optimization-based improvements, one type of improvement method is devoted to constructing more reasonable optimization objectives, such as SparseCEM with TVHTD. This type of improvement is often achieved by introducing a priori information. For example, SparseCEM introduces the sparsity of the targets, and TVHTD considers the spatial consistency of neighboring pixels in the optimization objective. Another type of improvement is to modify the constraints of the original optimization problem for a more reliable simulation of HTD. For example, CEM with Inequality Constraint introduces the inherent spectral variability of HSI into the modeling of constraints.

In statistical-based improvements, the CEM detector is often used as the basic detection unit, and the idea of machine learning methods is borrowed to ensemble the detectors. For example, hCEM is essentially a boosting-based detection method, while E-CEM is a detection method that combines boosting and bagging.

The relationship between the improvement methods is shown in Figure 21.16.

In recent years, the development of deep learning technology has brought new opportunities and challenges for the application of CEM algorithms, and researchers are actively exploring the combination of CEM detectors with deep learning-based HTD methods. How to extend and improve the optimization problem of CEM algorithms in the framework of deep learning or explore the integration of CEM detectors into advanced neural network architectures will become a hot spot for future research.

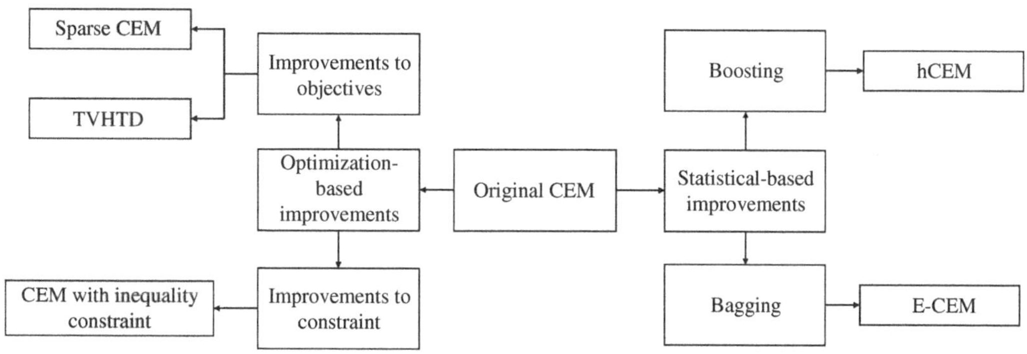

Figure 21.16 Relationships between CEM-based methods.

References

1 Farrand, W.H. and Harsanyi, J.C. (1997). Mapping the distribution of mine tailings in the Coeur d'Alene River Valley, Idaho, through the use of a constrained energy minimization technique. *Remote Sens. Environ.* 59 (1): 64–76.

2 Chang, C.I. and Heinz, D.C. (2000). Constrained subpixel target detection for remotely sensed imagery. *IEEE Trans. Geosci. Remote Sens.* 38 (3): 1144–1159.

3 Yang, S. and Shi, Z. (2014). SparseCEM and SparseACE for hyperspectral image target detection. *IEEE Geosci. Remote Sens. Lett.* 11 (12): 2135–2139.

4 Yang, S., Shi, Z., and Tang, W. (2015). Robust hyperspectral image target detection using an inequality constraint. *IEEE Trans. Geosci. Remote Sens.* 53 (6): 3389–3404.

5 Yang, S. and Shi, Z. (2016). Hyperspectral image target detection improvement based on total variation. *IEEE Trans. Image Process.* 25 (5): 2249–2258.

6 Zou, Z. and Shi, Z. (2016). Hierarchical suppression method for hyperspectral target detection. *IEEE Trans. Geosci. Remote Sens.* 54 (1): 330–342.

7 Zhao, R., Shi, Z., Zou, Z., and Zhang, Z. (2019). Ensemble-based cascaded constrained energy minimization for hyperspectral target detection. *Remote Sens* 11 (11): 1310.

8 Chang, C.I. (2024). Constrained energy minimization (CEM) for hyperspectral target detection: theory and generalizations. *IEEE Trans. Geosci. Remote Sens.* 62: 1–21.

9 Zhao, J., Wang, G., Zhou, B. et al. (2023). SRA-CEM: an improved CEM target detection algorithm for hyperspectral images based on subregion analysis. *IEEE J. Sel. Top. Appl. Earth Obs. Remote Sens.* 16: 6026–6037.

22

Hyperspectral Target Detection Based on Weighted Cauchy Distance Graph and Local Adaptive Collaborative Representation

Wei Li[1] *and Kun Gao*[2]

[1] *School of Information and Electronics, Beijing Institute of Technology, Beijing, China*
[2] *School of Optics and Photonics, Beijing Institute of Technology, Beijing, China*

22.1 Introduction

Hyperspectral target detection has great potential application value in many aspects, such as public safety, military reconnaissance, pollution monitoring, food hygiene, etc. However, due to the influence of the sun's position, angle conditions, atmospheric conditions, and other factors, the background spectrum is complex and changeable [1]. The Gaussian distribution detection model may not be satisfactory. In addition, background statistics are easily contaminated by abnormal noise, which leads to a high false alarm probability. Therefore, accurate hyperspectral target detection in complex background has become an arduous and challenging need in the field of remote sensing monitoring.

Target detection uses prior spectral knowledge of the target or background to find pixels with higher similarity in the image. This prior information can be obtained from laboratory measurements or extracted from images. Compared with anomaly detection, the target detection algorithm has a certain pertinence and can extract specific desired targets [2]. According to the level of information utilization, hyperspectral target detection algorithms are roughly divided into spectral detection algorithms and spatial-spectral detection algorithms.

Spectral detection algorithms include probabilistic spatial models, subspace models, and nonlinear models. The probability model assumes that the spectrum satisfies a certain probability statistical model. The Matching filter (MF) algorithm defined the target detection as a hypothesis testing problem, and it has a good detection result when the background is simple [3]. When the detection image is large, the inversion of the covariance matrix of the algorithm will require a large amount of computation. The constant false alarm detection algorithm spectrum matching filter algorithm was presented. Manolakis et al. proposed an adaptive spectral matching filter (ASMF) [4]. Krauts et al. developed the adaptive cosine estimation (ACE) by adding appropriate weighting factors to target noise and background noise covariance matrix [5] Farrand et al. realized a constrained energy minimization (CEM) algorithm. It highlights the target and suppresses the background by using a priori spectral constraints to minimize the output energy [6]. Geng et al. designed a weighted autocorrelation algorithm based on CEM (WCEM). Theiler et al. launched a covariance matrix estimation method for correcting the target signal [7]. The subspace model increases the contrast between the target and the background to achieve target detection. The orthogonal subspace projection (OSP) algorithm achieved background suppression by projecting image elements into the

Machine-Learning-Based Hyperspectral Image Processing, First Edition. Edited by Bing Zhang.

background orthogonal subspace and improved the signal-to-noise ratio (SNR) of the signal [8]. Low probability detection (LPD) employed the eigenvectors corresponding to the correlation matrix to construct orthogonal subspaces. Among them, the spectral vector belonging to the background is suppressed, and the target spectral vector is enhanced after projection [9]. Wang et al. obtained the unsupervised orthogonal subspace projection (UOSP) by the method of convex geometry analysis [10]. Estimating the virtual dimension accurately is the difficulty of the UOSP algorithm. On the basis of the pixel linear decomposition analysis method, Heinz et al. proposed the use of constrained least-squares for hyperspectral target detection [11]. Kwon et al. extended the existing linear detection algorithm through the nuclear method to their corresponding non-linear version [12]. However, the Gaussian radial basis kernel function is commonly used in the current nuclear method, and there is a lack of rules for selecting the kernel function. Zhang et al. applied the manifold learning method to hyperspectral target detection [13]. They embed sparse transformation manifolds into frames to enable dimensionality reduction of spectral images. In the spatial after the dimensionality reduction, the nearest neighbor of the target feature vector was calculated to achieve the hyperspectral target detection [14].

With the advancement of hyperspectral sensors, hyperspectral images have not only higher spectral resolution but also higher spatial resolution. At present, there are few algorithms that simultaneously employ spatial spectral-domain information to detect targets. There is still a lot of room for improvement in target detection by making full use of spatial and spectral information and combining the advantages [15]. In order to utilize the spatial neighborhood information, Li et al. launched a hyperspectral anomaly detection method with combined sparse and collaborative representation (CSCR). The opinion of the algorithm is to use the target library and the background library to represent test pixels to achieve target detection [16]. The tensor matching subspace detector treats hyperspectral image as a third-order tensor form to realize the joint utilization of multi-dimensional data information [17]. Yang et al. proposed sparse-spatial CEM (SSCEM), which introduced a total variational regularization term in the CEM algorithm and forced the output to be sparse through the L1 norm [18]. Although these algorithms use spatial information, the background model of the algorithm is fixed, which leads to poor robustness and a low detection probability. With the rise of deep learning, deep feature extraction has also been applied to hyperspectral target detection. The hyperspectral target detection network (HTD-NET) was developed [19]. The authors used the idea of pixel pairing to expand the amount of data and built a pixel similarity discrimination model. Shi et al. designed a new deep-space spectral network (DSSN) framework for unsupervised hyperspectral target detection [20]. This method uses classic detectors and edge-preserving filters to detect regions of interest. Cheng presented a hyperspectral target detection decomposition model based on background dictionary learning (DM-BDL) [21]. They divided the image to be measured into three parts: target, background, and noise. The smoothness of the background pixel space and the sparseness of the target pixel were used, and the background dictionary learning method of locality-constrained linear coding was adopted. Zhang et al. designed a sub-pixel target detection method based on supervised metric learning [22]. The algorithm maximized the distance between the target and the background, and then used similarity propagation constraints to link target pixels and positive samples, background pixels and negative samples to reduce false alarms. Among them, the manifold smoothness regularization method was adopted for positive samples.

In recent years, graph signal processing has been applied in many fields due to its ability to represent complex relationships between high-dimensional data. So far, graph-based methods have been applied to many fields, such as edge detection [23], gradient estimation [24], segmentation [25], etc. Graph theory has also recently been used to model relationships between samples

[26]. Considering that graphs can model complex backgrounds and make full use of background information, graph theory is considered for hyperspectral target detection. In order to overcome the shortcomings of existing algorithms such as poor background modeling, low spatial information utilization, and low detection probability, a weighted Cauchy distance Graph and local adaptive Collaborative Representation Detection (CGCRD) is proposed.

22.2 Related Works

22.2.1 Graph Signal Model

Graph signal models represent and handle high-dimensional data well. The most important thing for this model is to construct a weighting matrix [27]. In an undirected weighted matrix, $V$and E denote the vertex sets and edge sets, respectively. The edge sets E can form a weight matrix W. In an image, the vertex V represents each pixel. The edge E is the weight parameter of the edge between V_a and V_b [28, 29]. It describes the mutual relationship between two pixels x_a and x_b. When a and b are equal, W_{ab} is 0.

After obtaining the weight matrix, d_q in the degree matrix represents the sum of the element values of the qth column of W, namely $d_q = \sum_{p=1}^{N} W_{pq}$. The degree matrix is expressed as $D = \text{diag}(d_1, ..., d_N)$. The diag represents a diagonal matrix, p, q refer to row and column, N is the number of image pixels. The graph Laplace matrix is:

$$L_o = D - W \tag{22.1}$$

22.2.2 Collaborative Representation

The collaborative representation target detection (CRTD) algorithm is based on the spatial neighborhood of background pixels [30]. Different from the concept based on sparse representation, collaborative representation means the current pixel by linearly combining the spatial neighborhood pixels around the pixel. Finally, the desired solutions are obtained by minimizing the L_2 norm.

In a hyperspectral image, x represents the target pixel, N is the number of all pixels, and L is the number of bands. Here, s is the sum of the number of spatial pixels around$x$, and $X_s \in \mathbb{R}^{L\times s}$ represents local pixels. When solving the weight vector of the collaborative representation, it is transformed into a minimization problem:

$$\min \|x - X_s\omega\|_2^2 \tag{22.2}$$

where ω is the coefficient matrix. Adding the constraint restriction to ω, the objective function is rewritten as:

$$\arg\min_{\omega} \|x - X_s\omega\|_2^2 + \lambda\|\omega\|_2^2 \tag{22.3}$$

The parameter λ is the Lagrangian multiplier, so the objective function is replaced by the following formula:

$$\arg\min_{\omega} \left[\omega^T\left(X_s^T X_s + \lambda I\right)\omega - 2\omega^T X_s^T x\right] \tag{22.4}$$

The above formula is solved by:

$$\omega = \left(X_s^T X_s + \lambda\right)^{-1} X_s^T x \tag{22.5}$$

The target is obtained by calculating the residual between the actual value and the predicted value. The residual is expressed as:

$$r_{\mathrm{CRD}} = \|x - \hat{x}\|_2 = \|x - X_s\omega\|_2 \tag{22.6}$$

where x and $\hat{x}$ represent the actual and predicted values, respectively. I in Eqs. (22.4) and (22.5) is the unit matrix.

22.3 The Proposed Detection Methodology

The diagram of the proposed CGCRD is illustrated in Figure 22.1. Firstly, the Laplacian matrix based on the weighted Cauchy distance is calculated. The correlation between the prior target pixels and the background pixels is used to adjust the scale of the target and background in the whole graph model. The symmetric normalized Laplacian matrix is employed to replace the covariance matrix of the matched filter to achieve target detection. Secondly, an algorithm based on local adaptive collaborative representation is designed. The penalty coefficient is weighted by the local spatial Euclidean distance combined with the Pearson correlation coefficient, and then the detection result is obtained using the residual. Finally, the two strategies are fused to get the final detection result.

22.3.1 Weighted Cauchy Distance Graph Similarity Measure

Traditional detection methods are limited by the assumption of the Gaussian model and rarely consider the influence of the target on the model, which will have a certain impact on the detection results. The Graph is often used to represent data, it describes the complex structure of data, especially for high-dimensional data have obvious advantages.

In the graph model, the measure of the edge between two vertices needs to be calculated. Considering that the Cauchy function has been shown to effectively capture the distance of a graph [31],

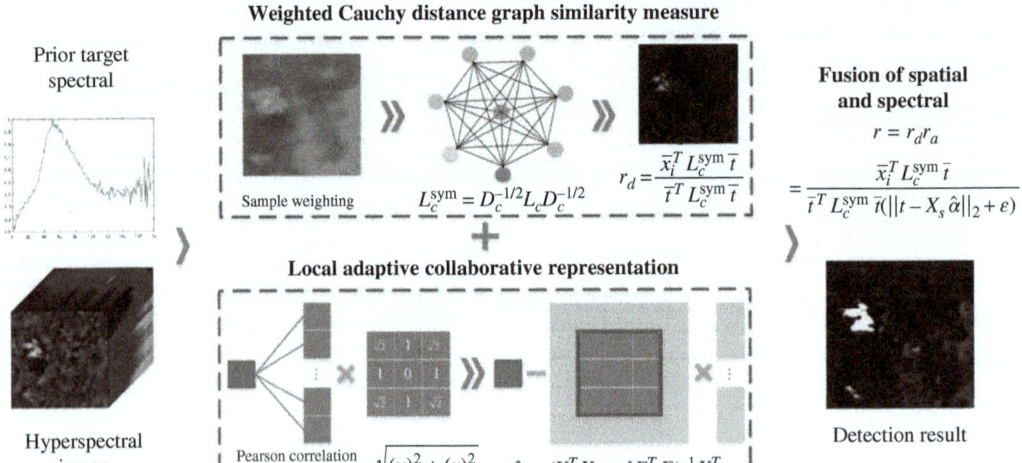

Figure 22.1 The diagram of the proposed CGCRD. Including weighted Cauchy distance Graph and local adaptive Collaborative Representation Detection.

the similarity or affinity of connected vertices can be better measured. Therefore, in order to better adapt to complex data and make full use of the correlation between bands, this method applies the Cauchy distance to the calculation of the graph edge weight matrix.

Considering a hyperspectral image has N pixels and L bands. The hyperspectral image is expressed as an $L \times N$ matrix: $X = (x_1, x_2, x_3, \ldots, x_N)$, $X \in \mathbb{R}^{L \times N}$. Assuming t ($t \in \mathbb{R}^{L \times 1}$) is the target pixel, the Cauchy distance between different bands of a pixel is derived as:

$$C(i) = \frac{1}{1 + \frac{l_g - l_h}{\bar{l}}} \tag{22.7}$$

where l_g and l_h represent the reflected energy of band g and band h, respectively. The $\bar{l}$ represents the mean value of the band, it is expressed as $\bar{l} = \frac{1}{L}\sum_{1}^{L} l_k$.

The adjacency matrix W of the sample set is considered to be the weighted average of the adjacency matrices of all pixels $x_i (i = 1, 2, \ldots, N)$. The subtle difference between the target spectrum under test and the prior target spectrum causes the filter results to be very different in the subsequent matched filter detection. Therefore, when calculating W, the influence of the target signal of interest t in W is as small as possible, and the influence of signal with a large difference from t in W is as large as possible. For different samples, the target and background image should be weighted to determine their contribution to W. The calculation formula of the correlation between the prior target spectrum and the background spectrum is as:

$$o_i = \|t - x_i\|_2 \tag{22.8}$$

where o_i is the Euclidean distance between the target and background. The weighted Cauchy distance for a single background pixel is used to construct the adjacency matrix, and its formula is expressed as:

$$W_c(i) = \frac{1}{1 + \frac{o_i (l_g - l_h)}{\bar{l}}} \tag{22.9}$$

where g and h are the index of spectral bands, l_g and l_h represent the reflected energy of band g and band h, respectively. Figure 22.2 illustrates the target and background spectral curves after

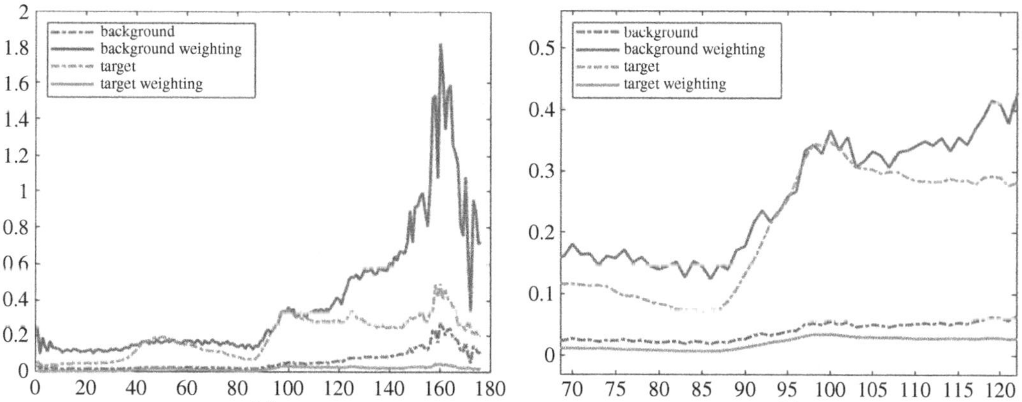

Figure 22.2 The target and background spectral curves after correlation weighting. (a) Full band. (b) Local band.

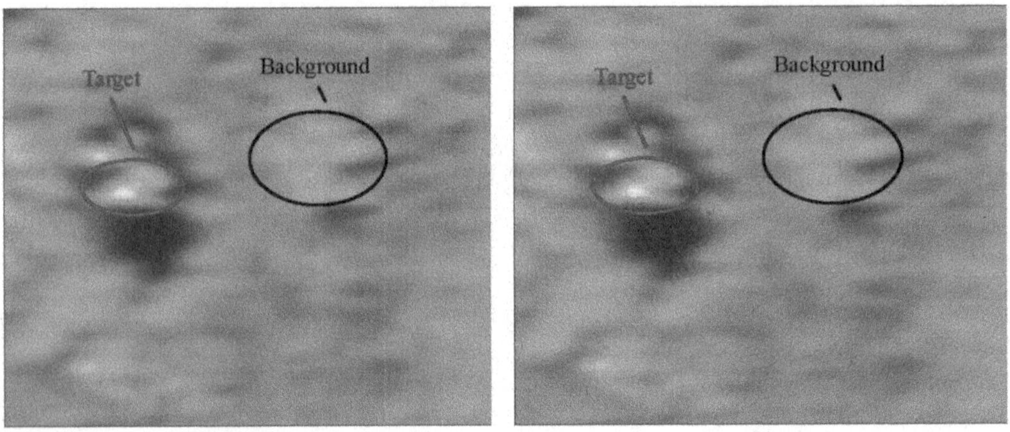

Figure 22.3 The maps of the sum of all bands of the hyperspectral image. (a) Original data. (b) Data after weighting.

correlation weighting. Figure 22.2 illustrates the target and background spectral curves after correlation weighting. The dashed and solid lines corresponding to the background represent the spectral curves before and after weighting, respectively. The other pair of curves represents the target spectral curves before and after weighting. It is found that the spectra of target pixels are suppressed and the spectra of background pixels are enhanced. Figure 22.3 illustrates the maps of the sum of all bands. Figure 22.3a and Figure 22.3b represent the original data and data after weighting, respectively. In Figure 22.3b, the target is suppressed and the background is enhanced.

The adjacency matrix of the whole image is obtained by weighted averaging of the adjacency matrix of each pixel, and the formula is stated as:

$$W_c = \frac{W_1 + \ldots + W_N}{N} \tag{22.10}$$

where N represents the number of all target pixels in the image. After the weight matrix is obtained, the degree matrix D_c is presented as:

$$D_c = \text{diag}(d_1, \ldots, d_q, \ldots, d_L) \tag{22.11}$$

where d_q represents the sum of the element values of the qth column of the weighting matrix W_c, L is the number of columns of the matrix W_c. The graph Laplacian matrix is calculated as:

$$L_c = D_c - W_c \tag{22.12}$$

The symmetric normalized Laplacian is denoted as:

$$L_c^{\text{sym}} = D_c^{-1/2} L_c D_c^{-1/2} \tag{22.13}$$

Generally, a random vector $x = [x_1, \ldots, x_L]$ satisfies a Gaussian Markov random field (MRF). The mean of the probability model of the graph structure $G = (V, E)$ is μ, and the precision matrix is $Q > 0$. The density function satisfies:

$$\begin{gathered} p(x) = (2\pi)^{-\frac{N}{2}} |Q|^{\frac{1}{2}} \exp\left(-\frac{1}{2}(x-\mu)^T Q (x-\mu)\right) \\ Q_{ij} \neq 0 \Leftrightarrow \{i,j\} \in E \qquad i \neq j \end{gathered} \tag{22.14}$$

where Q ($Q = \delta L$, δ is a scale factor) matrix represents the inverse of the multivariate covariance matrix [32].

Because the Laplace matrix is equivalent to the inverse of the multivariate covariance matrix. Applying the improved Laplacian matrix L_c to the matched filter detection makes it more robust and reduces the computational complexity of its covariance matrix inversion. The detection output in the spectral domain is described as:

$$r_d = \frac{\overline{x}_i^T L_c^{\mathrm{sym}} \overline{t}}{\overline{t}^T L_c^{\mathrm{sym}} \overline{t}} \tag{22.15}$$

where r_d is the detection result in the spectral domain. Here, $\overline{x}_i$ indicates the data to be measured after removing the mean, $\overline{t}$ represents the target of removing the mean.

22.3.2 Local Adaptive Collaborative Representation

The collaborative representation does not need to consider the background model and can make full use of the background information, so it is applied to the target detection in hyperspectral images. To further adjust the detection results, the Euclidean distance of the measured pixels and their correlation with the target spectrum is employed. This strategy uses a single-window collaborative representation to detect targets and reduce detection time. The target pixel t with the size of $L \times 1$ is approximated as:

$$\hat{t} = \alpha_1 x_1 + \alpha_2 x_2 + \dots + \alpha_s x_s = X_s \alpha \tag{22.16}$$

where $\hat{t}$ represents the estimated value of the pixel vector, X_s are the pixels in the window and is expressed as $X_s = [x_1, x_2, \dots, x_s]$. Here, α is the coefficient matrix, and it is expressed as $\alpha = [\alpha_1, \alpha_2, \dots, \alpha_s]^T$, where s represents the number of background pixels within dual-window (w) and is calculated by $s = w^2$.

Note that, X_s is adaptively adjusted for each test pixel. The a is obtained by the function:

$$\arg\min_{\alpha} \|t - X_s \alpha\|_2^2 + \lambda \|\alpha\|_2^2 \tag{22.17}$$

where X_s represents the purified background, λ is Lagrange multiplier. The weighted coefficient vector α is calculated as:

$$\hat{a} = \left(X_s^T X_s + \lambda I\right)^{-1} X_s^T t \tag{22.18}$$

where I is the unit matrix. The coefficients are small for those pixels being tested that have large differences from the prior pixels, so the penalty parameter must be increased for larger coefficients. Therefore, Euclidean distance combined with Pearson correlation coefficient is utilized to weight the penalty:

$$E = \begin{bmatrix} e_1 p_1 & \cdots & 0 \\ & \ddots & \\ \vdots & e_k p_k & \vdots \\ & & \ddots \\ 0 & \cdots & e_s p_s \end{bmatrix} \tag{22.19}$$

The position coordinates of x_i is represented as (0, 0). The coordinate of the $k$thpixel x_k ($k = 1, 2, \ldots, s$) in the local window s is (u, v). Then, the Euclidean distance between x_k and x_i is expressed by $e_k(p, q) = \sqrt{u^2 + v^2}$. The p_k is the derivative of $\rho_{\mathbf{tx}_k}$, and it is denoted as:

$$p_k = \frac{1}{\rho_{tx_k}} \tag{22.20}$$

The correlation coefficient ρ_{tx_k} between the kth pixel and the prior target pixel is stated as:

$$\rho_{tx_k} = \frac{\sum t^T x_k - \frac{\sum t \sum x_k}{L}}{\sqrt{\left(\sum x_k^T x_k - \frac{(\sum x_k)^2}{L}\right)\left(\sum t^T t - \frac{(\sum t)^2}{L}\right)}} \tag{22.21}$$

The objective function after adding Euclidean distance and Pearson correlation coefficient regularization is rewritten as:

$$\arg\min_{a} \|t - X_s\alpha\|_2^2 + \lambda\left\|E\alpha\right\|_2^2 \tag{22.22}$$

By using the Lagrange multiplier method, a final solution is obtained by:

$$\hat{\alpha} = \left(X_s^T X_s + \lambda E^T E\right)^{-1} X_s^T t \tag{22.23}$$

In target detection, the smaller the residual value, the closer to the target. The detection output is:

$$r_a = \frac{1}{\|t - X_s\hat{\alpha}\|_2 + \varepsilon} \tag{22.24}$$

where ε is a constant. It avoids having no solution when the denominator is 0 (residual is 0).

22.3.2.1 Spatial Spectral Fusion Detection

In order to use spectral and spatial information at the same time, this thesis adopts the method of fusion of spectral-domain information and spatial-domain information to achieve target detection. The final output is described as:

$$r = r_d r_a = \frac{\overline{x}_i^T L_c^{\text{sym}} \overline{t}}{\overline{t}^T L_c^{\text{sym}} \overline{t}\left(\|t - X_s\hat{\alpha}\|_2 + \varepsilon\right)} \tag{22.25}$$

If r exceeds the preset threshold, it is judged as the desired target pixel. In addition to that, r is determined to be the background pixel. The framework of the proposed CGCRD is summarized in Algorithm 22.1.

Algorithm 22.1 Main Steps of the Proposed CGCRD Algorithm

Input: X: The hyperspectral image; t: prior target pixels; λ: the Lagrange multiplier; w_{in}: the size of window.
Output: The detection result $r = [r_1, ..., r_N]$.
1: **for** $i = 1 ... N$ **do**
2: The similarity between the target spectrum and background spectrum is calculated by the Formula (22.8);
3: The adjacency matrix is calculated by Formula (22.10);
4: The Laplace matrix is calculated by Formula (22.13);
5: The detection output in the spectral domain is obtained by Formula (22.15);
6: The Euclidean distance combined with the Pearson correlation coefficient between prior target and background is calculated by Formula (22.19);
7: The coefficient of collaborative representation is obtained by Formula (22.23);
8: The detection output in the spatial domain is obtained by Formula (22.24);
9: The result of spatial-spectral detection is obtained by Formula (22.25);
10: end for

22.4 Experiments and Analysis

22.4.1 Parameters Analysis

A new BIT-HSI-I dataset has been collected to perform the experiments. We validate the effect of the proposed CGCRD using four different scenarios. To demonstrate the superiority of CGCRD, it is contrasted with existing seven superior methods. Seven algorithms compared are ACE [5], CEM [6], MF [3], ASMF [4], CSCR [16] SSCEM [18] and DM-BDL[21]. Next, the parameters and experimental results of the proposed algorithm are analyzed respectively.

By varying the parameter λ and the window size w_{in}, Figure 22.4a–d illustrate the area under the curve (AUC) of the proposed CGCRD. Figure 22.4a displays the AUC values under different λ and w_{in} for the wet grassland image. For example, when λ and w_{in} are selected as 10^{-4} and 15, respectively, the proposed CGCRD has the best detection performance with an AUC value of 0.9974. When w_{in} is selected as 5, the AUC value becomes smaller and drops to 0.9950. Figure 22.4b displays the AUC values under different λ and w_{in} for the dry grassland image. For example, when λ and $w_{in}$are selected as 10^{-1} and 3, respectively, the proposed CGCRD has the best detection performance with an AUC value of 0.9992. When w_{in} is selected as 9, the AUC value becomes smaller and drops to 0.9990. Figure 22.4c displays the AUC values under different λ and w_{in} for the shaded grassland image. For example, when λ and w_{in} are selected as 10^{-5} and 9, respectively, the proposed CGCRD has the best detection performance with an AUC value of 0.9990. When w_{in} is selected as 3, the AUC value becomes smaller and drops to 0.9882. Figure 22.4d displays the AUC values under different λ and w_{in} for the leaf ground image. For example, when λ and w_{in} are selected as 10^{-5} and 11, respectively, the proposed CGCRD has the best detection performance with an AUC value of 0.9941. When w_{in} is selected as 3, the AUC value becomes smaller and drops to 0.9714. Through the above analysis, it is found that the value of λ has little change in detection performance. The value of

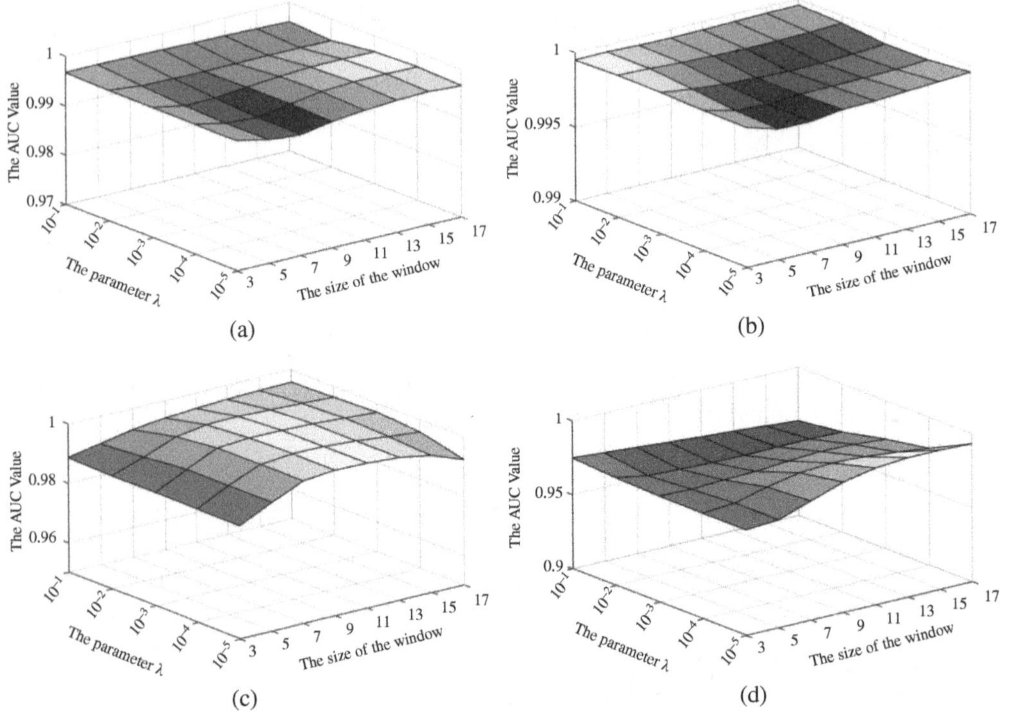

Figure 22.4 The AUC values for different λ and window size under different data sets. (a) Wet grassland. (b) Dry grassland. (c) Shaded grassland. (d) Leaf ground.

λ is set to 10^{-5}. The value of w_{in} is similar to the number of target pixels in the image. Its value is chosen based on the number of these pixels.

22.4.2 Detection Performance

To quantitatively and qualitatively compare the proposed method, a detection map, target background separation box, and receiver operating characteristic curve (ROC) are introduced. The detection map is a gray map. The brighter the pixel, the closer to the target.

The normalized values corresponding to the target and background locations in the detection probability are grouped into two groups. Dividable boxes represent statistical intervals of target and background normalized values as different colored boxes. The position of the horizontal line in the middle of each box is the median, and the upper and lower edges are the 75th and 25th of the maximum value of the data. The extremum of the detection result is represented by the "whisker" [33].

The abscissa and ordinate of the ROC curve are plotted with the probability of false detection (*PF*) and the probability of detection (*PD*), respectively. The closer the ROC is to the northwest corner of the figure, the higher the *PD* and the lower the *PF*, indicating that algorithm involved performance is more excellent. The AUC refers to the area enclosed by the ROC and the coordinate axis. It is expressed as:

$$\text{AUC} = \frac{1}{2} \times \sum_{i}^{W} (PF_i - PF_{i-1}) \times (PD_i + PD_{i-1}) \tag{22.26}$$

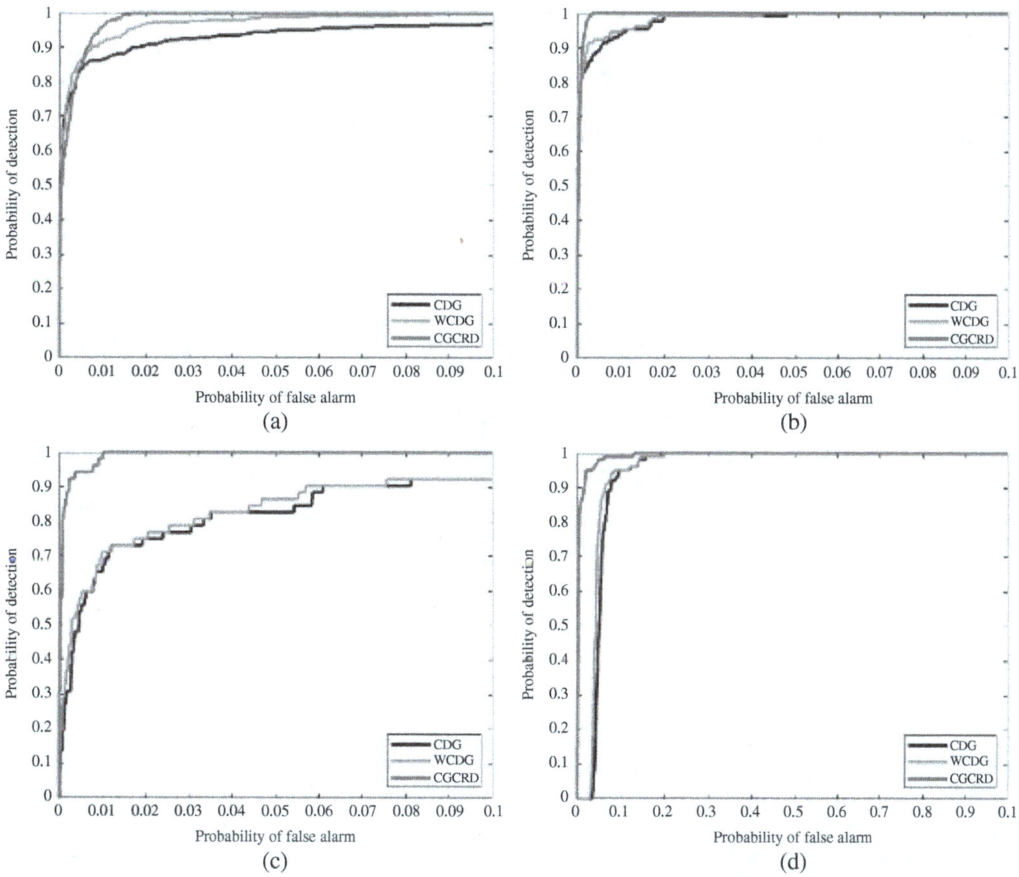

Figure 22.5 The ROC curves of the proposed CDG (Cauchy Distance Graph), WCDG (Weighted Cauchy Distance Graph) and CGCRD in different scenes. (a) Wet grassland. (b) Dry grassland. (c) Shaded grassland. (d) Leaf ground.

where *PD* is detection probability, *PF* is false alarm probability, *w* is the number of different thresholds. The *PD* denotes the percentage of correctly positioned target pixels to the whole number of target pixels actually possessed. The *PF* is the percentage of non-target pixels that are considered target pixels to the whole number of pixels. Under a certain *PF*, the higher the *PD*, the better the function of the algorithm used [34]. The *PD* and *PF* are calculated by:

$$PD = \frac{N_d}{N_t} \tag{22.27}$$

$$PF = \frac{N_f}{N} \tag{22.28}$$

where N_d, N_t, N_f and N indicate the correct number of pixels are detected, the real target pixels number of image, wrongly detected pixels, and all pixels of the image, respectively.

Figures 22.5 illustrate the results of visual detection by different algorithms in four scenarios. The proposed algorithm is able to identify more target pixels in the data sets of wet grass, dry grass, shaded grass, and leafy fields. Other comparison algorithms have poor detection performance. In Figure 22.6a–d, ACE, CEM, MF, ASMF detect fewer correct pixels. In Figure 22.6e–g, CSCR, SSCEM and DM-BDL detect more target pixels, but there are also many wrong target pixels. In

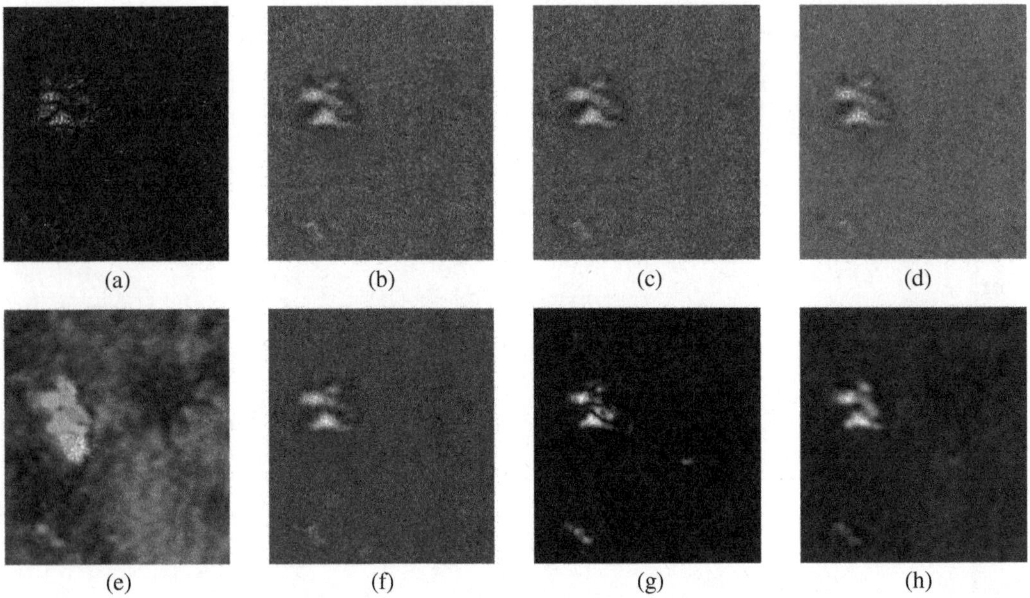

Figure 22.6 The detection results of eight methods in real wet grassland. (a) ACE. (b) CEM. (c) MF. (d) ASMF. (e) CSCR. (f) SSCEM. (g) DM-BDL. (h) CGCRD.

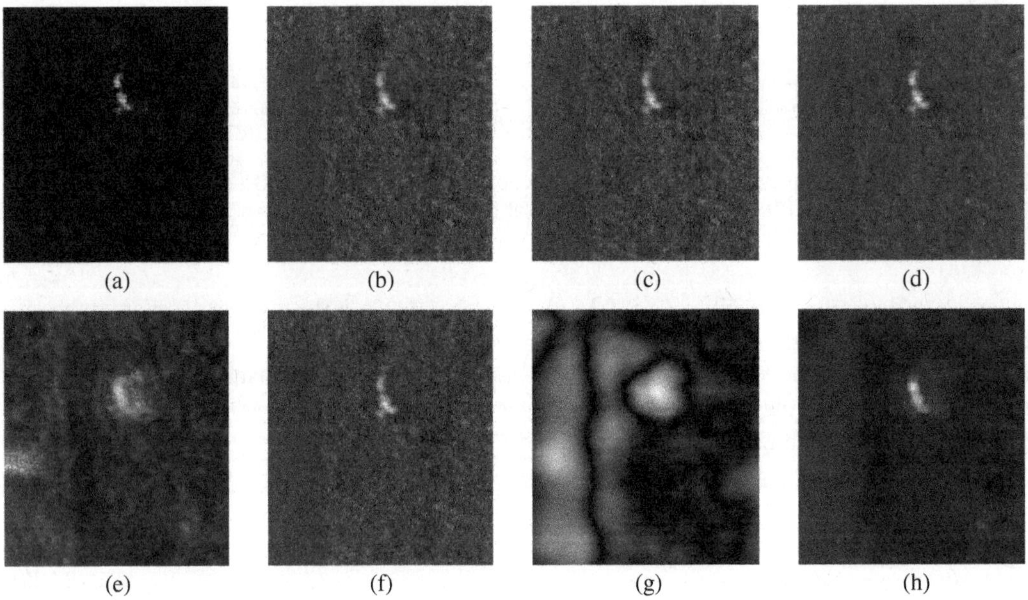

Figure 22.7 The detection results of eight methods in real dry grassland. (a) ACE. (b) CEM. (c) MF. (d) ASMF. (e) CSCR. (f) SSCEM. (g) DM-BDL. (h) CGCRD.

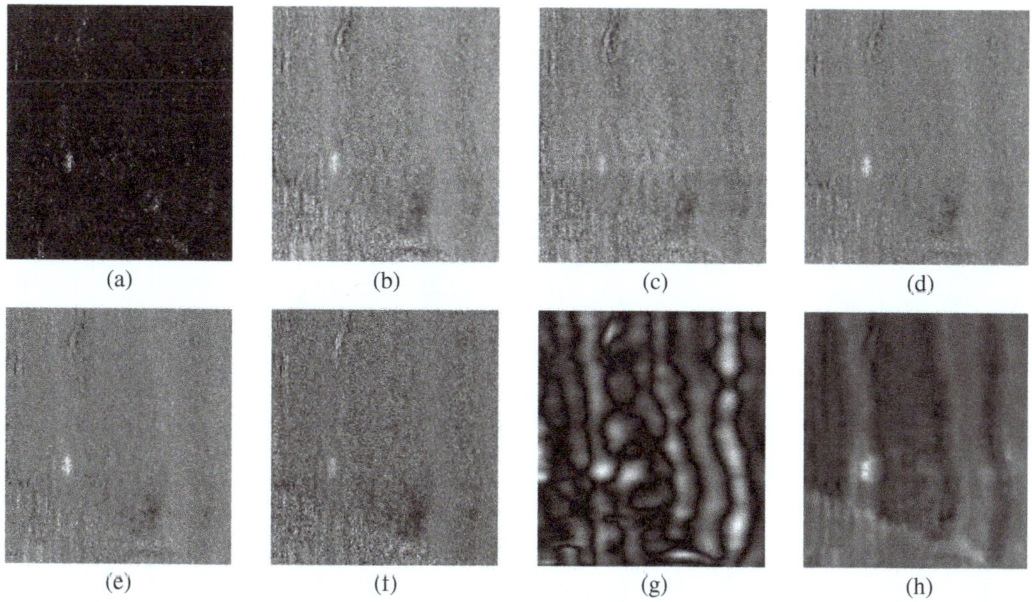

Figure 22.8 The detection results of eight methods in real shaded grassland. (a) ACE. (b) CEM. (c) MF. (d) ASMF. (e) CSCR. (f) SSCEM. (g) DM-BDL. (h) CGCRD.

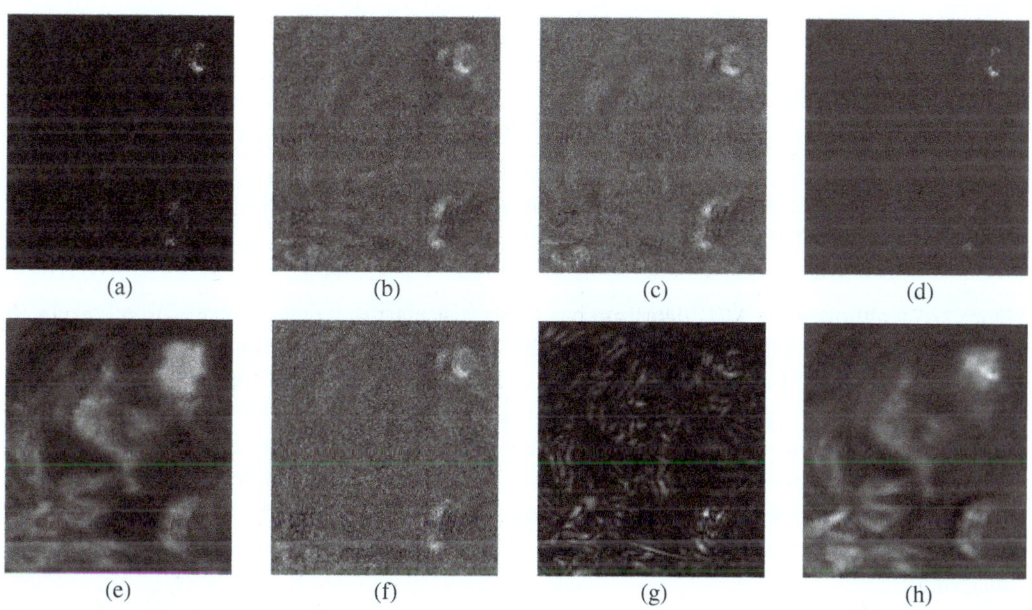

Figure 22.9 The detection results of eight methods in real leaf grassland. (a) ACE. (b) CEM. (c) MF. (d) ASMF. (e) CSCR. (f) SSCEM. (g) DM BDL. (h) CGCRD.

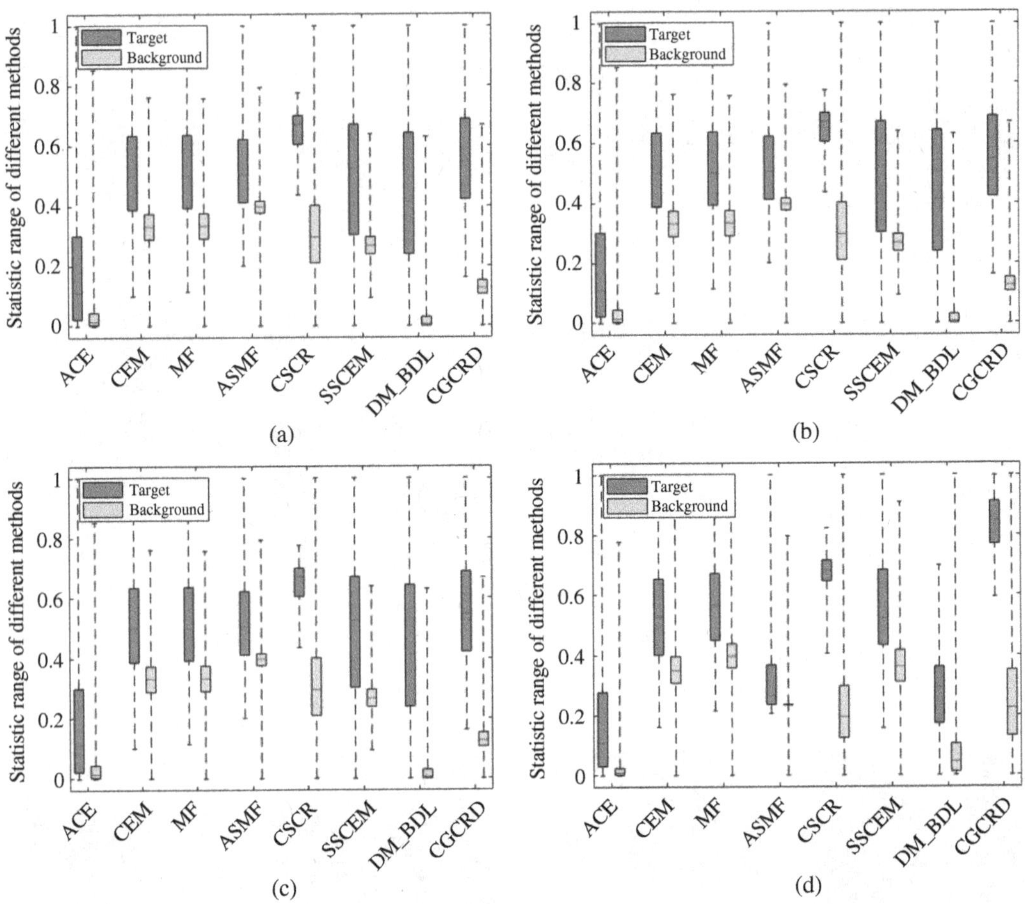

Figure 22.10 The statistical separability analysis with different detectors using four experimental data sets. (a) Wet grassland. (b) Dry grassland. (c) Shaded grassland. (d) Leaf ground.

Figure 22.7a, although the ACE algorithm has fewer false alarms, it detects fewer correct pixels. In Figure 22.7b–g, CEM, MF, ASMF, CSCR, SSCEM, and DM-BDL detect more wrong target pixels, and DM-BDL detects the most wrong pixels. In Figure 22.8a–f, ACE, CEM, MF, ASMF, CSCR, SSCEM detect fewer wrong target pixels and fewer correct target pixels. In Figure 22.8g, DM-BDL detects some correct pixels, and detect many wrong pixels. In Figure 22.9a,d,g, ACE, ASMF and DM-BDL hardly detect the target pixels. In Figure 22.9b–c,e–f, CEM, MF, CSCR and SSCEM detect fewer wrong target pixels and fewer correct target pixels. Therefore, the proposed CGCRD always has superior detection performance, which increases the separation of target and background.

In the separation box, the two boxplots represent the target probability area and the background probability area, respectively. The gap between the two boxplots represents the separability between the target and the background. In Fig. 22.10(a)–(d), CGCRD shows a larger gap between the target and background boxplots than the other algorithms, indicating better separability. This shows that the proposed CGCRD easily identifies the target from the background image.

The coordinates on the ROC curve indicate *PD* and *PF* at different thresholds. In Figure 22.11a, which is the wet grass image, when *PF* is are all 0.1, the *PD* corresponding to CGCRD is about 1.00. The *PD* of other methods (ACE, CEM, MF, ASMF, CSCR, SSCEM, DM-BDL) are 0.5394, 0.6909,

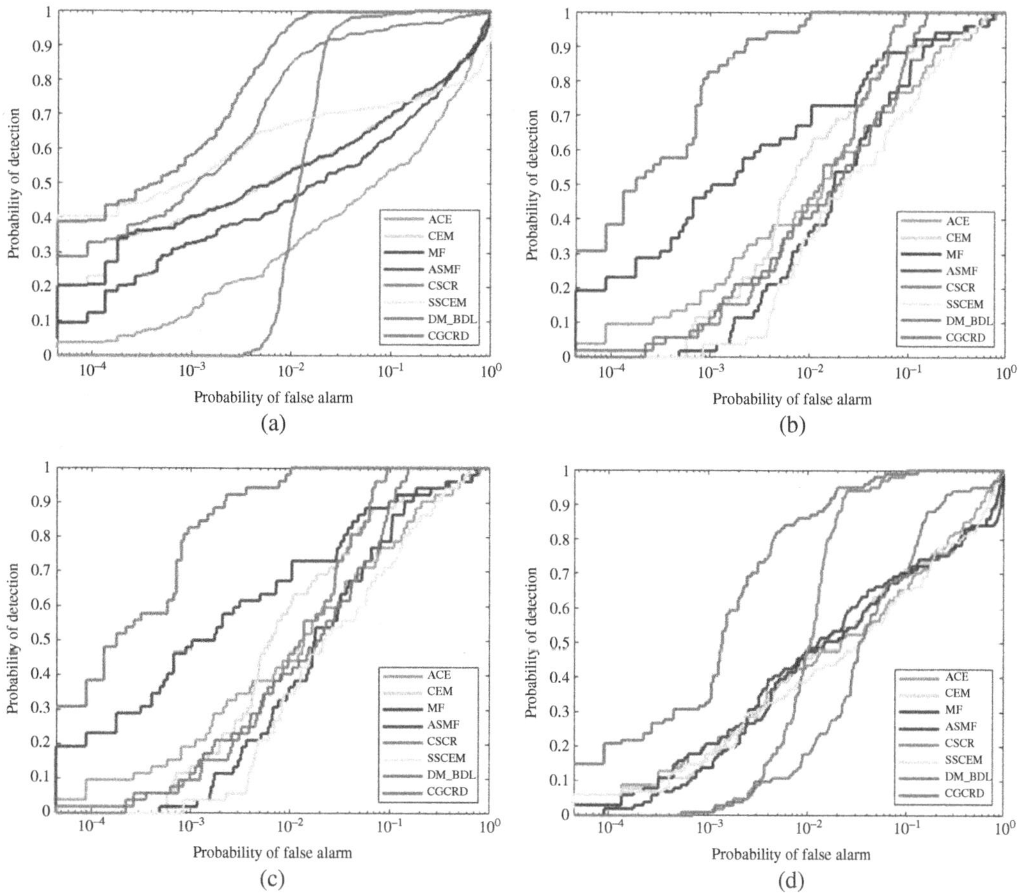

Figure 22.11 The ROC curve with different detectors using four experimental data sets. (a) Wet grassland. (b) Dry grassland. (c) Shaded grassland. (d) Leaf ground.

Table 22.1 AUC values of different detectors on four data sets.

Image	ACE	CEM	MF	ASMF	CSCR	SSCEM	DM-BDL	CGCRD
Wet grassland	0.7634	0.8296	0.8314	0.8217	0.9846	0.7976	0.9739	0.9974
Dry grassland	0.9489	0.9618	0.9634	0.9650	0.9968	0.9798	0,9705	0.9992
Shaded grassland	0.9164	0.9510	0.9280	0.9559	0.9764	0.9071	0.9620	0.9990
Leaf ground	0.8487	0.8137	0.8053	0.8162	0.9861	0.8253	0.8966	0.9941

0.6940, 0.6341, 0.9905, 0.7319, and 0.9558, respectively. From Figure 22.11b–d, when *PF* is 0.01, 0.01 and 0.1, the *PD* of CGCRD are 1.0, 0.9808 and 1.0, respectively. The maximum *PD* of other mentioned algorithms are 0.9147, 0.6731 and 0.9901 respectively. These results demonstrate the effectiveness of the proposed CGCRD.

Table 22.1 lists the AUC values of the eight comparison algorithms. The AUC values of CGCRD are 0.9974, 0.9992, 0.9990, and 0.9941 for these four scenarios, respectively. The optimal AUC values of the remaining algorithms in the four different scenarios are 0.9846, 0.9968, 0.9764, and 0.9861, respectively. These values are poor relative to the AUC values of CGCRD.

Table 22.2 Execution time of different detectors on four data sets (unit: seconds).

Image	ACE	CEM	MF	ASMF	CSCR	SSCEM	DM-BDL	CGCRD
Wet grassland	0.2031	0.0949	0.1302	1.3822	4.5834	231.0282	4.5004	29.9725
Dry grassland	0.1966	0.0839	0.1302	1.1616	4.4626	222.1655	7.0287	5.1503
Shaded grassland	0.1882	0.0825	0.1263	1.1656	8.0926	228.3280	5.4691	25.5902
Leaf ground	0.2140	0.0806	0.1330	1.2282	4.4288	203.2471	4.5716	67.1497

The running times of the eight detection algorithms are shown in Table 22.2. In four different scenarios, the time used by CGCRD is 29.9725, 5.1503, 25.5902, and 67.1497 seconds, respectively. The time consumption of CGCRD is mainly used for the local window calculation method. In addition, the time consumption of SSCEM is the largest. The computational efficiency of our proposed algorithm is also good. All test algorithms are performed with MATLAB on an Intel Core i7-8700 h CPU computer with 8Gb of computer memory.

22.5 Conclusion

In this manuscript, an effective hyperspectral target detection algorithm was proposed based on a weighted Cauchy distance graph and locally adaptive collaborative representation. The algorithm has employed the Laplacian matrix of weighted Cauchy distance to estimate background statistics, which improves the adaptability of the algorithm to complex data sets and reduces the calculation amount of covariance matrix estimation and inversion. Meanwhile, in order to fully utilize the local spatial information, an adaptive collaborative representation method was developed. It adopts the Euclidean distance combined with the Pearson correlation coefficient to adaptively penalize the collaborative representation coefficient, which can adjust the performance of the target detection. These experimental results show that the proposed CGCRD has better detection performance compared to other detection algorithms on four real hyperspectral images, and the detection performance of the proposed CGCRD is up to 30% higher than the comparison method using the collected data sets.

References

1 Hou, Z., Li, W., Li, L. et al. (2021). Hyperspectral change detection based on multiple morphological profiles. *IEEE Trans. Geosci. Remote Sens.* (60): 1–2.

2 Zhao, X., Li, W., Zhang, M. et al. (2020). Adaptive iterated shrinkage thresholding-based lp-norm sparse representation for hyperspectral imagery target detection. *Remote Sens.* 12 (23): 3991.

3 Manolakis, D., Lockwood, R., Cooley, T., and Jacobson, J. (2009). Is there a best hyperspectral detection algorithm?*Proc. SPIE*, pp. 733402. (eds. S. Sylvia, Shen, Paul E. Lewis. https://doi.org/10.1117/12.816917.

4 Manolakis, D.G., Shaw, G.A., and Keshava, N. (2000). Comparative analysis of hyperspectral adaptive matched filter detectors. *Algorithms for Multispectral, Hyperspectral, and Ultraspectral Imagery VI*, 4049, 2–17 (23 August 2000). Orlando, FL, USA: SPIE.

5 Kraut, S., Scharf, L.L., and Butler, R.W. (2005). The adaptive coherence estimator: a uniformly most-powerful-invariant adaptive detection statistic. *IEEE Trans. Signal Process.* 53 (2): 427–438.

6 Farrand, W.H. and Harsanyi, J.C. (1997). Maping the distribution of mine tailings in the Coeur d'Alene River Valley, Idaho, through the use of a constrained energy minimization technique. *Remote Sens. Environ.* 59 (1): 64–76.

7 Theiler, J. and Foy, B.R. (2006). Effect of signal contamination in matched-filter detection of the signal on a cluttered background. *IEEE Geosci. Remote Sens. Lett.* 3 (1): 98–102.

8 Harsanyi, J.C. and Chang, C.I. (1994). Hyperspectral image classification and dimensionality reduction: an orthogonal subspace projection approach. *IEEE Trans. Geosci. Remote Sens.* 32 (4): 779–785.

9 Harsanyi, J.C. (1993). *Detection and Classification Of Subpixel Spectral Signatures in Hyperspectral Image Sequences*. Baltimore County: University of Maryland.

10 Wang, C.M., Chen, C.C., Yang, S.C. et al. (2002). Unsupervised orthogonal subspace projection approach to magnetic resonance image classification. *Opt. Eng.* 41 (7): 1546–1557.

11 Heinz, D.C. (2001). Fully constrained least squares linear spectral mixture analysis method for material quantification in hyperspectral imagery. *IEEE Trans. Geosci. Remote Sens.* 39 (3): 529–545.

12 Kwon, H. and Nasrabadi, N.M. (2006). A comparative analysis of kernel subspace target detectors for hyperspectral imagery. *EURASIP J. Adv. Signal Process.* 2007: 1–3.

13 Zhang, L., Zhang, L., Tao, D., and Huang, X. (2013). Sparse transfer manifold embedding for hyperspectral target detection. *IEEE Trans. Geosci. Remote Sens.* 52 (2): 1030–1043.

14 Verdoja, F. and Grangetto, M. (2020). Graph Laplacian for image anomaly detection. *Mach. Vis. Appl.* 31 (1): 11.

15 Zhu, D., Du, B., and Zhang, L. (2019). Target dictionary construction-based sparse representation hyperspectral target detection methods. *IEEE J. Sel. Top. Appl. Earth Obs. Remote Sens.* 12 (4): 1254–1264.

16 Li, W., Du, Q., and Zhang, B. (2015). Combined sparse and collaborative representation for hyperspectral target detection. *Pattern Recogn.* 48 (12): 3904–3916.

17 Liu, Y., Gao, G., and Gu, Y. (2016). Tensor matched subspace detector for hyperspectral target detection. *IEEE Trans. Geosci. Remote Sens.* 55 (4): 1967–1974.

18 Yang, X., Chen, J., and He, Z. (2019). Sparse-spatial CEM for hyperspectral target detection. *IEEE J. Sel. Top. Appl. Earth Obs. Remote Sens.* 12 (7): 2184–2195.

19 Zhang, G., Zhao, S., Li, W. et al. (2020). HTD-net: a deep convolutional neural network for target detection in hyperspectral imagery. *Remote Sens* 12 (9): 1489.

20 Shi, Y., Li, J., Zheng, Y.B., and Li, Y. (2020). Hyperspectral target detection with RoI feature transformation and multiscale spectral attention. *IEEE Trans. Geosci. Remote Sens.* 59 (6): 5071–5084.

21 Cheng, T. and Wang, B. (2021). Decomposition model with background dictionary learning for hyperspectral target detection. *IEEE J. Sel. Top. Appl. Earth Obs. Remote Sens.* 8 (14): 1872–1884.

22 Zhang, L., Zhang, L., Tao, D. et al. (2013). Hyperspectral remote sensing image subpixel target detection based on supervised metric learning. *IEEE Trans. Geosci. Remote Sens.* 52 (8): 4955–4965.

23 Baterina, A.V. and Oppus, C. (2010). Image edge detection using ant colony optimization. *Wseas Trans. Signal Process.* 6 (2): 58–67.

24 Ravazzi, C., Coluccia, G., and Magli, E. (2017). Curl-constrained gradient estimation for image recovery from highly incomplete spectral data. *IEEE Trans. Image Process.* 26 (6): 2656–2668.

25 Boykov, Y. and Funka-Lea, G. (2006). Graph cuts and efficient ND image segmentation. *Int. J. Comput. Vis.* 70 (2): 109–131.

26 Sandryhaila A, Moura JM. Discrete signal processing on graphs: graph Fourier transform. *2013 IEEE International Conference on Acoustics, Speech and Signal Processing*, 6167–6710, Vancouver, BC, Canada (26 May 2013). IEEE.

27 Sandryhaila, A. and Moura, J.M. (2014). Big data analysis with signal processing on graphs: representation and processing of massive data sets with irregular structure. *IEEE Signal Process. Mag.* 31 (5): 80–90.

28 Yuan, Y., Ma, D., and Wang, Q. (2015). Hyperspectral anomaly detection by graph pixel selection. *IEEE Trans. Cybern.* 46 (12): 3123–3134.

29 Messinger DW, Albano J. A graph theoretic approach to anomaly detection in hyperspectral imagery. *2011 3rd Workshop on Hyperspectral Image and Signal Processing: Evolution in Remote Sensing (WHISPERS)*, 1–4, Lisbon, Portugal (6 June 2011). IEEE.

30 Li, W. and Du, Q. (2014). Collaborative representation for hyperspectral anomaly detection. *IEEE Trans. Geosci. Remote Sens.* 53 (3): 1463–1474.

31 Grady, L.J. and Polimeni, J.R. (2010). *Discrete Calculus: Applied Analysis on Graphs for Computational Science*. London: Springer.

32 Zhang, C. and Florêncio, D. (2012). Analyzing the optimality of predictive transform coding using graph-based models. *IEEE Signal Process. Lett.* 20 (1): 106–109.

33 Kwon, H. and Nasrabadi, N.M. (2007). Kernel spectral matched filter for hyperspectral imagery. *Int. J. Comput. Vis.* 71: 127–141.

34 Zhao, X., Hou, Z., Wu, X. et al. (2021). Hyperspectral target detection based on transform domain adaptive constrained energy minimization. *Int. J. Appl. Earth Obs. Geoinf.* 1 (103): 102461.

23

Weakly Supervised Learning-based Hyperspectral Image Anomaly/Target Detection

Weiying Xie[1], Xin Zhang[1], Yunsong Li[1], and Qian Du[2]

[1] *State Key Laboratory of Integrated Services Networks, Xidian University, Xi'an, China*
[2] *Department of Electrical and Computer Engineering, Mississippi State University, Mississippi State, MS, USA*

23.1 Introduction

With the growing demand for precise interpretation and the wide usage of hyperspectral imaging sensors, it has become urgent to distinguish anomalies from the background in hyperspectral images (HSIs) [1–3]. Hyperspectral anomalies are spectrally and spatially different from their surroundings in the absence of any priori information [4, 5]. Most existing hyperspectral anomaly detection (HAD) methods determine whether a testing point exhibits any irregularity from the estimated background. However, real HSIs are complex and highly imbalanced with large background and low occurrence probability of anomalies. Moreover, it is difficult to take all types of classes into consideration for background modelling. Therefore, the main challenge of HAD is to leverage the intrinsic, comprehensive, and real characteristic of the background only and distinguish the points that deviate from the background. The existing methods estimate the background in different ways. First and foremost, the Reed-Xiaoli (RX) detector [6], as a milestone, calculates the mean and variance of an entire image based on the assumption that the background obeys a multivariate Gaussian distribution. Obviously, such estimation is nonoptimal. Subsequently, variants of RX, such as local-RX (LRX) and kernel RX (KRX) [7, 8], have continuously been investigated. These extensions may relieve the stress on complete and precise estimation of the background in the absence of any priori information. Despite this, the problem has not been well solved since the background model was built from the samples mixed with anomalies and noise rather than true background samples. The representation-based methods are used in a wide range of application domains. Zhou et al. proposed a novel recurrent neural network for anomaly detection (called AnomalyNet) by deep feature learning [9], sparse representation, and dictionary learning in three joint neural processing blocks. Structured AutoEncoders are used for subspace clustering to preserve the local structure, and the StructAE learns representations to preserve both local and global structures [10]. For background modelling, the representation-based methods include collaborative representation [11–13], sparse representation [14–16], and low-rank representation (LRR) [17–19], which have grown from a specific niche to mainstream. Among them, the collaborative representation detector (CRD) estimated the background based on the assumption that each pixel in the background can be represented via a linear combination of neighbouring pixels within a sliding dual window [20]. The background joint sparse representation detection (BJSRD) models the background by selecting

Machine-Learning-Based Hyperspectral Image Processing, First Edition. Edited by Bing Zhang.

the most representative background bases for each local region [21]. The LRR-based detectors built the background model by leveraging the low-rank characteristic of the background. Concretely, the low-rank and sparse matrix decomposition (LRaSMD)-based Mahalanobis distance method for HAD (LSMAD) alleviates the anomaly contamination to a certain extent [22]. Li et al. proposed a detector called LSDM-MoG based on the LRR model in conjunction with the mixture of Gaussian (MoG) to better characterize data distribution [23]. Furthermore, the dictionary-based low-rank decomposition algorithms were applied on the background dictionary rather than the background itself [24, 25]. Thus, the performance of background estimation in these methods is highly correlated with the constructed background dictionary. Nevertheless, the dictionary constructed by traditional methods has a limited ability to characterize the real background, especially the complex background in HSIs. Deep neural networks have recently achieved unprecedented success in HSI interpretation due to their ability to learn complex data distributions without the demand of explicitly defining them [26–29]. Currently, DNNs have been extensively studied in HAD due to their powerful nonlinear and deep representational advantage. The sparse autoencoder (SAE), deep belief network (DBN), variational AE (VAE), and adversarial AE (AAE)-based HAD methods mainly focus on designing a feature extractor followed by a detector in an unsupervised way [30–33]. Besides, the DNNs, including generative adversarial network (GAN) and VAE, are used to directly give an anomaly score according to the reconstruction residual [34, 35]. Notably, the lack of priori information limits the detection performance. In addition to unsupervised approaches, supervised approaches, such as convolutional neural networks (CNNs), have been applied to HAD [36, 37]. It is worth noting that the DNNs-based HAD approaches in a supervised way rely on richly annotated samples. However, the correctness of annotation is questionable due to inaccurate priori information, which limits performance and flexibility in a wide range of practical applications. Compared to these methods, the adaptability of weakly supervised method makes it an attractive choice. With these considerations, we should construct a comprehensive and effective dictionary that best characterizes the underlying and intrinsic structure of complex background in HSIs draw support from the strong representational advantage of DNNs and optimize it to extract anomalies.

Target detection is also considered as a fundamental task and has received a surge of interest [39]. Essentially, target detection can be regarded as a problem of classification and localization which has been widely used spanning from civilian to military [40, 41]. A significant body of priori work exists within hyperspectral target detection. Traditionally, spectral difference between target and background is exploited to detect targets. Constrained energy minimization (CEM) [42], a classic hyperspectral target detection approach, imposes a constraint on target and background and builds a finite impulse response filter, which minimizes the filters output energy. Many extensions based on CEM have been investigated for hyperspectral target detection [43–45]. Among them, hierarchical CEM (hCEM) proposed by Zou and Shi is an improved method based on CEM [46], which is a hierarchical structure containing different layers of CEM detectors. The hCEM increases detection performance layer by layer through a hierarchical suppression process. Another typical target detection method is orthogonal subspaces projection (OSP) [47], which projects spectral vectors into an orthogonal subspace of background with the aim of maximizing the signal-to-noise ratio (SNR). A combined sparse and collaborative representation (CSCR)-based approach generates a detection output simply by using the difference between the representation residuals of target and background [11]. Other methods, such as adaptive coherence/cosine estimator (ACE) [48, 49], matched filter [50], and matched subspace detectors describe target detection as a hypothesis test problem [51]. Virtually, an HSI usually covers a large scale of ground scene, which contains various materials with different spectral properties. On this account, traditional target detection algorithms encounter many bottlenecks. For example, CEM estimates background with all pixels of an image, which ignores the influence of target pixels. Moreover, it is found to be difficult for OSP to construct background subspace accurately due to the complexity and diversity of HSIs. Recent developments in deep learning, shown to be highly capable of characterizing high-dimensional data. The DNNs can model complex data sets by extracting multiple layers of representation and abstraction. Thus, DNNs are expected to yield higher detection accuracy for HSIs than those traditional ones using shallow feature extractors [52–55]. Generative adversarial networks are promising deep learning models [56], which provide substantial advantages in learning input distributions with a min–max game. For example, by adding the learning of the inverse mapping which maps the data to a latent representation, the original GAN can be extended to bidirectional GAN (BiGAN) [33], which has been successfully used in anomaly detection. Another variant of GAN is known as adversarial autoencoder (AAE) [57], which imposes an arbitrary priori on the latent code to learn the input distribution adversarially. Several contemporary studies demonstrate that AAE is effective in generating an approximated data to the input, and can adapt well to various complex scenes [58–60]. A training set containing sufficient samples plays a significant role in the establishment of DNNs. Compared with the small area and low-probability target samples in HSIs, background occupying a larger area contains abundant samples. In virtue of its superior numbers, background samples are served as training data to establish a background estimation model in a weakly-supervised way [61]. Among the deep learning models mentioned above, AAE shows its potential in modelling background distribution. In [62], Xie et al. detected anomalies by learning the background distribution with an autoencoder and adversarial-learning-based background estimation model that is trained only on the background samples. Jiang et al. proposed an adversarial framework to learn a discriminative background reconstruction with anomaly targets being suppressed [34], such that an initial detection result can be generated by the residual between the original and reconstructed images. In establishing DNNs, a training set containing sufficient samples is crucial. Background samples, which occupy a larger area and are more abundant in HSIs compared to small area and low-probability target samples, can be leveraged as training data to establish background estimation models in a weakly-supervised manner. These advancements highlight the potential of deep learning approaches, particularly AAE, in improving target detection accuracy and background modelling in HSIs.

The wide deployment of cost-sensitive services and low-powered edge applications highlights the importance of computing load and memory footprint reduction [63–65]. Simplifying network design and reducing data dimensionare two prevalent approaches for removing redundancy [66–69]. Hyperspectral images (HSIs) describe various surface features by using solar reflectance in hundreds of spectral bands [19, 70, 71]. The resulted spectral redundancy is not conducive to downstream tasks, such as anomaly/target detection and classification [72–74]. Figure 23.1 shows the similarity between the 205 bands and the reference band. More than 60 bands achieve similarity greater than 0.9, and there are more than four-fifths with similarity over 0.5, which indicates the necessity of removing spectral redundancy through dimensionality reduction (DR). Band selection (BS) is an effective DR technique [75–78], solving the redundancy reduction problem in an interpretable way called "Take the essence, discard the dregs." BS explores a salient and representative subset from the original hyperspectral data without a detrimental impact on its performance on follow-up tasks. Instead of projecting data to a low-dimensional space, such as feature extraction (FE) [18–20], BS preserves the information of the original data in the physical sense. Roughly, there are two BS schemes: supervised and unsupervised. Due to more robust performance and higher application prospects, the latter one is preferred. Recently, there has been a surge of interest in clustering-based unsupervised or weakly-supervised BS methods [79–82]. Exemplified with optimal

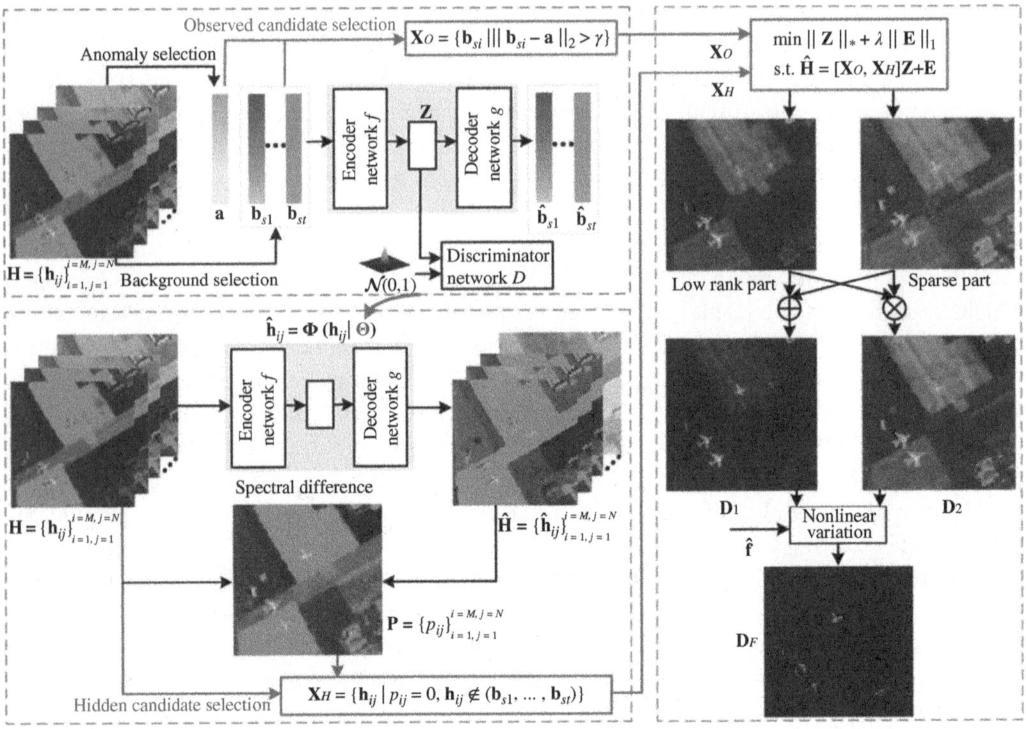

Figure 23.1 Schematic of the proposed WSLRR-based anomaly detection method.

clustering framework (OCF) and enhanced fast density-peak-based clustering (EFDPC) [83, 84], clustering based methods treat each band as individuals and cluster under some criteria. The most relevant band with other bands in each cluster is selected as a representative. However, this strategy fails to consider the global data properties and the relevance between bands. Besides, the information saliency is not evaluated, generating a BS result with significant individual differences but less effective content.

23.2 Weakly Supervised Hyperspectral Anomaly Detection (WSLRR)

Let $\mathbf{H} = \{\mathbf{h}_{ij}\}_{i=1 j=1}^{i=M j=N}$ denote a raw HSI, where $\mathbf{h}_{ij}$ is a spectral vector with L spectral channels, and its spatial position is represented by (i, j), M and N denote the length and width of the spatial dimension, respectively. Apparently, $\mathbf{H}$ is composed of anomaly and background which can be represented by $\mathbf{A}$ and $\mathbf{B}$, respectively:

$$\begin{aligned} \mathbf{A} &= [\mathbf{a}_1, \mathbf{a}_2, ..., \mathbf{a}_p] \\ \mathbf{B} &= [\mathbf{b}_1, \mathbf{b}_2, ..., \mathbf{b}_q] \end{aligned} \tag{23.1}$$

where $\mathbf{a}_i$ and $\mathbf{b}_i$ are respectively correspondent with anomaly spectral vector and background spectral vector.

Given that the total number of pixels in an HSI is equal to the number of pixels belonging to the anomaly and the background, we have $p + q = M \times N$. Then $\mathbf{H}$ is imported to a background estimation network. For clarity, the reconstructed HSI is denoted as $\hat{\mathbf{H}} = \left\{\hat{\mathbf{h}}_{ij}\right\}_{i=1,j=1}^{i=M,j=N}$, where $\hat{\mathbf{h}}_{ij}$ is the corresponding reconstructed spectral vector. Similarly, $\hat{\mathbf{H}}$ also can be divided into reconstructed anomaly $\hat{\mathbf{A}}$ and reconstructed background $\hat{\mathbf{B}}$:

$$\begin{aligned} \hat{\mathbf{A}} &= \left[\hat{\mathbf{a}}_1, \hat{\mathbf{a}}_2, \ldots, \hat{\mathbf{a}}_p\right] \\ \hat{\mathbf{B}} &= \left[\hat{\mathbf{b}}_1, \hat{\mathbf{b}}_2, \ldots, \hat{\mathbf{b}}_q\right]. \end{aligned} \tag{23.2}$$

Anomaly detection, ideally, can be conducted by checking the difference between $\mathbf{H}$ and $\hat{\mathbf{H}}$. However, it is difficult to extract each anomaly when estimating background in an unsupervised fashion. Namely, background training data is ambiguous, resulting in a weakly supervised network, which can also reconstruct anomalies. To further eliminate the influence of reconstructed anomalies, we resort to a low-rank representation method.

For $\hat{\mathbf{H}}$, reconstructed by the background estimation model, the background $\hat{\mathbf{B}}$ remains a low-rank property and has similar subspace structure as $\mathbf{B}$. On the other hand, pixels not obeying background distribution, have a low probability and account for only a very small part of the entire scene, indicating they have a sparse property. Thus, the reconstructed image can be regarded as corrupted background.

Dictionary construction is a key aspect of LRR. K observed background training samples are chosen to form the dictionary, depicted by:

$$\mathbf{X}_O = \left[\mathbf{x}_1, \mathbf{x}_2, \ldots, \mathbf{x}_K\right]. \tag{23.3}$$

However, the training data only characterize the background partially, which means the dictionary is incomplete. To satisfy the assumption that $\hat{\mathbf{B}}$ and $\mathbf{B}$ share a similar subspace structure, we comprehensively take the hidden learned data into consideration, denoted by $\mathbf{X}_H$. We refer to this new LRR method as dictionary-based LRR. The reconstructed $\hat{\mathbf{H}}$ can be formulated by the linear combination of the basis in the dictionary $\mathbf{X} = [\mathbf{X}_O, \mathbf{X}_H]$ with the weight matrix $\mathbf{Z}$. To find the one with the lowest rank from all representation candidates, an optimization problem is formulated as:

$$\begin{aligned} &\min \|\mathbf{Z}\|_* + \lambda \|\mathbf{E}\|_1 \\ &\text{s.t.} \hat{\mathbf{H}} = \mathbf{XZ} + \mathbf{E} \end{aligned} \tag{23.4}$$

where $\|\cdot\|_*$ and $\|\cdot\|_1$ denote the nuclear norm and the ℓ_1-norm of a matrix, respectively. Obviously, $\hat{\mathbf{H}}$ is decomposed into two parts, low-rank part $\mathbf{XZ}$ and sparse part $\mathbf{E}$, and these two parts are assumed to contribute to anomaly detection. The former provides a more accurate and more reliable difference with $\mathbf{H}$ compared to $\hat{\mathbf{H}}$. As shown in Figure 23.1, we need to address the problem of dictionary construction and make Eq. (23.4) convex with a weakly supervised background estimation model.

23.2.1 Weakly Supervised Background Learning

Background serves as a training set to encourage a weakly supervised background estimation model. In the following, we elaborate on how the background training data is obtained and how the background estimation model is established.

23.2.1.1 Unsupervised Background and Anomaly Selection

Searching pseudo-anomaly $\mathbf{A}_s$ and pseudo-background $\mathbf{B}_s$ is an essential task for further background learning and dictionary construction. Owing to the lack of priori knowledge, this task should be implemented in an unsupervised manner. Considering an intuitive but powerful assumption that anomalies in HSIs usually appear as small-size objects and are substantially different from the background, a joint filtering method is designed to separate background and anomalies initially.

As depicted in Figure 23.2, the joint filter comprises an attribute filter and a guided filter. The pixels with specific area properties or distinct spectral signatures are first detected with attribute filtering. Then, the result is refined with guided filtering to make full use of the spatial correlations among adjacent pixels. It is worth noting that principal component analysis (PCA) is applied to reduce the complexity of the joint filtering. With the 2-D image processed by PCA being denoted as $\mathbf{f}$, the joint filtering can be formulated as:

$$\hat{\mathbf{f}} = AG\{\mathbf{f}, \mathbf{g}, \alpha, \gamma, \omega, \theta\} \tag{23.5}$$

where $\hat{\mathbf{f}}$ is the initial detection result, AG symbolizes the joint filtering process, α and γ are the attribute thinnings and thickenings, respectively, and ω and θ are two parameters that control the smoothness of the guided filtering output. In our proposed method, the guided filter works in a self-guided case, in other words, the guidance image $\mathbf{g}$ is equal to $\mathbf{f}$.

The initial detection output is a matrix ranging from 0 to 1. It is difficult to separate background and anomaly precisely with only one threshold. To guarantee the validity of classification, a dual-threshold manner is applied. Concretely, a smaller threshold is configured to guarantee anomalies are rejected when background samples are searched. On the contrary, a greater one is set for anomaly searching. With the threshold-segmented images $\mathbf{S}^1$ and $\mathbf{S}^2$, anomaly selection and background selection are formulated as:

$$\begin{aligned} \mathbf{A}_s &= \left\{\mathbf{h}_{ij} \mid s_{ij}^1 = 1 \rightarrow (i,j)\right\} \\ \mathbf{B}_s &= \left\{\mathbf{h}_{ij} \mid s_{ij}^2 = 0 \rightarrow (i,j)\right\} \end{aligned} \tag{23.6}$$

where $s_{ij}^i \in \{1,0\}$ is the element at position (i, j) in $\mathbf{S}^i$.

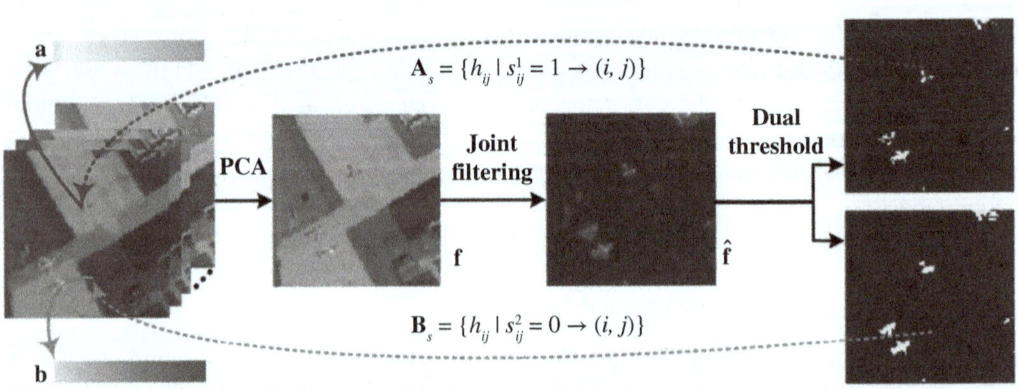

Figure 23.2 Procedure of initially searching anomaly and background in HSIs.

23.2.1.2 Background Estimation Model Establishment

$\mathbf{B}_s = [\mathbf{b}_{s1}, \mathbf{b}_{s2}, ..., \mathbf{b}_{st}]$ is fed into a spectral constrained Adversarial Autoencoder (AAE) network to encourage a background estimation model which can generate realistic-looking spectral vectors when input is background, whereas to synthesize a low-quality estimation when input is anomaly. As shown in Figure 4.1, AAE consists of three sub-neural networks: an encoder, a decoder and a discriminator functioning together to learn background spectral characteristics. The activation function of each architecture is the following sigmoid function:

$$f(x) = \frac{1}{1 + \exp(-x)}. \tag{23.7}$$

The whole training procedure is composed of the reconstruction stage and the adversarial stage, supplementing each other, which are elaborated below.

The reconstruction stage is to minimize the deviation between a reconstruction from the initial value as much as possible, carried out by an autoencoder consisting of encoder and decoder. Let $\mathbf{I}$ denote the hidden representation of $\mathbf{B}_s$ whereas $\hat{\mathbf{B}}_s$ is the reconstructed background. Hence, encoding process and decoding process can be expressed as:

$$\begin{aligned} \mathbf{I} &= f(\mathbf{W}^e\mathbf{B}_s + \delta^e) \\ \hat{\mathbf{B}}_s &= f\left(\mathbf{W}^d\mathbf{I} + \delta^d\right) \end{aligned} \tag{23.8}$$

respectively, where $\mathbf{W}^e$ and δ^e signify the weight matrix and the bias vector of the encoding layers, and $\mathbf{W}^d$ and δ^d function in the decoding procedure. Given the inherent spectral characteristics of spectral vectors, spectral distance (SD) based on the spectral angle mapper (SAM) is employed, instead of the common ℓ_2-norm or MSE, to constrain the input and renewed spectral vectors as:

$$\mathcal{L}_r = \frac{1}{\pi}\arccos\left(\frac{\mathbf{B}_s\hat{\mathbf{B}}_s}{\| \mathbf{B}_s \|_2 \| \hat{\mathbf{B}}_s \|_2}\right). \tag{23.9}$$

In the adversarial stage, as a generator G, the encoder concentrates on mapping the high-dimension HSI into a low-dimensional latent space, revealing the essential characteristics of the original spectral space. Adversarial training is introduced to impose the priori latent distribution $p_{\tilde{z}} \sim \mathcal{N}(0,1)$ to the latent feature z, and G intends to fool latent discriminator D with $z \sim q(z)$. Simultaneously, D strives to distinguish $z \sim q(z)$ from $\tilde{z} \sim p(\tilde{z})$ sampled from the priori distribution. Therefore, this forms a new optimization problem as:

$$\min_G \max_D \mathbb{E}[\log D(\mathcal{N}(0,1))] + \mathbb{E}[\log(1 - D(z)]. \tag{23.10}$$

With the two optimization objectives mentioned above, encoder, decoder and D are jointly learned for hundreds of epochs until the spectral constrained network converges. Then a background estimation model $\mathbf{\Phi}$ with parameter $\Theta = \{\mathbf{W}^e, \delta^e, \mathbf{W}^d, \delta^d\}$ is resulted in.

For a given $\mathbf{H} = [\mathbf{A}, \mathbf{B}] = \{\mathbf{h}_{ij}\}_{i=0, j=0}^{i=M, j=N}$, it is reconstructed by:

$$\hat{\mathbf{H}} = \mathbf{\Phi}(\mathbf{H} \mid \Theta) \tag{23.11}$$

Here, $\hat{\mathbf{H}} = [\hat{\mathbf{A}}, \hat{\mathbf{B}}]$. Considering the powerful background reconstruction capability of $\mathbf{\Phi}$, the distribution of $\hat{\mathbf{B}}$ approaches the real background distribution, whereas the exclusive features of anomaly are deprived of in $\hat{\mathbf{A}}$. This distinctive reconstruction is illustrated in Figure 23.3. Obviously, anomalies in HSIs are not well recovered, while background pixels are reconstructed with less reconstruction error. Then the anomalies can be detected by differencing $\hat{\mathbf{H}}$ and $\mathbf{H}$.

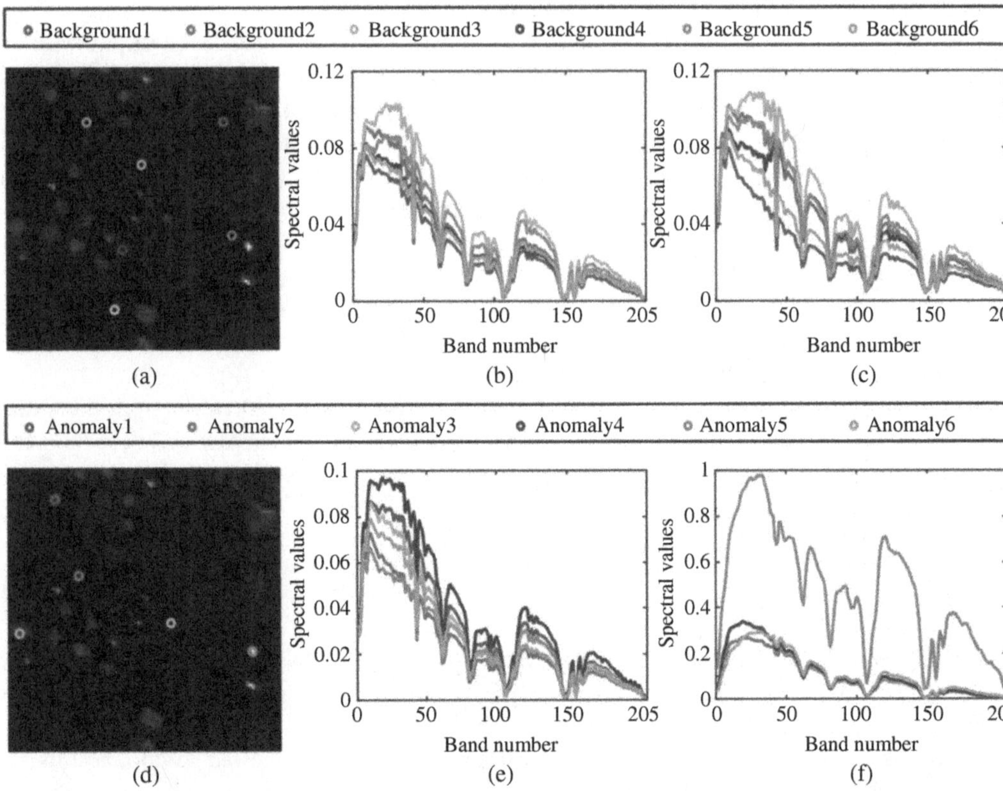

Figure 23.3 Procedure of initially searching anomaly and background in HSIs. (a) Locations of background samples in the original HSI. (b) Spectral curves of background samples in the original HSI. (c) Spectral curves of background samples in the reconstructed HSI. (d) Locations of anomalies in the original HSI. (e) Spectral curves of anomalies in the original HSI. (f) Spectral curves of anomalies in the reconstructed HSI.

23.2.2 Dictionary-based Low-rank Representation

The unsupervised background annotation introduces biases into the predict function $\mathbf{\Phi}$. In other words, some anomalies are reconstructed making against discriminative reconstruction. Based on the assumption that $\hat{\mathbf{A}}$ is sparse and $\hat{\mathbf{B}}$ has a low-rank property, further decomposition of $\hat{\mathbf{H}}$ with a dictionary-based LRR can tackle this issue. In the following, we elaborate on how the dictionary is constructed and how the dictionary-based low-rank representation problem is solved.

23.2.2.1 Dictionary Construction

On account of small size and low probability of anomalies, only a small fraction of spectral vectors in $\hat{\mathbf{H}}$ disobey the background distribution. Therefore $\hat{\mathbf{H}}$ is described as corrupted background. The complete dictionary includes observed training candidates and the learned hidden candidates.

Observed Candidate Selection: The background estimation model is carried out based on the background knowledge embodied in training set $\mathbf{B}_s = [\mathbf{b}_{s1}, \mathbf{b}_{s2}, ..., \mathbf{b}_{st}]$. Compared with the spectral vectors which do not participate in model learning, the reconstruction of $\mathbf{B}_s$ is expected to emulate the original training samples.

To form the observed training part $\mathbf{X}_O$, K most quintessential background spectral vectors are chosen according to threshold γ:

$$\mathbf{X}_O = \{\mathbf{b}_{si} \mid \| \mathbf{b}_{si} - \mathbf{a} \|_2 > \gamma\} \tag{23.12}$$

where $\mathbf{a}$ is an artificial anomaly calculated by taking the average of the vectors in $\mathbf{A}_s$.

Hidden Candidate Selection: Typically, the dictionary consists only of observed training data. However, the complexity and diversity of HSIs indicate that this strategy may not be optimal. By analysing and learning essential characteristics and immanency of the training data, the background estimation model can reconstruct the background samples including those excluded in the training set, i.e., the hidden learned data. These data contain some unique background features, providing a different perspective from the training data to depict the background. For a comprehensive description, both components are embraced in our dictionary construction. So, the dictionary-based LRR in this paper can be regarded as an "enhanced" LRR and behaves better than the LRR with an incomplete dictionary including only the observed training data.

The hidden learned candidates are searched according to the similarity map $\mathbf{P} = \left\{p_{ij}\right\}_{i=1,j=1}^{i=M,j=N}$, where p_{ij} is the spectral vector angle between $\mathbf{h}_{ij}$ and $\hat{\mathbf{h}}_{ij}$, calculated by:

$$p_{ij} = \frac{1}{\pi}\arccos\left(\frac{\mathbf{h}_{ij}^T\hat{\mathbf{h}}_{ij}}{\| \mathbf{h}_{ij} \|_2 \| \hat{\mathbf{h}}_{ij} \|_2}\right). \tag{23.13}$$

Here, p_{ij} varies from 0 to 1. As p_{ij} grows, the disparity between $\mathbf{h}_{ij}$ and $\hat{\mathbf{h}}_{ij}$ increases. When p_{ij} is small and $\mathbf{h}_{ij}$ is not involved in training set $\mathbf{B}_s$, and $\hat{\mathbf{h}}_{ij}$ is supposed to be reconstructed on learned knowledge. An appropriate threshold is configured to a binary $\mathbf{P}$, and the hidden learned candidates are selected by:

$$\mathbf{X}_H = \left\{\mathbf{h}_{ij} \mid p_{ij} = 0, \mathbf{h}_{ij} \notin (\mathbf{b}_{s1}, ..., \mathbf{b}_{st})\right\}. \tag{23.14}$$

Together, $\mathbf{X}_O$ and $\mathbf{X}_H$ offer the following LRR for a complete dictionary $\mathbf{X}$ to represent $\hat{\mathbf{H}}$.

23.2.2.2 Low-rank Representation

As stated earlier, it is a non-neglectful fact that the model is built in a weakly supervised way. To minimize the influence of reconstructed anomalies, LRR is implemented concerning the dictionary built in the last section.

In essence, LRR can be derived as the convex optimization problem mentioned in Eq. (23.4). The skinny Singular Value Decomposition (SVD) of column-stacked matrix $[\mathbf{X}_O, \mathbf{X}_H]$ is supposed to be:

$$[\mathbf{X}_O, \mathbf{X}_H] = \mathbf{U\Sigma V}^T \tag{23.15}$$

where matrix $\mathbf{V}$ can be partitioning by rows as $[\mathbf{V}_O; \mathbf{V}_H]$. It is easily to be derived as:

$$\mathbf{X}_O = \mathbf{U\Sigma V}_O^T; \qquad \mathbf{X}_H = \mathbf{U\Sigma V}_H^T. \tag{23.16}$$

Similarly, $\mathbf{Z}$ can be stacked vertically by two matrices, i.e., $\mathbf{Z} = [\mathbf{Z}_{O|H}; \mathbf{Z}_{H|O}]$. According to Eq. (23.16), the constraint of Eq. (23.4) can be rewritten as:

$$\begin{aligned}\hat{\mathbf{H}} &= [\mathbf{X}_O, \mathbf{X}_H]\mathbf{Z} + \mathbf{E}\\ &= \mathbf{X}_O\mathbf{Z}_{O|H} + \mathbf{X}_H\mathbf{Z}_{H|O} + \mathbf{E}\\ &= \mathbf{X}_O\mathbf{Z}_{O|H} + \mathbf{X}_H\mathbf{V}_H\mathbf{V}_O^T + \mathbf{E}\\ &= \mathbf{X}_O\mathbf{Z}_{O|H} + \mathbf{U\Sigma V}_H^T\mathbf{V}_H\mathbf{V}_O^T + \mathbf{E}\\ &= \mathbf{X}_O\mathbf{Z}_{O|H} + \mathbf{U\Sigma V}_H^T\mathbf{V}_H\Sigma^{-1}\mathbf{U}^T\mathbf{X}_O + \mathbf{E}\end{aligned} \tag{23.17}$$

Let $\mathbf{L}_{H|O} = \mathbf{U}\boldsymbol{\Sigma}\mathbf{V}_H^T\mathbf{V}_H\Sigma^{-1}\mathbf{U}^T$. The constraint can be described by a simple formulation as:

$$\hat{\mathbf{H}} = \mathbf{X}_O\mathbf{Z}_{O|H} + \mathbf{L}_{H|O}\mathbf{X}_O + \mathbf{E} \tag{23.18}$$

Given $\mathbf{X}_O$ and $\mathbf{X}_H$, the second term represented by $\mathbf{C}$ is fixed. Eq. (23.18) can be rewritten as:

$$\hat{\mathbf{H}} - \mathbf{C} = \mathbf{X}_O\mathbf{Z}_{O|H} + \mathbf{E} \tag{23.19}$$

Let $\mathbf{H}' = \hat{\mathbf{H}} - \mathbf{C}$, $\mathbf{X}' = \mathbf{X}_O$, and $\mathbf{Z}' = \mathbf{Z}_{O\,|\,H}$. Eq. (4.4) is equivalent to:

$$\begin{aligned} &\min \parallel \mathbf{Z}'\parallel_* + \lambda \parallel \mathbf{E}\parallel_1 \\ &\text{s.t.}\mathbf{H}' = \mathbf{X}'\mathbf{Z}' + \mathbf{E}. \end{aligned} \tag{23.20}$$

Compared with the original optimization problem described in Eq. (23.4), Eq. (23.20) can be executed with less computation. Specifically, in Eq. (23.20), simple matrix addition and subtraction are conducted to obtain $\mathbf{Z}'$ with smaller size, avoiding iterative optimization of a huge matrix. Depending on the purpose and environment, the optimization method of the problem depicted by Eq. (23.20) is accordingly different. In this paper, we choose the Augmented Lagrange Multiplier (ALM) method and introduce an auxiliary variable $\mathbf{J}$ as a split variable to replace $\mathbf{Z}'$. Therefore, the objective function becomes:

$$\begin{aligned} \min_{\mathbf{Z}',\mathbf{E},\mathbf{J},\mathbf{Y}_1,\mathbf{Y}_2} \quad & \parallel \mathbf{J}\parallel_* + \lambda \parallel \mathbf{E}\parallel_1 \\ & + \mathrm{tr}\left[\mathbf{Y}_1^T(\mathbf{H}' - \mathbf{X}'\mathbf{Z}' - \mathbf{E})\right] + \mathrm{tr}\left[\mathbf{Y}_2^T(\mathbf{Z}' - \mathbf{J})\right] \\ & + \frac{\mu}{2}\left(\parallel \mathbf{H}' - \mathbf{X}'\mathbf{Z}' - \mathbf{E}\parallel_F^2 + \parallel \mathbf{Z}' - \mathbf{J}\parallel_F^2\right) \end{aligned} \tag{23.21}$$

where tr[·] denotes the trace of a matrix, λ is the tradeoff parameter and $\mu > 0$ is the penalty parameter. The above problem is unconstrained and can be minimized for $\mathbf{J}$, $\mathbf{Z}'$ and $\mathbf{E}$, alternatingly, by fixing other variables, and then updating the Lagrange multipliers $\mathbf{Y}_1$ and $\mathbf{Y}_1$.

J step: Fix $\mathbf{Z}'$, $\mathbf{E}$ and update $\mathbf{J}$. The objective function with respect to $\mathbf{J}$ can be written as:

$$\begin{aligned} &\min_{\mathbf{J}} \parallel \mathbf{J}\parallel_* + \mathrm{tr}\left[\mathbf{Y}_2^T(\mathbf{Z}' - \mathbf{J})\right] + \frac{\mu}{2}\parallel \mathbf{Z}' - \mathbf{J}\parallel_F^2 \\ &= \min_{\mathbf{J}} \frac{1}{\mu}\parallel \mathbf{J}\parallel_* + \frac{1}{2}\parallel \mathbf{J} - \left(\mathbf{Z}' + \frac{\mathbf{Y}_2}{\mu}\right)\parallel_F^2 \end{aligned} \tag{23.22}$$

and can be solved by Lemma 3.2 in [38].

$\mathbf{Z}'$ step: Fix $\mathbf{J}$, $\mathbf{E}$ and update $\mathbf{Z}'$. The objective function with respect to $\mathbf{Z}'$ can be written as:

$$\begin{aligned} \min_{\mathbf{Z}'} \quad & \mathrm{tr}\left[\mathbf{Y}_1^T(\mathbf{H}' - \mathbf{X}'\mathbf{Z}' - \mathbf{E})\right] + \mathrm{tr}\left[\mathbf{Y}_2^T(\mathbf{Z}' - \mathbf{J})\right] \\ & + \frac{\mu}{2}\left(\parallel \mathbf{H}' - \mathbf{X}'\mathbf{Z}' - \mathbf{E}\parallel_F^2 + \parallel \mathbf{Z}' - \mathbf{J}\parallel_F^2\right) \end{aligned}$$

$$\mathbf{Z}' = \left(\mathbf{X}'^T\mathbf{X}' + \mathbf{I}\right)^{-1}\left[\frac{1}{\mu}\left(\mathbf{X}'^T\mathbf{Y}_1 - \mathbf{Y}_2\right) + \mathbf{X}'^T\mathbf{H}' - \mathbf{X}'^T\mathbf{E} + \mathbf{J}\right] \tag{23.23}$$

where $\mathbf{I}$ is an identity matrix.

E step: Fix $\mathbf{J}$,$\mathbf{Z}'$ and update $\mathbf{E}$. The objective function with respect to $\mathbf{E}$ can be written as:

$$\begin{aligned} &\min_{\mathbf{E}} \quad \lambda \parallel \mathbf{E}\parallel_1 + \mathrm{tr}\left[\mathbf{Y}_1^T(\mathbf{H}' - \mathbf{X}'\mathbf{Z}' - \mathbf{E})\right] \\ &\qquad + \frac{\mu}{2}\parallel \mathbf{H}' - \mathbf{X}'\mathbf{Z}' - \mathbf{E}\parallel_F^2 \\ &= \min_{\mathbf{E}} \frac{\lambda}{\mu}\parallel \mathbf{E}\parallel_1 + \frac{1}{2}\parallel \mathbf{E} - \left(\mathbf{H}' - \mathbf{X}'\mathbf{Z}' - \mu^{-1}\mathbf{Y}_1\right)\parallel_F^2. \end{aligned} \tag{23.24}$$

J step is solved via the Singular Value Thresholding (SVT) operator, while **E** step is solved by the shrinkage operator. When the convergence conditions:

$$\begin{aligned} &\| \mathbf{H}' - \mathbf{X}'\mathbf{Z}' - \mathbf{E}\|_\infty < \varepsilon \\ &\quad \| \mathbf{Z}' - \mathbf{J}\|_\infty < \varepsilon \end{aligned} \tag{23.25}$$

are satisfied, the lowest-rank coefficient matrix $\mathbf{Z}'$ is obtained. Here, $\| \cdot \|_\infty$ denotes the infinity norm and $\varepsilon = 10^{-3}$. According to Eq. (23.4), the reconstructed $\hat{\mathbf{H}} \in \mathbb{R}^{M \times N \times L}$ is decomposed into a low-rank background matrix **XZ** and a sparse anomaly matrix **E** which have an equal size to $\hat{\mathbf{H}}$. According to Eq. (23.19), the former is obtained by:

$$\mathbf{XZ} = \mathbf{X}'\mathbf{Z}' + \mathbf{C}. \tag{23.26}$$

With the aid of this decomposition, the anomalies undesirably reconstructed by the weakly supervised model are further separated from the background. It should be emphasized that **XZ** creates a greater gap than $\hat{\mathbf{H}}$ with **H** at the location of anomalies. The Euclidean Distance between **XZ** and **H** is measured to generate the low-rank part, identifying anomalies with fewer misses. To fully exploit the result of LRR, the sparse part is obtained by summing along each column of **E** and reformating into the same spatial dimension of a single image in HSI. By adding and multiplying these two parts, we can get two anomaly images $\mathbf{D}_1$ and $\mathbf{D}_2$. Then the final detection map $\mathbf{D}_F$ is obtained by transforming $\mathbf{D}_1$, $\mathbf{D}_2$ and initial detection result $\hat{\mathbf{f}}$ nonlinearly:

$$\mathbf{D}_F = \mathbf{D}_1 \left(1 - e^{\beta_1 \mathbf{D}_2}\right)\left(1 - e^{\beta_2 \hat{\mathbf{f}}}\right) \tag{23.27}$$

where β_1 and β_2 are positive parameters adjusting the shape of the nonlinear function.

23.2.3 Experiments of WSLRR

The visual detection results for four hyperspectral images (HSIs) are shown in Figure 23.4, accompanied by corresponding AUC values listed in Table 23.1. In the case of the Pavia data set (Figure 23.4a), the visual inspection reveals that anomalies are difficult to detect using RX [7],

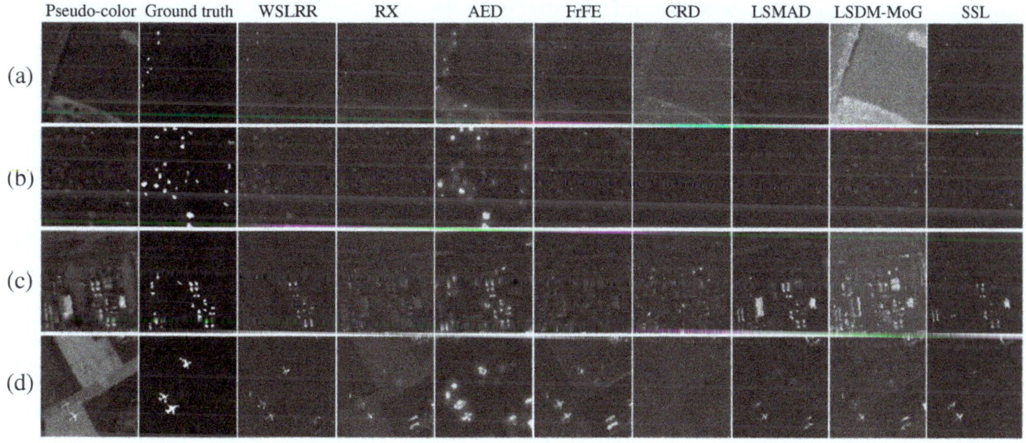

Figure 23.4 Scene images, ground truth maps, and detection maps of the compared methods. (a) Pavia. (b) LA-1. (c) LA-2. (d) San Diego.

Table 23.1 AUC values of the compared methods for experimental data sets.

	AUC values of (P_D, P_F)							
HSIs	**WSLRR**	**RX**	**AED**	**FrFE**	**CRD**	**LSMAD**	**LSDM-MoG**	**SSL**
Pavia	**0.9978**	0.9533	0.9950	0.9501	0.9009	0.9626	0.8827	0.9868
LA-1	**0.9962**	0.9886	0.9911	0.9813	0.9516	0.9835	0.9825	**0.9963**
LA-2	**0.9941**	0.9693	0.9845	0.9653	0.9304	0.9496	0.9511	0.9862
San Diego	**0.9931**	0.9404	0.9849	0.9784	0.6629	0.9763	0.9226	0.9849
Average	**0.9953**	0.9629	0.9887	0.9688	0.8615	0.9680	0.9347	0.9886
	AUC values of (P_F, τ)							
HSIs	**WSLRR**	**RX**	**AED**	**FrFE**	**CRD**	**LSMAD**	**LSDM-MoG**	**SSL**
Pavia	0.0008	0.0233	0.0438	0.0251	0.1124	0.0049	0.0687	**0.0004**
LA-1	0.0016	0.0114	0.0307	0.0117	**0.0012**	0.0014	0.0089	0.0017
LA-2	**0.0017**	0.0437	0.0306	0.0273	0.0445	0.0335	0.1839	0.0067
San Diego	**0.0023**	0.0589	0.0333	0.0486	0.0589	0.0140	0.0652	0.0063
Average	**0.0016**	0.0343	0.0346	0.0281	0.0134	0.0135	0.0817	0.0038

Attribute and Edge-preserving filtering-based anomaly Detection (AED) [85], Fractional Fourier Entropy (FrFE) [86], CRD [20], and LSDM-MoG due to interference from background features like the bridge [23]. Although LSMAD and SSL demonstrate superior background suppression [22], they struggle with accurately locating all anomalies, resulting in lower AUC values for (PD, PF) (0.9626 and 0.9868). Conversely, WSLRR achieves the highest AUC value of (PD, PF) (0.9978) by accurately locating anomalies while maintaining a low AUC value of (PF, τ) (0.0008).

Moving to the LA-1 data set (Figure 23.4b), AED shows good detection performance but fails to outline anomaly shapes accurately. RX, FrFE, and LSDM-MoG mistakenly detect background structures as anomalies, while CRD and LSMAD miss some anomaly information. SSL exhibits numerical advantages but lacks visual effectiveness. In contrast, WSLRR accurately identifies and outlines all anomalies, resulting in a high AUC value of (PD, PF) of 0.9962 while maintaining a low AUC value of (PF, τ) comparable to CRD and LSMAD.

For the LA-2 data set (Figure 23.4c), except for WSLRR, other detection maps exhibit cluttered backgrounds. WSLRR outperforms other methods significantly in terms of AUC values for (PD, PF) and (PF, τ), surpassing them by more than 0.975% and 93.773%, respectively.

In the San Diego data set (Figure 23.4d), WSLRR accurately locates airplanes with correct shapes, outperforming other methods with AUC values of 0.9931 and 0.0023. RX, FrFE, CRD, and LSDM-MoG fail to separate anomalous pixels from the background, while AED, LSMAD, and SSL retain the background at the expense of missing some anomalies.

Overall, WSLRR produces visually closest results to ground truth compared to other detectors, capable of detecting anomalies with different sizes and structural information. Numerically, for all scenes, the AUC values of (PD, PF) and (PF, τ) of WSLRR closely approximate the ideal values 1 and 0.

23.3 Weakly Supervised Hyperspectral Target Detection (BLTSC)

A weakly-supervised adversarial autoencoder, subject to a target suppression constraint, is proposed in this work for target detection. Due to scarce target samples, our method resorts to background learning, providing a new perspective to target detection. As depicted in Figure 23.5, the proposed background learning based on target suppression constraint (BLTSC) method consists of two main operations. First, the network is trained based on BLTSC to obtain unique background representation. Then, pinpoint targets with the trained model.

The BLTSC is adversarially trained on background samples only to reconstruct background as accurately as possible. Let the background training set be denoted as $\mathbf{H}_B$, which can be represented as $\mathbf{H}_B = [h_1 h_2 ... h_n]$. After training the network with abundant background samples, our approach can approximate background distribution. Then we test the trained model with a HSI, denoted by $\mathbf{H} \in \mathbb{R}^{M \times N \times L}$, and yield a discriminative reconstruction. The HSI can be divided into background spectra set $\mathbf{B}$ and target spectra set $\mathbf{T}$:

$$\begin{aligned} \mathbf{B} &= \left[\mathbf{b}_1^1, ..., \mathbf{b}_1^L, \mathbf{b}_2^1, ..., \mathbf{b}_2^L, \mathbf{b}_p^1, ..., \mathbf{b}_p^L\right] \\ \mathbf{T} &= \left[\mathbf{t}_1^1, ..., \mathbf{t}_1^L, \mathbf{t}_2^1, ..., \mathbf{t}_2^L, \mathbf{t}_q^L, ..., \mathbf{y}_q^q\right] \end{aligned} \tag{23.28}$$

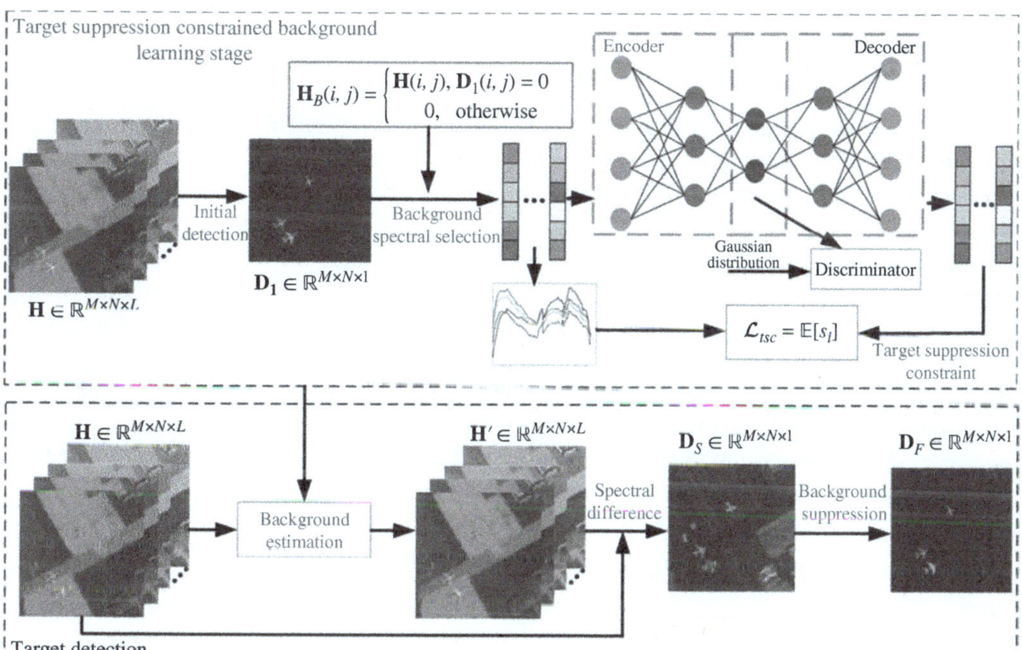

Figure 23.5 Schematic of the proposed BLTSC-based target detection method.

where $p + q = M \times N$. Similarly, the reconstructed HSI $\mathbf{H}' \in \mathbb{R}^{M\times N\times L}$ can also be divided into two components, reconstruced background $\mathbf{B}'$ and reconstructed target $\mathbf{T}'$:

$$\begin{aligned}\mathbf{B}' &= \left[\mathbf{b}_1'^1, \dots, \mathbf{b}_1'^L, \mathbf{b}_2'^1, \dots, \mathbf{b}_2'^L, \mathbf{b}_p'^1, \dots, \mathbf{b}_p'^L\right] \\ \mathbf{T}' &= \left[\mathbf{t}_1'^1, \dots, \mathbf{t}_1'^L, \mathbf{t}_2'^1, \dots, \mathbf{t}_2'^L, \mathbf{t}_q'^L, \dots, \mathbf{y}_q'^L\right].\end{aligned} \tag{23.29}$$

The trained model concentrates on reconstructing background, therefore, discriminative reconstruction is performed on the background and target samples. In our approach, Leaky Relu acts as the activation function:

$$f(x) = \begin{cases} x, & \text{if } x > 0 \\ \lambda x, & \text{if } x \le 0 \end{cases} \tag{23.30}$$

where $\lambda \sim U(l, u)$, $l < u$ and $u \in [0, 1)$. The background spectrum $\mathbf{b}_i$ and target spectrum $\mathbf{t}_i$ are considered as input, whereas $\mathbf{b}_i'$ and $\mathbf{t}_i'$ are the output. $\mathbf{l}_i^b$ denotes the hidden representation of the background spectrum $\mathbf{b}_i$. Hence the encoding and decoding process for background samples can be expressed as:

$$\begin{aligned}\mathbf{l}_i^b &= f(\mathbf{W}_h\mathbf{b}_i + \mathbf{a}_h) \\ \mathbf{b}_i' &= f\left(\mathbf{W}_o\mathbf{l}_i^b + \mathbf{a}_o\right)\end{aligned} \tag{23.31}$$

respectively. Similarly, for targets, the hidden representation of $\mathbf{t}_i$ is denoted by $\mathbf{l}_i^t$. Thus, the encoding and decoding process become:

$$\begin{aligned}\mathbf{l}_i^t &= f(\mathbf{W}_h\mathbf{t}_i + \mathbf{a}_h) \\ \mathbf{t}_i' &= f\left(\mathbf{W}_o\mathbf{l}_i^t + \mathbf{a}_o\right)\end{aligned} \tag{23.32}$$

respectively, where $\mathbf{W}_h$ and $\mathbf{a}_h$ denote the weight matrix and bias term of encoding layers, respectively, while $\mathbf{W}_o$ and $\mathbf{a}_o$ represent the weight matrix and bias term of decoding layers, respectively. With the optimization goal mentioned in Eq. (23.40), thousands of epochs are conducted until AAE converges. Then the parameters are fixed and used to reconstruct $\mathbf{H}'$.

The network, only trained on background samples, is expected to fail to reconstruct target samples as it is never trained on such examples. As illustrated in Figure 23.1, targets in HSIs are not well recovered, while background pixels are reconstructed with less reconstruction error, which indicates the model enhances discrimination between target and background with background learning. Additionally, a target suppression constraint is imposed on the training procedure to approximate background distribution as closely as possible. In contrast to the original HSI, the reconstructed one has an extremely similar background and more distinguishing target, which indicates that our model obtains a discriminative feature by learning the distribution of the training set. Then $\mathbf{H}$ and $\mathbf{H}'$ are compared pixel by pixel. The output $\mathbf{D}_S$ can be described as $\mathbf{D}_S = [\mathbf{d}_{s1}, \mathbf{d}_{s2}, \cdots \mathbf{d}_{sM\times N}]$, where $\mathbf{d}_{si}$ is the spectral distance between the ith pixel in $\mathbf{H}$ and $\mathbf{H}'$, calculated by:

$$\begin{aligned}\mathbf{d}_{si} &= \cos^{-1}\left(\frac{\mathbf{h}_i^T\mathbf{h}_i'}{(\|\mathbf{h}_i\|)(\|\mathbf{h}_i'\|)}\right) \\ &= \cos^{-1}\left(\frac{\mathbf{h}_i^T\mathbf{h}_i'}{\sqrt{(\mathbf{h}_i')^T\mathbf{h}_i'}\sqrt{\mathbf{h}_i^T\mathbf{h}_i)}}\right).\end{aligned} \tag{23.33}$$

Then, a distance map, containing distinguishable targets, is obtained.

23.3.1 Background Spectral Selection

A deep neural network architecture has shown to be highly capable of target detection based on massive volumes of training data. Targets are rare entities hence it is challenging to obtain their labels. Instead, background samples are far easier to acquire. With sufficient training samples, the model is capable to reconstruct background as realistically as possible and is conversely expected to have poor performance on target samples. During the training procedure, target suppression constraint is also imposed to aid AAE to learn more powerful background representation.

As noted, the motivation is to maximize the background reconstruction capability. The training set is only composed of background samples. In this work, the CEM is leveraged as a coarse detection approach to obtain the initial training set. Let the original HSI with L bands be denoted as $\mathbf{H} \in \mathbb{R}^{M\times N\times L}$, and the response of CEM filter is given by:

$$\begin{aligned}\mathbf{y} &= (\mathbf{w}^{*})^{T}\mathbf{H} \\ &= \frac{\mathbf{d}^{T}\mathbf{R}^{-1}}{\mathbf{d}\mathbf{R}^{-1}\mathbf{d}^{T}}\mathbf{H}\end{aligned} \tag{23.34}$$

where $\mathbf{R} = (1/N)\mathbf{H}\mathbf{H}^{T}$ represents the correlation matrix and $\mathbf{d}$ is a priori known target spectrum. By analyzing $\mathbf{D}_1 \in \mathbb{R}^{M\times N\times 1}$ reshaped from $\mathbf{y}$, we can locate background pixels roughly.

In the normalized initial detection result $\mathbf{D}_1$, the values of background and target incline to 0 and 1, respectively. To reject targets, a smaller threshold ϵ is configured to binary $\mathbf{D}_1$ while selecting background training samples by:

$$\mathbf{H}_D(i,j) = \begin{cases} \mathbf{H}(i,j), & \mathbf{D}_1(i,j) = 0 \\ 0, & \text{otherwise} \end{cases} \tag{23.35}$$

where $\mathbf{H}(i, j)$ represents the spectral vector at position (i, j). $\mathbf{H}_D$ is the collection of background samples selected from $\mathbf{H}$ according to $\mathbf{D}_1$. The background training set $\mathbf{H}_B = [h_1h_2 \ldots h_n]$ randomly samples 75% from $\mathbf{H}_D$.

23.3.2 Background Learning Based on Target Suppression Constraint

As mentioned above, the BLTSC aims to learn accurate background distribution. To achieve this, we propose to combine three losses (Adversarial, Target suppression constraint, Autoencoder), each of which contributes to better reconstruction. First, an adversarial loss for matching the distribution of the latent space with the priori distribution. Second, a target suppression constraint loss is adopted to ensure the network is only trained on background samples. Third, we evaluate performance with an autoencoder loss, which calculates the deviation between input samples and reconstructed output.

23.3.2.1 Adversarial Loss

AAE is known as a variant of Generative Adversarial Networks (GAN), which trains model in the adversarial regularization. AAE samples from the priori distribution to induce $q(\mathbf{z})$ to match $p(\mathbf{z})$. Different distributions of $q(\mathbf{z})$ will result in different kinds of models for various tasks. Each feature of $\mathbf{z}$ is excepted to be independent of each other and obey the known priori distribution $p(\mathbf{z})$. Inspired by existing anomaly detection models, we choose Gaussian distribution as the priori distribution. Two components of AAE, discriminator D and generator G are jointly trained. D aims to distinguish the true samples from the fake ones generated by the generator. Ultimately, $\min_G \max_D \mathcal{L}_{\text{adv}}$ is achieved, formulated as:

$$\mathcal{L}_{\text{adv}} = \mathbb{E}[\log D(\mathcal{N}(0,1))] + \mathbb{E}[\log(1 - D(z)] \tag{23.36}$$

where z is the latent representation of the input. With the minimization of $\mathcal{L}_{adv}$, an accurate generative reproduction of background distribution is guaranteed.

23.3.2.2 Target Suppression Constraint Loss

It is inevitable that the background samples obtained from coarse detection are ambiguous. To reconstruct the background sufficiently and reliably, the target suppression constraint loss is leveraged. This loss act as a criterion to eliminate the threat of potential target spectrum during the training phase. The Spectral Angle Mapper (SAM) $\mathbf{s}_i$ for every reconstructed background spectrum $\mathbf{h}_i'$ and $\mathbf{d}$, is calculated, resulting in $\mathbf{S} = [s_1 s_2 \dots s_n]$, where s_i is defined as:

$$\begin{aligned} \mathbf{s}_i &= \cos^{-1}\left(\frac{\mathbf{h}_i'^T \mathbf{d}}{(\| \mathbf{h}_i' \|)(\| \mathbf{d} \|)}\right) \\ &= \cos^{-1}\left(\frac{\mathbf{h}_i'^T \mathbf{d}}{\sqrt{(\mathbf{d})^T \mathbf{d}}\sqrt{\mathbf{h}_i'^T \mathbf{h}_i'})}\right). \end{aligned} \tag{23.37}$$

A smaller $\mathbf{s}_i$ indicates that the $\mathbf{h}_i'$ is most likely reconstructed by a target sample, that is, in all probability, the $\mathbf{h}_i$ is a target sample. The mean of $\mathbf{s}_i$ which smaller than pre-set threshold $\boldsymbol{\delta}$ should work as the target suppression constraint loss, i.e.,

$$\mathcal{L}_{\text{tsc}} = \mathbb{E}[\mathbf{s}_i], \quad \text{where} \quad s_i < \boldsymbol{\delta}. \tag{23.38}$$

23.3.2.3 Autoencoder Loss

Additionally, we define autoencoder loss to minimize the reconstruction error between input data $\mathbf{H}_B$ and reconstructed data $\mathbf{H}_B'$, encouraging encoder and decoder to approximate the real distribution, as:

$$\mathcal{L}_{\text{error}} = \sum_i \| \mathbf{h}_i - \mathbf{h}_i' \|_2 \tag{23.39}$$

where $\mathbf{h}_i'$ is the reconstructed spectrum corresponding to the input spectrum $\mathbf{h}_i$.

Taken together, the total loss is formulated as:

$$\mathcal{L} = \mathcal{L}_{\text{adv}} - \mathcal{L}_{\text{tsc}} + \mathcal{L}_{\text{error}}. \tag{23.40}$$

These three losses perform their respective functions and work together to optimize the model.

23.3.2.4 Target Detection

To finally detect targets, each pixel value $\mathbf{d}_{si}$ is transformed by multipling a nonnegative number $q(y_i)$ based on output of the coarse detection $\mathbf{y}$ as:

$$\mathbf{d}_{fi} = q(y_i)\mathbf{d}_{si}. \tag{23.41}$$

The nonlinear function $q(x)$ is used to suppress the undesired background spectra while keeping the target spectra unchanged. Considering that the target pixels in the distance map are much greater than the background, $q(x)$ should be able to maintain large values and remove small ones. Here, the nonlinear suppression function is defined as:

$$q(x) = \begin{cases} 1 - e^{-\lambda x}, & x \geq 0 \\ 0, & x < 0 \end{cases} \tag{23.42}$$

where λ is a positive parameter to adjust the suppression performance. Finally, the detection result $\mathbf{D}_F = [\mathbf{d}_{f1}, \mathbf{d}_{f2}, \cdots \mathbf{d}_{fM\times N}]$ is obtained.

In summary, the BLTSC method is implemented by following steps. Firstly, coarse detection is utilized to obtain initial training data. Secondly, a background learning based AAE network is trained to optimize the three losses mentioned in Section 1.2. Then the trained model is tested by the entire HSI, and the final target detection is achieved after applying a nonlinear scaling factor.

23.3.3 Experiments of BLTSC

The performance of the proposed BLTSC-based hyperspectral target detection is evaluated and compared with four widely used target detection algorithms, i.e., CEM, hCEM, CSCR, and ACE. For the experimental data sets, the reference maps, i.e., ground truths and detection results are shown in Figure 23.6. Obviously, the proposed BLTSC-AAE outperforms according to visual inspection. Besides, our proposed method can adapt to any targets with different sizes. For the typical detection method such as CEM, it is challenging to detect targets precisely while suppressing background. The hCEM is superior to CEM in suppressing background, however, the targets are far

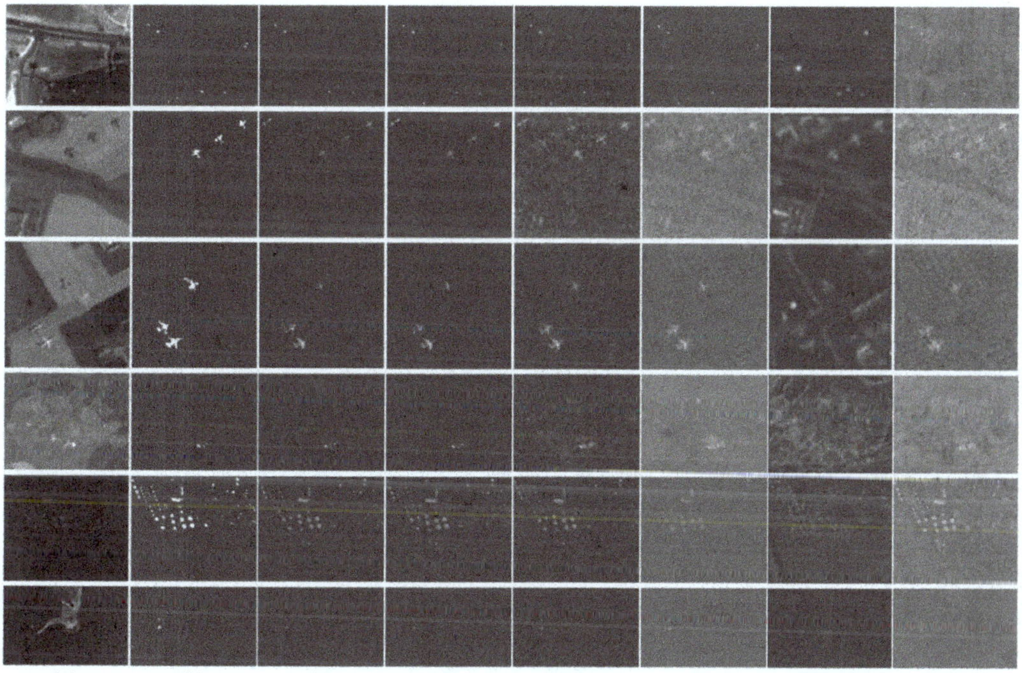

(a) (b) (c) (d) (e) (f) (g) (h)

Figure 23.6 Detection maps of different methods. (a) Scene images of HYDICE, two HSIs from San Diego, Cuprite, El Segundo, and Grand Isle data sets. (b) Reference map. (c) BLTSC-AAE. (d) BLTSC-SAE. (e) CEM. (f) hCEM. (g) CSCR. (h) ACE.

Table 23.2 AUC values of the compared methods for experimental data sets.

	AUC values of (P_D, P_F)					
HSIs	**BLTSC-AAE**	**BLTSC-SAE**	**CEM**	**hCEM**	**CSCR**	**ACE**
HYDICE	0.99433	0.99837	0.98243	**0.99976**	0.92561	0.98656
San Diego 1	**0.99340**	0.98831	0.96837	0.97915	0.92424	0.98177
San Diego2	**0.99566**	0.99518	0.95871	0.99241	0.86947	0.97327
Cuprite	**0.99995**	0.99992	0.99360	0.99986	0.70987	0.99982
El Segundo	**0.99193**	0.99124	0.99155	0.87147	0.71768	0.98726
Grand Isle	**0.99921**	0.99919	0.99881	0.99909	0.98363	0.99755
Average	**0.99575**	0.99543	0.98233	0.97362	0.85512	0.98770
	AUC values of (P_F, τ)					
HSIs	**BLTSC-AAE**	**BLTSC-SAE**	**CEM**	**hCEM**	**CSCR**	**ACE**
HYDICE	**0.00001**	0.00008	0.03010	0.00045	0.07600	0.24164
San Diego1	**0.00036**	0.00040	0.03570	0.27753	0.09832	0.34175
San Diego2	**0.00061**	0.00088	0.05881	0.00103	0.11221	0.19438
Cuprite	**0.00014**	0.00027	0.00124	0.29330	0.27443	0.33809
El Segundo	**0.00800**	0.01400	0.06732	0.17532	0.01607	0.26885
Grand Isle	**0.00066**	0.00081	0.01883	0.17575	0.01369	0.22916
Average	**0.00163**	0.00274	0.03718	0.15390	0.09845	0.26898

smaller and less than the background, which means some targets are easily rejected as uninterested information. CSCR and ACE cannot perform well for the targets containing structural information, and the background noise is unacceptable. On the contrary, the proposed BLTSC provides a more robust detection performance by expanding the difference between background and targets.

As reported in Table 23.2, the AUC scores of (PD, PF) and (PF, τ) of the proposed BLTSC-AAE method are approximate to ideal values 1 and 0 for all the scenes. The average AUC scores of (PD, PF) and (PF, τ) are 0.99575 and 0.00163, and they are superior to other methods numerically. Besides, to evaluate the compared methods more scientifically and rigorously, the nonlinear suppression mentioned in Section III-C is imposed on all the compared methods.

23.4 Rank-aware Hyperspectral Band Selection (R-GAN)

Let an HSI cube with B spectral bands and $N \times M$ pixels be defined as a three-way tensor $\mathcal{H} \in \mathbb{R}^{N \times M \times B}$. Let the (i, j, b)th entry be denoted as $\mathcal{H}_{ijb}$, and $\mathcal{H}(i, :, :)$, $\mathcal{H}(:, j, :)$, and $\mathcal{H}(:, :, b)$ represent the ith horizontal, jth lateral and bth frontal slice, respectively. Spatially, $\mathcal{H}$ consists of $N \times M$ spectral vectors $\mathcal{H} = \{\mathbf{h}_i\}_{i=1}^{N \times M}$. Along the band direction, the HSI can be regarded as a collection of B frontal slices, viz. band images $\mathcal{H} = \{\mathcal{H}(:, :, b)\}_{b=1}^{B}$. For convenience, it is abbreviated to $\mathcal{H} = \{\mathcal{H}_b\}_{b=1}^{B}$. In BS, $\mathcal{H}$ can be split into two categories, i.e., a remaining subset crammed with salient bands $\mathcal{I} = \{\mathcal{H}_{\mathcal{I}_1}, \mathcal{H}_{\mathcal{I}_2}, \cdots, \mathcal{H}_{\mathcal{I}_P}\} = \{\mathcal{I}_p\}_{p=1}^{P}$ and a subset, with redundancy and less saliency, to be discarded $\mathcal{U} = \{\mathcal{H}_{\mathcal{U}_1}, \mathcal{H}_{\mathcal{U}_2}, \cdots, \mathcal{H}_{\mathcal{U}_Q}\} = \{\mathcal{U}_q\}_{q=1}^{Q}$. Here, $\mathcal{I}_p$ and $\mathcal{U}_q$ are the indices of the pth selected and qth unselected band image, and $\mathcal{I} \cup \mathcal{U} = \mathcal{H}$, $\mathcal{I} \cap \mathcal{U} = \emptyset$, and $P + Q = B$.

In essence, BS involves two core issues: how many bands and which bands are preferred, i.e., to determine $\mathcal{I}_p$ and P. To solve these problems, BS is formulated as an optimization problem aiming to maximize the saliency of the reserved bands $\mathcal{I}$:

$$
\begin{aligned}
&\max_{\delta_b} \sum_{b=1}^{B} \delta_b \mathcal{R}(\mathcal{H}_b) \\
&\text{s.t.} \sum_{b=1}^{B} \delta_b = P
\end{aligned}
\tag{23.43}
$$

where δ_b is a pointer indicating if $\mathcal{H}_b$ is included in $\mathcal{I}$ ($\delta_b = 1$) or in $\mathcal{U}$ ($\delta_b = 0$). The saliency of each band is measured by $\mathcal{R}(\bullet)$. Solving the optimization problem in Eq. (23.43) is equivalent to removing Q redundant and less salient bands. Most of priori works calculate the related indicators and deteremine the saliency of band images using clustering, leading to the loss of global data properties and relevance between bands. In this paper, be virtue of the powerful ability of GAN in learning hierarchical and nonlinear features, a reasonable $\mathcal{R}(\bullet)$ is constructed. First, the original HSI $\mathcal{H}$ is fed into the network to generate the information-centralized latent feature $\mathcal{M} = \{\mathcal{M}_d\}_{d=1}^{D}$. Then, $\mathcal{M}$ is further refined in a rank-aware way consisting of two rank operations specific to current data. Finally, BS is induced by the refined feature $\mathcal{N} = \{\mathcal{N}_t\}_{t=1}^{T}$ through SSIM. SSIM captures the structural information which plays a pivotal role in human visual system (HSV). The larger SSIM is, the more similar $\mathcal{H}_b$ and informative $\mathcal{N}_t$ are, and the more salient $\mathcal{H}_b$ is. Then Eq. (23.43) can be reformulated as:

$$
\begin{aligned}
&\max_{\delta_b} \sum_{b=1}^{B} \sum_{t=1}^{T} \delta_b \text{SSIM}(\mathcal{N}_t, \mathcal{H}_b) \\
&\text{s.t.} \sum_{b=1}^{B} \delta_b = P
\end{aligned}
\tag{23.44}
$$

and the optimal band subset $\mathcal{I}$ can be obtained by:

$$\mathcal{I} = \{\mathcal{H}_b \mid \delta_b = 1\}.$$

The schematic of the proposed R-GAN is shown in Figure 23.7.

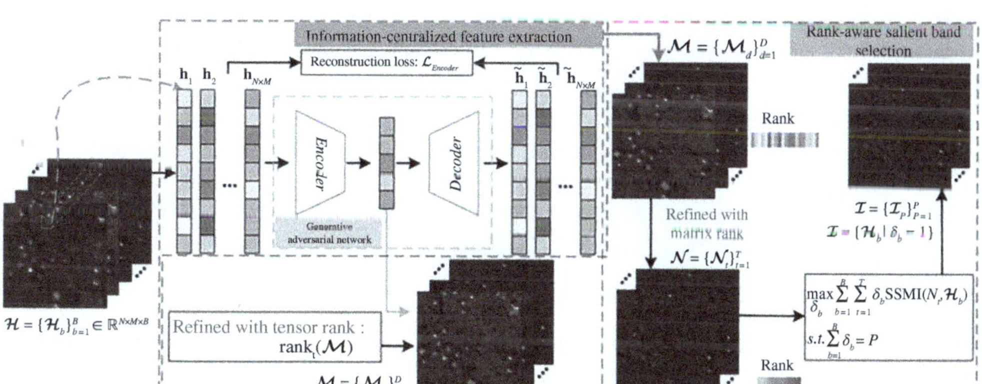

Figure 23.7 Schematic of the proposed R-GAN for BS in HSIs.

23.4.1 Information-centralized Feature Extraction

The sample adequacy of HSI makes it possible to model distribution with data-driven deep learning tools (an HSI of size 100 × 100 provides 10,000 training samples). Here, GAN is chosen to extract referential latent feature from B band images. Typically, GAN consists of a bowtie shaped generator G and a discriminator D in the latent space. However, such a structure often comes with a non-negligible reconstruction performance penalty. Thus, two discriminators D_s and D_z are added to enforce the alignment in the spectral and latent space, respectively. The GAN is trained by sovling the following optimization problem:

$$\arg\min_{\Theta_G}\max_{\Theta_{D_s},\Theta_{D_z}} \mathcal{L}_{\text{Adv}}(\Theta_G,\Theta_{D_s},\Theta_{D_z}) + \mathcal{L}_{\text{Recon}}(\Theta_G), \tag{23.45}$$

where Θ_G, Θ_{D_s}, and Θ_{D_z} denote the parameters of generator G, spectral discriminator D_s, and latent discriminator D_z, respectively. The first item is the adversarial loss and can be factorizated into two parts as follows:

$$\mathcal{L}_{\text{Adv}}(\Theta_G,\Theta_{D_s},\Theta_{D_z}) = \mathcal{L}_s(\Theta_G,\Theta_{D_s}) + \mathcal{L}_z(\Theta_G,\Theta_{D_z}), \tag{23.46}$$

where $\mathcal{L}_s(\Theta_G,\Theta_{D_s})$ is the spectral adversarial loss matching the distribution of the decoded spectral $p(\tilde{\mathbf{h}}_i)$ and the known input data distribution $p(\mathbf{h}_i)$:

$$\begin{aligned}\mathcal{L}_s(\Theta_G,\Theta_{D_s}) &= \mathbb{E}_{\mathbf{h}_i\sim p(\mathbf{h}_i)}[\log(D_s(\mathbf{h}_i,\Theta_{D_s}))]\\ &\quad + \mathbb{E}_{\tilde{\mathbf{h}}_i\sim p(\tilde{\mathbf{h}}_i)}\left[\log\left(1 - D_s\left(\tilde{\mathbf{h}}_i,\Theta_{D_s}\right)\right)\right].\end{aligned} \tag{23.47}$$

$\mathcal{L}_z(\Theta_G,\Theta_{D_z})$ is formulated in the similar fashion as Eq. (4.47) aiming to match distribution of the latent feature $p(\mathbf{z})$ with the priori distribution $p(\tilde{\mathbf{z}})$:

$$\begin{aligned}\mathcal{L}_z(\Theta_G,\Theta_{D_z}) &= \mathbb{E}_{\tilde{\mathbf{z}}\sim p(\tilde{\mathbf{z}})}\left[\log\left(D_z\left(\tilde{\mathbf{z}},\Theta_{D_z}\right)\right)\right]\\ &\quad + \mathbb{E}_{\mathbf{z}\sim p(\mathbf{z})}\left[\log\left(1 - D_z\left(\mathbf{z},\Theta_{D_z}\right)\right)\right].\end{aligned} \tag{23.48}$$

Here, $p(\tilde{\mathbf{z}})$ is recommended to be N(0, I).

Additionally, $\mathcal{L}_{\text{Recon}}(\Theta_G)$ is the reconstruction loss used to align the real input with the reconstructed output. Therefore, the reconstruction loss can be expressed by the MSE loss:

$$\mathcal{L}_{\text{Recon}}(\Theta_G) = \frac{1}{N\times M}\sum_{i=1}^{N\times M} \| \mathbf{h}_i - \tilde{\mathbf{h}}_i \|_2^2, \tag{23.49}$$

where $\tilde{\mathbf{h}}_i = G(\mathbf{h}_i,\Theta_G)$.

By optimizing Eq. (23.45) with stochastic gradient descent (SGD), we obtain the trained GAN $\boldsymbol{\Phi}(\Theta_G,\Theta_{D_s},\Theta_{D_z})$, where $\Theta_G = [\Theta_{\text{En}}, \Theta_{\text{De}}]$ and Θ_{En} and Θ_{De} are the parameters of encoder and decoder, respectively. The encoder is dedicated to map the high-dimensional HSI into a low-dimensional latent space, revealing the essential characteristics, i.e., the latent features:

$$\mathcal{M} = \text{Encoder}(\mathcal{H},\Theta_{\text{En}}) \tag{23.50}$$

23.4.2 Rank-aware Salient Band Selection

For the latent features, it is crucial to keep the sufficiency and conciseness of the contained information. Information insufficiency hinders the superiority of data-driven approach. On the contrary, information redundancy conflicts over the intention of BS. A linear algebraic measure, rank, turns to be an appropriate measurement for spectral saliency. Here, different data characteristics result in two rank calculation methods. First, the high-dimensional nature of $\mathcal{M}$ prefers global tensor tubal rank instead of calculating the rank of 2D matrix after being reshaped. For tensor $\mathcal{M} \in \mathbb{R}^{N\times M\times D}$, tensor tubal rank is defined as the number of nonzero singular tube of $\mathcal{S}$, where $\mathcal{S}$ is from the tensor singular value decomposition (t-SVD).

An illustration of the t-SVD of tensor $\mathcal{M}$. First, perform discrete fourier transformation (DFT) on every vector of $\mathcal{M}$ to obtain $\overline{\mathcal{M}}$. Then, compute each front slice of $\overline{\mathcal{U}}$, $\overline{\mathcal{S}}$ and $\overline{\mathcal{V}}$ from $\overline{\mathcal{M}}$ by SVD. Finally, $\mathcal{U}$, $\mathcal{S}$ and $\mathcal{V}$ are obtained via inverse DFT.

t-SVD shown in Figure 23.8 is solved with the aid of time-frequency domain conversion and factorizes a 3-D tensor into three components, including two orthogonal tensors, $\mathcal{U}$ and $\mathcal{V}$ and a f-diagonal tensor, $\mathcal{S}$:

$$\mathcal{M} = \mathcal{U} * \mathcal{S} * \mathcal{V}^*. \tag{23.51}$$

The tensor tubal rank $\text{rank}_t(\mathcal{M})$ can be defined as:

$$\text{rank}_t(\mathcal{M}) = \text{counts}\{i, \mathcal{S}(i, i, :) \neq 0\}. \tag{23.52}$$

Considering the property of inverse DFT:

$$\mathcal{S}(i, i, 1) = \frac{1}{n_3} \sum_{j=1}^{n_3} \overline{\mathcal{S}}(i, i, j). \tag{23.53}$$

Here, n_3 is the number of slices in $\mathcal{S}$. $\mathcal{S}(i, i, 1) = 0$ derives $\overline{\mathcal{S}}(i, i, j) = 0$ then $\mathcal{S}(i, i, j) = 0$ which indicates a zero-singular tube. Only $\mathcal{S}(i, i, 1) \neq 0$ contributes to the rank calculation. That is, the tensor tubal rank depends on the first slice $\mathcal{S}(i, i, 1)$ of $\mathcal{S}$:

$$\text{rank}_t(\mathcal{M}) = \text{counts}\{i, \mathcal{S}(i, i, 1) \neq 0\} \tag{23.54}$$

In accordance with rank, we can keep $\mathcal{M}$ informative and restrict its dimension to reduce the computation load.

With $\mathcal{M}$ of an appropriate dimension, local matrix rank is applied for further evaluation on each slice to find the most salient bands. Specifically, $\mathcal{M}$ is sorted by the rank of slice $\mathcal{M}_d$ and $\mathcal{N}$ is a collection of slices with top-T rank:***

$$\begin{aligned} \mathcal{M} &= \text{sort}(\mathcal{M}, \text{key} = \text{rank}(\mathcal{M}_d)) \\ \mathcal{N} &= \mathcal{M}[:, :, D-T : D] \end{aligned} \tag{23.55}$$

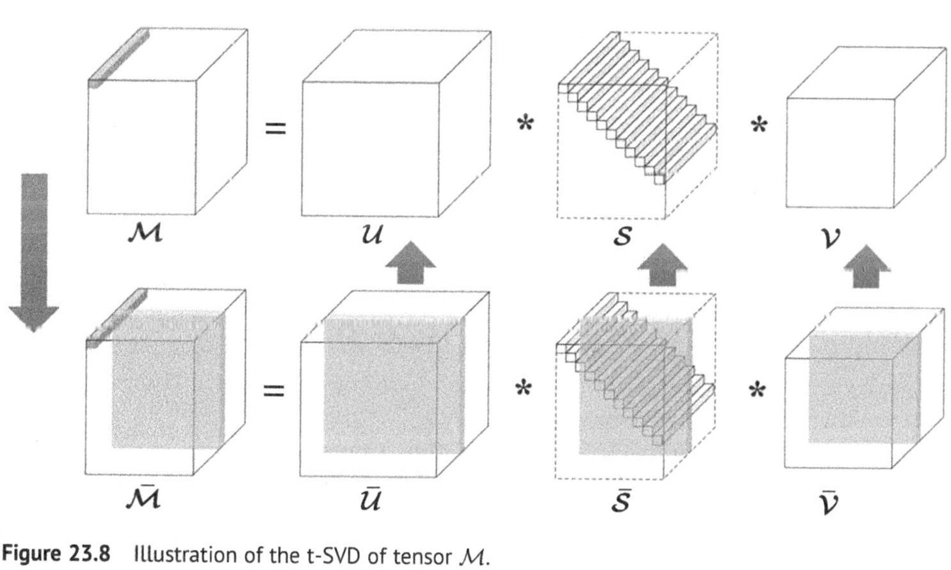

Figure 23.8 Illustration of the t-SVD of tensor $\mathcal{M}$.

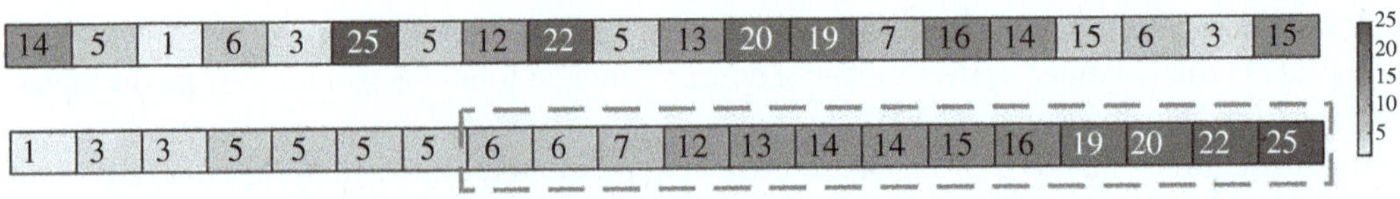

Figure 23.9 Illustration of salient slice selection. The shading intensity indicates the rank value tagged to the corresponding position.

The rationale lies in that a larger rank suggests a larger saliency. Figure 23.9 gives an intuitive illustration.

23.4.3 Mapping Saliency to Original Data Space

To obtain the final band selection result, the data-driven saliency is mapped to the original data space with SSIM as Eq. (23.44). In other words, $\mathcal{H}_b$ having the maximal SSIM with $\mathcal{N}_t$ is regarded as an alternative in the original data space. $\mathcal{H}_b$ is prioritized by the noise level before matching. Here, SSIM is adopted to evaluate the brightness, contrast, and structure to characterize the data for favorable human vision perception, which is defined as:

$$\begin{aligned} \text{SSIM} &= A{*}C{*}S \\ A &= \frac{2u_1u_2 + C_1}{u_1^2 + u_2^2 + C_1} \\ C &= \frac{2\sigma_1\sigma_2 + C_2}{\sigma_1^2 + \sigma_2^2 + C_2} \\ S &= \frac{\sigma_{12} + C_3}{\sigma_1\sigma_2 + C_3} \end{aligned} \tag{23.56}$$

where $u_1$and u_2 are the means of $\mathcal{N}_t$ and $\mathcal{H}_b$, respectively, σ_1 and σ_2 are the corresponding variances, σ_{12} is covariance, and C_1, C_2, and C_3 denote constants guaranteeing the validity of fraction. The larger SSIM between $\mathcal{N}_t$ and $\mathcal{H}_b$ is, the more salient $\mathcal{H}_b$ is, and the more likely $\mathcal{H}_b$ plays a critical role in subsequent tasks. Then the selected subset can be determined.

23.4.4 Experiments of R-GAN

Table 23.3 presents the anomaly detection performance. In the SD-1 data set, R-GAN demonstrates significant superiority across all studied band sizes except for 5. The subsets chosen by R-GAN outperform the baseline by at least 12.6% and 2.4% on SD-1 and SD-2, respectively. Although R-GAN trails behind the best-performing methods (BS-Net and EFPDC) by a mere 0.1% in peaked accuracy on SD-1 and SD-2, it exhibits remarkable performance overall. On the TC data set, all compared methods perform well, emphasizing minimizing accuracy loss as a reasonable criterion for determining the best band selection method. R-GAN ranks second in performance when the band size is 5, but its superiority becomes evident as the number of bands increases. In terms of peaked AUC, R-GAN surpasses the runner-up (BS-Net) by 0.1%. Similarly, R-GAN performs well on the GA data set across all band numbers, achieving higher global and peaked accuracy. The peaked performance of R-GAN outperforms FNGBS by 0.73%. On the LA data set, R-GAN maintains the highest accuracy across all data set scales, surpassing comparison methods like DSEBS and SBSS by 0.2%.

Regarding target detection performance in Table 23.4, R-GAN consistently outperforms other methods. On the SD-1 data set, R-GAN achieves the highest accuracy values across all subset scales,

Table 23.3 A JC values of the compared methods on experimental data sets for anomaly detection.

Dataset	No. of bands	Compared methods									Baseline
		R-GAN	DSEBS	EFPDC	OCF	SBSS	ASPS	SOPSRL	FNGBS	BS-Net	
SD-1	5	0.989 ± 0.002	0.967	0.955	0.961	0.984	0.975	0.973	0.972	**0.990**	0.864
	10	**0.982 ± 0.003**	0.977	0.968	0.966	0.978	0.953	0.973	0.968	0.980	
	15	**0.978 ± 0.003**	0.946	0.963	0.964	0.864	0.954	0.960	0.955	0.977	
	20	**0.974 ± 0.003**	0.973	0.965	0.963	0.969	0.951	0.966	0.960	**0.974**	
	25	**0.976 ± 0.002**	0.973	0.962	0.963	0.967	0.958	0.962	0.964	**0.976**	
	30	**0.973 ± 0.001**	0.972	0.955	0.968	0.962	0.959	0.958	0.953	**0.974**	
	Peaked AUC	0.989 ± 0.002	0.977	0.968	0.968	0.984	0.975	0.973	0.972	**0.990**	
	Low PFA Range	**2.7e-4 ± 0.0001**	0	4.5e-5	2.9e-5	1.3e-5	0	6.0e-5	1.1e-5	7.1e-5	9.1e-5
SD-2	5	0.985 ± 0.002	0.967	**0.986**	0.985	0.968	0.977	0.969	0.984	0.972	0.954
	10	**0.981 ± 0.001**	0.977	0.978	0.977	0.975	0.976	0.975	0.977	0.978	
	15	**0.979 ± 0.001**	0.971	0.975	0.974	0.973	0.976	0.974	0.974	**0.979**	
	20	**0.978 ± 0.001**	0.973	0.975	0.974	0.968	0.975	0.970	0.977	0.977	
	25	**0.978 ± 0.001**	0.973	0.974	0.975	0.966	0.969	0.973	0.975	0.977	
	30	**0.977 ± 0.000**	0.972	**0.977**	0.974	0.968	**0.977**	0.967	0.973	**0.977**	
	Peaked AUC	0.985 ± 0.002	0.977	**0.986**	0.985	0.975	0.977	0.975	0.984	0.978	
	Low PFA Range	**1.3e-3 ± 0.0001**	8.8e-4	4.8e-4	6.2e-4	3 2e-4	6.1e-4	4.0e-4	5.5e-4	5.6e-4	9.8e-4
TC	5	0.992 ± 0.002	0.988	0.981	0.985	**0.993**	0.990	0.985	0.986	0.994	0.992
	10	**0.995 ± 0.001**	0.992	0.987	0.990	0.993	0.994	0.993	0.982	0.992	
	15	**0.995 ± 0.001**	0.993	0.988	0.993	0.992	0.989	0.992	0.991	0.992	
	20	**0.995 ± 0.001**	0.992	0.989	0.993	0.991	0.990	0.992	0.990	0.992	

(Continued)

Table 23.3 (Continued)

Dataset	No. of bands	Compared methods									
		R-GAN	DSEBS	EFPDC	OCF	SBSS	ASPS	SOPSRL	FNGBS	BS-Net	Baseline
	25	**0.995 ± 0.000**	0.990	0.990	0.993	0.990	0.991	0.992	0.991	0.992	
	30	**0.995 ± 0.000**	0.991	0.991	0.993	0.991	0.991	0.993	0.993	0.991	
	Peaked AUC	**0.995 ± 0.000**	0.993	0.991	0.993	0.993	0.994	0.993	0.993	0.994	
	Low PFA Range	**7.2e-3 ± 0.0001**	0.006	0.005	0.006	0.005	0.007	0.006	0.005	0.006	0.005
GA	5	**0.968 ± 0.000**	0.899	0.958	0.947	0.968	0.957	0.958	0.952	0.842	0.951
	10	**0.970 ± 0.002**	0.962	0.938	0.946	0.970	0.957	0.942	0.941	0.969	
	15	**0.971 ± 0.002**	0.960	0.957	0.953	0.965	0.955	0.958	0.945	0.963	
	20	**0.971 ± 0.003**	0.963	0.967	0.968	0.967	0.951	0.956	0.959	0.963	
	25	**0.971 ± 0.003**	0.958	0.966	0.968	0.967	0.966	0.969	0.964	0.965	
	30	**0.970 ± 0.002**	0.965	0.968	0.965	0.965	0.964	0.965	0.959	0.965	
	Peaked AUC	**0.971 ± 0.002**	0.965	0.968	0.968	0.970	0.966	0.969	0.964	0.969	
	Low PFA Range	**1.2e-3 ± 0.0001**	7.9e-4	2.8e-4	5.0e-4	0.001	3.1e-4	8.3e-4	2.2e-4	4.7e-4	3.4e-4
LA	5	**0.992 ± 0.000**	0.990	0.975	0.976	0.990	0.978	0.979	0.977	0.969	0.989
	10	**0.988 ± 0.001**	0.986	0.981	0.984	0.987	0.982	0.985	0.987	0.982	
	15	**0.990 ± 0.001**	0.986	0.983	0.985	0.981	0.982	0.986	0.987	0.979	
	20	**0.990 ± 0.001**	0.986	0.982	0.984	0.980	0.981	0.985	0.984	0.989	
	25	**0.990 ± 0.000**	0.986	0.981	0.982	0.979	0.984	0.987	0.982	0.982	
	30	**0.991 ± 0.000**	0.985	0.982	0.982	0.979	0.983	0.987	0.981	0.984	
	Peaked AUC	**0.992 ± 0.000**	0.990	0.983	0.985	0.990	0.984	0.987	0.987	0.989	
	Low PFA Range	**4.5e-3 ± 0.0003**	0.004	0.003	0.003	0.003	0.004	0.004	0.003	0.002	0.003

Table 23.4 AUC values of the compared methods on experimental data sets for target detection.

Dataset	No. of Bands	Compared methods									Baseline
		R-GAN	DSEBS	EFPDC	OCF	SBSS	ASPS	SOPSRL	FNGBS	BS-Net	
SD-1	5	**0.998 ± 0.000**	0.974	**0.998**	0.990	0.997	0.990	0.991	0.989	0.994	1
	10	**0.999 ± 0.000**	0.984	0.997	0.997	**0.999**	0.993	0.998	0.997	0.994	
	15	**0.999 ± 0.000**	0.987	0.997	0.998	0.997	0.996	0.988	0.997	0.996	
	20	**0.999 ± 0.000**	0.998	0.998	0.998	0.998	0.996	0.998	0.997	0.998	
	25	**0.999 ± 0.000**	0.998	0.998	0.998	0.998	0.998	0.998	0.998	**0.999**	
	30	**0.999 ± 0.000**	0.998	0.998	**0.999**	0.998	**0.999**	0.998	0.998	**0.999**	
	Peaked AUC	**0.999 ± 0.000**	0.998	0.998	**0.999**	**0.999**	**0.999**	0.998	0.998	**0.999**	
	Low PFA Range	**9.1e-3 ± 7e-5**	0.003	0.008	0.005	0.008	0.004	0.006	0.004	0.008	0.009
TC	5	0.997 ± 0.001	0.994	0.970	0.985	**0.998**	0.995	0.988	0.992	0.995	1
	10	**0.999 ± 0.000**	0.994	0.984	0.989	0.998	0.996	0.991	0.977	0.995	
	15	**0.999 ± 0.000**	0.996	0.988	**0.999**	0.998	**0.999**	0.997	0.995	0.989	
	20	**0.999 ± 0.000**	0.995	0.998	**0.999**	**0.999**	0.984	0.998	0.998	0.990	
	25	**0.999 ± 0.000**	0.993	0.998	**0.999**	0.998	**0.999**	0.995	0.998	0.996	
	30	**0.999 ± 0.000**	0.996	**0.999**	**0.999**	0.995	**0.999**	**0.999**	**0.999**	0.998	
	Peaked AUC	**0.999 ± 0.000**	0.996	**0.999**	**0.999**	**0.999**	**0.999**	**0.999**	**0.999**	0.998	
	Low PFA Range	**9.0e-3 ± 6e-5**	0.008	0.007	0.008	0.008	0.008	0.008	0.008	0.008	0.010

even the worst performance of R-GAN on SD-1 exceeds 0.988, a level unmatched by other methods. Similarly, on the TC data set, R-GAN leads at different band scales except for 5, demonstrating integral superiorities that make it highly competitive.

In some military/defence application scenarios, the desired detector should be able to keep high PD when PFA is low, which is displayed as the ROC curve close to the upper left corner. As reported in Table 23.3, the AUC values with a low PFA range (1e − 4 and 1e − 2) outperform other methods and the baseline for all the experimental data sets. The corresponding ROC curves are illustrated in Figures 23.10 and 23.11. The proposed R-GAN envelopes other methods on SD and GA data sets and is a little lower than ASPS or DSEBS on TC and LA data sets, which indicates its competitiveness and effectiveness. The results of the target detection task are shown in Table 23.4 and Figure 23.12. The numerical superiority on the SD-1 data set is embodied in the ideal ROC curves in Figure 23.12a, which is above the comparison methods in the whole studied PFA range. For the TC data set, the AUC value of R-GAN is lower than the baseline, which is consistent with the ROC curves in Figure 23.12b. Except for the baseline, the ROC curve of R-GAN is only lower than FNGBS. In general, the proposed R-GAN performs well in the low PFA range on all the experimental data sets, which indicates it is a suitable BS method for the detection tasks in military/defence operations.

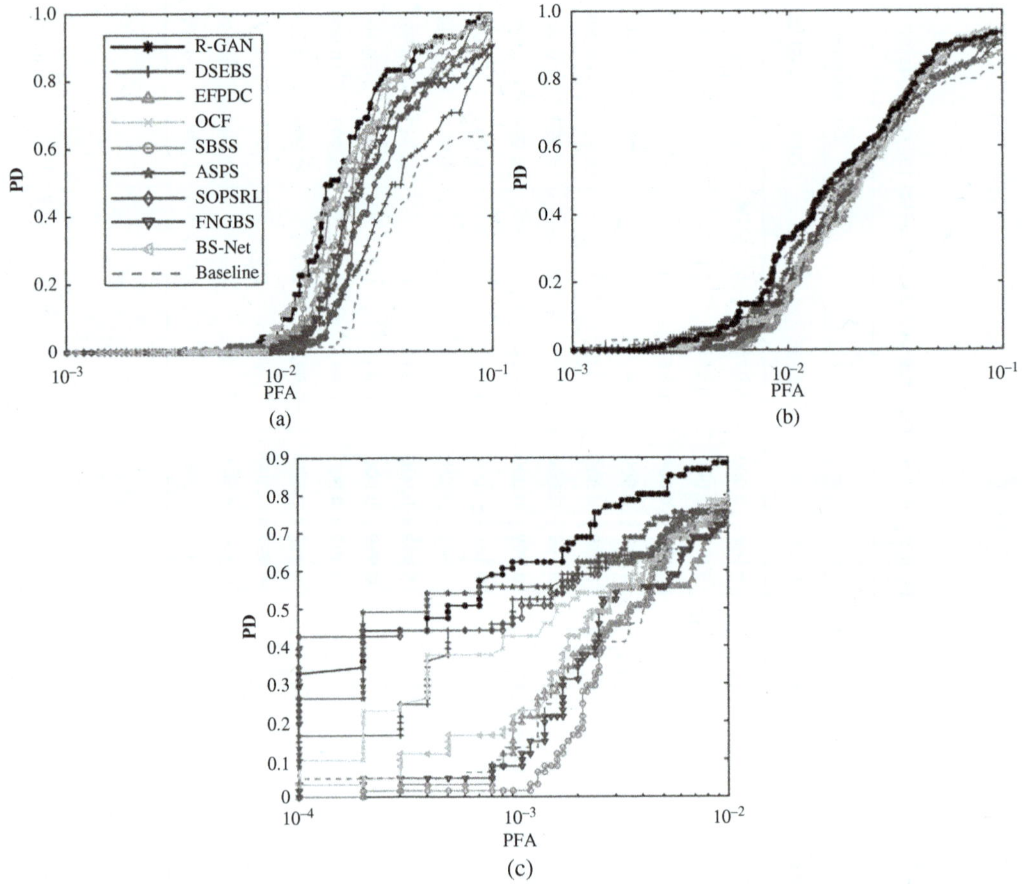

Figure 23.10 ROC curves (in low PFA range) of different methods on data sets. (a) SD-1. (b) SD-2. (c) TC.

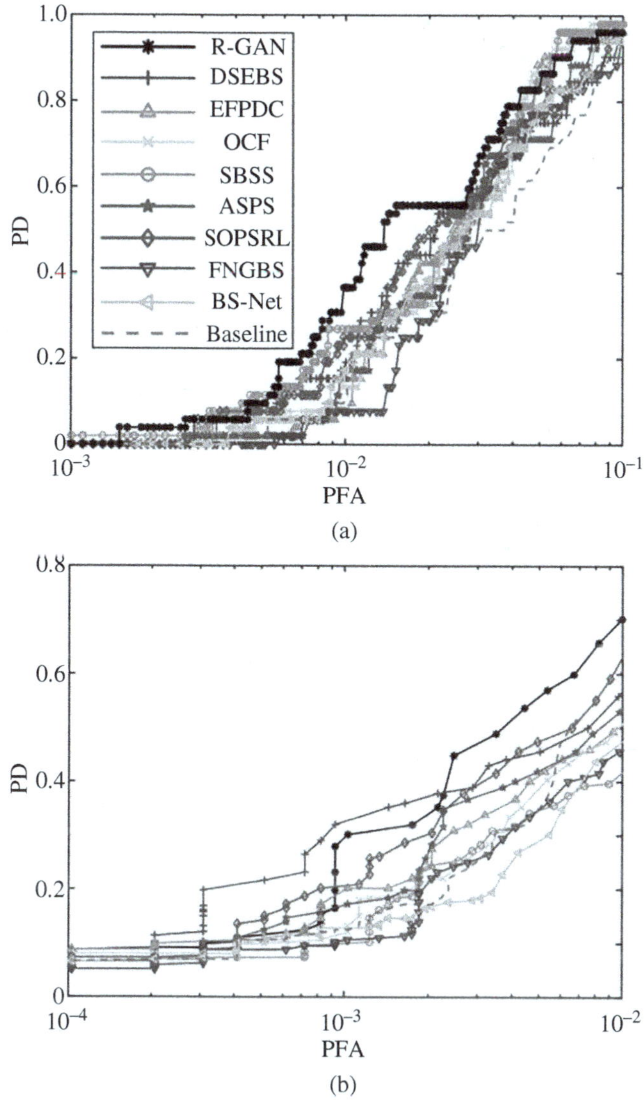

Figure 23.11 ROC curves (in low PFA range) of different methods on data sets. (a) GA. (b) LA.

23.5 Conclusions

In this chapter, we have explored the application of weakly supervised learning techniques to hyperspectral image (HSI) anomaly and target detection. Through the use of deep neural networks (DNNs) and generative adversarial networks (GANs), particularly adversarial autoencoders (AAEs), we have developed innovative methods for effective background modeling and accurate anomaly/target detection. Our approach also includes dimensionality reduction techniques, such as band selection (BS), which have proven effective in reducing spectral redundancy while maintaining the integrity of the data. The results from our experiments demonstrate the effectiveness of weakly supervised learning in improving target detection accuracy in HSIs, while also significantly

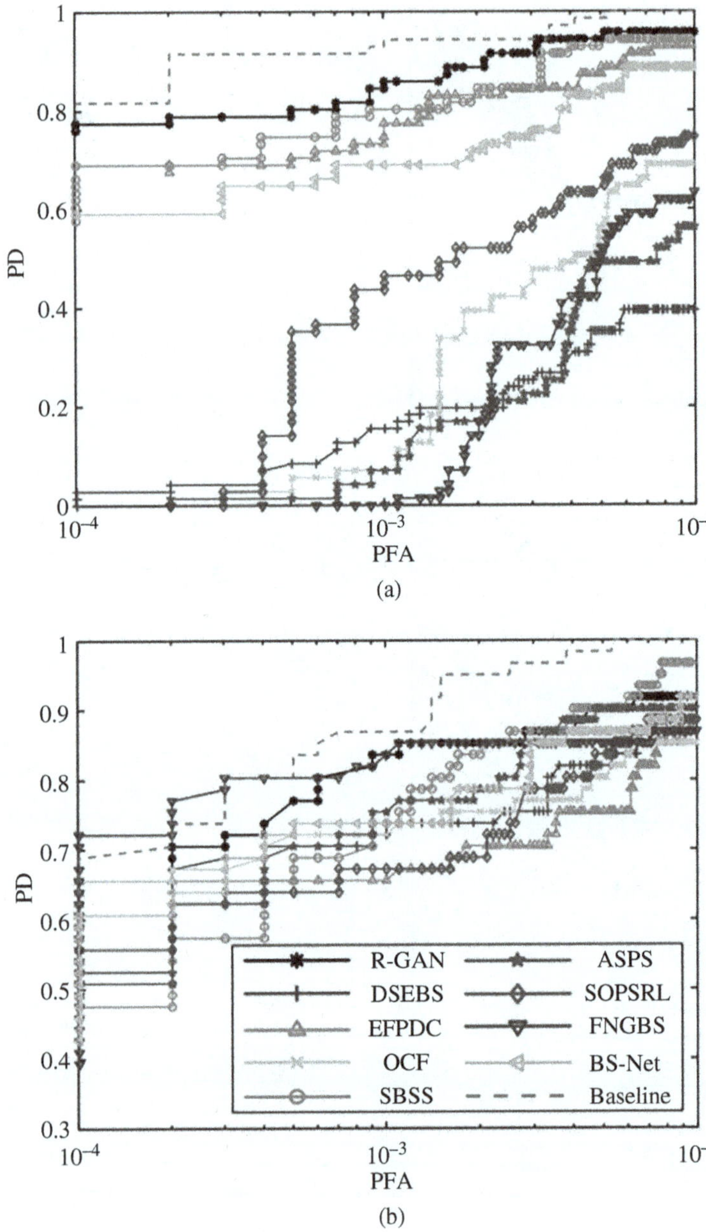

Figure 23.12 ROC curves (in low PFA range) of different methods on data sets. (a) SD-1. (b) TC.

reducing computational complexity. This dual achievement of accuracy and efficiency positions weakly supervised learning as a promising approach for real-world applications where both performance and resource constraints are critical.

As we move forward, the methodologies presented in this chapter pave the way for further research and practical applications in various domains, including remote sensing, environmental monitoring, and defense. The advancements in weakly supervised learning techniques discussed here have the potential to revolutionize the way we approach anomaly and target detection in hyperspectral imaging, making it more accessible and effective for a wide range of uses.

References

1 Sun, W., Tian, L., Xu, Y. et al. (2018). A randomized subspace learning based anomaly detector for hyperspectral imagery. *Remote Sens* 10 (3): 417.

2 Xie, W., Jiang, T., Li, Y. et al. (2019). Structure tensor and guided filtering-based algorithm for hyperspectral anomaly detection. *IEEE Trans. Geosci. Remote Sens.* 57 (7): 4218–4230.

3 Lu, X., Zhang, W., and Huang, J. (2020). Exploiting embedding manifold of autoencoders for hyperspectral anomaly detection. *IEEE Trans. Geosci. Remote Sens.* 58 (3): 1527–1537.

4 Manolakis, D., Truslow, E., Pieper, M. et al. (2014). Detection algorithms in hyperspectral imaging systems: an overview of practical algorithms. *IEEE Signal Process. Mag.* 31 (1): 24–33.

5 Li, S., Zhang, K., Duan, P., and Kang, X. (2020). Hyperspectral anomaly detection with kernel isolation forest. *IEEE Trans. Geosci. Remote Sens.* 58 (1): 319–329.

6 Reed, I.S. and Yu, X. (1990). Adaptive multiple-band CFAR detection of an optical pattern with unknown spectral distribution. *IEEE Trans. Acoust. Speech Signal Process.* 38 (10): 1760–1770.

7 Molero, J.M., Garzon, E.M., Garcia, I., and Plaza, A. (2013). Analysis and optimizations of global and local versions of the RX algorithm for anomaly detection in hyperspectral data. *IEEE J. Sel. Top. Appl. Earth Obs. Remote Sens.* 6 (2): 801–814.

8 Kwon, H. and Nasrabadi, N.M. (2005). Kernel RX-algorithm: a nonlinear anomaly detector for hyperspectral imagery. *IEEE Trans. Geosci. Remote Sens.* 43 (2): 388–397.

9 Zhou, J.T., Du, J., Zhu, H. et al. (2019). Anomalynet: an anomaly detection network for video surveillance. *IEEE Trans. Inf. Forensics Secur.* 14 (10): 2537–2550.

10 Peng, X., Feng, J., Xiao, S. et al. (2018). Structured autoencoders for subspace clustering. *IEEE Trans. Image Process.* 27 (10): 5076–5086.

11 Li, W., Du, Q., and Zhang, B. (2015). Combined sparse and collaborative representation for hyperspectral target detection. *Pattern Recogn.* 48 (12): 3904–3916.

12 Vafadar, M. and Ghassemian, H. (2018). Anomaly detection of hyperspectral imagery using modified collaborative representation. *IEEE Geosci. Remote Sens. Lett.* 15 (4): 577–581.

13 Su, H., Wu, Z., Du, Q., and Du, P. (2018). Hyperspectral anomaly detection using collaborative representation with outlier removal. *IEEE J. Sel. Top. Appl. Earth Obs. Remote Sens.* 11 (12): 5029–5038.

14 Zhang, L. and Cheng, B. (2020). Sparse representation and modified tensor projection for hyperspectral anomaly detection. *Infrared Phys. Technol.* 106: 103256.

15 Dundar, T. and Ince, T. (2019). Sparse representation-based hyperspectral image classification using multiscale super pixels and guided filter. *IEEE Geosci. Remote Sens. Lett.* 16 (2): 246–250.

16 Ou, X. et al. (2020). Hyperspectral image target detection via weighted joint k-nearest neighbour and multitask learning sparse representation. *IEEE Access* 8: 11503–11511.

17 Wang, Q., He, X., and Li, X. (2019). Locality and structure regularized low rank representation for hyperspectral image classification. *IEEE Trans. Geosci. Remote Sens.* 57 (2): 911–923.

18 Wang, S., Wang, X., Zhong, Y., and Zhang, L. (2020). Hyperspectral anomaly detection via locally enhanced low-rank prior. *IEEE Trans. Geosci. Remote Sens.* 58 (10): 6995–7009.

19 Song, S., Zhou, H., Gu, L. et al. (2020). Hyperspectral anomaly detection via tensor-based endmember extraction and low-rank decomposition. *IEEE Geosci. Remote Sens. Lett.* 17 (10): 1772–1776.

20 Li, W. and Du, Q. (2015). Collaborative representation for hyperspectral anomaly detection. *IEEE Trans. Geosci. Remote Sens.* 53 (3): 1463–1474.

21 Li, J., Zhang, H., Zhang, L., and Ma, L. (2015). Hyperspectral anomaly detection by the use of background joint sparse representation. *IEEE J. Sel. Top. Appl. Earth Obs. Remote Sens.* 8 (6): 2523–2533.

22 Zhang, Y., Du, B., Zhang, L., and Wang, S. (2016). A low-rank and sparse matrix decomposition-based Mahalanobis distance method for hyperspectral anomaly detection. *IEEE Trans. Geosci. Remote Sens.* 54 (3): 1376–1389.

23 Li, L., Li, W., Du, Q., and Tao, R. (2020). Low-rank and sparse decomposition with mixture of Gaussian for hyperspectral anomaly detection. *IEEE Trans. Cybern.* 51 (9): 4363–4372.

24 Xu, Y., Wu, Z., Li, J. et al. (2016). Anomaly detection in hyperspectral images based on low-rank and sparse representation. *IEEE Trans. Geosci. Remote Sens.* 54 (4): 1990–2000.

25 Qu, Y. et al. (2018). Hyperspectral anomaly detection through spectral unmixing and dictionary-based low-rank decomposition. *IEEE Trans. Geosci. Remote Sens.* 56 (8): 4391–4405.

26 Zhang, M., Li, W., Du, Q. et al. (2020). Feature extraction for classification of hyperspectral and LiDAR data using patch-to-patch CNN. *IEEE Trans. Cybern.* 50 (1): 100–111.

27 Jiang, K., Xie, W., Li, Y. et al. (2020). Semisupervised spectral learning with generative adversarial network for hyperspectral anomaly detection. *IEEE Trans. Geosci. Remote Sens.* 58 (7): 5224–5236.

28 Zhong, Z., Li, J., Clausi, D.A., and Wong, A. (2020). Generative adversarial networks and conditional random fields for hyperspectral image classification. *IEEE Trans. Cybern.* 50 (7): 3318–3329.

29 Li, X., Zhang, R., Wang, Q., and Zhang, H. (2021). Autoencoder constrained clustering with adaptive neighbors. *IEEE Trans. Neural Netw. Learn. Syst.* 32 (1): 443–449.

30 Zhao, C. and Zhang, L. (2018). Spectral-spatial stacked autoencoders based on low-rank and sparse matrix decomposition for hyperspectral anomaly detection. *Infrared Phys. Technol.* 92: 166–176.

31 Lei, J., Xie, W., Yang, J. et al. (2019). Spectral-spatial feature extraction for hyperspectral anomaly detection. *IEEE Trans. Geosci. Remote Sens.* 57 (10): 8131–8143.

32 Xie, W., Li, Y., Lei, J. et al. (2020). Hyperspectral band selection for spectral-spatial anomaly detection. *IEEE Trans. Geosci. Remote Sens.* 58 (5): 3426–3436.

33 Xie, W., Liu, B., Li, Y. et al. (2020). Spectral adversarial feature learning for anomaly detection in hyperspectral imagery. *IEEE Trans. Geosci. Remote Sens.* 58 (4): 2352–2365.

34 Jiang, T., Li, Y., Xie, W., and Du, Q. (2020). Discriminative reconstruction constrained generative adversarial network for hyperspectral anomaly detection. *IEEE Trans. Geosci. Remote Sens.* 58 (7): 4666–4679.

35 Lei, J., Fang, S., Xie, W., and Chang, C.-I. (2020). Discriminative reconstruction for hyperspectral anomaly detection with spectral learning. *IEEE Trans. Geosci. Remote Sens.* 58 (10): 7406–7417.

36 Li, W., Wu, G., and Du, Q. (2017). Transferred deep learning for anomaly detection in hyperspectral imagery. *IEEE Geosci. Remote Sens. Lett.* 14 (5): 597–601.

37 Song, S., Zhou, H., Yang, Y., and Song, J. (2019). Hyperspectral anomaly detection via convolutional neural network and low rank with density-based clustering. *IEEE J. Sel. Top. Appl. Earth Obs. Remote Sens.* 12 (9): 3637–3649.

38 Liu, G., Lin, Z., and Yong, Y. 2010. Robust subspace segmentation by low rank representation, *Proceedings of the 27th International Conference on Machine Learning*, Haifa, Israel (2010), 663–670.

39 Zhu, D., Du, B., and Zhang, L. (2019). Target dictionary construction-based sparse representation hyperspectral target detection methods. *IEEE J. Sel. Top. Appl. Earth Obs. Remote Sens.* 12 (4): 1254–1264.

40 Nasrabadi, N.M. (2014). Hyperspectral target detection: an overview of current and future challenges. *IEEE Signal Process. Mag.* 31 (1): 34–44.

41 Zhu, D., Du, B., and Zhang, L. (2019). Binary-class collaborative representation for target detection in hyperspectral images. *IEEE Geosci. Remote Sens. Lett.* 16 (7): 1100–1104.

42 Farrand, W.H. and Harsanyi, J.C. (1997). Mapping the distribution of mine tailings in the Coeur d'Alene River Valley, Idaho, through the use of a constrained energy minimization technique. *Remote Sens. Environ.* 59 (1): 64–76.

43 Zhao, R., Shi, Z., Zou, Z., and Zhang, Z. (2019). Ensemble-based cascaded constrained energy minimization for hyperspectral target detection. *Remote Sens* 11 (11): 1310.

44 Chen, S.-Y., Lin, C., Tai, C.-H., and Chuang, S.-J. (2018). Adaptive window-based constrained energy minimization for detection of newly grown tree leaves. *Remote Sens* 10 (1): 96.

45 Wang, T., Du, B., and Zhang, L. (2013). A kernel-based target-constrained interference-minimized filter for hyperspectral sub-pixel target detection. *IEEE J. Sel. Top. Appl. Earth Obs. Remote Sens.* 6 (2): 626–637.

46 Zou, Z. and Shi, Z. (2016). Hierarchical suppression method for hyperspectral target detection. *IEEE Trans. Geosci. Remote Sens.* 54 (1): 330–342.

47 Harsanyi, J.C. and Chang, C.-I. (1994). Hyperspectral image classification and dimensionality reduction: an orthogonal subspace projection approach. *IEEE Trans. Geosci. Remote Sens.* 32 (4): 779–785.

48 Kraut, S., Scharf, L.L., and McWhorter, L.T. (2001). Adaptive subspace detectors. *IEEE Trans. Signal Process.* 49 (1): 1–16.

49 Manolakis, D., Marden, D., and Shaw, G.A. (2003). Hyperspectral image processing for automatic target detection applications. *Lincoln Lab. J.* 14 (1): 79–116.

50 Fuhrmann, D.R., Kelly, E.J., and Nitzberg, R. (1992). A CFAR adaptive matched filter detector. *IEEE Trans. Aerosp. Electron. Syst.* 28 (1): 208–216.

51 Scharf, L.L. and Friedlander, B. (1994). Matched subspace detectors. *IEEE Trans. Signal Process.* 42 (8): 2146–2157.

52 Li, Y., Xie, W., and Li, H. (2017). Hyperspectral image reconstruction by deep convolutional neural network for classification. *Pattern Recogn.* 63: 371–383.

53 Yang, X., Ye, Y., Li, X. et al. (2018). Hyperspectral image classification with deep learning models. *IEEE Trans. Geosci. Remote Sens.* 56 (9): 5408–5423.

54 Venkatesan, R. and Prabu, S. (2019). Hyperspectral image features classification using deep learning recurrent neural networks. *J. Med. Syst.* 43 (7): 216.

55 Pan, B., Shi, Z., and Xu, X. (2018). Mugnet: deep learning for hyperspectral image classification using limited samples. *ISPRS J. Photogramm. Remote Sens.* 145: 108–119.

56 Goodfellow, I.J., Pouget-Abadie, J., Mirza, M. et al. (2014). Generative adversarial nets. In: *Advances in Neural Information Processing Systems*, vol. 27 (ed. Z. Ghahramani, M. Welling, C. Cortes, et al.).

57 Makhzani, A., Shlens, J., Jaitly, N. et al. (2015). Adversarial autoencoders. *arXiv preprint* arXiv:1511.05644.

58 Li, N. and Chang, F. (2019). Video anomaly detection and localization via multivariate Gaussian fully convolution adversarial autoencoder. *Neurocomputing* 369: 92–105.

59 Xiao, Y., Xiao, D., Hu, B., and Shi, C. 2018. ANE: network embedding via adversarial autoencoders, *2018 IEEE International Conference on Big Data and Smart Computing (BigComp)*, 66–73, Shanghai, China (15–17 January 2018). IEEE.

60 Xie, W., Lei, J., Liu, B. et al. (2019). Spectral constraint adversarial autoencoders approach to feature representation in hyperspectral anomaly detection. *Neural Netw.* 119: 222–234.

61 Chalapathy, R. and Chawla, S. (2019). Deep learning for anomaly detection: a survey. *arXiv preprint* arXiv:1901.03407.

62 Xie, W., Liu, B., Li, Y. et al. (2020). Autoencoder and adversariallearning-based semisupervised background estimation for hyperspectral anomaly detection. *IEEE Trans. Geosci. Remote Sens.* 58 (8): 5416–5427.

63 Yang, Z. et al., 2020. CARS: continuous evolution for efficient neural architecture search, *Proceedings of the IEEE/CVF Conference on Computer Vision and Pattern Recognition (CVPR)*, Seattle, WA, USA (13–19 June 2020), 1826–1835.

64 Lin, S. et al. 2019. Towards optimal structured CNN pruning via generative adversarial learning, *2019 IEEE/CVF Conference on Computer Vision and Pattern Recognition (CVPR)*, Long Beach, CA, USA (15–20 June 2020), 2785–2794.

65 You, H. et al. 2020. ShiftAddNet: a ardware-inspired deep network, *Proceedings of the 34th International Conference on Neural Information Processing Systems* (6–12 December 2020), 2771–2783.

66 Tang, Y. et al. 2021. Manifold regularized dynamic network pruning, *2021 IEEE/CVF Conference on Computer Vision and Pattern Recognition (CVPR)*, 5018–5028, Nashville, TN, USA (20–25 June 2021), IEEE.

67 Tang, Y. et al. (2020). SCOP: scientific control for reliable neural network pruning. *Adv. Neural Inf. Proces. Syst.* 33: 10939–10947. arXiv:2010.10732.

68 Lam, R.R., Zahm, O., Marzouk, Y.M., and Willcox, K.E. (2020). Multifidelity dimension reduction via active subspaces. *SIAM J. Sci. Comput.* 42 (2): A929–A956.

69 Su, P., Liu, D., Li, X., and Liu, Z. (2018). A saliency-based band selection approach for hyperspectral imagery inspired by scale selection. *IEEE Geosci. Remote Sens. Lett.* 15 (4): 572–576.

70 Zhu, Z., Hou, J., Chen, J. et al. (2021). Hyperspectral image super-resolution via deep progressive zero-centric residual learning. *IEEE Trans. Image Process.* 30: 1423–1438.

71 Zhao, R., Wang, Q., Fu, J., and Ren, L. (2020). Exploiting block-sparsity for hyperspectral Kronecker compressive sensing: a tensor-based Bayesian method. *IEEE Trans. Image Process.* 29: 1654–1668.

72 Li, Z. and Zhang, Y. (2021). Hyperspectral anomaly detection via image super-resolution processing and spatial correlation. *IEEE Trans. Geosci. Remote Sens.* 59 (3): 2307–2320.

73 Song, X., Zou, L., and Wu, L. (2021). Detection of subpixel targets on hyperspectral remote sensing imagery based on background endmember extraction. *IEEE Trans. Geosci. Remote Sens.* 59 (3): 2365–2377.

74 Hang, R., Li, Z., Liu, Q. et al. (2021). Hyperspectral image classification with attention-aided CNNs. *IEEE Trans. Geosci. Remote Sens.* 59 (3): 2281–2293.

75 Dou, Z., Gao, K., Zhang, X. et al. (2021). Band selection of hyperspectral images using attention-based autoencoders. *IEEE Geosci. Remote Sens. Lett.* 18 (1): 147–151.

76 Wei, X., Zhu, W., Liao, B., and Cai, L. (2019). Scalable one-pass self-representation learning for hyperspectral band selection. *IEEE Trans. Geosci. Remote Sens.* 57 (7): 4360–4374.

77 Sui, C., Li, C., Feng, J., and Mei, X. (2020). Unsupervised manifold-preserving and weakly redundant band selection method for hyperspectral imagery. *IEEE Trans. Geosci. Remote Sens.* 58 (2): 1156–1170.

78 Yang, H., Du, Q., Su, H., and Sheng, Y. (2011). An efficient method for supervised hyperspectral band selection. *IEEE Geosci. Remote Sens. Lett.* 8 (1): 138–142.

79 Su, H., Yang, H., Du, Q., and Sheng, Y. (2011). Semisupervised band clustering for dimensionality reduction of hyperspectral imagery. *IEEE Geosci. Remote Sens. Lett.* 8 (6): 1135–1139.

80 Su, H., Du, P., and Du, Q. (2012). Semi-supervised dimensionality reduction using orthogonal projection divergence-based clustering for hyperspectral imagery. *Proc. SPIE Opt. Eng.* 51 (11): 111715.

81 Su, H. and Du, Q. (2012). Hyperspectral band clustering and band selection for urban land cover classification. *Geocarto Int.* 27 (5): 395–411.

82 Sun, W., Peng, J., Yang, G., and Du, Q. Correntropy-based sparse spectral clustering for hyperspectral band selection. *IEEE Geosci. Remote Sens. Lett.* 17 (3): 484–488.

83 Wang, Q., Zhang, F., and Li, X. (2018). Optimal clustering framework for hyperspectral band selection. *IEEE Trans. Geosci. Remote Sens.* 56 (10): 5910–5922.

84 Jia, S., Tang, G., Zhu, J., and Li, Q. (2016). A novel ranking-based clustering approach for hyperspectral band selection. *IEEE Trans. Geosci. Remote Sens.* 54 (1): 88–102.

85 Kang, X., Zhang, X., Li, S. et al. (2017). Hyperspectral anomaly detection with attribute and edge-preserving filters. *IEEE Trans. Geosci. Remote Sens.* 55 (10): 5600–5611.

86 Tao, R., Zhao, X., Li, W. et al. (2019). Hyperspectral anomaly detection by fractional Fourier entropy. *IEEE J. Sel. Top. Appl. Earth Obs. Remote Sens.* 12 (12): 4920–4929.

24

Hyperspectral Anomaly Detection via Background-separable Mode

Bing Tu[1], Xianchang Yang[2], Jun Li[3], Antonio Plaza[4], and Kaiyuan Chen[1]

[1] The Institute of Optics and Electronics, the State Key Laboratory Cultivation Base of Atmospheric Optoelectronic Detection and Information Fusion, Jiangsu International Joint Laboratory on Meteorological Photonics and Optoelectronic Detection, and Jiangsu Engineering Research Center for Intelligent Optoelectronic Sensing Technology of Atmosphere, Nanjing University of Information Science and Technology, Nanjing, China

[2] School of Information Science and Engineering, Hunan Institute of Science and Technology, Yueyang, China

[3] School of Computer Science and Hubei Key Laboratory of Intelligent Geo-Information Processing, University of Geosciences Wuhan, China

[4] Hyperspectral Computing Laboratory, Department of Technology of Computers and Communications, Escuela Politécnica, University of Extremadura, Cáceres, Spain

24.1 Hyperspectral Anomaly Detection Using Dual Window Density

In this section we introduce (for the first time in the literature) the intrinsic image decomposition (IID) into HSI anomaly detection. IID is a well-known problem in computer vision [1–5]. The HSIs comprise two main components: (i) the spectral reflectance component, which is determined by the material and (ii) the shading component, which is not only caused by the illumination conditions and the scene geometry, but also by the reflected solar radiation and thermal radiation of ground objects. Recently, a low-rank IID (LRIID) model [6] has been proposed, which extends the Retinex theory [7] to the multispectral IID domain. Inspired by this approach, and assuming that the Retinex theory also holds on the HSI domain, in this article we adapt the LRIID model to be suitable for recovering the reflectance and shading components from HSIs. In our context, the reflectance component is used for HSI anomaly detection and the shading component is removed. In order to exploit the reflectance component, we propose a new dual window density (DWD)-based anomaly detector that is based on the density peak clustering (DPC) algorithm [8]. In particular, the use of the reflectance component (with pure and highly discriminative spectral features) brings significant benefits to HSI anomaly detection (in general) and to our newly developed DWD. Specifically, our DWD performs adaptive density integration by using inner and outer windows to detect anomalies.

The newly proposed HSI anomaly detection method is based on two main ideas. First, a Retinex-based IID (RIID) model is used to extract the reflectance component and remove the shading component, in order to obtain pure and discriminative features. Figure 24.1 graphically illustrates the IID operation. Second, in order to avoid the Gaussian distribution assumption (and the contamination of the background statistics), and further detect anomalies with different sizes. Figure 24.2 provides a schematic of DWD. Hereinafter, the newly developed HSI anomaly detection method is referred to as R-DWD.

Machine-Learning-Based Hyperspectral Image Processing, First Edition. Edited by Bing Zhang.

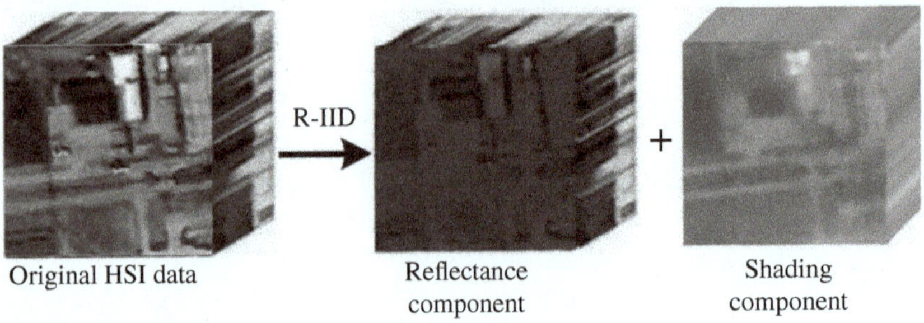

Figure 24.1 Graphical illustration of the RIID model.

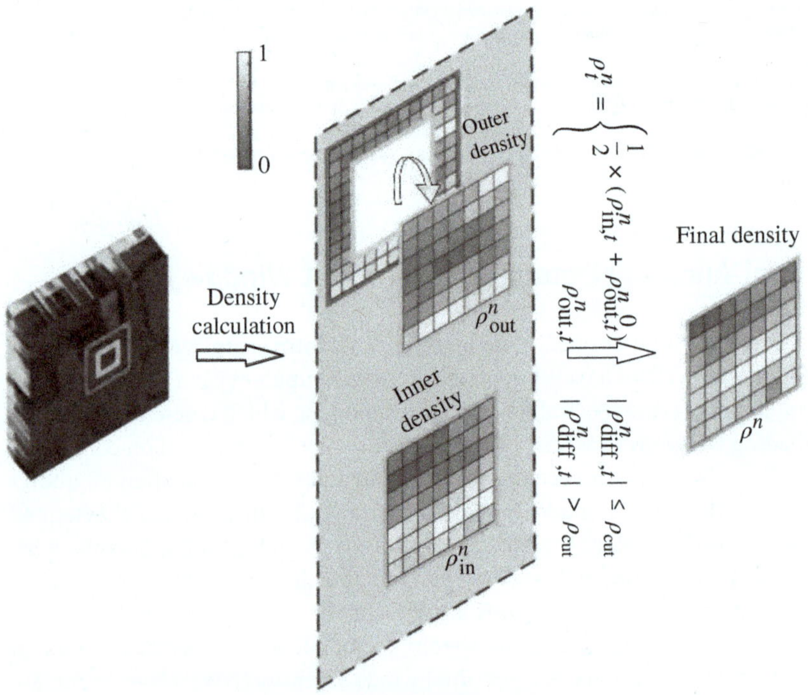

Figure 24.2 Schematic of the proposed DWD detector.

24.1.1 Related Work

In this section, we briefly revisit some related works, including the RX anomaly detector, the LRIID model, and the DPC algorithm.

24.1.1.1 RX Detector

The RX is one of the most typical hyperspectral anomaly detection methods which is defined as

$$RX(\mathbf{x}) = (\mathbf{x} - \mu)^T \Gamma^{(-1)} (\mathbf{x} - \mu) \tag{24.1}$$

where $\mathbf{x}$ is a test pixel, μ and Γ are the mean and covariance matrix of the global image, respectively. $RX(\boldsymbol{x})$ is the output of RX, which is the Mahalanobis distance, equivalent to the standard deviation away from the mean.

24.1.1.2 LRIID

Let a HSI be denoted as $\mathbf{X} = [\mathbf{x}_1, ..., \mathbf{x}_i, ..., \mathbf{x}_I] \in \mathbb{R}^{I \times D}$, where I and D are, respectively, the number of pixels and the number of spectral bands. In the IID problem, each pixel $\mathbf{x}_i$ can be modeled as the product of a reflectance component $\mathbf{r}_i$ and a shading component $\mathbf{s}_i$ as follows:

$$\mathbf{x}_i = \mathbf{r}_i. * \mathbf{s}_i. \tag{24.2}$$

The LRIID extends the Retinex theory to the multispectral IID domain as follows.

1) When the reflectance difference between two pixels is significant, the Retinex assumes that the difference between such pixels is mainly caused by the reflectance component (the shading tends to be consistent). This leads to $\mathbf{s}_i = \mathbf{s}_j$, which can also be written as $\mathbf{x}_i. * \mathbf{r}_j = \mathbf{x}_j. * \mathbf{r}_i$. We can define an energy function E_{sc} as follows:

$$E_{\text{sc}} = \sum_{i,j \in \mathrm{N}} \left|\left|w_{i,j}\left(\mathbf{x}_i. * \mathbf{r}_j - \mathbf{x}_j. * \mathbf{r}_i\right)\right|\right|^2 \tag{24.3}$$

where N is a neighborhood set (in which only horizontally adjacent and vertically adjacent pixels are considered) and $w_{i,\,j}$ contains the weights that reflect the similarity between the two pixels.

2) When the reflectance difference between two pixels is small, the Retinex assumes that the difference between the two pixels is mainly caused by the shading component (the reflectance tends to be consistent). This leads to $\mathbf{r}_i = \mathbf{r}_j$ and the energy function E_{rc} can be defined as follows:

$$E_{\text{rc}} = \sum_{i,j \in \mathrm{N}} \left|\left|v_{i,j}\left(\mathbf{r}_i - \mathbf{r}_j\right)\right|\right|^2 \tag{24.4}$$

where $v_{i,\,j}$ contains the weights that reflect the similarity between the two pixels. The LRIID introduces a low-rank basis for the reflectance, denoted as matrix $\mathbf{B}_r$, and the reflectance vectors can be linearly represented as $\mathbf{r}_i = \mathbf{B}_r\tilde{\mathbf{r}}_i$. The energy functions in 24.3 and 24.4 can be now separately written as:

$$\begin{aligned} E_{\text{sc}} &= \sum_{i,j \in \mathrm{N}} \left|\left|w_{i,j}\left(\mathbf{L}_i\mathbf{B}_r\tilde{\mathbf{r}}_j - \mathbf{L}_j\mathbf{B}_r\tilde{\mathbf{r}}_i\right)\right|\right|^2 \\ E_{\text{rc}} &= \sum_{i,j \in \mathrm{N}} \left|\left|v_{i,j}\left(\mathbf{B}_r\tilde{\mathbf{r}}_i - \mathbf{B}_r\tilde{\mathbf{r}}_j\right)\right|\right|^2 \end{aligned} \tag{24.5}$$

where $\mathbf{L}_i$ is a diagonal matrix composed of spectral elements of $\mathbf{x}_i$. In order to avoid the ambiguity of the IID problem, LRIID also provides another solution with a generic constraint on the coefficient sum as $\mathbf{M}\tilde{\mathbf{R}} = \mathbf{C}$, where $\tilde{\mathbf{R}}$ consists of $\tilde{\mathbf{r}}$ for all pixels. The energy functions can now be combined (in matrix form) as follows:

$$E_r = \left|\left|\mathbf{W}_{\mathbf{L},\mathbf{B}_r}\tilde{\mathbf{R}}\right|\right|^2 + \lambda_1\left|\left|\mathbf{V}_{\mathbf{B}_r}\tilde{\mathbf{R}}\right|\right|^2 + \lambda_2\left|\left|\mathbf{M}_r\tilde{\mathbf{R}} - \mathbf{C}\right|\right|^2 \tag{24.6}$$

where $\mathbf{W}_{\mathbf{L},\mathbf{B}_r}$ are jointly determined by the neighborhood set N, the weight $w_{i,j}$, the reflectance basis $\mathbf{B}_r$, and the spectral vector $\mathbf{x}_i$. Likewise, $\mathbf{V}_{\mathbf{B}_r}$, λ_1 and λ_2 are the weights that allow combining the three functions. When the shading base matrix $\mathbf{B}_s$ is known, the energy function can be formulated as follows (for a more detailed description of the LRIID model, we refer readers to the work [6]):

$$E_s = \left\|\mathbf{W}_{\mathbf{B}_s}\tilde{\mathbf{S}}\right\|^2 + \lambda_1 \left\|\mathbf{V}_{\mathbf{L},\mathbf{B}_s}\tilde{\mathbf{S}}\right\|^2 + \lambda_2 \left\|\mathbf{M}_s\tilde{\mathbf{S}} - \mathbf{C}\right\|^2 \tag{24.7}$$

24.1.1.3 DPC

In this section, we briefly describe the DPC algorithm (a detailed description is available in [9]). It relies on the Euclidean distance between two pixels $\mathbf{x}_i$ and $\mathbf{x}_j$, computed as follows:

$$d_{ij} = \left\|\mathbf{x}_i - \mathbf{x}_j\right\|. \tag{24.8}$$

The local density, ρ_i, of pixel $\mathbf{x}_i$ can then be defined [10] as

$$\rho_i = \sum_j \exp\left[\left(-\frac{d_{ij}}{d_c}\right)^2\right] \tag{24.9}$$

where d_c is the specified cutoff distance that indicates the radius of the search region, and is specified to control the weight degradation rate.

24.1.2 RIID

We apply the RIID to obtain the pure reflectance component in HSIs, with the aim of capturing material reflectance properties. Our assumption is that Retinex theory still plays a role in HSI data. Given the amount of evidence already available about the low rank nature of the reflectance space [6], a low-dimensional subspace of $\mathbf{X} \in \mathbb{R}^{I\times D}$ (designated by $\mathbf{X}' \in \mathbb{R}^{I\times D'}$) is firstextracted for subsequent processing. In order to keep the low rank nature, we use isometric sampling for band selection. Next, we introduce the assumptions of Retinex theory in HSI data. By adopting the weights w_{ij} and v_{ij}, we combine these two relations as follows:

$$w_{ij}\mathbf{x}_i .* \mathbf{r}_j + v_{ij}\mathbf{r}_i = w_{ij}\mathbf{x}_j .* \mathbf{r}_i + v_{ij}\mathbf{r}_j \tag{24.10}$$

where w_{ij} and v_{ij} are determined by a normalized cosine distance formulated as

$$d_{\mathbf{x}_i,\mathbf{x}_j} = 1 - \frac{\mathbf{x}_i \cdot \mathbf{x}_j}{|\mathbf{x}_i||\mathbf{x}_j|}. \tag{24.11}$$

As introduced in [6]

$$w_{ij} = \frac{1}{1 + e^{\alpha\left(d_{\mathbf{x}_i,\mathbf{x}_j} - \beta\right)}}, v_{ij} = 1 - w_{ij} \tag{24.12}$$

where α and β are the parameters of the sigmoid function. In our implementation, we assume that $\mathbf{x}_j$ denotes the pixels in the local window $\mathbf{W}_i$ of WI × WI, centered on pixel $\mathbf{x}_i$. The relation in 24.1 can now be written as follows:

$$\mathbf{r}_i = \sum_{j\in\mathbf{W}_i} \frac{v_{ij}\mathbf{r}_j - w_{ij}\mathbf{x}_i .* \mathbf{r}_j}{v_{ij} - w_{ij}\mathbf{x}_j}. \tag{24.13}$$

The resulting shading and reflectance components can be obtained by optimizing the following energy function:

$$E(\mathbf{r}_i, \mathbf{s}_i) = \sum_{i \in \mathbf{X}'} \left(\mathbf{r}_i - \sum_{j \in \mathbf{W}_i} \frac{v_{ij}\mathbf{r}_j - w_{ij}\mathbf{x}_i. * \mathbf{r}_j}{v_{ij} - w_{ij}\mathbf{x}_j} \right)^2 + \sum_{i \in \mathbf{X}'} \left(\frac{\mathbf{x}_i.}{\mathbf{s}_i - \mathbf{r}_i} \right)^2. \tag{24.14}$$

Let **R** and **S** be the matrices of the reflectance component $\mathbf{r}_i$ and the shading component $\mathbf{s}_i$, respectively. The shading component is not taken into account in this article, since it does not directly reflect the material features.

24.1.3 DWD Anomaly Detector

Specifically, we use the DPC to compute the density in local windows [11]. The resulting IID reflectance matrix $\mathbf{R} = [\mathbf{r}_1, ..., \mathbf{r}_i, ..., \mathbf{r}_I] \in \mathbb{R}^{I \times D'}$ is divided into N local windows, with T pixels represented as $\mathbf{Y}^n = [\mathbf{r}_1^n, ..., \mathbf{r}_t^n, ..., \mathbf{r}_T^n]$.For two pixels under test, that is, $\mathbf{r}_i^n$ and $\mathbf{r}_j^n$, belonging to the nth window, the Euclidean distance can be calculated as follows:

$$d_{ij}^n = \left\| \mathbf{r}_i^n - \mathbf{r}_j^n \right\|. \tag{24.15}$$

In this way, we can obtain a distance matrix $\mathbf{D}^n = [\mathbf{d}_1^n, ..., \mathbf{d}_t^n, ...\mathbf{d}_T^n]$, where the column $\mathbf{d}_t^n = d_{t1}^n, ..., d_{tt}^n, ..., d_{tT}^n$ denotes the distance between the tth pixel, $\mathbf{r}_t^n$, and all pixels under test within the nth window. Then, the upper triangular element s in matrix $\mathbf{D}^n$ are extracted and sorted as vector **d** in an ascending order. The cutoff distance d_c can be estimated as follows:

$$d_c = \mathbf{d}([T(T-1) \cdot P\%]) \tag{24.16}$$

where $[\cdot]$ represents the integer operation, P is a free-control parameter, and $P\%$ is the percentage which determines the position of d_c in d. Consequently, the local density of the pixels under test in the n-th window can be computer with (24.9). For convenience of the subsequent analysis, (24.9) is rewritten into an average form as follows:

$$\varrho\mathbf{P}^n = \frac{1}{T}\sum_{t=1}^{T} \exp\left[\left(-\frac{\mathbf{D}^n}{d_c} \right)^2 \right] \tag{24.17}$$

where $\varrho\mathbf{P}$ is the capital form of ρ and $\varrho\mathbf{P}^n$ is the density matrix of the n-th window.

Anomalies in images vary in size, and relying solely on density from a single window for detection can cause false positives. For example, in Figure 24.3, a 3×3 pixel target in a 12×12 pixel window has low density and is correctly identified as an anomaly. However, in a 4×4 pixel window, the target density increases, leading to misidentification. To mitigate this, a dual window operation is employed, allowing for accurate density computation that accounts for the relative size of the target to the background, enhancing anomaly detection by better characterizing the pixel density under test.

Specifically, the dual window refers to an inner window with a size of $W_{\text{in}} \times W_{\text{in}}$ and an outer window with size of $W_{\text{out}} \times W_{\text{out}}$, in which the outer window is centered on the inner window. The densities obtained in the n-th inner and outer windows are denoted ad the matrices $\varrho\mathbf{P}_{\text{in}}^n$ and $\varrho\mathbf{P}_{\text{out}}^n$, respectively. We note that $\varrho\mathbf{P}_{\text{out}}^n$ only consists of the densities of the center $W_{\text{in}} \times W_{\text{in}}$ pixels, which are extracted from the entire outer windows. The outer windows are treated as a pure background, assuming anomalies appear only in the inner windows. However, as dual windows

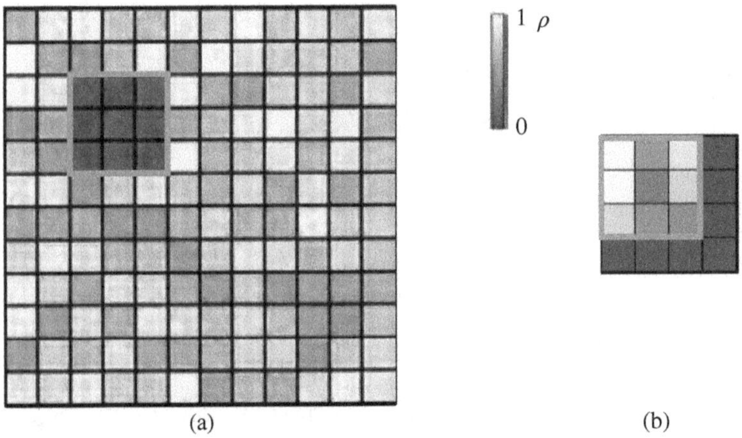

Figure 24.3 Density of the same target in different windows. (a) 3 × 3 target in a 12 × 12 window. (b) 3 × 3 target in a 4 × 4 window.

move across the image, anomalies often fall outside or cross inner window boundaries. To address this, a strategy is devised to eliminate interference from such anomalies, which is as follows.

Using Eq. (24.6), we compute the distance matrix D for pixels in an outer window, where D is symmetric and each row or column represents distances between a pixel and all others. Summing D by row or column yields vector d, indicating how much each pixel deviates from the background. Pixels are ranked by d, with the top 10% considered anomalies. The remaining 90%, deemed as background, are used to compute an average pixel vector u, which replaces the anomalies. This refines the pixel set for subsequent density calculations, reducing interference from anomalies outside or crossing inner window boundaries.

Then for a certain pixel under test $\mathbf{r}_t^n$, $\rho_{\text{in},t}^n$ and $\rho_{\text{out},t}^n$ are (separately) its density in the inner window and its density in the outer window, so that one of the following scenarios may appear.

If $\rho_{\text{in},t}^n$ and $\rho_{\text{out},t}^n$ are both relatively low, there should be an anomalous target with small size in the inner window, and $\mathbf{r}_t^n$ is supposed to be an anomalous pixel (e.g., pixel 1 in Figure 24.4). Here, $\rho_{\text{in},t}^n$ and $\rho_{\text{out},t}^n$ will be combined for detection.

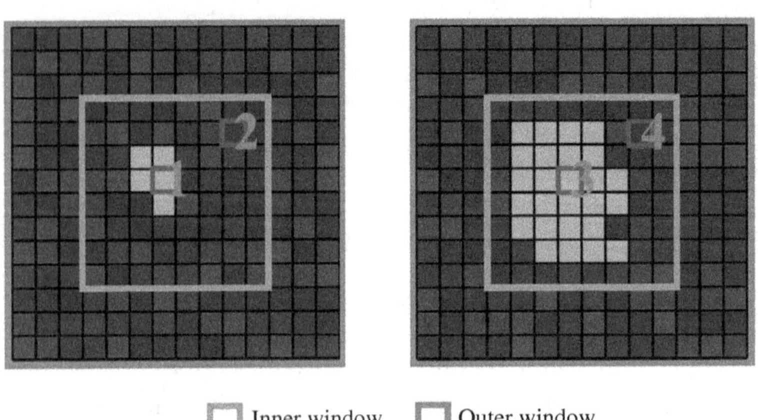

Figure 24.4 Illustration of four possible scenarios in anomaly detection.

If $\rho_{\text{in},t}^n$ and $\rho_{\text{out},t}^n$ are both relatively high, there should be an anomalous target with small size or no anomalies in the inner window, and $\mathbf{r}_t^n$ is supposed to be a normal background pixel (e.g., pixel 2 in Figure 24.4). Here, $\rho_{\text{in},t}^n$ and $\rho_{\text{out},t}^n$ will be combined for detection.

If $\rho_{\text{in},t}^n$ is relatively high and $\rho_{\text{out},t}^n$ is relatively low, there should be an anomalous target with large size in inner window and $\mathbf{r}_t^n$ is supposed to be an anomalous pixel (e.g., pixel 3 in Figure 24.4). Here, $\rho_{\text{out},t}^n$ will be used for detection.

If $\rho_{\text{in},t}^n$ is relatively low and $\rho_{\text{out},t}^n$ is relatively high, there should be an anomalous target with large size in the inner window an $\mathbf{r}_t^n$ is supposed to be a normal background pixel (e.g., pixel 4 in Figure 24.4). Here, $\rho_{\text{out},t}^n$ will be used for detection.

Let us define $\varrho\mathbf{P}_{\text{diff}}^n = \varrho\mathbf{P}_{\text{out}}^n - \varrho\mathbf{P}_{\text{in}}^n$ as the difference density matrix between $\varrho\mathbf{P}_{\text{in}}^n$ and $\varrho\mathbf{P}_{\text{out}}^n$, and $\rho_{\text{diff},t}^n$ is the element of $\varrho\mathbf{P}_{\text{diff}}^n$, namely the difference value between the density of $\mathbf{r}_t^n$ in the outer window and in the inner window. When $\rho_{\text{in},t}^n$ and $\rho_{\text{out},t}^n$ are both relatively low or high, the absolute value of $\rho_{\text{diff},t}^n$ tends to be large. As a result, we can decide which density to be used for each pixel under test in the inner window as follows:

$$\rho_t^n = \begin{cases} \frac{1}{2}\left(\rho_{\text{in},t}^n + \rho_{\text{out},t}^n\right), & |\, \rho_{\text{diff},t}^n \,| \le \rho_{\text{cut}} \\ \rho_{\text{out},t}^n, & |\, \rho_{\text{diff},t}^n \,| > \rho_{\text{cut}} \end{cases} \tag{24.18}$$

where ρ_{cut} is the cutoff density, set as 3×10^{-3} in this article. Then, in order to obtain a separable density distribution, we propose the following method:

$$\rho_t^n = \rho_t^n \cdot \exp\left(\frac{d_c^n}{d_{tk}^n} - 1\right) \tag{24.19}$$

where d_c^n is the cut-off distance of the nth inner window, d_{tk}^n is the distance between pixel $\mathbf{r}_t^n$ and $\mathbf{r}_k^n$, and $\mathbf{r}_k^n$ is the pixel with the highest density in the nth inner window. Finally, the density is normalized by the tanh function as follows:

$$\rho_t^n = \frac{\exp(\rho_t^n) - \exp(\rho_t^n)}{\exp(\rho_t^n) + \exp(\rho_t^n)}. \tag{24.20}$$

$\varrho\mathbf{P}^n$ is the final density of the nth inner window. A density map can be constructed for the whole image by combining the local densities of all of the N windows. Anomalies can be determined using the final density map. Due to the fact that anomalies are usually rare and exhibit low density in the image, if the density of a pixel under test is smaller than a given threshold, the pixel under test will be determined as an anomaly.

24.1.4 Experimental Results

24.1.4.1 Experimental Setup

Experiments were performed on the Airport-Beach-Urban (ABU) data set. In order to conduct an exhaustive quantitative evaluation, we use receiver operating characteristic (ROC) curves [12] and the area under the curve (AUC) as our metrics for evaluating the detection performance of different methods. Due to the different spatial and spectral characteristics of the considered images, we report different parameter settings for the proposed R-DWD method when applied to the different images considered in our experiment, as shown in Table 24.1.

Table 24.1 Parameter setting for the proposed R-DWD method in each analyzed image.

Images	*Win*	*Wout*	P	α	β
Airport-(1)	11	35	1	1300	10^{-3}
Airport-(2)	20	34	1	3000	10^{-5}
Airport-(3)	7	35	1	9000	5×10^{-4}
Airport-(4)	15	23	5	11,000	5×10^{-4}
Beach-(1)	14	34	4	13,000	5×10^{-6}
Beach-(2)	6	12	21	1000	10^{-4}
Beach-(3)	19	35	5	7000	10^{-3}
Beach-(4)	16	34	5	1000	5×10^{-3}
Urban-(1)	5	13	20	1000	5×10^{-5}
Urban-(2)	21	35	30	1000	5×10^{-4}
Urban-(3)	14	28	19	1000	5×10^{-3}
Urban-(4)	13	35	30	1000	5×10^{-3}
Urban-(5)	21	35	17	11,000	5×10^{-4}

24.1.4.2 Detection Performance

In this section, the proposed R-DWD method is compared to five widely used anomaly detection methods: the RX detector [13], the LRX detector [13], the CRD detector [14], the local kernel RX (L-KRX) detector [15], the low-rank and sparse matrix decomposition (LRaSMD)-based Mahalanobis distance detector (LSMAD) [16], and the density measurement-based SDBP detector [17]. Table 24.2 shows the detection performance in terms of the AUC score for each compared method. The best score for each row is highlighted in bold. It can be seen that the proposed R-DWD method obtains the highest AUCs compared to other methods in most of the considered images. And the volatility of the AUC for the R-DWD method is also smaller than for the other tested methods, which reveals a better stability of our newly developed R-DWD. Figure 24.5–Figure 24.7 show the detection maps obtained by the different tested methods on the Airport, Beach, and Urban-scenes. As can be intuitively seen, the R-DWD provides the best detection maps.

24.1.4.3 Summary

This article introduces a new HSI anomaly detection method called R-DWD. Our method is composed of main ingredients: the RIID and the DWD-based anomaly detector. The RIID is adapted from the low rank multispectral IID model, called LRIID, which can effectively extract the reflectance component of HSIs for anomaly detection purposes. In order to exploit this reflectance component for anomaly detection purposes, a DWD is proposed that circumvents the Gaussian assumption of the distribution of the background in HSIs, improving the calculation of background statistics. The dual window operation of DWD exhibits the ability to detect anomalies with varying sizes and accurately recognize their shape. Our experimental results, conducted on a large database of HSIs including airport, beach, and urban scenes, demonstrate the superiority of the proposed method with regards to state-of the-art competitors. As with any new approach, there are still some unresolved issues that may present challenges over time. Specifically, the proposed method still

Table 24.2 AUC scores obtained on the ABU Data set by the R-DWD, O-DWD, DWD, RX, LRX, CRD, L-KRX, LSMAD and SDBP anomaly detection methods.

				Airport scene					
Images	**R-DWD**	**O-DWD**	**DWD**	**RX**	**LRX**	**CRD**	**L-KRX**	**LSMAD**	**SDBP**
Airport-(1)	0.9716	0.9518	**0.9723**	0.8281	0.9665	0.9665	0.9005	0.8720	0.9615
Airport-(2)	**0.9940**	0.9856	0.9876	0.8404	0.9744	0.9874	0.8590	0.9018	0.9842
Airport-(3)	0.9732	0.9568	**0.9804**	0.9288	0.9564	0.9559	0.8680	0.9225	0.9662
Airport-(4)	**0.9986**	0.9940	0.9955	0.9526	0.9757	0.8740	0.9592	0.9588	0.9930
Average	**0.9844**	0.9721	0.9839	0.8874	0.9682	0.9459	0.8966	0.9132	0.9762
				Beach scene					
Images	**R-DWD**	**O-DWD**	**DWD**	**RX**	**LRX**	**CRD**	**L-KRX**	**LSMAD**	**SDBP**
Beach-(1)	0.9931	0.9903	0.9895	0.9807	0.9956	0.9916	0.9753	0.9737	**0.9959**
Beach-(2)	**0.9903**	0.9736	**0.9903**	0.9106	0.9777	0.9416	0.9012	0.9133	0.9876
Beach-(3)	**0.9999**	0.9998	0.9998	**0.9999**	0.9997	0.9996	0.9997	**0.9999**	**0.9999**
Beach-(4)	**0.9871**	0.9609	0.9866	0.9538	0.9391	0.9561	0.9771	0.9528	0.9763
Average	**0.9926**	0.9812	0.9915	0.9915	0.9780	0.9722	0.9633	0.9599	0.9899
				Urban scene					
Images	**R-DWD**	**O-DWD**	**DWD**	**RX**	**LRX**	**CRD**	**L-KRX**	**LSMAD**	**SDBP**
Urban-(1)	0.9851	0.9675	0.9867	0.9907	0.9968	0.9948	0.9885	0.9904	**0.9989**
Urban-(2)	0.9958	0.9737	0.9956	0.9946	0.9231	0.9410	0.9959	0.9951	**0.9984**
Urban-(3)	**0.9970**	0.9812	0.9962	0.9513	0.9800	0.9696	0.9816	0.9657	0.9946
Urban-(4)	0.9911	0.9531	0.9903	0.9887	0.9696	0.9816	0.9928	0.9864	**0.9972**
Urban-(5)	0.9711	0.9582	0.9744	0.9692	0.9538	0.9521	0.9638	0.9668	**0.9877**
Average	0.9880	0.9667	0.9885	0.9789	0.9646	0.9665	0.9808	0.9809	**0.9954**

produces a certain number of false alarms in the detection result, and the parameter setting of our algorithm is laborious. These aspects deserve further research and improvements in future work. We are also planning on developing an efficient implementation of the proposed approach by resorting to high performance computing architectures such as graphics processing units (GPUs).

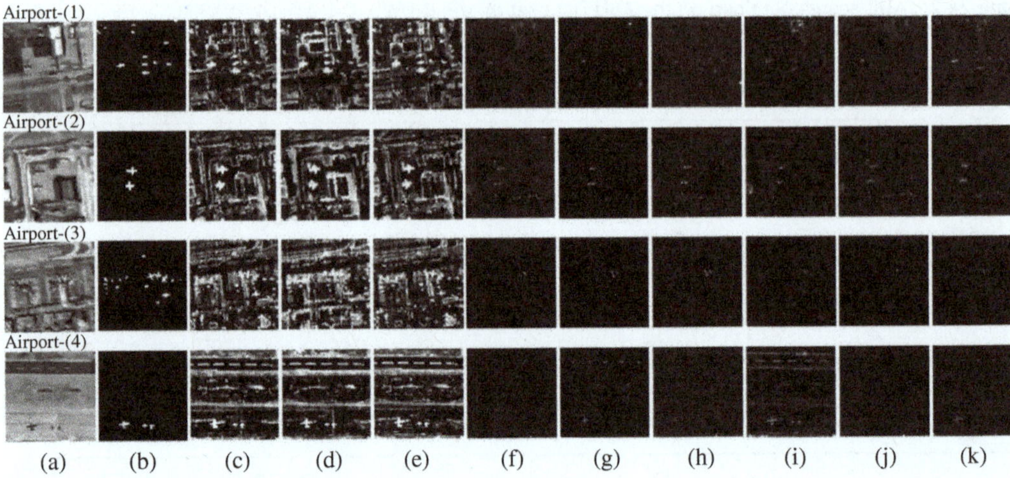

Figure 24.5 Detection maps obtained by the different tested methods on the Airport scene. (a) Grayscale composite of the HSI. (b) Reference map showing the targets to be detected. (c) Result of the R-DWD method. (d) Result of the O-DWD method. (e) Result of the DWD method. (f) Result of the RX method. (g) Result of the LRX method. (h) Result of the CRD method. (i) Result of the L-KRX method. (j) Result of the LSMAD method. (k) Result of the SDBP method.

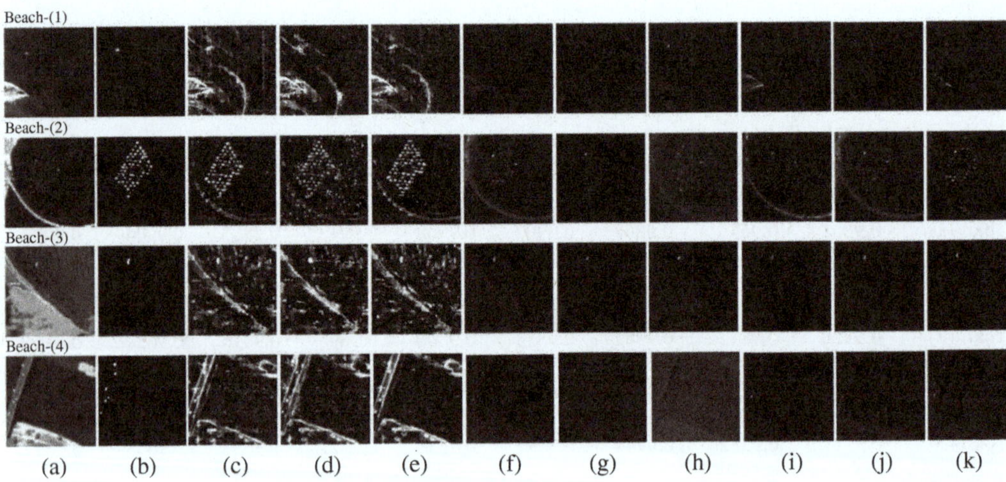

Figure 24.6 Detection maps obtained by the different tested methods on the Beach scene. (a) Grayscale composite of the HSI. (b) Reference map showing the targets to be detected. (c) Result of the R-DWD method. (d) Result of the O-DWD method. (e) Result of the DWD method. (f) Result of the RX method. (g) Result of the LRX method. (h) Result of the CRD method. (i) Result of the L-KRX method. (j) Result of the LSMAD method. (k) Result of the SDBP method.

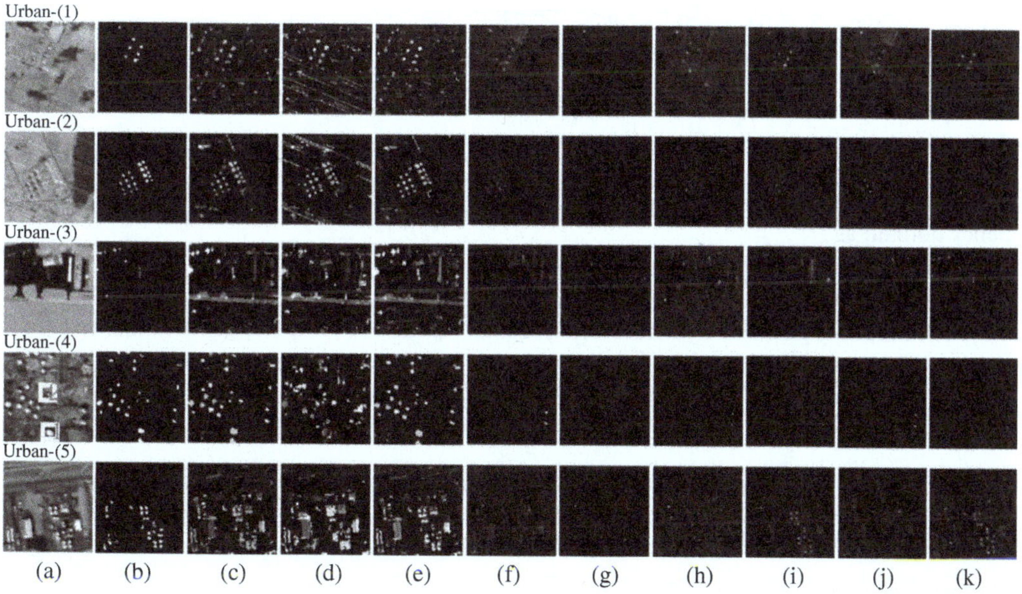

Figure 24.7 Detection maps obtained by the different tested methods on the Urban scene. (a) Grayscale composite of the HSI. (b) Reference map showing the targets to be detected. (c) Result of the R-DWD method. (d) Result of the O-DWD method. (e) Result of the DWD method. (f) Result of the RX method. (g) Result of the LRX method. (h) Result of the CRD method. (i) Result of the L-KRX method. (j) Result of the LSMAD method. (k) Result of the SDBP method.

24.2 Hyperspectral Anomaly Detection Using Reconstruction Fusion of Quaternion Frequency Domain Analysis

In this part, we propose a new HAD method using reconstruction fusion based on FT and QFT [18]. To elucidate the motivations and principles of our proposed method, we elaborate the following two basic ideas from phenomenon to theory. First, we illustrate that spikes in the amplitude spectrum correspond to the background, and a Gaussian low-pass filter performing on the amplitude spectrum is equivalent to an anomaly detector. Second, we illustrate that the phase spectrum is critical information to perceive the spatial saliency of anomalies.

24.2.1 Background Modeling in Frequency Domain

An image is a 2-D discrete signal, while an HSI is a series of 2-D images stacked along with spectral bands. The rich diagnostic features of HSIs can be reflected in the spectral value difference of all pixels in any band. Naturally, we use 2-D FT for frequency domain analysis of HSIs. The 2-D FT has a very definite physical meaning in image processing. It essentially transforms the image intensity distribution into the frequency distribution. The frequency of a 2-D image can measure the extent of change in local regions. In general, smooth regular changes are low-frequency components, while dramatically irregular changes are high-frequency components. In HSIs, the background is presented in periodic repeating patterns that change smoothly and regularly. Thus, the frequency contains important information about the background and anomalies.

24.2.1.1 Background Modeling in Frequency Domain

Given an image $\in\mathbb{R}^{M\times N}$, the 2-D FT is defined as

$$\mathbf{F}(u,v)=\frac{1}{\mathrm{MN}}\sum_{n=0}^{N-1}\sum_{m=0}^{M-1}\mathbf{I}(m,n)e^{-2\pi i\left(\frac{mu}{M}+\frac{nv}{N}\right)} \tag{24.21}$$

where $\mathbf{F}$ refers to the frequency domain representation of $\mathbf{I}$, which is a complex matrix in the frequency domain as

$$\mathbf{F}=\mathbf{Real}+i\mathbf{Imaginary} \tag{24.22}$$

where $\mathbf{Real}$ and $\mathbf{Imaginary}$ are the real and imaginary parts of F, respectively. Its amplitude and phase-angle form is

$$\mathbf{F}(u,v)=\mathbf{A}(u,v)e^{i\mathbf{P}(u,v)} \tag{24.23}$$

where the amplitude spectrum is given as

$$\mathrm{A}=\sqrt{\mathbf{Real}^2+\mathbf{Imaginary}^2} \tag{24.24}$$

and the phase spectrum is given as

$$\mathrm{P}=\arctan\left(\frac{\mathbf{Imaginary}}{\mathbf{Real}}\right). \tag{24.25}$$

Then, the 2-D inverse FT (IFT) is defined as

$$\begin{aligned}\mathbf{I}(m,n)&=\sum_{v=0}^{N-1}\sum_{u=0}^{M-1}\mathbf{F}(u,v)e^{2\pi i\left(\frac{um}{M}+\frac{vn}{N}\right)}\\&=\mathcal{F}^{-1}\left[\mathbf{A}(u,v)e^{i\mathbf{P}(u,v)}\right].\end{aligned} \tag{24.26}$$

In the following, we use $\mathcal{F}$ and $\mathcal{F}^{-1}$ to denote FT and IFT, respectively.

In images, especially those with simple backgrounds, the amplitude spectrum's energy is mostly concentrated in low frequencies, with very low high-frequency energy, hindering frequency domain analysis. To address this, we use the log amplitude spectrum calculated by $\mathbf{L}=\log 1+\mathbf{A}$ for analysis. Figure 24.8 illustrates the log amplitude spectrum of an image in 2-D, 1-D, and 3-D forms. The 1-D form is a cross-section of the 2-D spectrum, while the 3-D form is a surface plot. These forms facilitate easier observation of frequency distribution due to their value axes. In Figure 24.8(d), the x-axis represents frequency and the y-axis amplitude. When the zero-frequency component is centered, the amplitude spectrum becomes symmetric, with frequency increasing further from the origin. In natural images, amplitude typically decreases at high frequencies.

The amplitude spectrum represents frequency distribution. In [19], it was shown that spikes in the amplitude spectrum of a 1-D signal indicate non-saliency. Here, we demonstrate that such spikes correspond to the background in 2-D images. Figure 24.9(a) shows five image signals where different numbers of periodic patterns (elliptical boxes) and a constant anomaly (rectangular box) are embedded. Figure 24.9 (b) shows their corresponding 3-D-form and 1-D-form log amplitude spectrum, respectively. Image 1, having no components, shows no spectrum response. From images 2 to 5, as periodic patterns increase, sharper spectrum spikes appear, especially in image 4 with 169 patterns. The definition of *sharpness* introduced in [19] was adopted, defined as

$$\gamma(\mathbf{x})=\|\mathbf{x}-\mathbf{h}\otimes\mathbf{x}\|_\infty \tag{24.27}$$

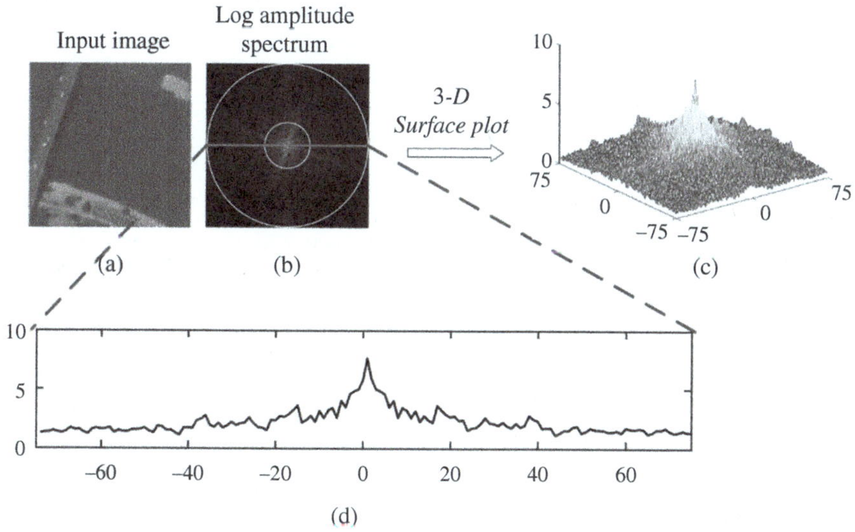

Figure 24.8 Illustration of the image log amplitude spectrum. (a) Input image. (b) 2-D log amplitude spectrum. (c) Surface plot of (b). (d) 1-D cross section of (b).

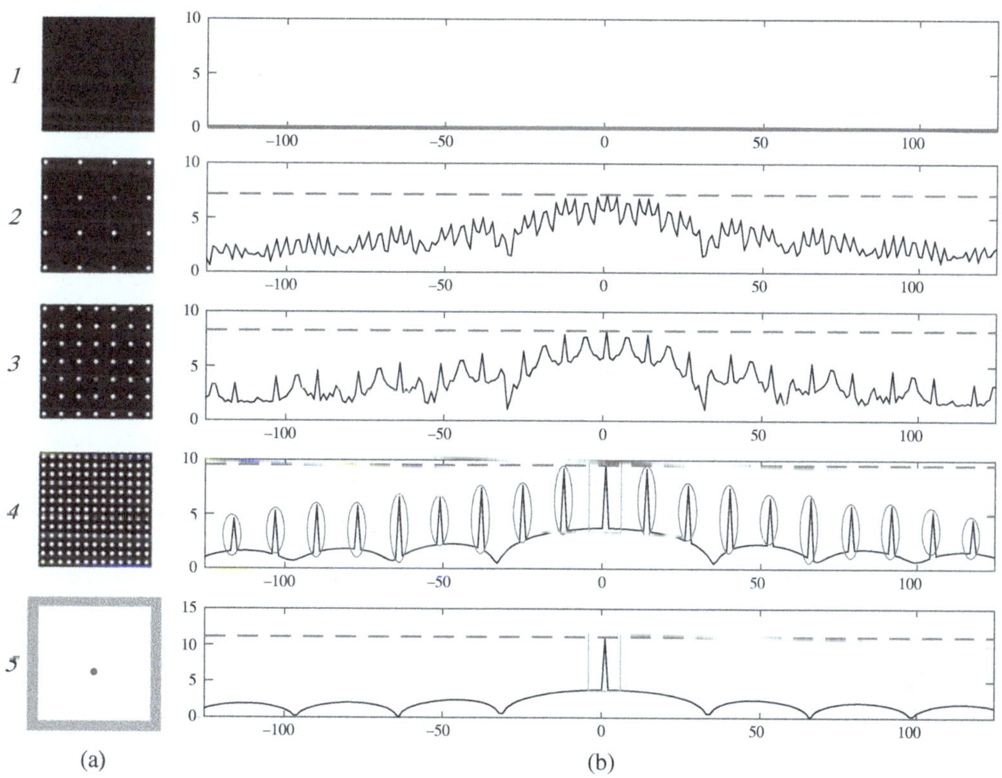

Figure 24.9 Example of that periodic patterns corresponds to sharp spikes of amplitude spectrum. (a) Left: images with different number of repeated cycles. (b) Middle and right: corresponding 3-D-form and 1-D-form amplitude spectrum.

where **x** represent a 1-D-form amplitude spectrum, **h** is a 1-D low-pass Gaussian kernel, and $\gamma(\mathbf{X})$ denotes the *sharpness* of **x**. The sharper the original spike, the more it is filtered by the Gaussian kernel with fixed scale. The sharpness values of the five spectrums in Figure 24.9 are 0, 1.8957, 2.8468, 4.8384, and 6.1152, respectively.

In the amplitude spectrum of image 4, multiple spikes are visible. The spike at the zero-frequency component (rectangular box) corresponds to a single circle's repeating pattern, while other spikes (elliptical boxes) correspond to patterns of multiple neighboring circles. Image 5, with circles filling the space, shows only one spike due to a uniform repeating pattern. For theoretical justification of this fact, we take 1-D periodic signal $f(t)$ with frequency of $n\omega_1$ as an example. Because of FT separability, the discussion is easily extended to 2-D. Suppose that

$$f(t) = \sum_{n=-\infty}^{+\infty} F(n)e^{jn\omega_1 t} \tag{24.28}$$

where

$$F(n) = \frac{1}{T}\int_{-\frac{T}{2}}^{\frac{T}{2}} f(t)e^{-jn\omega_1 t}dt. \tag{24.29}$$

Then, the FT of $f(t)$ is

$$\mathcal{F}(w) = 2\pi \sum_{n=-\infty}^{\infty} F(n)\delta(\omega - n\omega_1) \tag{24.30}$$

where

$$\delta(\omega - n\omega_1) = \begin{cases} 1, & \text{if} \omega = n\omega_1 \\ 0, & \text{otherwise} \end{cases} \tag{24.31}$$

is the unit Dirac delta function. According to (24.30), it is clear that the frequency spectrum of the periodic signal $f(t)$ consists of infinite Dirac delta spikes, resulting in an extremely large amplitude at the frequency of $n\omega_1$. In practice, the Dirac delta functions in (24.30) will be replaced by sinc functions because the signal to be processed is finite, but the spectrum of the periodic signal is still with very sharp spikes.

From the above-mentioned analysis, we can conclude that the periodic patterns correspond to the spikes of the amplitude spectrum. In Figure 24.10, we take a widely used HSI (Gulfport) for HAD [20] as example. After the original image illustrated in Figure 24.10 (a) is divided into small patches, it can be found that the patches with anomalies (airplanes) are significantly different from the other patches, while the others (the patches in the background area) belong to two or three major classes, and the patches in each class are highly similar, as illustrated in Figure 24.10 (b). That is further to say that the background appears as periodic patterns in HAD. Thus, the background can be modeled in the frequency domain as the spikes of the amplitude spectrum.

24.2.1.2 From Filtered Amplitude Reconstruction to Anomaly Detection Map

At this point, we establish the correspondence between the background and the spikes of the amplitude spectrum. Then by filtering the spikes in the frequency domain, the background will be suppressed and the anomalies will be extracted in the spatial domain. This is formulated as follows:

$$\mathbf{A}_s = \mathcal{G}_\sigma \otimes \mathbf{A} \tag{24.32}$$

where $\mathcal{G}_\sigma \in \mathbb{R}^{M_g \times N_g}$ is a Gaussian low-pass kernel with standard deviation σ, given by $\mathcal{G}(m,n) = 1/(2\pi\sigma^2)e^{-(m^2+n^2)/(2\sigma^2)}$. $\otimes$ denotes the convolution operation; and $\mathbf{A}_s$ is the filtered

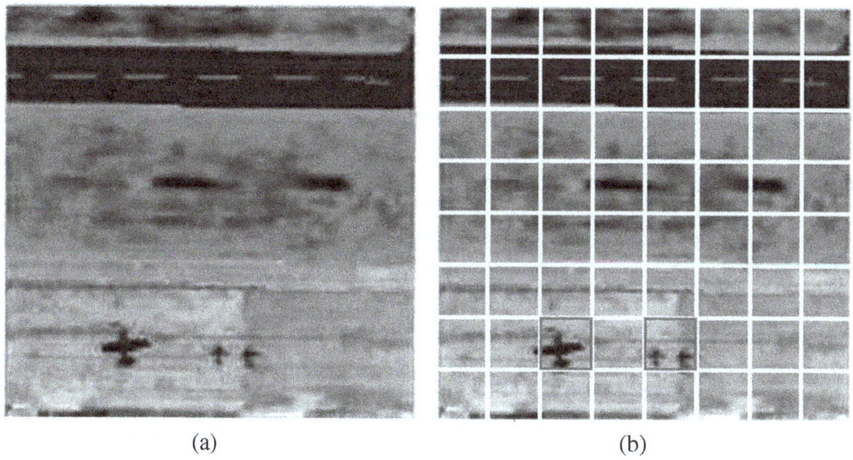

Figure 24.10 Example of background periodic patterns. (a, b) Right: collection of small patches of the left HSI.

amplitude spectrum. Using $\mathbf{A}_s$ and original phase $\mathbf{P}$, the initial anomaly detection map MFAR in spatial domain can be obtained by IFT

$$\mathbf{M}_{\text{FAR}} = \left|\mathcal{F}^{-1}\left(\mathbf{A}_s e^{i\mathbf{P}}\right)\right| \tag{24.33}$$

where $|\cdot|$ represents modulo operation.

Figure 24.11 (a) demonstrates a synthetic image with a gray-filled rectangular anomaly against a background of repeated white-filled circles. An anomaly detector should highlight this distinct rectangle. Figure 24.11 (b) shows the image's amplitude spectrum in 3-D and 1-D forms, revealing spikes corresponding to the background. After the Gaussian low-pass filtering with $\sigma = 1$, the

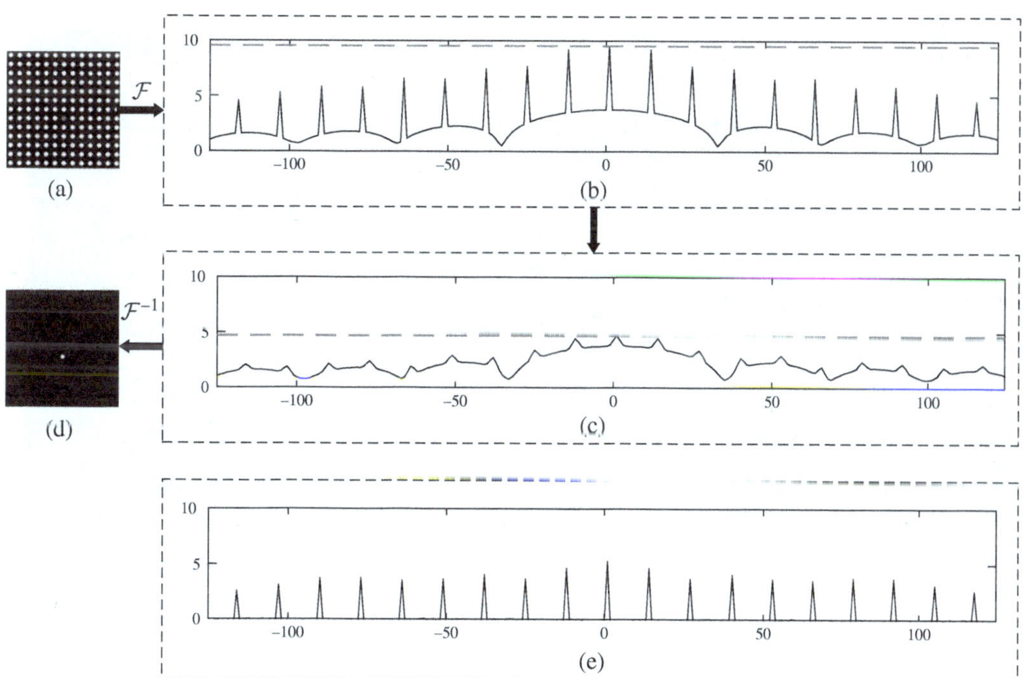

Figure 24.11 (a–e) Example of the suppression of periodic patterns using spectrum filtering.

filtered amplitude spectrum is depicted in Figure 24.11 (c), with Figure 24.11 (d) showing an anomaly map where anomalies are preserved against a suppressed background. Figure 24.11 (e) displays frequency components removed by the filter, indicating that Gaussian low-pass filtering on the amplitude spectrum effectively acts as an anomaly detector.

24.2.2 Reconstruction Fusion of Fourier Transform

Figure 24.12 illustrates synthetic images with periodic backgrounds and a gray triangle anomaly in the first column, and their ground truth in the second column. The third row shows the initial detection map using FAR with $\sigma = 10$. In simple backgrounds (image 1), the anomaly is clearly detected with the background well suppressed. However, in more complex backgrounds (images 2 and 3), while the anomaly remains prominent, other details, especially edges between different periodic backgrounds, are also highlighted. These detection results may include both anomalies and non-anomalous aperiodic variations. To address this, we propose using phase-only reconstruction (POR) of FT to enhance FAR results.

24.2.2.1 Phase-only Reconstruction

Before the fusion of FAR and POR, we first discuss what the phase spectrum represents. We provide examples using 1-D signal $s(t)$ to indicate the underlying principle and intrinsic rules of the phase spectrum. Because of FT separability, the discussion is easily extended to 2-D. let the FT of $s(t)$ be

$$\mathcal{F}(\omega) = \frac{1}{\sqrt{2\pi}} \int_{-\infty}^{+\infty} s(t) e^{-i\omega t} dt = \mathcal{A}(\omega) e^{i\mathcal{P}(\omega)} \tag{24.34}$$

where $\mathcal{P}(\omega)$ is the phase of $s(t)$. Then, the POR of $s(t)$ is given by $\mathcal{POR}(s) = \mathcal{F}^{-1}\left[e^{i\mathcal{P}(\omega)}\right]$.

Figure 24.13 demonstrates 1-D signal phase-only reconstruction (POR). Figure 24.13 (a) shows 1-D periodic signals with embedded anomalies, and Figure 24.13 (b) displays their

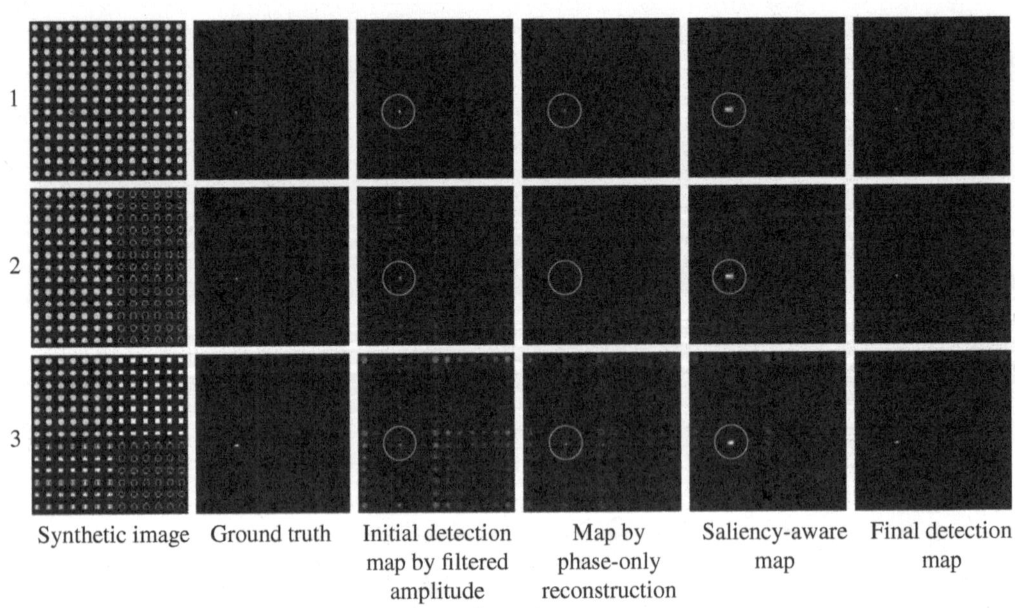

Figure 24.12 Example of reconstruction fusion of FT for anomaly detection.

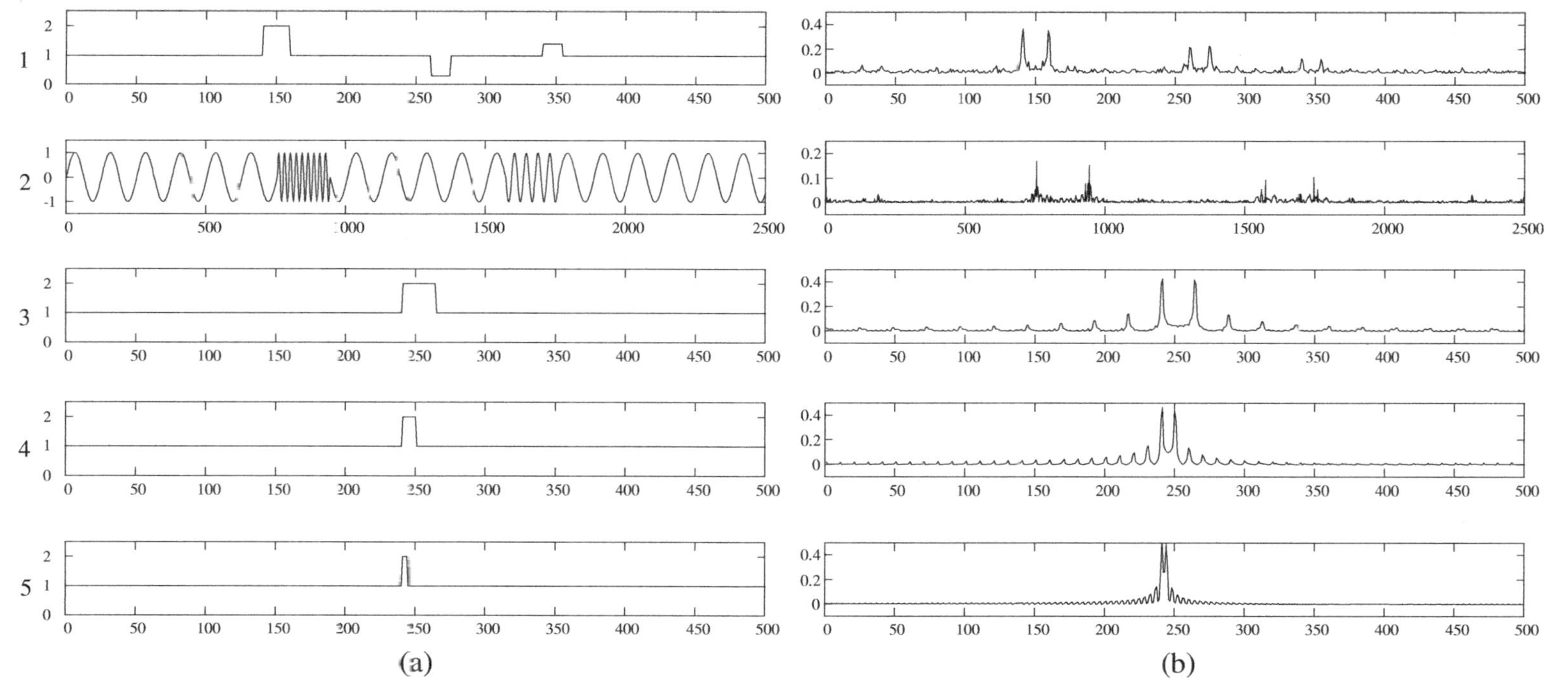

Figure 24.13 Examples of 1-D signal POR. (a) Left: original signal. (b) Right: reconstructed signal with POR.

POR-reconstructed signals, plotted using |POR(s)| for clarity. Signal 1 illustrates a straight line with three embedded pulses (anomalies); reconstruction highlights maximum peaks at signal edges. Signal 2, a sinusoidal periodic signal, features short segment anomalies due to frequency differences. POR highlights these segment edges while suppressing the background. According to Castlman [21], the amplitude spectrum quantifies periodic components, while the phase spectrum determines their positions. Low periodicity or abrupt changes highlight targets in POR, indicating anomaly locations. As anomaly size decreases (signals 3 to 5), the reconstruction's highlighted area shifts from edges to entire anomalies, relevant for hyperspectral image detection where anomalies are small but distinct from the background.

For FT of images, the map of POR $\mathbf{M}_{\text{POR}}$ is formulated as

$$\mathbf{M}_{\text{POR}} = \left|\mathcal{F}^{-1}\left(e^{i\mathbf{P}}\right)\right|. \tag{24.35}$$

As shown in Figure 24.12 the maps obtained by POR (the fourth column) can also detect the anomalies. So POR can also be regarded as an anomaly detector in a sense. However, there are some differences between the results of POR and FAR. When compared with FAR, POR suppressed the background better but reduced the significance of the anomaly. Next, we will discuss the justification of this.

According to (24.23), we can rewrite (24.35) as

$$\mathbf{M}_{\text{POR}} = \left|\mathcal{F}^{-1}\left(\frac{\mathbf{F}}{\mathbf{A}}\right)\right| = \left|\mathcal{F}^{-1}\left[\mathbf{A}_{\text{unit}}e^{i\mathbf{P}}\right]\right|. \tag{24.36}$$

From (24.36), we can conclude that POR is actually the IFT with the unified amplitude spectrum $\mathbf{A}_{\text{unit}}$ where the amplitude value equals 1 for all frequency components. In fact, the unified amplitude spectrum $\mathbf{A}_{\text{unit}}$ is the limiting case of the filtered amplitude spectrum $\mathbf{A}_{\mathbf{s}}$. In other words, when the value of σ for the Gaussian kernel is extremely large, the filtered amplitude spectrum tends to be uniform. And we can explain why POR can detect anomalies and produce greater suppression (both for background and anomalies). The reason is that there is no spike in $\mathbf{A}_{\text{unit}}$ and the POR carries out high-frequency component emphasis, resulting in the prominence of aperiodic areas.

24.2.2.2 Reconstruction Fusion for Anomaly Detection

For HAD, both anomaly emphasis and background suppression are important. From the discussion, we know that FAR and POR can complement each other in anomaly emphasis and background suppression. Therefore, we propose a HAD method based on reconstruction fusion of FT (RFFT). However, as the role of enhancing background suppression, the map by POR is not ideal (as shown in the fourth column of Figure 24.12). As a result, before the fusion of the FAR and POR, the POR is successively enhanced by square operation and Gaussian filtering as follows:

$$\tilde{\mathbf{M}}_{\text{POR}} = \mathcal{G}_{\sigma} \otimes \mathbf{M}_{\text{POR}}^{2} \tag{24.37}$$

where the square operation is to further suppress the background, and the Gaussian filtering is to increase the spatial saliency region of anomalies. For convenience, the Gaussian kernel used in (24.36) is the same one used in FAR. As shown in the fifth column of Figure 24.12, the enhanced POR ($\tilde{\mathbf{M}}_{\text{POR}}$) can effectively improve background suppression. In addition, anomalies are also enhanced but their details (such as shapes) are not preserved. Thus, $\tilde{\mathbf{M}}_{\text{POR}}$ can be regarded as a saliency-aware map perceiving anomaly targets. At this point, we can simply realize reconstruction fusion through the product of $\mathbf{M}_{\text{FAR}}$ and $\tilde{\mathbf{M}}_{\text{POR}}$ as

$$\mathbf{M}_{\text{RFFT}} = \mathbf{M}_{\text{FAR}} \odot \tilde{\mathbf{M}}_{\text{POR}} \tag{24.38}$$

where ⊙ represent elementwise production and $\mathbf{M}_{\text{RFFT}}$ is the final detection map. The last column of Figure 24.12 shows the final detection map obtained by RFFT. Compared with the initial anomaly map by FAR and saliency-aware map by POR, the detection effect by reconstruction fusion is obviously improved.

24.2.3 Multiscale and Multifeature Processing Using Quaternion Fourier Transform

In this section, we go further and make possible improvements to RFFT. Specifically, due to the variability of anomaly scale and spectral feature in HSIs, we adopt the quaternion Fourier transform (QFT) [18] additionally to the standard FT, for conducting multiscale and multifeature processing in a parallel way, to obtain the frequency domain representation of HSIs.

The size of the receptive field is basically the same at different scales.

24.2.3.1 Quaternion Fourier Transform

Different from FT which takes a real matrix (each element is a real number) as input, the input of the QFT is a quaternion matrix that is specified to be a quaternion [18]. Each element of the quaternion matrix is a quaternion number. Given a quaternion image (quaternion matrix)

$$\mathbf{I}_q = \mathbf{I}_{q,0} + \mathbf{I}_{q,1}i + \mathbf{I}_{q,2}j + \mathbf{I}_{q,3}k \tag{24.39}$$

where $\mathbf{I}_{q,0}$, $\mathbf{I}_{q,1}$, $\mathbf{I}_{q,2}$, and $\mathbf{I}_{q,3}$ are real matrix, and $i^2 = j^2 = k^2 = ijk = -1, i \perp j, i \perp k, j \perp k, k = ij$. The doscrete QFT of $\mathbf{I}_q$ is defined as

$$\mathbf{F}_q(u, v) = \frac{1}{\sqrt{\text{MN}}} \sum_{n=0}^{N-1} \sum_{m=0}^{M-1} \mathbf{I}_q(m, n) e^{-\mu 2\pi\left(\frac{mu}{M} + \frac{nv}{N}\right)} \tag{24.40}$$

where μ is a pure quaternion and $\mu^2 = -1$. $\mathbf{F}_q$ is the frequency domain representation of $\mathbf{I}_q$, which is also a quaternion matrix. Its amplitude spectrum $\mathbf{A}_q$, phase spectrum $\mathbf{P}_q$, and eigenaxis $\mathcal{X}$ are given as

$$\mathbf{A}_q = \sqrt{\mathbf{Real}_q^2 + \mathbf{Imaginary}_q^2} \tag{24.41}$$

$$\mathbf{P}_q = \arctan\left(\frac{\mathbf{Imaginary}_q}{\mathbf{Real}_q}\right) \tag{24.42}$$

and

$$\mathcal{X} = \frac{\text{Imaginary}_q}{\left\|\text{Imaginary}_q\right\|} \tag{24.43}$$

where $\mathbf{Real}_q$ and $\mathbf{Imaginary}_q$ represent the real part and imaginry part of $\mathbf{F}_q$, respectively. The inverse QFT (IQFT) is defined as

$$\mathbf{I}_q(m, n) = \mathcal{F}_q^{-1}\left[\mathbf{A}_q(u, v) e^{\mathcal{X}\mathbf{P}_q(u,v)}\right]. \tag{24.44}$$

24.2.3.2 Multiscale-based Quaternion Matrix

Scale variation of anomaly targets poses a challenge in hyperspectral anomaly detection due to differing target shapes and sizes. The RFFT detector's scale is dictated by the input HSI's resolution: low resolution corresponds to a large scale, ignoring details, while high resolution highlights finer details. Figure 24.14 demonstrates that with a fixed reference system, the saliency-aware map

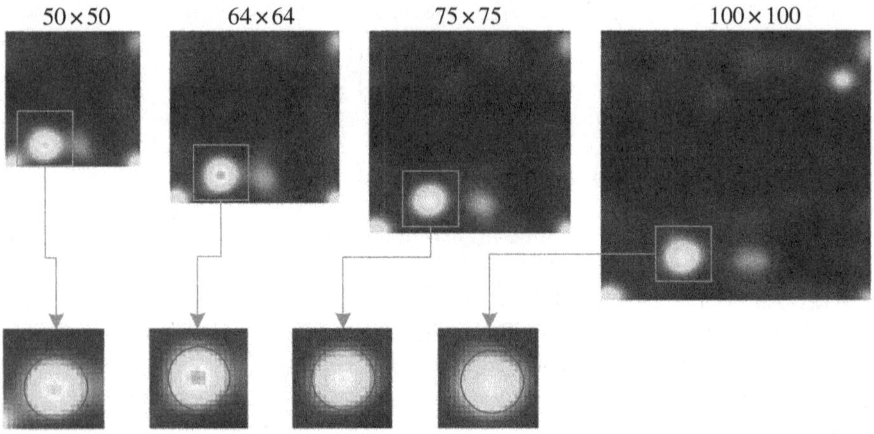

Figure 24.14 Example of size of receptive field by the enhanced POR in different image scales.

(enhanced POR) perceives target sizes consistently across scales, indicating a fixed receptive field for the RFFT detector. Thus, multiscale analysis can enhance RFFT's anomaly detection performance by accommodating different scales and improving sensitivity to varying target sizes.

To construct a multiscale-based quaternion HSI for QFT, the HSI is resized to different scales. Each band forms a quaternion matrix. Figure 24.15 illustrates this process, using four scales: the original and three downsampled versions. Redundant spectral information at each scale is reduced using the optimal clustering framework (OCF) method [22], which selects representative bands via clustering and ranking. The selected bands, totaling *Nd*, are upsampled to a uniform size, either matching or slightly larger than the original HSI. Despite having identical final sizes, the images maintain different scales due to the downsampling and upsampling process. Then, the multiscale-based quaternion matrix is constructed as

$$\mathbf{I}_{\mathrm{Ms}} = w_1\mathbf{Ms}_1 + w_2\mathbf{Ms}_2 \cdot i + w_3\mathbf{Ms}_3 \cdot j + w_4\mathbf{Ms}_4 \cdot k \tag{24.45}$$

where $\mathbf{Ms}_1 - \mathbf{Ms}_4$ is a band of the HSI at different scales and $\mathbf{I}_{\mathrm{Ms}}$ represents the quaternion matrix for the band. $\mathbf{S}_1$ corresponds to the original scale. $w_1 - w_4$ is weight controlling the contribution of different scale. In this article, we use $w_1 = 0.7$ and $w_2 = w_3 = w_4 = 0.1$ as default weights for multiscale-based quarternion matrix.

24.2.3.3 Multifeature-based Quaternion Matrix

The quaternion matrix can also be considered as the combination of multiple features. In this article, we use different spatial and spectral features to construct quaternion matrices for frequency domain analysis of HSIs. These features include spectral, PCA [23], orthogonal total variation component analysis (OTVCA) [24], and locality preserving projection (LPP) [25] features. Since these features cover multiple aspects (spectral information, spatial information, and manifold learning) of HSI characterization, it is reasonable to integrate them to construct a quaternion matrix for anomaly detection. For spectral feature, the number of band is reduced to Nd by the band selection method OCF. For PCA, OTVCA, and LPP, the number of bands of extracted features is consistent with spectral feature. The construction of multifeature-based quaternion HSI is shown in Figure 24.16. Then, the multifeature-based quaternion matrix is constructed as

$$\mathbf{I}_{\mathrm{Mf}} = w_1\mathbf{Mf}_1 + w_2\mathbf{Mf}_2 \cdot i + w_3\mathbf{Mf}_3 \cdot j + w_4\mathbf{Mf}_4 \cdot k \tag{24.46}$$

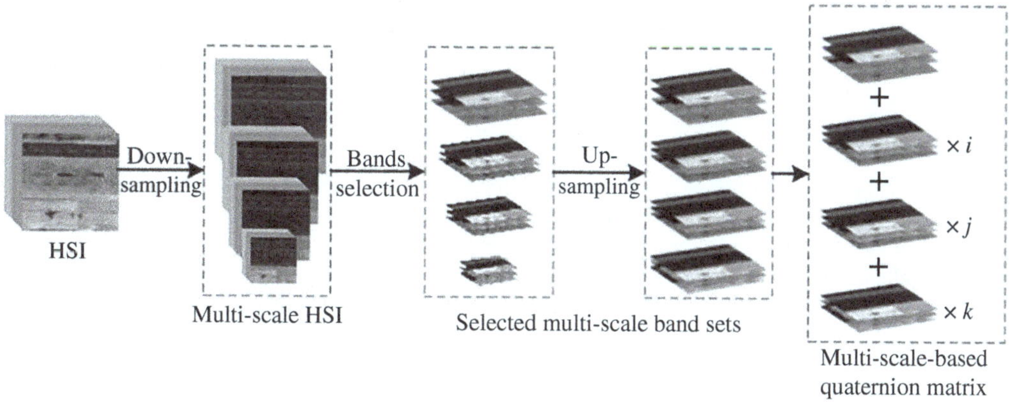

Figure 24.15 Procedure for the construction of multiscale-based quaternion matrix.

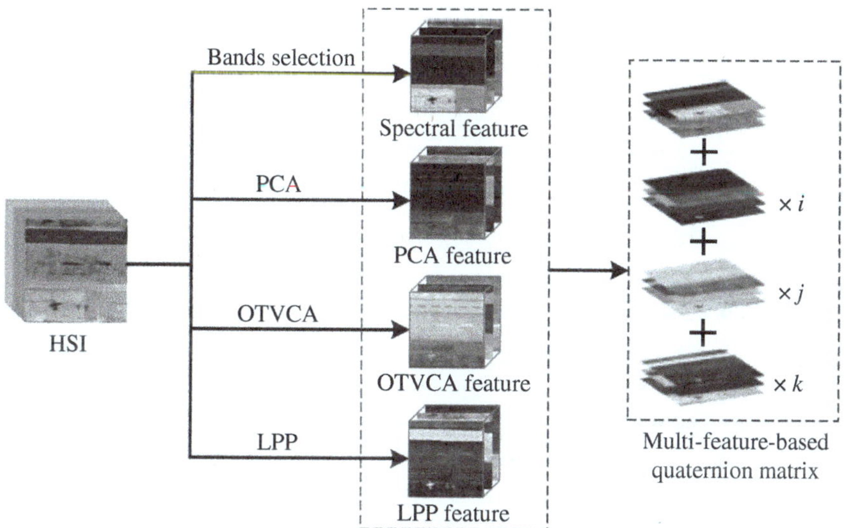

Figure 24.16 Procedure for the construction of multifeature-based quaternion matrix.

where $\mathbf{Mf}_1 - \mathbf{Mf}_4$ is a band of different features and $\mathbf{I}_{\mathrm{Mf}}$ represents the quaternion matrix for the band. For multifeature-based quaternion matrix, we assume that all features contribute equally. So all weights are set to 0.25 as default (Table 24.3).

24.2.3.4 Reconstruction Fusion of Quaternion Fourier Transform for Anomaly Detection

We can now define the reconstruction fusion of quaternion Fourier transform (RFQFT) using multiscale- and multifeature-based quaternion matrices. According to 24.32, 24.33, (24.35), 24.37, and (24.38), the RFFT can be reformulated as

$$\boldsymbol{M}_{\mathrm{RFFT}} = \boldsymbol{M}_{\mathrm{SAR}} \odot \tilde{\boldsymbol{M}}_{\mathrm{POR}} = \left|\mathcal{F}^{-1}\left[(\mathcal{G}_{\sigma} \otimes \boldsymbol{A})\mathrm{e}^{\mathrm{i}\boldsymbol{P}}\right]\right| \odot \left[\mathcal{G}_{\sigma} \otimes \left|\mathcal{F}^{-1}\left(\mathrm{e}^{\mathrm{i}\boldsymbol{P}}\right)\right|^{2}\right] \tag{24.47}$$

Table 24.3 Descriptions of the Gulfport, Pavia, Texas Coast and San Diego data sets.

Features\data sets	Gulfport	Pavia	Texas Coast	San Diego
Spatial resolution (m/pixel)	3.4	1.3	17.2	3.5
Spatial size	100 × 100	150 × 150	100 × 100	100 × 100
Wavelength range (μm)	Unknown	0.43–0.86	0.45–1.35	0.37–2.51
Number of spectral bands	191	102	207	189
Proportion of aomaly (%)s	0.60	0.30	1.55	1.34
Sensor	AVIRIS	ROSIS-03	AVIRIS	AVIRIS
Captured place	Gulfport	Pavia	Texas Coast	San Diego

where **A**, **P** are the amplitude and phase spectrums of FT, respectively; $\mathcal{G}_\sigma$ is the Gaussian kernel. Further according to (20) and (24), the RFQFT is formulated as

$$\boldsymbol{M}_{\mathrm{RFQFT}} = \boldsymbol{M}_{\mathrm{QSAR}} \odot \tilde{\boldsymbol{M}}_{\mathrm{POR}} = \left|\mathcal{F}_{\mathrm{q}}^{-1}\left[(\mathcal{G}_\sigma \otimes \boldsymbol{A}_{\mathrm{q}})e^{\mathcal{X}\boldsymbol{P}_{\mathrm{q}}}\right]\right| \odot \left[\mathcal{G}_\sigma \otimes \left|\mathcal{F}_{\mathrm{q}}^{-1}\left(e^{\mathcal{X}\boldsymbol{P}_{\mathrm{q}}}\right)\right|^2\right] \tag{24.48}$$

where $\boldsymbol{A}_q$, $\boldsymbol{P}_q$, and $\mathcal{X}$ are the amplitude, phase, and eigenaxis spectrums of QFT, respectively; MQFAR and MQPOR are the filtered amplitude reconstruction and the enhanced POR (saliency-aware map) of QFT, respectively.

Let $\mathbf{X} \in \mathbb{R}^{M\times N\times B}$ be the original HSI and $\{\mathbf{X}^k\}_{k=1}^{B} \in \mathbb{R}^{M\times N}$ be its set of bands, where M, N, and B are length, width, and number of bands, respectively. For the RFFT, the input is the HSI after band selection by using the OCF method, which is denoted as $\hat{\mathbf{X}} \in \mathbb{R}^{M\times N\times N_d}$, where $N_d < B$ is the number of bands after band selection. According to the quaternion matrix used, RFQFT can be divided into multiscale-based RFQFT (MsRFQFT) and multifeature-based RFQFT (MfRFQFT). The input of MsRFQFT is the multiscale-based quaternion HSI denoted as $\mathbf{X}_{q-\mathrm{Ms}} \in \mathbb{R}^{M\times N\times N_d}$. The input of MfRFQFT is the multifeature-based quaternion HSI denoted as $\mathbf{X}_{q-\mathrm{Mf}} \in \mathbb{R}^{M\times N\times N_d}$. For RFFT, each band ($\mathbf{X}^k$) is a real matrix, while for MsRFQFT and MfRFQFT, each band ($\mathbf{X}^k_{q-\mathrm{Ms}}$ and $\mathbf{X}^k_{q-\mathrm{Mf}}$) is a quaternion matrix. Since the RFFT, MsRFQFT, and MfRFQFT all perform frequency domain analysis band by band, the reconstruction fusion is conducted with the averaged FAR and the averaged enhanced POR over the results of all bands as

$$\mathcal{O}\mathbf{M}_{\mathrm{RFFT}} = \frac{1}{{N_d}^2}\sum_{k=1}^{N_d}\mathbf{M}^k_{\mathrm{FAR}} \odot \sum_{k=1}^{N_d}\tilde{\mathbf{M}}^k_{\mathrm{POR}} \tag{24.49}$$

$$\mathcal{O}\mathbf{M}_{\mathrm{MsRFQFT}} = \frac{1}{{N_d}^2}\sum_{k=1}^{N_d}\mathbf{M}^k_{\mathrm{MsQFAR}} \odot \sum_{k=1}^{N_d}\tilde{\mathbf{M}}^k_{\mathrm{MsQPOR}} \tag{24.50}$$

and

$$\mathcal{O}\mathbf{M}_{\mathrm{MfRFQFT}} = \frac{1}{{N_d}^2}\sum_{k=1}^{N_d}\mathbf{M}^k_{\mathrm{MfQFAR}} \odot \sum_{k=1}^{N_d}\tilde{\mathbf{M}}^k_{\mathrm{MfQPOR}} \tag{24.51}$$

where $\mathbf{M}^k_{\mathrm{FAR}}(\tilde{\mathbf{M}}^k_{\mathrm{POR}})$, $\mathbf{M}^k_{\mathrm{MsQFAR}}(\tilde{\mathbf{M}}^k_{\mathrm{MsQPOR}})$, and $\mathbf{M}^k_{\mathrm{MfQFAR}}(\tilde{\mathbf{M}}^k_{\mathrm{MfQPOR}})$ are the FAR (POR) of $\mathbf{X}^k$, $\mathbf{X}^k_{q-\mathrm{Ms}}$ and $\mathbf{X}^k_{q-\mathrm{Mf}}$, respectively; $\mathcal{O}\mathbf{M}_{\mathrm{RFFT}}$, $\mathcal{O}\mathbf{M}_{\mathrm{MsRFQFT}}$, and $\mathcal{O}\mathbf{M}_{\mathrm{MfRFQFT}}$, respectively. Figure 24.17 presents the flowchart of our proposed RFFT, MsRFQFT, and MfRFQFT hyperspectral anomaly detection methods.

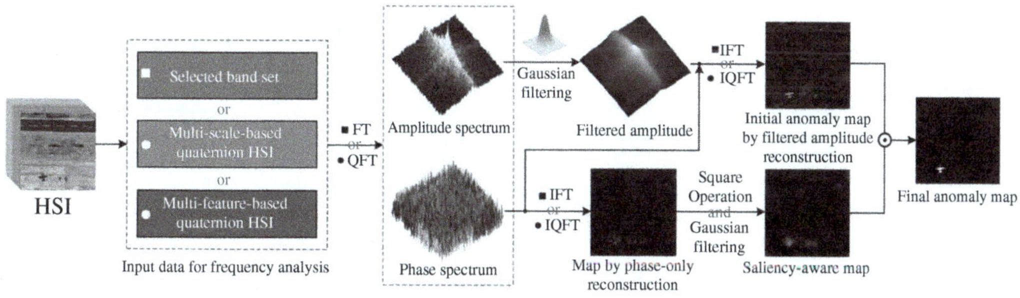

Figure 24.17 Flowchart of our proposed RFFT, MsRFQFT, and MfRFQFT hyperspectral anomaly detection methods. For RFFT, the input is the selected band set. For MsRFQFT, the input is the multiscale-based quaternion HSI. For the MfRFQFT, the input is the multifeature-based quaternion HSI. RFFT uses FT for frequency domain analysis, while MsRFQFT and MfRFQFT use QFT.

24.2.4 Experiments

The proposed anomaly detection methods were evaluated with four real-scene HSI data sets, i.e., the Gulfport image, Pavia City image, Texas Coast image, and San Diego image. All four images were selected from the ABU data set.

24.2.4.1 Evaluation Criteria

In addition to ROC and AUC, the false detection probability (FDP) was also used. The threshold value of FDP considered in this article was determined by the ratio of anomaly pixels in the image, defined as

$$\text{FDP} = \frac{\text{FD}}{\text{CD} + \text{FD}} \tag{24.52}$$

where CD and FD are the number of pixels of the correct detection and false detection, respectively. The smaller the FDP, the better the background suppression. To further quantitatively study the ability of proposed methods to separate anomalies and backgrounds, we employed separability maps for evaluation.

24.2.4.2 Detection Performance

Five state-of-the-art detectors were employed for comparison, including the GRX [13], LRX [13], CRD [14], LSMAD [14], and FrFE [23] methods. The parameter settings for different methods on different data sets are listed in Table 24.4. We used binary detection maps to discuss the detection performance of the proposed method, as shown in Figure 24.18. Binary detection maps are created by segmenting grayscale detection maps using a threshold based on the anomaly pixel proportion. For example, Gulfport's 0.60% anomaly proportion sets a 99.4% threshold. These maps display detected anomalies at this level, with correct detections (CD), missed detections (MD), and false detections (FD) shown for analysis. CD accurately identifies anomalies, MD misses them, and FD mistakenly flags background. The RFFT, MsRFQFT, and MfRFQFT methods significantly reduce MD and FD, effectively suppressing the background while highlighting anomalies.

Figure 24.19 illustrates ROC curves for different methods on different data sets. On the Gulfport and Pavia data sets, the ROC curves of the proposed RFFT, MsRFQFT, and MfRFQFT methods were almost always above the ROC curves of the other comparison methods. The AUC and FDP scores are provided in Table 24.5. Obviously, the proposed RFFT, MsRFQFT, and MfRFQFT methods were significantly superior to other comparison methods in terms of AUC and FDP.

Table 24.4 Parameter setting for different methods on different datasets.

Methods\ Images	Gulfport	Pavia	Texas Coast	San Diego
GRX	\	\	\	\
LRX	$(w_{in}, w_{out}) = (21,23)$	$(w_{in}, w_{out}) = (23,31)$	$(w_{in}, w_{out}) = (21,23)$	$(w_{in}, w_{out}) = (17,31)$
CRD	$(w_{in}, w_{out}) = (21,27)$	$(w_{in}, w_{out}) = (7,9)$	$(w_{in}, w_{out}) = (25,31)$	$(w_{in}, w_{out}) = (15,19)$
LSMAD	$(k, r) = (0.006,21)$	$(k, r) = (0.003,27)$	$(k, r) = (0.0115,8)$	$(k, r) = (0.0134,2)$
FrFE	order = 0.9	order = 1	order = 1	order = 1.1
RFFT	$(\sigma, N_d) = (3.6,3)$	$(\sigma, N_d) = (1.2,3)$	$(\sigma, N_d) = (1.2,3)$	$(\sigma, N_d) = (4,3)$
MsRFQFT	$(\sigma, N_d) = (10,3)$	$(\sigma, N_d) = (1.6,3)$	$(\sigma, N_d) = (1.4,3)$	$(\sigma, N_d) = (6.8,3)$
MfRFQFT	$(\sigma, N_d) = (3.6,6)$	$(\sigma, N_d) = (1.2,6)$	$(\sigma, N_d) = (0.8,6)$	$(\sigma, N_d) = (0.8,3)$

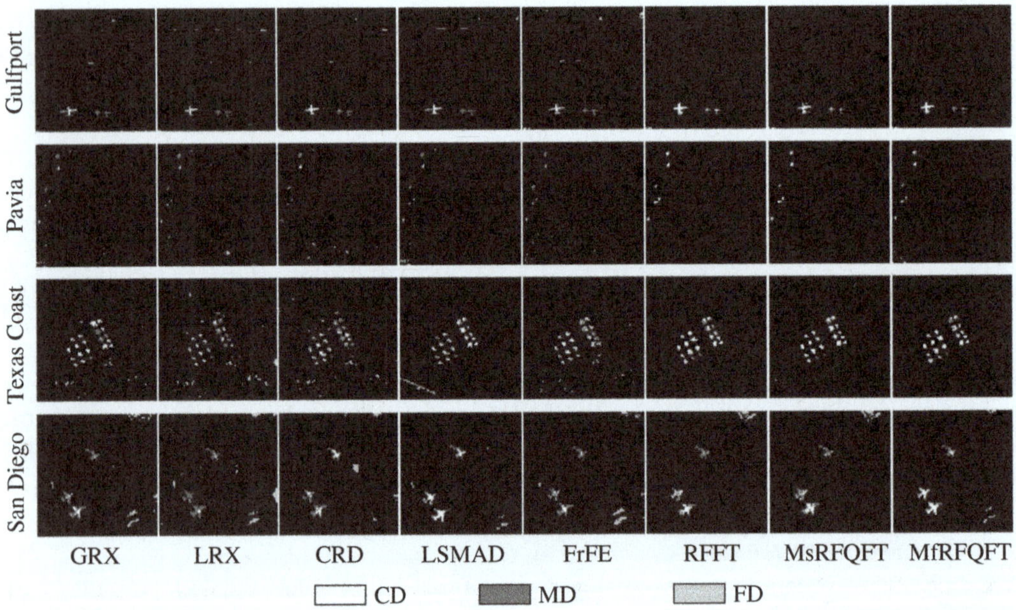

Figure 24.18 Binary anomaly detection maps obtained by the GRX, LRX, CRD, LSMAD, FrFE, RFFT, MsRFQFT, and MfRFQFT methods on the Gulfport, Pavia, Texas Coast, and San Diego data sets. White, dark gray, and light gray represent correct detection, missed detection, and false detection, respectively.

Table 24.5 also reports the computational time of the comparison detectors. The experiments were conducted on a computer with a 3.7-GHz CPU and a 32-GB memory. Obviously, the proposed RFFT is a very fast detector, taking only 0.068, 0.059, 0.078, and 0.068 s on the Gulfport, Pavia, Texas Coast, and San Diego data sets, respectively. In addition, by comparing MfRFQFT with RFFT and MsRFQFT, it can be known that the calculation consumption of MfRFQFT mainly comes from different feature extraction processes. Although multiscale and multifeature optimization increase the computation cost of RFFT, MsRFQFT and MfRFQFT are still much more efficient than other

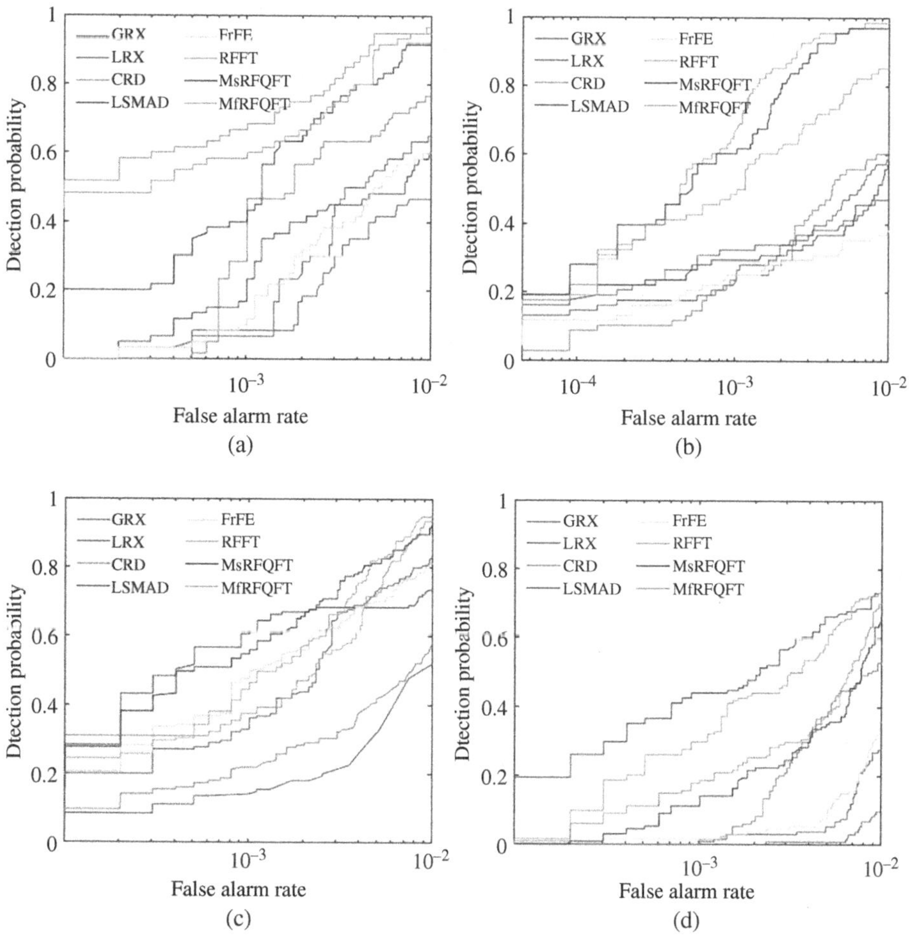

Figure 24.19 ROC curves of the GRX, LRX, CRD, LSMAD, FrFE, RFFE, MsRFQFT, and MfRFQFT methods on different data sets. (a) Gulfport. (b) Pavia. (c) Texas Coast. (d) San Diego.

comparison methods except RX. This illustrates the feasibility of the proposed methods in actual anomaly detection applications.

24.2.5 Summary

Anomaly detection for HSI is very conventional and important. But its performance is far from satisfying. In this article, a new hyperspectral anomaly detection method based on frequency domain analysis is proposed. We first establish the correspondence between the background in spatial domain and the spikes of the amplitude spectrum in frequency domain. Then, two inverse Fourier transforms, i.e., filtering amplitude reconstruction and POR, are fused to enhance background suppression. Moreover, multiscale and multifeature analysis based on quaternion Fourier transform further improves the robustness of anomaly detection performance. To evaluate the proposed method, we have conducted experiments on widely used hyperspectral data sets and demonstrated the superiority of the proposed method with regard to state-of-the-art competitors. As for future work, it would be interesting to investigate the combination of multiple spatial scale and multiple filtering scale methods.

Table 24.5 AUC scores, FDP scores, and the execution time of the GRX, LRX, CRD, LSMAD, FRFE, RFFE, MsRFQFT, and MfRFQFT methods, the value marked in bold is the best score, and the value underlined is the second best score.

	Gulfport			Pavia			Texas Coast			San Diego			Average	
Images Methods	**AUC**	**FDP**	**Time/s**	**AUC**	**FDP**	**Time/s**	**AUC**	**FDP**	**Time/s**	**AUC**	**FDP**	**Time/s**	**AUC**	**FDP**
GRX	0.9525	0.6500	0.044	0.9538	0.6618	0.042	0.9945	0.2903	0.042	0.9402	0.7239	0.046	0.9602	0.5815
LRX	0.9903	0.5333	32.424	0.9739	0.6618	34.659	0.9432	0.5226	36.991	0.9153	0.8826	52.668	0.9557	0.6496
CRD	0.9938	0.4167	111.093	0.9553	0.7059	21.130	0.9817	0.4968	137.925	0.9805	0.5299	46.606	0.9778	0.5373
LSMAD	0.9878	0.5500	5.982	0.9720	0.6912	7.993	0.9887	0.3161	6.843	0.9798	0.3582	5.811	0.9821	0.4789
FrFE	0.9849	0.6000	13.903	0.8962	0.7059	12.004	0.9678	0.3032	15.506	0.9788	0.6940	13.723	0.9569	0.5758
RFFT	0.9981	0.2667	0.068	0.9986	0.3382	0.059	0.9961	0.2839	0.078	0.9816	0.4925	0.068	0.9936	0.3453
MsRFQFT	0.9945	0.3500	0.249	0.9984	0.3824	0.173	0.9962	0.2258	0.272	0.9872	0.5299	0.256	0.9941	0.3720
MfRFQFT	0.9977	0.3333	1.676	0.9954	0.4265	9.950	0.9967	0.2581	1.680	0.9909	0.3881	1.722	0.9952	0.3515

24.3 Ensemble Entropy Metric for Hyperspectral Anomaly Detection

This section presents a novel technique for hyperspectral anomaly detection, incorporating an innovative perspective rooted in information theory to effectively leverage these concepts. The primary objective is to modify system entropy. Anomaly pixels' rarity and low occurrence probabilities in images are widely acknowledged in anomaly detection. Leveraging this, we proposed a new anomaly detection approach based on information entropy analysis to fully consider this property. Information entropy, quantifying a system's information content with event probabilities, can serve as a metric of anomaly conspicuousness when appropriate system definitions are established for pixels with known occurrence probabilities. The overall architecture of our anomaly detector is illustrated in Figure 24.20. Detailed steps will be described in subsequent sections.

24.3.1 Density Peak Clustering (DPC) Algorithm and Entropy in Information Theory

24.3.1.1 DPC Algorithm

The density peak clustering (DPC) algorithm proposed by Rodriguez and Laio [8] is a data-driven adaptive clustering algorithm. For each pixel $\mathbf{x}_i$ in the data set, the distance d_{ij} between $\mathbf{x}_i$ and other pixels $\mathbf{x}_j$ is first computed as follows:

$$d_{ij} = \left\|\mathbf{x}_i - \mathbf{x}_j\right\|_2 \tag{24.53}$$

where $\|\cdot\|_2$ denotes the $\mathbf{L}_2$ norm. The value of d_{ij} measures the similarity between two pixels $\mathbf{x}_i$ and $\mathbf{x}_j$. The smaller the distance, the more similar the two pixels are, and vice versa.

For $\mathbf{x}_i$, the density and distance parameters of $\mathbf{x}_i$ are defined according to the d_{ij} set. To reduce the error of density estimation caused by the number of pixels around the pixel to be measured, the Gaussian radial basis function (GBF) is used to define the density [10]. According to the definition of GBF, the density ρ_i of pixel $\mathbf{x}_i$ is defined as

$$\rho_i = \sum_j \exp\left[\left(-\frac{d_{ij}}{d_c}\right)^2\right] \tag{24.54}$$

where d_c is the specified cutoff distance that determines the radius of the scale of similarity measurement. The value of density ρ_i is determined by the number of pixels with similar spectral features to pixel $\mathbf{x}_i$. The higher the density ρ_i is, the more similar pixels to $\mathbf{x}_i$ are. If pixel $\mathbf{x}_i$ is taken as the center, the set size of similar pixels around it will be large in the distance space and vice versa.

For any pixel $\mathbf{x}_i$ in the data set, according to its density ρ_i and densities of other pixels ρ_j, the distance parameter is defined as

$$\delta_i - \begin{cases} \min\limits_{j:\rho_j > \rho_i}\left(d_{ij}\right), & \exists \rho_i < \rho_j \\ \max\limits_{j}\left(d_{ij}\right), & \text{others} \end{cases} \tag{24.55}$$

where δ_i reflects the significance of pixel $\mathbf{x}_i$ as the cluster center. When the density of pixel $\mathbf{x}_i$ is the maximum, δ_i takes the maximum value in the set of d_{ij}. On the contrary, if the density of pixel $\mathbf{x}_j$ is larger than that of pixel $\mathbf{x}_i$, then δ_i takes the minimum distance between $\mathbf{x}_j$ and $\mathbf{x}_i$. In this article, we adopt the density definition in DPC to evaluate the occurrence probability for each pixel.

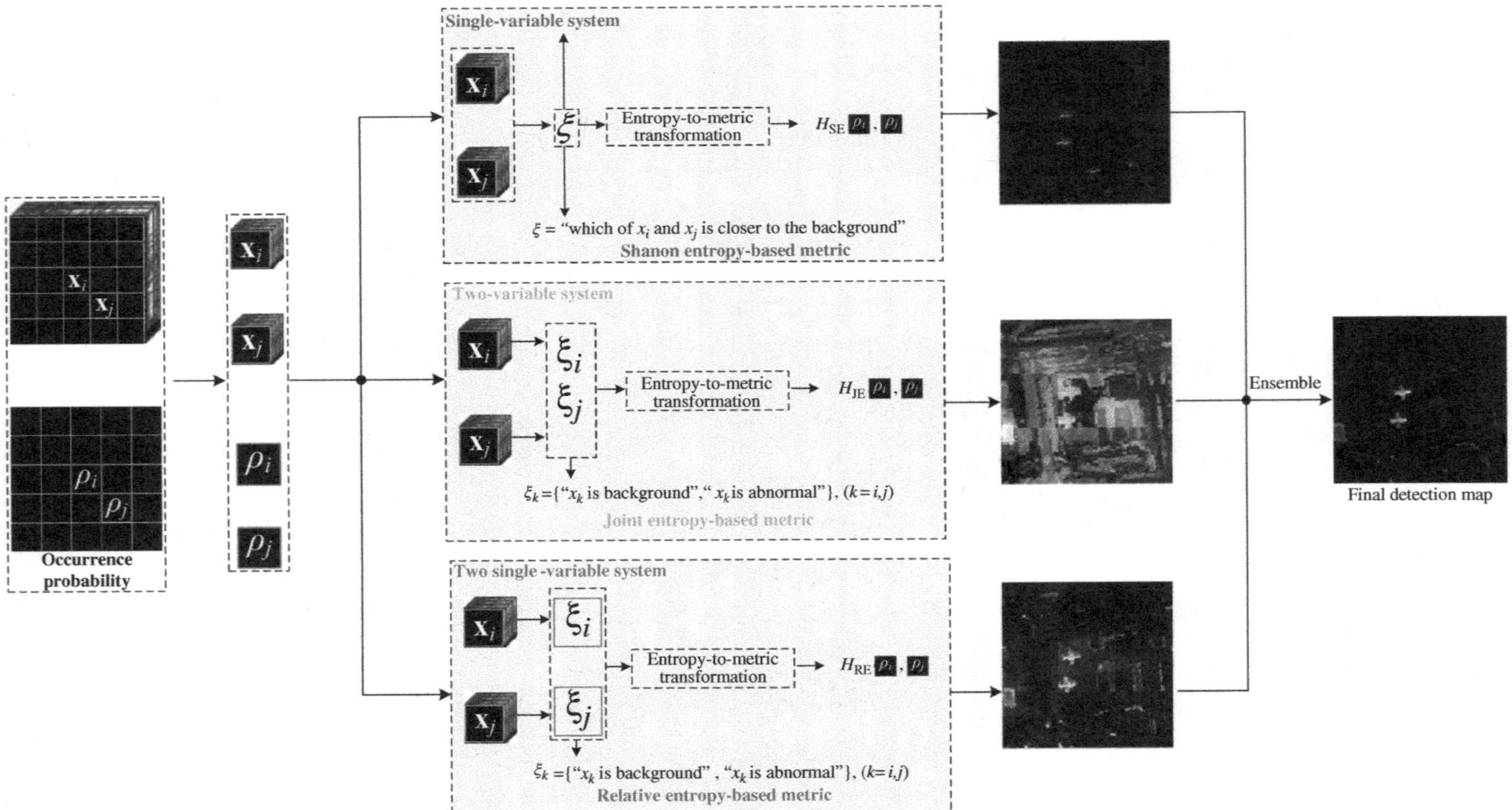

Figure 24.20 Schematic of the ensemble entropy metric-based anomaly detector.

24.3.1.2 Entropy in Information Theory

Entropy, a fundamental concept in physics, is widely applied in various fields. In statistical physics, it is known as physical entropy, while information theory refers to it as information entropy. In 1-D random systems, information entropy, also called SE, measures system information or uncertainty. For 2-D systems, derived concepts like JE and RE are based on information entropy. JE quantifies uncertainty in a 2-D system with simultaneous events, while RE compares information entropy differences in separate systems. This section transforms SE, JE, and RE into metrics for assessing anomaly conspicuousness from distinct perspectives and integrates them into an ensemble entropy metric-based detector (EEMD) detailed in the following section.

24.3.2 Ensemble Entropy Metric-based Detector (EEMD)

Combined anomalies, rare targets with unique spectral features and low occurrence probabilities, are ideal for exception detection. To effectively utilize these properties, determining each pixel's occurrence probability in the image is crucial. Introducing information entropy, a measure of a system's information content based on event probabilities, into anomaly detection allows for differentiation between background and anomaly by leveraging pixel occurrence probabilities. The goal is to convert system entropy into measurable metrics of anomaly visibility using occurrence probabilities. Figure 24.21 illustrates this concept, showing background pixels with occurrence probabilities of 0.95 and 0.9 as light gray points, and an anomaly pixel with a 0.1 occurrence probability as a dark gray point. The entropy between the anomaly and background pixels is significantly lower than that between two background pixels, demonstrating the effectiveness of occurrence probabilities in distinguishing background from anomaly pixels.

However, the entropy calculation in Figure 24.21 is merely a mechanical application of the formula without clear interpretability or concrete meaning. To address this limitation and effectively tackle anomaly detection, valid system definitions for individual pixels and between pixels are essential. Therefore, two tasks must be completed: constructing pixel occurrence probabilities and defining valid systems for the specific detection problem. Furthermore, to enhance detection performance, three types of entropy definitions in information theory (SE, JE, and RE) are considered with multiple perspectives for system construction.

24.3.2.1 Construction of Occurrence Probability

Let $\mathbf{X} \in \mathbb{R}^{I \times D}$ be a hyperspectral image with I pixels with D spectral bands. Since the DPC process requires computing the distance matrix among pixels, processing the entire image at once requires a large amount of memory and a very high time consumption. Therefore, in our implementation, the **HSI** $\mathbf{X}$ is first divided into a certain number of nonoverlapping blocks with size $w_P \times w_P$ and

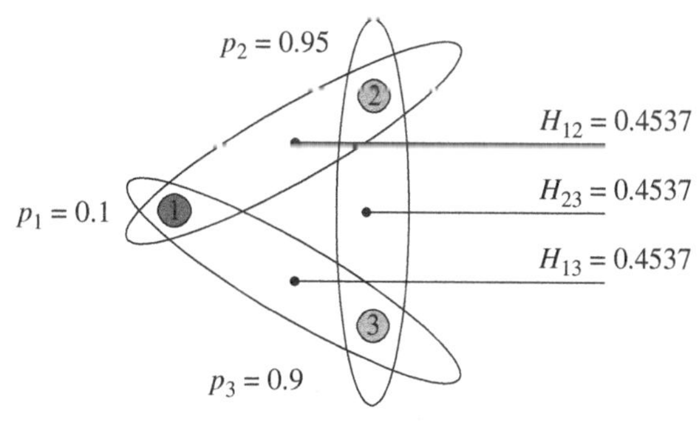

Figure 24.21 Simple illustration of the motivation. The light gray and dark gray points represent the background and anomaly pixels, respectively. $P_i (i = 1, 2, 3)$ is the occurrence probability. The entropy H is calculated by the SE, i.e., $H_{ij} = -\Sigma_{k=ij} p(x_k) \log p(x_k)$, where $\{p(\mathbf{x}_k)\}_{k=i,j} = \{(P_k/(P_i + P_j))\}_{k=i,j}$.

the DPC is then conducted on each block in sequence. This process can be simply described as follows:

$$\rho = \mathrm{DPC}(X, \omega_{\rho}, r_c) \tag{24.56}$$

where DPC(·) is the DPC operation, $w_{\mathcal{P}}$ is the block size and r_c controls the cutoff distance d_c. To be specific, let $\mathbf{D}$ be the distance matrix for the block. We extract the upper triangular elements of $\mathbf{D}$ and sort them as vector $\mathbf{d}$ in ascending order. Then, we have $d_c = \mathbf{d}([T(T-1)\cdot r_c\%])$, where $T = w_{\mathcal{P}} \times w_{\mathcal{P}}$ and $r_c\%$ is the percentage, which determines the position of d_c in $\mathbf{d}$. $\rho = \rho_{ii=1}^{I} \in \mathbb{R}^{I\times 1}$ (values range from 0 to 1) is the output density vector composed of each pixel density, namely the occurrence probability for each pixel. In this article, the initial background probability refers to the probability that a certain pixel is a background pixel. It is obvious that the occurrence probability is proportional to the background probability of pixels. To some extent, the initial background probability can be represented directly by the occurrence probability.

24.3.2.2 Realization of Entropy-based Metrics

In order to obtain the anomaly score (anomaly conspicuousness) with entropy-based metrics for each pixel under test (PUT), a sliding window operation is adopted. For each PUT $\mathbf{x} \in \mathbb{R}^{D\times 1}$, the surrounding pixels within the window (of the size of $w_e \times w_e$), centered at the PUT $\mathbf{x}$, are used to jointly calculate the anomaly score of $\mathbf{x}$ by evaluating the similarity between them, based on the assumption that most of the surrounding pixels are normal (background) pixels. It is worth mentioning that the use of an inner and outer window is suggested in many works [14, 26] to achieve a more robust detection result. In such a strategy, only the samples inside the outer window and outside the inner window are collected, while the pixels inside the inner window are treated as anomalies similar to the central PUT, which may interfere with the reconstruction error. However, our experiments show that, when the window size w_e is large enough, the effect of whether using a hollow (inner and outer) window strategy or not is negligible in our method. Consequently, in order to simplify the algorithm and avoid additional parameter settings, we adopt a sliding window strategy with a single window. In addition, for each PUT $\mathbf{x}_i (i = 1, 2, ..., I)$ with the initial background probability (occurrence probability) ρ_j, the surrounding pixels are given by $\mathbf{x}_{jj=1}^{w_e \times w_e}$ with the corresponding initial background probability $\rho_{jj=1}^{w_e \times w_e}$.

After discussing the above aspects, we now design three different entropy metrics based on three kinds of entropy concepts in information theory and then integrate them into an ensemble metric for anomaly detection. The anomaly detector based on the set entropy metric is shown in Figure 24.20.

1) *SE-Based Metric:* The SE describes the indeterminacy (i.e., the average amount of information source) of a random variable. In order to implement this concept, we first define a random variable (single-variable system) and then make a logical derivation as follows. Consider the random variable

$$\begin{aligned} \xi &= \text{“Which of } \mathbf{x}_i \text{ and } \mathbf{x}_j \text{ is closer to } \mu\text{”} \\ &= \{\mathbf{x}_i, \mathbf{x}_j\} \end{aligned} \tag{24.57}$$

where μ is the mean of the surrounding pixel set $\mathbf{x}_{jj=1}^{w_e \times w_e - 1}$ and is viewed as a background pixel vector because the surrounding pixels are assumed to be background pixels. Therefore, a PUT close to μ is equivalent to the fact that the PUT tends to be background, that is, the probability of the PUT being close to μ is equal to that of the PUT being background. According to this, we can obtain

$$p(\xi = \mathbf{x}_k) = p(\mathbf{x}_k \text{ is background}) = p_k, (k = i,j). \tag{24.58}$$

Then, the SE of the random variable ξ can be written as follows:

$$H_{\mathrm{SE}^{ij}} = -\sum_{k=i,j} p(\mathbf{x}_k) \log_p(\mathbf{x}_k) \tag{24.59}$$

where $\{p(\mathbf{x}_k)\}_{k=i,j} = \{\rho_k/(\rho_i + \rho_j)\}_{k=i,j}$ is the normalized background probability between $\mathbf{x}_i$ and $\mathbf{x}_j$. This step is to ensure that the sum of the probabilities of the two is equal to 1 to match the definition of SE.

According to the maximum entropy theorem, the more uniform the probability distribution of the random variable is, the larger the SE is. When the probability of each event is equal, the maximum SE will be obtained, that is, the higher the similarity between ρ_i and ρ_j, the larger the $H_{\mathrm{SE}}{}^{ij}$. Now, we can reinterpret (24.59) as a metric that measures the similarity between ρ_i and ρ_j (equivalent to the similarity between $\mathbf{x}_i$ and $\mathbf{x}_j$). Thus, the similarity between the PUT $\mathbf{x}_i$ and the surrounding pixels (background) set $\mathbf{x}_{jj=1}^{\omega_e \times \omega_e - 1}$ is defined by

$$H_{\mathrm{SE}^i} = \frac{1}{\omega_e \times \omega_e - 1} \sum_{j=1}^{\omega_e \times \omega_e - 1} H_{\mathrm{SE}^{ij}} \tag{24.60}$$

2) *JE-Based Metric:* Different from the SE-based metric (SED) where $\mathbf{x}_i$ and $\mathbf{x}_j$ are regarded as two random events of a random variable, here, $\mathbf{x}_i$ and $\mathbf{x}_j$ are defined as two independent random variables in a two-variable system, and their similarity is described by the degree of random system chaos. Specifically, two independent random variables are defined as

$$\begin{aligned}\xi_k &= \text{Is } \mathbf{x}_k \text{ background or abnormal} \\ &= \{\text{"}\mathbf{x}_k \text{ is background", "}\mathbf{x}_k \text{ abnormal"}\} \\ (k &= i,j)\end{aligned} \tag{24.61}$$

According to the initial background probability ρ, we can have

$$p = (\text{"}\mathbf{x}_k \text{ is background"}) = \rho_k, \quad (k = i,j) \tag{24.62}$$

and

$$p = (\text{"}\mathbf{x}_k \text{ abnormal"}) = 1 - \rho_k, (k = i,j) \tag{24.63}$$

For the two-variable random system composed by the two random variables ξ_i and ξ_j, a joint probability distribution needs to be constructed. Since our method starts with the spectral and density properties of the pixels without considering the spatial correlation among them, whether a pixel is background or abnormal is irrelevant to other pixels. Hence, ξ_i and ξ_j are pairwise independent variables. Consequently, with the marginal distribution from Formulas (24.62) and (24.63), we can easily compute the joint probability distribution of ξ_i and ξ_j, as shown in Figure 24.29. For convenience, we use ξ_{k1} and ξ_{k2} to refer to the events "$\mathbf{x}_k$ is background" and "$\mathbf{x}_k$ is abnormal" ($k = i, j$), respectively, in Figure 24.22.

Now, the JE of the random system composed by ξ_i and ξ_j is expressed as follows:

$$H_{\mathrm{JI}^{ij}} = -\sum_{u \in \xi_i} \sum_{v \in \xi_j} p(u,v) \log_p p(u,v) \tag{24.64}$$

ξ_j \ ξ_i	ξ_{i1}	ξ_{i2}	Marginal distribution of ξ_j
ξ_{j1}	$p(\xi_{i1}, \xi_{j1})$ $= p_i \times p_j$	$p(\xi_{i2}, \xi_{j1})$ $= p_j - p(\xi_{i1}, \xi_{j1})$ $= p_j(1 - p_i)$	p_j
ξ_{j2}	$p(\xi_{i1}, \xi_{j2})$ $= p_i - p(\xi_{i1}, \xi_{j1})$ $= p_i(1 - p_j)$	$p(\xi_{i2}, \xi_{j2})$ $= (1 - p_i) \times (1 - p_j)$	$1 - p_j$
Marginal distribution of ξ_i	p_i	$1 - p_i$	

Figure 24.22 Construction of the joint probability distribution. ξ_{k1} and ξ_{k2} refer to the events "$\mathbf{x}_k$ is background" and "$\mathbf{x}_k$ is abnormal" ($k = i,j$), respectively.

where $\xi_i = \{\xi_{i1},\xi_{i1}\}$ and $\xi_j = \{\xi_{j1},\xi_{j1}\}$. The maximum entropy theorem is also applicable to JE. This means that a more uniform joint probability distribution $p(u,v)$ leads to a larger JE $H_{\mathrm{JE}}{}^{ij}$. According to Figure 24.22, we know that the uniformity of joint distribution is positively correlated with that of marginal distribution. In addition, the more uniform the marginal distribution means that both ρ_i and ρ_j tend to be close to 0.5 (i.e., the density of $\mathbf{x}_i$ and $\mathbf{x}_j$ tends to be the same, and $\mathbf{x}_i$ and $\mathbf{x}_j$ are similar. As a result, (24.64) can also be viewed as a metric evaluating the similarity between $\mathbf{x}_i$ and $\mathbf{x}_j$, and the similarity between $\mathbf{x}_i$ and $\mathbf{x}_{jj=1}^{w_e \times w_e - 1}$ is defined as follows:

$$H_{\mathrm{JE}^i} = \frac{1}{\omega_e \times \omega_e - 1} \sum_{j=1}^{\omega_e \times \omega_e - 1} H_{\mathrm{JE}^{ij}}. \tag{24.65}$$

3) *RE-Based Metric:* RE is a measure of the difference between two probability distributions P and Q. The divergence is used to measure the average additional number of bits required to encode samples from P using Q-based coding. Typically, P is the true distribution of data, and Q is the theoretical distribution, model distribution, or approximate distribution of P, that is to say, RE can measure the distance between two random distributions. When two random distributions are the same, their RE is zero. When the difference between two random distributions increases, their RE will also increase.

In the foregoing, we have defined two random variables (viewed as two single-variable systems here) ξ_i and ξ_j and given their probability distribution. Then, the RE between ξ_i and ξ_j is given by

$$H_{\mathrm{RE}^{ij}} = -\sum_{t=1}^{2} p(\xi_{jt}) \log \frac{p(\xi_{jt})}{p(\xi_{it})} \tag{24.66}$$

According to simple reasoning, the distance between the probability distributions of ξ_i and ξ_j is equivalent to the distance between the normal probabilities of $\mathbf{x}_i$ and $\mathbf{x}_j$ (namely, the density of $\mathbf{x}_i$ and $\mathbf{x}_j$). Consequently, (24.66) can be transformed into a distance metric of two pixels $\mathbf{x}_i$ and $\mathbf{x}_j$. As a result, we have

$$H_{\mathrm{JE}^i} = \frac{1}{\omega_e \times \omega_e - 1} \sum_{j=1}^{\omega_e \times \omega_e - 1} H_{\mathrm{RE}^{ij}}. \tag{24.67}$$

which is the distance between the PUT $\mathbf{x}_i$ and its surrounding pixels $\mathbf{x}_{jj=1}^{w_e \times w_e - 1}$.

24.3.2.3 Ensemble Entropy Metric-based Detector for Anomaly Detection

The three previously mentioned entropy-based metrics involve the integration of three distinct entropy concepts into the assessment of the similarity between the PUTs and their surrounding pixels. This is achieved by constructing random variables and systems, and deriving their internal relations from various perspectives.

1) The SED treats two pixels as random events within a random variable (single-variable system) and transforms their original background probabilities into event probabilities. In line with the maximum entropy theorem, the uniformity of the probability distribution of this random variable is evaluated using information entropy.
2) The JE-based metric (JED) establishes two random variables for two pixels, computes the Joint Entropy (JE) of the random system formed by these variables, and subsequently translates the JE into a measure of the similarity of the initial background probabilities.
3) The RE-based metric (RED) directly computes the dissimilarity between the probability distributions of these two random variables, considering it as the distinction in initial background probabilities between the pixels.

Unfortunately, as shown in Figure 24.23, the detection results of SED can highlight some anomalies but with several false detections; the JED can detect the anomaly completely, but it has little background suppression ability; and the RED has better background suppression, but the anomaly emphasis is worse than SED. Therefore, each metric has its drawbacks, leading to detection performance less than ideal when used alone. This section integrates the three individual metrics as an EEMD to obtain more robust detection results. Let HSE refer to the matrix consisting of the element HSEi of all pixels, likewise HJE and HRE. After normalizing HSE, HJE, and HRE to 0~1, we define OHSE = E − HSE, OHJE = E − HJE, and OHRE = HRE as the anomaly scores obtained by the SED, JED, and RED, respectively, where E is a matrix with element values of 1 and the same size as HSE, HJE, and HRE.

We first adopt the sum rule for the integration of the individual metrics as follows:

$$^{O}\mathbf{OR} = \frac{1}{3}\left(^{O}\mathbf{H}_{\mathrm{SE}} + {}^{O}\mathbf{H}_{\mathrm{JE}} + {}^{O}\mathbf{H}_{\mathrm{RE}}\right) \tag{24.68}$$

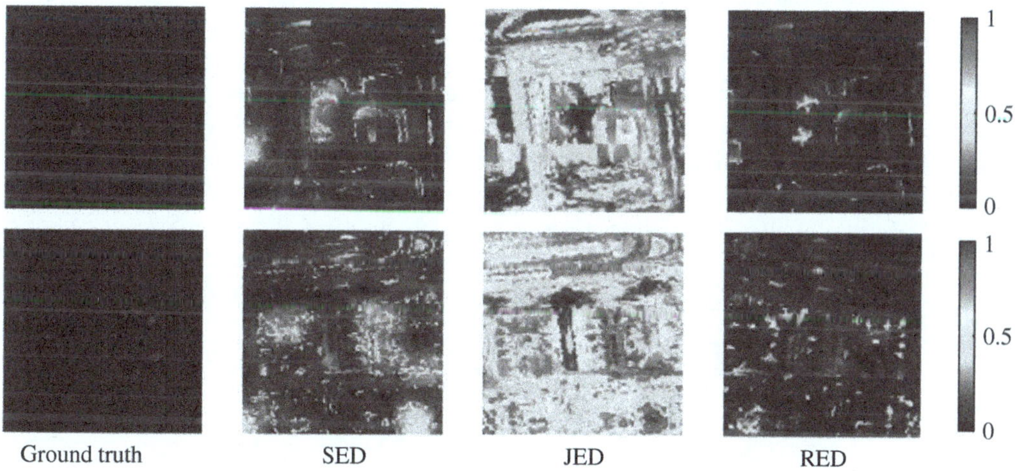

Figure 24.23 Anomaly map obtained by the SED, JED, and RED, respectively. Taking ABU-airport (b) and (c) for examples.

This operation is a simple bagging model averaging multiple anomaly scores, which can also be viewed as a soft max pooling over the anomaly scores. The sum rule here implements the logical "OR" operation, namely a disjunction of all anomalies of the individual metrics. It can effectively reduce the missed detection rate, that is, improve the detection rate.

Second, the product rule is also considered as follows:

$$^{O}\mathbf{AND} = {}^{O}\mathbf{H}_{\mathbf{SE}} \times {}^{O}\mathbf{H}_{\mathbf{JE}} \times {}^{O}\mathbf{H}_{\mathbf{RE}} \tag{24.69}$$

which can be understood as the logical "AND" operation whose result is true only when all conditions are true. It implements conjunction of all anomalies of the individual metrics, which can effectively reduce the false alarm rate, based on that a PUT is an anomaly only when it is judged to be abnormal by each of the individual metrics.

We then generate ensemble entropy-based metric by combining the sum- and product-rule integrations of the three individual metrics, which is formulated as

$$^{O}\mathbf{EEMD} = \mathcal{W} \bullet * {}^{O}\mathbf{OR}^{3} + (\mathbf{E} - \mathcal{W}) \bullet * {}^{O}\mathbf{AND} \tag{24.70}$$

where ^{O}EEMD is the final anomaly map and $\mathcal{W}$ is a weight map (where each element ranges from 0 to 1) controlling the contribution of the sum and product rules. Furthermore, we propose an image standard deviation-based strategy to automatically determine the weight map $\mathcal{W}$

$$\tilde{\mathcal{W}} = \underset{\mathcal{W}}{\operatorname{argmin}} \mathrm{STD}\left({}^{O}\mathbf{EEMD}\right) \tag{24.71}$$

where STD(^{O}EEMD) calculates the image standard deviation of the ^{O}EEMD that can be understood as a grayscale image. This strategy is motivated by: in an ideal anomaly map, the anomaly regions would be assigned higher values, and the background of the image would be largely suppressed. Therefore, we expect values in the histogram of the anomaly map to be clustered around a specific value. Thus, according to the definition of the standard deviation of the images, the standard deviation of a desirable anomaly map will be very small.

Conventional image standard deviation relies on histograms, ignoring spatial structure. Figure 24.24 shows that images with identical histograms, despite chaotic spatial structures, have the same standard deviation. To reduce chaos in anomaly detection maps, spatial structure is considered. Inspired by [19], we introduce an improved standard deviation definition where pixel intensity considers neighboring values. This is achieved using spatial filters, specifically a low-pass Gaussian kernel, followed by computing the standard deviation on the filtered anomaly map. Consequently, the new standard deviation is defined as: $\mathrm{STD}_{2-D}(\mathcal{A}) = \mathrm{STD}(g \star \mathcal{A})$, where g is a lowpass Gaussian kernel. Second, we employ a border avoidance strategy [27] to avoid anomaly maps with a strong border response. The border effect factor α is defined as: given an anomaly map $\mathcal{A}$, $\alpha = \sum\sum \mathcal{G}(n,m) \cdot \mathcal{N}(A(n,m))$, where $\mathcal{G}$ is a Gaussian mask of the same size as $\mathcal{A}$, and

Figure 24.24 Binary images with the same histogram, but with different spatial structures.

$\mathcal{G}(n, m) = 1$. $\mathcal{N}(\cdot)$ is used to normalize $\mathcal{A}$ so that the summation of all the pixel values is 1. Consequently, $\tilde{\mathcal{W}}$ in (24.71) is revised as follows:

$$\tilde{\mathcal{W}} = \underset{\mathcal{W}}{\mathrm{argmin}} \alpha^{-1} \mathrm{STD}_{2-D}\left({}^{O}\mathbf{EEMD}\right) \tag{24.72}$$

In this method, the interior point algorithm is adopted for optimizing the weight map $\mathcal{W}$. However, if we directly optimize all the pixels of the whole weight map in (24.72), the number of independent variables (equal to the number of pixels) to be optimized will be very large, leading to expensive computing consumption and memory requirements. For example, a 100×100 anomaly map leads to 10,000 independent variables. We use the blocking strategy as shown in Figure 24.25 to address this problem, where the anomaly map is divided into several $N \times N$ blocks, and the pixels in the same block are given the same weight value.

In our implementation, we set $N = 10$ for the ABU data set and $N = 25$ for the Viareggio data set, and these data sets will be described in the experimental part. Moreover, the edge padding can be used to deal with the case that the edge length of the image cannot be divided by N. Based on this, $\mathcal{W}$ is optimized, and then, the final anomaly map ^{O}EEMD is obtained for anomaly detection purposes. The proposed method is summarized in Algorithm 24.1.

Algorithm 24.1 EEMD
Inputs: The HSI **X**; Parameters ω_p, r_c and ω_e
Output: Anomaly map ${}^{O}\mathbf{EEMD}$ of **X**.
1: Construct the occurrence probability vector $\boldsymbol{\rho}$ of **X** according to (4)
2: Compute the anomaly map by the SE-based metric, ${}^{O}\mathbf{HSE}$, according to (7) and (8)
3: Compute the anomaly map by the JE-based metric, ${}^{O}\mathbf{HJE}$, according to (12) and (13)
4: Compute the anomaly map by the RE-based metric, ${}^{O}\mathbf{HRE}$, according to (14) and (15)
5: Obtain the logical "*OR*" detection map, ${}^{O}\mathbf{OR}$, by (16)
6: Obtain the logical "*AND*" detection map, ${}^{O}\mathbf{AND}$, by (17)
7: Optimize the weight map $\mathcal{W}$ according to (20)
8: Combine ${}^{O}\mathbf{OR}$ and ${}^{O}\mathbf{AND}$ by (18) to obtain the final Anomaly map ${}^{O}\mathbf{EEMD}$
9: **return** ${}^{O}\mathbf{EEMD}$

24.3.3 Experiments

The ABU and Viareggio data sets were selected for experiments. The proposed EEMD is compared with other widely used anomaly detection methods, including the GRX [13], LRX [13], LSMAD [16], CRD [14], DCR [28], and MoG [29]. We report the optimal parameters settings used for the experiments in Table 24.6. From the observations in Table 24.6 and the ground truth in Figure 24.26–Figure 24.28, we can infer that there is a significant relationship between the optimal

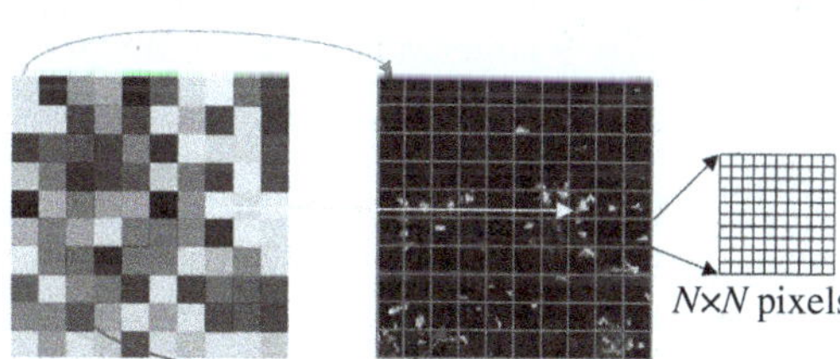

Figure 24.25 Sketch map for the blocking strategy.

Table 24.6 Optimal parameters settings for the proposed EEMD method according to the highest AUC scores of (P_d,P_f).

Images\Parmeters		w_p	r_c	w_e
ABU-airport	(a)	35	2	13
	(b)	33	8	17
	(c)	35	2	15
	(d)	15	17	35
ABU-beach	(a)	9	30	11
	(b)	31	10	13
	(c)	21	30	15
	(d)	19	11	21
ABU-urban	(a)	23	7	9
	(b)	29	30	5
	(c)	27	10	17
	(d)	35	30	17
	(e)	21	17	17

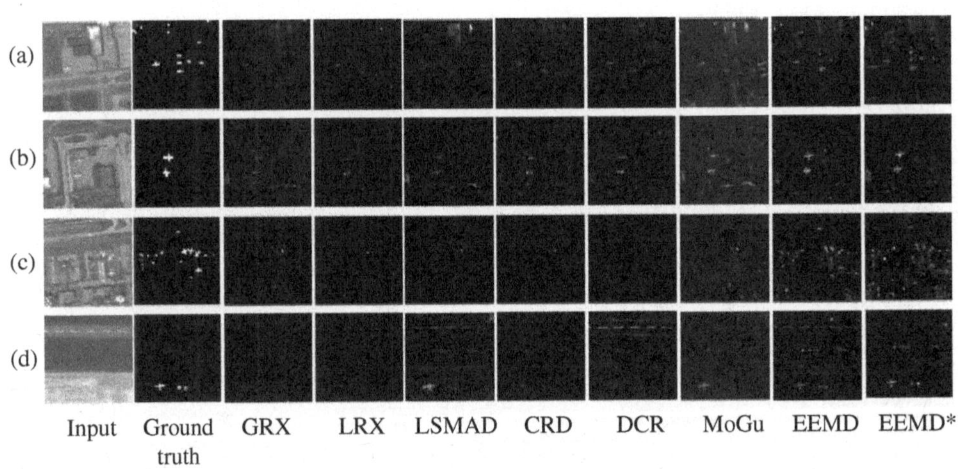

Figure 24.26 Detection result maps by the GRX, LRX, LSMAD, CRD, DCR, MOG, and proposed EEMD methods for the ABU-airport scene. (a) ABU-airport. (b) ABU-airport. (c) ABU-airport. (d) ABU-airport.

w_p and the size and quantity of anomaly targets. Anomalous targets with larger size or quantity usually lead to a larger value of the optimal w_p.

1) *Experiment on the ABU Data set:* Table 24.7 shows the AUC scores of (P_d,P_f) by different anomaly detection methods on each image (noting that, EEMD* refers to the EEMD using optimal parameters). On the whole, the average AUC scores of (P_d,P_f) by the EEMD over each of the three scenes are higher than other comparison methods, especially in airport and beach scenes, which are 0.0126 and 0.0229 higher than that of the second (obtained by the CRD and LSMAD,

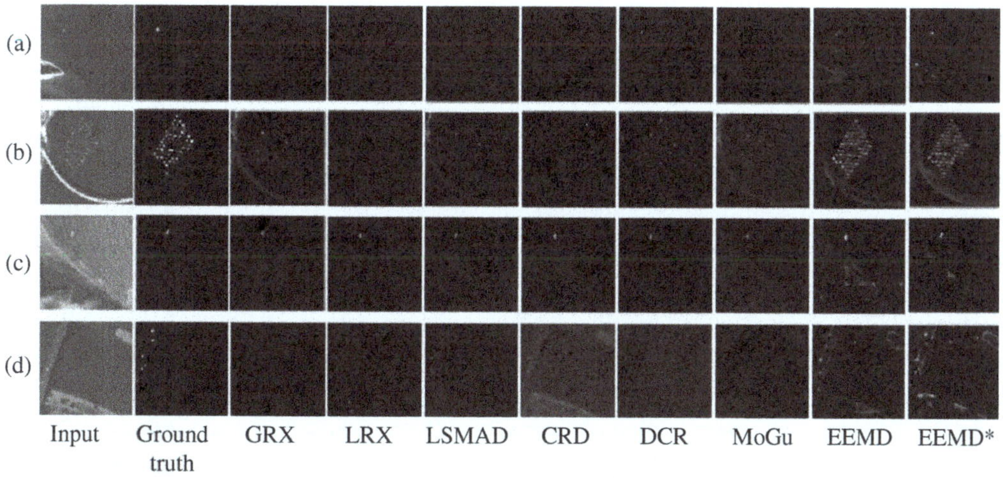

Figure 24.27 Detection result maps by the GRX, LRX, LSMAD, CRD, DCR, MOG, and proposed EEMD methods for the ABU-beach scene. (a) ABU-beach. (b) ABU-beach. (c) ABU-beach. (d) ABU-beach.

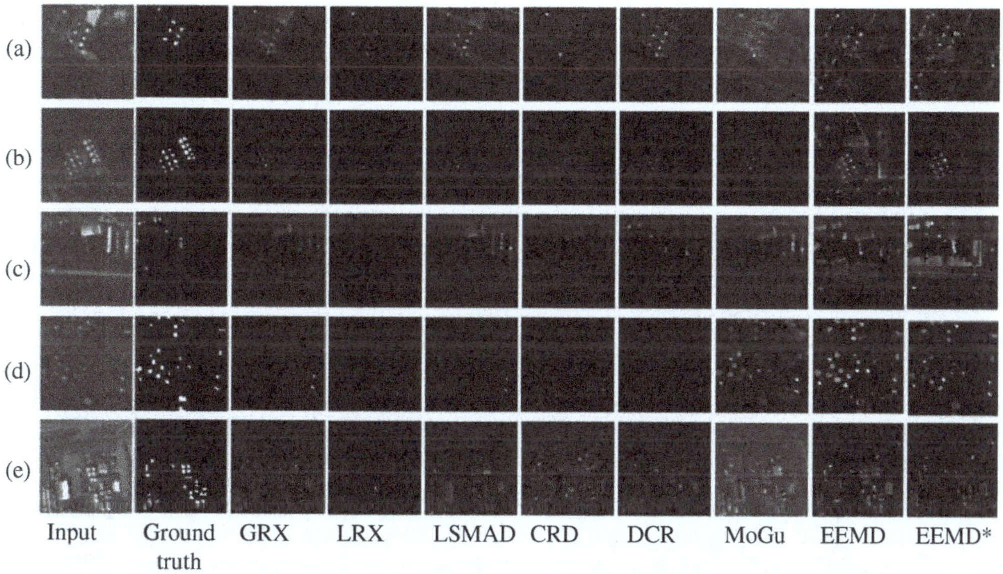

Figure 24.28 Detection result maps by the GRX, LRX, LSMAD, CRD, DCR, MOG, and proposed EEMD methods for the ABU-urban scene. (a) ABU-urban. (b) ABU-urban. (c) ABU-urban. (d) ABU-urban. (e) ABU-urban.

respectively). Therefore, we can conclude that, benefitted from the ensemble entropy metric strategy we proposed, the EEMD can achieve a quite competitive detection performance. The result detection maps obtained by different methods are shown in Figure 24.26–Figure 24.28. As can be seen visually, the EEMD can better recover anomalies of different sizes and shapes by suppressing background and highlighting anomalies.

Table 24.7 AUC scores of (P_d, P_f) on the ABU data set for different Hyperspectral anomaly detection methods.

Images\Methods		RX	LRX	LSMA	CRD	DCR	MoG	EEMD	EEMD*
ABU-airport	(a)	0.8219	0.9666	0.8377	0.9512	**0.9668**	0.8398	0.9586	0.9767
	(b)	0.8404	0.9489	0.9195	0.9694	0.9460	0.8601	**0.9910**	0.9950
	(c)	0.9288	0.9410	0.9397	0.9580	0.9532	0.9125	**0.9759**	0.9850
	(d)	0.9526	0.9537	0.9873	0.9834	0.9346	0.9433	**0.9870**	0.9972
	Average	0.8859	0.9526	0.9211	0.9655	0.9501	0.8889	**0.9781**	0.9885
ABU-beach	(a)	0.9807	**0.9980**	0.9768	0.9891	0.9913	0.9908	0.9916	0.9968
	(b)	0.9106	0.9755	0.9054	0.9249	0.9590	0.9243	**0.9894**	0.9912
	(c)	**0.9999**	**0.9999**	0.9996	0.9997	**0.9999**	0.9998	**0.9999**	0.9999
	(d)	0.9538	0.9314	**0.9726**	0.8751	0.7919	0.8804	0.9650	0.9867
	Average	0.9613	0.9762	0.9636	0.9472	0.9355	0.9496	**0.9865**	0.9937
ABU-urban	(a)	0.9907	0.9807	0.9830	0.9851	0.9865	0.9846	**0.9891**	0.9895
	(b)	0.9946	0.8538	0.9840	0.9541	0.9662	**0.9848**	0.9575	0.9914
	(c)	0.9513	0.9459	0.9641	0.9579	0.9802	0.9305	**0.9829**	0.9924
	(d)	0.9887	0.8534	0.9814	0.9687	**0.9902**	0.9811	0.9825	0.9929
	(e)	0.9692	0.8811	0.9610	0.9529	0.9652	0.9525	**0.9773**	0.9807
	Average	0.9789	0.9030	0.9747	0.9637	0.9777	0.9667	**0.9779**	0.9894

2) *Experiment on the Viareggio data set:* The proposed method is further evaluated on the Viareggio data set. Since the size and number of bands of the Viareggio data set are much larger than those of the ABU data set, the parameters used for the Viareggio data set should be different. For the LRX, CRD, and DCR, w_{in} and w_{out} are set to (7,25), (7,27), and (5,21), respectively. For the MoG, the default parameters suggested in [4] are used. For the EEMD, we set $w_p = 39$, $r_c = 1$, and $w_e = 25$ here. Figure 24.29 shows the detection maps obtained by different methods.

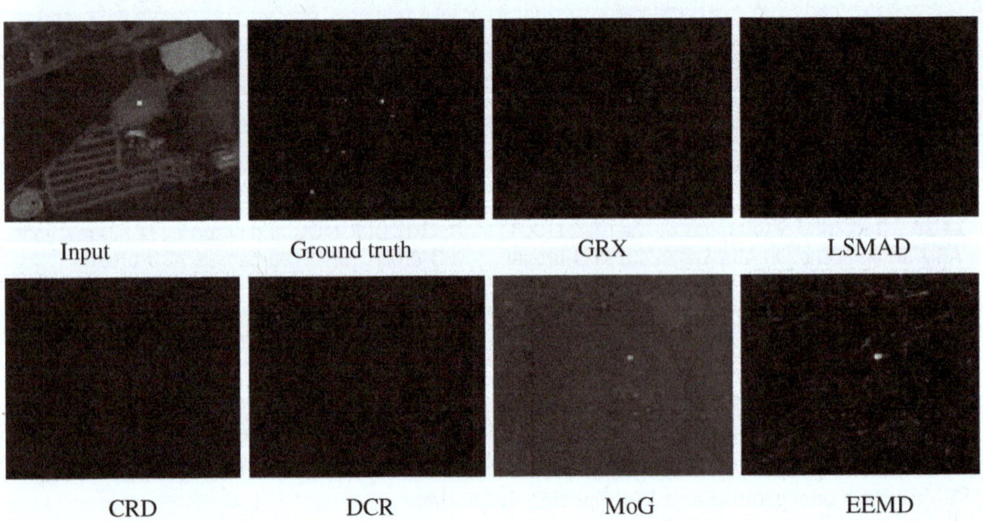

Figure 24.29 Detection result maps by the GRX, LRX, LSMAD, CRD, DCR, MOG, and proposed EEMD methods on the Viareggio data set.

Table 24.8 AUC scores of (P_d,P_f) and execution time on the Viareggio data set for different hyperspectral anomaly detection methods.

	RX	LRX	CRD	DCR	MoG	EEMD
AUC	0.8593	0.9568	0.9609	0.9532	0.9280	0.9698
Time/s	4.9	5649.0	17196.9	2882.1	1176.7	155.1

As the size of the image increases, the proportion of anomaly targets decreases, which increases the difficulty of detection. All the comparison methods, including EEMD, can only detect the largest abnormal target effectively. In addition, compared with other methods, EEMD can highlight the anomaly most. Table 24.8 shows the AUC scores and execution time for different detectors. The EEMD performs best compared to other methods, whose AUC is 0.9698. According to the execution time, the EEMD is much faster than other methods accepted RX.

24.3.4 Summary

This article proposed a new EEMD for hyperspectral anomaly detection, which is based on the entropy analysis of the system in information theory. The main idea of the proposed method is transforming the system entropy into three metrics evaluating the anomaly score of pixels, by considering the SE, JE, and RE and correspondingly establishing the systems. Our ensemble strategy for the three individual entropy-based metrics can not only improve the detection rate but also reduce the false alarm rate. Our experimental results, conducted on the ABU data set and the Viareggio data set, demonstrate the superiority of the proposed method with regard to state-of-the-art competitors. As with any new approach, there are still some unresolved issues that may present challenges over time. Specifically, the proposed method still produces some false alarms in the detection result. These aspects deserve further research and improvements in future work. We are also planning on developing an efficient implementation of the proposed approach by resorting to high-performance computing architectures such as graphics processing units (GPUs).

References

1 Tappen, M.F., Freeman, W.T., and Adelson, E.H. (2005). Recovering intrinsic images from a single image. *IEEE Trans. Pattern Anal. Mach. Intell.* 27 (9): 1459 1472.

2 Bousseau, A., Paris, S., and Durand, F. (2009). User-assisted intrinsic images. *ACM Trans. Graph.* 28 (5): 1–10.

3 Grosse, R., Johnson, M.K., Adelson, E.H., and Freeman, W.T. 2009. Ground truth data set and baseline evaluations for intrinsic image algorithms. *2009 IEEE 12th International Conference on Computer Vision*, 2335–2342, Kyoto, Japan (29 September 2009). IEEE.

4 Shen, L., Yeo, C., and Hua, B.-S. (2013). Intrinsic image decomposition using a sparse representation of reflectance. *IEEE Trans. Pattern Anal. Mach. Intell.* 35 (12): 2904–2915.

5 Zhao, Q., Tan, P., Dai, Q. et al. (2012). A closedform solution to Retinex with nonlocal texture constraints. *IEEE Trans. Pattern Anal. Mach. Intell.* 34 (7): 1437–1444.

6 Huang, Q. et al. June 2018. Multispectral image intrinsic decomposition via subspace constraint, *2018 IEEE/CVF Conference on Computer Vision and Pattern Recognition*, Salt Lake City, UT, USA (18–23 June 2018). IEEE.

7 Land, E.H. and McCann, J.J. (1971). Lightness and Retinex theory. *J. Opt. Soc. Am. A* 61 (1): 1.

8 Rodriguez, A. and Laio, A. (2014). Machine learning. Clustering by fast search and find of density peaks. *Science* 344 (6191): 1492–1496.

9 Taitano, Y.P., Geier, B.A., and Bauer, K.W. (2010). A locally adaptable iterative RX detector. *EURASIP J. Adv. Signal Process.* December 2010 (1): 1–10.

10 Sun, K., Geng, X., and Ji, L. (2015). Exemplar component analysis: a fast band selection method for hyperspectral imagery. *IEEE Geosci. Remote Sens. Lett.* 12 (5): 998–1002.

11 Yang, X., He, L., and Lu, H. (2009). A clustering algorithm for data sets with different densities. *2009 International Conference on Computer Technology and Development*, 504–507, Kota Kinabalu, Malaysia (13–15 November 2009). IEEE.

12 Kerekes, J. (2008). Receiver operating characteristic curve confidence intervals and regions. *IEEE Geosci. Remote Sens. Lett.* 5 (2): 251–255.

13 Reed, I.S. and Yu, X. (1990). Adaptive multiple-band CFAR detection of an optical pattern with unknown spectral distribution. *IEEE Trans. Acoust. Speech Signal Process.* 38 (10): 1760–1770.

14 Li, W. and Du, Q. (2015). Collaborative representation for hyperspectral anomaly detection. *IEEE Trans. Geosci. Remote Sens.* 53 (3): 1463–1474.

15 Kwon, H. and Nasrabadi, N.M. (2005). Kernel RX-algorithm: a nonlinear anomaly detector for hyperspectral imagery. *IEEE Trans. Geosci. Remote Sens.* 43 (2): 388–397.

16 Zhang, Y., Du, B., Zhang, L., and Wang, S. (2016). A low-rank and sparse matrix decomposition-based Mahalanobis distance method for hyperspectral anomaly detection. *IEEE Trans. Geosci. Remote Sens.* 54 (3): 1376–1389.

17 Tu, B., Li, N., Liao, Z. et al. (2019). Hyperspectral anomaly detection via spatial density background purification. *Remote Sens* 11: 2618.

18 Ell, T. (1993). Quaternion-Fourier transforms for analysis of two-dimensional linear time-invariant partial differential systems. *Proceedings of 32nd IEEE Conference on Decision and Control*, 1830–1841, San Antonio, TX, USA (15–17 December 1993). IEEE.

19 Li, J., Levine, M.D., An, X. et al. (2013). Visual saliency based on scale-space analysis in the frequency domain. *IEEE Trans. Pattern Anal. Mach. Intell.* 35 (4): 996–1010.

20 Kang, X., Zhang, X., Li, S. et al. (2017). Hyperspectral anomaly detection with attribute and edge-preserving filters. *IEEE Trans. Geosci. Remote Sens.* 55 (10): 5600–5611.

21 Castleman, K.R. (1996). *Digital Image Processing*. Upper Saddle River, NJ: Prentice-Hall.

22 Wang, Q., Zhang, F., and Li, X. (2018). Optimal clustering framework for hyperspectral band selection. *IEEE Trans. Geosci. Remote Sens.* 56 (10): 5910–5922.

23 Jolliffe, I.T. (2003). Principal component analysis. *Technometrics* 45 (3): 276.

24 Rasti, B., Ulfarsson, M.O., and Sveinsson, J.R. (2016). Hyperspectral feature extraction using total variation component analysis. *IEEE Trans. Geosci. Remote Sens.* 54 (12): 6976–6985.

25 He, X. and Niyogi, P. (2003). Locality preserving projections. *Proceedings of the 17th International Conference on Neural Information Processing Systems*, Whistler British Columbia Canada (9 December 2003), 153–160.

26 Banerjee, A., Burlina, P., and Diehl, C. (2006). A support vector method for anomaly detection in hyperspectral imagery. *IEEE Trans. Geosci. Remote Sens.* 44 (8): 2282–2291.

27 Zhang, L., Tong, M.H., Marks, T.K. et al. (2008). SUN: a Bayesian framework for saliency using natural statistics. *J. Vis.* 8 (7): 1–20.

28 Zhang, G., Li, N., Tu, B. et al. (2020). Hyperspectral anomaly detection via dual collaborative representation. *IEEE J. Sel. Top. Appl. Earth Obs. Remote Sens.* 13: 4881–4894.

29 Li, L., Li, W., Du, Q., and Tao, R. (2020). Low-rank and sparse decomposition with mixture of Gaussian for hyperspectral anomaly detection. *IEEE Trans. Cybern.* 51 (9): 4363–4372.

25

Spectral Change Analysis for Multitemporal Change Detection in Hyperspectral Remote Sensing Images

Sicong Liu[1], Kecheng Du[1], Xiaohua Tong[1], and Peijun Du[2]

[1] *College of Surveying and Geo-Informatics, Tongji University, Shanghai, China*
[2] *School of Geography and Ocean Science, Nanjing University, Nanjing, China*

25.1 Introduction

For decades, Earth Observation (EO) satellites have provided a unique method observing our living planet from space. The revisit property of EO satellites has resulted in the creation of extensive archives containing multitemporal images. This allows for the monitoring of land surface changes in wide geographical areas according to both long-term (e.g., yearly) and short-term (e.g., daily) observations. The detection and understanding of changes occurred in the multitemporal images is essential for the study of global change, environmental evolution and anthropogenic phenomena [1]. Change Detection (CD) is the process designed to identify changes occurred on the same geographical area at different observation times [1, 2]. CD techniques have been widely and successfully employed in numerous remote sensing applications (e.g., environmental monitoring, agriculture, disaster monitoring) over the past few decades, particularly in the context of multitemporal remote sensing spectral images [2–5].

As technology is constantly updated, the growing availability of hyperspectral data brings remote sensing into a high spectral resolution era. Hyperspectral sensors take images with a very high spectral resolution (e.g., 10 nm) over a wide spectral range (e.g., 400–2500 nm). In change detection, this important property allows one to potentially detect small spectral variations that are usually not detectable in multispectral (MS) images due to the poor spectral representation (i.e., generally sufficient for representing only the major abrupt changes) [6]. However, due to the special characteristics of hyperspectral images, many change detection algorithms applied to MS and other images are not applicable to hyperspectral images. Thus, more targeted algorithms need to be proposed. Firstly, due to the influence of atmosphere and illumination factors, it is possible to identify the same object with different spectra and different objects with the same spectrum phenomena in hyperspectral images. This introduces new challenges to hyperspectral change detection. In addition, the spatial resolution of commonly used hyperspectral images is usually higher than 30 m/pixel, which limits the spatial information that can be extracted from them. Many traditional change detection algorithms, which primarily utilize spatial information, are difficult to apply to hyperspectral images [7, 8]. Therefore, the development of more suitable change detection methods for hyperspectral images becomes an important and urgent task.

Machine-Learning-Based Hyperspectral Image Processing, First Edition. Edited by Bing Zhang.

In recent decades, exhaustive investigations on change detection topic have been conducted on hyperspectral images. These investigations have considered a range of techniques, including manual thresholding [9], automatic modeling and thresholding techniques [10], clustering [11], and other specific approaches [12–14]. The most commonly used traditional unsupervised change detection methods include change vector analysis (CVA) [15], iterative reweighted multivariate alteration detection (IR-MAD) [16], temporal-principal components analysis (TPCA) [17], the slow feature analysis (SFA) [18], where clustering and thresholding are mainly change determination methods [11, 19] for determining specific change information. Among all unsupervised CD methods, a cluster of the most popular and widely used techniques is the CVA-based methods. The original CVA was proposed to analyze the possible multiple types of changes in different band combinations in bitemporal remote sensing images [10, 15]. However, it still has the problem of detecting incomplete changes that occur in all spectral bands. To overcome this drawback, an improved version of the method, named compressed change vector analysis (C^2VA), was proposed. In this method, the spectral change vectors (SCVs) were compressed and projected in a 2-D polar coordinate domain [20]. A sequential spectral change vector analysis (S^2CVA) method was then proposed to further optimize the compressed representation in the 2D polar according to the calculation of an adaptive reference vector in each of the spectral projections [21]. In addition, with the continuous development of computer technology, supervised change detection methods based on machine learning classifiers have become an important direction. Different classifiers, such as Support Vector Machine (SVM), Extreme Learning Machine (ELM), and Nearest Neighbor Classifier (KNN) have shown their applicability and effectiveness in various CD applications [22, 23]. The incorporation of a priori information into these supervised CD methods typically results in higher accuracy. For instance, an object-based approach to urban area CD has been proposed, which employs rotation forest (RoF) [24] to obtain more precise CD results. An integrated classifier is proposed, in which multiple classifiers are used in combination in order to obtain more accurate CD results [25, 26].

The emergence of deep learning based CD methods, has led to a significant improvement in the accuracy, efficiency, and automation of hyperspectral CD methods based on deep learning models [26–28]. In contrast, unsupervised traditional CD methods, rely on manual feature extraction, which is often based on a priori knowledge and tends to extract shallow change features. However, deep unsupervised CD methods typically utilize potential multi-layer change feature extraction implemented through deep learning models, such as Deep Change Vector Analysis (DCVA) [29] and Deep Slow Feature Analysis (DSFA) [30], which can extract deep change vectors by deep learning network. Similarly, deep learning models are extensively used for supervised CD. Supervised hyperspectral CD methods based on deep network models are capable of more effectively suppressing CD-irrelevant spatial and spectral information in hyperspectral data, resulting in higher accuracy CD results [31]. For example, a novel spectral and spatial attention network (S^2AN) for hyperspectral-based CD is proposed to focus on extracting CD-relevant information, which comprises several spectral attention modules and Gaussian spatial attention modules [31]. A three-directions spectral-spatial convolution neural network (TDSSC) is proposed to relieve the massive noise and data redundancy issues in hyperspectral images for CD task [32]. By extracting one-dimensional spectral features and two-dimensional spatial-spectral features, this work achieves network lightweighting and reduces noise interference while improving CD accuracy. A multipath convolutional long short-term memory (LSTM) multipath convolutional long short-term memory neural network (MP-ConvLSTM) is proposed for the extraction of multiscale temporal-spatial-spectral features from bitemporal hyperspectral images. This network takes advantage of LSTM and convolutional neural network (CNN) through a parallel architecture to learn multilevel temporal dependencies is proposed for extracting. The ConvLSTM exhibits a better trade-off between complexity and accuracy than other networks in general [33]. A hyperspectral change detection method based on a simplified 3-D convolutional autoencoder (S3DCAECD) is proposed to extract deep spectral-spatial features from bitemporal hyperspectral images without any prior information [34]. An end-to-end residual self-calibrated network (RSCNet) is proposed to increase the accuracy of hyperspectral CD, which adaptively builds interspatial and inter-spectral dependencies [35]. Multiscale feature extraction and fusion networks are proposed to capture the rich spatial details of complex objects and learn fine changes [36, 37]. To enhance the discriminative capability of spectral-spatial features, spectral and spatial attention [31], and self-attention mechanisms have been integrated into CNNs [38], which makes the network concentrate on the significant information which is more relevant to CD. A triplet temporal attention mechanism is constructed by introducing the difference-temporal features in the transformer structure to fully utilize temporal dependencies for enhanced feature expression [39]. Numerous approaches have been developed to address the dependence of deep learning methods on labeled data, which can be categorized into semi-supervised and unsupervised techniques. For example, semi-supervised methods leverage a limited set of labeled samples to extract feature representations from a larger pool of unlabeled data. This includes techniques such as graph convolutional networks, transfer learning, and active learning, all aimed at enhancing semi-supervised classification [40]. A novel semi-supervised deep learning model assumes the dual roles of teacher and student, learning from labeled and unlabeled samples through weak-to-strong consistency training [41]. Unsupervised methods leverage unsupervised networks like autoencoders [42], and networks based-on pseudolabels or self-supervised learning to avoid manual annotation [43]. A network for unsupervised domain adaptive hyperspectral CD is constructed, exploiting labeled source domain information to achieve accurate CD on unlabeled target domains through cyclically updated samples [44]. The aforementioned hyperspectral-CD methods, which employ deep learning models for automatic CD, have achieved considerable success.

25.2 Related Works

25.2.1 The Standard C²VA

First, we formalize the multiple-change detection problem for multi/hyperspectral images. Let $\mathbf{X}_1$ and $\mathbf{X}_2$ be two co-registered multi/hyperspectral images acquired over the same geographical area at times t_1 and t_2, respectively. The multitemporal difference image $\mathbf{X}_D$ (the Spectral Change Vector (SCV) associated with each pixel) is computed by subtracting the two images pixel by pixel, i.e.,

$$\mathbf{X}_D = \mathbf{X}_2 - \mathbf{X}_1 \tag{25.1}$$

Let $\Omega = \{\omega_n, \Omega_C\}$ be the set of all classes in $\mathbf{X}_D$, where ω_n is the no-change class and $\Omega_C = \{\omega_{C_1}, \omega_{C_2}, ..., \omega_{C_K}\}$ is the set of the K possible change classes. The considered CD problem can be defined as to detect all changed pixels (Ω_C) and to separate them into multiple change classes $\{\omega_{C_1}, \omega_{C_2}, ..., \omega_{C_K}\}$.

In the standard C²VA method, a compressed change representation in a 2-D polar domain is defined by two change variables, i.e., the magnitude ρ and the direction α [20]:

$$\rho = \sqrt{\sum_{b=1}^{B} \left(\mathbf{X}_D^b\right)^2} \tag{25.2}$$

$$\alpha = \arccos\left[\frac{1}{\sqrt{B}}\left(\sum_{b=1}^{B} \mathbf{X}_D^b \bigg/ \sqrt{\sum_{b=1}^{B} \left(\mathbf{X}_D^b\right)^2}\right)\right] \tag{25.3}$$

where $\mathbf{X}_D^b$ is the b-th ($b = 1, \ldots, B$) component of $\mathbf{X}_D$ and B is the number of spectral channels of the considered images (i.e., the dimensionality of SCVs). The magnitude ρ is defined based on the popular Euclidean distance [6]. It measures the total contribution of spectral change brightness, whereas it is not sensitive to the shape of spectral vectors. The angle distance α is measured by the Spectral Angle Distance (SAD) [45], which is widely used in several hyperspectral application fields for material identification, classification, etc. [45–47]. SAD measures the similarity between two given spectral signatures, especially focusing on the shape of the spectrum.

Variables ρ and α define a 2-D polar coordinate domain D [20] as:

$$D = \{\rho \in [0, \rho_{\max}] \text{ and } \alpha \in [0, \pi]\} \tag{25.4}$$

where $\rho_{\max}$ is the maximum value of ρ. All the SCVs in $\mathbf{X}_D$ can be represented in a 2-D semicircle scattergram. This scattergram allows one to easily visualize multidimensional change information in a 2-D feature space. However, the compression from a B-D space into a 2-D space results in a loss of information and thus in ambiguity on the detection of different kinds of changes.

In the C^{2}VA framework, the multiple-change detection problem is addressed according to two steps [20]:

1) Set threshold T_ρ along ρ variable to divide the whole semicircle of the C^{2}VA representation domain into two parts, i.e., SC$_n$ and SA$_c$, which are related to the unchanged (ω_n) and changed (Ω_C) SCVs, respectively:

$$\mathrm{SC}_n = \{\rho, \alpha | 0 \le \rho < \mathrm{T}_\rho \text{ and } 0 \le \alpha \le \pi\} \tag{25.5}$$

$$\mathrm{SA}_c = \{\rho, \alpha | \mathrm{T}_\rho \le \rho \le \rho_{\max} \text{ and } 0 \le \alpha \le \pi\} \tag{25.6}$$

2) Separate multiple-change classes ($\omega_{C_1}, \ldots, \omega_{C_K}$) along the direction α by analyzing the semiannulus SA$_c$. Multiple angular thresholds $T_{\alpha,k}$ ($k = 1, \ldots, K - 1$) can be defined to find K annular sectors (each corresponding to a change) inside SA$_c$:

$$S_k = \{\rho, \alpha | \mathrm{T}_\rho \le \rho < \rho_{\max} \text{ and } T_{\alpha,k} \le \alpha \le T_{\alpha,k+1}\}\frac{1}{2} \tag{25.7}$$

where $0 \le T_{\alpha,k} < T_{\alpha,k+1} \le \pi$.

Note that the thresholds T_ρ and T_α can be detected manually or automatically according to one of the various methods proposed in the literature [48–51].

25.2.2 Problems and Challenges

C^{2}VA has been demonstrated to be an effective approach for dealing with MS images [1, 20, 52]. Due to the limited spectral resolution of MS images, the direction variable α is a suitable representation for generally effective to represent the relatively few abrupt changes that are visible in MS data, and it does not suffer from the loss of information associated with the compressed representation. However, in the hyperspectral-CD case, the finer spectral resolution results in a high number of changes that can be detected [53]. Thus, the compressed representation of many spectral channels in one variable α leads to a high probability of ambiguous description of changes, which may result in highly overlapped clusters in the C^{2}VA representation.

In multitemporal hyperspectral images, we can distinguish between two kinds of hierarchically related changes [53]: (i) major changes, which have a significant spectral difference with respect to both the no-change class and the other change classes; (ii) subtle changes, whose SCVs are similar to those of an associated major change, but statistically significantly differ from each other in some portions of the spectrum. When subtle changes inside a major change are present, due to a high similarity among their SCVs, the α variable defined on the basis of a fixed unit reference vector $\mathbf{R} = [1/\sqrt{B},..., 1/\sqrt{B}]$ (as the one derived in (25.3), [20]) is likely to be ineffective for their discrimination. To overcome this drawback, a robust definition of the reference vector **R** (and thus the change variable α) should be designed. This definition should optimize the separation of changes and provide a meaningful change visualization in a hierarchical and adaptive way, thus enabling the representation and discovery of as many changes present in the hyperspectral images as possible.

Accordingly, let use recall that the angle distance α between SCVs in $\mathbf{X}_D$ and a generic reference vector **R** is defined as:

$$\alpha = \arccos\left[\left(\sum_{b=1}^{B}(\mathbf{X}_D^b\mathbf{R}^b)\Bigg/\sqrt{\sum_{b=1}^{B}(\mathbf{X}_D^b)^2\sum_{b=1}^{B}(\mathbf{R}^b)^2}\right)\right], \quad \alpha \in [0, \pi] \tag{25.8}$$

where R^b is the b-th component of the reference vector **R**. Due to the fact that α is invariant to the multiplicative scaling [45], the reference **R** in (25.8) actually can be extended to any constant vector $\mathbf{R} = [a,..., a]$, where $a > 0$ and $a \in \mathfrak{R}$.

25.3 Spectral Change Analysis in Hyperspectral Images

25.3.1 Sequential Spectral Change Vector Analysis (S²CVA)

Due to the high-dimensionality of the feature space, the presence of noisy channels and redundant information in hyperspectral images, some potential small spectral variations are difficult to detect by C²VA. Thus, Sequential Spectral Change Vector Analysis (S²CVA) [21] is designed to be sensitive to the small spectral variations that can be identified in hyperspectral images but usually are not detectable in MS images. The iterative hierarchical scheme enables the discovery and identification of each subset of changes through S²CVA. The approach is interactive and semi-automatic, allowing for the detailed study of the structure of changes hidden in the variations of the spectral signatures according to a top-down procedure. A novel 2-D Adaptive Spectral Change Vector Representation (ASCVR) is proposed for the visualization of changes. The ASCVR will be updated automatically at each iteration until the smallest spectral variation subset is identified.

25.3.1.1 Proposed 2-D Adaptive Spectral Change Vector Representation (ASCVR)

Similarly to C²VA, the proposed ASCVR [21] technique is designed in a 2-D feature space. The main reason for using a 2-D rather than a high-dimensional feature space is that in this way it is easy to visualize the change clusters and their numbers. In contrast to the fixed reference vector **R** employed in C²VA [20], the proposed ASCVR is designed to adaptively define the most suitable reference vector **R** for analyzing the multiple changes at each considered hierarchical level. The selection of **R** and the change representation are directly derived based on the statistic distribution of the input SCVs. Consequently, the proposed ASCVR is totally unsupervised.

The proposed ASCVR is defined by the change magnitude ρ (which is the same as defined in C^2VA (25.2)) and the compressed change direction α (which represents the spectral angle distance between a given SCV in $\mathbf{X}_D$ and a reference vector $\mathbf{R}$ (25.8)). Different values of angle distance measure indicate different kinds of changes. At different levels of the proposed hierarchical analysis, a new reference vector $\mathbf{R}$ is defined for each specific portion of the SCV feature space associated with the considered change cluster. In greater detail, the first eigenvector that corresponds to the maximum eigenvalue of the data covariance matrix of the SCVs associated with the considered cluster j at level i (i.e., $P_{i,j}$) is adopted as the reference vector. The selection of the first eigenvector is motivated by the desire for a 2-D change representation that preserves as much as possible the spectral variations of the considered SCVs in a low-dimensional feature space that can be easily managed. In the proposed ASCVR, this vector shows a direction that maximizes the variance of the measurement on α, thus resulting in an adaptive and effective representation of the hidden change patterns in the considered SCVs. The procedure for adaptively defining the reference vector $\mathbf{R}_{i,j}$ for a considered generic cluster $P_{i,j}$ in the hierarchy is as follows. Let us consider the covariance matrix $\mathbf{A}_{i,j}$ of $\mathbf{x}_{i,j}$ (denoted as the SCVs in $P_{i,j}$):

$$\mathbf{A}_{i,j} = \mathrm{cov}\left(\mathbf{x}_{i,j}\right) = E\left[\left(\mathbf{x}_{i,j} - E\left[\mathbf{x}_{i,j}\right]\right)\left(\mathbf{x}_{i,j} - E\left[\mathbf{x}_{i,j}\right]\right)^T\right] \tag{25.9}$$

where $E[\mathbf{x}_{i,j}]$ is the expectation of $\mathbf{x}_{i,j}$ and $\mathbf{A}_{i,j}$ is the $B \times B$ dimensional covariance matrix that represents $\mathbf{x}_{i,j}$ by means of the eigenvectors and eigenvalues, which are calculated according to (25.10):

$$\mathbf{A}_{i,j} \cdot \mathbf{V}_{i,j} = \mathbf{V}_{i,j} \cdot \mathbf{W}_{i,j} \tag{25.10}$$

$\mathbf{W}_{i,j}$ is a diagonal matrix where the eigenvalues are sorted in descending order (i.e., $\lambda_{i,j}^1 > \lambda_{i,j}^2 > \ldots > \lambda_{i,j}^B$) in the diagonal. The magnitude of eigenvalues reflects the amount of data variance that is captured by the corresponding eigenvectors. Let $\mathbf{V}_{i,j} = \left[\mathbf{V}_{i,j}^1, \mathbf{V}_{i,j}^2, \ldots, \mathbf{V}_{i,j}^B\right]$ be the matrix of eigenvectors. The reference vector $\mathbf{R}_{i,j}$ for computing $\alpha_{i,j}$ in (25.8) is selected as the first eigenvector $\mathbf{V}_{i,j}^1$ that corresponds to the largest eigenvalue $\lambda_{i,j}^1$:

$$\mathbf{R}_{i,j} = \mathbf{V}_{i,j}^1 = \begin{pmatrix} v_1 \\ v_2 \\ \vdots \\ v_B \end{pmatrix}_{i,j} \tag{25.11}$$

Accordingly, the two change variables for the SCVs of the cluster $P_{i,j}$ are defined as follows:

$$\begin{cases} \rho_{i,j} = \sqrt{\sum_{b=1}^{B} \left(\mathbf{x}_{i,j}^b\right)^2} \\ \alpha_{i,j} = \arccos\left[\left(\sum_{b=1}^{B} \left(\mathbf{x}_{i,j}^b R_{i,j}^b\right)\right) \Big/ \sqrt{\sum_{b=1}^{B} \left(\mathbf{x}_{i,j}^b\right)^2 \sum_{b=1}^{B} \left(\mathbf{R}_{i,j}^b\right)^2}\right] \end{cases} \tag{25.12}$$

The related 2-D representation domain $\mathbf{D}_{i,j}$ is defined as:

$$\mathbf{D}_{i,j} = \left\{\rho_{i,j} \in \left[0, \rho_{i,j}^{\max}\right] \text{ and } \alpha_{i,j} \in [0, \pi]\right\} \tag{25.13}$$

It should be noted that the use of the first eigenvector does not guarantee the maximum discriminability in all cases. However, this is an effective choice for an adaptive 2-D visualization of the latent change information.

25.3.1.2 Proposed Sequential Spectral Change Vector Analysis (S^{2}CVA)

The intrinsic adaptive characteristic of the proposed ASCVR can be exploited to represent either the whole or a portion of the SCV space. Accordingly, the challenging hyperspectral-CD problem can be addressed hierarchically by the proposed S^{2}CVA. The main idea is that a sequence of ASCVR scattergrams can be obtained for representing SCVs in different specific spectral significance levels, thus SCVs that are associated with different change classes can be gradually separated following the sequential analysis. The block scheme of the proposed S^{2}CVA method is shown in Figure 25.1 [21].

The process begins at the initial level L_0 of the hierarchy, where P_0 is the initial change cluster obtained by thresholding the ρ variable. Then the sequential technique focuses on the P_0 (i.e., SCVs that belong to Ω_C) in order to identify the possible kinds of changes. At level L_1, if more than one homogenous cluster $P_{1,1}, P_{1,2}, \ldots, P_{1,J_1}$ is observed, changes must be discriminated and separated among each other. The procedure then moves to the next level L_2, focusing on each single cluster in $\{P_{1,1}, P_{1,2}, \ldots, P_{1,J_1}\}$ to continue the iterative change analysis by re-projecting the SCVs of each cluster in its corresponding new ASCVR domain. This process is designed to identify any potential changes at this level of representation. The ASCVR scheme, as previously defined, is employed for each considered change cluster, resulting in the generation of corresponding 2-D change representations. $D_{1,j}$ are built through the automatic updating of the references, $\mathbf{R}_{1,j}$ (and thus $\alpha_{1,j}$), in accordance with the SCVs $x_{1,j}$ in $P_{1,j}$ ($j = 1, \ldots, J_1$). By considering the intrinsic properties of SCVs that SCVs belonging to a given change class exhibit homogeneous behaviors on the change variables. Consequently, a single cluster is expected to be observed on their representation domain. On the contrary, presence of different clusters that can be discriminated in the ASCVR scattergram indicates the potential for different kinds of changes. A manual procedure is applied interactively by the user. For each observed change cluster, a discrimination boundary is manually defined, which is structured as a polygon in the software prototype. It should be noted that boundaries are selected independently for each observed change cluster. At a given level of S^{2}CVA, the homogeneity is evaluated manually. Convergence is reached when only a single homogenous change cluster is observed in the scattergram. The cluster is finally associated with a change class in $\{\omega_{C_1}, \omega_{C_2}, \ldots, \omega_{C_K}\}$ and the SCVs of that change class are inversely mapped into the image space to generate the CD map. The whole CD procedure is completed when each representation of

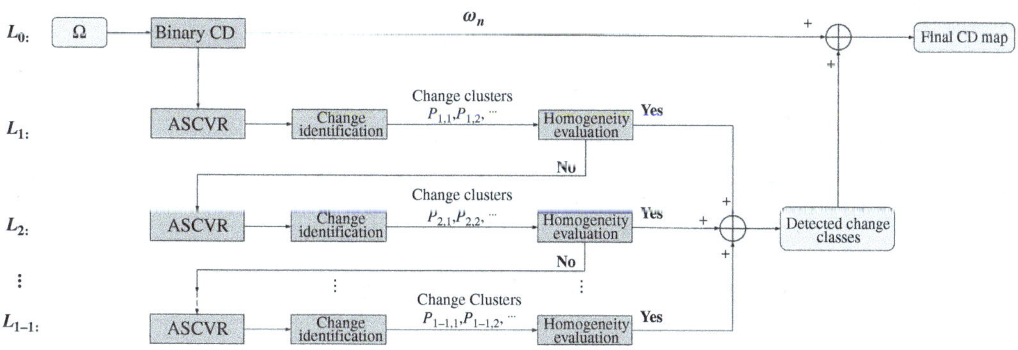

Figure 25.1 Block scheme of the proposed S^{2}CVA step. *Source:* Liu et al. [21]/with permission of IEEE.

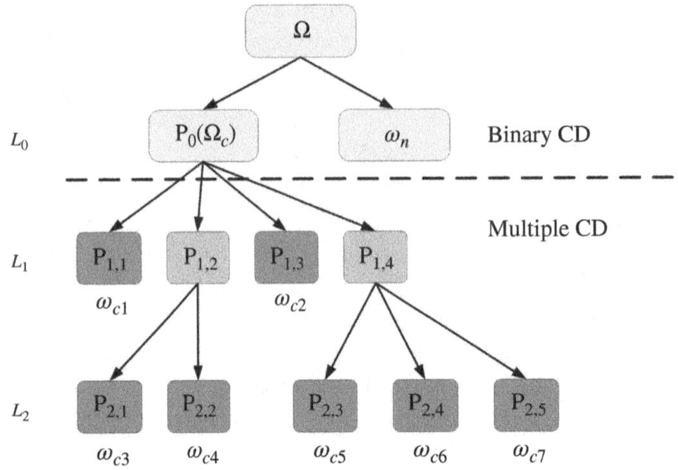

Figure 25.2 Example of the obtained three-level hierarchical tree by the proposed S^2CVA approach, where seven leaf nodes are detected as change classes and one as the no-change class. *Source:* Liu et al. [21]/with permission of IEEE.

the considered specific portion of SCVs in the hierarchy achieves convergence. The whole S^2CVA hierarchy can be conceptualized as a tree structure (see an example in Figure 25.2). The final multiple-change detection map is the union of all the identified change classes $\{\omega_{C_1}, \omega_{C_2}, ..., \omega_{C_K}\}$ and the extracted no-change class ω_n (i.e., the union of all the leaf nodes in the tree). It is important to note that by following the proposed sequential analysis, the original global change representation and optimization problem is decomposed into several local sub-problems at different levels. This allows for the detection of many potential changes hierarchically, taking into account different levels of spectral change significance.

The proposed S^2CVA method enables users to engage in effective interactions with change representation and discovery (in the 2-D representation domain), and change extraction (in the original image domain). At the conclusion of the process, the obtained hierarchical tree provides a comprehensive description of the major and subtle changes present in the considered hyperspectral multitemporal images and their parental relations.

25.3.2 Intrinsic Image Decomposition Based Spectral Change Analysis

Hyperspectral images make it possible for CD performance with enhanced discrimination of changes. However, the shadow and abnormal spectral variations caused by illumination and other external environmental factors in hyperspectral images may impact on the hyperspectral CD performances. The intrinsic image decomposition (IID) model can decompose the hyperspectral temporal difference image into two parts: real change and pseudo change information. In particular, the spectral reflecting component is selected as a kind of pure spectral feature used to enhance the CD performance in multitemporal hyperspectral images [54, 55].

25.3.2.1 Hyperspectral Image Band Grouping

A hyperspectral difference image cannot be used directly as the input in an optimization-based intrinsic image decomposition (IID) algorithm due to its high dimension and wide wavelength range. Therefore, we adopt a dimensional reduction and grouping strategy [54] before the IID feature extraction.

Theoretically, an IID algorithm requires a natural optical image as an input, which records the spectral reflection characteristics of the scene. Owing to this reason, some dimensionality reduction methods that preserve only statistical properties but not physical properties, such as principal components analysis (PCA) and independent component analysis (ICA) are unsuitable. To this end, a straightforward band grouping and fusion approach is employed. In particular, the original N-dimensional hyperspectral difference image is initially partitioned into M equal-sized subsets of adjacent spectral bands, and then the bands within each subset are fused based on the averaging operation. This can be expressed as follows:

$$\tilde{X}_m = \frac{\sum_{n=1}^{N_m} X_m^n}{N_m} \tag{25.14}$$

where m is the m-th subset, X_m^n represents the n-th band of the hyperspectral difference image in the m-th subset. $\tilde{X}_m$ is the m-th fused band ($m = 1, \ldots, M$), M is the number of groups in $\mathbf{X}_D$ and N_m is the number of total bands in the m-th subset. $\mathbf{X}_D$ is the hyperspectral difference image. $\tilde{X}$ is the dimensional reduction result on hyperspectral difference image which is the superposition of $\tilde{X}_m$ ($m = 1, \ldots, M$).

In order to meet the fitting condition of optimization-based IID that the wavelengths of the input data channels are similar, $\tilde{X}$ are divided into M/Z groups:

$$\tilde{X} = \begin{Bmatrix} G^1 \\ G^2 \\ \cdots \\ G^{M/Z} \end{Bmatrix} \tag{25.15}$$

where Z represents the number of bands in each subgroup, G^l is the lth subgroup ($l = 1, \ldots, M/Z$). Note that in each subgroup, the adjacent bands satisfy the condition of the optimization-based method. Then, these subgroups are decomposed with the optimization-based IID method, respectively, and finally M-dimensional fused features are extracted.

25.3.2.2 Intrinsic Image Decomposition on Difference Image

The original IID model used for color images can be expressed as follows:

$$I_a = U_a Q_a \tag{25.16}$$

where a refers to the a-th pixel, $I_a = \left(I_a^\varepsilon, I_a^\gamma, I_a^\beta\right)$, $U_a = \left(U_a^\varepsilon, U_a^\gamma, U_a^\beta\right)$, $\varepsilon, \gamma, \beta$ represent the red, green and blue channels of a color image. This formula indicates that a pixel vector of color image can be decomposed into spectral reflection component U and brightness component Q. Specifically, Q is determined by some factors such as ambient lighting and shadow, which are not directly related to the material of ground objects. In contrast, pixel value of U has a direct relationship with the ground object material. Therefore, IID features that represent more accurate spectral reflection components are potential for the next step hyperspectral-CD.

In a bitemporal CD case, a hyperspectral difference image is obtained by subtracting two times hyperspectral images, the illumination conditions of each single hyperspectral image will impact the accuracy of CD. In fact, different illumination conditions will produce different shadow shapes on hyperspectral difference images. It is therefore difficult to eliminate or weaken the influence of shadows, which will lead to an increase in commission errors. Therefore, the IID method can be employed to decompose the hyperspectral difference image into two distinct categories: the real change area and the pseudo change area. The former is likely to be influenced by shadow and abnormal spectral variations, whereas the latter is not. The IID model for a subgroup in the hyperspectral difference image G^l can be expressed as follows:

$$G_a^l \approx U_a^l Q_a^l \tag{25.17}$$

where a refers to the a-th pixel, and G_a^l is the vector of a-th pixel in group G^l. U^l in (25.17) is a Z-dimensional vector which represents the real change information that will be used in CD as IID features, whereas Q^l is the pseudo change information which will be eliminated.

In order to solve (25.17), researchers have proposed various solutions in recent years. The optimization-based method is adopted to calculate the U and Q two matrices. It is defined based on the assumption that the change in scene lighting or shadow will only result in proportional changes to the pixel values of different channels. Therefore, the brightness component Q and reflection component U of the image can be calculated by optimizing the following energy function:

$$\mathrm{E}(U,Q) = \sum \left(U_p - \sum_{q \in \zeta_p} \chi_{\mathrm{pq}} U_q \right)^2 + \sum_{p \in I} \left(G_p^l / Q_p - U_p \right)^2 \tag{25.18}$$

where $\chi_{\mathrm{pq}} = e^{-\left[(Y_p - Y_q)^2 / \sigma_{pY}^2 + \mathrm{Arc}(G_p^l, G_q^l)^2 / \sigma_{pA}^2 \right]}$, $U_p = \sum_{q \in \zeta_p} \chi_{\mathrm{pq}} U_q$. ζ_p is a local window with a size of $(2o+1) \times (2o-1)$ around pixel p (o is the radius of the window); Y means the intensity image which can be calculated by averaging all bands; $\mathrm{Arc}\left(G_p^l, G_q^l\right) = \arccos\left(G_p^1 G_q^1 + G_p^2 G_q^2 + \ldots + G_p^Z G_q^Z\right)$ is the angle between pixel vectors G_p^l and G_q^l, σ_{pA}^2 and σ_{pY}^2 is obtained by calculating variances of the angle and pixel values in the local window. More details readers can refer to [56]. The procedure for extracting IID features from hyperspectral difference images is illustrated in Figure 25.3.

Finally, a supervised classifier will be selected to assess the performance of the extracted IID features in CD.

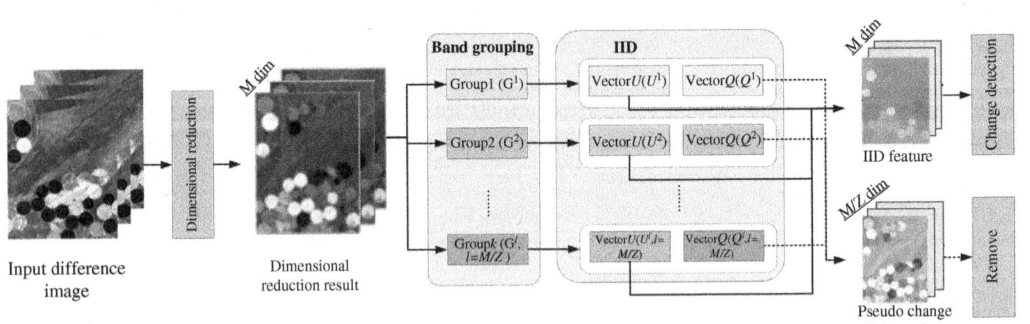

Figure 25.3 The process of extracting IID features from hyperspectral difference image. *Source:* Du and Liu [55]/with permission of SPIE.

25.4 Experimental Setup

25.4.1 Setup for S^2CVA

Experiments were performed on the Umatilla and Yancheng data sets. The binary CD based on the S^2CVA feature space is performed by the Expectation Maximization (EM) algorithm to calculate the threshold automatically. Then, the separation based on the change cluster subsets is implemented by manual discrimination.

25.4.2 Setup for IID Based Spectral Change Analysis

For the extraction of IID features, the feature dimension M and band number Z of each group are two important parameters, which are finally defined as $M = 24$, $Z = 4$ for both data sets. 10% samples from the available reference maps of Yancheng and Umatilla data sets are selected as training samples. Then IID features with different parameters are generated and imported into the classifier. Popular classifier support vector machine (SVM) is selected for HS CD task based on IID features. The radial basis function (RBF) kernel is selected with fivefold cross-validation, and the parameter gamma is defined as 2^{-6}. Note that any other supervised classifier can be applied to generate an accurate multi-class CD map. Furthermore, to avoid the uncertainty caused by the random selection of training samples, each experiment was repeated 10 times to take the average of the accuracy indices.

25.5 Results and Analysis

25.5.1 Umatilla Data Set

25.5.1.1 HS CD Results Based on S^2CVA

Figure 25.4a depicts the scattergram of all SCVs in the standard S^2CVA feature space. In the binary CD step (L_0), the threshold T_ρ was automatically estimated yielded a value of 1.4855 (see the semicircle in Figure 25.4a). Four clusters within the general Ω_c class (P_0) were identified and separated into $P_{1,1}$, ..., $P_{1,4}$ according to the defined discrimination boundaries in Figure 25.4a, which are defined in black polygons. Subsequently, the processing proceeded to the next level (i.e., L_1) and concentrated on each identified cluster $P_{1,1}$, ..., $P_{1,4}$ with the objective of investigating the spectral homogeneity and further exploring the potential presence of multiple changes in the re-projection in the ASCVR scattergram. The reference vectors $\mathbf{R}_{1,j}$ (i.e., $\alpha_{1,j}$, $j = 1$, ..., 4) were automatically derived for each considered specific cluster, thus generating a 2-D representation for each of them. The corresponding six scattergrams $\mathbf{D}_{1,j} - \mathbf{D}_{1,4}$ are illustrated in Figure 25.4 from b to e. It is evident that two of the four clusters (i.e., $P_{1,2}$, $P_{1,3}$) exhibited a single homogeneous class in their corresponding representation domains (see Figure 25.4c and d). These homogeneous clusters were associated with different change classes. The two discriminable clusters observed in the representation of $P_{1,1}$ and in $P_{1,4}$ (i.e., Figure 25.4b and e, respectively) were further analyzed and separated in the next level L_2. In this level, both clusters appeared as a single homogenous cluster on the corresponding ASCVR scattergram $\mathbf{D}_{2,j} - \mathbf{D}_{2,4}$ (see Figure 25.4f–i). Therefore, six change classes were successfully identified according to the proposed sequential analysis, with two identified at level L_1 and four at level L_2.

The resulting hierarchical tree of the considered CD-HS problem is shown in Figure 25.5. The correspondences between the identified clusters and the reference change classes were as follows:

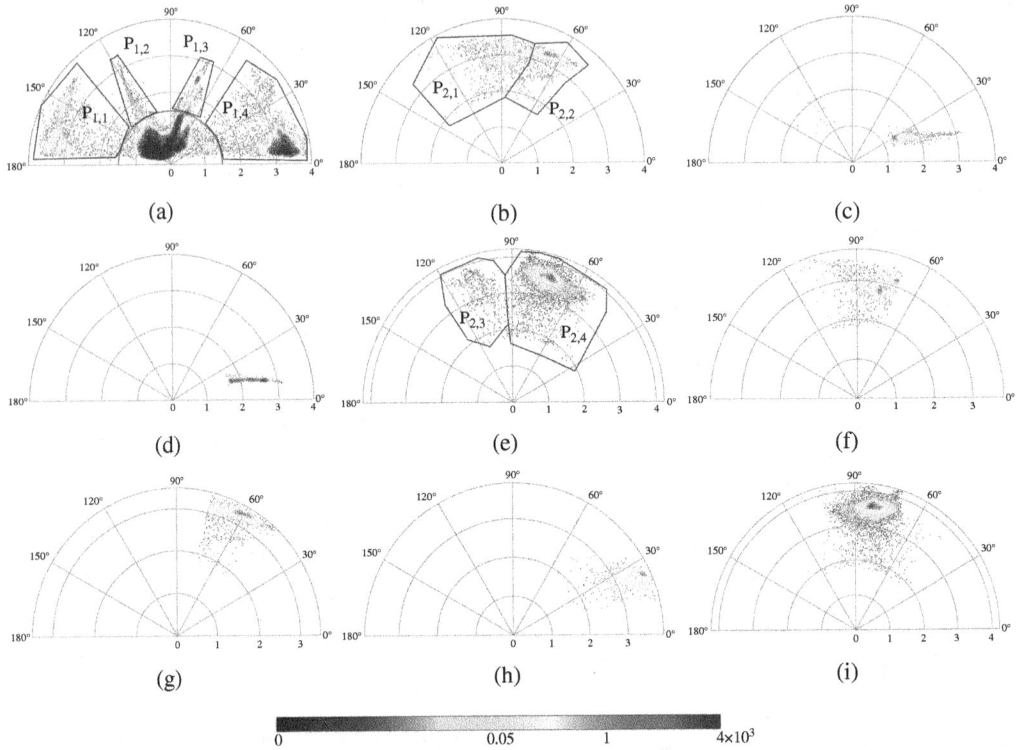

Figure 25.4 The sequence of ASCVR scattergrams represents changes at different levels of the S^2CVA hierarchy. The binary CD decision threshold is defined as the semicircle, whereas discrimination boundaries are represented by black polygons. The final detected change classes are those that obtain a single homogenous cluster in their corresponding representation scattergrams. (a) S^2CVA_M. (b) $\mathbf{D}_{1,1}$. (c) $\mathbf{D}_{1,2}$. (d) $\mathbf{D}_{1,3}$. (e) $\mathbf{D}_{1,4}$. (f) $\mathbf{D}_{2,1}$. (g) $\mathbf{D}_{2,2}$. (h) $\mathbf{D}_{2,3}$. (i) $\mathbf{D}_{2,4}$.

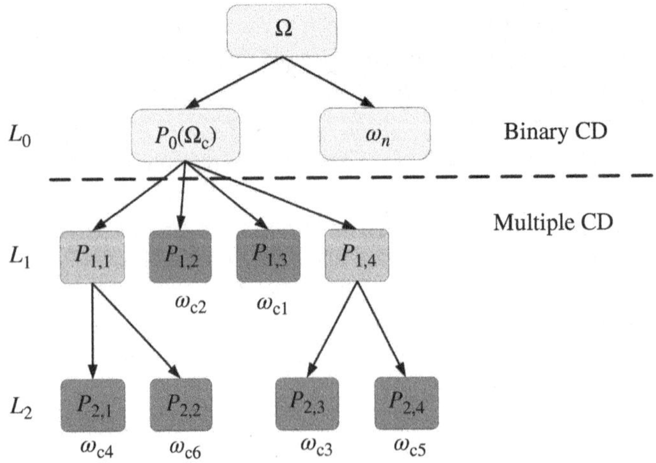

Figure 25.5 The three-level hierarchical tree obtained by the proposed S^2CVA_M method. The nodes highlighted in dotted rectangles represent the final detected changes.

L_0: $\Omega = \{\omega_n, \Omega_c(P_O)\}$; L_1: $P_{1,1} = \{\omega_{C_4}, \omega_{C_6}\}$, $P_{1,2} = \omega_{C_2}$, $P_{1,3} = \omega_{C_1}$, $P_{1,4} = \{\omega_{C_3}, \omega_{C_5}\}$; L_2: $P_{2,1} = \omega_{C_4}$, $P_{2,2} = \omega_{C_6}$, $P_{2,3} = \omega_{C_3}$ and $P_{2,4} = \omega_{C_5}$.

C^{2}VA [20] and Improved C^{2}VA (IC^{2}VA) [52] were selected as the methods of comparison. The qualitative and quantitative comparisons of the CD results obtained by the other considered reference methods are shown in Figure 25.6 and Table 25.1, respectively. The accuracy indices included in Table 25.1 are the Overall Accuracy (OA) and Kappa Coefficient (Kappa), according to the available reference map. The highest values for the OA and Kappa coefficient were obtained by S^{2}CVA in HS-CD experiments.

25.5.1.2 HS CD Results Based on IID Features

The detailed results obtained on the Umatilla data set with 10% training set are presented in Table 25.2. And the best results are highlighted in bold. To evaluate the validity of IID features

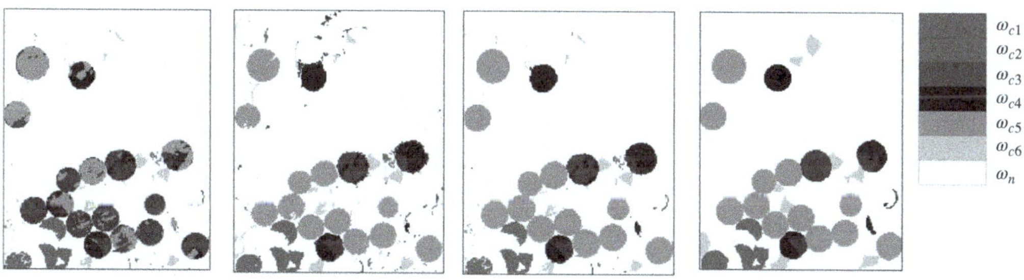

(a) (b) (c) (d)

Figure 25.6 CD maps obtained by (a) C^{2}VA; (b) IC^{2}VA; (c) S^{2}CVA. (d) change reference map. Different changes are represented by varying grayscale intensities, and the no-change is in white.

Table 25.1 Comparison results obtained by different unsupervised methods.

Method	OA	Kappa
C^{2}VA	0.8673	0.6691
IC^{2}VA	0.9373	0.8434
S^{2}CVA	0.9497	0.8729

Table 25.2 SVM Change detection numeric results based on different features with 10% training set (mean ± stand deviation).

Features (dimensionality)	OA	Kappa
HSI (159)	0.9609 ± 0.0044	0.9026 ± 0.0100
Conv_HSI (159)	0.9633 ± 0.0017	0.9090 ± 0.0041
HSI_PCA (10)	0.9592 ± 0.0029	0.8972 ± 0.0065
Conv_HSI_PCA (10)	0.9632 ± 0.0024	0.9083 ± 0.0055
EMAPs (60)	0.9659 ± 0.0024	0.9148 ± 0.0057
IID features (24)	$\mathbf{0.9750 \pm 0.0023}$	$\mathbf{0.9365 \pm 0.0055}$

in the HS CD task, the original HS image and four other popular features were employed for comparison, including the HS image with PCA (HIS_PCA), the HS image with 2D convolution (Conv_HSI), the HS image with 2D convolution and PCA (Conv_HSI_PCA), and the Extended Multi-attribute Profile (EMAP) [57]. It can be observed that the CD performance of IID features outperforms that of all other spectral features (i.e., HSI and HSI_PCA) and spatial-spectral features (i.e., Conv_HSI, Conv_HSI_PCA, and EMAPs) on the data set. In order to qualitatively compare the results, CD maps obtained by different methods are shown in Figure 25.7. It can be seen that the CD results generated by the proposed IID features exhibit more precise and regular edge information of change classes. In particular, the CD results of obtained from the Umatilla data set demonstrate a reduction in noise points and misclassification errors, which may be the presence of pseudo changes resulting from shadow and abnormal spectral variations.

25.5.2 Yancheng Data Set

25.5.2.1 HS CD Results Based on S^{2}CVA

Figure 25.8 illustrates the results of Yancheng data set obtained through S^{2}CVA algorithm. As shown in Figure 25.8a, the threshold T_ρ was estimated at 0.9038, and five clusters within the general Ω_c class (P_0) were manually identified and separated in the 2D feature space ($P_{1,1}$, ..., $P_{1,5}$). The corresponding five represented scattergrams $\mathbf{D}_{1,1} - \mathbf{D}_{1,5}$ are illustrated in Figure 25.8 from b to f.

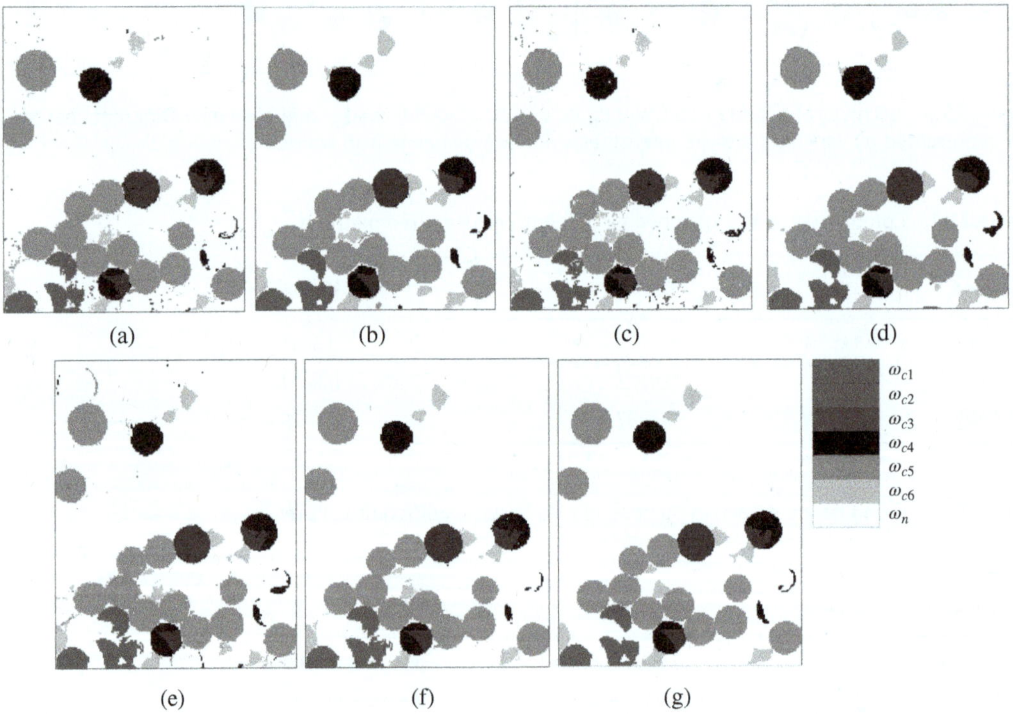

Figure 25.7 Multiclass CD results obtained by using different features: (a) original HSI, (b) Conv_HSI, (c) HSI_PCA, (d) Conv_HSI PCA, (e) EMAPs, (f) IID features and (g) reference map (six change classes are represented by varying grayscale intensities, and the no-change class is shown in white).

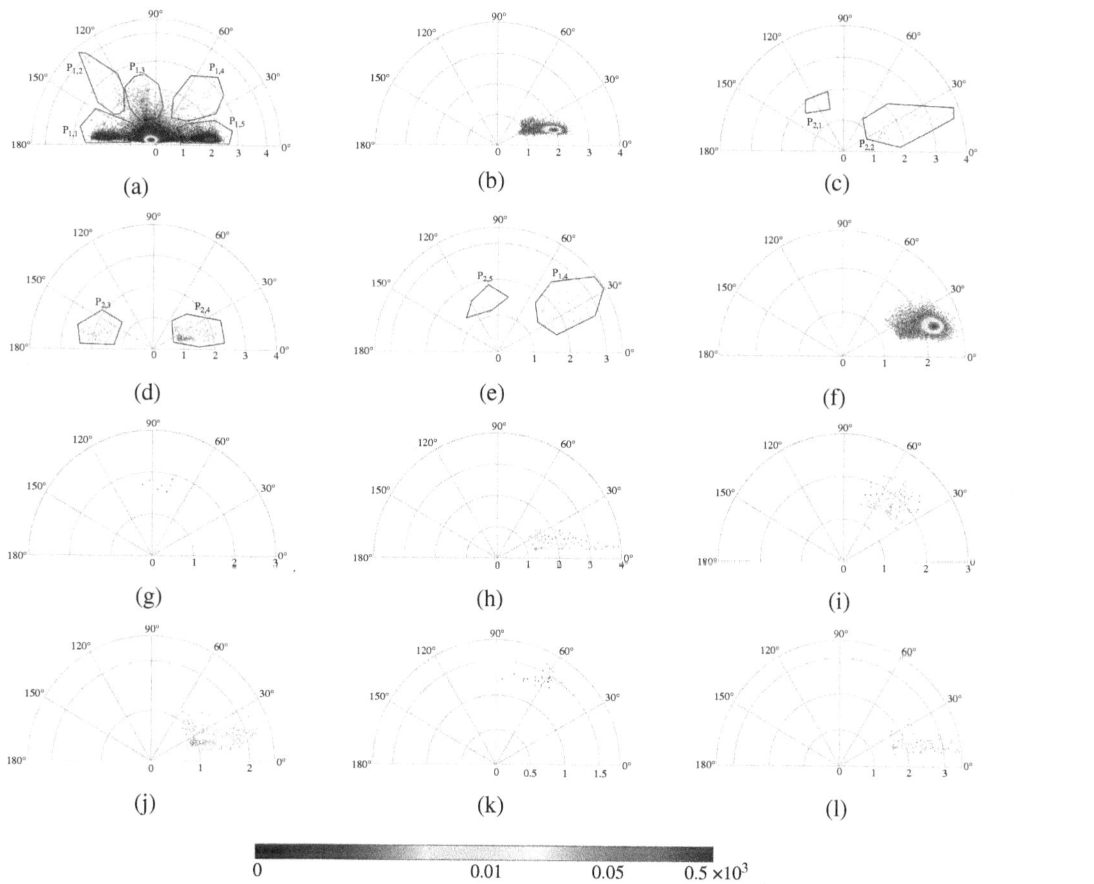

Figure 25.8 The sequence of ASCVR scattergrams represents changes at different levels of the S^2CVA hierarchy. Binary CD decision threshold is defined by the semicircle, whereas discrimination boundaries as black polygons. The final detected change classes are those obtaining a single homogenous cluster in their corresponding representation scattergrams. (a) S^2CVA_M. (b) $\mathbf{D}_{1,1}$. (c) $\mathbf{D}_{1,2}$. (d) $\mathbf{D}_{1,3}$. (e) $\mathbf{D}_{1,4}$. (f) $\mathbf{D}_{1,5}$. (g) $\mathbf{D}_{2,1}$. (h) $\mathbf{D}_{2,2}$. (i) $\mathbf{D}_{2,3}$. (j) $\mathbf{D}_{2,4}$. (k) $\mathbf{D}_{2,5}$. (l) $\mathbf{D}_{2,6}$.

And the two discriminable clusters observed in the representation of $P_{1,2}$, $P_{1,3}$ and in $P_{1,4}$ were further analyzed and separated into $P_{2,1}$ to $P_{2,6}$ (see in Figure 25.8g–l).

However, due to the presence of three change classes with very few pixels (ω_{C_2}, ω_{C_4} and ω_{C_5}), which have no obvious cluster center in the 2D polar coordinate region, the manually identified clusters in step L_0 may contain some no-change pixels or samples of the other change classes. Thus, by manual discrimination, the hierarchal tree of the considered CD-HS problem is shown in Figure 25.9. The correspondence between the identified clusters and the reference change classes is as follows: L_0: $\Omega = \{\omega_n, \Omega_c(P_0)\}$; L_1: $P_{1,1} = \omega_{C_1}$, $P_{1,2} = \{\omega_{C_1}, \omega_{C_3}\}$, $P_{1,3} = \{\omega_{C_4}, \omega_n\}$, $P_{1,4} = \{\omega_{C_2}, \omega_{C_5}\}$, $P_{1,5} = \omega_{C_2}$, L_2: $P_{2,1} = \omega_{C_1}$, $P_{2,2} = \omega_{C_3}$, $P_{2,3} = \omega_{C_4}$, $P_{2,4} = \omega_n$, $P_{2,5} = \omega_{C_2}$ and $P_{2,4} = \omega_{C_5}$.

The qualitative and quantitative comparisons of the CD results obtained by the other considered reference methods are shown in Figure 25.10 and Table 25.3. The highest OA and Kappa values for HS-CD experiments were obtained by S^2CVA.

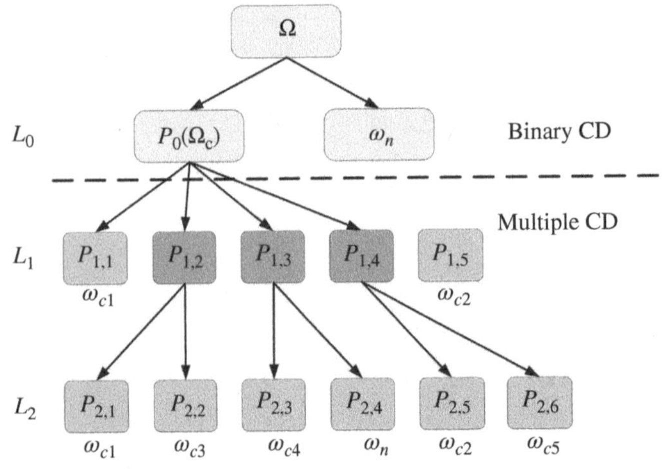

Figure 25.9 The three-level hierarchical tree obtained by the proposed S^2CVA_M method. Nodes highlighted in dotted rectangles are the final detected changes.

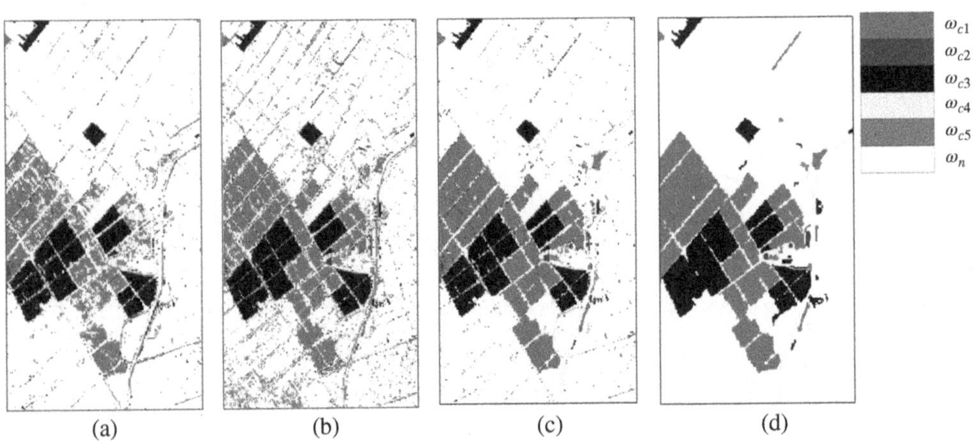

Figure 25.10 CD maps obtained by (a) C^2VA; (b) IC^2VA; (c) S^2CVA, and (d) change reference map. Different changes are represented by varying grayscale intensities, and the no-change class is in white.

Table 25.3 Comparison results obtained by different unsupervised methods.

Method	OA	Kappa
C^2VA	0.8926	0.7481
IC^2VA	0.8259	0.6384
S^2CVA	0.9434	0.8650

25.5.2.2 HS CD Results Based on IID Features

For Yancheng data set, 10% samples were also selected randomly as the training set. Quantitative evaluation metrics and the CD results are illustrated in Table 25.4 and Figure 25.11. And the best results are highlighted in bold. The CD results generated by the proposed IID features have the

Table 25.4 SVM Change detection numeric results based on different features with 10% training set (mean ± stand deviation).

Features (dimensionality)	OA	Kappa
HSI (159)	0.9604 ± 0.0018	0.9017 ± 0.0041
Conv_HSI (159)	0.9670 ± 0.0012	0.9180 ± 0.0029
HSI_PCA (10)	0.9621 ± 0.0017	0.9048 ± 0.0041
Conv_HSI_PCA (10)	0.9679 ± 0.0006	0.9201 ± 0.0013
EMAPs (60)	0.9683 ± 0.0016	0.9208 ± 0.0039
IID features (24)	**0.9756 ± 0.0017**	**0.9386 ± 0.0041**

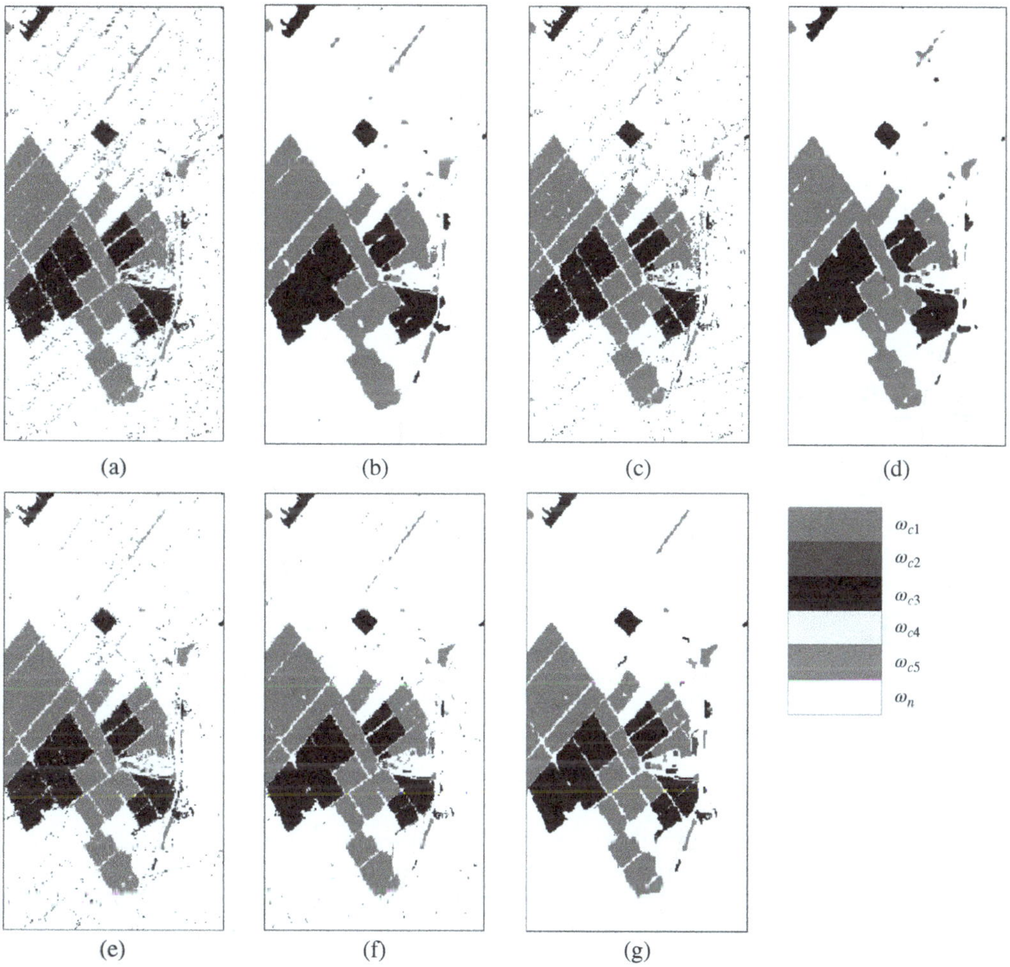

Figure 25.11 Multiclass CD results obtained by using different features: (a) original HSI, (b) Conv_HSI, (c) HSI_PCA, (d) Conv_HSI PCA, (e) EMAPs, (f) IID features and (g) reference map (six change classes are represented by varying grayscale intensities, and no-change class is shown in white).

highest OA and Kappa values. Compared with other features (as shown in Figure 25.11a–e), CD result based on IID feature (Figure 25.11f) maintains more accurate information about the boundaries of the changing region and eliminates most of the noise in CD results which is caused by pseudo change information.

25.6 Conclusion

The very high spectral resolution of HS images provides the basis for weak spectral change detection. However, due to the special characteristics of HS images, many CD algorithms applied to MS and other images are not applicable to HS images. In this chapter, we reviewed the current development of CD methods based on HS images, including traditional unsupervised CD methods, supervised CD methods based on machine learning models, and the CD methods based on deep learning models. In particular, we focused on the perspective of effective change feature extraction to find solutions to the important multi-class CD problem based on HS images. Accordingly, two approaches were proposed, including S^2CVA and IID-based CD method. By extracting compressed feature representations of change vectors in the 2D polar coordinate domain, S^2CVA provides a clearly visualized way to easily perform multi-class CD tasks. The IID algorithm is able to extract the spatial-spectral information and eliminate the interference information of shadows and lights, and improve the accuracy of pixel-level CD by combining with machine learning models. Experimental results obtained on two real multispectral data sets covering agricultural and artificial construction areas confirmed the effectiveness of the proposed approaches in terms of higher CD accuracy compared to the reference methods.

Acknowledgement

This work was supported in part by the National Natural Science Foundation of China under Grants 42071324 and by the Shanghai Rising-Star Program (21QA1409100), and by the Fundamental Research Funds for the Central Universities (22120240318).

References

1 Bruzzone, L. and Bovolo, F. (2013). A novel framework for the design of change-detection systems for very-high-resolution remote sensing images. *Proc. IEEE* 101 (3): 609–630.

2 Singh, A. (1 June 1989). Review article digital change detection techniques using remotely-sensed data. *Int. J. Remote Sens.* 10 (6): 989–1003.

3 Coppin, P., Jonckheere, I., Nackaerts, K. et al. (1 May 2004). Digital change detection methods in ecosystem monitoring: a review. *Int. J. Remote Sens.* 25: 1565–1596.

4 Lu, D., Mausel, P., Brondízio, E. et al. (1 June 2004). Change detection techniques. *Int. J. Remote Sens.* 25 (12): 2365–2401.

5 Coppin, P.R. and Bauer, M.E. (1 April 1996). Digital change detection in forest ecosystems with remote sensing imagery. *Remote Sens. Rev.* 13 (3-4): 207–234.

6 Chang, C.-I. (2003). *Hyperspectral Imaging: Techniques for Spectral Detection and Classification.* New York: Plenum Publishing Co.

7 Landgrebe, D. (2002). Hyperspectral image data analysis. *IEEE Signal Process. Mag.* 19 (1): 17–28.

8 Bioucas-Dias, J.M., Plaza, A., Camps-Valls, G. et al. (2013). Hyperspectral remote sensing data analysis and future challenges. *IEEE Geosci. Remote Sens. Mag.* 1 (2): 6–36.

9 Adar, S., Shkolnisky, Y., and Ben Dor, E. (16 February 2014). A new approach for thresholding spectral change detection using multispectral and hyperspectral image data, a case study over Sokolov, Czech Republic. *Int. J. Remote Sens.* 35 (4): 1563–1584.

10 Bovolo, F. and Bruzzone, L. (2007). A theoretical framework for unsupervised change detection based on change vector analysis in the polar domain. *IEEE Trans. Geosci. Remote Sens.* 45 (1): 218–236.

11 Li, Y., Ren, J., Yan, Y. et al. (1 May 2022). Unsupervised change detection in hyperspectral images using principal components space data clustering. *J. Phys. Conf. Ser.* 2278 (1): 012021.

12 Wu, C., Du, B., and Zhang, L. (2013). A subspace-based change detection method for hyperspectral images. *IEEE J. Sel. Top. Appl. Earth Obs. Remote Sens.* 6 (2): 815–830.

13 Meola, J., Eismann, M.T., Moses, R.L. et al. (2011). Detecting changes in hyperspectral imagery using a model-based approach. *IEEE Trans. Geosci. Remote Sens.* 49 (7): 2647–2661.

14 Nielsen, A.A. (2007). The regularized iteratively reweighted MAD method for change detection in multi- and hyperspectral data. *IEEE Trans. Image Process.* 16 (2): 463–478.

15 Marinelli, D., Bovolo, F., and Bruzzone, L. (2019). A novel change detection method for multitemporal hyperspectral images based on binary hyperspectral change vectors. *IEEE Trans. Geosci. Remote Sens.* 57 (7): 4913–4928.

16 Wang, B., Choi, S.-K., Han, Y.-K. et al. (3 August 2015). Application of IR-MAD using synthetically fused images for change detection in hyperspectral data. *Remote Sens. Lett.* 6 (8): 578–586.

17 Vanessa, O.-R., Miguel, V.-R., and Badrinath, R. (2006). Change detection in hyperspectral imagery using temporal principal components. In: *Algorithms and Technologies for Multispectral, Hyperspectral, and Ultraspectral Imagery*, vol. 6233 (ed. S.S. Shen and P.E. Lewis), 368–377. Orlando (Kissimmee), FL.

18 Wu, C., Du, B., and Zhang, L. (2014). Slow feature analysis for change detection in multispectral imagery. *IEEE Trans. Geosci. Remote Sens.* 52 (5): 2858–2874.

19 Sumaiya, M.N., Shantha, R., and Kumari, S. (1 February 2017). Gabor filter based change detection in SAR images by KI thresholding. *Optik* 130: 114–122.

20 Bovolo, F., Marchesi, S., and Bruzzone, L. (2012). A framework for automatic and unsupervised detection of multiple changes in multitemporal images. *IEEE Trans. Geosci. Remote Sens.* 50 (6): 2196–2212.

21 Liu, S., Bruzzone, L., Bovolo, F. et al. (2015). Sequential spectral change vector analysis for iteratively discovering and detecting multiple changes in hyperspectral images. *IEEE Trans. Geosci. Remote Sens.* 53 (8): 4363–4378.

22 Volpi, M., Tuia, D., Bovolo, F. et al. (1 February 2013). Supervised change detection in VHR images using contextual information and support vector machines. *Int. J. Appl. Earth Obs. Geoinf.* 20: 77–85.

23 Tu, B., Wang, J., Kang, X. et al. (2018). KNN-based representation of superpixels for hyperspectral image classification. *IEEE J. Sel. Top. Appl. Earth Obs. Remote Sens.* 11 (11): 4032–4047.

24 Feng, W., Sui, H., Tu, J. et al. (2018). A novel change detection approach for multi-temporal high-resolution remote sensing images based on rotation forest and coarse-to-fine uncertainty analyses. *Remote Sens* 10: 1015.

25 Tan, K., Zhang, Y., Wang, X. et al. (2019). Object-based change detection using multiple classifiers and multi-scale uncertainty analysis. *Remote Sens* 11: 359.

26 Liu, S., Du, K., Zheng, Y., et al. (2023). Remote sensing change detection technology in the era of artificial intelligence: inheritance development and challenges. *National Remote Sens. Bulletin* 27 (9): 1975–1987.

27 Huang, F., Yu, Y., and Feng, T. (1 January 2019). Hyperspectral remote sensing image change detection based on tensor and deep learning. *J. Vis. Commun. Image Represent.* 58: 233–244.

28 Khelifi, L. and Mignotte, M. (2020). Deep learning for change detection in remote sensing images: comprehensive review and meta-analysis. *IEEE Access* 8: 126385–126400.

29 Saha, S., Bovolo, F., and Bruzzone, L. (2019). Unsupervised deep change vector analysis for multiple-change detection in VHR images. *IEEE Trans. Geosci. Remote Sens.* 57 (6): 3677–3693.

30 Du, B., Ru, L., Wu, C. et al. (2019). Unsupervised deep slow feature analysis for change detection in multi-temporal remote sensing images. *IEEE Trans. Geosci. Remote Sens.* 57 (12): 9976–9992.

31 Gong, M., Jiang, F., Qin, A.K. et al. (2022). A spectral and spatial attention network for change detection in hyperspectral images. *IEEE Trans. Geosci. Remote Sens.* 60: 1–14.

32 Zhan, T., Song, B., Sun, L. et al. (2021). TDSSC: a three-directions spectral–spatial convolution neural network for hyperspectral image change detection. *IEEE J. Sel. Top. Appl. Earth Obs. Remote Sens.* 14: 377–388.

33 Shi, C., Zhang, Z., Zhang, W. et al. (2022). Learning multiscale temporal–spatial–spectral features via a multipath convolutional LSTM neural network for change detection with hyperspectral images. *IEEE Trans. Geosci. Remote Sens.* 60: 1–16.

34 Zhao, C., Cheng, H., and Feng, S. (2022). A spectral–spatial change detection method based on simplified 3-D convolutional autoencoder for multitemporal hyperspectral images. *IEEE Geosci. Remote Sens. Lett.* 19: 1–5.

35 Wang, L., Wang, L., Wang, Q. et al. (2022). RSCNet: a residual self-calibrated network for hyperspectral image change detection. *IEEE Trans. Geosci. Remote Sens.* 60: 1–17.

36 Yang, Y., Qu, J., Xiao, S. et al. (March 2022). A deep multiscale pyramid network enhanced with spatial–spectral residual attention for hyperspectral image change detection. *IEEE Trans. Geosci. Remote Sens.* 60: 1–13.

37 Luo, F., Zhou, T., Liu, J. et al. (January 2023). Multiscale diff-changed feature fusion network for hyperspectral image change detection. *IEEE Trans. Geosci. Remote Sens.* 61: 1–13.

38 Li, Y., Ren, J., Yan, Y. et al. (May 2023). CBANet: an end-to-end cross-band 2-D attention network for hyperspectral change detection in remote sensing. *IEEE Trans. Geosci. Remote Sens.* 61: 1–11.

39 Wang, X., Zhao, K., Zhao, X. et al. (March 2023). TriTF: a triplet transformer framework based on parents and brother attention for hyperspectral image change detection. *IEEE Trans. Geosci. Remote Sens.* 61: 1–13.

40 Zhao, X., Li, S., Geng, T. et al. (2024). GTransCD: graph transformer-guided multitemporal information united framework for hyperspectral image change detection. *IEEE Trans. Geosci. Remote Sens.* 62: 1–13.

41 Huang, Y., Zhang, L., Qi, W. et al. (February 2024). Semi-supervised hypermatch-driven cross temporal and spatial interaction transformer for hyperspectral change detection. *IEEE J. Sel. Top. Appl. Earth Obs. Remote Sens.* 17: 6426–6443.

42 Sun, J., Liu, J., and Xiao, L. (April 2023). Intrinsic decomposition model-guided two-stream coupled autoencoder for unsupervised hyperspectral image change detection. *IEEE Geosci. Remote Sens. Lett.* 20: 1–5.

43 Xu, Y., Xiao, S., Qu, J. et al. (2024). Parallel compared-and-stacked pyramid transformer network for unsupervised hyperspectral change detection. *IEEE Trans. Geosci. Remote Sens.* 62: 1–14.

44 Qu, J., Zhao, J., Dong, W. et al. (2024). Feature mutual representation-based graph domain adaptive network for unsupervised hyperspectral change detection. *IEEE Trans. Geosci. Remote Sens.* 62: 1–14.

45 Keshava, N. (2004). Distance metrics and band selection in hyperspectral processing with applications to material identification and spectral libraries. *IEEE Trans. Geosci. Remote Sens.* 42 (7): 1552–1565.

46 Chein, I.C. (2000). An information-theoretic approach to spectral variability, similarity, and discrimination for hyperspectral image analysis. *IEEE Trans. Inf. Theory* 46 (5): 1927–1932.

47 Sohn, Y.-S., Rebello, N.S.J.P.E., and Sensing, R. (2002). Supervised and unsupervised spectral angle classifiers. *Photogramm. Eng. Remote. Sens.* 68: 1271–1282.

48 Du, P., Liu, S., Bruzzone, L., et al. (2012), Target-driven change detection based on data transformation and similarity measures. *2012 IEEE International Geoscience and Remote Sensing Symposium*, Munich, Germany (22–27 July 2012). IEEE.

49 Ghosh, A., Mishra, N.S., and Ghosh, S. (15 February 2011). Fuzzy clustering algorithms for unsupervised change detection in remote sensing images. *Inf. Sci.* 181 (4): 699–715.

50 Bruzzone, L. and Serpico, S.B. (1997). An iterative technique for the detection of land-cover transitions in multitemporal remote-sensing images. *IEEE Trans. Geosci. Remote Sens.* 35 (4): 858–867.

51 Bruzzone, L. and Prieto, D.F. (2000). Automatic analysis of the difference image for unsupervised change detection. *IEEE Trans. Geosci. Remote Sens.* 38 (3): 1171–1182.

52 Bovolo, F., and Bruzzone, L. (2011). An adaptive thresholding approach to multiple-change detection in multispectral images. *2011 IEEE International Geoscience and Remote Sensing Symposium*, 233–236, Vancouver, BC, Canada (24–29 July 2011). IEEE.

53 Liu, S., Bruzzone, L., Bovolo, F. et al. (2015). Hierarchical unsupervised change detection in multitemporal hyperspectral images. *IEEE Trans. Geosci. Remote Sens.* 53 (1): 244–260.

54 Kang, X., Li, S., Fang, L. et al. (2015). Intrinsic image decomposition for feature extraction of hyperspectral images. *IEEE Trans. Geosci. Remote Sens.* 53 (4): 2241–2253.

55 Du, K. and Liu, S. (2021). Hyperspectral image change detection based on intrinsic image decomposition feature extraction. *Image and Signal Process. Evol. Remote Sens. XXVII* 11862: 1186215.

56 Shen, J., Yang, X., Li, X. et al. (2013). Intrinsic image decomposition using optimization and user scribbles. *IEEE Trans. Cybern.* 43 (2): 425–436.

57 Dalla Mura, M., Atli Benediktsson, J., Waske, B. et al. (6 December 2010). Extended profiles with morphological attribute filters for the analysis of hyperspectral data. *Int. J. Remote Sens.* 31 (22): 5975–5991.

26

Challenges and Future Directions

Bing Zhang, He Sun, and Ruitong Du

Aerospace Information Research Institute, Chinese Academy of Sciences, Beijing, China

26.1 Challenges and Future Directions in Hyperspectral Image Denoising

Hyperspectral image (HSI) denoising remains a critical yet challenging task in remote sensing and computer vision, primarily due to the complex nature of mixed noise and the high-dimensional structure of hyperspectral data. Despite significant advancements in model-driven, data-driven, and hybrid model-data-driven approaches, several unresolved challenges persist, limiting the practical applicability of existing methods. Addressing these challenges requires a nuanced understanding of the interplay between noise characteristics, computational efficiency, generalization capabilities, and the integration of domain-specific knowledge. Future directions must focus on bridging gaps between theoretical frameworks and real-world scenarios while leveraging emerging technologies to enhance robustness, adaptability, and interpretability.

26.1.1 Challenges

26.1.1.1 Improving Generalization Across Diverse Noise Distributions

One of the foremost challenges lies in improving the generalization ability of denoising algorithms. Existing methods often exhibit strong performance on simulated datasets or specific types of noise but struggle to adapt to the diverse noise distributions encountered in real-world HSIs. For instance, noise types such as Gaussian, Poisson, stripe, impulse, and deadline noise often coexist, with varying intensities across spectral bands. Model-driven methods like BM4D or LRTV, while effective in preserving structural details, rely heavily on handcrafted priors and regularization terms that may not generalize across heterogeneous scenes. Data-driven approaches, such as HSID-CNN or SSGN, face similar limitations when trained on datasets with noise distributions that differ from real-world conditions. Even hybrid methods like DSSBP, which combine model-based priors with deep learning, show instability when applied to HSIs with unknown noise characteristics. Future efforts must prioritize the development of adaptive frameworks capable of dynamically adjusting to varying noise levels and types. This could involve self-supervised learning paradigms that infer noise statistics directly from corrupted data or meta-learning strategies to transfer knowledge across diverse HSI domains. Additionally, incorporating uncertainty quantification into denoising models

Machine-Learning-Based Hyperspectral Image Processing, First Edition. Edited by Bing Zhang.

could enhance reliability, allowing algorithms to flag regions where noise removal is uncertain, thereby preventing over-smoothing or artifact generation.

26.1.1.2 Balancing Model-driven and Data-driven Methodologies

Another critical challenge is the effective integration of model-driven and data-driven strategies. While model-data-driven methods like NMF-DPR or LR-Net have demonstrated promising results by fusing physical priors with neural networks, their current implementations often lack a cohesive balance between interpretability and flexibility. Model-driven approaches excel in leveraging domain-specific knowledge, such as spectral low-rankness or spatial nonlocal similarity, but suffer from high computational complexity and parameter sensitivity. Conversely, data-driven methods offer end-to-end optimization and efficiency but require large volumes of labeled training data and risk overfitting to synthetic noise patterns. Future research should explore tighter couplings between these paradigms, such as embedding physical degradation models directly into neural architectures or designing physics-informed loss functions that guide learning without rigid constraints. For example, unfolding iterative optimization algorithms into deep networks could preserve interpretability while enabling data-adaptive parameter tuning. Furthermore, advancements in transformer-based architectures, which inherently capture long-range dependencies, could be tailored to exploit the spectral-spatial correlations in HSIs, combining the strengths of nonlocal mean strategies with the scalability of deep learning.

26.1.2 Future Directions

26.1.2.1 Unsupervised Learning with Spectral-spatial Priors

The scarcity of noise-free HSI training data poses a persistent bottleneck for supervised data-driven methods. While unsupervised and self-supervised techniques like DHP or SURE-CNN mitigate this issue by leveraging the intrinsic structure of noisy data, they often neglect critical priors such as spectral sparsity or global low-rankness. Future directions must emphasize the development of unsupervised frameworks that harmonize data-driven flexibility with model-driven insights. Techniques like deep image prior (DIP), which exploit the implicit regularization of neural networks, could be enhanced by incorporating spectral-spatial constraints derived from tensor factorization or total variation models. Additionally, generative models such as diffusion models or adversarial networks might be adapted to synthesize realistic noise-free HSIs, enabling the creation of large-scale training datasets without relying on costly acquisitions. Semi-supervised learning could also play a role, where limited labeled data is supplemented with pseudo-labels generated from model-driven denoising outputs, creating a feedback loop to refine both paradigms.

26.1.2.2 Lightweight Architectures and Real-time Processing

Computational efficiency and real-time processing remain significant hurdles, particularly for large-scale HSIs. Model-driven methods like low-rank tensor factorization or nonlocal mean algorithms often involve iterative optimization procedures that scale poorly with data size. Data-driven approaches, while faster during inference, require substantial computational resources for training and may not be deployable on edge devices. Future work should focus on lightweight architectures, such as knowledge distillation or neural architecture search, to compress complex models without sacrificing performance. Techniques like patch-based processing or band selection could reduce dimensionality upfront, while hardware-software co-design strategies might optimize memory usage for hyperspectral cubes. Moreover, the integration of quantum computing or parallel processing frameworks could revolutionize computationally intensive tasks like tensor decomposition, enabling real-time denoising for applications such as airborne surveillance or environmental monitoring.

26.1.2.3 Task-specific Optimization and Explainable AI

Advancing HSI denoising requires closer alignment with downstream tasks such as classification, anomaly detection, or material identification. Current denoising pipelines often operate in isolation, neglecting the interplay between noise removal and feature preservation critical for subsequent analyses. For instance, over-smoothing during denoising might erase subtle spectral signatures essential for mineral mapping. Future methods should adopt a holistic perspective, jointly optimizing denoising and high-level vision tasks through multi-task learning or end-to-end systems. Embedding classification or segmentation losses into the denoising objective could ensure that restored HSIs retain discriminative features. Furthermore, explainable AI techniques could shed light on how denoising impacts task-specific metrics, guiding the development of application-aware algorithms.

In conclusion, the path forward for HSI denoising lies in transcending traditional boundaries between models and data, embracing adaptability, and fostering synergy with real-world applications. By addressing challenges in generalization, integration, scalability, and task-specific optimization, the next generation of denoising methods will not only enhance image quality but also unlock the full potential of hyperspectral imaging across scientific and industrial domains.

26.2 Challenges and Future Directions in Hyperspectral (HS) and Multispectral (MS) Image Fusion

26.2.1 Challenges

26.2.1.1 Spectral-spatial Trade-off and Artifact Suppression

HS images provide rich spectral information but suffer from low spatial resolution, while MS images offer finer spatial details at the cost of limited spectral bands. Balancing these attributes without introducing artifacts – such as spectral distortion in vegetation indices or blurring in urban structures – remains a persistent challenge. For instance, deep learning (DL) models like convolutional neural networks (CNNs) often prioritize spatial enhancement, inadvertently suppressing subtle spectral features critical for applications like mineral identification or crop stress detection. The inherent heterogeneity between HS and MS sensors (e.g., differing bandpass filters or noise profiles) further complicates seamless fusion, leading to mismatched spectral responses in fused outputs.

26.2.1.2 Data Misalignment and Geometric Registration

HS and MS images are frequently acquired from separate platforms (e.g., airborne HS sensors paired with satellite MS imagers) or at different times, resulting in geometric misalignment. Sub-pixel registration errors propagate through fusion pipelines, causing spatial ghosting or spectral aberrations. Traditional registration methods, reliant on feature matching or affine transformations, struggle with large-scale datasets or complex terrains. DL-based approaches, while promising, often assume perfect co-registration during training, limiting their adaptability to real-world scenarios where temporal or spatial discrepancies are unavoidable (e.g., seasonal vegetation changes affecting ground control points).

26.2.1.3 Generalization Across Sensors and Environments

Most fusion models are trained on specific sensor pairs (e.g., Hyperion HS with Sentinel-2 MS) and fail to generalize to unseen configurations, such as fusion between PRISMA HS and Landsat MS data. Variations in spectral band positions, spatial resolutions, or noise characteristics degrade performance, necessitating retraining with extensive labeled datasets – a resource-intensive process. Additionally, environmental factors like atmospheric conditions (e.g., haze, cloud cover) or illumination changes introduce non-linear distortions that challenge model robustness, particularly in unsupervised frameworks.

26.2.1.4 High Computational Complexity and Memory Demands

HS datasets, often comprising hundreds of spectral bands, impose significant computational burdens on DL architectures. Training 3D-CNNs or transformer-based models for HS-MS fusion requires specialized hardware (e.g., GPUs with large VRAM), limiting accessibility for real-time or edge-computing applications. Techniques like band selection or dimensionality reduction can mitigate this but risk discarding diagnostically valuable spectral information. Moreover, memory-intensive operations (e.g., gradient calculations in GANs) hinder scalability for large-area mosaics or time-series analysis.

26.2.1.5 Lack of High-quality Ground Truth for Supervision

Supervised DL methods rely on paired HS-MS images with perfectly aligned high-resolution HS references, which are rarely available in practice. Synthetic datasets, generated by degrading high-resolution HS images, fail to capture real-world sensor noise or environmental variability, leading to overfitted models. Unsupervised and self-supervised approaches, though promising, often produce suboptimal results due to the absence of explicit spectral fidelity constraints, especially in complex scenes with mixed land covers.

26.2.2 Future Directions

26.2.2.1 Unsupervised and Self-supervised Learning Paradigms

To address the scarcity of real-world training pairs, future work should prioritize unsupervised frameworks that learn fusion rules directly from unpaired HS and MS data. Generative models like CycleGAN or diffusion models can simulate realistic spectral-spatial relationships without requiring ground truth. Self-supervised pretext tasks – such as predicting masked spectral bands or reconstructing degraded MS images from HS inputs – could leverage inherent data correlations to improve generalization. For example, contrastive learning might align latent representations of HS and MS patches from the same geographic region, enhancing cross-modal feature compatibility.

26.2.2.2 Physics-guided Deep Learning Architectures

Integrating physical principles into DL models can enhance interpretability and enforce spectral consistency. Hybrid frameworks might combine model-based techniques (e.g., matrix factorization or spectral unmixing) with neural networks to preserve physically plausible constraints. For instance, an unrolled optimization network could iteratively refine fusion results using handcrafted priors (e.g., spectral smoothness) alongside learned features. Additionally, embedding sensor-specific response functions or radiative transfer models into the network architecture could improve adaptability across diverse imaging systems.

26.2.2.3 Attention Mechanisms and Multi-scale Fusion

Attention-based models, such as vision transformers (ViTs) or squeeze-and-excitation networks, can dynamically weight spectral bands and spatial regions based on their diagnostic importance. Cross-modal attention modules might prioritize MS-derived edges in urban areas while emphasizing HS spectral features in agricultural zones. Multi-scale architectures, incorporating pyramid pooling or wavelet transforms, could capture both global context (e.g., land-cover patterns) and local details (e.g., crop boundaries), reducing artifacts at resolution boundaries.

26.2.2.4 Lightweight and Adaptive Networks for Edge Deployment

Developing compact models (e.g., via neural architecture search or knowledge distillation) is critical for deploying HS-MS fusion on drones or satellites. Techniques like quantization, pruning, or tensor factorization can reduce parameter counts without sacrificing accuracy. Adaptive networks might dynamically adjust computational pathways based on input complexity – for example, applying shallow layers to homogeneous landscapes and deeper networks for heterogeneous urban scenes – to optimize resource usage.

26.2.2.5 Cross-sensor Harmonization and Domain Adaptation

Generalizable fusion frameworks must accommodate varying sensor characteristics. Meta-learning approaches could train models to rapidly adapt to new HS-MS sensor pairs with minimal fine-tuning. Domain adaptation techniques, such as adversarial training or feature alignment, might bridge gaps between source (e.g., laboratory-calibrated) and target (e.g., field-acquired) datasets. Open-source repositories of multi-sensor HS-MS pairs, annotated with metadata (e.g., illumination angles, atmospheric conditions), would facilitate benchmarking and model validation.

26.2.2.6 Integration with Downstream Applications

Moving beyond pixel-level metrics, future research should align fusion objectives with application-specific goals. For instance, loss functions could prioritize spectral bands critical for wildfire risk assessment or water quality monitoring. Joint fusion-classification frameworks might co-optimize feature extraction and land-cover mapping, ensuring fused data directly enhance end-task performance. Collaborative efforts with domain experts (e.g., ecologists, agronomists) will ensure fusion models address real-world needs, such as detecting invasive species or monitoring post-disaster recovery.

In conclusion, HS-MS image fusion stands at the intersection of technological innovation and practical utility, offering transformative potential for environmental monitoring and resource management. Overcoming current limitations demands a synergistic approach – melding advances in DL with domain knowledge, sensor physics, and computational efficiency. By prioritizing adaptive, interpretable, and scalable solutions, the next generation of fusion models will unlock hyperspectral imaging's full potential, bridging the gap between laboratory precision and global-scale Earth observation.

26.3 Challenges and Future Directions in NMF-based Hyperspectral Unmixing

NMF-based unmixing has emerged as a powerful technique for hyperspectral image (HSI) analysis. Despite its success, several challenges remain, particularly in handling computational complexity, scalability, nonlinear spectral mixing, and interpretability. Many NMF-based unmixing methods exhibit high computational costs, especially when applied to large-scale datasets. The iterative nature of NMF optimization, often involving complex constraints such as sparsity and robustness, results in significant processing time, limiting its feasibility for large hyperspectral scenes. Moreover, Real-time processing of hyperspectral data remains a major challenge for NMF-based approaches due to their reliance on iterative updates and high-dimensional matrix computations.

Traditional NMF assumes a linear mixing model, which is often insufficient for real-world scenarios involving multiple scattering interactions, terrain effects, and atmospheric distortions. While NMF provides physically meaningful endmember and abundance representations, its interpretability is still limited by the constraints and factorization strategies used. Developing explainable NMF architectures by integrating transparency-driven regularization techniques or uncertainty quantification methods can improve model interpretability.

26.4 Challenges and Future Directions in Knowledge Graph-enhanced Hyperspectral Unmixing

In the future, we will develop more effective EP algorithms based on this framework. Additional constraints will be introduced and tested. Robust learning provides a good way to recover endmember. However, the quality of the selected pixels plays an important role on in performance. Thus, the spatial relationship of the pixels and the spectral features will be further considered. Finally, this is our first attempt to embed the knowledge graph into the unmixing model. In the next step, we will introduce more geographic knowledge to enrich our knowledge graph and improve reasoning capability. The integration of knowledge graphs with deep learning is poised to facilitate unmixing processes with enhanced efficiency and precision.

26.5 Challenges and Future Directions in Numerical Model-guided Nonlinear Hyperspectral Unmixing

Numerical model-guided nonlinear unmixing methods provide a straightforward and effective way to physically interpret the nonlinear mixing effects, revealing the land covers' spectral constituents and spatial distributions in hyperspectral remote sensing images. However, considerable challenges are present in processing hyperspectral data with the increasing amount and complexity, and meeting the requirements for more refined real quantitative applications. In-depth research must be explored to develop nonlinear unmixing methods with higher computational efficiency and accuracy, richer interpretation capabilities, and generalization ability for a wider range of application scenarios.

Firstly, given the high computational complexity of nonlinear unmixing, real-time processing data with higher resolutions and larger scenarios is intractable. Specifically, GCBAE transforms the complex nonlinear unmixing problem into a simple linear one, and its computational complexity is affected by the number of endmembers. The computational burden of KBU mainly comes from the kernel-based operations highly dependent on the data size. The computational complexity of updating major variables in BNLSU is $O(mn^3)$ where m and n are the numbers of pixels and bands, respectively. Therefore, to satisfy the requirement of real-time unmixing hyperspectral data on board or edge devices, it is important to develop faster nonlinear unmixing methods by employing parallel computing architecture and high-performance hardware in the future.

Secondly, integrating high-dimensional multi-source multi-modal data, domain knowledge, and advanced deep learning techniques to build an intelligent and universal nonlinear unmixing framework can be very challenging. A highly promising research domain could be the investigation of large artificial intelligent models for multi-source remote sensing image unmixing. The advantages of numerical model-guided physical interpretation and deep neural networks-driven data learning integrated into such models can promote intelligent and reliable applications for precise unmixing and effectively generalize unmixing to different remote sensing datasets.

Finally, nonlinear unmixing theories and methods for complex nature scenarios such as estuarine and coastal water bodies and related applications are rarely studied, and reliable ground truth of real hyperspectral remote sensing data for validating unmixing performance is usually inaccessible. Consequently, in light of specific application tasks, it is of significance to develop advanced unmixing techniques for interpreting the intricate radiative transfer processes in various natural scenarios. Moreover, combined with real hyperspectral remote sensing images labeled with in-situ collected data, simulated hyperspectral data generated by deep generative models considering nonlinear unmixing and spectral variability have a great potential to provide reliable datasets for quantitative unmixing research.

26.6 Challenges and Future Directions in Hyperspectral Image Classification

Hyperspectral image (HSI) classification has a wide range of applications across various fields due to its ability to capture rich spectral information. In agriculture, HSI is used for crop monitoring, disease detection, and soil composition analysis, enabling precision farming and sustainable agricultural practices. In environmental monitoring, it helps in identifying land cover changes, detecting pollution, and assessing deforestation. Remote sensing and urban planning leverage HSI for infrastructure analysis, vegetation mapping, and land-use classification. Additionally, in geology and mineral exploration, hyperspectral classification assists in identifying rock compositions and mineral deposits, improving resource extraction efficiency. Medical imaging has also benefited from hyperspectral classification, enabling non-invasive disease diagnosis and tissue analysis by differentiating biological materials based on their spectral signatures.

Despite its vast potential, hyperspectral image classification faces several challenges that hinder its widespread adoption. One major issue is high dimensionality, as HSI data contains hundreds of spectral bands, leading to increased computational costs and the risk of the "curse of dimensionality." Another challenge is limited labeled data, as acquiring high-quality ground truth for hyperspectral datasets is expensive and labor-intensive, making supervised learning approaches difficult to scale. Additionally, variability in atmospheric and illumination conditions affects spectral consistency, requiring robust preprocessing techniques. The integration of deep learning and self-supervised methods is promising but demands significant computational resources and explainability improvements. Future research should focus on efficient feature extraction, domain adaptation, and hybrid modeling approaches to enhance the generalization and interpretability of HSI classification models.

26.7 Chapter on Challenges and Future Directions in Hyperspectral Target Detection

Over the past three decades, there has been a sustained increase in research activity within the domain of hyperspectral detection. We undertake a comprehensive examination of the field by systematically reviewing and synthesizing a wide array of scholarly references, research findings, and pertinent materials to elucidate the current dynamics of hyperspectral detection. In particular, this analysis identifies several critical phases in the development of the field, assessing their respective strengths and weaknesses to uncover potential patterns of evolution and avenues for improvements. Additionally, we provide a summary of anticipated future trends and further highlight key technological challenges that must be addressed to advance the field effectively.

26.7.1 Signal Processing Stage

Algorithms for hyperspectral detection that rely on signal processing have demonstrated efficacy in analyzing hyperspectral images (HSIs) characterized by monotonous distributions and a limited number of land cover classes. These signal processing-based approaches typically employ specific model assumptions to evaluate HSIs, mathematically modeling the processed data to formulate detection response criteria, which are then used to compute the output of the algorithms [1, 2]. The advantages of these conventional algorithms in practical applications stem from their robust theoretical foundations, well-defined mechanisms, and high interpretability, which contribute to their low computational demands and straightforward development and integration processes. Nonetheless, the performance of these algorithms is contingent upon the compatibility between the model assumptions and the actual hyperspectral data. When the model employed does not accurately reflect the characteristics of the data being analyzed, traditional algorithms struggle to extract deep-level features from HSI data, thereby failing to accommodate the complexities of land cover distributions found in real-world scenarios. This mismatch can lead to a substantial decline in detection performance [3].

26.7.2 Machine Learning Stage

The mathematical modeling of complex real HSIs is employed to extract deep-level features. Traditional algorithms, constrained by specific model assumptions, often struggle to fully capture the rich information present in HSIs. To address such limitations, machine learning techniques have been introduced to improve the extraction of data features [4]. Consequently, machine learning approaches have increasingly gained prominence in hyperspectral detection, leading to numerous successful applications and the emergence of derivative theoretical advancements. These include representation reconstruction, metric learning, kernel methods, tensor decomposition, and deep learning, which have become focal points for subsequent research. However, despite their robust analytical capabilities for hyperspectral data, machine-learning-based methods typically require certain conditions to be effective. Factors such as stringent validation requirements, the quality of training datasets, sensitivity to parameters, and computational complexity during implementation significantly influence detection outcomes, thereby constraining their practical applicability [5, 6].

26.7.3 Deep Learning Stage

In light of the numerous challenges associated with detection tasks using extensive hyperspectral remote sensing data that contain a wealth of information, deep learning, as an advanced and prominent subset of machine learning, facilitates the automatic learning of higher-order features through the training of multi-layered network architectures. Deep learning-based approaches effectively extract detailed land cover information from large datasets for detection purposes [7, 8], capitalizing on their distinctive strengths in managing diverse, multi-dimensional, and highly complex data [9]. A variety of networks with differing structures and functionalities, along with their derivative adaptations, continue to emerge, leading to significant enhancements in the processing and analysis of HSIs, thereby advancing high-precision detection capabilities within this domain. Nonetheless, many deep learning methodologies primarily concentrate on data-driven learning, often neglecting the integration of mechanistic knowledge, which can compromise interpretability. Additionally, the substantial demands for quality training data and computational resources during network development pose significant limitations on their generalizability in real-world applications [10, 11].

The advancement of hyperspectral detection is evidently interconnected and mutually reinforcing across its various stages. To date, a range of detection algorithms, grounded in diverse theoretical frameworks, model assumptions, and research focal points, have matured to effectively tackle the challenges posed by the complexity and variability of land cover distributions in real-world scenarios, as well as the constraints introduced by unfavorable factors during hyperspectral imaging. As the demand for hyperspectral detection technology continues to grow in critical areas such as livelihood engineering and national defense security, it becomes essential to evaluate related research from both theoretical and practical application perspectives. As a result, there is an increasing emphasis on enhancing algorithm performance in terms of computational efficiency, memory usage, and detection accuracy.

The shift from model-driven to data-driven methodologies represents a significant evolution in the fundamental principles guiding theoretical innovation, scheme formulation, and algorithm development in hyperspectral detection. This transition not only advances the overall growth of the field but also opens up new avenues for future research endeavors. In the future, the evolution of hyperspectral detection is anticipated to extend beyond traditional disciplinary boundaries, embracing integrative and complementary approaches. This will involve leveraging the extensive theoretical frameworks emerging from interdisciplinary domains such as hyperspectral remote sensing, signal theory, and machine learning. Consequently, innovative analytical models and algorithmic systems tailored to the specific characteristics of hyperspectral data will be developed, facilitating intelligent interpretation of remote sensing information to fulfill the demands for high-precision detection. Thus, it is essential to consider both theoretical advancements and practical applications in order to enhance the overall significance and utility of related research.

References

1 Manolakis, D. and Shaw, G. (January 2002). Detection algorithms for hyperspectral imaging applications. *IEEE Signal Process. Mag.* 19 (1): 29–43.

2 Matteoli, S., Diani, M., and Corsini, G. (July 2010). A tutorial overview of anomaly detection in hyperspectral images. *IEEE Aerosp. Electron. Syst. Mag.* 25 (7): 5–28.

3 Stein, D.W.J., Beaven, S.G., Hoff, L.E. et al. (January 2002). Anomaly detection from hyperspectral imagery. *IEEE Signal Process. Mag.* 19 (1): 58–69.

4 Xu, Y., Zhang, L., Du, B. et al. (April 2022). Hyperspectral anomaly detection based on machine learning: an overview. *IEEE J. Sel. Top. Appl. Earth Obs. Remote Sens.* 15: 3351–3364.

5 Li, W. and Du, Q. (March 2015). Collaborative representation for hyperspectral anomaly detection. *IEEE Trans. Geosci. Remote Sens.* 53 (3): 1463–1474.

6 Chen, Y., Nasrabadi, N.M., and Tran, T.D. (July 2011). Sparse representation for target detection in hyperspectral imagery. *IEEE J. Sel. Top. Signal Process.* 5 (3): 629–640.

7 Shinde, P.P. and Shah, S. (2018). A review of machine learning and deep learning applications. *2018 Fourth International Conference on Computing Communication Control and Automation (ICCUBEA)*, 1–6, Pune, India (16–18 August 2018). IEEE.

8 Zhang, G., Zhao, S., Li, W. et al. (May 2020). HTD-net: a deep convolutional neural network for target detection in hyperspectral imagery. *Remote Sens* 12 (9): 1489.

9 Hu, X., Xie, C., Fan, Z. et al. (April 2022). Hyperspectral anomaly detection using deep learning: a review. *Remote Sens* 14 (9).

10 Li, W., Wu, G., and Du, Q. (May 2017). Transferred deep learning for anomaly detection in hyperspectral imagery. *IEEE Geosci. Remote Sens. Lett.* 14 (5): 597–601.

11 Zhu, D., Du, B., and Zhang, L. (November 2020). Two-stream convolutional networks for hyperspectral target detection. *IEEE Trans. Geosci. Remote Sens.* 59: 6907–6921.

Index

Note: Page numbers in **bold** indicate tables, and *italicized* page numbers indicate figures.

Machine-Learning-Based Hyperspectral Image Processing, First Edition. Edited by Bing Zhang.

e

i

j

k

t

u

Printed in the USA/Agawam, MA
June 30, 2026

907142.012